A-Z TYNE and

C000178947

CONTENTS

REFERENCE

Motorway	**A1(M)**	Car Park Selected	**P**
A Road	A1	Church or Chapel	†
Proposed		City Wall (Large Scale Only)	⊓⊔⊓⊔⊓
B Road	B1288	Cycleway	🚲
Dual Carriageway		Fire Station	■
Tunnel	A19	Hospital	Ⓗ
One-way Street	→	House Numbers Selected Roads	13 8 4
Traffic flow on A Roads is also indicated by a heavy line on the driver's left.	→	Information Centre	𝒊
Restricted Access		National Grid Reference	⁴20
Pedestrianized Road		Park & Ride	Kingston Park P+
Track / Footpath		Police Station	▲
Residential Walkway		Post Office	★
Railway	Level Crossing Heritage Sta. Tunnel Station	Toilet	▽
		with Facilities for the Disabled	▽
Metro Line	**M** Tunnel	Viewpoint	⋇ ☀
Local Authority Boundary		Educational Establishment	◰
Posttown Boundary		Hospital or Hospice	◰
Postcode Boundary within Posttowns		Industrial Building	◰
Built-up Area	MILL ST.	Leisure or Recreational Facility	◰
		Place of Interest	◰
		Public Building	◰
Map Continuation	54 Large Scale City Centre 4	Shopping Centre or Market	◰
		Other Selected Buildings	◰

SCALES

Map Pages 8-181	Map Pages 4-5	Map Pages 6-7
1:14,908 4¼ inches (10.8 cm) to 1 mile 6.7 cm to 1 km	1:10,560 6 inches (15.24 cm) to 1 mile 9.47 cm to 1 km	1:7,454 8½ inches (21.6 cm) to 1 mile 13.42 cm to 1 km
0 ¼Mile	0 ⅛ ¼ Mile	0 ⅛ ¼ Mile
0 250 500 Metres	0 250 Metres	0 250 Metres

Copyright of Geographers' A-Z Map Company Ltd.

Head Office:
Fairfield Road, Borough Green, Sevenoaks, Kent TN15 8PP
Telephone: 01732 781000

www.a-zmaps.co.uk

Copyright © Geographers' A-Z Map Co. Ltd. 2004

Ordnance Survey® This product includes mapping data licensed from Ordnance Survey® with the permission of the Controller of Her Majesty's Stationery Office.

© Crown Copyright 2004. Licence number 100017302

EDITION 2 2004

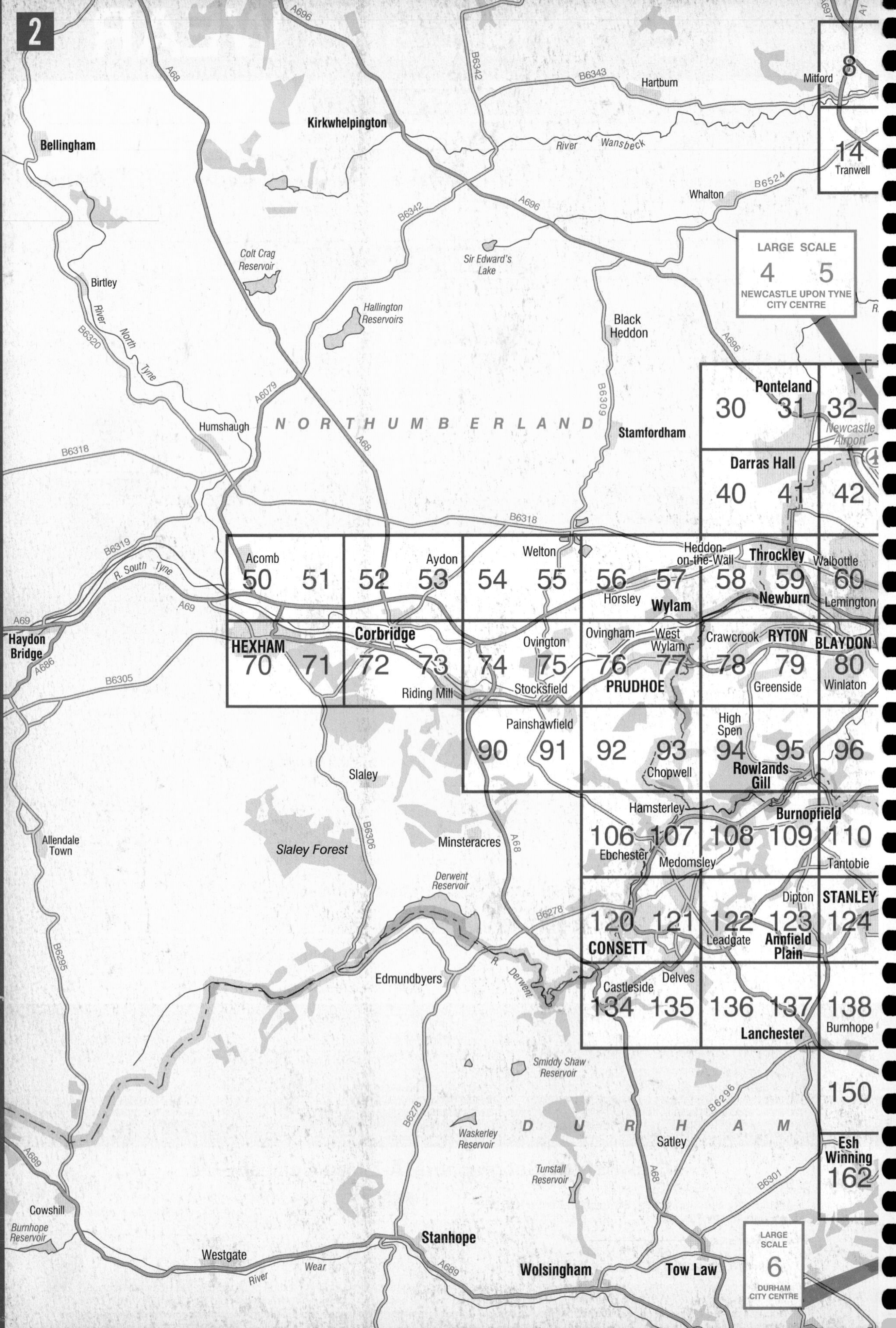
Bellingham
Kirkwhelpington
Hartburn
Mitford
8
14
Tranwell
River Wansbeck
Whalton
Colt Crag Reservoir
Sir Edward's Lake
Birtley
Hallington Reservoirs
LARGE SCALE
4 5
NEWCASTLE UPON TYNE CITY CENTRE
Black Heddon
River North Tyne
Ponteland
30 31 32
Newcastle Airport
Humshaugh
NORTHUMBERLAND
Stamfordham
Darras Hall
40 41 42
R. South Tyne
Acomb
Aydon
Welton
Heddon-on-the-Wall
Throckley
Walbottle
50 51 52 53 54 55 56 57 58 59 60
Horsley
Wylam
Newburn
Lemington
Haydon Bridge
HEXHAM
Corbridge
Ovington
Ovingham
West Wylam
Crawcrook
RYTON
BLAYDON
70 71 72 73 74 75 76 77 78 79 80
Riding Mill
Stocksfield
PRUDHOE
Greenside
Winlaton
Painshawfield
High Spen
90 91 92 93 94 95 96
Chopwell
Rowlands Gill
Slaley
Hamsterley
Burnopfield
Allendale Town
Slaley Forest
Minsteracres
106 107 108 109 110
Ebchester
Medomsley
Tantobie
Derwent Reservoir
Dipton
STANLEY
120 121 122 123 124
CONSETT
Leadgate
Annfield Plain
Edmundbyers
R. Derwent
Castleside
Delves
134 135 136 137 138
Lanchester
Burnhope
Smiddy Shaw Reservoir
150
DURHAM
Satley
Waskerley Reservoir
Esh Winning
162
Tunstall Reservoir
Cowshill
Burnhope Reservoir
Stanhope
LARGE SCALE
6
DURHAM CITY CENTRE
Westgate
River Wear
Wolsingham
Tow Law
A696
A68
B6342
B6343
A697
A1
B6524
B6320
A6079
B6309
B6318
B6319
A69
A686
B6305
B6306
B6278
B6295
B6296
A689
B6301

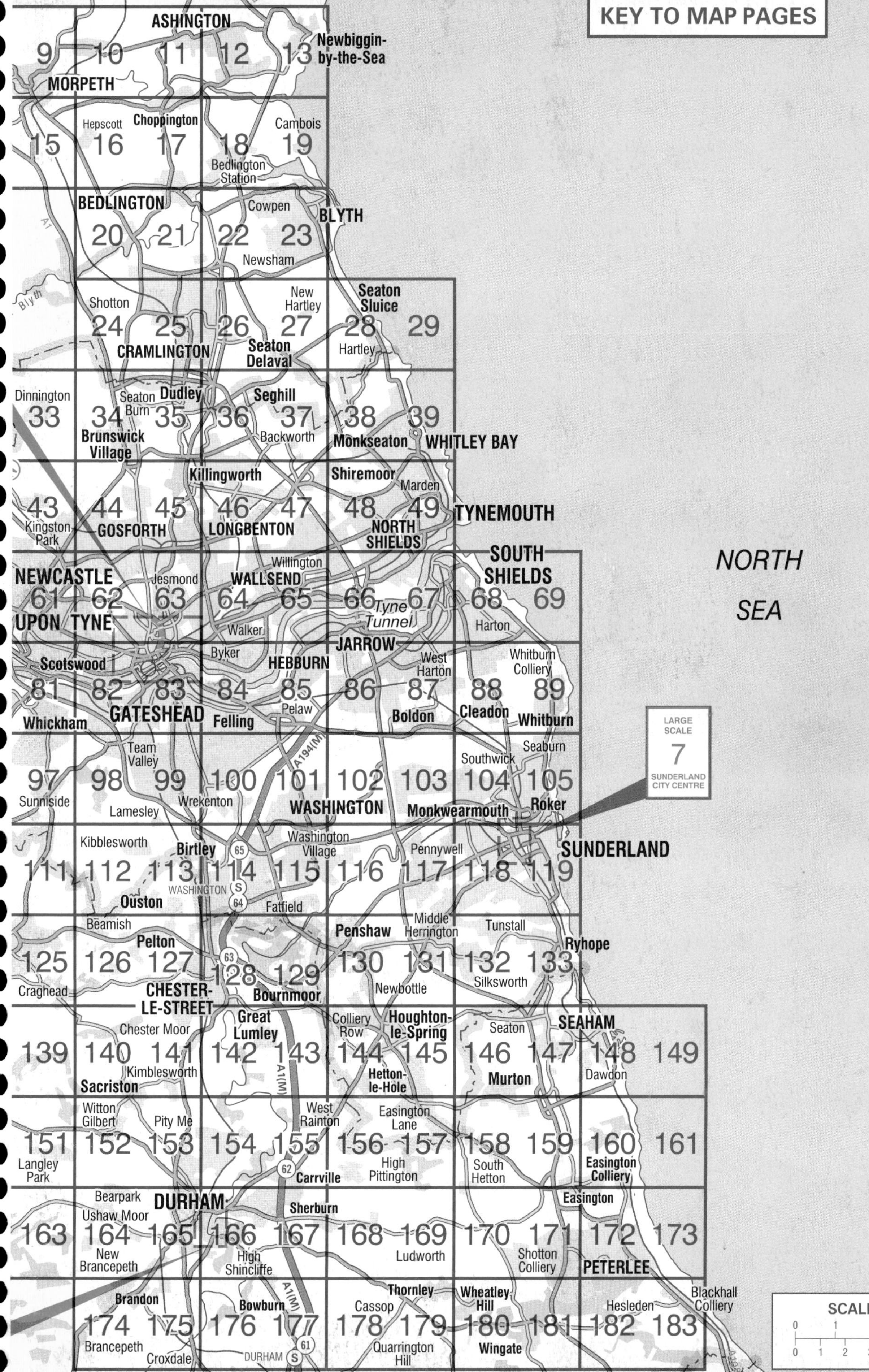

ASHINGTON
9 10 11 12 13 Newbiggin-by-the-Sea
MORPETH

Hepscott Choppington Cambois
15 16 17 18 19
Bedlington Station

BEDLINGTON Cowpen BLYTH
20 21 22 23
Newsham

Shotton New Hartley Seaton Sluice
24 25 26 27 28 29
CRAMLINGTON Seaton Delaval Hartley

Dinnington Seaton Burn Dudley Seghill
33 34 35 36 37 38 39
Brunswick Village Backworth Monkseaton WHITLEY BAY

Killingworth Shiremoor
43 44 45 46 47 48 49 TYNEMOUTH
Kingston Park GOSFORTH LONGBENTON Marden NORTH SHIELDS

NEWCASTLE Jesmond Willington WALLSEND SOUTH SHIELDS
61 62 63 64 65 66 67 68 69
UPON TYNE Walker Tyne Tunnel Harton

Scotswood Byker HEBBURN West Harton Whitburn Colliery
81 82 83 84 85 86 87 88 89
Whickham GATESHEAD Felling Pelaw Boldon Cleadon Whitburn

Team Valley Southwick Seaburn
97 98 99 100 101 102 103 104 105
Sunniside Lamesley Wrekenton WASHINGTON Monkwearmouth Roker

LARGE SCALE 7 SUNDERLAND CITY CENTRE

Kibblesworth Birtley Washington Village Pennywell SUNDERLAND
111 112 113 114 115 116 117 118 119
Ouston Fatfield

Beamish Pelton Middle Herrington Tunstall Ryhope
125 126 127 128 129 130 131 132 133
Craghead CHESTER-LE-STREET Bournmoor Newbottle Silksworth

Chester Moor Great Lumley Colliery Row Houghton-le-Spring Seaton SEAHAM
139 140 141 142 143 144 145 146 147 148 149
Sacriston Kimblesworth Hetton-le-Hole Murton Dawdon

Witton Gilbert Pity Me West Rainton Easington Lane
151 152 153 154 155 156 157 158 159 160 161
Langley Park High Pittington South Hetton Easington Colliery

Bearpark DURHAM Sherburn Easington
163 164 165 166 167 168 169 170 171 172 173
Ushaw Moor New Brancepeth High Shincliffe Ludworth Shotton Colliery PETERLEE

Brandon Bowburn Thornley Wheatley Hill Hesleden Blackhall Colliery
174 175 176 177 178 179 180 181 182 183
Brancepeth Croxdale DURHAM Quarrington Hill Wingate

Cassop

Kelloe

NORTH SEA

SCALE
0 1 2 Miles
0 1 2 3 Kilometres

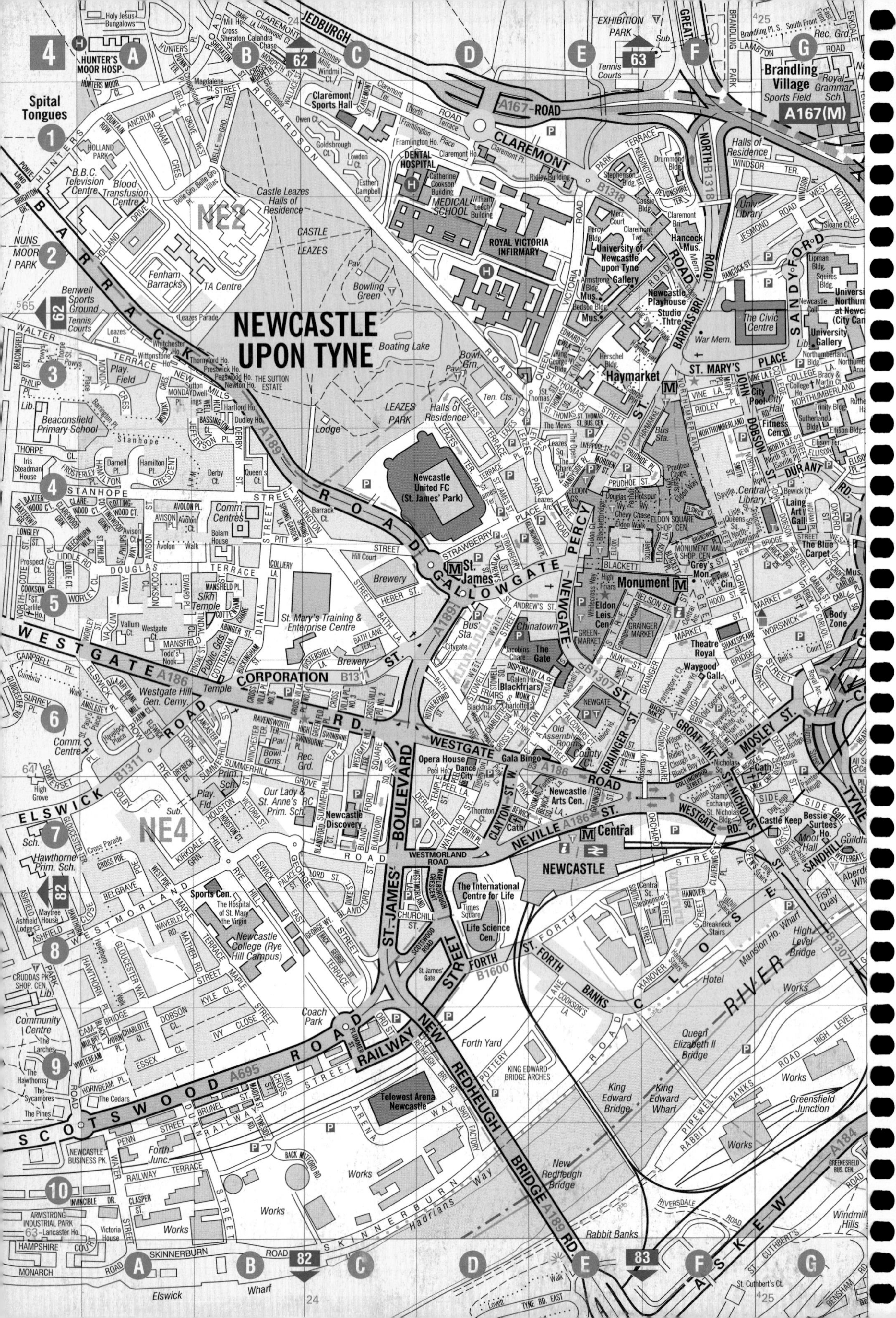
4
A
B
C
D
E
F
G
1
2
3
4
5
6
7
8
9
10
62
63
82
83
24
25
NEWCASTLE UPON TYNE
NE2
NE4
Spital Tongues
HUNTER'S MOOR HOSP.
Holy Jesus Bungalows
EXHIBITION PARK
Tennis Courts
Brandling Village
Sports Field
Royal Grammar Sch.
A167(M)
A167 ROAD
CLAREMONT
Claremont Sports Hall
DENTAL HOSPITAL
MEDICAL SCHOOL
ROYAL VICTORIA INFIRMARY
Halls of Residence
Univ. Library
B.B.C. Television Centre
Blood Transfusion Centre
NUNS MOOR PARK
Castle Leazes Halls of Residence
CASTLE LEAZES
Fenham Barracks
TA Centre
Bowling Green
Boating Lake
Benwell Sports Ground
Tennis Courts
University of Newcastle upon Tyne
Hancock Mus.
Newcastle Playhouse
Studio Thtre
The Civic Centre
War Mem.
University Gallery
BARRAS BRI.
ST. MARY'S PLACE
Haymarket
THE SUTTON ESTATE
LEAZES PARK
Halls of Residence
Lodge
Beaconsfield Primary School
Play. Field
Newcastle United FC (St. James' Park)
Brewery
St. James
GALLOWGATE
PERCY
NEWGATE
ELDON SQUARE SHOP. CEN.
Chinatown
The Gate
Monument
Grey's Mon.
City Pool
City Hall
Fitness Cen.
Central Library
Laing Art Gall.
The Blue Carpet
Eldon Leis. Cen
GRAINGER MARKET
Theatre Royal
Waygood Gall.
Body Zone
Comm. Centres
Sikh Temple
St. Mary's Training & Enterprise Centre
Westgate Hill Gen. Cemy.
WESTGATE ROAD A186
CORPORATION ST. B1311
Temple
Comm. Centre
Blackfriars
Opera House
Dance City
Gala Bingo
Newcastle Arts Cen.
Old Assembly Rooms
County Ct.
Cath.
Castle Keep
Bessie Surtees Ho.
Moot Hall
Central
NEWCASTLE
ELSWICK
Hawthorne Prim. Sch.
Our Lady & St. Anne's RC Prim. Sch.
Newcastle Discovery
Rec. Grd.
BOULEVARD
WESTMORLAND ROAD
ST. JAMES' STREET
The International Centre for Life
Times Square
Life Science Cen.
Sports Cen.
The Hospital of St. Mary the Virgin
Newcastle College (Rye Hill Campus)
CRUDDAS PARK SHOP. CEN.
Community Centre
SCOTSWOOD ROAD A695
RAILWAY
Coach Park
Forth Yard
KING EDWARD BRIDGE ARCHES
Telewest Arena Newcastle
CLOSE
RIVER
High Level Bridge
Queen Elizabeth II Bridge
King Edward Bridge
King Edward Wharf
Works
Greensfield Junction
NEWCASTLE BUSINESS PK.
Forth Junc.
Hadrians Way
SKINNERBURN ROAD
New Redheugh Bridge
REDHEUGH BRIDGE RD. A189
Rabbit Banks
ARMSTRONG INDUSTRIAL PARK
Elswick
Wharf
ASKEW RD
A184
Windmill Hills
St. Cuthbert's Ct.
Fish Quay

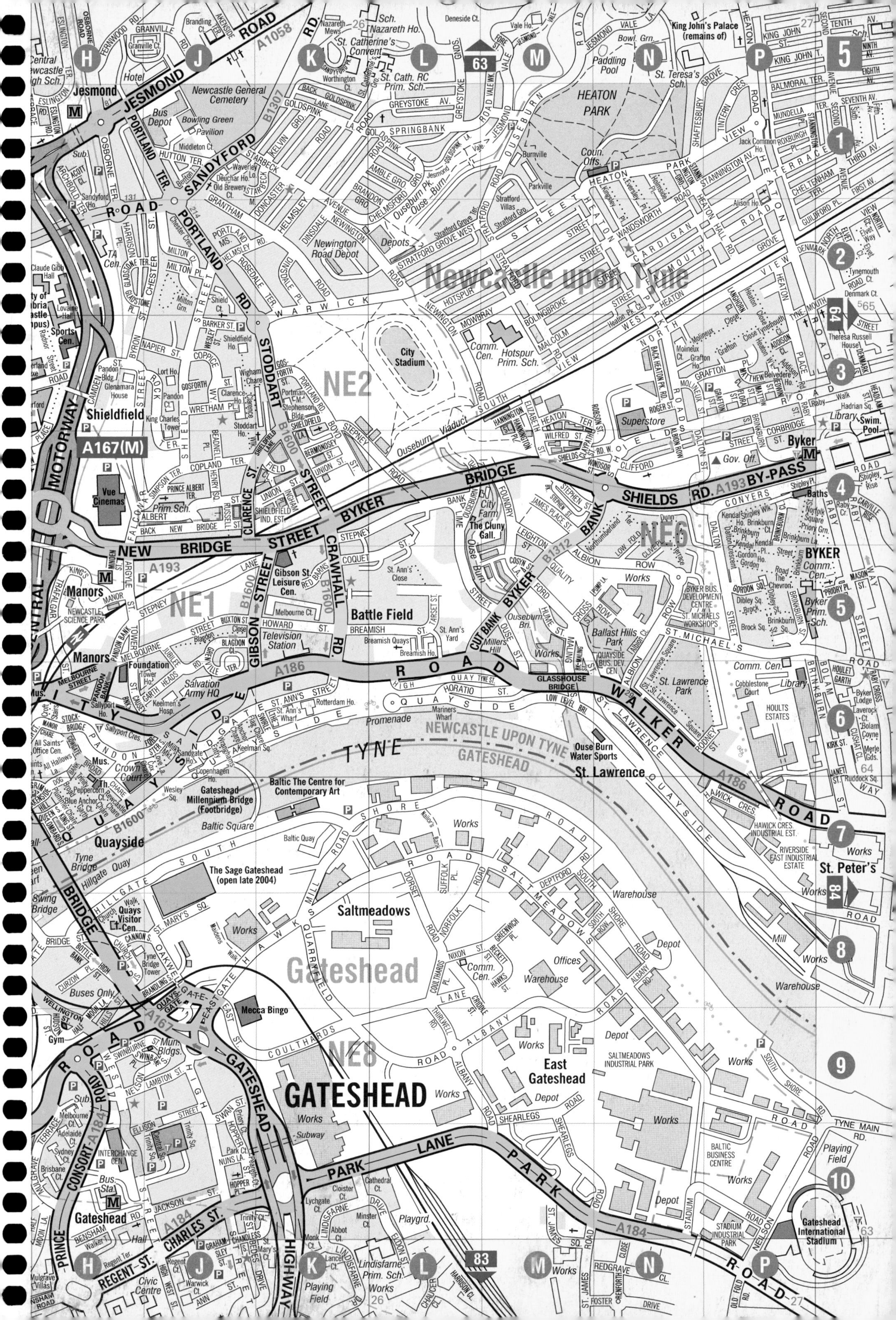
Newcastle upon Tyne
Gateshead
GATESHEAD
Jesmond
Shieldfield
Manors
Quayside
Byker
BYKER
Saltmeadows
East Gateshead
St. Lawrence
St. Peter's
NE1
NE2
NE6
NE8
TYNE
NEWCASTLE UPON TYNE
GATESHEAD
HEATON PARK
City Stadium
Newcastle General Cemetery
Vue Cinemas
Battle Field
Gibson St. Leisure Cen.
Television Station
Salvation Army HQ
The Cluny Gall.
City Farm
Ballast Hills Park
St. Lawrence Park
Superstore
Baltic The Centre for Contemporary Art
Gateshead Millennium Bridge (Footbridge)
The Sage Gateshead (open late 2004)
Mecca Bingo
Gateshead International Stadium
Ouse Burn Water Sports
King John's Palace (remains of)
Paddling Pool
Hotspur Prim. Sch.
Newington Road Depot
Ouseburn Viaduct
Byker Prim. Sch.
Saltmeadows Industrial Park
Baltic Business Centre
Stadium Industrial Park
Hawick Cres. Industrial Est.
Riverside East Industrial Estate
Hoults Estates
Quays Visitor Cen.
Civic Centre
Lindisfarne Prim. Sch.
JESMOND ROAD
SANDYFORD ROAD
PORTLAND ROAD
STODDART STREET
NEW BRIDGE STREET
BYKER BRIDGE
SHIELDS RD. BY-PASS
CITY ROAD
QUAYSIDE
WALKER ROAD
SOUTH SHORE ROAD
PARK LANE
PARK ROAD
GATESHEAD HIGHWAY
CENTRAL MOTORWAY
A167(M)
A1058
A186
A193
A184
A167
B1600
B1307
B1312
63
64
83
84
H
J
K
L
M
N
P
1
2
3
4
5
6
7
8
9
10

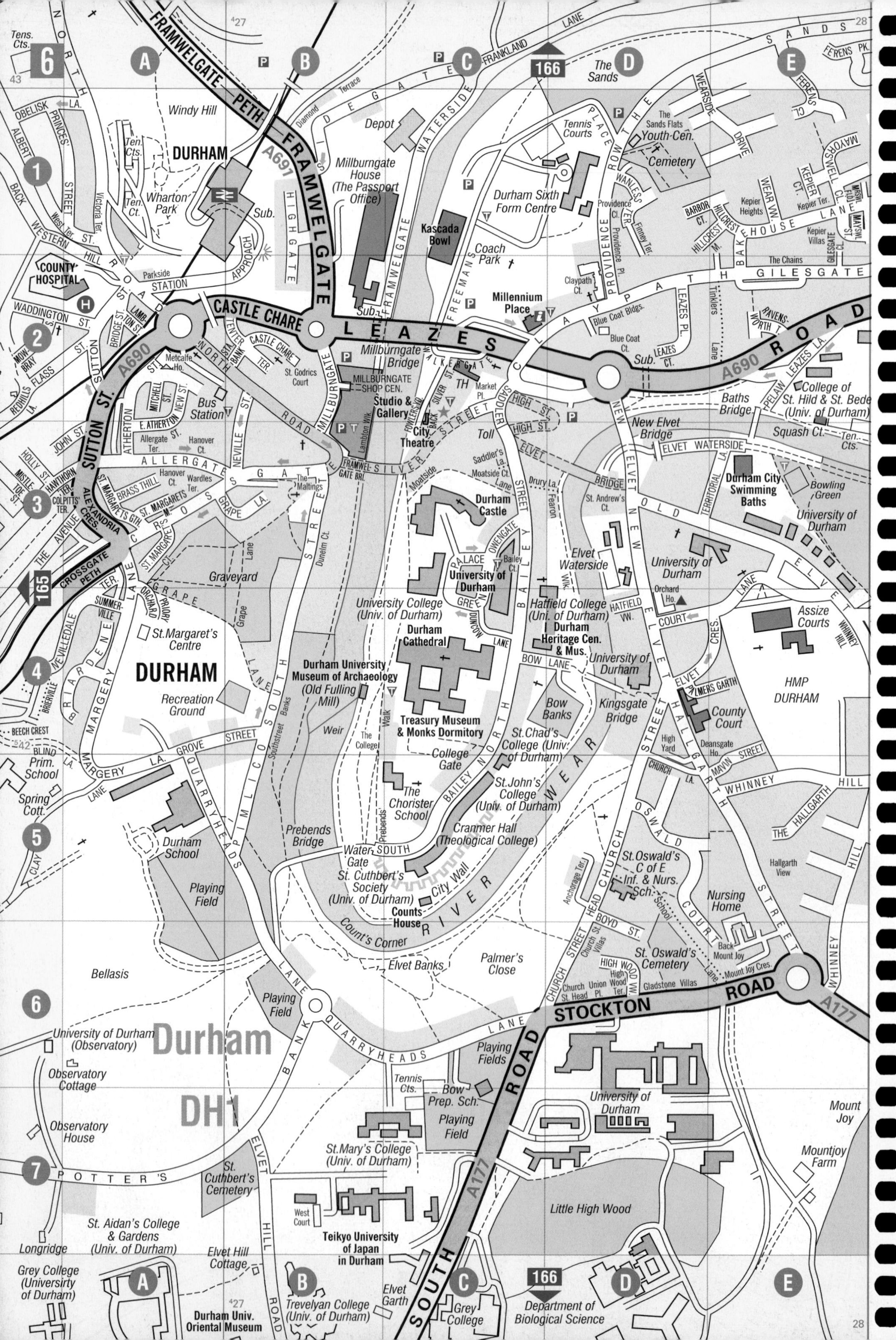
6
Durham
DH1
DURHAM
Windy Hill
Wharton Park
COUNTY HOSPITAL
CASTLE CHARE
LEAZES
CLAYPATH
FRAMWELGATE
FRAMWELGATE PETH
A691
A690
A177
LEAZES ROAD
SUTTON ST.
Millburngate House (The Passport Office)
Depot
Kascada Bowl
Coach Park
Durham Sixth Form Centre
Millennium Place
Millburngate Bridge
MILLBURNGATE SHOP CEN.
Studio & Gallery
City Theatre
Bus Station
Market Pl.
Toll
Durham Castle
University of Durham
University College (Univ. of Durham)
Durham Cathedral
Durham University Museum of Archaeology (Old Fulling Mill)
Treasury Museum & Monks Dormitory
Hatfield College (Uni. of Durham)
Durham Heritage Cen. & Mus.
Elvet Waterside
New Elvet Bridge
Durham City Swimming Baths
Bowling Green
College of St. Hild & St. Bede (Univ. of Durham)
Baths Bridge
Squash Ct.
Assize Courts
HMP DURHAM
County Court
Kingsgate Bridge
Bow Banks
St.Chad's College (Univ. of Durham)
St.John's College (Univ. of Durham)
Cranmer Hall (Theological College)
College Gate
The Chorister School
Prebends Bridge
Water Gate
St. Cuthbert's Society (Univ. of Durham)
City Wall
Counts House
Count's Corner
RIVER WEAR
Elvet Banks
Palmer's Close
St.Margaret's Centre
Graveyard
Recreation Ground
Weir
Durham School
Playing Field
Prim. School
Spring Cott.
Bellasis
University of Durham (Observatory)
Observatory Cottage
Observatory House
POTTER'S BANK
St. Cuthbert's Cemetery
St. Aidan's College & Gardens (Univ. of Durham)
Longridge
Grey College (University of Durham)
Elvet Hill Cottage
Durham Univ. Oriental Museum
Trevelyan College (Univ. of Durham)
Elvet Garth
Grey College
Teikyo University of Japan in Durham
West Court
St.Mary's College (Univ. of Durham)
Bow Prep. Sch.
Playing Fields
QUARRYHEADS LANE
STOCKTON ROAD
SOUTH ROAD
Little High Wood
Department of Biological Science
Mountjoy Farm
Mount Joy
Hallgarth View
Nursing Home
St. Oswald's Cemetery
St.Oswald's C of E Inf. & Nurs. Sch.
Gladstone Villas
The Sands
The Sands Flats
Youth Cen.
Cemetery
Tennis Courts
Kepier Heights
Kepier Villas
The Chains
GILESGATE
Providence Row
WHINNEY HILL
HALLGARTH STREET
NEW ELVET
OLD ELVET
CHURCH STREET
165
166
28

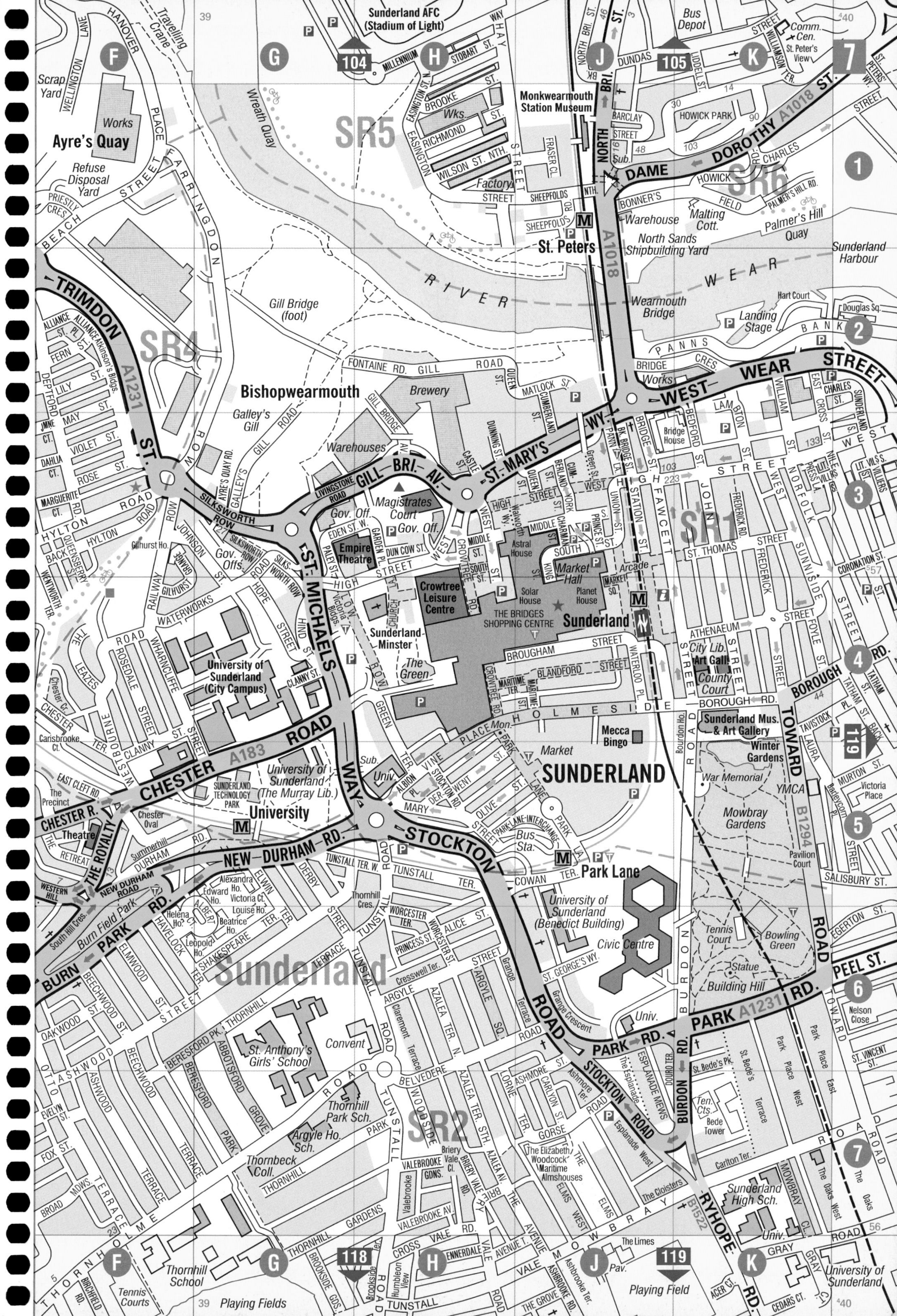

Sunderland AFC (Stadium of Light)
104
105
Bus Depot
Comm. Cen.
St. Peter's View
7
F
G
H
J
K
Travelling Crane
Scrap Yard
Works
Ayre's Quay
Refuse Disposal Yard
Wreath Quay
SR5
Monkwearmouth Station Museum
Wks.
Factory
HOWICK PARK
DAME DOROTHY ST.
A1018
SR6
Warehouse
Malting Cott.
Palmer's Hill Quay
North Sands Shipbuilding Yard
St. Peters
Sunderland Harbour
RIVER WEAR
Gill Bridge (foot)
Wearmouth Bridge
Hart Court
Douglas Sq.
Landing Stage
1
2
3
4
5
6
7
TRIMDON
A1231
SR4
Bishopwearmouth
Galley's Gill
Brewery
Warehouses
Magistrates Court
Gov. Off.
Empire Theatre
WEST WEAR STREET
Bridge House
SR1
Astral House
Market Hall
Crowtree Leisure Centre
Solar House
Planet House
THE BRIDGES SHOPPING CENTRE
Sunderland
Sunderland Minster
The Green
City Lib. Art Gall.
County Court
University of Sunderland (City Campus)
Sunderland Mus. & Art Gallery
Winter Gardens
Mecca Bingo
SUNDERLAND
Market
119
War Memorial
YMCA
Mowbray Gardens
CHESTER ROAD
A183
University of Sunderland (The Murray Lib.)
SUNDERLAND TECHNOLOGY PARK
University
Chester Oval
Theatre
ST. MICHAELS WAY
STOCKTON ROAD
NEW DURHAM RD.
Bus Sta.
Park Lane
Pavilion Court
University of Sunderland (Benedict Building)
Civic Centre
Tennis Court
Bowling Green
Statue
Building Hill
BURN PARK RD.
Burn Field Park
Sunderland
St. Anthony's Girls' School
Convent
PARK RD.
PARK A1231 RD.
B1294
TOWARD ROAD
PEEL ST.
Nelson Close
Thornhill Park Sch.
SR2
Argyle Ho. Sch.
Thornbeck Coll.
The Elizabeth Woodcock Maritime Almshouses
Bede Tower
Sunderland High Sch.
Univ.
The Cloisters
B1522
RYHOPE RD.
118
Thornhill School
Tennis Courts
Playing Fields
Playing Field
The Limes
Pav.
University of Sunderland
39
40
56
57

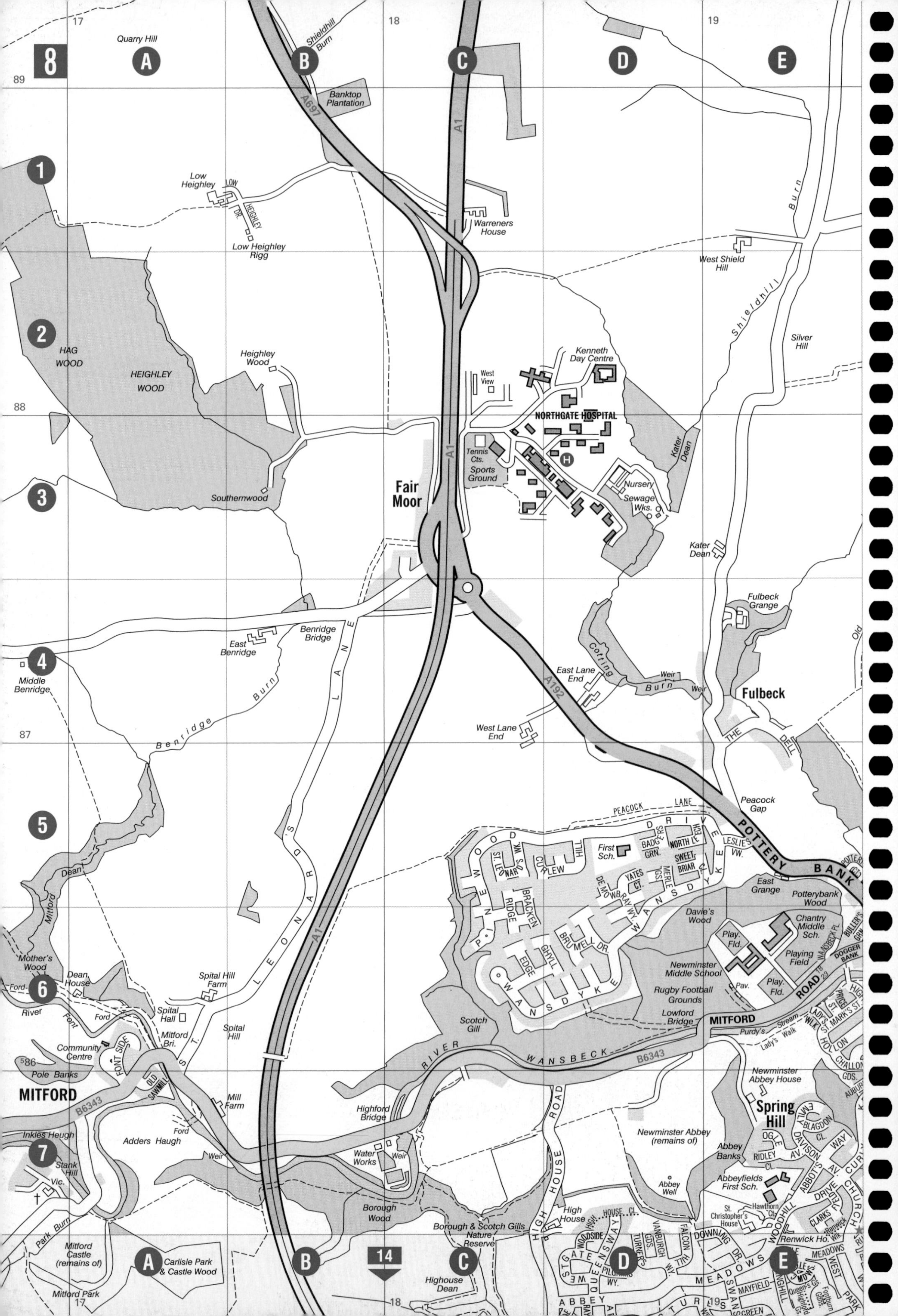
8
Quarry Hill
Shieldhill Burn
Banktop Plantation
A697
A1
Low Heighley
Heighley Dr.
Warreners House
Low Heighley Rigg
West Shield Hill
HAG WOOD
HEIGHLEY WOOD
Heighley Wood
Kenneth Day Centre
West View
NORTHGATE HOSPITAL
Silver Hill
Shieldhill
Burn
Tennis Cts.
Sports Ground
Kater Dean
Fair Moor
Nursery
Sewage Wks.
Southernwood
Kater Dean
Fulbeck Grange
East Benridge
Benridge Bridge
Middle Benridge
Cotting Burn
East Lane End
Weir
Fulbeck
A192
Benridge Burn
West Lane End
The Dell
Leonard's Lane
Peacock Gap
Peacock Lane
Pottery Bank
Pinewood Drive
First Sch.
North Ridge
Leslies Vw.
Curlew Hill
Badg. Grn.
Sweet Briar
Yates Ct.
Merle Gs.
Wansdyke
East Grange
Potterybank Wood
Bracken Ridge
Mitford Dean
Davie's Wood
Chantry Middle Sch.
Play. Fld.
Playing Field
Brumell Dr.
Ghyll Edge
Mother's Wood
Dean House
Newminster Middle School
Spital Hill Farm
Rugby Football Grounds
Play. Fld.
Pav.
Ford
River Font
Spital Hall
Mitford Bri.
Lowford Bridge
Mitford Road
Scotch Gill
Purdy's Stream
Lady's Walk
Community Centre
Spital Hill
River Wansbeck
B6343
Pole Banks
Font Side
Newminster Abbey House
MITFORD
Old Sawmill
Mill Farm
Highford Bridge
High House Road
Spring Hill
B6343
Inkles Heugh
Ford
Adders Haugh
Newminster Abbey (remains of)
Blagdon Cl.
Stank Hill
Vic.
Weir
Water Works
Weir
Abbey Banks
Ogle
Ridley Av.
Davison Av.
Abbey Well
Abbeyfields First Sch.
Abbot's Way
Park Burn
Borough Wood
High House
St. Christopher's House
Hawthorn Ct.
Woodhill Drive
Church
Mitford Castle (remains of)
Borough & Scotch Gills Nature Reserve
High House Cl.
Woodside
Queensway
Turner's
Vanburgh Wy.
Falcon Hill
Downing Dr.
Clarks
Renwick Ho.
Carlisle Park & Castle Wood
14
Highouse Dean
Westgate
Pilgrims Wy.
Meadows
Mayfield
Swans
Abbey
Mitford Park
Queen's Gs.
Fontburn Gdns.
West Park
A B C D E
1 2 3 4 5 6 7
17 18 19
86 87 88 89

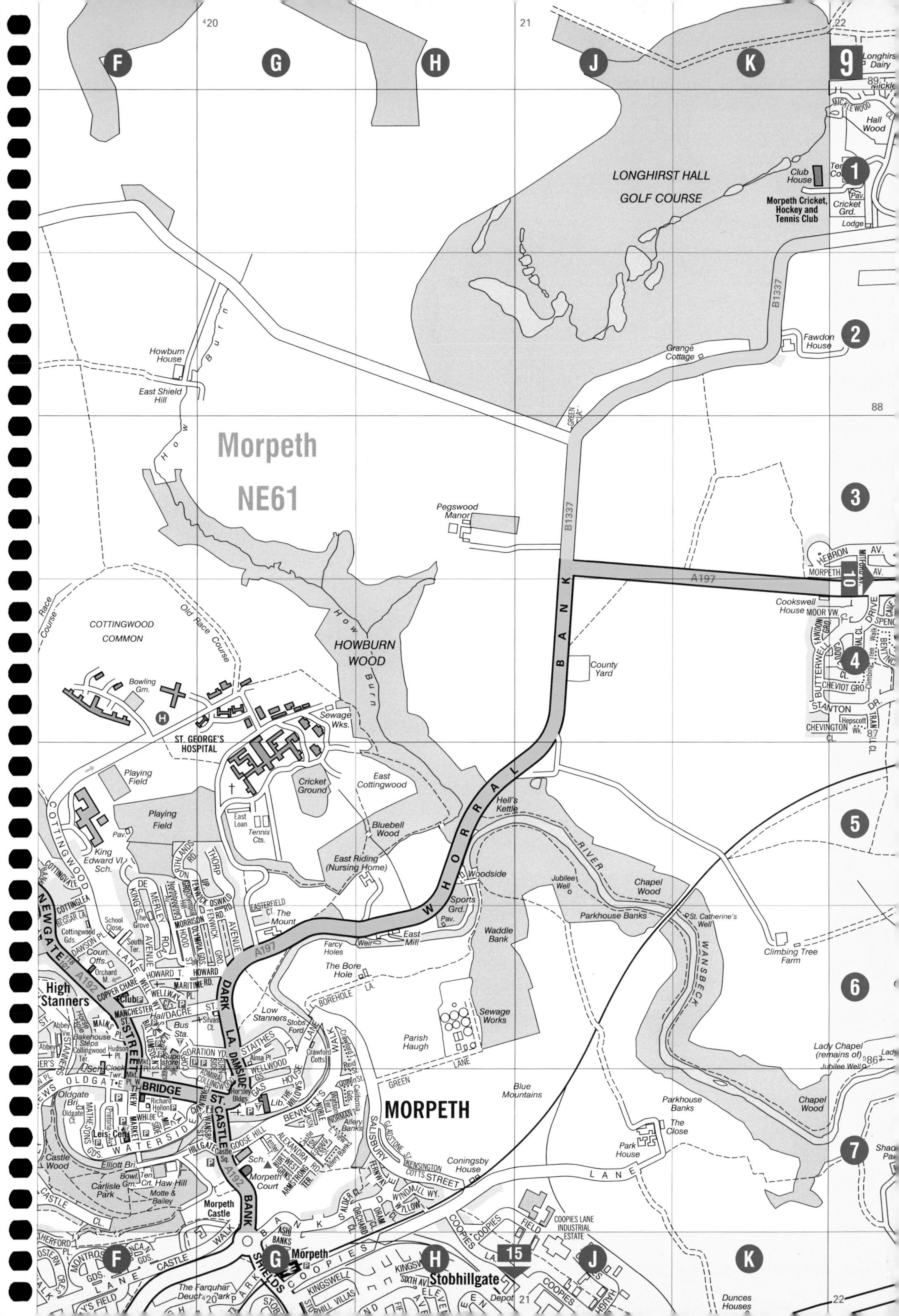
9
F
G
H
J
K
420
21
22
89
88
87
86
Longhirst Dairy
Hall Wood
LONGHIRST HALL
GOLF COURSE
Club House
Morpeth Cricket, Hockey and Tennis Club
Cricket Grd.
Pav.
Lodge
B1337
Fawdon House
Grange Cottage
Howburn House
East Shield Hill
How Burn
Morpeth
NE61
Pegswood Manor
GREEN LA.
HEBRON AV.
MORPETH AV.
A197
10
Cookswell House
MOOR VW.
BUTTERWELL
CHEVIOT GRO.
STANTON DR.
CHEVINGTON CL.
Hepscott Wk.
Race Course
COTTINGWOOD COMMON
Old Race Course
HOWBURN WOOD
County Yard
Bowling Grn.
Sewage Wks.
ST. GEORGE'S HOSPITAL
Playing Field
Cricket Ground
East Cottingwood
WHORRAL BANK
Hell's Kettle
Tennis Cts.
East Loan
Bluebell Wood
East Riding (Nursing Home)
King Edward VI Sch.
COTTINGWOOD
Woodside
Jubilee Well
RIVER WANSBECK
Chapel Wood
Sports Grd.
Parkhouse Banks
St. Catherine's Well
Waddle Bank
Climbing Tree Farm
EASTERFIELD CT.
The Mount
East Mill
Farcy Holes
Weir
NEWGATE
A192
High Stanners
COPPER CHARE
HOWARD T.
MARITIME RD.
WELLWAY
DACRE
The Bore Hole
BOREHOLE LA.
Sewage Works
Low Stanners
Stobs Ford
Bus Sta.
DARK LA.
DAMSIDE
STAITHES LA.
WELLWOOD GDS.
Parish Haugh
BRIDGE ST.
OLDGATE
Lib.
GREEN LANE
Blue Mountains
Lady Chapel (remains of)
Jubilee Well
Chapel Wood
Parkhouse Banks
The Close
MORPETH
WATERSIDE
Leis. Cen.
CASTLE SQ.
GOOSE HILL
Sch.
Morpeth Court
Castle Wood
Elliott Bri.
Carlisle Park
Haw Hill
Motte & Bailey
CASTLE BANK
Morpeth Castle
SALISBURY ST.
GLADSTONE ST.
KENSINGTON COTTS.
Coningsby House
Park House
LANE
COOPIES LANE INDUSTRIAL ESTATE
15
COOPIES
Morpeth
Stobhillgate
CASTLE WALK
BANK
SHIELDS
KINGSWELL
Depot
Dunces Houses
Shaw Park
1
2
3
4
5
6
7

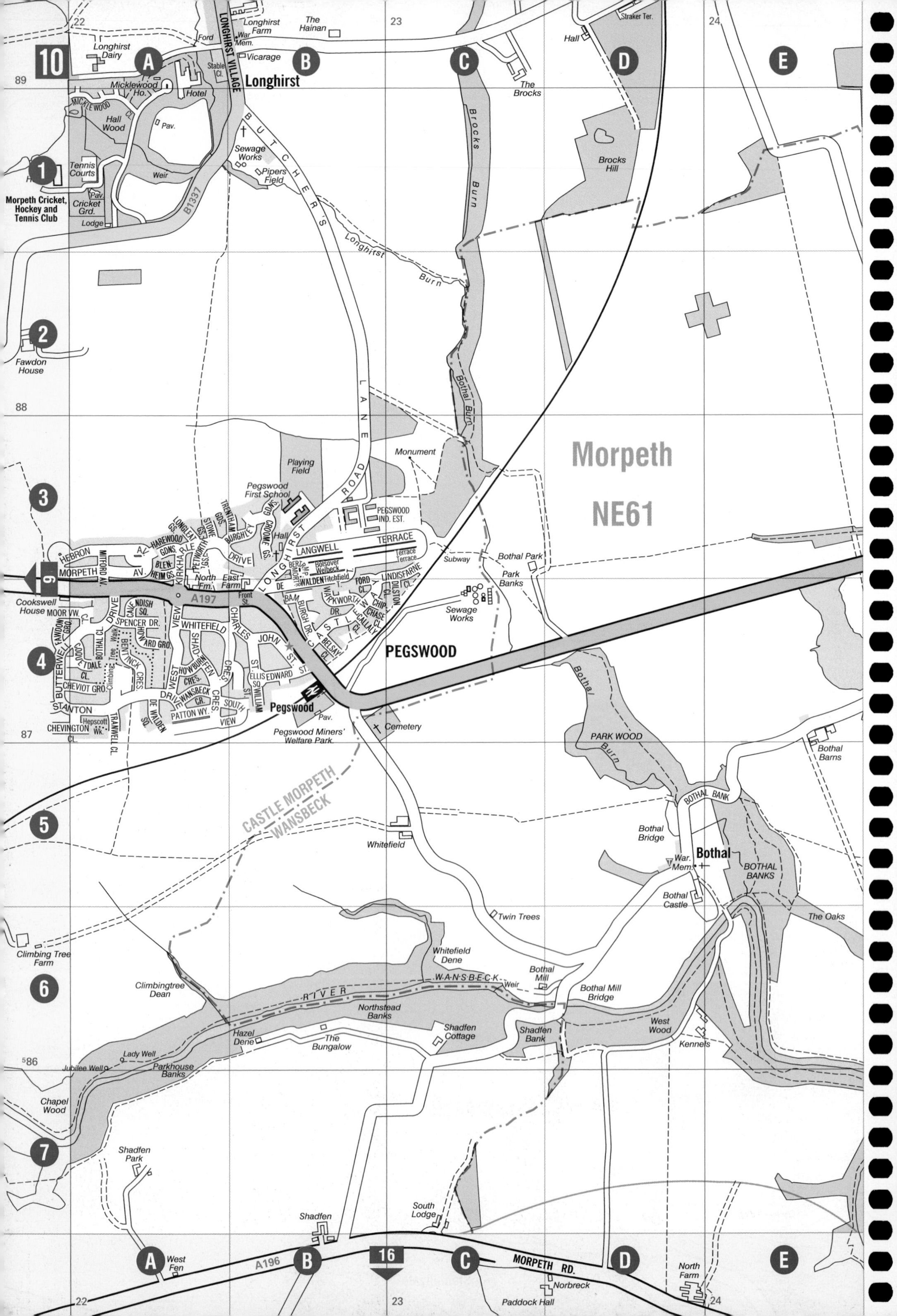
10
Longhirst
Longhirst Farm
The Hainan
Longhirst Dairy
Longhirst Village
War Mem.
Vicarage
Stable Cl.
Ford
Micklewood Ho.
Hotel
Micklewood Cl.
Hall Wood
Pav.
Tennis Courts
Weir
Sewage Works
Pipers Field
Butcher's Lane
Longhirst Road
B1337
Morpeth Cricket, Hockey and Tennis Club
Cricket Grd.
Lodge
Fawdon House
The Brocks
Brocks Burn
Brocks Hill
Hall
Straker Ter.
Longhirst Burn
Bothal Burn
Monument
Playing Field
Pegswood First School
Pegswood Ind. Est.
Langwell Terrace
Morpeth
NE61
Subway
Bothal Park
Park Banks
Sewage Works
PEGSWOOD
Pegswood
Pegswood Miners' Welfare Park
Cemetery
A197
Hebron
Mitford Av.
Morpeth Av.
Cookswell House
Moor Vw.
Whitefield
Charles St.
John St.
Edward St.
William St.
Ellis Sq.
Castle Morpeth
Wansbeck
Whitefield
Park Wood
Bothal Bank
Bothal Barns
Bothal Bridge
Bothal
War. Mem.
Bothal Banks
Bothal Castle
The Oaks
Twin Trees
Whitefield Dene
Bothal Mill
Weir
River Wansbeck
Bothal Mill Bridge
Climbing Tree Farm
Climbingtree Dean
Northstead Banks
Hazel Dene
The Bungalow
Shadfen Cottage
Shadfen Bank
West Wood
Kennels
Lady Well
Jubilee Well
Parkhouse Banks
Chapel Wood
Shadfen Park
Shadfen
South Lodge
West Fen
A196
Morpeth Rd.
16
North Farm
Norbreck
Paddock Hall
Stanton
Chevington Cl.
Tranwell Cl.
Patton Wy.
South View
De Walden Sq.
Wansbeck Cr.
Cheviot Gro.
Howburn Cres.
Bentinck Cres.
Spencer Dr.
Cavendish Sq.
Bothal Cl.
Butterwell
A B C D E
1 2 3 4 5 6 7
22 23 24
89 88 87 86
9

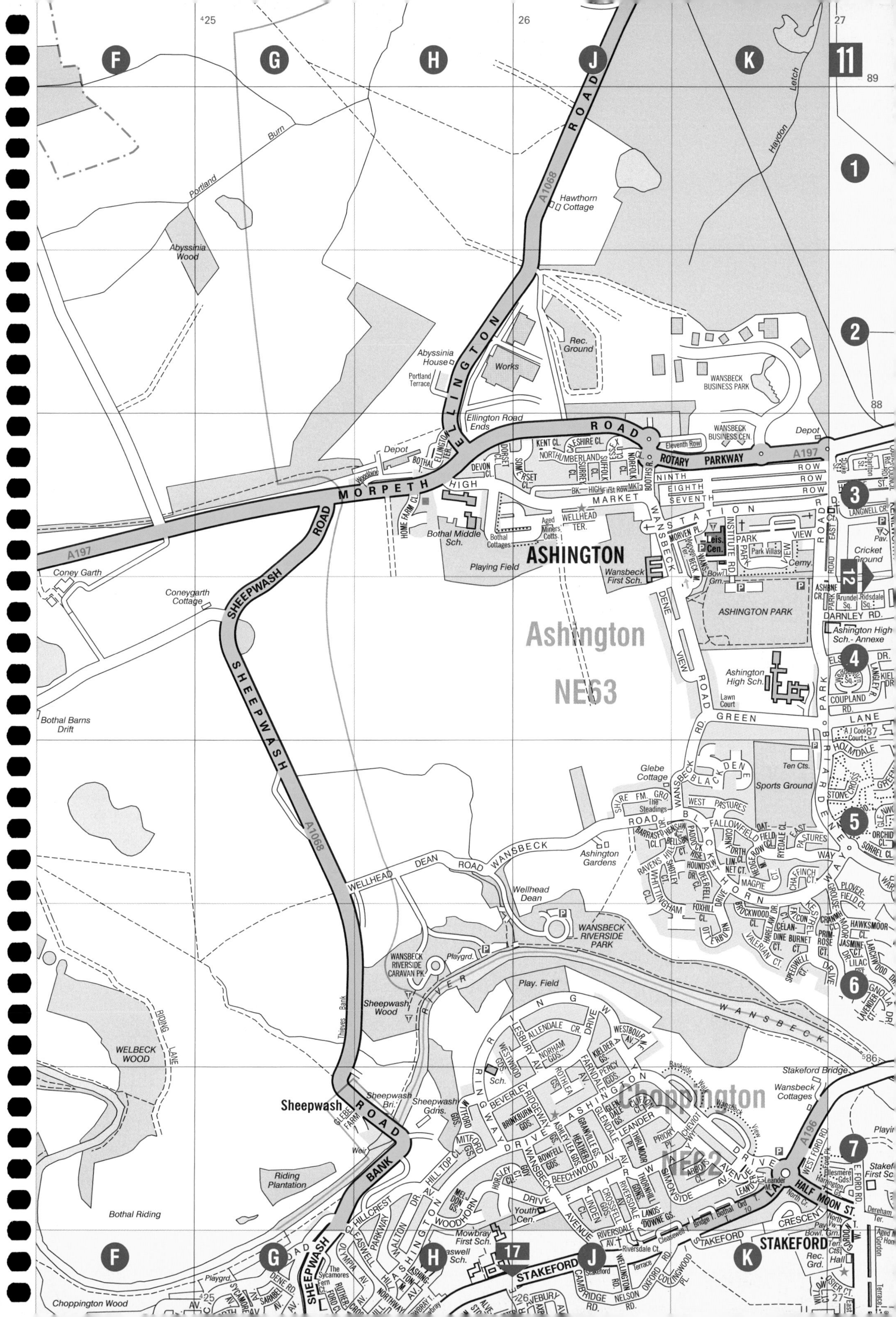

F
G
H
J
K
Abyssinia Wood
Hawthorn Cottage
Rec. Ground
Works
WANSBECK BUSINESS PARK
WANSBECK BUSINESS CEN.
ROTARY PARKWAY
A197
MORPETH ROAD
ELLINGTON ROAD
A1068
SHEEPWASH ROAD
ASHINGTON
Ashington
NE63
Bothal Middle Sch.
Playing Field
Wansbeck First Sch.
ASHINGTON PARK
Ashington High Sch.
Ashington High Sch.- Annexe
Cricket Ground
Sports Ground
Coney Garth
Coneygarth Cottage
Bothal Barns Drift
Glebe Cottage
WANSBECK RIVERSIDE PARK
WANSBECK RIVERSIDE CARAVAN PK.
Sheepwash Wood
Wellhead Dean
Ashington Gardens
RIVER WANSBECK
WELBECK WOOD
Sheepwash
Riding Plantation
Bothal Riding
Choppington Wood
Choppington
NE62
Stakeford Bridge
Wansbeck Cottages
STAKEFORD
Mowbray First Sch.
Youth Cen.
A196
HALF MOON ST.

12
17

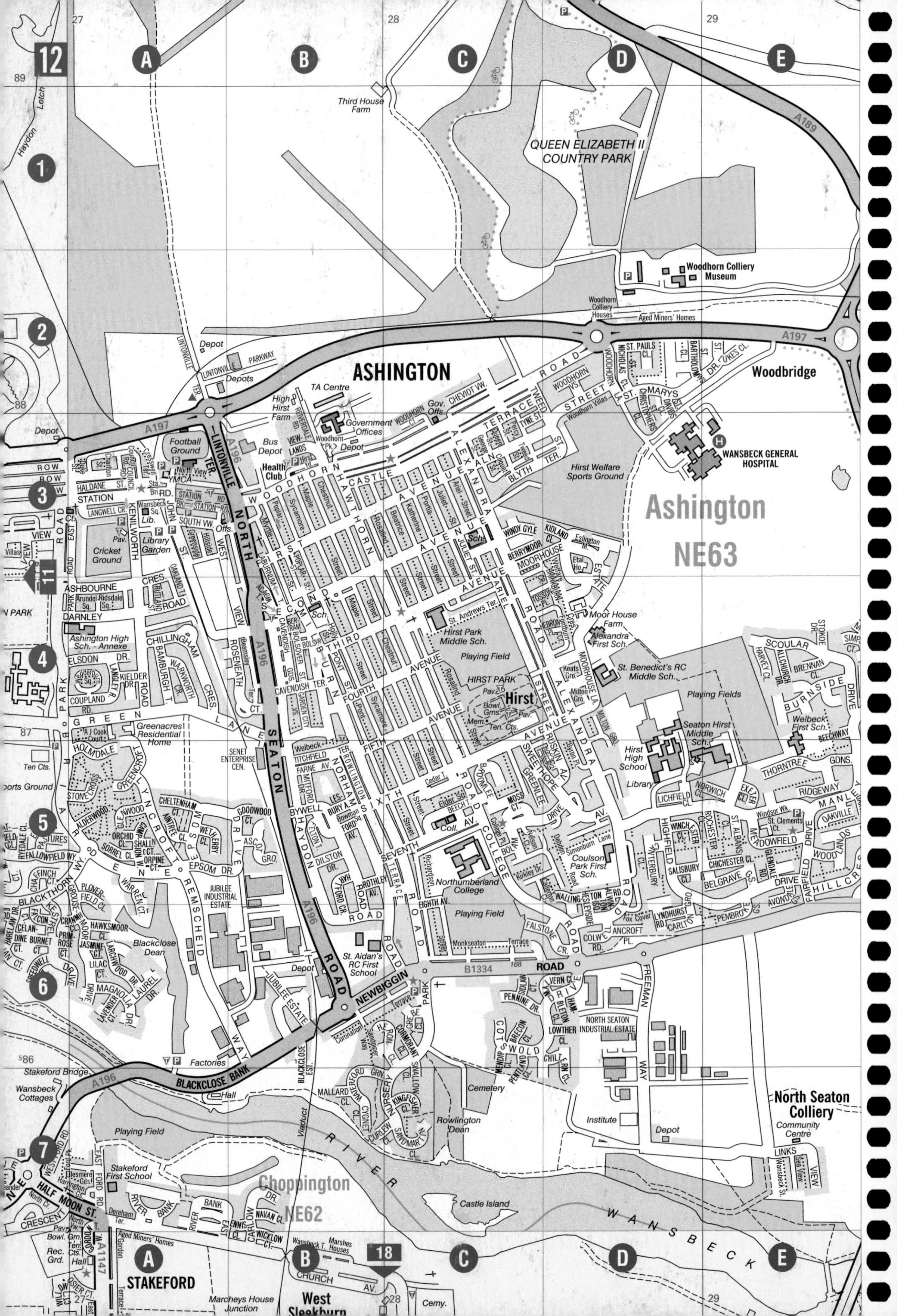
ASHINGTON
Ashington
NE63
QUEEN ELIZABETH II
COUNTRY PARK
Woodhorn Colliery
Museum
WANSBECK GENERAL
HOSPITAL
Woodbridge
Hirst Welfare
Sports Ground
Hirst Park
Middle Sch.
Playing Field
HIRST PARK
Hirst
Northumberland
College
North Seaton
Colliery
Choppington
NE62
STAKEFORD
West
Sleekburn
RIVER
WANSBECK
Castle Island
Rowlington
Dean
Cemetery
Blackclose
Dean
JUBILEE
INDUSTRIAL
ESTATE
NORTH SEATON
INDUSTRIAL ESTATE
St. Benedict's RC
Middle Sch.
Seaton Hirst
Middle
Sch.
Hirst
High
School
Playing Fields
Alexandra
First Sch.
Moor House
Farm
Coulson
Park First
Sch.
St. Aidan's
RC First
School
Stakeford
First School
Ashington High
Sch. - Annexe
Greenacres
Residential
Home
Football
Ground
Cricket
Ground
Library
Garden
Government
Offices
TA Centre
Third House
Farm
A197
A196
A189
A1147
B1334
NEWBIGGIN ROAD
SEATON ROAD
NORTH SEATON ROAD
LINTONVILLE TER.
BLACKCLOSE BANK
HALF MOON ST.
Stakeford Bridge
Wansbeck
Cottages
Playing Field
Institute
Depot
Community
Centre
Marcheys House
Junction
Cemy.
11
18
27
28
29
89
88
87
86

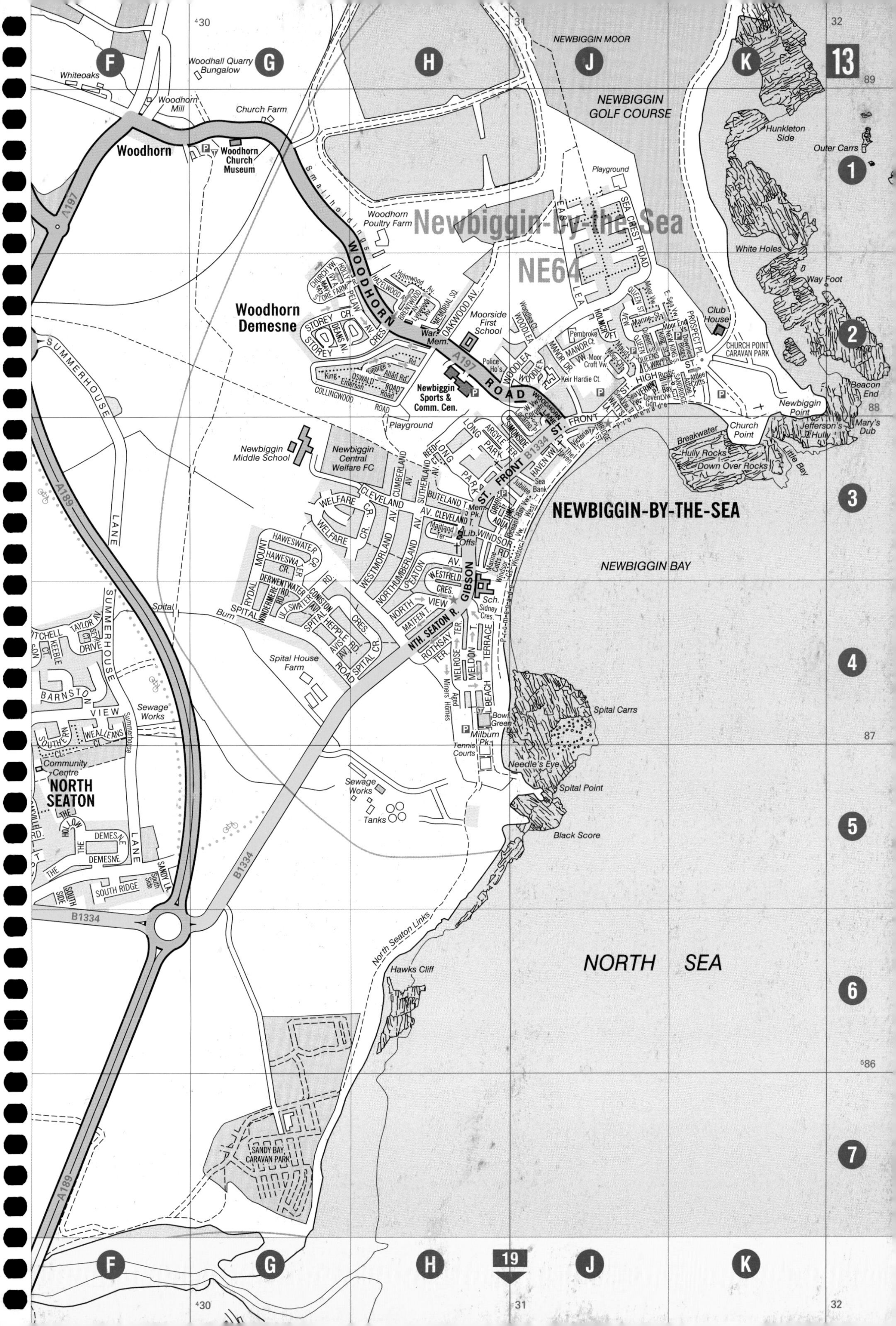

Newbiggin-by-the-Sea
NE64
NEWBIGGIN-BY-THE-SEA
NEWBIGGIN BAY
NORTH SEA
NEWBIGGIN MOOR
NEWBIGGIN GOLF COURSE
Woodhorn
Woodhorn Church Museum
Woodhorn Mill
Woodhall Quarry Bungalow
Whiteoaks
Church Farm
Woodhorn Poultry Farm
Woodhorn Demesne
WOODHORN ROAD
Moorside First School
War Mem.
Police Ho's.
Newbiggin Sports & Comm. Cen.
Playground
Newbiggin Middle School
Newbiggin Central Welfare FC
Club House
CHURCH POINT CARAVAN PARK
Church Point
Newbiggin Point
Breakwater
Hully Rocks
Down Over Rocks
Jefferson's Hully
Mary's Dub
Little Bay
Beacon End
Way Foot
White Holes
Hunkleton Side
Outer Carrs
Spital Carrs
Needle's Eye
Spital Point
Black Score
Hawks Cliff
North Seaton Links
Spital House Farm
Sewage Works
Tanks
Bowl. Green
Milburn Pk.
Tennis Courts
Aged Miners' Homes
NORTH SEATON
Community Centre
SANDY BAY CARAVAN PARK
SUMMERHOUSE LANE
NTH. SEATON R.
GIBSON ST.
FRONT ST.
A197
A189
B1334
Spital Burn

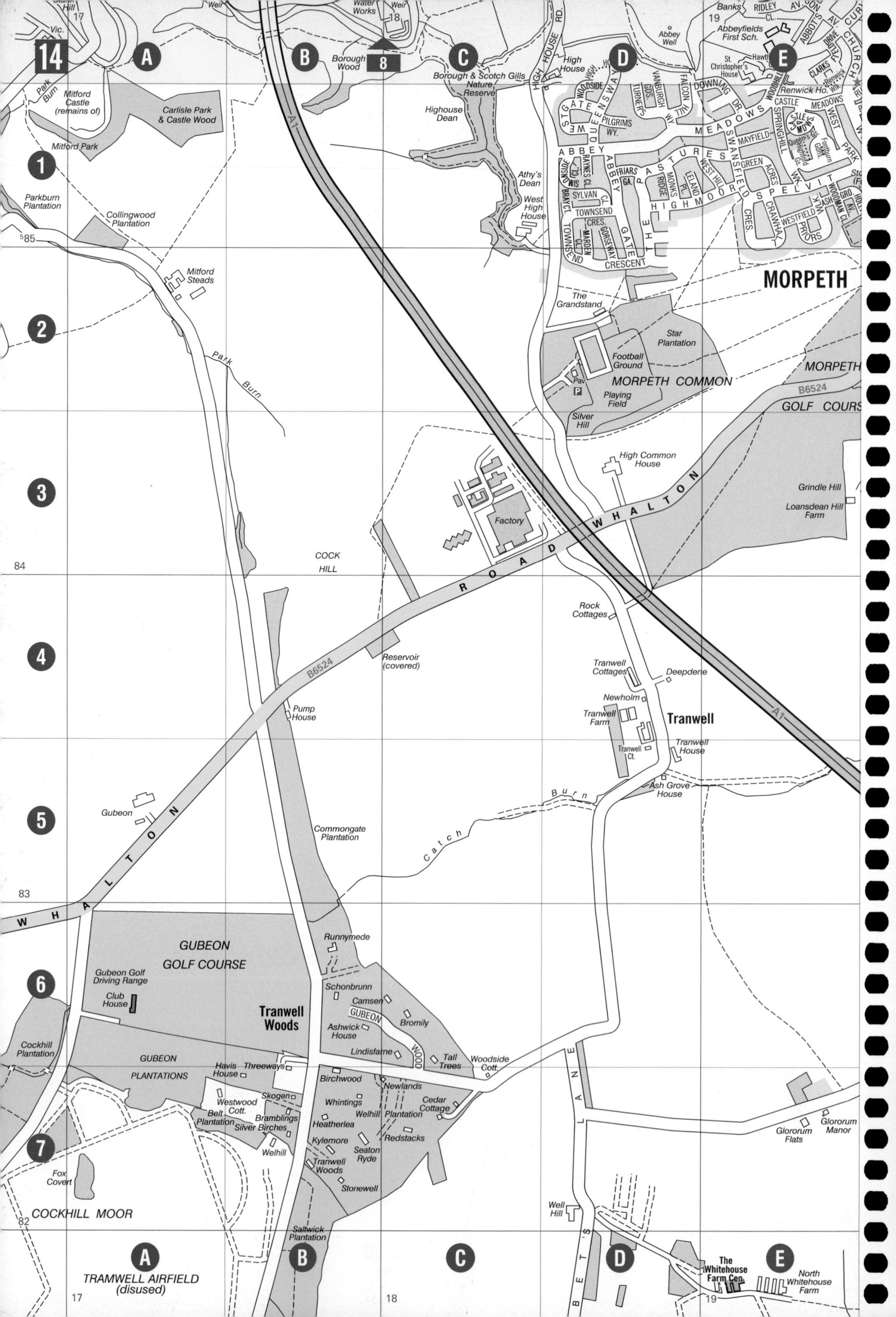

14

A B Borough Wood 8 C Borough & Scotch Gills Nature Reserve D E

Weir Water Works Weir 18

Park Burn Vic. Hill 17

Mitford Castle (remains of) Carlisle Park & Castle Wood

Mitford Park

1

Parkburn Plantation Collingwood Plantation

585

Mitford Steads

2

Park Burn

High House Rd. High House Abbey Well Banks 19 Abbeyfields First Sch. RIDLEY AV. CHURCH ABBOTT'S DRIVE CLARKS CASTLE MEADOWS WEST PARK

St. Christopher's House Renwick Ho. Hawth

WOODSIDE VANBURGH FALCON DOWNING SILES MON Queen's Gt. Penbury Cont.

WEST GATE QUEENS ABBEY RAYNES CL. GODS PILGRIMS WY. TURNER'S MAYFIELD SPRINGHILL THIRLMERE WOODMAN CL. STO

Highhouse Dean Athy's Dean West High House ABBEY GATE SYLVAN TOWNSEND WIS CRES. MARDEN FRIARS GA. MONKS RIDGE LELAND WEST HILL GREEN ACRES CRAWHALL ASH GRO.

HIGHMOOR TOWNSEND GORSEMN. PASTURES MEADOWS SPELVIT WESTFIELD PRIORS WEST

MARDEN CRESCENT P HIGHMOOR ABBEY GATE SWANSFIELD CRES.

MORPETH

The Grandstand Football Ground Star Plantation MORPETH

2

3

COCK HILL Factory High Common House Grindle Hill Loansdean Hill Farm

84 Pav P Playing Field Silver Hill MORPETH COMMON B6524 GOLF COURS

ROAD WHALTON

3

Rock Cottages

4

B6524 Reservoir (covered) Tranwell Cottages Deepdene A1

Pump House Newholm Tranwell Farm **Tranwell** Tranwell House

Tranwell Ct.

WHALTON Gubeon Commongate Plantation Catch Burn Ash Grove House

5

83

6

GUBEON GOLF COURSE Runnymede

Gubeon Golf Driving Range Club House Schonbrunn Camsen GUBEON Bromily

Tranwell Woods Ashwick House Lindisfarne WOOD Tall Trees Woodside Cott.

GUBEON PLANTATIONS Havis House Threeways Birchwood Newlands LANE

Cockhill Plantation Westwood Cott. Skogen Whitings Welhill Cedar Cottage Plantation Redstacks Glororum Flats Glororum Manor

7

Belt Plantation Silver Birches Bramblings Heatherlea Kylemore Seaton Ryde

Fox Covert Welhill Tranwell Woods Stonewell Well Hill

82 **COCKHILL MOOR**

A **TRAMWELL AIRFIELD** (disused) 17 B Saltwick Plantation 18 C D BEET'S LANE E **The Whitehouse Farm Cen.** North Whitehouse Farm 19

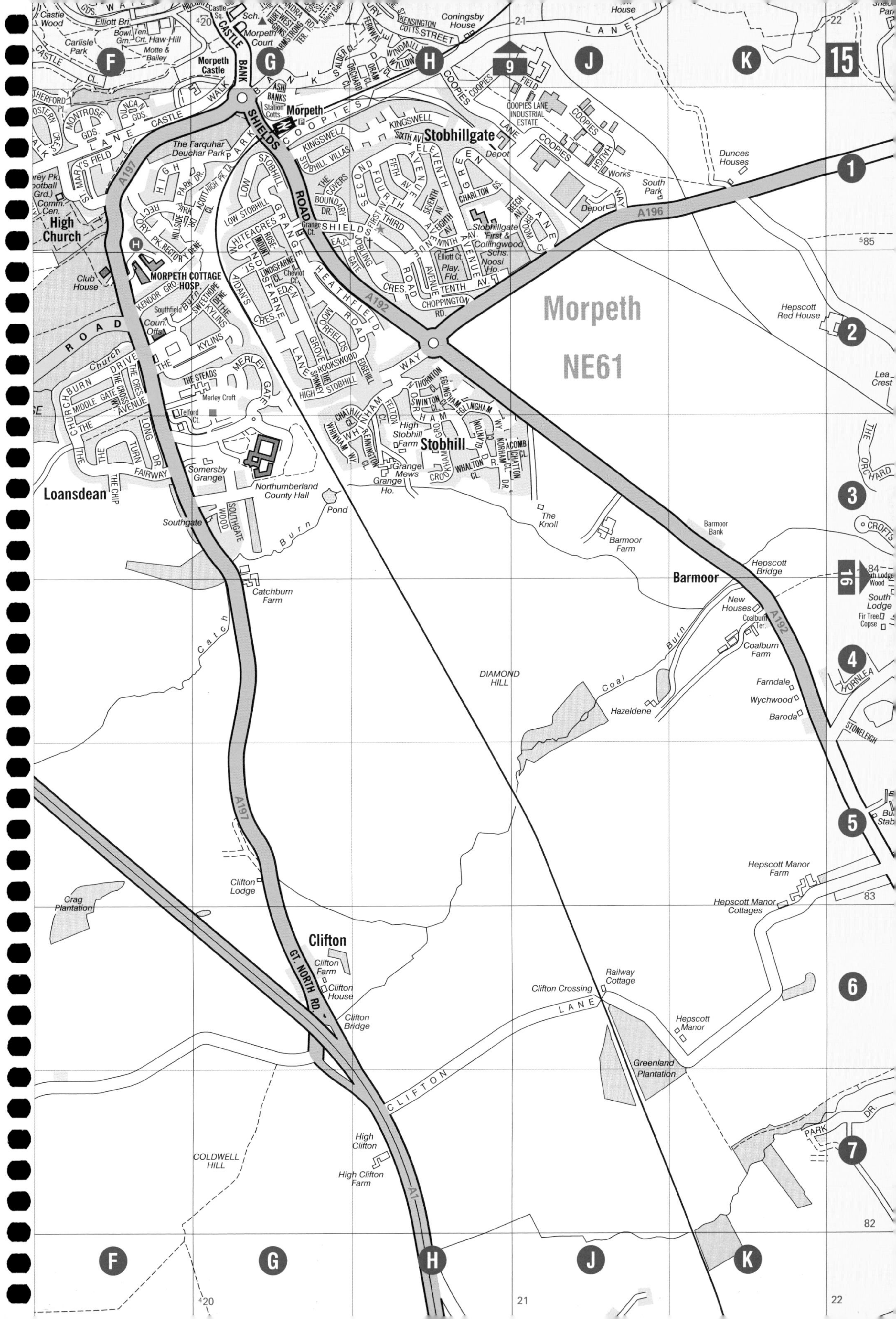
15
F
G
H
J
K
9
16
1
2
3
4
5
6
7
20
21
22
585
84
83
82
Castle Wood
Elliott Bri.
Bowl. Ten. Grn.
Crt. Haw Hill
Motte & Bailey
Carlisle Park
Castle Cl.
Morpeth Castle
Castle Bank
Castle Sq.
Sch.
Morpeth Court
Burt Ter.
West Grns.
Armstrong Rd.
Alder Cl.
Orchard Cl.
Oram Cl.
Windmill Willow
Fernway
Coningsby House
Kensington Cotts.
Street
Lane
House
Ash Banks
Station Cotts.
Morpeth
Coopies
Coopies Field
Coopies Lane Industrial Estate
Coopies Haugh
Works
Dunces Houses
South Park
Kingswell
Sixth Av.
Stobhillgate
Depot
Charlton Gs.
Beech Av.
Broom Lane
A196
Montrose Gds.
Duncan Gds.
Castle
Walk
Lane
St. Mary's Field
The Farquhar Deuchar Park
Park
Shields Road
A197
High Park Dr.
Acott High Pk. Ter.
Comm. Cen.
High Church
Hillside
Rectory Pk.
Rectory Dene
Low Stobhill
Stobhill Villas
The Covers
Boundary Dr.
Second
Fourth
Fifth Av.
Eleventh Avenue
Seventh Av.
Eighth Av.
Ninth Av.
Third
Green
First Av.
Stobhillgate First & Collingwood Schs.
Noosi Ho.
Elliott Ct.
Play. Fld.
Tenth
Choppington Rd.
Whiteacres
Mount Rose
Grange
Grange Ct.
Shields
Jobling
Gate
Cres.
Road
Avenue
Lindisfarne Cl.
Cheviot Cl.
Eden
St. Aidan's
Heathfield Road
A192
Club House
Morpeth Cottage Hosp.
Kendor Gro.
Burn
Southfield
Sweethope Dene
The Kylins
Coun. Offs.
Road
Church
Drive
Churchburn
The Cres.
The Cross
Middle Gate Wy.
Avenue
The Steads
Merley Gate
Merley Croft
Telford Ct.
Long Dr.
The Turn
Fairway
The Chip
Loansdean
Morrfields
Grove
The Spinney
Lane
Rookswood
High Stobhill
Edgehill
Way
Thornton Cl.
Eglingham
Swinton Cl.
Whinham
Chathill Cl.
Felton Cl.
Rennington Cl.
High Stobhill Farm
Stobhill
Crookham Gro.
Glanton Cl.
Norham Cl.
Acomb Cl.
Chatton Cl.
Whalton Cl.
Dr.
Grange Mews
Grange Ho.
Somersby Grange
Northumberland County Hall
Southgate Wood
Southgate
Pond
Burn
Morpeth
NE61
Hepscott Red House
Lea Crest
The Orchard
Crofts
The Knoll
Barmoor Farm
Barmoor Bank
Barmoor
Hepscott Bridge
South Lodge Wood
South Lodge
Fir Tree Copse
New Houses
Coalburn Ter.
Coalburn Farm
Catchburn Farm
Catch
Burn
Coal
Diamond Hill
Hazeldene
Farndale
Wychwood
Baroda
Hornlea
Stoneleigh
Hepscott Manor Farm
Hepscott Manor Cottages
Clifton Lodge
Crag Plantation
Clifton
Clifton Farm
Clifton House
Gt. North Rd.
Clifton Bridge
Clifton Crossing
Railway Cottage
Lane
Hepscott Manor
Greenland Plantation
Clifton
High Clifton
High Clifton Farm
A1
Coldwell Hill
Park
Dr.

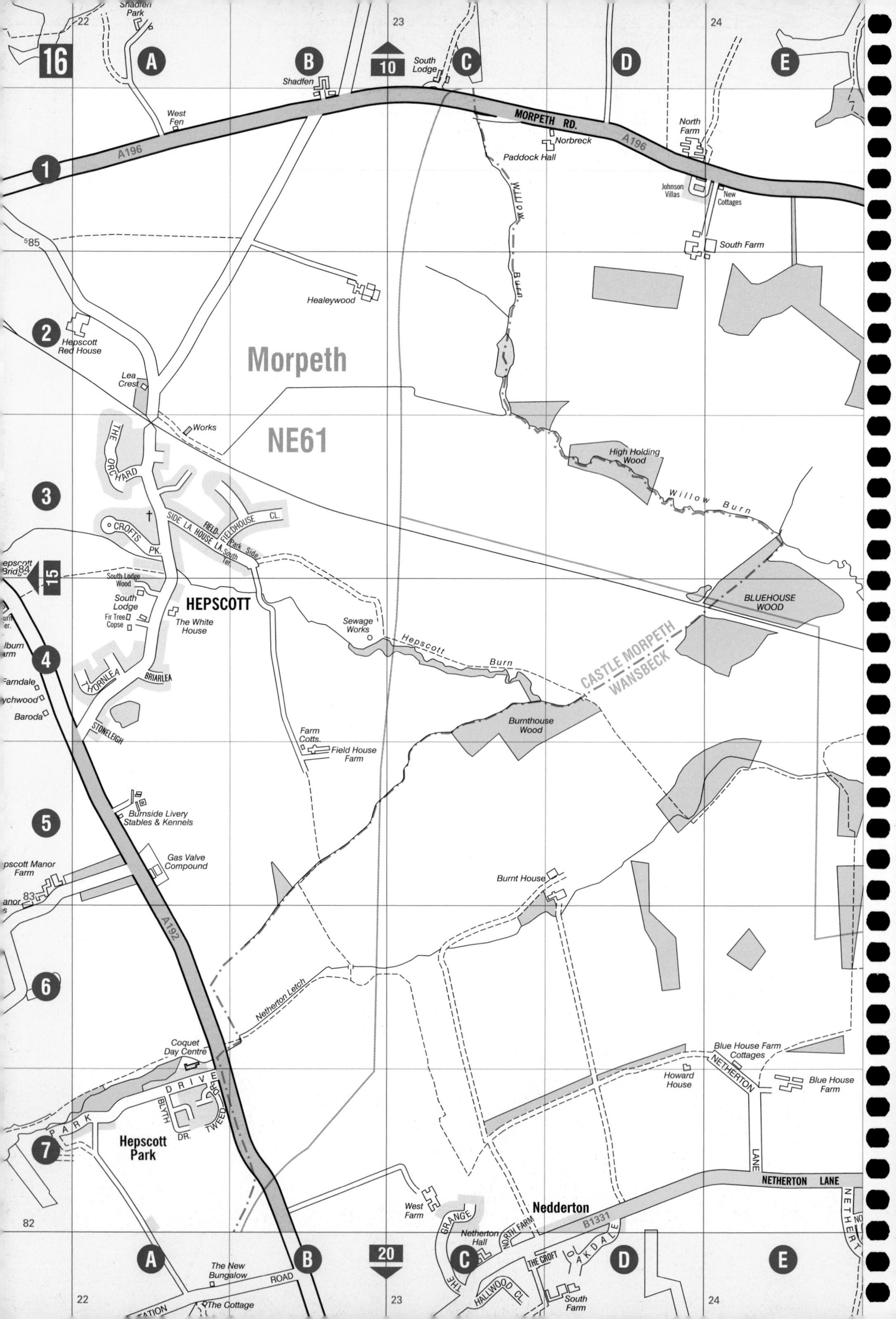

16
10
15
20
Shadfen Park
West Fen
A196
Shadfen
South Lodge
MORPETH RD.
Norbreck
Paddock Hall
North Farm
Johnson Villas
New Cottages
South Farm
Willow Burn
Healeywood
Hepscott Red House
Morpeth
Lea Crest
Works
NE61
High Holding Wood
THE ORCHARD
CROFTS PK.
SIDE LA.
FIELD HOUSE LA.
FIELDHOUSE CL.
Park Side
South Ter.
South Lodge Wood
South Lodge
Fir Tree
Copse
HEPSCOTT
The White House
Sewage Works
Hepscott Burn
BLUEHOUSE WOOD
CASTLE MORPETH
WANSBECK
HORNLEA
BRIARLEA
STONELEIGH
Farndale
Baroda
Burnthouse Wood
Farm Cotts.
Field House Farm
Burnside Livery Stables & Kennels
Gas Valve Compound
A192
Burnt House
Netherton Letch
Coquet Day Centre
DRIVE
BLYTH DR.
TWEED DR.
PARK
Hepscott Park
Blue House Farm Cottages
Howard House
NETHERTON LANE
Blue House Farm
West Farm
Nedderton
GRANGE
Netherton Hall
NORTH FARM
B1331
THE CROFT
OAKDALE
HALLWOOD CL.
South Farm
The New Bungalow
ROAD
The Cottage
22
23
24
82
83
84
85

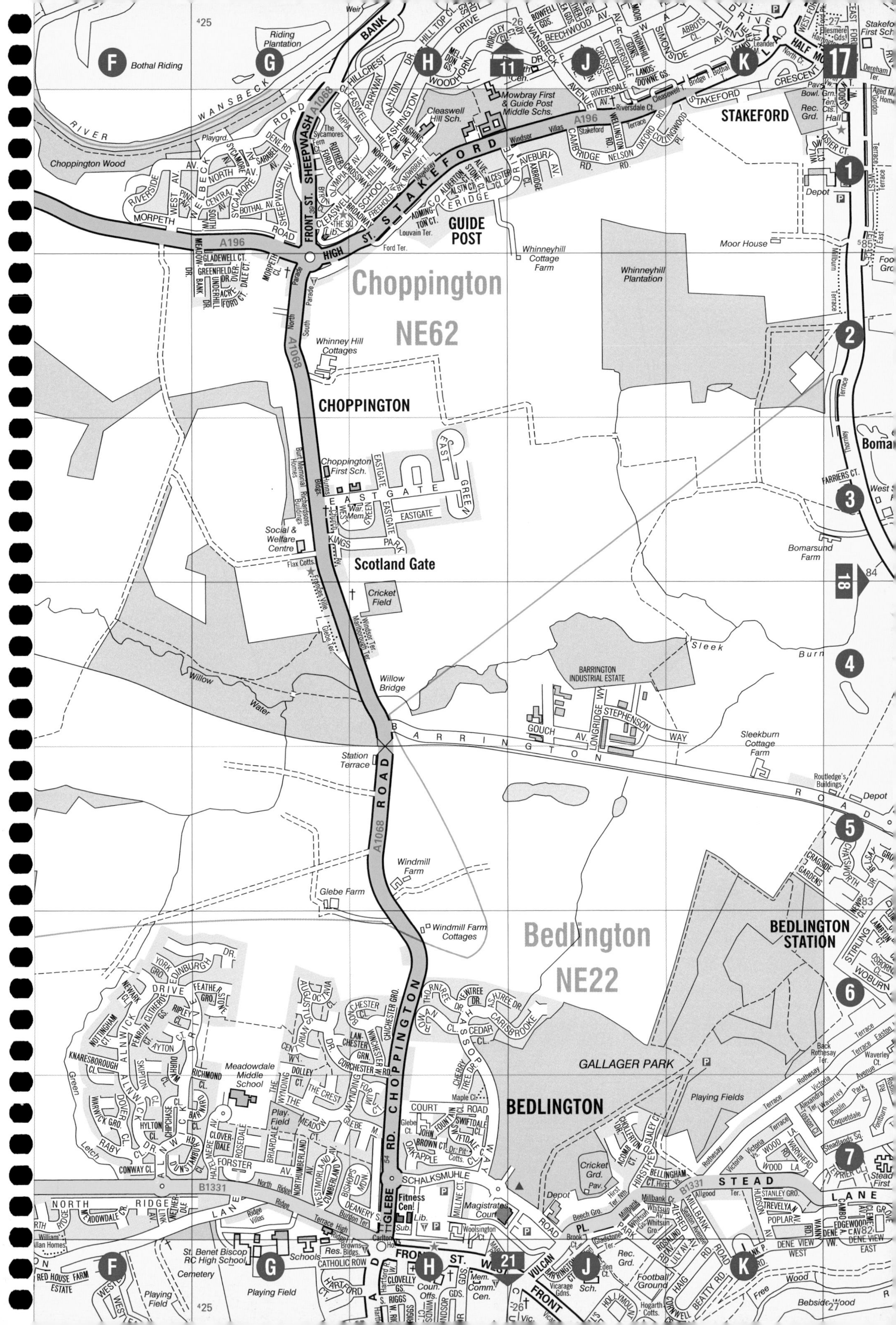

17
Choppington
NE62
CHOPPINGTON
STAKEFORD
GUIDE POST
Scotland Gate
Bedlington
NE22
BEDLINGTON
BEDLINGTON STATION
GALLAGER PARK
BARRINGTON INDUSTRIAL ESTATE
Choppington Wood
Bothal Riding
Riding Plantation
Whinneyhill Plantation
Whinneyhill Cottage Farm
Moor House
Bomarsund Farm
Sleekburn Cottage Farm
Windmill Farm
Windmill Farm Cottages
Glebe Farm
Willow Bridge
Station Terrace
Meadowdale Middle School
St. Benet Biscop RC High School
Cemetery
Playing Field
Playing Fields
Cricket Field
Choppington First Sch.
Social & Welfare Centre
Mowbray First & Guide Post Middle Schs.
Cleaswell Hill Sch.
Magistrates Court
Fitness Cen.
RED HOUSE FARM ESTATE
A196
A1068
B1331
BARRINGTON ROAD
CHOPPINGTON ROAD
STAKEFORD
SHEEPWASH BANK
11
18
21

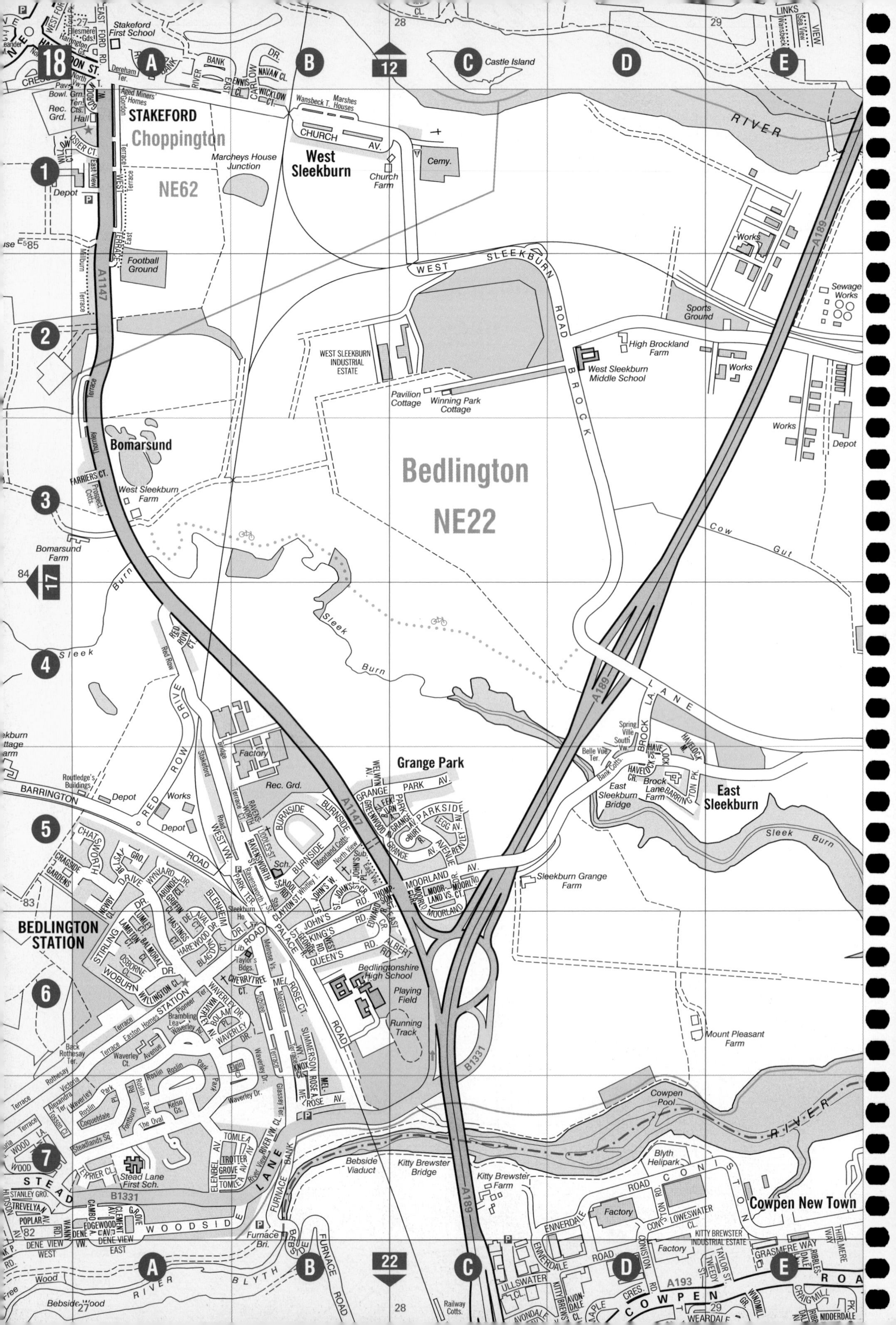
12
Castle Island
STAKEFORD
Choppington
NE62
West Sleekburn
Marcheys House Junction
Church Farm
Cemy.
Football Ground
RIVER
WEST SLEEKBURN ROAD
Sports Ground
Sewage Works
Works
High Brockland Farm
West Sleekburn Middle School
WEST SLEEKBURN INDUSTRIAL ESTATE
Pavilion Cottage
Winning Park Cottage
Depot
Bomarsund
West Sleekburn Farm
Bomarsund Farm
Bedlington
NE22
Cow Gut
17
Sleek Burn
A1147
A189
Grange Park
East Sleekburn
East Sleekburn Bridge
Brock Lane Farm
Sleekburn Grange Farm
BARRINGTON ROAD
RED ROW DRIVE
Rec. Grd.
Factory
BEDLINGTON STATION
Bedlingtonshire High School
Playing Field
Running Track
Mount Pleasant Farm
Cowpen Pool
RIVER
B1331
Bebside Viaduct
Kitty Brewster Bridge
Kitty Brewster Farm
Blyth Helipark
CONISTON ROAD
Cowpen New Town
KITTY BREWSTER INDUSTRIAL ESTATE
Stead Lane First Sch.
WOODSIDE
Furnace Bri.
FURNACE ROAD
RIVER BLYTH
Bebside Wood
22
COWPEN ROAD
A193
Railway Cotts.

12
17
22

31   32

WANSBECK

SANDY BAY CARAVAN PARK

30

East View   Cambois House
Cambois Farm Cottages   Wayside Cottages
Oma House
Cambois Links

1

⁵85

South View

West Vw.

North Vw. Ter.
Wembley Cs.   Wembley Ter.
Foundry
Playing Field

Works

Bernicea

2

Maw   Burn

Depot

Mawburn House

NORTH SEA

3

84

Reservoir

Cambois First Sch.

War Mem.

Retd Miners Homes/Schuring Ter.

Cambois

Unity Ter.   Ridley Ter.

NORTH-FIELD
SANDFIELD RD.
WATERFIELD RD.
WILSON AVENUE
Harbour Vw.

Factory

Cow Gut

4

West Bridge St.

5

The Rockers

Tidal Basin

Battleship Wharfe Reclamation Site

Mooring Stages

6

Green Skeer

WANSBECK
BLYTH VALLEY

Slipway
Boating Yard
Factory Point

Jetty

North Blyth

Jetty

Jetty
Landing Stage

Worsdell St. Dales
GRAY ST.

North Beach

B L Y T H

Jetty
Landing Stages

Blyth

BLYTH INDUSTRIAL ESTATE

Works

COWLEY ROAD

SPENCER ROAD

NE24

TA Centre

Depot

SPENCER CT.

A193

R I V E R

North Side Steithes

Jetty

Warehouse

7

BUTT... INW MFRE IWY.
JOHN ST.
BEECHER ST.
Edendale Cs.
EDENDALE
Glaston Ho.
Rec. Grd. Meldon Ho.

D

COWPEN ROAD
MALVINS
COWPEN

AV.
ALWINTON
Blyth Crematorium
30
ALWINTON CT.
AYSON
ALWINTON AVENUE
ROAD

TEMPLE

AVENUE
POPLAR
WILLOW
CHESTNUT
SYCAMORE
MILLIE CS.
LINKS

B1329
HODGSON'S

CRAWFORD ST.
BEBSIDE

COWPEN ST.
PORTLAND ST.
CHURCH

AVENUE
Play Fld.
The Gables
Babies Hosp.
ANNS ROW

THOMPSON ST.
DISRAELI ST.
SALISBURY

THE BROADWAY
REGENT ST.
GLADSTONE ST.
KELWIN ST.
ATHLONE ST.
BOYNE ST.

STREET
GOSCHEN ST.
KERRY
BURT ST.
ALBERT ST.
YORK ST.

WIMBOURNE QUAY

Warehouse

BLYTH HARBOUR

Works

BLYTH

Depot

Jetty
Jetties

82

32

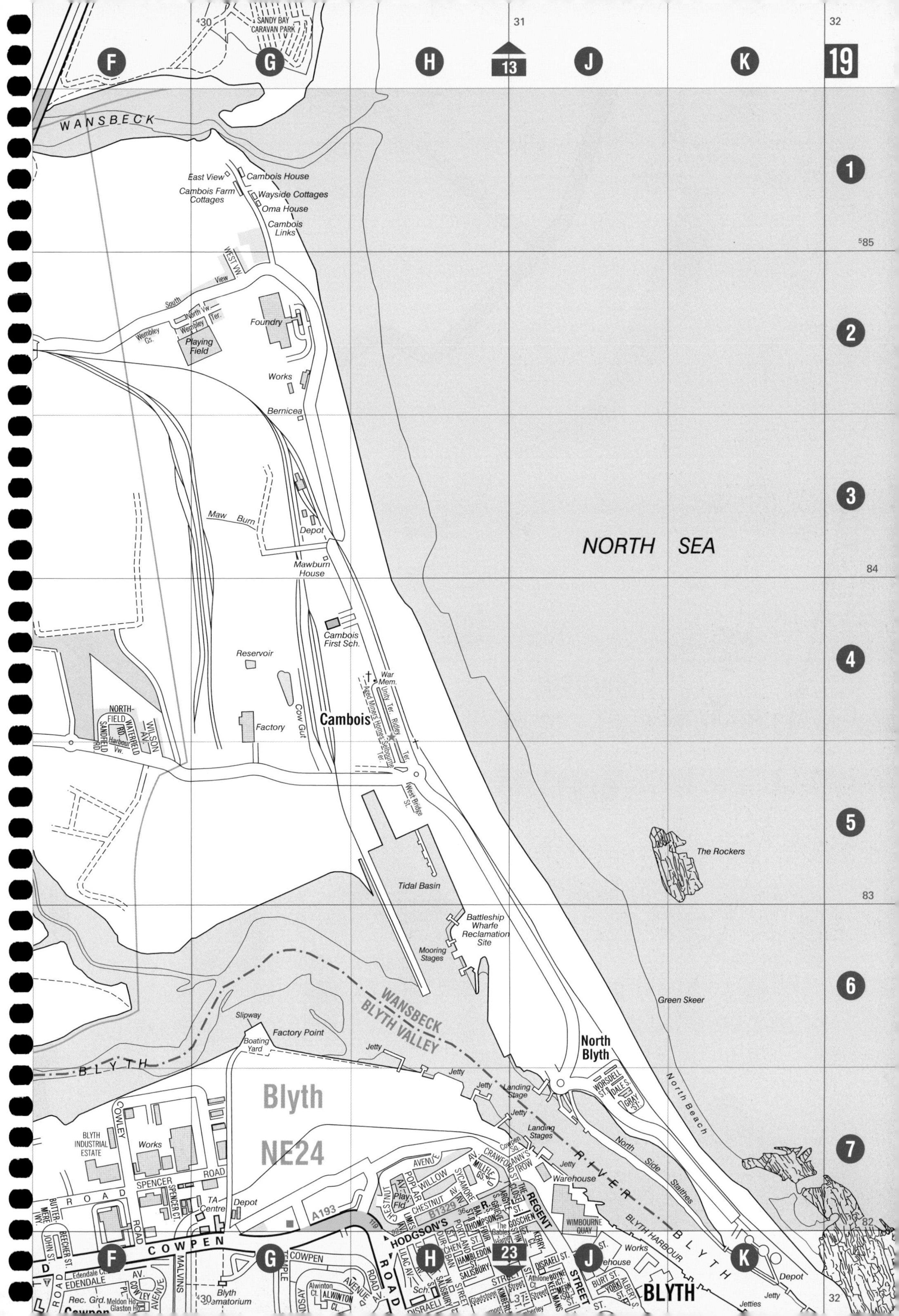

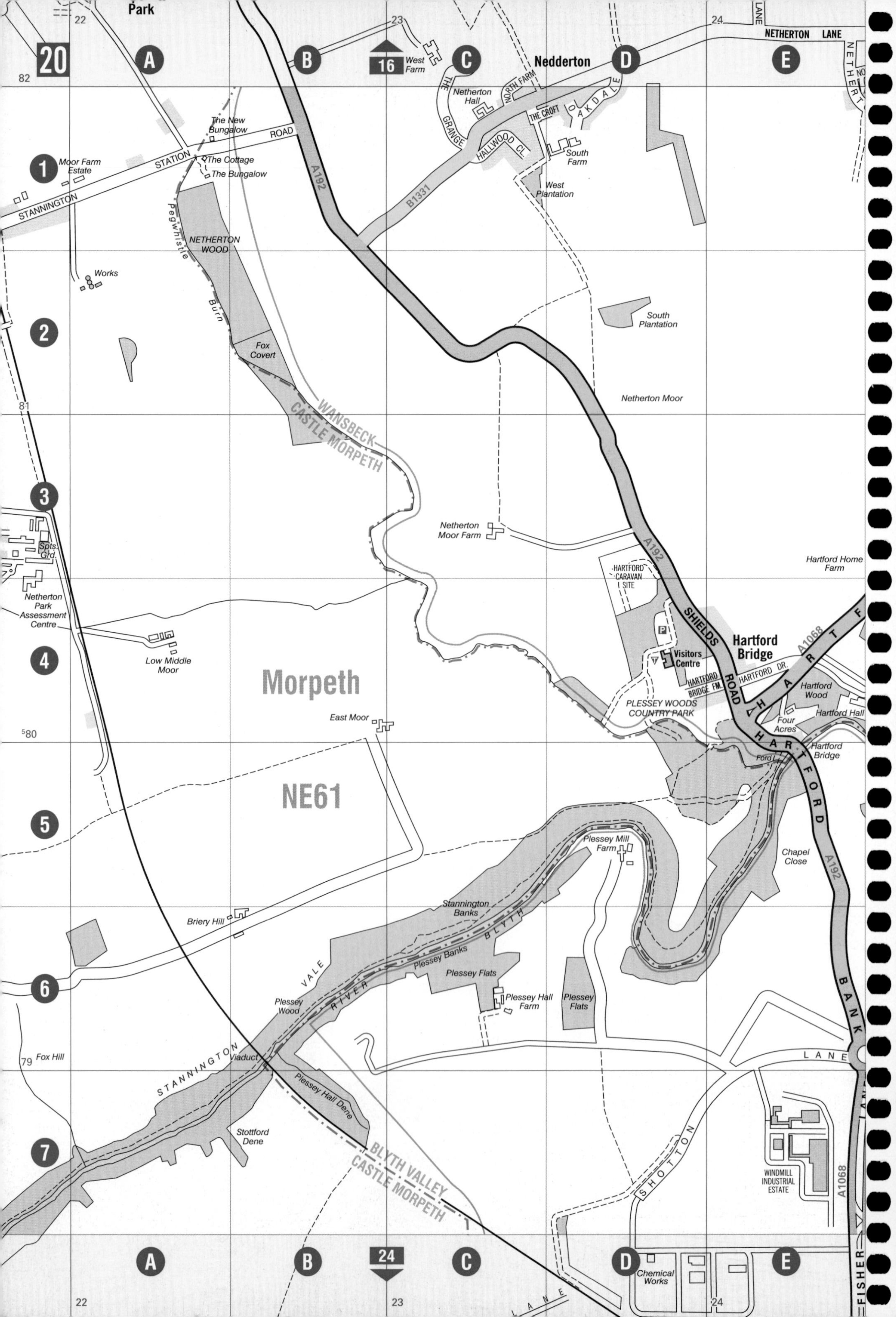

Park
Nedderton
NETHERTON LANE
West Farm
Netherton Hall
NORTH FARM
THE GRANGE
OAKDALE
THE CROFT
HALLWOOD CL.
South Farm
West Plantation
B1331
A192
The New Bungalow
STATION ROAD
The Cottage
The Bungalow
Moor Farm Estate
STANNINGTON
Pegwhistle Burn
NETHERTON WOOD
Works
Fox Covert
South Plantation
Netherton Moor
WANSBECK
CASTLE MORPETH
Netherton Moor Farm
HARTFORD CARAVAN SITE
Hartford Home Farm
Spts. Grd.
Netherton Park Assessment Centre
Low Middle Moor
SHIELDS ROAD
Hartford Bridge
Visitors Centre
HARTFORD BRIDGE FM.
HARTFORD DR.
A1068
HARTFORD
Hartford Wood
Hartford Hall
Four Acres
Hartford Bridge
Ford
Morpeth
East Moor
PLESSEY WOODS COUNTRY PARK
NE61
Plessey Mill Farm
Chapel Close
Stannington Banks
Briery Hill
BLYTH
Plessey Banks
Plessey Flats
VALE
RIVER
Plessey Wood
Plessey Hall Farm
Plessey Flats
BANK
Fox Hill
Viaduct
STANNINGTON
Plessey Hall Dene
LANE
Stottford Dene
SHOTTON
WINDMILL INDUSTRIAL ESTATE
BLYTH VALLEY
CASTLE MORPETH
Chemical Works
FISHER LANE

16
24

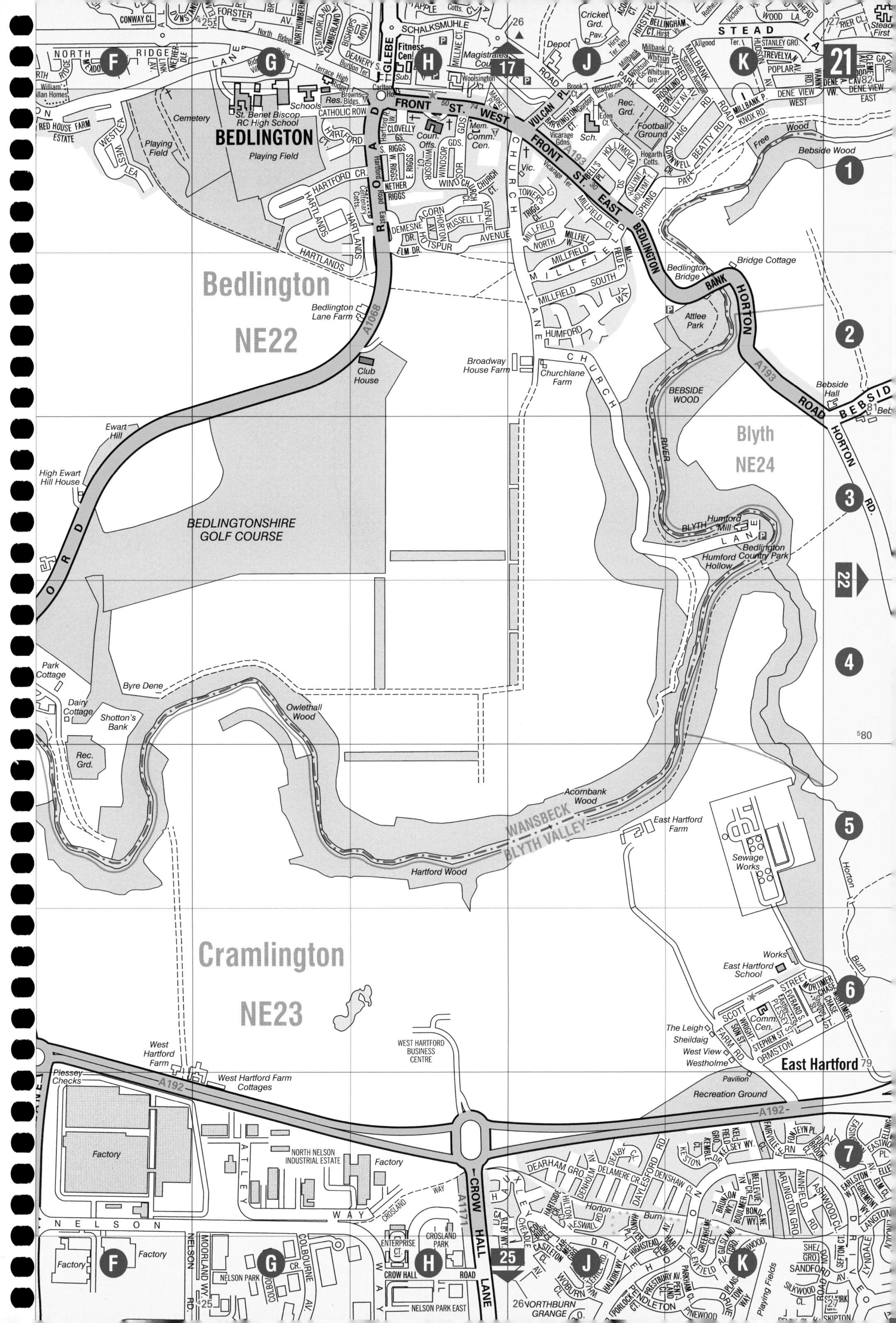

21
17
22
25
BEDLINGTON
Bedlington
NE22
Blyth
NE24
Cramlington
NE23
East Hartford
FRONT ST. WEST
FRONT ST. EAST
GLEBE
SCHALKSMUHLE
NORTH RIDGE
STEAD LA.
MILLBANK
HAIG RD.
BEATTY RD.
VULCAN PL.
CATHOLIC ROW
HARTFORD CR.
HARTLANDS
ACORN AV.
HOTSPUR
DEMESNE DR.
ELM DR.
AVENUE
CHURCH LANE
MILLFIELD
MILLFIELD SOUTH
HUMFORD
BEDLINGTON BANK
HORTON ROAD
BEBSIDE
A193
A1068
A192
A1171
St. Benet Biscop RC High School
Schools
Cemetery
Playing Field
Coun. Offs.
Comm. Cen.
Magistrates Court
Fitness Cen.
Cricket Grd. Pav.
Rec. Grd.
Football Ground
Sch.
Bebside Wood
Bridge Cottage
Bedlington Bridge
Attlee Park
BEBSIDE WOOD
Bebside Hall
Bedlington Lane Farm
Club House
Broadway House Farm
Churchlane Farm
Ewart Hill
High Ewart Hill House
BEDLINGTONSHIRE GOLF COURSE
RIVER BLYTH
Humford Mill
Bedlington Country Park
Humford Hollow
Park Cottage
Byre Dene
Dairy Cottage
Shotton's Bank
Rec. Grd.
Owlethall Wood
Acornbank Wood
WANSBECK
BLYTH VALLEY
Hartford Wood
East Hartford Farm
Sewage Works
Horton Burn
Works
East Hartford School
SCOTT ST.
STREET
MORTIMER CHASE
ORMSTON
STEPHEN ST.
FARM RD.
The Leigh
Sheildaig
West View
Westholme
Pavilion
Recreation Ground
West Hartford Farm
West Hartford Farm Cottages
WEST HARTFORD BUSINESS CENTRE
Plessey Checks
Factory
NORTH NELSON INDUSTRIAL ESTATE
ATLEY WAY
CROSLAND WAY
NELSON
NELSON PARK
NELSON PARK EAST
ENTERPRISE CT.
CROSLAND PARK
CROW HALL ROAD
CROW HALL LANE
MOORLAND WY.
COLBOURNE AV.
DEARHAM GRO.
DELAMERE CR.
DENSHAW CL.
DAYLESFORD RD.
HORTON
NORTHBURN GRANGE
PENDLETON
Playing Fields
SANDFORD
ARLINGTON GRO.
ANNFIELD RD.
FONTEYN PL.
F
G
H
J
K
1
2
3
4
5
6
7

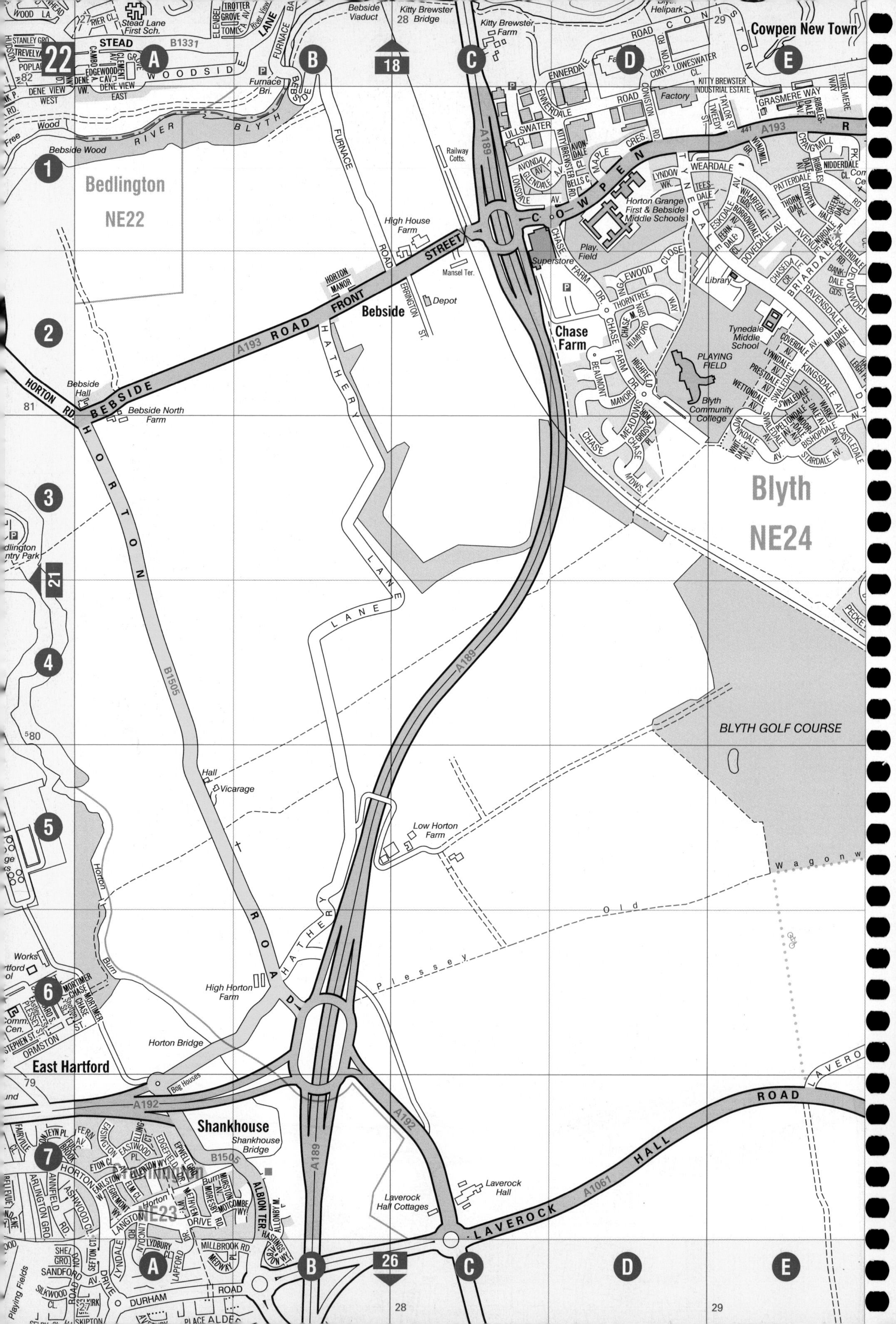
Cowpen New Town
Bedlington
NE22
Blyth
NE24
BLYTH GOLF COURSE
Bebside
Chase Farm
East Hartford
Shankhouse
Shankhouse Bridge
Bebside Wood
Bebside Viaduct
Kitty Brewster Bridge
Kitty Brewster Farm
KITTY BREWSTER INDUSTRIAL ESTATE
Stead Lane First Sch.
Furnace Bri.
RIVER BLYTH
Railway Cotts.
High House Farm
Mansel Ter.
Depot
HORTON MANOR
FRONT STREET
A193 ROAD
BEBSIDE
HORTON RD.
Bebside Hall
Bebside North Farm
Superstore
Play. Field
Horton Grange First & Bebside Middle Schools
Library
Tynedale Middle School
PLAYING FIELD
Blyth Community College
HATHERY LANE
HORTON ROAD
B1505
A189
Hall
Vicarage
Low Horton Farm
High Horton Farm
Horton Bridge
Bog Houses
Old Plessey
Wagonway
Laverock Hall
Laverock Hall Cottages
LAVEROCK HALL ROAD
A1061
A192
B1331
COWPEN
Factory
Works
Playing Fields
18
21
26
28
29
81
80
79
A B C D E
1 2 3 4 5 6 7

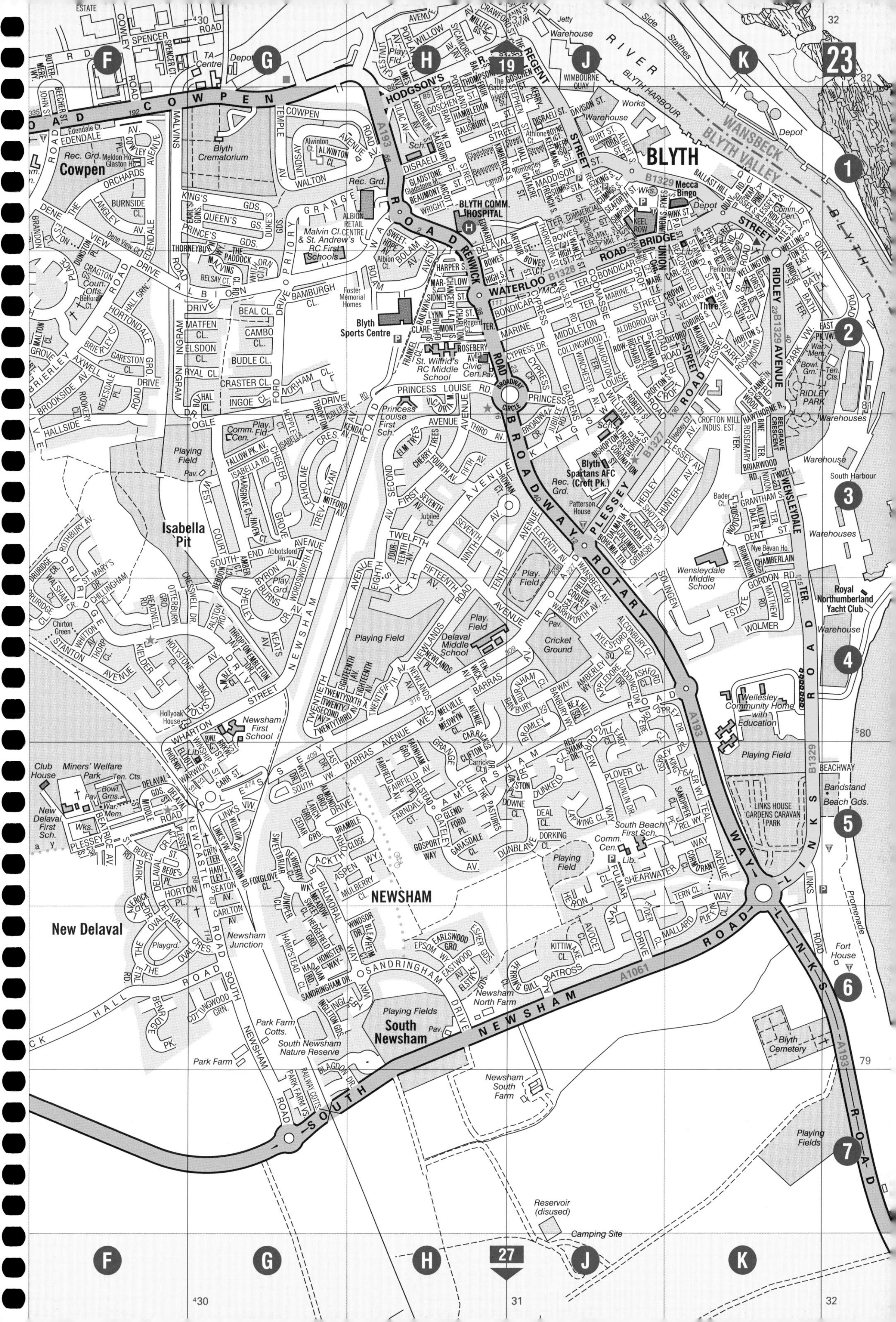
23
BLYTH
Cowpen
NEWSHAM
South Newsham
New Delaval
Isabella Pit
F
G
H
J
K
1
2
3
4
5
6
7
19
27
430
31
32
82
81
580
79
COWPEN ROAD
RENWICK ROAD
BROADWAY
ROTARY WAY
SOUTH NEWSHAM ROAD
LINKS ROAD
NEWSHAM ROAD
SOUTH NEWCASTLE ROAD
WATERLOO ROAD
BRIDGE STREET
RIDLEY AVENUE
PLESSEY ROAD
WENSLEYDALE TER.
BARRAS AVENUE
PRINCESS LOUISE RD.
RIVER BLYTH
BLYTH HARBOUR
WANSBECK
BLYTH VALLEY
A193
A1061
B1329
B1328
B1327
Blyth Crematorium
BLYTH COMM. HOSPITAL
Blyth Sports Centre
Foster Memorial Homes
St. Wilfrid's RC Middle School
Civic Cen.
Princess Louise First Sch.
Blyth Spartans AFC (Croft Pk.)
Patterson House
Rec. Grd.
Play. Field
Playing Field
Delaval Middle School
Cricket Ground
Newsham First School
Miners' Welfare Park
Club House
New Delaval First Sch.
Newsham Junction
Park Farm
Park Farm Cotts.
South Newsham Nature Reserve
Playing Fields
Newsham North Farm
Newsham South Farm
Reservoir (disused)
Camping Site
Blyth Cemetery
Fort House
Promenade
Bandstand
Beach Gds.
LINKS HOUSE GARDENS CARAVAN PARK
South Beach First Sch.
Wellesley Community Home with Education
Royal Northumberland Yacht Club
Wensleydale Middle School
Warehouse
Warehouses
South Harbour
RIDLEY PARK
CROFTON MILL INDUS. EST.
Mecca Bingo
KEEL ROW
Thtre
Depot
Works
WIMBOURNE QUAY
Jetty
Side Staithes
Malvin Cl. & St. Andrew's RC First Schools
ALBION RETAIL CENTRE
Hollyoak House
Chirton Green
Abbotsford Ho.

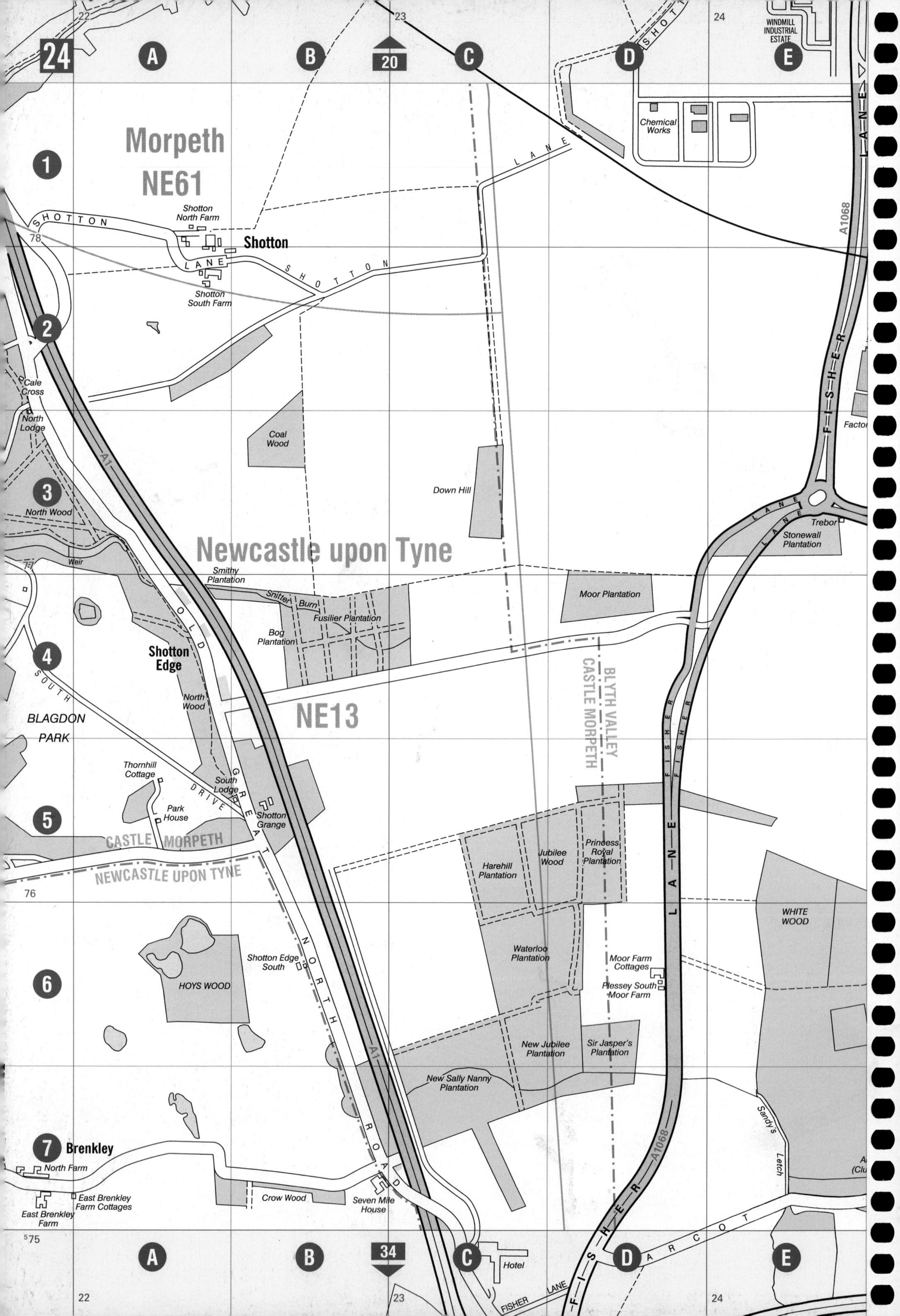

24

Morpeth
NE61

A · B · **20** · C · D · E

Newcastle upon Tyne

Shotton North Farm

Shotton

Shotton South Farm

SHOTTON LANE

LANE

A1

Cale Cross

North Lodge

Coal Wood

Down Hill

Chemical Works

WINDMILL INDUSTRIAL ESTATE

A1068

FISHER LANE

Factor

North Wood

Weir

Smithy Plantation

Snifter Burn

Fusilier Plantation

Bog Plantation

Moor Plantation

Trebor

Stonewall Plantation

Shotton Edge

North Wood

OLD

NE13

SOUTH

BLAGDON PARK

Thornhill Cottage

Park House

South Lodge

Shotton Grange

GREAT DRIVE

BLYTH VALLEY

CASTLE MORPETH

Harehill Plantation

Jubilee Wood

Princess Royal Plantation

FISHER LANE

CASTLE MORPETH

NEWCASTLE UPON TYNE

76

Shotton Edge South

HOYS WOOD

NORTH ROAD A1

Waterloo Plantation

New Jubilee Plantation

New Sally Nanny Plantation

Sir Jasper's Plantation

Moor Farm Cottages

Plessey South Moor Farm

WHITE WOOD

Sandy's Letch

A (Clu

Brenkley

North Farm

East Brenkley Farm Cottages

East Brenkley Farm

Crow Wood

Seven Mile House

Hotel

FISHER LANE

A1068

ARCOT

A · B · **34** · C · D · E

22 · 23 · 24

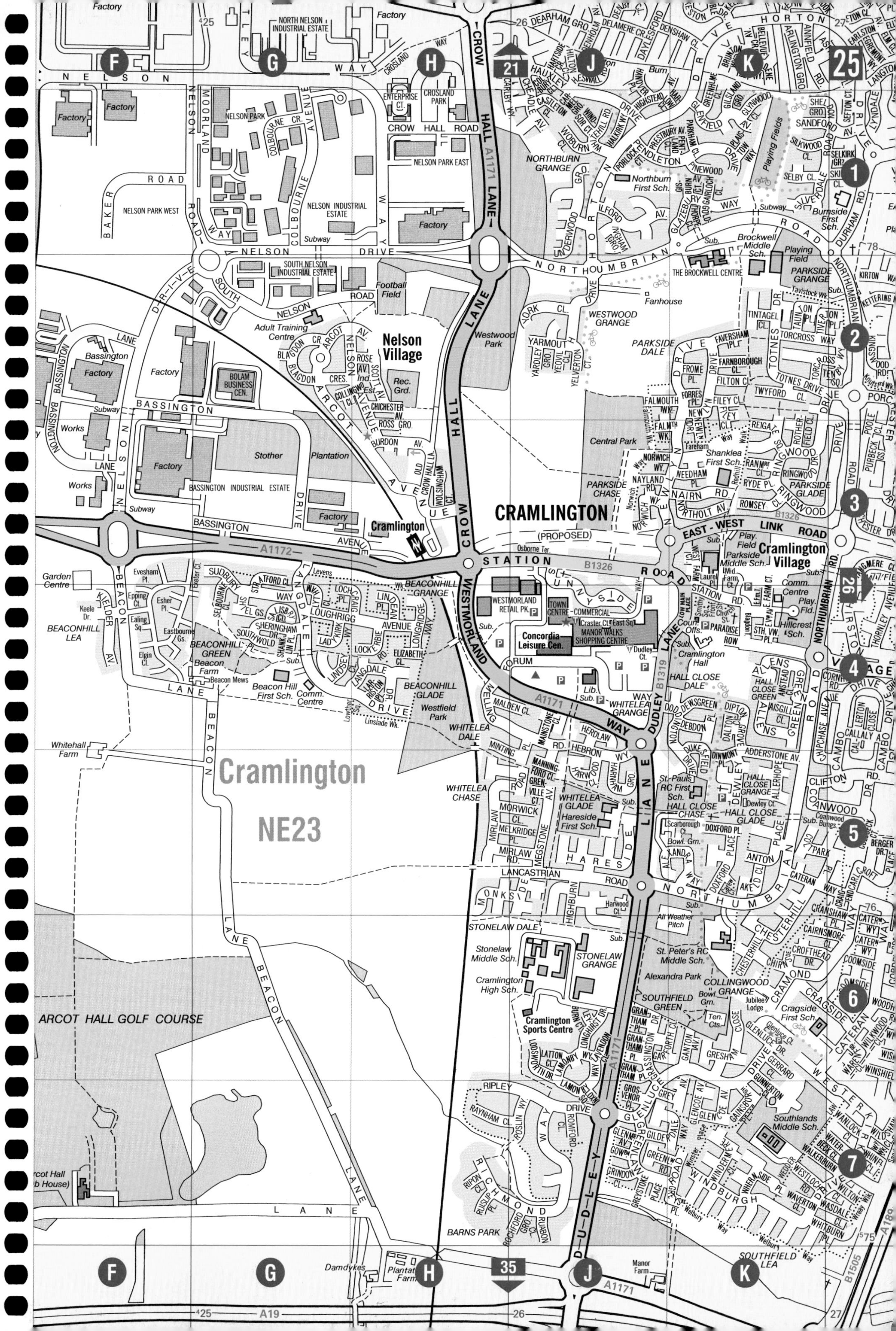

25
CRAMLINGTON
Cramlington
NE23
Nelson Village
Cramlington Village
NORTH NELSON INDUSTRIAL ESTATE
NELSON PARK
NELSON PARK WEST
NELSON PARK EAST
NELSON INDUSTRIAL ESTATE
SOUTH NELSON INDUSTRIAL ESTATE
BASSINGTON INDUSTRIAL ESTATE
ENTERPRISE CT.
CROSLAND PARK
CROW HALL ROAD
NELSON WAY
NELSON DRIVE
NELSON ROAD
BAKER ROAD
MOORLAND WAY
COLBOURNE AVENUE
COLBOURNE CR.
CROSLAND WAY
CROW HALL LANE
A1171
A1172
A19
B1326
B1319
B1505
NORTHUMBRIAN ROAD
NORTHUMBRIAN WAY
STATION ROAD
EAST - WEST LINK ROAD
(PROPOSED)
DUDLEY LANE
WESTMORLAND WAY
BEACON LANE
BASSINGTON AVENUE
BASSINGTON LANE
BASSINGTON DRIVE
ARCOT AVENUE
HORTON DRIVE
Factory
Works
Subway
Stother
Plantation
Football Field
Adult Training Centre
Rec. Grd.
BOLAM BUSINESS CEN.
Westwood Park
WESTWOOD GRANGE
PARKSIDE DALE
PARKSIDE CHASE
PARKSIDE GLADE
PARKSIDE GRANGE
Central Park
NORTHBURN GRANGE
Northburn First Sch.
Brockwell Middle Sch.
THE BROCKWELL CENTRE
Playing Field
Playing Fields
Burnside First Sch.
Fanhouse
Shanklea First Sch.
Parkside Middle Sch.
Comm. Centre
Play. Fld.
Hillcrest Sch.
WESTMORLAND RETAIL PK.
TOWN CENTRE
COMMERCIAL
MANOR WALKS SHOPPING CENTRE
Concordia Leisure Cen.
FORUM
Cramlington Hall
HALL CLOSE DALE
HALL CLOSE GREEN
HALL CLOSE GRANGE
HALL CLOSE CHASE
HALL CLOSE GLADE
BEACONHILL GRANGE
BEACONHILL GREEN
BEACONHILL GLADE
BEACONHILL LEA
Beacon Farm
Beacon Hill First Sch.
Comm. Centre
Westfield Park
Garden Centre
Whitehall Farm
WHITELEA GRANGE
WHITELEA DALE
WHITELEA CHASE
WHITELEA GLADE
Hareside First Sch.
St. Pauls RC First Sch.
STONELAW DALE
STONELAW GRANGE
Stonelaw Middle Sch.
Cramlington High Sch.
Cramlington Sports Centre
All Weather Pitch
St. Peter's RC Middle Sch.
Alexandra Park
SOUTHFIELD GREEN
COLLINGWOOD GRANGE
Cragside First Sch.
Southlands Middle Sch.
SOUTHFIELD LEA
BARNS PARK
ARCOT HALL GOLF COURSE
Arcot Hall (Club House)
Damdykes
Plantation Farm
Manor Farm
Cramlington
F
G
H
J
K
1
2
3
4
5
6
7
21
26
35

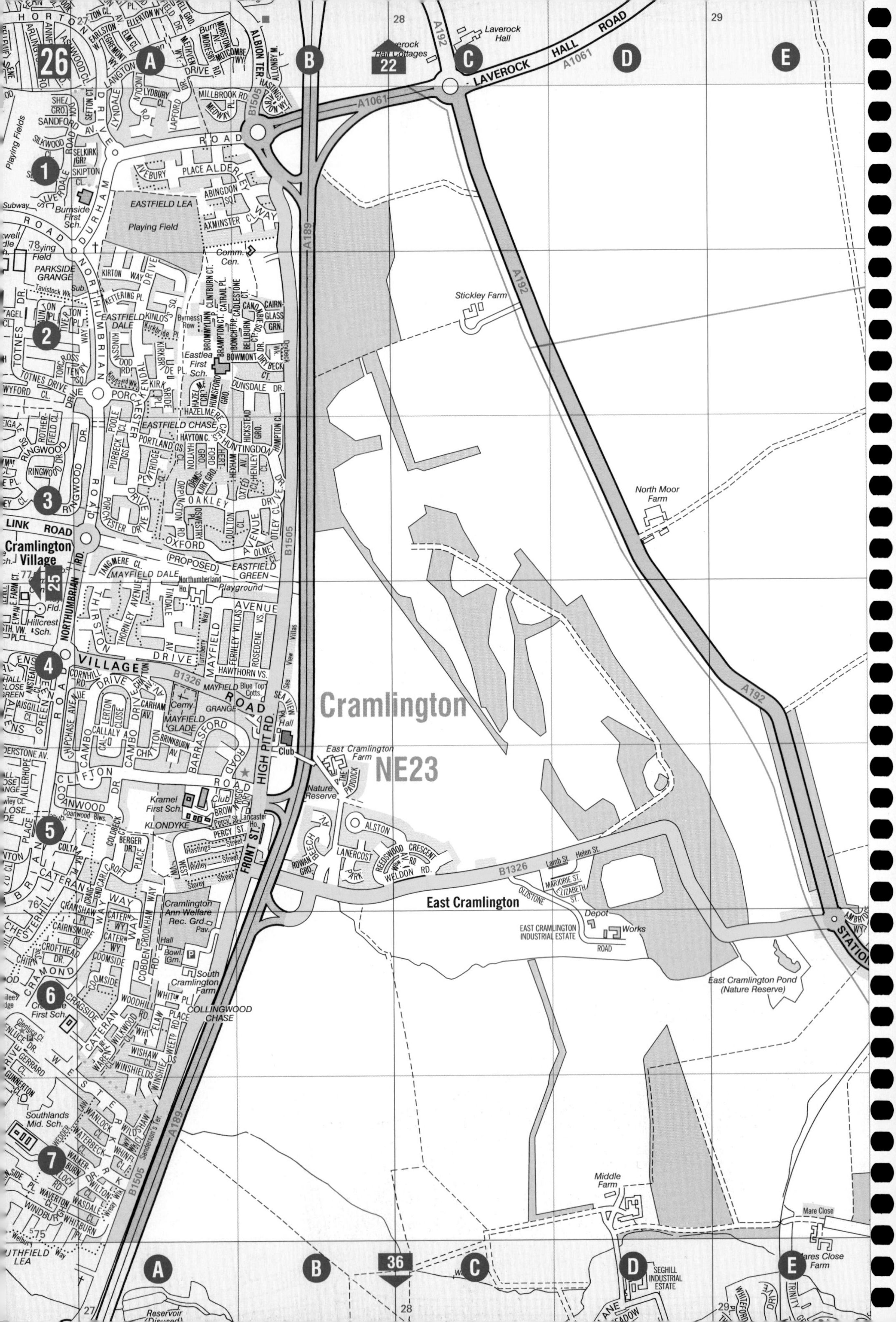
Cramlington
NE23
East Cramlington
Cramlington Village
Laverock Hall
Stickley Farm
North Moor Farm
East Cramlington Farm
Nature Reserve
East Cramlington Pond (Nature Reserve)
EAST CRAMLINGTON INDUSTRIAL ESTATE
Middle Farm
Mares Close Farm
SEGHILL INDUSTRIAL ESTATE
LAVEROCK HALL ROAD
A1061
A192
A189
B1505
B1326
HIGH PIT RD.
FRONT ST.
LINK ROAD
VILLAGE ROAD
NORTHUMBRIAN RD.
EASTFIELD LEA
Playing Field
Playing Fields
Burnside First Sch.
Eastlea First Sch.
Kramel First Sch.
KLONDYKE
Cramlington Ann Welfare Rec. Grd.
South Cramlington Farm
COLLINGWOOD CHASE
Southlands Mid. Sch.
Hillcrest Sch.
Cemy.
Reservoir (Disused)
28
29
27
22
25
36

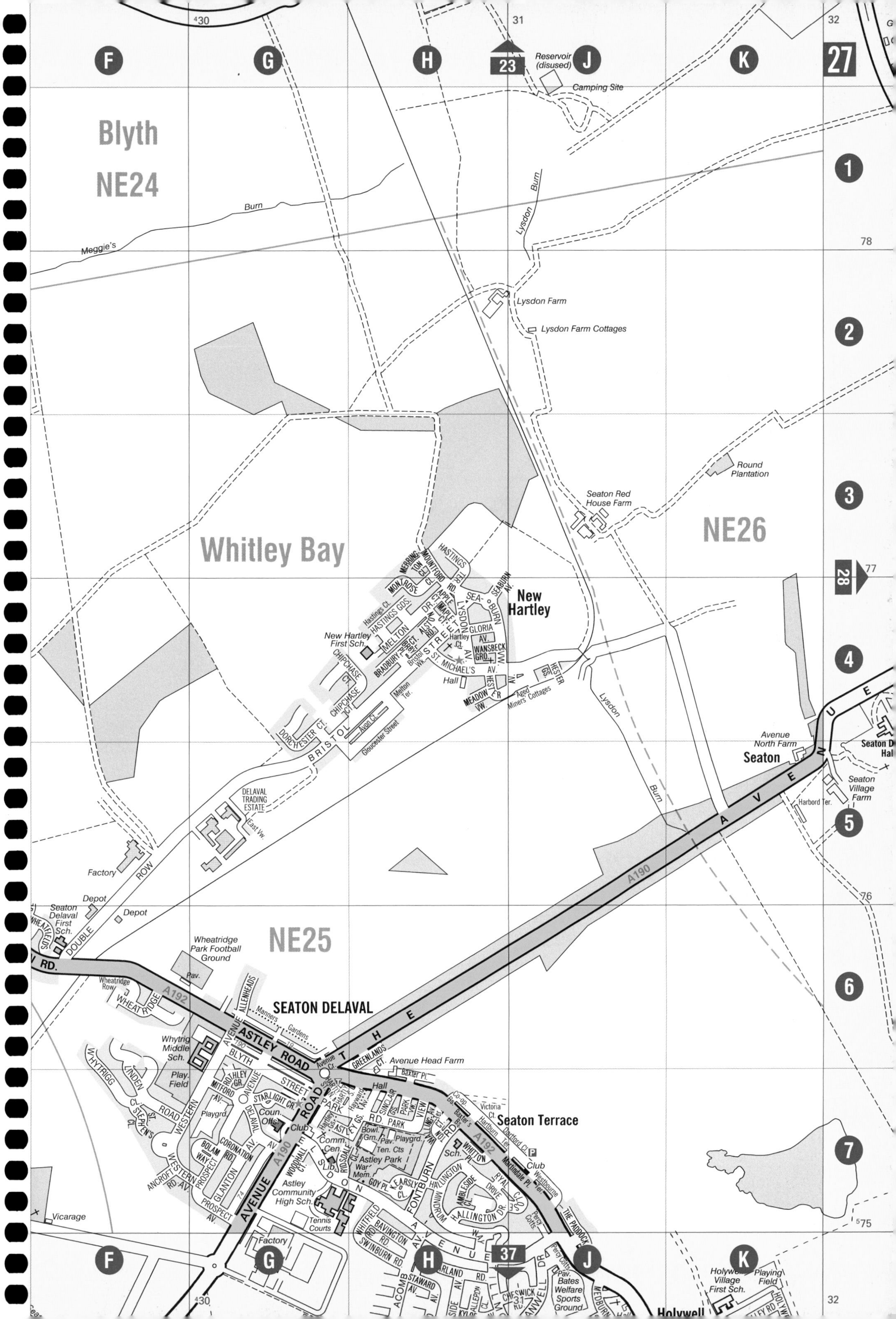

Reservoir
(disused)

Camping Site

1

Blyth

NE24

Burn

78

Meggie's

Lysdon Burn

Lysdon Farm

2

Lysdon Farm Cottages

Round
Plantation

3

Seaton Red
House Farm

NE26

Whitley Bay

HASTINGS

MEBURN

MONTROSE

TOM

MUMFORD

RD.

SEA-

SEABURN

BURN

New
Hartley

Hastings Ct.

HASTINGS GDS.

MELTON

DR.

GLORIA

AV.

New Hartley
First Sch.

CHIPCHASE

BRADBURY

WANSBECK
GRO.

4

Bristol St.

ST.

HESTER

Hartley

CHIPCHASE
CT.

BRISTOL

ST. MICHAEL'S

MEADOW
VW.

HESTER

Avenue
North Farm

Seaton

Seaton D
Hal

DORCHESTER CT.

Angel Ct.

Melton
Ter.

Hall

Aged
Miners' Cottages

Lysdon

Seaton
Village
Farm

Harbord Ter.

5

Gloucester Street

DELAVAL
TRADING
ESTATE

East Vw.

Lysdon
Burn

A190

76

Factory

ROW

Depot

Depot

Seaton
Delaval
First Sch.

WHEATHEADS

DOUBLE

NE25

Wheatridge
Park Football
Ground

THE

NE25

AVENUE

6

RY RD.

A192

WHEATRIDGE

Wheatridge
Row

Pav.

SEATON DELAVAL

ASTLEY ROAD

Manners
Gardens

ALLENHEADS

Avenue

GREENLANDS

CT.

Avenue Head Farm

Whytrigg
Middle
Sch.

BLYTH

STREET

Baxter Pl.

WHYTRIGG

LINDEN

Play.
Field

ROTHLEY GR.

MITFORD

STARLIGHT CR.

Coun.
Offs.

Playgrd.

Club

ASTLY

RD.

PARK

PARK
VIEW

SINCLAIR

Victoria

Seaton Terrace

ROAD

Club

STEPHEN'S
CL.

WESTERN

ROAD

DELAVAL

CORONATION
RD.

AV.

Comm.
Cen.

Astley Park

Ten. Cts.

Pav.

Playgrd.

SCH.

WHITTON

A192

RYAL

Harbottle Pl.

Wethorpe

7

BOLAM

AV.

Club

ANCROFT

WESTERN

RD.

PROSPECT

GLANTON

A190

WOODHALL

WOODHALL

SLD.N

War
Mem.

WHITFIELD

EARSLYBURN

WHITTON

HALLINGTON DR.

TYNE

The Pad

Vicarage

AV.

AVENUE

PROSPECT
AV.

Astley Community
High Sch.

Tennis
Courts

BAVINGTON
RD.

FONTBURN

AV.

HILLSIDE

WAY

Pav.
Bates
Welfare
Sports
Ground

Holywell
Village
First Sch.

Holywell
Playing
Field

Factory

SWINBURN RD.

STAWARD

ACOMB

ALLENDON

CHESWICK DR.

KYLOE

 CANWELL

WEDBURN

HOLYWELL

430

Holywell

31

32

31

32

75

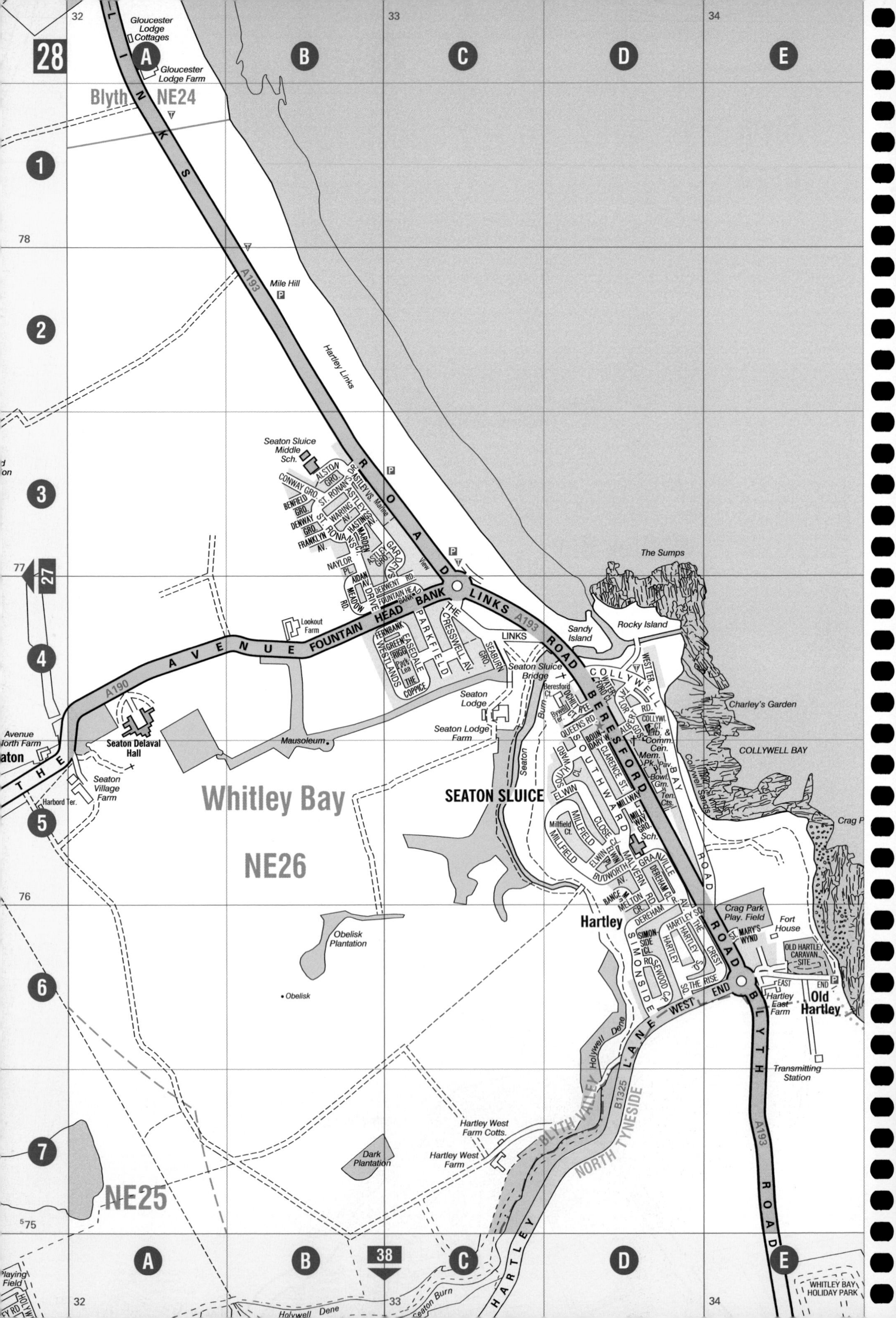

32   33   34

A   B   C   D   E

Blyth NE24

Gloucester
Lodge
Cottages
Gloucester
Lodge Farm

1

78

Mile Hill

2

Hartley Links

A193

Seaton Sluice
Middle Sch.

3

CONWAY GRO
BENFIELD GRO
DENWAY GRO
FRANKLYN AV.
ALSTON GRO
ST. RONAN'S
ASTLEY VS. Mains
WARING AV.
HASTINGS
BRENNANS
NAYLOR PL
AIDAN AV.
MEADOW RD.
DERWENT RD.
FOUNTAIN THE BANKS
ASTLEY GRO
GARDEN'S
VIEW RD.

27

77

4

AVENUE   FOUNTAIN HEAD   BANK   LINKS   ROAD   A193

A190

Lookout Farm
FERNBANK
WESTLANDS
GREEN'S
BRIGG
EASEDALE
PARKFIELD
THE COPPICE
THE CRESSWELL AV.
SEABURN GRO
SEABURN
LINKS
Seaton Sluice
Bridge
Seaton Lodge
Beresford Ct.
Byewell Ter.
WHILL
COLLYWELL
WESTER
CT.
TAYLOR
COLLYWI. RD.
COLL. Lib. &
Comm. Cen.
Mem. Pk
Pav
Bowl
Grn.
St. Ter.
Cts.

The Sumps

Sandy
Island   Rocky Island

Charley's Garden

COLLYWELL BAY

Avenue
North Farm
eaton

Seaton Delaval Hall

Seaton Village Farm

Harbord Ter.

Mausoleum.

Seaton Lodge
Farm

Seaton Burn

QUEENS RD.
SOUTH WARD
CLARENCE ST.
ELWIN
BERESFORD
MILLWAY
MILLWAY GRO.
Sch.
GRANVILLE
DEREHAM CT.
BANCE
MELTON
DEREHAM
ELWIN
CLOSE
MILLFIELD
BUDWORTH AV.
Millfield
Ct.
Millfield

Crag P

Whitley Bay

NE26

SEATON SLUICE

Hartley

Collywell Stairs

5

76

Obelisk
Plantation

Obelisk

Dene

HARTLEY
SIMON
SIDE
SQ.
SEWOOD Cp.
SIMONSIDE
THE CREST
HARTLEY
SQ.
HARTLEY
SQ.
THE RISE
WEST END
St. Mary's
Wynd
Crag Park
Play. Field
Fort
House
East
Hartley
END
EAST
Old Hartley
East
Farm
Old Hartley
CARAVAN
SITE

6

ROAD
BLYTH
A193

NE25

Dark
Plantation

Hartley West
Farm Cotts.

Hartley West
Farm

BLYTH VALLEY
NORTH TYNESIDE
HARTLEY
LANE
WEST
END
Holywell

B1325

Transmitting
Station

7

75

A   B   C   D   E

38

32   33   34

FY RD
Playing
Field

Holywell Dene   Seaton Burn

WHITLEY BAY
HOLIDAY PARK

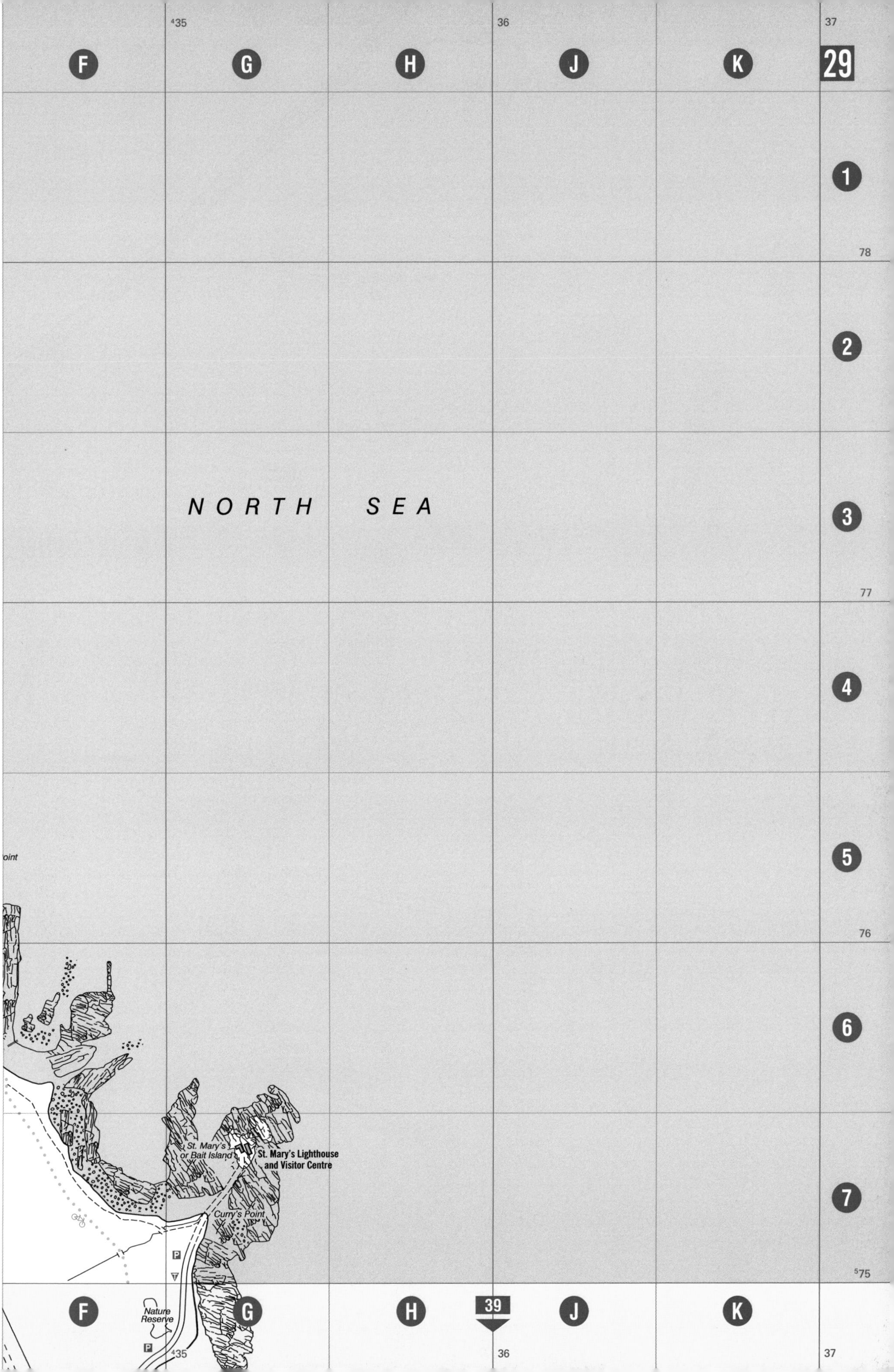

⁴35 36 37

1

78

2

NORTH SEA

3

77

4

oint

5

76

6

St. Mary's or Bait Island
St. Mary's Lighthouse and Visitor Centre

Curry's Point

7

P
▽

⁵75

Nature Reserve
P
⁴35 36 37

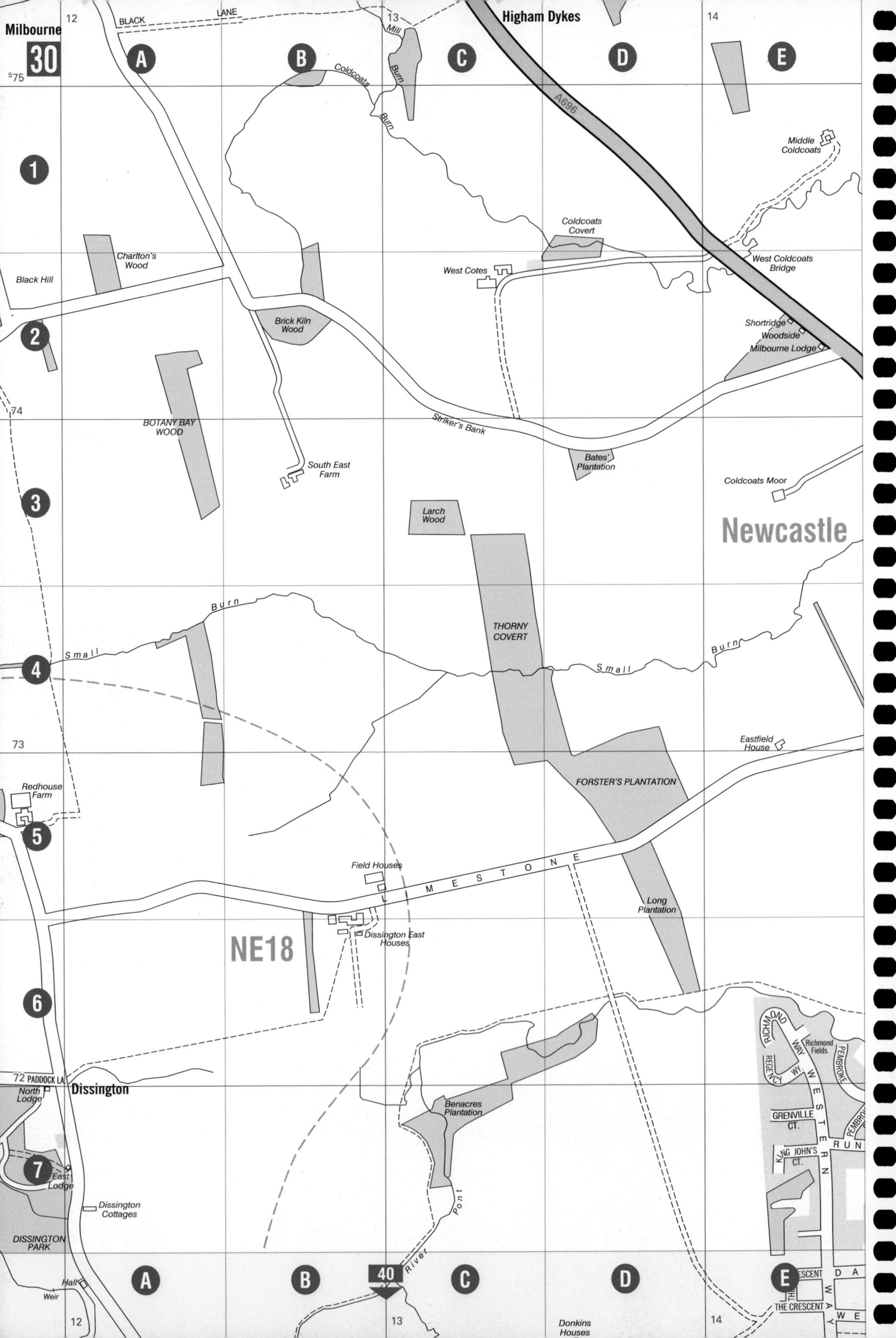

Milbourne

30

⁵75

Higham Dykes

Newcastle

NE18

BLACK LANE

Coldcoats Burn

Mill Burn

A696

Middle Coldcoats

Charlton's Wood

Black Hill

Coldcoats Covert

West Cotes

West Coldcoats Bridge

Brick Kiln Wood

Shortridge
Woodside
Milbourne Lodge

BOTANY BAY WOOD

Striker's Bank

Bates' Plantation

Coldcoats Moor

South East Farm

Larch Wood

THORNY COVERT

Burn

Small Burn

Small Burn

Eastfield House

FORSTER'S PLANTATION

Redhouse Farm

Field Houses

LIMESTONE

Long Plantation

Dissington East Houses

RICHMOND WAY
Richmond Fields

REGENCY WY
PEMBROKE

WESTERN

GRENVILLE CT.

PADDOCK LA.
North Lodge
Dissington

Benacres Plantation

RUN

KING JOHN'S CT.

East Lodge

Dissington Cottages

DISSINGTON PARK

Hall

Weir

Pont

River Pont

40

Donkins Houses

THE CRESCENT

DA

WE

12

13

14

74

73

72

12

13

14

A B C D E

A B C D E

1 2 3 4 5 6 7

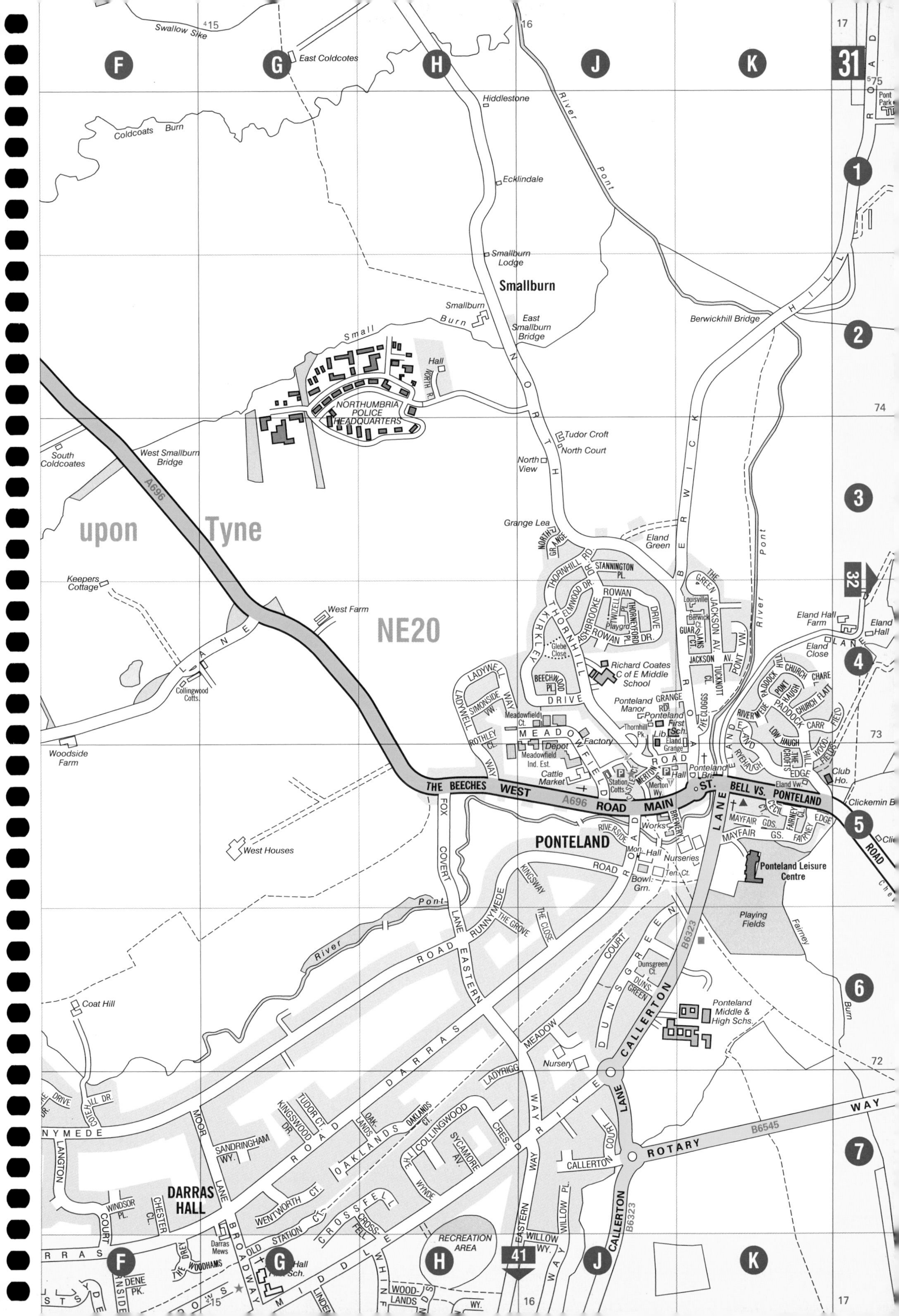
Swallow Sike
East Coldcotes
Hiddlestone
Coldcoats Burn
River Pont
Ecklindale
Smallburn Lodge
Smallburn
Smallburn Burn
East Smallburn Bridge
Berwickhill Bridge
Small Burn
Hall
NORTH R.
NORTHUMBRIA POLICE HEADQUARTERS
NORTH ROAD
Tudor Croft
North Court
North View
South Coldcoates
West Smallburn Bridge
A696
upon Tyne
Grange Lea
Eland Green
BERWICK ROAD
Keepers Cottage
West Farm
NE20
STANNINGTON PL.
THORNHILL RD.
ROWAN DRIVE
ELMWOOD DR.
ASHBROOKE
TWIZELL PL.
THORNEYFORD PL.
ROWAN DR.
Playgro.
THE GREEN
JACKSON AV.
Louisville
Berwick Ct.
GUARDIANS CT.
JACKSON AV.
PONT VW.
TUCKNOTT CT.
Eland Hall Farm
Eland Hall
Eland Close
ELAND LANE
KIRKLEY
THORNHILL
Glebe Close
Richard Coates C of E Middle School
Collingwood Cotts.
BEECHWOOD PL.
DRIVE
LADYWELL WAY
SIMONSIDE VW.
LADYWELL
Ponteland Manor
GRANGE RD.
Ponteland First Sch.
Meadowfield Ct.
Thornhill Pk.
Lib.
Eland Grange
THE CLOGGS
CHURCH CHARE
PADDOCK
PONT HAUGH
CHURCH FLAT
RIVERMEDE
CARR FIELD
LOW HAUGH
THE CROFTS
HILL WOOD
FIELDS
Woodside Farm
ROTHLEY CT.
MEADOWFIELD
Factory
Depot
Meadowfield Ind. Est.
Cattle Market
Station Cotts.
CASTLE
MERTON
ROAD
Hall
Merton Wy.
Ponteland Bri.
RYEHAUGH
EDGE
Club Ho.
Eland Vw.
Clickemin B
THE BEECHES
WEST ROAD
MAIN
ST.
BELL VS.
PONTELAND
FOX COVERT LANE
RIVERSIDE
Works
BREWERY LA.
LANE
MAYFAIR GDS.
CECIL CT.
FAIRNEY CL.
MAYFAIR GS.
FAIRNEY EDGE
ROAD
PONTELAND
West Houses
Mon. Hall
Nurseries
Ten. Ct.
Ponteland Leisure Centre
ROAD
KINGSWAY
Bowl. Grn.
Pont
Playing Fields
Fairney
RUNNYMEDE
THE GROVE
THE CLOSE
River
ROAD
EASTERN
COURT
DUNSGREEN
Dunsgreen Ct.
DUNS. GREEN
B6323
CALLERTON
Ponteland Middle & High Schs.
Burn
Coat Hill
DARRAS
MEADOW
Nursery
LADYRIGG
DRIVE
WAY
B6545
ROTARY
LANE
COURT
CALLERTON
TUDOR CT.
KINGSWOOD DR.
OAK LANDS
OAKLANDS CT.
OAKLANDS
COLLINGWOOD
SYCAMORE AV.
CRES.
COTEHILL DR.
RUNNYMEDE
MOOR
SANDRINGHAM WY.
LANGTON
THE WYNDE
WILLOW PL.
DARRAS HALL
WINDSOR PL.
CHESTER CL.
COURT
LANE
WENTWORTH CT.
CROSSFELL
CROSS FELL
STATION CT.
RECREATION AREA
EASTERN
WILLOW WY.
41
Darras Mews
BROADWAY
OLD
WOODHAMS
THE DREY
Hall
First Sch.
DENE PK.
MIDDLE DRIVE
WHINFELL
WOODLANDS
WY.
F
G
H
J
K
1
2
3
4
5
6
7
32
15
16
17
74
73
72
75

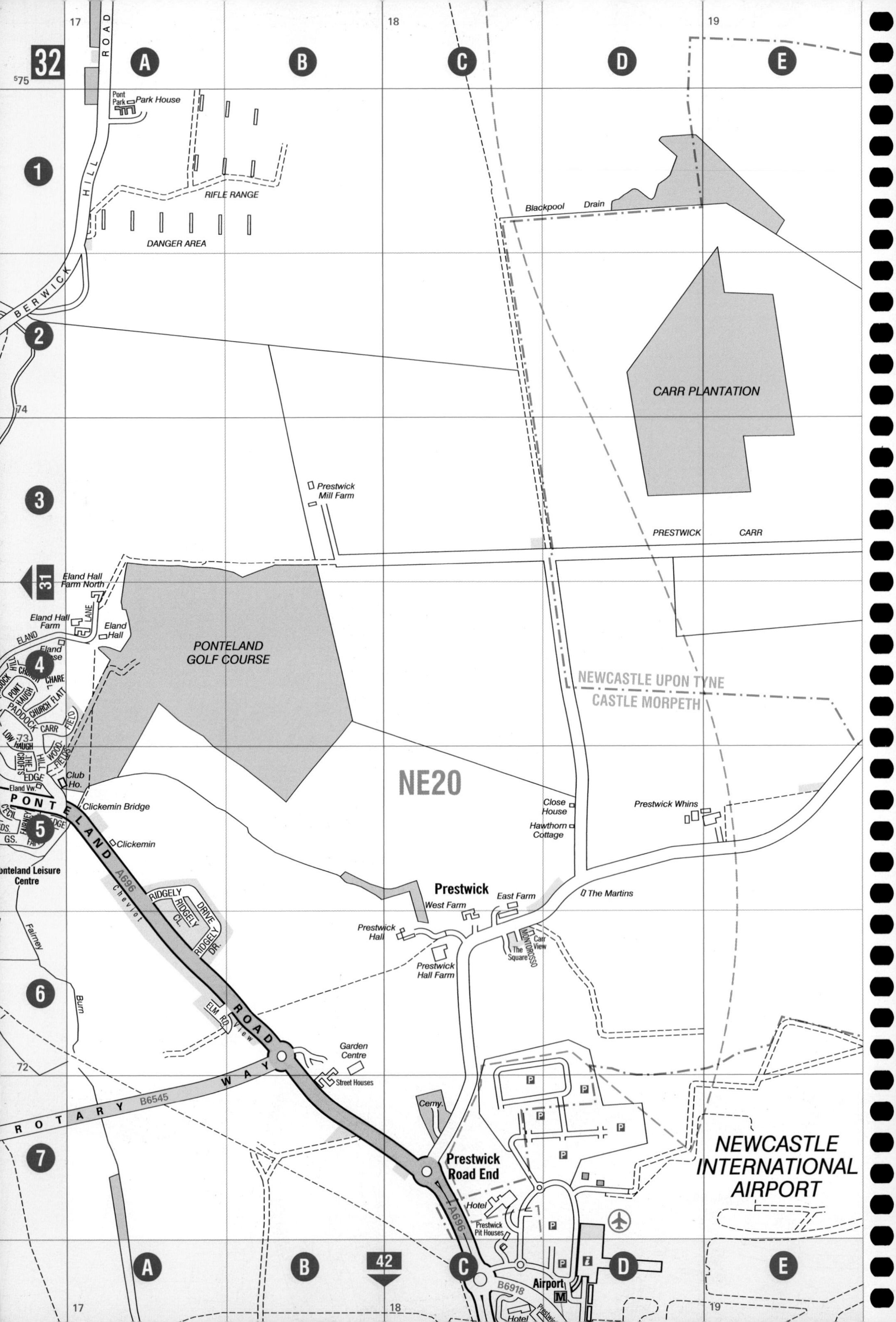
Pont Park
Park House
RIFLE RANGE
DANGER AREA
HILL ROAD
BERWICK
Blackpool Drain
CARR PLANTATION
Prestwick Mill Farm
PRESTWICK CARR
Eland Hall Farm North
Eland Hall Farm
Eland Hall
PONTELAND GOLF COURSE
NEWCASTLE UPON TYNE
CASTLE MORPETH
NE20
Close House
Hawthorn Cottage
Prestwick Whins
The Martins
Club Ho.
Clickemin Bridge
Clickemin
PONTELAND ROAD
A696
Chevlot View
Ponteland Leisure Centre
Fairney
Burn
RIDGELY DRIVE
RIDGELY CL.
RIDGELY DR.
ELM RD.
Prestwick
East Farm
West Farm
Prestwick Hall
Prestwick Hall Farm
The Square
Carr View
MONTROSSO
Garden Centre
Street Houses
ROTARY WAY
B6545
Cemy.
Prestwick Road End
Hotel
Prestwick Pit Houses
B6918
Airport
NEWCASTLE INTERNATIONAL AIRPORT
CHURCH FLAT
CHARE
PADDOCK
CARR
FIELD
LOW HAUGH
THE CROFTS
HILL
WOOD FIELDS
EDGE
Eland Vw.
PONT HAUGH
ELAND
31
42

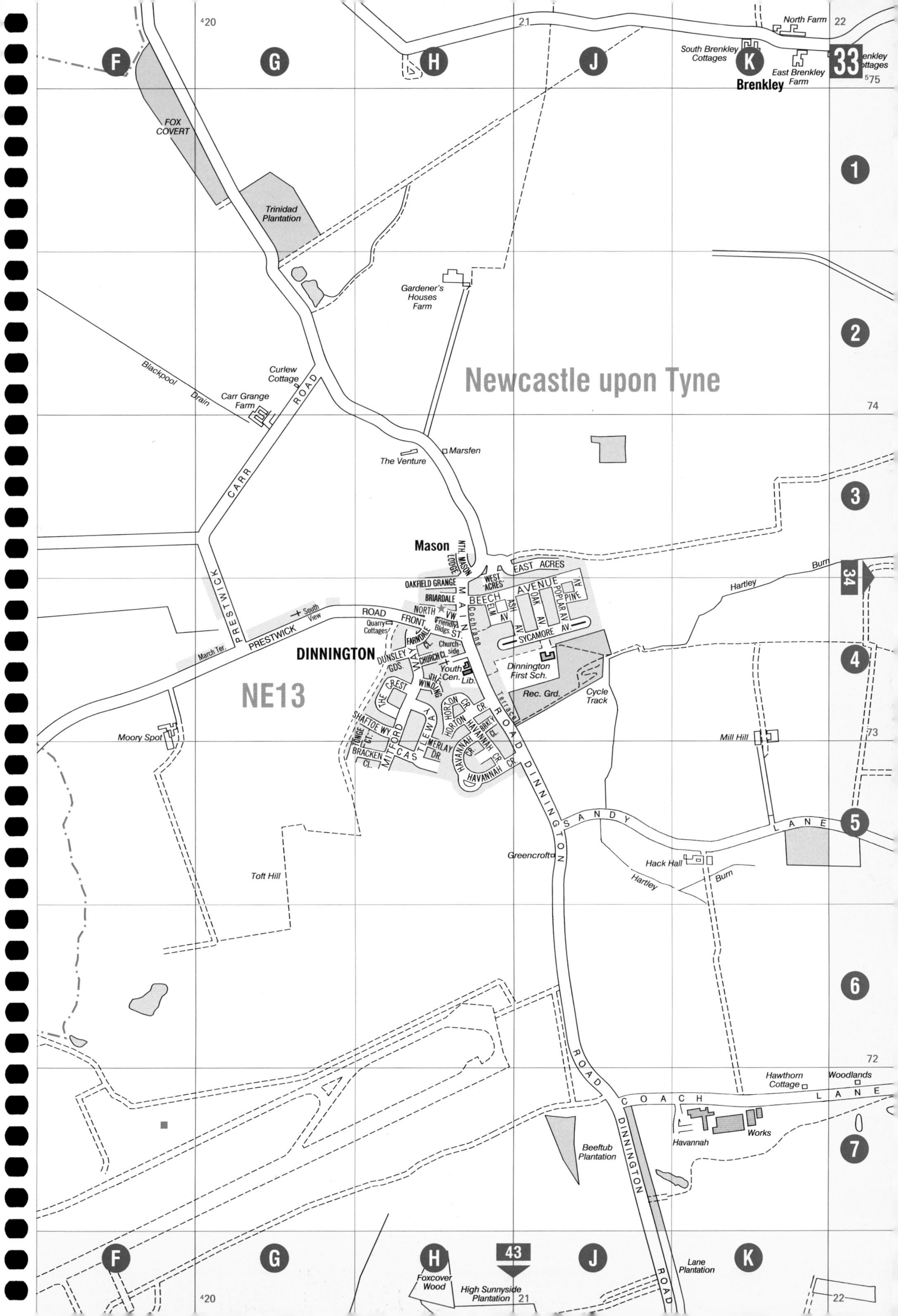

North Farm

South Brenkley
Cottages

Brenkley
Cottages

East Brenkley
Farm

Brenkley

⁵75

1

FOX
COVERT

Trinidad
Plantation

2

Gardener's
Houses
Farm

Newcastle upon Tyne

74

Blackpool Drain

Curlew
Cottage

Carr Grange
Farm

CARR ROAD

The Venture

Marsfen

3

Mason

NTH. MASON

EAST ACRES

WEST
ACRES

Hartley

Burn

34

OAKFIELD GRANGE

BRIARDALE

BEECH AVENUE

ELM AV. ASH AV. OAK AV. POPLAR AV. PINE AV.

LODGE

MAIN

ROAD

South
View

FRONT

NORTH

VW

Friendly
Bldgs. ST.

SYCAMORE AV.

PRESTWICK ROAD

Quarry
Cottages

Cochrane

March Ter.

PRESTWICK WAY

DINNINGTON

Church Cl.

Church
side

Youth
Cen. Lib.

DUNSLEY
GDS.

FARNDALE

CL.

Dinnington
First Sch.

NE13

THE CREST

WINDING

WAY

Rec. Grd.

Cycle
Track

4

Moory Spot

SHAFTOE WY

MITFORD

CASTLEWAY

MERLAY DR.

HORTON CR.

HAVANNAH CR.

BIRTLEY CL.

Terrace

ROAD

Mill Hill

73

YONGE CT.

BRACKEN CL.

HAVANNAH CR.

HAVANNAH CR.

DINNINGTON

5

Greencroft

Hartley

Hack Hall

Burn

SANDY LANE

Toft Hill

6

72

Hawthorn
Cottage

Woodlands

Beeftub
Plantation

DINNINGTON ROAD

COACH

Havannah

Works

LANE

7

Foxcover
Wood

High Sunnyside
Plantation

Lane
Plantation

⁴20

21

22

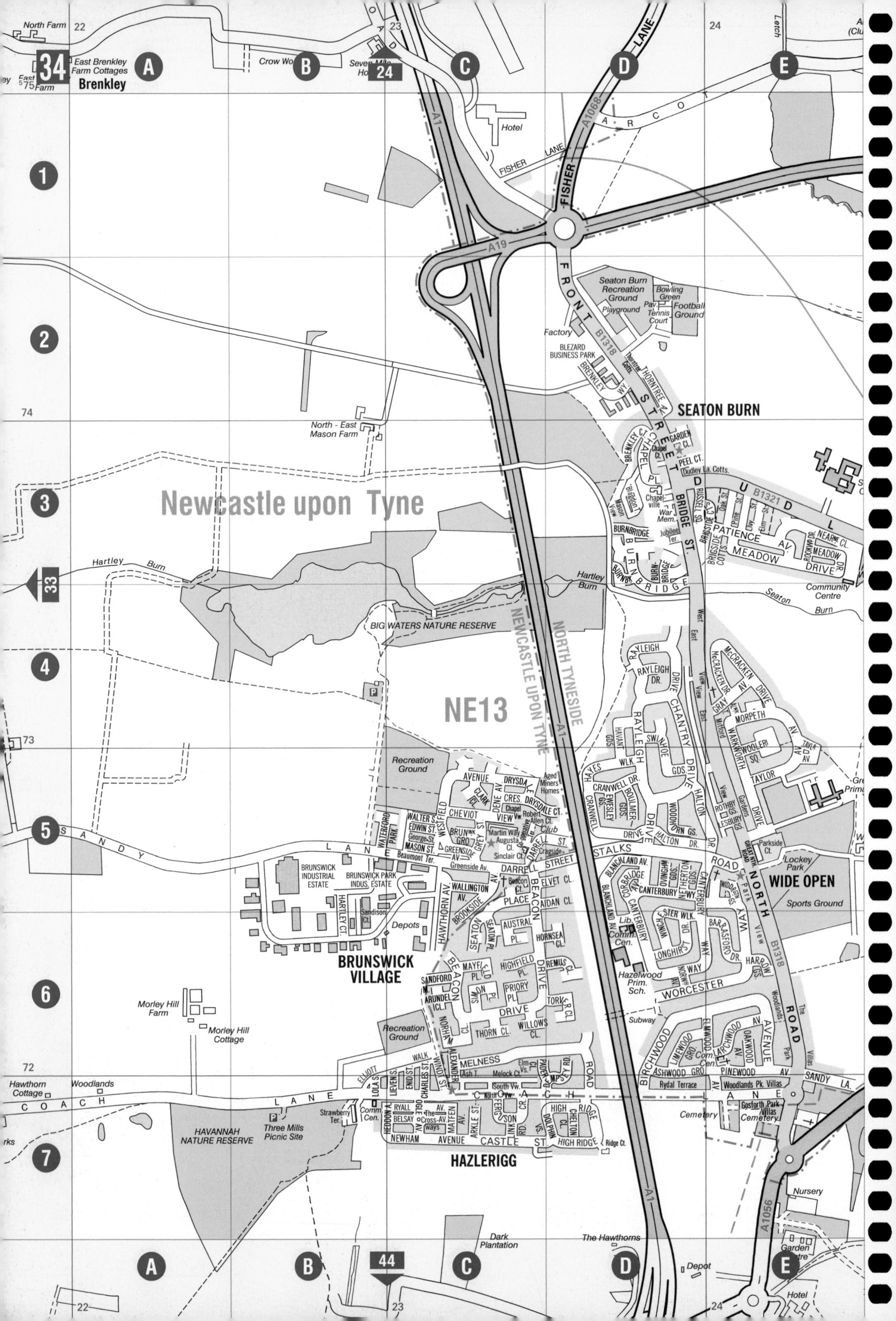
Brenkley
Seaton Burn
Newcastle upon Tyne
NE13
Big Waters Nature Reserve
Brunswick Village
Wide Open
Hazlerigg
Havannah Nature Reserve
Three Mills Picnic Site
North Tyneside
Newcastle upon Tyne
North Farm
East Brenkley Farm Cottages
Crow Wood
Seven Mile House
Hotel
Fisher Lane
Arcot Lane
Front Street
Bridge St.
Seaton Burn Recreation Ground
Bowling Green
Football Ground
Tennis Court
Playground
Factory
Blezard Business Park
North - East Mason Farm
Hartley Burn
Seaton Burn
Community Centre
Patience
Meadow Drive
Rayleigh Drive
Chantry Drive
Halton Drive
Morpeth Av.
Warkworth
Taylor
Recreation Ground
Aged Miners Homes
Sandy Lane
Brunswick Industrial Estate
Brunswick Park Indus. Estate
Depots
Darrell Street
Stalks Road
North Road
Canterbury Way
Worcester Way
Hazelwood Prim. Sch.
Lib. Comm. Cen.
Subway
Lockey Park
Sports Ground
Woodlands Pk. Villas
Rydal Terrace
Cemetery
Gosforth Park Villas Cemetery
Morley Hill Farm
Morley Hill Cottage
Hawthorn Cottage
Woodlands
Coach Lane
Strawberry Ter.
Comm. Cen.
Castle St.
High Ridge
Newham Avenue
Recreation Ground
Dark Plantation
The Hawthorns
Depot
Nursery
Garden Centre
Hotel
A1
A19
A1068
B1318
B1321
A1056
24
33
44
34

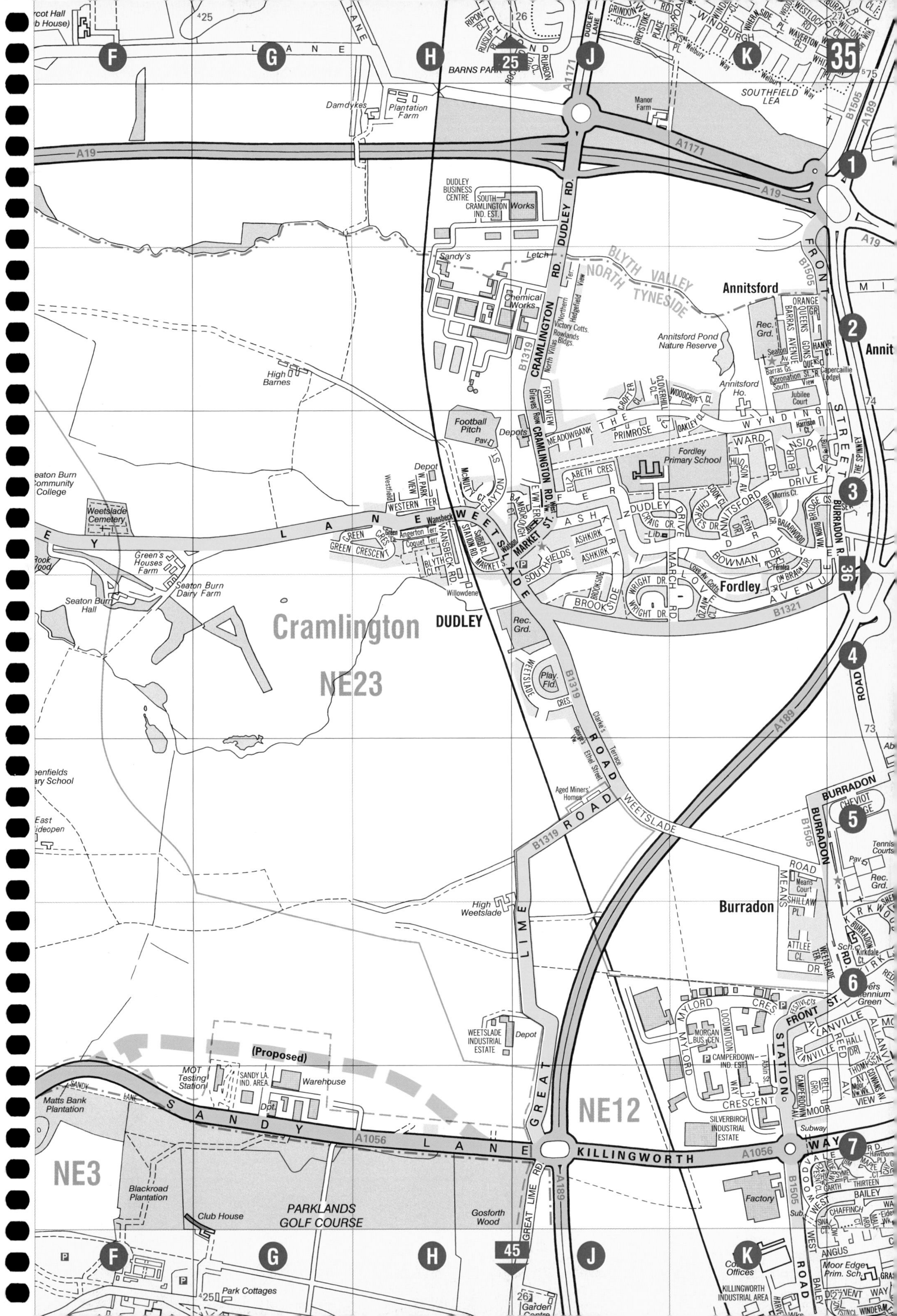
35
F
G
H
J
K
LANE
BARNS PARK
25
26
Damdykes
Plantation Farm
Manor Farm
SOUTHFIELD LEA
A19
A1171
B1505
A189
DUDLEY BUSINESS CENTRE
SOUTH CRAMLINGTON IND. EST.
Works
DUDLEY RD.
Sandy's
Letch
BLYTH VALLEY
NORTH TYNESIDE
Chemical Works
CRAMLINGTON RD.
B1319
High Barnes
Annitsford
Annitsford Pond Nature Reserve
Rec. Grd.
Capercaillie Lodge
Jubilee Court
Annitsford Ho.
FRONT STREET
THE SPINNEY
Football Pitch
Pav.
Depots
MEADOWBANK
THE PRIMROSE
WYNDING
Fordley Primary School
WARD
BURNSIDE AV.
HUDSON AV.
DRIVE
Depot
W. PARK VIEW
WESTERN TER.
McNULTY CT.
CLAYTON ST.
ELIZABETH CRES.
FERN
DUDLEY DRIVE
CRAIG CR.
Lib.
ANNITSFORD DR.
BURRADON R.
Seaton Burn Community College
Weetslade Cemetery
LANE
WEETSLADE
WANSBECK RD.
GREEN CRESCENT
Angerton Terr.
Coquet Terr.
STATION RD.
MARKET ST.
ASHKIRK
SOUTHFIELDS
BOWMAN DR.
AVENUE
LOVE AV.
Fordley
36
B1321
Green's Houses Farm
Seaton Burn Dairy Farm
Seaton Burn Hall
Willowdene
BROOKSIDE
WRIGHT DR.
MARCH RD.
Cramlington
DUDLEY
Rec. Grd.
NE23
Play. Fld.
WEETSLADE CRES.
ROAD
Clarke's Terrace
Ethel Street
Aged Miners' Homes
B1319 ROAD
WEETSLADE
BURRADON
CHEVIOT
BURRADON ROAD
Tennis Courts
Rec. Grd.
Means Court
SHILLAW PL.
Burradon
High Weetslade
LIME
ATTLEE CL.
Sch.
Kirkdale Cl.
WEETSLADE TER.
Millennium Green
MYLORD CRES.
MORGAN BUS. CEN.
LOCOMOTION WAY
CAMPERDOWN IND. EST.
FRONT ST.
STATION
ALLANVILLE
WEETSLADE INDUSTRIAL ESTATE
Depot
(Proposed)
MOT Testing Station
SANDY LA. IND. AREA
Warehouse
Dpt.
Matts Bank Plantation
SANDY LANE
A1056
GREAT
NE12
CRESCENT
SILVERBIRCH INDUSTRIAL ESTATE
Subway
WAY
KILLINGWORTH
NE3
Blackroad Plantation
Club House
PARKLANDS GOLF COURSE
Gosforth Wood
GREAT LIME RD.
Factory
THIRTEEN
BAILEY
ANGUS
45
Park Cottages
Council Offices
KILLINGWORTH INDUSTRIAL AREA
Moor Edge Prim. Sch.
WEST BAILEY
ROAD
Garden Centre

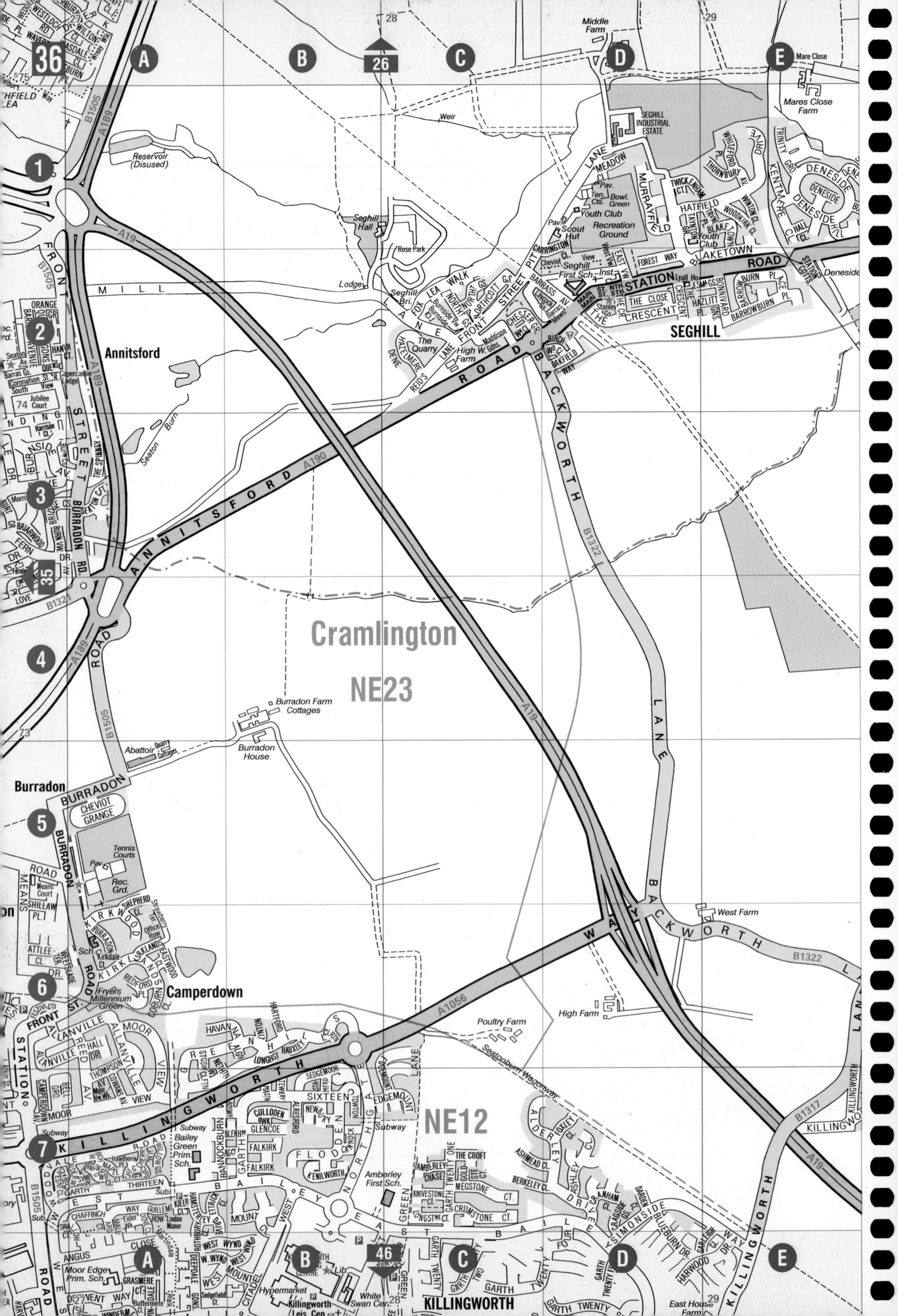
A
B
C
D
E
26
28
29
Middle Farm
Mare Close
Mares Close Farm
SEGHILL INDUSTRIAL ESTATE
Weir
Reservoir (Disused)
Seghill Hall
Rose Park
Lodge
Seghill Bri.
The Quarry
High W. Farm
Annitsford
ANNITSFORD ROAD
A190
A19
A189
B1505
B1321
B1322
B1317
A1056
BACKWORTH LANE
STATION ROAD
BLAKETOWN
SEGHILL
Youth Club
Recreation Ground
Scout Hut
Seghill First Sch.
Seaton Burn
35
Cramlington
NE23
Burradon Farm Cottages
Burradon House
Abattoir
Quarry Cottages
Burradon
BURRADON ROAD
CHEVIOT GRANGE
Tennis Courts
Rec. Grd.
West Farm
BACKWORTH
WAY
Camperdown
Fryers Millennium Green
High Farm
Poultry Farm
Seatonburn Waggonway
KILLINGWORTH ROAD
NE12
Subway
Bailey Green Prim. Sch.
Amberley First Sch.
Moor Edge Prim. Sch.
Hypermarket
Killingworth Leis. Cen.
White Swan Cen.
46
KILLINGWORTH
East House Farm
Deneside
1
2
3
4
5
6
7
73
74
75

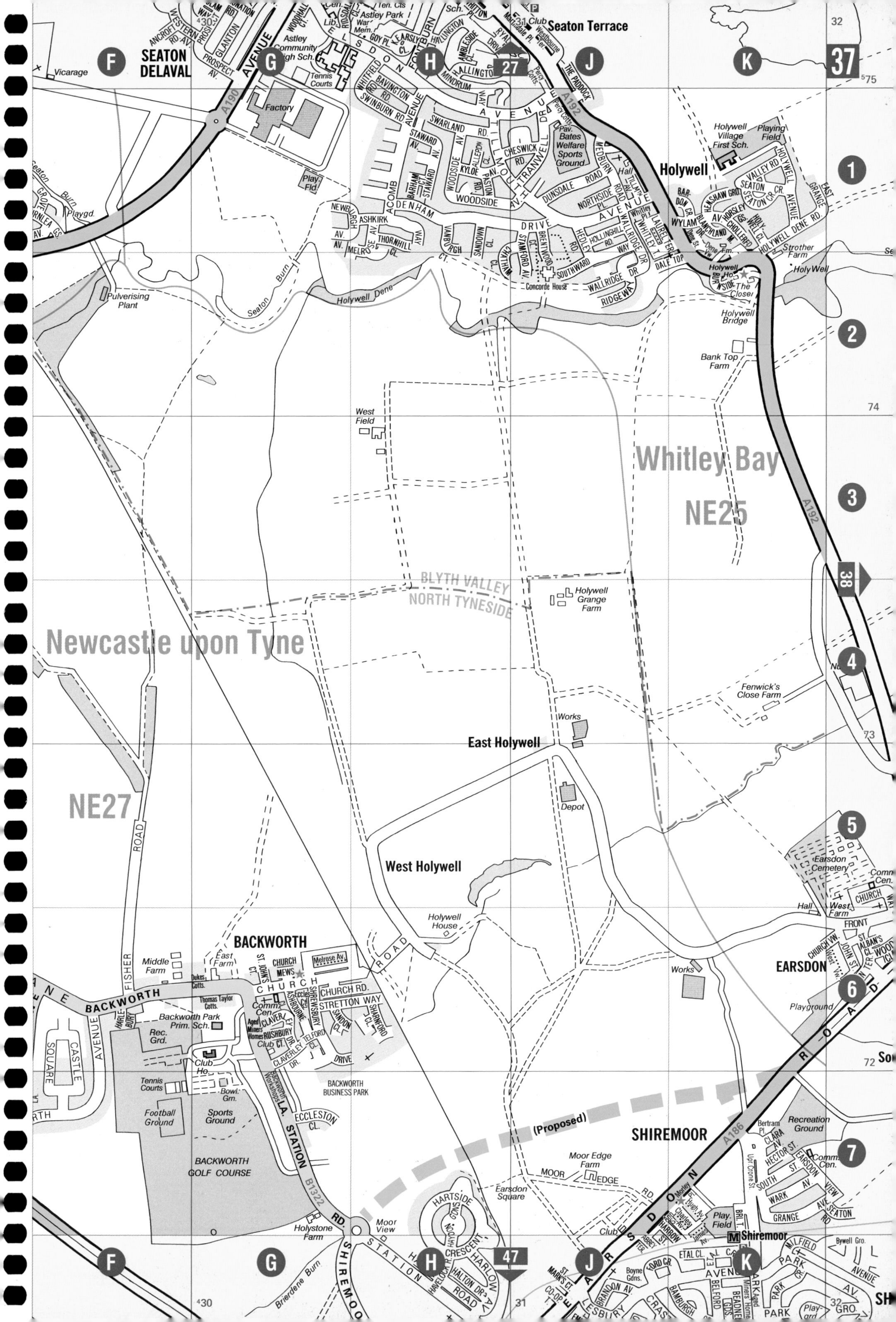

F SEATON DELAVAL **G** **H** 27 **J** **K** 37

Vicarage

Holywell

Whitley Bay
NE25

BLYTH VALLEY
NORTH TYNESIDE

Newcastle upon Tyne

Holywell
Grange
Farm

Fenwick's
Close Farm

East Holywell

NE27

Depot

West Holywell

Earsdon
Cemetery

Hall

West
Farm

CHURCH

Holywell
House

EARSDON

Works

BACKWORTH

Middle
Farm

East
Farm

CHURCH
MEWS

Melrose Av.

Comms
Cen.

Aged
Miners
Homes

Backworth Park
Prim. Sch.

Rec.
Grd.

Thomas Taylor
Cotts.

Dukes
Cotts.

STRETTON WAY

Club
Ho.

Tennis
Courts

Bowl.
Grn.

Football
Ground

Sports
Ground

BACKWORTH
BUSINESS PARK

BACKWORTH
GOLF COURSE

Holystone
Farm

Moor
View

(Proposed)

Moor Edge
Farm

MOOR

EDGE

Earsdon
Square

Playground

SHIREMOOR

Recreation
Ground

Comm.
Cen.

Shiremoor

HARTSIDE

F **G** **H** 47 **J** **K**

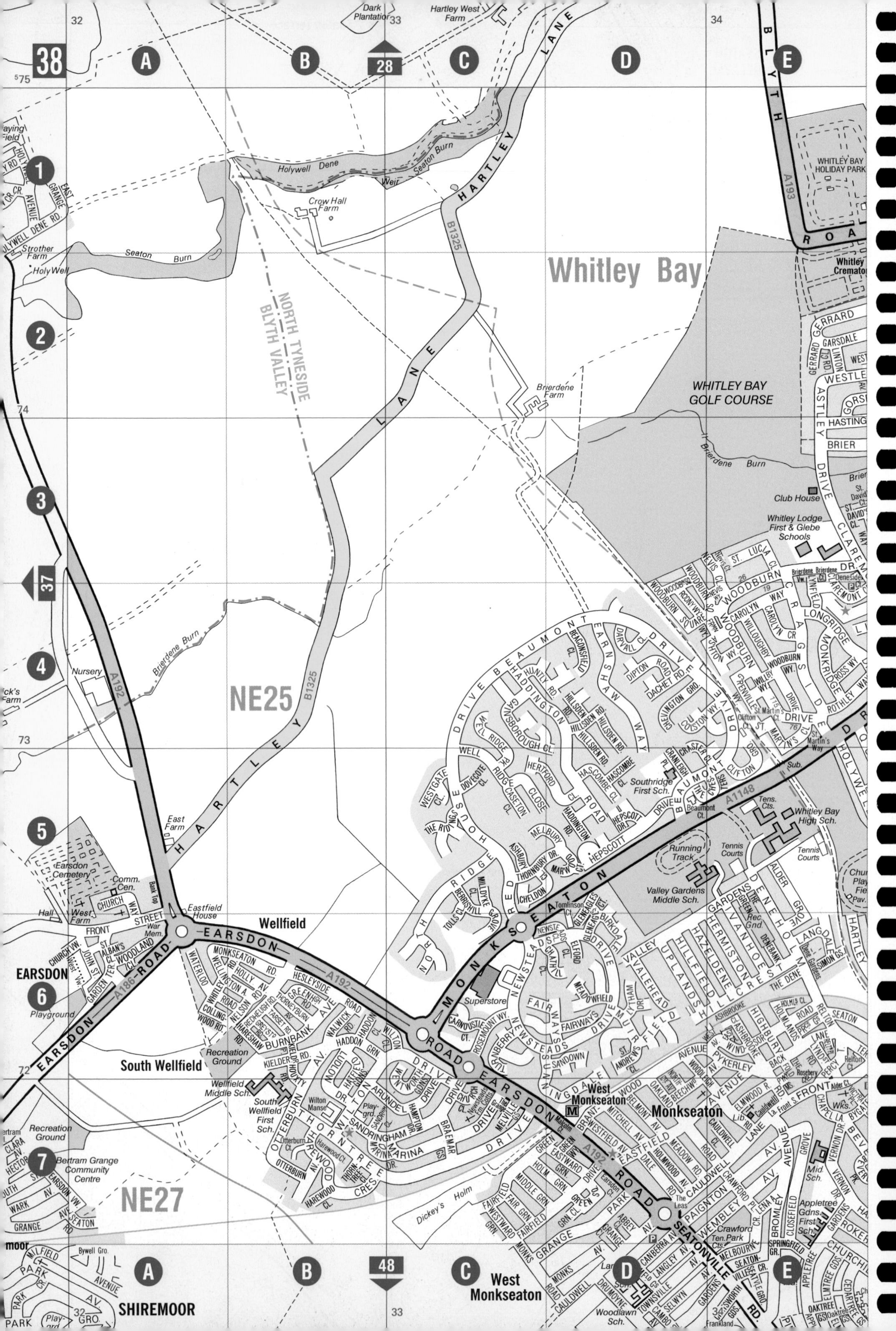

38
28
37
48
A
B
C
D
E
1
2
3
4
5
6
7
32
33
34
74
73
72
575
Dark Plantation
Hartley West Farm
HARTLEY LANE
B1325
Holywell Dene
Seaton Burn
Weir
Crow Hall Farm
Strother Farm
Holy Well
NORTH TYNESIDE
BLYTH VALLEY
Whitley Bay
WHITLEY BAY HOLIDAY PARK
A193
BLYTH ROAD
Whitley Crematorium
Brierdene Farm
WHITLEY BAY GOLF COURSE
Brierdene Burn
Club House
Whitley Lodge First & Glebe Schools
Nursery
A192
NE25
East Farm
Earsdon Cemetery
Comm. Cen.
CHURCH WAY
Hall
West Farm
FRONT STREET
War Mem.
Eastfield House
Wellfield
EARSDON ROAD
A186
EARSDON
Playground
South Wellfield
Recreation Ground
Wellfield Middle Sch.
South Wellfield First Sch.
Superstore
MONKSEATON DRIVE
A1148
Southridge First Sch.
Running Track
Tennis Courts
Whitley Bay High Sch.
Valley Gardens Middle Sch.
West Monkseaton
Monkseaton
Recreation Ground
Bertram Grange Community Centre
NE27
Dickey's Holm
SEATONVILLE RD.
Crawford Ten. Park
Appletree Gdns First Sch.
Mid. Sch.
SHIREMOOR
West Monkseaton
Woodlawn Sch.

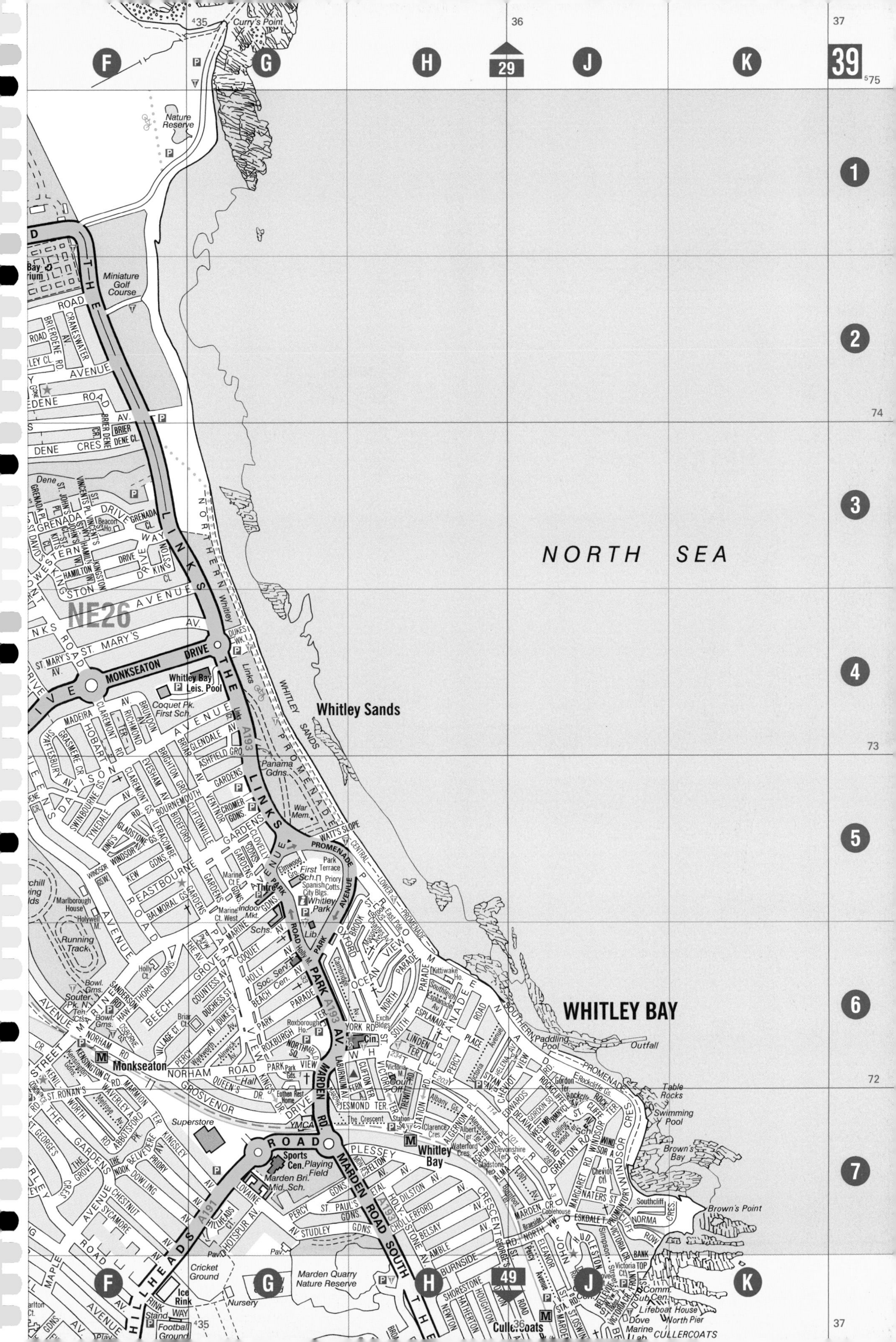

F
G
H
J
K
29
36
37
1
2
3
4
5
6
7
74
73
72
Curry's Point
Nature Reserve
Miniature Golf Course
NORTH SEA
NE26
Whitley Sands
WHITLEY BAY
Whitley Bay Leis. Pool
Coquet Pk. First Sch.
THE LINKS
MONKSEATON DRIVE
ST. MARY'S AV.
NORTHERN PROMENADE
WHITLEY SANDS PROMENADE
Panama Gdns.
War Mem.
WATT'S SLOPE
CENTRAL LOWER PROMENADE
Whitley Park
Spanish City Blgs.
First Sch.
Park Terrace
Priory Cotts.
Indoor Mkt.
Lib.
Kittiwake Ho.
Southleigh
ESPLANADE
Paddling Pool
Outfall
Table Rocks
Swimming Pool
Brown's Bay
Brown's Point
Southcliff
Monkseaton
Marlborough House
Running Track
Bowl. Grns.
Superstore
YMCA
Sports Cen.
Playing Field
Marden Bri. Mid. Sch.
Marden Quarry Nature Reserve
Cricket Ground
Ice Rink
Football Ground
Nursery
Whitley Bay
Cullercoats
49
Lifeboat House
North Pier
CULLERCOATS
PARK AVENUE
PARK ROAD
MARDEN ROAD SOUTH
HILLHEADS ROAD
A191
A193
GROSVENOR DRIVE
NORHAM ROAD
EASTBOURNE GARDENS
MARINE AVENUE
PLESSEY GDNS.

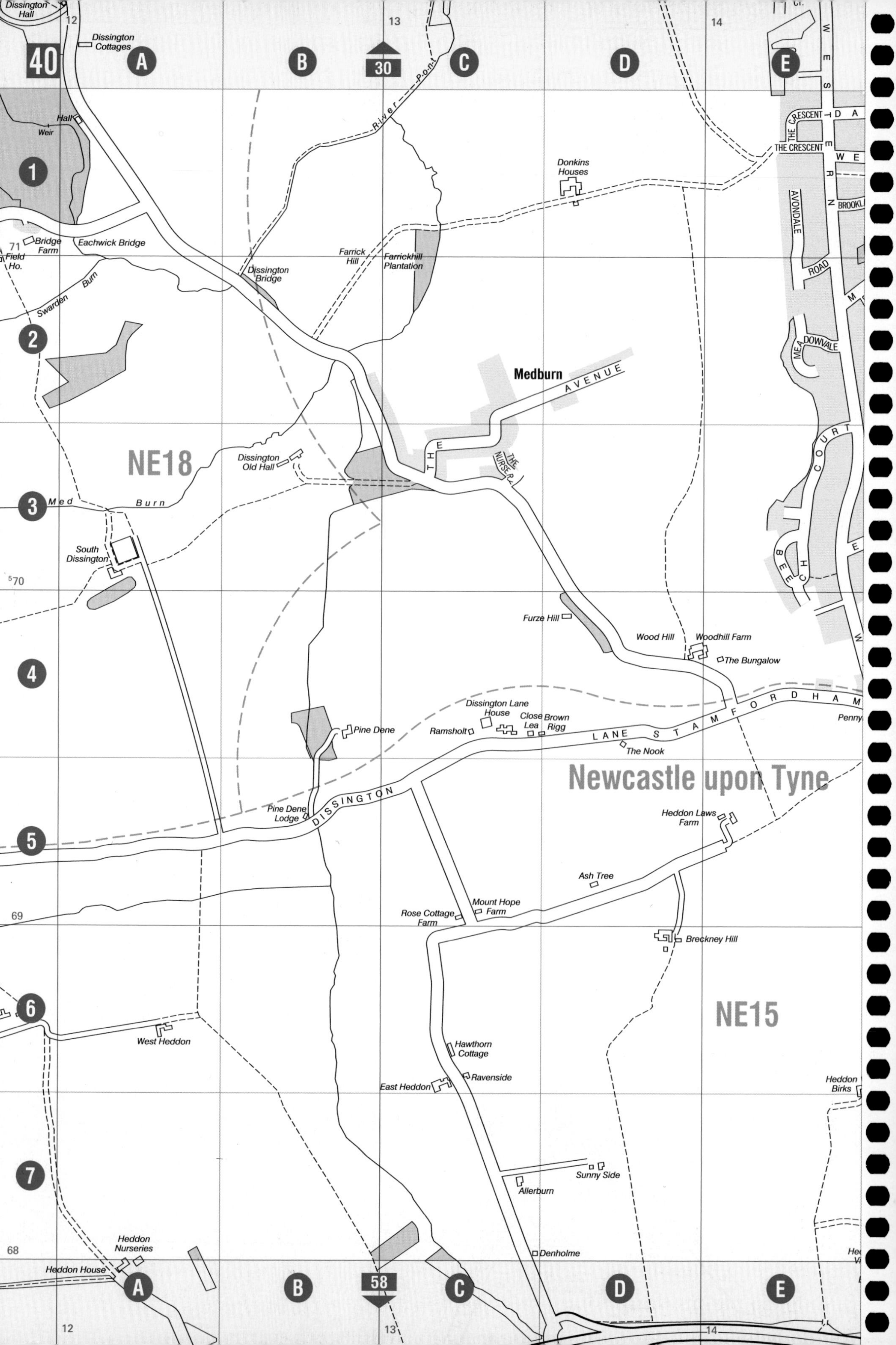

40
A
B
C
D
E
30
58
12
13
14
71
70
69
68
1
2
3
4
5
6
7
Dissington Hall
Dissington Cottages
Hall
Weir
Bridge Farm
Eachwick Bridge
Field Ho.
Swarden Burn
River Pont
Dissington Bridge
Farrick Hill
Farrickhill Plantation
Donkins Houses
THE CRESCENT
AVONDALE
ROAD
BROOKL
MEADOWVALE
COURT
BEECH
Medburn
AVENUE
THE NURSERY
NE18
Dissington Old Hall
Med Burn
South Dissington
Furze Hill
Wood Hill
Woodhill Farm
The Bungalow
Dissington Lane House
Close Lea
Brown Rigg
Ramsholt
Pine Dene
STAMFORDHAM
LANE
The Nook
Penny
Newcastle upon Tyne
Heddon Laws Farm
Pine Dene Lodge
DISSINGTON
Ash Tree
Mount Hope Farm
Rose Cottage Farm
Breckney Hill
West Heddon
NE15
Hawthorn Cottage
Ravenside
East Heddon
Heddon Birks
Sunny Side
Allerburn
Heddon Nurseries
Heddon House
Denholme

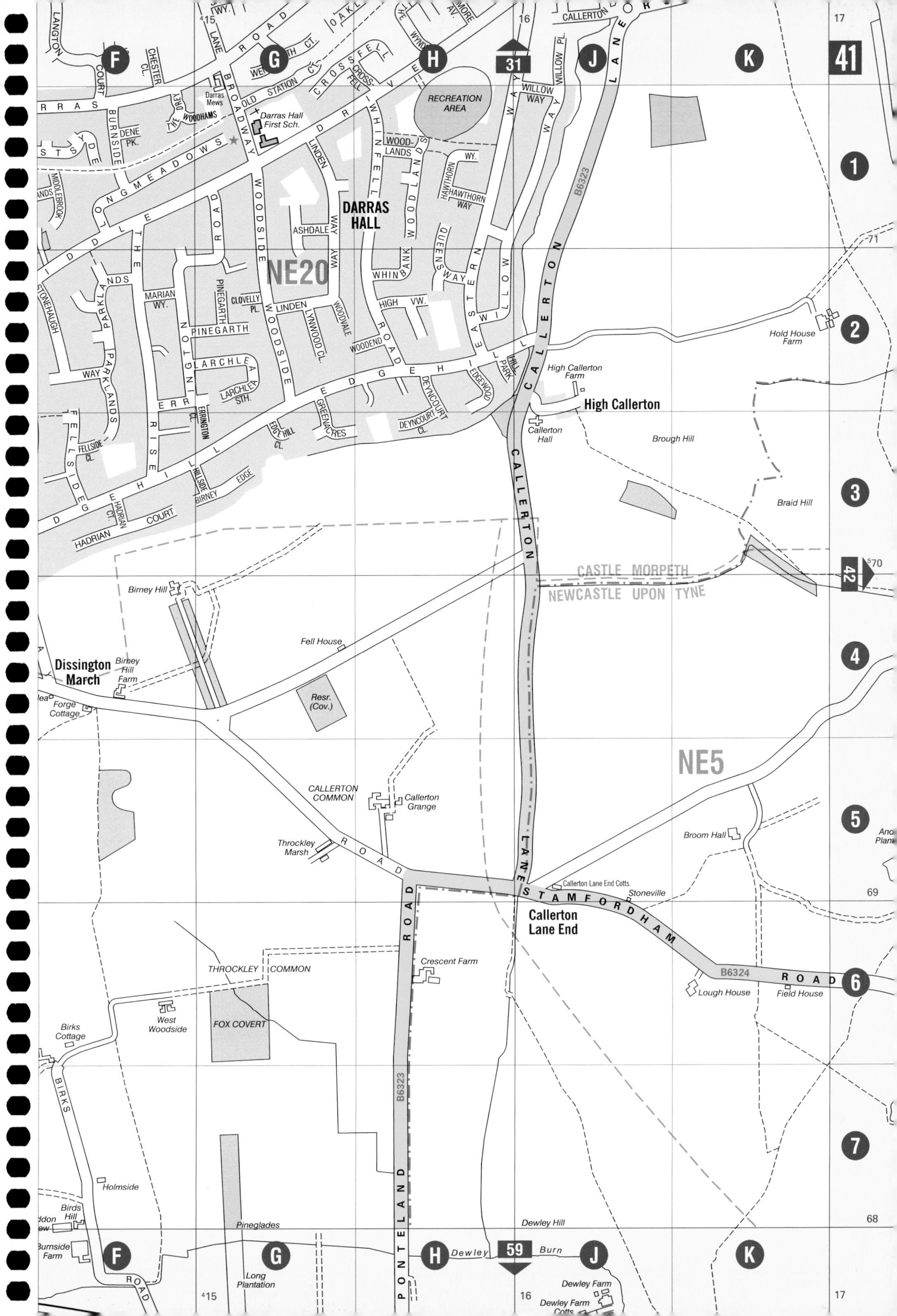

DARRAS HALL
NE20
NE5
High Callerton
Dissington March
Callerton Lane End
CASTLE MORPETH
NEWCASTLE UPON TYNE
RECREATION AREA
Darras Hall First Sch.
Darras Mews
High Callerton Farm
Callerton Hall
Brough Hill
Hold House Farm
Braid Hill
Birney Hill
Fell House
Birney Hill Farm
Forge Cottage
Resr. (Cov.)
CALLERTON COMMON
Callerton Grange
Throckley Marsh
Broom Hall
Callerton Lane End Cotts.
Stoneville
Crescent Farm
THROCKLEY COMMON
FOX COVERT
West Woodside
Birks Cottage
Lough House
Field House
Holmside
Birds Hill
Burnside Farm
Pineglades
Long Plantation
Dewley Hill
Dewley Burn
Dewley Farm
Dewley Farm Cotts
CALLERTON LANE
STAMFORDHAM ROAD
PONTELAND ROAD
B6323
B6324
31
42
59

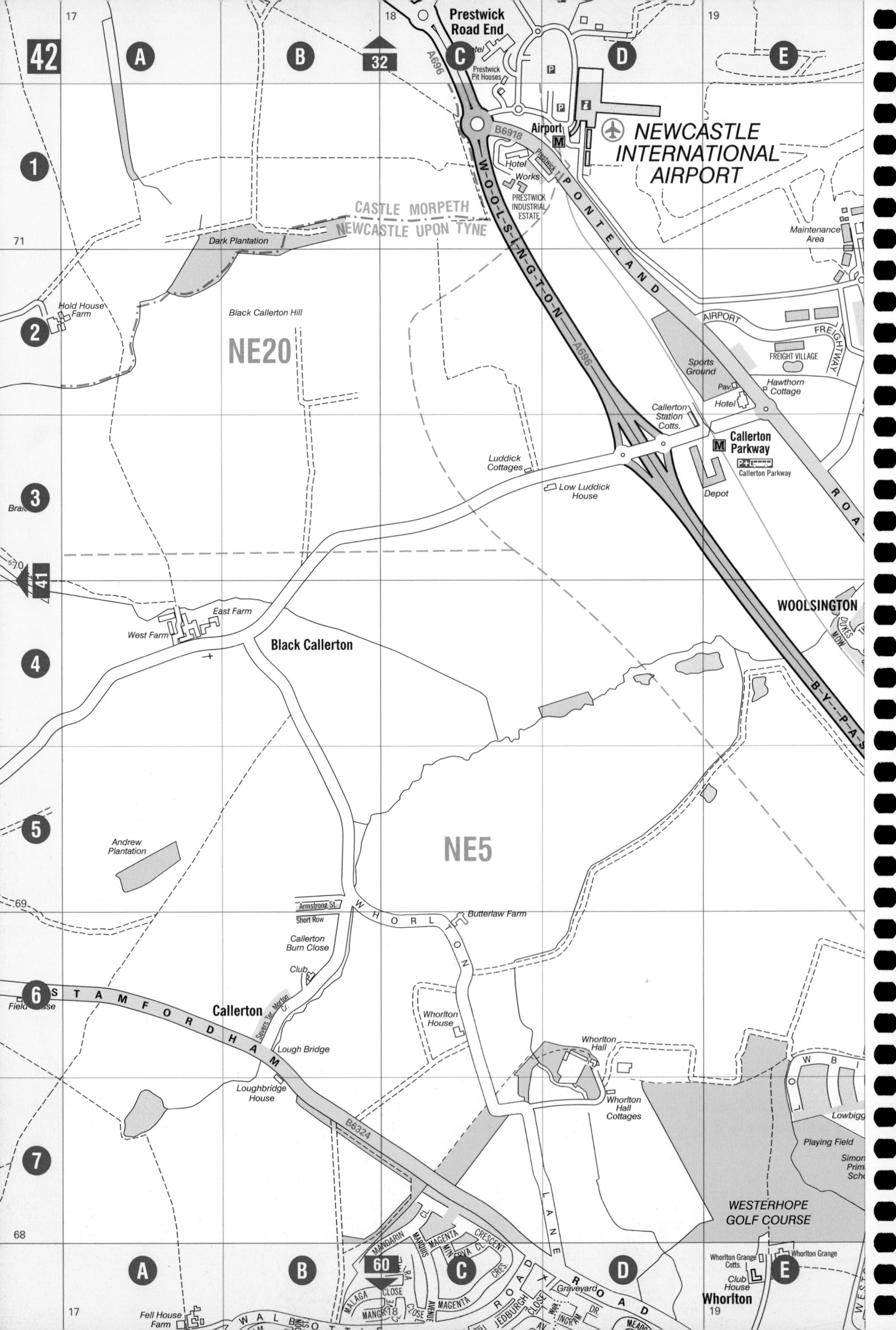
17
18
19
A
B
C
D
E
32
Prestwick Road End
Prestwick Pit Houses
A696
B6918
Airport
NEWCASTLE INTERNATIONAL AIRPORT
Hotel
Works
PRESTWICK INDUSTRIAL ESTATE
CASTLE MORPETH
NEWCASTLE UPON TYNE
WOOLSINGTON
PONTELAND
Maintenance Area
71
Dark Plantation
Hold House Farm
Black Callerton Hill
NE20
AIRPORT
FREIGHTWAY
FREIGHT VILLAGE
Sports Ground
Pav
Hawthorn Cottage
Hotel
Callerton Station Cotts.
Callerton Parkway
Luddick Cottages
Low Luddick House
Depot
ROAD
70
41
WOOLSINGTON
DUKES MDW
East Farm
West Farm
Black Callerton
BY-PASS
Andrew Plantation
NE5
69
Armstrong St.
Short Row
WHORLTON
Butterlaw Farm
Callerton Burn Close
Club
STAMFORDHAM
Callerton
Severs Ter.
Morton Cr.
Whorlton House
Lough Bridge
Whorlton Hall
Loughbridge House
Whorlton Hall Cottages
B6324
Lowbigg
Playing Field
WESTERHOPE GOLF COURSE
68
60
MANDARIN CL.
MARQUIS
MAGENTA
MINERVA CL.
CRESCENT
CRES.
LANE
ROAD
Graveyard
Whorlton Grange Cotts.
Whorlton Grange
Club House
Whorlton
MALAGA
CLOSE
MANGROVE
AVENUE
JEDBURGH
CLOSE
INGRAM
DR.
Fell House Farm
WALBOTTLE
1
2
3
4
5
6
7

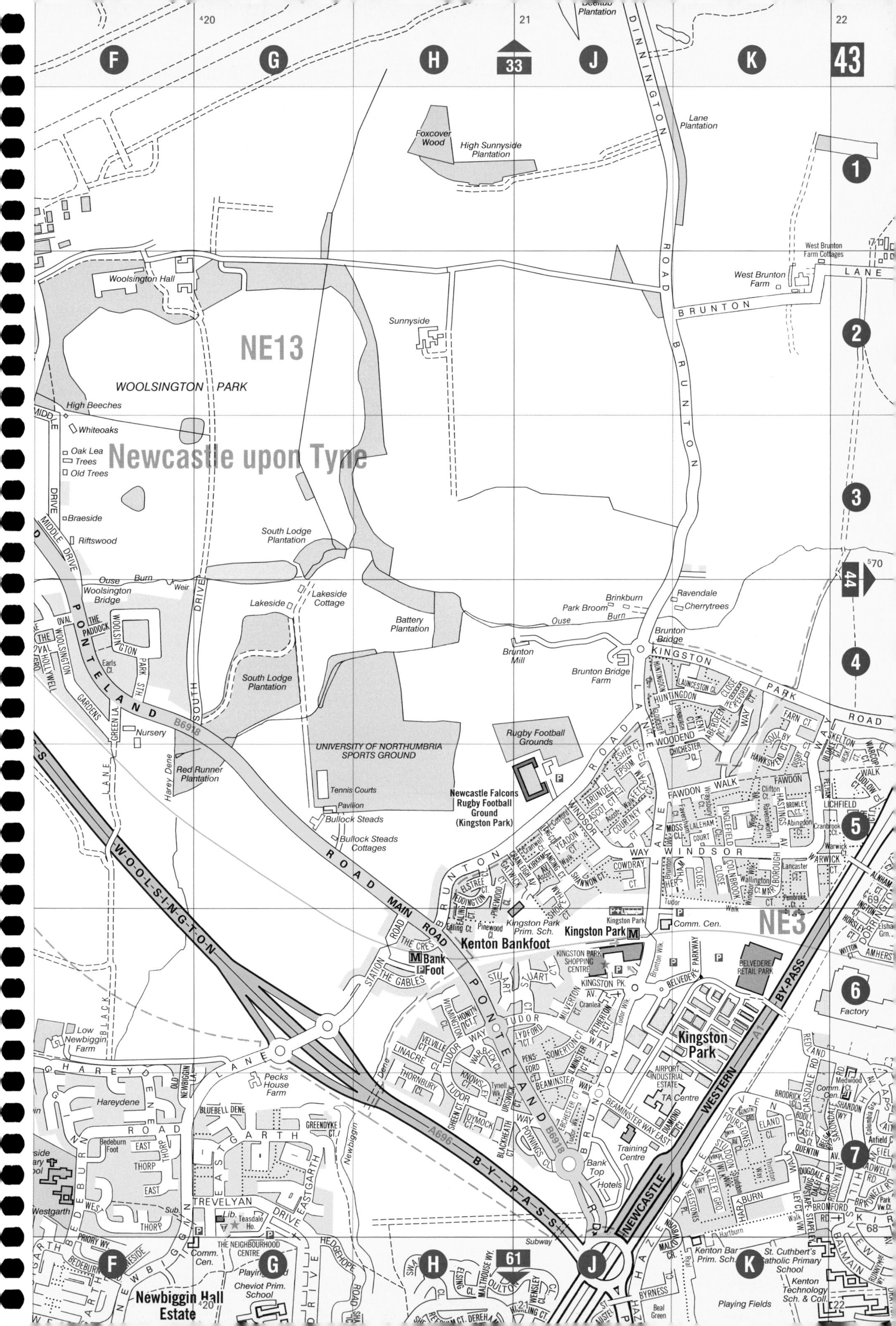
F
G
H
J
K
33
44
61
NE13
NE3
Newcastle upon Tyne
WOOLSINGTON PARK
Woolsington Hall
High Beeches
Whiteoaks
Oak Lea
Trees
Old Trees
Braeside
Riftswood
Foxcover Wood
High Sunnyside Plantation
Lane Plantation
Sunnyside
West Brunton Farm Cottages
West Brunton Farm
BRUNTON LANE
DINNINGTON ROAD
BRUNTON
South Lodge Plantation
Ouse Burn
Woolsington Bridge
Weir
Lakeside
Lakeside Cottage
Battery Plantation
Park Broom
Brinkburn
Ravendale
Cherrytrees
Brunton Bridge
Brunton Mill
Brunton Bridge Farm
KINGSTON PARK ROAD
Rugby Football Grounds
UNIVERSITY OF NORTHUMBRIA SPORTS GROUND
Tennis Courts
Pavilion
Bullock Steads
Bullock Steads Cottages
Newcastle Falcons Rugby Football Ground (Kingston Park)
Nursery
Harey Dene
Red Runner Plantation
PONTELAND ROAD
WOOLSINGTON BY-PASS
Kingston Park Prim. Sch.
Kingston Park
Kenton Bankfoot
Bank Foot
Comm. Cen.
KINGSTON PARK SHOPPING CENTRE
BELVEDERE RETAIL PARK
Factory
Kingston Park
AIRPORT INDUSTRIAL ESTATE
TA Centre
Training Centre
Bank Top
Hotels
Low Newbiggin Farm
HAREY DENE
Hareydene
Pecks House Farm
Bedeburn Foot
Westgarth
TREVELYAN DRIVE
Lib.
Teasdale Ho.
THE NEIGHBOURHOOD CENTRE
Cheviot Prim. School
Newbiggin Hall Estate
Subway
Kenton Bar Prim. Sch.
St. Cuthbert's Catholic Primary School
Kenton Technology Sch. & Coll.
Playing Fields
Beal Green
NEWCASTLE WESTERN BY-PASS
A1
A696
B6918

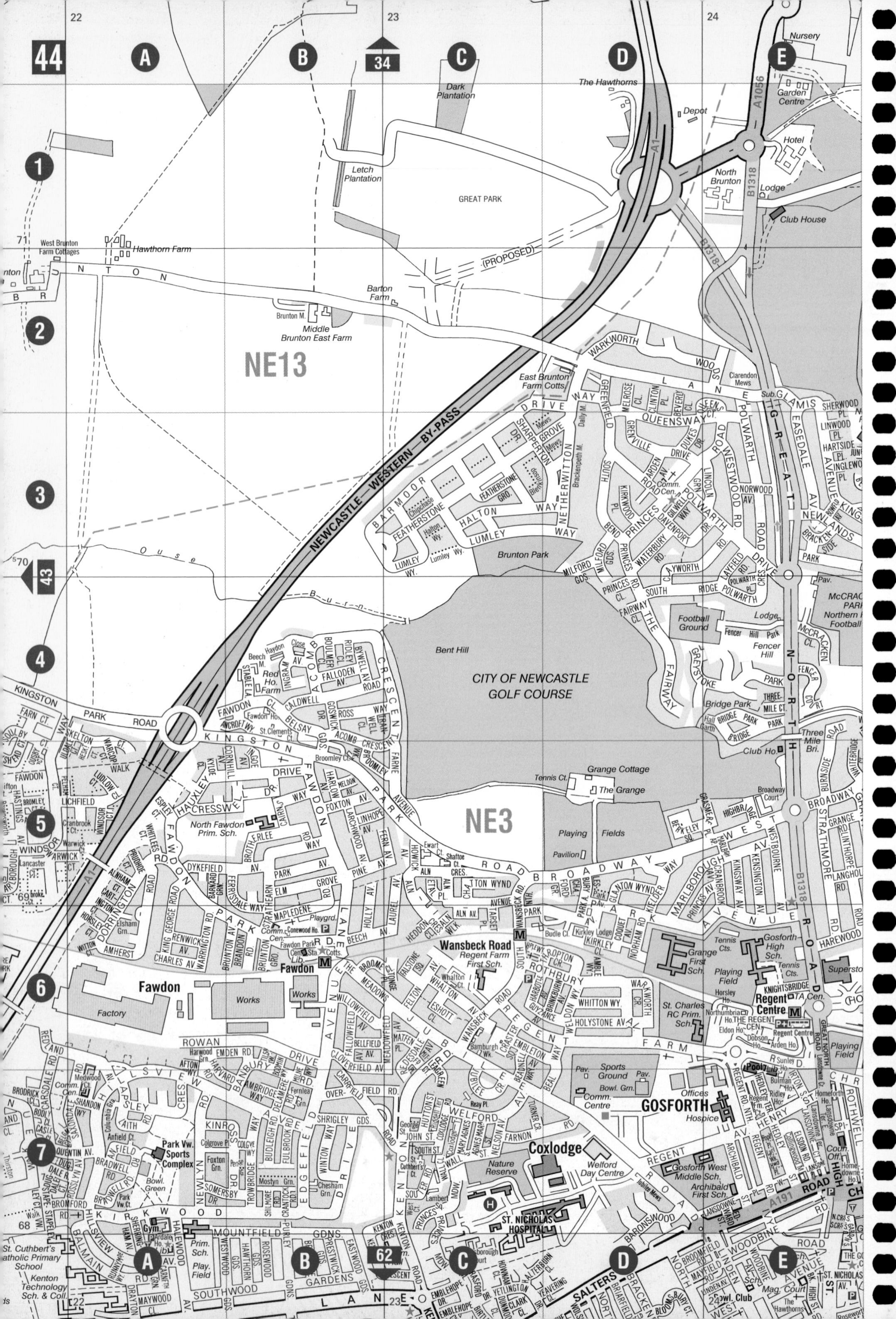

22
23
24
A
B
C
D
E
1
2
3
4
5
6
7
34
43
62
Dark Plantation
Letch Plantation
GREAT PARK
The Hawthorns
Depot
Nursery
Garden Centre
Hotel
North Brunton
Lodge
Club House
West Brunton Farm Cottages
Hawthorn Farm
Barton Farm
Brunton M.
Middle Brunton East Farm
(PROPOSED)
NE13
NEWCASTLE WESTERN BY-PASS
East Brunton Farm Cotts.
Clarendon Mews
Brunton Park
Ouse Burn
Bent Hill
CITY OF NEWCASTLE GOLF COURSE
Football Ground
Fencer Hill
Bridge Park
Three Mile Bri.
Club Ho.
Grange Cottage
The Grange
Tennis Ct.
NE3
Playing Fields
Pavilion
North Fawdon Prim. Sch.
KINGSTON PARK ROAD
Fawdon
Factory
Works
Wansbeck Road
Regent Farm First Sch.
Grange First Sch.
Gosforth High Sch.
Regent Centre
Superstore
St. Charles RC Prim. Sch.
Sports Ground
Comm. Centre
GOSFORTH
Hospice
Offices
Coxlodge
Welford Day Centre
Nature Reserve
ST. NICHOLAS HOSPITAL
Gosforth West Middle Sch.
Archibald First Sch.
Park Vw. Sports Complex
St. Cuthbert's Catholic Primary School
Kenton Technology Sch. & Coll.
Bowl. Club
Playing Field
McCRACKEN PARK Northern Football
A1
A1056
B1318
A191

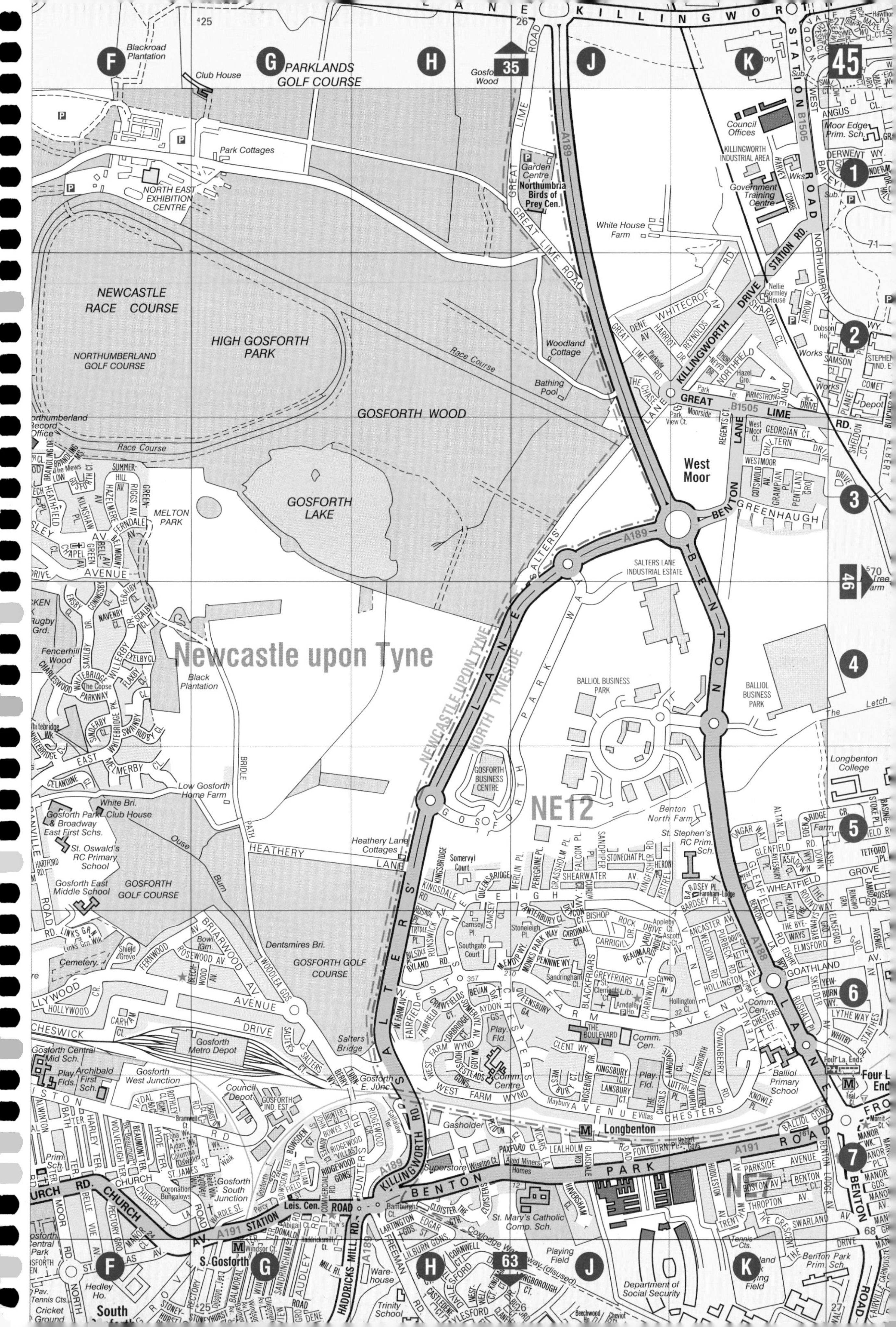
45
35
46
63
KILLINGWORTH
PARKLANDS GOLF COURSE
Blackroad Plantation
Club House
Gosforth Wood
Park Cottages
NORTH EAST EXHIBITION CENTRE
Garden Centre
Northumbria Birds of Prey Cen.
Council Offices
KILLINGWORTH INDUSTRIAL AREA
Government Training Centre
White House Farm
NEWCASTLE RACE COURSE
HIGH GOSFORTH PARK
NORTHUMBERLAND GOLF COURSE
Race Course
Woodland Cottage
Bathing Pool
GOSFORTH WOOD
Northumberland Record Office
GREAT LIME ROAD
A189
B1505
STATION ROAD
KILLINGWORTH DRIVE
West Moor
MELTON PARK
GOSFORTH LAKE
BENTON LANE
SALTERS LANE INDUSTRIAL ESTATE
Rugby Grd.
Fencerhill Wood
Newcastle upon Tyne
Black Plantation
BALLIOL BUSINESS PARK
NEWCASTLE UPON TYNE
NORTH TYNESIDE
GOSFORTH BUSINESS CENTRE
NE12
Longbenton College
Low Gosforth Home Farm
Benton North Farm
St. Stephen's RC Prim. Sch.
Gosforth Park & Broadway East First Schs.
White Bri. Club House
St. Oswald's RC Primary School
Heathery Lane Cottages
HEATHERY LANE
Gosforth East Middle School
GOSFORTH GOLF COURSE
Ouse Burn
Dentsmires Bri.
GOSFORTH GOLF COURSE
Cemetery
A188
Comm. Cen.
Balliol Primary School
Four Lane Ends
Gosforth Metro Depot
Salters Bridge
Gosforth Central Mid Sch.
Archibald First Sch.
Gosforth West Junction
Council Depot
GOSFORTH IND. EST.
Gosforth E. Junc.
Gasholder
Longbenton
A191
BENTON PARK ROAD
NE7
Superstore
Aged Miners' Homes
Gosforth South Junction
Coronation Bungalows
Leis. Cen.
STATION ROAD
S. Gosforth
St. Mary's Catholic Comp. Sch.
Playing Field
Department of Social Security
Benton Park Prim. Sch.
Hedley Ho.
Cricket Ground
Trinity School
Ware-house
South
F
G
H
J
K
1
2
3
4
5
6
7

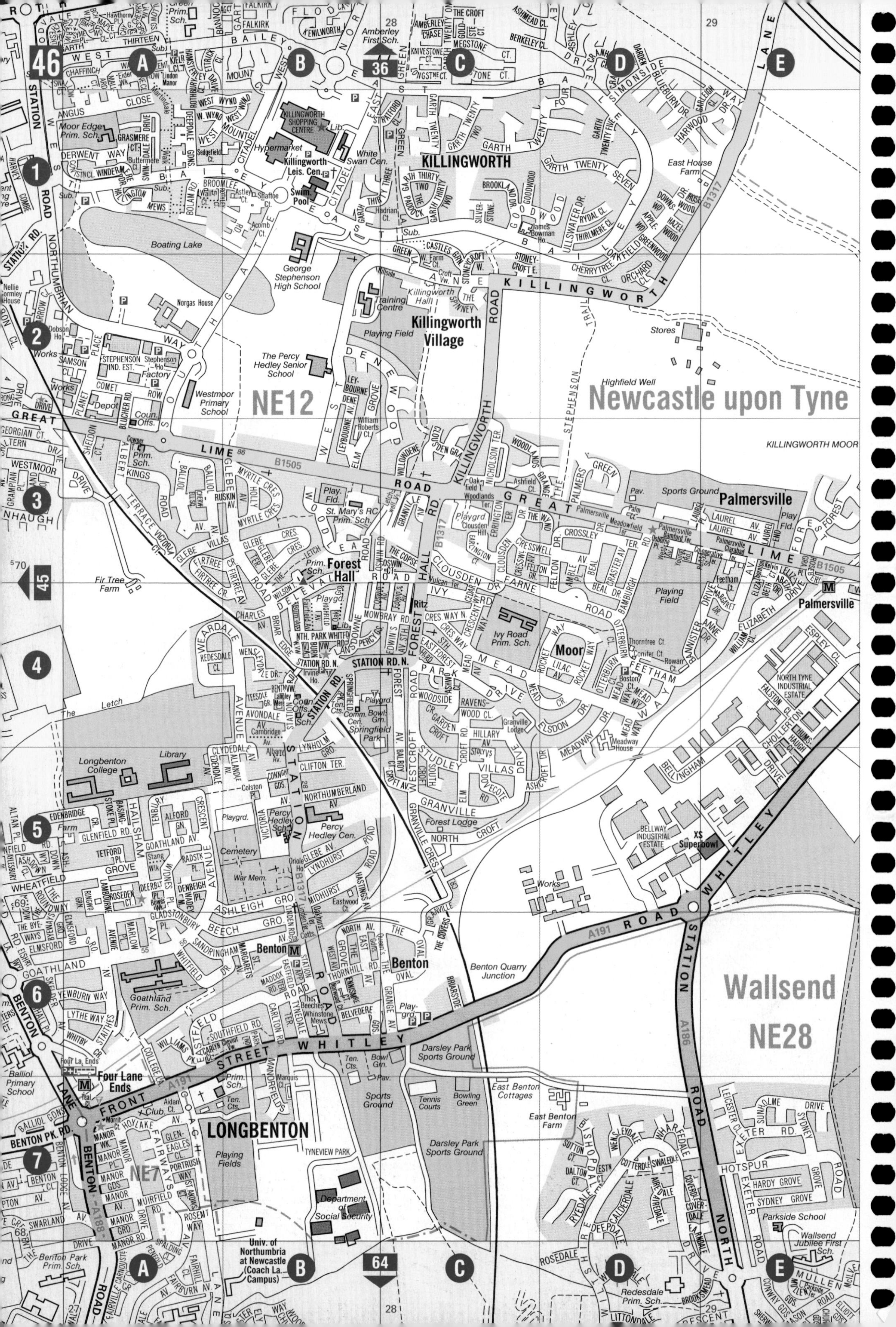
36
KILLINGWORTH
Killingworth Shopping Centre
Hypermarket
Killingworth Leis. Cen.
Swim. Pool
White Swan Cen.
Boating Lake
George Stephenson High School
Norgas House
Training Centre
Killingworth Hall
Killingworth Village
Playing Field
The Percy Hedley Senior School
Westmoor Primary School
Stephenson Ind. Est.
NE12
Newcastle upon Tyne
KILLINGWORTH MOOR
Highfield Well
Stores
East House Farm
Moor Edge Prim. Sch.
GREAT LIME ROAD
B1505
KILLINGWORTH ROAD
FOREST HALL RD.
B1317
Sports Ground
Palmersville
Forest Hall
Ivy Road Prim. Sch.
Moor
Playing Field
Fir Tree Farm
45
The Letch
Library
Longbenton College
Springfield Park
NORTH TYNE INDUSTRIAL ESTATE
BELLWAY INDUSTRIAL ESTATE
XS Superbowl
Percy Hedley Cen.
Cemetery
War Mem.
Benton
Benton Quarry Junction
WHITLEY ROAD
A191
STATION ROAD
A186
Wallsend
NE28
Goathland Prim. Sch.
Four Lane Ends
FRONT STREET
Darsley Park Sports Ground
East Benton Cottages
East Benton Farm
LONGBENTON
Playing Fields
Tennis Courts
Bowling Green
TYNEVIEW PARK
Department of Social Security
NE7
BENTON LANE
A188
Balliol Primary School
Benton Park Prim. Sch.
Univ. of Northumbria at Newcastle (Coach La. Campus)
64
Redesdale Prim. Sch.
Parkside School
Wallsend Jubilee First Sch.
A B C D E
1 2 3 4 5 6 7
27 28 29

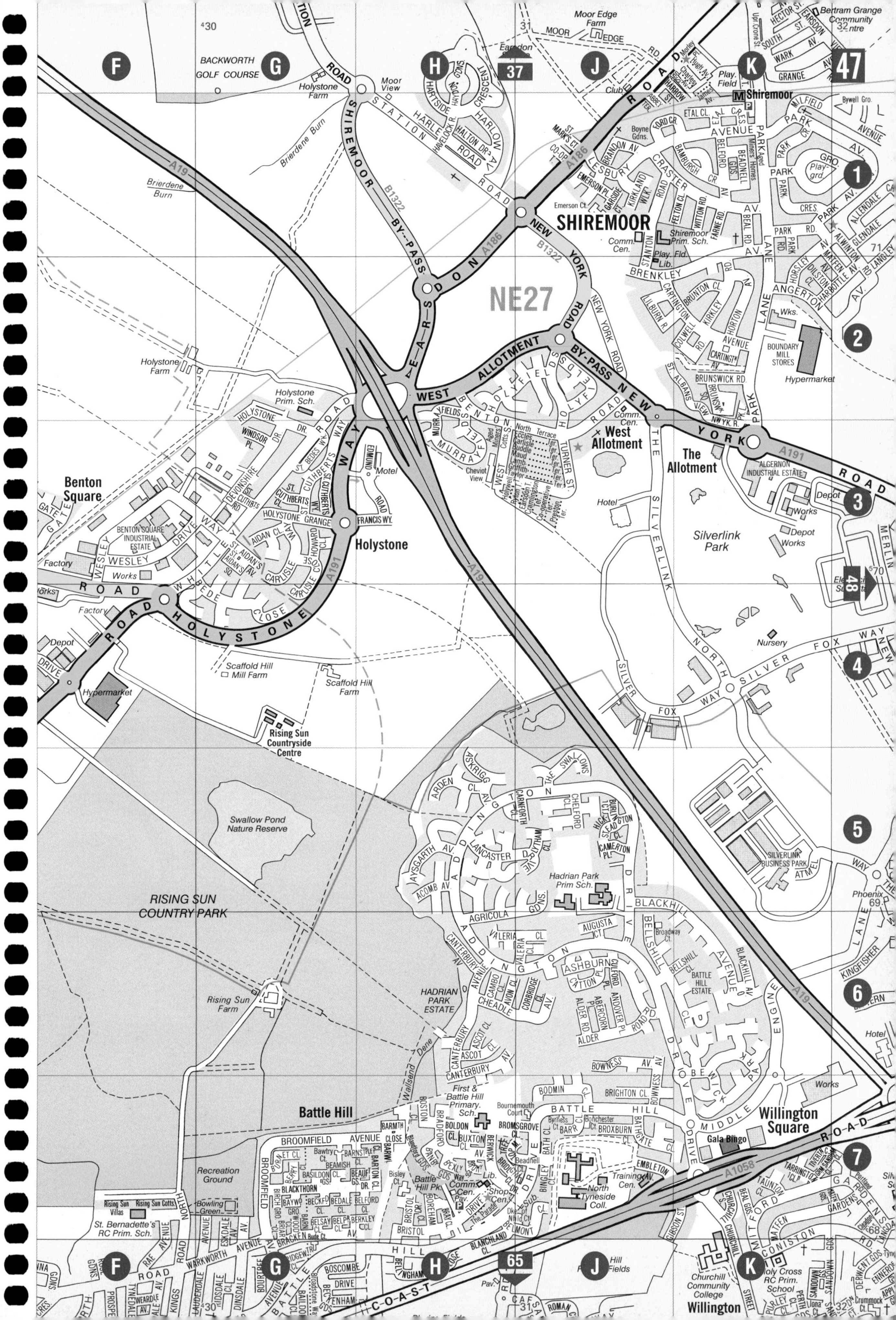
F
G
H
J
K
1
2
3
4
5
6
7
37
48
65
BACKWORTH GOLF COURSE
Holystone Farm
Moor View
Moor Edge Farm
MOOR EDGE
Earsdon
Bertram Grange Community Centre
Shiremoor
SHIREMOOR
Shiremoor Prim. Sch.
Comm. Cen.
Play. Fld.
Lib.
Emerson Ct.
Boyne Gdns.
NE27
SHIREMOOR BY-PASS
EARSDON ROAD
STATION ROAD
WEST ALLOTMENT
NEW YORK ROAD
NEW YORK BY-PASS
Brierdene Burn
Holystone Farm
Holystone Prim. Sch.
HOLYSTONE WAY
HOLYSTONE ROAD
Benton Square
BENTON SQUARE INDUSTRIAL ESTATE
Factory
Works
Depot
Hypermarket
Holystone
Motel
West Allotment
Comm. Cen.
The Allotment
ALGERNON INDUSTRIAL ESTATE
Hotel
Silverlink Park
SILVERLINK
SILVER FOX WAY
Nursery
Depot
Works
BOUNDARY MILL STORES
Hypermarket
Wks.
Scaffold Hill Mill Farm
Scaffold Hill Farm
Rising Sun Countryside Centre
Swallow Pond Nature Reserve
RISING SUN COUNTRY PARK
Rising Sun Farm
SILVERLINK BUSINESS PARK
Phoenix
Hadrian Park Prim Sch.
HADRIAN PARK ESTATE
BATTLE HILL ESTATE
Broadway Ct.
Works
Hotel
Battle Hill
First & Battle Hill Primary Sch.
Bournemouth Court
Battle Hill Pk.
Comm. Cen.
Shop. Cen.
Training Cen.
North Tyneside Coll.
Willington Square
Gala Bingo
Recreation Ground
Bowling Green
Rising Sun Villas
Rising Sun Cotts
St. Bernadette's RC Prim. Sch.
Hill Fields
Churchill Community College
Willington
Holy Cross RC Prim. School
COAST ROAD
BATTLE HILL DRIVE
MIDDLE DRIVE
BROOMFIELD AVENUE
ADDINGTON DRIVE
BLACKHILL AVENUE
WARKWORTH AVENUE
A19
A186
A191
A1058
B1322

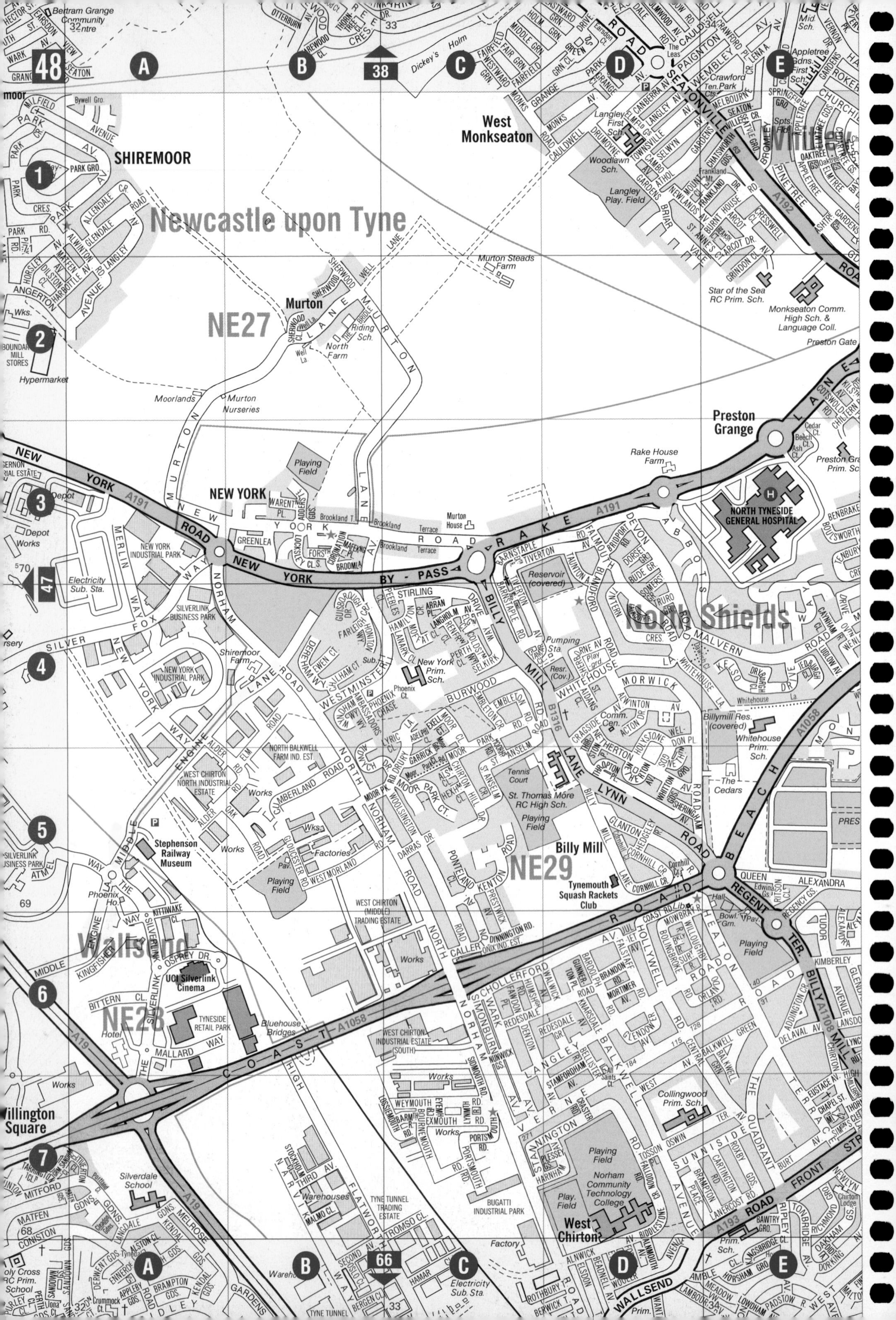

A
B
C
D
E
38
47
66
1
2
3
4
5
6
7
Newcastle upon Tyne
NE27
NE28
NE29
SHIREMOOR
West Monkseaton
Murton
NEW YORK
Preston Grange
North Shields
Billy Mill
Wallsend
West Chirton
Willington Square
Bertram Grange Community Centre
Dickey's Holm
Langley First Sch.
Woodlawn Sch.
Langley Play. Field
Murton Steads Farm
Star of the Sea RC Prim. Sch.
Monkseaton Comm. High Sch. & Language Coll.
Preston Gate
Riding Sch.
North Farm
Moorlands
Murton Nurseries
Playing Field
Rake House Farm
NORTH TYNESIDE GENERAL HOSPITAL
Preston Grange Prim. Sch.
Murton House
NEW YORK INDUSTRIAL PARK
Electricity Sub. Sta.
SILVERLINK BUSINESS PARK
Shiremoor Farm
Reservoir (covered)
Pumping Sta.
New York Prim. Sch.
Phoenix Ct.
NORTH BALKWELL FARM IND. EST.
WEST CHIRTON NORTH INDUSTRIAL ESTATE
Comm. Cen.
Billymill Res. (covered)
Whitehouse Prim. Sch.
The Cedars
Tennis Court
St. Thomas More RC High Sch.
Stephenson Railway Museum
Factories
Works
Tynemouth Squash Rackets Club
WEST CHIRTON (MIDDLE) TRADING ESTATE
UCI Silverlink Cinema
TYNESIDE RETAIL PARK
Bluehouse Bridges
Hotel
WEST CHIRTON INDUSTRIAL ESTATE (SOUTH)
Collingwood Prim. Sch.
Norham Community Technology College
Silverdale School
Warehouses
TYNE TUNNEL TRADING ESTATE
BUGATTI INDUSTRIAL PARK
Electricity Sub. Sta.
Holy Cross RC Prim. School
Hypermarket
BOUNDARY MILL STORES
NEW YORK ROAD
A191
NEW YORK BY-PASS
RAKE LANE
BILLY MILL LANE
B1316
COAST ROAD
A1058
A19
A192
A193
A108
BEACH ROAD
MIDDLE ENGINE LANE
NORHAM ROAD
NORTH ROAD
WALLSEND ROAD
FRONT STREET
TYNE TUNNEL

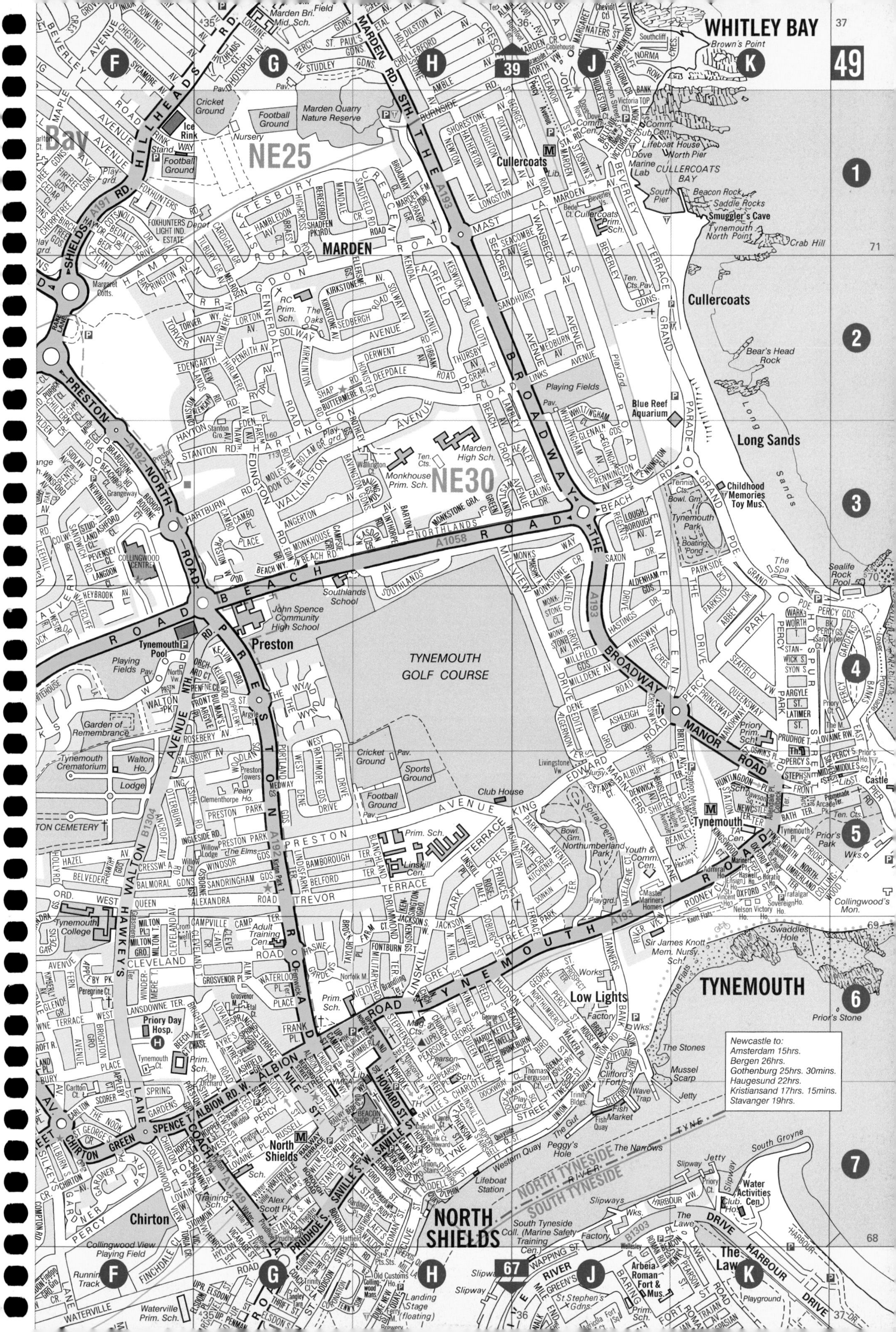

WHITLEY BAY
49
37
NE25
NE30
Bay
Cullercoats
CULLERCOATS BAY
Marden Quarry Nature Reserve
Cricket Ground
Football Ground
Ice Rink
FOXHUNTERS LIGHT IND. ESTATE
MARDEN
Marden High Sch.
Monkhouse Prim. Sch.
Playing Fields
Blue Reef Aquarium
Long Sands
Childhood Memories Toy Mus.
Tynemouth Park
Brown's Point
Beacon Rock
Saddle Rocks
Smuggler's Cave
Tynemouth North Point
Crab Hill
Bear's Head Rock
Sealife Rock Pool
The Spa
Southlands School
John Spence Community High School
Preston
Tynemouth Pool
TYNEMOUTH GOLF COURSE
Sports Ground
Club House
Northumberland Park
Tynemouth Crematorium
PRESTON CEMETERY
Tynemouth College
Priory Day Hosp.
Castle
Prior's Park
Collingwood's Mon.
TYNEMOUTH
Prior's Stone
Low Lights
Clifford Fort
Fish Quay
Trinity Bldgs.
The Narrows
South Groyne
Water Activities Cen.
Newcastle to:
Amsterdam 15hrs.
Bergen 26hrs.
Gothenburg 25hrs. 30mins.
Haugesund 22hrs.
Kristiansand 17hrs. 15mins.
Stavanger 19hrs.
NORTH TYNESIDE
SOUTH TYNESIDE
RIVER TYNE
NORTH SHIELDS
North Shields
Chirton
Collingwood View Playing Field
Lifeboat Station
South Tyneside Coll. (Marine Safety Training Cen.)
Arbeia Roman Fort & Mus.
The Lawe
Waterville Prim. Sch.
BROADWAY
BEACH ROAD
A1058
A193
A192
A191
B1304
PRESTON ROAD
TYNEMOUTH ROAD
HAWKEY'S LANE
MANOR ROAD
GRAND PARADE
39
67
F
G
H
J
K
1
2
3
4
5
6
7
71
70
69
68

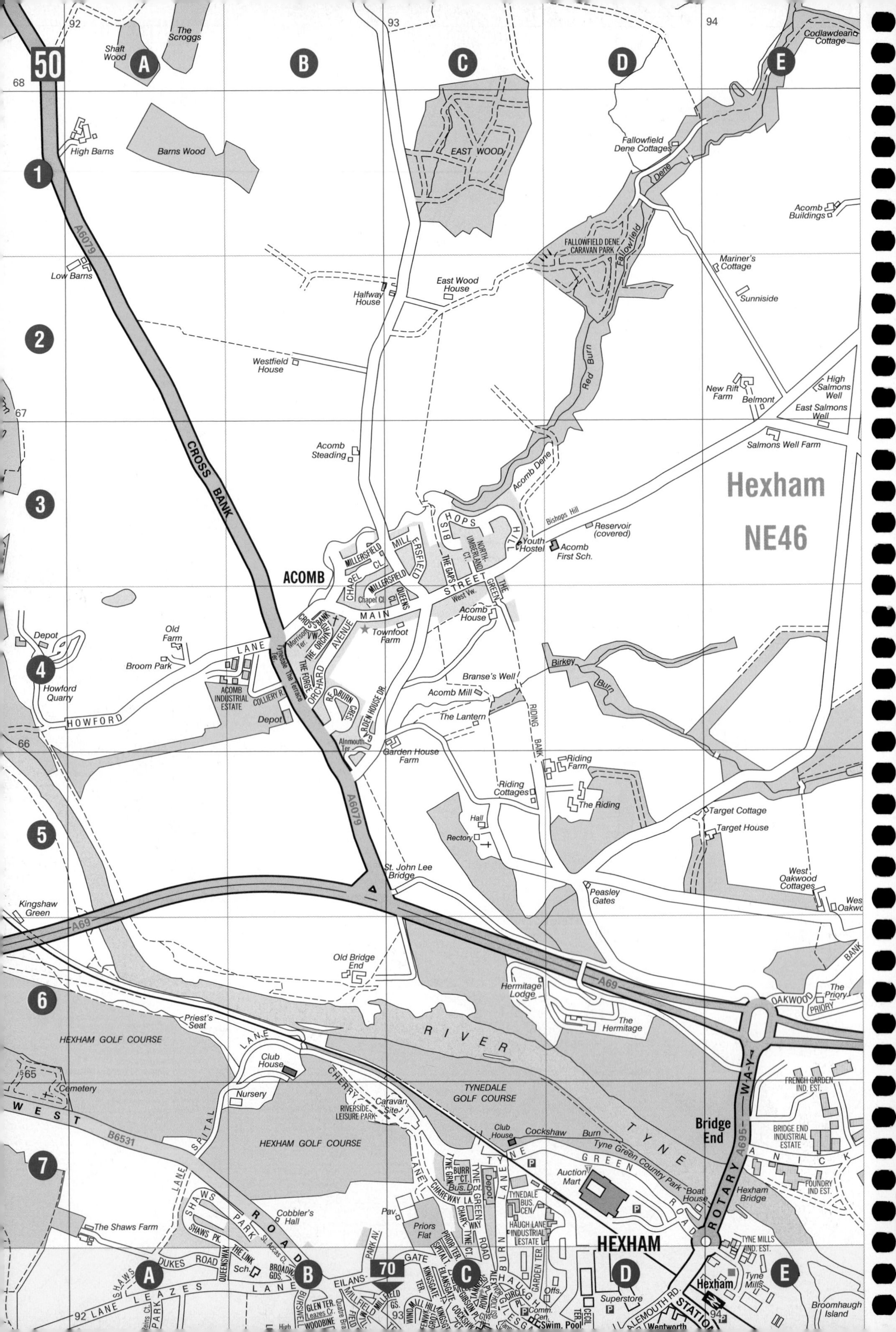

A
B
C
D
E
1
2
3
4
5
6
7
92
93
94
68
67
66
65
Shaft Wood
The Scroggs
Codlawdean Cottage
High Barns
Barns Wood
EAST WOOD
Fallowfield Dene Cottages
Dene
Acomb Buildings
FALLOWFIELD DENE CARAVAN PARK
Fallowfield
Mariner's Cottage
Low Barns
Halfway House
East Wood House
Sunniside
Westfield House
Red Burn
New Rift Farm
Belmont
High Salmons Well
East Salmons Well
A6079
CROSS BANK
Acomb Steading
Salmons Well Farm
Acomb Dene
Hexham
NE46
BISHOPS HILL
Bishops Hill
Reservoir (covered)
Youth Hostel
Acomb First Sch.
MILLERSFIELD
CHAPEL CL.
MILL
ERSFIELD
NORTH UMBERLAND CT.
THE GAPS
ACOMB
MILLERSFIELD
CHAPEL
QUEENS CT.
STREET
THE GREEN
West Vw.
Chapel Cl.
MAIN
Acomb House
Townfoot Farm
Old Farm
Depot
LANE
CROSS BANK
Morrison Ter.
THE ORCHARD
AVENUE
Tynedale Ter.
The Terrace
THE FORGE
ORCHARD
Broom Park
Birkey
Burn
Branse's Well
Howford Quarry
ACOMB INDUSTRIAL ESTATE
COLLIERY R.
Acomb Mill
REDBURN CRES.
ARDEN HOUSE DR.
RIDING BANK
HOWFORD
Depot
The Lantern
Alnmouth Ter.
Garden House Farm
Riding Farm
Riding Cottages
The Riding
Target Cottage
Target House
Hall
Rectory
A6079
St. John Lee Bridge
West Oakwood Cottages
Peasley Gates
Kingshaw Green
A69
Old Bridge End
BANK
Hermitage Lodge
A69
The Priory
OAKWOOD
PRIORY
The Hermitage
Priest's Seat
HEXHAM GOLF COURSE
RIVER
Club House
LANE
CHERRY
TYNEDALE GOLF COURSE
Cemetery
Nursery
Caravan Site
RIVERSIDE LEISURE PARK
WAY
FRENCH GARDEN IND. EST.
WEST
SPITAL
B6531
HEXHAM GOLF COURSE
Club House
Cockshaw
Burn
Tyne Green Country Park
TYNE
Bridge End
BRIDGE END INDUSTRIAL ESTATE
A695
ANICK
GREEN
Auction Mart
Boat House
FOUNDRY IND EST.
SHAWS PARK
ROAD
Cobbler's Hall
Pav.
Priors Flat
TYNEDALE BUS. CEN.
HAUGH LANE INDUSTRIAL ESTATE
ROTARY
Hexham Bridge
The Shaws Farm
SHAWS PK.
QUEENSWAY
THE LINK
St. Aidans Cl.
DUKES
ROAD
Sch.
BROADWAY GDS.
PARK AV.
GATE
70
HEXHAM
Superstore
TYNE MILLS IND. EST.
Tyne Mills
Hexham
SHAWS
LEAZES
LANE
EILANS
GLEN TER.
Leazes Cr.
WOODBINE
Offs.
Comm. Cen.
Swim. Pool
ALEMOUTH RD.
STATION
Wentworth
Broomhaugh Island

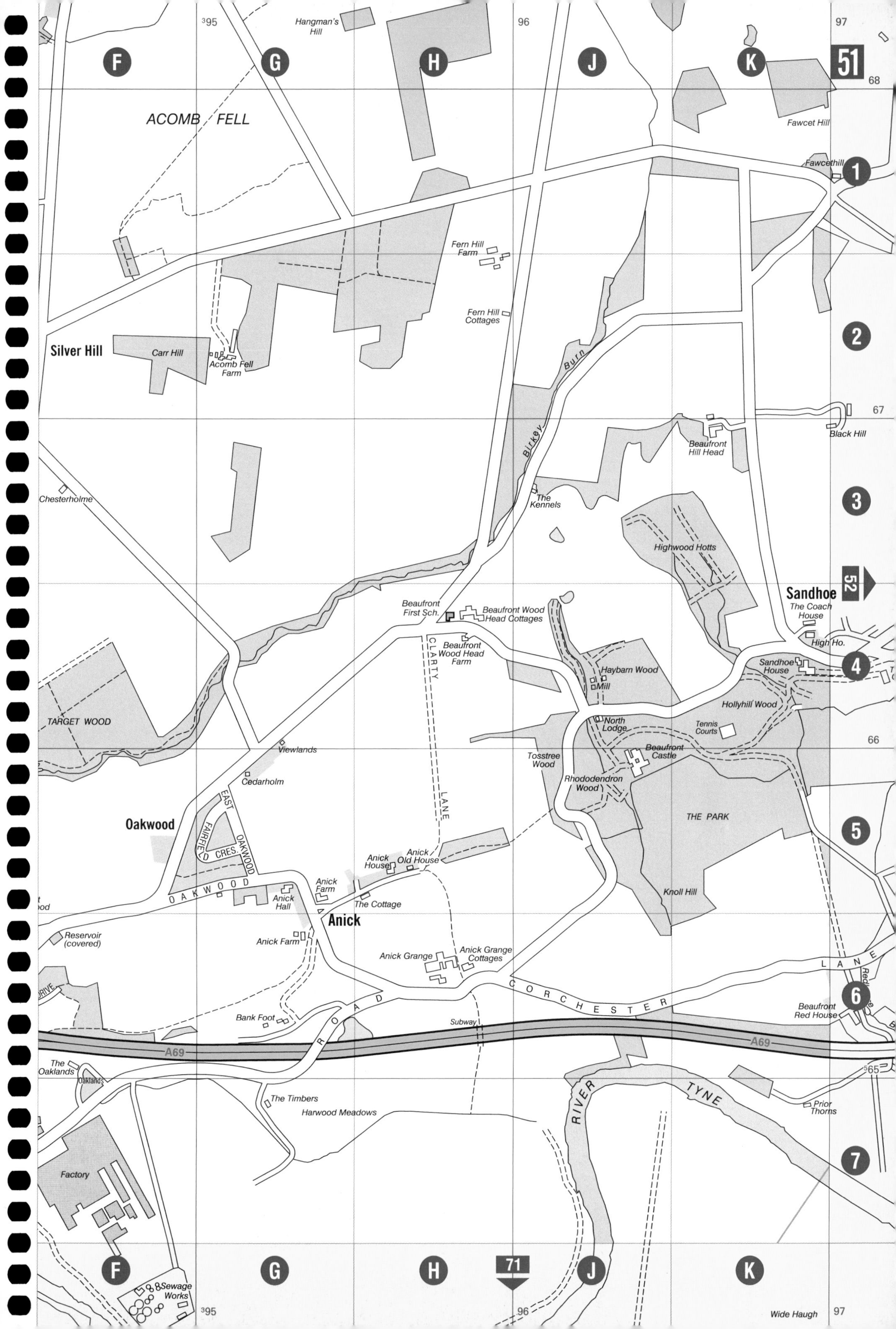

ACOMB FELL

Hangman's Hill

Fawcet Hill

51

Fawcethill

1

Silver Hill

Carr Hill

Fern Hill Farm

Fern Hill Cottages

Acomb Fell Farm

Birkey Burn

2

Black Hill

67

Beaufront Hill Head

Chesterholme

The Kennels

3

Highwood Hotts

Sandhoe

52

The Coach House

High Ho.

Beaufront First Sch.

Beaufront Wood Head Cottages

Beaufront Wood Head Farm

Haybarn Wood

Mill

Sandhoe House

4

TARGET WOOD

Viewlands

Cedarholm

North Lodge

Tennis Courts

Hollyhill Wood

66

Oakwood

EAST FAIRFIE CRES

OAKWOOD

Tosstree Wood

Rhododendron Wood

Beaufront Castle

THE PARK

5

Anick House

Anick Old House

CLARTY LANE

OAKWOOD ROAD

Anick Farm

Anick Hall

Anick

The Cottage

Knoll Hill

Reservoir (covered)

Anick Farm

Anick Grange

Anick Grange Cottages

CORCHESTER

LANE

Red

Beaufront Red House

6

DRIVE

Bank Foot

Subway

A69

A69

65

The Oaklands

Oaklands

The Timbers

Harwood Meadows

RIVER TYNE

Prior Thorns

7

Factory

Sewage Works

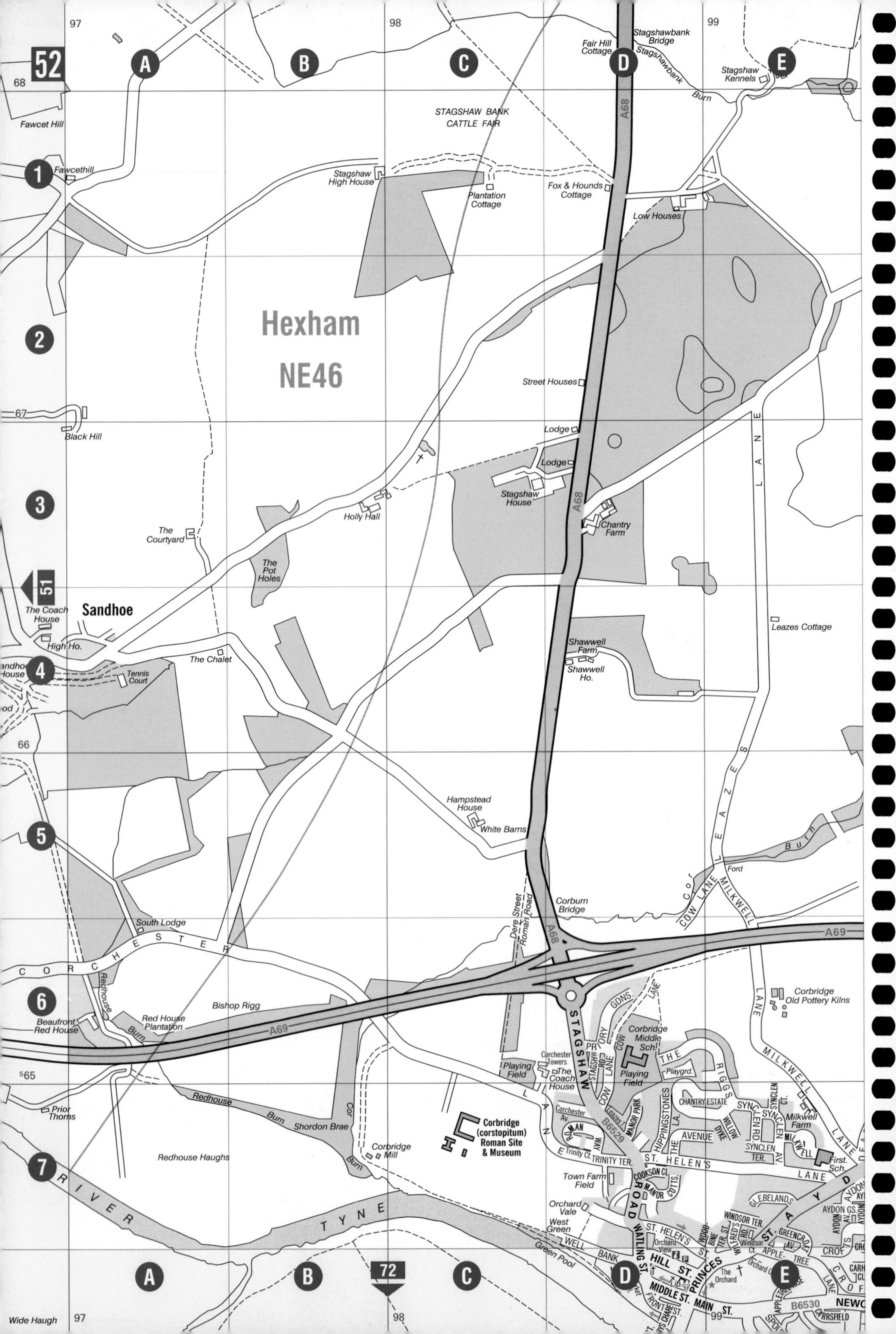
Hexham
NE46
Sandhoe
Fawcet Hill
Fawcethill
Black Hill
The Coach House
High Ho.
Tennis Court
The Chalet
The Courtyard
The Pot Holes
Holly Hall
Stagshaw High House
Plantation Cottage
STAGSHAW BANK CATTLE FAIR
Fair Hill Cottage
Stagshawbank Bridge
Stagshawbank Burn
Stagshaw Kennels
Fox & Hounds Cottage
Low Houses
Street Houses
Lodge
Lodge
Stagshaw House
Chantry Farm
Leazes Cottage
Shawwell Farm
Shawwell Ho.
Hampstead House
White Barns
Corburn Bridge
Dere Street Roman Road
Ford
Cor Burn
COW LANE
MILKWELL
LEAZES LANE
South Lodge
CORCHESTER
Redhouse
Beaufront Red House
Red House Plantation
Bishop Rigg
A68
A69
B6529
Corbridge Old Pottery Kilns
Corchester Towers
Playing Field
The Coach House
Corbridge Middle Sch.
Playing Field
Playgrd.
THE RIGGS
CHANTRY ESTATE
AVENUE
SYNCLEN
Milkwell Farm
First. Sch.
Corbridge (corstopitum) Roman Site & Museum
Corbridge Mill
Redhouse Burn
Shordon Brae
Prior Thorns
Redhouse Haughs
RIVER TYNE
Town Farm Field
Orchard Vale
West Green
Green Pool
Trinity Cl.
TRINITY TER.
ST. HELEN'S LANE
COOKSON CL.
MANOR COTTS.
STAGSHAW ROAD
GLEBELANDS
WINDSOR TER.
AYDON RD
AYDON GS.
GREENCROFT AV.
APPLE-TREE
ST. HELEN'S ST.
WATLING ST.
HILL ST.
PRINCES ST.
MIDDLE ST.
MAIN ST.
FRONT ST.
The Orchard
Lib.
B6530
Wide Haugh
97
98
99
68
67
66
65
51
72

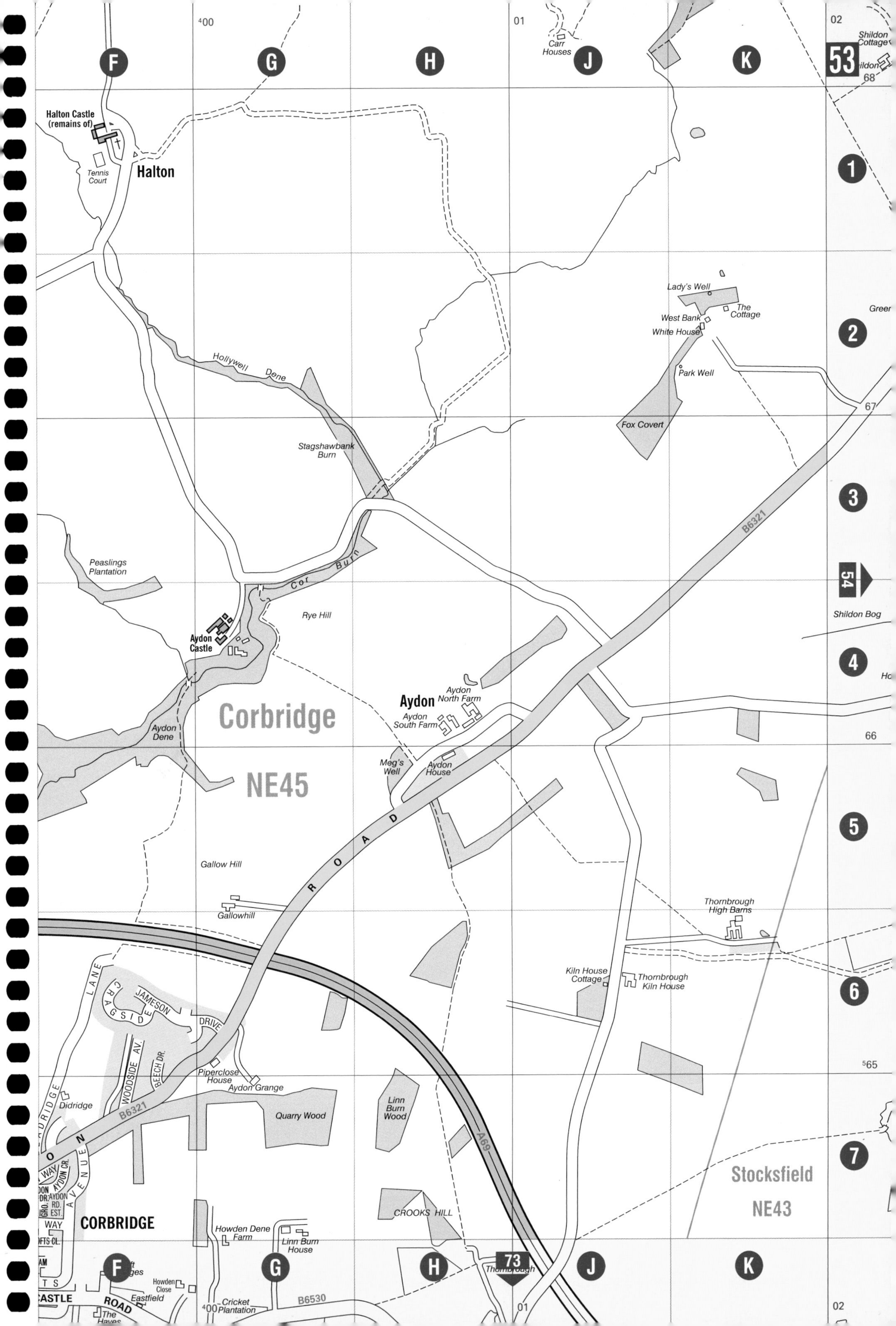
Halton Castle (remains of)
Tennis Court
Halton
Carr Houses
Shildon Cottage
Hollywell Dene
Stagshawbank Burn
Lady's Well
The Cottage
West Bank
White House
Park Well
Fox Covert
Peaslings Plantation
Cor Burn
Rye Hill
Aydon Castle
Aydon
Aydon North Farm
Aydon South Farm
Corbridge
NE45
Aydon Dene
Meg's Well
Aydon House
B6321
ROAD
Shildon Bog
Gallow Hill
Gallowhill
Thornbrough High Barns
Kiln House Cottage
Thornbrough Kiln House
LANE
CRAGSIDE
JAMESON
DRIVE
WOODSIDE AV.
BEECH DR.
Piperclose House
Aydon Grange
Didridge
Quarry Wood
Linn Burn Wood
A69
Stocksfield
NE43
CROOKS HILL
CORBRIDGE
Howden Dene Farm
Linn Burn House
Howden Close
Eastfield
Cricket Plantation
B6530
Thornbrough
CASTLE
ROAD
The Hayes
AYDON CR.
AYDON RD. EST.
AVENUE
WAY
Green
400
01
02
68
67
66
565
F G H J K
1 2 3 4 5 6 7

54
73

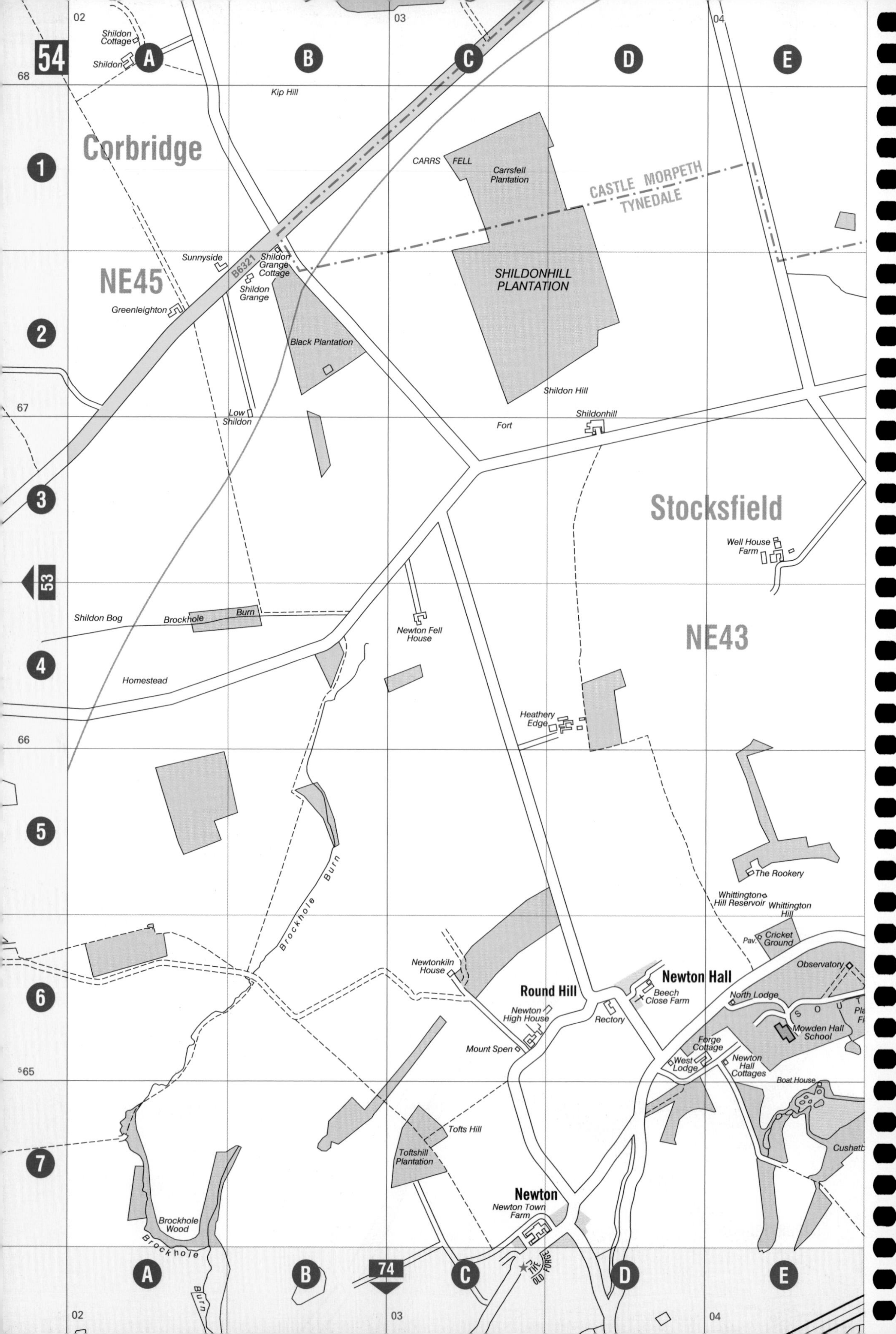
A
B
C
D
E
02
03
04
68
67
66
565
1
2
3
4
5
6
7
Shildon Cottage
Shildon
Kip Hill
Corbridge
CARRS FELL
Carrsfell Plantation
CASTLE MORPETH
TYNEDALE
Sunnyside
Shildon Grange Cottage
B6321
NE45
Shildon Grange
Greenleighton
SHILDONHILL PLANTATION
Black Plantation
Shildon Hill
Low Shildon
Fort
Shildonhill
Stocksfield
Well House Farm
53
Shildon Bog
Brockhole
Burn
Newton Fell House
NE43
Homestead
Heathery Edge
The Rookery
Whittington Hill Reservoir
Whittington Hill
Brockhole Burn
Pav.
Cricket Ground
Newtonkiln House
Observatory
Newton Hall
Round Hill
Beech Close Farm
North Lodge
Newton High House
Rectory
Mowden Hall School
Mount Spen
Forge Cottage
West Lodge
Newton Hall Cottages
Boat House
Tofts Hill
Toftshill Plantation
Cushatb
Newton
Newton Town Farm
Brockhole Wood
Brockhole
Burn
74
THE OLD FORGE

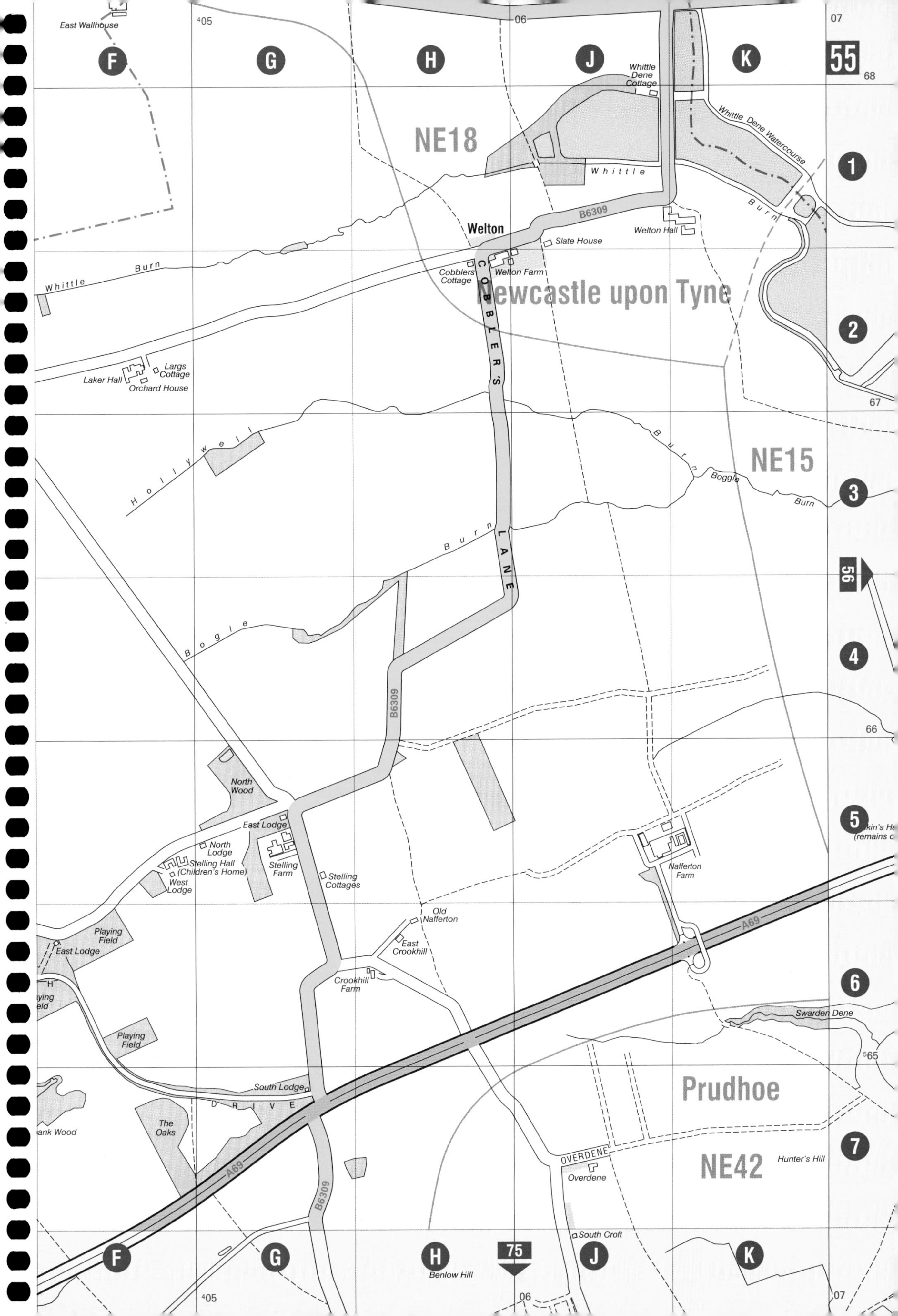
East Wallhouse
405
06
07
F
G
H
J
K
68
Whittle Dene Cottage
Whittle Dene Watercourse
NE18
Whittle
Burn
B6309
Welton
Welton Hall
Slate House
Whittle Burn
Cobblers Cottage
Welton Farm
Newcastle upon Tyne
COBBLER'S LANE
Laker Hall
Largs Cottage
Orchard House
67
Hollywell
Burn
NE15
Boggle Burn
Burn
Bogle
B6309
66
North Wood
East Lodge
North Lodge
Stelling Hall (Children's Home)
West Lodge
Stelling Farm
Stelling Cottages
Nafferton Farm
Old Nafferton
East Crookhill
Crookhill Farm
Playing Field
East Lodge
Playing Field
A69
Swarden Dene
565
South Lodge
DRIVE
The Oaks
Prudhoe
OVERDENE
Overdene
NE42
Hunter's Hill
A69
B6309
South Croft
Benlow Hill
405
06
07
1
2
3
4
5
6
7

56

75

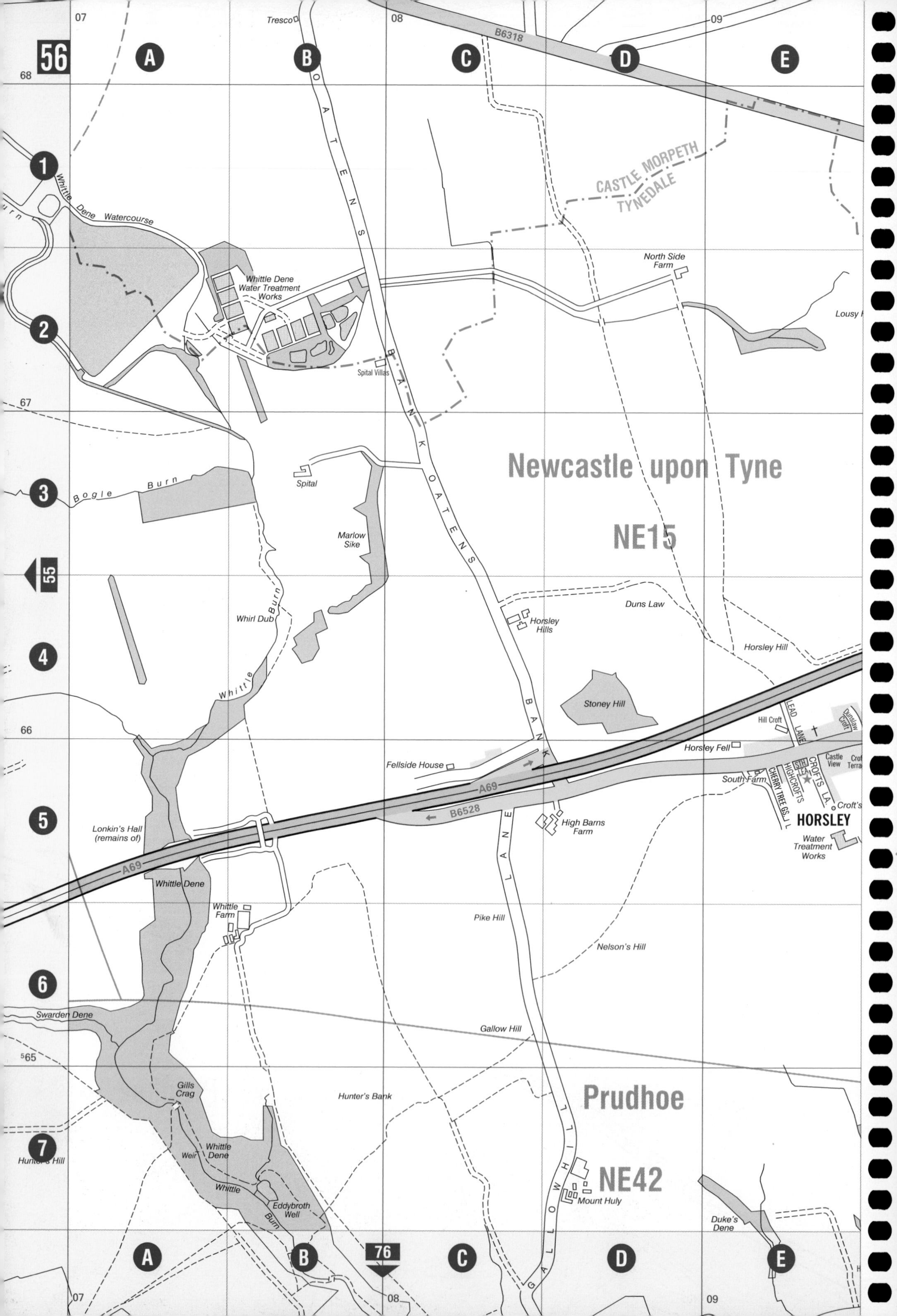
Tresco
B6318
CASTLE MORPETH
TYNEDALE
Whittle Dene Watercourse
Whittle Dene Water Treatment Works
Spital Villas
North Side Farm
Lousy H
Newcastle upon Tyne
NE15
Bogle Burn
Spital
Marlow Sike
OATENS BANK
Whirl Dub
Burn
Whittle
Duns Law
Horsley Hills
Horsley Hill
Stoney Hill
Hill Croft
LEAD LANE
Dunslaw Croft
Horsley Fell
Fellside House
Castle View
Croft Terra
South Farm
CHERRY TREE GS.
HIGHCROFTS
CROFTS LA.
Croft's
HORSLEY
Water Treatment Works
A69
B6528
High Barns Farm
Lonkin's Hall (remains of)
Whittle Dene
Whittle Farm
Pike Hill
Nelson's Hill
Swarden Dene
Gallow Hill
Gills Crag
Hunter's Bank
Prudhoe
Whittle Dene
Weir
Whittle
Burn
Eddybroth Well
Hunter's Hill
NE42
Mount Huly
GALLOWHILL LANE
Duke's Dene
07
08
09
68
67
66
565
A B C D E
1 2 3 4 5 6 7
55
76

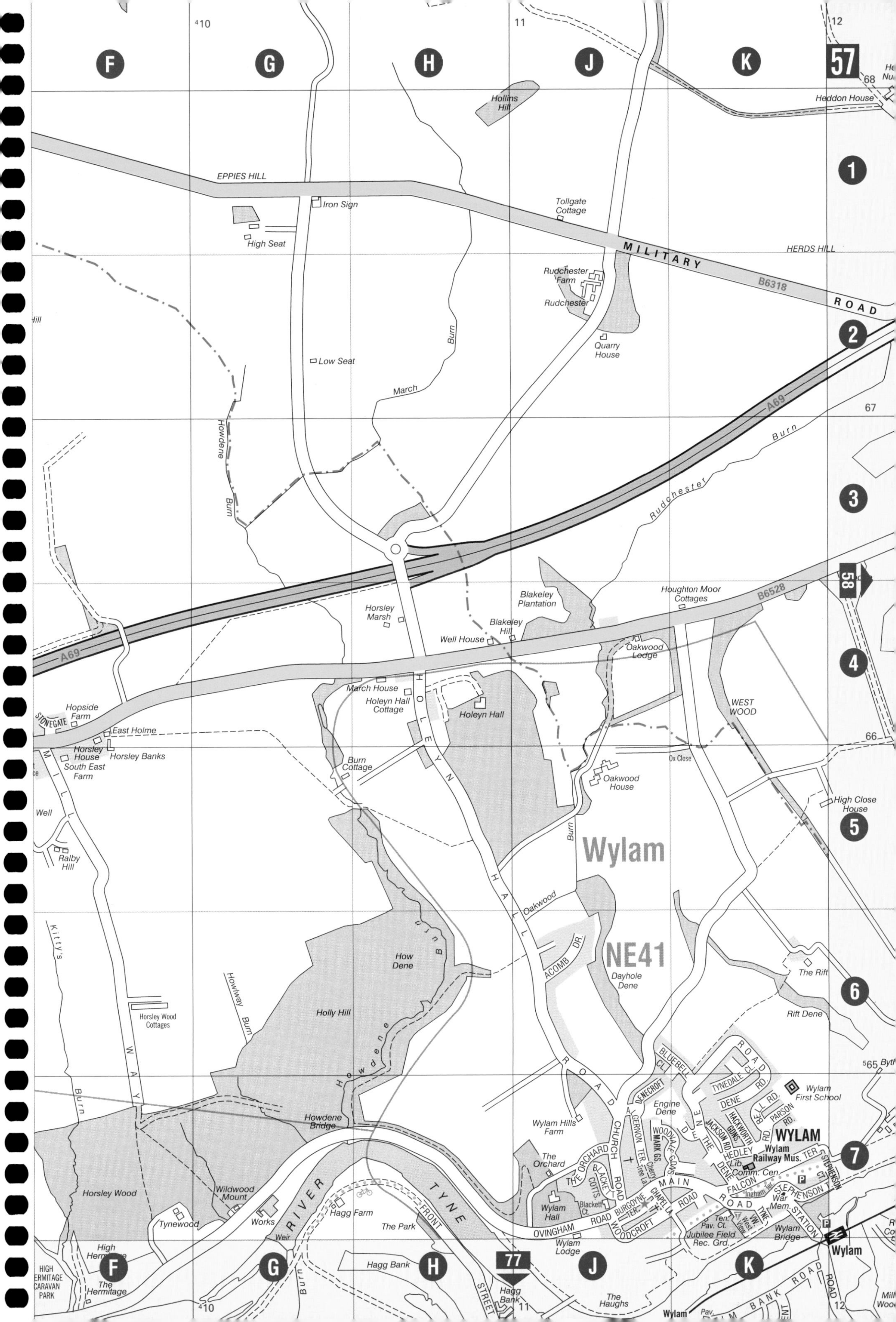
57
F
G
H
J
K
410
11
12
Heddon House
Hollins Hill
EPPIES HILL
Iron Sign
High Seat
Tollgate Cottage
MILITARY
ROAD
B6318
HERDS HILL
Rudchester Farm
Rudchester
Quarry House
Low Seat
March
Burn
Howdene
Burn
A69
Rudchester
Burn
67
58
Blakeley Plantation
Houghton Moor Cottages
B6528
Horsley Marsh
Blakeley Hill
Well House
Oakwood Lodge
A69
Hopside Farm
STOWEGATE
March House
Holeyn Hall Cottage
Holeyn Hall
WEST WOOD
East Holme
Horsley House
Horsley Banks
South East Farm
Burn Cottage
Ox Close
Oakwood House
66
High Close House
Well
Ralby Hill
Wylam
Kitty's
Oakwood
NE41
How Dene
Howlway Burn
ACOMB DR.
Dayhole Dene
The Rift
Rift Dene
Horsley Wood Cottages
Holly Hill
Howdene
Burn
BLUEBELL CL.
ROAD
TYNEDALE CL.
DENE RD.
DENECROFT
Engine Dene
Wylam First School
Wylam Hills Farm
ALGERNON TER.
MARK GS.
WOODVALE GDNS.
THE DENE
JACKSON RD.
HACKWORTH GDNS.
BELL RD.
PARSON RD.
WYLAM
Howdene Bridge
CHURCH
HEDLEY
Wylam Railway Mus.
TER.
The Orchard
THE ORCHARD
Lib.
Comm. Cen.
STEPHENSON
Horsley Wood
Wildwood Mount
RIVER
TYNE
BLACKETT COTTS.
MAIN
FALCON
Ingham Ter.
Works
Hagg Farm
Wylam Hall
Blackett Ct.
BURGOYNE TER.
CHAPEL LA.
ROAD
STEPHENSON
War Mem.
Tynewood
FRONT
The Park
OVINGHAM
ROAD
WOODCROFT
Ten. Pav. Ct.
TYNE VIEW
West View
STATION
Wylam Bridge
Weir
Jubilee Field Rec. Grd.
Wylam Lodge
Wylam
High Hermitage
HIGH HERMITAGE CARAVAN PARK
The Hermitage
Burn
Hagg Bank
77
STREET
Hagg Bank
11
The Haughs
BANK
ROAD
Wylam
Pav.
410
12
5
6
7
1
2
3
4
565
Byth

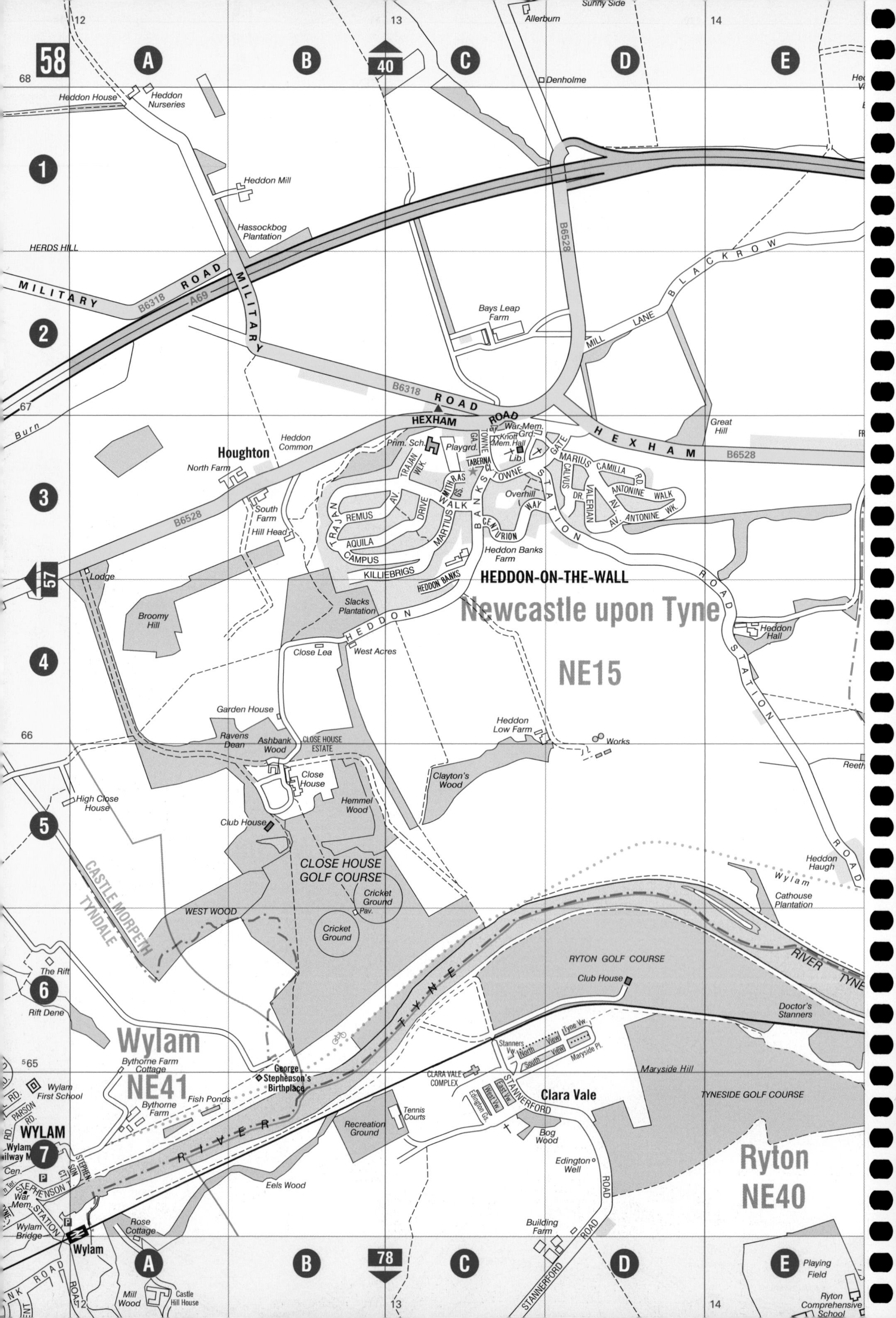

A
B
C
D
E
40
78
57
12
13
14
68
67
66
65
Heddon House
Heddon Nurseries
Heddon Mill
Hassockbog Plantation
HERDS HILL
MILITARY ROAD
B6318
A69
Allerburn
Sunny Side
Denholme
B6528
Bays Leap Farm
MILL LANE
BLACKROW
HEXHAM ROAD
Great Hill
Houghton
North Farm
Heddon Common
Prim. Sch.
Playgrd.
War Mem. Grd.
Knott Mem. Hall
Lib.
TABERNA CL.
TOWNE GA.
TOWNE
MARIUS
CAMILLA RD.
CALVUS DR.
VALERIAN AV.
ANTONINE WALK
ANTONINE WK.
Overhill
WAY
STATION ROAD
CENTURION
TRAJAN WLK.
MITHRAS GS.
WALK
REMUS
TRAJAN AV.
DRIVE
MARTIUS
AQUILA
CAMPUS
KILLIEBRIGS
HEDDON BANKS
BANKS
Heddon Banks Farm
HEDDON-ON-THE-WALL
Newcastle upon Tyne
NE15
South Farm
Hill Head
Lodge
Broomy Hill
Slacks Plantation
HEDDON
Close Lea
West Acres
Heddon Hall
Garden House
Ravens Dean
Ashbank Wood
CLOSE HOUSE ESTATE
Close House
Heddon Low Farm
Works
Clayton's Wood
High Close House
Hemmel Wood
Club House
CLOSE HOUSE GOLF COURSE
Cricket Ground
Pav.
CASTLE MORPETH
TYNDALE
WEST WOOD
Heddon Haugh
Wylam
Cathouse Plantation
RIVER TYNE
RYTON GOLF COURSE
The Rift
Rift Dene
Doctor's Stanners
Wylam
NE41
Bythorne Farm Cottage
George Stephenson's Birthplace
Wylam First School
Fish Ponds
Bythorne Farm
WYLAM
Wylam Railway M
Stanners Vw.
North View
Tyne Vw.
South View
Maryside Pl.
CLARA VALE COMPLEX
West Vw.
East Vw.
Edington Gs.
STANNERFORD
Clara Vale
Maryside Hill
TYNESIDE GOLF COURSE
Tennis Courts
Recreation Ground
Bog Wood
Edington Well
Ryton
NE40
Eels Wood
Rose Cottage
Wylam Bridge
STEPHENSON
STATION
War Mem.
Wylam
Building Farm
STANNERFORD ROAD
Mill Wood
Castle Hill House
Playing Field
Ryton Comprehensive School
Reeth

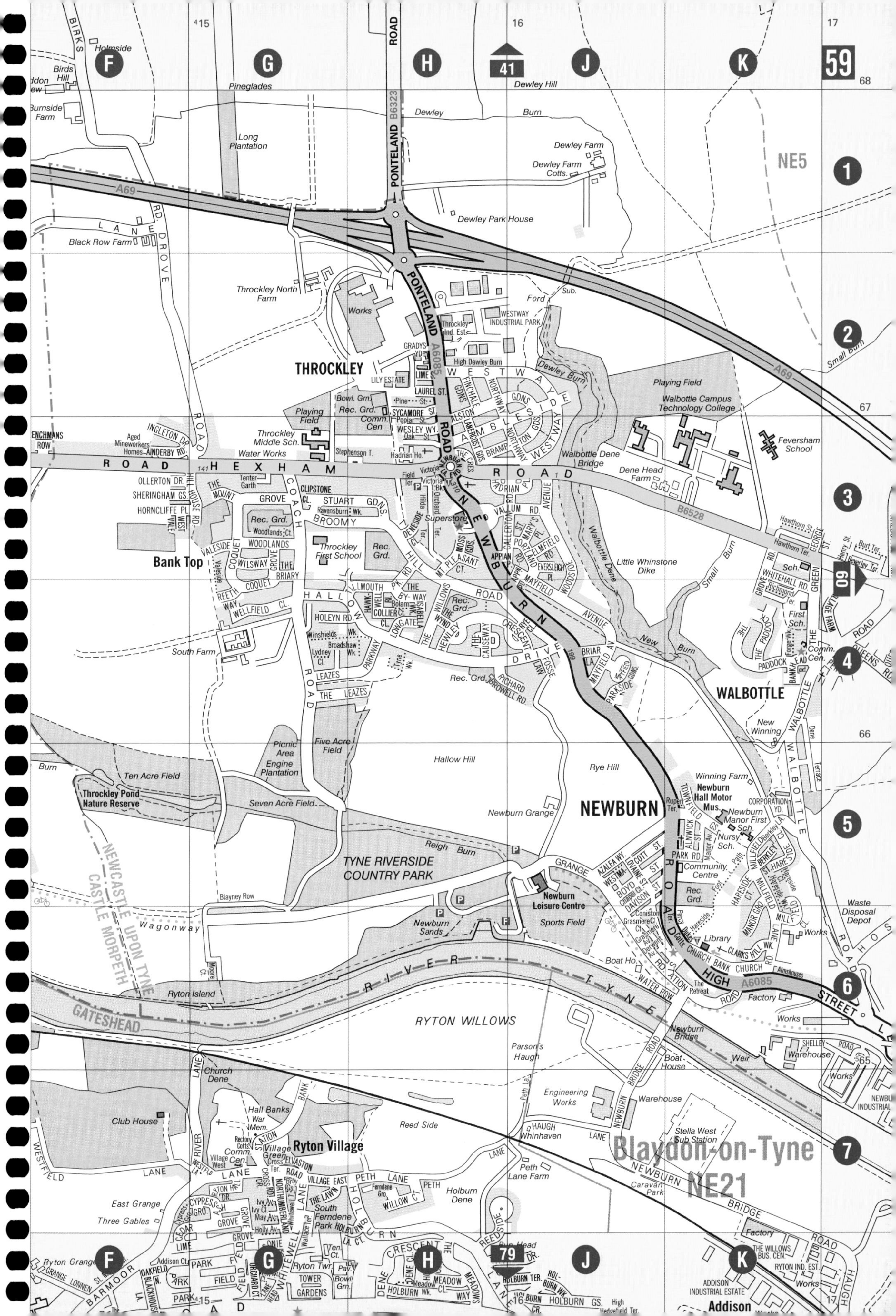

59
41
60
79
F
G
H
J
K
415
16
17
68
67
66
65
1
2
3
4
5
6
7
NE5
Blaydon-on-Tyne
NE21
THROCKLEY
NEWBURN
WALBOTTLE
Bank Top
Ryton Village
Addison
Holmside
Birds Hill
Burnside Farm
Pineglades
Long Plantation
Dewley Hill
Dewley
Burn
Dewley Farm
Dewley Farm Cotts.
Dewley Park House
Black Row Farm
Throckley North Farm
Works
Ford
Sub.
WESTWAY INDUSTRIAL PARK
Throckley Ind. Est.
High Dewley Burn
Playing Field
Walbottle Campus Technology College
Feversham School
Small Burn
A69
PONTELAND ROAD
B6323
A6085
B6528
HEXHAM ROAD
NEWBURN ROAD
Throckley Middle Sch.
Water Works
Aged Mineworkers Homes
Walbottle Dene Bridge
Dene Head Farm
Throckley First School
Superstore
Walbottle Dene
Little Whinstone Dike
South Farm
Rec. Grd.
Picnic Area
Engine Plantation
Five Acre Field
Hallow Hill
Rye Hill
Ten Acre Field
Throckley Pond Nature Reserve
Seven Acre Field
Newburn Grange
Reigh Burn
TYNE RIVERSIDE COUNTRY PARK
Blayney Row
Wagonway
NEWCASTLE UPON TYNE
CASTLE MORPETH
GATESHEAD
Newburn Leisure Centre
Sports Field
Newburn Sands
Ryton Island
RIVER TYNE
Boat Ho.
Newburn Hall Motor Mus.
Winning Farm
New Winning
Newburn Manor First Sch.
Nursy. Sch.
Community Centre
Library
The Retreat
HIGH STREET
Waste Disposal Depot
Works
Factory
RYTON WILLOWS
Parson's Haugh
Newburn Bridge
Boat House
Weir
SHELLEY ROAD
Warehouse
Engineering Works
Stella West Sub Station
Church Dene
Hall Banks
War Mem.
Club House
Reed Side
HAUGH LANE
Whinhaven
Peth Lane Farm
Holburn Dene
Caravan Park
NEWBURN BRIDGE ROAD
East Grange
Three Gables
Ryton Grange
South Ferndene Park
Ryton Twr.
TOWER GARDENS
Bowl. Grn.
THE WILLOWS BUS. CEN.
RYTON IND. EST.
ADDISON INDUSTRIAL ESTATE
NEWBURN INDUSTRIAL

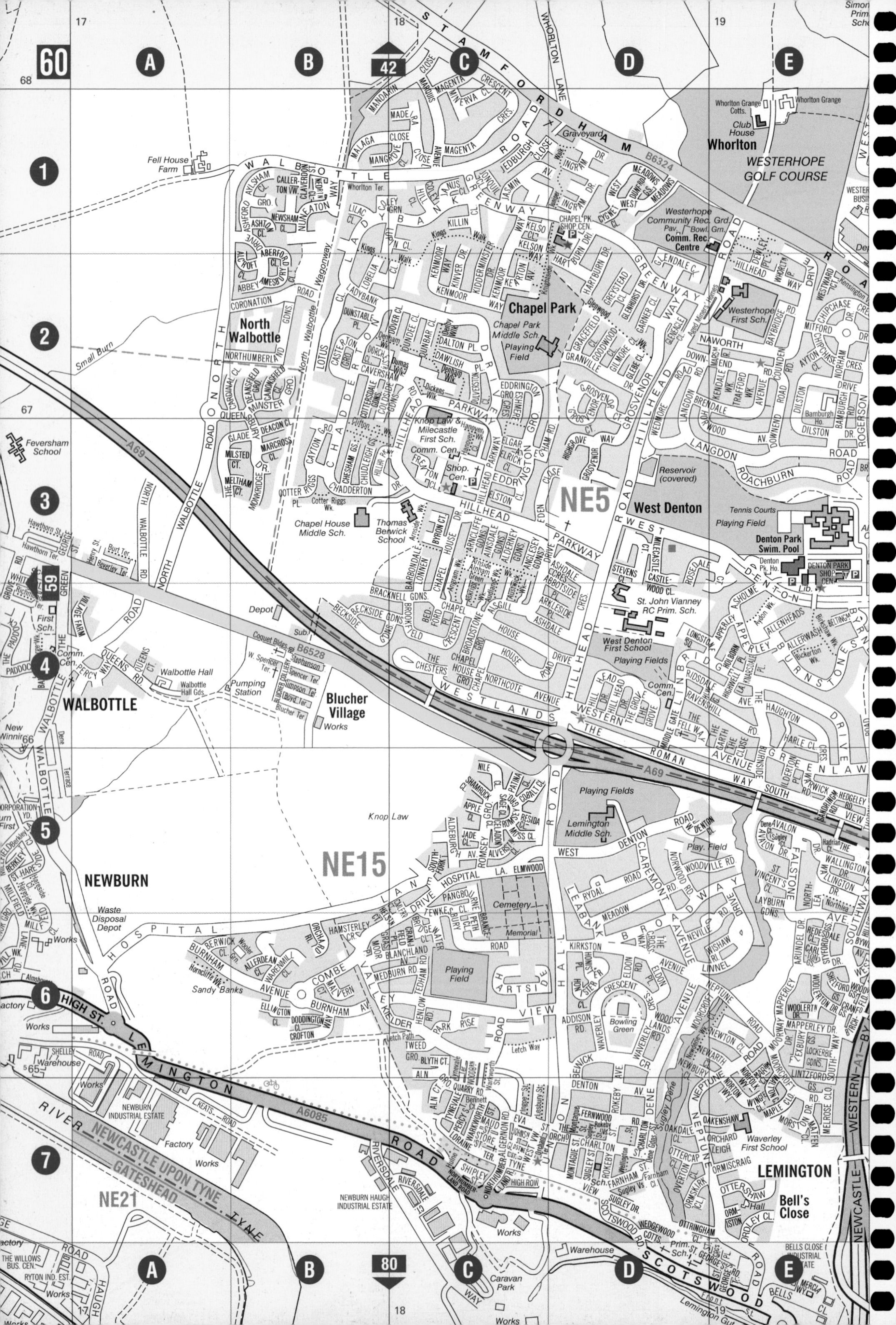

60
17
18
19
A
B
C
D
E
42
80
59
1
2
3
4
5
6
7
68
67
66
65
STAMFORD
WHORLTON LANE
Whorlton Grange Cotts.
Whorlton Grange
Club House
Whorlton
WESTERHOPE GOLF COURSE
B6324
Graveyard
Fell House Farm
WALBOTTLE ROAD
Whorlton Ter.
North Walbottle
North Walbottle Wagonway
Small Burn
NORTHUMBERLAND GDNS.
CORONATION
Feversham School
Chapel Park
Chapel Park Middle Sch.
Playing Field
CHAPEL PK. SHOP CEN.
Westerhope Community Rec. Grd.
Pav.
Bowl. Grn.
Comm. Rec. Centre
Westerhope First Sch.
Aged Miners' Homes
NAWORTH
LANGDON
ROACHBURN
Reservoir (covered)
West Denton
Tennis Courts
Playing Field
Denton Park Swim. Pool
Denton Pk. Ho.
DENTON PARK SHOP CEN.
Lib.
NE5
Knop Law & Milecastle First Sch.
Comm. Cen.
Shop. Cen.
HILLHEAD PARKWAY
WEST DENTON
Cotter Riggs Wk.
Chapel House Middle Sch.
Thomas Berwick School
St. John Vianney RC Prim. Sch.
West Denton First School
Playing Fields
A69
Depot
Sub.
Coquet Bldgs.
B6528
Pumping Station
Walbottle Hall
Walbottle Hall Gds.
Blucher Village
Works
WALBOTTLE
First Sch.
New Winning
WESTLANDS
WESTERN
THE ROMAN WAY
AVENUE
Playing Fields
Lemington Middle Sch.
Play. Field
Knop Law
NE15
NEWBURN
Waste Disposal Depot
HOSPITAL
HOSPITAL LANE
Cemetery
Memorial
Playing Field
Sandy Banks
Bowling Green
HIGH ST.
LEMINGTON
A6085
NEWBURN INDUSTRIAL ESTATE
Factory
RIVER TYNE
NEWCASTLE UPON TYNE
GATESHEAD
NE21
NEWBURN HAUGH INDUSTRIAL ESTATE
ROAD
Waverley First School
LEMINGTON
Bell's Close
BELLS CLOSE INDUSTRIAL ESTATE
WESTERN
A1
NEWCASTLE
SCOTSWOOD
Prim. Sch.
Warehouse
Caravan Park
THE WILLOWS BUS. CEN.
RYTON IND. EST.
Works

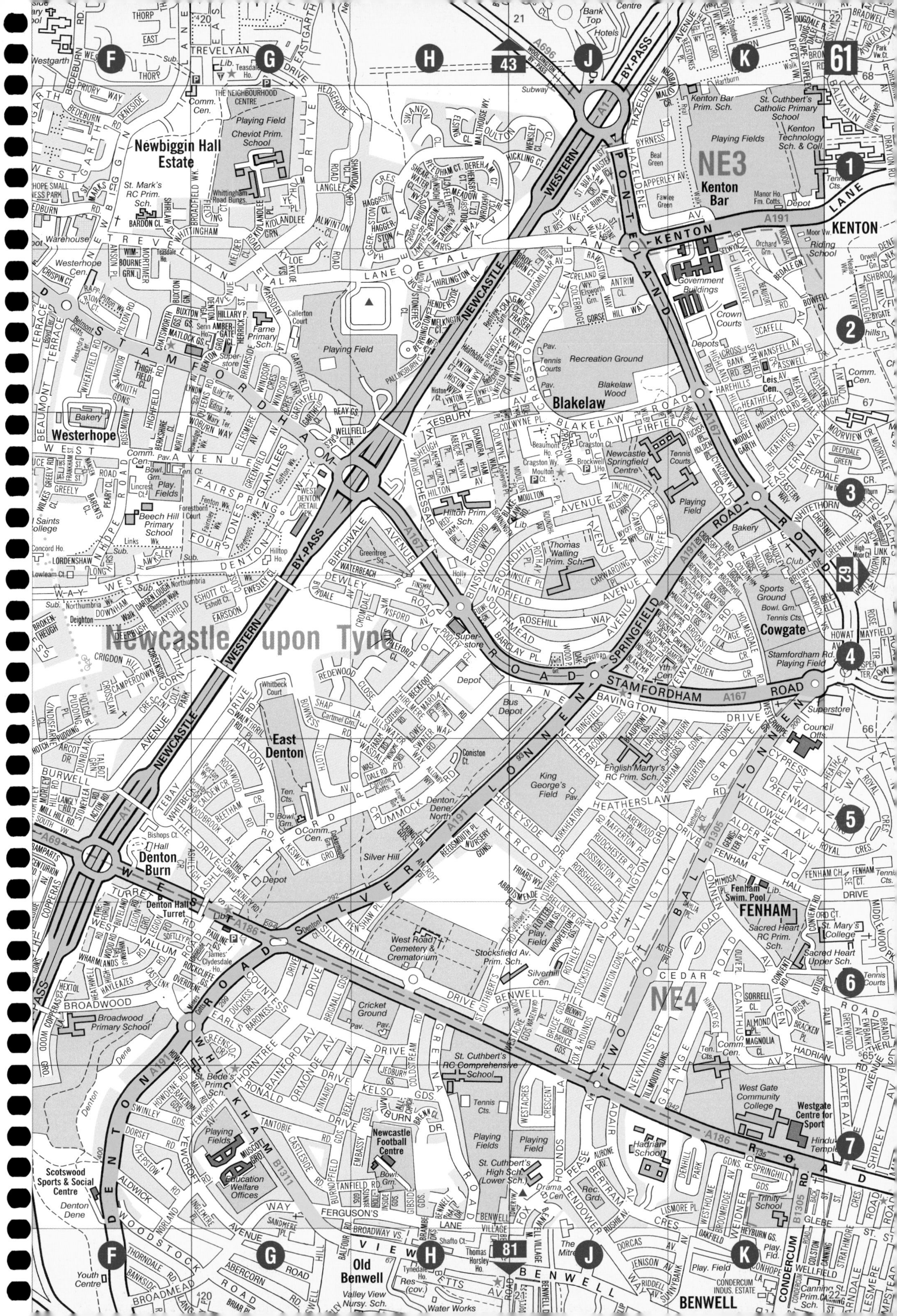
61
43
62
81
F
G
H
J
K
1
2
3
4
5
6
7
NE3
NE4
Newcastle upon Tyne
Newbiggin Hall Estate
Westerhope
Kenton Bar
KENTON
Blakelaw
Cowgate
East Denton
Denton Burn
FENHAM
Old Benwell
BENWELL
WESTERN BY-PASS
NEWCASTLE
A1
A69
A191
A167
A186
A696
B1305
B1311
KENTON LANE
STAMFORDHAM ROAD
SILVER LONNEN
SLATYFORD LANE
WEST ROAD
WESTERHOPE ROAD
DENTON ROAD
WHICKHAM VIEW
TWO BALL LONNEN
SPRINGFIELD ROAD
PONTELAND ROAD
TREVELYAN
Cheviot Prim. School
St. Mark's RC Prim. Sch.
Farne Primary Sch.
Beech Hill Primary School
Playing Field
Recreation Ground
Blakelaw Wood
Newcastle Springfield Centre
Hilton Prim. Sch.
Thomas Walling Prim. Sch.
Government Buildings
Crown Courts
St. Cuthbert's Catholic Primary School
Kenton Technology Sch. & Coll.
Kenton Bar Prim. Sch.
Riding School
Sports Ground
Stamfordham Rd. Playing Field
King George's Field
English Martyr's RC Prim. Sch.
Fenham Swim. Pool
Sacred Heart RC Prim. Sch.
Sacred Heart Upper Sch.
St. Mary's College
West Road Cemetery & Crematorium
Stocksfield Av. Prim. Sch.
Silverhill Cen.
Silver Hill
Cricket Ground
St. Cuthbert's RC Comprehensive School
St. Cuthbert's High Sch. (Lower Sch.)
Newcastle Football Centre
Education Welfare Offices
Broadwood Primary School
Scotswood Sports & Social Centre
Denton Dene
West Gate Community College
Westgate Centre for Sport
Hindu Temple
Hadrian School
Trinity School
St. Bede's Prim. Sch.
Denton Hall Turret
Bus Depot
Superstore
Council Offs.
Valley View Nursy. Sch.
Water Works
CONDERCUM INDUS. ESTATE

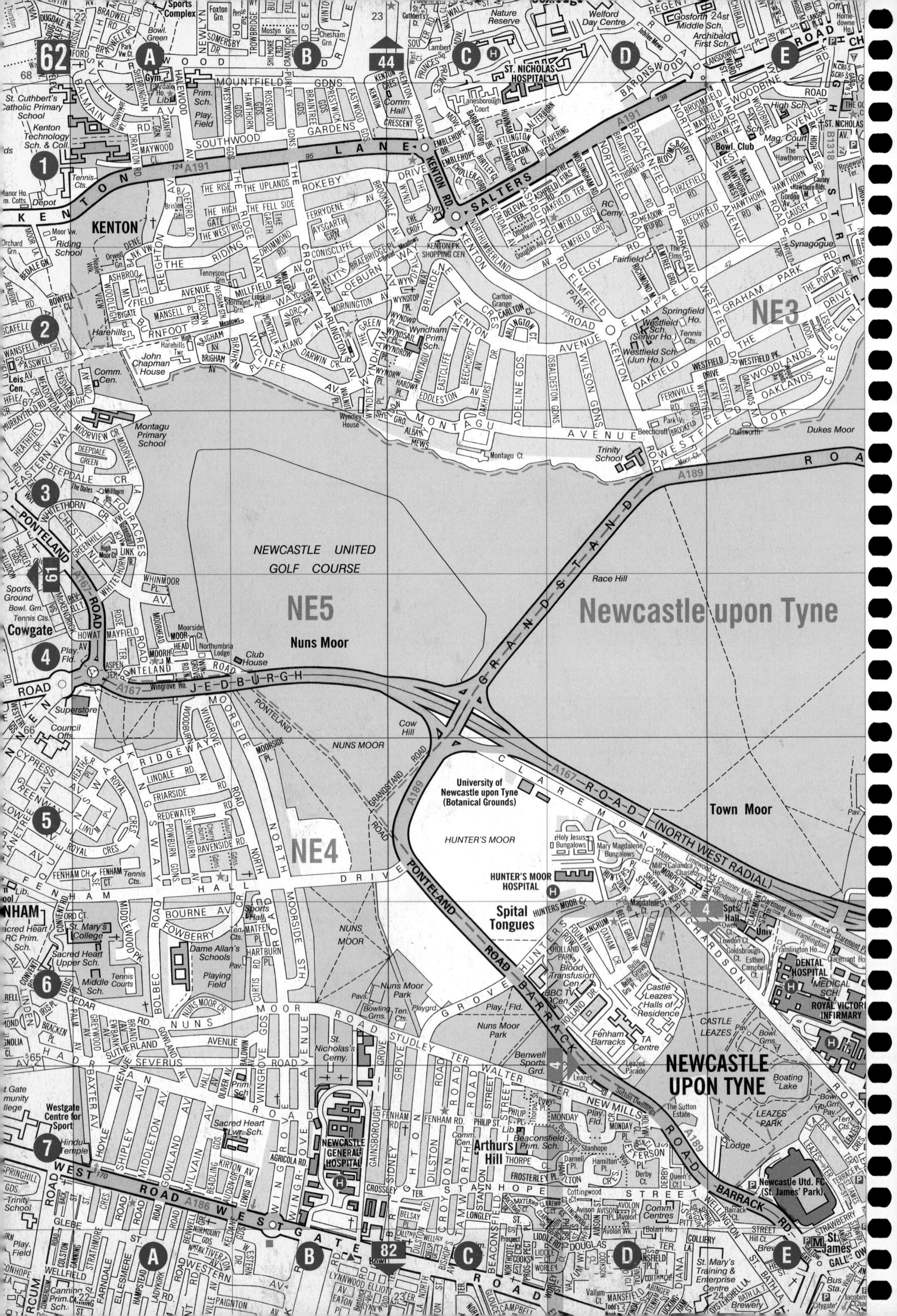

44
61
82
4
A
B
C
D
E
1
2
3
4
5
6
7
KENTON
Kenton Technology Sch. & Coll.
St. Cuthbert's Catholic Primary School
Sports Complex
Nature Reserve
Welford Day Centre
Gosforth Middle Sch.
Archibald First Sch.
ST. NICHOLAS HOSPITAL
KENTON LANE
A191
SALTERS
KENTON RD.
Comm. Hall
Kenton Pk. Shopping Cen.
Riding School
John Chapman House
Wyndham Prim. Sch.
Montagu Primary School
MONTAGU AVENUE
Trinity School
Dukes Moor
Westfield Sch. (Senior Ho.)
Westfield Sch. (Jun Ho.)
Springfield Ho.
NE3
RC Cemy.
Synagogue
High Sch.
Bowl. Club
NEWCASTLE UNITED GOLF COURSE
NE5
Nuns Moor
Race Hill
Newcastle upon Tyne
GRANDSTAND ROAD
A189
JEDBURGH ROAD
A167
PONTELAND ROAD
Cowgate
Club House
Cow Hill
NUNS MOOR
University of Newcastle upon Tyne (Botanical Grounds)
HUNTER'S MOOR
HUNTER'S MOOR HOSPITAL
CLAREMONT ROAD
(NORTH WEST RADIAL)
Town Moor
NE4
FENHAM HALL DRIVE
Spital Tongues
Dame Allan's Schools
St. Mary's College
Sacred Heart Upper Sch.
Sacred Heart RC Prim. Sch.
Nuns Moor Park
St. Nicholas's Cemy.
Benwell Sports Grd.
Fenham Barracks
Castle Leazes Halls of Residence
Blood Transfusion Cen.
BBC TV Cen.
DENTAL HOSPITAL
MEDICAL SCH.
ROYAL VICTORIA INFIRMARY
CASTLE LEAZES
Boating Lake
LEAZES PARK
NEWCASTLE UPON TYNE
Newcastle Utd. FC (St. James' Park)
St. James
NEWCASTLE GENERAL HOSPITAL
Arthurs Hill
Beaconsfield Prim. Sch.
Westgate Centre for Sport
Hindu Temple
WEST ROAD
A186
WESTGATE ROAD
BARRACK ROAD
STANHOPE STREET
St. Mary's Training & Enterprise Centre
Brewery
Bus Sta.

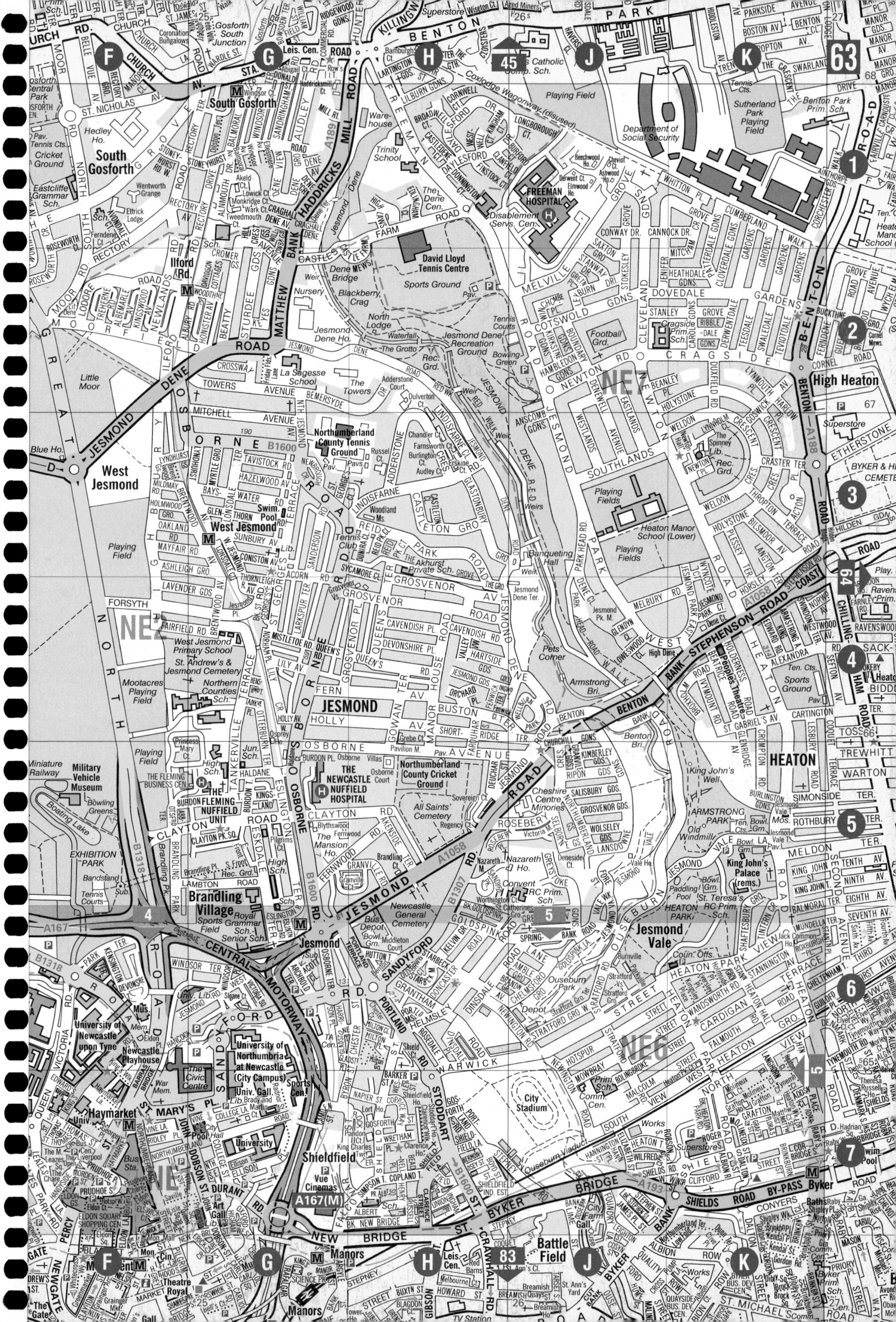

63
F
G
H
J
K
1
2
3
4
5
6
7
45
64
83
South Gosforth
Gosforth South Junction
Benton Park
Freeman Hospital
David Lloyd Tennis Centre
Jesmond Dene
High Heaton
NE7
West Jesmond
Jesmond
Northumberland County Tennis Ground
NE2
Heaton
Military Vehicle Museum
Exhibition Park
The Newcastle Nuffield Hospital
Northumberland County Cricket Ground
Brandling Village
Jesmond Vale
NE6
Heaton Park
Armstrong Park
King John's Palace (rems.)
City Stadium
University of Newcastle upon Tyne
Newcastle Playhouse
The Civic Centre
University of Northumbria at Newcastle (City Campus)
Haymarket
Shieldfield
Vue Cinemas
A167(M)
Manors
Battle Field
Byker
Theatre Royal
Jesmond Dene Road
Osborne Road
Central Motorway
Benton Bank
Stephenson Road
Coast Road
Shields Road
Byker Bridge
New Bridge St.
Great North Road
Haddricks Mill Road
Matthew Bank
Jesmond Road
Heaton Road
Benton Road
A188
A189
A1058
A167
A193
B1600
B1307
B1318
Ilford Rd.
Sports Ground
Heaton Manor School (Lower)
Newcastle General Cemetery
All Saints' Cemetery
Ouseburn Viaduct

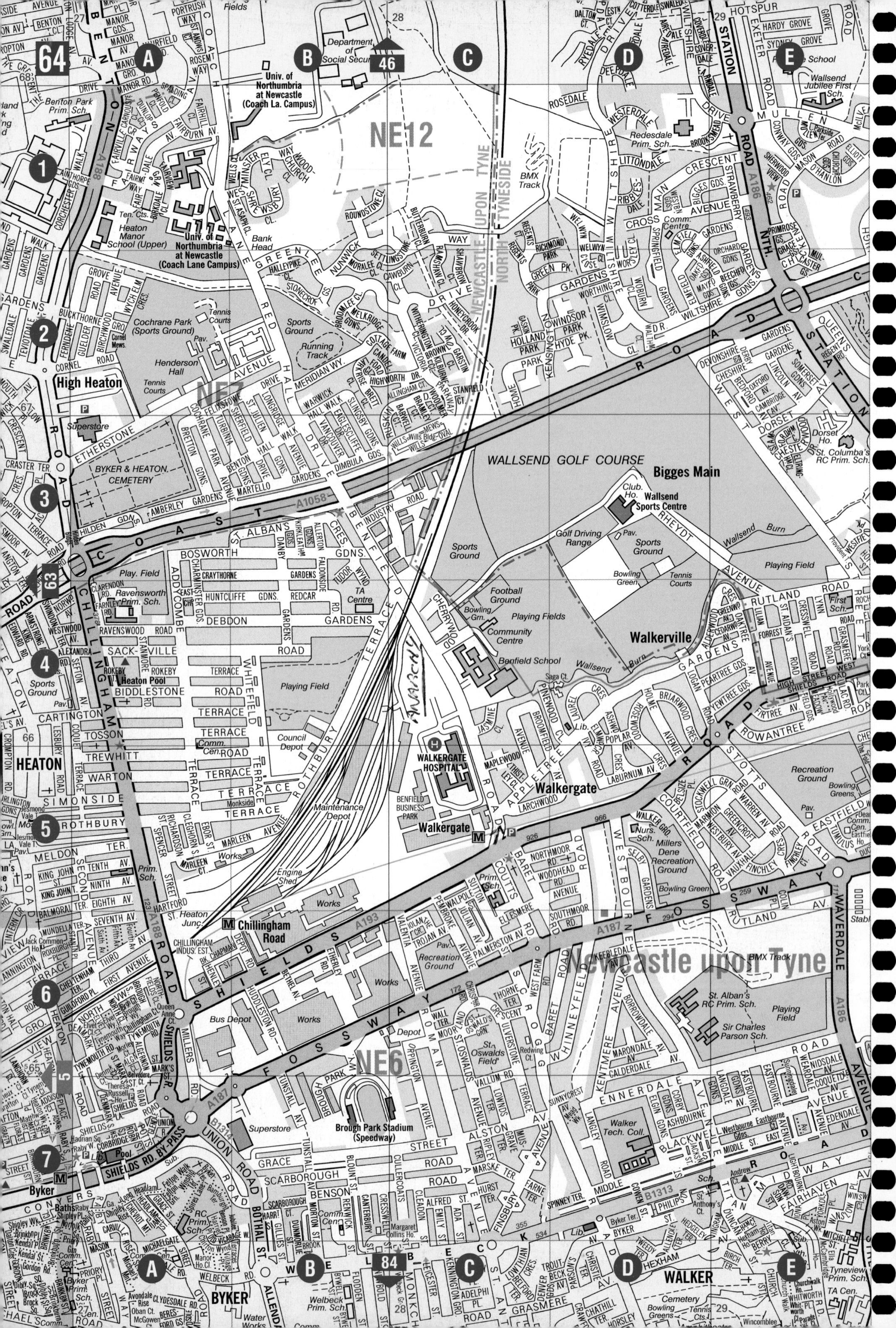
NE12
NE7
NE6
High Heaton
HEATON
Byker
BYKER
WALKER
Walkergate
Walkerville
Bigges Main
Newcastle upon Tyne
WALLSEND GOLF COURSE
BYKER & HEATON CEMETERY
WALKERGATE HOSPITAL
Brough Park Stadium (Speedway)
Univ. of Northumbria at Newcastle (Coach La. Campus)
Heaton Manor School (Upper)
Cochrane Park (Sports Ground)
Henderson Hall
Ravensworth Prim. Sch.
Heaton Pool
Benfield School
Community Centre
Wallsend Sports Centre
Redesdale Prim. Sch.
Walker Tech. Coll.
St. Alban's RC Prim. Sch.
Sir Charles Parson Sch.
Chillingham Road
COAST ROAD
SHIELDS ROAD
FOSSWAY
CHILLINGHAM ROAD
BENFIELD ROAD
STATION ROAD
WAVERDALE AVENUE
46
63
84
5
A
B
C
D
E
1
2
3
4
5
6
7

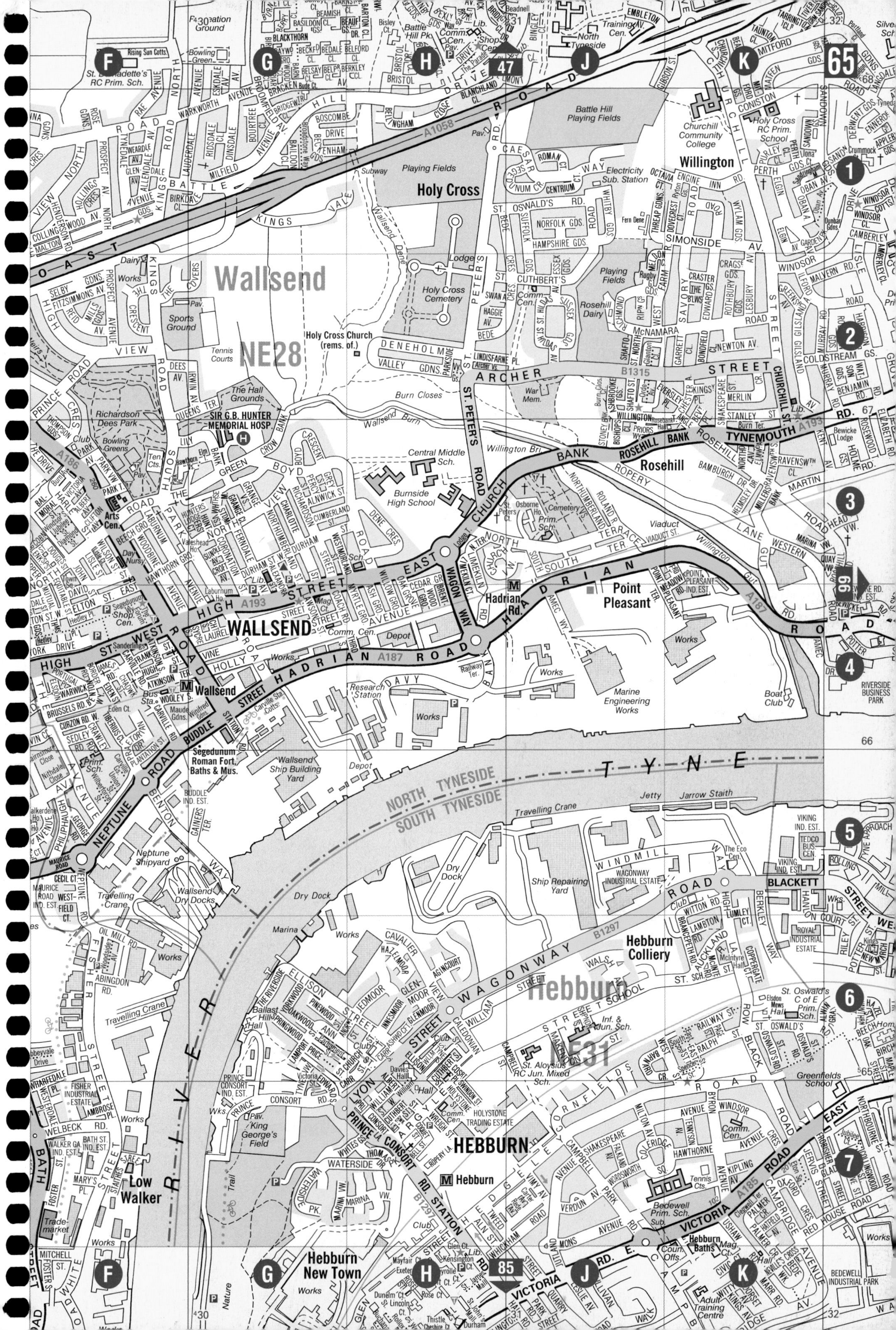
F
G
H
J
K
47
85
66
1
2
3
4
5
6
7
Wallsend
NE28
WALLSEND
Holy Cross
Willington
Rosehill
Point Pleasant
Hebburn
NE31
HEBBURN
Hebburn Colliery
Hebburn New Town
Low Walker
Battle Hill Playing Fields
Churchill Community College
Holy Cross RC Prim. School
Holy Cross Cemetery
Holy Cross Church (rems. of.)
Richardson Dees Park
Sports Ground
SIR G.B. HUNTER MEMORIAL HOSP.
Central Middle Sch.
Burnside High School
Segedunum Roman Fort, Baths & Mus.
Wallsend Ship Building Yard
Neptune Shipyard
Wallsend Dry Docks
Marine Engineering Works
Ship Repairing Yard
WAGONWAY INDUSTRIAL ESTATE
VIKING IND. EST.
RIVERSIDE BUSINESS PARK
BEDEWELL INDUSTRIAL PARK
HOLYSTONE TRADING ESTATE
FISHER INDUSTRIAL ESTATE
BUDDLE IND. EST.
PRINCE CONSORT IND. EST.
King George's Field
St. Aloysius RC Jun. Mixed Sch.
Bedewell Prim. Sch.
Greenfields School
St. Oswald's C of E Prim. Sch.
Hebburn Baths
Adult Training Centre
NORTH TYNESIDE
SOUTH TYNESIDE
T Y N E
RIVER
COAST ROAD
A1058
A193
A187
A186
A185
B1315
B1297
HIGH STREET WEST
HIGH STREET EAST
HADRIAN ROAD
CHURCH BANK
ROSEHILL BANK
TYNEMOUTH RD.
ARCHER STREET
ST. PETER'S ROAD
WAGON WAY
BUDDLE ROAD
NEPTUNE ROAD
WAGONWAY
VICTORIA RD. E.
STATION RD.
PRINCE CONSORT
BLACKETT STREET
Hadrian Rd.
Wallsend
Hebburn
Travelling Crane
Jarrow Staith
Dry Dock

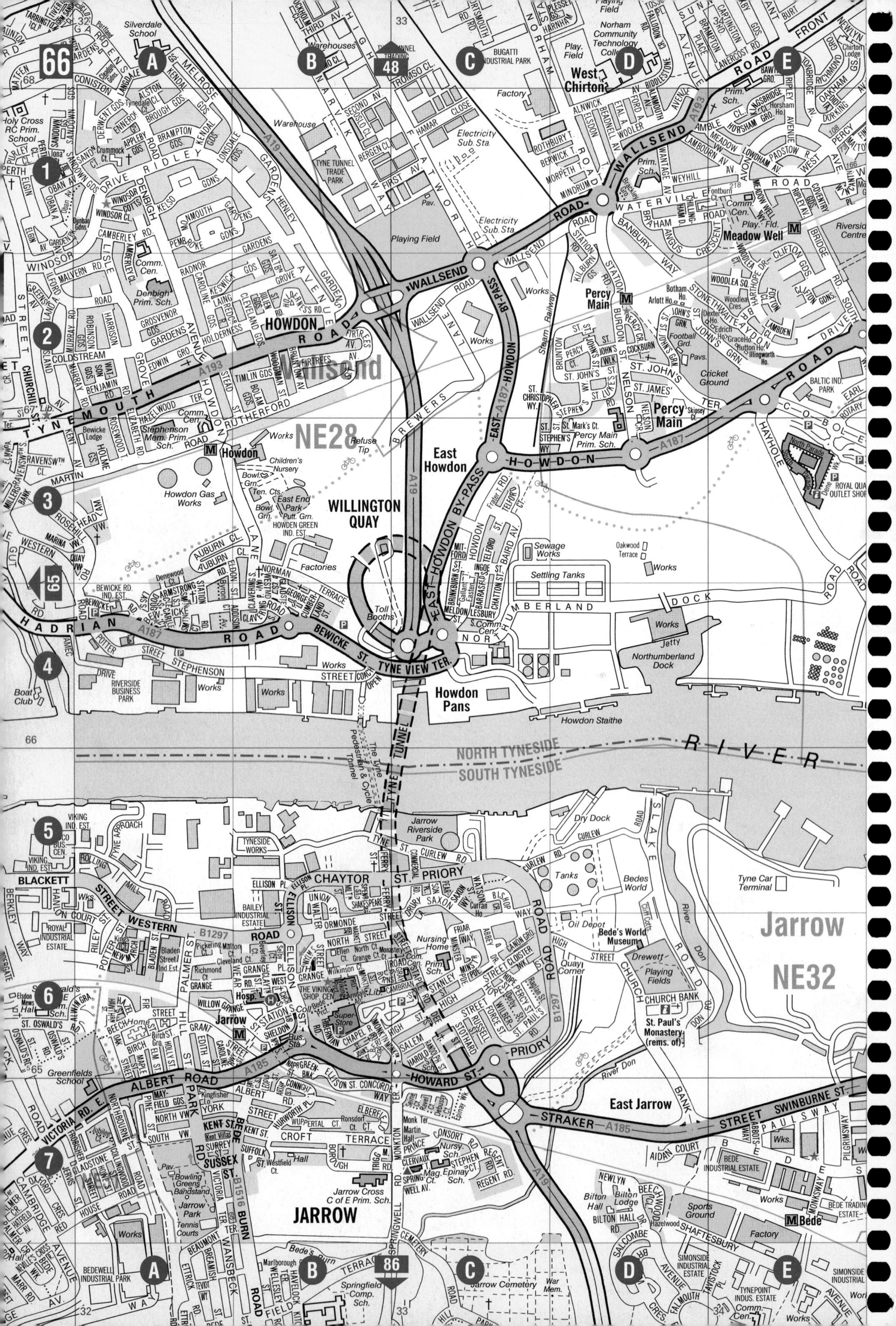
66
48
65
86
NE28
NE32
Wallsend
HOWDON
Howdon
WILLINGTON QUAY
East Howdon
Percy Main
Meadow Well
West Chirton
Howdon Pans
Jarrow
JARROW
East Jarrow
BLACKETT
NORTH TYNESIDE
SOUTH TYNESIDE
RIVER
TYNE TUNNEL
The Tyne Pedestrian & Cycle Tunnel
NORTHUMBERLAND DOCK
Northumberland Dock
Howdon Staithe
Jetty
Settling Tanks
Sewage Works
Toll Booths
Refuse Tip
Howdon Gas Works
East End Park
HOWDEN GREEN IND. EST.
RIVERSIDE BUSINESS PARK
BEWICKE RD. IND. EST.
Boat Club
TYNE TUNNEL TRADE PARK
BUGATTI INDUSTRIAL PARK
Norham Community Technology College
Silverdale School
Holy Cross RC Prim. School
Denbigh Prim. Sch.
Stephenson Mem. Prim. Sch.
Children's Nursery
Percy Main Prim. Sch.
Cricket Ground
Football Grd.
BALTIC IND. PARK
ROYAL QUAYS OUTLET SHOPS
Oakwood Terrace
Electricity Sub. Sta.
Playing Field
Jarrow Riverside Park
TYNESIDE WORKS
VIKING IND. EST.
ROYAL INDUSTRIAL ESTATE
BAILEY INDUSTRIAL ESTATE
Bladen Street Ind. Est.
Dry Dock
Tanks
Bedes World
Bede's World Museum
Oil Depot
Quay Corner
Tyne Car Terminal
Drewett Playing Fields
St. Paul's Monastery (rems. of)
River Don
Nursing Home
Super Store
THE VIKING SHOP. CEN.
Hosp.
Bus Sta.
Greenfields School
Kingfisher Ct.
Bowling Greens Bandstand
Jarrow Park
Tennis Courts
Jarrow Cross C of E Prim. Sch.
BEDEWELL INDUSTRIAL PARK
Springfield Comp. Sch.
Jarrow Cemetery
War Mem.
Bilton Hall
Bilton Lodge
Sports Ground
BEDE INDUSTRIAL ESTATE
BEDE TRADING ESTATE
SIMONSIDE INDUSTRIAL ESTATE
TYNEPOINT INDUS. ESTATE
Bede
A19
A187
A193
A185
B1297
B1516
TYNEMOUTH ROAD
WALLSEND ROAD
HADRIAN ROAD
HOWDON ROAD
EAST HOWDON BY-PASS
NORHAM ROAD
TYNE VIEW TER.
BEWICKE ST.
STEPHENSON STREET
ALBERT ROAD
HOWARD ST.
STRAKER STREET
SWINBURNE ST.
WESTERN ROAD
CHAYTOR ST.
PRIORY ROAD
SLAKE ROAD
CHURCH BANK
SPRINGWELL RD.
BEDE BURN ROAD
VICTORIA RD. E.
FRONT ROAD
WATERVILLE ROAD
COBLE DENE

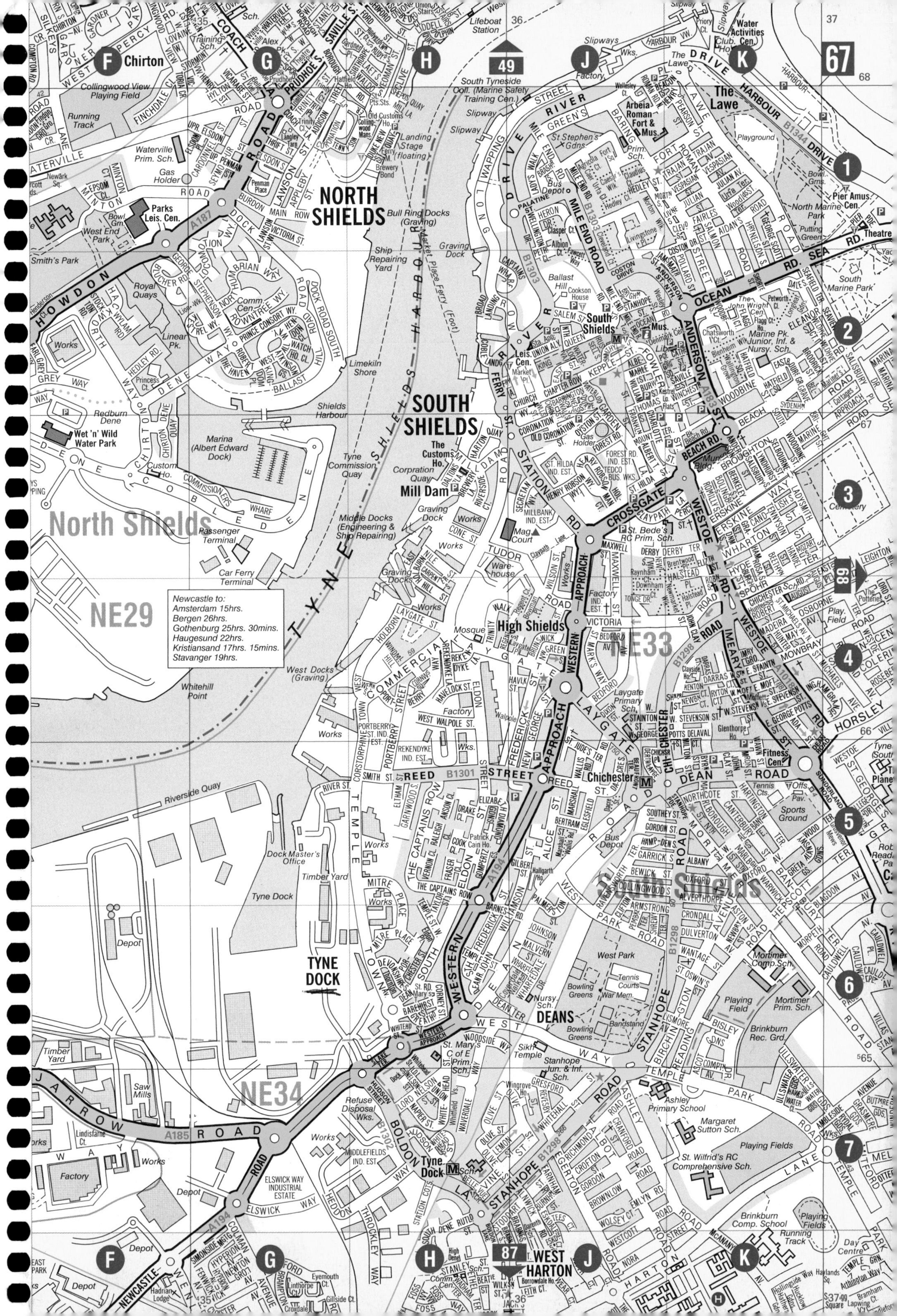
49
87
68
Chirton
NORTH SHIELDS
SOUTH SHIELDS
North Shields
South Shields
TYNE DOCK
High Shields
Chichester
DEANS
WEST HARTON
The Lawe
Mill Dam
NE29
NE33
NE34
RIVER TYNE
SHIELDS HARBOUR
Newcastle to:
Amsterdam 15hrs.
Bergen 26hrs.
Gothenburg 25hrs. 30mins.
Haugesund 22hrs.
Kristiansand 17hrs. 15mins.
Stavanger 19hrs.
Royal Quays
Marina (Albert Edward Dock)
Wet 'n' Wild Water Park
Passenger Terminal
Car Ferry Terminal
Tyne Dock
Timber Yard
Arbeia Roman Fort & Mus.
South Marine Park
North Marine Park
West Park
Mortimer Comp. Sch.
St. Wilfrid's RC Comprehensive Sch.
Brinkburn Comp. School
HOWDON ROAD
JARROW ROAD
WESTERN APPROACH
OCEAN RD.
SEA RD.
STANHOPE ROAD
DEAN ROAD
WESTOE RD.
CROSSGATE
LAYGATE
BOLDON LA.
TEMPLE PARK
HARTON LANE
HORSLEY
F
G
H
J
K
1
2
3
4
5
6
7
36
37
35
65
66
67
68

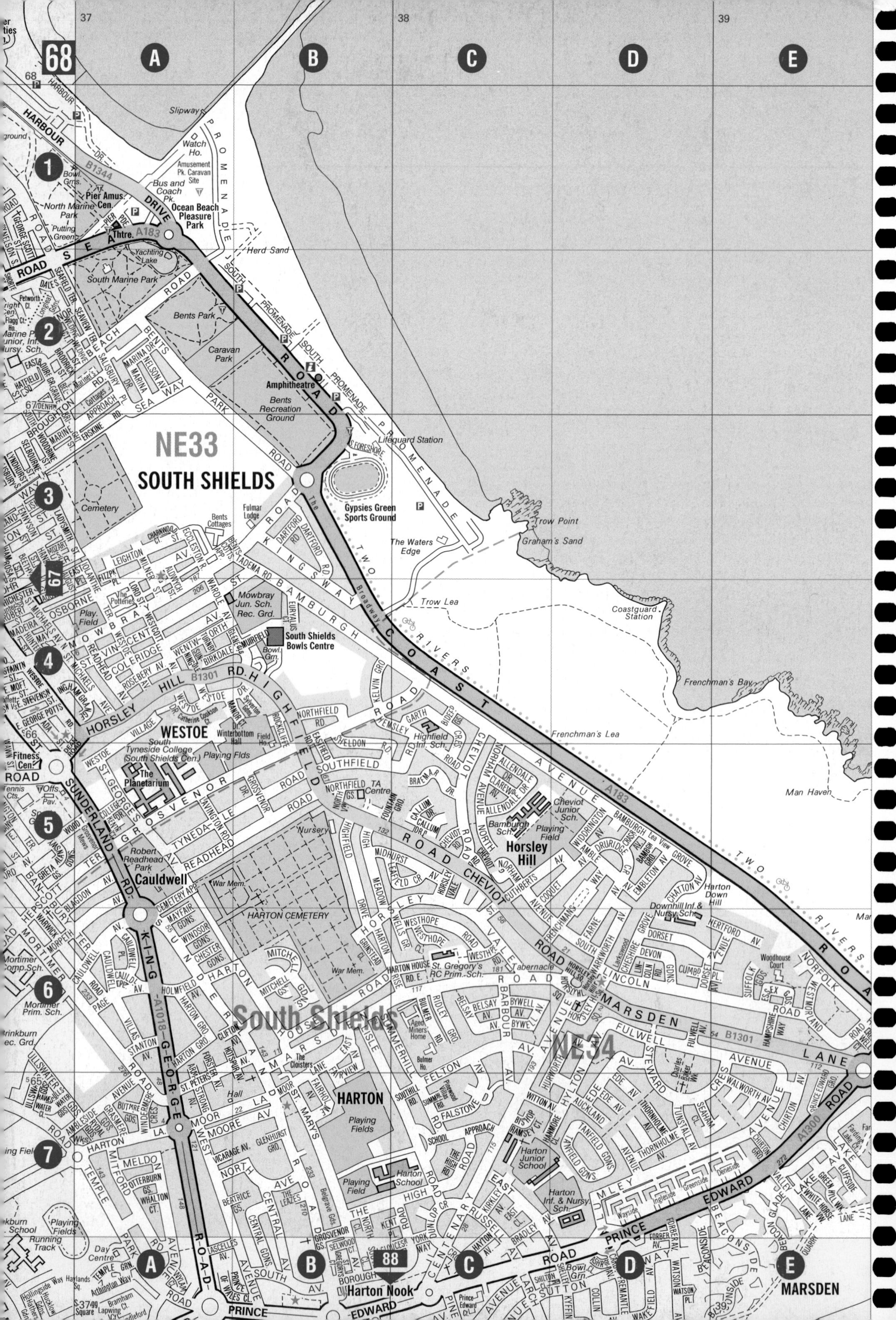

37
38
39
A
B
C
D
E
1
2
3
4
5
6
7
NE33
SOUTH SHIELDS
NE34
South Shields
WESTOE
HARTON
Horsley Hill
Cauldwell
Harton Nook
MARSDEN
Ocean Beach Pleasure Park
Pier Amus. Cen.
North Marine Park
South Marine Park
Bents Park
Caravan Park
Amphitheatre
Bents Recreation Ground
Gypsies Green Sports Ground
Lifeguard Station
Herd Sand
Trow Point
Graham's Sand
Trow Lea
Coastguard Station
Frenchman's Bay
Frenchman's Lea
Man Haven
South Shields Bowls Centre
Mowbray Jun. Sch. Rec. Grd.
Highfield Inf. Sch.
Cheviot Junior Sch.
Bamburgh Sch.
Harton Down Hill
Downhill Inf.& Nursy.Sch.
South Tyneside College (South Shields Cen.)
The Planetarium
Robert Readhead Park
HARTON CEMETERY
War Mem.
St. Gregory's RC Prim. Sch.
Harton School
Harton Junior School
Harton Inf. & Nursy. Sch.
Playing Fields
Mortimer Comp.Sch.
Mortimer Prim. Sch.
Cemetery
Slipway
Watch Ho.
Amusement Pk. Caravan Site
Bus and Coach Pk.
Yachting Lake
The Waters Edge
Fulmar Lodge
Bents Cottages
Woodhouse Court
HARBOUR DRIVE
SEA ROAD
B1344
A183
B1301
A1018
A1300
COAST ROAD
PROMENADE
BROADWAY
KINGSWAY
BAMBURGH AV.
HORSLEY HILL RD.
SUNDERLAND RD.
KING GEORGE ROAD
PRINCE EDWARD ROAD
MARSDEN ROAD
CHEVIOT ROAD
HARTON HOUSE RD.
HIGHFIELD RD.
FULWELL AV.
HARTON LANE
GROSVENOR RD.
READHEAD AV.
WESTOE RD.
67
88

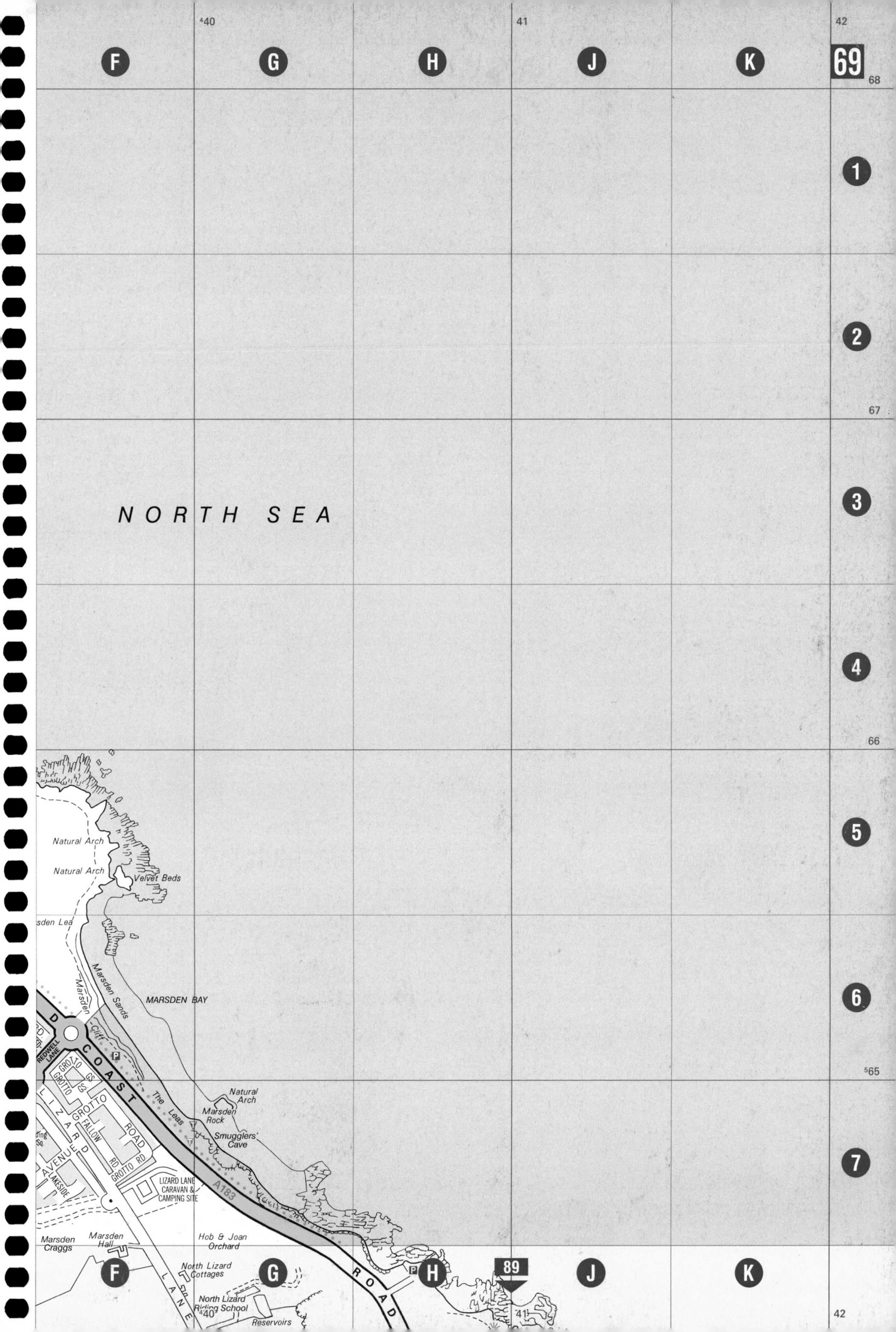
F
G
H
J
K
1
2
3
4
5
6
7
NORTH SEA
Natural Arch
Natural Arch
Velvet Beds
MARSDEN BAY
Marsden Sands
Natural Arch
Marsden Rock
Smugglers' Cave
The Leas
COAST
ROAD
A183
LIZARD LANE CARAVAN & CAMPING SITE
GROTTO ROAD
LIZARD
AVENUE
Marsden Craggs
Marsden Hall
Hob & Joan Orchard
North Lizard Cottages
North Lizard Riding School
Reservoirs
LANE
89

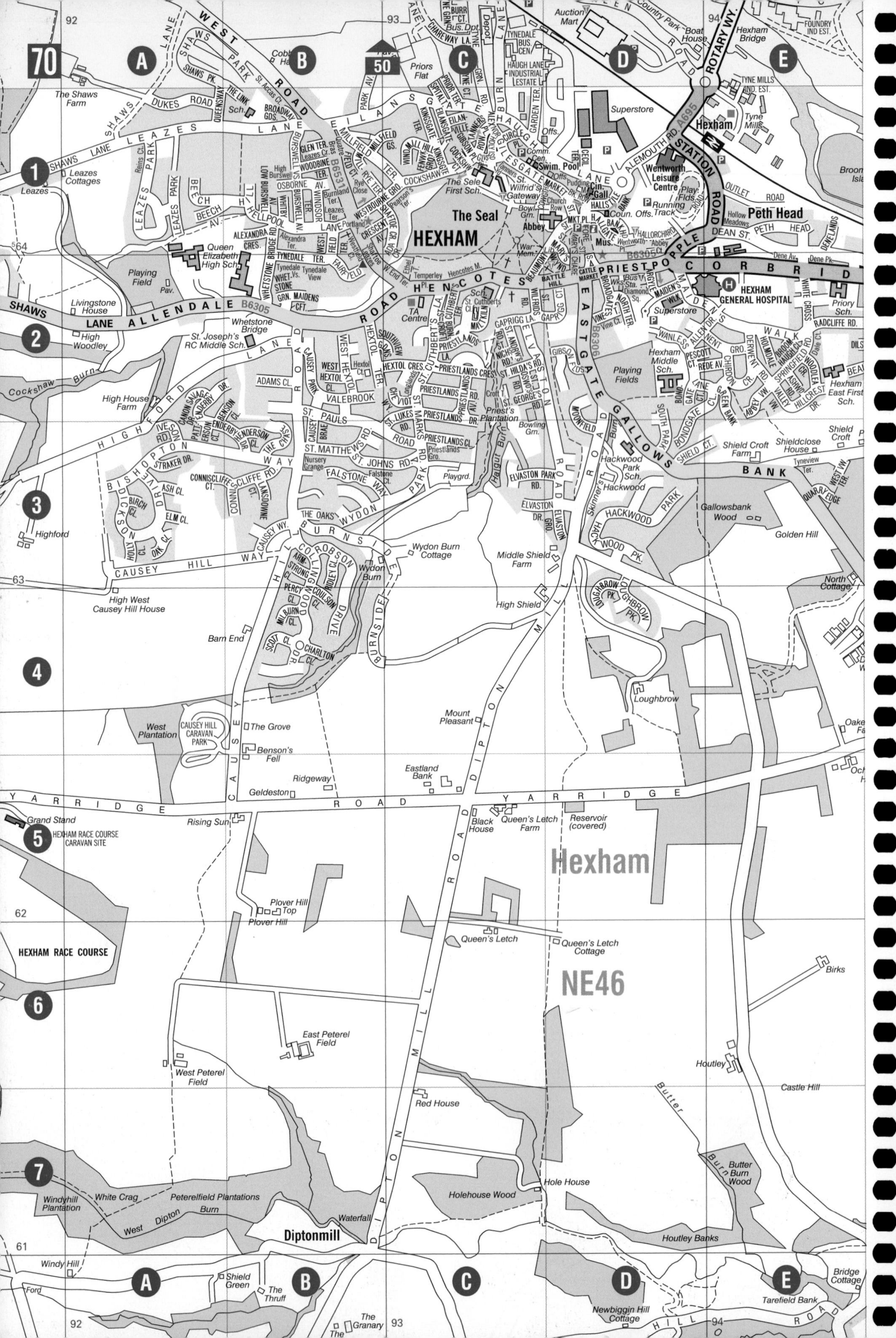
50
HEXHAM
The Seal
Hexham
NE46
HEXHAM GENERAL HOSPITAL
HEXHAM RACE COURSE
HEXHAM RACE COURSE CARAVAN SITE
Grand Stand
Peth Head
Priors Flat
Superstore
Wentworth Leisure Centre
Queen Elizabeth High Sch.
Hexham Middle Sch.
Hexham East First Sch.
Priory Sch.
St. Joseph's RC Middle Sch.
The Sele First Sch.
Hackwood Park Sch.
Abbey
Swim. Pool
Playing Field
Playing Fields
The Shaws Farm
Leazes Cottages
Livingstone House
High Woodley
High House Farm
Highford
High West Causey Hill House
Barn End
Wydon Burn Cottage
Middle Shield Farm
High Shield
Loughbrow
Mount Pleasant
West Plantation
CAUSEY HILL CARAVAN PARK
The Grove
Benson's Fell
Ridgeway
Eastland Bank
Geldeston
Rising Sun
Black House
Queen's Letch Farm
Reservoir (covered)
Plover Hill Top
Plover Hill
Queen's Letch
Queen's Letch Cottage
Birks
East Peterel Field
West Peterel Field
Red House
Houtley
Castle Hill
Butter Burn Wood
Hole House
Holehouse Wood
Windyhill Plantation
White Crag
Peterelfield Plantations
West Dipton Burn
Waterfall
Diptonmill
Houtley Banks
Windy Hill
Shield Green
The Thruff
The Granary
Newbiggin Hill Cottage
Tarefield Bank
Bridge Cottage
Golden Hill
North Cottage
Gallowsbank Wood
Shield Croft Farm
Shieldclose House
Auction Mart
Hexham Bridge
Tyne Mills
TYNE MILLS IND. EST.
FOUNDRY IND EST.
YARRIDGE ROAD
DIPTON MILL ROAD
CAUSEY HILL WAY
ALLENDALE ROAD
SHAWS LANE
HIGHFORD LANE
HENCOTES
PRIESTPOPPLE
CORBRIDGE ROAD
STATION ROAD
ROTARY WY.
GALLOWS BANK
EASTGATE
WEST ROAD
EILANSGATE
B6305
B6306
B6531
A695
92
93
94
64
63
62
61
A
B
C
D
E
1
2
3
4
5
6
7

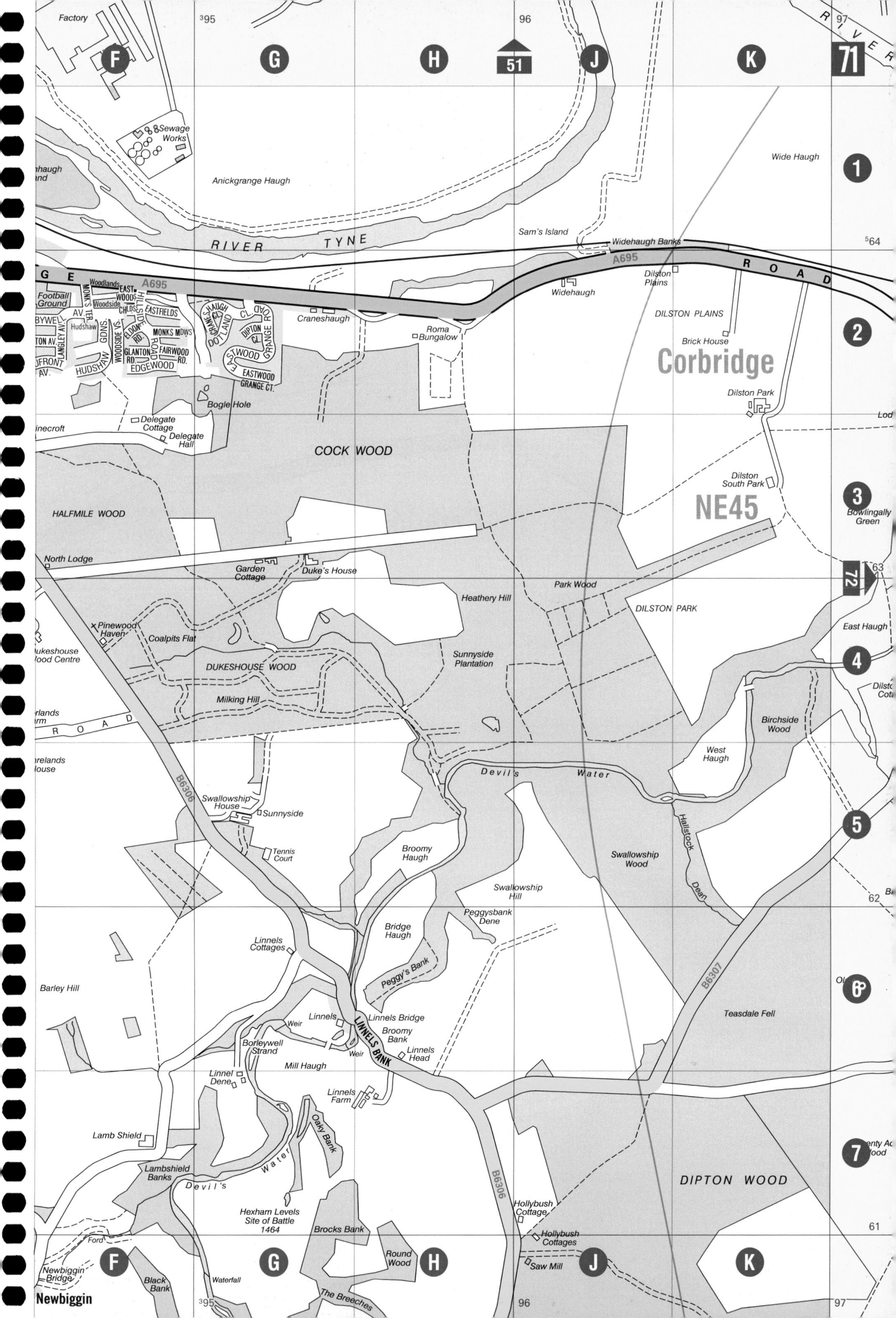

Factory
Sewage Works
Anickgrange Haugh
RIVER TYNE
Sam's Island
Widehaugh Banks
Wide Haugh
A695
ROAD
Widehaugh
Dilston Plains
Craneshaugh
Roma Bungalow
DILSTON PLAINS
Brick House
Corbridge
Dilston Park
Bogle Hole
Delegate Cottage
Delegate Hall
COCK WOOD
Dilston South Park
NE45
HALFMILE WOOD
Bowlingally Green
North Lodge
Garden Cottage
Duke's House
Park Wood
Heathery Hill
DILSTON PARK
East Haugh
Pinewood Haven
Coalpits Flat
DUKESHOUSE WOOD
Sunnyside Plantation
Milking Hill
Birchside Wood
West Haugh
Devil's Water
B6306
Swallowship House
Sunnyside
Tennis Court
Broomy Haugh
Hallstock Dean
Swallowship Wood
Swallowship Hill
Peggysbank Dene
Bridge Haugh
Linnels Cottages
Peggy's Bank
B6307
Barley Hill
Teasdale Fell
Linnels
Linnels Bridge
Weir
Broomy Bank
Borleywell Strand
LINNELS BANK
Linnels Head
Mill Haugh
Linnel Dene
Linnels Farm
Oaky Bank
Lamb Shield
Lambshield Banks
Devil's Water
DIPTON WOOD
Hexham Levels Site of Battle 1464
Hollybush Cottage
Hollybush Cottages
Brocks Bank
Round Wood
Saw Mill
Ford
Newbiggin Bridge
Black Bank
Waterfall
Newbiggin
The Breeches

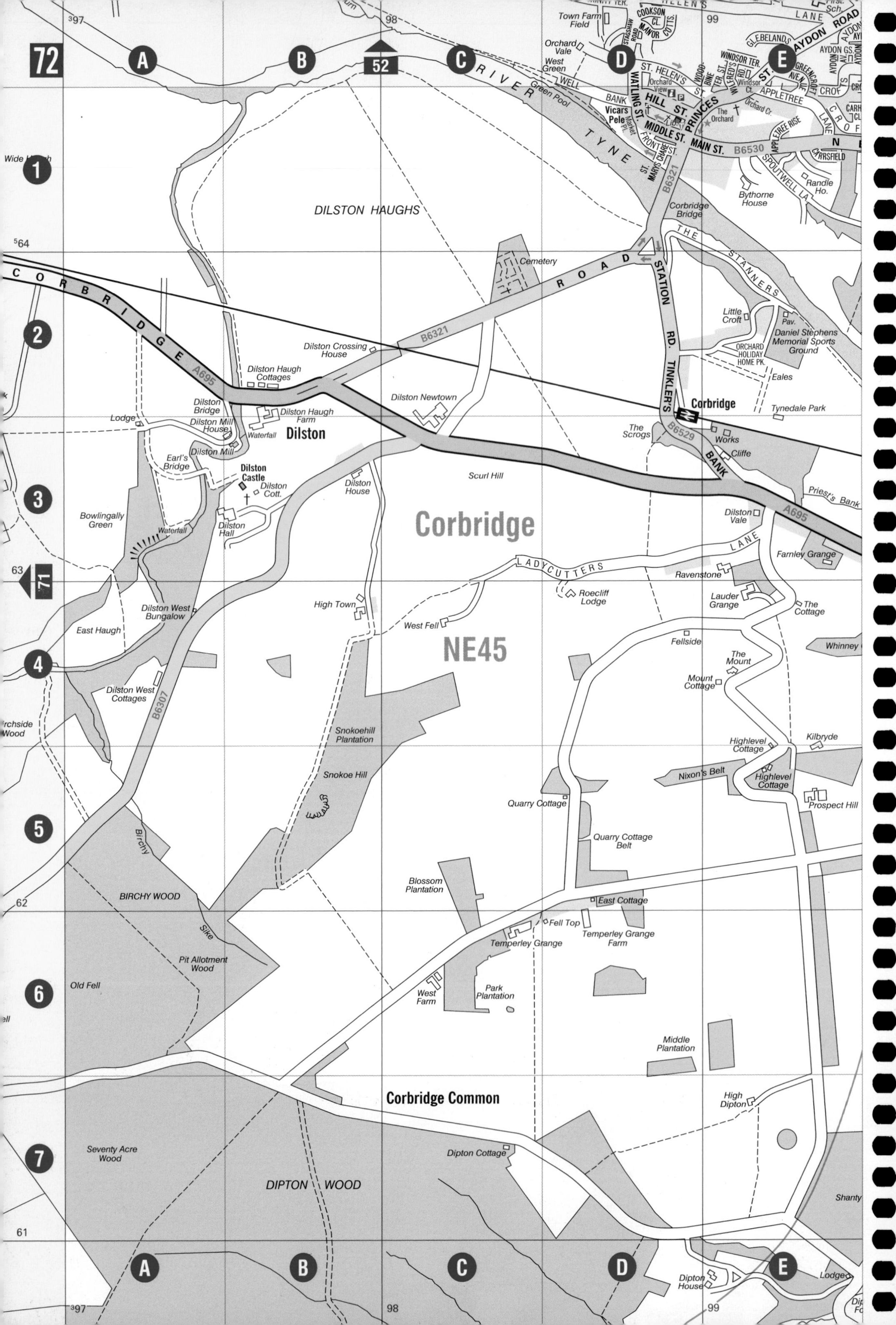
52
71
A
B
C
D
E
1
2
3
4
5
6
7
397
98
99
564
63
62
61
RIVER TYNE
Green Pool
DILSTON HAUGHS
Wide Haugh
Town Farm Field
COOKSON CL.
MANOR COTTS.
STAGSHAW ROAD
Orchard Vale
West Green
WELL BANK
ST. HELEN'S
WOODBINE ST
LANE
AYDON ROAD
GLEBELANDS
WINDSOR TER.
WILFRED'S RD
TER. ST.
AYDON GS.
GREENCROFT AVENUE
APPLETREE
CROFT
Orchard View
HILL ST.
WATLING ST.
Vicars Pele
Market Pl.
PRINCES ST.
MIDDLE ST.
MAIN ST.
B6530
FRONT ST.
ST. MARYS CHARE
The Orchard
Orchard Cr.
APPLETREE RISE
CARRSFIELD
SPOUTWELL LA.
Randle Ho.
Bythorne House
Corbridge Bridge
B6321
THE STANNERS
Cemetery
CORBRIDGE ROAD
STATION RD.
TINKLER'S BANK
Little Croft
Pav.
Daniel Stephens Memorial Sports Ground
ORCHARD HOLIDAY HOME PK.
Eales
Corbridge
Tynedale Park
Dilston Crossing House
Dilston Haugh Cottages
A695
Dilston Newtown
Dilston Bridge
Dilston Haugh Farm
Lodge
Dilston Mill House
Dilston Mill
Waterfall
Dilston
The Scrogs
B6529
Works
Cliffe
Earl's Bridge
Dilston Castle
Dilston Cott.
Dilston House
Scurl Hill
Priest's Bank
Bowlingally Green
Dilston Hall
Corbridge
Dilston Vale
Farnley Grange
LADYCUTTERS LANE
Ravenstone
Roecliff Lodge
Lauder Grange
The Cottage
Dilston West Bungalow
High Town
West Fell
East Haugh
NE45
Fellside
Whinney
The Mount
Mount Cottage
Dilston West Cottages
B6307
rchside Wood
Snokoehill Plantation
Snokoe Hill
Highlevel Cottage
Kilbryde
Nixon's Belt
Prospect Hill
Quarry Cottage
Quarry Cottage Belt
Birchy
BIRCHY WOOD
Sike
Blossom Plantation
East Cottage
Fell Top
Temperley Grange
Temperley Grange Farm
Pit Allotment Wood
Old Fell
West Farm
Park Plantation
Middle Plantation
Corbridge Common
High Dipton
Seventy Acre Wood
Dipton Cottage
DIPTON WOOD
Shanty
Dipton House
Lodge

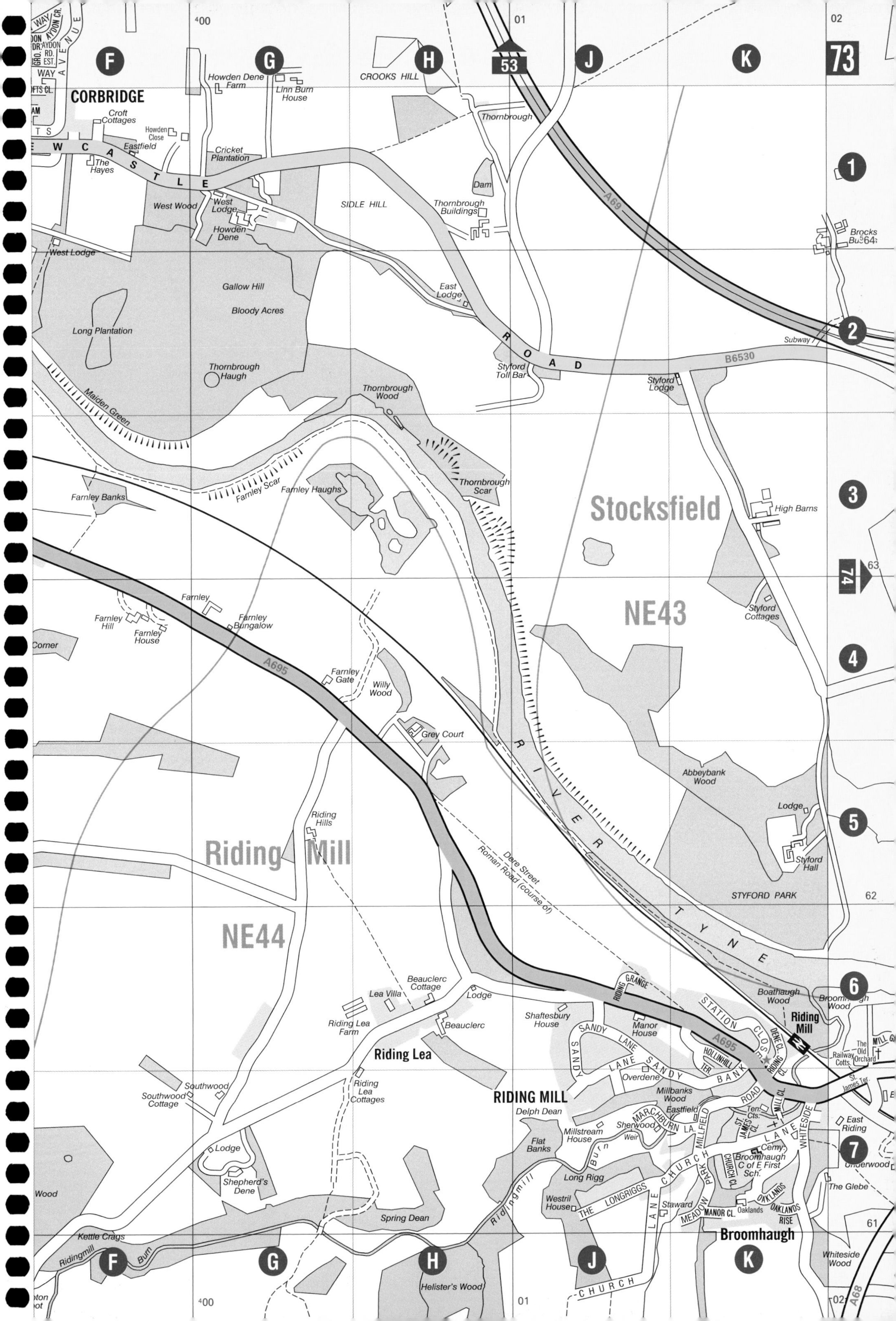
CORBRIDGE
Croft Cottages
Howden Close
Eastfield
The Hayes
Howden Dene Farm
Linn Burn House
CROOKS HILL
53
Thornbrough
Cricket Plantation
NEWCASTLE ROAD
West Wood
West Lodge
Howden Dene
SIDLE HILL
Dam
Thornbrough Buildings
A69
Brocks Bus
West Lodge
Gallow Hill
Bloody Acres
Long Plantation
East Lodge
Subway
B6530
Thornbrough Haugh
Styford Toll Bar
Styford Lodge
Thornbrough Wood
Maiden Green
Farnley Scar
Farnley Haughs
Thornbrough Scar
Farnley Banks
Stocksfield
High Barns
74
NE43
Farnley
Farnley Hill
Farnley House
Farnley Bungalow
Styford Cottages
Corner
A695
Farnley Gate
Willy Wood
Grey Court
RIVER TYNE
Abbeybank Wood
Lodge
Riding Hills
Riding Mill
Styford Hall
Dere Street Roman Road (course of)
STYFORD PARK
NE44
Beauclerc Cottage
Lea Villa
Lodge
Boathaugh Wood
Broomhaugh Wood
RIDING GRANGE
STATION
Riding Mill
Shaftesbury House
SANDY LANE
Manor House
CLOSE
DENE CL.
Riding Lea Farm
Beauclerc
HOLLINHILL TER.
RIDING CL.
Railway Cotts.
The Old Orchard
Riding Lea
Overdene
BANK
Southwood
Southwood Cottage
Riding Lea Cottages
RIDING MILL
Millbanks Wood
ROAD
MILL CL.
St. James Ter.
Delph Dean
Eastfield
Ten. Cts.
East Riding
Millstream House
Sherwood
MARCHBURN LA.
MILLFIELD
ST. JAMES CL.
WHITESIDE
Weir
Flat Banks
Burn
LANE
Cemy.
Lodge
CHURCH
Broomhaugh C of E First Sch.
Underwood
Long Rigg
CHURCH CL.
Shepherd's Dene
PARK
OAKLANDS
The Glebe
Westril House
THE LONGRIGGS
Staward
Wood
Spring Dean
Ridingmill
MEADOW
MANOR CL.
Oaklands
OAKLANDS RISE
Broomhaugh
Kettle Crags
Ridingmill Burn
Whiteside Wood
Helister's Wood
CHURCH
A68
F G H J K
1 2 3 4 5 6 7
400 01 02 61 62 63 64

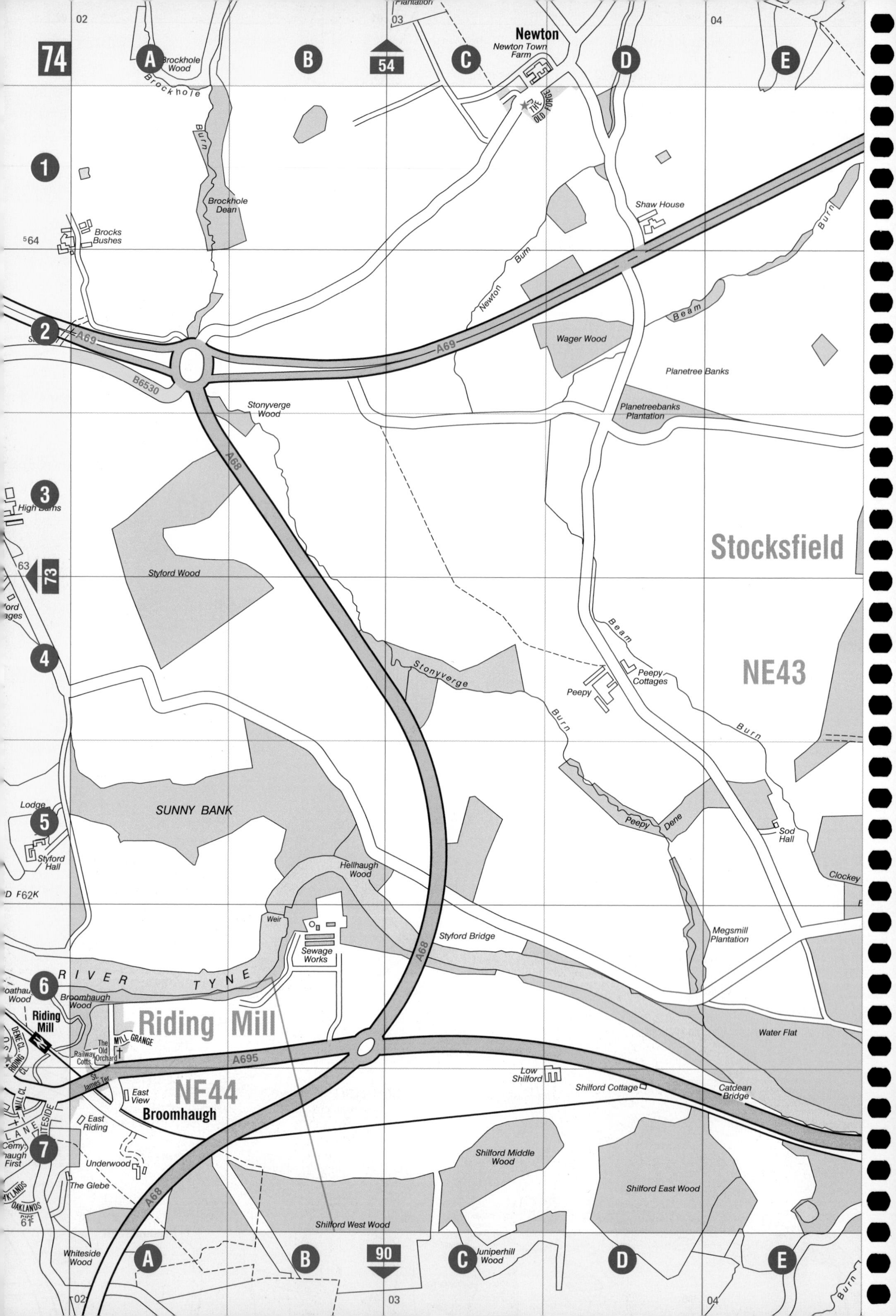
Newton
Newton Town Farm
THE OLD FORGE
Brockhole Wood
Brockhole
Burn
Brockhole Dean
Brocks Bushes
Shaw House
Newton Burn
Beam
Wager Wood
Planetree Banks
Planetreebanks Plantation
A69
B6530
A68
Stonyverge Wood
High Barns
Styford Wood
Stocksfield
Beam
Peepy
Peepy Cottages
NE43
Stonyverge
Burn
Burn
SUNNY BANK
Lodge
Styford Hall
Peepy Dene
Sod Hall
Hellhaugh Wood
Clockey
Weir
Sewage Works
Styford Bridge
Megsmill Plantation
RIVER TYNE
Broomhaugh Wood
Riding Mill
MILL GRANGE
The Old Orchard
Railway Cotts
Water Flat
A695
Low Shilford
Shilford Cottage
Catdean Bridge
St. James Ter.
East View
NE44
Broomhaugh
East Riding
Underwood
Shilford Middle Wood
Shilford East Wood
The Glebe
OAKLANDS
Shilford West Wood
Whiteside Wood
Juniperhill Wood
Burn
54
73
90
A B C D E
1 2 3 4 5 6 7
02 03 04
564 63 61

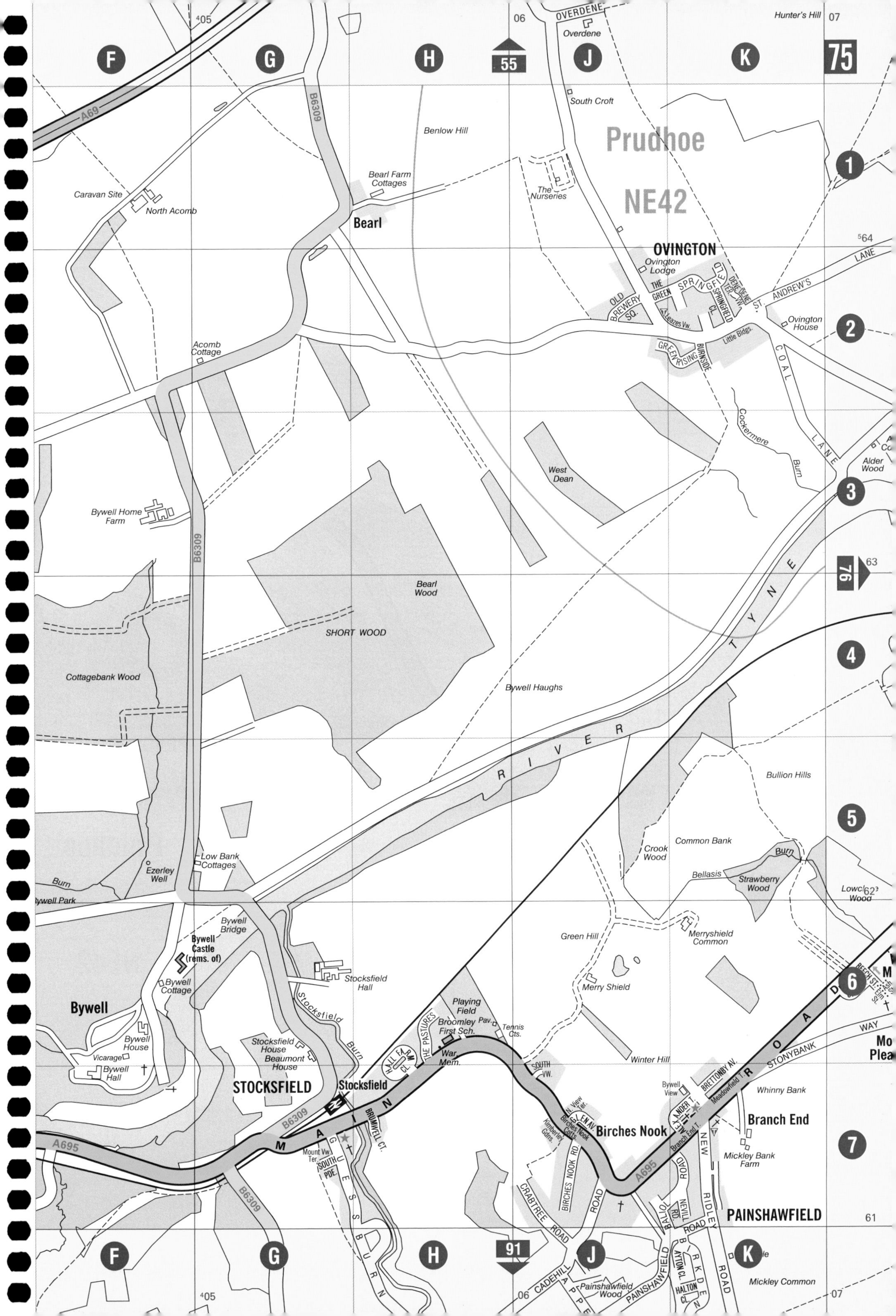

Hunter's Hill
Overdene
South Croft
Prudhoe
NE42
Benlow Hill
Bearl Farm Cottages
Caravan Site
North Acomb
Bearl
The Nurseries
OVINGTON
Ovington Lodge
Ovington House
OLD BREWERY SQ.
THE GREEN
SPRINGFIELD
SPRINGFIELD CL.
Leazes Vw.
GREEN RISING
BURNSIDE
Little Bldgs.
ST. ANDREW'S LANE
COAL LANE
Acomb Cottage
Cockermere Burn
West Dean
Alder Wood
Bywell Home Farm
Bearl Wood
SHORT WOOD
Cottagebank Wood
Bywell Haughs
RIVER TYNE
Bullion Hills
Common Bank
Crook Wood
Bellasis
Strawberry Wood
Burn
Lowcl Wood
Low Bank Cottages
Ezerley Well
Bywell Park
Bywell Bridge
Bywell Castle (rems. of)
Bywell Cottage
Green Hill
Merryshield Common
Merry Shield
Stocksfield Hall
Stocksfield Burn
Bywell
Bywell House
Vicarage
Bywell Hall
Stocksfield House
Beaumont House
STOCKSFIELD
Stocksfield
Playing Field
Pav.
Tennis Cts.
Broomley First Sch.
THE PASTURES
HALL FARM CL.
War Mem.
SOUTH VW.
Winter Hill
Bywell View
BRETTONBY AV.
Meadowfield T.
STONYBANK WAY
Whinny Bank
Branch End
Birches Nook
GLEN AV.
N. View Ter.
Birches Nook Cotts.
Kimberley Gdns.
BIRCHES NOOK RD.
CRABTREE ROAD
ROAD
MAIN ROAD
A695
B6309
A69
BRUMWELL CT.
GUESSBURN
Mount Vw. Ter.
SOUTH PDE.
Mickley Bank Farm
NEW RIDLEY ROAD
NEVILL RD.
BALIOL ROAD
PAINSHAWFIELD
Painshawfield Wood
PAINSHAWFIELD ROAD
CADEHILL
BIRKDENE
AYTON CL.
HALTON CL.
Mickley Common
BEECH ST.
F G H J K
1 2 3 4 5 6 7
55
76
91
405 06 07 564 63 623 61

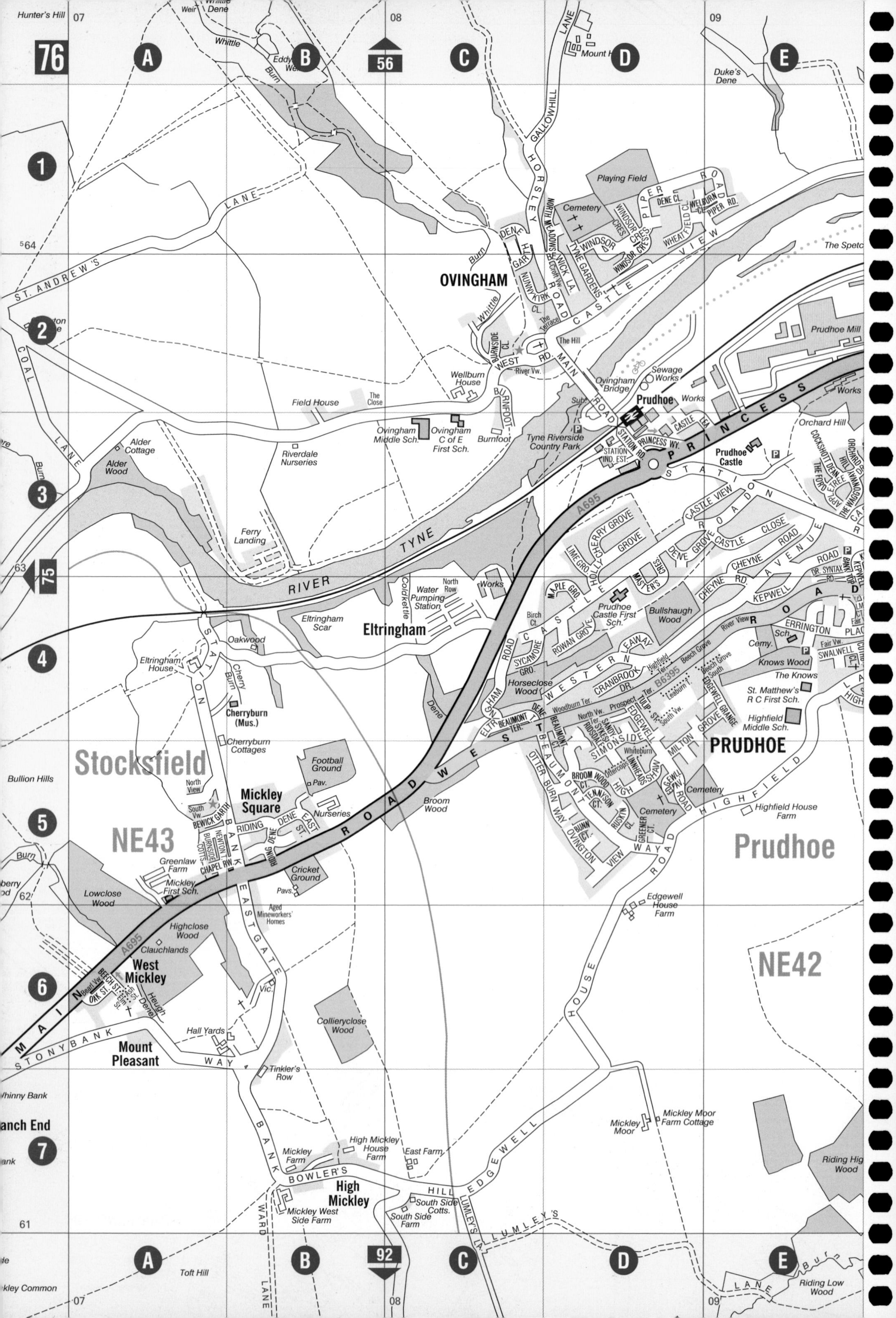
76
56
75
92
OVINGHAM
Prudhoe
PRUDHOE
Stocksfield
NE43
NE42
Mickley Square
Eltringham
West Mickley
Mount Pleasant
High Mickley
RIVER TYNE
Playing Field
Cemetery
Prudhoe Mill
Prudhoe Castle
Tyne Riverside Country Park
Ovingham Bridge
Sewage Works
Ovingham Middle Sch.
Ovingham C of E First Sch.
Burnfoot
Wellburn House
Field House
Riverdale Nurseries
Alder Cottage
Alder Wood
Ferry Landing
Eltringham Scar
Water Pumping Station
Oakwood
Eltringham House
Cherryburn (Mus.)
Cherryburn Cottages
Football Ground
Nurseries
Cricket Ground
Mickley First Sch.
Greenlaw Farm
Lowclose Wood
Highclose Wood
Clauchlands
Hall Yards
Tinkler's Row
Collieryclose Wood
Broom Wood
Horseclose Wood
Prudhoe Castle First Sch.
Bullshaugh Wood
Knows Wood
The Knows
St. Matthew's R C First Sch.
Highfield Middle Sch.
Highfield House Farm
Edgewell House Farm
Mickley Moor
Mickley Moor Farm Cottage
Riding High Wood
Riding Low Wood
Mickley Farm
High Mickley House Farm
East Farm
Mickley West Side Farm
South Side Farm
South Side Cotts.
Orchard Hill
Duke's Dene
Hunter's Hill
Bullion Hills
Toft Hill
ST. ANDREW'S LANE
COAL LANE
STATION BANK
EASTGATE BANK
STONYBANK WAY
BOWLER'S HILL
EDGEWELL HOUSE ROAD
PRINCESS WAY
A695
B6395
WEST ROAD
MAIN ROAD
CASTLE VIEW
STATION ROAD
HIGHFIELD ROAD
LUMLEY'S LANE
WARD LANE
GALLOWHILL LANE

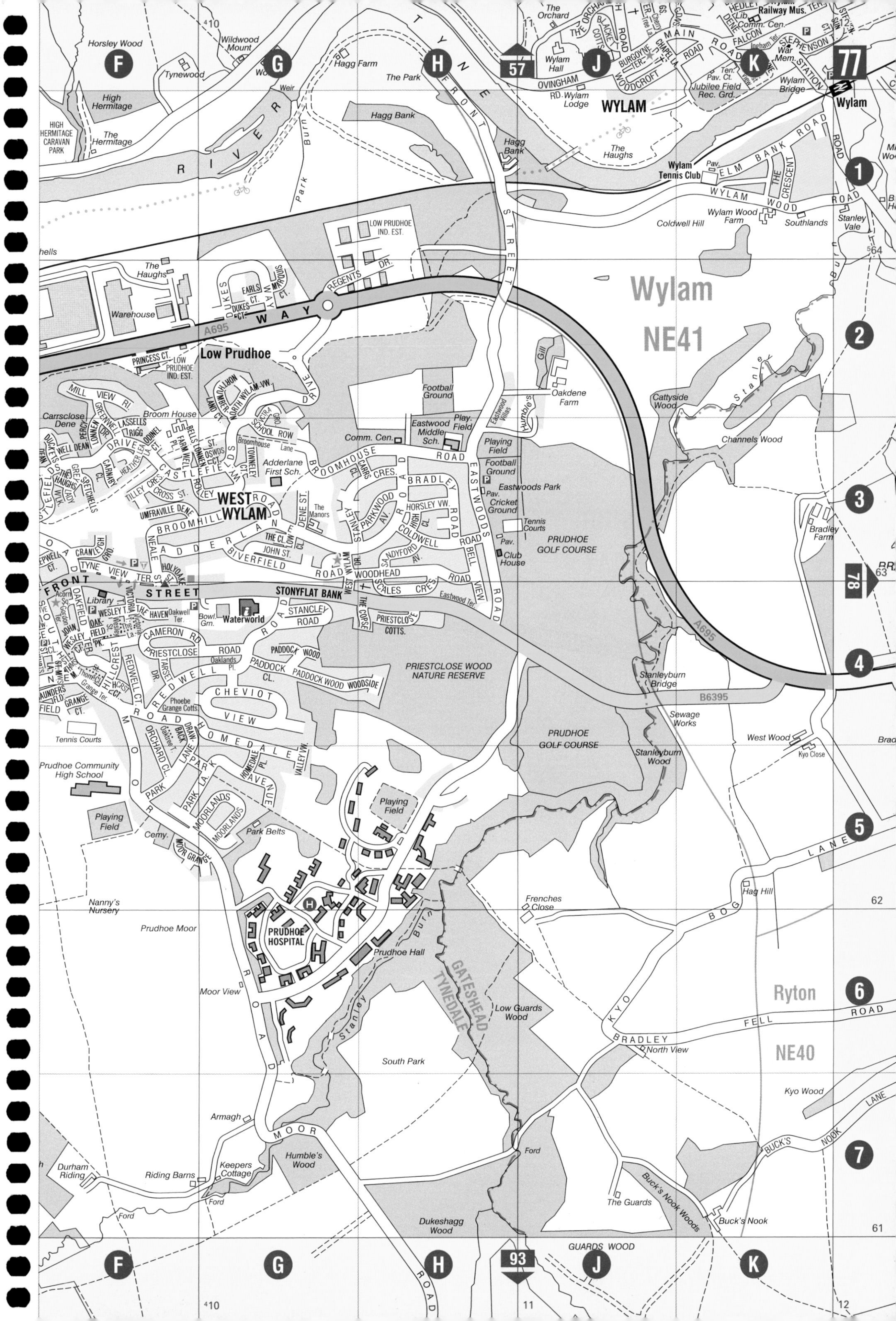
77
57
93
78
F
G
H
J
K
1
2
3
4
5
6
7
410
11
12
64
63
62
61
Horsley Wood
Wildwood Mount
Tynewood
High Hermitage
The Hermitage
HIGH HERMITAGE CARAVAN PARK
Weir
RIVER TYNE
Hagg Farm
The Park
Hagg Bank
Park Burn
The Orchard
Railway Mus.
Comm. Cen.
Wylam Hall
OVINGHAM RD.
Wylam Lodge
BURGOYNE TER.
WOODCROFT
MAIN ROAD
FALCON
STEPHENSON T.
STATION
War Mem.
Jubilee Field Rec. Grd.
Pav. Ct.
Ten. Ct.
Wylam Bridge
Wylam
WYLAM
The Haughs
Wylam Tennis Club
ELM BANK ROAD
THE CRESCENT
WYLAM WOOD ROAD
Wylam Wood Farm
Southlands
Coldwell Hill
Stanley Vale
FRONT STREET
LOW PRUDHOE IND. EST.
The Haughs
Warehouse
DUKES CT.
EARLS CT.
MARQUIS CT.
REGENTS DR.
WAY
A695
PRINCESS CT.
Low Prudhoe
Wylam
NE41
Gill
Oakdene Farm
Football Ground
Play. Field
Eastwood Middle Sch.
Comm. Cen.
Playing Field
Football Ground
Eastwoods Park
Pav.
Cricket Ground
Tennis Courts
Club House
PRUDHOE GOLF COURSE
Cattyside Wood
Stanley Burn
Channels Wood
Bradley Farm
MILL VIEW RI.
Carrsclose Dene
Broom House
LASSELLS RIGG
SCHOOL ROW
Broomhouse Lane
BROOMHOUSE ROAD
Adderlane First Sch.
CASTLEFIELDS
WEST WYLAM
BROOMHILL ROAD
UMFRAVILLE DENE
ADDERLANE
BIVERFIELD ROAD
JOHN ST.
THE CL.
DENE ST.
The Manors
STANLEY TER.
PARKWOOD AV.
CARRS CRES.
BRADLEY ROAD
HORSLEY VW.
COLDWELL ROAD
SANDYFORD AV.
WOODHEAD ROAD
BELL VIEW
EASTWOODS ROAD
TYNE VIEW TER.
CRANLEIGH GRO.
FRONT STREET
STONYFLAT BANK
SCALES CRES.
Eastwood Ter.
Library
Acorn Sq.
OAKFIELD
WESLEY T.
THE HAVEN
Oakwell Ter.
Bowl. Grn.
Waterworld
STANCLEY ROAD
PRIESTCLOSE COTTS.
THE COPSE
CAMERON RD.
PRIESTCLOSE ROAD
Oaklands Pl.
PADDOCK WOOD
PADDOCK CL.
PADDOCK WOOD
WOODSIDE
PRIESTCLOSE WOOD NATURE RESERVE
Stanleyburn Bridge
B6395
Sewage Works
REDWELL
CHEVIOT VIEW
Phoebe Grange Cotts
HOMEDALE ROAD
HILLCREST
REDWELL CT.
GRANGE CT.
SAUNDERS FLD.
Tennis Courts
ORCHARD CL.
BACK LANE
DRAW
PARK LANE
HOMEDALE PL.
AVENUE
VALLEY VW.
MOORLANDS
Prudhoe Community High School
Playing Field
Cemy.
Park Belts
Playing Field
MOOR GRANGE
PRUDHOE GOLF COURSE
Stanleyburn Wood
West Wood
Kyo Close
LANE
Hag Hill
BOG
Nanny's Nursery
Prudhoe Moor
PRUDHOE HOSPITAL
Prudhoe Hall
Frenches Close
GATESHEAD
TYNEDALE
Moor View
ROAD
Low Guards Wood
South Park
KYO
BRADLEY FELL ROAD
North View
Ryton
NE40
Kyo Wood
Armagh
MOOR
Humble's Wood
Durham Riding
Riding Barns
Keepers Cottage
Ford
BUCK'S NOOK LANE
The Guards
Buck's Nook Woods
Buck's Nook
Dukeshagg Wood
GUARDS WOOD

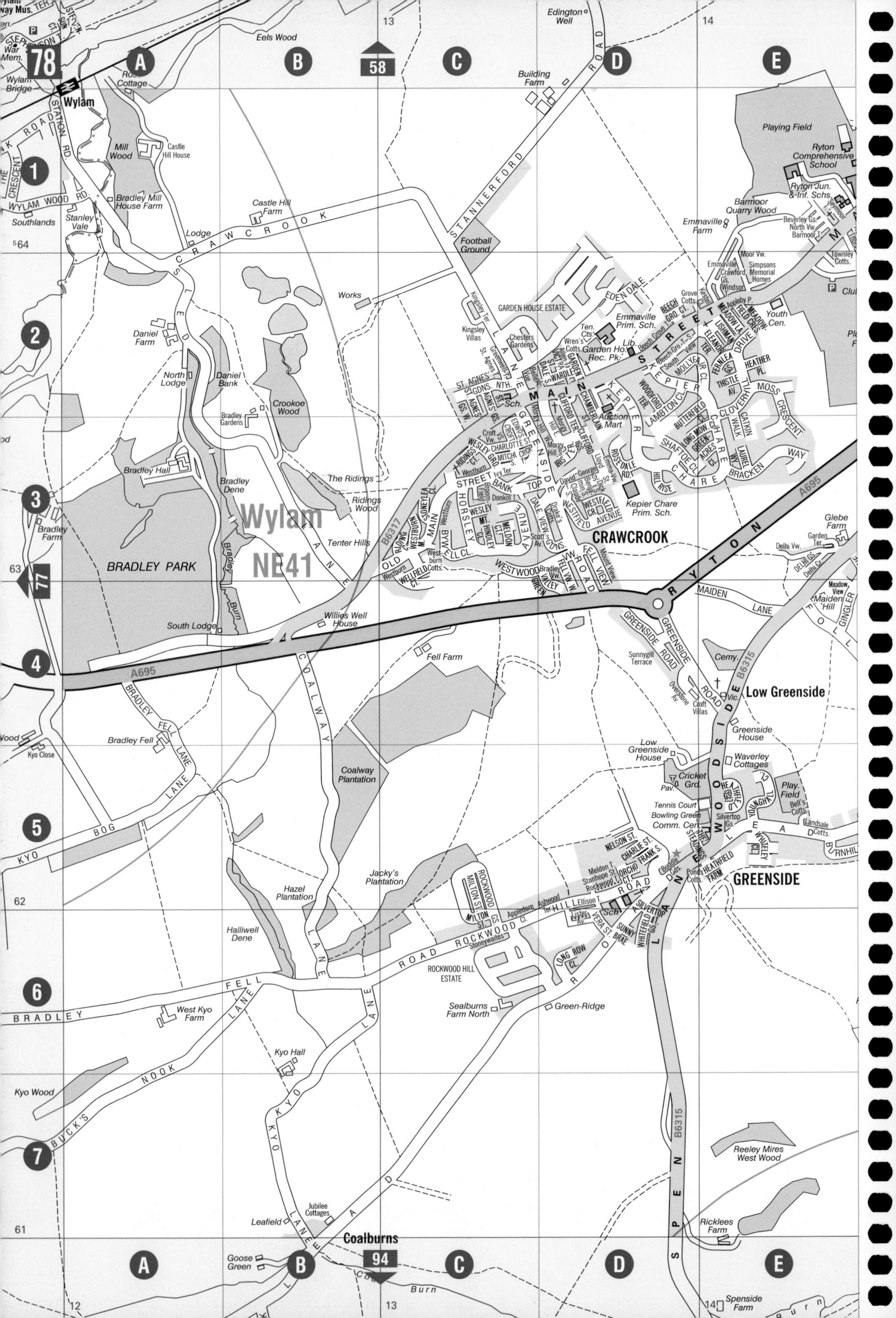

78
Wylam
Wylam Bridge
War Mem.
STATION RD.
Eels Wood
Rose Cottage
13
14
58
A
B
C
D
E
Edington Well
Building Farm
ROAD
Mill Wood
Castle Hill House
Bradley Mill House Farm
Castle Hill Farm
WYLAM WOOD RD.
CRESCENT
Stanley Vale
Southlands
Lodge
CRAWCROOK
STANNERFORD
Football Ground
Playing Field
Ryton Comprehensive School
Ryton Jun. & Inf. Schs.
Barmoor Quarry Wood
Emmaville Farm
Moor Vw.
Simpsons Memorial Homes
Youth Cen.
Club
Works
GARDEN HOUSE ESTATE
EDEN DALE
Emmaville Prim. Sch.
Kingsley Villas
Chesters Gardens
Garden Ho. Rec. Pk.
Lib.
MAIN
STREET
KEPIER
CHARE
Daniel Farm
North Lodge
Daniel Bank
Crookoe Wood
Bradley Gardens
Bradley Hall
Bradley Dene
The Ridings
Ridings Wood
Tenter Hills
Wylam
NE41
Auction Mart
Kepier Chare Prim. Sch.
CRAWCROOK
MOSS CRESCENT
BRACKEN WAY
BRADLEY PARK
Bradley Farm
63
77
South Lodge
Willies Well House
Fell Farm
RYTON
A695
B6317
Glebe Farm
Delhi Vw.
MAIDEN LANE
Maiden Hill
Cemy.
Sunnygill Terrace
GREENSIDE ROAD
Low Greenside
Greenside House
Low Greenside House
Waverley Cottages
Cricket Grd.
Play. Field
Tennis Court
Bowling Green
Comm. Cen.
Bradley Fell
BRADLEY FELL LANE
COALWAY
Coalway Plantation
Kyo Close
BOG LANE
KYO
Jacky's Plantation
Hazel Plantation
ROCKWOOD HILL ROAD
ROCKWOOD HILL ESTATE
GREENSIDE
Halliwell Dene
62
Sealburns Farm North
Green-Ridge
BRADLEY FELL ROAD
West Kyo Farm
Kyo Hall
NOOK LANE
BUCK'S
Kyo Wood
KYO LANE
Reeley Mires West Wood
SPEN LANE
B6315
Jubilee Cottages
Leafield
Coalburns
94
Goose Green
Ricklees Farm
61
12
Burn
Spenside Farm
1
2
3
4
5
6
7

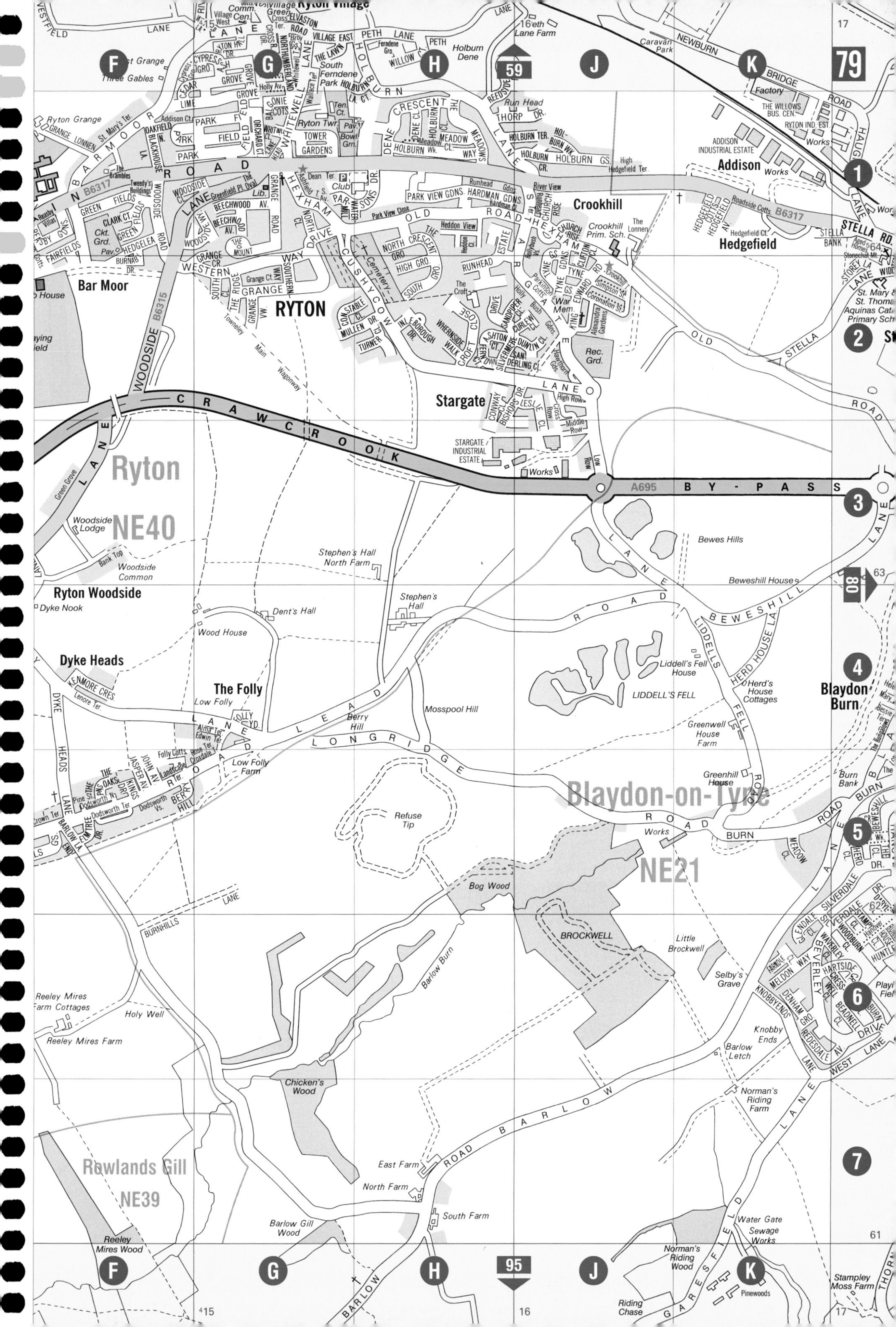
79
Ryton Village
Newburn Bridge Road
Caravan Park
Factory
The Willows Bus. Cen.
Ryton Ind. Est.
Addison Industrial Estate
Addison
Works
Holburn Dene
16'eth Lane Farm
Run Head
Thorp Dr.
Holburn Ter.
Holburn Gs.
High Hedgefield Ter.
Crookhill
Crookhill Prim. Sch.
The Lonnen
Hedgefield
Hedgefield Ct.
Roadside Cotts.
B6317
Stella Rd.
Stella Bank
St. Mary & St. Thomas Aquinas Cath. Primary Sch.
Old Stella Road
Ryton Grange
Grange Lonnen
St. Mary's Ter.
Barmoor Lane
Ryton Twr.
Tower Gardens
Holburn Wk.
Meadow Cl.
Meadows Way
Dean Ter.
Club
Park View Gdns.
Hardman Gdns.
Runhead Gdns.
River View
Old Road
Heddon View
North Crescent
High Gro.
Runhead Estate
Church Rise
Hexham Road
Lib.
Grange Road
Hexham Old Road
Cushycow Lane
Cemetery
Bar Moor
Western Way
Grange Way
RYTON
Stargate
Stargate Lane
Stargate Industrial Estate
Works
Rec. Grd.
War Mem.
Woodside Lane
B6315
Crawcrook Lane
A695 By-Pass
Ryton
NE40
Woodside Lodge
Woodside Common
Bank Top
Green Grove
Ryton Woodside
Dyke Nook
Stephen's Hall North Farm
Stephen's Hall
Dent's Hall
Wood House
Dyke Heads
Kenmore Cres.
Lenore Ter.
The Folly
Low Folly
Folly Yd.
Low Folly Farm
Berry Hill
Lead Road
Longridge Road
Mosspool Hill
Bewes Hills
Beweshill House
Beweshill Road
Herd House La.
Liddell's Fell House
Liddell's Fell
Herd's House Cottages
Greenwell House Farm
Greenhill House
Liddells Fell Road
Blaydon-on-Tyne
Blaydon Burn
Burn Bank
Burn Road
Works
NE21
Refuse Tip
Bog Wood
Brockwell
Little Brockwell
Selby's Grave
Barlow Burn
Burnhills Lane
Reeley Mires Farm Cottages
Holy Well
Reeley Mires Farm
Chicken's Wood
Knobby Ends
Barlow Letch
Norman's Riding Farm
Barlow Road
West Lane
East Farm
North Farm
South Farm
Barlow Gill Wood
Rowlands Gill
NE39
Reeley Mires Wood
Water Gate Sewage Works
Norman's Riding Wood
Garesfield Lane
Pinewoods
Riding Chase
Stampley Moss Farm
Barlow
59
80
95
F G H J K
1 2 3 4 5 6 7
15 16 17 61 62 63 64

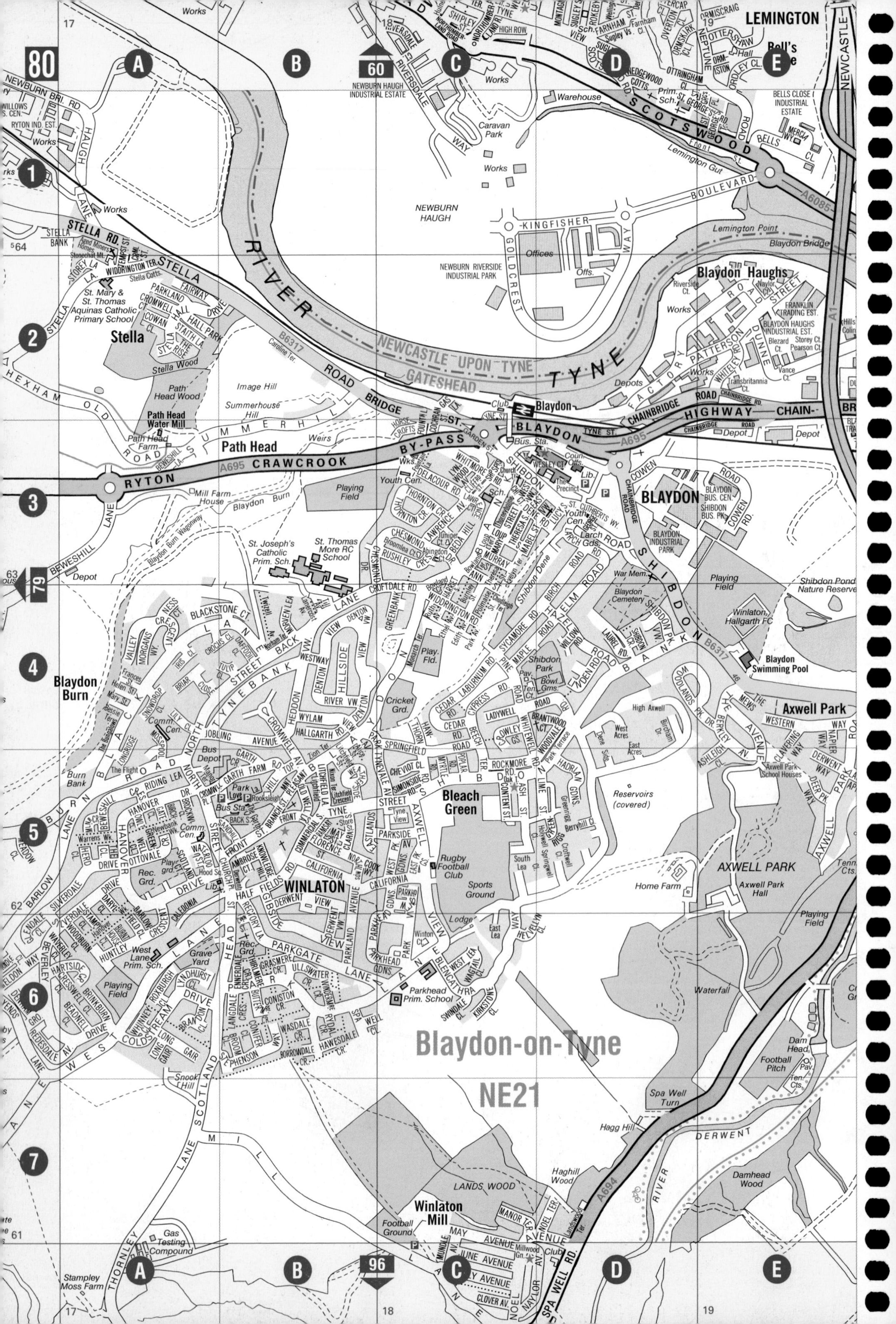
LEMINGTON
NEWCASTLE
Bell's Close
BELLS CLOSE INDUSTRIAL ESTATE
NEWBURN HAUGH INDUSTRIAL ESTATE
60
Works
Caravan Park
Warehouse
SCOTSWOOD ROAD
Lemington Gut
BOULEVARD
A6085
NEWBURN HAUGH
KINGFISHER WAY
GOLDCREST
Offices
NEWBURN RIVERSIDE INDUSTRIAL PARK
Lemington Point
Blaydon Bridge
Blaydon Haughs
FRANKLIN TRADING EST.
BLAYDON HAUGHS INDUSTRIAL EST.
A1
RIVER TYNE
NEWCASTLE UPON TYNE
GATESHEAD
FACTORY ROAD
PATTERSON
Depots
CHAINBRIDGE ROAD
HIGHWAY
Blaydon
BLAYDON
TYNE ST.
A695
Depot
NEWBURN BRI. RD
RYTON IND. EST.
HAUGH LANE
STELLA RD.
STELLA BANK
WIDDRINGTON TER.
Stella Cotts.
St. Mary & St. Thomas Aquinas Catholic Primary School
Stella
Stella Wood
HEXHAM OLD ROAD
Path Head Wood
Image Hill
Summerhouse Hill
Path Head Water Mill
Path Head Farm
Path Head
B6317
BRIDGE ROAD
SUMMERHILL
Weirs
BY-PASS
RYTON CRAWCROOK
A695
RYTON
Mill Farm House
Blaydon Burn
Playing Field
Youth Cen.
St. Joseph's Catholic Prim. Sch.
St. Thomas More RC School
BEWESHILL LANE
79
Depot
BLAYDON
BLAYDON BUS. CEN.
SHIBDON BUS. PK.
BLAYDON INDUSTRIAL PARK
COWEN RD.
Shibdon Dene
Larch Road
War Mem.
Blaydon Cemetery
SHIBDON BANK
Playing Field
Shibdon Pond Nature Reserve
Winlaton, Hallgarth FC
Blaydon Swimming Pool
Axwell Park
Blaydon Burn
CROFTDALE RD.
BLACKSTONE CT.
BACK STREET
TYNEBANK
Play. Fld.
Cricket Grd.
Shibdon Park
High Axwell
West Acres
East Acres
Reservoirs (covered)
Bus Depot
Bleach Green
WINLATON
Rugby Football Club
Sports Ground
Home Farm
AXWELL PARK
Axwell Park Hall
Playing Field
Burn Bank
West Lane Prim. Sch.
Grave Yard
Playing Field
Parkhead Prim. School
Waterfall
Blaydon-on-Tyne
NE21
Snook Hill
WEST LANE
SCOTLAND LANE
MILL LANE
Spa Well Turn
Hagg Hill
DERWENT
RIVER
Haghill Wood
LANDS WOOD
Damhead Wood
A694
Winlaton Mill
Football Ground
96
Gas Testing Compound
Stampley Moss Farm
THORNLEY LANE
SPA WELL RD.
Dam Head
Football Pitch
17
18
19
63
62
61
564

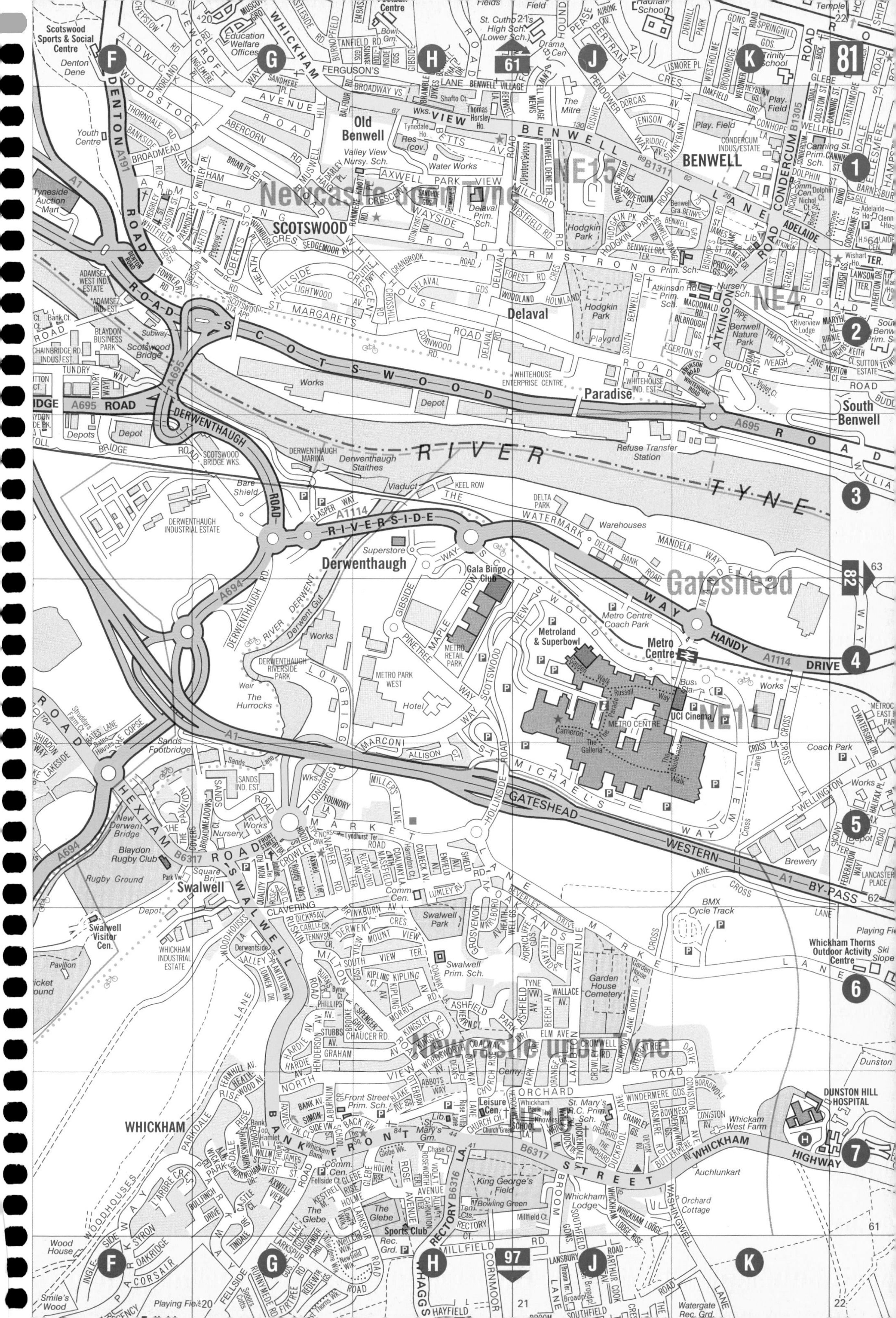
F
G
H
J
K
61
1
2
3
4
5
6
7
82
97
Scotswood Sports & Social Centre
Denton Dene
Youth Centre
Tyneside Auction Mart
Education Welfare Offices
WHICKHAM
Old Benwell
Valley View Nursy. Sch.
Water Works
Delaval Prim. Sch.
St. Cuthbert's High Sch. (Lower Sch.)
Drama Cen
The Mitre
BENWELL
Play. Field
CONDERCUM INDUS. ESTATE
Canning St. Prim. Sch.
Newcastle upon Tyne
SCOTSWOOD
NE15
NE4
Hodgkin Park
Delaval
Benwell Nature Park
Riverview Lodge
Atkinson Rd. Prim. Sch.
Nursery Sch.
South Benwell
Paradise
WHITEHOUSE ENTERPRISE CENTRE
Works
Depot
Depots
ADAMSEZ WEST IND. ESTATE
BLAYDON BUSINESS PARK
CHAINBRIDGE RD. INDUS. EST.
Scotswood Bridge
SCOTSWOOD ROAD
A695
A1
A191
DENTON ROAD
RIVER TYNE
DERWENTHAUGH MARINA
Derwenthaugh Staithes
Refuse Transfer Station
Bare Shield
Viaduct
KEEL ROW
DELTA PARK
Warehouses
DERWENTHAUGH INDUSTRIAL ESTATE
RIVERSIDE WAY
A7114
Superstore
Derwenthaugh
Gala Bingo Club
Gateshead
Metroland & Superbowl
Metro Centre Coach Park
Metro Centre
HANDY DRIVE
A1114
METRO RETAIL PARK
DERWENTHAUGH RIVERSIDE PARK
METRO PARK WEST
Hotel
Weir
The Hurrocks
UCI Cinema
NE11
METRO CENTRE
The Galleria
Cameron Walk
Russell Way
Coach Park
Brewery
GATESHEAD WESTERN BY-PASS
Sands Footbridge
SANDS IND. EST.
New Derwent Bridge
Blaydon Rugby Club
Rugby Ground
Swalwell
Swalwell Visitor Cen.
WHICKHAM INDUSTRIAL ESTATE
Pavilion
Swalwell Park
Swalwell Prim. Sch.
BMX Cycle Track
Whickham Thorns Outdoor Activity Centre
Ski Slope
Garden House Cemetery
Cemy.
Front Street Prim. Sch.
Leisure Cen.
St. Mary's R.C. Prim. Sch.
DUNSTON HILL HOSPITAL
Whickam West Farm
Auchlunkart
Orchard Cottage
WHICKHAM HIGHWAY
FRONT STREET
B6317
King George's Field
Bowling Green
The Glebe
Sports Club
Whickham Lodge
Wood House
Smile's Wood
Playing Field
Watergate Rec. Grd.

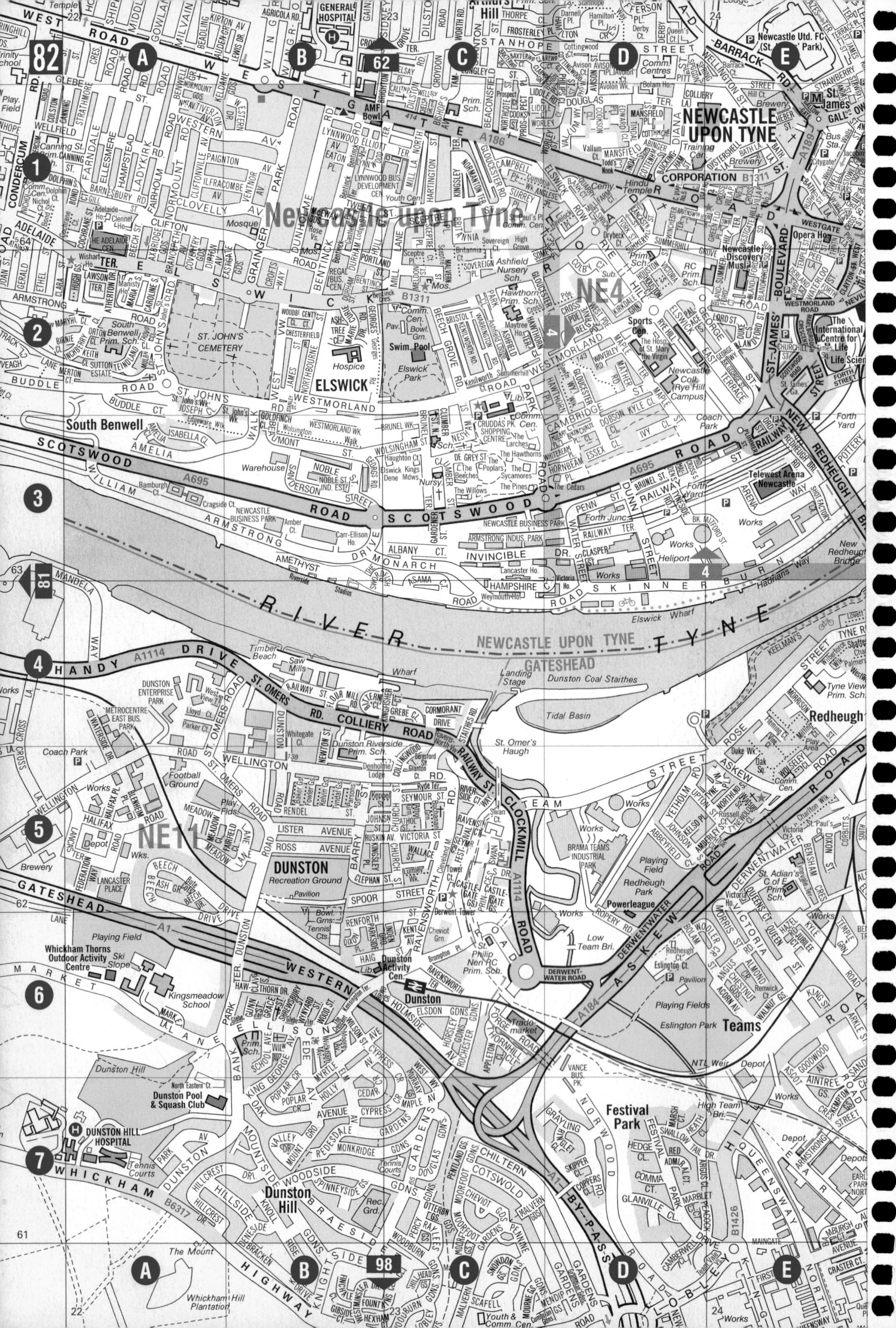

82
A
B
C
D
E
1
2
3
4
5
6
7
62
98
81
4
NEWCASTLE UPON TYNE
Newcastle upon Tyne
NE4
NE11
ELSWICK
South Benwell
DUNSTON
Dunston Hill
Redheugh
Teams
Festival Park
Arthur's Hill
GENERAL HOSPITAL
Newcastle Utd. FC (St. James' Park)
St. James
WEST ROAD
WESTGATE ROAD
A186
SCOTSWOOD ROAD
A695
RIVER TYNE
NEWCASTLE UPON TYNE
GATESHEAD
Dunston Coal Staithes
Tidal Basin
St. Omer's Haugh
Elswick Wharf
New Redheugh Bridge
Telewest Arena Newcastle
Newcastle Discovery Mus.
Opera Ho.
The International Centre for Life
Newcastle Coll. (Rye Hill Campus)
ST. JOHN'S CEMETERY
Elswick Park
Swim. Pool
Hospice
NEWCASTLE BUSINESS PARK
ARMSTRONG INDUS. PARK
Heliport
HANDY DRIVE
A1114
ST. OMERS RD.
COLLIERY ROAD
DUNSTON ENTERPRISE PARK
METROCENTRE EAST BUS. PARK
Coach Park
Football Ground
Dunston Riverside Prim. Sch.
Recreation Ground
CLOCKMILL ROAD
TEAM STREET
BRAMA TEAMS INDUSTRIAL PARK
Redheugh Park
Playing Field
Powerleague
DERWENTWATER ROAD
ASKEW ROAD
A184
GATESHEAD
WESTERN
A1
Whickham Thorns Outdoor Activity Centre
Kingsmeadow School
Dunston Hill
Dunston Pool & Squash Club
DUNSTON HILL HOSPITAL
WHICKHAM HIGHWAY
B6317
Dunston Activity Cen.
Dunston
Trade market
Low Team Bri.
Eslington Park
Playing Fields
A1 BY-PASS ROAD
B1426
QUEENSWAY
The Mount
Whickham Hill Plantation
22
23
24
61

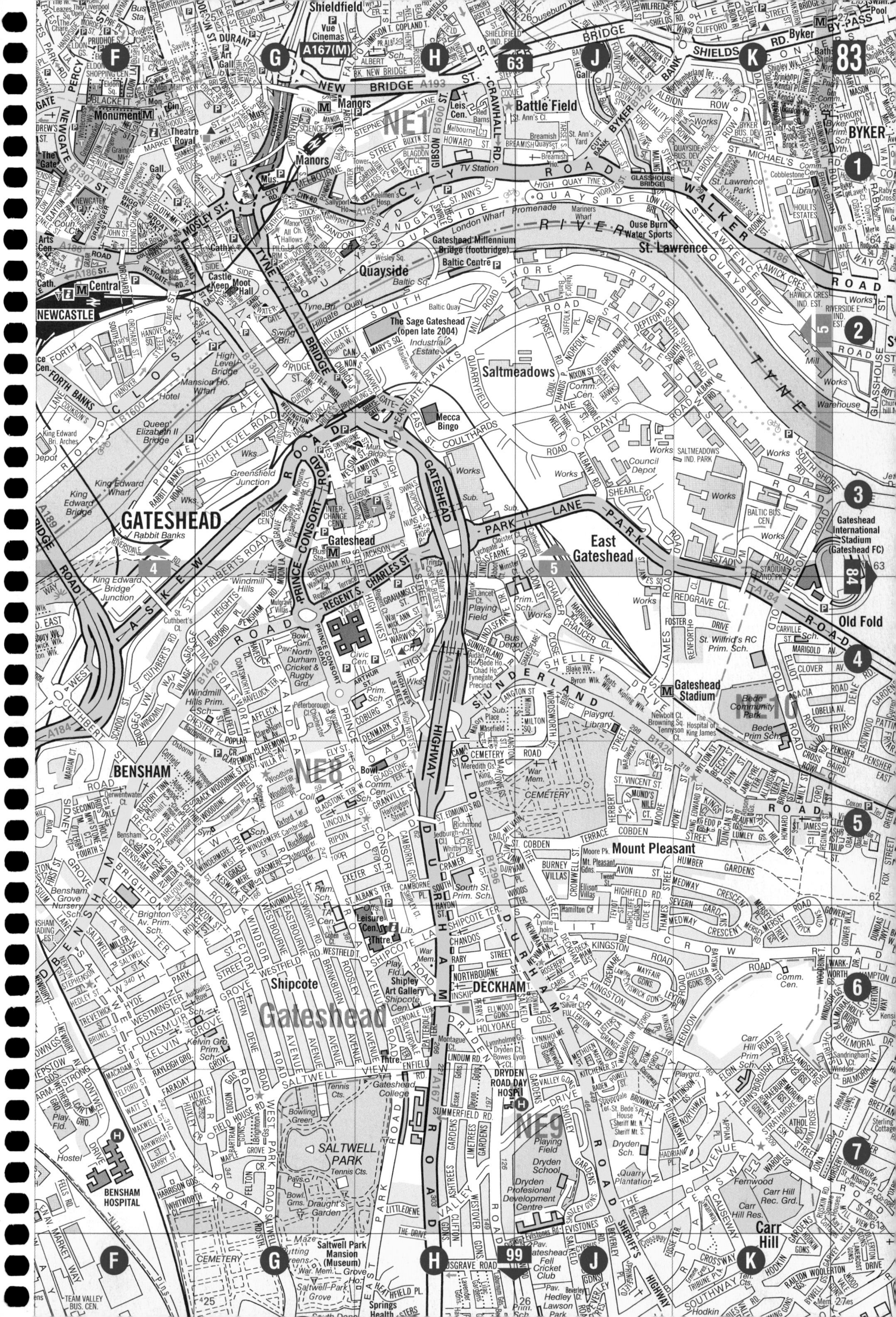

Shieldfield
Vue Cinemas
A167(M)
F
G
H
63
J
K
BYKER
Byker
NEW BRIDGE A193
Manors
NE1
Battle Field
Monument
Theatre Royal
Central
NEWCASTLE
Quayside
Gateshead Millennium Bridge (footbridge)
Baltic Centre
Ouse Burn Water Sports
St. Lawrence
RIVER
TYNE
Tyne Bri.
The Sage Gateshead (open late 2004)
Industrial Estate
Saltmeadows
Mecca Bingo
High Level Bridge
Queen Elizabeth II Bridge
King Edward Bridge
King Edward Wharf
Greensfield Junction
GATESHEAD
Rabbit Banks
Gateshead
East Gateshead
SALTMEADOWS IND. PARK
Council Depot
Gateshead International Stadium (Gateshead FC)
84
Old Fold
4
5
BENSHAM
NE8
Civic Cen.
North Durham Cricket & Rugby Grd.
Bus Depot
Gateshead Stadium
NE10
Bede Community Park
Mount Pleasant
CEMETERY
Shipcote
Gateshead
DECKHAM
Leisure Cen.
Shipley Art Gallery
Gateshead College
DRYDEN ROAD DAY HOSP.
NE9
SALTWELL PARK
Saltwell Park Mansion (Museum)
BENSHAM HOSPITAL
Dryden Professional Development Centre
Carr Hill
Carr Hill Rec. Grd.
Quarry Plantation
99
Gateshead Fell Cricket Club
CEMETERY
TEAM VALLEY BUS. CEN.
1
2
3
4
5
6
7
25
26
27
61
62
63
64

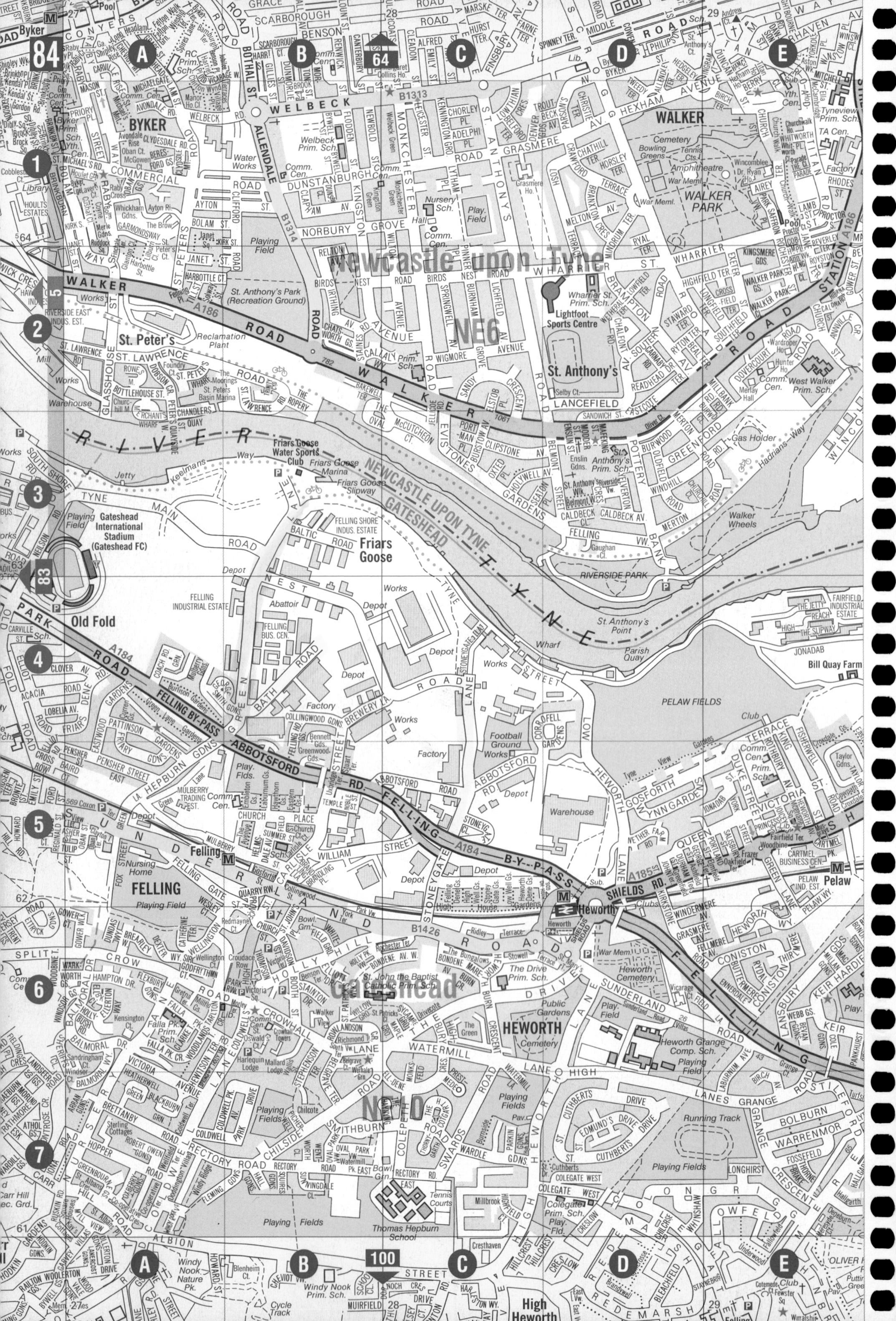

84
64
100
83
5
A
B
C
D
E
1
2
3
4
5
6
7
BYKER
WALKER
WALKER PARK
Newcastle upon Tyne
NE6
St. Anthony's
Lightfoot Sports Centre
St. Peter's
RIVER
TYNE
NEWCASTLE UPON TYNE
GATESHEAD
Friars Goose
Friars Goose Water Sports Club
Gateshead International Stadium (Gateshead FC)
Old Fold
FELLING
Felling
Gateshead
HEWORTH
Heworth
NE10
PELAW FIELDS
Pelaw
Bill Quay Farm
RIVERSIDE PARK
St. Anthony's Point
Walker Wheels
Gas Holder
West Walker Prim. Sch.
Heworth Cemetery
Heworth Grange Comp. Sch.
Thomas Hepburn School
Windy Nook Nature Pk.
Windy Nook Prim. Sch.
High Heworth
WALKER ROAD
FELLING BY-PASS
SHIELDS RD.
WELBECK
A186
A184
A185
B1313
B1314
B1426
St. Anthony's Park (Recreation Ground)
FELLING INDUSTRIAL ESTATE
FELLING SHORE INDUS. ESTATE
FAIRFIELD INDUSTRIAL ESTATE
CARTMEL BUSINESS CEN.
PELAW IND. EST.
MULBERRY TRADING EST.
RIVERSIDE EAST INDUS. EST.
Running Track
Playing Fields

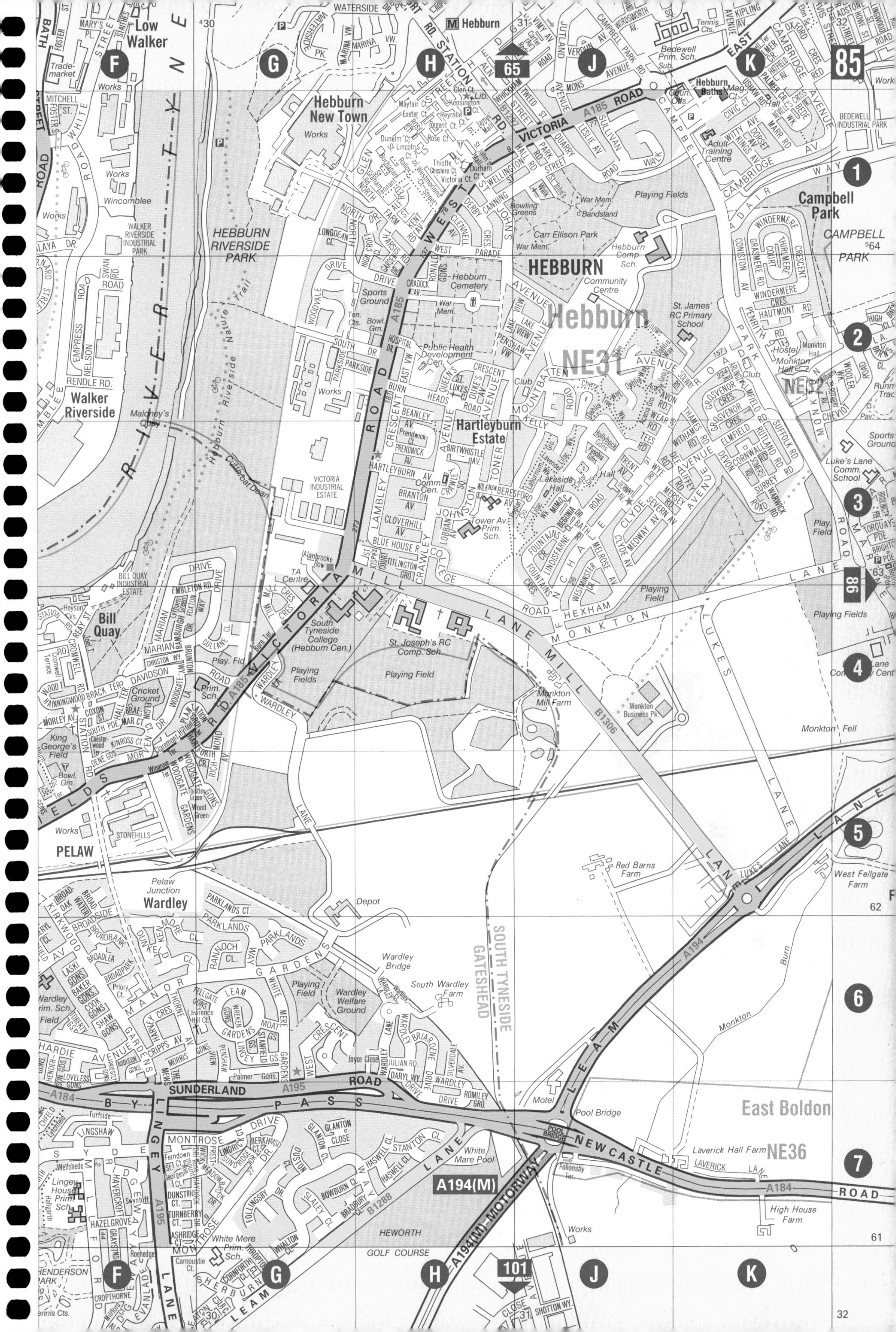

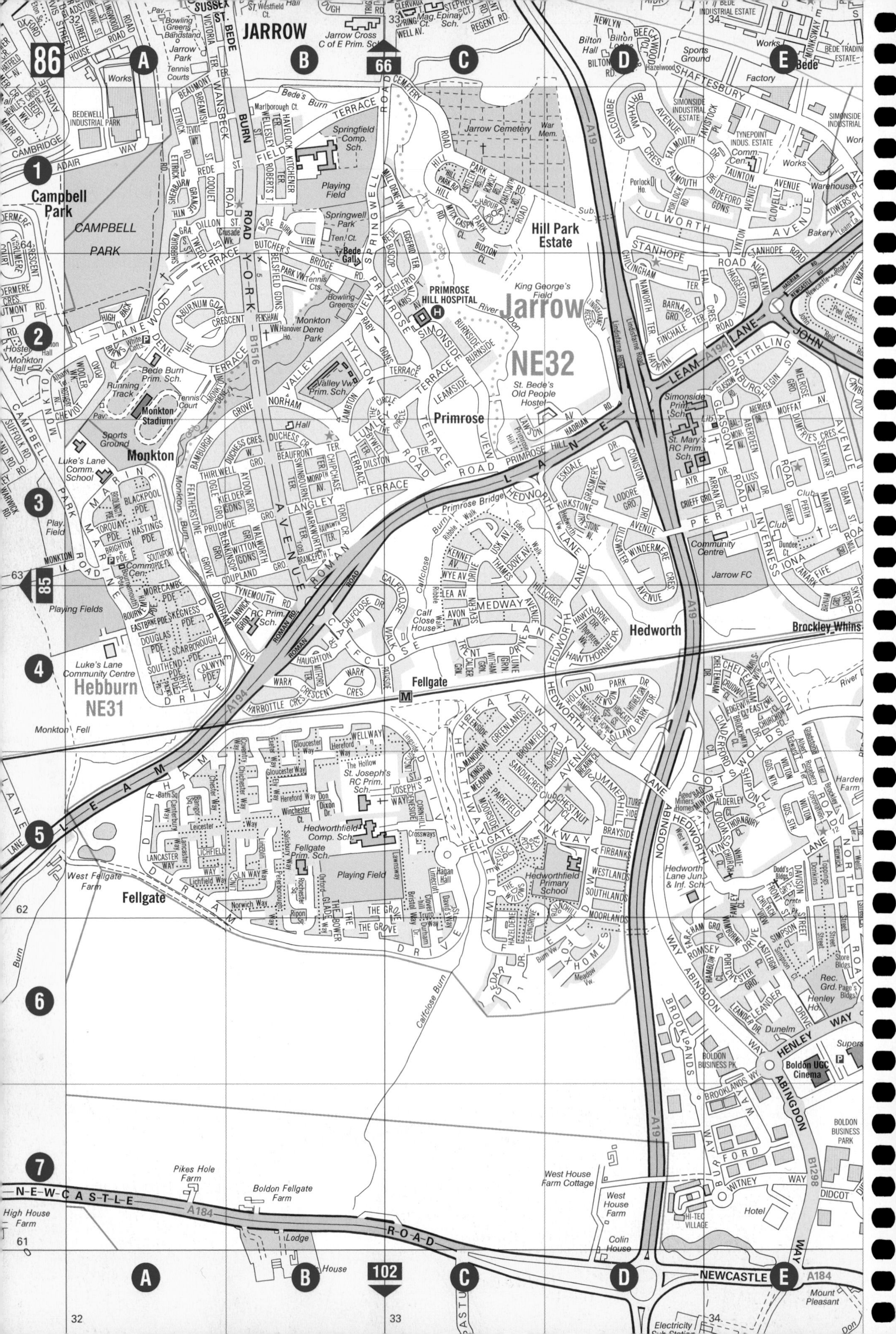
JARROW
Jarrow Cross C of E Prim. Sch.
66
A
B
C
D
E
1
2
3
4
5
6
7
Campbell Park
CAMPBELL PARK
Bedewell Industrial Park
Works
Springfield Comp. Sch.
Playing Field
Springwell Park
Bede Gall.
Jarrow Cemetery
War Mem.
Hill Park Estate
Primrose Hill Hospital
King George's Field
Jarrow
NE32
River Don
St. Bede's Old People Hostel
Primrose
Valley Vw Prim. Sch.
Monkton Dene Park
Bede Burn Prim. Sch.
Running Track
Monkton Stadium
Sports Ground
Monkton
Luke's Lane Comm. School
Play. Field
Playing Fields
Luke's Lane Community Centre
Hebburn NE31
Monkton Fell
85
RC Prim. Sch.
Calf Close House
Fellgate
Hedworth
Jarrow FC
Community Centre
Simonside Prim. Sch.
St. Mary's RC Prim. Sch.
Simonside Industrial Estate
Tynepoint Indus. Estate
Bede Trading Estate
Bede
Sports Ground
Bilton Hall
Brockley Whins
St. Joseph's RC Prim. Sch.
Hedworthfield Comp. Sch.
Fellgate Prim. Sch.
Playing Field
Hedworthfield Primary School
Hedworth Lane Jun. & Inf. Sch.
Aged Miners Homes
West Fellgate Farm
Fellgate
Calfclose Burn
Boldon Business Pk
Boldon UGC Cinema
Boldon Business Park
Hi-Tec Village
Hotel
West House Farm Cottage
West House Farm
Colin House
Pikes Hole Farm
Boldon Fellgate Farm
High House Farm
Lodge
102
NEWCASTLE ROAD
A184
A19
A194
B1516
B1298
LEAM LANE
YORK AVENUE
DURHAM DRIVE
ABINGDON WAY
HEDWORTH LANE
FELLGATE AVENUE
Harden Farm
Mount Pleasant
Electricity Sub Station
32
33
34
61
62
63
64

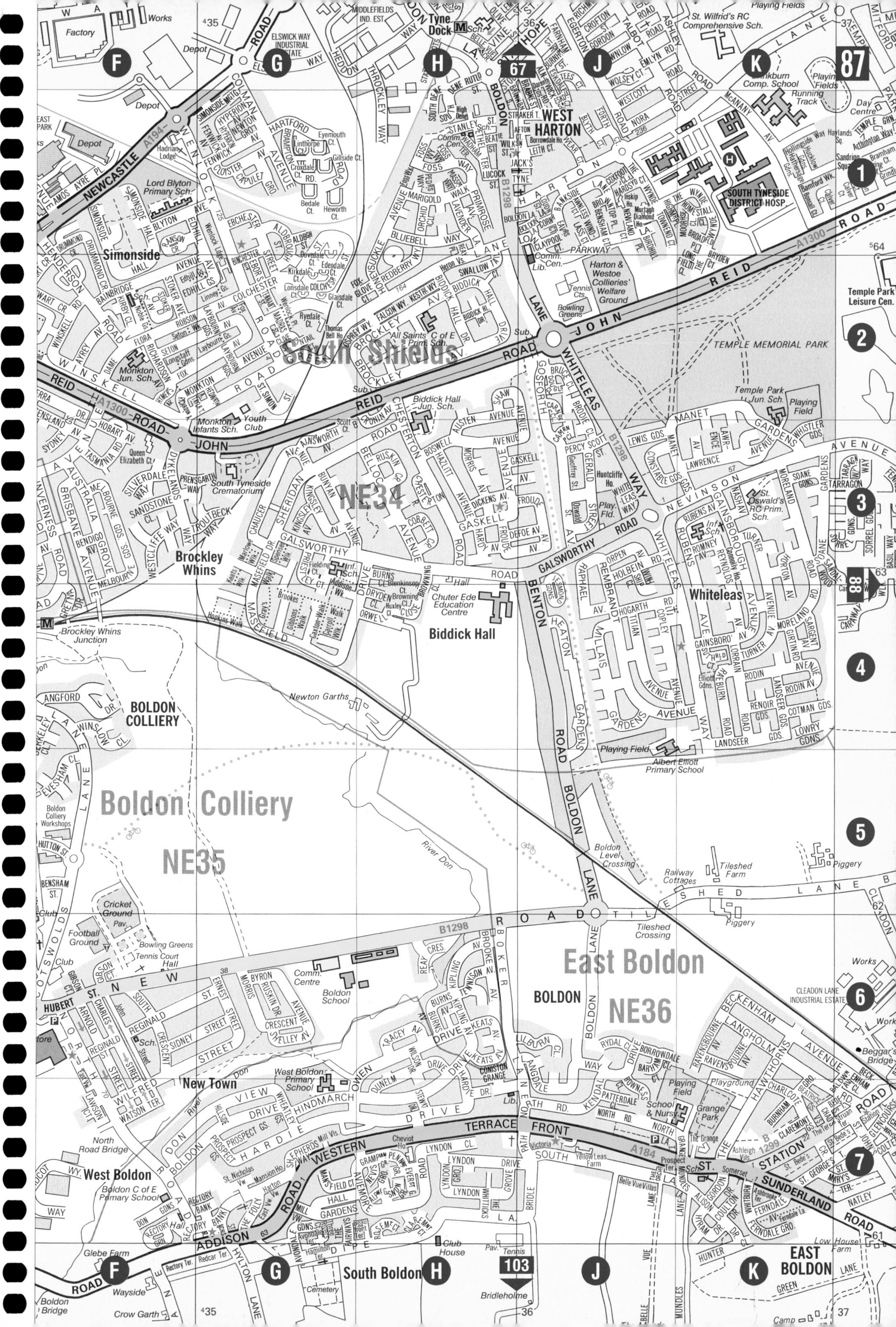

87
67
88
103
F
G
H
J
K
1
2
3
4
5
6
7
435
36
37
564
63
62
61
38
57
Factory
Works
Depot
ELSWICK WAY INDUSTRIAL ESTATE
MIDDLEFIELDS IND. EST
Tyne Dock
St. Wilfrid's RC Comprehensive Sch.
Playing Fields
Harton Comp. School
Running Track
Day Centre
WEST HARTON
SOUTH TYNESIDE DISTRICT HOSP.
Lord Blyton Primary Sch.
Simonside
Hadrian Lodge
NEWCASTLE ROAD
A194
COLEMAN ROAD
BOLDON LANE
B1298
JOHN REID ROAD
A1300
Temple Park Leisure Cen.
TEMPLE MEMORIAL PARK
Harton & Westoe Collieries' Welfare Ground
Tennis Cts.
Bowling Greens
South Shields
All Saints C of E Prim. Sch.
Monkton Jun. Sch.
Monkton Infants Sch.
Youth Club
Biddick Hall Jun. Sch.
Temple Park Jun. Sch.
Playing Field
St. Oswald's RC Prim. Sch.
South Tyneside Crematorium
Queen Elizabeth Ct.
NE34
Brockley Whins
Chuter Ede Education Centre
Biddick Hall
Whiteleas
WHITELEAS WAY
BENTON ROAD
GALSWORTHY ROAD
Huntcliffe Ho.
Play. Fld.
Brockley Whins Junction
Newton Garths
BOLDON COLLIERY
Boldon Colliery
Boldon Colliery Workshops
NE35
River Don
Playing Field
Albert Elliott Primary School
BOLDON LANE
Boldon Level Crossing
Railway Cottages
Tileshed Farm
Piggery
TILESHED LANE
Tileshed Crossing
Cricket Ground
Football Ground
Bowling Greens
Tennis Court
Hall
Club
NEW ROAD
B1298
BROKER AV.
Comm. Centre
Boldon School
East Boldon
BOLDON
NE36
Works
CLEADON LANE INDUSTRIAL ESTATE
Beggar's Bridge
New Town
West Boldon Primary School
Playing Field
Playground
School & Nursy.
Grange Park
The Grange
North Road Bridge
West Boldon
Boldon C of E Primary School
WESTERN TERRACE
FRONT ST.
A184
STATION RD.
SUNDERLAND ROAD
B1299
Victoria
Yellow Leas Farm
Belle Vue Villas
Cheviot Ho.
Club House
Pav.
Tennis
ADDISON ROAD
Glebe Farm
Wayside
Boldon Bridge
Crow Garth
Cemetery
South Boldon
Bridleholme
Low House Farm
EAST BOLDON
HUNTER
GREEN LANE

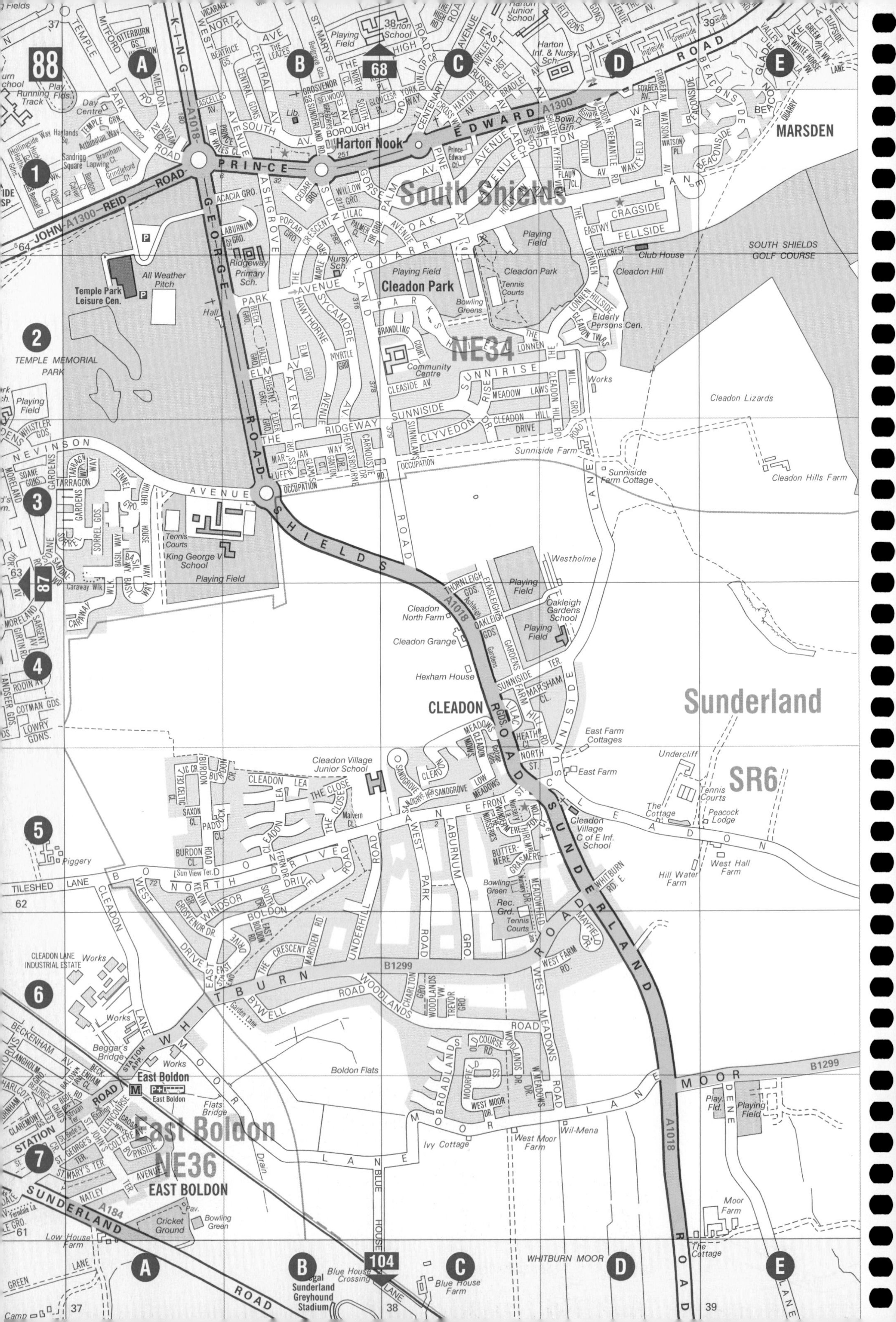
South Shields
Harton Nook
MARSDEN
SOUTH SHIELDS GOLF COURSE
Club House
Cleadon Hill
Cleadon Park
Playing Field
Tennis Courts
Bowling Greens
Elderly Persons Cen.
NE34
Community Centre
Works
Cleadon Lizards
Sunniside Farm
Sunniside Farm Cottage
Cleadon Hills Farm
Temple Park Leisure Cen.
All Weather Pitch
Hall
TEMPLE MEMORIAL PARK
Ridgeway Primary Sch.
Nursy Sch.
King George V School
Tennis Courts
Westholme
Oakleigh Gardens School
Cleadon North Farm
Cleadon Grange
Hexham House
CLEADON
Sunderland
East Farm Cottages
East Farm
Undercliff
SR6
Tennis Courts
The Cottage
Peacock Lodge
West Hall Farm
Hill Water Farm
Cleadon Village Junior School
Cleadon Village C of E Inf. School
Piggery
Bowling Green
Rec. Grd.
CLEADON LANE INDUSTRIAL ESTATE
Works
Beggar's Bridge
East Boldon
Flats Bridge
Boldon Flats
East Boldon
NE36
EAST BOLDON
Cricket Ground
Bowling Green
Pav.
Low House Farm
Ivy Cottage
West Moor Farm
Wil-Mena
Play. Fld.
Playing Field
Moor Farm
The Cottage
WHITBURN MOOR
Blue House Crossing
Blue House Farm
Sunderland Greyhound Stadium
Harton School
Harton Junior School
Harton Inf. & Nursy. Sch.
Day Centre
Running Track
Playing Field
Lib.
A1300
A1018
A184
B1299
KING GEORGE ROAD
PRINCE EDWARD ROAD
JOHN REID ROAD
NEVINSON AVENUE
SHIELDS ROAD
SUNDERLAND ROAD
CLEADON LANE
WHITBURN ROAD
MOOR LANE
TILESHED LANE
STATION ROAD
QUARRY LANE
SUNDERLAND LANE
68
87
104
A
B
C
D
E
1
2
3
4
5
6
7
37
38
39
61
62
63
64

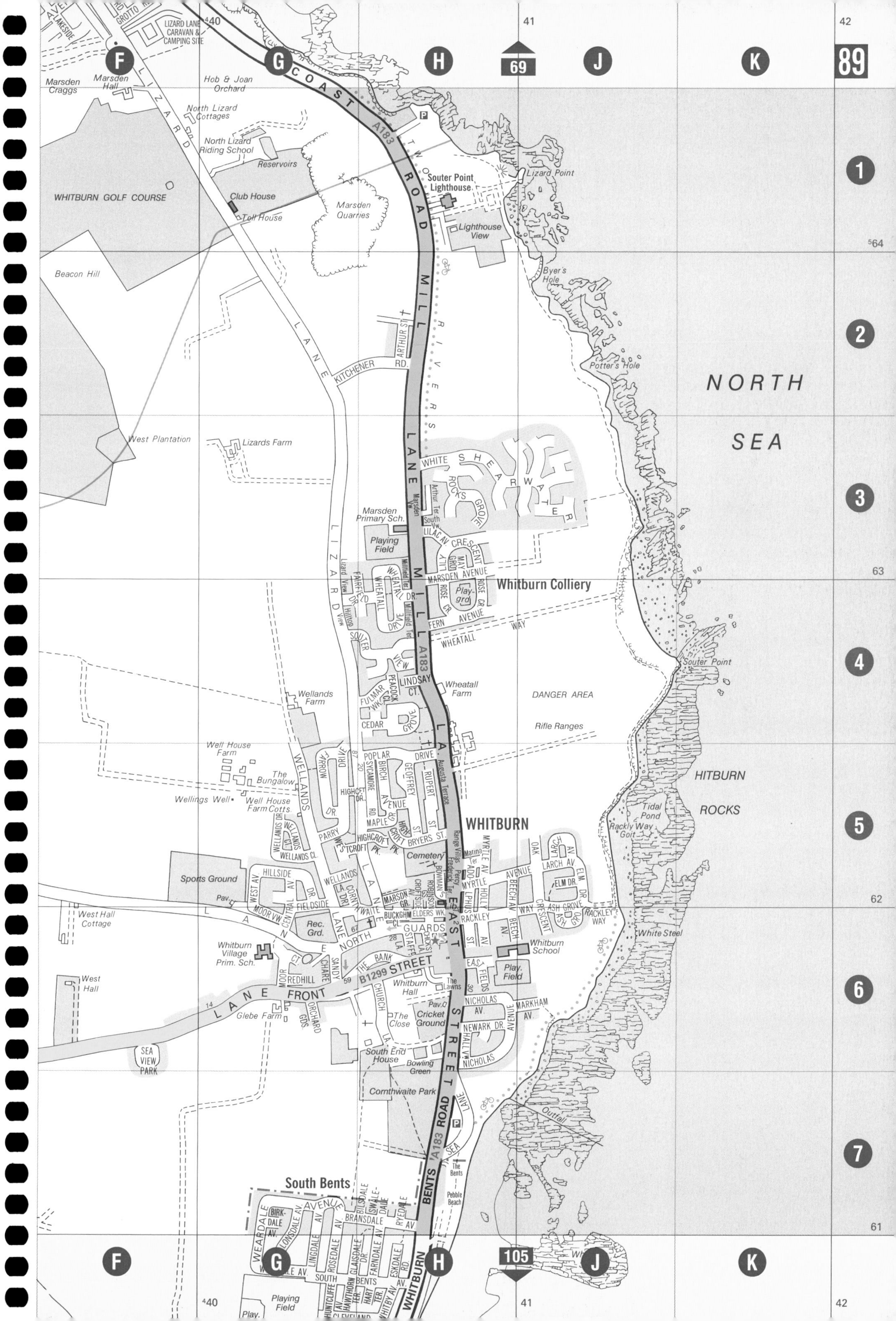

NORTH SEA
WHITBURN
Whitburn Colliery
South Bents
WHITBURN GOLF COURSE
Marsden Craggs
Marsden Hall
Hob & Joan Orchard
North Lizard Cottages
North Lizard Riding School
Reservoirs
Club House
Toll House
Marsden Quarries
Souter Point Lighthouse
Lighthouse View
Lizard Point
Byer's Hole
Potter's Hole
Beacon Hill
West Plantation
Lizards Farm
LIZARD LANE CARAVAN & CAMPING SITE
COAST ROAD
MILL LANE
A183
TWO RIVERS
KITCHENER RD.
WHITE ROCKS GROVE
SHEARWATER
Marsden Primary Sch.
Playing Field
MARSDEN AVENUE
FERN AVENUE
WHEATALL WAY
WHEATALL DR.
SOUTER VIEW
LINDSAY CT.
Wheatall Farm
DANGER AREA
Rifle Ranges
Souter Point
Wellands Farm
Well House Farm
The Bungalow
Wellings Well
Well House Farm Cotts.
WELLANDS LANE
POPLAR DRIVE
Augusta Terrace
HITBURN ROCKS
Tidal Pond
Rackly Way Goit
White Steel
Sports Ground
West Hall Cottage
Cemetery
EAST STREET
Whitburn School
Play. Field
Whitburn Village Prim. Sch.
West Hall
Glebe Farm
SEA VIEW PARK
B1299 STREET
FRONT
NORTH GUARDS
Whitburn Hall
The Lawns
Cricket Ground
The Close
South End House
Bowling Green
Cornthwaite Park
NICHOLAS AV.
NEWARK DR
MARKHAM AV.
SEA LANE
Outfall
The Bents
Pebble Beach
BENTS ROAD
WHITBURN
WEARDALE AV.
BIRKDALE AV.
LONSDALE AV.
AVENUE
BRANSDALE AV.
RYEDALE
SOUTH BENTS AV.
Playing Field
F G H J K
1 2 3 4 5 6 7
69
105
440 41 42
564 63 62 61

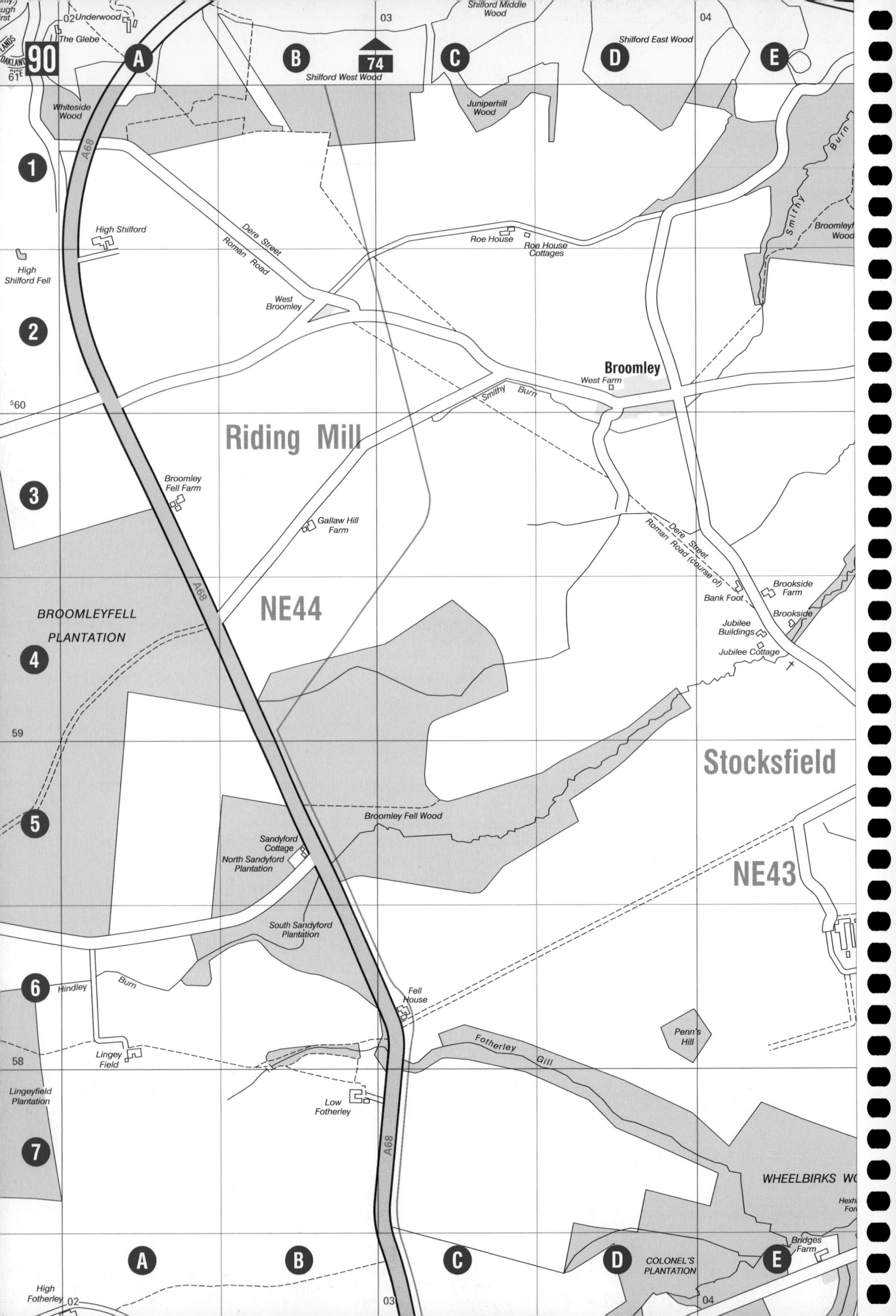

90

Underwood
The Glebe
Shilford Middle Wood
Shilford West Wood
Shilford East Wood
Juniperhill Wood
Broomley Wood
Smithy Burn

A B 74 C D E

Whiteside Wood

1

High Shilford
Dere Street
Roman Road
Roe House
Roe House Cottages

High Shilford Fell

2
West Broomley
Broomley
West Farm

⁵60

Riding Mill
Smithy Burn

3
Broomley Fell Farm
Gallaw Hill Farm
Dere Street
Roman Road (course of)
Brookside Farm
Bank Foot
Brookside

NE44
BROOMLEYFELL PLANTATION
Jubilee Buildings
Jubilee Cottage

4

59

Stocksfield

5
Sandyford Cottage
North Sandyford Plantation
Broomley Fell Wood

NE43

South Sandyford Plantation

6
Hindley
Burn
Fell House

58
Lingey Field
Penn's Hill

Lingeyfield Plantation
Fotherley Gill

Low Fotherley

7
WHEELBIRKS WO

A B C D COLONEL'S PLANTATION E
Bridges Farm

High Fotherley 02 03 04

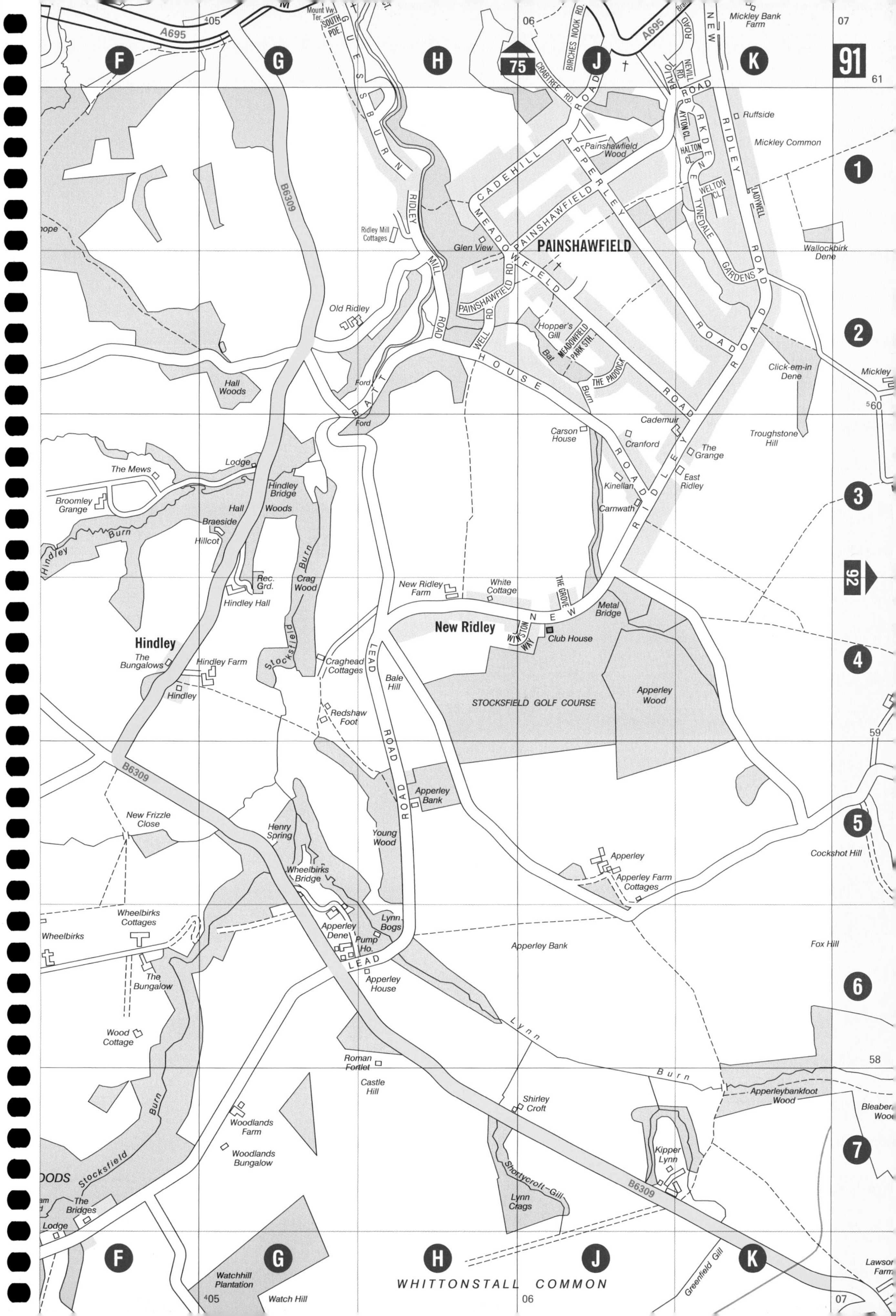

F   **G**   **H**   **75**   **J**   **K**   07

A695

Mount Vw. Ter.
SOUTH PDE

Mickley Bank Farm

61

Ruffside

Mickley Common

1

Wallockbirk Dene

GUESSBURN

RIDLEY MILL ROAD

Ridley Mill Cottages

CADEHILL ROAD

Painshawfield Wood

HALTON CL

RKDEN

AYTON CL

NEVILL RD.

BALLO... RD.

WELTON CL

TYNEDALE

RIDLEY ROAD

LADYWELL

Glen View

Old Ridley

MEADOWFIELD RD.

PAINSHAWFIELD RD.

PAINSHAWFIELD

Hall Woods

WELL RD.

MILL ROAD

BATT

Ford

Ford

Hopper's Gill

MEADOWFIELD PARK STH.

Bal.

THE PADDOCK

Carson House

Cademuir

GARDENS

Click-em-in Dene

Mickley

560

2

Cranford

The Grange

Troughstone Hill

Kinellan

East Ridley

Carnwath

HOUSE

The Mews

Lodge

Hindley Bridge

Woods

Broomley Grange

Hall

Braeside

Hindley Hall

Hillcot

Rec. Grd.

Crag Wood

ROADDLEY

New Ridley Farm

White Cottage

THE GROVE

Metal Bridge

3

92 ▶

59

Hindley

The Bungalows

Hindley

Hindley Farm

Craghead Cottages

Bale Hill

Redshaw Foot

New Ridley

WINTON WAY

Club House

Apperley Wood

4

B6309

New Frizzle Close

Henry Spring

Wheelbirks Bridge

Young Wood

LEAD ROAD

Apperley Bank

STOCKSFIELD GOLF COURSE

Cockshot Hill

5

Wheelbirks Cottages

Wheelbirks

The Bungalow

Apperley Dene

Pump Ho.

Lynn Bogs

Apperley House

Apperley Bank

Apperley

Apperley Farm Cottages

Fox Hill

6

Wood Cottage

LEAD ROAD

Roman Fortlet

Castle Hill

Lynn

Burn

58

Apperleybankfoot Wood

Woodlands Farm

Woodlands Bungalow

Shirley Croft

Shortycroft Gill

B6309

Kipper Lynn

Bleaber Wood

7

Stocksfield

WOODS

The Bridges

Lodge

Lynn Crags

Greenfield Gill

Lawson

F   **G**   **H**   **J**   **K**

Watchhill Plantation

405

Watch Hill

WHITTONSTALL COMMON

06

07

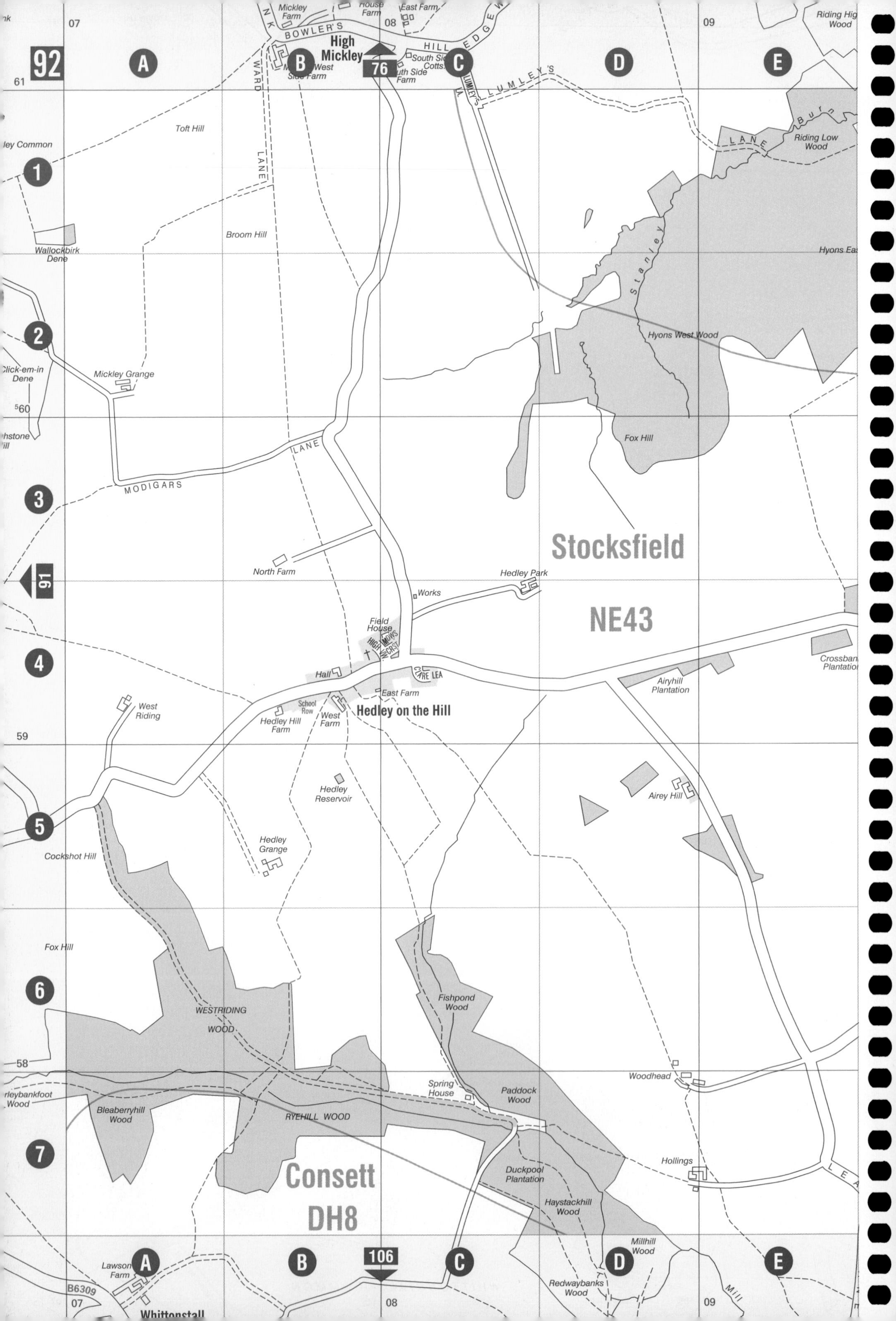
92
07
08
09
A
B
C
D
E
61
Mickley Farm
House Farm
East Farm
BOWLER'S
HILL
EDGE
High Mickley
76
South Side Cotts.
South Side Farm
West Side Farm
WARD LANE
LUMLEY'S
Riding High Wood
Toft Hill
Riding Low Wood
Burn
LANE
1
Broom Hill
Stanley
Wallockbirk Dene
Hyons East
2
Hyons West Wood
Click-em-in Dene
Mickley Grange
560
Fox Hill
LANE
MODIGARS
3
Stockstfield
North Farm
Hedley Park
91
Works
NE43
Field House
HIGH VW
MDWS
CRST
4
Hall
CLARE LEA
Crossbank Plantation
Airyhill Plantation
East Farm
West Riding
School Row
West Farm
Hedley on the Hill
Hedley Hill Farm
59
Hedley Reservoir
Airey Hill
5
Hedley Grange
Cockshot Hill
Fox Hill
6
Fishpond Wood
WESTRIDING WOOD
58
Woodhead
Paddock Wood
Spring House
Bleaberryhill Wood
RYEHILL WOOD
7
Hollings
Consett DH8
Duckpool Plantation
Haystackhill Wood
Millhill Wood
106
Lawson Farm
B6309
Redwaybanks Wood
Mill
Whittonstall

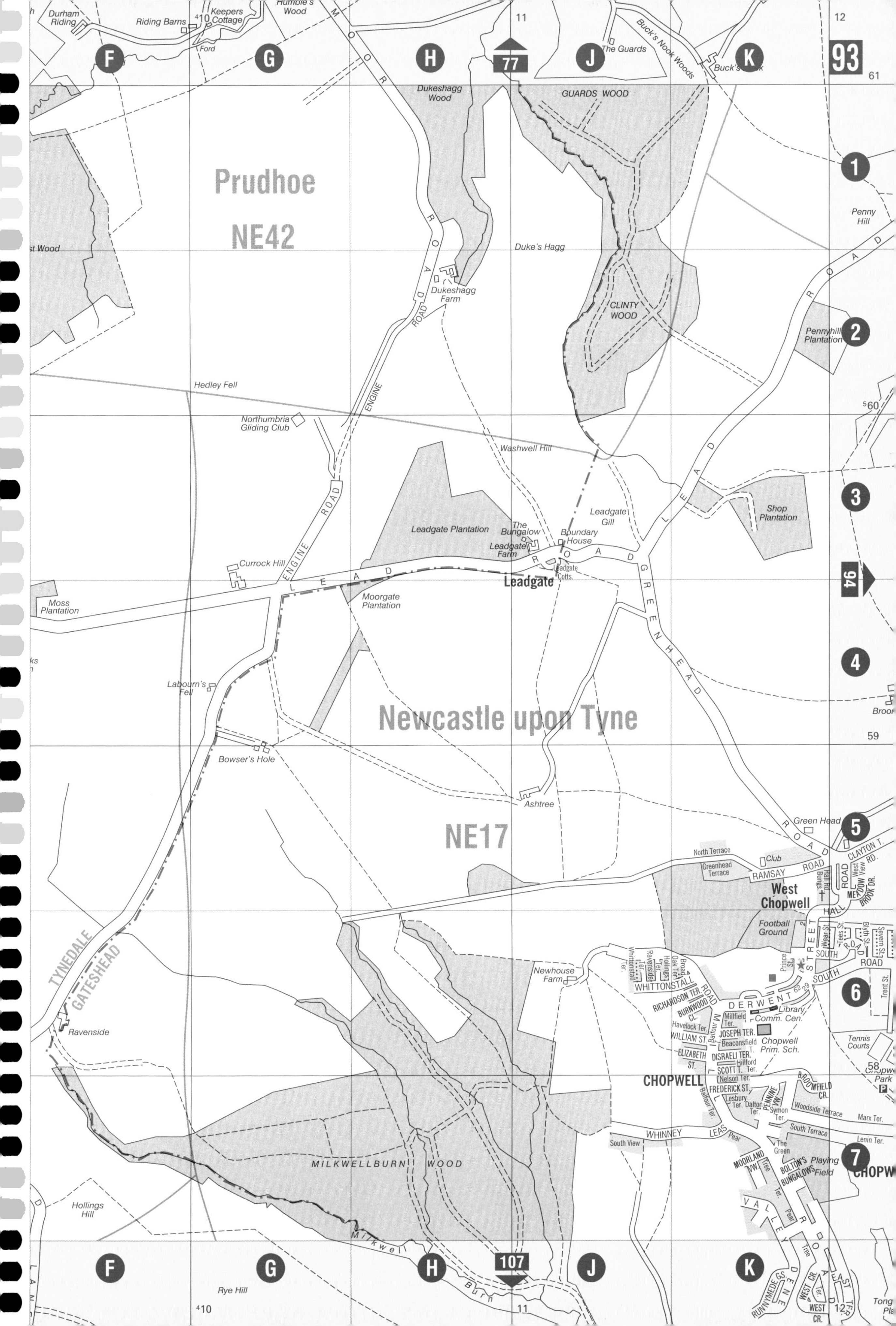

Durham Riding
Riding Barns
Keepers Cottage
Ford
Humble's Wood
The Guards
Buck's Nook Woods
77
GUARDS WOOD
Dukeshagg Wood
Prudhoe
NE42
Penny Hill
Duke's Hagg
Dukeshagg Farm
CLINTY WOOD
Pennyhill Plantation
Hedley Fell
Northumbria Gliding Club
ENGINE ROAD
Washwell Hill
Shop Plantation
Leadgate Gill
Leadgate Plantation
The Bungalow
Boundary House
Leadgate Farm
Curlock Hill
LEAD ROAD
Leadgate Cotts.
Leadgate
94
Moss Plantation
Moorgate Plantation
GREENHEAD ROAD
Labourn's Fell
Newcastle upon Tyne
Bowser's Hole
Ashtree
Green Head
NE17
North Terrace
Greenhead Terrace
Club
RAMSAY ROAD
West Chopwell
Football Ground
HALL ROAD
SOUTH ROAD
TYNEDALE
GATESHEAD
Newhouse Farm
WHITTONSTALL ROAD
DERWENT ST.
Library Comm. Cen.
RICHARDSON TER.
BURNWOOD CL.
JOSEPH TER.
WILLIAM ST.
Chopwell Prim. Sch.
Tennis Courts
ELIZABETH ST.
DISRAELI TER.
SCOTT T.
Ravenside
CHOPWELL
Nelson Ter.
FREDERICK ST.
Chopwell Park
Woodside Terrace
Marx Ter.
South Terrace
Lenin Ter.
WHINNEY LEAS
South View
The Green
MILKWELLBURN WOOD
MOORLAND VW.
BOLTON'S BUNGALOWS
Playing Field
CHOPW
Hollings Hill
VALLEY DENE
Milkwell Burn
107
Rye Hill
RUNNYMEDE GS.
WEST CR.
EAST TER.
F
G
H
J
K
1
2
3
4
5
6
7
11
12
410
560
59
58
61

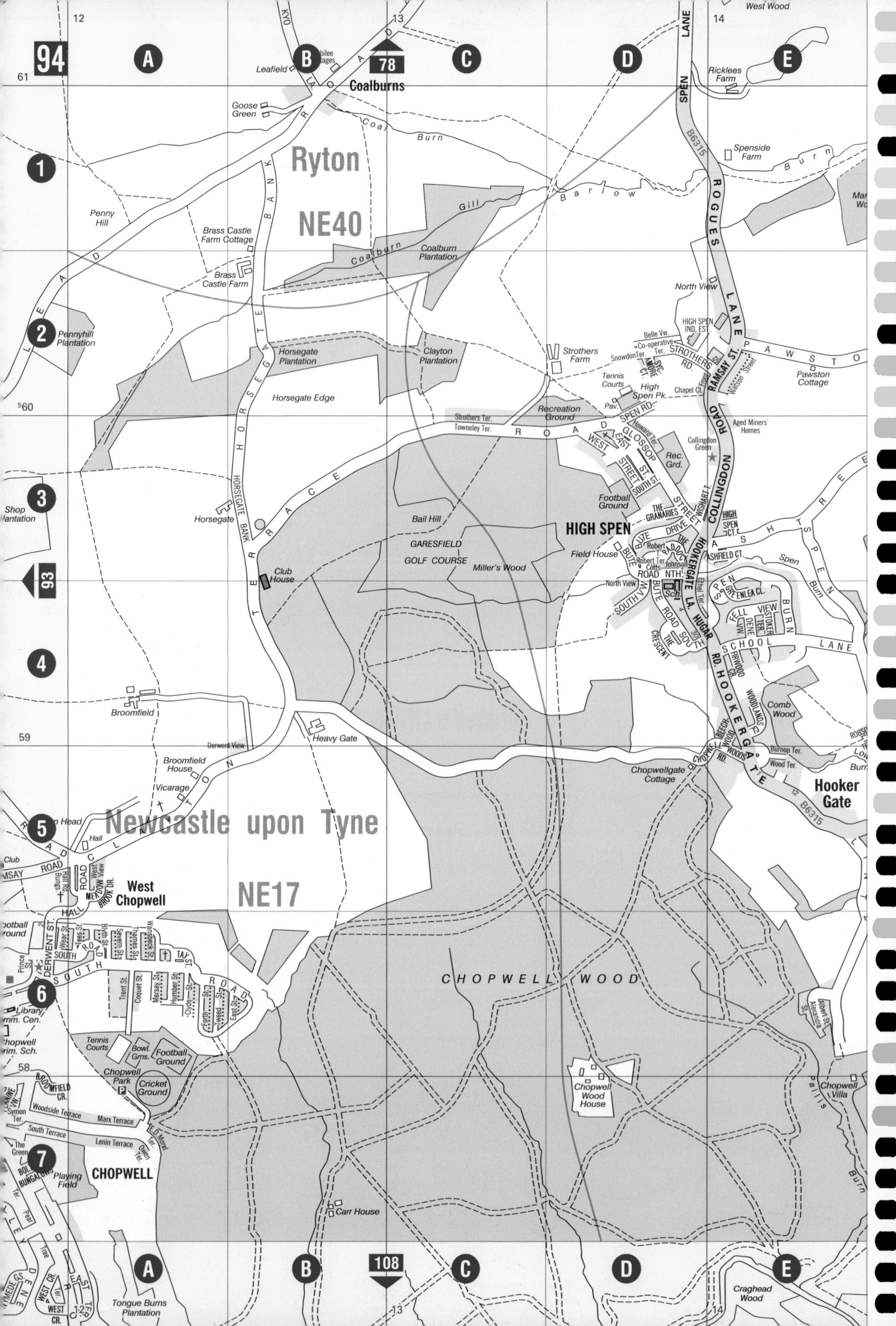

Ryton
NE40
Coalburns
Leafield
Goose Green
Coal Burn
Penny Hill
Brass Castle Farm Cottage
Brass Castle Farm
Barlow Gill
Coalburn Plantation
Pennyhill Plantation
Horsegate Plantation
Clayton Plantation
Horsegate Edge
Strothers Farm
Recreation Ground
Ricklees Farm
Spenside Farm
West Wood
North View
HIGH SPEN IND. EST.
Pawston Cottage
Aged Miners' Homes
Collingdon Green
Rec. Grd.
Football Ground
HIGH SPEN
Field House
Horsegate
Bail Hill
GARESFIELD GOLF COURSE
Miller's Wood
Club House
Shop Plantation
Broomfield
Heavy Gate
Broomfield House
Vicarage
Chopwellgate Cottage
Hooker Gate
Comb Wood
Newcastle upon Tyne
NE17
West Chopwell
CHOPWELL WOOD
Chopwell Wood House
Chopwell Villa
Tennis Courts
Bowl. Grns.
Football Ground
Chopwell Park
Cricket Ground
Library
Comm. Cen.
Chopwell Prim. Sch.
CHOPWELL
Playing Field
Carr House
Tongue Burns Plantation
Craghead Wood
B6315
HORSEGATE BANK
TERRACE ROAD
ROGUES LANE
COLLINGDON ROAD
HOOKERGATE LANE
HOOKERGATE RD.
SPEN LANE
SCHOOL LANE
PAWSTON

78
93
108

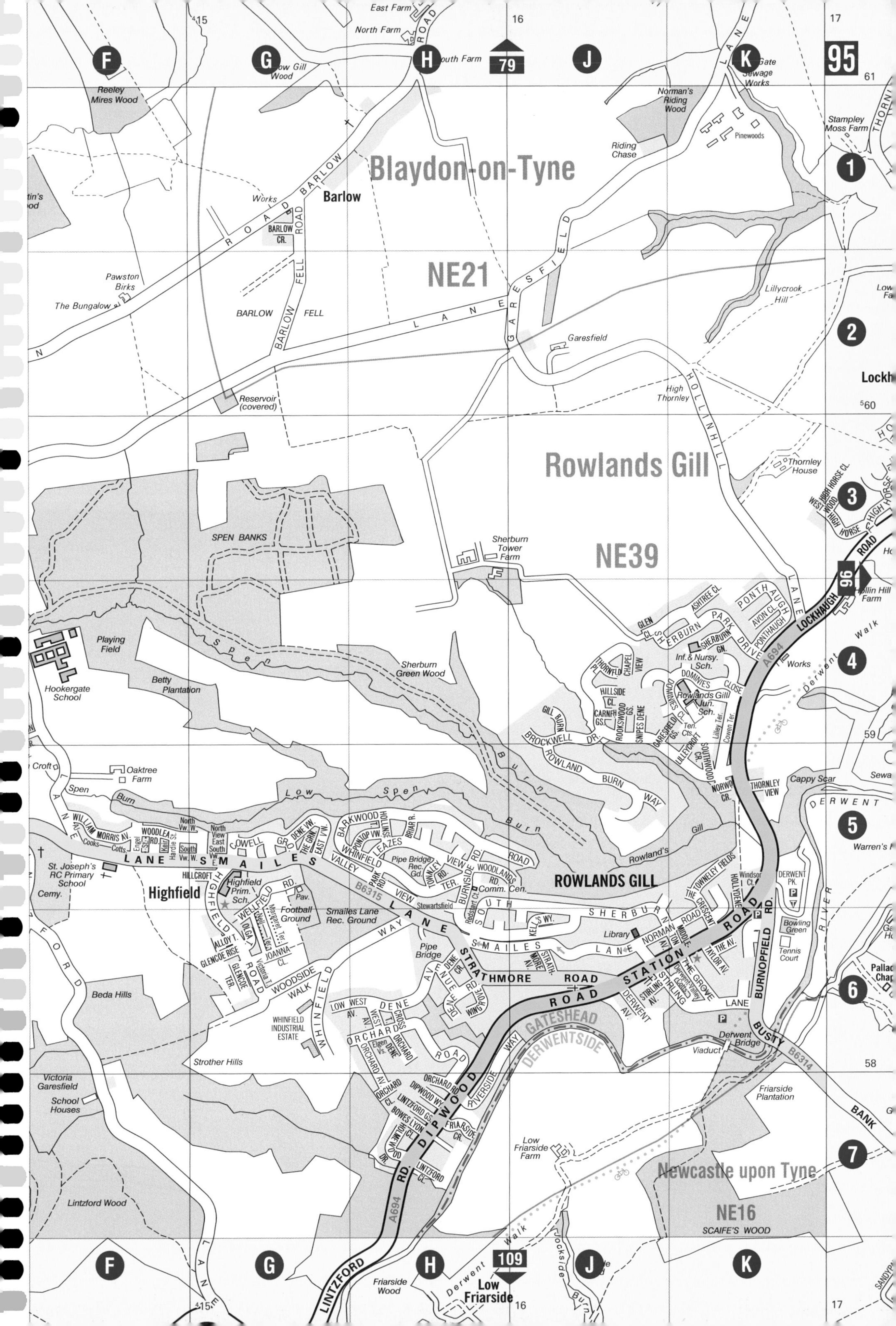
Blaydon-on-Tyne
Barlow
NE21
Rowlands Gill
NE39
ROWLANDS GILL
Highfield
Newcastle upon Tyne
NE16
79
109
96
Reeley Mires Wood
Low Gill Wood
East Farm
North Farm
South Farm
Gate Sewage Works
Norman's Riding Wood
Riding Chase
Pinewoods
Stampley Moss Farm
Works
BARLOW CR.
Pawston Birks
The Bungalow
BARLOW FELL
Garesfield
Lillycrook Hill
High Thornley
Reservoir (covered)
Thornley House
SPEN BANKS
Sherburn Tower Farm
Hollin Hill Farm
Playing Field
Hookergate School
Betty Plantation
Sherburn Green Wood
Inf. & Nursy. Sch.
Rowlands Gill Jun. Sch.
Works
Oaktree Farm
Croft
Cappy Scar
Warren's Hill
St. Joseph's RC Primary School
Cemy.
Highfield Prim. Sch.
Pav.
Football Ground
Smailes Lane Rec. Ground
Pipe Bridge Rec. Gd.
Comm. Cen.
Library
Stewartsfield
Pipe Bridge
Bowling Green
Tennis Court
Beda Hills
WHINFIELD INDUSTRIAL ESTATE
Strother Hills
Victoria Garesfield
School Houses
Derwent Bridge
Viaduct
Friarside Plantation
Low Friarside Farm
Lintzford Wood
SCAIFE'S WOOD
Friarside Wood
Low Friarside
Derwent Walk
SMAILES LANE
STATION ROAD
STRATHMORE ROAD
LINTZFORD RD.
DIPWOOD RD.
LOCKHAUGH ROAD
BUSTY BANK
GATESHEAD DERWENTSIDE
A694
B6315
B6314

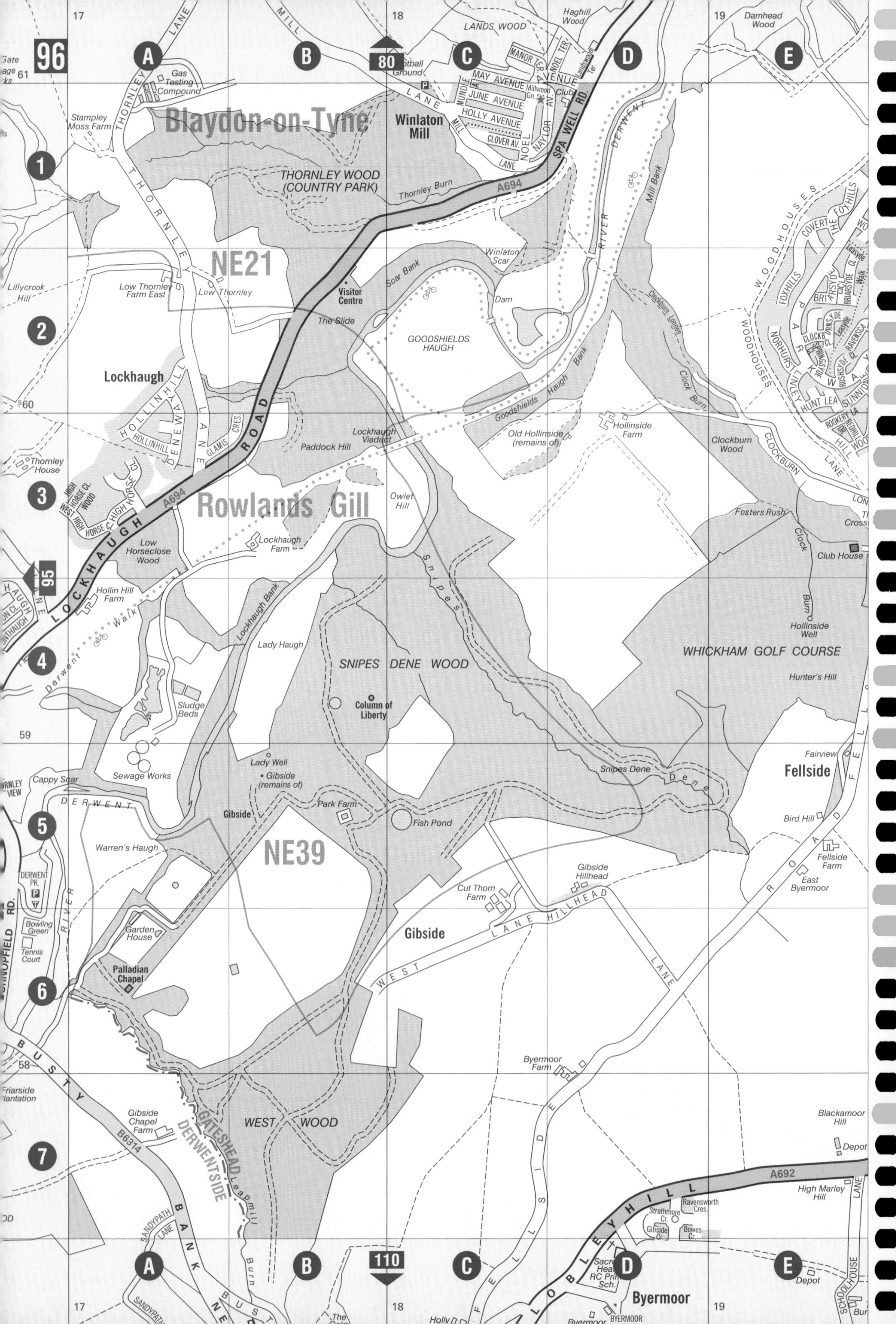
Blaydon-on-Tyne
Winlaton Mill
THORNLEY WOOD (COUNTRY PARK)
NE21
Lockhaugh
Rowlands Gill
GOODSHIELDS HAUGH
Visitor Centre
Lockhaugh Viaduct
Paddock Hill
Owlet Hill
Lockhaugh Farm
Low Horseclose Wood
Hollin Hill Farm
Low Thornley Farm East
Low Thornley
Stampley Moss Farm
Gas Testing Compound
LANDS WOOD
Haghill Wood
Damhead Wood
Winlaton Scar
Scar Bank
The Slide
Dam
Old Hollinside (remains of)
Hollinside Farm
Clockburn Wood
Fosters Rush
Club House
Hollinside Well
WHICKHAM GOLF COURSE
Hunter's Hill
Fairview
Fellside
Bird Hill
Fellside Farm
East Byermoor
SNIPES DENE WOOD
Column of Liberty
Lady Haugh
Lady Well
Gibside (remains of)
Gibside
Park Farm
Fish Pond
Snipes Dene
NE39
Sludge Beds
Sewage Works
Cappy Scar
Warren's Haugh
Garden House
Palladian Chapel
Cut Thorn Farm
Gibside Hillhead
Gibside
Byermoor Farm
WEST WOOD
Gibside Chapel Farm
GATESHEAD
DERWENTSIDE
Blackamoor Hill
Depot
High Marley Hill
A692
LOBLEY HILL
Byermoor
A694
LOCKHAUGH ROAD
SPA WELL RD.
THORNLEY LANE
HILLHEAD LANE
WEST LANE
FELLSIDE ROAD
BUSTY BANK
B6314
Lillycrook Hill
Thornley House
Friarside Plantation

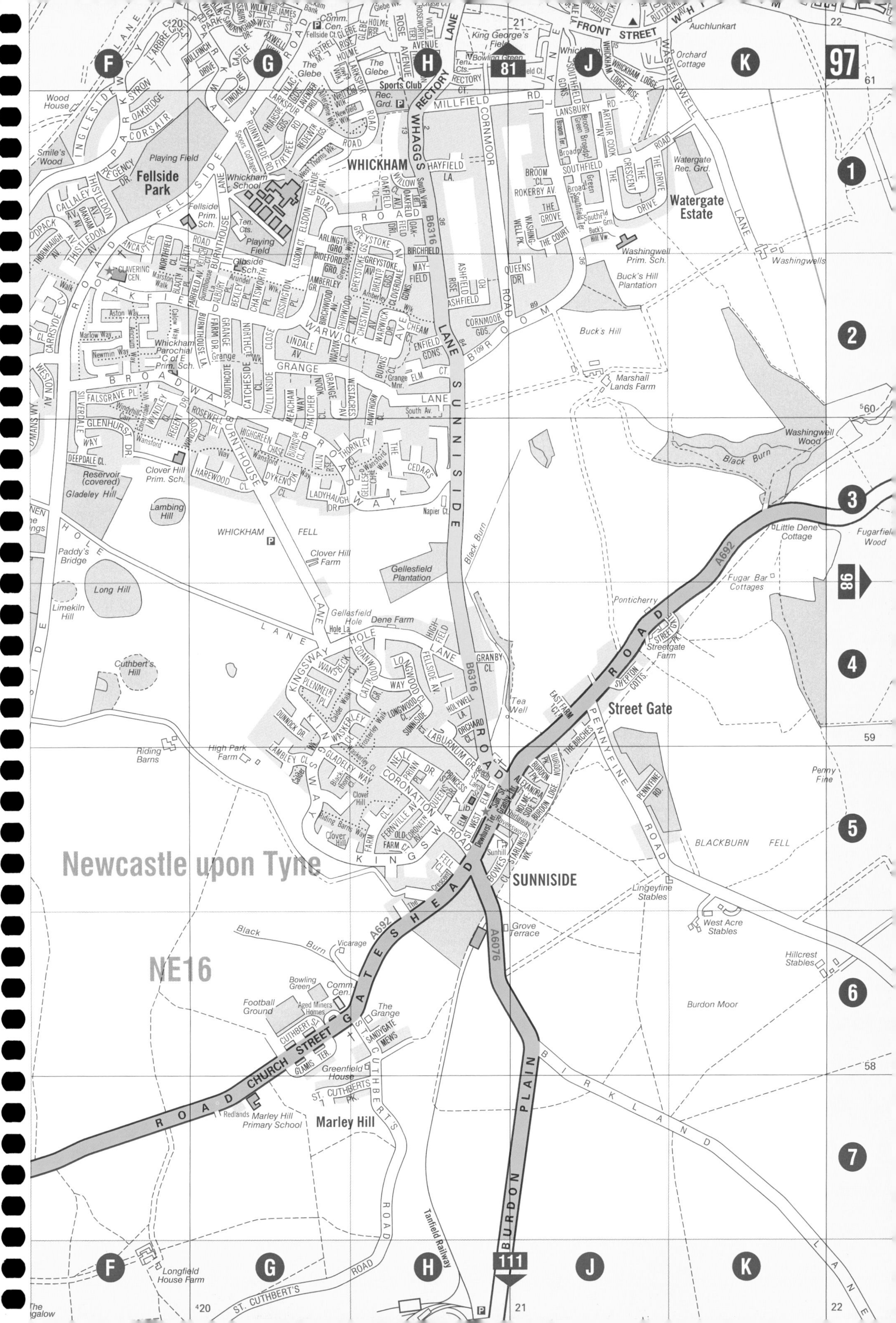
97
F
G
H
J
K
1
2
3
4
5
6
7
81
86
111
20
21
22
61
560
59
58
WHICKHAM
Fellside Park
Playing Field
Whickham School
Fellside Prim. Sch.
Watergate Estate
Watergate Rec. Grd.
Sports Club
Rec. Grd.
The Glebe
King George's Field
Bowling Green
FRONT STREET
Auchlunkart
Orchard Cottage
Wood House
Smile's Wood
Washingwell Prim. Sch.
Buck's Hill Plantation
Buck's Hill
Washingwells
Marshall Lands Farm
Washingwell Wood
Black Burn
Whickham Parochial C of E Prim. Sch.
Clover Hill Prim. Sch.
Reservoir (covered)
Gladeley Hill
Lambing Hill
WHICKHAM FELL
Clover Hill Farm
Gellesfield Plantation
Paddy's Bridge
Long Hill
Limekiln Hill
Cuthbert's Hill
Gellesfield Hole
Dene Farm
Tea Well
Street Gate
Streetgate Farm
Fugar Bar Cottages
Little Dene Cottage
Fugarfield Wood
Ponticherry
Riding Barns
High Park Farm
Penny Fine
BLACKBURN FELL
SUNNISIDE
Newcastle upon Tyne
NE16
Lingeyfine Stables
West Acre Stables
Hillcrest Stables
Burdon Moor
Grove Terrace
Vicarage
Bowling Green
Comm. Cen.
Football Ground
Aged Miners Homes
The Grange
Greenfield House
Marley Hill Primary School
Marley Hill
Redlands
Longfield House Farm
Tanfield Railway
FELLSIDE ROAD
BROADWAY
SUNNISIDE LANE
SUNNISIDE ROAD
WHAGGS LANE
RECTORY LANE
MILLFIELD RD
CORNMOOR ROAD
BROOM LANE
WASHINGWELL LANE
HOLE LANE
KINGSWAY
GATESHEAD ROAD
CHURCH STREET
ROAD
BURDON PLAIN
BIRKLAND LANE
PENNYFINE ROAD
ST. CUTHBERT'S ROAD
A692
A6076
B6316

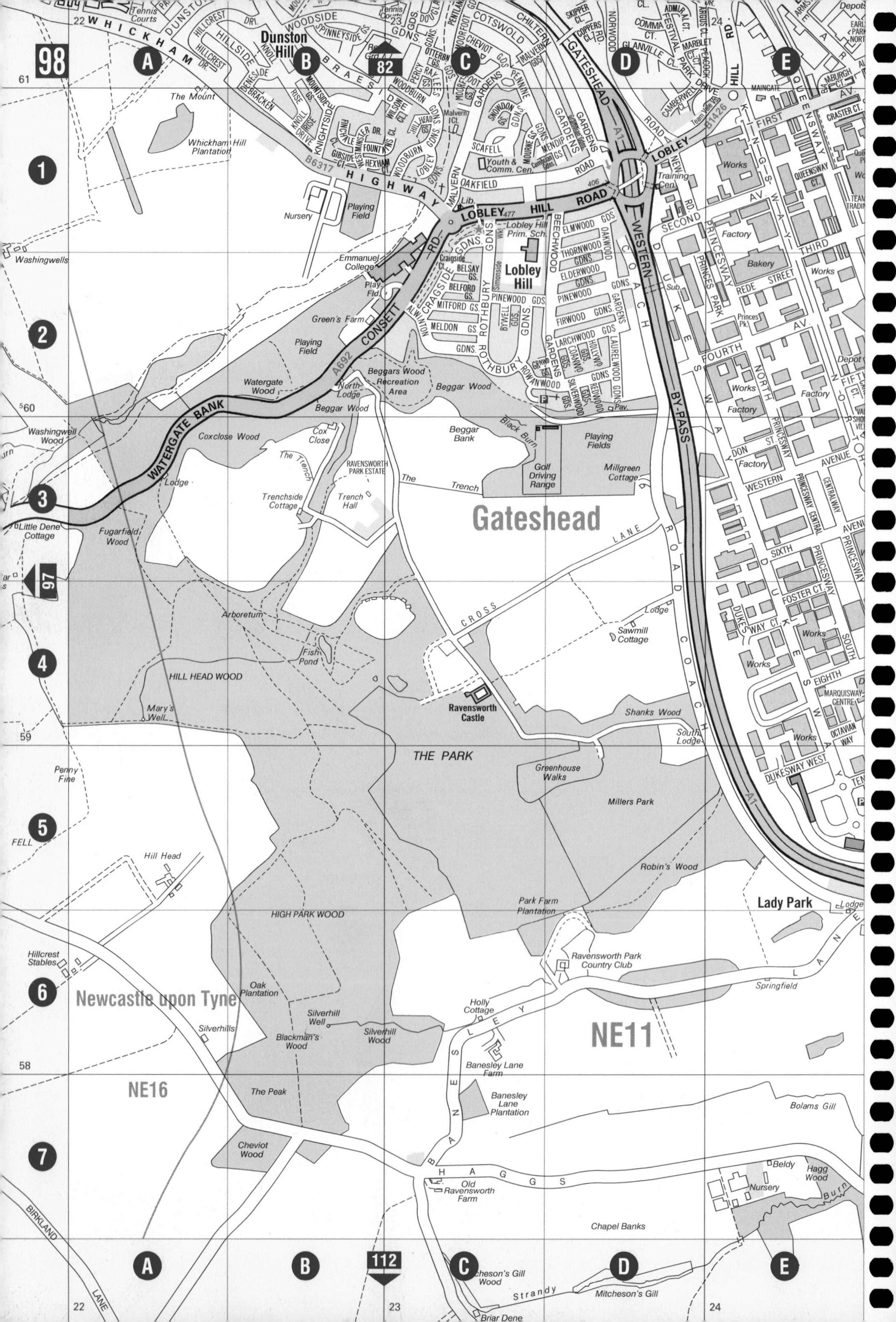
Dunston Hill
Lobley Hill
Gateshead
Whickham Hill Plantation
The Mount
Washingwells
Washingwell Wood
Coxclose Wood
Watergate Wood
Fugarfield Wood
Little Dene Cottage
Green's Farm
Playing Field
Emmanuel College
Beggars Wood Recreation Area
Beggar Wood
Beggar Bank
Golf Driving Range
Playing Fields
Millgreen Cottage
Ravensworth Park Estate
Trench Hall
Trenchside Cottage
Cox Close
The Trench
Arboretum
Fish Pond
HILL HEAD WOOD
Mary's Well
Ravensworth Castle
THE PARK
Greenhouse Walks
Millers Park
Shanks Wood
South Lodge
Sawmill Cottage
Robin's Wood
Lady Park
Park Farm Plantation
Ravensworth Park Country Club
Springfield
HIGH PARK WOOD
Hill Head
Penny Fine
Hillcrest Stables
Oak Plantation
Newcastle upon Tyne
Silverhill Well
Silverhills
Blackman's Wood
Silverhill Wood
Holly Cottage
NE11
NE16
Banesley Lane Farm
Banesley Lane Plantation
The Peak
Cheviot Wood
Bolams Gill
Old Ravensworth Farm
Beldy
Hagg Wood
Nursery
Chapel Banks
Mitcheson's Gill Wood
Mitcheson's Gill
Strandy
Briar Dene
Birkland Lane
Whickham Highway
Lobley Hill Road
Consett Rd.
Watergate Bank
Western By-Pass
Coach Road
Cross Lane
Banesley Lane
Haggs Lane
Dukesway
Princesway
Kingsway
Team Valley
A1
A692
B6317
B1426
82
97
112
A B C D E
1 2 3 4 5 6 7
22 23 24
61 560 59 58

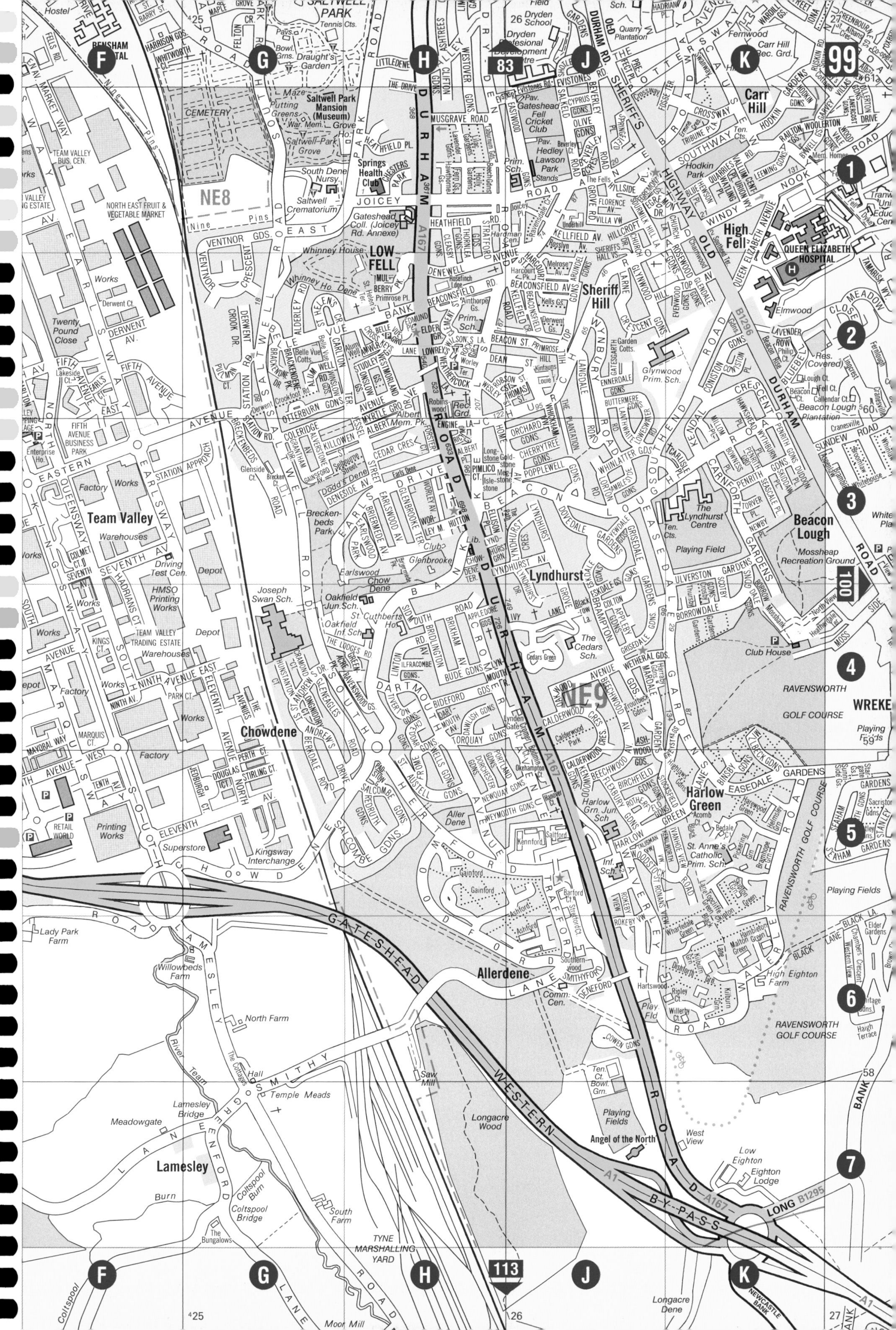

99
83
100
113
NE8
NE9
Saltwell Park Mansion (Museum)
Low Fell
Team Valley
Chowdene
Lyndhurst
Sheriff Hill
Carr Hill
High Fell
Queen Elizabeth Hospital
Beacon Lough
Harlow Green
Allerdene
Lamesley
Angel of the North
Ravensworth Golf Course
Team Valley Trading Estate
North East Fruit & Vegetable Market
Gateshead Western By-Pass
Durham Road
Tyne Marshalling Yard
Longacre Wood

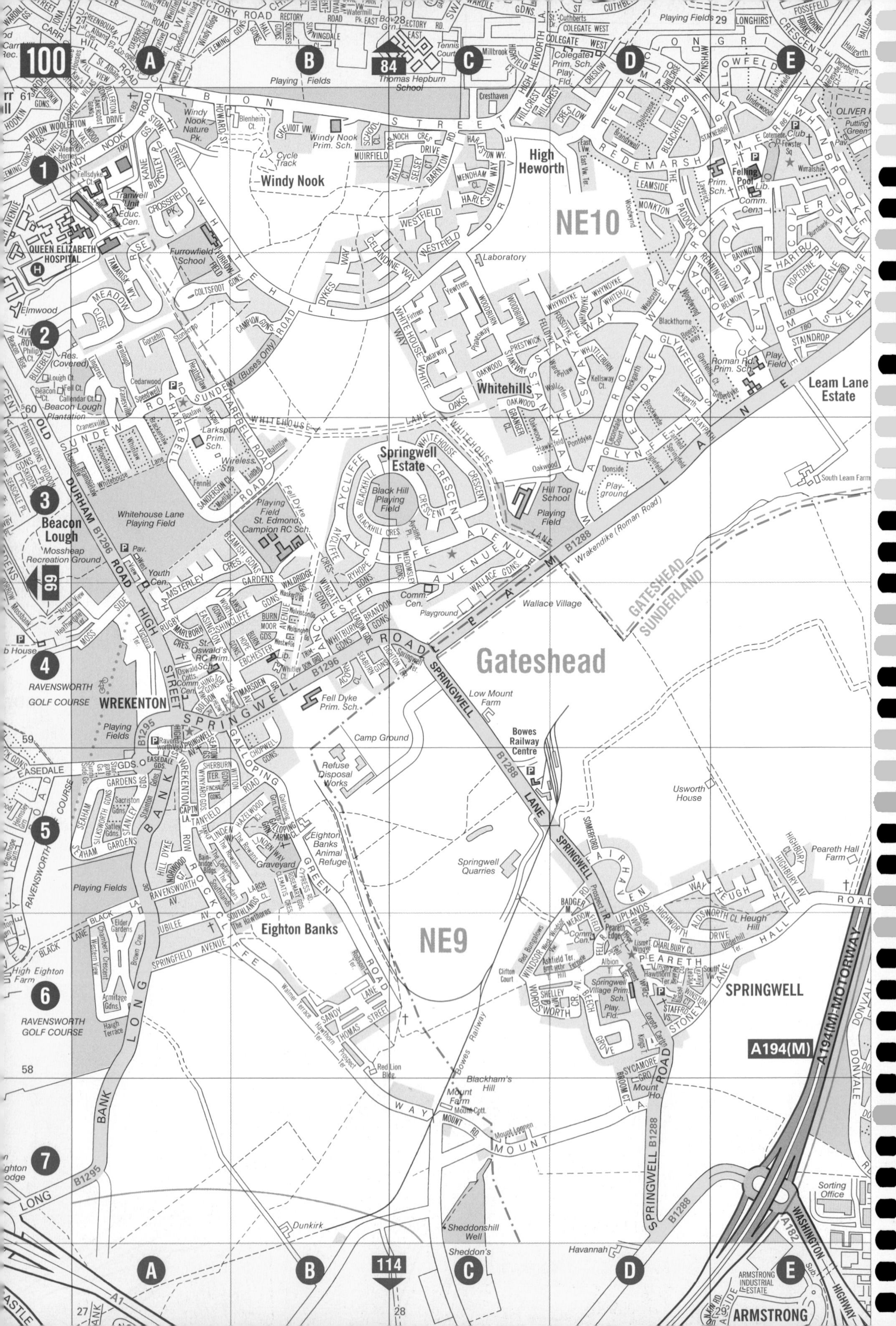
Windy Nook
High Heworth
NE10
Whitehills
Springwell Estate
Leam Lane Estate
Beacon Lough
Wrekenton
Gateshead
Eighton Banks
NE9
SPRINGWELL
ARMSTRONG
A194(M)
84
99
114

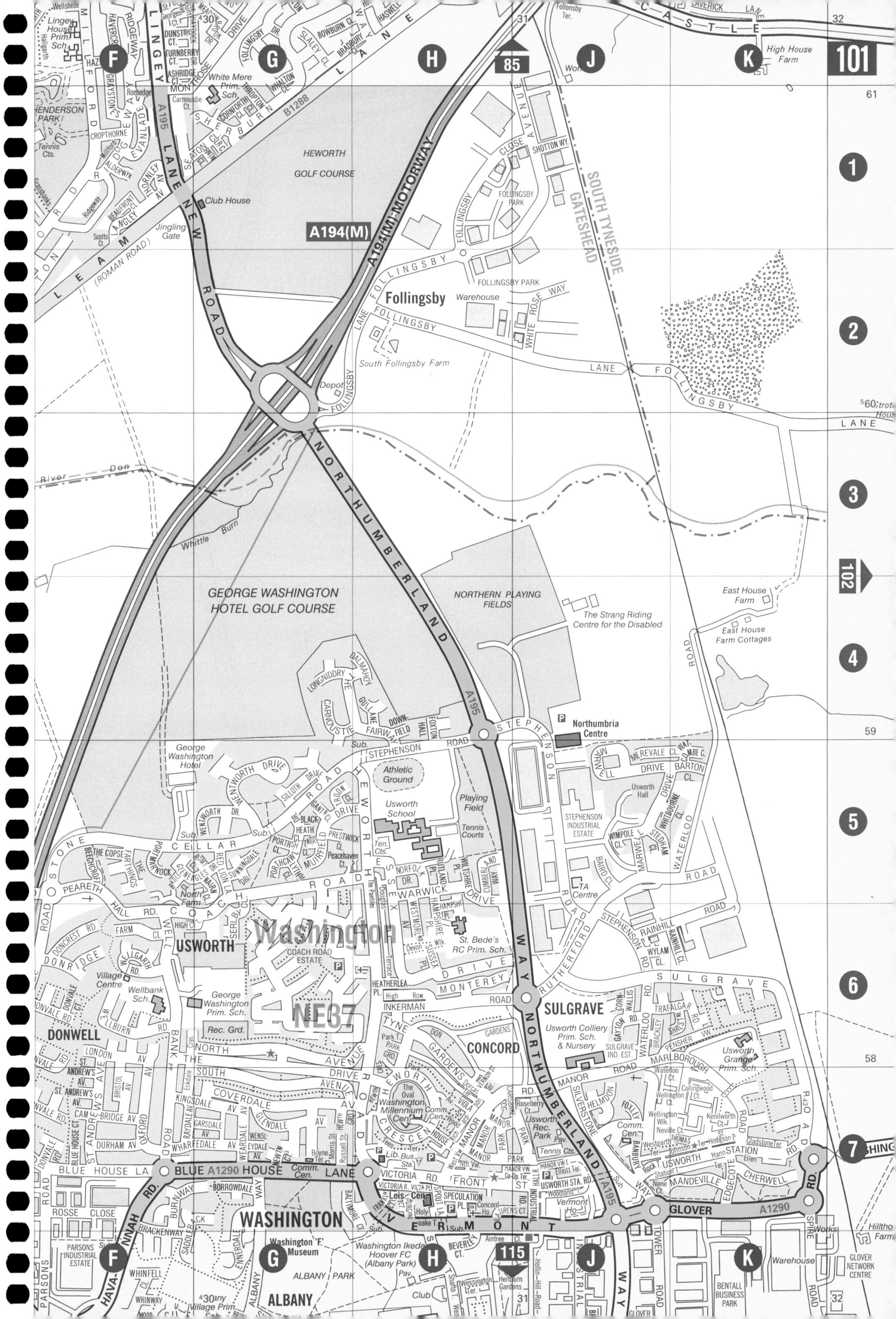
F
G
H
J
K
85
31
32
61
60
59
58
1
2
3
4
5
6
7
102
115
High House Farm
CASTLE
LAVERICK LANE
Follonsby Ter.
Lingey House Prim. Sch.
HENDERSON PARK
Tennis Cts.
CROPTHORNE
LINGEY LANE
NEW ROAD
A195
White Mere Prim. Sch.
SHERBURN
B1288
HEWORTH GOLF COURSE
Club House
Jingling Gate
LEAM
(ROMAN ROAD)
A194(M)
A194(M) MOTORWAY
FOLLINGSBY PARK
SHOTTON WY.
SOUTH TYNESIDE
GATESHEAD
FOLLINGSBY PARK
Follingsby
Warehouse
WHITE ROSE WAY
FOLLINGSBY LANE
South Follingsby Farm
Depot
LANE
River Don
Whittle Burn
NORTHUMBERLAND ROAD
GEORGE WASHINGTON HOTEL GOLF COURSE
NORTHERN PLAYING FIELDS
The Strang Riding Centre for the Disabled
East House Farm
East House Farm Cottages
Northumbria Centre
STEPHENSON ROAD
George Washington Hotel
WENTWORTH DRIVE
Athletic Ground
Usworth School
Playing Field
Tennis Courts
Usworth Hall
STEPHENSON INDUSTRIAL ESTATE
CELLAR
THE COPSE
PEARETH HALL RD.
COACH ROAD
North Farm
TA Centre
WARWICK
St. Bede's RC Prim. Sch.
Washington
USWORTH
COACH ROAD ESTATE
DONRIDGE
Village Centre
Wellbank Sch.
George Washington Prim. Sch.
Rec. Grd.
NE37
MONTEREY
INKERMAN
SULGRAVE
Usworth Colliery Prim. Sch. & Nursery
SULGRAVE IND. EST.
CONCORD
DONWELL
NORTH AVENUE
SOUTH DRIVE
COVERDALE AV
MARLBOROUGH
Usworth Grange Prim. Sch.
The Oval
Washington Millennium Cen.
HEWORTH CRESCENT
Usworth Rec. Park
Tennis Cts.
MANOR
BLUE HOUSE LA
BLUE A1290 HOUSE LANE
Comm. Cen.
VICTORIA RD.
FRONT ST.
Leis. Cen.
SPECULATION PL
USWORTH STATION RD.
GLOVER
A1290
WASHINGTON
VERMONT
PARSONS INDUSTRIAL ESTATE
Washington 'F' Museum
Washington Ikeda Hoover FC (Albany Park)
ALBANY PARK
ALBANY
WHINFELL
TOWER ROAD
Warehouse
BENTALL BUSINESS PARK
GLOVER NETWORK CENTRE
Hilltho Farm
Hertburn Gardens
Albany Village Prim.

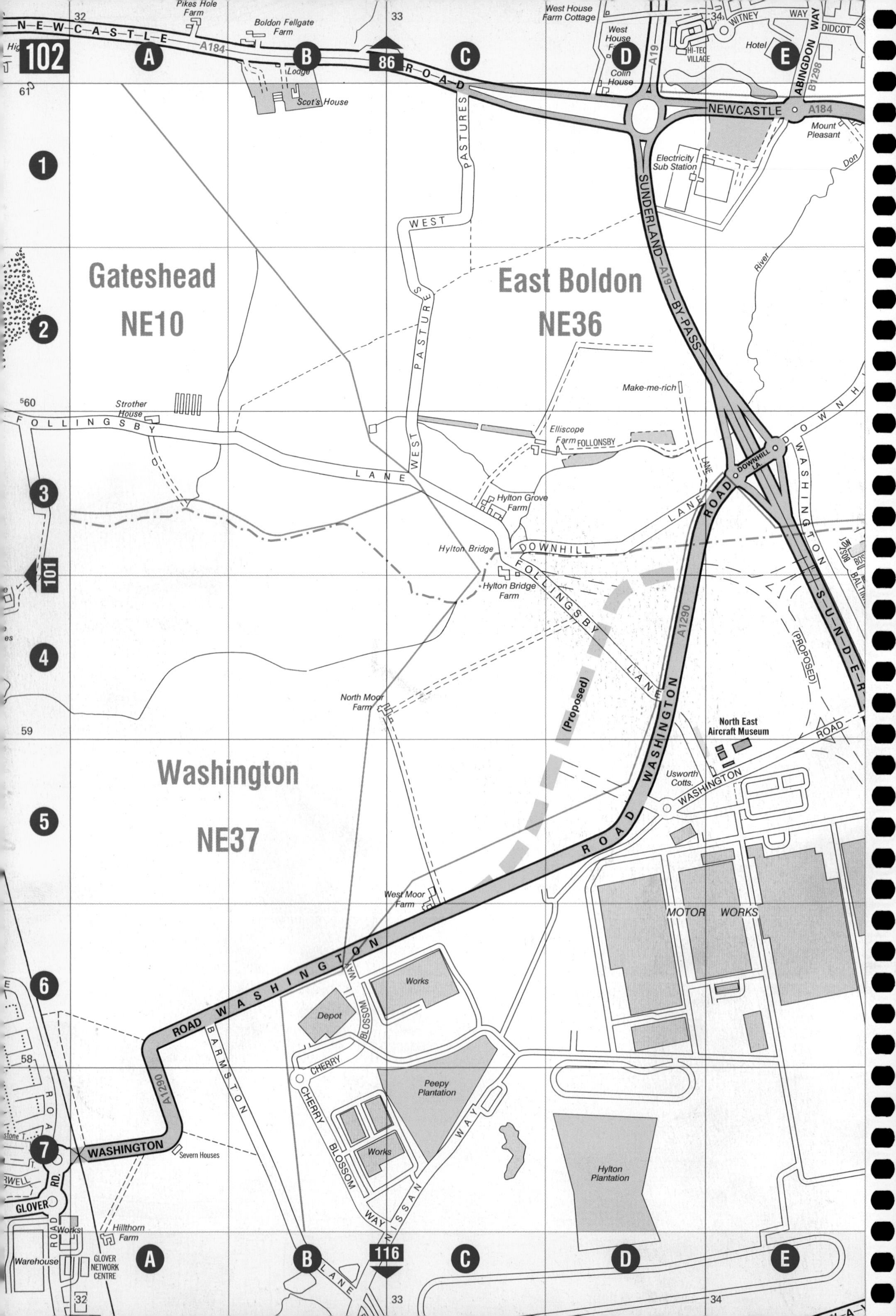

NEWCASTLE ROAD
A184
Pikes Hole Farm
Boldon Fellgate Farm
Lodge
Scot's House
West House Farm Cottage
West House Farm
Colin House
A19
WITNEY WAY
DIDCOT
ABINGDON WAY
B1298
HI-TEC VILLAGE
Hotel
NEWCASTLE
A184
Mount Pleasant
Electricity Sub Station
River Don
WEST PASTURES
SUNDERLAND A19 BY-PASS
Gateshead
NE10
East Boldon
NE36
Make-me-rich
Strother House
FOLLINGSBY LANE
Elliscope Farm
FOLLONSBY LANE
DOWNHILL LA.
WASHINGTON ROAD
Hylton Grove Farm
Hylton Bridge
DOWNHILL LANE
Hylton Bridge Farm
FOLLINGSBY LANE
A1290
(PROPOSED)
(Proposed)
North Moor Farm
North East Aircraft Museum
Washington
NE37
Usworth Cotts.
WASHINGTON ROAD
West Moor Farm
MOTOR WORKS
WASHINGTON ROAD
A1290
Works
Depot
BLOSSOM WAY
BARMSTON LANE
CHERRY BLOSSOM WAY
Peepy Plantation
Works
NISSAN WAY
Hylton Plantation
WASHINGTON
Severn Houses
GLOVER ROAD
Hillthorn Farm
Works
Warehouse
GLOVER NETWORK CENTRE

86
101
116

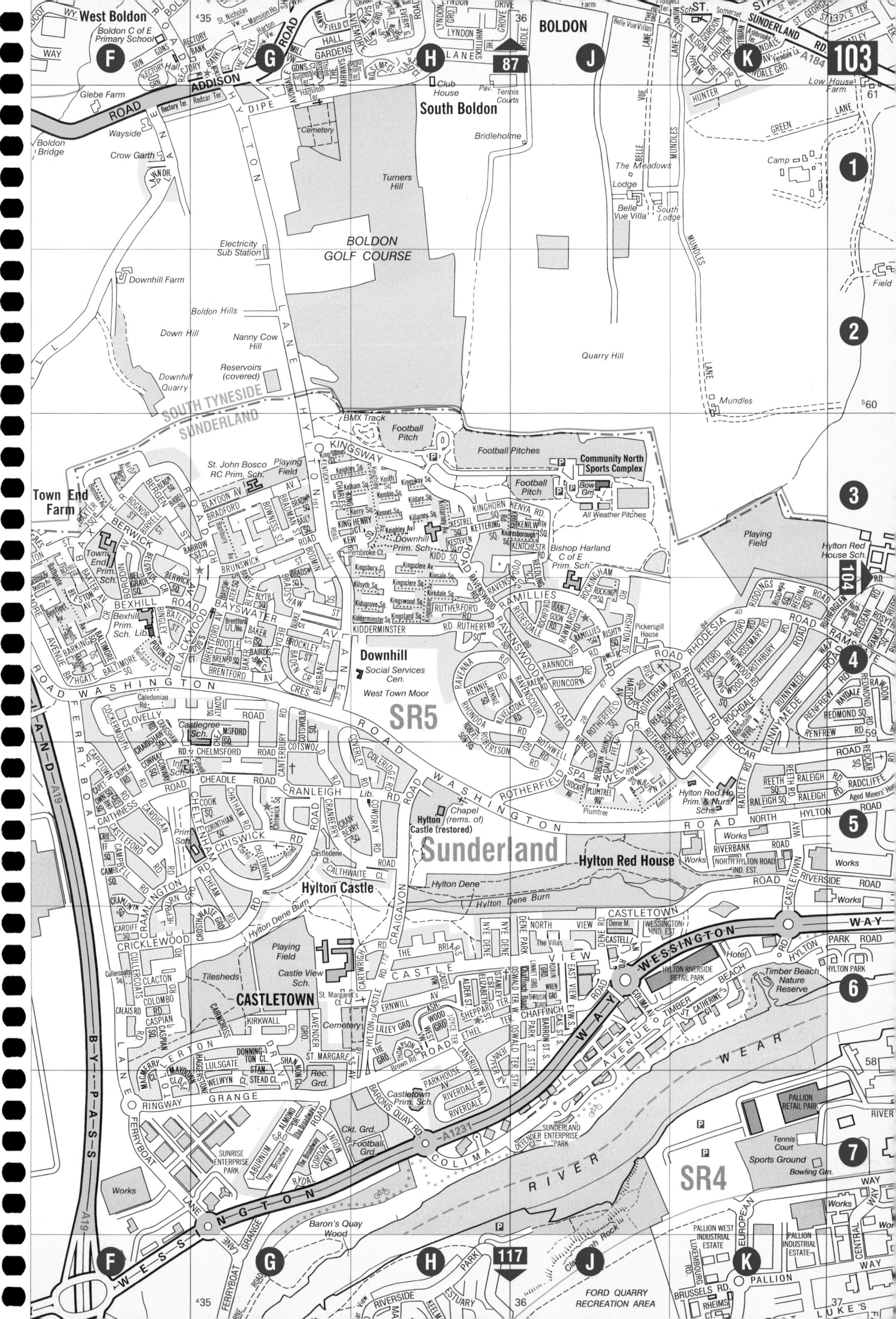
West Boldon
Boldon C of E Primary School
BOLDON
South Boldon
ADDISON ROAD
Glebe Farm
Boldon Bridge
Wayside
Crow Garth
Club House
Tennis Courts
Bridleholme
Cemetery
Turners Hill
BOLDON GOLF COURSE
Electricity Sub Station
Downhill Farm
Boldon Hills
Down Hill
Nanny Cow Hill
Reservoirs (covered)
Downhill Quarry
SOUTH TYNESIDE
SUNDERLAND
The Meadows
Lodge
Belle Vue Villa
South Lodge
MUNDLES LANE
Mundles
Quarry Hill
Camp
Field
Low House Farm
SUNDERLAND RD.
A184
GREEN LANE
HYLTON LANE
BMX Track
Football Pitch
Football Pitches
Community North Sports Complex
All Weather Pitches
Playing Field
Hylton Red House Sch.
St. John Bosco RC Prim. Sch.
Town End Farm
Town End Prim. Sch.
Bexhill Prim. Sch.
Downhill Prim. Sch.
Bishop Harland C of E Prim. Sch.
Pickersgill House
Downhill
Social Services Cen.
West Town Moor
SR5
WASHINGTON ROAD
Castlegree Sch.
Hylton Castle (restored)
Chapel (rems. of)
Sunderland
Hylton Red House
Hylton Red Ho. Prim. & Nurs. Schs.
Hylton Dene
Hylton Dene Burn
Hylton Castle
Playing Field
Castle View Sch.
Tilesheds
CASTLETOWN
Cemetery
Castletown Prim. Sch.
Rec. Grd.
Ckt. Grd.
Football Grd.
SUNRISE ENTERPRISE PARK
Works
SUNDERLAND ENTERPRISE PARK
WESSINGTON WAY
A1231
A19
BY-PASS
HYLTON RIVERSIDE RETAIL PARK
Timber Beach Nature Reserve
HYLTON PARK
RIVERSIDE ROAD
NORTH HYLTON ROAD IND. EST.
RIVER WEAR
Baron's Quay Wood
PALLION RETAIL PARK
Tennis Court
Sports Ground
Bowling Grn.
SR4
PALLION WEST INDUSTRIAL ESTATE
PALLION INDUSTRIAL ESTATE
FORD QUARRY RECREATION AREA
Claxheugh Rock
87
104
117
F G H J K
1 2 3 4 5 6 7

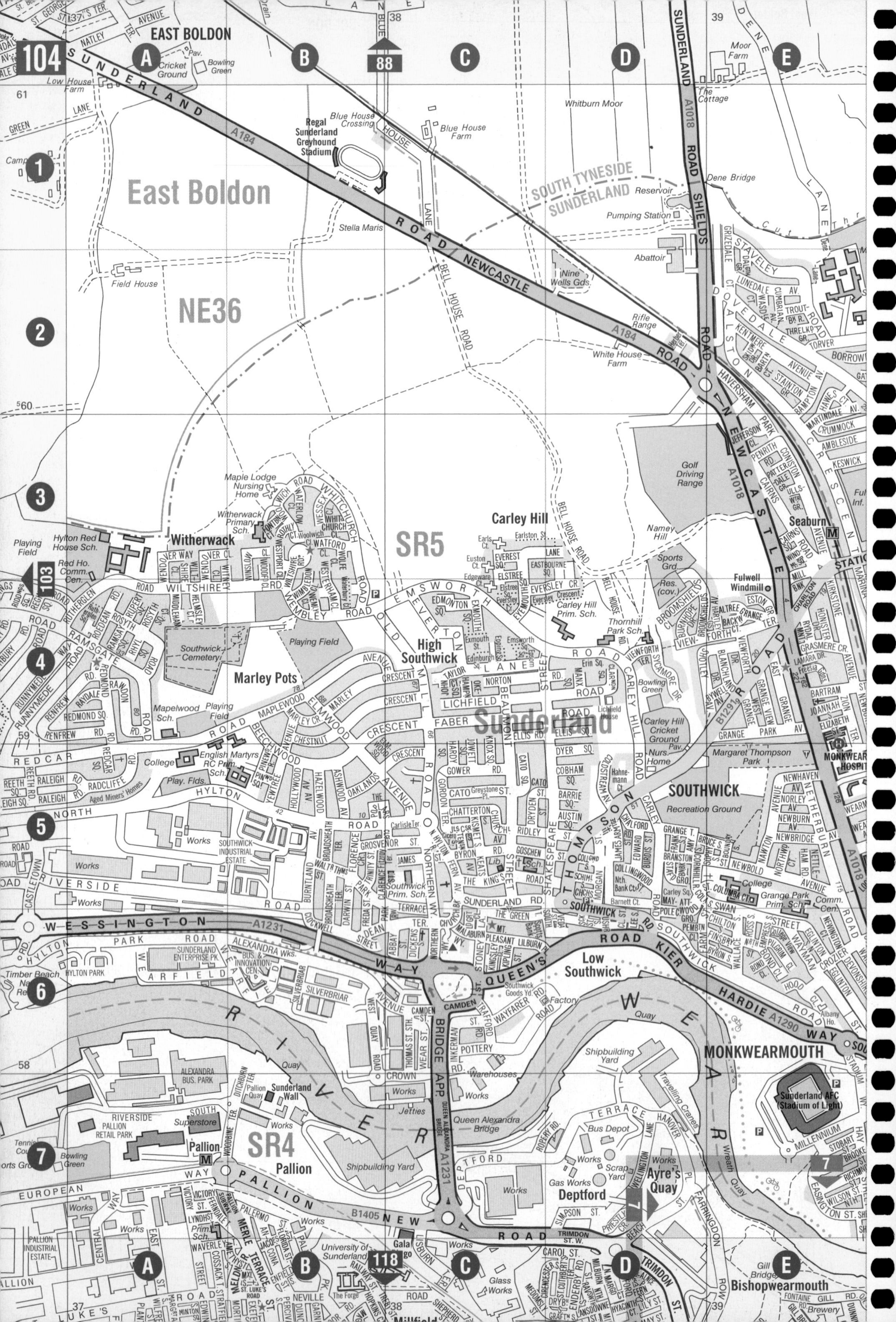

104
EAST BOLDON
East Boldon
NE36
88
103
118
Regal Sunderland Greyhound Stadium
Blue House Crossing
Blue House Farm
Whitburn Moor
SOUTH TYNESIDE
SUNDERLAND
Reservoir
Pumping Station
Dene Bridge
Moor Farm
The Cottage
Stella Maris
Field House
Abattoir
Nine Wells Gds.
Rifle Range
White House Farm
SUNDERLAND ROAD
NEWCASTLE ROAD
SHIELDS ROAD
A184
A1018
A1231
A1290
B1405
Golf Driving Range
Maple Lodge Nursing Home
Witherwack Primary Sch.
Witherwack
Hylton Red House Sch.
Red Ho. Comm. Cen.
Playing Field
Carley Hill
SR5
Carley Hill Prim. Sch.
Thornhill Park Sch.
Namey Hill
Sports Grd.
Fulwell Windmill
Seaburn
Southwick Cemetery
Marley Pots
High Southwick
Mapelwood Sch.
English Martyrs RC Prim. Sch.
College
Aged Miners' Homes
Sunderland
Carley Hill Cricket Ground
Margaret Thompson Park
SOUTHWICK
Recreation Ground
MONKWEARMOUTH HOSPITAL
SOUTHWICK INDUSTRIAL ESTATE
Works
Southwick Prim. Sch.
Grange Park Prim. Sch.
Comm. Cen.
WESSINGTON WAY
QUEEN'S ROAD
KIER HARDIE WAY
SUNDERLAND ENTERPRISE PK.
ALEXANDRA BUS. & INNOVATION CEN.
HYLTON PARK
Timber Beach Nature Reserve
Low Southwick
Southwick Goods Yd.
RIVER WEAR
MONKWEARMOUTH
Sunderland AFC (Stadium of Light)
Shipbuilding Yard
Travelling Cranes
ALEXANDRA BUS. PARK
RIVERSIDE PALLION RETAIL PARK
Superstore
Pallion
SR4
Sunderland Wall
Queen Alexandra Bridge
Bus Depot
Scrap Yard
Gas Works
Deptford
Ayre's Quay
PALLION INDUSTRIAL ESTATE
University of Sunderland
Gala Bingo
Glass Works
Gill Bridge
Bishopwearmouth
Brewery
The Forge
Millfield

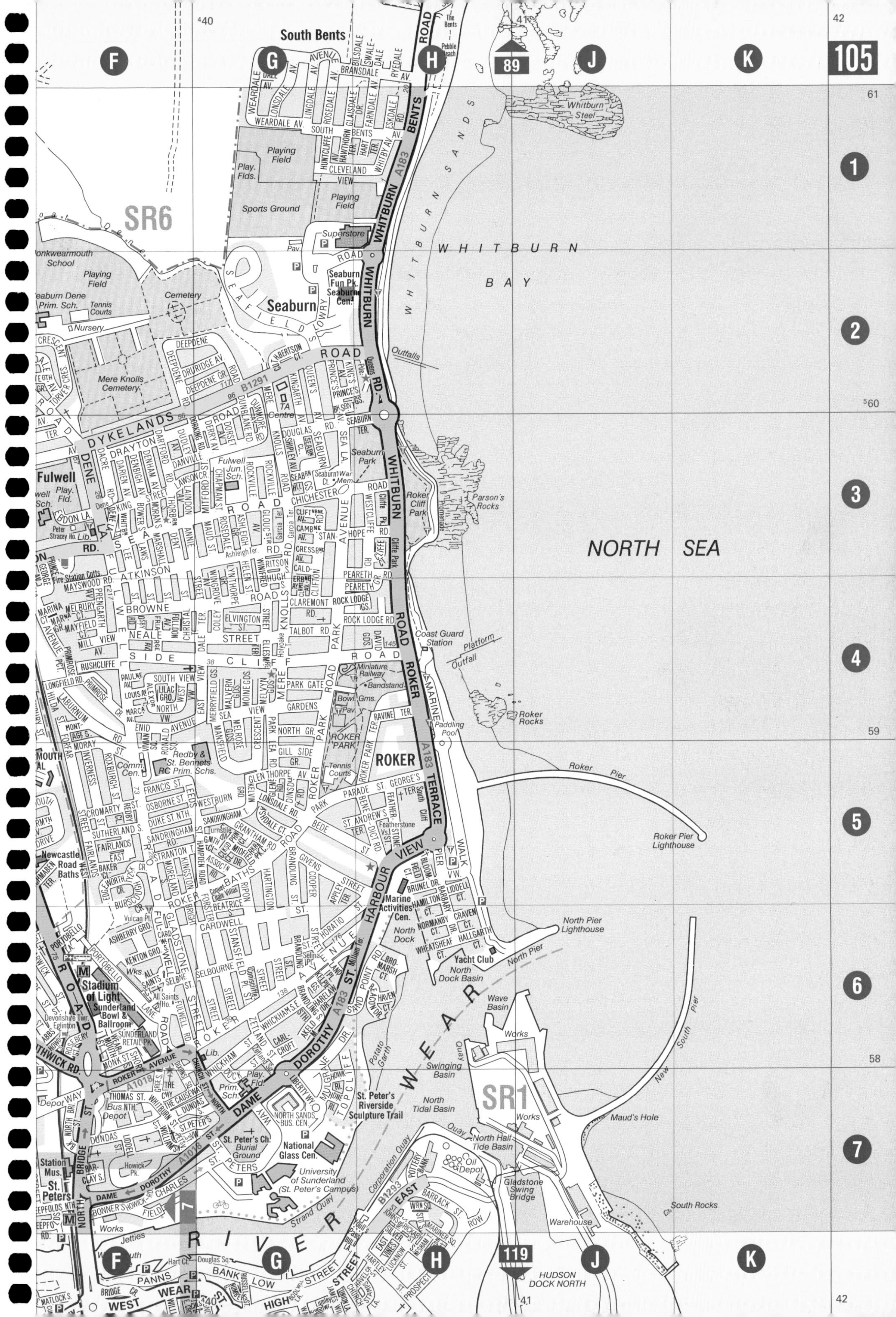
South Bents
The Bents
Pebble Beach
89
Whitburn Steel
SR6
Monkwearmouth School
Playing Field
Play. Flds.
Sports Ground
Superstore
Seaburn
Seaburn Fun Pk.
Seaburn Cen.
Seaburn Dene Prim. Sch.
Tennis Courts
Cemetery
Nursery
Mere Knolls Cemetery
WHITBURN SANDS
WHITBURN BAY
Outfalls
WHITBURN ROAD
WHITBURN BENTS
A183
SEA ROAD
DYKELANDS ROAD
B1291
Fulwell
Fulwell Jun. Sch.
TA Centre
Seaburn Park
Seaburn War Mem.
Roker Cliff Park
Promenade
Parson's Rocks
NORTH SEA
Peter Stracey Ho. Lib.
Fire Station Cotts
Coast Guard Station
Platform
Outfall
Miniature Railway
Bandstand
Bowl. Gms.
Pav.
ROKER PARK
Tennis Courts
ROKER
ROKER TERRACE
MARINE WALK
Paddling Pool
Roker Rocks
Roker Pier
Roker Pier Lighthouse
Redby & St. Bennets RC Prim. Schs.
Comm. Cen.
Newcastle Road Baths
HARBOUR VIEW
Featherstone
Marine Activities Cen.
North Dock
Yacht Club
North Dock Basin
North Pier
North Pier Lighthouse
Stadium of Light
Sunderland Bowl & Ballroom
SUNDERLAND RETAIL PK.
All Saints Ho.
Wave Basin
Works
Swinging Basin
New South Pier
Maud's Hole
DOROTHY ST.
DAME DOROTHY
A1018
Lib.
Play. Fld.
Prim. Sch.
Bus Depot
St. Peter's Riverside Sculpture Trail
NORTH SANDS BUS. CEN.
St. Peter's Ch. Burial Ground
National Glass Cen.
University of Sunderland (St. Peter's Campus)
Potato Garth
North Tidal Basin
SR1
Works
North Hall Tide Basin
Oil Depot
Gladstone Swing Bridge
Corporation Quay
Strand Quay
B1293
Station Mus.
St. Peters
Howick Pk.
RIVER WEAR
Jetties
Works
Warehouse
South Rocks
119
HUDSON DOCK NORTH
F
G
H
J
K
1
2
3
4
5
6
7
440
41
42
61
560
59
58

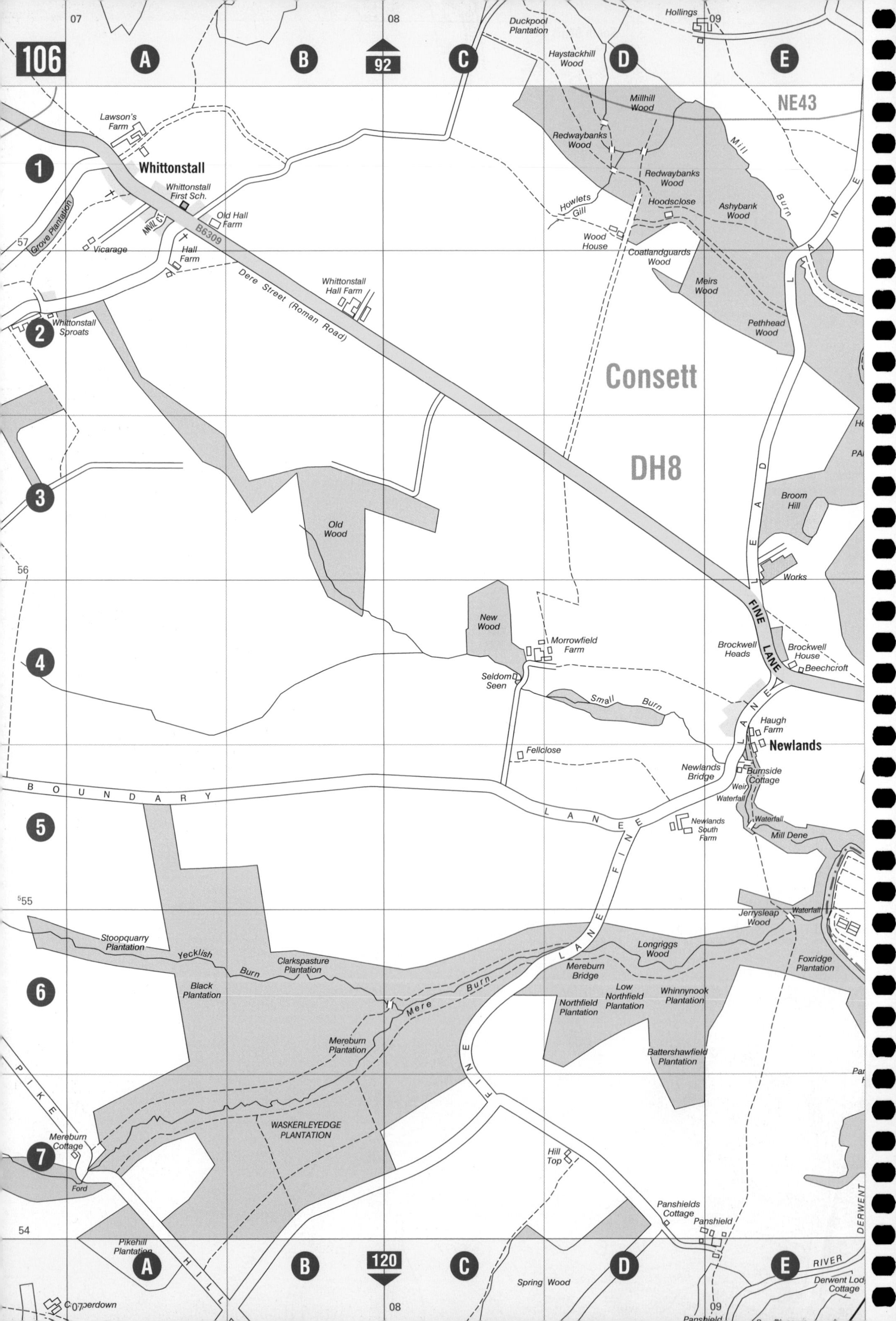

07
08
09
A
B
C
D
E
92
120
1
2
3
4
5
6
7
57
56
55
54
Hollings
Duckpool Plantation
Haystackhill Wood
NE43
Millhill Wood
Redwaybanks Wood
Redwaybanks Wood
Mill Burn
Lawson's Farm
Whittonstall
Whittonstall First Sch.
Old Hall Farm
Grove Plantation
Anvil Cl.
B6309
Vicarage
Hall Farm
Howlets Gill
Hoodsclose
Ashybank Wood
Wood House
Coatlandguards Wood
Dere Street (Roman Road)
Whittonstall Hall Farm
Meirs Wood
Whittonstall Sproats
Pethhead Wood
Consett
DH8
Lead Lane
Broom Hill
Old Wood
Works
Fine Lane
New Wood
Morrowfield Farm
Brockwell Heads
Brockwell House
Beechcroft
Seldom Seen
Small Burn
Haugh Farm
Newlands
Fellclose
Newlands Bridge
Burnside Cottage
Weir
Waterfall
Boundary Lane
Fine Lane
Newlands South Farm
Waterfall
Mill Dene
Jerrysleap Wood
Waterfall
Stoopquarry Plantation
Yecklish Burn
Clarkspasture Plantation
Longriggs Wood
Foxridge Plantation
Black Plantation
Mereburn Bridge
Low Northfield Plantation
Whinnynook Plantation
Northfield Plantation
Mere Burn
Mereburn Plantation
Battershawfield Plantation
Pike Hill
Fine Lane
WASKERLEYEDGE PLANTATION
Mereburn Cottage
Ford
Hill Top
Panshields Cottage
Panshield
Derwent
River
Pikehill Plantation
Spring Wood
Derwent Lodge Cottage
Copperdown
Panshield

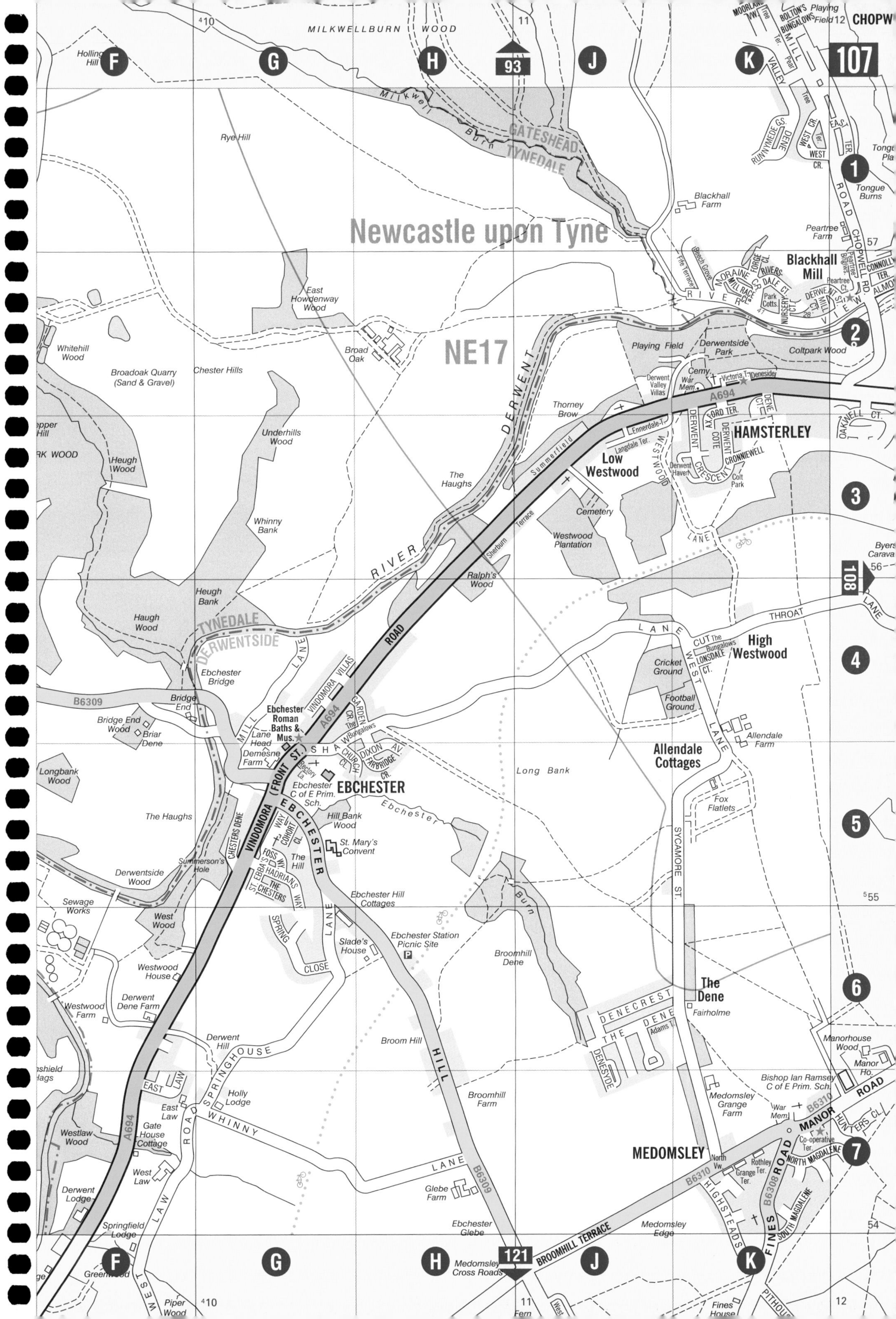

F **G** **H** **93** **J** **K** CHOPW

MILKWELLBURN WOOD

Moorland Vw
Bolton's Playing Field 12

Newcastle upon Tyne

GATESHEAD
TYNEDALE

Rye Hill

Hollings Hill

Blackhall Farm

Blackhall Mill

NE17

East Howdenway Wood

Whitehill Wood

Broadoak Quarry (Sand & Gravel)

Chester Hills

Broad Oak

Playing Field

Derwentside Park

Coltpark Wood

Underhills Wood

Derwent Valley Villas

War Mem

Cemy

Victoria

Deneside

Thorney Brow

HAMSTERLEY

Pepper Hill

PARK WOOD

Heugh Wood

Whinny Bank

The Haughs

Ennerdale T.

Langdale Ter.

Low Westwood

Colt Park

CRONNIEWELL

OAKWELL CT.

DERWENT

Cemetery

Westwood Plantation

RIVER

Ralph's Wood

Sherburn Terrace

Heugh Bank

Haugh Wood

CUT

The Bungalows

LONSDALE CT.

High Westwood

Byers Caravan

TYNEDALE
DERWENTSIDE

Ebchester Bridge

B6309

Bridge End

Cricket Ground

WEST LANE

Allendale Farm

Bridge End Wood

Briar Dene

Longbank Wood

Ebchester Roman Baths & Mus.

VINDOMORA VILLAS

GARDEN CR.

The Bungalows

DIXON CL.

Lane Head

Demesne Farm

CHURCH CL.

ARBRIDGE CR.

Allendale Cottages

Football Ground

Fox Flatlets

EBCHESTER

Ebchester C of E Prim. Sch.

Ebchester

Long Bank

The Haughs

CHESTERS DENE

VINDOMORA

EBCHESTER

Hill Bank Wood

St. Mary's Convent

SYCAMORE ST.

The Hill

The Chesters

HADRIAN'S WAY

FOSS WAY

CONORT CL.

ST. ERRA

Derwentside Wood

Summerson's Hole

SPRING

Ebchester Hill Cottages

Broomhill Dene

West Wood

Sewage Works

Westwood House

CLOSE

Slade's House

Ebchester Station Picnic Site

HILL

The Dene

Fairholme

DENECREST

THE DENE

Manorhouse Wood

Derwent Dene Farm

Westwood Farm

Westlaw Wood

SPRINGHOUSE

Derwent Hill

Broom Hill

Broomhill Farm

DENESYDE

Manor Ho.

Bishop Ian Ramsey C of E Prim. Sch.

shield Hags

EAST LAW

Holly Lodge

Medomsley Grange Farm

War Mem

MANOR ROAD

HUNTERS CL.

Gate House Cottage

East Law

WHINNY

Co-operative Ter.

North Vw

Derwent Lodge

WEST LAW ROAD

A694

West Law

LANE

B6309

MEDOMSLEY

B6310

Rothley Ter.

Grange Ter.

North Magdalene

South Magdalene

HIGHSTEADS

FINES ROAD

PITHOU

Springfield Lodge

Glebe Farm

Medomsley Edge

Greenwell

Piper Wood

Ebchester Glebe

F **G** **H** **121** Medomsley Cross Roads **J** BROOMHILL TERRACE **K**

Fern

Fines House

1

2

3

4

5

6

7

108

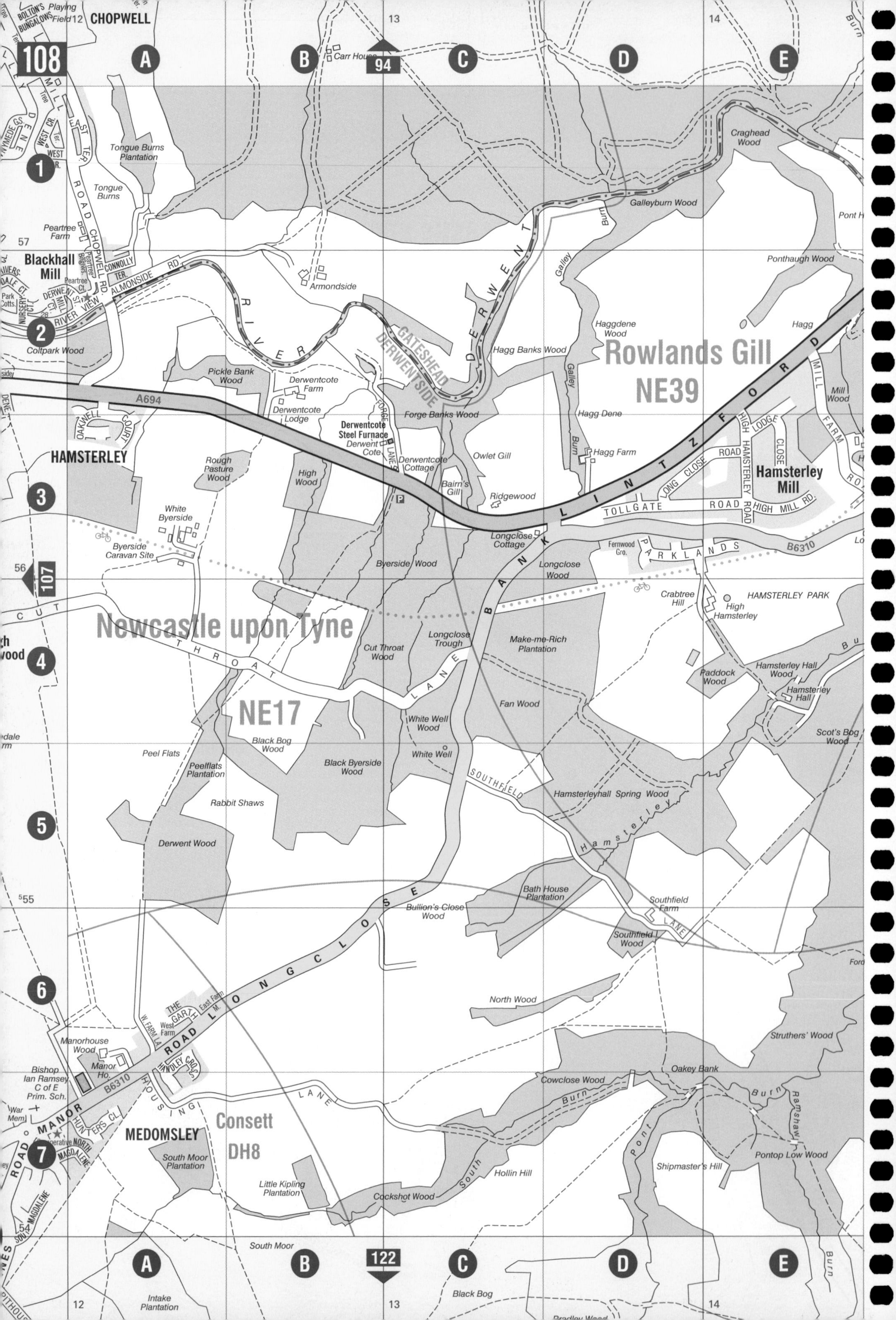
108
CHOPWELL
Playing Field
BOLTON'S BUNGALOWS
Carr House
94
A
B
C
D
E
13
14
12
Tongue Burns Plantation
Tongue Burns
Peartree Farm
Blackhall Mill
CHOPWELL RD.
CONNOLLY TER.
ALMONSIDE RD.
RIVER VIEW
DERWENT ST.
Coltpark Wood
EAST TER.
ROAD
WEST CR.
WEST TER.
Craghead Wood
Galleyburn Wood
Pont H
Ponthaugh Wood
Armondside
RIVER DERWENT
GATESHEAD
DERWENTSIDE
Galley Burn
Haggdene Wood
Hagg Banks Wood
Hagg
Rowlands Gill
NE39
LINTZFORD RD
MILL FARM
Mill Wood
Pickle Bank Wood
Derwentcote Farm
Derwentcote Lodge
A694
OAKWELL COURT
HAMSTERLEY
Derwentcote Steel Furnace
Derwent Cote
FORGE LANE
Derwentcote Cottage
Forge Banks Wood
Hagg Dene
Hagg Farm
Owlet Gill
HIGH HAMSTERLEY ROAD
LODGE CLOSE
LONG CLOSE
ROAD
Hamsterley Mill
Rough Pasture Wood
High Wood
Bairn's Gill
Ridgewood
TOLLGATE ROAD
HIGH MILL RD.
White Byerside
Byerside Caravan Site
Longclose Cottage
BANK
Fernwood Gro.
PARKLANDS
B6310
Byerside Wood
Longclose Wood
56
107
CUT THROAT LANE
Newcastle upon Tyne
Crabtree Hill
High Hamsterley
HAMSTERLEY PARK
Longclose Trough
Cut Throat Wood
Make-me-Rich Plantation
Hamsterley Hall Wood
Paddock Wood
Hamsterley Hall
NE17
White Well Wood
Fan Wood
Scot's Bog Wood
Peel Flats
Black Bog Wood
White Well
Black Byerside Wood
Peelflats Plantation
SOUTHFIELD
Hamsterleyhall Spring Wood
Rabbit Shaws
Hamsterley
Derwent Wood
Bath House Plantation
55
LONGCLOSE ROAD
Bullion's Close Wood
Southfield Farm
LANE
Southfield Wood
North Wood
THE GARTH
East Farm
West Farm
W. FARM LA.
Struthers' Wood
Manorhouse Wood
Manor Ho.
HANDLEY CROSS
Oakey Bank
Bishop Ian Ramsey C of E Prim. Sch.
B6310
HOUSING LANE
Cowclose Wood
Burn
Ramshaw
War Meml
MANOR ROAD
HUNTERS CL.
MEDOMSLEY
Consett
DH8
NORTH MAGDALENE
SOUTH MAGDALENE
South Moor Plantation
Pont
Shipmaster's Hill
Pontop Low Wood
Hollin Hill
South Burn
Little Kipling Plantation
Cockshot Wood
South Moor
122
Black Bog
Intake Plantation
Bradley Wood
Ford

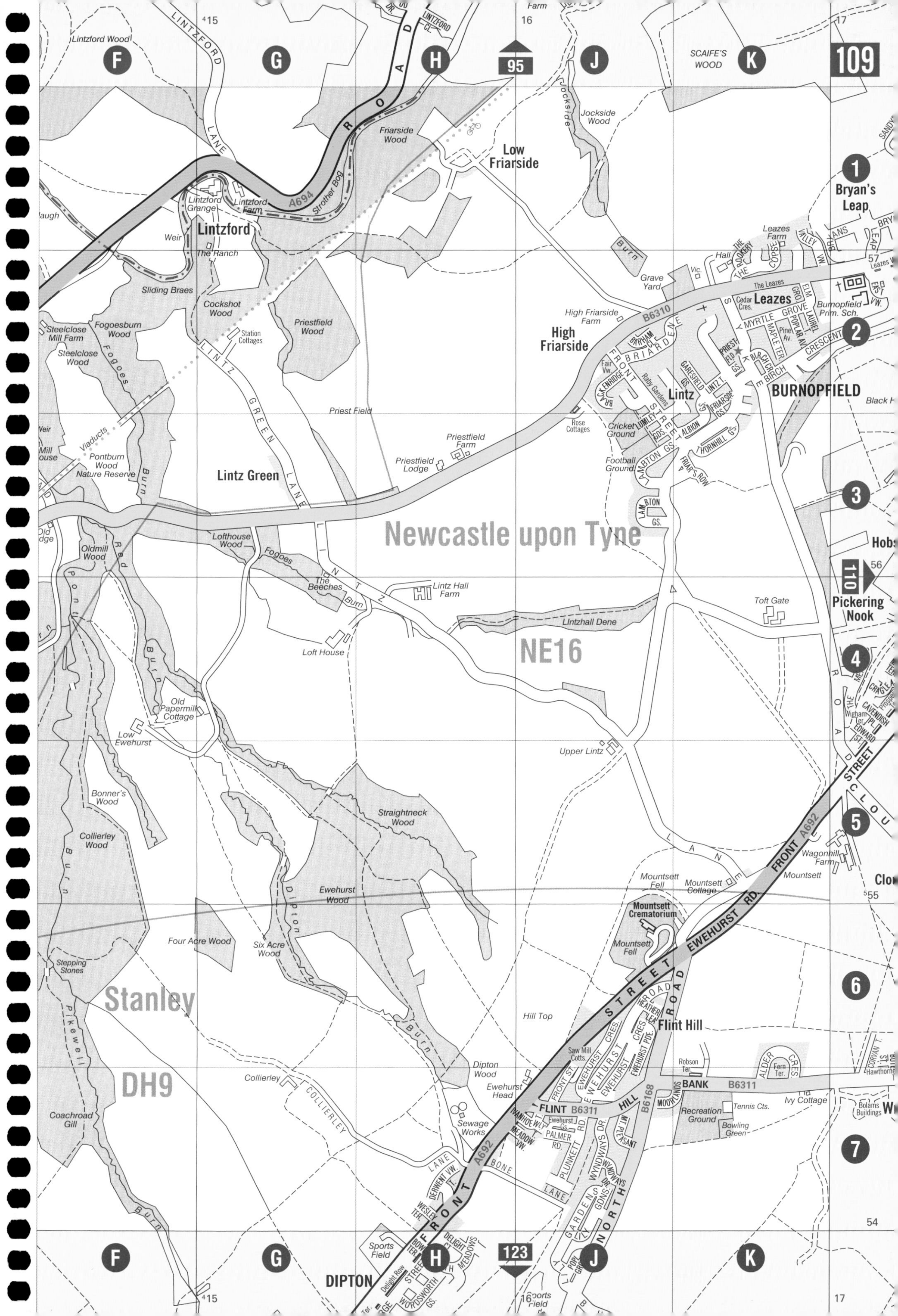

Lintzford Wood
SCAIFE'S WOOD
95
Jockside Wood
Friarside Wood
Low Friarside
Bryan's Leap
Lintzford Grange
Lintzford Farm
Lintzford
Weir
The Ranch
Strother Bog
A694
Leazes Farm
Sliding Braes
Cockshot Wood
Grave Yard
Leazes
Burnopfield Prim. Sch.
Steelclose Mill Farm
Fogoesburn Wood
Station Cottages
Priestfield Wood
High Friarside Farm
High Friarside
B6310
Steelclose Wood
Lintz
BURNOPFIELD
Priest Field
Rose Cottages
Cricket Ground
Football Ground
Viaducts
Pontburn Wood
Nature Reserve
Priestfield Farm
Priestfield Lodge
Lintz Green
Newcastle upon Tyne
Lofthouse Wood
Oldmill Wood
The Beeches
Lintz Hall Farm
110
Pickering Nook
Toft Gate
Lintzhall Dene
Loft House
NE16
Old Papermill Cottage
Low Ewehurst
Upper Lintz
Bonner's Wood
Straightneck Wood
Collierley Wood
Wagonhill Farm
Mountsett Fell
Mountsett Cottage
Mountsett
Ewehurst Wood
Mountsett Crematorium
Four Acre Wood
Six Acre Wood
Stepping Stones
Mountsett Fell
Stanley
Hill Top
Flint Hill
Saw Mill Cotts.
Robson Ter.
Dipton Wood
Ewehurst Head
Collierley
BANK B6311
DH9
FLINT B6311
Tennis Cts.
Ivy Cottage
Bolams Buildings
Recreation Ground
Bowling Green
Coachroad Gill
Sewage Works
EWEHURST RD.
FRONT STREET
A692
Sports Field
123
DIPTON

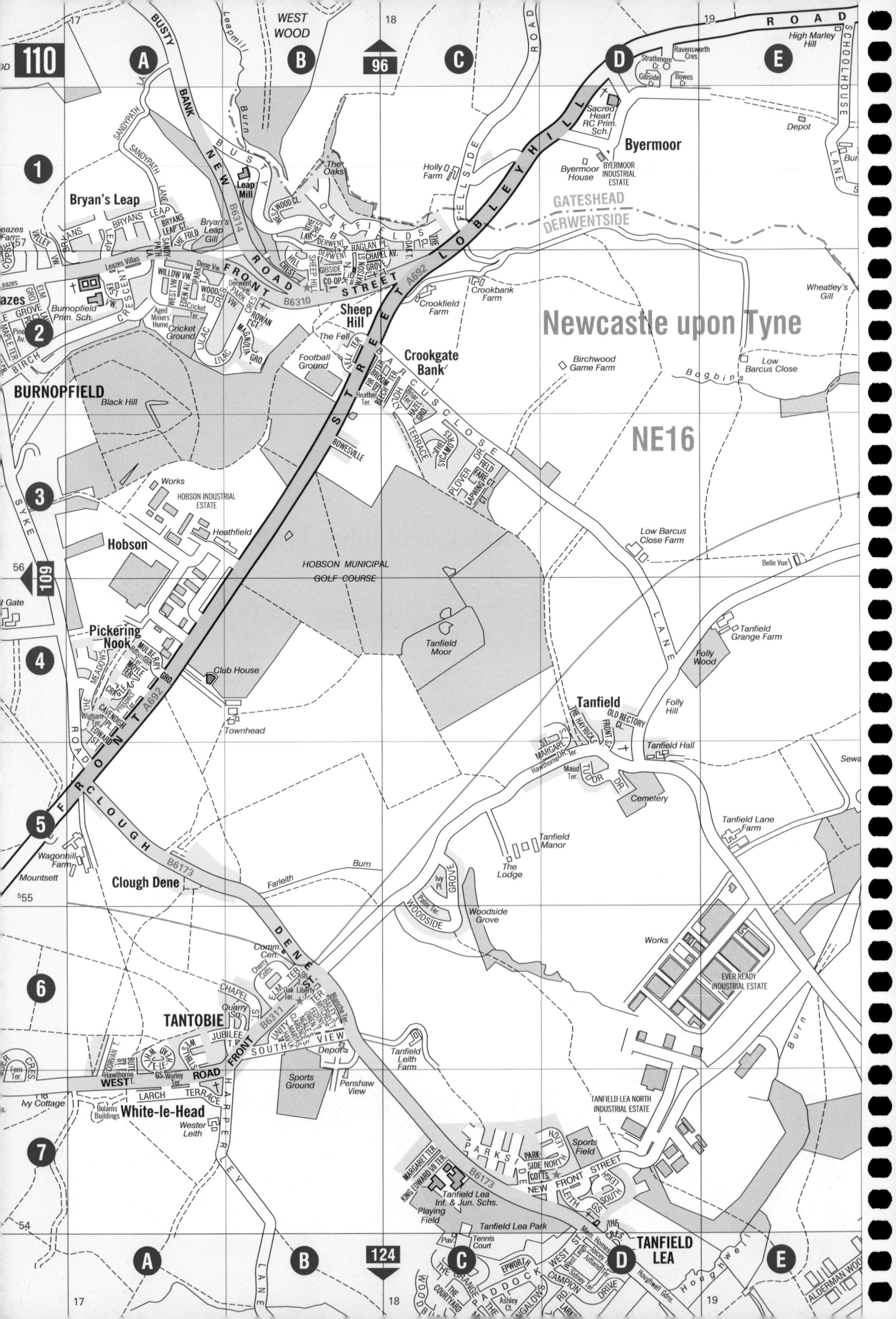

A **B** 96 **C** **D** **E**

WEST WOOD

Newcastle upon Tyne

NE16

1

Bryan's Leap

Leap Mill

The Oaks

Holly Farm

Strathmore Cr.
Gibside Cr.
Bowes Cr.

Ravensworth Cres.

High Marley Hill

Depot

Sacred Heart RC Prim. Sch.

Byermoor House
Byermoor Industrial Estate

Byermoor

GATESHEAD
DERWENTSIDE

Leazes Farm

Leazes
Leazes Villas

Dene Vw.
Willow Vw.

Burnopfield Prim. Sch.

Aged Miners' Home

Cricket Ground

2

Sheep Hill

Crookgate Bank

The Fell

Football Ground

Bowesville

Crookfield Farm

Crookbank Farm

Birchwood Game Farm

Low Barcus Close

Bogbins

Wheatley's Gill

BURNOPFIELD

Black Hill

3

Works

Hobson Industrial Estate

Heathfield

Hobson

Low Barcus Close Farm

Belle Vue

4

Pickering Nook

Club House

Townhead

HOBSON MUNICIPAL GOLF COURSE

Tanfield Moor

Tanfield Grange Farm

Folly Wood

Folly Hill

Tanfield

The Haynings
Old Rectory Cl.
Tanfield Hall

Margaret St.
Hawthorne Dr.
Maud Ter.
Tudor Dr.

Cemetery

Tanfield Manor

The Lodge

Tanfield Lane Farm

5

Wagonhill Farm

Mountsett

B6173

Clough Dene

Farleith

Burn

Woodside Grove

Works

EVER READY INDUSTRIAL ESTATE

6

Comm. Cen.
Cherry Cotts.

CHAPEL
Quarry

TANTOBIE

JUBILEE T.

Elm Ter.
Oak Liberty Ter.

Depot

Tanfield Leith Farm

Sports Ground

Penshaw View

Tanfield Lea North Industrial Estate

7

WEST
LARCH TERRACE

Ivy Cottage

Bolams Buildings

White-le-Head

Wester Leith

Sports Field

Tanfield Lea Inf. & Jun. Schs. Playing Field

Tanfield Lea Park

Pav.

Tennis Court

New Front Street

TANFIELD LEA

A 17 **B** 124 **C** 18 **D** **E** 19

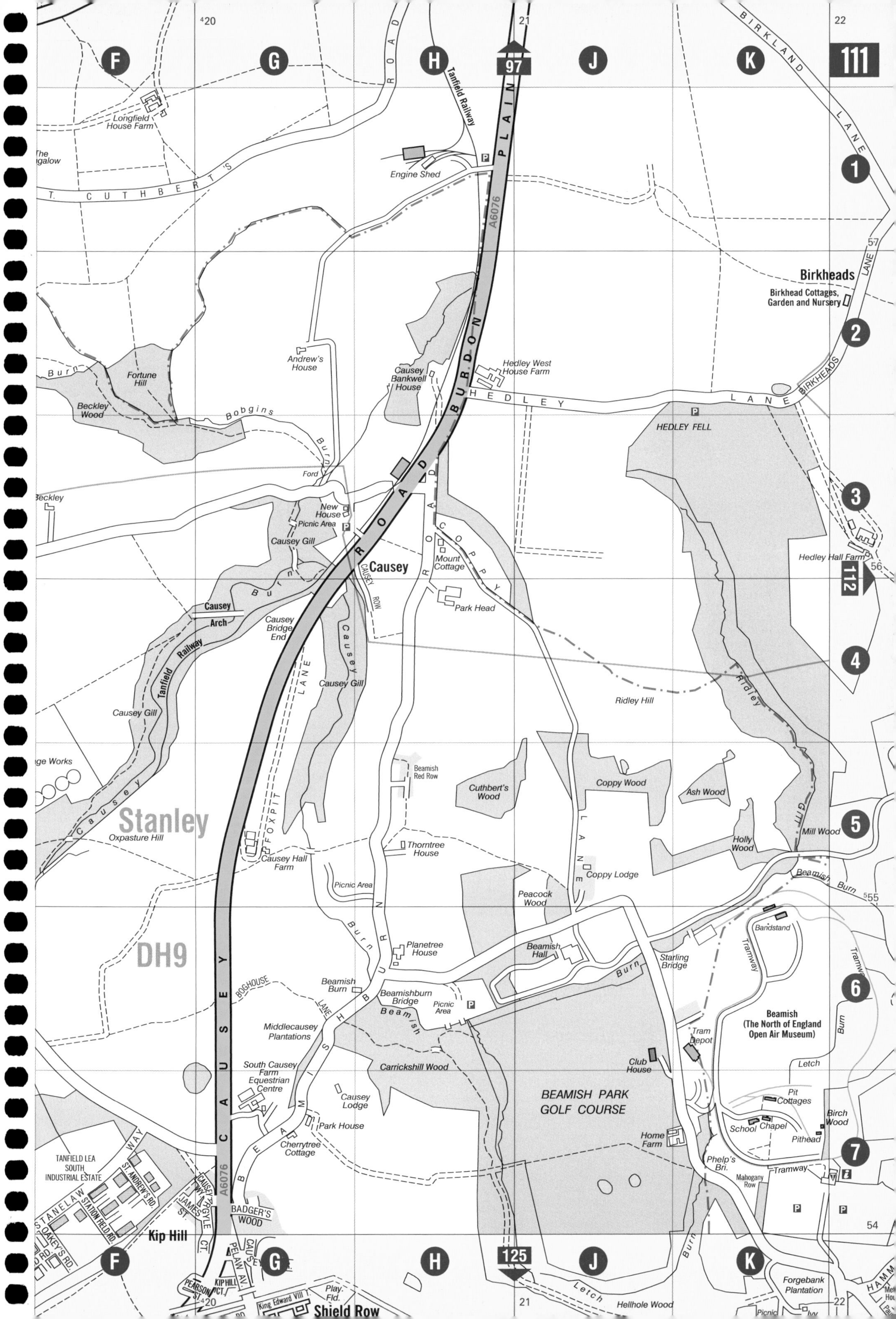

F
G
H
J
K
97
125
112
Longfield House Farm
Tanfield Railway
Engine Shed
ST. CUTHBERT'S ROAD
BIRKLAND LANE
Birkheads
Birkhead Cottages, Garden and Nursery
BIRKHEADS LANE
Fortune Hill
Beckley Wood
Bobgins Burn
Andrew's House
Causey Bankwell House
Hedley West House Farm
HEDLEY LANE
HEDLEY FELL
BURDON PLAIN ROAD
A6076
Ford
New House
Picnic Area
Causey Gill
Causey
Mount Cottage
COPPY ROAD
Park Head
Hedley Hall Farm
Causey Arch
Causey Bridge End
CAUSEY ROW
Tanfield Railway
Causey Burn
Causey Gill
Ridley Hill
Ridley Gill
Beamish Red Row
Cuthbert's Wood
Coppy Wood
Ash Wood
Holly Wood
Mill Wood
Stanley
Oxpasture Hill
FOXPIT LANE
Causey Hall Farm
Thorntree House
Coppy Lodge
Picnic Area
Peacock Wood
Beamish Burn
DH9
Planetree House
Beamish Hall
Starling Bridge
Bandstand
Tramway
BOGHOUSE LANE
Beamish Burn
Beamishburn Bridge
Picnic Area
Middlecausey Plantations
Beamish (The North of England Open Air Museum)
Tram Depot
Club House
Letch
Carrickshill Wood
South Causey Farm Equestrian Centre
BEAMISH PARK GOLF COURSE
Pit Cottages
Causey Lodge
Park House
School
Chapel
Birch Wood
Pithead
Home Farm
Cherrytree Cottage
Phelp's Bri.
Mahogany Row
Tramway
TANFIELD LEA SOUTH INDUSTRIAL ESTATE
STANELAW WAY
ST. ANDREW'S RD.
STATION FIELD RD.
OAKEY'S RD.
CAUSEY WAY
ARGYLE ST.
JAMES ST.
CAUSEY ROAD
BADGER'S WOOD
Kip Hill
PELAW AV.
KIP HILL CT.
PEARSON ST.
King Edward VIII T.
Play. Fld.
Shield Row
Letch
Hellhole Wood
Forgebank Plantation
HAMM

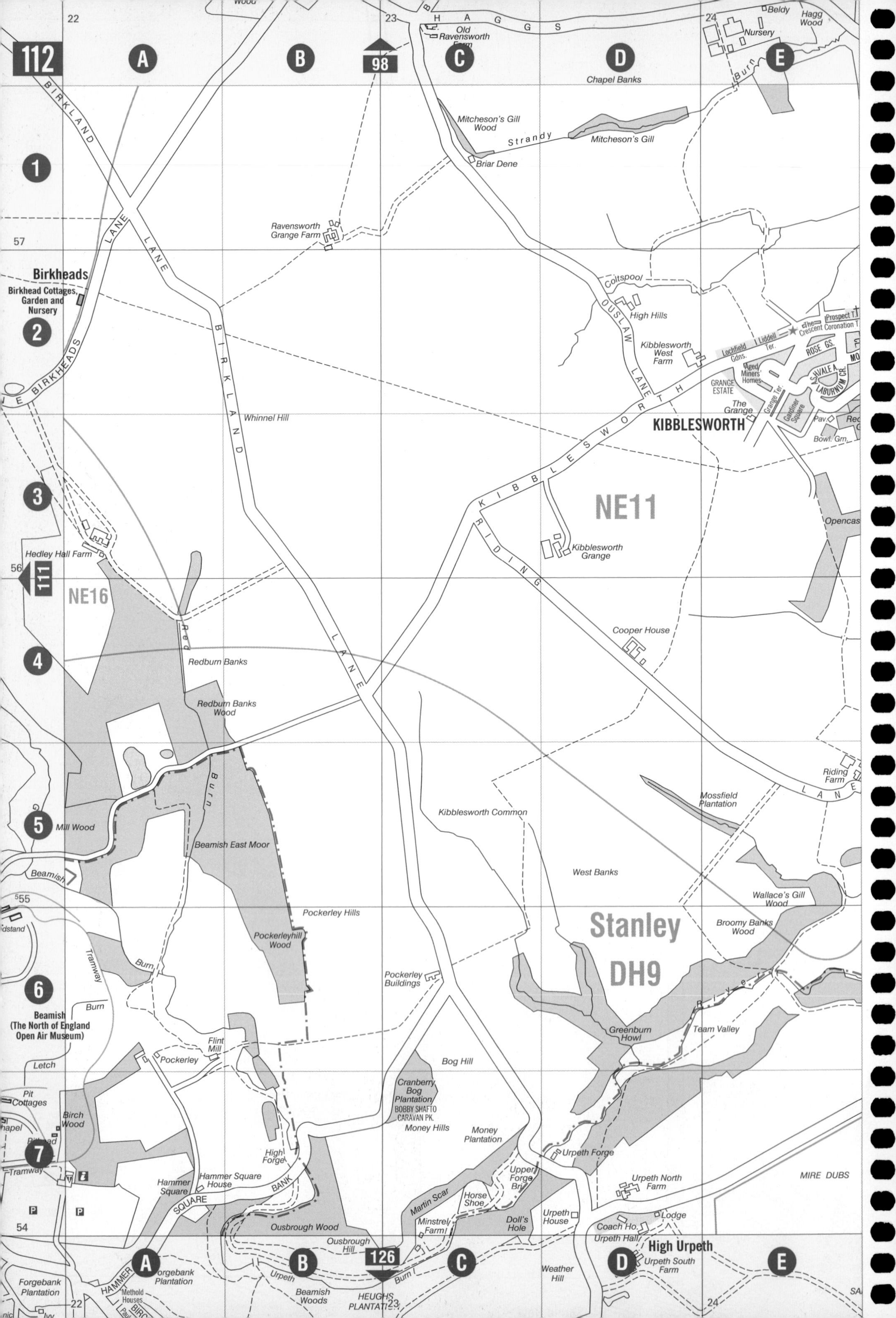

HAGGS
Old Ravensworth Farm
Beldy
Hagg Wood
Nursery
Chapel Banks
Burn
Mitcheson's Gill Wood
Strandy
Mitcheson's Gill
Briar Dene
BIRKLAND LANE
Ravensworth Grange Farm
Birkheads
Birkhead Cottages, Garden and Nursery
BIRKHEADS LANE
Coltspool
OUSLAW LANE
High Hills
Kibblesworth West Farm
Lochfield Gdns.
Liddell Ter.
The Crescent
Prospect T.
Coronation T.
ROSE GS.
Aged Miners' Homes
ASHVALE A.
LABURNUM CR.
GRANGE ESTATE
Grange Ter.
Gardiner Square
The Grange
KIBBLESWORTH
Pav.
Bowl. Grn.
Whinnel Hill
KIBBLESWORTH
NE11
Kibblesworth Grange
RIDING LANE
Opencast
Hedley Hall Farm
NE16
Red Burn
Cooper House
Redburn Banks
Redburn Banks Wood
Riding Farm
Mossfield Plantation
Kibblesworth Common
Mill Wood
Beamish East Moor
Beamish
West Banks
Wallace's Gill Wood
Pockerley Hills
Broomy Banks Wood
Stanley DH9
Pockerleyhill Wood
Tramway
Pockerley Buildings
Beamish (The North of England Open Air Museum)
Burn
Greenburn Howl
Team Valley
Flint Mill
Pockerley
Letch
Bog Hill
Pit Cottages
Birch Wood
Cranberry Bog Plantation
BOBBY SHAFTO CARAVAN PK.
Money Hills
Money Plantation
High Forge
Urpeth Forge
Tramway
Hammer Square
Hammer Square House
SQUARE BANK
Upper Forge Bri.
Urpeth North Farm
MIRE DUBS
Martin Scar
Horse Shoe
Minstrel Farm
Doll's Hole
Urpeth House
Lodge
Ousbrough Wood
Coach Ho.
Urpeth Hall
High Urpeth
Ousbrough Hill
Urpeth South Farm
Forgebank Plantation
Weather Hill
Urpeth
Burn
Beamish Woods
HEUGHS PLANTATION
HAMMER
Methold Houses

98
111
126

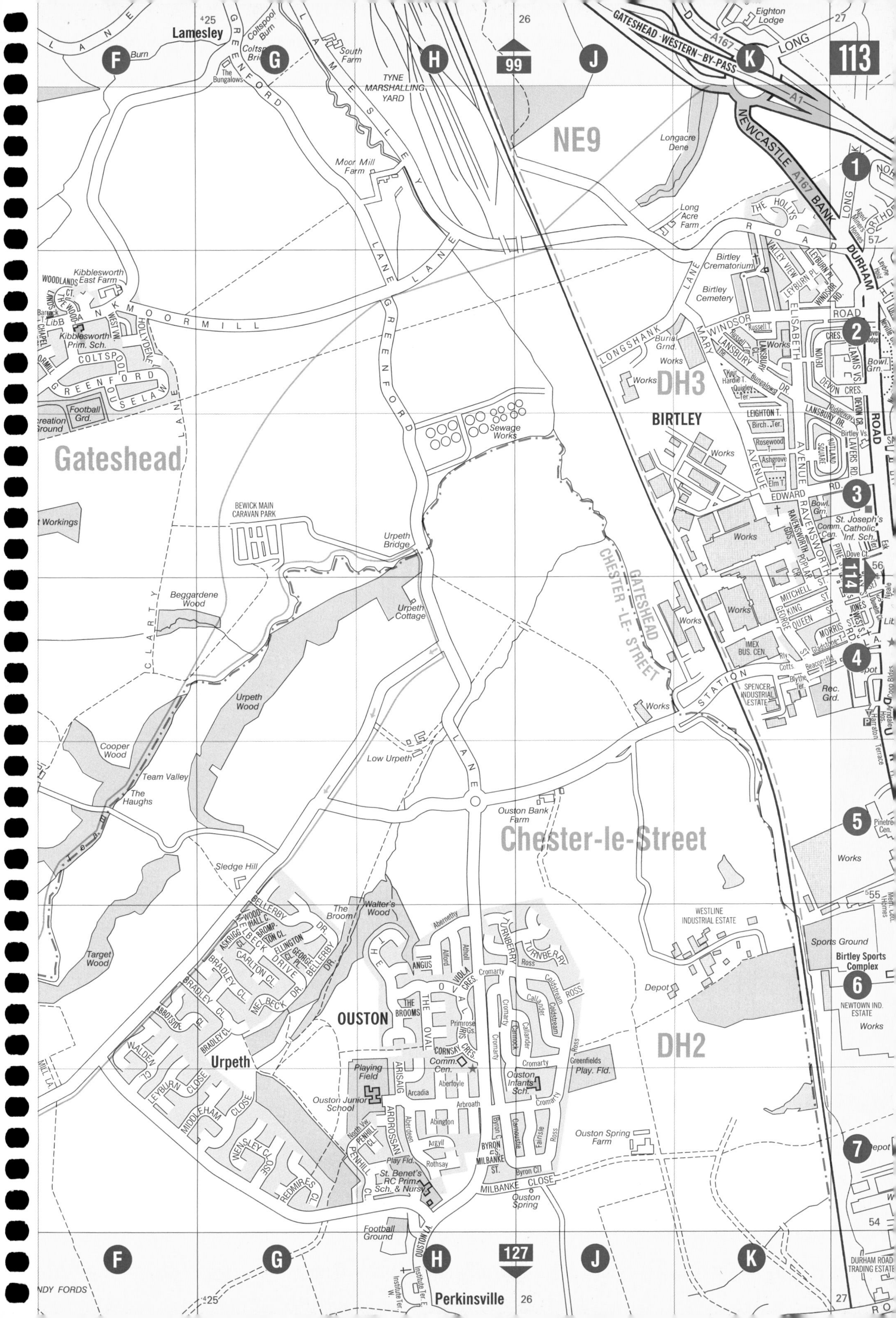

Lamesley
Greenford
Coltspool Burn
South Farm
Tyne Marshalling Yard
Gateshead Western By-Pass
Eighton Lodge
Long Bank
A167
A1
Newcastle Bank
NE9
Longacre Dene
Moor Mill Farm
Long Acre Farm
The Hollys
Birtley Crematorium
Birtley Cemetery
Durham Road
Kibblesworth East Farm
Woodlands
Kibblesworth Prim. Sch.
Moormill Lane
Lamesley Lane
Longshank Lane
Burial Grnd.
Works
DH3
Birtley
Windsor
Lansbury Dr.
Elisabeth Avenue
Mary Avenue
Devon Cres.
Leighton T.
Birch Ter.
Rosewood T.
Ashgrove T.
Elm T.
Rutland Square
Lavers Rd.
Edward Rd.
Football Grd.
Recreation Ground
Gateshead
Sewage Works
Bewick Main Caravan Park
Urpeth Bridge
Urpeth Cottage
Ravensworth
St. Joseph's Catholic Inf. Sch.
Mitchell St.
King St.
Queen St.
George St.
Morris St.
Jones St.
IMEX Bus. Cen.
Beggardene Wood
Clarty Lane
Urpeth Wood
Gateshead
Chester-le-Street
Station Lane
Spencer Industrial Estate
Rec. Grd.
Harraton Terrace
Cooper Wood
Team Valley
The Haughs
Low Urpeth
Ouston Bank Farm
Chester-le-Street
Pinetree Cen.
Works
Sledge Hill
Target Wood
The Broom
Walter's Wood
Bellerby Dr.
Westline Industrial Estate
Sports Ground
Birtley Sports Complex
Newtown Ind. Estate
Depot
Turnberry
Ross
Cromarty
Angus
The Oval
The Brooms
Ouston
Melbeck Dr.
Bradley Cl.
Abbotside Cl.
Walden Cl.
Urpeth
Playing Field
Comm. Cen.
Ouston Infants Sch.
Greenfields Play. Fld.
DH2
Ouston Junior School
Leyburn Close
Middleham Close
Wensley Cl.
Redmires Cl.
Ardrossan
Penhill Cl.
Arisaig
Arcadia
Aberfoyle
Arbroath
Abington
Argyll
Rothsay
Byron Cl.
Milbanke St.
Milbanke Close
Ouston Spring
Ouston Spring Farm
St. Benet's RC Prim. Sch. & Nurs.
Football Ground
Ouston La.
Perkinsville
Institute Ter. E.
Institute Ter. W.
Durham Road Trading Estate
Mill La.
99
127
114
F G H J K
1 2 3 4 5 6 7
425 26 27
57 56 55 54

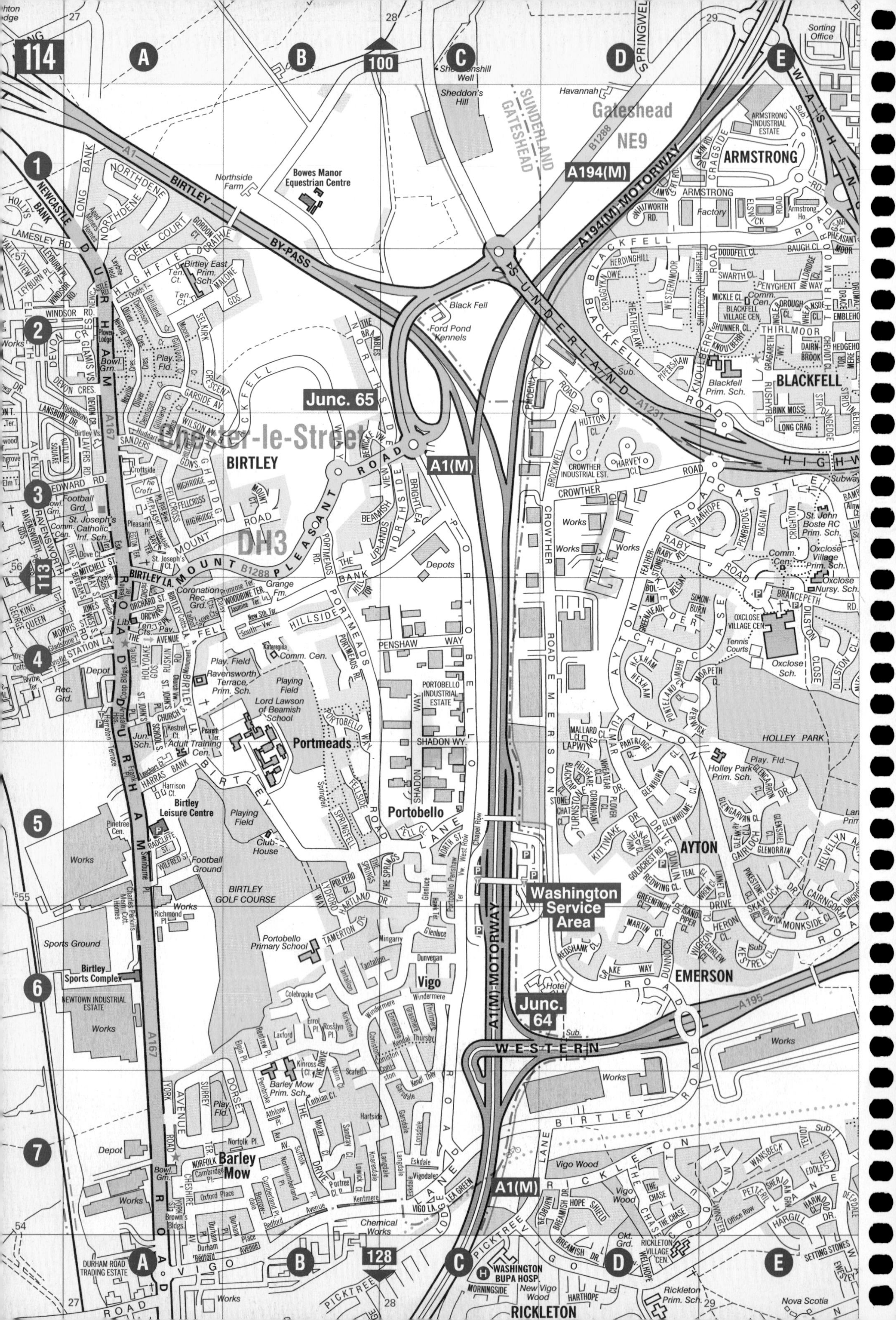
114
100
128
113
A
B
C
D
E
1
2
3
4
5
6
7
27
28
29
55
56
54
Gateshead
NE9
SUNDERLAND
GATESHEAD
ARMSTRONG
BLACKFELL
BIRTLEY
Chester-le-Street
DH3
Portmeads
Portobello
AYTON
EMERSON
Vigo
Barley Mow
RICKLETON
Sheddon's Hill
Havannah
Sorting Office
Armstrong Industrial Estate
Bowes Manor Equestrian Centre
Northside Farm
Black Fell
Ford Pond Kennels
A194(M)
A194(M) MOTORWAY
A1(M)
A1(M) MOTORWAY
Junc. 65
Junc. 64
A1
BIRTLEY BY-PASS
A167
DURHAM ROAD
B1288
A1231
A195
SUNDERLAND ROAD
NEWCASTLE BANK
LONG BANK
NORTHDENE
DENE COURT
HIGHFIELD
Birtley East Prim. Sch.
PLEASANT ROAD
MOUNT ROAD
BIRTLEY LA.
NORTHSIDE
PORTOBELLO ROAD
PORTMEADS RD.
PENSHAW WAY
PORTOBELLO INDUSTRIAL ESTATE
SHADON WY.
Depots
Crowther Industrial Est.
CROWTHER ROAD
EMERSON ROAD
Blackfell Prim. Sch.
BLACKFELL ROAD
Oxclose Village Cen.
Oxclose Sch.
Oxclose Village Prim. Sch.
Oxclose Nursy. Sch.
St. John Boste RC Prim. Sch.
HOLLEY PARK
Holley Park Prim. Sch.
Washington Service Area
St. Joseph's Catholic Inf. Sch.
Ravensworth Terrace Prim. Sch.
Lord Lawson of Beamish School
Adult Training Cen.
Birtley Leisure Centre
Birtley Golf Course
Football Ground
Club House
Playing Field
Sports Ground
Birtley Sports Complex
Newtown Industrial Estate
Works
Depot
Portobello Primary School
Barley Mow Prim. Sch.
Chemical Works
Vigo Wood
WESTERN
BIRTLEY LANE
RICKLETON WAY
VIGO LANE
PICKTREE LANE
Rickleton Village Cen.
Rickleton Prim. Sch.
WASHINGTON BUPA HOSP.
New Vigo Wood
Durham Road Trading Estate
Nova Scotia
SETTING STONES

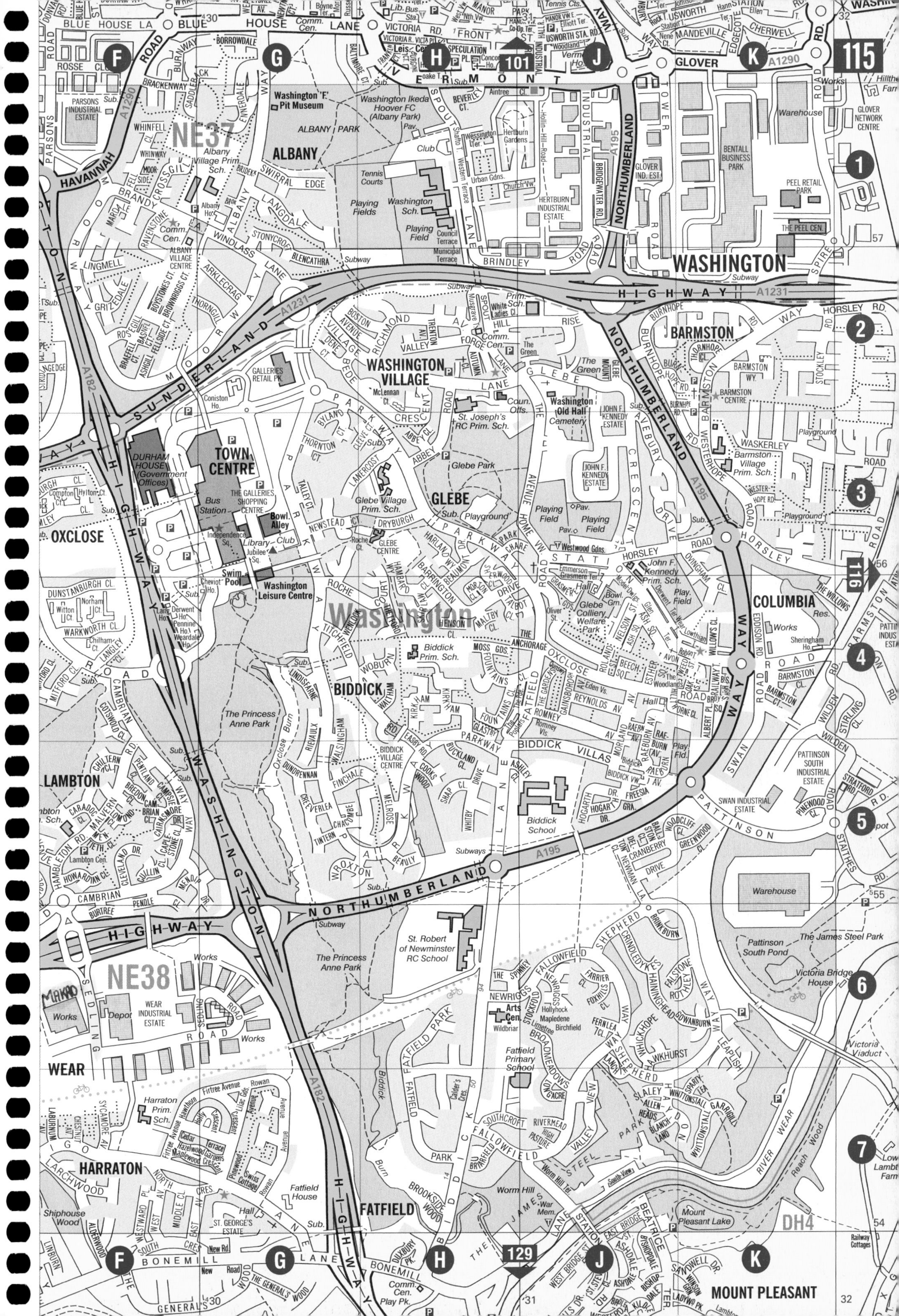
115
WASHINGTON
NE37
NE38
DH4
ALBANY
WASHINGTON VILLAGE
TOWN CENTRE
GLEBE
OXCLOSE
BIDDICK
BARMSTON
COLUMBIA
LAMBTON
WEAR
HARRATON
FATFIELD
MOUNT PLEASANT
Washington
BLUE HOUSE LANE
GLOVER
HAVANNAH ROAD
SUNDERLAND HIGHWAY
NORTHUMBERLAND WAY
NORTHUMBERLAND HIGHWAY
WASHINGTON HIGHWAY
HIGHWAY
A1231
A1290
A195
A182
PARKWAY
OXCLOSE ROAD
BIDDICK VILLAS
PATTINSON ROAD
BONEMILL LANE
RIVER WEAR
Washington 'F' Pit Museum
Washington Ikeda Hoover FC (Albany Park)
Albany Village Prim. Sch.
Washington Sch.
Playing Fields
DURHAM HOUSE (Government Offices)
THE GALLERIES SHOPPING CENTRE
Bus Station
Washington Leisure Centre
Washington Old Hall
Glebe Park
Glebe Village Prim. Sch.
Biddick Prim. Sch.
Biddick School
The Princess Anne Park
St. Robert of Newminster RC School
John F. Kennedy Prim. Sch.
Barmston Village Prim. Sch.
BENTALL BUSINESS PARK
PEEL RETAIL PARK
THE PEEL CEN.
GLOVER NETWORK CENTRE
GLOVER IND. EST.
HERTBURN INDUSTRIAL ESTATE
PARSONS INDUSTRIAL ESTATE
WEAR INDUSTRIAL ESTATE
PATTINSON SOUTH INDUSTRIAL ESTATE
SWAN INDUSTRIAL ESTATE
The James Steel Park
Pattinson South Pond
Victoria Bridge House
Victoria Viaduct
Fatfield Primary School
Harraton Prim. Sch.
Worm Hill
Mount Pleasant Lake
Shiphouse Wood
Fatfield House
101
116
129
F G H J K
1 2 3 4 5 6 7
30 31 32
54 55 56 57

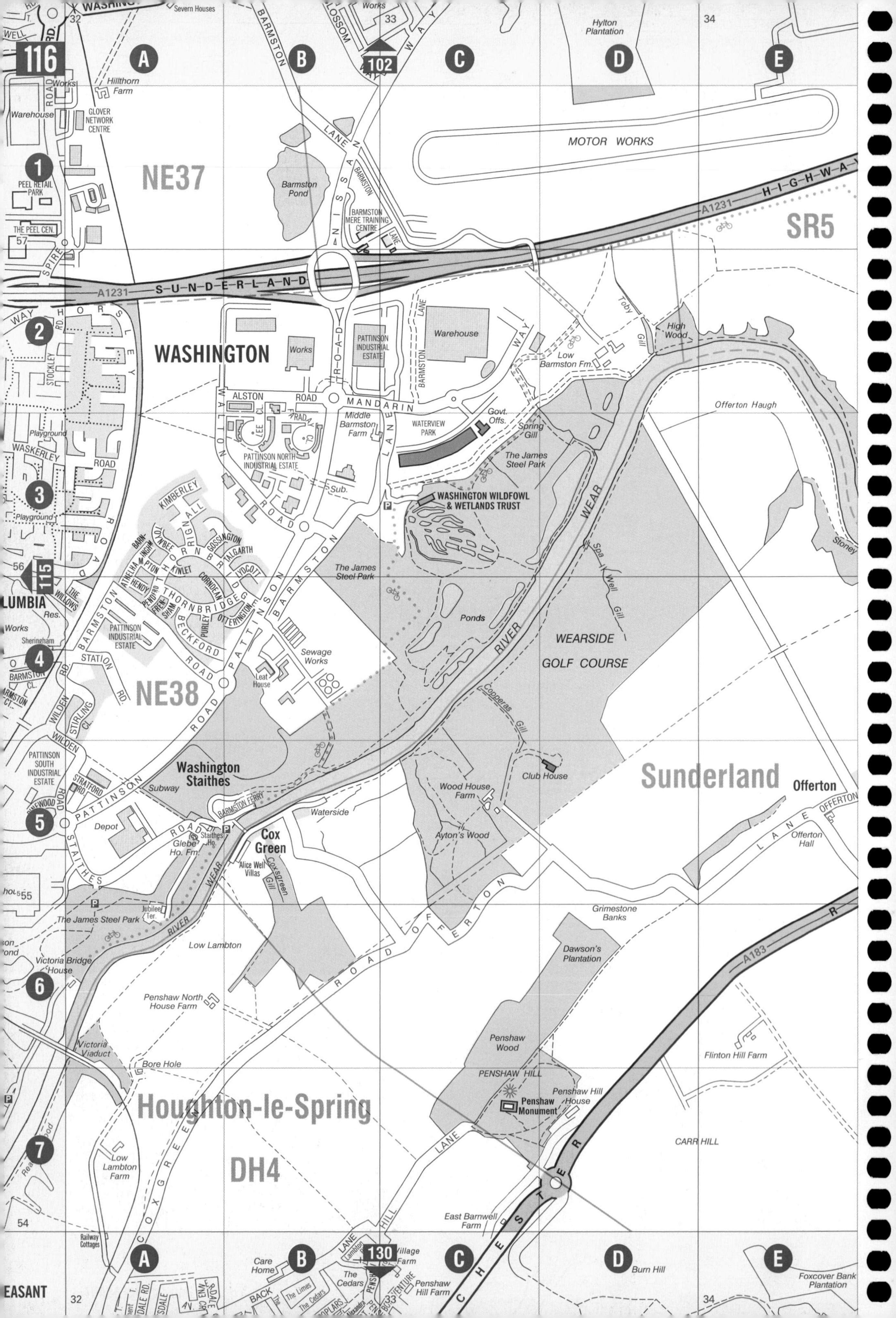

WASHINGTON
NE37
NE38
SR5
DH4
Sunderland
Houghton-le-Spring
Offerton
Cox Green
Washington Staithes
MOTOR WORKS
Hylton Plantation
Barmston Pond
Severn Houses
Hillthorn Farm
GLOVER NETWORK CENTRE
PEEL RETAIL PARK
THE PEEL CEN.
Warehouse
Works
BARMSTON MERE TRAINING CENTRE
PATTINSON INDUSTRIAL ESTATE
PATTINSON NORTH INDUSTRIAL ESTATE
PATTINSON SOUTH INDUSTRIAL ESTATE
Middle Barmston Farm
WATERVIEW PARK
Govt. Offs.
Low Barmston Fm.
High Wood
Toby Gill
Spring Gill
The James Steel Park
WASHINGTON WILDFOWL & WETLANDS TRUST
Ponds
Sewage Works
Leat House
WEARSIDE GOLF COURSE
Spa Well Gill
Copperas Gill
Club House
Wood House Farm
Ayton's Wood
Waterside
Alice Well Villas
Coxgreen Gill
RIVER WEAR
Offerton Haugh
Stoney
Offerton Hall
Grimestone Banks
Dawson's Plantation
Penshaw Wood
PENSHAW HILL
Penshaw Monument
Penshaw Hill House
Flinton Hill Farm
CARR HILL
East Barnwell Farm
Burn Hill
Foxcover Bank Plantation
Low Lambton
Penshaw North House Farm
Victoria Bridge House
Victoria Viaduct
Bore Hole
Low Lambton Farm
Railway Cottages
Care Home
The Cedars
Penshaw Hill Farm
Village Farm
Depot
Subway
Glebe Ho. Fm.
Staithes Ho.
Jubilee Ter.
A1231
SUNDERLAND HIGHWAY
A183
CHESTER ROAD
OFFERTON LANE
COXGREEN
LANE
PENSHAW
BARMSTON FERRY
MANDARIN WAY
ALSTON ROAD
WALTON ROAD
FARADAY CL.
LEE CL.
BARMSTON LANE
BARMSTON ROAD
BARMSTON WAY
PATTINSON ROAD
STAITHES ROAD
WILDEN RD.
STIRLING CL.
STATION RD.
STRATFORD RD.
BECKFORD
THORNBRIDGE
KIMBERLEY
GOSSINGTON
TALGARTH
LYDCOTT
CORNDEAN
OTTERINGTON
PURLEY
KINLET
HENDY
ATHELHAMPTON
FRENSHAM
PENDRO
TOWBEE
BARNINGHAM
RIGNALL
HORSLEY ROAD
STOCKLEY RD.
WASKERLEY ROAD
Playground
LUMBIA
Res.
Sheringham
THE WILLOWS
SPIRE
WASHINGTON
Sub.
Hylton
Works
102
115
130
A B C D E
1 2 3 4 5 6 7
32 33 34
54 55 56 57

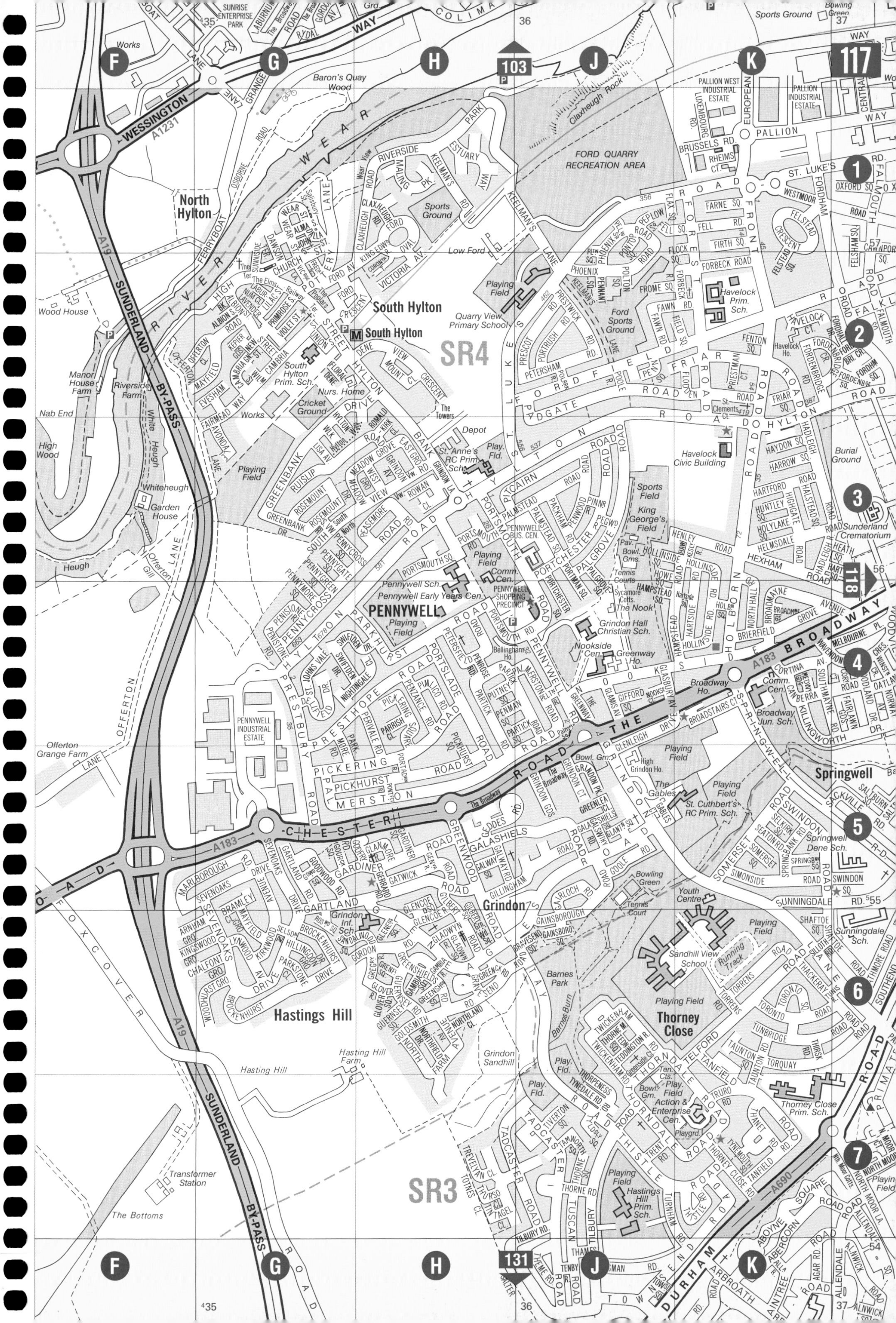

117
103
118
131
F
G
H
J
K
1
2
3
4
5
6
7
35
36
37
SR4
SR3
North Hylton
South Hylton
PENNYWELL
Grindon
Hastings Hill
Thorney Close
Springwell
RIVER WEAR
WESSINGTON WAY
A1231
SUNDERLAND BY-PASS
A19
CHESTER ROAD
A183
THE BROADWAY
DURHAM ROAD
A690
FORD QUARRY RECREATION AREA
Claxheugh Rock
Baron's Quay Wood
PALLION WEST INDUSTRIAL ESTATE
PALLION INDUSTRIAL ESTATE
PENNYWELL INDUSTRIAL ESTATE
SUNRISE ENTERPRISE PARK
Sunderland Crematorium
Burial Ground
Havelock Civic Building
Havelock Prim. Sch.
Quarry View Primary School
South Hylton Prim. Sch.
St. Anne's RC Prim. Sch.
Pennywell Sch.
Pennywell Early Years Cen.
Grindon Hall Christian Sch.
Broadway Jun. Sch.
St. Cuthbert's RC Prim. Sch.
Springwell Dene Sch.
Sunningdale Sch.
Sandhill View School
Thorney Close Prim. Sch.
Hastings Hill Prim. Sch.
Grindon Inf. Sch.
King George's Field
Wood House
Manor House Farm
Riverside Farm
Nab End
High Wood
Whiteheugh
Garden House
Offerton Grange Farm
Hasting Hill Farm
Hasting Hill
Transformer Station
The Bottoms
Grindon Sandhill
Barnes Park
Low Ford
FOXCOVER ROAD

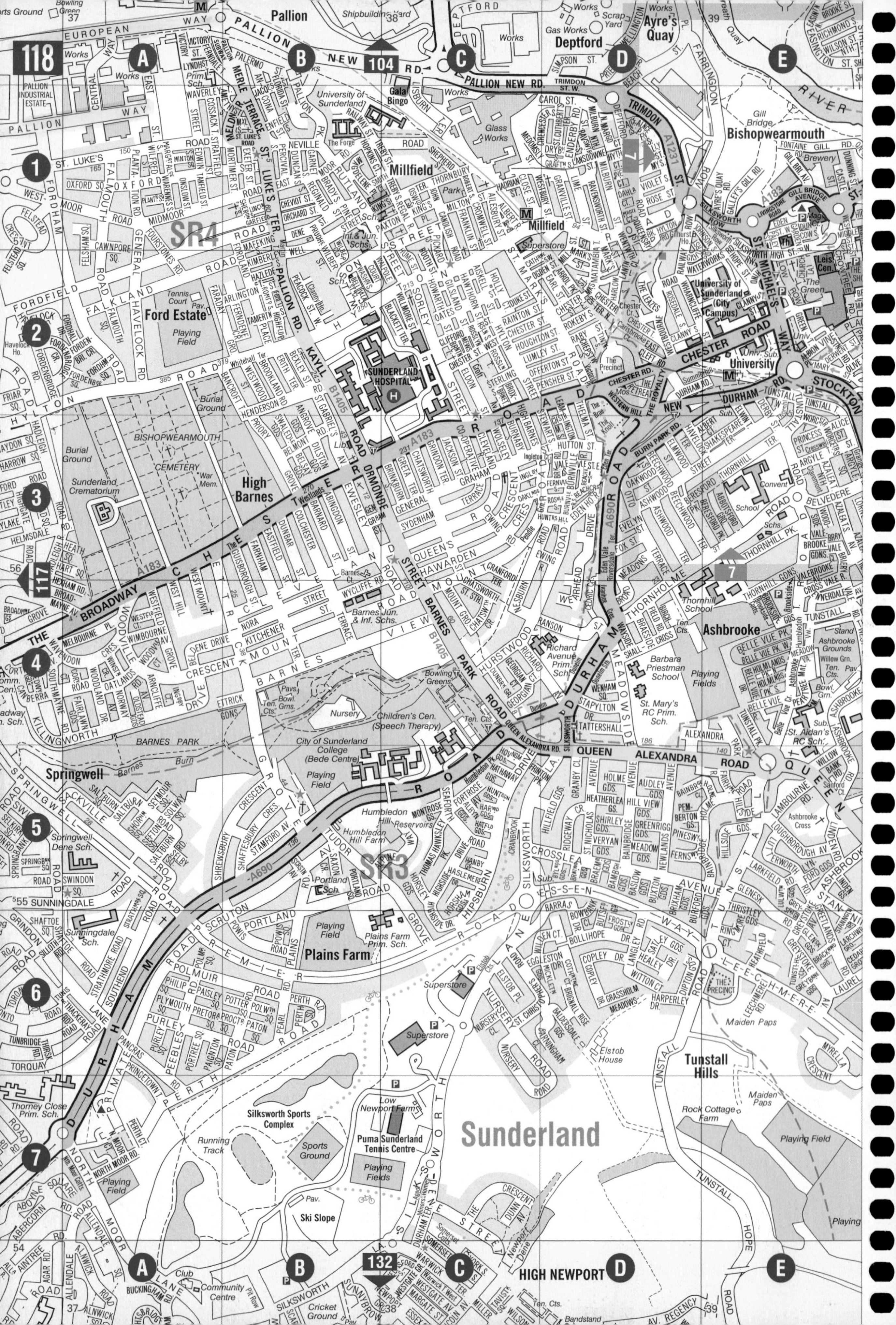

118
104
132
117
7
A
B
C
D
E
1
2
3
4
5
6
7
Pallion
Deptford
Ayre's Quay
Bishopwearmouth
Millfield
Ford Estate
High Barnes
Springwell
Plains Farm
Ashbrooke
Tunstall Hills
Sunderland
HIGH NEWPORT
SR4
SR3
PALLION NEW RD.
EUROPEAN WAY
PALLION INDUSTRIAL ESTATE
University of Sunderland
Gala Bingo
Glass Works
Gas Works
Shipbuilding Yard
RIVER
Gill Bridge
Brewery
University of Sunderland (City Campus)
CHESTER ROAD
University
STOCKTON
SUNDERLAND HOSPITAL
Superstore
BISHOPWEARMOUTH CEMETERY
Burial Ground
Sunderland Crematorium
Tennis Court
Playing Field
THE BROADWAY
CHESTER ROAD
DURHAM ROAD
QUEEN ALEXANDRA ROAD
BARNES PARK
City of Sunderland College (Bede Centre)
Humbledon Hill Reservoirs
Humbledon Hill Farm
Nursery
Children's Cen. (Speech Therapy)
Richard Avenue Prim. Sch.
Barbara Priestman School
St. Mary's RC Prim. Sch.
St. Aidan's RC Sch.
Thornhill School
Convent
School
Springwell Dene Sch.
Sunningdale Sch.
Portland Sch.
Plains Farm Prim. Sch.
Thorney Close Prim. Sch.
Silksworth Sports Complex
Running Track
Sports Ground
Puma Sunderland Tennis Centre
Playing Fields
Low Newport Farm
Ski Slope
Elstob House
Rock Cottage Farm
Maiden Paps
THE PRECINCT
Community Centre
Cricket Ground
Bandstand
A183
A690
A1231
B1405

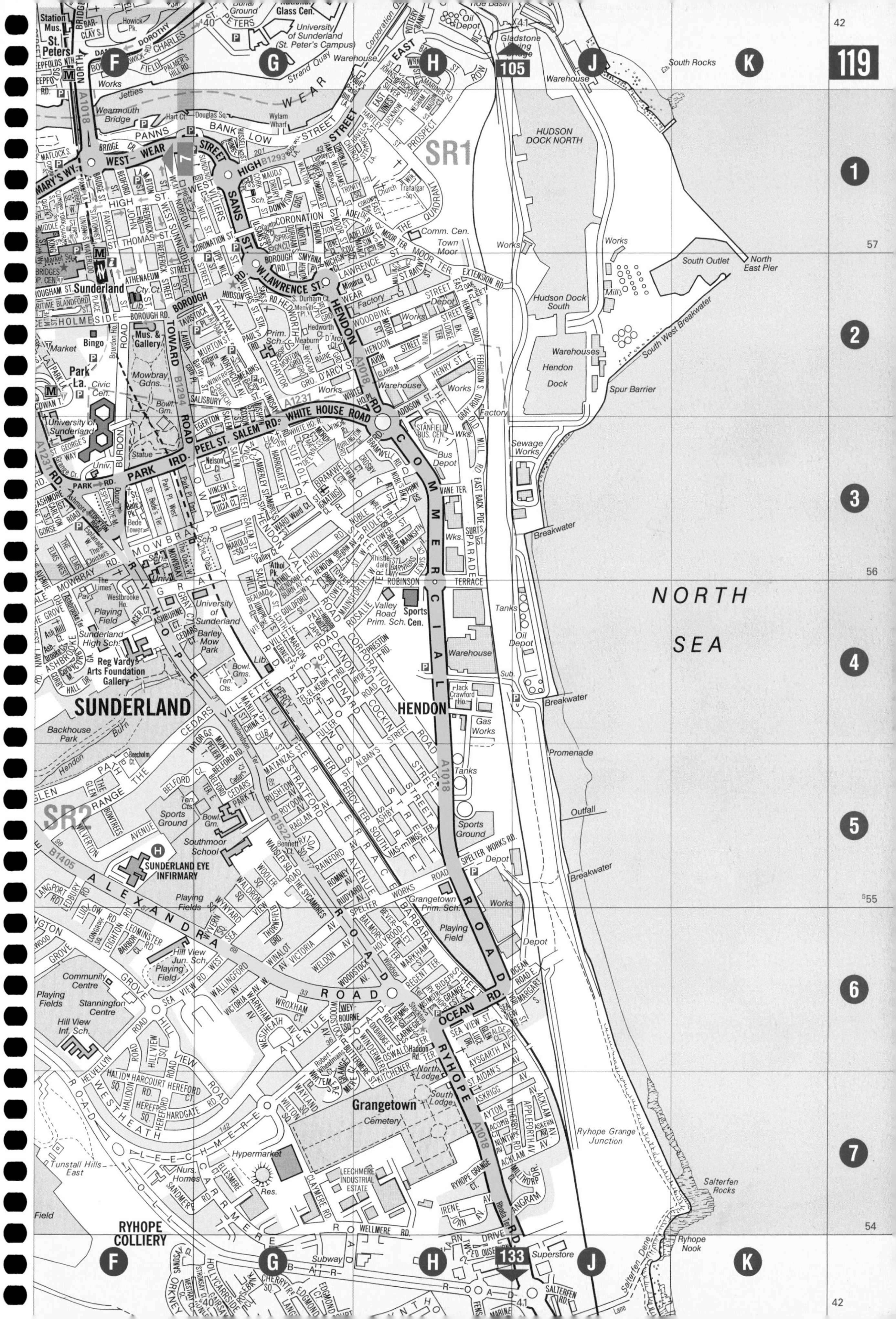
NORTH
SEA
SUNDERLAND
Sunderland
HENDON
Grangetown
RYHOPE
COLLIERY
SR1
SR2
105
133
F
G
H
J
K
1
2
3
4
5
6
7
42
57
56
55
54
Station Mus.
St. Peters
University of Sunderland (St. Peter's Campus)
National Glass Cen.
Gladstone Swing Bridge
Oil Depot
South Rocks
Warehouse
Strand Quay
Wearmouth Bridge
Jetties
Works
WEAR
HUDSON DOCK NORTH
Hudson Dock South
Hendon Dock
Warehouses
Spur Barrier
South West Breakwater
South Outlet
North East Pier
Mills
Comm. Cen.
Town Moor
Church
Trafalgar Sq.
Mus. & Gallery
Mowbray Gdns.
Park La.
Civic Cen.
University of Sunderland
Market
Bingo
Cty. Ct.
Lib.
Factory
Depot
Sewage Works
Bus Depot
Breakwater
Tanks
Oil Depot
Sub.
Jack Crawford Ho.
Gas Works
Promenade
Outfall
Sports Ground
Sports Cen.
Valley Road Prim. Sch.
Warehouse
Barley Mow Park
Sunderland High Sch.
Reg Vardy Arts Foundation Gallery
Backhouse Park
Southmoor School
SUNDERLAND EYE INFIRMARY
Playing Fields
Hill View Jun. Sch.
Community Centre
Stannington Centre
Hill View Inf. Sch.
Grangetown Prim. Sch.
Grangetown Cemetery
North Lodge
South Lodge
Hypermarket
LEECHMERE INDUSTRIAL ESTATE
Nurs. Homes
Res.
Tunstall Hills East
Ryhope Grange Junction
Salterfen Rocks
Ryhope Nook
Salterfen Dene
Superstore
Subway
HIGH ST. WEST
WEST WEAR STREET
HIGH STREET EAST
LOW STREET
BOROUGH RD.
TOWARD ROAD
PARK RD.
PEEL ST.
SALEM RD.
WHITE HOUSE ROAD
HENDON RD.
COMMERCIAL ROAD
ROBINSON TERRACE
HENDON ROAD
OCEAN RD.
RYHOPE ROAD
ALEXANDRA ROAD
HENDON VALLEY ROAD
VILLETTE ROAD
CEDARS
THE GLEN
SEA VIEW RD. WEST
LEECHMERE
TOLL BAR RD.
A1018
A1231
B1293
B1294
B1405
B1522

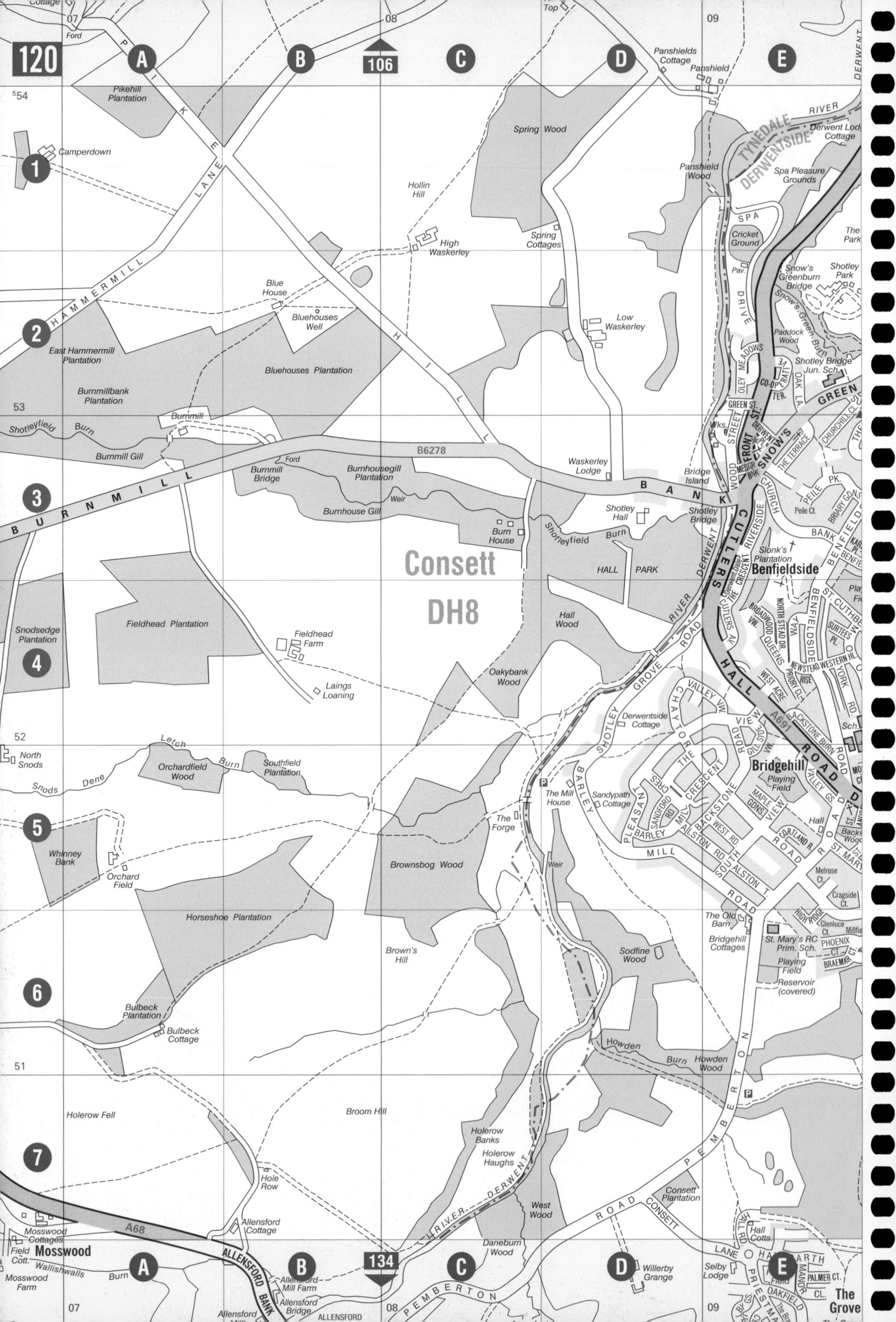

106
Pikehill Plantation
Camperdown
Pike Lane
Hammermill
East Hammermill Plantation
Burnmillbank Plantation
Burnmill
Shotleyfield Burn
Burnmill Gill
Burnmill Bank
B6278
Burnmill Bridge
Burnhousegill Plantation
Burnhouse Gill
Ford
Weir
Blue House
Bluehouses Well
Bluehouses Plantation
Hill
Hollin Hill
High Waskerley
Spring Wood
Spring Cottages
Low Waskerley
Waskerley Lodge
Panshields Cottage
Panshield
Panshield Wood
Bridge Island
Shotley Hall
Shotley Bridge
Burn House
Hall Park
Hall Wood
Consett
DH8
Snodsedge Plantation
Fieldhead Plantation
Fieldhead Farm
Laings Loaning
Oakybank Wood
North Snods
Letch Burn
Orchardfield Wood
Southfield Plantation
Snods Dene
Whinney Bank
Orchard Field
Horseshoe Plantation
Brownsbog Wood
Brown's Hill
The Forge
The Mill House
Weir
Bulbeck Plantation
Bulbeck Cottage
Holerow Fell
Broom Hill
Holerow Banks
Holerow Haughs
Hole Row
Allensford Cottage
A68
Mosswood Cottages
Field Cott.
Mosswood
Mosswood Farm
Wallishwalls Burn
Allensford Bank
Allensford Mill Farm
Allensford Bridge
Allensford
134
Pemberton Road
Daneburn Wood
West Wood
River Derwent
Consett Road
Consett Plantation
Willerby Grange
Selby Lodge
Hall Cotts.
Lane
Sodfine Wood
Howden Burn
Howden Wood
Derwentside Cottage
Sandypath Cottage
Shotley Grove Road
Barley Mill Road
Pleasant
Sandford Rd.
The Crescent
Backstone
West Rd.
Alston Rd.
South Alston T.
Bridgehill
Playing Field
Maple Gdns.
View
Portland R.
Melrose Ct.
Cragside Ct.
High Ridge
Glenluce Ct.
St. Mary's RC Prim. Sch.
Phoenix Ct.
Braemar
Playing Field
Reservoir (covered)
The Old Barn
Bridgehill Cottages
Chaytor Rd.
Valley Vw.
Gillside Vw.
Hall Road
A691
Backstone Burn Rd.
Valley Gs.
Hall
Sch.
Benfieldside
Slonk's Plantation
The Crescent
Cutlers Av.
Cutlers Bank
Riverside
Broadwood Vw.
Queens
North Stead Dr.
Way
Benfieldside
Newstead
Western Hl.
Prior Cl.
Rise
West Acre
Surtees Pl.
York Rd.
St. Cuthbert
Church Bank
Peile Pk.
Peile Ct.
Briary Gdns.
Benfield
Snow's Green
The Terrace
Churchill Cl.
Wks.
Green St.
Front St.
Derwent Pl.
Mesgr. Bnk.
Wood Street
Oley Meadows
Co-op Ter.
Pratt Ter.
Oak La.
Shotley Bridge Jun. Sch.
Paddock Wood
Snow's Green Burn
Snow's Greenburn Bridge
Shotley Park
The Park
Cricket Ground
Pav.
Drive
Spa
Spa Pleasure Grounds
Tyndale
Derwentside
River Derwent
Derwent Lodge Cottage
The Grove
Palmer Ct.
Oakfield
Priestman
Manor
Hall Garth
Top
Ford
07
08
09
54
53
52
51

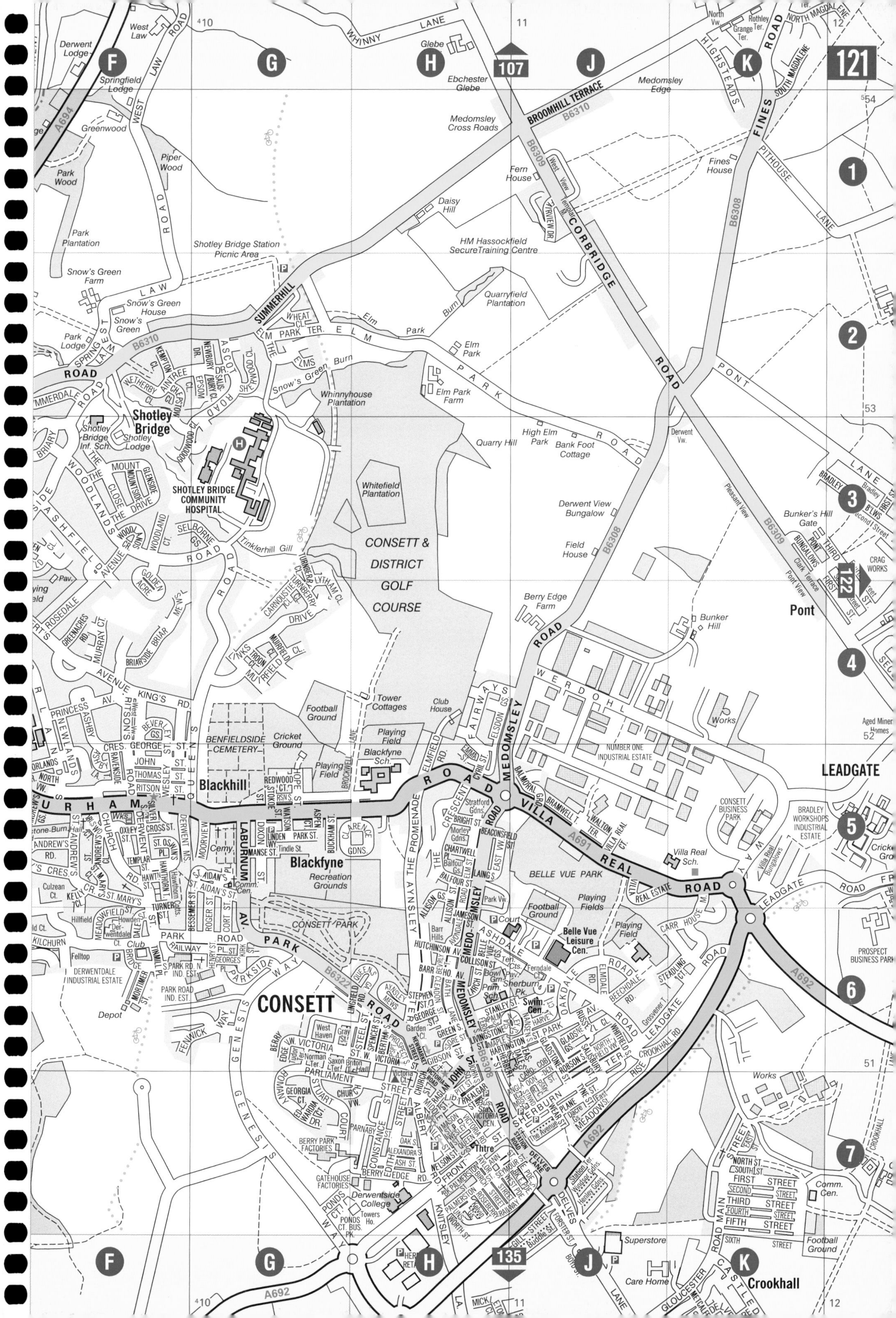

F G H **107** J K

West Law

Derwent Lodge

Springfield Lodge

Glebe

Ebchester Glebe

Medomsley Edge

North Vw.

Rothley Grange Ter.

NORTH MAGDALENE

SOUTH MAGDALENE

HIGHSTEADS

FINES ROAD

Greenwood

Piper Wood

Medomsley Cross Roads

Fern House

West View

CORBRIDGE ROAD

Fines House

PITHOUSE LANE

1

Park Plantation

Daisy Hill

554

Snow's Green Farm

HM Hassockfield Secure Training Centre

PONT

53

2

SUMMERHILL

WHEAT CL.

ELM PARK TER.

ELM PARK

Quarryfield Plantation

Burn

Elm Park

ELM PARK ROAD

Elm Park Farm

Derwent Vw.

B6308

Snow's Green House

Snow's Green

ASCOT CL.

High Elm Park

Quarry Hill

Bank Foot Cottage

BRADLEY LANE

Bradley Blws.

Second Street

3

Shotley Bridge

B6310

Shotley Bridge Inf. Sch.

Shotley Lodge

B6309

Derwent View Bungalow

BUNGALOWS

PONT

Third First

Clara Terrace

Bunker's Hill Gate

CRAG WORKS

SHOTLEY BRIDGE COMMUNITY HOSPITAL

Whitefield Plantation

Field House

Pleasant View

Pont View

122

Pont

Tinklerhill Gill

CONSETT & DISTRICT GOLF COURSE

Berry Edge Farm

Bunker Hill

4

Aged Miner Homes

52

Football Ground

Tower Cottages

Club House

FAIRWAYS

MEDOMSLEY ROAD

WERDOHL

Works

NUMBER ONE INDUSTRIAL ESTATE

LEADGATE

Cricket Ground

Playing Field

Blackfyne Sch.

Consett Business Park

BRADLEY WORKSHOPS INDUSTRIAL ESTATE

5

BENFIELDSIDE CEMETERY

Playing Field

Blackhill

THE PROMENADE

ELMFIELD RD.

CRESCENT

VILLA REAL

BALMORAL GRO.

WALTON TER.

Villa Real Sch.

VILLA REAL ROAD

Consett

Cricket Gro.

DURHAM ROAD

Blackfyne

Recreation Grounds

BELLE VUE PARK

CARR HOUSE M.

LEADGATE ROAD

A692

PROSPECT BUSINESS PARK

6

CONSETT PARK

Football Ground

Playing Fields

Belle Vue Leisure Cen.

Playing Field

51

Derwentdale Industrial Estate

Depot

PARK ROAD

B6322

Park Road Ind. Est.

CONSETT

Swim. Cen.

Works

7

Derwentside College

Towers Ho.

Thtre

DELVES LANE

A692

Comm. Cen.

Superstore

Football Ground

F G H **135** J K

Crookhall

A692

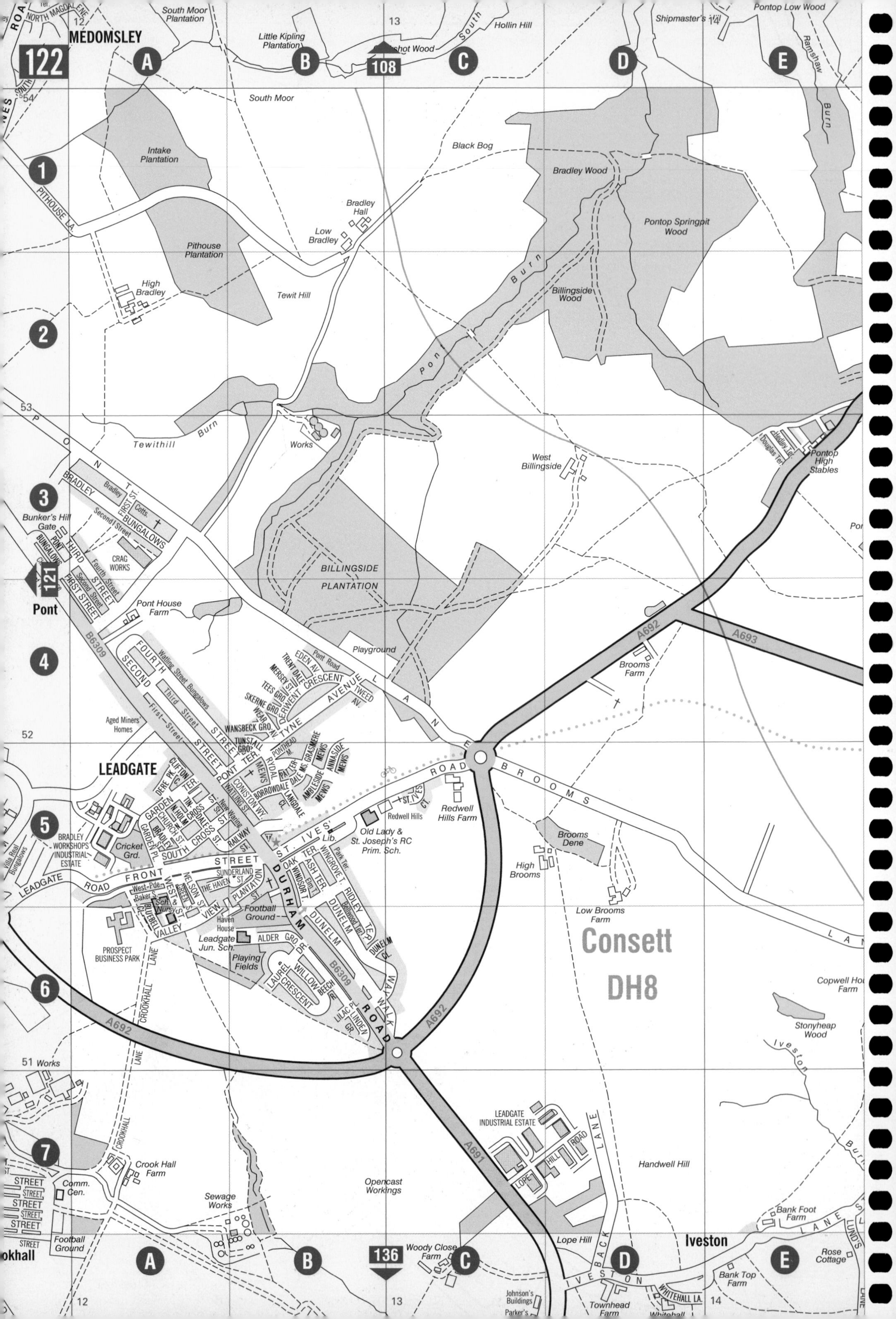
MEDOMSLEY
South Moor Plantation
Little Kipling Plantation
Hollin Hill
Shipmaster's Hill
Pontop Low Wood
108
South Moor
Intake Plantation
Black Bog
Bradley Wood
Ramshaw Burn
Pontop Springpit Wood
PITHOUSE LA.
Bradley Hall
Low Bradley
Pithouse Plantation
High Bradley
Tewit Hill
Billingside Wood
Pont Burn
Tewithill Burn
Works
West Billingside
Pontop High Stables
Bunker's Hill Gate
BRADLEY BUNGALOWS
CRAG WORKS
BILLINGSIDE PLANTATION
121
Pont
Pont House Farm
B6309
Playground
A692
A693
Brooms Farm
PONT LANE
Aged Miners' Homes
LEADGATE
ROAD
BROOMS LANE
Redwell Hills
Redwell Hills Farm
Old Lady & St. Joseph's RC Prim. Sch.
Lib.
Brooms Dene
High Brooms
BRADLEY WORKSHOPS INDUSTRIAL ESTATE
Cricket Grd.
LEADGATE ROAD
FRONT STREET
DURHAM ROAD
Football Ground
Haven House
Leadgate Jun. Sch.
Playing Fields
PROSPECT BUSINESS PARK
CROOKHALL LANE
Low Brooms Farm
Consett
DH8
Copwell House Farm
Stonyheap Wood
Iveston Burn
A692
A691
LEADGATE INDUSTRIAL ESTATE
BACK LANE
Handwell Hill
Crook Hall Farm
Comm. Cen.
Sewage Works
Opencast Workings
Football Ground
Bank Foot Farm
Lope Hill
Iveston
Rose Cottage
Woody Close Farm
136
Bank Top Farm
IVESTON LA.
WHITEHALL LA.
Townhead Farm
Johnson's Buildings
Parker's

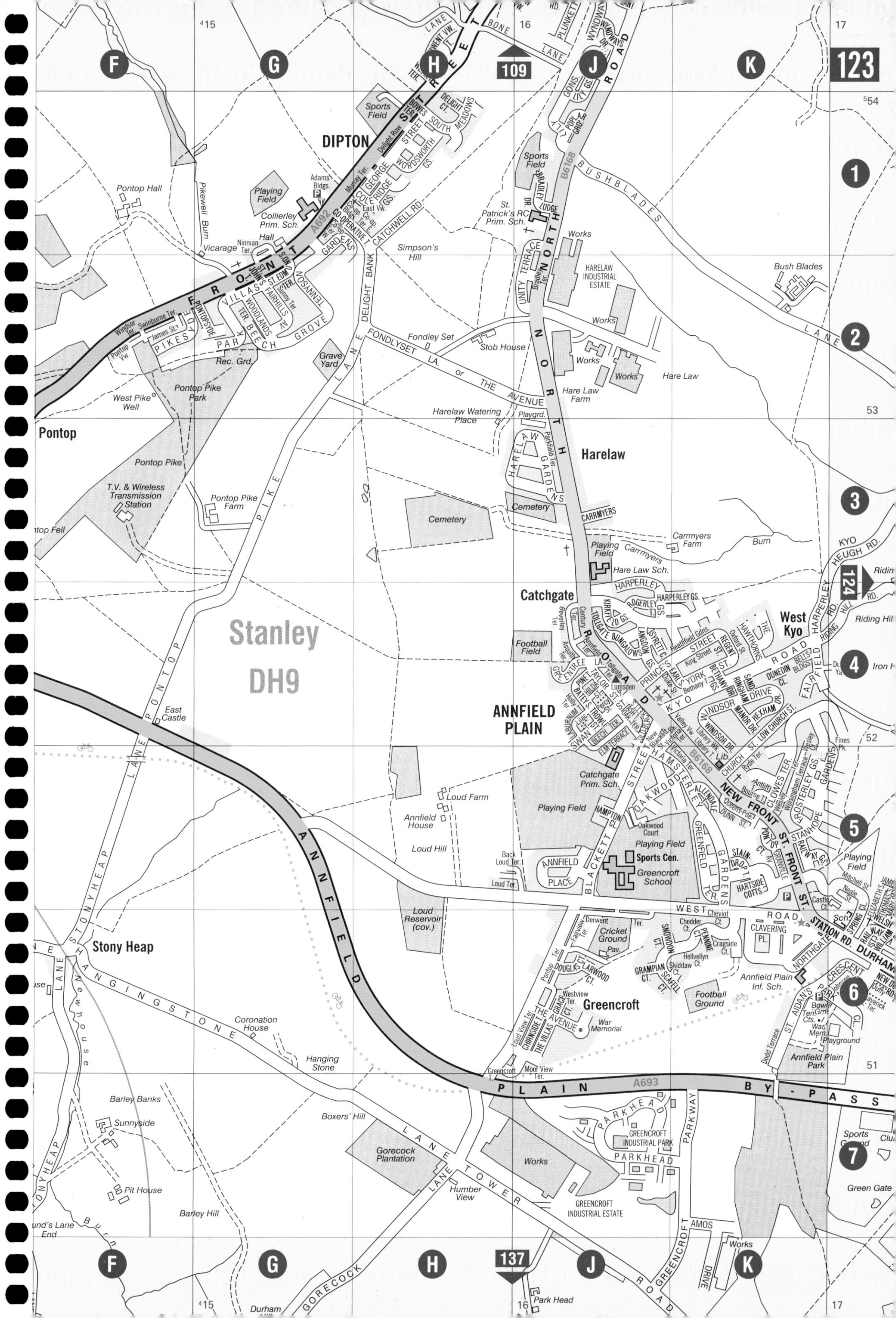

DIPTON
Pontop
Stanley
DH9
Harelaw
Catchgate
ANNFIELD PLAIN
West Kyo
Greencroft
Stony Heap
FRONT STREET
NORTH ROAD
B6168
A692
A693
ANNFIELD PLAIN BY-PASS
FONDLYSET LA. or THE AVENUE
PONTOP PIKE LANE
DELIGHT BANK LANE
STONYHEAP LANE
HANGINGSTONE LANE
TOWER ROAD
GORECOCK LANE
GREENCROFT ROAD
WEST ROAD
KYO ROAD
NEW FRONT ST.
BUSHBLADES LANE
KYO HEUGH RD.
HARPERLEY RD.
RIDING HILL RD.
STATION RD.
DURHAM
Pontop Hall
Pikewell Burn
Playing Field
Collierley Prim. Sch.
Vicarage
Sports Field
Simpson's Hill
St. Patrick's RC Prim. Sch.
Works
HARELAW INDUSTRIAL ESTATE
Bush Blades
Fondley Set
Stob House
Grave Yard
Hare Law
Hare Law Farm
West Pike Well
Pontop Pike Park
Pontop Pike
T.V. & Wireless Transmission Station
Pontop Pike Farm
Rec. Grd.
Harelaw Watering Place
Cemetery
Carrmyers Farm
Burn
Hare Law Sch.
Football Field
East Castle
Catchgate Prim. Sch.
Loud Farm
Annfield House
Loud Hill
Sports Cen.
Greencroft School
Loud Reservoir (cov.)
Cricket Ground
Football Ground
Annfield Plain Inf. Sch.
Annfield Plain Park
War Memorial
Coronation House
Hanging Stone
Barley Banks
Sunnyside
Boxers' Hill
Gorecock Plantation
Pit House
Barley Hill
Humber View
GREENCROFT INDUSTRIAL PARK
GREENCROFT INDUSTRIAL ESTATE
Park Head
Green Gate
Iron H
109
124
137
F G H J K
1 2 3 4 5 6 7
415 16 17
54 53 52 51

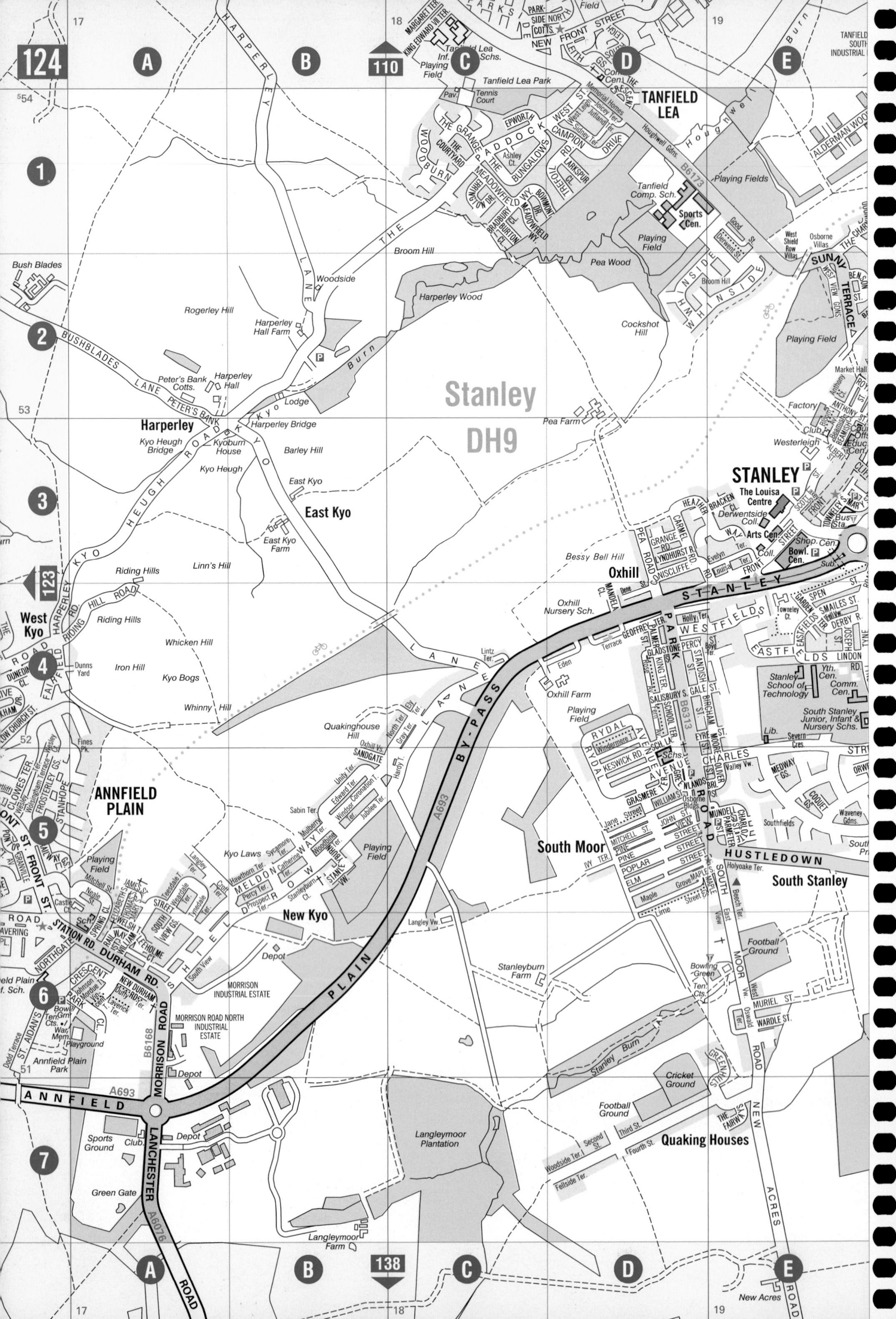

Stanley
DH9
TANFIELD LEA
STANLEY
Harperley
East Kyo
West Kyo
ANNFIELD PLAIN
New Kyo
Oxhill
South Moor
South Stanley
Quaking Houses
Tanfield Lea Park
Broom Hill
Harperley Wood
Pea Wood
Cockshot Hill
Rogerley Hill
Harperley Hall Farm
Harperley Hall
Peter's Bank Cotts.
Kyo Lodge
Harperley Bridge
Kyo Heugh Bridge
Kyoburn House
Barley Hill
Kyo Heugh
East Kyo
East Kyo Farm
Pea Farm
Bessy Bell Hill
Riding Hills
Linn's Hill
Whicken Hill
Iron Hill
Kyo Bogs
Whinny Hill
Dunns Yard
Bush Blades
Woodside
Quakinghouse Hill
Kyo Laws
Oxhill Farm
Oxhill Nursery Sch.
Stanleyburn Farm
Langleymoor Plantation
Langleymoor Farm
Green Gate
MORRISON INDUSTRIAL ESTATE
MORRISON ROAD NORTH INDUSTRIAL ESTATE
Annfield Plain Park
Tanfield Comp. Sch.
Sports Cen.
Playing Field
Playing Fields
Football Ground
Cricket Ground
Stanley School of Technology
South Stanley Junior, Infant & Nursery Schs.
The Louisa Centre
Derwentside Coll.
Arts Cen.
New Acres
BUSHBLADES LANE
HARPERLEY LANE
KYO HEUGH ROAD
RIDING HILL ROAD
KYO LANE
STANLEY BY-PASS
ANNFIELD PLAIN
MORRISON ROAD
LANCHESTER ROAD
DURHAM RD.
STATION RD.
FRONT ST.
PARK ROAD
SOUTH MOOR ROAD
HUSTLEDOWN
WESTFIELDS
EASTFIELDS
NEW ACRES ROAD
A693
A6076
B6168
B6173
B6313

110
123
138

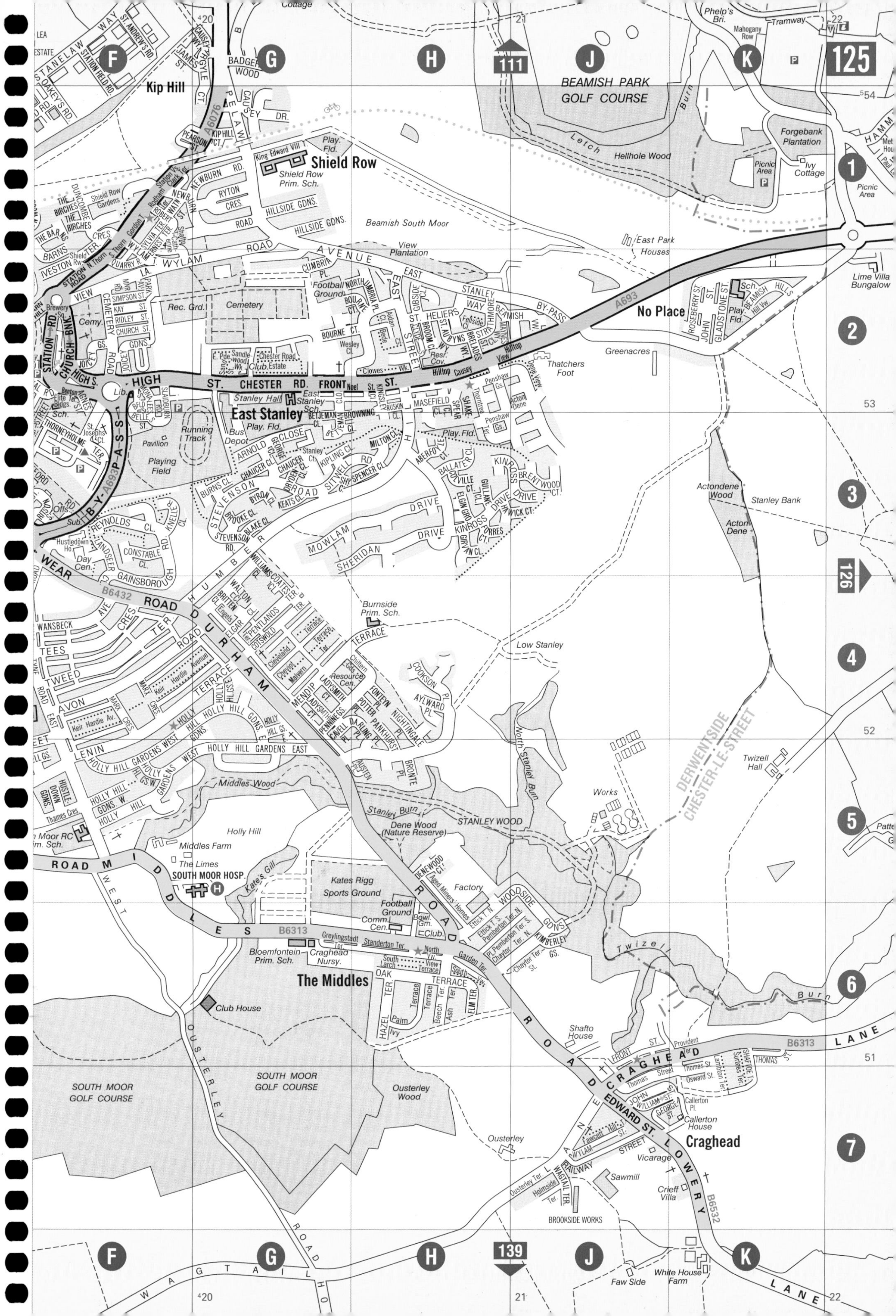
F
G
H
J
K
111
BEAMISH PARK
GOLF COURSE
Kip Hill
Shield Row
Shield Row
Prim. Sch.
King Edward VIII
Play. Fld.
Beamish South Moor
Hellhole Wood
Forgebank
Plantation
Picnic
Area
Ivy
Cottage
East Park
Houses
View
Plantation
Lime Villa
Bungalow
No Place
Greenacres
Thatchers
Foot
A693
A6076
A693
HIGH ST. CHESTER RD. FRONT ST.
STANLEY BY-PASS
East Stanley
Stanley Hall
Rec. Grd.
Cemetery
Cemy.
Running
Track
Pavilion
Playing
Field
Bus
Depot
Actondene
Wood
Acton
Dene
Stanley Bank
126
Burnside
Prim. Sch.
Low Stanley
B6432
DURHAM ROAD
WEAR ROAD
Resource
Cen.
Twizell
Hall
DERWENTSIDE
CHESTER-LE-STREET
Works
Middles Wood
Holly Hill
Middles Farm
The Limes
SOUTH MOOR HOSP.
Kate's Gill
Stanley Burn
Dene Wood
(Nature Reserve)
STANLEY WOOD
North Stanley Burn
Kates Rigg
Sports Ground
Football
Ground
Factory
Comm.
Cen.
B6313
MIDDLES ROAD
Bloemfontein
Prim. Sch.
Craghead
Nursy.
The Middles
Club House
Twizell Burn
Shafto
House
CRAGHEAD LANE
B6313
Callerton
House
Craghead
SOUTH MOOR
GOLF COURSE
SOUTH MOOR
GOLF COURSE
Ousterley
Wood
Ousterley
OUSTERLEY ROAD
Vicarage
Sawmill
Crieff
Villa
BROOKSIDE WORKS
B6532
LOWERY LANE
EDWARD ST.
139
WAGTAIL ROAD
Faw Side
White House
Farm
1
2
3
4
5
6
7
54
53
52
51
420
21
22

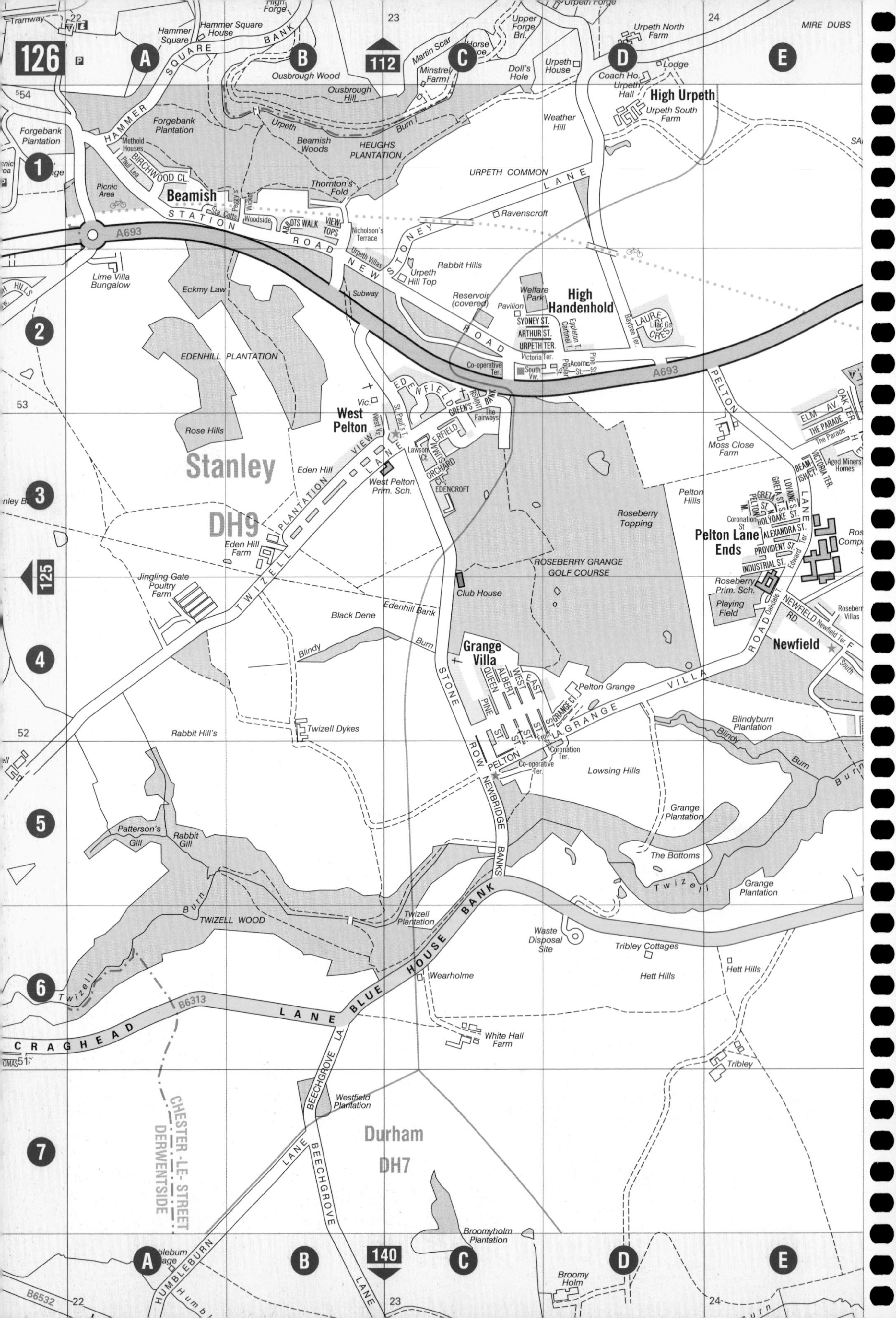

Beamish
Forgebank Plantation
Ousbrough Wood
Urpeth Burn
Beamish Woods
HEUGHS PLANTATION
Thornton's Fold
HAMMER SQUARE BANK
Hammer Square
Hammer Square House
Martin Scar
Minstrel Farm
Upper Forge Bri.
Doll's Hole
Urpeth House
Urpeth North Farm
Coach Ho.
Lodge
Urpeth Hall
High Urpeth
Urpeth South Farm
Weather Hill
MIRE DUBS
URPETH COMMON
LANE
Ravenscroft
STATION ROAD
NEW STONEY ROAD
A693
Nicholson's Terrace
Urpeth Villas
Urpeth Hill Top
Rabbit Hills
Lime Villa Bungalow
Eckmy Law
Subway
Reservoir (covered)
Welfare Park
Pavilion
High Handenhold
SYDNEY ST.
ARTHUR ST.
URPETH TER.
Victoria Ter.
Co-operative Ter.
South Vw.
Acorne St.
Pine St.
Baytree Ter.
LAUREL CRES.
Lilac Gs
EDENHILL PLANTATION
Rose Hills
Stanley
DH9
West Pelton
Vic.
Eden Hill
PLANTATION VIEW
LANE
West Pelton Prim. Sch.
ORCHARD CT.
EDENCROFT
The Fairways
Moss Close Farm
Pelton Hills
PELTON LANE
ELM AV.
OAK TER.
THE PARADE
Aged Miners Homes
VICTORIA TER.
Pelton Lane Ends
ALEXANDRA ST.
PROVIDENT ST.
INDUSTRIAL ST.
HOLYOAKE ST.
Rosebery Prim. Sch.
Playing Field
Roseberry Topping
ROSEBERRY GRANGE GOLF COURSE
Club House
Eden Hill Farm
Jingling Gate Poultry Farm
TWIZELL LANE
Black Dene
Edenhill Bank
Blindy Burn
Grange Villa
STONE ROW
QUEEN ST.
ALBERT ST.
PINE ST.
WEST ST.
EAST ST.
GRANGE CT.
Pelton Grange
GRANGE VILLA ROAD
NEWFIELD RD.
Newfield
Rosebery Villas
Twizell Dykes
Rabbit Hill's
PELTON
Co-operative Ter.
Coronation Ter.
Lowsing Hills
Blindyburn Plantation
Blindy Burn
Grange Plantation
The Bottoms
Twizell
Patterson's Gill
Rabbit Gill
TWIZELL WOOD
Burn
NEWBRIDGE BANKS
Twizell Plantation
BLUE HOUSE BANK
Waste Disposal Site
Tribley Cottages
Hett Hills
Wearholme
B6313
CRAGHEAD LANE
White Hall Farm
Tribley
BEECHGROVE LA.
Westfield Plantation
Durham
DH7
CHESTER-LE-STREET
DERWENTSIDE
BEECHGROVE LANE
Broomyholm Plantation
HUMBLEBURN LANE
Broomy Holm
B6532
Urpeth Forge
High Forge
Tramway
Picnic Area
Methold Houses
BIRCHWOOD CL.
Paul Lea
Sta. Cotts
Woodside
ABBOTS WALK
VIEW TOPS
Peggy's Wicket
112
125
140

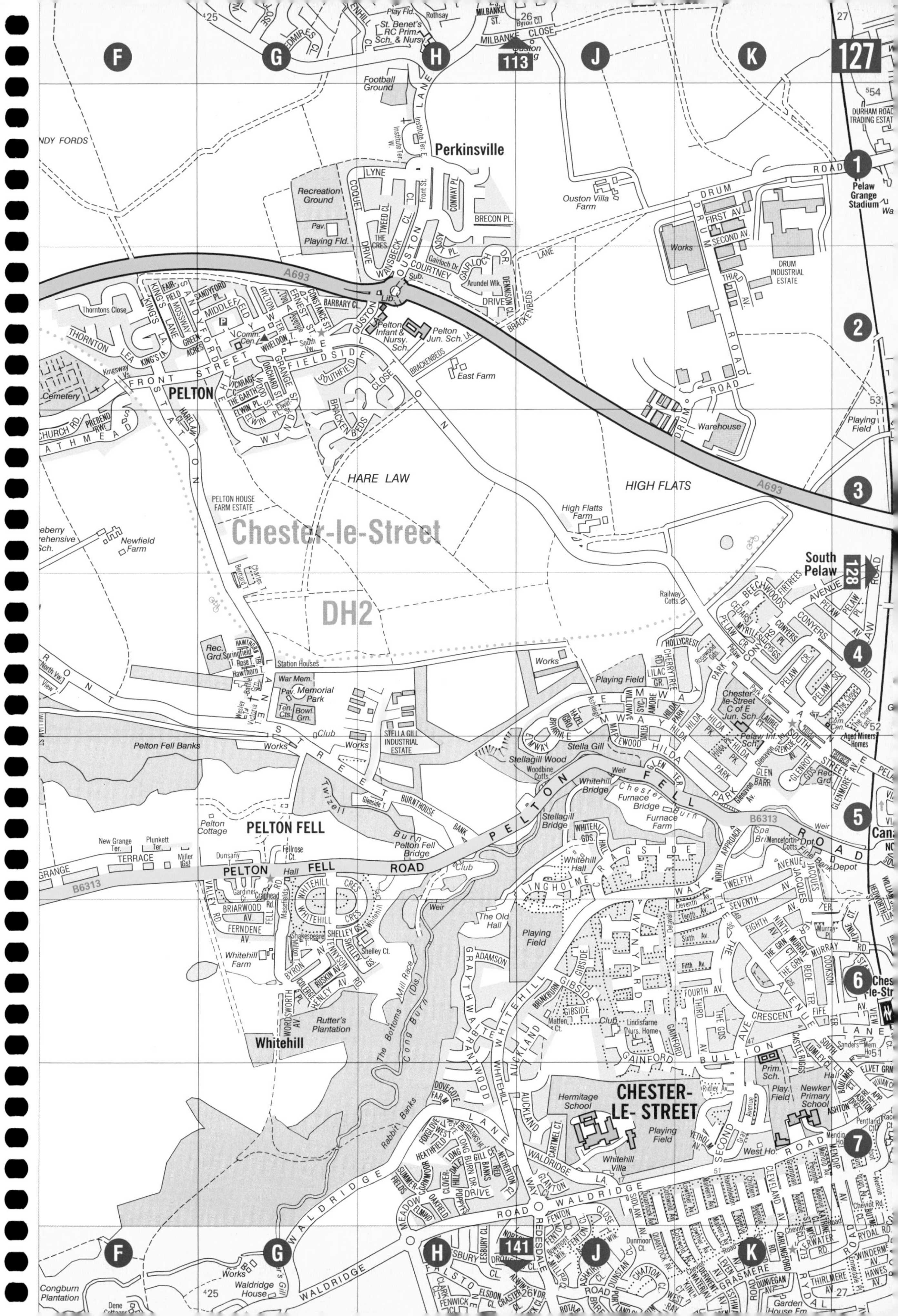
F
G
H
J
K
113
141
128
1
2
3
4
5
6
7
Perkinsville
PELTON
PELTON FELL
Whitehill
CHESTER-
LE- STREET
Chester-le-Street
DH2
South
Pelaw
HARE LAW
HIGH FLATS
A693
B6313
FRONT STREET
PELTON FELL ROAD
WALDRIDGE ROAD
WALDRIDGE LANE
DRUM ROAD
DRUM INDUSTRIAL ESTATE
Works
Warehouse
Pelaw Grange Stadium
Ouston Villa Farm
High Flatts Farm
East Farm
Newfield Farm
Whitehill Farm
Pelton Cottage
Rutter's Plantation
The Bottoms
Cong Burn
Rabbit Banks
Pelton Fell Banks
Stellagill Wood
Stella Gill
STELLA GILL INDUSTRIAL ESTATE
Memorial Park
War Mem.
Station Houses
Recreation Ground
Playing Fld.
Football Ground
Cemetery
PELTON HOUSE FARM ESTATE
Pelton Infant & Nursy. Sch.
Pelton Jun. Sch.
St. Benet's RC Prim. Sch. & Nursy.
Chester-le-Street C of E Jun. Sch.
Hermitage School
Newker Primary School
Whitehill Villa
Whitehill Hall
The Old Hall
Lindisfarne Nurs. Home
Furnace Farm
Chester Furnace Bridge
Whitehill Bridge
Stellagill Bridge
Pelton Fell Bridge
Waldridge House
Congburn Plantation
Dene Cottages
Railway Cotts.
Aged Miners Homes
Playing Field
Depot
DURHAM ROAD TRADING ESTATE

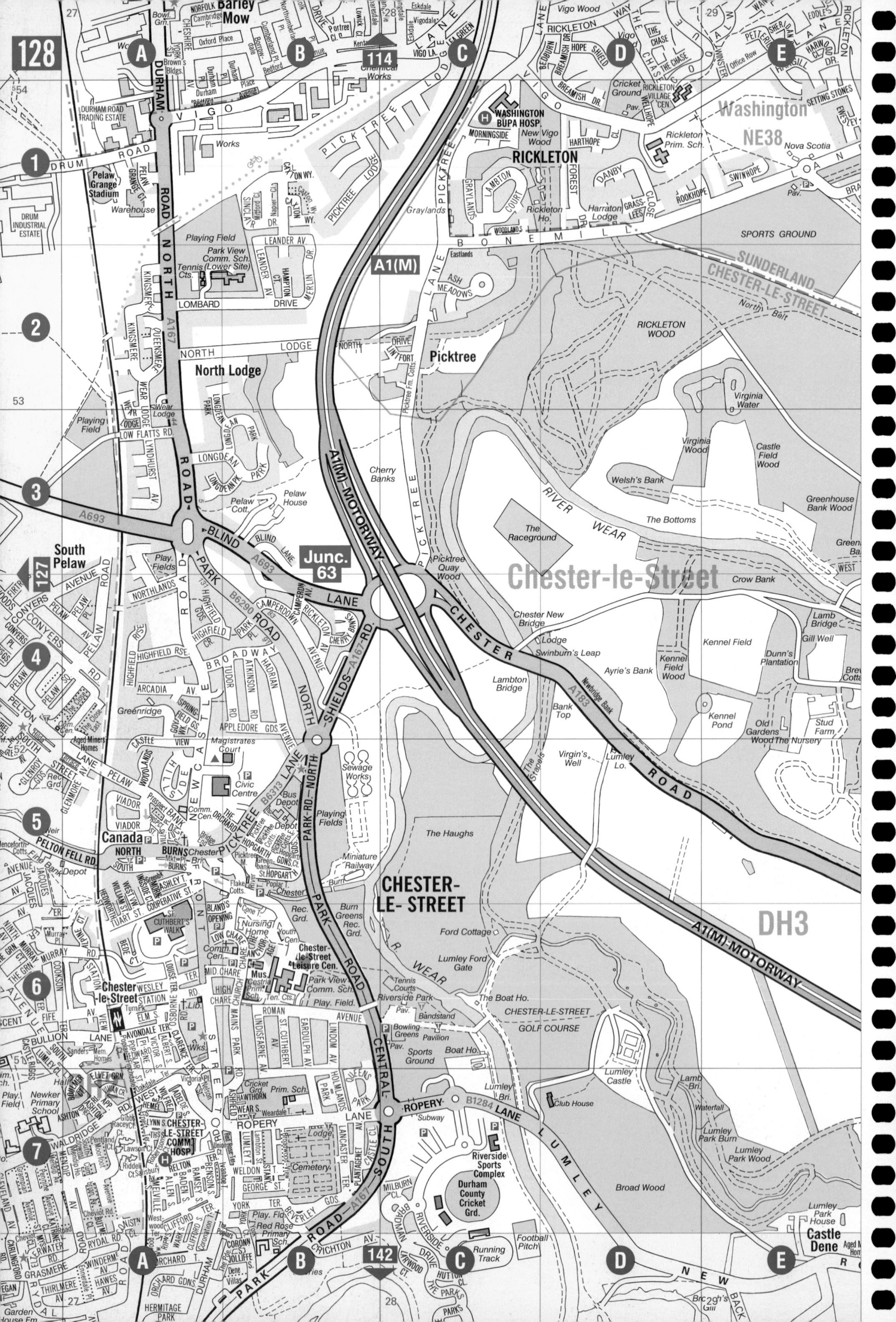
114
Barley Mow
Rickleton
Washington
NE38
Washington BUPA Hosp.
Rickleton Prim. Sch.
Nova Scotia
Sports Ground
Durham Road Trading Estate
Pelaw Grange Stadium
Drum Industrial Estate
Playing Field
Park View Comm. Sch.
A1(M)
Sunderland
Chester-le-Street
North Lodge
Picktree
Rickleton Wood
Virginia Water
Virginia Wood
Castle Field Wood
Welsh's Bank
Cherry Banks
Pelaw House
River Wear
The Raceground
The Bottoms
Greenhouse Bank Wood
South Pelaw
127
Junc. 63
A1(M) Motorway
Picktree Quay Wood
Chester-le-Street
Crow Bank
Chester New Bridge
Lamb Bridge
Gill Well
Kennel Field
Dunn's Plantation
Swinburn's Leap
Ayrie's Bank
Kennel Field Wood
Lambton Bridge
Bank Top
Kennel Pond
Old Gardens Wood
Stud Farm
The Nursery
Magistrates Court
Civic Centre
Sewage Works
Virgin's Well
Lumley Lo.
Chester Road
Canada
The Haughs
Miniature Railway
Chester-le-Street
DH3
Ford Cottage
Lumley Ford Gate
Chester-le-Street Leisure Cen.
Chester-le-Street Station
The Boat Ho.
Chester-le-Street Golf Course
Riverside Park
Bandstand
Bowling Greens Pavilion
Sports Ground
Boat Ho.
Lumley Castle
Lamb Bri.
Club House
Waterfall
Lumley Park Burn
Lumley Park Wood
Broad Wood
Newker Primary School
Chester-le-Street Comm. Hosp.
Riverside Sports Complex
Durham County Cricket Grd.
Running Track
Football Pitch
Lumley Park House
Castle Dene
Red Rose Primary Sch.
142
Lumley New Road
Park Road South
Park Road Central
Park Road North
Durham Road
Vigo Lane
Bonemill Lane
Picktree Lane
Blind Lane
North Lodge Drive
A167
A693
A183
B6290
B6313
B1284
Ropery Lane
Pelton Fell Rd.
Front Street

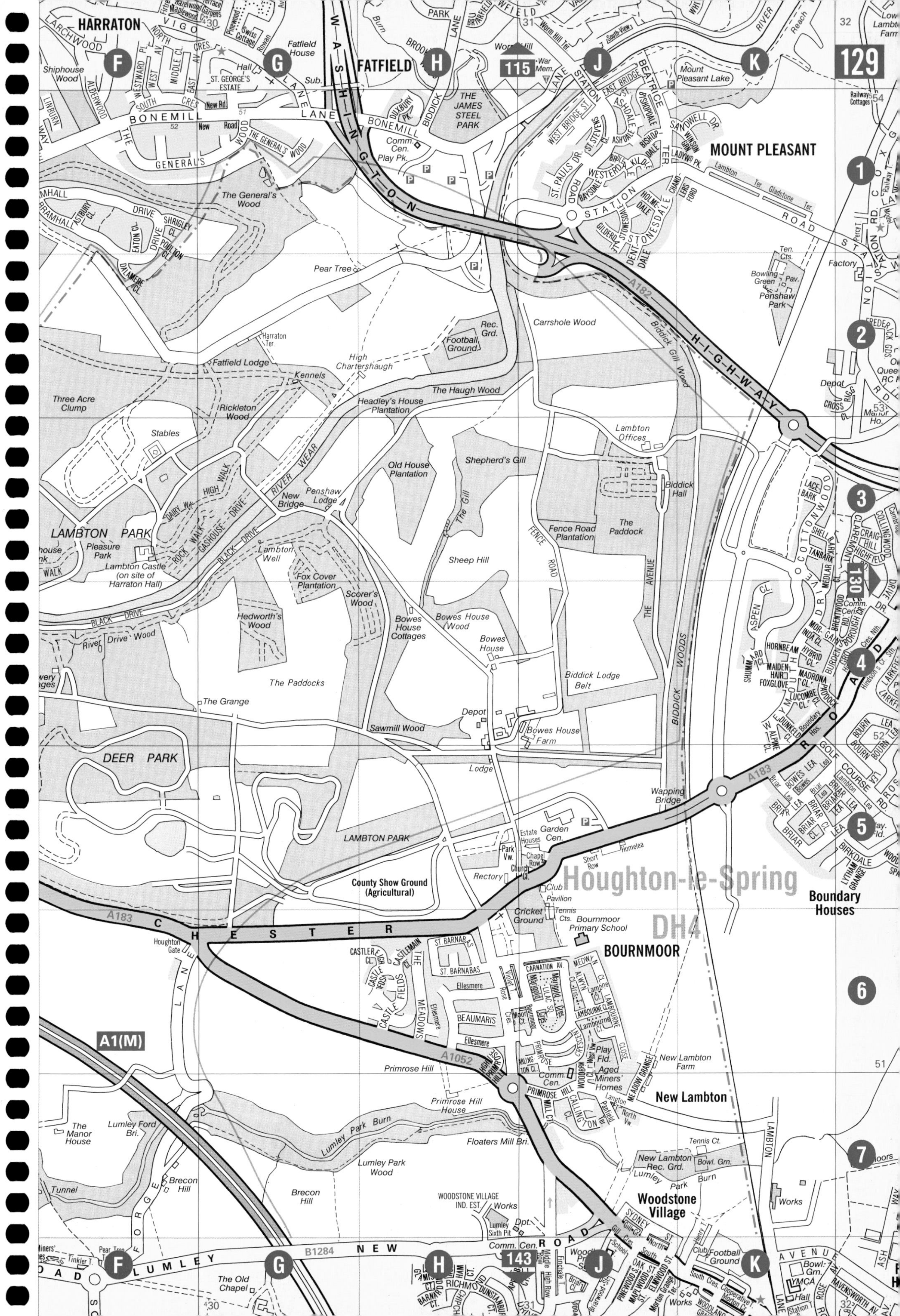
HARRATON
FATFIELD
MOUNT PLEASANT
LAMBTON PARK
DEER PARK
Houghton-le-Spring
DH4
BOURNMOOR
New Lambton
Woodstone Village
Boundary Houses
115
130
143
F
G
H
J
K
1
2
3
4
5
6
7
A1(M)
A182
A183
A1052
B1284
WASHINGTON HIGHWAY
CHESTER ROAD
LUMLEY NEW ROAD
STATION ROAD
BONEMILL LANE
GENERAL'S WOOD
Fatfield House
Shiphouse Wood
St. George's Estate
The James Steel Park
Comm. Cen.
Play Pk.
Worm Hill
War Mem.
Mount Pleasant Lake
Railway Cottages
The General's Wood
Pear Tree
Carrshole Wood
Rec. Grd.
Football Ground
Harraton Ter.
Fatfield Lodge
High Chartershaugh
Kennels
The Haugh Wood
Three Acre Clump
Rickleton Wood
Headley's House Plantation
Stables
Old House Plantation
Shepherd's Gill
Lambton Offices
Biddick Hall
Biddick Gill Wood
Penshaw Park
Bowling Green
Pav.
Ten. Cts.
Factory
Depot
Manor Ho.
River Wear
New Bridge
Penshaw Lodge
The Gill
Fence Road Plantation
The Paddock
Lambton Well
Fox Cover Plantation
Scorer's Wood
Sheep Hill
Lambton Castle (on site of Harraton Hall)
Pleasure Park
Hedworth's Wood
Bowes House Cottages
Bowes House Wood
Bowes House
Biddick Lodge Belt
The Paddocks
The Grange
Depot
Sawmill Wood
Bowes House Farm
Biddick Woods
The Avenue
Lodge
Wapping Bridge
River Drive Wood
Black Drive
Estate Houses
Garden Cen.
Park Vw.
Chapel Row
Short Row
Homelea
Rectory
Church Cl.
County Show Ground (Agricultural)
Club Pavilion
Tennis Cts.
Cricket Ground
Bournmoor Primary School
Houghton Gate
Primrose Hill
Primrose Hill House
Play Fld.
Aged Miners' Homes
New Lambton Farm
Floaters Mill Bri.
Lumley Park Burn
Lumley Park Wood
The Manor House
Lumley Ford Bri.
Brecon Hill
Tunnel
Woodstone Village Ind. Est.
Works
Lumley Sixth Pit
Tennis Ct.
New Lambton Rec. Grd.
Bowl. Grn.
Football Ground
The Old Chapel
YMCA
Hall
Golf Course Rd.
Cottonwood
Claremont
Craig Hill
Highfield
Sunnybank
Weymouth
Station Rd.

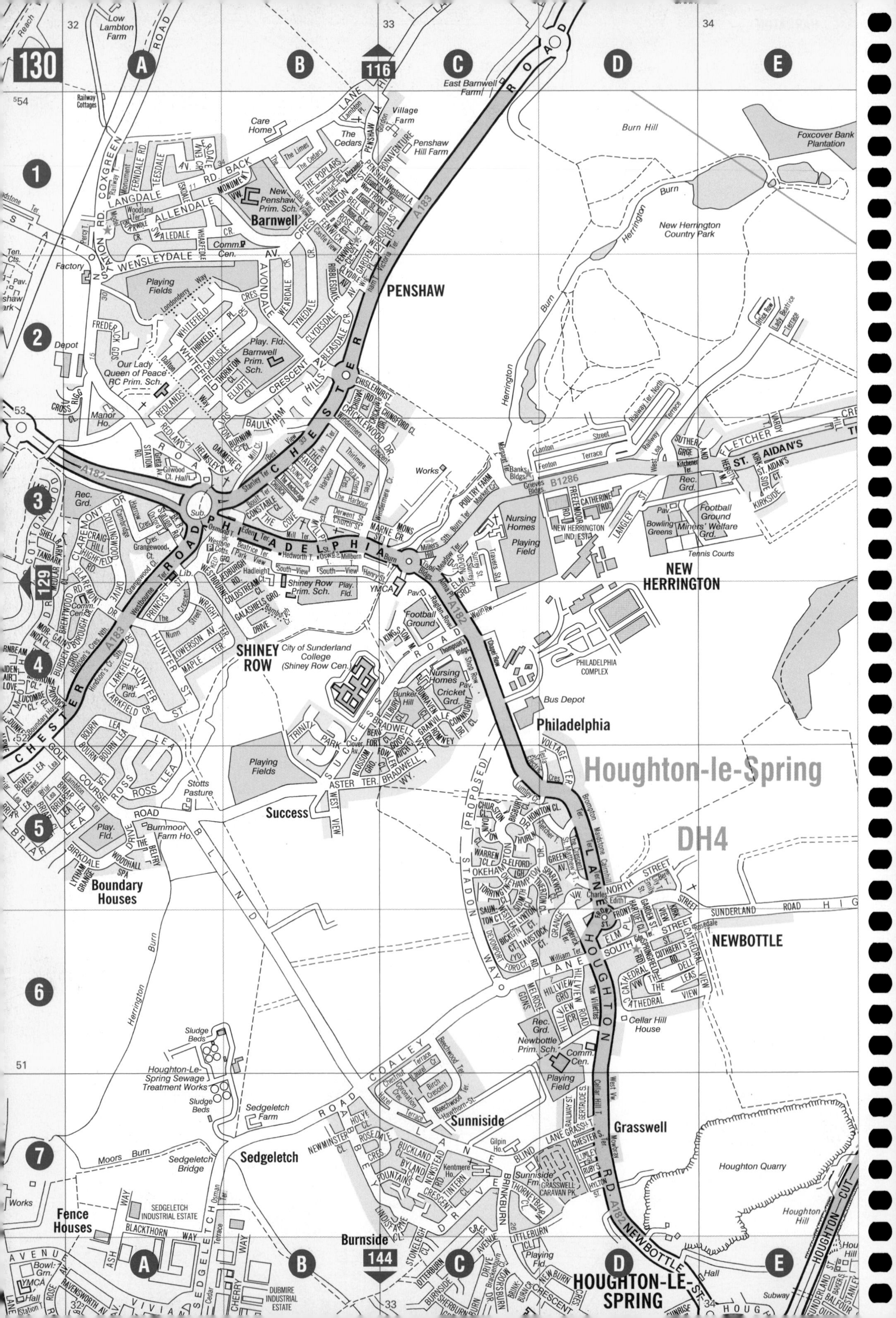

116
129
144
Low Lambton Farm
East Barnwell Farm
Village Farm
Penshaw Hill Farm
The Cedars
Care Home
Burn Hill
Foxcover Bank Plantation
New Herrington Country Park
Herrington Burn
Barnwell
New Penshaw Prim. Sch.
PENSHAW
Playing Fields
Our Lady Queen of Peace RC Prim. Sch.
Play. Fld. Barnwell Prim. Sch.
Manor Ho.
Depot
Factory
Railway Cottages
Comm. Cen.
A182
A183
B1286
CHESTER ROAD
PHILADELPHIA
Rec. Grd.
Works
Nursing Homes
Playing Field
NEW HERRINGTON IND. EST.
Football Ground
Bowling Greens
Miners' Welfare Grd.
Tennis Courts
NEW HERRINGTON
ST. AIDAN'S TER.
Shiney Row Prim. Sch.
YMCA
SHINEY ROW
City of Sunderland College (Shiney Row Cen.)
Football Ground
Cricket Grd.
PHILADELPHIA COMPLEX
Bus Depot
Philadelphia
Houghton-le-Spring
DH4
Playing Fields
Stotts Pasture
Success
Burnmoor Farm Ho.
Boundary Houses
NEWBOTTLE
SUNDERLAND ROAD
Cellar Hill House
Rec. Grd.
Newbottle Prim. Sch.
Comm. Cen.
Playing Field
Sludge Beds
Houghton-le-Spring Sewage Treatment Works
Sedgeletch Farm
Sunniside
Grasswell
Moors Burn
Sedgeletch Bridge
Sedgeletch
Houghton Quarry
Houghton Hill
SEDGELETCH INDUSTRIAL ESTATE
Fence Houses
Works
Burnside
GRASSWELL CARAVAN PK.
DUBMIRE INDUSTRIAL ESTATE
HOUGHTON-LE-SPRING
HOUGHTON CUT
Subway
Hall

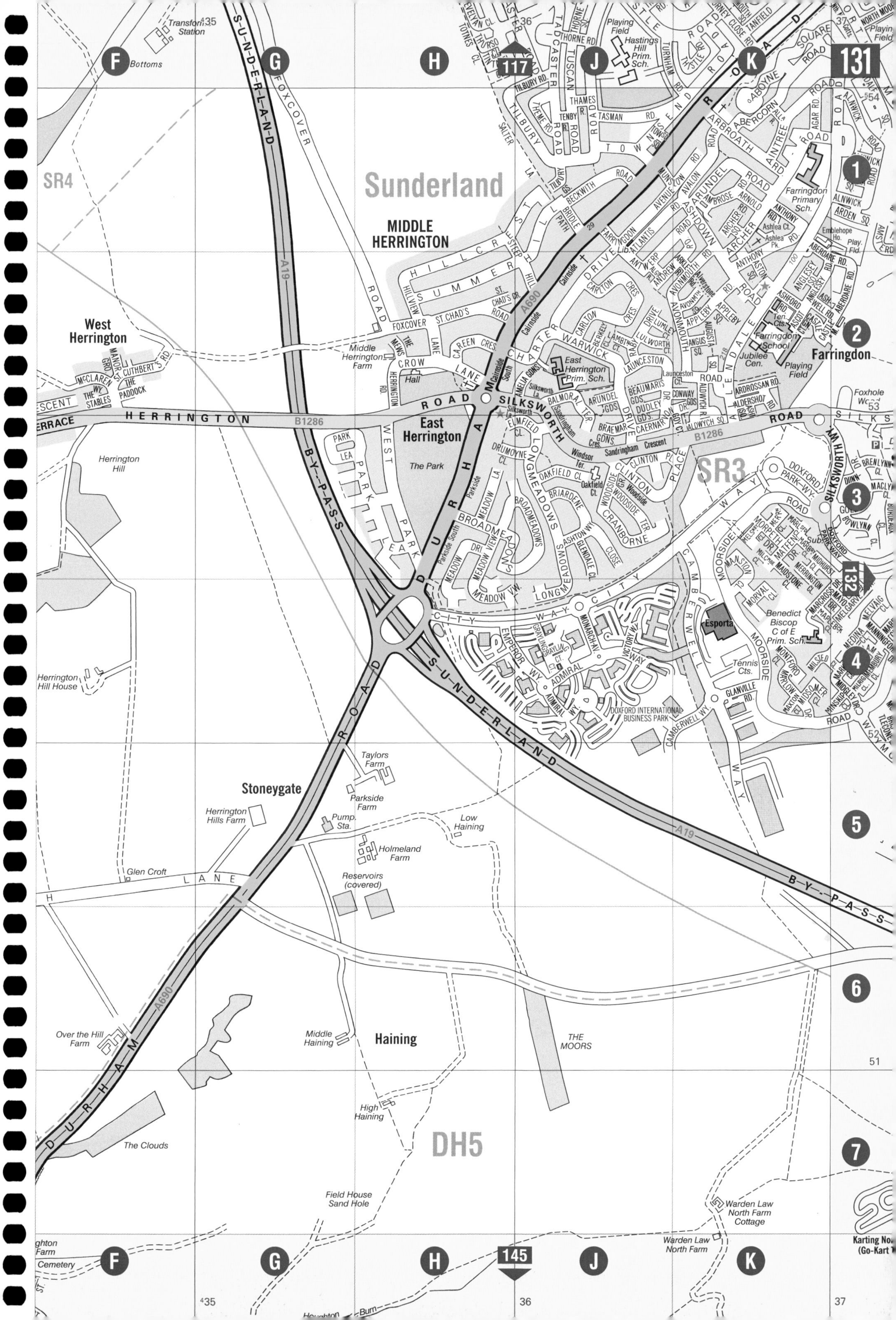
Sunderland
MIDDLE HERRINGTON
West Herrington
East Herrington
SILKSWORTH
Farringdon
Stoneygate
Haining
SR4
SR3
DH5
HERRINGTON ROAD
B1286
SUNDERLAND BY-PASS
A19
DURHAM ROAD
A690
CITY WAY
DOXFORD INTERNATIONAL BUSINESS PARK
Esporta
East Herrington Prim. Sch.
Farringdon Primary Sch.
Farringdon School
Jubilee Cen.
Hastings Hill Prim. Sch.
Benedict Biscop C of E Prim. Sch.
Herrington Hill
Herrington Hill House
Herrington Hills Farm
Glen Croft
Taylors Farm
Parkside Farm
Holmeland Farm
Reservoirs (covered)
Low Haining
Middle Haining
High Haining
Over the Hill Farm
The Clouds
THE MOORS
Field House Sand Hole
Warden Law North Farm Cottage
Warden Law North Farm
Middle Herrington Farm
The Park
Transformer Station
Bottoms
Karting North (Go-Kart)
Houghton Burn
117
132
145
F
G
H
J
K
1
2
3
4
5
6
7
435
36
37
51
52
53
54

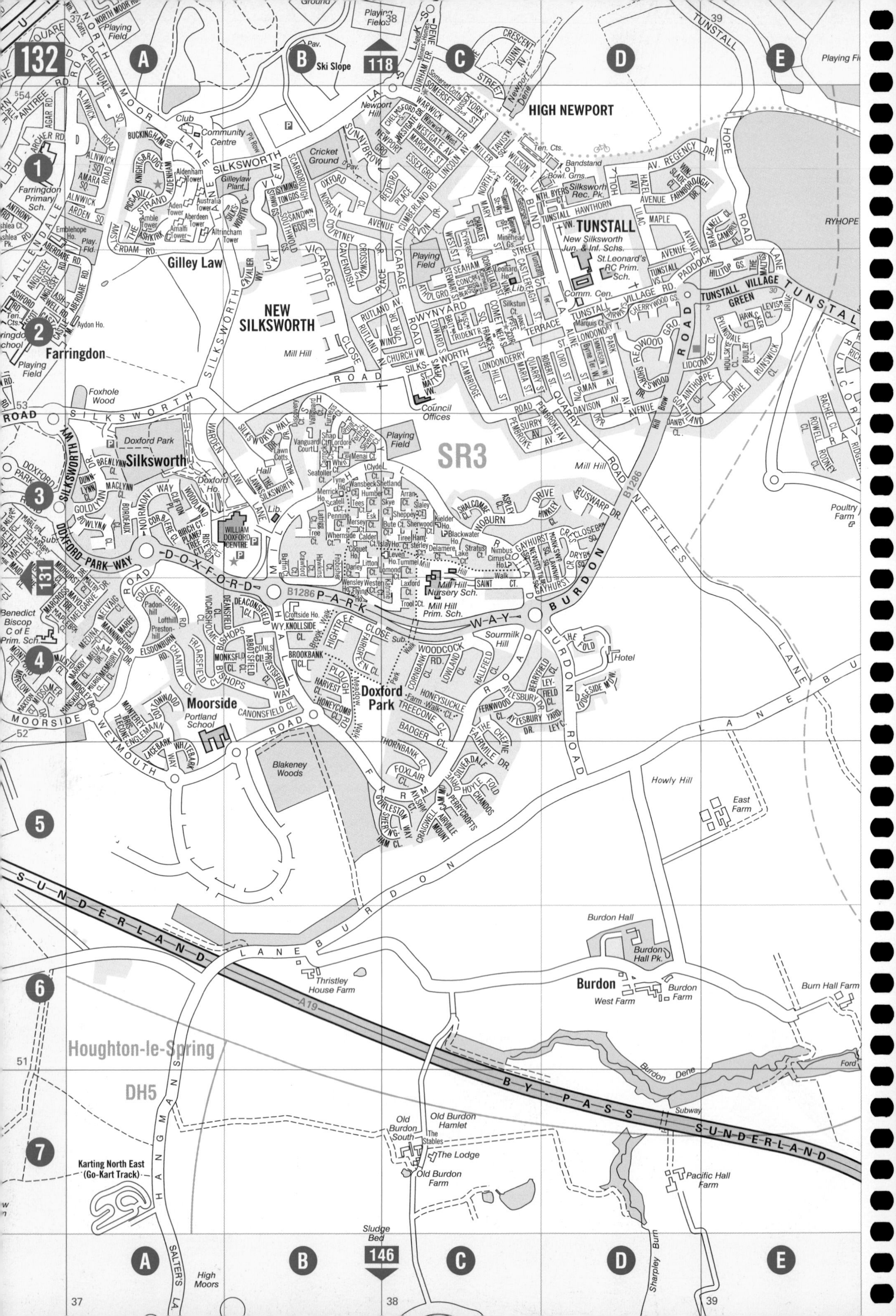
A
B
C
D
E
118
Ski Slope
HIGH NEWPORT
Newport Dene
Community Centre
SILKSWORTH LANE
Cricket Ground
Gilley Law
NEW SILKSWORTH
TUNSTALL
New Silksworth Jun. & Inf. Schs.
St.Leonard's RC Prim. Sch.
Comm. Cen.
Silksworth Rec. Pk.
Bandstand
RYHOPE
TUNSTALL VILLAGE GREEN
Farringdon Primary Sch.
Farringdon
Mill Hill
Foxhole Wood
Doxford Park
Silksworth
Council Offices
SR3
Playing Field
WILLIAM DOXFORD CENTRE
Mill Hill Nursery Sch.
Mill Hill Prim. Sch.
DOXFORD PARK WAY
B1286
BURDON ROAD
NETTLES LANE
Poultry Farm
Hotel
Sourmilk Hill
Benedict Biscop C of E Prim. Sch.
Moorside
Portland School
Doxford Park
Blakeney Woods
Howly Hill
East Farm
BURDON LANE
SUNDERLAND BY-PASS
A19
Burdon Hall
Burdon Hall Pk.
Thristley House Farm
Burdon
West Farm
Burdon Farm
Burn Hall Farm
Houghton-le-Spring
DH5
Burdon Dene
Ford
Subway
Old Burdon South
Old Burdon Hamlet
The Stables
The Lodge
Old Burdon Farm
Pacific Hall Farm
Karting North East (Go-Kart Track)
HANGMANS LANE
Sludge Bed
146
131
High Moors
SALTER'S LA.
Sharpley Burn
1
2
3
4
5
6
7
37
38
39
54
53
52
51

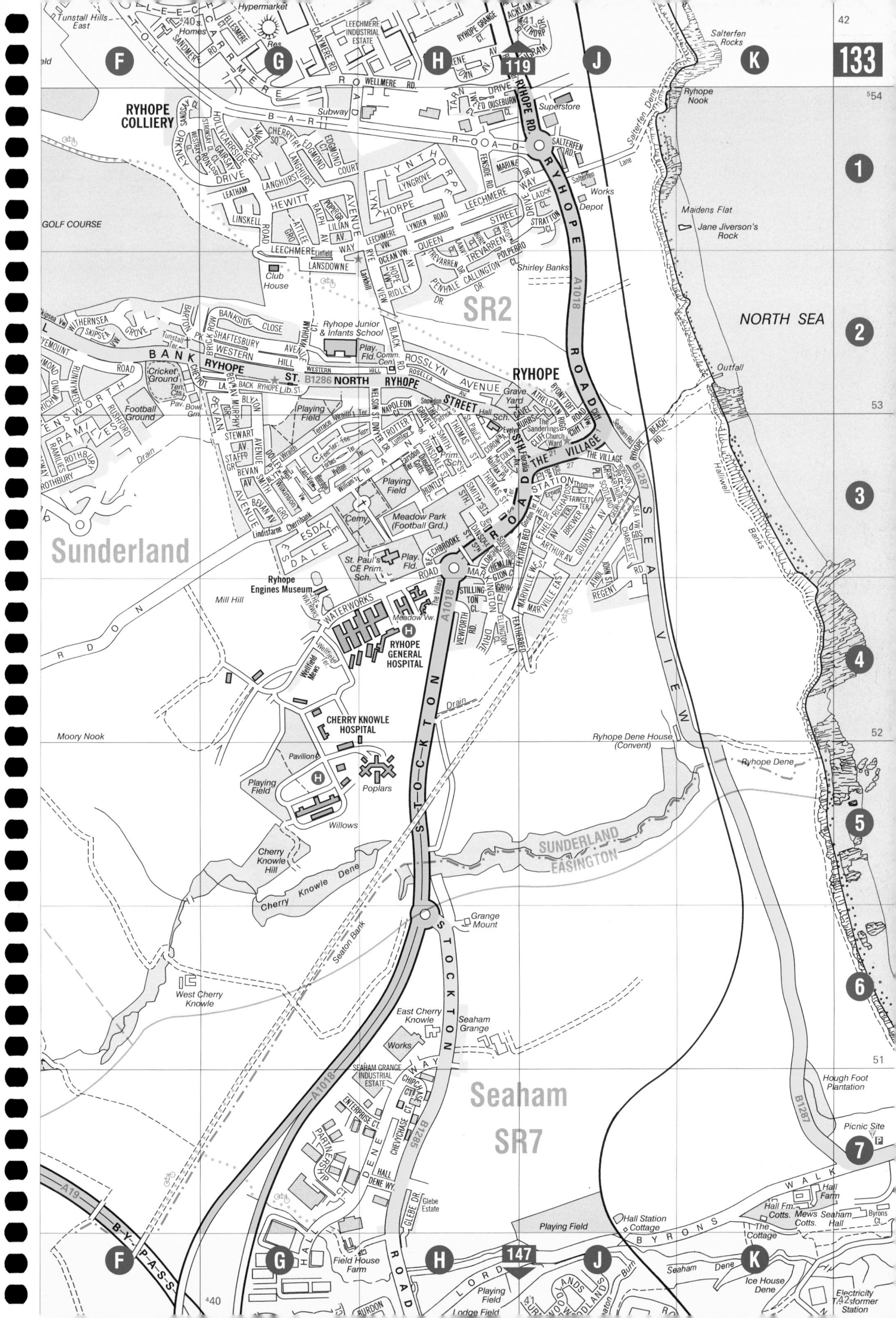
F
G
H
J
K
119
147
42
54
53
52
51
1
2
3
4
5
6
7
440
441
Tunstall Hills East
Hypermarket
Homes
Res.
LEECHMERE INDUSTRIAL ESTATE
RYHOPE GRANGE CT.
Salterfen Rocks
RYHOPE COLLIERY
Subway
Superstore
Ryhope Nook
Salterfen Dene
SALTERFEN RD.
Salterfen Works
Depot
GOLF COURSE
Maidens Flat
Jane Jiverson's Rock
Club House
Shirley Banks
SR2
NORTH SEA
Ryhope Junior & Infants School
Play. Fld.
Comm. Cen.
Outfall
RYHOPE
Cricket Ground
Ten. Cts.
Pav.
Bowl. Grn.
Football Ground
Playing Field
Grave Yard
The Sanderlings
Church Ward
Drain
Playing Field
Cemy.
Meadow Park (Football Grd.)
Sunderland
St. Paul's CE Prim. Sch.
Ryhope Engines Museum
Mill Hill
RYHOPE GENERAL HOSPITAL
Meadow Vw.
CHERRY KNOWLE HOSPITAL
Moory Nook
Ryhope Dene House (Convent)
Ryhope Dene
Pavilion
Playing Field
Poplars
Willows
SUNDERLAND
EASINGTON
Cherry Knowle Hill
Cherry Knowle Dene
Grange Mount
Seaton Bank
West Cherry Knowle
East Cherry Knowle
Seaham Grange
Works
SEAHAM GRANGE INDUSTRIAL ESTATE
Seaham
SR7
Hough Foot Plantation
Picnic Site
Hall Farm
Hall Fm. Cotts.
Mews Cotts.
Seaham Hall
The Cottage
Hall Station Cottage
Playing Field
Glebe Estate
Field House Farm
Seaham Dene
Ice House Dene
Electricity Transformer Station
Playing Field
Lodge Field
RYHOPE ROAD
STOCKTON ROAD
SEA VIEW
BYRONS WALK
A19 BY-PASS
A1018
B1286
B1287
B1285

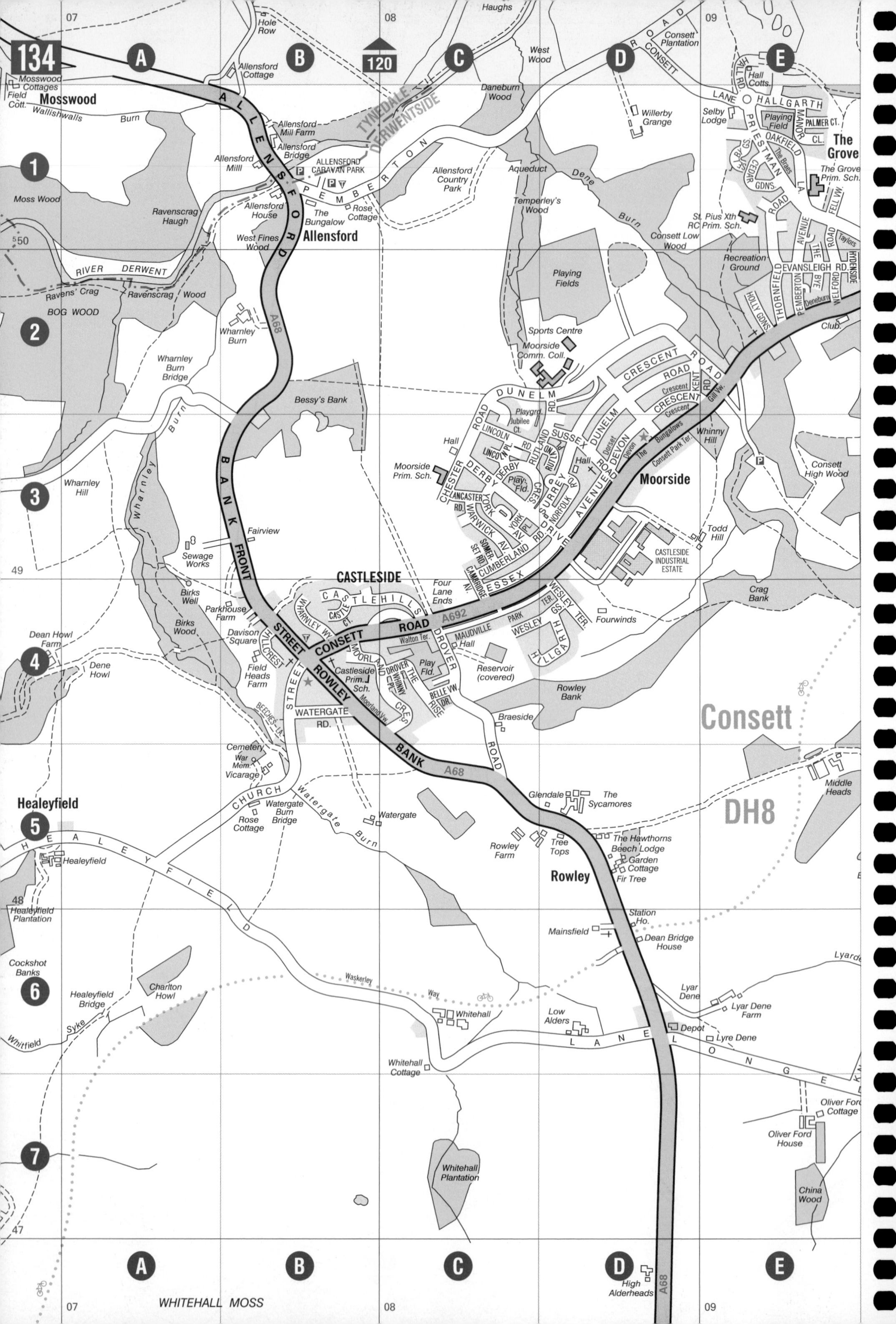

07
08
09
A
B
C
D
E
1
2
3
4
5
6
7
50
49
48
47
120
Haughs
Hole Row
Consett Plantation
West Wood
Allensford Cottage
Mosswood Cottages
Field Cott.
Mosswood
Wallishwalls
Burn
Allensford Mill Farm
Allensford Bridge
Allensford Mill
ALLENSFORD CARAVAN PARK
TYNEDALE
DERWENTSIDE
Daneburn Wood
Willerby Grange
Hall Cotts.
Selby Lodge
Playing Field
HALLGARTH
MANOR
PALMER CT.
CL.
OAKFIELD
PRIESTMAN
The Grove
The Grove Prim. Sch.
CEDAR GDNS.
The Braes
FELL VW.
HALL RD.
LANE
CONSETT
ROAD
Moss Wood
Ravenscrag Haugh
PEMBERTON
Allensford House
The Bungalow
Rose Cottage
Allensford Country Park
Aqueduct
Dene
Burn
Temperley's Wood
St. Pius Xth RC Prim. Sch.
Consett Low Wood
West Fines Wood
Allensford
RIVER DERWENT
Ravens' Crag
Ravenscrag Wood
BOG WOOD
ALLENSFORD
A68
Playing Fields
Recreation Ground
AVENUE
THE
ROAD
Taylors
HYDESIDE
EVANSLEIGH RD.
THORNFIELD
PEMBERTON
BYE
WELFORD
Deneburn
HOLLY GDNS.
Club
Wharnley Burn
Sports Centre
Moorside Comm. Coll.
Wharnley Burn Bridge
CRESCENT
ROAD
KENT RD.
Gill Vw.
Crescent
DUNELM
RD.
Bessy's Bank
Playgrd.
Jubilee Ct.
Hall
LINCOLN
RUTLAND
SUSSEX
Dorset
DEVON
Devon
The Bungalows
Consett Park Ter.
Whinny Hill
Consett High Wood
Moorside Prim. Sch.
CHESTER
DERBY
Play. Fld.
SURREY
NORFOLK
AVENUE
Moorside
Wharnley Hill
BANK FRONT
LANCASTER
WARWICK
YORK AV.
CUMBERLAND RD.
DRIVE
Todd Hill
CASTLESIDE INDUSTRIAL ESTATE
Fairview
Sewage Works
SOMER. SET RD.
CAMBRIDGE AV.
ESSEX
Crag Bank
CASTLESIDE
CASTLEHILLS
Four Lane Ends
A692
WESLEY TER.
Birks Well
Parkhouse Farm
Birks Wood
Dean Howl Farm
Dene Howl
Davison Square
HILLCREST
Field Heads Farm
WHARNLEY WY.
CASTLE CT.
CONSETT ROAD
Walton Ter.
MAUDVILLE
PARK
WESLEY
GS.
HALLGARTH
Fourwinds
Hall
Reservoir (covered)
STREET
ROWLEY
MOORLAND
DROVER
Castleside Prim. Sch.
Play Fld.
THE RISE
BELLE VW.
DR.
WHINNY PL.
CRES.
Moorland Vw.
Rowley Bank
BEECHES LA.
WATERGATE RD.
Braeside
ROAD
Consett
Cemetery
War Mem.
Vicarage
BANK
A68
Middle Heads
Healeyfield
CHURCH
Watergate Burn Bridge
Rose Cottage
Watergate
Glendale
The Sycamores
DH8
HEALEYFIELD
Healeyfield
Rowley Farm
Tree Tops
The Hawthorns
Beech Lodge
Garden Cottage
Fir Tree
Rowley
Healeyfield Plantation
Station Ho.
Mainsfield
Dean Bridge House
Cockshot Banks
Charlton Howl
Waskerley Way
Lyardene
Healeyfield Bridge
Lyar Dene
Lyar Dene Farm
Whitehall
Low Alders
Depot
Lyre Dene
Whitfield
Syke
LONG LANE
Whitehall Cottage
Oliver Ford Cottage
Oliver Ford House
Whitehall Plantation
China Wood
High Alderheads
WHITEHALL MOSS

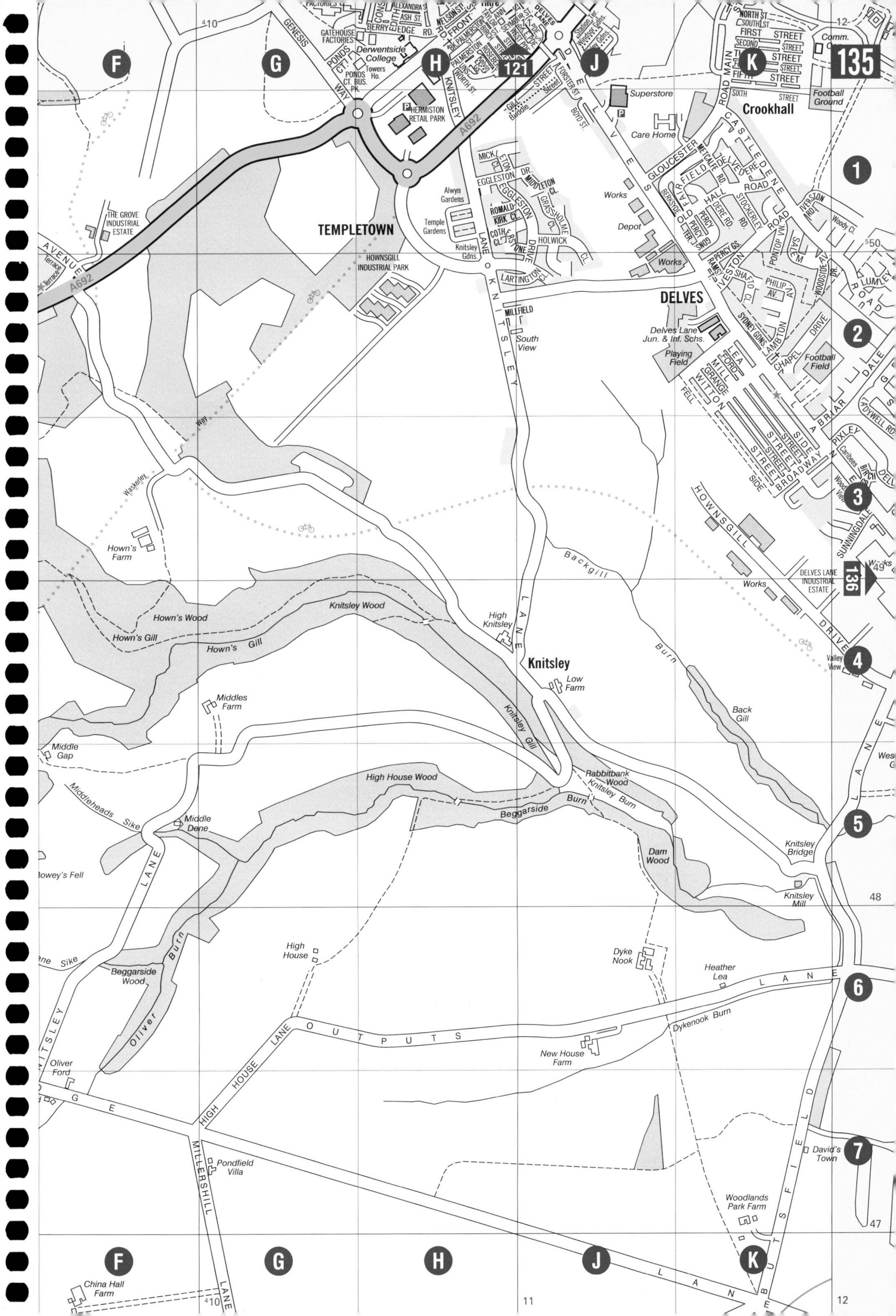

135
121
136
TEMPLETOWN
DELVES
Crookhall
Knitsley
HERMISTON RETAIL PARK
HOWNSGILL INDUSTRIAL PARK
THE GROVE INDUSTRIAL ESTATE
DELVES LANE INDUSTRIAL ESTATE
Derwentside College
GATEHOUSE FACTORIES
Superstore
Care Home
Works
Depot
Delves Lane Jun. & Inf. Schs.
Playing Field
Football Field
Football Ground
A692
GENESIS WAY
KNITSLEY LANE
DELVES LANE
HOWNSGILL DRIVE
BROADWAY
CASTLEDENE ROAD
GLOUCESTER ROAD
Alwyn Gardens
Temple Gardens
Knitsley Gdns.
MILLFIELD
South View
Hown's Farm
Hown's Wood
Hown's Gill
Knitsley Wood
High Knitsley
Low Farm
Middles Farm
Middle Gap
Middleheads Sike
Middle Dene
Bowey's Fell
High House Wood
Knitsley Gill
Rabbitbank Wood
Knitsley Burn
Beggarside Burn
Dam Wood
Back Gill
Backgill Burn
Knitsley Bridge
Knitsley Mill
Valley View
Beggarside Wood
Oliver Burn
Oliver Ford
High House
Dyke Nook
Heather Lea
OUTPUTS LANE
HIGH HOUSE LANE
Dykenook Burn
New House Farm
MILLERSHILL LANE
Pondfield Villa
David's Town
Woodlands Park Farm
BUTSFIELD LANE
China Hall Farm
Waskerley Way
F
G
H
J
K
1
2
3
4
5
6
7
10
11
12
47
48
49
50

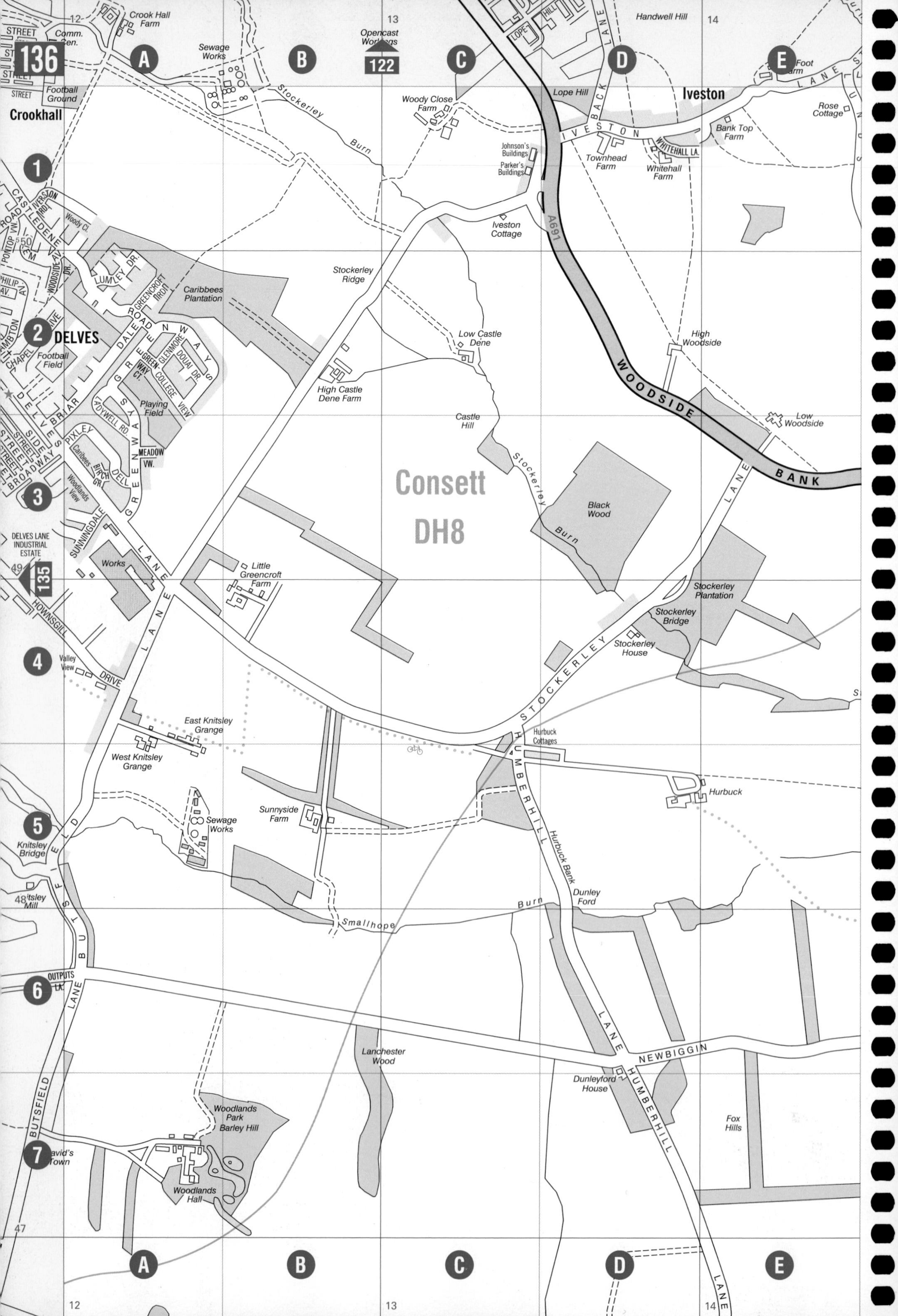

136

A   **B**   **122**   **C**   **D**   **E**

Crookhall

Comm. Cen.
Football Ground
Sewage Works
Crook Hall Farm
Handwell Hill

1

Woody Close Farm
Lope Hill
Iveston
Foot Farm
Rose Cottage

Johnson's Buildings
Parker's Buildings
Townhead Farm
Whitehall LA.
Bank Top Farm
WHITEHALL LA.
Whitehall Farm

CASTLESIDE ROAD
IVERSON VW.
WOODSIDE DR.
PONTOP TOP
PHILIP AV.
Woody Cl.
Stockerley Burn

Iveston Cottage
A691

Stockerley Ridge

2 **DELVES**

Caribbees Plantation
LUMLEY DR.
GREENCROFT ROAD
DALE ROAD
NWAY
GLENMORE WAY CT.
DOUAI DR.
GREEN COLLEGE VIEW
Low Castle Dene
High Woodside

Football Field
Chapel
Playing Field
High Castle Dene Farm
WOODSIDE
Castle Hill
Black Wood
Low Woodside
BANK

3

CARIBBEES
BROADWAY
DELVES STREET
DELVES SIDE STREET
BRIAR
PIXLEY
BIRCH GR.
DELL GR.
LADYWELL RD.
MEADOW VW.
Woodlands View
Caribbees

Consett
DH8

Stockerley Burn
Stockerley Plantation
Stockerley Bridge

DELVES LANE INDUSTRIAL ESTATE
SUNNINGDALE
Works
GREENWAY LANE
Little Greencroft Farm
Stockerley House
HOWNSGILL
135

4

Valley View
DRIVE
East Knitsley Grange
STOCKERLEY
Hurbuck Cottages
Hurbuck
HUMBERHILL

West Knitsley Grange
Sunnyside Farm
Hurbuck Bank

5

Knitsley Bridge
BUTSFIELD LANE
Sewage Works
Smallhope Burn
Dunley Ford

Knitsley Mill

6

OUTPUTS LA.
Lanchester Wood
NEWBIGGIN
Dunleyford House
HUMBERHILL LANE
Fox Hills

7

David's Town
BUTSFIELD LANE
Woodlands Park Barley Hill
Woodlands Hall

A   **B**   **C**   **D**   **E**

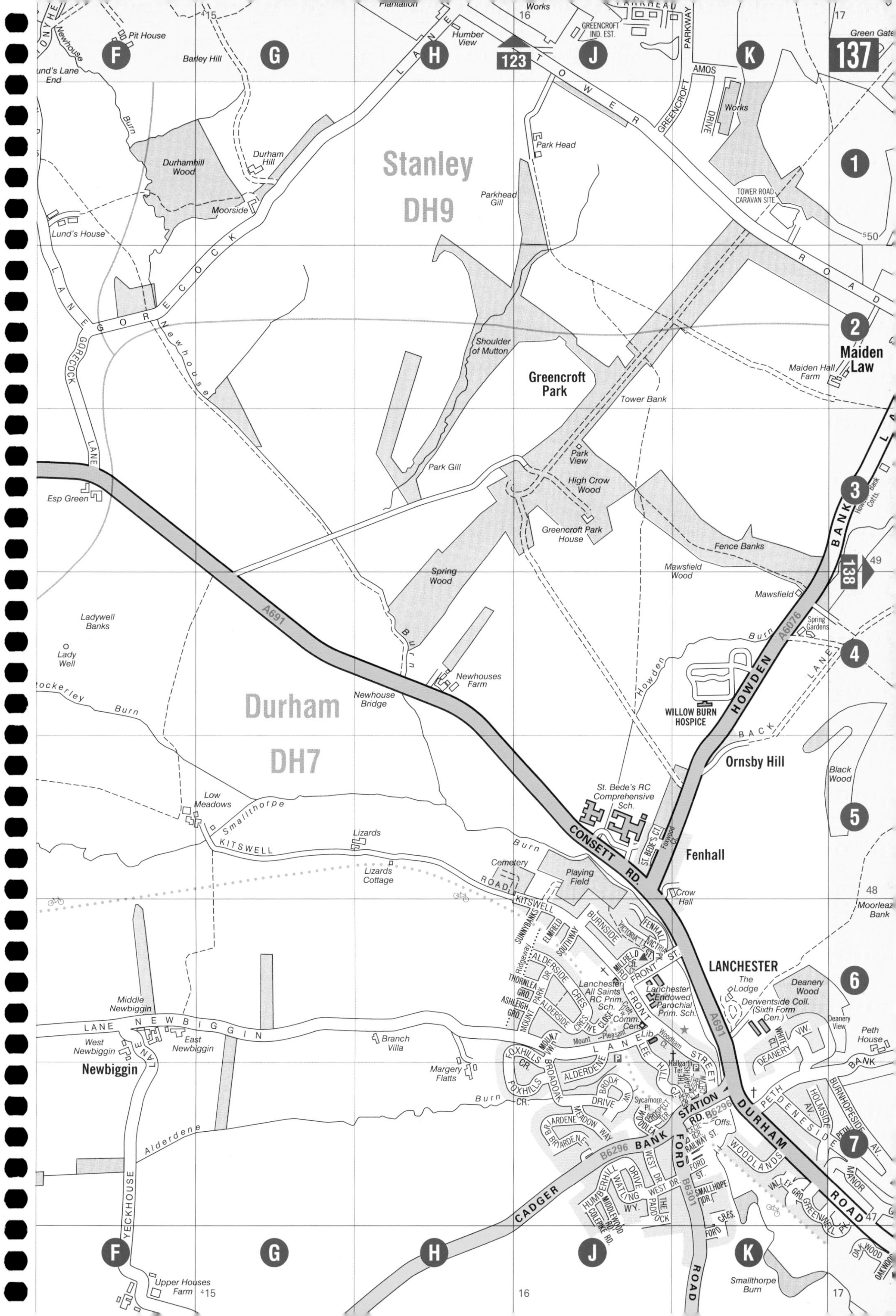
Stanley
DH9
Durham
DH7
Greencroft Park
Maiden Law
Ornsby Hill
Fenhall
LANCHESTER
Newbiggin
Pit House
Barley Hill
Lund's Lane End
Durhamhill Wood
Durham Hill
Moorside
Lund's House
Humber View
GREENCROFT IND. EST.
Works
Park Head
Parkhead Gill
TOWER ROAD CARAVAN SITE
Shoulder of Mutton
Tower Bank
Maiden Hall Farm
Esp Green
Park Gill
Park View
High Crow Wood
Greencroft Park House
Fence Banks
Spring Wood
Mawsfield Wood
Mawsfield
Spring Gardens
Ladywell Banks
Lady Well
Newhouses Farm
Newhouse Bridge
WILLOW BURN HOSPICE
Black Wood
St. Bede's RC Comprehensive Sch.
Low Meadows
Lizards
Lizards Cottage
Cemetery
Playing Field
Crow Hall
Moorleaze Bank
The Lodge
Deanery Wood
Derwentside Coll. (Sixth Form Cen.)
Peth House
Middle Newbiggin
West Newbiggin
East Newbiggin
Branch Villa
Margery Flatts
Lanchester All Saints RC Prim. Sch.
Lanchester Endowed Parochial Prim. Sch.
Comm. Cen.
Lib.
Upper Houses Farm
Smallthorpe Burn
A691
A6076
B6296
B6301
GORECOCK LANE
TOWER ROAD
HOWDEN BANK
CONSETT RD.
KITSWELL ROAD
NEWBIGGIN LANE
YECKHOUSE LANE
CADGER BANK
DURHAM ROAD
STATION RD.
FORD ROAD
BACK LANE
123
138

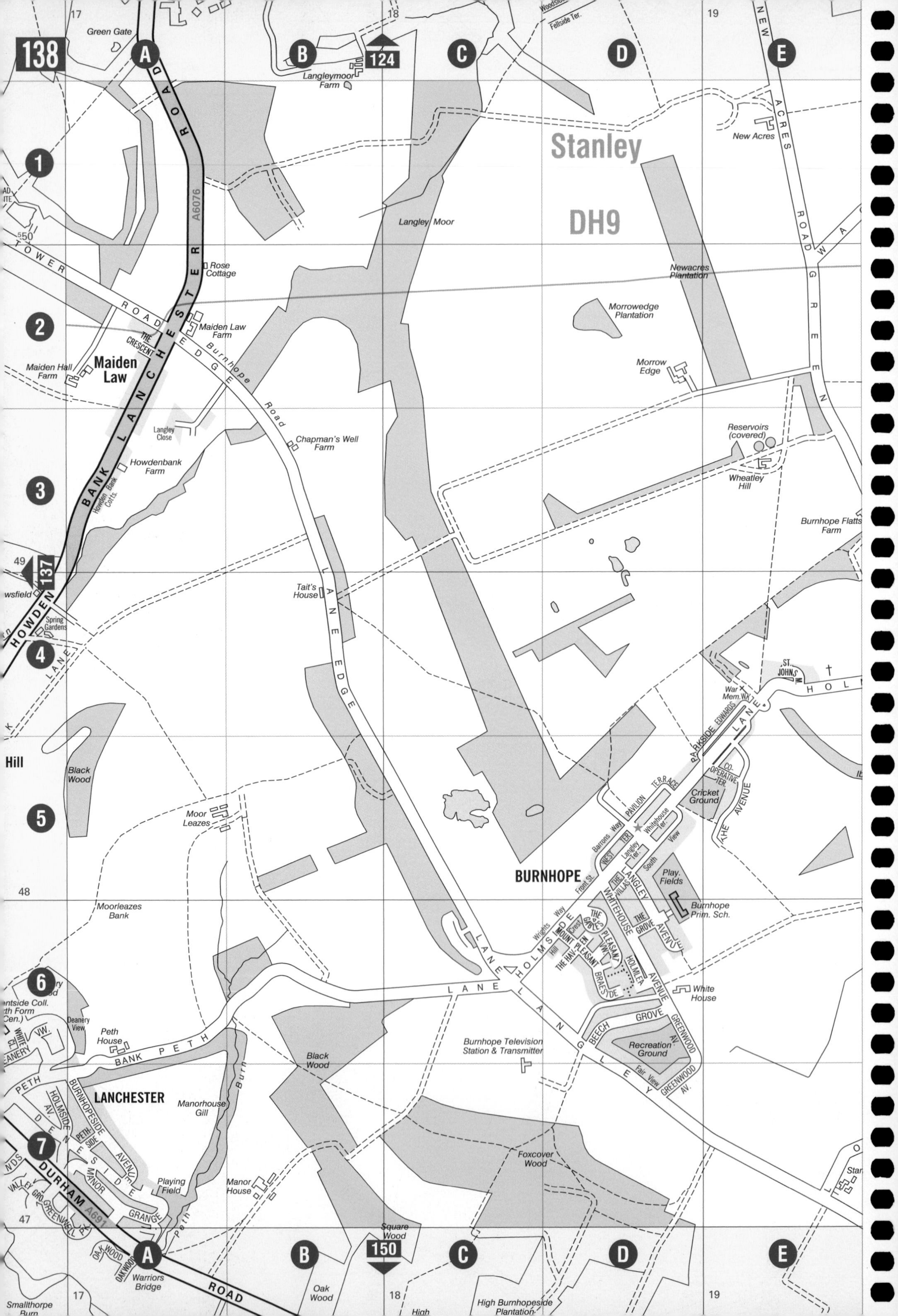

A
B
C
D
E
17
18
19
124
Green Gate
Langleymoor Farm
Woodside
Fellside Ter.
NEW ACRES ROAD
New Acres
Stanley
DH9
1
2
3
4
5
6
7
50
49
48
47
TOWER ROAD
LANCHESTER ROAD
A6076
Langley Moor
Rose Cottage
Newacres Plantation
Morrowedge Plantation
Maiden Law Farm
THE CRESCENT
Maiden Hall Farm
Maiden Law
EDGE
Burnhope Road
Morrow Edge
GREEN
Langley Close
Chapman's Well Farm
Reservoirs (covered)
Wheatley Hill
Howdenbank Farm
BANK LANCHESTER
Howden Bank Cotts.
Burnhope Flatts Farm
137
Tait's House
LANE EDGE
HOWDEN
Spring Gardens
LANE
ST. JOHN'S
War Mem.
HOLMSIDE
PARKSIDE
EDWARDS
LANE
CO-OPERATIVE TER.
Hill
Black Wood
PAVILION TERRACE
Cricket Ground
THE AVENUE
Moor Leazes
Barrons Way
WEST TER.
Whitehouse Ter.
South View
Langley Ter.
Play. Fields
BURNHOPE
Front St.
THE VILLAS
LANGLEY
WHITEHOUSE
THE GROVE
AVENUE
Burnhope Prim. Sch.
Moorleazes Bank
Wrights Way
THE GARTH
Crest
MOUNT PLEASANT
PLEASANT VIEW
Hill
THE HAVEN
BRAESIDE
HOLMLEA
AVENUE
HOLMSIDE LANE
White House
Deanery View
Sixth Form Cen.
WHITE CL
DEANERY VW.
Peth House
BANK PETH
BEECH
GROVE
GREENWOOD AV.
Recreation Ground
Burnhope Television Station & Transmitter
LANGLEY
Fair View
GREENWOOD AV.
Black Wood
PETH
LANCHESTER
Manorhouse Gill
Burn
HOLMSIDE AV.
BURNHOPESIDE
PETH-SIDE
DENE
AVENUE
SIDE
MANOR
Foxcover Wood
DURHAM
A691
Playing Field
Manor House
VALLEY GRO.
GREENWELL PK.
GRANGE
Peth
Square Wood
150
OAK WOOD
OAKWOOD
Warriors Bridge
ROAD
Oak Wood
High
High Burnhopeside Plantation
Smallthorpe Burn

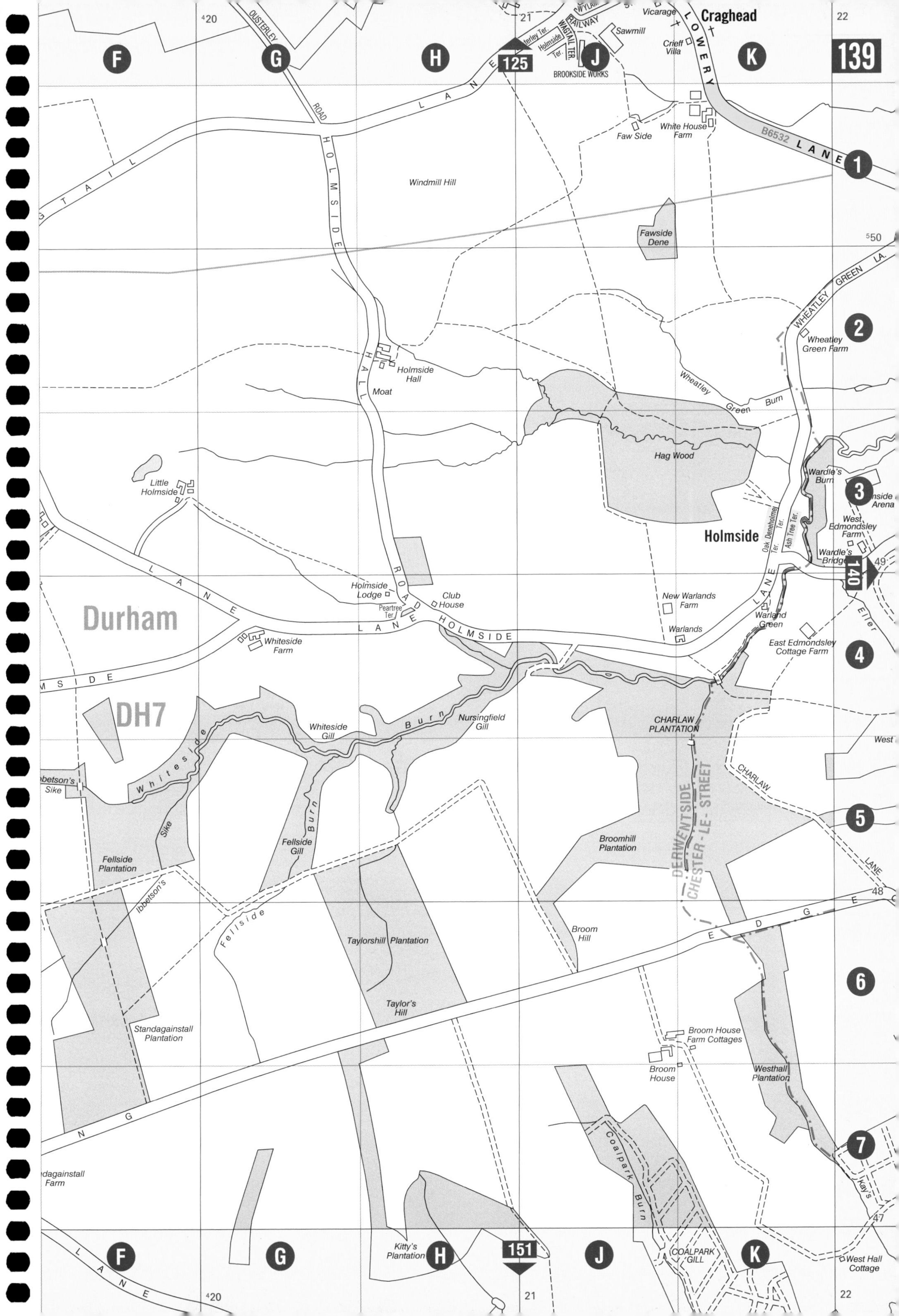

Craghead
Vicarage
Sawmill
Crieff Villa
BROOKSIDE WORKS
OUSTERLEY
ROAD
HOLMSIDE
LANE
LOWERY
B6532 LANE
Faw Side
White House Farm
Windmill Hill
Fawside Dene
WHEATLEY GREEN LA.
Wheatley Green Farm
Wheatley Green Burn
Holmside Hall
Moat
Hag Wood
Little Holmside
Wardle's Burn
West Edmondsley Farm
Wardle's Bridge
Holmside
Oak Deneholme Ter.
Ash Tree Ter.
Holmside Lodge
Club House
Peartree Ter.
New Warlands Farm
Warland Green
Warlands
Durham
HOLMSIDE LANE
Whiteside Farm
East Edmondsley Cottage Farm
DH7
Whiteside Gill
Whiteside Burn
Nursingfield Gill
CHARLAW PLANTATION
CHARLAW LANE
Ibbetson's Sike
Whiteside Sike
Fellside Gill
Fellside Plantation
Broomhill Plantation
DERWENTSIDE
CHESTER-LE-STREET
Ibbetson's
Fellside
EDGE LANE
Broom Hill
Taylorshill Plantation
Taylor's Hill
Standagainstall Plantation
Broom House Farm Cottages
Broom House
Westhall Plantation
Coalpark Burn
Standagainstall Farm
Kitty's Plantation
COALPARK GILL
West Hall Cottage
Kay's
F G H J K
1 2 3 4 5 6 7
420 21 22 550 49 48 47
125 140 151

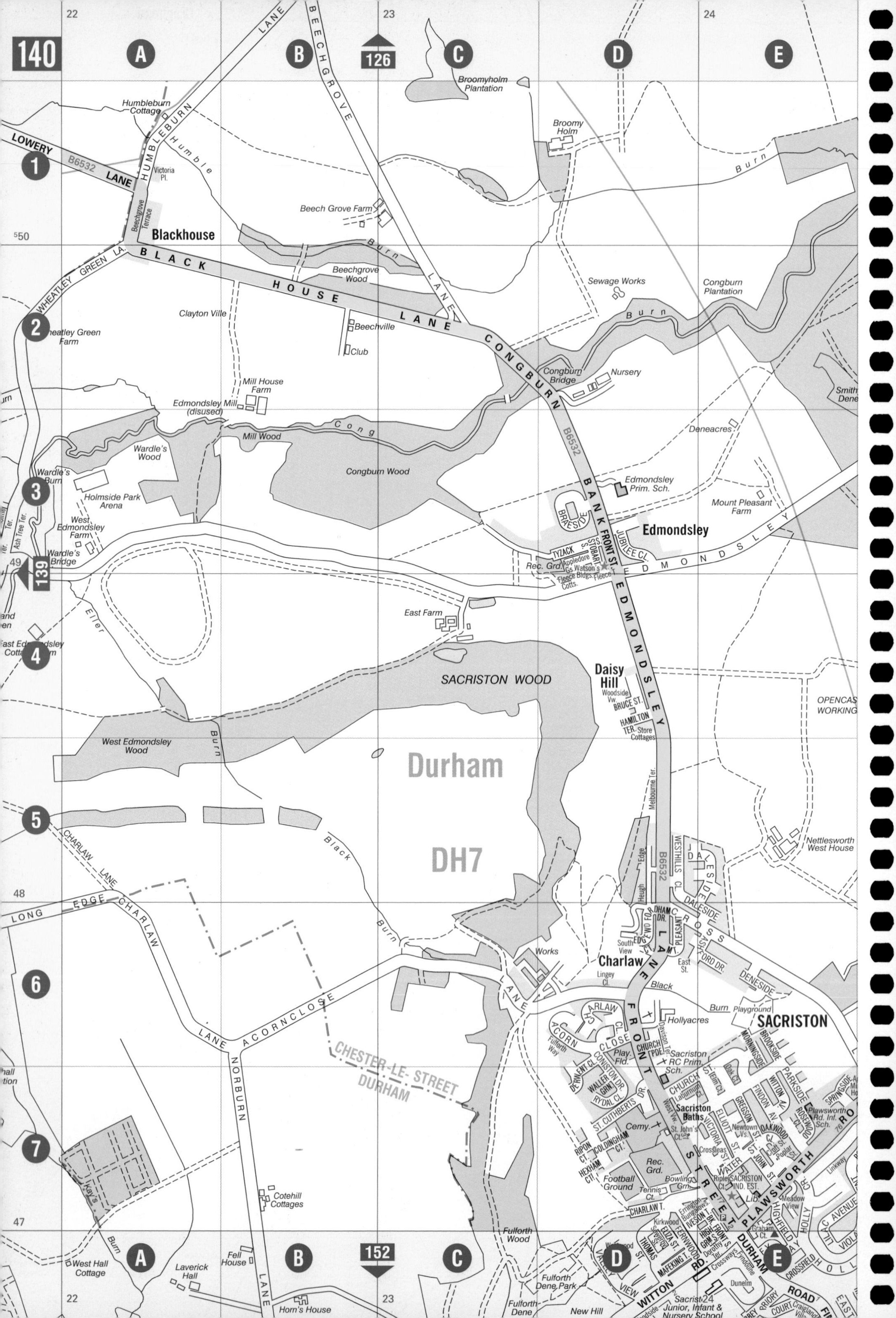

A
B
C
D
E
1
2
3
4
5
6
7
22
23
24
126
139
152
550
49
48
47
LOWERY LANE
B6532
HUMBLEBURN LANE
Humbleburn Cottage
Humble Burn
Victoria Pl.
Beechgrove Terrace
Blackhouse
BLACK HOUSE LANE
WHEATLEY GREEN LA.
Wheatley Green Farm
BEECH GROVE LANE
Beech Grove Farm
Beechgrove Wood
Broomyholm Plantation
Broomy Holm
Sewage Works
Congburn Plantation
Clayton Ville
Beechville
Club
CONGBURN
Congburn Bridge
Nursery
Mill House Farm
Edmondsley Mill (disused)
Mill Wood
Cong Burn
Congburn Wood
Wardle's Wood
Wardle's Burn
Holmside Park Arena
West Edmondsley Farm
Wardle's Bridge
Ash Tree Ter.
Deneacres
Edmondsley Prim. Sch.
Mount Pleasant Farm
Smith Dene
BANK
FRONT ST.
BRAESIDE
JUBILEE CL.
Edmondsley
EDMONDSLEY
TYZACK
STOBART ST.
Appledore
Gs Watson's
Rec. Grd.
Fleece Bldgs.
Fleece
Cotts.
East Farm
Eller
East Edmondsley Cottage
SACRISTON WOOD
Daisy Hill
Woodside Vw.
BRUCE ST.
HAMILTON TER.
Store Cottages
OPENCAST WORKING
West Edmondsley Wood
Durham
DH7
Melbourne Ter.
Black Burn
CHARLAW LANE
LONG EDGE
WESTHILLS CL.
DALESIDE
Heugh Edge
Nettlesworth West House
DURHAM DR.
PLEASANT
CROSS
ASHFORD DR.
South View
East St.
Charlaw
Works
Lingey Cl.
DENESIDE
Playground
SACRISTON
ACORNCLOSE LANE
NORBURN LANE
ACORN CLOSE
CHARLAW CL.
Fulforth Way
Hollyacres
Play. Fld.
CHURCH PDE.
Davison Ter.
Sacriston RC Prim. Sch.
CHESTER-LE-STREET
DURHAM
DERWENT CL.
CONISTON DR.
WALLER GRNT.
RYDAL CL.
ST. CUTHBERTS DR.
Cemy.
Sacriston Baths
St. John's Cl.
ELLIOTT ST.
GREGSON
FINDON AV.
WITTON AV.
PARKSIDE
ROSEWOOD CL.
OAKWOOD
MORNINGSIDE
BROOKSIDE
SPRINGSIDE
Plawsworth Rd. Inf. Sch.
PLAWSWORTH ROAD
RIPON CT.
COLDINGHAM CT.
HEXHAM CT.
Rec. Grd.
Football Ground
Tennis Ct.
Bowling Grn.
Crossleas
VICTORIA ST.
WATER ST.
SACRISTON IND. EST.
Lib.
FRONT STREET
Cotehill Cottages
CHARLAW T.
Kirkwood
ELIZA ST.
THOMAS ST.
MAFEKING T.
FERNWOOD
WITTON RD.
VALLEY VIEW
HOLLY
HIGHFIELD
LILAC AVENUE
CROSSFIELD
Dunelm
PRIORY COURT
DURHAM ROAD
Kay's
West Hall Cottage
Laverick Hall
Fell House
Horn's House
Fulforth Wood
Fulforth Dene Park
Fulforth Dene
New Hill
Sacriston Junior, Infant & Nursery School

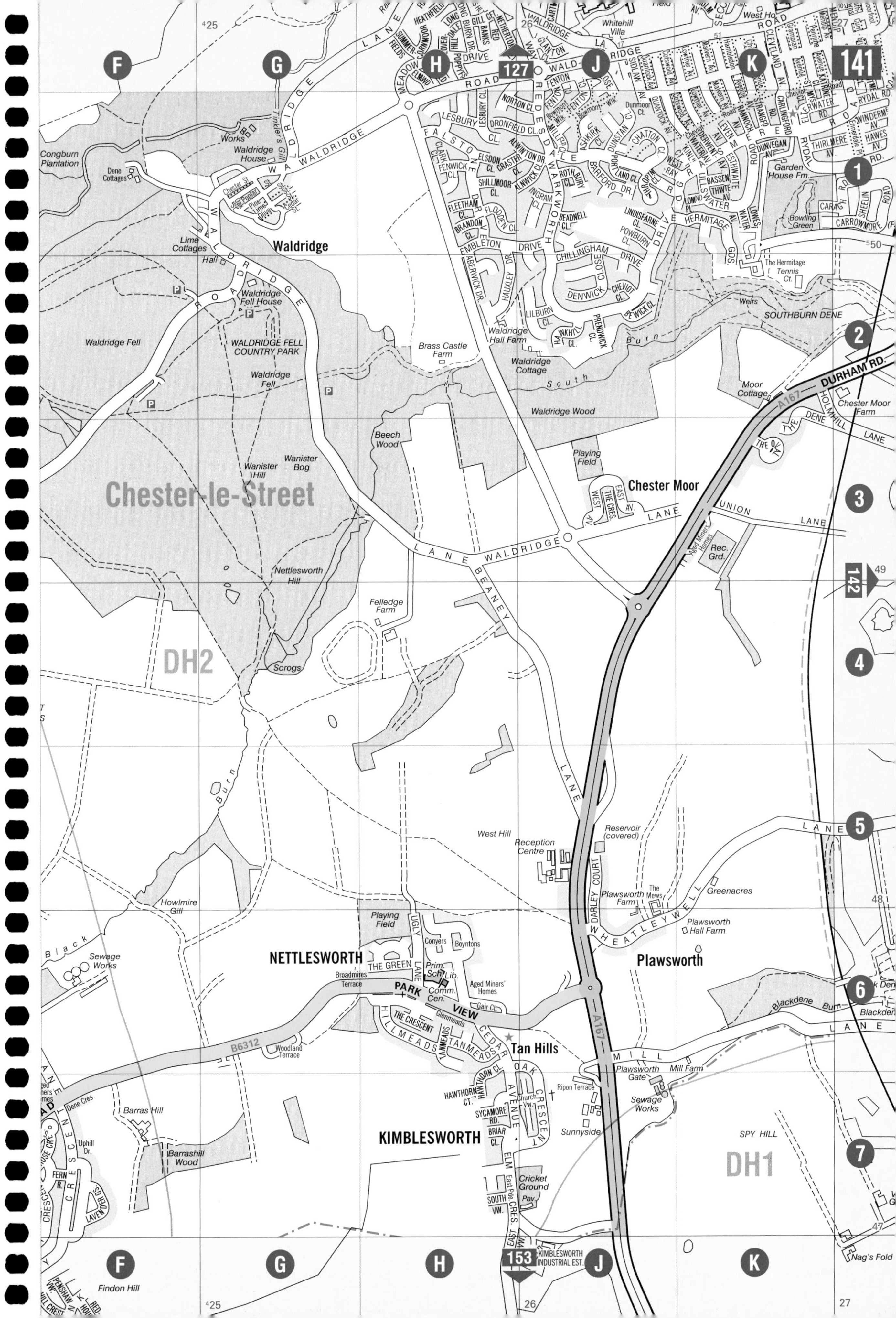
127
Waldridge
Chester-le-Street
Waldridge Fell
WALDRIDGE FELL
COUNTRY PARK
Waldridge Fell
Wanister Hill
Wanister Bog
Nettlesworth Hill
Scrogs
DH2
Congburn Plantation
Dene Cottages
Works
Waldridge House
Lime Cottages
Hall
Waldridge Fell House
Tinkler's Gill
Brass Castle Farm
Beech Wood
Felledge Farm
Waldridge Hall Farm
Waldridge Cottage
Waldridge Wood
South Burn
SOUTHBURN DENE
Weirs
The Hermitage
Tennis Ct.
Garden House Fm.
Bowling Green
Moor Cottage
Chester Moor Farm
Chester Moor
Playing Field
DURHAM RD.
A167
UNION LANE
Rec. Grd.
Aged Miners' Homes
WALDRIDGE LANE
BEANEY LANE
HOLMHILL LANE
142
West Hill
Reception Centre
Reservoir (covered)
DARLEY COURT
Plawsworth Farm
The Mews
Greenacres
Plawsworth Hall Farm
WHEATLEY WELL LANE
Plawsworth
Howlmire Gill
Black Burn
Sewage Works
NETTLESWORTH
Playing Field
Conyers
Boyntons
THE GREEN
UGLY LANE
Prim. Sch.
Lib.
Comm. Cen.
Aged Miners' Homes
Broadmires Terrace
PARK VIEW
B6312
Woodland Terrace
HILLMEADS
THE CRESCENT
TANMEADS
Glenmeads
Gair Ct.
CEDAR
Tan Hills
MILL LANE
Plawsworth Gate
Mill Farm
Sewage Works
Ripon Terrace
Sunnyside
Blackdene Burn
Barras Hill
Barrashill Wood
KIMBLESWORTH
HAWTHORN CT.
SYCAMORE RD.
BRIAR CL.
OAK CRESCENT
AVENUE
Church Vw.
ELM
Cricket Ground
Pav.
SOUTH VW.
EAST VW.
KIMBLESWORTH INDUSTRIAL EST.
153
SPY HILL
DH1
Nag's Fold
Findon Hill
Dene Cres.
Uphill Dr.
FERN R.
CRESCENT
LAVENDER GDS.
WALDRIDGE ROAD
MEADOW DR.
WEST HO.
CLEVELAND AV.
RYDAL RD.
CARROWMORE
HERMITAGE GDS.
DRIVE
EMBLETON DRIVE
CHILLINGHAM DRIVE
DENWICK CL.
WARKWORTH
REDESDALE
FALSTONE
LESBURY
Whitehill Villa
F
G
H
J
K
1
2
3
4
5
6
7
425
26
27
50
49
48
47

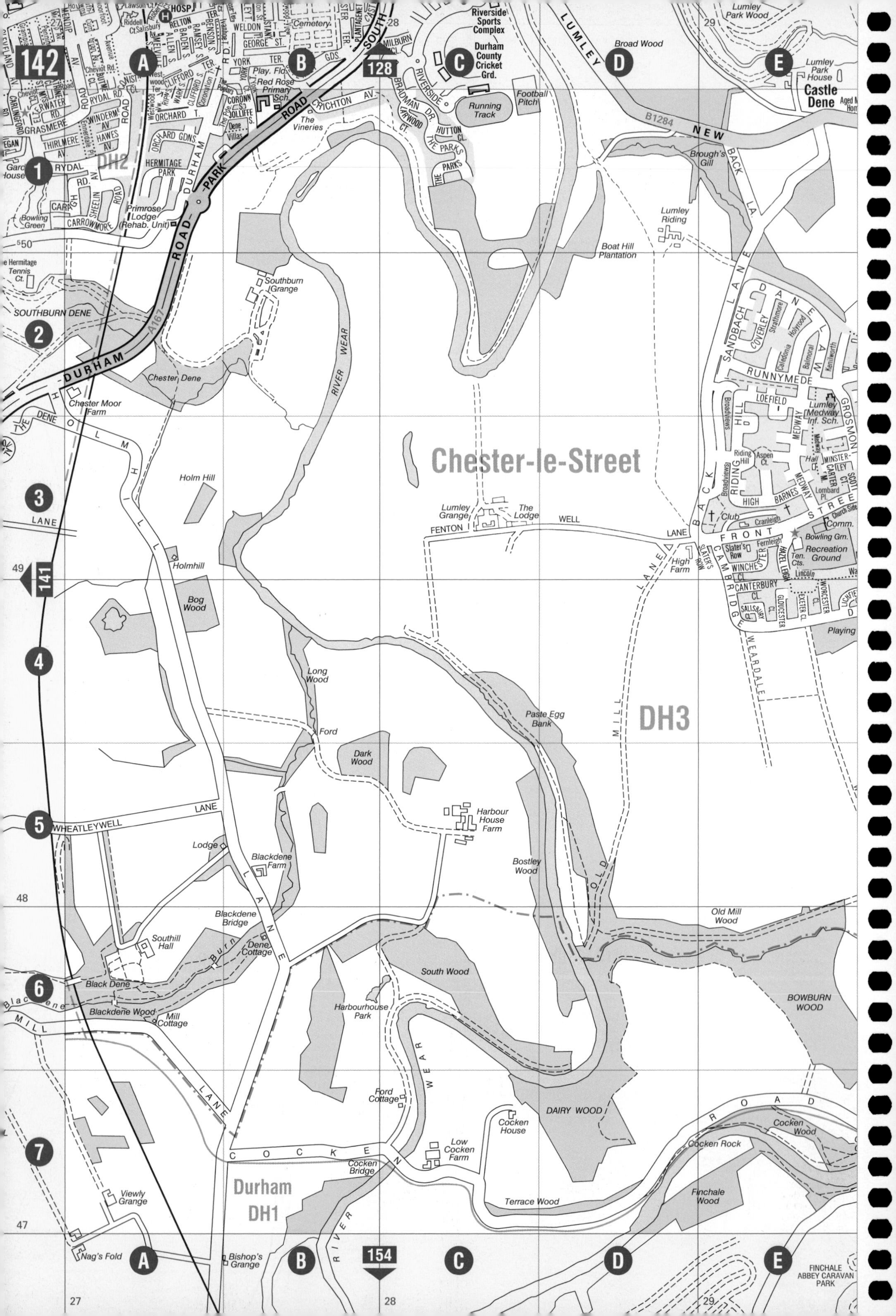
Chester-le-Street
DH2
DH3
Durham
DH1
Riverside Sports Complex
Durham County Cricket Grd.
Running Track
Football Pitch
Broad Wood
Lumley Park Wood
Lumley Park House
Castle Dene
B1284
NEW
LUMLEY
Brough's Gill
Lumley Riding
Boat Hill Plantation
Red Rose Primary Sch.
Play. Fld.
Cemetery
The Vineries
Primrose Lodge (Rehab. Unit)
Southburn Grange
SOUTHBURN DENE
The Hermitage Tennis Ct.
Chester Dene
Chester Moor Farm
DURHAM ROAD
PARK ROAD
SOUTH
A167
RIVER WEAR
Holm Hill
Holmhill
Bog Wood
Long Wood
Ford
Dark Wood
Harbour House Farm
Paste Egg Bank
Bostley Wood
Lumley Grange
The Lodge
FENTON WELL LANE
High Farm
MILL LANE
OLD
Lumley Medway Inf. Sch.
Bowling Grn.
Recreation Ground
Ten. Cts.
Playing
Comm.
WEARDALE
WHEATLEYWELL LANE
Lodge
Blackdene Farm
Blackdene Bridge
Southill Hall
Dene Cottage
Black Dene
Blackdene Wood
Mill Cottage
MILL LANE
South Wood
Harbourhouse Park
Old Mill Wood
BOWBURN WOOD
Ford Cottage
Cocken House
DAIRY WOOD
Low Cocken Farm
Cocken Bridge
COCKEN ROAD
Cocken Rock
Cocken Wood
Finchale Wood
Terrace Wood
Viewly Grange
Nag's Fold
Bishop's Grange
FINCHALE ABBEY CARAVAN PARK
128
141
154
27
28
29
47
48
49
550

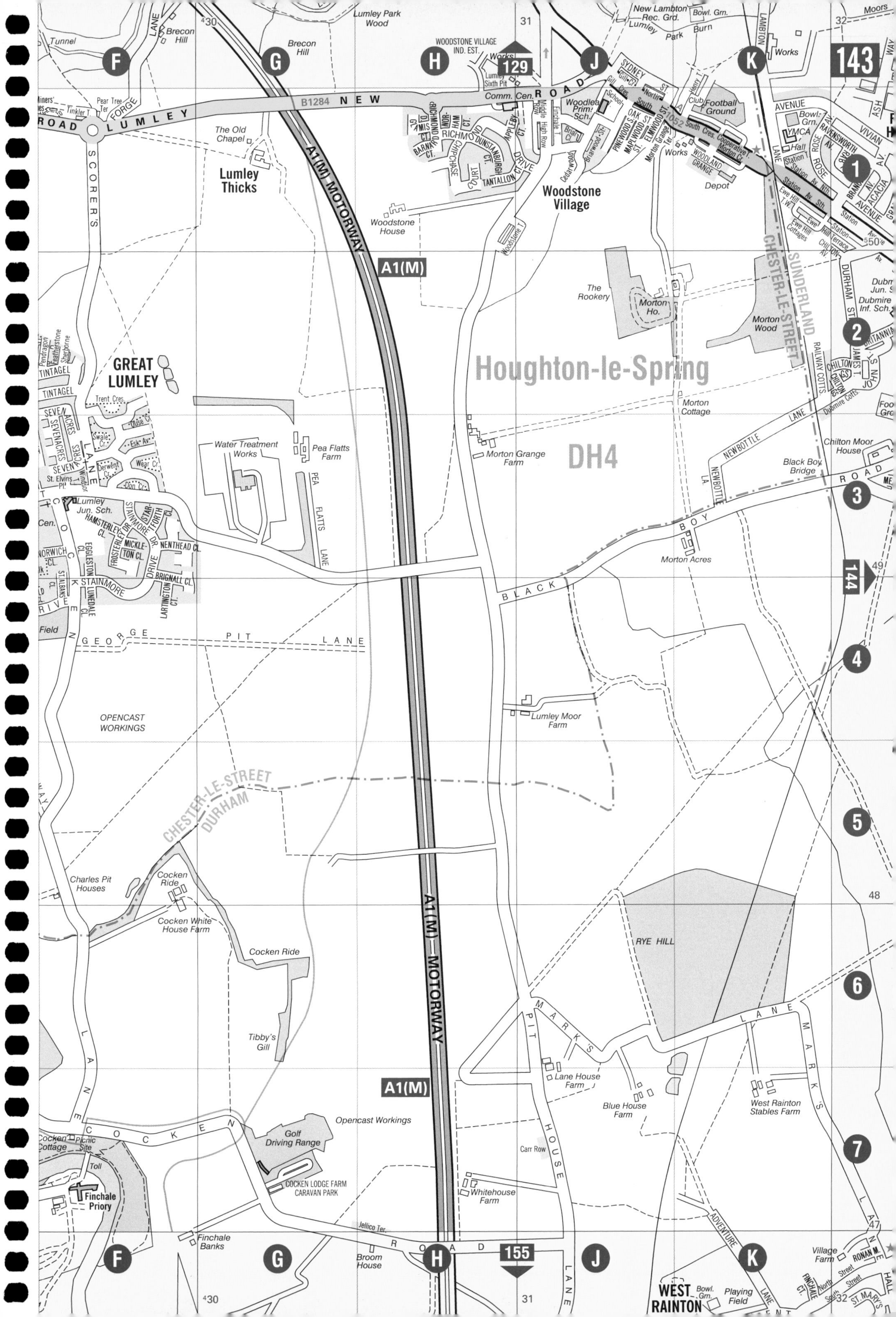

Houghton-le-Spring
DH4
GREAT LUMLEY
Lumley Thicks
Woodstone Village
WEST RAINTON
A1(M) MOTORWAY
A1(M)
NEW ROAD
B1284
LUMLEY ROAD
SCORER'S LANE
BLACK BOY ROAD
GEORGE PIT LANE
PEA FLATTS LANE
NEWBOTTLE LANE
COCKEN ROAD
COCKEN LANE
PIT HOUSE LANE
MARK'S LANE
SUNDERLAND
CHESTER-LE-STREET
DURHAM
Lumley Park Wood
Brecon Hill
WOODSTONE VILLAGE IND. EST.
The Old Chapel
Woodstone House
Water Treatment Works
Pea Flatts Farm
Morton Grange Farm
The Rookery
Morton Ho.
Morton Wood
Morton Cottage
Chilton Moor House
Black Boy Bridge
Morton Acres
Lumley Moor Farm
OPENCAST WORKINGS
Charles Pit Houses
Cocken Ride
Cocken White House Farm
Tibby's Gill
RYE HILL
Lane House Farm
Blue House Farm
West Rainton Stables Farm
Opencast Workings
Golf Driving Range
COCKEN LODGE FARM CARAVAN PARK
Carr Row
Whitehouse Farm
Finchale Priory
Finchale Banks
Broom House
Jellico Ter.
Village Farm
Playing Field
Lumley Jun. Sch.
Woodlea Prim. Sch.
Football Ground
Depot
Dubmire Inf. Sch.
New Lambton Rec. Grd.
Lumley Park Burn
129
144
155

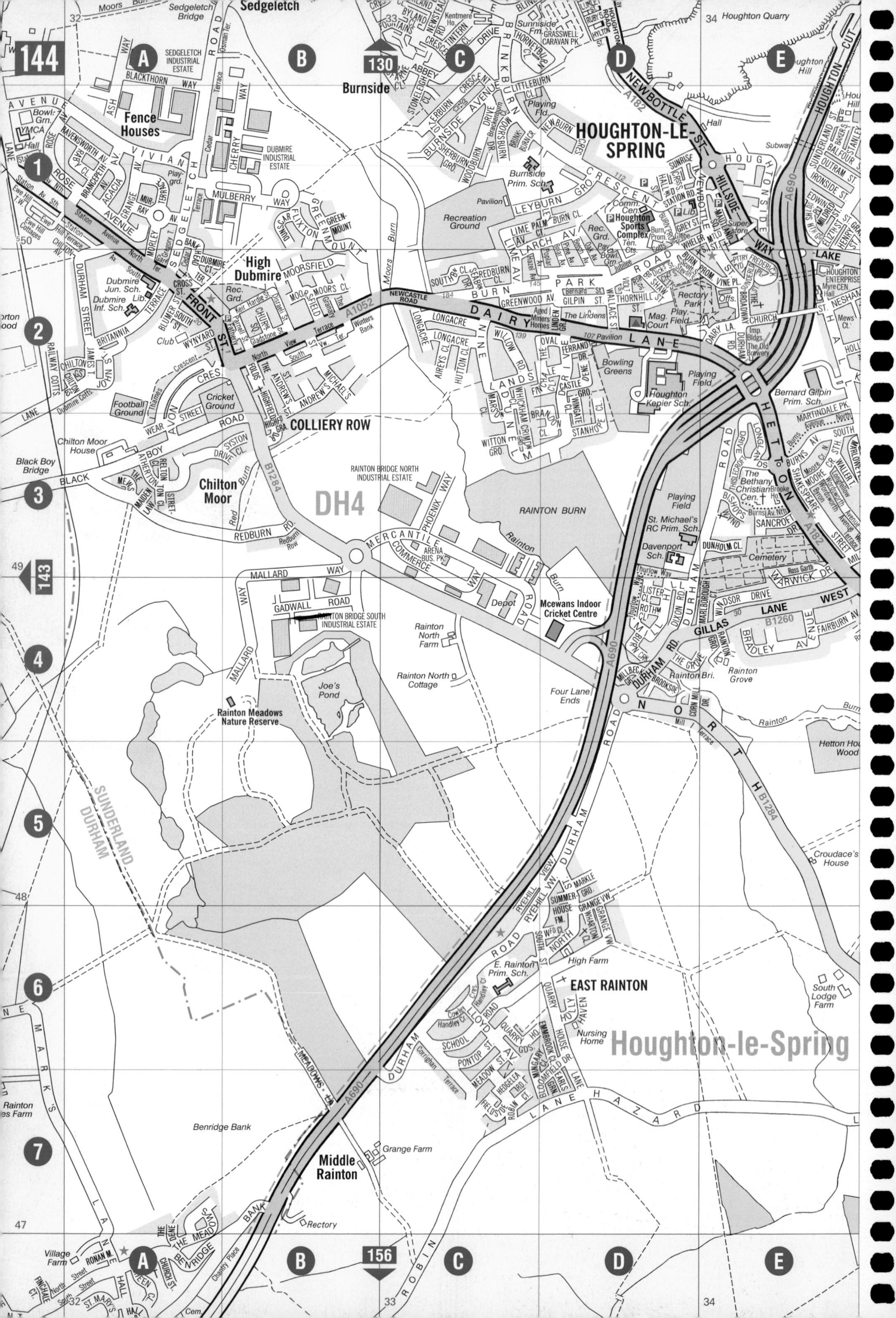
144
130
156
143
A
B
C
D
E
1
2
3
4
5
6
7
Sedgeletch
Sedgeletch Bridge
SEDGELETCH INDUSTRIAL ESTATE
Burnside
Houghton Quarry
Fence Houses
DUBMIRE INDUSTRIAL ESTATE
HOUGHTON-LE-SPRING
High Dubmire
Recreation Ground
Burnside Prim. Sch.
Houghton Sports Complex
NEWBOTTLE ST.
HOUGHTON CUT
A690
A182
A1052
NEWCASTLE ROAD
DAIRY LANE
FRONT ST.
COLLIERY ROW
Chilton Moor
Black Boy Bridge
Football Ground
Cricket Ground
DH4
RAINTON BRIDGE NORTH INDUSTRIAL ESTATE
RAINTON BURN
MERCANTILE
PHOENIX WAY
ARENA BUS. PK.
MALLARD WAY
GADWALL ROAD
RAINTON BRIDGE SOUTH INDUSTRIAL ESTATE
B1284
Mcewans Indoor Cricket Centre
Depot
Raintom North Farm
Raintom North Cottage
Joe's Pond
Rainton Meadows Nature Reserve
Four Lane Ends
Houghton Kepier Sch.
Bowling Greens
Playing Field
St. Michael's RC Prim. Sch.
Davenport Sch.
Cemetery
GILLAS LANE WEST
B1260
Rainton Bri.
Rainton Grove
NORTH ROAD
Hetton House Wood
Bernard Gilpin Prim. Sch.
The Bethany Christian Cen.
SUNDERLAND
DURHAM
Crowdace's House
RYEHILL VW.
SUMMERHOUSE FM.
E. Rainton Prim. Sch.
EAST RAINTON
High Farm
Nursing Home
South Lodge Farm
Houghton-le-Spring
HAZARD LANE
Benridge Bank
Grange Farm
Middle Rainton
Rectory
Village Farm
Rainton Farm
ROBIN LANE
32
33
34
47
48
49
50

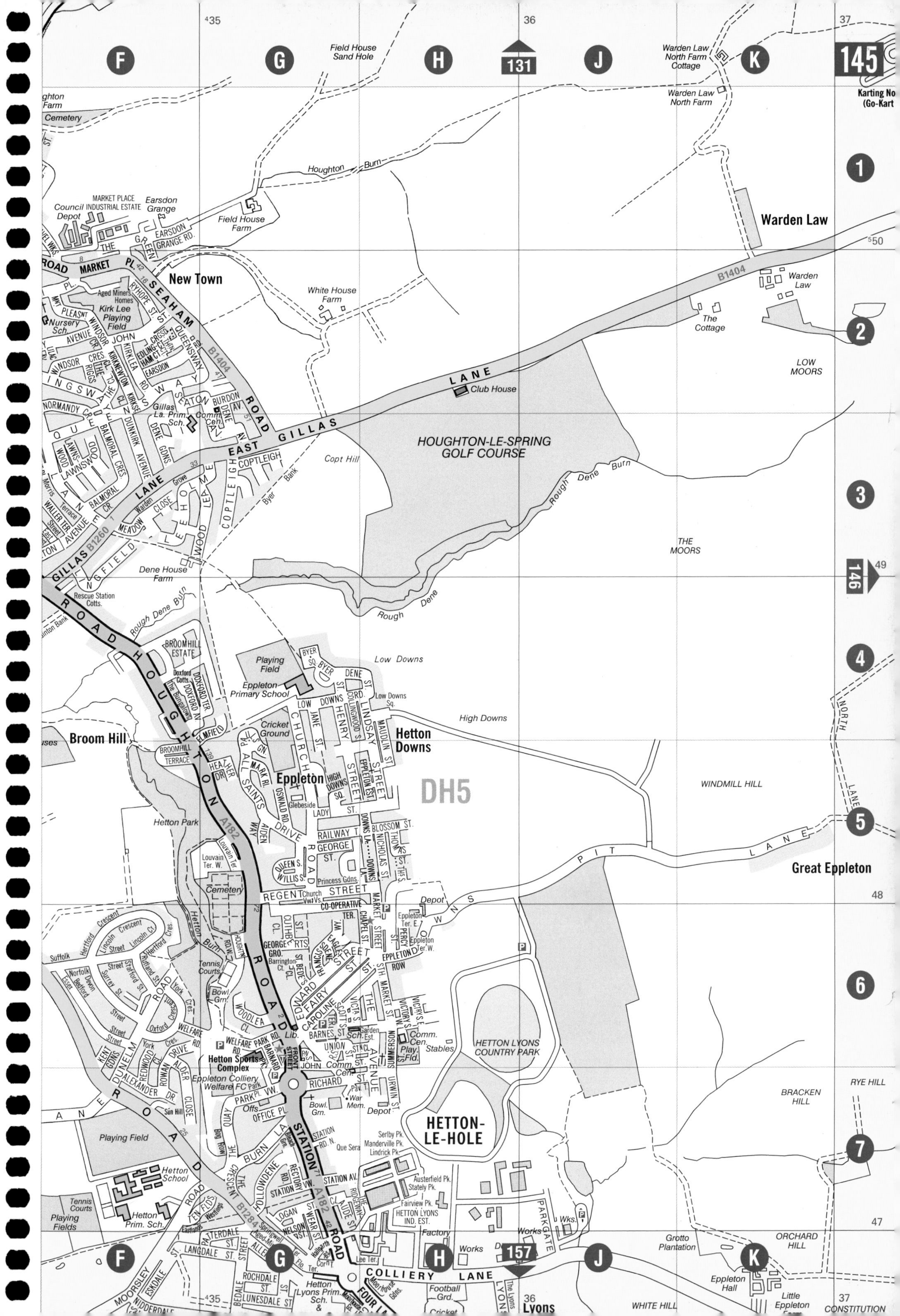

F
G
H
J
K
131
Field House Sand Hole
Warden Law North Farm Cottage
Warden Law North Farm
Karting No (Go-Kart
Cemetery
Houghton Burn
MARKET PLACE INDUSTRIAL ESTATE
Council Depot
Earsdon Grange
Field House Farm
EARSDON GRANGE RD.
Warden Law
MARKET PL.
SEAHAM ROAD
New Town
B1404
White House Farm
Warden Law
The Cottage
Aged Miners Homes
Kirk Lee Playing Field
LOW MOORS
EAST GILLAS LANE
Club House
HOUGHTON-LE-SPRING GOLF COURSE
Copt Hill
Rough Dene Burn
THE MOORS
Dene House Farm
Rescue Station Cotts.
146
Rough Dene
Low Downs
BROOMHILL ESTATE
Playing Field
Eppleton Primary School
High Downs
Broom Hill
Cricket Ground
Hetton Downs
Eppleton
DH5
WINDMILL HILL
HOUGHTON ROAD
Hetton Park
A182
PIT LANE
Great Eppleton
Cemetery
REGENT STREET
DOWNS LANE
HETTON LYONS COUNTRY PARK
Hetton Sports Complex
Eppleton Colliery Welfare FC Park
RYE HILL
BRACKEN HILL
HETTON-LE-HOLE
STATION ROAD
Playing Field
Hetton School
Hetton Prim. Sch.
HETTON LYONS IND. EST.
Grotto Plantation
ORCHARD HILL
157
COLLIERY LANE
Eppleton Hall
Little Eppleton
Lyons
WHITE HILL
CONSTITUTION

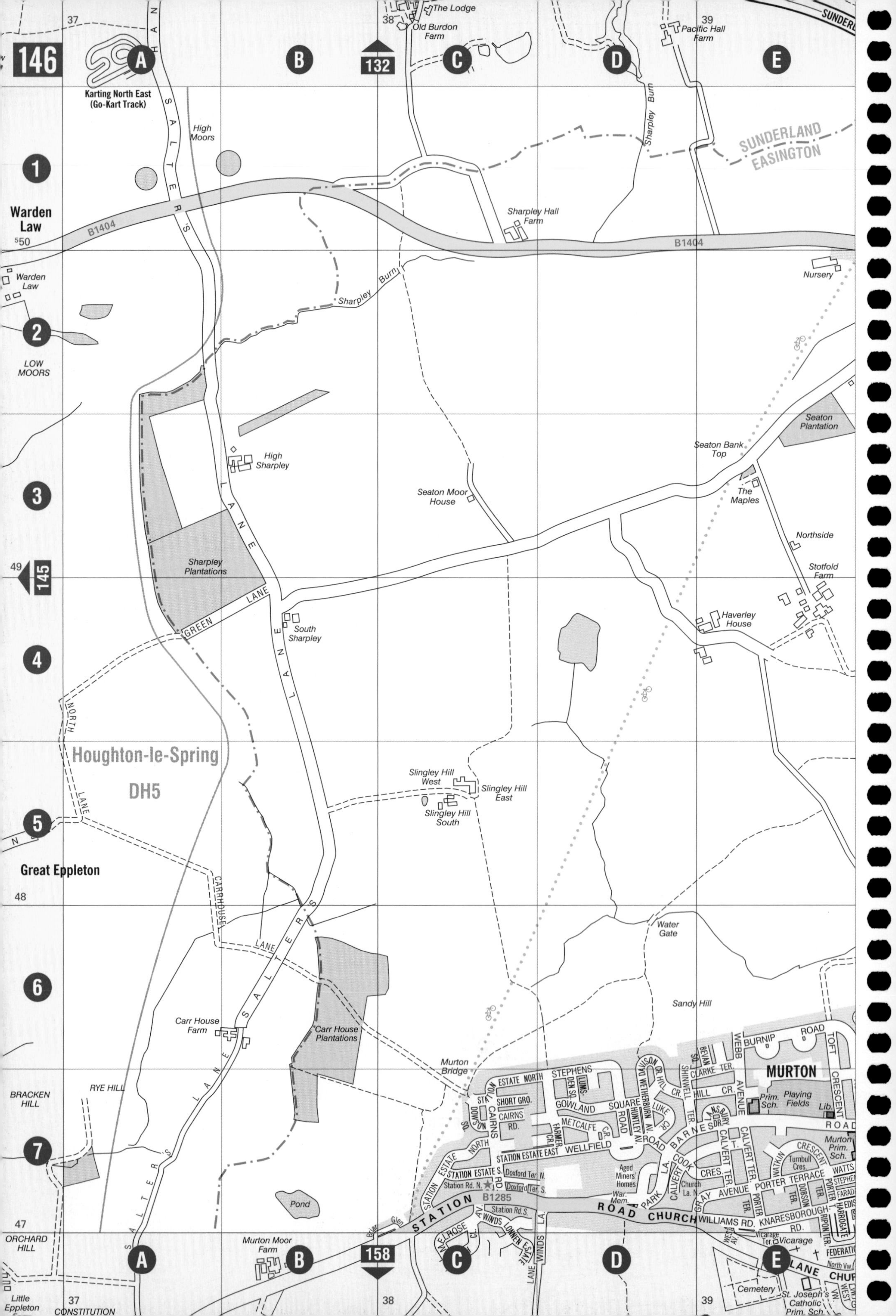
Karting North East (Go-Kart Track)
High Moors
Warden Law
B1404
Sharpley Hall Farm
Sharpley Burn
The Lodge
Old Burdon Farm
Pacific Hall Farm
SUNDERLAND
EASINGTON
Nursery
LOW MOORS
High Sharpley
Seaton Plantation
Seaton Bank Top
The Maples
Seaton Moor House
Northside
Stotfold Farm
Sharpley Plantations
GREEN LANE
SALTERS LANE
South Sharpley
Haverley House
NORTH LANE
CARRHOUSE LANE
Houghton-le-Spring
DH5
Slingley Hill West
Slingley Hill East
Slingley Hill South
Great Eppleton
Water Gate
Sandy Hill
Carr House Farm
Carr House Plantations
Murton Bridge
BRACKEN HILL
RYE HILL
MURTON
Playing Fields
Prim. Sch.
Lib.
Murton Prim. Sch.
STATION ROAD
CHURCH LANE
B1285
Pond
Aged Miners' Homes
War. Mem.
Vicarage
ORCHARD HILL
Murton Moor Farm
Cemetery
St. Joseph's Catholic Prim. Sch.
Little Eppleton
CONSTITUTION

132
145
158

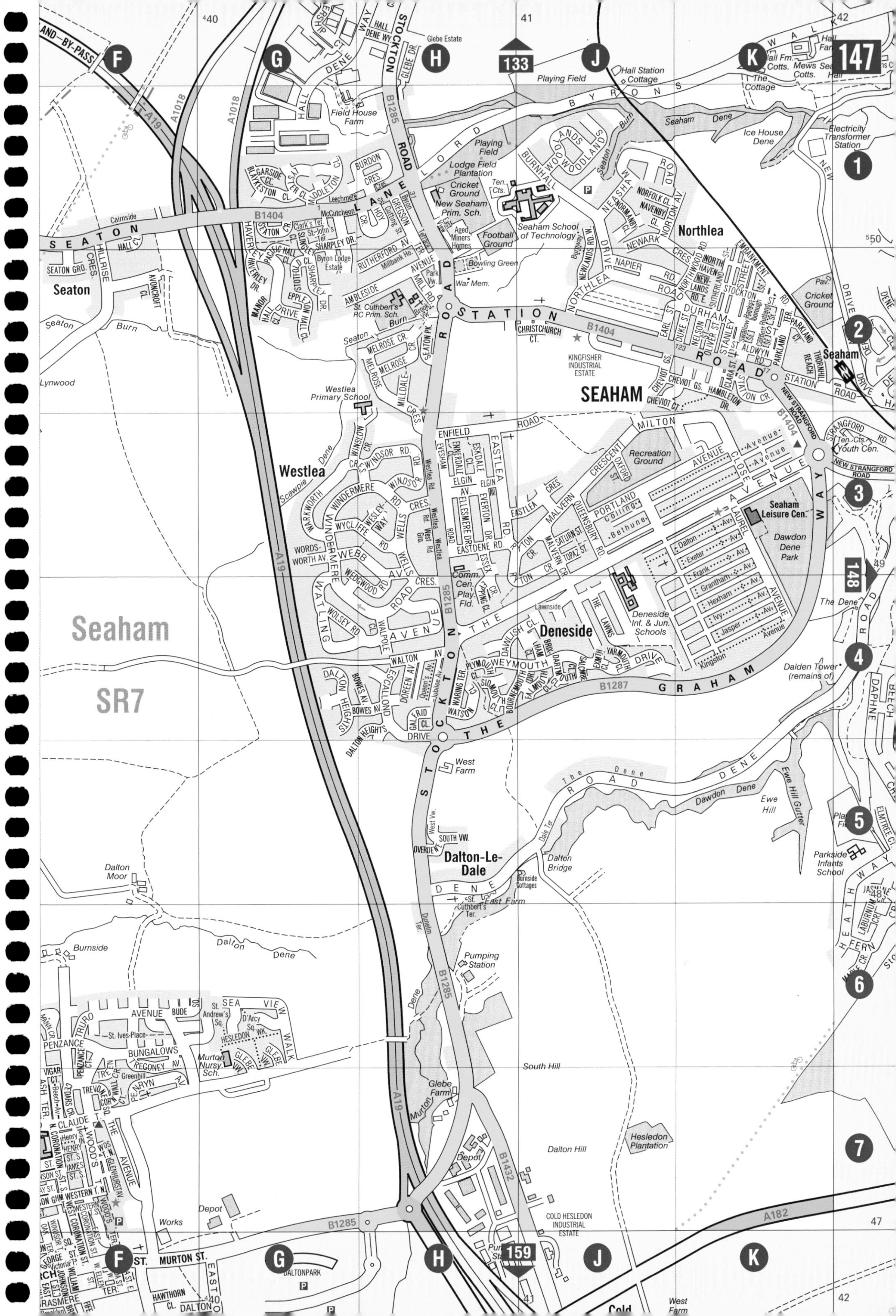
SEAHAM
Seaham
SR7
Northlea
Westlea
Deneside
Seaton
Dalton-Le-Dale
Seaham Leisure Cen.
Dawdon Dene Park
Recreation Ground
Seaham School of Technology
New Seaham Prim. Sch.
KINGFISHER INDUSTRIAL ESTATE
COLD HESLEDON INDUSTRIAL ESTATE
Deneside Inf. & Jun. Schools
Westlea Primary School
St. Cuthbert's RC Prim. Sch.
Parkside Infants School
Dalden Tower (remains of)
Hesledon Plantation
Dalton Hill
South Hill
Glebe Farm
Pumping Station
West Farm
Lodge Field Plantation
Cricket Ground
Football Ground
Playing Field
Seaham Dene
Dawdon Dene
Dalton Dene
Ewe Hill
A19
A182
B1404
B1285
B1287
B1432
A1018
133
148
159

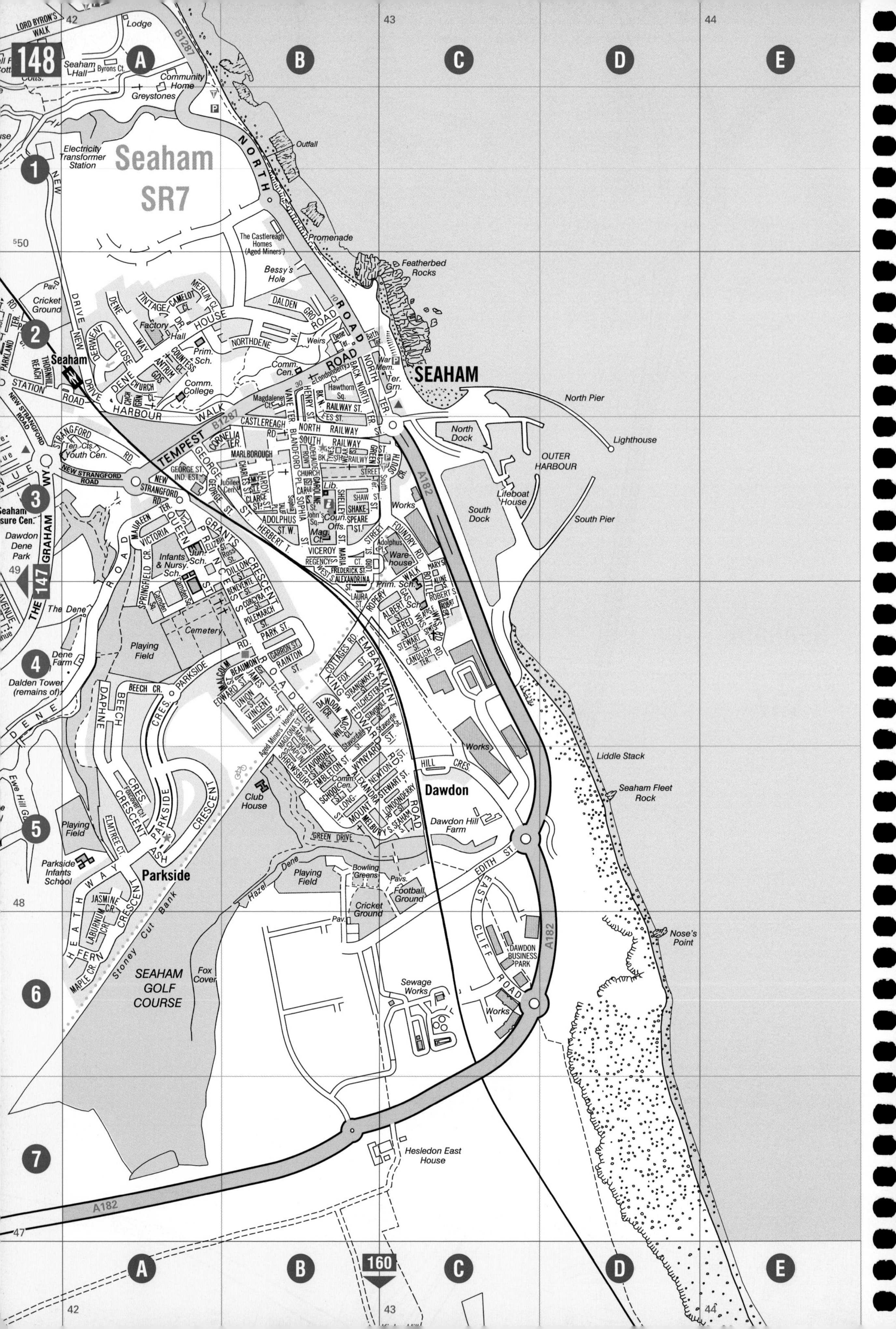

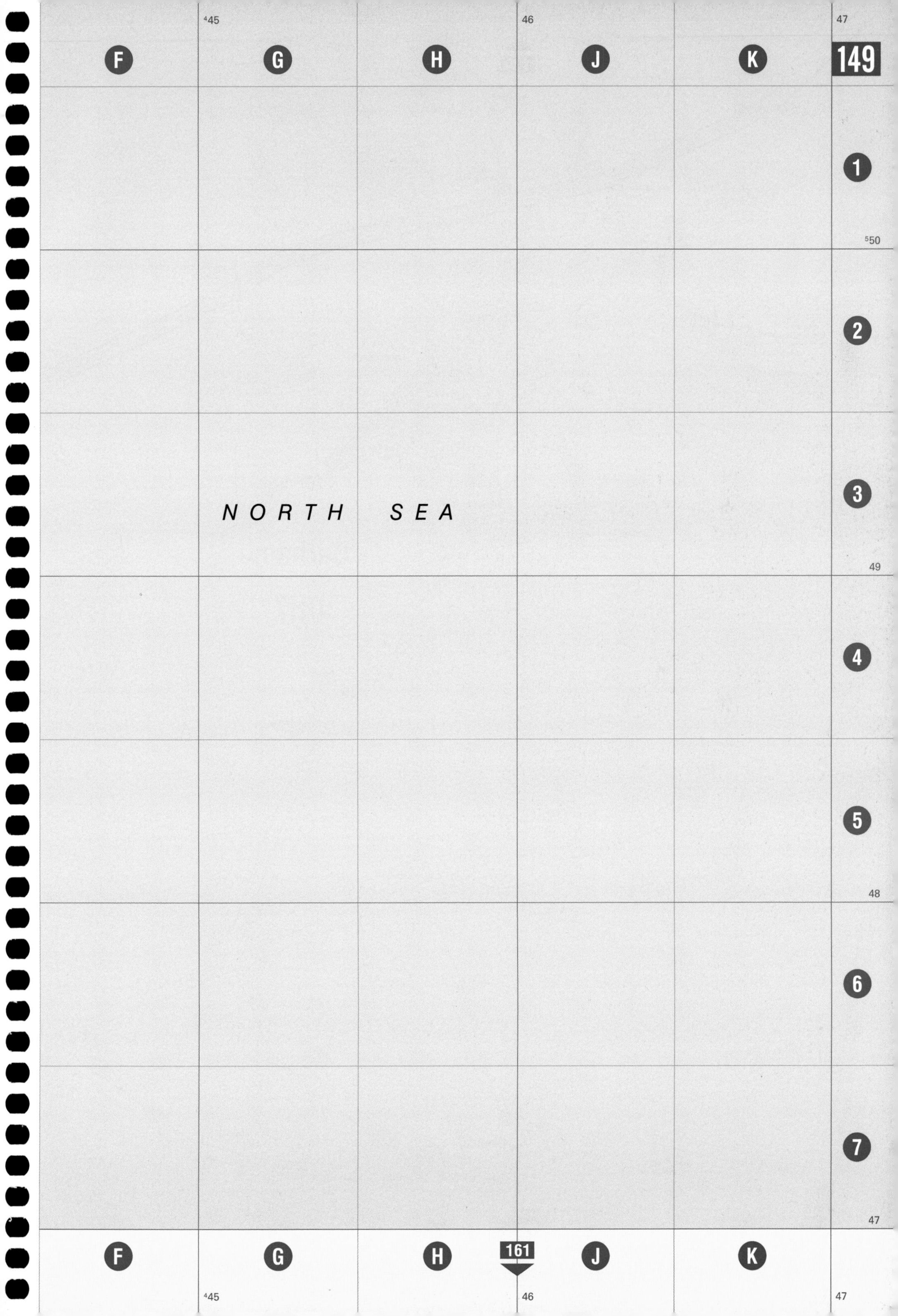
149
445
46
47
F
G
H
J
K
1
2
3
4
5
6
7
550
49
48
47
NORTH SEA
161
F
G
H
J
K
445
46
47

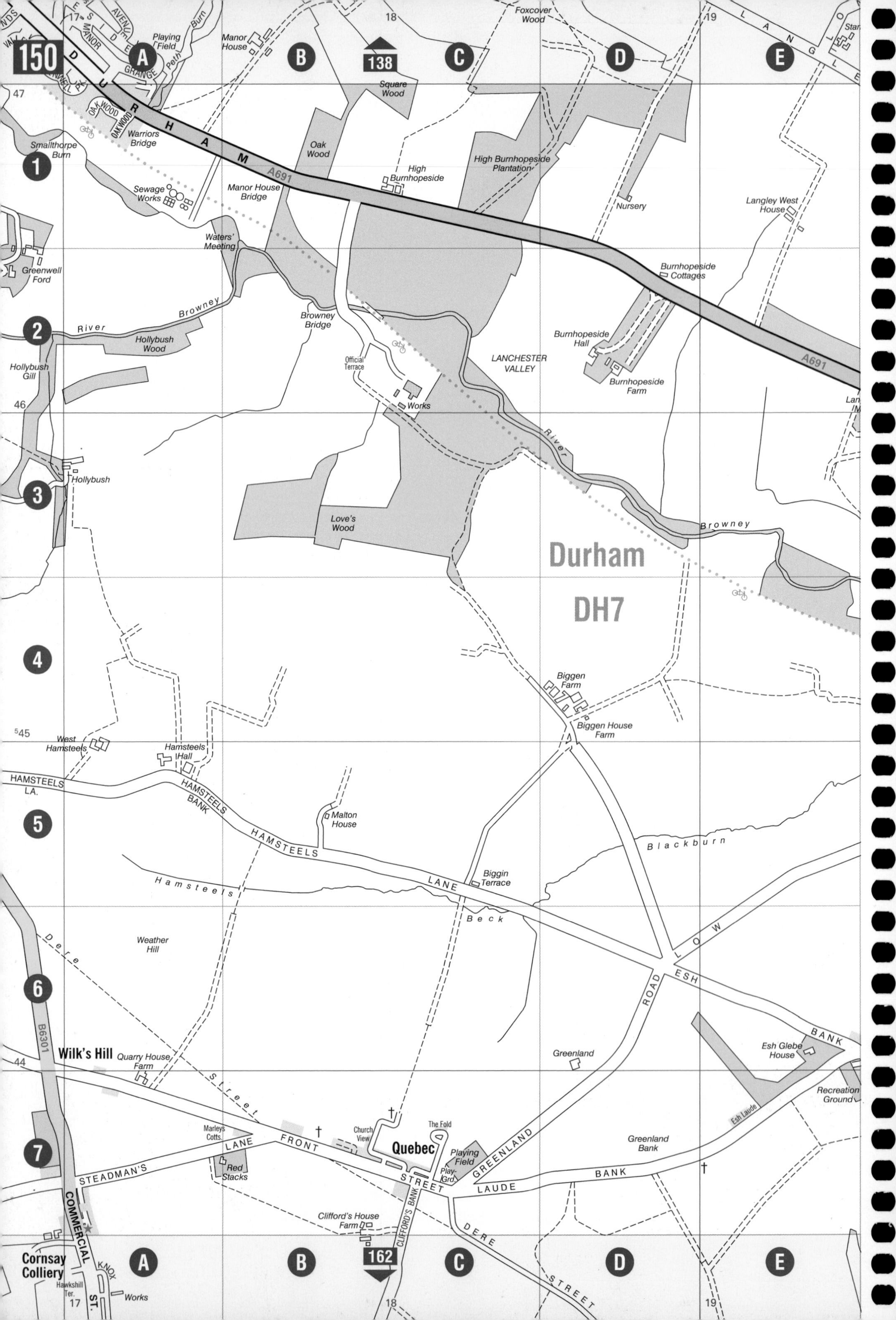

138
162
A
B
C
D
E
1
2
3
4
5
6
7
17
18
19
47
46
45
44
Playing Field
Manor House
Foxcover Wood
Square Wood
Oak Wood
Smallthorpe Burn
Warriors Bridge
DURHAM
A691
High Burnhopeside
High Burnhopeside Plantation
Sewage Works
Manor House Bridge
Nursery
Langley West House
Waters' Meeting
Greenwell Ford
Burnhopeside Cottages
River Browney
Hollybush Wood
Browney Bridge
Burnhopeside Hall
Burnhopeside Farm
Hollybush Gill
Official Terrace
LANCHESTER VALLEY
Works
Hollybush
Love's Wood
Durham
DH7
Biggen Farm
Biggen House Farm
West Hamsteels
Hamsteels Hall
HAMSTEELS LA.
HAMSTEELS BANK
Malton House
HAMSTEELS LANE
Blackburn
Biggin Terrace
Hamsteels Beck
Weather Hill
Dere Street
LOW ESH BANK
ROAD
B6301
Wilk's Hill
Quarry House Farm
Greenland
Esh Glebe House
Recreation Ground
Marleys Cotts.
Church View
The Fold
Quebec
Playing Field
Play Grd
Esh Laude
Greenland Bank
STEADMAN'S LANE
FRONT STREET
Red Stacks
GREENLAND
LAUDE BANK
COMMERCIAL
CLIFFORD'S BANK
Clifford's House Farm
DERE STREET
Cornsay Colliery
KNOX ST.
Hawkshill Ter.
Works

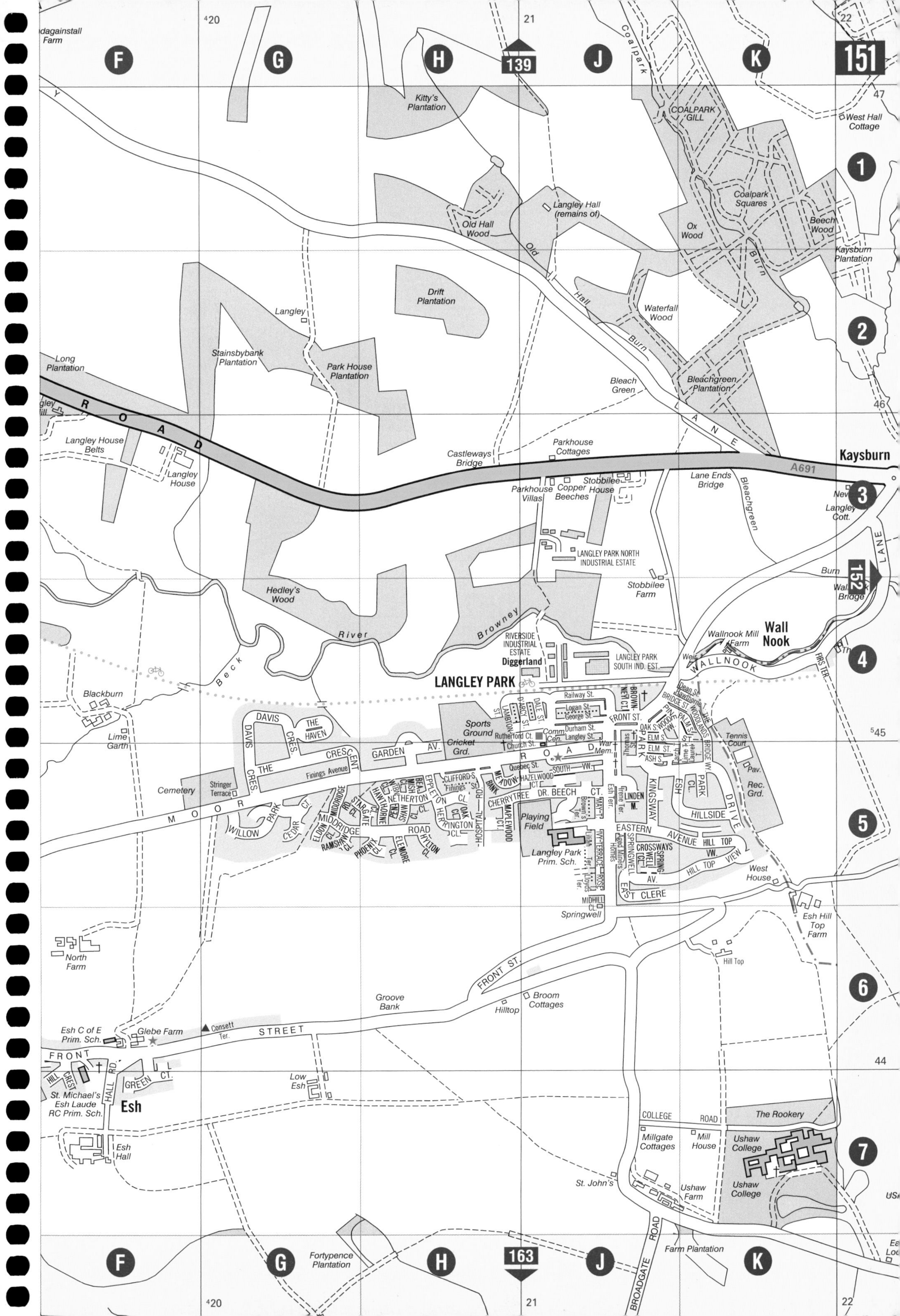
139
152
163
Kitty's Plantation
Coalpark Gill
West Hall Cottage
Langley Hall (remains of)
Old Hall Wood
Ox Wood
Coalpark Squares
Beech Wood
Kaysburn Plantation
Drift Plantation
Langley
Waterfall Wood
Stainsbybank Plantation
Park House Plantation
Long Plantation
Bleach Green
Bleachgreen Plantation
Langley House Belts
Langley House
Castleways Bridge
Parkhouse Cottages
Kaysburn
A691
Lane Ends Bridge
Parkhouse Villas
Copper Beeches
Stobbilee House
Langley Cott.
LANGLEY PARK NORTH INDUSTRIAL ESTATE
Stobbilee Farm
Hedley's Wood
River Browney
Wallnook Mill Farm
Wall Nook
Wall Bridge
RIVERSIDE INDUSTRIAL ESTATE
Diggerland
LANGLEY PARK SOUTH IND. EST.
LANGLEY PARK
Blackburn
Lime Garth
Sports Ground
Cricket Grd.
Tennis Court
Pav.
Rec. Grd.
Cemetery
Stringer Terrace
Playing Field
Langley Park Prim. Sch.
West House
Springwell
Esh Hill Top Farm
Hill Top
North Farm
Groove Bank
Hilltop
Broom Cottages
Esh C of E Prim. Sch.
Glebe Farm
Consett Ter.
Low Esh
St. Michael's Esh Laude RC Prim. Sch.
Esh
Esh Hall
The Rookery
Millgate Cottages
Mill House
Ushaw College
St. John's
Ushaw Farm
Fortypence Plantation
Farm Plantation
BROADGATE ROAD
MOOR ROAD
FRONT STREET
COLLEGE ROAD

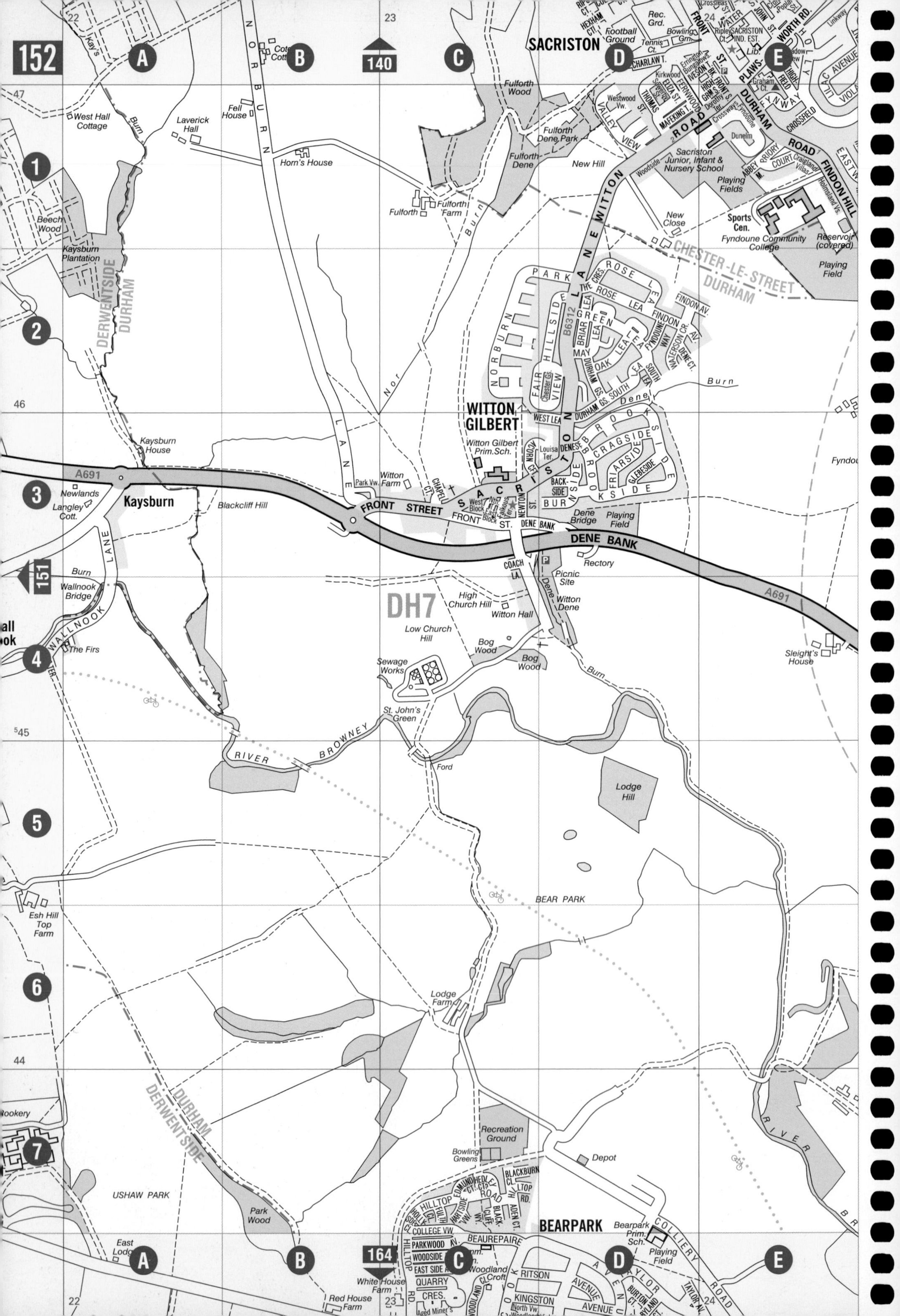

SACRISTON
WITTON GILBERT
Kaysburn
BEARPARK
DH7
A691
FRONT STREET
DENE BANK
B6312
WITTON LANE
NORBURN LANE
CHESTER-LE-STREET
DURHAM
DERWENTSIDE
DURHAM ROAD
FINDON HILL
Fulforth Wood
Fulforth Dene Park
Fulforth Dene
New Hill
Fulforth Farm
Fulforth
Horn's House
Laverick Hall
Fell House
West Hall Cottage
Beech Wood
Kaysburn Plantation
Kaysburn House
Newlands
Langley Cott.
Blackcliff Hill
Wallnook Bridge
The Firs
Witton Farm
Witton Gilbert Prim.Sch.
Dene Bridge
Playing Field
Rectory
Picnic Site
Witton Dene
High Church Hill
Witton Hall
Low Church Hill
Bog Wood
Sewage Works
St. John's Green
RIVER BROWNEY
Ford
Lodge Hill
BEAR PARK
Esh Hill Top Farm
Lodge Farm
Recreation Ground
Bowling Greens
Depot
USHAW PARK
Park Wood
East Lodge
White House Farm
Red House Farm
Bearpark Prim. Sch.
Playing Field
Sleight's House
Sacriston Junior, Infant & Nursery School
Playing Fields
Sports Cen.
Fyndoune Community College
Reservoir (covered)
Playing Field
New Close
Football Ground
Rec. Grd.
Tennis Ct.
Bowling Grn.
Lib.
SACRISTON IND. EST.
COLLIERY ROAD

140
151
164

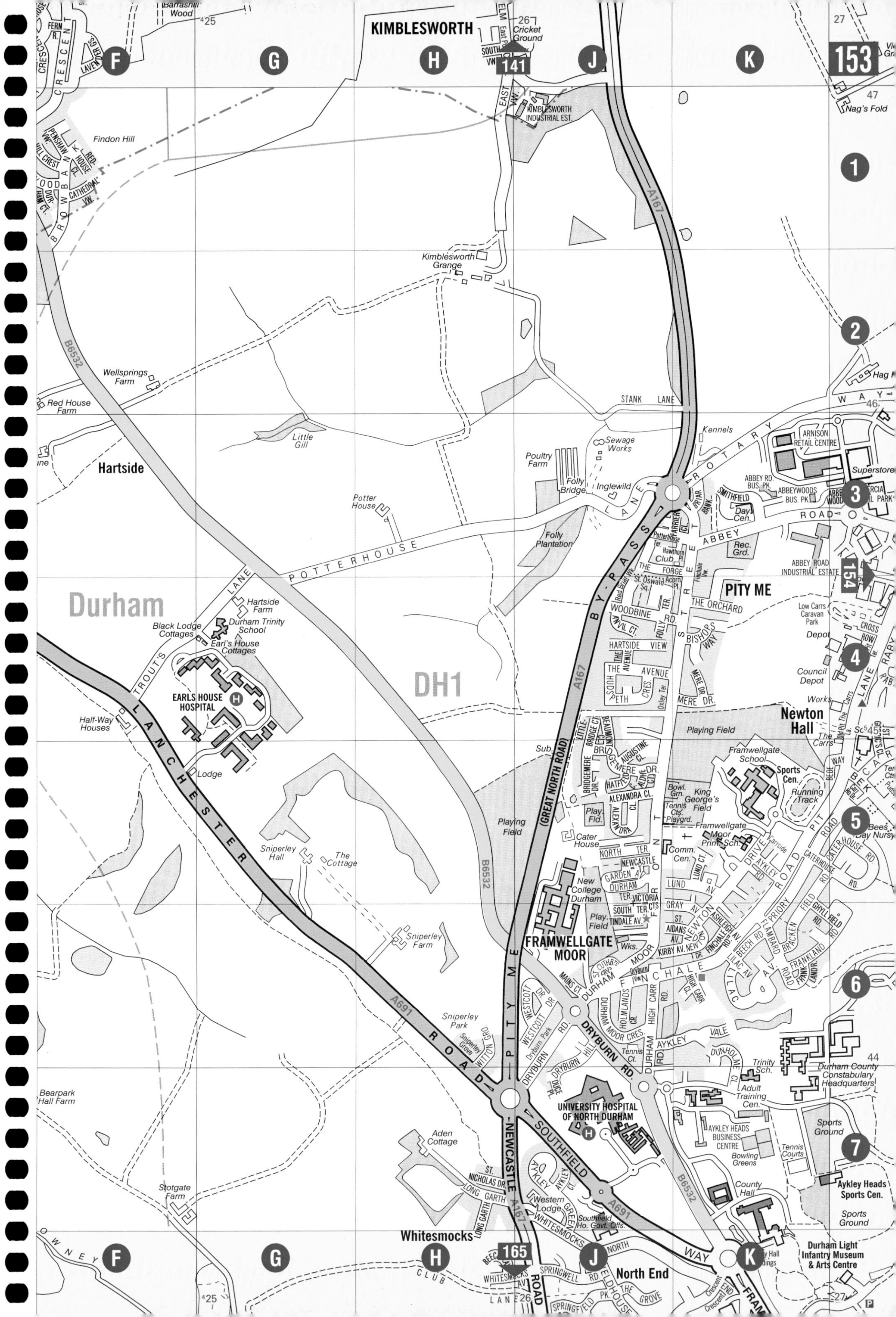

KIMBLESWORTH

F　G　H　141　J　K

1

2

3

154

4

5

6

7

Nag's Fold

Cricket Ground

KIMBLESWORTH INDUSTRIAL EST.

Findon Hill

Kimblesworth Grange

STANK LANE

Hag

Wellsprings Farm

Red House Farm

Hartside

Little Gill

Sewage Works

Kennels

Poultry Farm

Folly Bridge

Inglewild

ARNISON RETAIL CENTRE

Superstore

ABBEY RD. BUS. PK.

ABBEYWOODS BUS. PK.

Day Cen.

Potter House

Folly Plantation

POTTERHOUSE LANE

ABBEY ROAD

Rec. Grd.

ABBEY ROAD INDUSTRIAL ESTATE

PITY ME

Low Carrs Caravan Park

Depot

CROSS ROW

Durham

Hartside Farm

Durham Trinity School

Black Lodge Cottages

Earl's House Cottages

WOODBINE

HARTSIDE VIEW

BISHOPS WAY

Council Depot

Works

DH1

EARLS HOUSE HOSPITAL

THE AVENUE

MERE DR.

Newton Hall

The Carrs

Half-Way Houses

Lodge

Playing Field

Framwellgate School

Sports Cen.

Running Track

Bees Day Nursy.

Sniperley Hall

The Cottage

Playing Field

BRIDGEMERE DR.

AUGUSTINE

ALEXANDRA CL.

Bowl. Grn.

King George's Field

Tennis Cts. Playgrd.

Framwellgate Moor Prim.Sch.

CATERHOUSE RD.

Sniperley Farm

Play. Fld.

Cater House

NORTH TER.

NEWCASTLE GARDEN

New College Durham

VICTORIA SOUTH TER. CTS.

TINDALE AV.

GRAY ST.

LUND AV.

LUND CT.

PRIORY RD.

FIELD

GHYLL FIELD RD.

FRAMWELLGATE MOOR

ST. AIDANS AV.

KIRBY AV.

NEWTON

ASHLEIGH

BEECH AV.

LILAC

Sniperley Park

MAINS CT.

DURHAM

DURHAM MOOR CRES.

HOLMLANDS CRES.

DURHAM HIGH CARR RD.

AYKLEY

DUNHOLME CT.

Trinity Sch.

VALE

Durham County Constabulary Headquarters

Bearpark Hall Farm

DRYBURN RD.

Tennis Ct.

DRYBURN HILL

Adult Training Cen.

Sports Ground

Aden Cottage

ST. NICHOLAS DR.

Dryburn Park

UNIVERSITY HOSPITAL OF NORTH DURHAM

AYKLEY HEADS BUSINESS CENTRE

Bowling Greens

Tennis Courts

Stotgate Farm

LONG GARTH

Western Lodge

AYKLEY GREEN

Southfield Ho. Govt. Offs.

County Hall

Aykley Heads Sports Cen.

Sports Ground

F　G　**Whitesmocks**　H　165　J　**North End**　K

Durham Light Infantry Museum & Arts Centre

WHITESMOCKS

SPRINGWELL RD.

NEWCASTLE RD.

SOUTHFIELD

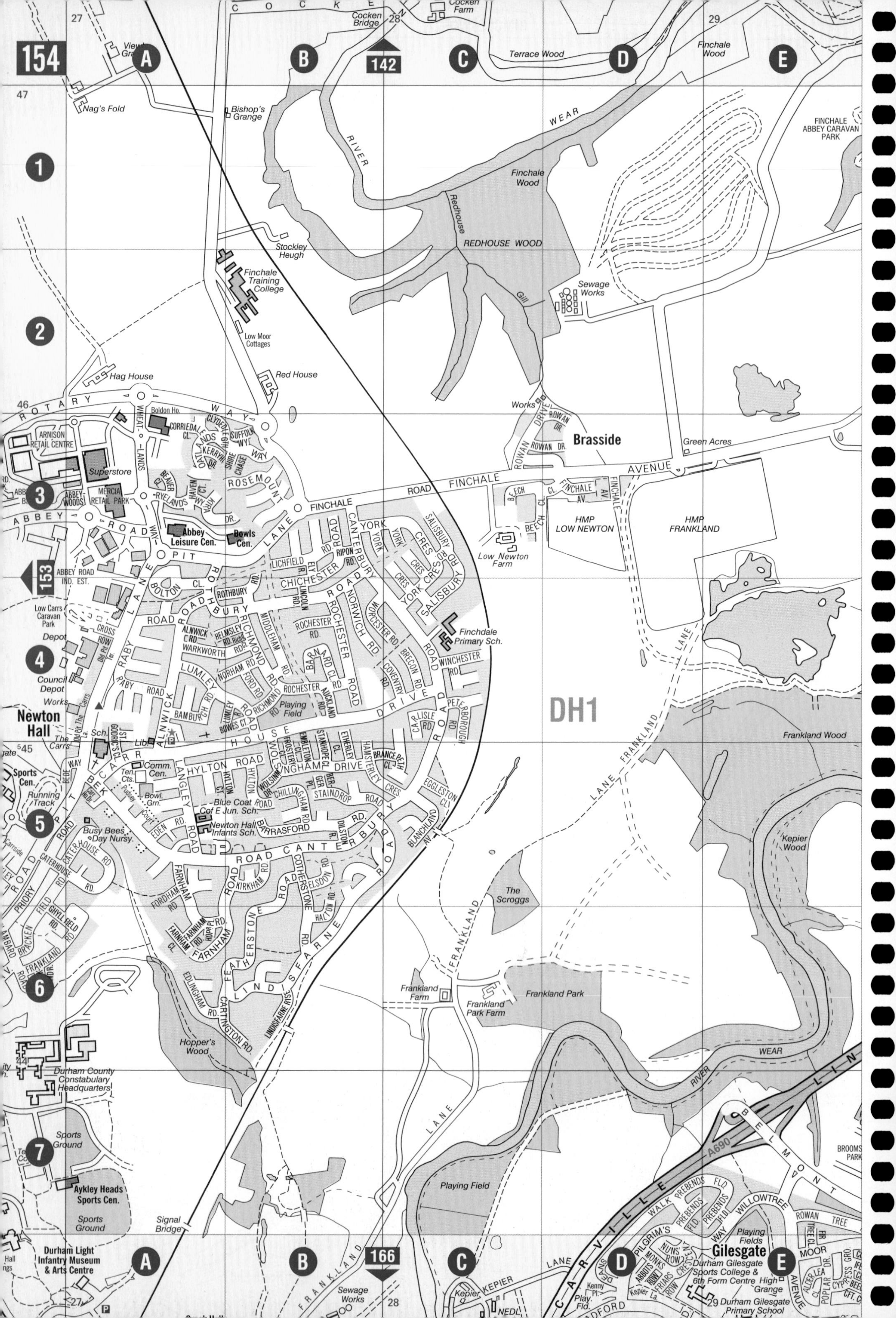

A
B
C
D
E
1
2
3
4
5
6
7
142
153
166
DH1
Cocken Bridge
Cocken Farm
Terrace Wood
Finchale Wood
Nag's Fold
Bishop's Grange
RIVER WEAR
FINCHALE ABBEY CARAVAN PARK
Finchale Wood
Redhouse
REDHOUSE WOOD
Stockley Heugh
Finchale Training College
Sewage Works
Gill
Low Moor Cottages
Hag House
Red House
Works
ROTARY WAY
Boldon Ho.
Brasside
Green Acres
ARNISON RETAIL CENTRE
Superstore
MERCIA RETAIL PARK
ROSEMOUNT
FINCHALE ROAD
FINCHALE AVENUE
HMP LOW NEWTON
HMP FRANKLAND
Low Newton Farm
ABBEY ROAD
Abbey Leisure Cen.
Bowls Cen.
PIT LANE
ABBEY ROAD IND. EST.
Low Carrs Caravan Park
Depot
Council Depot
Works
Finchdale Primary Sch.
Newton Hall
Playing Field
HOUSE DRIVE
Lib
Sch.
The Carrs
Sports Cen.
Running Track
Comm. Cen.
Ten. Cts.
Bowl. Grn.
Blue Coat C of E Jun. Sch.
Newton Hall Infants Sch.
Busy Bees Day Nursy.
CANTERBURY ROAD
LINDISFARNE
Frankland Wood
Kepier Wood
The Scroggs
FRANKLAND LANE
Frankland Farm
Frankland Park Farm
Frankland Park
Hopper's Wood
WEAR
RIVER
Durham County Constabulary Headquarters
Sports Ground
Aykley Heads Sports Cen.
Sports Ground
Signal Bridge
Playing Field
Durham Light Infantry Museum & Arts Centre
Sewage Works
BROOMS PARK
A690
CARVILLE LINK
BELMONT
WILLOWTREE
ROWAN TREE
Gilesgate
Playing Fields
Durham Gilesgate Sports College & 6th Form Centre
High Grange
Durham Gilesgate Primary School
KEPIER LANE
Kepier

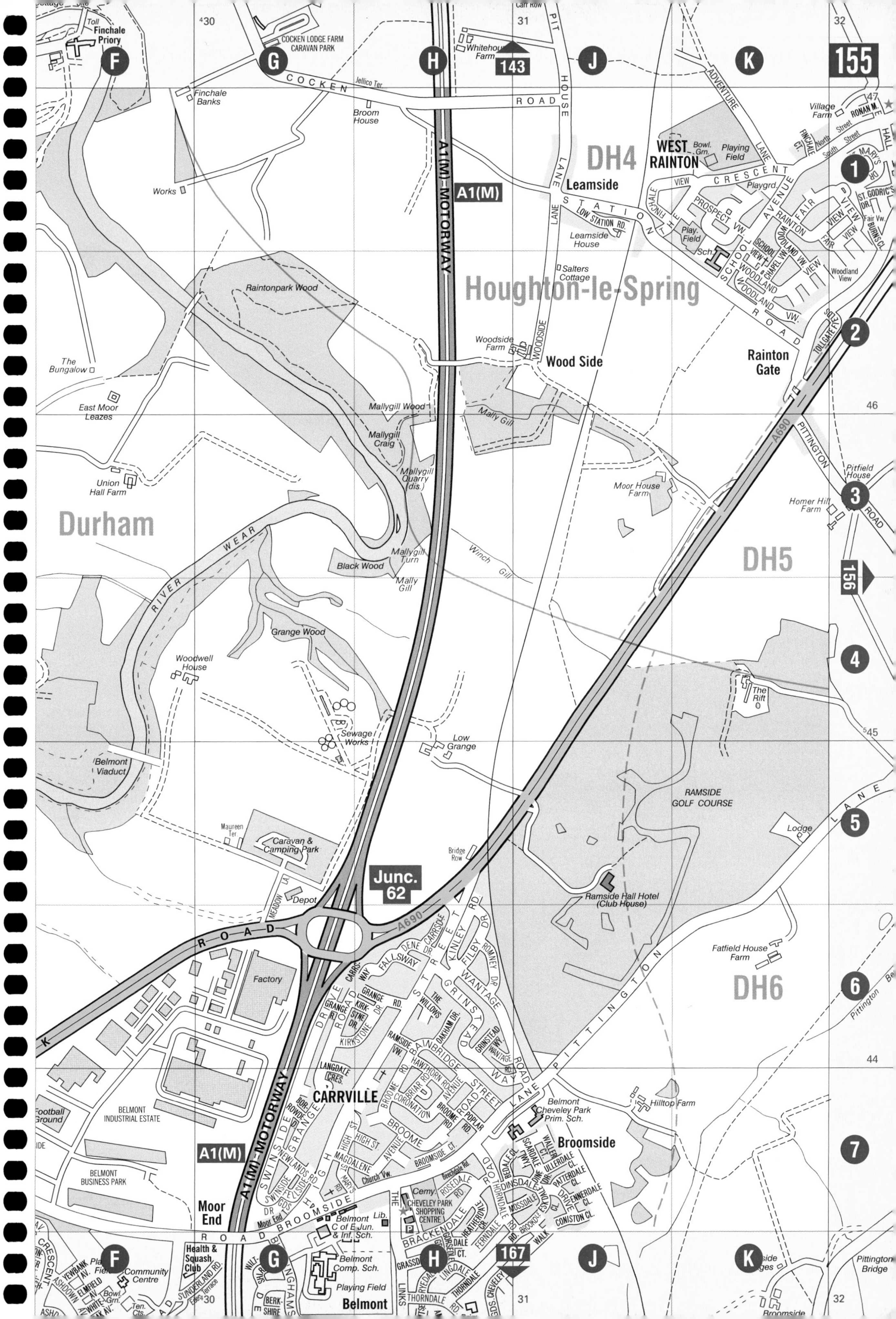

Finchale Priory
COCKEN LODGE FARM CARAVAN PARK
Whitehouse Farm
COCKEN ROAD
Finchale Banks
Broom House
PIT HOUSE LANE
DH4
WEST RAINTON
Playing Field
Leamside
A1(M)
A1(M) MOTORWAY
Works
STATION ROAD
LOW STATION RD.
Leamside House
Salters Cottage
Raintonpark Wood
Houghton-le-Spring
Woodside Farm
Wood Side
Rainton Gate
The Bungalow
East Moor Leazes
Mallygill Wood
Mally Gill
Mallygill Craig
Mallygill Quarry (dis.)
Pitfield House
Homer Hill Farm
Union Hall Farm
Moor House Farm
Durham
RIVER WEAR
Black Wood
Mallygill Turn
Winch Gill
DH5
Grange Wood
Woodwell House
The Rift
Sewage Works
Low Grange
Belmont Viaduct
RAMSIDE GOLF COURSE
Lodge
Maureen Ter
Caravan & Camping Park
Bridge Row
Junc. 62
Ramside Hall Hotel (Club House)
Depot
A690
Fatfield House Farm
Factory
DH6
PITTINGTON LANE
CARRVILLE
Football Ground
BELMONT INDUSTRIAL ESTATE
Belmont Cheveley Park Prim. Sch.
Hilltop Farm
Broomside
BELMONT BUSINESS PARK
Moor End
CHEVELEY PARK SHOPPING CENTRE
Belmont C of E Jun. & Inf. Sch.
Health & Squash Club
Community Centre
Belmont Comp. Sch.
Playing Field
Belmont
Pittington Bridge

143
156
167

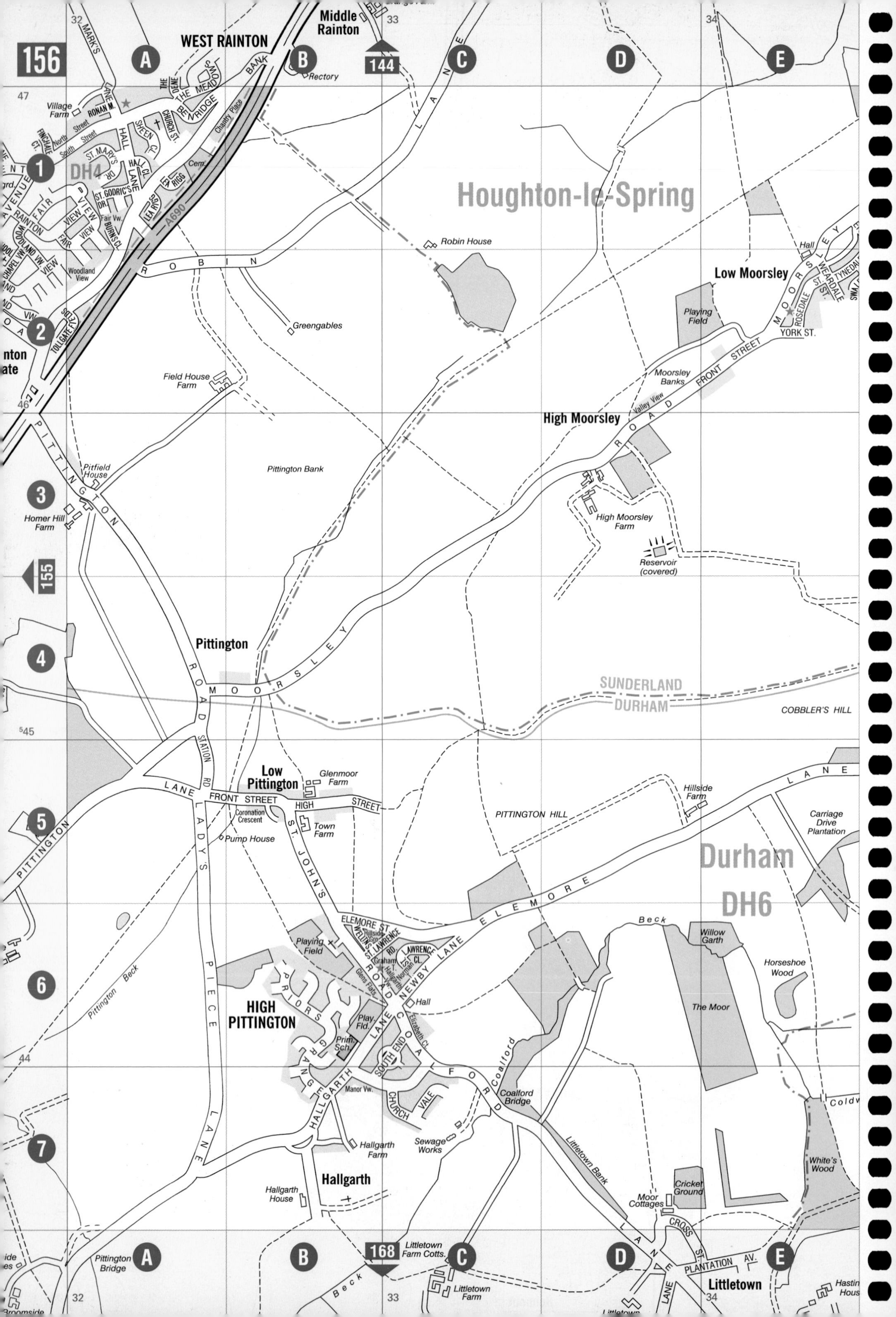

WEST RAINTON

Middle Rainton

144

A   B   C   D   E

Rectory

Village Farm

RONAH M.

DH4

1

Houghton-le-Spring

Robin House

Low Moorsley

Playing Field

Hall

YORK ST.

Woodland View

2

Moorsley Banks

Field House Farm

Greengables

High Moorsley

Valley View

Pittington House

3

Pitfield House

Pittington Bank

High Moorsley Farm

Homer Hill Farm

155

Reservoir (covered)

Pittington

4

SUNDERLAND

DURHAM

COBBLER'S HILL

45

Low Pittington

Glenmoor Farm

Hillside Farm

Carriage Drive Plantation

PITTINGTON HILL

Coronation Crescent

Town Farm

Durham DH6

Pump House

5

Beck

Willow Garth

Playing Field

Horseshoe Wood

ELEMORE ST.

LAWRENCE CL.

The Moor

6

Pittington Beck

HIGH PITTINGTON

Hall

Play Fld.

Prim. Sch.

Manor Vw.

44

Coalford Bridge

7

Hallgarth Farm

Sewage Works

Littletown Bank

Moor Cottages

Cricket Ground

White's Wood

Hallgarth House

Hallgarth

Coldw

CROSS ST.

A   B   C   D   E

Pittington Bridge

168

Littletown Farm Cotts.

Littletown Farm

PLANTATION AV.

Littletown

Hastin House

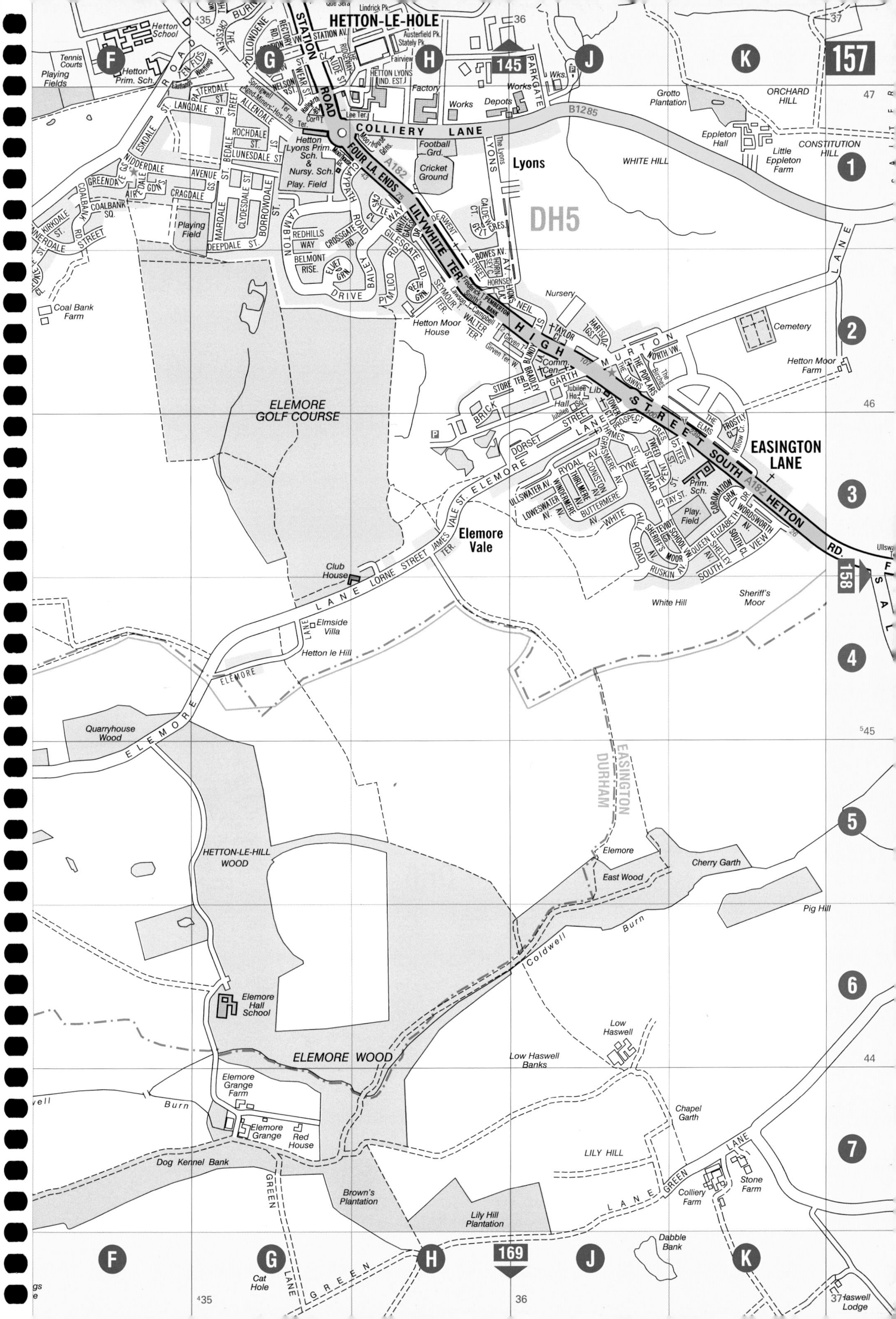

157
HETTON-LE-HOLE
Hetton School
Tennis Courts
Playing Fields
Hetton Prim. Sch.
STATION ROAD
STATION AV.
Lindrick Pk.
Austerfield Pk.
Stately Pk.
Fairview
HETTON LYONS IND. EST.
Factory
Works
Depots
Wks.
PARKGATE
145
COLLIERY LANE
B1285
Grotto Plantation
ORCHARD HILL
Eppleton Hall
Little Eppleton Farm
CONSTITUTION HILL
WHITE HILL
Lyons
Football Grd.
Cricket Ground
Hetton Lyons Prim. Sch. & Nursy. Sch.
Play. Field
FOUR LA. ENDS
A182
LILYWHITE TER.
ROCHDALE ST.
LUNESDALE ST.
LANGDALE ST.
PATTERDALE ST.
ALLENDALE
ESKDALE
NIDDERDALE AVENUE
GREENDALE
COALBANK SQ.
KIRKDALE ST.
CRAGDALE
MARDALE
CLYDESDALE ST.
BORROWDALE ST.
DEEPDALE ST.
Playing Field
LAMBTON
REDHILLS WAY
BELMONT RISE
CROSSGATE RD.
BAILEY DRIVE
PIMLICO
GILESGATE RD.
DH5
Nursery
Coal Bank Farm
Hetton Moor House
SEYMOUR TER.
WALTER TER.
HIGH STREET SOUTH
MURTON
NORTH VW.
THE POPLARS
THE LAWNS
Cemetery
Hetton Moor Farm
STORE TER.
BRICK GARTH
Comm. Cen.
Lib.
Hall
Jubilee Ho.
PROSPECT
THE ELMS
FROSTLY CL.
Willow Ct.
EASINGTON LANE
ELEMORE GOLF COURSE
DORSET STREET
ELEMORE LANE
RYDAL AV.
CONISTON AV.
GRASMERE AV.
THIRLMERE AV.
WINDERMERE AV.
ULLSWATER AV.
LOWESWATER AV.
BUTTERMERE AV.
TYNE ST.
TAMAR ST.
TAY ST.
Prim. Sch.
Play. Field
CORONATION
WORDSWORTH AV.
HETTON RD.
WHITE HILL ROAD
SHERIFF'S MOOR AV.
TEVIOT
SCHOOL VW.
QUEEN ELIZABETH DR.
SHELLEY AV.
SOUTH VIEW
RUSKIN AV.
SOUTH
Elemore Vale
JAMES ST.
VALE TER.
LORNE STREET
Club House
White Hill
Sheriff's Moor
158
Elmside Villa
Hetton le Hill
ELEMORE
Quarryhouse Wood
EASINGTON
DURHAM
HETTON-LE-HILL WOOD
Elemore
East Wood
Cherry Garth
Pig Hill
Coldwell Burn
Elemore Hall School
Low Haswell
Low Haswell Banks
ELEMORE WOOD
Elemore Grange Farm
Elemore Grange
Red House
Dog Kennel Bank
Chapel Garth
LILY HILL
GREEN LANE
Colliery Farm
Stone Farm
Brown's Plantation
Lily Hill Plantation
Dabble Bank
Cat Hole
169
Haswell Lodge
F
G
H
J
K
1
2
3
4
5
6
7
435
36
37
47
46
545
44

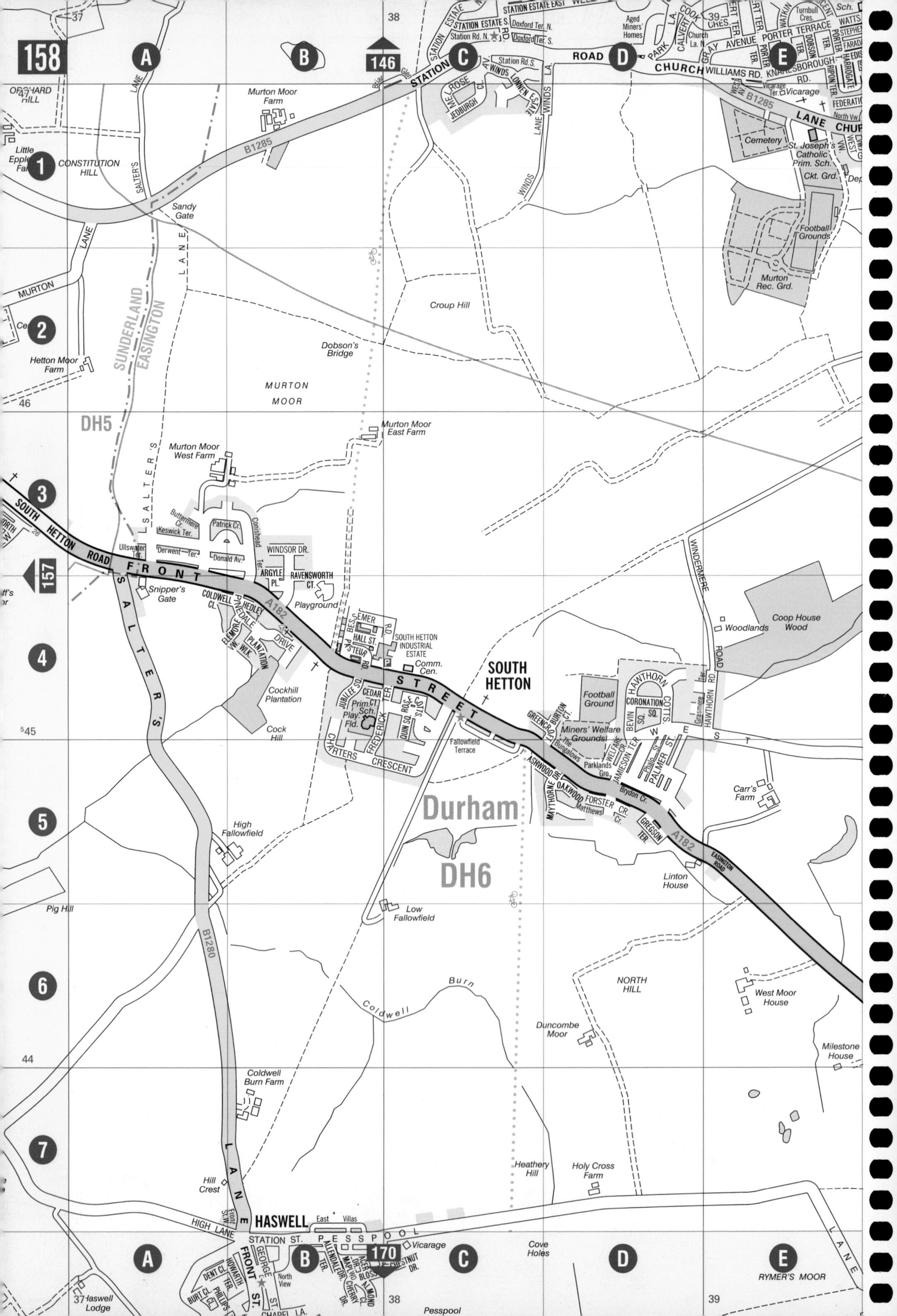

146
157
170
SOUTH HETTON
HASWELL
Durham
DH5
DH6
MURTON MOOR
Murton Moor Farm
Murton Moor East Farm
Murton Moor West Farm
CONSTITUTION HILL
Sandy Gate
Croup Hill
Dobson's Bridge
Hetton Moor Farm
SUNDERLAND
EASINGTON
SOUTH HETTON ROAD
FRONT STREET
SALTER'S LANE
STATION ROAD
CHURCH LANE
WINDS LANE
B1285
A182
B1280
SOUTH HETTON INDUSTRIAL ESTATE
Comm. Cen.
Playground
Snipper's Gate
Cockhill Plantation
Cock Hill
CHARTERS CRESCENT
Football Ground
Miners' Welfare Grounds
CORONATION SQ.
HAWTHORN SQ.
WEST ST
Fallowfield Terrace
High Fallowfield
Low Fallowfield
Linton House
Carr's Farm
Coop House Wood
Woodlands
WINDERMERE ROAD
HAWTHORN RD.
EASINGTON ROAD
NORTH HILL
West Moor House
Milestone House
Duncombe Moor
Coldwell Burn
Coldwell Burn Farm
Pig Hill
Heathery Hill
Holy Cross Farm
Hill Crest
HIGH LANE
STATION ST.
PESSPOOL LANE
Cove Holes
RYMER'S MOOR
Haswell Lodge
Pesspool
Cemetery
St. Joseph's Catholic Prim. Sch.
Ckt. Grd.
Football Grounds
Murton Rec. Grd.
Aged Miners' Homes
Vicarage

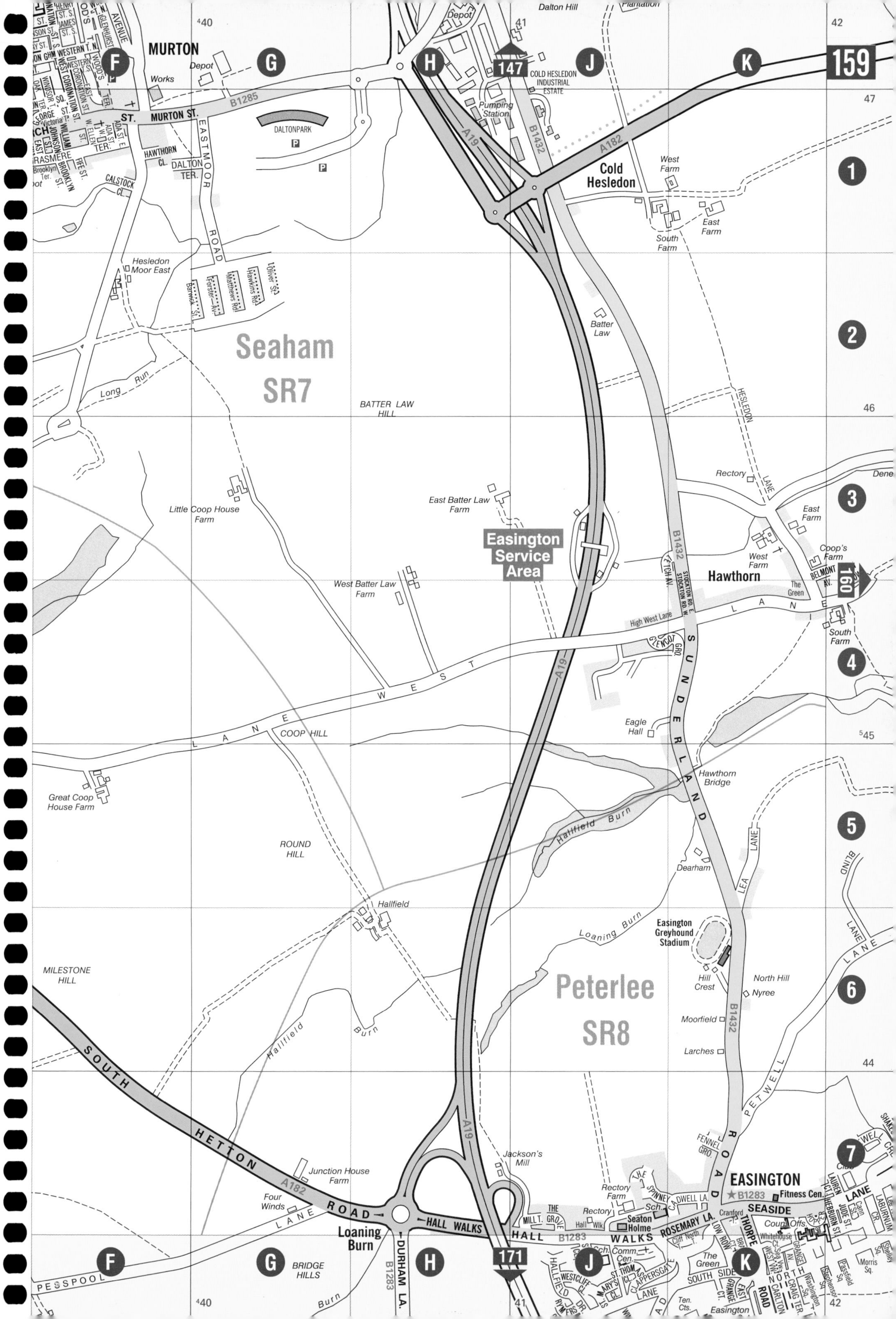

159
MURTON
Depot
Works
MURTON ST.
B1285
DALTONPARK
EASTMOOR ROAD
HAWTHORN CL.
DALTON TER.
CALSTOCK CL.
COLD HESLEDON INDUSTRIAL ESTATE
Pumping Station
Dalton Hill
147
A19
B1432
A182
Cold Hesledon
West Farm
East Farm
South Farm
Hesledon Moor East
Barwick St.
Forster Av.
Matthews Rd.
Hawkins Rd.
Oliver St.
Seaham
SR7
Long Run
BATTER LAW HILL
Batter Law
HESLEDON LANE
Rectory
East Farm
Little Coop House Farm
East Batter Law Farm
Easington Service Area
West Batter Law Farm
West Farm
Coop's Farm
Hawthorn
The Green
BELMONT AV.
160
High West Lane
STOCKTON RD. E.
STOCKTON RD. W.
South Farm
WEST LANE
COOP HILL
SUNDERLAND ROAD
Eagle Hall
Great Coop House Farm
Hawthorn Bridge
Hallfield Burn
ROUND HILL
Dearham
LEA LANE
BLIND LANE
Hallfield
Loaning Burn
Easington Greyhound Stadium
MILESTONE HILL
Hill Crest
North Hill
Nyree
Peterlee
SR8
Moorfield
Larches
PETWELL
SOUTH HETTON ROAD
A182
FENNEL GRO.
Jackson's Mill
Junction House Farm
Four Winds
EASINGTON
B1283
Fitness Cen.
Rectory Farm
Rectory
Seaton Holme
SEASIDE LANE
ROSEMARY LA.
HALL WALKS
Loaning Burn
DURHAM LA.
171
PESSPOOL LANE
BRIDGE HILLS
The Green
SOUTH SIDE
THORPE ROAD
NORTH CRAIG TER.
Easington
F
G
H
J
K
1
2
3
4
5
6
7
440
41
42
47
46
545
44

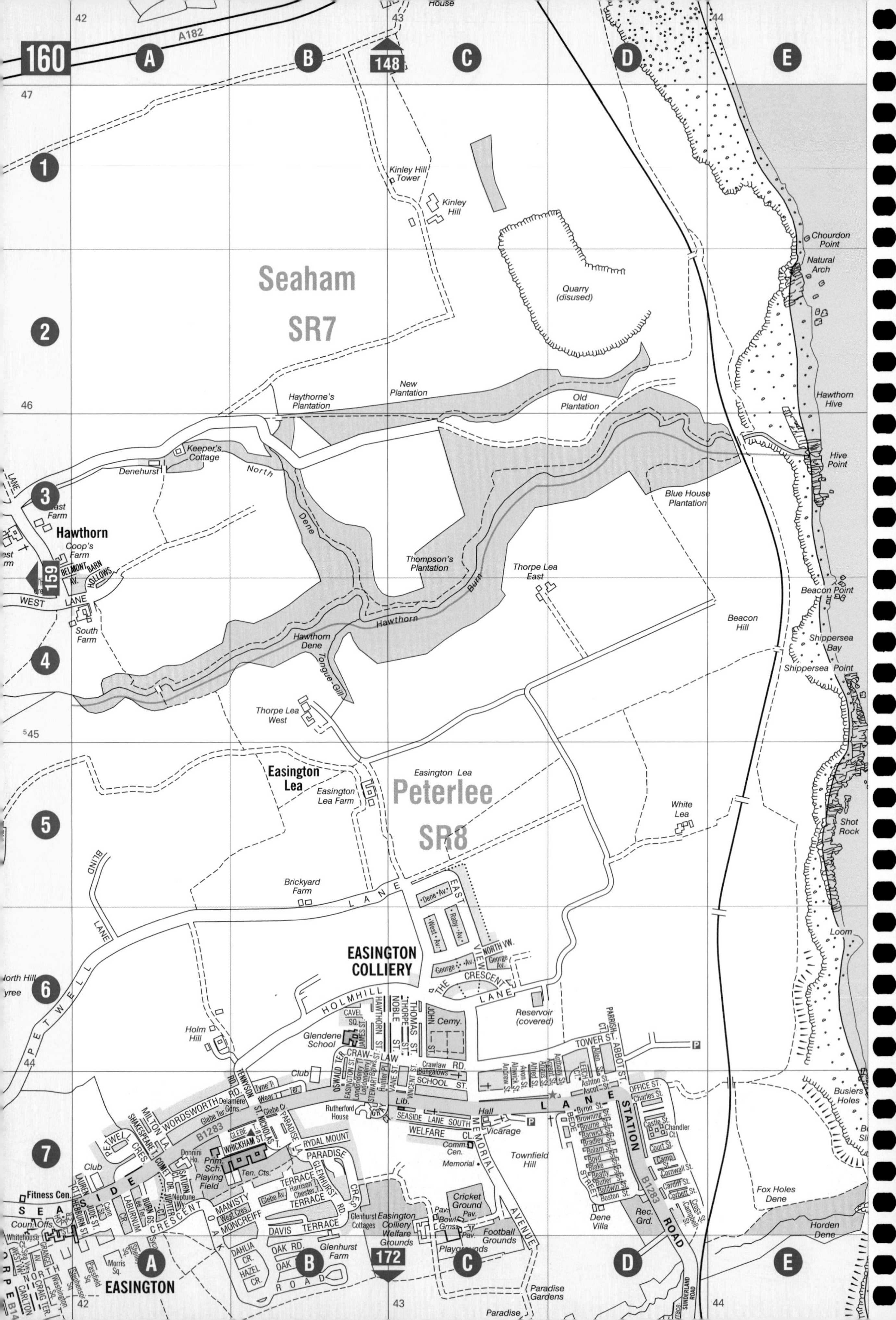

A182

A   B   148   C   D   E

Seaham

SR7

Kinley Hill Tower

Kinley Hill

Quarry (disused)

Chourdon Point

Natural Arch

New Plantation

Haythorne's Plantation

Old Plantation

Hawthorn Hive

Keeper's Cottage

North

Denehurst

Dene

Blue House Plantation

Hive Point

East Farm

Hawthorn

Coop's Farm

BELMONT AV.

BARN HOLLOWS

159

WEST   LANE

Thompson's Plantation

Burn

Thorpe Lea East

Beacon Point

West Farm

South Farm

Hawthorn

Beacon Hill

Shippersea Bay

Hawthorn Dene

Tongue Gill

Shippersea Point

Thorpe Lea West

Easington Lea

Easington Lea

Easington Lea Farm

Peterlee

SR8

White Lea

Shot Rock

Brickyard Farm

LANE

Dene Av.

EAST

Rabn' Av.

West Av.

North VW.

North Hill

Tyree

BLIND

LANE

PETWELL

LANE

George Av.

George Av.

EASINGTON COLLIERY

THE

CRESCENT

LANE

Reservoir (covered)

Loom

HOLMHILL

Holm Hill

CAVEL SQ.

HAWTHORN ST.

NOBLE ST.

THORPE ST.

THOMAS ST.

JOHN ST.

Cemy.

PARRISH ST.

ABBOTT ST.

TOWER ST.

Busiers Holes

Glendene School

CRAW LAW

Crawlaw Bungalows

JOHN ST.

VINCENT ST.

Crawlaw RD.

SCHOOL ST.

Alfred St.

LEECH

Ashton St.

OFFICE ST.

OSWALD TER

Club

Tyne Ter.

Wear Ter.

Glebe Cr.

STEPHENSON

Lib.

LANE

STATION

Charles St.

Avon St.

Alnwick St.

Andrew St.

Byron St.

Browning St.

Bourne St.

Barwick St.

Bradley St.

Bolam St.

Blake St.

Burke St.

Castle St.

Chandler Ct.

Cardiff St.

Camp St.

Cornwall St.

Court St.

Fox Holes Dene

WORDSWORTH RD.

SHAKESPEARE

MILTON

COMET DR.

Glebe Ter Gdns.

Delamere

GLEBE

ST. NICHOLAS ST.

Rutherford House

Hall

Vicarage

Beatty St.

Boyd St.

Baldwin St.

Boston St.

B1283

WHICKHAM ST.

Donnini Ho.

Prim. Sch. Playing Field

Ten. Cts.

PARADISE

RYDAL MOUNT

SEASIDE LANE SOUTH

WELFARE

MEMORIAL CL.

Comm. Cen.

Memorial

Townfield Hill

Dene Villa

Rec. Grd.

B1283

SUNDERLAND ROAD

STATION ROAD

Horden Dene

Fitness Cen.

Club

WREN CR.

HEBRON ST.

SEASIDE

Count Offs

Whitehouse

Morris Sq.

LAURENCE ST.

LAURELS

NORTH

CARLTON

CRAIG ST.

B1...

PETWELL CRES.

LABURNUM

COM ROAD

SATURN

Neptune

MANISTY

West Cres.

MONCREIFF

DAHLIA CR.

HAZEL CR.

OAK RD.

OAK

ROAD

DAVIS TERRACE

GLENHURST CRES.

Harrison Chester TERRACE

Glebe Av.

PARADISE TERRACE

Glenhurst Farm

Glenhurst Cottages

Easington Colliery Welfare Grounds

172

Cricket Ground

Pav.

Bowl'g Grn

Pav.

Football Grounds

Playgrounds

AVENUE

Paradise Gardens

Paradise

EASINGTON

A   B   172   C   D   E

42   43   44

45 46 47

47

1

2

46

3

N O R T H   S E A

4

545

5

6

44

Fox Holes

7

445 46 47

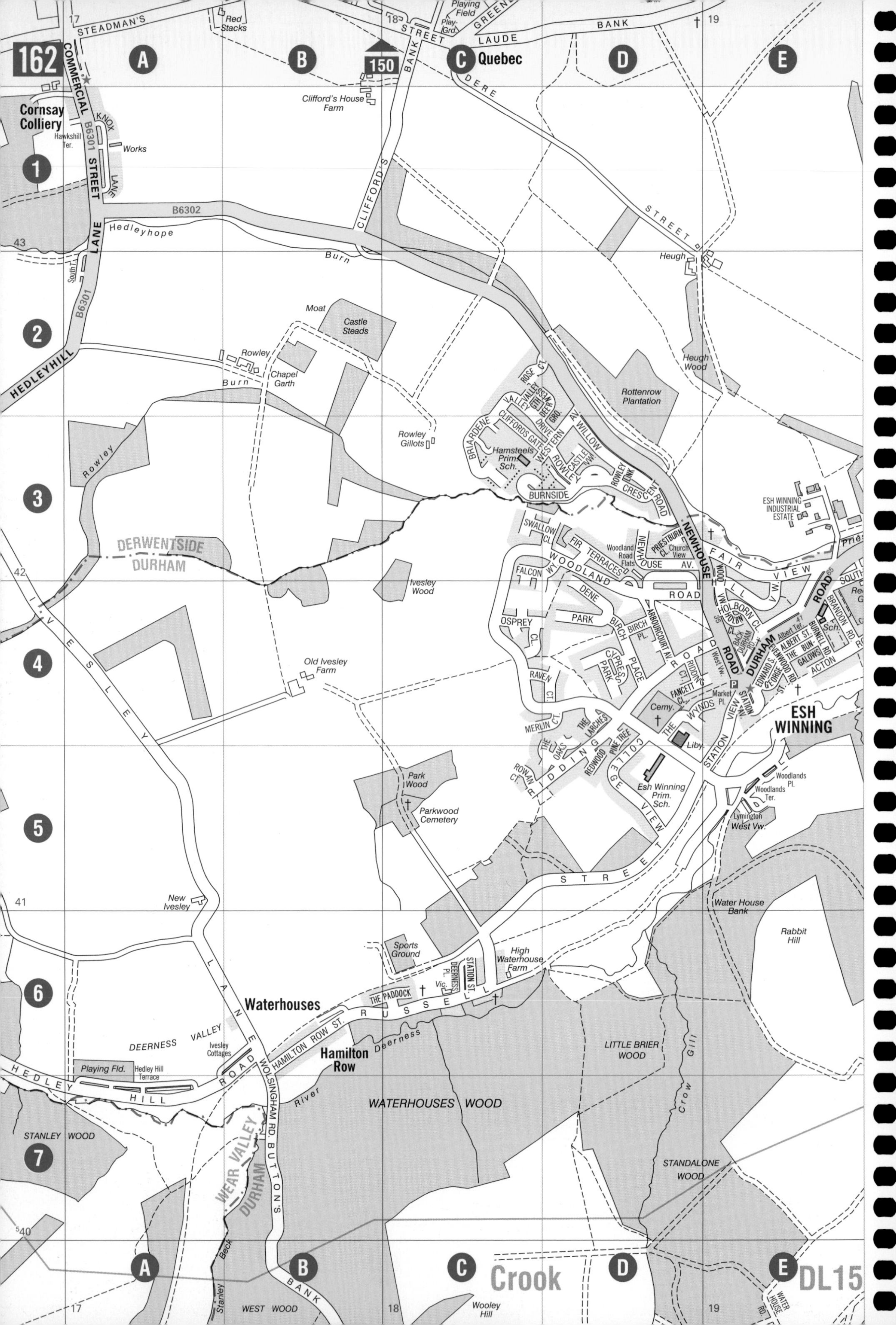

Cornsay Colliery

A   B   C   Quebec   D   E

DERWENTSIDE DURHAM

ESH WINNING INDUSTRIAL ESTATE

ESH WINNING

Waterhouses

Hamilton Row

WATERHOUSES WOOD

STANLEY WOOD

LITTLE BRIER WOOD

STANDALONE WOOD

Rabbit Hill

WEST WOOD

Wooley Hill

A   B   C   Crook   D   E   DL15

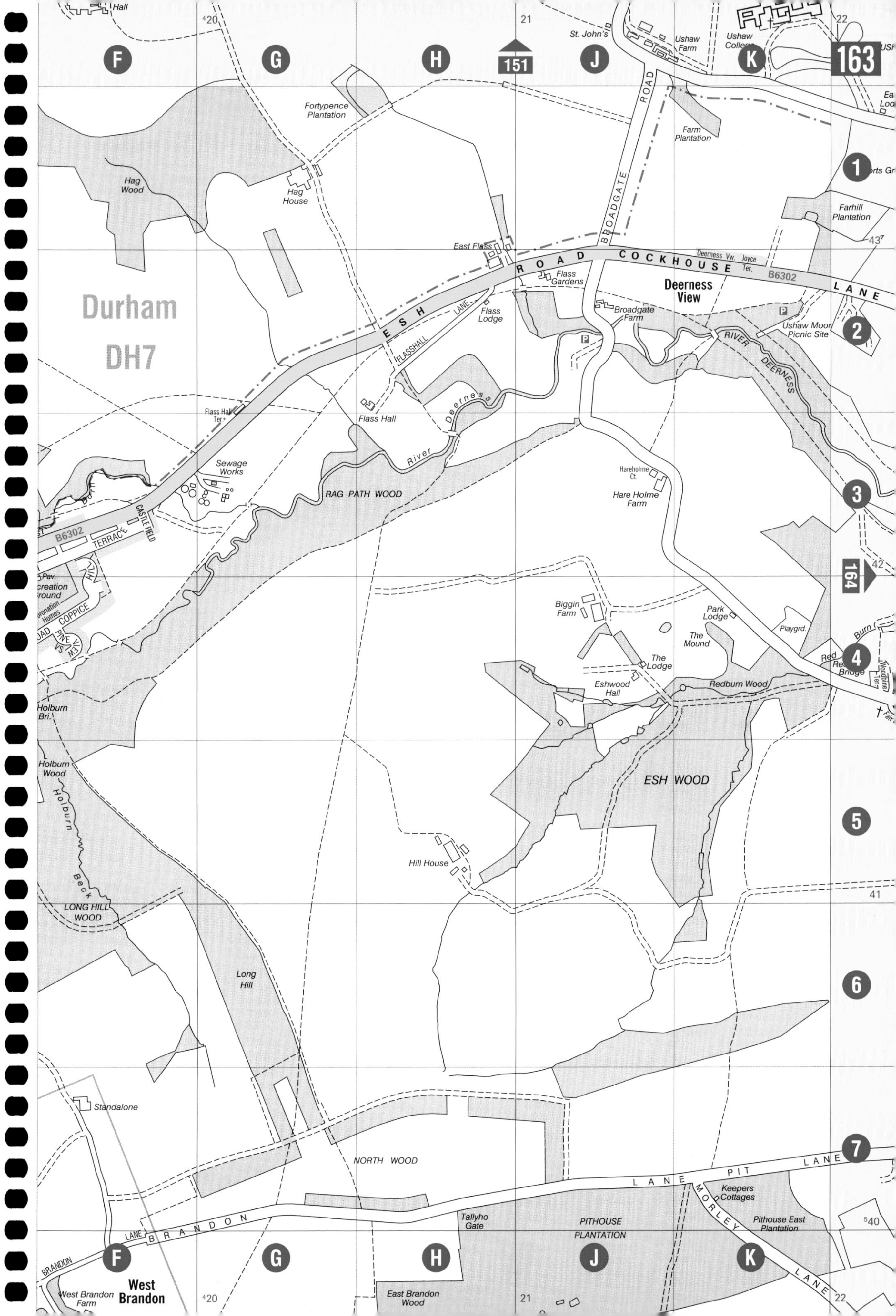

Durham
DH7
Fortypence Plantation
Hag Wood
Hag House
East Flass
ESH ROAD COCKHOUSE LANE
B6302
BROADGATE ROAD
St. John's
Ushaw Farm
Ushaw College
Farm Plantation
Farhill Plantation
Deerness Vw.
Joyce Ter.
Deerness View
Flass Gardens
Flass Lodge
FLASSHALL LANE
Broadgate Farm
Ushaw Moor Picnic Site
RIVER DEERNESS
River Deerness
Flass Hall
Flass Hall Ter.
Sewage Works
RAG PATH WOOD
Hareholme Ct.
Hare Holme Farm
CASTLE FIELD
TERRACE
HILL
COPPICE
PINE VIEW
Pav.
Recreation Ground
Coronation Homes
Biggin Farm
Park Lodge
The Mound
Playgrd.
The Lodge
Eshwood Hall
Redburn Wood
Red Re Bridge
Woodbine Ter.
Holburn Bri.
Holburn Wood
Holburn Beck
ESH WOOD
Hill House
LONG HILL WOOD
Long Hill
Standalone
NORTH WOOD
BRANDON LANE
PIT LANE
MORLEY LANE
Keepers Cottages
Tallyho Gate
PITHOUSE PLANTATION
Pithouse East Plantation
West Brandon Farm
West Brandon
East Brandon Wood

151
164

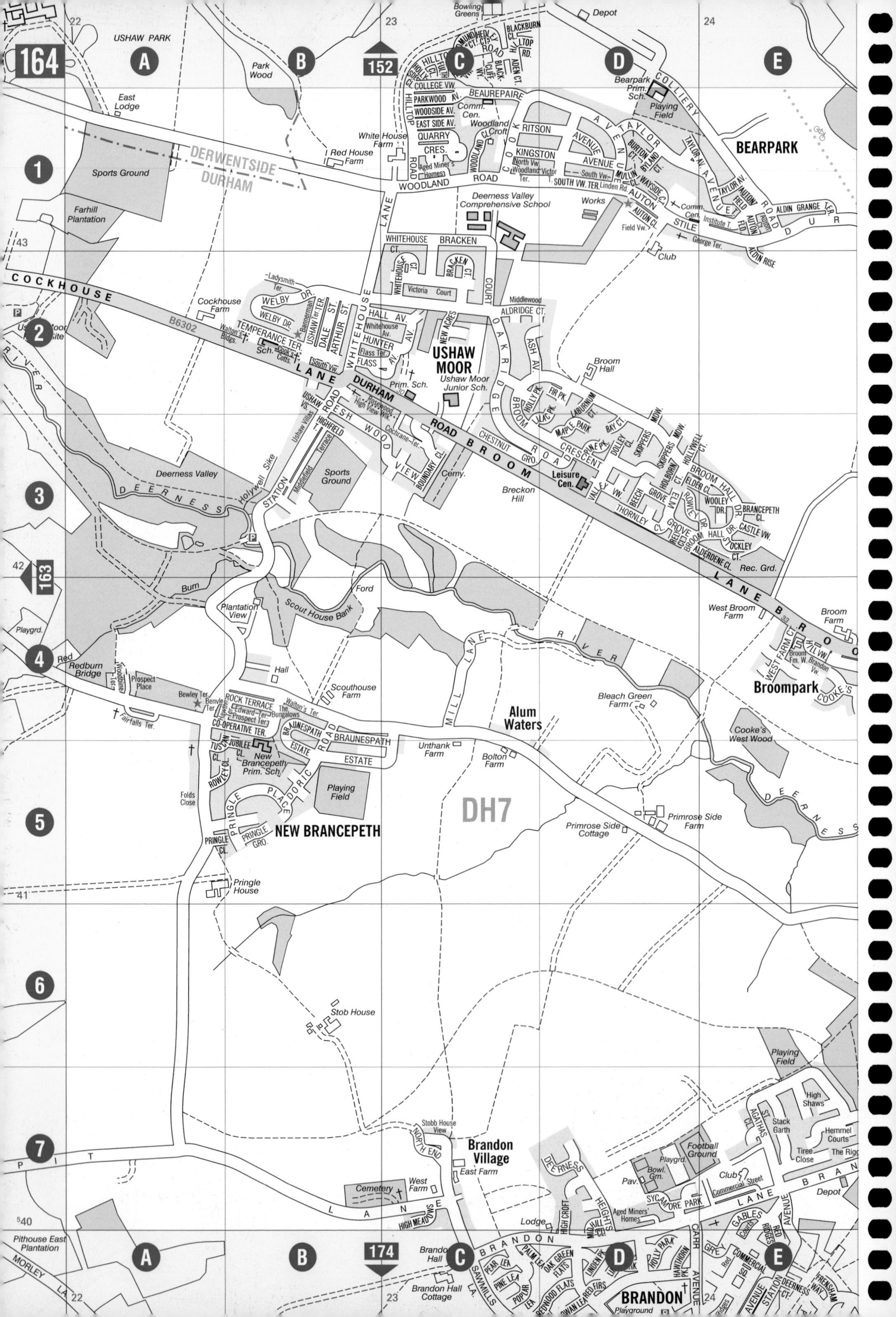
152
174
163
A
B
C
D
E
1
2
3
4
5
6
7
22
23
24
43
42
41
40
USHAW PARK
Park Wood
East Lodge
Bowling Greens
Depot
BLACKBURN CL.
HILLTOP RD.
COLLEGE VW.
PARKWOOD AV.
WOODSIDE AV.
EAST SIDE AV.
QUARRY CRES.
BEAUREPAIRE
Comm. Cen.
Woodland Croft
Bearpark Prim. Sch.
Playing Field
COLLIERY
BEARPARK
White House Farm
Red House Farm
Aged Miner's Homes
RITSON
KINGSTON
AVENUE
TAYLOR
North Vw.
Woodland Ter.
Victor T.
South Vw.
SOUTH VW. TER.
Linden Rd.
DERWENTSIDE
DURHAM
Sports Ground
Farhill Plantation
WOODLAND ROAD
Deerness Valley Comprehensive School
Works
AUTON STILE
AUTON CL.
Field Vw.
ALDIN GRANGE TER.
Institute T.
George Ter.
ALDIN RISE
Club
WHITEHOUSE CT.
BRACKEN CT.
BRACKEN COURT
Victoria Court
Middlewood
ALDRIDGE CT.
COCKHOUSE
Ladysmith Ter.
WELBY DR.
Cockhouse Farm
B6302
TEMPERANCE TER.
Walton's Bldgs.
Sch.
Cook's Cotts.
USHAW TER.
DALE
ARTHUR ST.
WHITEHOUSE
HALL AV.
Whitehouse Av.
HUNTER
Flass Ter.
FLASS
NEW ACRES
USHAW MOOR
Ushaw Moor Junior Sch.
Prim. Sch.
ASH AV.
OAKRIDGE
Broom Hall
HOLLY PK.
FIR PK.
LAURNUM CT.
MAPLE PARK
BAY CT.
LANE
DURHAM ROAD
BROOM
ESH WOOD VIEW
HIGHFIELD
Rosewood
High View Wlk.
Cochrane Ter.
Ushaw Villas
BOUNDARY CL.
CHESTNUT GRO.
BROOM ROAD CRESCENT
Leisure Cen.
SKIPPERS MDW.
HOLLYWELL CT.
DOLLEY CL.
Deerness Valley
Holywell Sike
STATION
Sports Ground
Cemy.
Breckon Hill
VALLEY VW.
BEECH GROVE
THORNLEY CL.
ELM GROVE
ELDER CL.
WOOLEY DR.
BRANCEPETH CL.
CASTLE VW.
OCKLEY CT.
ALDERDENE CL.
Rec. Grd.
Burn
Plantation View
Scout House Bank
Ford
West Broom Farm
Broom Farm
WEST FARM CT.
HILL VW.
Broom Fm. W.
Brandon Vw.
Broompark
COOKE'S
Playgrd.
Red
Redburn Bridge
Woodbine Ter.
Prospect Place
Bewley Ter.
Benvie Ter.
Fairfalls Ter.
Hall
ROCK TERRACE
Edward Ter.
Prospect Ter.
The Bungalows
Walton's Ter.
CO-OPERATIVE TER.
Scouthouse Farm
MILL LANE
Alum Waters
Bleach Green Farm
RIVER
Cooke's West Wood
BRAUNESPATH ESTATE
JUBILEE CL.
TUSCAN CL.
ROWLEY CL.
New Brancepeth Prim. Sch.
DORIC ROAD
Playing Field
Unthank Farm
Bolton Farm
Folds Close
PRINGLE PLACE
PRINGLE GRO.
PRINGLE CL.
NEW BRANCEPETH
DH7
Primrose Side Cottage
Primrose Side Farm
DEERNESS
Pringle House
Stob House
Playing Field
High Shaws
ST. AGATHAS
Stack Garth
Hemmel Courts
Tiree Close
The Rigg
Stobb House View
NORTH END
Brandon Village
East Farm
Football Ground
Playgrd.
Bowl. Grn.
Pav.
Club
Commercial Street
LANE
BRAN
Depot
PIT
Cemetery
West Farm
LANE
HIGH MEADOWS
Lodge
HIGH CROFT
HEIGHTS
Aged Miners' Homes
SYCAMORE PARK
CARR AVENUE
AVENUE
Pithouse East Plantation
MORLEY LA.
Brandon Hall
Brandon Hall Cottage
BRANDON
SAWMILLS LA.
PEAR LEA
PINE LEA
PALM LEA
OAK GREEN FLATS
POPLAR LEA
REDWOOD FLATS
ROWAN LEA
REDFIRS
LINDEN PK.
HOLLY PARK
HAWTHORN PK.
GREY
BRANDON
Playground
COMMERCIAL
STATION AVENUE
DEERNESS CT.
FRENSHAM WAY

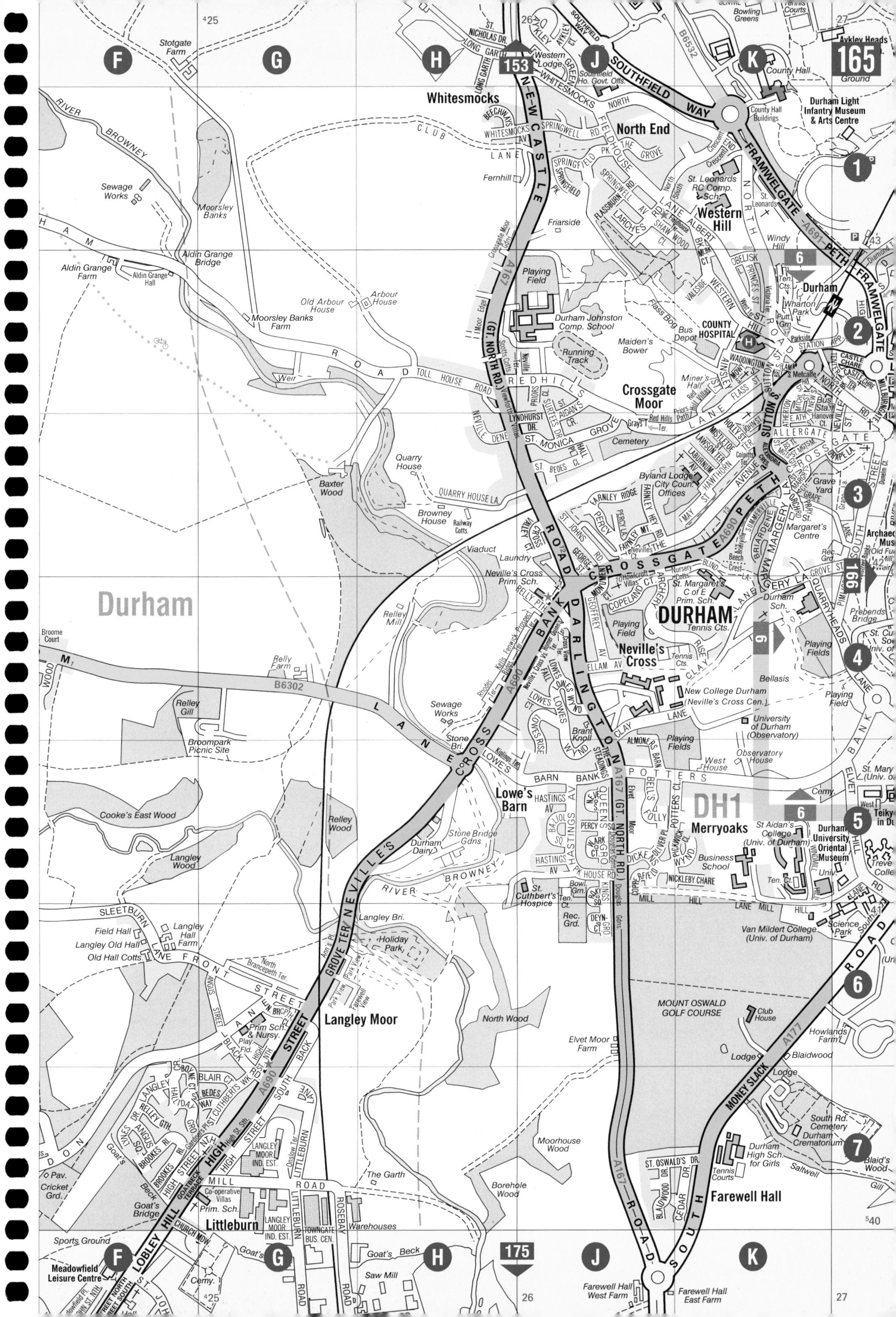
F
G
H
J
K
153
Stotgate Farm
Bowling Greens
Aykley Heads
Ground
County Hall
Whitesmocks
Western Lodge
Southfield Ho. Govt. Offs.
SOUTHFIELD WAY
North End
County Hall Buildings
Durham Light Infantry Museum & Arts Centre
RIVER BROWNEY
Sewage Works
Moorsley Banks
Fernhill
Friarside
St. Leonards RC Comp. Sch.
Western Hill
FRAMWELGATE
PETH
Windy Hill
Aldin Grange Bridge
Aldin Grange Farm
Aldin Grange Hall
Playing Field
Durham Johnston Comp. School
Old Arbour House
Arbour House
Moorsley Banks Farm
Running Track
Maiden's Bower
Bus Depot
COUNTY HOSPITAL
Durham
Wharton Park
Weir
TOLL HOUSE ROAD
REDHILLS
Crossgate Moor
Miner's Hall
Cemetery
Quarry House
Baxter Wood
QUARRY HOUSE LA
Browney House
Railway Cotts.
Byland Lodge City Coun. Offices
Grave Yard
St. Margaret's Centre
Viaduct
Laundry
Neville's Cross Prim. Sch.
CROSSGATE
St. Margaret's C of E Prim. Sch.
Durham Sch.
Prebends Bridge
Durham
Relley Mill
Broome Court
DURHAM
Tennis Cts.
Playing Field
Neville's Cross
Playing Fields
Relly Farm
B6302
M1
Relley Gill
Sewage Works
New College Durham (Neville's Cross Cen.)
Bellasis
University of Durham (Observatory)
Stone Bri.
Brant Knoll
Playing Fields
Broompark Picnic Site
Observatory House
West House
Lowe's Barn
DH1
Merryoaks
Cooke's East Wood
Relley Wood
Durham Dairy
Stone Bridge Gdns
St Aidan's College (Univ. of Durham)
Durham University Oriental Museum
Langley Wood
Business School
RIVER BROWNEY
St. Cuthbert's Hospice
Rec. Grd.
Van Mildert College (Univ. of Durham)
Science Park
Field Hall
Langley Hall Farm
Langley Old Hall
Old Hall Cotts.
Langley Bri.
Holiday Park
North Brancepeth Ter.
FRONT STREET
MOUNT OSWALD GOLF COURSE
Club House
Howlands Farm
Langley Moor
North Wood
Prim Sch. & Nursy.
Elvet Moor Farm
Lodge
Blaidwood
MONEY SLACK
South Rd. Cemetery
Durham Crematorium
Moorhouse Wood
Durham High Sch. for Girls
Tennis Courts
Saltwell
Blaid's Wood
Cricket Grd.
Goat's Bridge
MILL ROAD
The Garth
Borehole Wood
Co-operative Villas
Prim. Sch.
Littleburn
LANGLEY MOOR IND. EST.
TOWNGATE BUS. CEN.
Warehouses
Farewell Hall
Sports Ground
Meadowfield Leisure Centre
Goat's Beck
Saw Mill
Cemy.
175
Farewell Hall West Farm
Farewell Hall East Farm
A167
A690
A691
A177
B6532
1
2
3
4
5
6
7
425
26
27
540

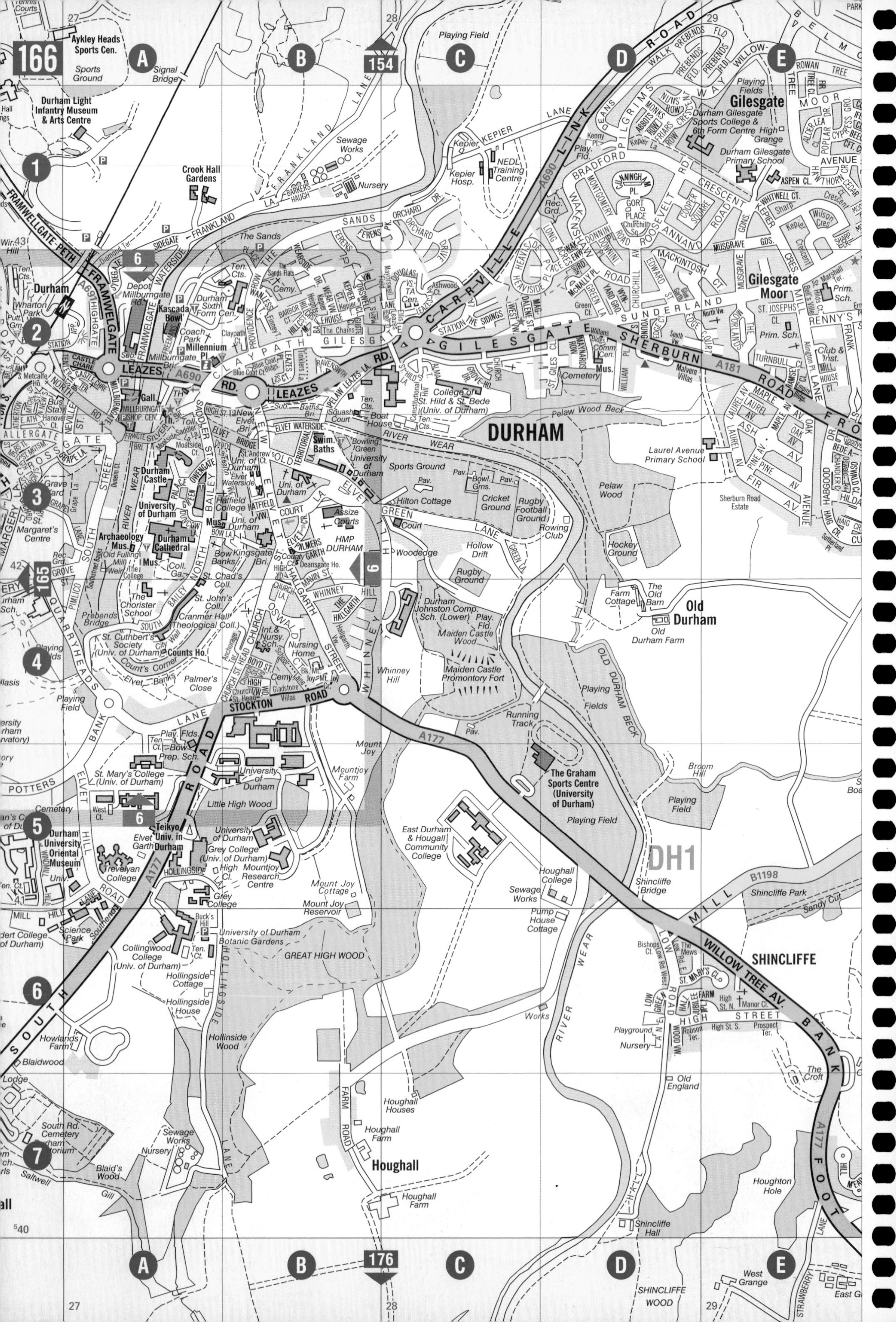

Aykley Heads Sports Cen.
Sports Ground
Signal Bridge
Durham Light Infantry Museum & Arts Centre
Playing Field
154
Sewage Works
Crook Hall Gardens
Nursery
Kepier Hosp.
NEDL Training Centre
FRANKLAND LANE
SIDEGATE
FRAMWELLGATE PETH
FRAMWELLGATE
The Sands
WATERSIDE
Durham
Durham Sixth Form Cen.
Kascada Bowl
Millburngate Ho.
Millennium Pl.
Coach Park
CLAYPATH
GILESGATE
LEAZES
LEAZES RD.
A690
A691
CARRVILLE LINK ROAD
A690
PILGRIMS' WAY
BRADFORD CRESCENT
Gilesgate
Durham Gilesgate Sports College & 6th Form Centre
High Grange
Durham Gilesgate Primary School
Playing Fields
Gilesgate Moor
SHERBURN ROAD
A181
SUNDERLAND ROAD
Cemetery
Mus.
College of St. Hild & St. Bede (Univ. of Durham)
Pelaw Wood Beck
DURHAM
RIVER WEAR
Sports Ground
Boat House
Swim. Baths
Cricket Ground
Rugby Football Ground
Rowing Club
Hilton Cottage
Court
Assize Courts
HMP DURHAM
Woodedge
Hollow Drift
Rugby Ground
Pelaw Wood
Hockey Ground
Laurel Avenue Primary School
Sherburn Road Estate
Durham Castle
University of Durham
Durham Cathedral
Archaeology Mus.
Bow Banks
Kingsgate Bri.
St. Chad's Coll.
St. John's Coll.
Cranmer Hall Theological Coll.
The Chorister School
Prebends Bridge
St. Cuthbert's Society (Univ. of Durham)
Counts Ho.
Count's Corner
Palmer's Close
St. Margaret's Centre
Durham Johnston Comp. Sch. (Lower)
Play. Fld.
Maiden Castle Wood
Maiden Castle Promontory Fort
Whinney Hill
Farm Cottage
The Old Barn
Old Durham
Old Durham Farm
OLD DURHAM BECK
Playing Fields
Running Track
The Graham Sports Centre (University of Durham)
Playing Field
Broom Hill
STOCKTON ROAD
A177
Mount Joy
Mountjoy Farm
University of Durham
Little High Wood
St. Mary's College (Univ. of Durham)
Ustinov College
Teikyo Univ. in Durham
Grey College (Univ. of Durham)
Mountjoy Research Centre
Durham University Oriental Museum
Trevelyan College
Science Park
Grey College
Collingwood College (Univ. of Durham)
Hollingside Cottage
Hollingside House
University of Durham Botanic Gardens
GREAT HIGH WOOD
Mount Joy Cottage
Mount Joy Reservoir
East Durham & Hougall Community College
Houghall College
Sewage Works
Pump House Cottage
DH1
Shincliffe Bridge
B1198
Shincliffe Park
Sandy Cut
SHINCLIFFE
WILLOW TREE AV.
BANK FOOT
HIGH STREET
Playground
Nursery
Old England
The Croft
Works
RIVER WEAR
Howlands Farm
Hollinside Wood
Blaidwood
Lodge
South Rd. Cemetery
Sewage Works
Nursery
Blaid's Wood
Saltwell Gill
Houghall Houses
Houghall Farm
Houghall
Houghall Farm
FARM ROAD
HOLLINGSIDE LANE
Shincliffe Hall
Houghton Hole
West Grange
SHINCLIFFE WOOD
STRAWBERRY LANE
176
A B C D E
1 2 3 4 5 6 7
27 28 29
165

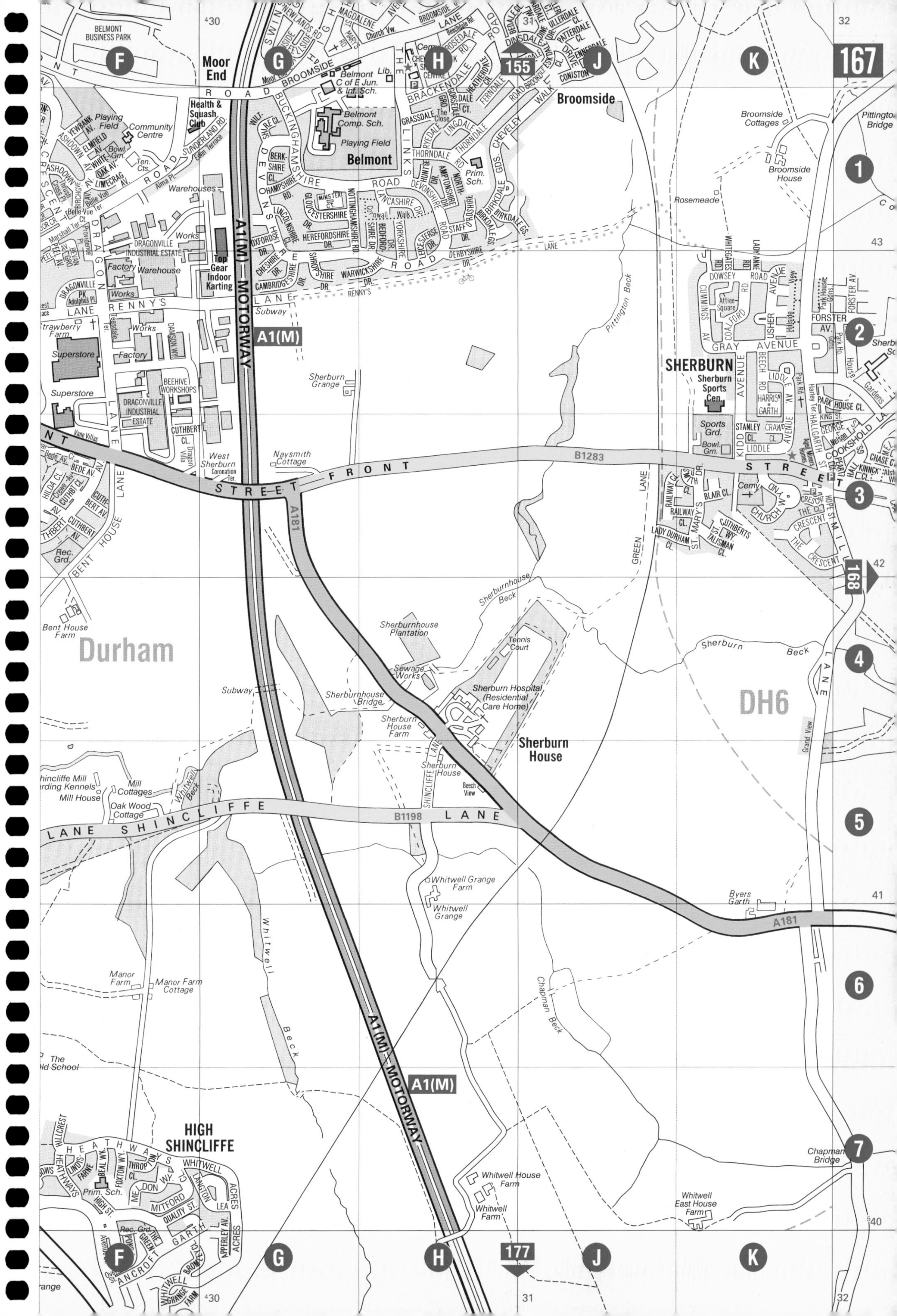
BELMONT BUSINESS PARK
Moor End
Broomside
Belmont
SHERBURN
Sherburn Sports Cen.
A1(M) MOTORWAY
FRONT STREET
B1283
A181
SHINCLIFFE LANE
B1198
Durham
DH6
Sherburn Grange
Naysmith Cottage
Sherburnhouse Plantation
Sherburn Hospital (Residential Care Home)
Sherburn House
Sherburn House Farm
Sherburnhouse Bridge
Whitwell Grange Farm
Whitwell Grange
Whitwell House Farm
Whitwell Farm
Whitwell East House Farm
Byers Garth
Chapman Bridge
HIGH SHINCLIFFE
Bent House Farm
Manor Farm
Manor Farm Cottage
Mill House
Oak Wood Cottage
Mill Cottages
DRAGONVILLE INDUSTRIAL ESTATE
Top Gear Indoor Karting
Broomside Cottages
Broomside House
Rosemeade
Pittington Bridge
Pittington Beck
Sherburn Beck
Sherburnhouse Beck
Chapman Beck
Whitwell Beck
155
168
177

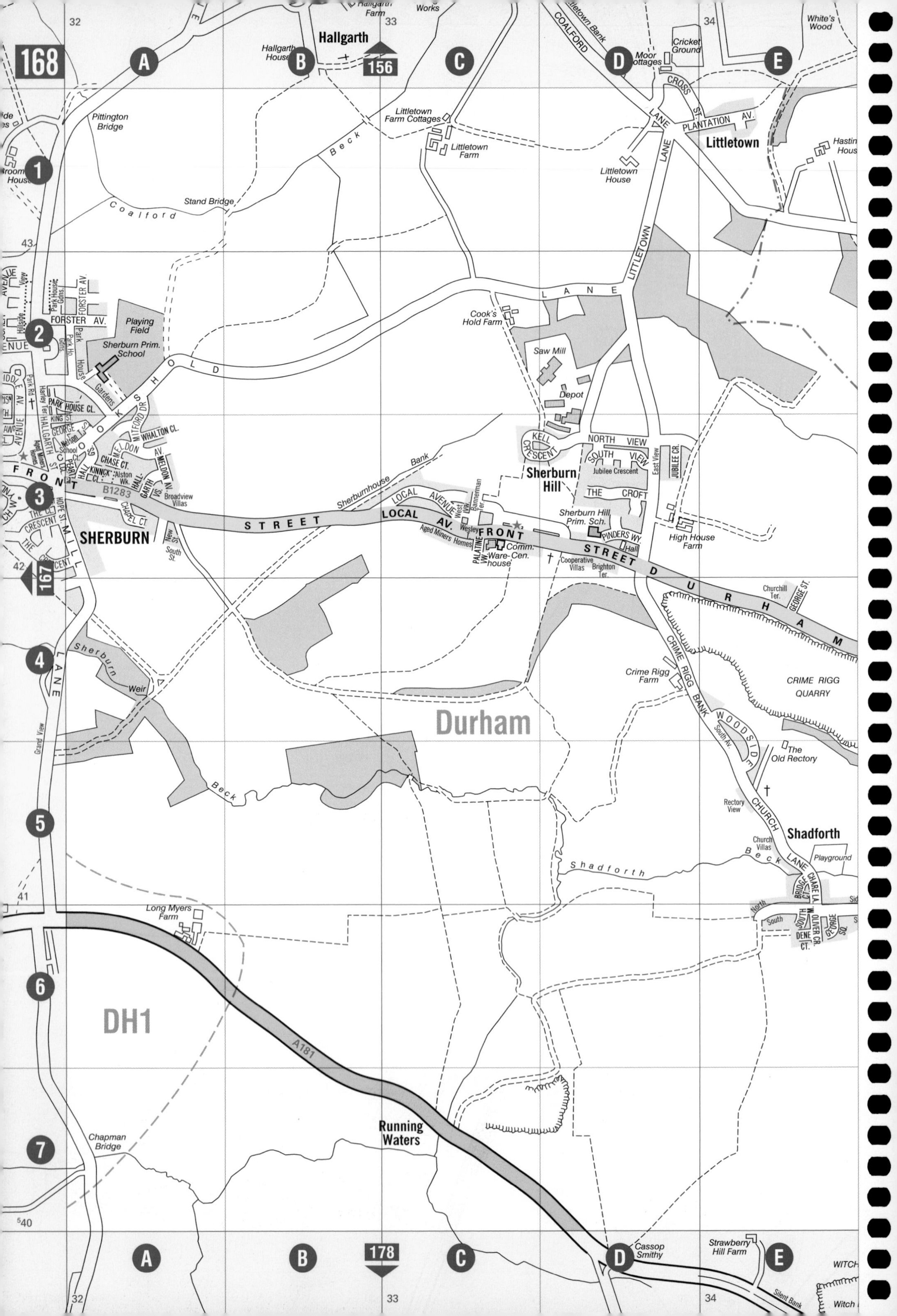
Hallgarth
Hallgarth House
Hallgarth Farm
Works
156
Pittington Bridge
Littletown Farm Cottages
Littletown Farm
Beck
Stand Bridge
Coalford
COALFORD
Moor Cottages
Cricket Ground
CROSS ST.
PLANTATION AV.
LANE
Littletown
Littletown House
White's Wood
LITTLETOWN LANE
LANE
Cook's Hold Farm
Saw Mill
Depot
SHOTS HOLD
FORSTER AV.
Playing Field
Sherburn Prim. School
Park House Gardens
PARK HOUSE CL.
MITFORD DR.
WHALTON CL.
MELDON AV.
CHASE CT.
KINNCK CL.
Alston Wk.
HALL GARTH
Broadview Villas
KELL CRESCENT
NORTH VIEW
SOUTH VIEW
Jubilee Crescent
East View
JUBILEE CR.
Sherburn Hill
THE CROFT
Sherburn Hill Prim. Sch.
PINDERS WY.
High House Farm
FRONT STREET
B1283
SHERBURN
CHAPEL CT.
New St.
South St.
Sherburnhouse Bank
LOCAL AVENUE
LOCAL AV.
West Wk.
Bannerman Ter.
Wesley
Aged Miners Homes
PALATINE W.
Comm. Cen.
Ware-house
Cooperative Villas
Brighton Ter.
FRONT STREET DURHAM
Churchill Ter.
GEORGE ST.
HOPE ST.
MILL
THE CRESCENT
167
Sherburn
Weir
LANE
Grand View
Crime Rigg Farm
CRIME RIGG BANK
CRIME RIGG QUARRY
WOODSIDE
South Av.
The Old Rectory
Rectory View
CHURCH LANE
Shadforth
Church Villas
Beck
Playground
Shadforth
Durham
Beck
Long Myers Farm
DH1
A181
Running Waters
Chapman Bridge
Cassop Smithy
Strawberry Hill Farm
Silent Bank
Witch
178
32
33
34
43
42
41
540

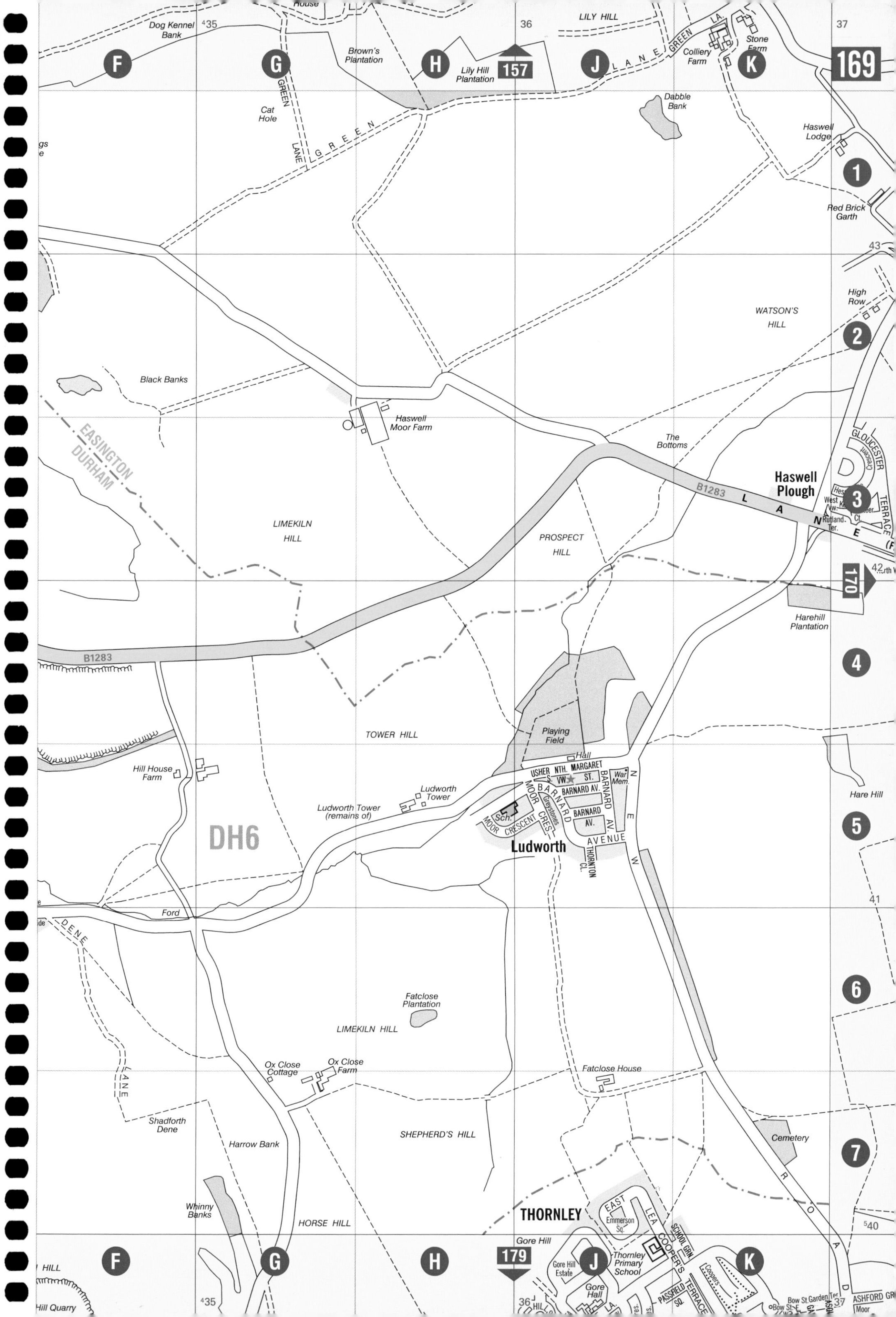

F G H 157 J K 169

1

Dog Kennel
Bank 435

LILY HILL

Colliery
Farm

Stone
Farm

Haswell
Lodge

Brown's
Plantation

Cat
Hole

Lily Hill
Plantation

Dabble
Bank

Red Brick
Garth

43

WATSON'S
HILL

High
Row

2

Black Banks

Haswell
Moor Farm

The
Bottoms

Haswell
Plough

GLOUCESTER

3

170

Hes.
West
Vw.

N

Rutland.
Ter.

E

42

LIMEKILN
HILL

PROSPECT
HILL

B1283

L A N E

Harehill
Plantation

B1283

4

TOWER HILL

Playing
Field

Hare Hill

Hill House
Farm

Ludworth
Tower

USHER NTH. MARGARET
ST.

Hall

BARNARD AV.

War
Mem.

DH6

Ludworth Tower
(remains of)

MOOR CRESCENT

BARNARD

MOOR

Sch.

Ludworth

BARNARD
AV.

AVENUE

THORNTON
CL.

N
E
W

5

41

Ford

DENE

Fatclose
Plantation

Fatclose House

6

LIMEKILN HILL

Ox Close
Cottage

Ox Close
Farm

Shadforth
Dene

LANE

SHEPHERD'S HILL

Cemetery

7

Harrow Bank

Whinny
Banks

THORNLEY

EAST

Fatclose House

HORSE HILL

Gore Hill

179

Emmerson
Sq.

Gore Hill
Estate

LEA COOPER'S

SCHOOL GRN

J

Thornley
Primary
School

K

HILL

Gore
Hall

PASSFIELD
SQ.

TERRACE

Bow St. Garden Ter.

Bow St. E.

ASHFORD GR

Moor

Hill Quarry

435

36

540

37

F G H J K

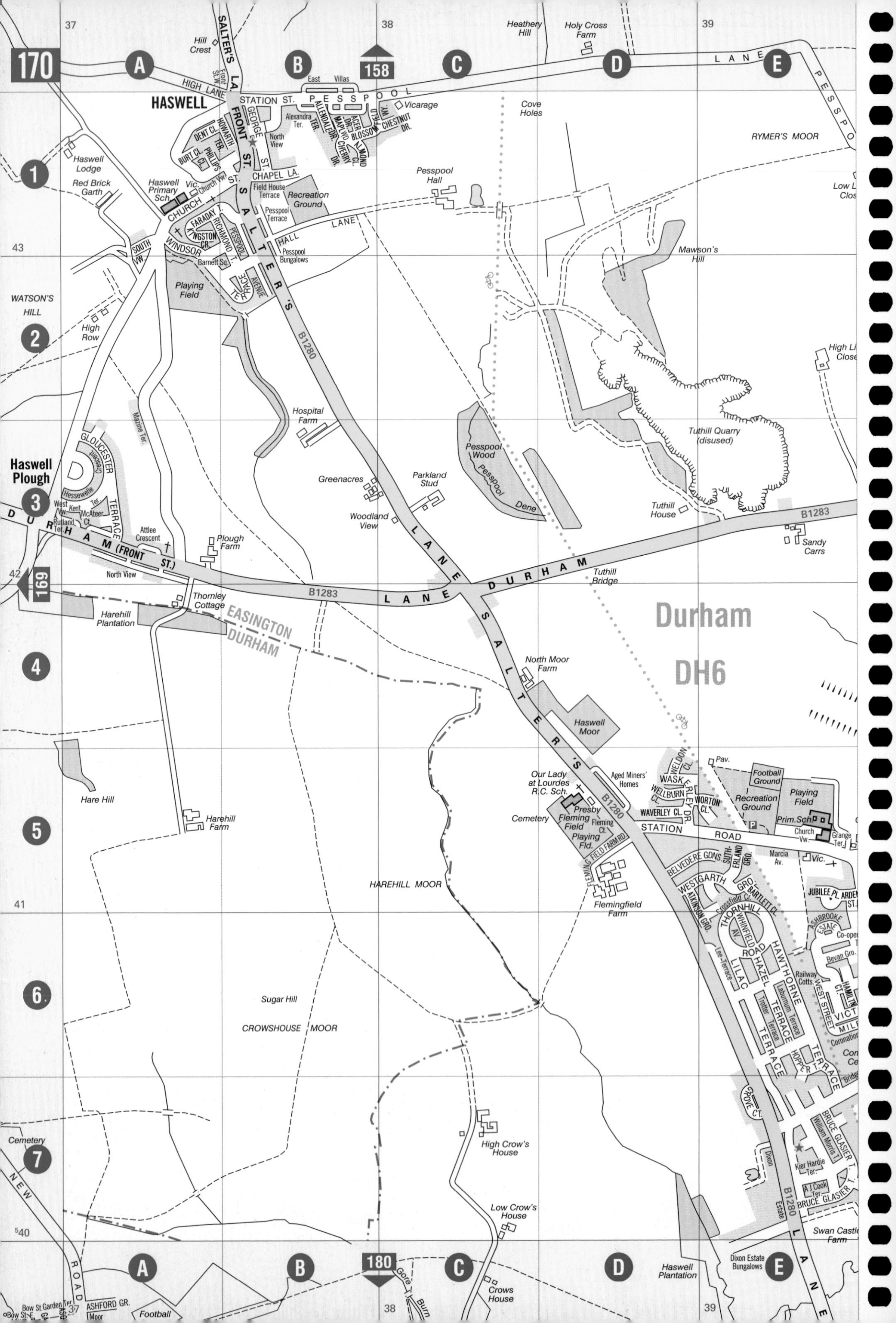

37   A   38   B   158   C   D   39   E

HASWELL

Hill Crest
SALTER'S LA.
HIGH LANE
Heathery Hill
Holy Cross Farm
LANE PESSPOOL

1
Haswell Lodge
Red Brick Garth
STATION ST.
PESSPOOL
East Villas
Vicarage
Cove Holes
RYMER'S MOOR

DENT CL.
HOWARTH TER.
BURT CL.
PHILLIPS T.
GEORGE ST.
FRONT ST.
ALEXANDRA TER.
ALLENDALE DR.
ACACIA
BLOSSOM
CHESTNUT DR.
MAY RD.
CHERRY DR.
RICHMOND CL.
North View
Pesspool Hall
Low L... Close

Haswell Primary Sch.
Vic.
Church Vw.
CHAPEL LA.
Field House Terrace
Recreation Ground

CHURCH
FARADAY T.
KINGSTON CR.
RICHMOND T.
PESSPOOL T.
HALL LANE
Pesspool Terrace

WINDSOR
SOUTH VW.
Barnett Sq.
TERRACE
AVENUE
Pesspool Bungalows

43   Mawson's Hill

WATSON'S HILL
2   High Row
Playing Field
B1280
High Li... Close

Mazine Ter.
Hospital Farm
Pesspool Wood
Tuthill Quarry (disused)

GLOUCESTER
TERRACE
Hesswelle
Greenacres
Parkland Stud
Pesspool Dene
Tuthill House
B1283

Haswell Plough
3
D
West Vw.
Kent Ter.
Rutland Ter.
McAteer Ct.
Attlee Crescent
Plough Farm
Woodland View
LANE   DURHAM
Sandy Carrs

DURHAM (FRONT ST.)
North View
B1283   SALTER'S   LANE   DURHAM
Tuthill Bridge
42   169

Thornley Cottage
Harehill Plantation
EASINGTON
DURHAM
North Moor Farm

4   Durham
DH6
Haswell Moor

Hare Hill
Harehill Farm
Our Lady at Lourdes R.C. Sch.
Aged Miners' Homes
WELDON CL.
WASK...
Pav.
Football Ground
Playing Field

5
Cemetery
Presby
Fleming Field Playing Fld.
Fleming Ct.
WELLBURN CL.
WAVERLEY CL.
ERLEY CR.
WORTON CL.
STATION   ROAD
Recreation Ground
Prim. Sch.
Church Vw.
Grange Ter.
Vic.
B1280
FLEMING FIELD FARM RD.

41   BELVEDERE GDNS.
WESTGARTH
SUTHERLAND GRO.
BARTLETT CL.
Marcia Av.
JUBILEE PL.
ARDEN ST.
Flemingfield Farm
ATKINSON GRO.
THORNHILL ROAD
WHINFIELD CL.
HAZEL TERRACE
LILAC TERRACE
HAWTHORNE TERRACE
Cossfield Gro.
ASHBROOKE ESTATE
Co-oper...
Bevan Gro.
Railway Cotts.
WEST STREET

HAREHILL MOOR
6   Sugar Hill
CROWSHOUSE MOOR
Lee Terrace
Laburnum Terrace
Trotter Terrace
VICT...
MILL...
TERRACE
UPPER TERRACE
Coronation...
Con... Ce...

7
Cemetery
High Crow's House
GROVE CT.
BRUCE GLASIER
William Morris...
Kier Hardie Ter.
Dixon...
A.J.Cook Ter.
BRUCE GLASIER Estate

NEW... ROAD
Low Crow's House
Swan Castle Farm

40   A   38   B   180   C   D   39   E
Bow St. Garden...
ASHFORD GR.
Bow St.
37   Football
Crows House
Gore Burn
Haswell Plantation
Dixon Estate Bungalows
LANE

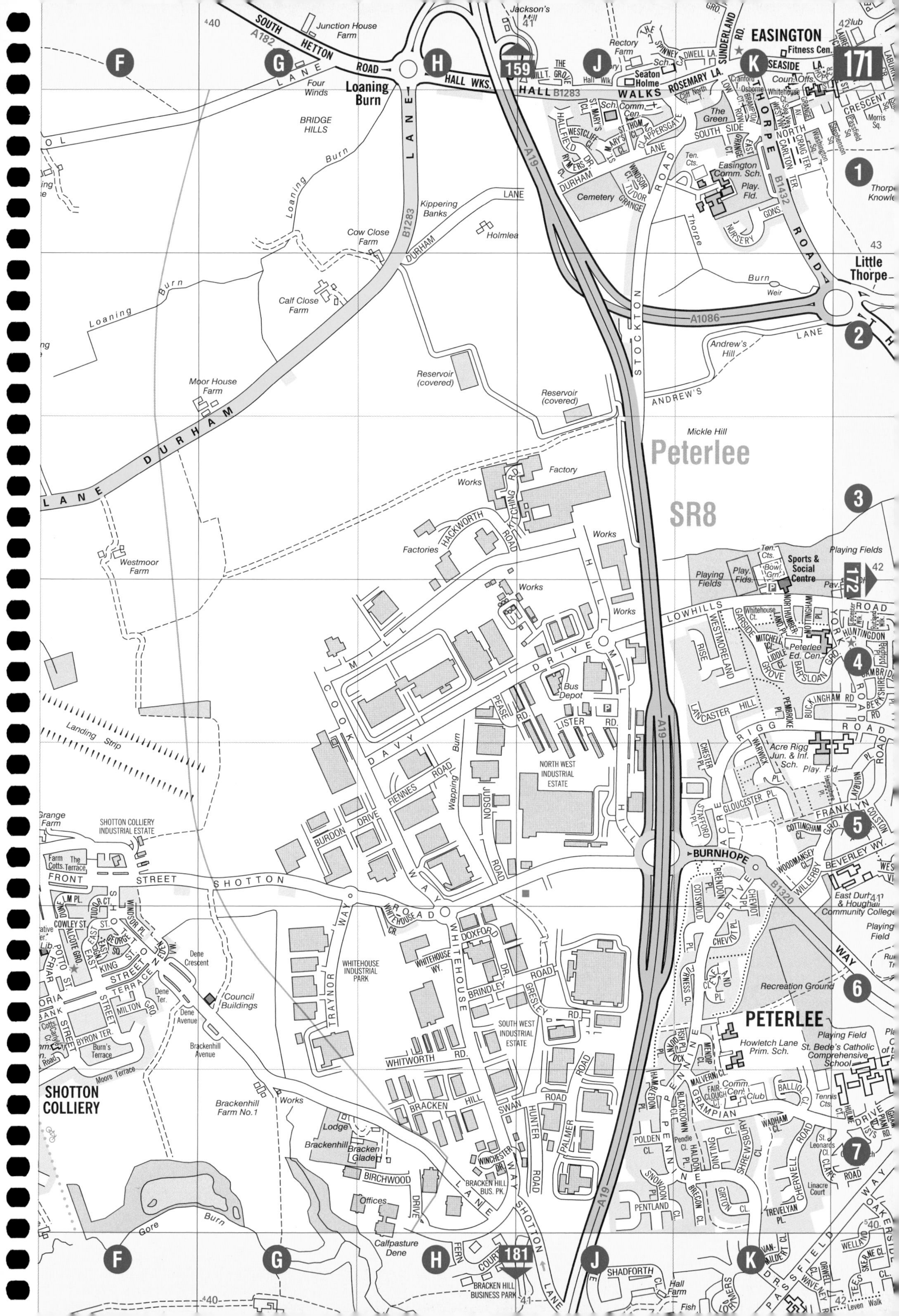
EASINGTON
Loaning Burn
Little Thorpe
Peterlee
SR8
PETERLEE
SHOTTON COLLIERY
SOUTH HETTON ROAD
HALL WALKS
DURHAM LANE
NORTH WEST INDUSTRIAL ESTATE
SOUTH WEST INDUSTRIAL ESTATE
WHITEHOUSE INDUSTRIAL PARK
SHOTTON COLLIERY INDUSTRIAL ESTATE
Sports & Social Centre
Peterlee Ed. Cen.
Acre Rigg Jun. & Inf. Sch.
Howletch Lane Prim. Sch.
St. Bede's Catholic Comprehensive School
East Durham & Houghall Community College
Easington Comm. Sch.
Recreation Ground
Council Buildings
Bus Depot
Landing Strip
Reservoir (covered)
Mickle Hill
Andrew's Hill
Calf Close Farm
Cow Close Farm
Moor House Farm
Westmoor Farm
Junction House Farm
Brackenhill Farm No.1
Calfpasture Dene
BRACKEN HILL BUS. PK.
159
172
181

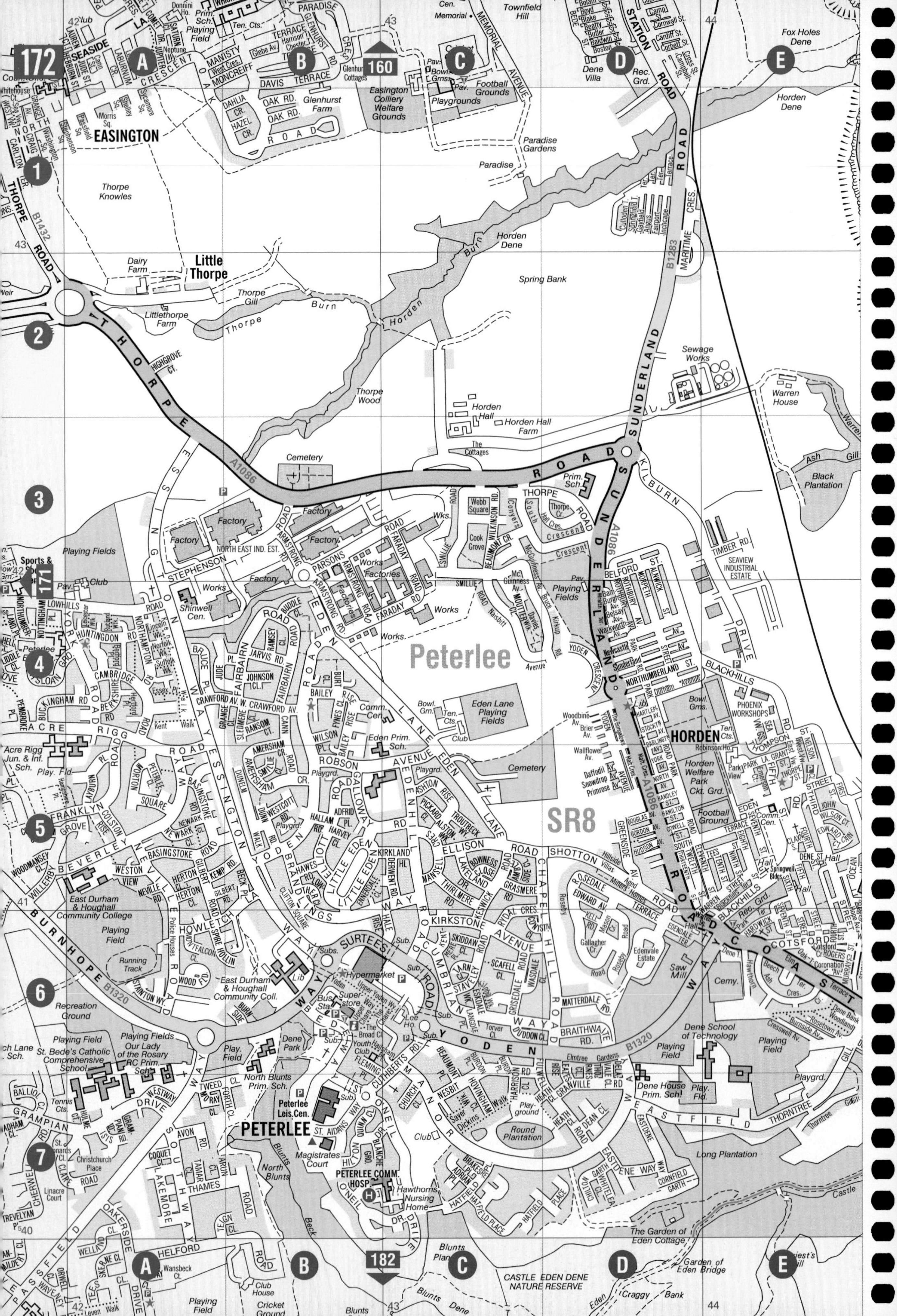
160
EASINGTON
SEASIDE
Easington Colliery Welfare Grounds
Glenhurst Farm
Football Grounds
Playgrounds
Townfield Hill
Memorial
DAVIS TERRACE
OAK RD.
MEMORIAL AVENUE
STATION ROAD
Dene Villa
Rec. Grd.
Fox Holes Dene
Horden Dene
Paradise Gardens
Paradise
Thorpe Knowles
THORPE ROAD
B1432
Little Thorpe
Dairy Farm
Thorpe Gill
Littlethorpe Farm
Thorpe Burn
Horden Burn
Horden Dene
Spring Bank
SUNDERLAND ROAD
B1283
MARITIME CRES.
Sewage Works
Warren House
Thorpe Wood
Horden Hall
Horden Hall Farm
The Cottages
Cemetery
A1086
Ash Gill
Black Plantation
KILBURN
Prim. Sch.
Factory
Works
Playing Fields
Sports & Social Club
171
NORTH EAST IND. EST.
STEPHENSON
ARMSTRONG ROAD
PARSONS
FARADAY RD
Webb Square
Cook Grove
SEAVIEW INDUSTRIAL ESTATE
TIMBER RD.
Shinwell Cen.
Peterlee
Eden Lane Playing Fields
HORDEN
Horden Welfare Park Ckt. Grd.
Football Ground
PHOENIX WORKSHOPS
BLACKHILLS RD
NORTHUMBERLAND ST.
Acre Rigg Jun. & Inf. Sch.
ACRE RIGG ROAD
CRAWFORD AV.
ROBSON AVENUE
Eden Prim. Sch.
EDEN LANE
ESSINGTON WAY
SR8
Cemetery
SHOTTON ROAD
Miners Homes
Edenvale Estate
Saw Mill
Cemy.
COAST ROAD
COTSFORD
East Durham & Houghall Community College
Playing Field
Running Track
BURNHOPE WAY
B1320
Recreation Ground
YODEN WAY
SURTEES
Hypermarket
Superstore
Bus Sta.
Dene Park
East Durham & Houghall Community Coll.
Playing Fields
St. Bede's Catholic Comprehensive School
Our Lady of the Rosary RC Prim. Sch.
North Blunts Prim. Sch.
Peterlee Leis.Cen.
PETERLEE
Magistrates Court
PETERLEE COMM. HOSP.
Hawthorns Nursing Home
Round Plantation
Dene House Prim. Sch.
Dene School of Technology
EASTFIELD ROAD
THORNTREE
Long Plantation
The Garden of Eden Cottage
Garden of Eden Bridge
CASTLE EDEN DENE NATURE RESERVE
Blunts Dene
Craggy Bank
Club House
Cricket Ground
Playing Field
Wansbeck Ct.
HELFORD
OAKERSIDE DRIVE
GRAMPIAN
Christchurch Place
Linacre Court
182
A
B
C
D
E
1
2
3
4
5
6
7
41
42
43
44
40

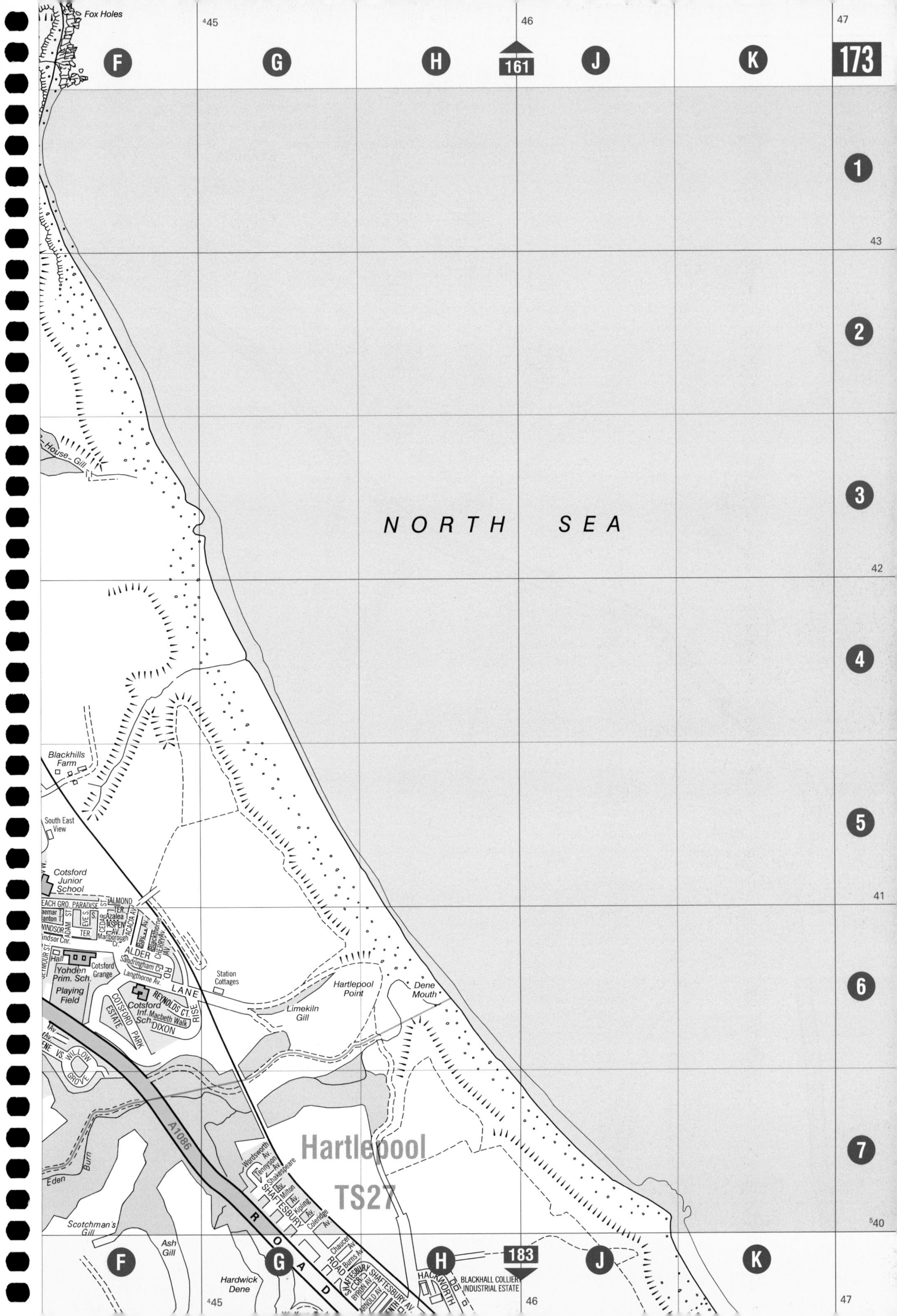

Fox Holes

1

43

2

NORTH SEA

3

42

4

Blackhills
Farm

South East
View

5

41

Cotsford
Junior
School

BEACH GRO. PARADISE
Braemar T
lanton T
WINDSOR
indsor Cnr.
TALMOND
TER.
Azalea
ASPEN
AV.
ACACIA AV.
CEDAR
BIRCH AV.
EVE S.
TER.
Blackthorne
Marlborough
Ct.
ALDER
Sandringham Cl.
Langthorne Av.
Station
Cottages

Hall
Yohden
Prim. Sch.
Cotsford
Grange
LANE
REYNOLDS CT.
Cotsford
Inf. Macbeth Walk
Sch
DIXON
Playing
Field
COTSFORD PARK
ESTATE
RISE

Hartlepool
Point
Dene
Mouth

6

Limekiln
Gill

AV.
ENE VS
GROV
WILLOW

Burn
Eden

A1086

Wordsworth
Av.
Tennyson
St
Shakespeare
St

Milton
Av.
Kipling
Av.

**Hartlepool
TS27**

7

Chaucer
Burns Av.
SHAFTESBURY AV.
BYRON AV.
REYNOLD AV.
Coleridge
Av.

ROAD
SHAFTESBURY

Scotchman's
Gill

Ash
Gill

Hardwick
Dene

HACKWORTH
BLACKHALL COLLIER
INDUSTRIAL ESTATE

⁵40

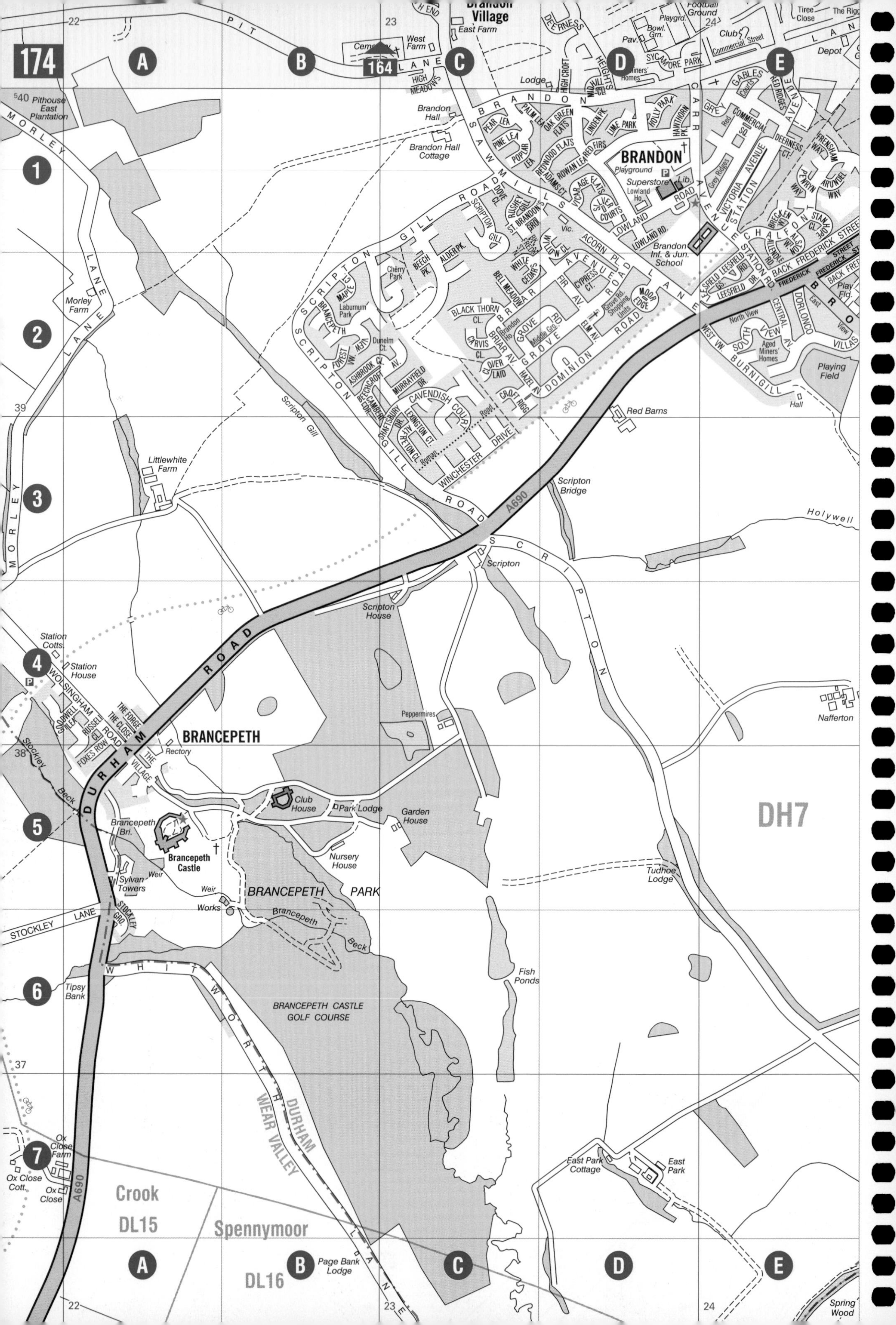
Brandon Village
East Farm
West Farm
Cemetery
164
PIT LANE
HIGH MEADOWS
DEERNESS HEIGHTS
Playgrd.
Football Ground
Bowl. Grn.
Pav.
Club
Commercial Street
SYCAMORE PARK
Miners' Homes
Tiree Close
The Rigg
Depot
Lodge
HIGH CROFT
MIDHILL CL.
GABLES
Courts
RED RIDGES
AVENUE
Pithouse East Plantation
MORLEY LANE
Brandon Hall
Brandon Hall Cottage
BRANDON LANE
SAW MILLS LANE
PEAR LEA
PALM LEA
OAK GREEN FLATS
LINDEN PK.
LIME PARK
HOLLY PARK
HAWTHORN PK.
CARR AVENUE
GREY
COMMERCIAL
DEERNESS CT.
FRENSHAM WAY
PINE LEA
POPLAR LEA
REDWOOD FLATS
ROWAN LEA
RED FIRS
BRANDON
Playground
Superstore
Lib.
Lowland Ho.
Grey Ridges
VICTORIA AVENUE
STATION AVENUE
PENRYN WAY
ARUNDEL WAY
ADAMS CT.
VICAR AGE FLATS
SILVER COURTS
LOWLAND ROAD
LOWLAND RD.
SCRIPTON GILL ROAD
DOVE CL.
SCRIPTON GILL
RUSHEY GILL
ST. BRANDON'S GRO.
Vic.
WILLOW CL.
ACORN PL.
AVENUE ROAD
Brandon Inf. & Jun. School
CHALFONT
BRECKEN
ALLENDALE RD.
STANHOPE CL.
STATION RD.
BACK FREDERICK STREET
FREDERICK STREET
LEESFIELD LEESFIELD GS. RD.
LEESFIELD DR.
BRANDON
Cherry Park
BEECH PK.
ALDER PK.
WHITE CEDARS
CYPRESS CT.
FIR AV.
BELL MEADOW
MAPLE
Laburnum Park
BRANCEPETH
BLACK THORN CL.
Grove Rd. Shopping Units
MOOR EDGE
Play. Fld.
DORLONCO
East View
VILLAS
North View
SOUTH VIEW
CENTRAL AV.
WEST VW.
Aged Miners' Homes
BURNIGILL
Playing Field
Hall
FOREST VW.
Dunelm Ct.
ASHBROOK CL.
AV.
Brandon Ho.
GROVE RD.
Middle Gro.
ELM AV.
CARVIS CL.
BRIAR AV.
GROVE
DOMINION ROAD
CLOVER LAID
HAZEL AV.
MURRAYFIELD DR.
BEECHCROFT
CAMBERLEY
CROFT RIGG
CAVENDISH COURT
SHAFTSBURY DR.
LEXINGTON CT.
Rowan Road
WINCHESTER DRIVE
Red Barns
Scripton Gill
Littlewhite Farm
Morley Farm
Scripton Bridge
ROAD
A690
Holywell
SCRIPTON
Scripton
Scripton House
DURHAM ROAD
Station Cotts.
Station House
WOLSINGHAM ROAD
GOODWELL LEA
RUSSELL CL.
THE FORGE
THE CLOSE
FOXES ROW
THE VILLAGE
Rectory
BRANCEPETH
Peppermires
Nafferton
DH7
Stockley Beck
Club House
Park Lodge
Garden House
Brancepeth Bri.
Brancepeth Castle
Nursery House
Sylvan Towers
Weir
Works
BRANCEPETH PARK
Brancepeth Beck
Tudhoe Lodge
STOCKLEY LANE
STOCKLEY GRO.
WHITWORTH LANE
Tipsy Bank
Fish Ponds
BRANCEPETH CASTLE GOLF COURSE
WEAR VALLEY
DURHAM
Ox Close Farm
Ox Close Cott.
Ox Close
East Park Cottage
East Park
Crook DL15
Spennymoor DL16
Page Bank Lodge
Spring Wood
A B C D E
1 2 3 4 5 6 7
22 23 24
540 39 38 37

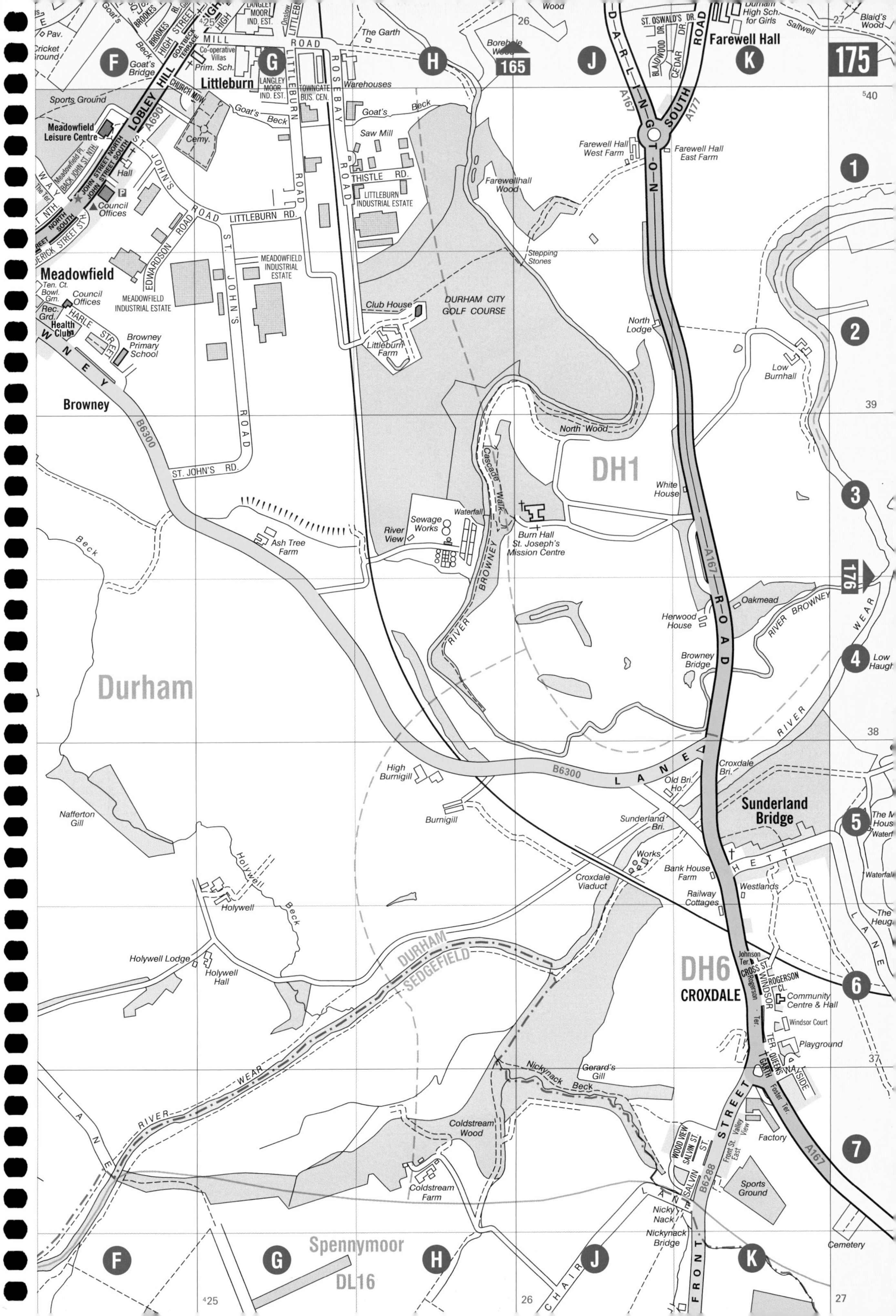

Meadowfield
Littleburn
Browney
Durham
DH1
DH6
CROXDALE
Sunderland Bridge
Spennymoor
DL16
Farewell Hall
Meadowfield Leisure Centre
Sports Ground
Goat's Bridge
Goat's Beck
Co-operative Villas
Prim. Sch.
Cemy.
Council Offices
Health Club
Browney Primary School
MEADOWFIELD INDUSTRIAL ESTATE
LITTLEBURN INDUSTRIAL ESTATE
LANGLEY MOOR IND. EST.
TOWNGATE BUS. CEN.
Warehouses
Saw Mill
The Garth
Borehole Wood
165
176
Farewell Hall West Farm
Farewell Hall East Farm
Farewellhall Wood
Stepping Stones
DURHAM CITY GOLF COURSE
Club House
Littleburn Farm
North Lodge
Low Burnhall
North Wood
White House
Cascade Walk
Waterfall
Sewage Works
River View
Burn Hall St. Joseph's Mission Centre
Ash Tree Farm
RIVER BROWNEY
Oakmead
Herwood House
Browney Bridge
RIVER WEAR
Low Haugh
Croxdale Bri.
Old Bri. Ho.
B6300 LANE
High Burnigill
Burnigill
Sunderland Bri.
Works
Bank House Farm
Westlands
Railway Cottages
Croxdale Viaduct
Nafferton Gill
Holywell
Holywell Beck
Holywell Lodge
Holywell Hall
DURHAM SEDGEFIELD
Community Centre & Hall
Windsor Court
Playground
Nickynack Beck
Gerard's Gill
Coldstream Wood
Coldstream Farm
Factory
Sports Ground
Nicky Nack
Nickynack Bridge
Cemetery
FRONT STREET
CHAIR
LANE
A167
A177
A690
B6288
DARLINGTON ROAD SOUTH
ST. JOHN'S ROAD
LITTLEBURN RD.
LITTLEBURN ROAD
ROSEBAY ROAD
THISTLE RD.
EDWARDSON ROAD
MILL ROAD
LOBLEY HILL
HIGH STREET
HARLE STREET
F
G
H
J
K
1
2
3
4
5
6
7
540
39
38
37
425
26
27

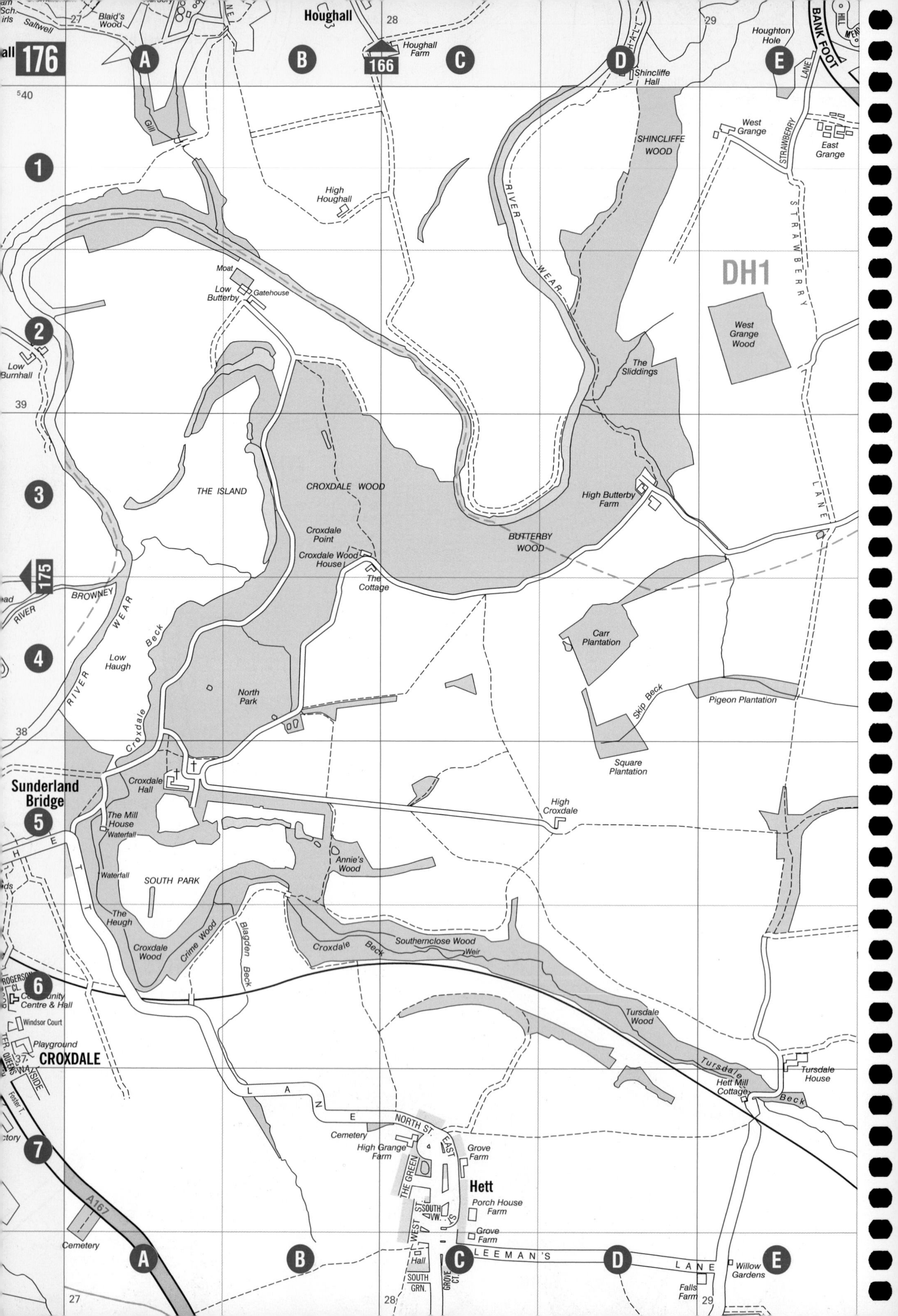

DH1

Saltwell
Blaid's Wood
Sch.
irls

Gill

High Houghall

Houghall Farm

Shincliffe Hall

SHINCLIFFE WOOD

West Grange

East Grange

STRAWBERRY LANE

Houghton Hole

BANK FOOT
HILL

RIVER WEAR

Moat
Low Butterby
Gatehouse

West Grange Wood

Low Burnhall

THE ISLAND

CROXDALE WOOD

The Sliddings

Croxdale Point

Croxdale Wood House

BUTTERBY WOOD

High Butterby Farm

BROWNEY

RIVER WEAR

Low Haugh

North Park

The Cottage

Carr Plantation

Skip Beck

Pigeon Plantation

Square Plantation

High Croxdale

Croxdale Beck

Sunderland Bridge

Croxdale Hall

The Mill House
Waterfall

Waterfall

SOUTH PARK

The Heugh

Croxdale Wood

Crime Wood

Blagden Beck

Annie's Wood

Croxdale Beck

Southernclose Wood

Weir

Tursdale Wood

ROGERSON CL.
Community Centre & Hall

Windsor Court

Playground

CROXDALE

TR QUEENS WAY SIDE
Foster T.

ctory

A167

Cemetery

Tursdale Beck

Tursdale House

Hett Mill Cottage

LANE

Cemetery

High Grange Farm

NORTH ST.

THE GREEN

Grove Farm

EAST ST.

Hett

Porch House Farm

WEST ST.
SOUTH VW.
SOUTH ST.

Grove Farm

Hall
SOUTH GRN.

GROVE CT.

LEEMAN'S LANE

Willow Gardens

Falls Farm

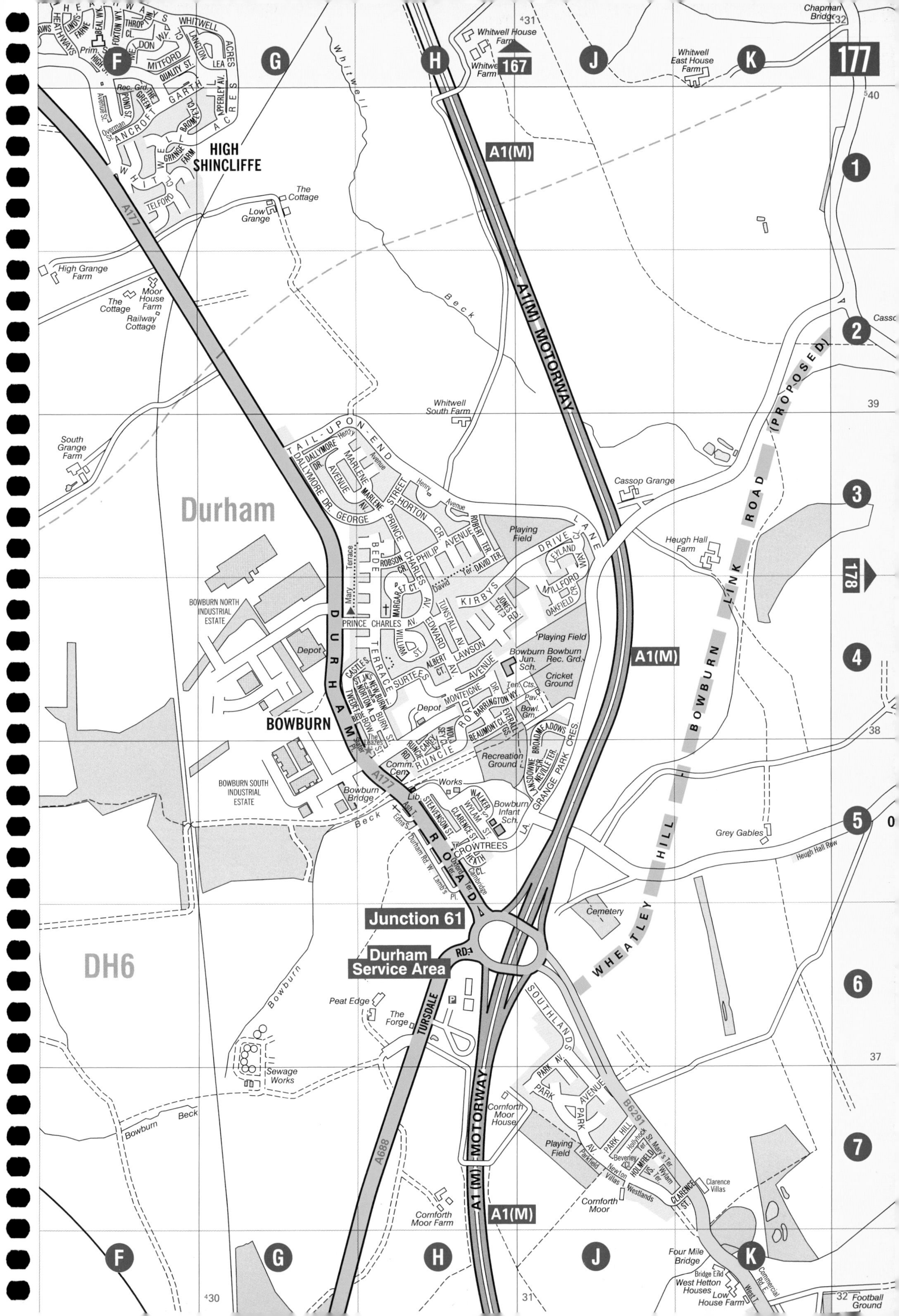
HIGH SHINCLIFFE
Durham
BOWBURN
BOWBURN NORTH INDUSTRIAL ESTATE
BOWBURN SOUTH INDUSTRIAL ESTATE
DH6
A1(M) MOTORWAY
A1(M)
A177
A688
B6291
Junction 61
Durham Service Area
DURHAM ROAD
TURSDALE RD.
BOWBURN LINK ROAD (PROPOSED)
WHEATLEY HILL
Whitwell House Farm
Whitwell East House Farm
Chapman Bridge
The Cottage
Low Grange
High Grange Farm
The Cottage
Moor House Farm
Railway Cottage
South Grange Farm
Whitwell South Farm
Cassop Grange
Heugh Hall Farm
Grey Gables
Heugh Hall Row
Cemetery
Playing Field
Recreation Ground
Cricket Ground
Bowburn Jun. Sch.
Bowburn Rec. Grd.
Bowburn Infant Sch.
Bowburn Bridge
Depot
Works
Comm. Cen.
Peat Edge
The Forge
Sewage Works
Bowburn Beck
Cornforth Moor House
Cornforth Moor Farm
Cornforth Moor
Clarence Villas
Four Mile Bridge
Bridge End
West Hetton Houses
Low House Farm
Football Ground
TAIL-UPON-END
DALLYMORE DR.
MARLENE AVENUE
PRINCE CHARLES AV.
PHILIP AVENUE
KIRBYS DRIVE
LANE
EDWARD AV.
TUNSTALL AV.
LAWSON AVENUE
SURTEES TERRACE
MONTEIGNE DR.
BARRINGTON WY.
BEAUMONT CL.
RUNCIE RD.
CROWTREES
GRANGE PARK CRES.
LANSDOWNE RD.
SOUTHLANDS
PARK AV.
PARK AVENUE
PARK HILL
CLARENCE ST.
Westlands
Newton Villas
Whitwell
Beck
F
G
H
J
K
1
2
3
4
5
6
7
167
178

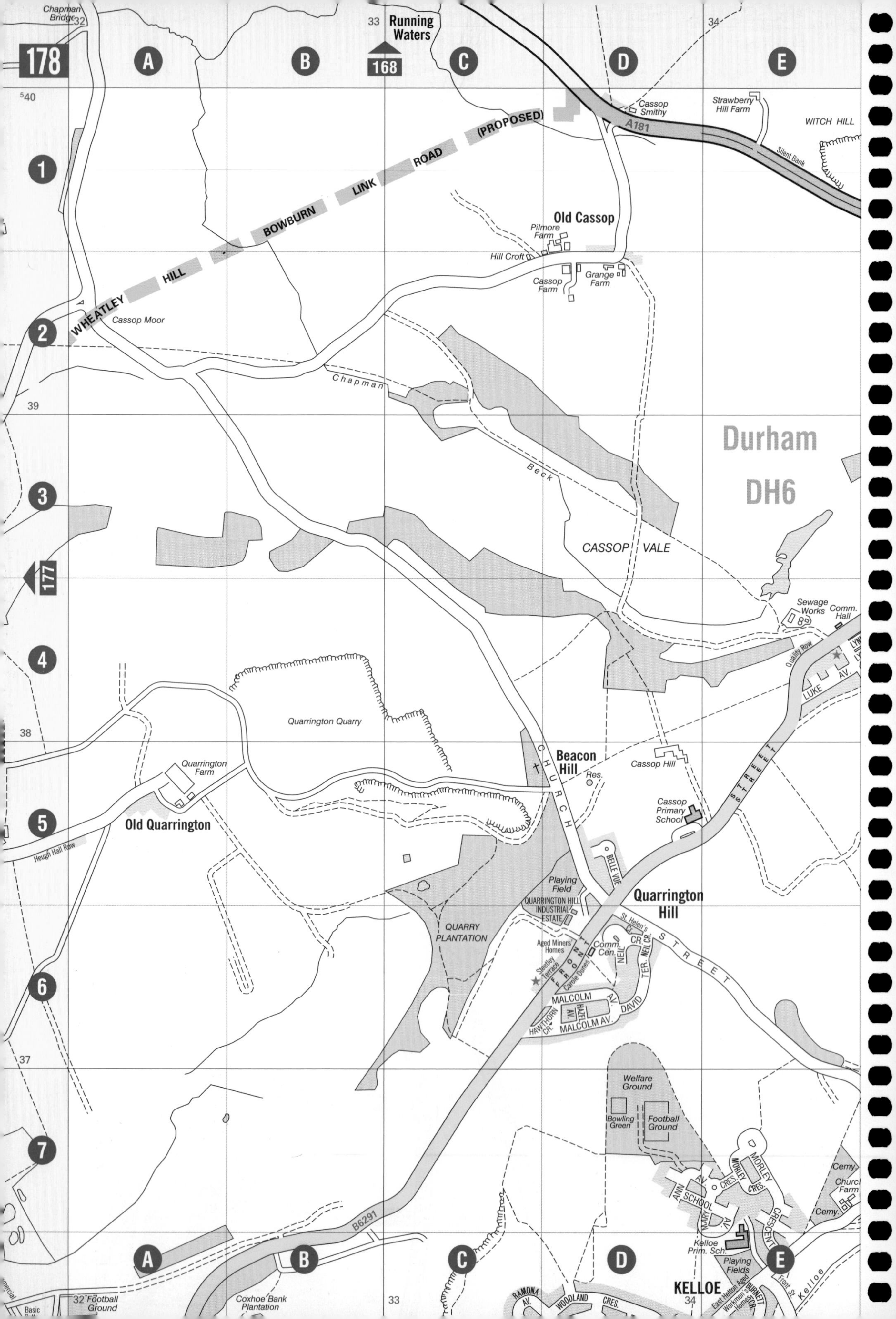

A B 168 C D E

33 Running Waters

1

Cassop Smithy
Strawberry Hill Farm
WITCH HILL
A181
Silent Bank

Old Cassop
Pilmore Farm
Hill Croft
Cassop Farm
Grange Farm

BOWBURN LINK ROAD (PROPOSED)
WHEATLEY HILL

2

Cassop Moor

39

Chapman

Beck

Durham
DH6

3

177

CASSOP VALE

Sewage Works
Comm. Hall

4

Quarrington Quarry

38

Quarrington Farm

Beacon Hill
CHURCH STREET
Res.
Cassop Hill
Cassop Primary School

5

Old Quarrington
Heugh Hall Row

Quarrington Hill
BELLE VUE

Playing Field
QUARRINGTON HILL INDUSTRIAL ESTATE
QUARRY PLANTATION

St. Helen's CR.
NEIL CR.
TER. NEIL CR.
DAVID
STREET

6

Aged Miners Homes
Shelter Terrace
Carole Dunes
Comm. Cen.
FRONT STREET
MALCOLM AV.
HAWTHORN CR.
HAZEL AV.
MALCOLM AV.

37

Welfare Ground
Bowling Green
Football Ground

7

MORLEY AV.
MORLEY CRES.
Cemy.
Church Farm
Cemy.

Basic

ANN AV.
SCHOOL AV.
WYATT AV.
CRESCENT
Front St.
Kelloe Prim. Sch.
Playing Fields
East Helton Aged Workmen Homes
BURNETT STREET

A B C D E

B6291

32 Football Ground
Coxhoe Bank Plantation
33
RAMONA AV.
WOODLAND CRES.
KELLOE
34
Kelloe

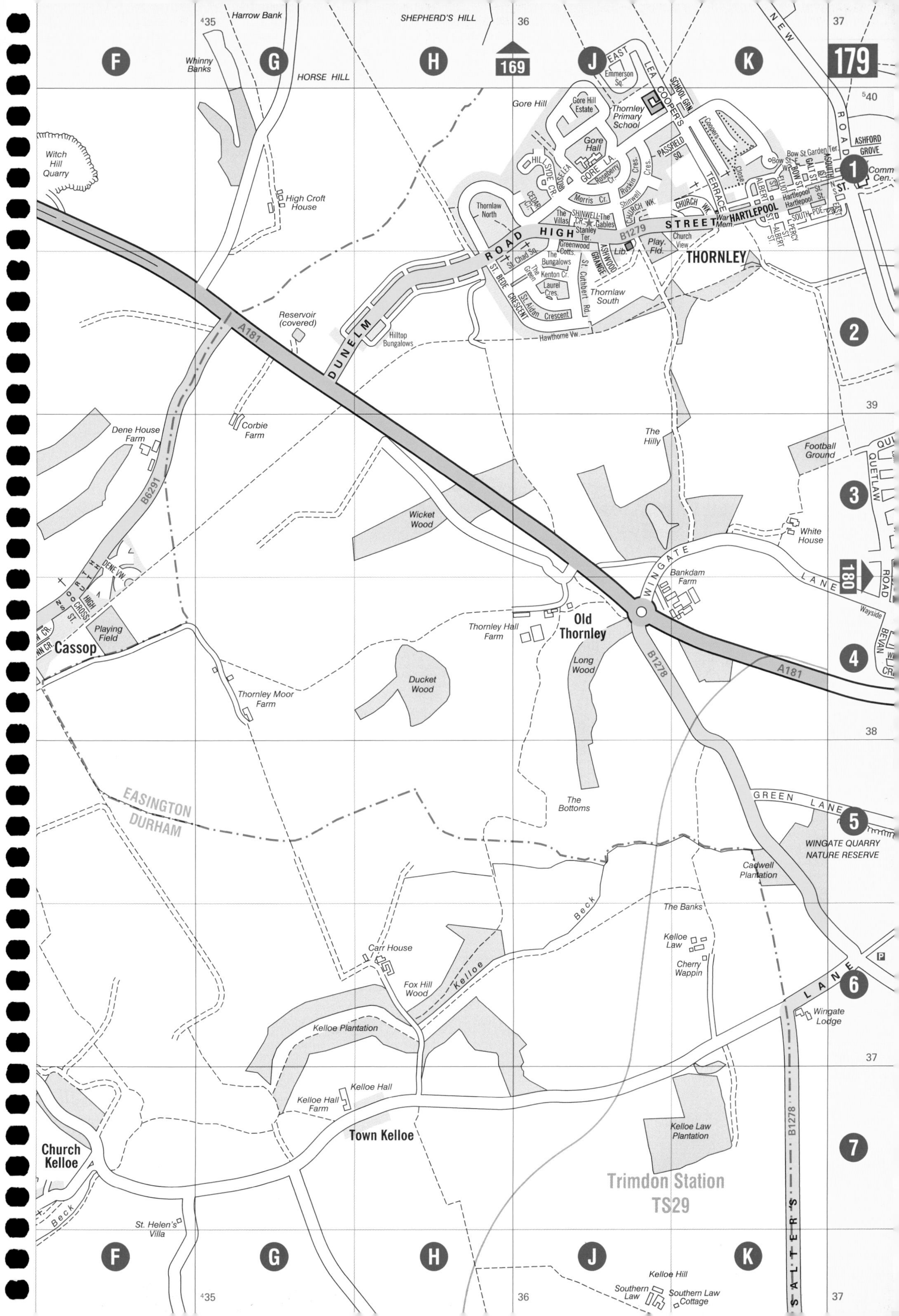

F **G** **H** **J** **K**

Harrow Bank
SHEPHERD'S HILL
⁴35
36
169
EAST
⁵40
37
Emmerson Sq.
Whinny Banks
HORSE HILL
Gore Hill
Bow St Garden Ter
ASHFORD GROVE
Gore Hill Estate
Thornley Primary School
Witch Hill Quarry
Gore Hall
1 Comm. Cen.
High Croft House
Thornlaw North
Rosebury
Hartlepool
HIGH
ROAD
THORNLEY
Thornlaw South
The Villas
SHINWELL The Gables
Stanley Ter.
Greenwood Cotts.
The Bungalows
Kenton Cr.
Laurel Cres.
Play. Fld.
Church View
War Mem.
HARTLEPOOL
STREET
2
39
Hawthorne Vw.
Thornlaw Crescent
Reservoir (covered)
A181
DUNELM
Hilltop Bungalows
Dene House Farm
Corbie Farm
The Hilly
Football Ground
White House
3
QUI QUETLAW
Wicket Wood
Bankdam Farm
WINGATE LANE
180 ROAD
Wayside
BEVAN CR
4
Cassop
Playing Field
Thornley Moor Farm
Thornley Hall Farm
Old Thornley
Long Wood
Ducket Wood
A181
38
EASINGTON DURHAM
The Bottoms
GREEN LANE
5
WINGATE QUARRY NATURE RESERVE
Cadwell Plantation
B1278
Beck
The Banks
Kelloe Law
Kelloe
Carr House
Cherry Wappin
6
Fox Hill Wood
Kelloe Plantation
Wingate Lodge
37
LANE
Kelloe Hall
Kelloe Hall Farm
Town Kelloe
Kelloe Law Plantation
7
Church Kelloe
Trimdon Station TS29
SALTER'S
B1278
St. Helen's Villa
Beck
F **G** **H** **J** **K**
⁴35
36
Kelloe Hill
Southern Law
Southern Law Cottage
37

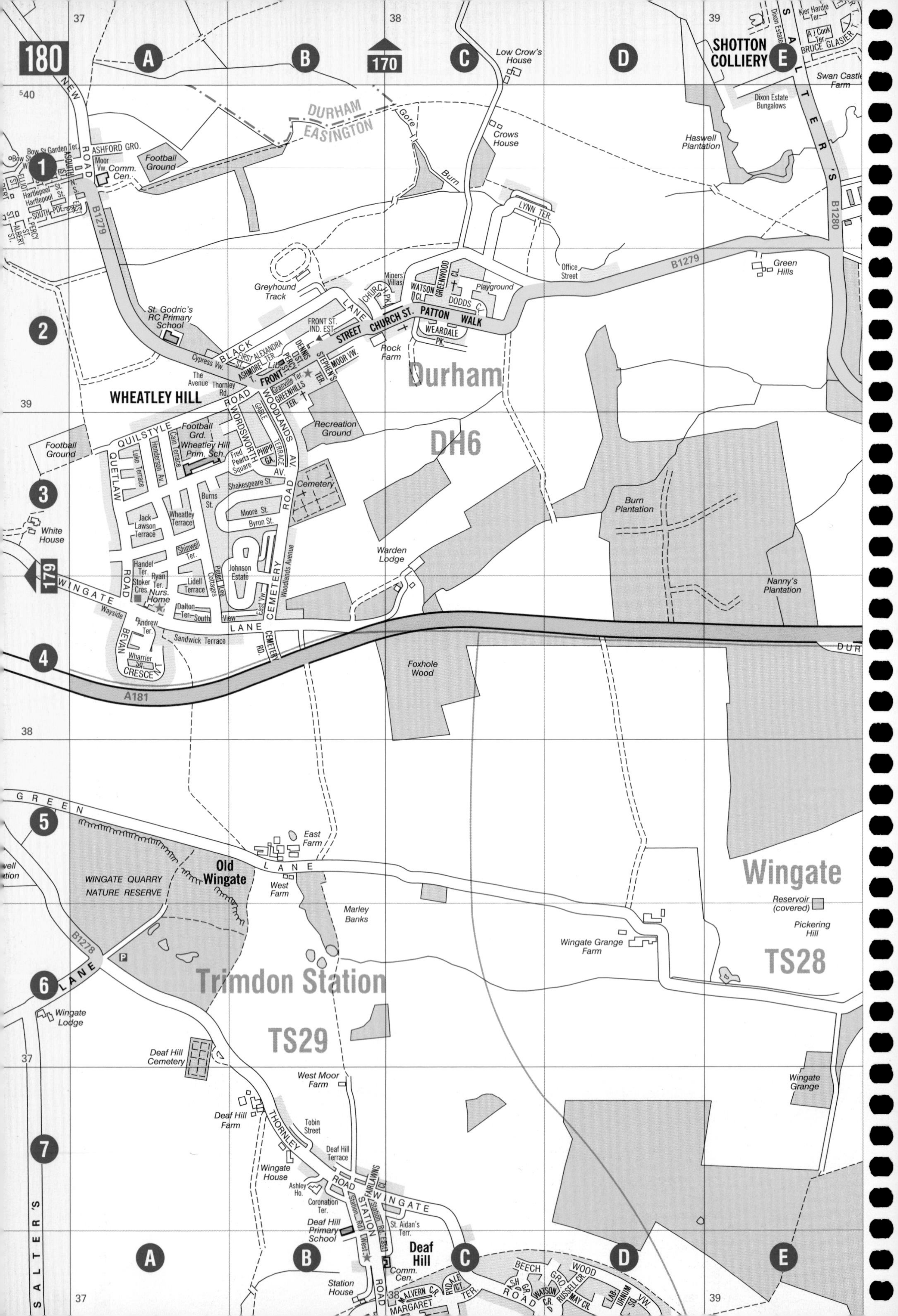

170
179
SHOTTON COLLIERY
WHEATLEY HILL
Durham
DH6
Wingate
TS28
Trimdon Station
TS29
Old Wingate
Deaf Hill
DURHAM
EASINGTON
B1279
B1280
B1278
A181
NEW ROAD
BLACK LANE
FRONT STREET
CHURCH ST.
PATTON WALK
WINGATE LANE
GREEN LANE
THORNLEY ROAD
STATION ROAD
SALTER'S
Low Crow's House
Crows House
Swan Castle Farm
Dixon Estate Bungalows
Haswell Plantation
Greyhound Track
St. Godric's RC Primary School
Football Ground
Recreation Ground
Cemetery
Wheatley Hill Prim. Sch.
White House
Warden Lodge
Burn Plantation
Nanny's Plantation
Foxhole Wood
Green Hills
Rock Farm
Office Street
Playground
East Farm
West Farm
Marley Banks
WINGATE QUARRY NATURE RESERVE
Wingate Grange Farm
Reservoir (covered)
Pickering Hill
Wingate Grange
Wingate Lodge
Deaf Hill Cemetery
West Moor Farm
Deaf Hill Farm
Tobin Street
Deaf Hill Terrace
Wingate House
Ashley Ho.
Coronation Ter.
Deaf Hill Primary School
St. Aidan's Terr.
Comm. Cen.
Station House

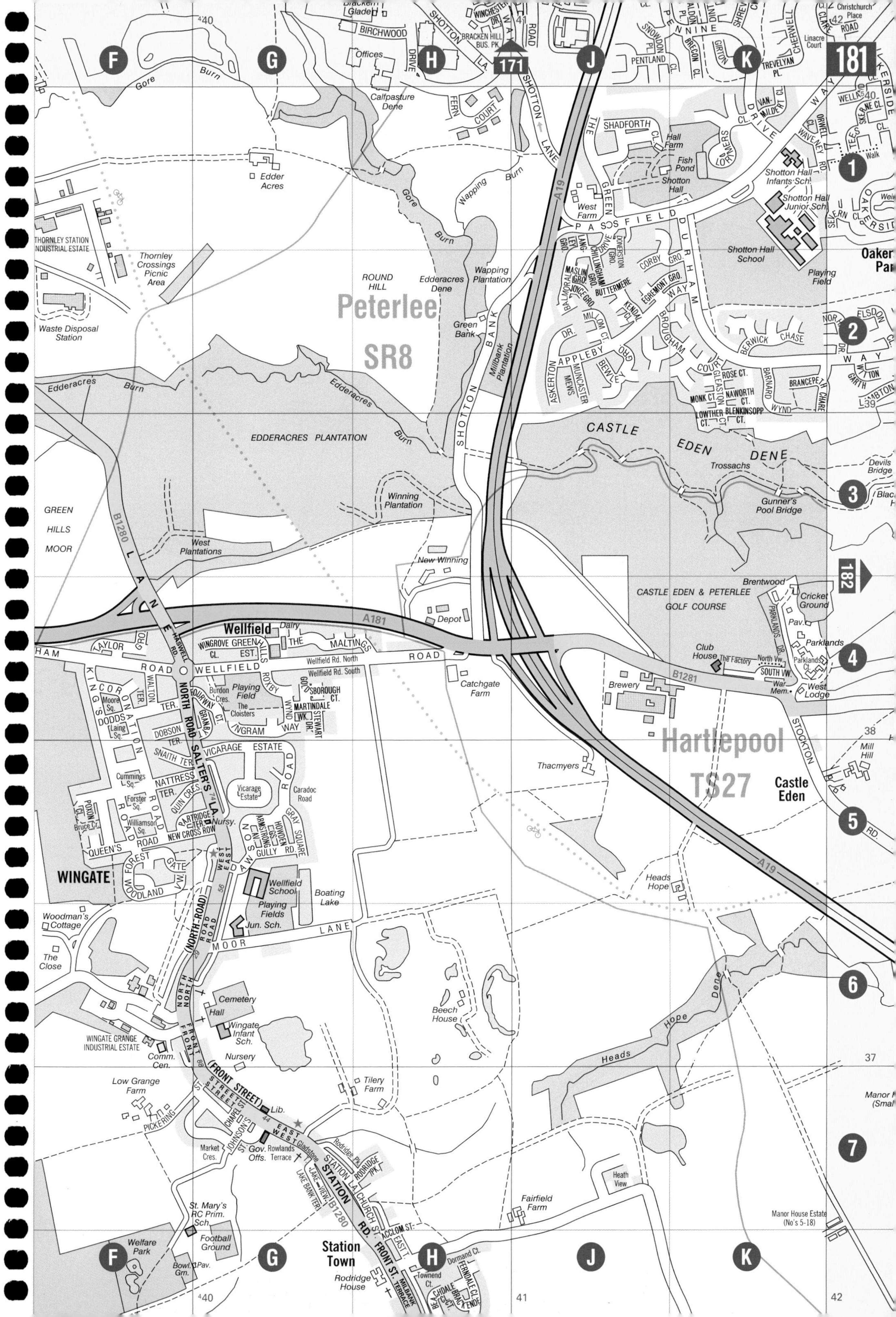
Peterlee
SR8
Hartlepool
TS27
WINGATE
Wellfield
Castle Eden
Station Town
CASTLE EDEN DENE
EDDERACRES PLANTATION
CASTLE EDEN & PETERLEE GOLF COURSE
GREEN HILLS MOOR
ROUND HILL
Edderacres Dene
Wapping Plantation
Green Bank
Millbank Plantation
Winning Plantation
West Plantations
New Winning
Depot
Catchgate Farm
Thacmyers
Heads Hope
Beech House
Tilery Farm
Fairfield Farm
Heath View
Brewery
Club House
Cricket Ground
Parklands
West Lodge
Mill Hill
Brentwood
Trossachs
Gunner's Pool Bridge
Devils Bridge
Shotton Hall School
Shotton Hall Infants Sch.
Shotton Hall Junior Sch.
Playing Field
Shotton Hall
Fish Pond
Hall Farm
West Farm
Calfpasture Dene
Edder Acres
Offices
BRACKEN HILL BUS. PK.
THORNLEY STATION INDUSTRIAL ESTATE
Thornley Crossings Picnic Area
Waste Disposal Station
Wellfield School
Playing Fields
Boating Lake
Jun. Sch.
Woodman's Cottage
The Close
Cemetery
Hall
Wingate Infant Sch.
Nursery
WINGATE GRANGE INDUSTRIAL ESTATE
Comm. Cen.
Low Grange Farm
Lib.
Gov. Offs.
Market Cres.
St. Mary's RC Prim. Sch.
Football Ground
Welfare Park
Bowl Grn.
Pav.
Rodridge House
Manor House Estate (No's 5-18)
A19
A181
B1280
B1281
171
182

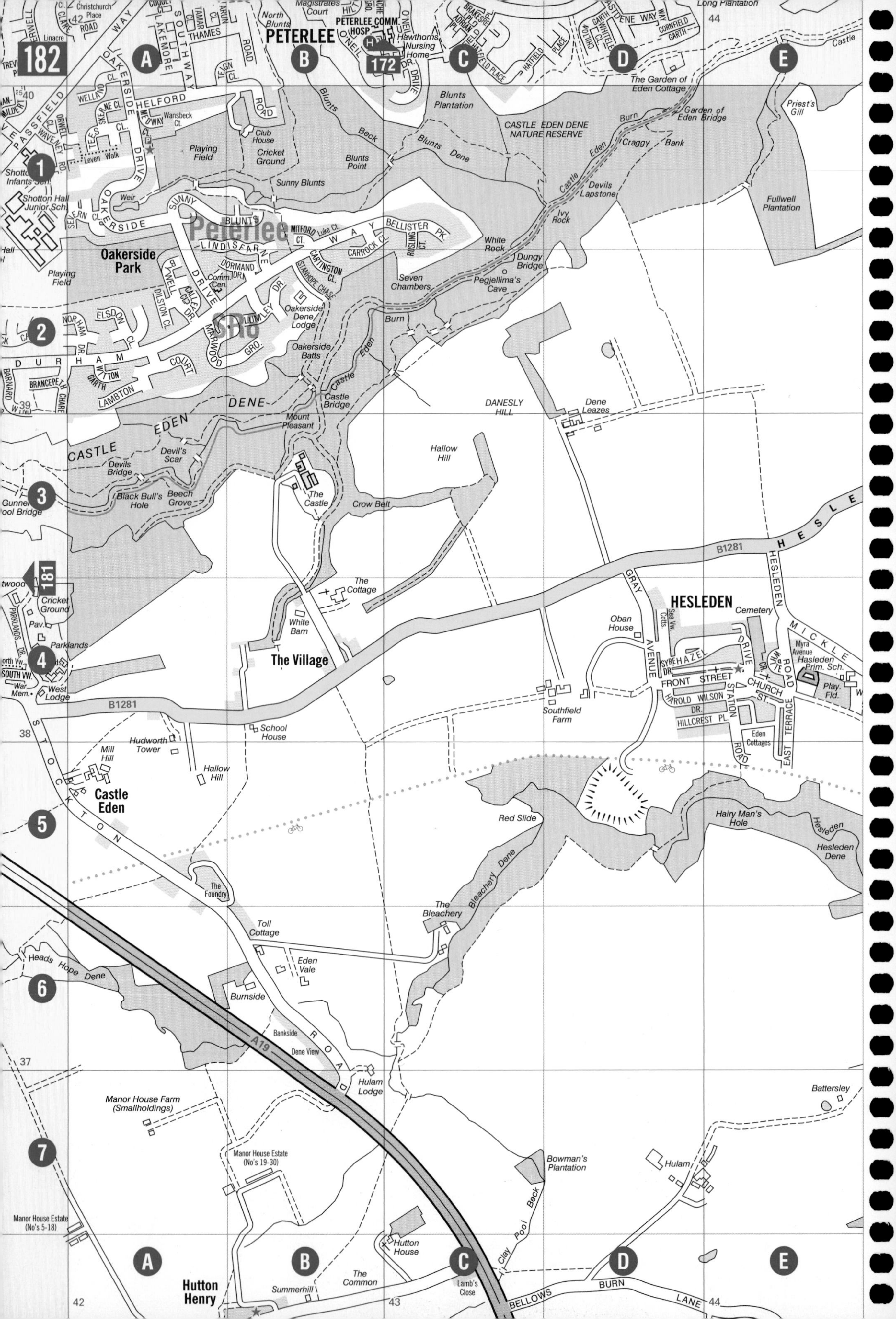
PETERLEE
PETERLEE COMM. HOSP.
Hawthorns Nursing Home
172
Blunts Plantation
CASTLE EDEN DENE NATURE RESERVE
The Garden of Eden Cottage
Garden of Eden Bridge
Long Plantation
Priest's Gill
Fullwell Plantation
Playing Field
Club House
Cricket Ground
Blunts Point
Sunny Blunts
Craggy Bank
Devils Lapstone
Ivy Rock
White Rock
Dungy Bridge
Pegjellima's Cave
Seven Chambers
Oakerside Park
Peterlee
Oakerside Dene Lodge
Oakerside Batts
Castle Bridge
Mount Pleasant
CASTLE EDEN DENE
Devils Bridge
Devil's Scar
Black Bull's Hole
Beech Grove
Gunner Pool Bridge
The Castle
Crow Belt
DANESLY HILL
Dene Leazes
Hallow Hill
The Cottage
White Barn
The Village
HESLEDEN
Oban House
Cemetery
Hasleden Prim. Sch.
Play. Fld.
Southfield Farm
Eden Cottages
Cricket Ground
Parklands
West Lodge
War Mem.
B1281
School House
Hudworth Tower
Mill Hill
Hallow Hill
Castle Eden
Red Slide
Hairy Man's Hole
Hesleden Dene
Bleachery Dene
The Bleachery
The Foundry
Toll Cottage
Eden Vale
Heads Hope Dene
Burnside
Bankside
Dene View
A19
Hulam Lodge
Manor House Farm (Smallholdings)
Manor House Estate (No's 19-30)
Manor House Estate (No's 5-18)
Battersley
Bowman's Plantation
Clay Pool Beck
Hulam
Hutton House
Hutton Henry
The Common
Summerhill
Lamb's Close
BELLOWS BURN LANE
181

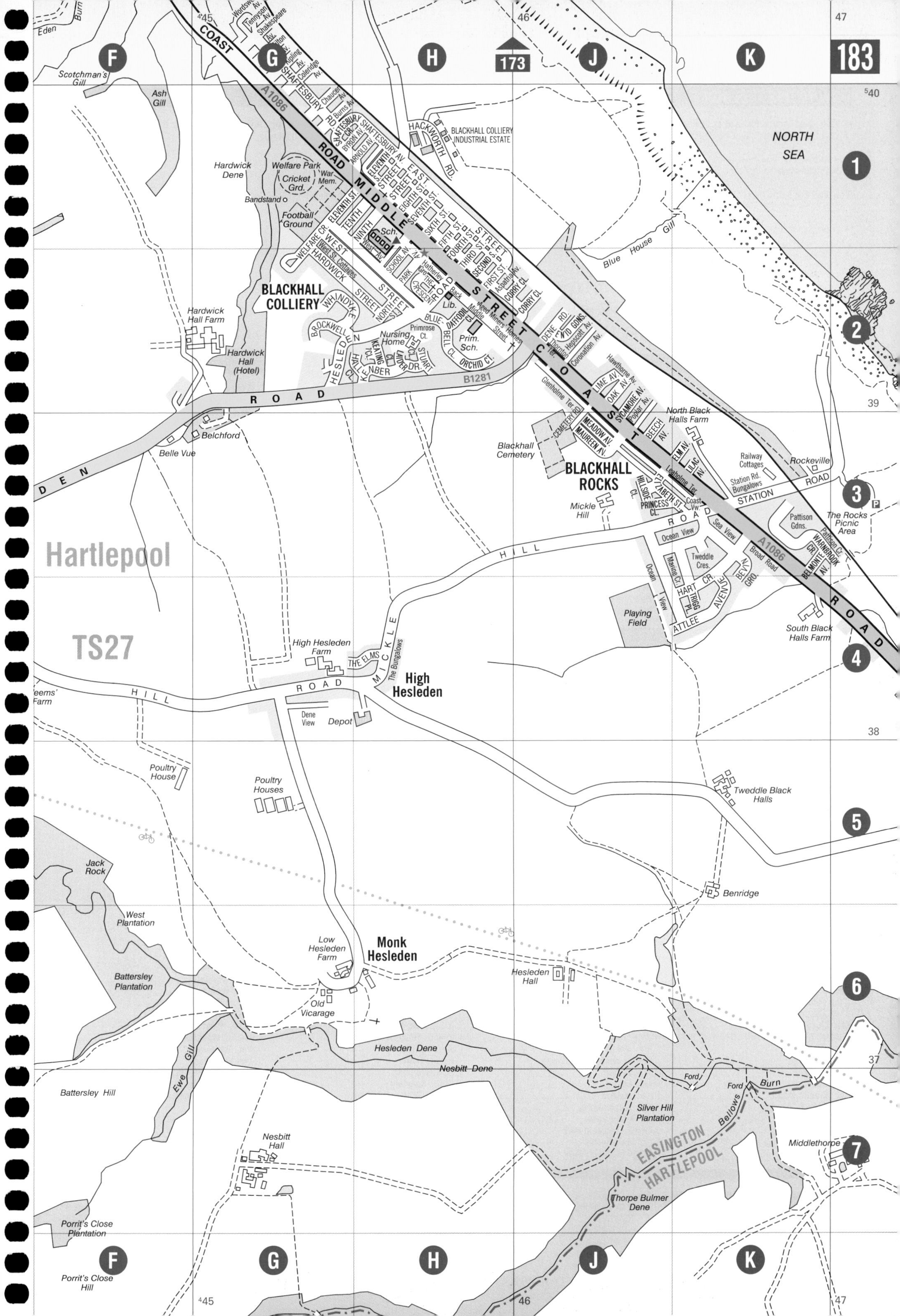

173
NORTH SEA
BLACKHALL COLLIERY
BLACKHALL ROCKS
High Hesleden
Monk Hesleden
Hartlepool
TS27
COAST ROAD
MIDDLE STREET
A1086
B1281
HESLEDEN ROAD
HILL ROAD
MICKLE HILL ROAD
STATION ROAD
BLACKHALL COLLIERY INDUSTRIAL ESTATE
Hardwick Dene
Welfare Park
Cricket Grd.
War Mem.
Bandstand
Football Ground
Hardwick Hall Farm
Hardwick Hall (Hotel)
Belchford
Belle Vue
Scotchman's Gill
Ash Gill
Eden Burn
Blue House Gill
Blackhall Cemetery
North Black Halls Farm
Railway Cottages
Rockeville
Station Rd. Bungalows
The Rocks Picnic Area
Mickle Hill
Playing Field
South Black Halls Farm
High Hesleden Farm
Dene View
Depot
Poultry House
Poultry Houses
Tweddle Black Halls
Benridge
Jack Rock
West Plantation
Battersley Plantation
Low Hesleden Farm
Old Vicarage
Hesleden Hall
Hesleden Dene
Nesbitt Dene
Ford
Burn
Silver Hill Plantation
Bellows
EASINGTON
HARTLEPOOL
Thorpe Bulmer Dene
Middlethorpe
Battersley Hill
Ewe Gill
Nesbitt Hall
Porrit's Close Plantation
Porrit's Close Hill
F G H J K
1 2 3 4 5 6 7
445 46 47
540 39 38 37

INDEX

Including Streets, Places & Areas, Industrial Estates, Selected Flats & Walkways,
Stations and Selected Places of Interest.

HOW TO USE THIS INDEX

1. Each street name is followed by its Postcode District and then by its Locality abbreviation(s) and then by its map reference; e.g. **Abbey Dr.** DH4: Hou S . . . 7B **130** is in the DH4 Postcode District and the Houghton-le-Spring Locality and is to be found in square 7B on page **130**. The page number is shown in bold type.

2. A strict alphabetical order is followed in which Av., Rd., St., etc. (though abbreviated) are read in full and as part of the street name; e.g. **Acornclose La.** appears after **Acorn Cl.** but before **Acorn Cft.**

3. Streets and a selection of flats and walkways too small to be shown on the maps, appear in the index with the thoroughfare to which it is connected shown in brackets; e.g. **Abbey Vw. Yd.** *NE61: Mor* . . . *6E 8 (off Buller's Grn.)*

4. Addresses that are in more than one part are referred to as not continuous.

5. Places and areas are shown in the index in BLUE TYPE and the map reference is to the actual map square in which the town centre or area is located and not to the place name shown on the map; e.g. **ACOMB** . . . **4B 50**

6. An example of a selected place of interest is Arbeia Roman Fort & Mus. 1J 67

7. An example of a station is Blaydon Station (Rail) . . . 2C 80. Included are Rail **(Rail)** and Metro **(Metro)**.

8. Map references shown in brackets; e.g **Abbotsford Gro.** SR2: Sund . . . 3E **118** (6G **7**) refer to entries that also appear on the large scale pages **4-7**.

GENERAL ABBREVIATIONS

App. : Approach	**Ct.** : Court	**Info.** : Information	**Prom.** : Promenade
Arc. : Arcade	**Cres.** : Crescent	**Intl.** : International	**Ri.** : Rise
Av. : Avenue	**Cft.** : Croft	**La.** : Lane	**Rd.** : Road
Bk. : Back	**Dr.** : Drive	**Lit.** : Little	**Shop.** : Shopping
Blvd. : Boulevard	**E.** : East	**Lwr.** : Lower	**Sth.** : South
Bri. : Bridge	**Ent.** : Enterprise	**Mnr.** : Manor	**Sq.** : Square
Bldg. : Building	**Est.** : Estate	**Mans.** : Mansions	**Sta.** : Station
Bldgs. : Buildings	**Fld.** : Field	**Mkt.** : Market	**St.** : Street
Bungs. : Bungalows	**Flds.** : Fields	**Mdw.** : Meadow	**Ter.** : Terrace
Bus. : Business	**Gdn.** : Garden	**Mdws.** : Meadows	**Twr.** : Tower
Cvn. : Caravan	**Gdns.** : Gardens	**M.** : Mews	**Trad.** : Trading
Cen. : Centre	**Gth.** : Garth	**Mt.** : Mount	**Up.** : Upper
Chu. : Church	**Ga.** : Gate	**Mus.** : Museum	**Va.** : Vale
Chyd. : Church Yard	**Gt.** : Great	**Nth.** : North	**Vw.** : View
Circ. : Circle	**Grn.** : Green	**No.** : Number	**Vs.** : Villas
Cl. : Close	**Gro.** : Grove	**Pde.** : Parade	**Vis.** : Visitors
Coll. : College	**Hgts.** : Heights	**Pk.** : Park	**Wlk.** : Walk
Cnr. : Corner	**Ho.** : House	**Pas.** : Passage	**W.** : West
Cott. : Cottage	**Ho's** : Houses	**Pl.** : Place	**Yd.** : Yard
Cotts. : Cottages	**Ind.** : Industrial	**Pct.** : Precinct	

LOCALITY ABBREVIATIONS

Acomb : **Acomb**	Dur : **Durham**	Lead : **Leadgate**	Seg : **Seghill**
Ann P : **Annfield Plain**	Eas : **Easington**	Leam : **Leamside**	Shad : **Shadforth**
Ash : **Ashington**	Eas L : **Easington Lane**	Lem : **Lemington**	Sher : **Sherburn**
Ayd : **Aydon**	E Bol : **East Boldon**	Loan : **Loansdean**	Shir : **Shiremoor**
Back : **Backworth**	E Cram : **East Cramlington**	Longb : **Longbenton**	Shot B : **Shotley Bridge**
Beam : **Beamish**	E Har : **East Hartford**	M'sly : **Medomsley**	Shot C : **Shotton Colliery**
Bed : **Bedlington**	E Her : **East Herrington**	Mic : **Mickley**	S Het : **South Hetton**
Bir : **Birtley**	E Sle : **East Sleekburn**	Mil : **Milbourne**	S Shi : **South Shields**
B Col : **Blackhall Colliery**	Ebc : **Ebchester**	Mit : **Mitford**	S'wck : **Southwick**
Bla T : **Blaydon-on-Tyne**	Edm : **Edmondsley**	Monk : **Monkwearmouth**	Spri : **Springwell**
Bly : **Blyth**	Esh W : **Esh Winning**	Mor : **Morpeth**	Stly : **Stanley**
Bol C : **Boldon Colliery**	Fair M : **Fair Moor**	Mur : **Murton**	Stoc : **Stocksfield**
Bow : **Bowburn**	Gate : **Gateshead**	Nel V : **Nelson Village**	Sund : **Sunderland**
B'don : **Brandon**	Gos : **Gosforth**	Newb S : **Newbiggin-by-the-Sea**	Sun : **Sunniside**
Bras : **Brasside**	Gt Lum : **Great Lumley**	New B : **New Brancepeth**	Swa : **Swalwell**
B End : **Bridge End**	G'sde : **Greenside**	Newc T : **Newcastle upon Tyne**	Tan L : **Tanfield Lea**
B'ley : **Broomley**	Ham C : **Hamsterley Colliery**	News : **Newsham**	Thor : **Thornley**
Bru V : **Brunswick Village**	Ham M : **Hamsterley Mill**	New S : **New Silksworth**	Thro : **Throckley**
B'hpe : **Burnhope**	H Bri : **Hartford Bridge**	Newt : **Newton**	Tra W : **Tranwell Woods**
Burn : **Burnopfield**	Has : **Haswell**	N Sea : **North Seaton**	Trim S : **Trimdon Station**
Cal : **Callerton**	Heb : **Hebburn**	N Shi : **North Shields**	Tud V : **Tudhoe Village**
Camb : **Cambois**	Hed W : **Heddon-on-the-Wall**	Ous : **Ouston**	Ush M : **Ushaw Moor**
Carr : **Carrville**	Hed : **Hedley**	O'ham : **Ovingham**	Usw : **Usworth**
Cass : **Cassop**	Hep : **Hepscott**	Peg : **Pegswood**	Walk : **Walker**
Cas E : **Castle Eden**	Hes : **Hesleden**	Pelt : **Pelton**	W'snd : **Wallsend**
C'sde : **Castleside**	Hett : **Hett**	Pen : **Penshaw**	Wash : **Washington**
C'twn : **Castletown**	Hett H : **Hetton-le-Hole**	Pet : **Peterlee**	Wat : **Waterhouses**
Cha P : **Chapel Park**	Hex : **Hexham**	Plaw : **Plawsworth**	Well : **Wellfield**
Ches S : **Chester-le-Street**	H Pitt : **High Pittington**	Pon : **Ponteland**	Welt : **Welton**
Chop : **Choppington**	H Shin : **High Shincliffe**	Pru : **Prudhoe**	W Bol : **West Boldon**
C'wl : **Chopwell**	H Spen : **High Spen**	Quar H : **Quarrington Hill**	W Rai : **West Rainton**
Cle : **Cleadon**	Hir : **Hirst**	Rid M : **Riding Mill**	W Sle : **West Sleekburn**
C Dene : **Clough Dene**	H'wll : **Holywell**	Row G : **Rowlands Gill**	Whe H : **Wheatley Hill**
Con : **Consett**	Hor : **Horsley**	Ryh : **Ryhope**	Whi : **Whickham**
Cor : **Corbridge**	Hou S : **Houghton-le-Spring**	Ryton : **Ryton**	Whit : **Whitburn**
Cow : **Cowpen**	Jar : **Jarrow**	Sac : **Sacriston**	Whit B : **Whitley Bay**
Coxh : **Coxhoe**	Kel : **Kelloe**	Sand : **Sandhoe**	W'stll : **Whittonstall**
Cra : **Cramlington**	Ken : **Kenton**	Sco G : **Scotland Gate**	Wide O : **Wide Open**
Crox : **Croxdale**	Kib : **Kibblesworth**	S'hm : **Seaham**	Win : **Wingate**
Din : **Dinnington**	Kil : **Killingworth**	Sea : **Seaton**	Wit G : **Witton Gilbert**
Dip : **Dipton**	Lam P : **Lambton Park**	Sea B : **Seaton Burn**	Wood : **Woodhorn**
Dud : **Dudley**	Lan : **Lanchester**	Sea D : **Seaton Delaval**	Wool : **Woolsington**
Dun : **Dunston**	Lang P : **Langley Park**	Sea S : **Seaton Sluice**	Wylam : **Wylam**

A

Abbay St. SR5: S'wck 6C **104**
Abbey Cl. NE25: Whit B 7D **38**
  NE38: Wash 3H **115**
Abbey Ct. NE8: Gate 5H **83**

Abbey Ct. NE46: Hex 2D **70**
Abbey Dr. DH4: Hou S 7B **130**
  NE5: Cha P 2B **60**
  NE30: N Shi 4K **49**
  NE32: Jar 6C **66**
Abbeyfield Cl. NE8: Gate 5D **82**
Abbey Ga. NE61: Mor 1D **14**

Abbey Leisure Cen. 3A **154**
Abbey Mdws. NE61: Mor 1D **14**
Abbey M. DH7: Sac 1E **152**
Abbey Rd. DH1: Dur 3K **153**
  NE38: Wash 3H **115**
Abbey Rd. Bus. Pk. DH1: Dur 3K **153**
Abbey Rd. Ind. Est. DH1: Dur 3K **153**

Abbey Ter. NE27: Shir 1J **47**
  NE61: Mor 6F **9**
Abbeyvale Dr. NE6: Walk 6F **65**
Abbey Vw. NE46: Hex 2E **70**
  NE61: Mor 6F **9**
Abbey Vw. Yd. *NE61: Mor* 6E **8**
          (off Buller's Grn.)

Abbeywoods—Alexandra Ter.

Abbeywoods DH1: Dur 3A 154
Abbeywoods Bus. Pk. DH1: Dur 3K 153
Abbot Ct. NE8: Gate 3H 83 (10K 5)
Abbots Cl. NE62: Chop 7K 11
Abbotsfield Cl. SR3: New S 4B 132
Abbotsford Gro. SR2: Sund 3E 118 (6G 7)
Abbotsford Ho. NE24: Bly 3G 23
Abbotsford Pk. NE25: Whit B 7F 39
Abbotsford Rd. NE10: Gate 5B 84
Abbotsford Ter. NE2: Newc T 5F 63
Abbotside Cl. DH9: Ous 6F 113
Abbotside Pl. NE5: Cha P 4D 60
Abbotsmeade Cl. NE5: Newc T 5H 61
Abbots Row DH1: Dur 1D 166
Abbot St. SR8: Eas 6D 160
Abbots Wlk. DH9: Beam 1B 126
Abbots Way NE16: Whi 7H 81
NE29: N Shi 3D 48
NE61: Mor .7E 8
Abbotsway NE32: Jar 7E 66
Abbs St. SR5: S'wck 6F 105
Abercorn Pl. NE28: W'snd 6J 47
Abercorn Rd. NE15: Newc T 1G 81
SR3: E Her 1K 131
Abercrombie Pl. NE5: Newc T 3H 61
Aberdare Rd. SR3: E Her 2A 132
Aberdeen DH2: Ous 7H 113
Aberdeen Ct. NE3: Ken 4K 43
Aberdeen Dr. NE32: Jar 2E 86
Aberdeen Twr. SR3: E Her 1A 132
Aberford Cl. NE5: Cha P 1B 60
Aberfoyle DH2: Ous 7H 113
Aberfoyle Ct. DH9: Stly 3H 125
Abernethy DH2: Ous 6H 113
Aberwick Dr. DH2: Ches S 2H 141
Abigail Ct. NE3: Gos 7G 45
Abingdon Ct. NE3: Ken 5K 43
NE21: Bla T 3C 80
Abingdon Rd. NE6: Walk 6F 65
Abingdon Sq. NE23: Cra 1A 26
Abingdon St. SR4: Sund 3B 118
Abingdon Way NE35: Bol C 5D 86
Abinger St. NE4: Newc T 1D 82 (5B 4)
Abington DH2: Ous 7H 113
Aboyne Sq. SR3: E Her 7K 117
Acacia Av. DH4: Hou S 1A 144
SR8: Pet .6F 173
Acacia Gro. NE31: Heb 2J 85
NE34: S Shi 1B 88
Acacia Rd. NE10: Gate 4K 83
Acacia Ter. NE63: Hir 4B 12
Acanthus Av. NE4: Newc T 6K 61
Acclom St. TS28: Win 7H 181
Acer Ct. SR2: Sund 4F 119 (7K 7)
Acer Dr. DH6: Has 1B 170
Acklam Av. SR2: Sund 7J 119
ACOMB 4B 50
Acomb Av. NE25: Sea D 1H 37
NE28: W'snd 5H 47
Acomb Cl. NE61: Hep 3J 15
Acomb Ct. NE9: Gate 5K 99
NE12: Kil .1B 46
NE22: Bed .7J 17
SR2: Sund 7H 119
Acomb Cres. NE3: Ken 4B 44
Acomb Dr. NE41: Wylam 6J 57
Acomb Gdns. NE5: Newc T 5J 61
Acomb Ind. Est. NE46: Acomb 4B 50
Acorn Av. NE8: Gate 6E 82
NE22: Bed .1H 21
Acorn Cl. DH7: Sac 6D 140
NE9: Gate 4B 100
Acornclose La. DH7: Sac 6B 140
Acorn Cft. DH7: Wit G 3C 152
Acorn Pl. DH1: Dur 4J 153
DH7: B'don 1D 174
Acorn Rd. NE2: Newc T 3G 63
Acorn Sq. NE42: Pru 4F 77
Acorn St. DH2: Beam 2D 126
Acreford Ct. NE62: Chop 2G 17
Acre Rigg Rd. SR8: Pet 5K 171
Acton Dene DH9: Stly 2J 125
Acton Dr. NE29: N Shi 4D 48
Acton Pl. NE7: Newc T 3K 63
Acton Rd. DH7: Esh W 4E 162
NE5: Newc T 5F 61
Ada Cres. NE46: Hex 1C 70
Adair Av. NE15: Newc T 7J 61
Adair Way NE31: Heb 1K 85
Adams Bldgs. DH9: Dip 1G 123
Adamsez Ind. Est. NE15: Newc T 2F 81
Adamsez W. Ind. Est.
NE15: Newc T 2F 81
Adamson DH2: Ches S 6H 127
Adams Ter. DH8: M'sly 6J 107
Adam St. SR8: Pet 6F 173
Ada St. NE6: Walk 7C 64
NE33: S Shi 4K 67
Ada St. E. SR7: Mur 1F 159
Ada St. W. SR7: Mur 1F 159
Adderlane Rd. NE42: Pru 3F 77
Adderstone Av. NE23: Cra 5K 25
Adderstone Ct. NE2: Newc T 2H 63
Adderstone Cres. NE2: Newc T 3H 63
Adderstone Gdns. NE29: N Shi 3B 48
Addington Cres. NE29: N Shi 6E 48
Addington Dr. NE24: News 4J 23
NE28: W'snd 5H 47
ADDISON 1K 79
Addison Cl. NE6: Newc T 7K 63 (3P 5)
Addison Ct. NE28: W'snd 4B 66
NE40: Ryton 1F 79
Addison Gdns. NE10: Gate 6F 85
Addison Ind. Est. NE21: Bla T 1K 79
Addison Rd. NE6: Newc T 7K 63 (3P 5)
NE15: Lem .6D 60
NE36: W Bol 7G 87
Addison St. NE29: N Shi 1G 67
SR2: Sund 2H 119
Addison Wlk. NE34: S Shi 4G 87
Addycombe Ter. NE6: Newc T 3A 64
Adelaide Cen., The NE4: Newc T 1A 82
Adelaide Cl. SR1: Sund 1H 119
Adelaide Ct. NE8: Gate 3G 83 (9H 5)
Adelaide Ho. NE4: Newc T 1A 82
Adelaide Pl. SR1: Sund 1H 119
Adelaide Row SR7: S'hm 3B 148
Adelaide St. DH3: Ches S 7A 128
Adelaide Ter. NE4: Newc T 1K 81
Adeline Gdns. NE3: Ken 3C 62
Adelphi Cl. NE29: N Shi 4C 48
Adelphi Pl. NE6: Walk 1C 84
Aden Ct. DH7: Ush M 7C 152
Aden Twr. SR3: E Her 1A 132
Adfrid Pl. SR8: Pet 5B 172
Admington Ct. NE62: Chop 1H 17
Admiral Collingwood Ct.
NE61: Mor 7G 9
Admiral Ho. NE30: N Shi 5K 49
Admiral Way SR3: E Her 4J 131
Adolphus Pl. DH1: Dur 2F 167
SR7: S'hm 3C 148
Adolphus St. SR6: Whit 5H 89
Adolphus St. W. SR7: S'hm 3B 148
Adrian Pl. SR8: Pet 7C 172
Adventure La. DH4: W Rai 7K 143
Affleck St. NE8: Gate 4G 83
Afton Ct. NE34: S Shi 1J 87
Afton Way NE3: Ken 6A 44
Agar Rd. SR3: E Her 1K 131
Aged Miners' Cotts. NE25: Sea D 4J 27
NE42: Pru .5D 76
(off Edgewell Rd.)
NE63: Ash 3J 11
NE27: Shir .3H 47
Aged Miners' Homes DH2: Ches S 5A 128
(Pelaw Bank)
DH2: Ches S 3K 141
(Union La.)
DH2: Pelt .3E 126
DH2: Plaw 6H 141
DH3: Gt Lum 1F 143
DH4: Hou S 2C 144
DH4: Hou S 3B 130
(off Chester Rd.)
DH5: Hett H 1G 157
DH5: Hou S 2F 145
DH6: Quar H 6D 178
DH6: Sher 3K 167
(Hallgarth St.)
DH6: Sher 3C 168
(Local Av.)
DH6: Shot C 5D 170
DH7: B'don 2E 174
(Burnigill)
DH7: B'don 7D 164
(Deerness Hgts.)
DH7: Lang P 5J 151
DH7: Sac .7E 140
DH7: Ush M 1C 164
DH8: Lead 4A 122
DH9: Stly .5H 125
NE5: Newc T 2D 60
NE7: Longb .7J 45
NE11: Kib .2E 112
NE12: Dud .5J 35
NE13: Bru V 5C 34
NE16: Burn 2A 110
NE16: Sun .6G 97
NE21: Bla T 1A 80
NE24: Camb 4H 19
NE25: Sea D 7H 27
(off Ryal Cl.)
NE27: Back 6G 37
NE27: Shir .1K 47
NE34: S Shi 6C 68
NE35: Bol C 5D 86
NE39: H Spen 3E 94
NE40: Ryton 2J 79
(off Stargate La.)
NE62: Chop 1A 18
NE63: Wood 2D 12
NE64: Newb S 4H 13
SR2: Ryh .2G 133
(off Cheviot La.)
SR3: New S 7C 118
SR5: C'twn 5A 104
SR7: Mur .7D 146
SR7: S'hm 1H 147
Aged Miners' Homes SR7: S'hm 5B 148
SR8: Pet .5D 172
TS27: B Col 2H 183
Aged Mineworkers' Homes
NE15: Thro .3F 59
NE43: Mic .6B 76
Agincourt NE12: Kil 7B 36
NE31: Heb .6H 65
Agnes Maria St. NE3: Gos 7C 44
Agnes St. DH9: Stly 2F 125
Agricola Ct. NE33: S Shi 1J 67
Agricola Gdns. NE28: W'snd 6H 47
Agricola Rd. NE4: Newc T 7B 62
Aidan Av. NE26: Sea S 4B 28
Aidan Cl. DH9: Stly 2H 125
NE13: Wide O 5C 34
NE27: Longb 3G 47
Aidan Ct. NE7: Newc T 7A 46
NE32: Jar .7D 66
Aidan Ho. NE8: Gate 4H 83
Aidan Wlk. NE3: Gos 7F 45
Aiden Way DH5: Hett H 5G 145
Ailesbury St. SR4: Sund 1C 118
Ainderby Rd. NE15: Thro 3F 59
Ainsdale Gdns. NE5: Cha P 3C 60
Ainsley St. DH1: Dur 2K 165
Ainslie Pl. NE5: Newc T 4J 61
Ainsworth Av. NE34: S Shi 3G 87
Ainthorpe Cl. SR3: New S 2D 132
Ainthorpe Gdns. NE7: Newc T 1K 63
NE9: Gate .2H 99
Aintree Cl. NE37: Wash 1H 115
NE63: Ash .5A 12
Aintree Dr. DH8: Shot B 2F 121
Aintree Gdns. NE8: Gate 2K 83
Aintree Rd. SR3: E Her 1K 131
Airedale NE28: W'snd 7D 46
Airedale Gdns. DH5: Hett H 1F 157
Aireys Cl. DH4: Hou S 2C 144
Airey Ter. NE6: Walk 1E 84
NE8: Gate .5F 83
Airport Freightway NE13: Wool 2E 42
Airport Ind. Est. NE3: Ken 6J 43
Airport Station (Metro) 1D 42
Airville Mt. SR3: New S 5C 132
Aisgill Cl. NE23: Cra 4K 25
Aisgill Dr. NE5: Cha P 4C 60
Aiskell St. SR4: Sund 2C 118
A J Cook Ct. NE63: Ash 4A 12
A J Cooks Cotts. NE39: Row G 5F 95
A J Cook Ter. DH6: Shot C 7E 170
Akeld Cl. NE23: Cra 5K 25
Akeld Ct. NE3: Gos 1G 63
Akeld M. SR6: Monk 6G 105
Akenside Hill NE1: Newc T 2G 83 (7H 5)
Akenside Ter. NE2: Newc T 5H 63 (1J 5)
Alanbrooke Row NE31: Heb 3G 85
Alansway Gdns. NE33: S Shi 5K 67
ALBANY 1G 115
Albany Av. NE12: Longb 5B 46
Albany Ct. NE4: Newc T 3C 82
Albany Gdns. NE26: Whit B 7H 39
Albany Ho. NE37: Wash 1G 115
SR5: S'wck 6E 104
Albany M. NE3: Ken 3C 62
Albany Rd. NE8: Gate 3J 83 (9L 5)
Albany St. E. NE33: S Shi 5K 67
Albany St. W. NE33: S Shi 5K 67
Albany Ter. NE32: Jar 2K 85
Albany Village Cen.
NE37: Wash 2F 115
Albany Way NE37: Wash 1G 115
Albatross Way NE24: News 6J 23
Albemarle Av. NE2: Gos 2F 63
Albemarle St. NE33: S Shi 2J 67
Albert Av. NE28: W'snd 3F 65
Albert Ct. DH6: Bow 4H 177
SR2: Sund 3E 118 (6G 7)
Albert Dr. NE9: Gate 3H 99
Albert Edward Ter. NE35: Bol C 4E 86
Albert Pl. NE9: Gate 3H 99
NE38: Wash 4K 115
Albert Rd. DH8: Con 7H 121
NE22: Bed .6C 18
NE26: Sea S 4D 28
NE32: Jar .6B 66
(Chapel Rd.)
NE32: Jar .7A 66
(Park Rd., not continuous)
SR4: Sund 1C 118
Albert St. DH1: Dur 1K 165 (1A 6)
DH2: Pelt .4C 126
DH3: Ches S 6A 128
DH6: Thor 1K 179
DH7: Esh W 4E 162
DH9: Stly .3E 124
NE2: Newc T 7H 63 (4J 5)
NE24: Bly 1J 23
NE31: Heb .6H 65
NE39: C'wl .6E 94
SR7: S'hm 4C 148
Albert Ter. DH7: Esh W 4E 162
NE12: Longb 3A 46
NE26: Whit B 7H 39
NE33: S Shi 3J 67
Albion Ct. NE6: Newc T 1K 83 (5N 5)
NE24: Cow .2H 23
NE33: S Shi 1J 67
Albion Gdns. NE16: Burn 3K 109
Albion Pl. SR1: Sund 2E 118 (5H 7)
Albion Retail Cen. NE24: Cow 1H 23
Albion Rd. NE29: N Shi 6G 49
NE30: N Shi 6G 49
Albion Rd. W. NE29: N Shi 7G 49
Albion Row NE6: Newc T 1J 83 (5M 5)
(not continuous)
Albion St. NE10: Gate 1A 100
SR4: Sund 2G 117
Albion Ter. NE9: Spri 6D 100
NE23: Cra .7B 22
NE29: N Shi 6G 49
Albion Way NE23: Cra 1B 26
NE24: Bly, Cow 2G 23
Albion Yd. NE1: Newc T 1F 83 (6E 4)
Albury Pk. Rd. NE30: N Shi 5J 49
Albury Pl. NE16: Whi 2G 97
Albury Rd. NE2: Gos 2F 63
Albyn Gdns. SR3: Sund 5C 118
Alcester Cl. NE62: Chop 1H 17
Alconbury Cl. NE24: News 4J 23
Alcote Gro. DH6: Shot C 6F 171
Alcroft Cl. NE5: Cha P 2B 60
Aldborough St. NE24: Bly 2J 23
Aldbrough Cl. SR2: Ryh 3H 133
Aldbrough St. NE34: S Shi 1G 87
Aldeburgh Av. NE15: Lem 5C 60
Aldenham Gdns. NE30: N Shi 3J 49
Aldenham Rd. SR3: E Her 1A 132
Aldenham Twr. SR3: E Her 1A 132
Alder Av. NE4: Newc T 5K 61
Alder Cl. DH5: Hett H 7F 145
NE61: Mor 7G 9
Alder Ct. NE25: Whit B 7E 38
Alder Cres. DH9: Tan L 7K 109
Alderdene DH7: Lan 7J 137
Alderdene Cl. DH7: Ush M 3E 164
Alder Gro. DH8: Lead 6B 122
NE25: Whit B 5E 38
Alderlea Cl. DH1: Dur 1E 166
Alderley Cl. NE35: Bol C 5E 86
SR2: Sund 6H 119
Alderley Dr. NE12: Kil 7C 36
Alderley Rd. NE9: Gate 2G 99
Alderley Way NE23: Cra 1A 26
Alderman Wood Rd. DH9: Tan L 1E 124
Alderney Gdns. NE5: Cha P 3C 60
Alder Pk. DH7: B'don 2C 174
Alder Rd. NE28: W'snd 6J 47
NE29: N Shi 5A 48
SR8: Pet .6F 173
Aldershot Rd. SR3: E Her 2K 131
Aldershot Sq. SR3: E Her 2K 131
Alderside Cres. DH7: Lan 6J 137
Alder St. SR5: C'twn 6H 103
Alderton Ct. NE62: Chop 1H 17
Alder Way NE12: Kil 7A 36
Alderwood NE8: Gate 5F 83
NE38: Wash 1F 129
NE63: Ash .5A 12
Alderwood Cres. NE6: Walk 4D 64
Alderwyk NE10: Gate 1F 101
Aldhome Ct. DH1: Dur 5J 153
Aldin Grange Hall DH7: Ush M 2F 165
Aldin Grange Ter. DH7: Ush M 1E 164
Aldin Ri. DH7: Ush M 2E 164
Aldridge Ct. DH7: Ush M 2C 164
Aldsworth Cl. NE9: Spri 6D 100
Aldwick Rd. NE15: Newc T 7F 61
Aldwych Dr. NE29: N Shi 5B 48
Aldwych Rd. SR3: E Her 2K 131
Aldwych Sq. SR3: E Her 3K 131
Aldwych St. NE33: S Shi 3A 68
Alemouth Rd. NE46: Hex 1D 70
Alexander Dr. DH5: Hett H 7F 145
Alexander Pl. NE46: Hex 1C 70
Alexander Ter. NE13: Bru V 6C 34
NE43: Stoc .7K 75
SR6: Monk 4F 105
Alexandra Av. SR5: Sund 6B 104
Alexandra Bus. Pk. SR4: Sund 7A 104
Alexandra Cl. DH1: Dur 5J 153
Alexandra Cres. NE46: Hex 1B 70
Alexandra Dr. NE16: Swa 6J 81
Alexandra Gdns. NE29: N Shi 6E 48
NE40: Ryton 2J 79
Alexandra Ho. SR2: Sund 5G 7
Alexandra Pk. SR3: Sund 4D 118
Alexandra Pl. *NE61: Mor 7G 9*
(off Alexandra Rd.)
Alexandra Rd. NE6: Newc T 4K 63
NE8: Gate .4G 83
NE61: Mor 7G 9
NE63: Hir 3C 12
Alexandra St. DH2: Pelt 3E 126
DH8: Con .7H 121
NE28: W'snd 3G 65
NE39: C'wl .6E 94
Alexandra Ter. DH4: Pen 1B 130
DH6: Has .1B 170
DH6: Whe H 2B 180

Alexandra Ter.—Arden Cl.

Alexandra Ter. NE5: Newc T 2F 61
NE9: Spri 6D 100
NE16: Sun 5J 97
NE22: Bed 7K 17
NE26: Whit B 7H 39
NE46: Hex 1B 70
Alexandra Way NE23: Cra 5J 25
Alexandria Cres. DH1: Dur 3K 165 (3A 6)
Alexandrina St. SR7: S'hm 3B 148
Alford DH2: Ous 6H 113
Alford Grn. NE12: Longb 5A 46
Alfred Av. NE22: Bed 7K 17
Alfred St. NE6: Walk 7C 64
NE24: Bly 3J 23
NE31: Heb 1H 85
SR7: S'hm 4C 148
SR8: Eas 6C 160
Alfred St. E. SR7: S'hm 4C 148
Alfreton Cl. DH7: B'don 3C 174
Algernon NE12: Kil 6B 36
Algernon Cl. NE6: Newc T 6A 64
Algernon Ct. *NE6: Newc T 6A 64*
(off Algernon Rd.)
Algernon Ind. Est. NE27: Shir 3K 47
Algernon Pl. NE26: Whit B 7H 39
Algernon Rd. NE6: Newc T 6A 64
NE15: Lem 7C 60
Algernon Ter. NE30: N Shi 4J 49
NE41: Wylam 7J 57
Algiers Rd. SR3: E Her 2J 131
Alice St. NE21: Bla T 5B 80
NE33: S Shi 5J 67
SR2: Sund 3E 118 (6H 7)
Alice Well Vs. SR4: Pen 5B 116
Aline St. SR3: New S 2D 132
SR7: S'hm 3C 148
Alington Pl. DH1: Dur 2E 166
Alison Dr. NE36: E Bol 7K 87
Alison Ho. NE6: Newc T 2P 5
Allandale Av. NE12: Longb 5B 46
Allan Rd. NE64: Newb S 2H 13
Allanville NE12: Kil 6K 35
All Church NE15: Newc T 7H 61
Allchurch Dr. NE63: N Sea 4E 12
Allen Av. NE11: Gate 7E 82
Allendale Av. NE28: W'snd 1F 65
ALLENDALE COTTAGES 5K 107
Allendale Cres. DH4: Pen 1A 130
NE27: Shir 1A 48
NE62: Chop 6J 11
Allendale Dr. NE34: S Shi 5C 68
Allendale Pl. NE30: N Shi 5K 49
Allendale Rd. DH7: B'don 1E 174
NE6: Newc T 1B 84
NE24: Bly 3K 23
NE46: Hex 2A 70
SR3: E Her 2K 131
Allendale Sq. SR3: E Her 7A 118
Allendale St. DH5: Hett H 1G 157
Allendale Ter. DH6: Has 1B 170
DH9: Ann P 5K 123
NE6: Walk 1D 84
Allen Dr. NE46: Hex 2D 70
Allenheads NE5: Newc T 4E 60
NE25: Sea D 6G 27
NE38: Wash 7J 115
ALLENSFORD 1B 134
Allensford Bank DH8: C'sde 1B 134
Allensford Cvn. Pk. DH8: C'sde 1B 134
Allensford Country Pk. 1C 134
Allens Grn. NE23: Cra 4K 25
Allen St. DH3: Ches S 7A 128
SR8: Eas 6D 160
Allen Ter. NE40: Ryton 2D 78
Allerdean Cl. NE15: Lem 6B 60
NE25: Sea D 1H 37
ALLERDENE 6J 99
Allerdene Wlk. NE16: Whi 1G 97
Allergate DH1: Dur 3K 165 (3A 6)
Allergate Ter. DH1: Dur 3A 6
Allerhope NE23: Cra 5K 25
Allerton Gdns. NE6: Newc T 3B 64
Allerton Pl. NE16: Whi 2F 97
Allerwash NE5: Newc T 4E 60
Allery Banks NE61: Mor 7G 9
Allgood Ter. NE22: Bed 7K 17
All Hallows La. NE1: Newc T 1G 83 (6H 5)
Allhusen Ter. NE8: Gate 5K 83
Alliance Pl. SR4: Sund 1D 118 (2F 7)
Alliance St. SR4: Sund 1D 118 (2F 7)
Allingham Ct. NE7: Newc T 2C 64
Allison Ct. NE11: Dun 5H 81
Allison Gdns. DH8: Con 6H 121
Allison St. DH8: Con 6H 121
Alloa Rd. SR3: E Her 1K 131
Allonby M. NE23: Cra 7B 22
Allonby Way NE5: Newc T 5H 61
ALLOTMENT, THE 3K 47
Alloy Ter. NE39: Row G 6G 95
All Saints Cen. NE1: Newc T 6G 4
All Saints Ct. NE29: N Shi 6D 48
SR6: Monk 6F 105
All Saints Dr. DH5: Hett H 5G 145
All Saints Ho. SR6: Monk 6F 105
All Saints Office Cen. NE1: Newc T 6H 5
Allwork Ter. NE16: Whi 7H 81
Alma Pl. DH1: Dur 1F 167
DH4: Hou S 4C 130
NE26: Whit B 7H 39
NE29: N Shi 6G 49
NE61: Mor 6G 9
Alma St. SR4: Sund 1G 117
Alma Ter. *DH1: Dur 4J 165*
(off Neville's Cross Bank)
DH1: Dur 2C 166
NE40: G'sde 4G 79
Almond Cl. DH6: Has 1B 170
Almond Cres. NE8: Gate 6E 82
Almond Dr. SR5: C'twn 7G 103
Almond Gro. NE24: News 5G 23
Almond Pl. NE4: Newc T 6K 61
Almond Ter. SR8: Pet 5F 173
Almoners Barn DH1: Dur 5J 165
Almonside Rd. NE17: C'wl 2A 108
Almshouses NE15: Thro 6K 59
Aln Av. NE3: Ken 5C 44
Aln Ct. NE15: Lem 7C 60
Aln Cres. NE3: Ken 5C 44
Aln Gro. NE15: Lem 6C 60
Alnham Ct. NE3: Ken 5A 44
Alnham Grn. NE5: Cha P 3C 60
Alnmouth Av. NE29: N Shi 1D 66
Alnmouth Dr. NE3: Gos 1G 63
Alnmouth Ter. NE46: Acomb 4B 50
Aln St. NE31: Heb 7H 65
(not continuous)
NE63: Hir 3C 12
Aln Wlk. NE3: Ken 6C 44
Alnwick Av. NE26: Whit B 6G 39
NE29: N Shi 1D 66
Alnwick Cl. DH2: Ches S 1J 141
NE16: Whi 7G 81
Alnwick Ct. NE38: Wash 3F 115
Alnwick Dr. NE22: Bed 7F 17
Alnwick Gro. NE32: Jar 4B 86
Alnwick Rd. DH1: Dur 4A 154
NE34: S Shi 7J 67
SR3: E Her 1A 132
Alnwick Sq. SR3: E Her 1A 132
Alnwick St. NE15: Thro 5K 59
NE28: W'snd 3G 65
SR8: Eas 6C 160
SR8: Pet 3D 172
Alnwick Ter. NE13: Wide O 4E 34
Alpine Cl. DH4: Hou S 4K 129
Alpine Ct. DH2: Ches S 6A 128
Alpine Gro. NE36: W Bol 7H 87
Alpine Way SR3: Sund 5C 118
Alresford NE12: Kil 7B 36
Alston Av. NE6: Walk 7C 64
NE23: E Cram 5B 26
Alston Cl. NE28: W'snd 1A 66
NE29: N Shi 5C 48
Alston Cres. SR6: Monk 2E 104
Alstone Ct. NE62: Chop 1H 17
Alston Gdns. NE15: Thro 3H 59
Alston Gro. NE26: Sea S 3B 28
Alston Rd. DH8: Con 5D 120
NE25: Sea D 4H 27
NE38: Wash 2B 116
Alston St. NE8: Gate 5E 82
Alston Ter. DH8: Con 5E 120
Alston Wlk. DH6: Sher 3A 168
SR8: Pet 5C 172
Alston Way DH7: B'don 1E 174
Altan Pl. NE12: Longb 5K 45
Altree Grange SR5: S'wck 4E 104
Altrincham Twr. SR3: E Her 1A 132
ALUM WATERS 4C 164
Alum Well NE9: Gate 2H 99
Alum Well Rd. NE9: Gate 2G 99
(Carlton Ter.)
NE9: Gate 2H 99
(Cross Keys La.)
Alverston Cl. NE15: Lem 5C 60
Alverstone Av. NE9: Gate 3G 99
Alverstone Rd. SR3: E Her 2K 131
Alverthorpe St. NE33: S Shi 5K 67
Alveston Cl. NE62: Chop 1H 17
Alwin NE38: Wash 7E 114
Alwin Grange NE31: Heb 6K 65
Alwinton Av. NE29: N Shi 4D 48
Alwinton Cl. NE5: Newc T 1G 61
NE24: Cow 1G 23
Alwinton Ct. NE24: Cow 1G 23
Alwinton Dr. DH2: Ches S 1J 141
Alwinton Gdns. NE11: Gate 2C 98
Alwinton Rd. NE27: Shir 1A 48
Alwinton Sq. NE63: Hir 5D 12
Alwinton Ter. NE3: Gos 7F 45
Alwyn Cl. DH4: Hou S 6J 129
Alwyn Gdns. DH8: Con 1H 135
Amalfi Twr. SR3: E Her 1A 132
Amara Sq. SR3: E Her 1A 132
Ambassadors Way NE29: N Shi 4B 48
Amber Ct. NE4: Newc T 3B 82
NE24: Bly 3G 23
Ambergate Cl. NE5: Newc T 2G 61
Amberley Chase NE12: Kil 7C 36
Amberley Cl. NE28: W'snd 1A 66
Amberley Gdns. NE7: Newc T 3A 64
Amberley Gro. NE16: Whi 2G 97
Amberley St. NE8: Gate 5D 82
SR2: Sund 3G 119
Amberley St. Sth. SR2: Sund 3G 119
Amberley Wlk. NE16: Whi 2H 97
Amberley Way NE24: News 4J 23
Amble Av. NE25: Whit B 7H 39
NE34: S Shi 5D 68
Amble Cl. NE24: Bly 4G 23
NE29: N Shi 1D 66
Amble Gro. NE2: Newc T 6J 63 (1L 5)
Amble Pl. NE12: Longb 3D 46
Ambleside NE15: Thro 3H 59
Ambleside Av. NE34: S Shi 7A 68
SR7: S'hm 2G 147
Ambleside Cl. NE25: Sea D 7H 27
SR8: Pet 5C 172
Ambleside Gdns. NE9: Gate 3J 99
Ambleside Grn. NE5: Newc T 5H 61
Ambleside M. DH8: Lead 5B 122
Ambleside Ter. SR6: Monk 3E 104
Amble Twr. SR3: E Her 1A 132
Amble Way NE3: Gos 6D 44
Ambridge Way NE3: Ken 7B 44
NE25: Sea D 6E 26
Ambrose Ct. NE21: Bla T 5B 80
Ambrose Pl. NE6: Walk 7F 65
Ambrose Rd. SR3: E Her 1K 131
Amec Dr. NE28: W'snd 4K 65
Amec Way NE28: W'snd 4J 65
Amelia Cl. NE4: Newc T 3A 82
Amelia Gdns. SR3: E Her 2J 131
Amelia Wlk. NE4: Newc T 3A 82
(not continuous)
Amen Cnr. NE1: Newc T 2G 83 (7G 4)
Amersham Cres. SR8: Pet 5B 172
Amersham Pl. NE5: Newc T 3H 61
Amersham Rd. NE24: News 5H 23
Amesbury Cl. NE5: Cha P 2B 60
Amethyst Rd. NE4: Newc T 3B 82
Amethyst St. SR4: Sund 1B 118
AMF Bowling
Newcastle 1B 82
Washington 3G 115
Amherst Rd. NE3: Ken 6A 44
Amos Ayre Pl. NE34: S Shi 1F 87
Amos Dr. DH9: Ann P 7K 123
Amphitheatre 2B 68
Amsterdam Rd. SR3: E Her 1A 132
Amusement Pk. Cvn. Site
NE33: S Shi 1A 68
Amy St. SR5: S'wck 5D 104
Ancaster Av. NE12: Longb 6K 45
Ancaster Rd. NE16: Whi 1F 97
Anchorage Ter. DH1: Dur 4B 166 (5D 6)
Anchorage, The DH3: Ches S 6B 128
DH4: Hou S 3B 130
NE38: Wash 4J 115
Anchor Chare NE1: Newc T 6J 5
Ancona St. SR4: Sund 7B 104
Ancroft Av. NE29: N Shi 5F 49
Ancroft Gth. DH1: H Shin 1F 177
Ancroft Pl. NE5: Newc T 5H 61
NE63: Hir 6D 12
Ancroft Rd. NE25: Sea D 7F 27
Ancroft Way NE3: Ken 4B 44
Ancrum St. NE2: Newc T 6D 62 (1A 4)
Ancrum Way NE16: Whi 2F 97
Anderson St. NE33: S Shi 2K 67
Anderson St. Nth. NE33: S Shi 2J 67
Andover Pl. NE28: W'snd 6J 47
Andrew Ct. NE6: Walk 7E 64
Andrew Rd. SR3: E Her 2J 131
Andrew's La. SR8: Eas 2J 171
Andrew St. SR8: Eas 7C 160
Andrew Ter. DH6: Whe H 4A 180
Anfield Ct. NE3: Ken 7A 44
Anfield Rd. NE3: Ken 7A 44
Angelica Cl. DH8: Con 7J 121
Angel of the North 7J 99
Angerton Av. NE27: Shir 2K 47
NE30: N Shi 3G 49
Angerton Gdns. NE5: Newc T 5K 61
Angerton Ter. NE23: Dud 3H 35
Anglesey Gdns. NE5: Cha P 3C 60
Anglesey Pl. NE4: Newc T 1D 82 (6A 4)
Anglesey Rd. SR3: E Her 2K 131
Anglesey Sq. SR3: E Her 2K 131
Angle Ter. NE28: W'snd 3K 65
Angram Dr. SR2: Sund 7J 119
Angram Wlk. NE5: Cha P 3C 60
Angrove Gdns. SR4: Sund 3B 118
Angus DH2: Ous 6H 113
Angus Cl. NE12: Kil 1A 46
Angus Rd. NE8: Gate 6E 82
Angus Sq. DH7: B'don 7F 165
SR3: E Her 2K 131
Angus St. DH7: B'don 6G 165
SR8: Eas 6C 160
Angus Ter. SR8: Eas 1D 172
ANICK 5G 51
Anick Rd. NE46: B End 7E 50
Anker's House Mus. 6B 128
Annand Rd. DH1: Dur 1D 166
Annaside M. DH8: Lead 5B 122
Ann Av. DH6: Kel 7D 178
Anne Dr. NE12: Longb 4E 46
Annfield Pl. DH9: Ann P 5J 123
ANNFIELD PLAIN 6K 123
Annfield Plain By-Pass
DH9: Ann P 5G 123
Annfield Rd. NE23: Cra 7K 21
Annfield Ter. DH9: Ann P 4J 123
Annie St. SR6: Monk 3F 105
ANNITSFORD 2K 35
Annitsford Dr. NE23: Dud 3K 35
Annitsford Pond Nature Reserve 2K 35
Annitsford Rd. NE23: Seg 3A 36
Ann's Pl. DH7: B'don 6G 165
Ann's Row NE24: Bly 7J 19
Ann St. DH8: Con 7H 121
NE8: Gate 4H 83 (10J 5)
NE21: Bla T 3C 80
NE27: Shir 7J 37
NE31: Heb 6G 65
Annville Cres. NE6: Walk 2E 84
Ann Wlk. NE6: Walk 2E 84
Anscomb Gdns. NE7: Newc T 3J 63
Anson Cl. NE33: S Shi 5H 67
Anson Pl. NE5: Newc T 2F 61
Anson St. NE8: Gate 5K 83
Anstead Cl. NE23: Cra 4K 25
Anthony Ct. DH9: Stly 2E 124
Anthony Rd. SR3: E Her 1K 131
Anthony St. DH9: Stly 2E 124
SR8: Eas 6D 160
Antliff Ter. DH9: Ann P 5K 123
Antonine Wlk. NE15: Hed W 3D 58
Anton Pl. NE23: Cra 5K 25
Antrim Cl. NE5: Newc T 2J 61
Antrim Gdns. SR7: S'hm 2A 148
Antwerp Rd. SR3: E Her 2J 131
Anvil Ct. DH1: Dur 4J 153
DH8: W'stll 1A 106
Apperley NE5: Newc T 4E 60
Apperley Av. DH1: H Shin 1G 177
NE3: Ken 1J 61
Apperley Rd. NE43: Stoc 1J 91
Appian Pl. NE9: Gate 7K 83
NE15: Thro 3H 59
(not continuous)
Appleby Ct. DH4: Hou S 1H 143
NE12: Longb 6J 45
NE29: N Shi 7F 49
Appleby Gdns. NE9: Gate 4J 99
NE28: W'snd 1A 66
Appleby Pk. NE29: N Shi 6F 49
Appleby Pl. NE40: Ryton 2E 78
Appleby Rd. SR3: E Her 2K 131
Appleby Sq. SR3: E Her 2K 131
Appleby St. NE29: N Shi 1G 67
Appleby Way SR8: Pet 2J 181
Apple Cl. NE15: Lem 5C 60
Apple Ct. NE25: Sea D 4H 27
Appledore Cl. NE40: G'sde 6C 78
Appledore Gdns. DH3: Ches S 4B 128
DH7: Edm 3D 140
NE9: Gate 4H 99
Appledore Rd. NE24: News 4J 23
Appleforth Av. SR2: Sund 7J 119
Appleton Cl. NE11: Gate 6C 82
Apple Tree Dr. NE42: Pru 3E 76
Appletree Gdns. NE6: Walk 5C 64
NE25: Whit B 1E 48
Appletree La. NE45: Cor 1E 72
Appletree Ri. NE45: Cor 1E 72
Applewood NE12: Kil 1D 46
Appley Ter. SR6: Monk 5G 105
Apsley Cres. NE3: Ken 7A 44
Aqua Ter. NE64: Newb S 3H 13
Aquila Dr. NE15: Hed W 3B 58
Arbeia Roman Fort & Mus. 1J 67
Arbourcourt Av. DH7: Esh W 4D 162
Arbroath DH2: Ous 7H 113
Arbroath Rd. SR3: E Her 1K 131
Arcade Pk. NE30: N Shi 5K 49
Arcade, The *NE24: Bly 2J 23*
(off Waterloo Rd.)
NE30: N Shi 5K 49
Arcadia DH2: Ous 7H 113
Arcadia Av. DH3: Ches S 4A 128
Arcadia Ter. NE24: Bly 3J 23
Archbold Ter. NE2: Newc T 6G 63 (1H 5)
Archer Rd. SR3: E Her 1K 131
Archer Sq. SR3: E Her 1K 131
Archer St. NE28: W'snd 2H 65
Archer Vs. NE28: W'snd 2H 65
Archery Ri. DH1: Dur 4J 165
Archibald St. NE3: Gos 7E 44
Arcot Av. NE23: Nel V 2G 25
NE25: Whit B 1E 48
Arcot Dr. NE5: Newc T 5F 61
NE25: Whit B 1E 48
Arcot La. NE23: Dud, Sea B 1D 34
Arcot Ter. NE24: Bly 1H 23
Ardale Ho. NE3: Ken 1A 62
Arden Av. NE3: Gos 3D 44
Arden Cl. NE28: W'snd 5H 47

Arden Cres.—Auton Ct.

Arden Cres. NE5: Newc T 4K 61
Arden Ho. NE3: Gos 6E 44
Arden Sq. SR3: E Her 1A 132
Arden St. DH6: Shot C 5E 170
Ardrossan DH2: Ous 7H 113
Ardrossan Rd. SR3: E Her 2K 131
Arena Bus. Pk. DH4: Hou S 3C 144
Arena Way NE4: Newc T 3E 82 (9C 4)
Argent St. SR8: Eas 6D 160
Argus Cl. NE11: Gate 7D 82
Argyle Ct. DH9: Stly 7G 111
Argyle Pl. DH6: S Het 3B 158
NE29: N Shi 6G 49
Argyle Sq. SR2: Sund 3E 118 (6H 7)
Argyle St. NE1: Newc T 1G 83 (5H 5)
NE24: Bly 7H 19
NE30: N Shi 4K 49
NE31: Heb 7H 65
SR2: Sund 3E 118 (6H 7)
Argyle Ter. NE29: N Shi 4G 49
NE46: Hex 2D 70
NE64: Newb S 3H 13
Argyll DH2: Ous 7H 113
Ariel St. NE63: Hir 3C 12
(Juliet St.)
NE63: Hir 4C 12
(St Andrew's Ter.)
Arisaig DH2: Ous 7H 113
Arklecrag NE37: Wash 2G 115
Arkle Rd. SR3: E Her 2K 131
Arkleside Pl. NE5: Cha P 4D 60
Arkle St. NE8: Gate 6E 82
NE13: Bru V 7C 34
Arkwright St. NE8: Gate 7F 83
Arlington Av. NE3: Ken 2B 62
Arlington Cl. DH4: Hou S 6J 129
Arlington Ct. NE3: Ken 2C 62
Arlington Gro. NE16: Whi 1G 97
NE23: Cra 7K 21
Arlington Rd. NE31: Heb 2K 85
Arlington St. SR4: Sund 2B 118
Arlott Ho. NE29: N Shi 2D 66
Armitage Gdns. NE9: Spri 6A 100
ARMSTRONG 1E 114
Armstrong Av. NE6: Newc T 4K 63
NE34: S Shi 7A 68
TS28: Win 5G 181
Armstrong Bldg. NE1: Newc T 2E 4
Armstrong Cl. NE46: Hex 3B 70
Armstrong Dr. NE12: Kil 2K 45
Armstrong Ho. NE37: Wash 1E 114
Armstrong Ind. Est.
NE37: Wash 1E 114
Armstrong Ind. Pk.
NE4: Newc T 3C 82 (10A 4)
(not continuous)
Armstrong Rd. NE4: Newc T 1F 81
NE15: Newc T 1F 81
NE28: W'snd 4A 66
NE37: Wash 1D 114
SR8: Pet 3B 172
Armstrong St. NE5: Cal 5B 42
NE8: Gate 7E 82
(not continuous)
Armstrong Ter. NE33: S Shi 6J 67
NE61: Mor 7G 9
Arncliffe Av. SR4: Sund 4A 118
Arncliffe Gdns. NE5: Cha P 3C 60
Arndale Arc. NE32: Jar 6B 66
Arndale Ho. NE3: Ken 7A 44
NE12: Longb 6J 45
Arndale Sq. *NE12: Longb 6J 45*
(off Greyfriars La.)
Arnham Gro. SR4: Sund 6F 117
Arnison Retail Cen. DH1: Dur 3K 153
Arnold Av. TS27: B Col 1H 183
Arnold Cl. DH9: Stly 3G 125
Arnold Rd. SR3: E Her 1K 131
Arnold St. NE35: Bol C 6F 87
Arnside Wlk. NE5: Cha P 3C 60
(not continuous)
Arran Ct. SR3: New S 3C 132
Arran Dr. NE32: Jar 3E 86
Arran Gdns. NE10: Gate 7A 84
Arran Pl. NE29: N Shi 4C 48
Arras La. SR1: Sund 1G 119
Arrol Pk. SR4: Sund 2D 118
Arrow Cl. NE12: Kil 2K 45
Arthington Way NE34: S Shi 1A 88
Arthur Av. SR2: Ryh 3J 133
Arthur Cook Av. NE16: Whi 1J 97
ARTHURS HILL 7C 62
Arthur St. DH2: Beam 2C 126
DH7: Ush M 2B 164
NE8: Gate 4H 83
NE24: Bly 1J 23
(not continuous)
NE32: Jar 7B 66
SR2: Ryh 3J 133
SR6: Whit 2H 89
Arthur Ter. SR6: Whit 3H 89
Arun Cl. SR8: Pet 7A 172
Arundale Ho's. DH3: Bir 4A 114
Arundel Cl. NE13: Wide O 6C 34
NE22: Bed 5A 18
Arundel Ct. NE3: Ken 5J 43
NE12: Longb 6J 45
Arundel Dr. NE15: Lem 6E 60
NE25: Whit B 7B 38
Arundel Gdns. NE9: Gate 2J 99
SR3: E Her 2J 131
Arundel Rd. SR3: E Her 1K 131
Arundel Sq. NE63: Ash 4A 12
Arundel Wlk. DH2: Ous 2H 127
NE16: Whi 2G 97
Arundel Way DH7: B'don 1E 174
Asama Ct. NE4: Newc T 3C 82
(not continuous)
Ascot Cl. NE28: W'snd 6H 47
Ascot Ct. NE3: Ken 5J 43
SR3: E Her 2K 131
(not continuous)
Ascot Cres. NE8: Gate 6E 82
Ascot Gdns. NE34: S Shi 6K 67
Ascot Gro. NE63: Ash 5B 12
Ascot Pl. DH2: Ous 1H 127
Ascot Rd. DH8: Shot B 2G 121
Ascot St. SR8: Eas 7D 160
Ascott Ct. NE12: Longb 6J 45
Ascot Wlk. NE3: Ken 5J 43
Ash Av. DH1: Dur 3E 166
DH7: Ush M 2C 164
NE13: Din 4H 33
Ash Banks NE61: Mor 1G 15
Ashberry Gro. SR6: Monk 6F 105
Ashbourne Av. NE6: Walk 7D 64
Ashbourne Cl. NE27: Back 6G 37
Ashbourne Cres. NE63: Ash 4K 11
Ashbourne Rd. NE32: Jar 1C 86
Ashbrook Cl. DH7: B'don 2B 174
ASHBROOKE 4E 118
Ashbrooke NE25: Whit B 6E 38
Ashbrooke Cl. NE25: Whit B 6E 38
Ashbrooke Cres. SR2: Sund 4F 119
Ashbrooke Cross SR2: Sund 5E 118
Ashbrooke Dr. NE20: Pon 4J 31
Ashbrooke Est. DH6: Shot C 6E 170
Ashbrooke Gdns.
NE28: W'snd 2J 65
Ashbrooke Mt. SR2: Sund 4E 118
Ashbrooke Range SR2: Sund 5E 118
Ashbrooke Rd. SR2: Sund 4E 118 (7J 7)
Ashbrooke St. NE3: Ken 2A 62
Ashbrooke Ter. NE36: E Bol 7K 87
SR2: Sund 4F 119 (7J 7)
Ashburne Ct. SR2: Sund 4F 119
Ashburn Rd. NE28: W'snd 6J 47
Ashburton Rd. NE3: Gos 1C 62
Ashbury NE25: Whit B 5C 38
Ashby Cres. DH8: Shot B 4F 121
Ashby La. DH8: Shot B 5F 121
Ashby St. SR2: Sund 5H 119
Ash Cl. NE46: Hex 3A 70
Ash Ct. NE29: N Shi 3E 48
Ash Cres. SR7: S'hm 5A 148
SR8: Pet 6E 172
Ashcroft Dr. NE12: Longb 5C 46
Ashdale DH4: Pen 1J 129
NE20: Pon 1G 41
Ashdale Ct. SR6: Monk 5G 105
Ashdale Cres. NE5: Cha P 3D 60
Ashdale Rd. DH8: Con 6H 121
Ashdown Av. DH1: Dur 1F 167
Ashdown Cl. NE12: Longb 5K 45
Ashdown Rd. SR3: E Her 1K 131
Ashdown Way NE12: Longb 5K 45
Asher St. NE10: Gate 5A 84
Ashfield DH8: Shot B 3F 121
NE32: Jar 5D 86
Ashfield Av. NE16: Whi 6J 81
Ashfield Cl. NE4: Newc T 2C 82 (8A 4)
Ashfield Ct. NE39: H Spen 3E 94
Ashfield Gdns. NE28: W'snd 2D 64
Ashfield Gro. NE26: Whit B 5G 39
NE29: N Shi 6G 49
Ashfield Lodge NE4: Newc T 2C 82 (8A 4)
Ashfield Pk. NE16: Whi 6H 81
Ashfield Ri. NE16: Whi 2H 97
Ashfield Rd. NE3: Gos 1C 62
NE16: Whi 2H 97
Ashfield Ter. DH3: Ches S 7B 128
NE9: Spri 6D 100
NE10: Gate 5D 84
NE40: Ryton 1G 79
Ashford NE9: Gate 5J 99
Ashford Cl. NE24: News 4J 23
NE29: N Shi 3F 49
Ashford Dr. DH7: Sac 6E 140
Ashford Gro. DH6: Thor 1A 180
NE5: Cha P 1B 60
Ashford Rd. SR3: E Her 2K 131
Ashgill NE37: Wash 2F 115
Ashgrove DH2: Ches S 7H 127
Ash Gro. NE11: Dun 5A 82
NE28: W'snd 4H 65
NE40: Ryton 7G 59
NE61: Mor 1E 14
SR6: Whit 5J 89
TS29: Trim S 7C 180
Ashgrove Av. NE34: S Shi 1B 88
Ashgrove Ter. DH3: Bir 3K 113
NE8: Gate 5G 83
Ash Hill Ct. SR2: Sund 4F 119
ASHINGTON 7A 22
Ashington Dr. NE62: Chop 1H 17
Ashington Leisure Cen. 3K 11
Ashington M. NE62: Chop 1H 17
Ashkirk NE23: Dud 3J 35
SR3: E Her 1A 132
Ashkirk Cl. DH2: Ches S 1J 141
Ashkirk Way NE25: Sea D 1H 37
Ashlea Ct. SR3: E Her 1K 131
Ashlea Pk. SR3: E Her 1K 131
Ashleigh DH2: Ches S 4J 127
Ashleigh Av. DH1: Dur 6K 153
Ashleigh Cl. NE21: Bla T 5E 80
Ashleigh Cres. NE5: Newc T 5G 61
Ashleigh Gdns. SR6: Cle 4C 88
Ashleigh Gro. DH7: Lan 6J 137
NE2: Newc T 3F 63
NE12: Longb 5B 46
NE30: N Shi 4J 49
SR6: Monk 3G 105
Ashleigh Rd. NE5: Newc T 5G 61
Ashleigh Ter. SR6: Monk 3G 105
Ashleigh Vs. NE36: E Bol 7K 87
Ashley Cl. NE12: Kil 7D 36
NE38: Wash 5J 115
Ashley Ct. DH9: Tan L 1C 124
Ashley Gdns. NE62: Chop 7J 11
Ashley Ho. TS29: Trim S 7B 180
Ashley Rd. NE34: S Shi 7J 67
Ashley Ter. DH3: Ches S 5A 128
Ashmead Cl. NE12: Kil 7C 36
Ash Mdws. NE38: Wash 2C 128
Ashmore St. SR2: Sund 3F 119 (7J 7)
Ashmore Ter. DH6: Whe H 2B 180
SR2: Sund 3F 119 (6J 7)
Asholme NE5: Newc T 4E 60
Ashridge Cl. NE34: S Shi 1D 88
Ashridge Ct. NE10: Gate 7F 85
Ash Sq. NE38: Wash 4J 115
Ash St. DH7: Lang P 5J 151
DH8: Con 7H 121
NE21: Bla T 5C 80
NE43: Mic 6A 76
Ash Ter. DH6: Bow 5H 177
DH8: Lead 5B 122
DH9: Ann P 4J 123
DH9: Stly 6H 125
DH9: Tan L 6B 110
NE13: Bru V 6C 34
SR7: Mur 7F 147
Ashton Cl. NE5: Cha P 1B 60
Ashton Ct. NE40: Ryton 2H 79
Ashton Downe DH2: Ches S 7A 128
Ashton Ri. DH2: Ches S 7A 128
SR8: Pet 5C 172
Ashton St. SR8: Eas 7D 160
Ashton Way NE26: Whit B 4E 38
SR3: E Her 3J 131
Ashtree Cl. NE4: Newc T 2B 82
NE39: Row G 4K 95
Ashtree Dr. NE22: Bed 6H 17
Ashtree Gdns. NE25: Whit B 1E 48
Ashtree La. NE21: Bla T 3E 94
NE39: H Spen, Row G 3E 94
Ashtrees Gdns. NE9: Gate 7H 83
Ash Tree Ter. DH7: Edm 3K 139
Ashvale Av. NE11: Kib 2E 112
Ash Way DH4: Hou S 1A 144
Ashwell Rd. SR3: E Her 2K 131
Ashwood *DH3: Ches S 7B 128*
(off George St.)
DH6: S Het 5C 158
Ashwood Av. SR5: S'wck 5B 104
Ashwood Cl. NE12: Longb 4C 46
NE23: Cra 7K 21
Ashwood Cres. NE6: Walk 4D 64
Ashwood Cft. NE31: Heb 6H 65
Ashwood Gdns. NE9: Gate 4J 99
Ashwood Grange DH6: Thor 2J 179
Ashwood Gro. NE13: Wide O 6D 34
SR5: C'twn 6H 103
Ashwood Ho. NE7: Newc T 1J 63
Ashwood Rd. NE46: Hex 2E 70
Ashwood St. SR2: Sund 3D 118 (7F 7)
Ashwood Ter. NE40: G'sde 5D 78
SR2: Sund 3D 118 (7F 7)
Askern Av. SR2: Sund 7J 119
Askerton Dr. SR8: Pet 2J 181
Askew Rd. NE8: Gate 6D 82
(Derwentwater Rd.)
NE8: Gate 4F 83 (10F 4)
(St Cuthbert's Rd.)
Askew Rd. W. NE8: Gate 5E 82
(not continuous)
Askrigg Av. NE28: W'snd 5H 47
SR2: Sund 7H 119
Askrigg Cl. DH2: Ous 6G 113
Askrigg Wlk. NE5: Cha P 4C 60
Aspatria Av. TS27: B Col 2H 183
Aspen Av. SR8: Pet 6F 173
Aspen Cl. DH1: Dur 1E 166
DH4: Hou S 4K 129
Aspen Ct. DH3: Gt Lum 3E 142
DH8: Con 5G 121
SR3: New S 3A 132
Aspenlaw NE9: Gate 3A 100
Aspen Ter. NE5: Newc T 4A 62
Aspen Way NE24: News 5G 23
Aspley Cl. SR3: New S 3C 132
Asquith St. DH6: Thor 1K 179
Asquith Ter. DH9: Ann P 4J 123
Association Rd. SR6: Monk 5G 105
Astbury Cl. NE38: Wash 1F 129
Aster Pl. NE4: Newc T 6J 61
Aster Ter. DH4: Hou S 5B 130
Astley Ct. NE12: Kil 1B 46
Astley Dr. NE26: Whit B 2E 38
Astley Gdns. NE25: Sea D 7G 27
NE26: Sea S 3B 28
(not continuous)
Astley Gro. NE26: Sea S 3B 28
Astley Rd. NE25: Sea D 6G 27
Astley St. NE23: E Har 6K 21
Astley Vs. NE26: Sea S 3B 28
Aston Sq. SR3: E Her 2K 131
Aston St. NE33: S Shi 6K 67
Aston Wlk. NE6: Walk 7E 64
Aston Way NE16: Whi 2F 97
Astral Ho. SR1: Sund 3J 7
Athelhampton NE38: Wash 3A 116
Athelstan Rigg SR2: Ryh 2J 133
Athenaeum St. SR1: Sund 2F 119 (4K 7)
Atherton Dr. DH4: Hou S 3A 144
NE4: Newc T 2A 82
Atherton St. DH1: Dur 3K 165 (3A 6)
Athlone Ct. *NE24: Bly 1J 23*
(off Disraeli St.)
Athlone Pl. DH3: Bir 7B 114
Athol Gdns. NE9: Gate 7K 83
NE25: Whit B 1D 48
SR2: Ryh 3J 133
Athol Grn. NE11: Dun 5C 82
Athol Gro. SR3: New S 2C 132
Athol Ho. *NE20: Pon 5K 31*
(off Callerton La.)
Atholl DH2: Ous 6H 113
Athol Pk. SR2: Sund 3G 119
Athol Rd. SR2: Sund 3G 119
Athol St. NE11: Dun 5C 82
Athol Ter. SR2: Sund 3G 119
Atkinson Gdns. NE29: N Shi 2G 67
Atkinson Gro. DH6: Shot C 5D 170
Atkinson Rd. DH3: Ches S 4B 128
NE4: Newc T 2K 81
SR6: Monk 3F 105
Atkinson's Bldgs. SR4: Sund 2F 7
Atkinson St. NE28: W'snd 4F 65
Atkinson Ter. NE4: Newc T 1K 81
NE28: W'snd 4F 65
Atkin St. NE12: Kil 7K 35
Atlantis Fitness Cen. *6B 84*
(off Coldwell St.)
Atlantis Rd. SR3: E Her 1J 131
Atlas Gym *7H 101*
(off Front St.)
Atley Way NE23: Nel V 7G 21
Atmel Way NE28: W'snd 5K 47
Attlee Av. TS27: B Col 4K 183
Attlee Cl. NE23: Dud 6K 35
Attlee Cotts. NE64: Newb S 2K 13
Attlee Cres. DH6: Has 3A 170
Attlee Gro. SR2: Ryh 1G 133
Attlee Sq. DH6: Sher 2K 167
Attlee Ter. NE64: Newb S 2K 13
Attwood Gro. SR5: S'wck 6D 104
Aubone Av. NE15: Newc T 7J 61
Auburn Cl. NE28: W'snd 3A 66
Auburn Gdns. NE4: Newc T 5A 62
Auburn Pl. NE61: Mor 7E 8
Auckland DH2: Ches S 7J 127
Auckland Av. NE34: S Shi 7D 68
Auckland Rd. DH1: Dur 4B 154
NE31: Heb 6K 65
Auckland Ter. NE32: Jar 2E 86
Auden Gro. NE4: Newc T 7A 62
Audland Wlk. NE5: Cha P 4C 60
Audley Ct. NE2: Newc T 3H 63
Audley Gdns. SR3: Sund 5D 118
Audley Rd. NE3: Gos 1G 63
Audouins Row NE8: Gate 6F 83
Augusta Ct. NE28: W'snd 6J 47
Augusta Sq. SR3: E Her 2K 131
(not continuous)
Augusta Ter. SR6: Whit 5H 89
Augustine Cl. DH1: Dur 5J 153
August Pl. NE33: S Shi 4K 67
Augustus Dr. NE22: Bed 6G 17
Austen Av. NE34: S Shi 3H 87
Austen Pl. DH9: Stly 5H 125
Austerfield Pk. DH5: Hett H 7H 145
Austin Sq. SR5: S'wck 5D 104
Australia Gro. NE34: S Shi 3F 87
Australia Twr. SR3: E Her 1A 132
Austral Pl. NE13: Wide O 6C 34
Austwick Wlk. NE5: Cha P 4C 60
Auton Cl. DH7: Ush M 1D 164
Auton Ct. DH7: Ush M 1E 164

Auton Fld. DH7: Ush M 1E 164	Aycliffe Pl. NE9: Gate 3C 100	Back Riggs NE61: Mor 6F 9	Balmoral Gro. DH8: Con 5J 121
Auton Fld. Ter. DH7: Ush M ...1E 164	AYDON 4H 53	Bk. Rothesay Ter. NE22: Bed ...6K 17	Balmoral St. NE28: W'snd 3F 65
Auton Stile DH7: Ush M 1D 164	Aydon Av. NE45: Cor 7E 52	Back Row NE16: Whi 7G 81	Balmoral Ter. NE3: Gos 1G 63
Autumn Cl. NE38: Wash 2H 115	Aydon Castle 4G 53	NE46: Hex 1D 70	NE6: Newc T 6K 63 (1P 5)
Avalon Dr. NE15: Lem 5E 60	Aydon Cres. NE45: Cor 7F 53	Bk. Ryhope St. SR2: Ryh 2G 133	SR2: Sund 6H 119
Avalon Rd. SR3: E Her 1K 131	Aydon Dr. NE45: Cor 7F 53	Bk. St George's Ter. NE2: Newc T ..4G 63	SR3: E Her 2J 131
Avebury Av. NE62: Chop 1J 17	Aydon Gdns. NE12: Longb 6H 45	Bk. Seaburn Ter. SR6: Monk ...2G 105	Balmoral Way NE10: Gate 7A 84
Avebury Dr. NE38: Wash 3J 115	NE45: Cor 7F 53	Bk. Shipley Rd. NE30: N Shi ...5K 49	NE45: Cor 7E 52
Avebury Pl. NE23: Cra 1A 26	Aydon Gro. NE32: Jar 3B 86	Bk. Silver St. DH1: Dur 2C 6	NEWS 5G 23
Avenue Cres. NE25: Sea D 6G 27	NE45: Cor 7E 52	Bk. Sth. Railway St. SR7: S'hm ...3B 148	Balroy Ct. NE12: Longb 5C 46
Avenue Rd. NE8: Gate 6H 83	Aydon Ho. SR3: E Her 2A 132	Bk. Station Rd. NE63: Ash 3A 12	Baltic Bus. Cen. NE8: Gate ..3K 83 (10P 5)
NE25: Sea D 7G 27	Aydon Rd. NE30: N Shi 3J 49	Bk. Stephen St. NE6: Newc T ..7J 63 (4M 5)	Baltic Cen. for Contemporary Art
Avenues, The NE11: Gate 4G 99	NE45: Ayd, Cor 7E 52	Backstone Burn DH8: Shot B 4E 120	..........2H 83 (7K 5)
Avenue St. DH1: H Shin 1F 177	Aydon Rd. Est. NE45: Cor 7F 52	Backstone Rd. DH8: Con 5E 120	Baltic Ind. Pk. NE29: N Shi ...2E 66
Avenue Ter. NE25: Sea D 7H 27	Aydon Wlk. NE5: Newc T 4E 60	Back St. NE21: Bla T 5B 80	Baltic Quay NE8: Gate 2H 83 (7K 5)
SR2: Sund 4E 118 (7H 7)	Aydon Way NE45: Cor 7E 52	Bk. Victoria Ter. DH9: Ann P ...4K 123	Baltic Rd. NE10: Gate 3B 84
Avenue, The DH1: Dur 3J 165 (3A 6)	Aykley Ct. DH1: Dur 7J 153	Backview Ct. SR5: S'wck 4E 104	Baltimore Av. SR5: C'twn 4E 102
(Crossgate Peth)	Aykley Grn. DH1: Dur 7J 153	Bk. Western Hill Dur ...1K 165 (1A 6)	Baltimore Ct. NE37: Wash 7G 101
DH1: Dur 4J 153	Aykley Heads Bus. Cen. DH1: Dur ..7K 153	(off Halstead Pl.)	Baltimore Sq. SR5: C'twn 4F 103
(Hudspeth Cres.)	Aykley Heads Sports Cen. 7A 154	Bk. Westoe Rd. NE33: S Shi ...3K 67	(not continuous)
DH2: Ches S 6K 127	Aykley Rd. DH1: Dur 5K 153	Bk. Woodbine St. NE8: Gate ...5G 83	Bamborough Ct. NE23: Dud 3J 35
DH2: Pelt 2G 127	Aykley Va. DH1: Dur 6J 153	BACKWORTH 6G 37	Bamborough Ter. NE30: N Shi ...5G 49
DH3: Bir 4A 114	Aylesbury Dr. SR3: New S 4C 132	Backworth Bus. Pk. NE27: Back ...7G 37	Bambro St. SR2: Sund 3G 119
DH3: Lam P 4J 129	Aylesbury Pl. NE12: Longb 5K 45	Backworth La. NE27: Seg 2D 36	Bamburgh Av. NE33: S Shi 4B 68
DH5: Hett H 6H 145	Aylesford Sq. NE24: News 4J 23	Backworth Ter. NE27: Shir 3H 47	NE34: S Shi 4B 68
DH6: Whe H 2A 180	Aylsham Cl. NE5: Cha P 1B 60	(off West St.)	SR8: Pet 4D 172
DH7: B'hpe 5E 138	Aylsham Ct. SR3: New S 5C 132	Backworth Workshops NE27: Back ..7G 37	Bamburgh Cl. NE24: Bly 2G 23
DH8: Con 7J 121	Aylward Pl. NE3: Stly 4H 125	Baden Cres. SR5: C'twn 4G 103	NE38: Wash 3E 114
DH9: Ann P 6J 123	Aylyth Pl. NE3: Ken 2B 62	Baden Powell St. NE9: Gate 7J 83	Bamburgh Ct. NE4: Newc T 3A 82
(Chirnside Ter.)	Aynsley M. DH8: Con 6H 121	Baden St. DH3: Ches S 7A 128	NE7: Newc T 7H 45
DH9: Ann P, Dip 2A 123	Aynsley Ter. DH8: Con 5H 121	Bader Cl. SR3: New S 3K 23	NE11: Gate 7E 82
(Fondlyset La.)	Ayr Dr. NE32: Jar 3D 86	Badger Cl. SR3: New S 4C 132	Bamburgh Cres. DH4: Hou S 4B 130
NE9: Gate 7J 83	AYRE'S QUAY 7D 104 (1F 7)	Badger M. NE9: Spri 5D 100	NE27: Shir 1K 47
NE10: Gate 5B 84	Ayre's Quay Rd. SR1: Sund ...1E 118 (3G 7)	Badgers Grn. NE61: Mor 5D 8	Bamburgh Dr. NE10: Gate 4F 85
NE20: Pon 3C 40	Ayre's Ter. NE29: N Shi 6G 49	Badgers Wood DH9: Stly 7G 111	NE28: W'snd 3K 65
NE21: Bla T 4E 80	Ayrey Av. NE34: S Shi 2F 87	Badminton Cl. NE35: Bol C 5D 86	NE61: Peg 4B 10
NE25: Sea D 6H 27	Aysgarth Av. NE28: W'snd 5H 47	Baffin Cl. SR3: New S 3B 132	Bamburgh Gdns. SR3: Sund 5D 118
NE26: Sea D, Sea S 6H 27	SR2: Sund 6H 119	Baildon Cl. NE28: W'snd 1G 65	Bamburgh Gro. NE32: Jar 3A 86
NE26: Whit B 6G 39	Aysgarth Grn. NE3: Ken 1B 62	Bailey Ct. DH1: Dur 3C 6	NE34: S Shi 5D 68
NE28: W'snd 4F 65	AYTON 5D 114	Bailey Ind. Est. NE32: Jar 5B 66	Bamburgh Ho. NE5: Newc T 2E 60
NE38: Wash 3J 115	Ayton Av. SR2: Sund 7H 119	Bailey Ri. SR8: Pet 4B 172	Bamburgh Rd. DH1: Dur 4A 154
NE39: Row G 6K 95	Ayton Cl. NE5: Newc T 2E 60	Bailey Sq. SR5: C'twn 3G 103	NE5: Newc T 2E 60
NE45: Cor 7D 52	NE43: Stoc 1K 91	Bailey St. DH9: Tan L 6B 110	NE12: Longb 4D 46
NE61: Loan 3F 15	Ayton Ct. NE22: Bed 6F 17	Bailey Way DH5: Hett H 2H 157	Bamburgh Ter. NE6: Newc T 7A 64
SR2: Sund 3F 119 (7H 7)	Ayton Ri. NE6: Newc T 1A 84	Bainbridge Av. NE34: S Shi 2F 87	NE63: Ash 4A 12
SR7: Mur 7F 147	Ayton Rd. NE38: Wash 4D 114	SR3: Sund 5D 118	Bamburgh Wlk. NE3: Gos 6C 44
SR7: S'hm 4H 147	Ayton St. NE6: Newc T 1A 84	Bainbridge Bldgs. NE9: Spri ...5A 100	Bamford Ter. NE12: Longb 3D 46
Avenue Vivian DH4: Hou S 1K 143	Azalea Av. SR2: Sund 3E 118 (7H 7)	Bainbridge Holme Cl. SR3: Sund ..5D 118	Bamford Wlk. NE34: S Shi 1K 87
Aviemore Rd. NE36: W Bol 7H 87	Azalea Ter. SR8: Pet 6F 173	Bainbridge Holme Rd. SR3: Sund ..5E 118	Bampton Av. SR6: Monk 2E 104
Avis Av. NE64: Newb S 4G 13	Azalea Ter. Nth. SR2: Sund ..3E 118 (6H 7)	Bainbridge St. DH1: Carr 6H 155	Banbury NE37: Usw 7J 101
Avison St. NE4: Newc T 7D 62 (4A 4)	Azalea Ter. Sth. SR2: Sund ..3E 118 (7H 7)	Bainford Av. NE15: Newc T 7G 61	Banbury Av. SR5: C'twn 3G 103
Avison Pl. NE4: Newc T 7D 62 (4A 4)	Azalea Way NE15: Thro 5J 59	Baird Av. NE28: W'snd 3C 66	Banbury Gdns. NE28: W'snd 7H 47
Avison St. NE4: Newc T 1D 82 (5A 4)		Baird Cl. NE37: Usw 5J 101	Banbury Rd. NE3: Ken 7B 44
Avocet Cl. NE24: News 6J 23		Baird Ct. NE10: Gate 5A 84	Banbury Ter. NE33: S Shi 5K 67
Avolon Ct. NE4: Newc T 7D 62 (4A 4)	**B**	Baird St. SR5: C'twn 4G 103	NE34: S Shi 5K 67
Avolon Pl. NE4: Newc T 7D 62 (4A 4)		Bakehouse La. DH1: Dur ...2B 166 (2E 6)	Banbury Way NE24: News 4J 23
Avolon Wlk. NE4: Newc T 1D 82 (5A 4)	Bk. Albion Rd. NE30: N Shi 6G 49	Baker Gdns. NE10: Gate 6F 85	NE29: N Shi 1D 66
Avon Av. NE29: N Shi 1E 66	Bk. Albion St. SR4: Sund 2G 117	NE11: Dun 5B 82	Bancroft Ter. SR4: Sund 2B 118
NE32: Jar 4C 86	Bk. Beach Rd. NE33: S Shi 3K 67	Baker Rd. NE23: Nel V 1F 25	Banesley La. NE11: Gate, Kib ...7C 98
Avon Cl. NE28: W'snd 6H 47	Bk. Beaumont Ter. NE3: Gos 7F 45	Baker Sq. SR5: C'twn 4G 103	Banff St. SR5: C'twn 3G 103
NE39: Row G 4K 95	Bk. Bridge St. SR1: Sund 3J 7	Baker St. DH5: Hou S 1E 144	Bangor Sq. NE32: Jar 5A 86
Avon Ct. NE25: Sea D 4H 27	Bk. Chapman St. NE6: Walk 6A 64	DH8: Lead 5A 122	Bank Av. NE16: Whi 7G 81
Avon Cres. DH4: Hou S 3A 144	Bk. Croft Rd. NE24: Bly 2J 23	SR5: C'twn 4G 103	Bank Cotts. NE22: E Sle 5D 18
Avoncroft Cl. SR7: S'hm, Sea ...2F 147	Bk. Durham Rd. DH7: Esh W 4E 162	Bakewell Ter. NE6: Walk 2B 84	Bank Ct. NE21: Bla T 2F 81
Avondale SR4: Sund 3G 117	Bk. East Pde. DH8: Con 7J 121	Baldersdale Gdns. SR3: Sund ...6D 118	NE30: N Shi 7H 49
Avondale Av. DH4: Pen 2B 130	Bk. Ecclestone Rd. NE33: S Shi ...4A 68	Baldwin Av. NE4: Newc T 6B 62	Bankdale Gdns. NE24: Cow 2E 22
NE12: Longb 4B 46	(off Mowbray Rd.)	NE36: E Bol 7A 88	Bank Foot DH1: H Shin 6E 166
NE24: Cow 1C 22	Bk. Frederick St. Nth. DH7: B'don ..2E 174	Baldwin St. SR8: Eas 7D 160	Bank Foot Station (Metro) 6H 43
Avondale Cl. NE24: Cow 1D 22	(Leesfield Dr.)	Balfour Gdns. DH8: Con 5H 121	Bankhead NE46: Hex 1D 70
Avondale Ct. NE3: Gos 1F 63	DH7: B'don 1C 174	Balfour Rd. NE15: Newc T 1G 81	Bankhead Rd. NE15: Thro 4K 59
Avondale Gdns. NE36: W Bol ...1G 103	(St Brandon's Gro.)	(not continuous)	Bankhead Ter. DH4: Hou S 1A 144
NE63: N Sea 5E 12	Bk. Frederick St. Sth. DH7: B'don ..2E 174	Balfour St. DH5: Hou S 1E 144	Banks Bldgs. DH4: Hou S 3C 130
Avondale Ri. NE6: Newc T 1A 84	Bk. Front St. DH7: Sac 7E 140	DH8: Con 5H 121	Banks Holt DH2: Ches S 7H 127
Avondale Rd. DH8: Con 6H 121	Bk. George St. NE4: Newc T ..2E 82 (8C 4)	NE8: Gate 5F 83	Bankside NE61: Mor 7G 9
NE6: Newc T 1A 84	Bk. Goldspink La.	NE24: Bly 7H 19	TS27: Cas E 6B 182
NE20: Pon 1E 40	NE2: Newc T 6H 63 (1K 5)	Balfour Ter. NE17: C'wl 6K 93	Bankside Cl. SR2: Ryh 2G 133
Avondale Ter. DH3: Ches S 6A 128	Bk. Hawthorn Rd. W. NE3: Gos ...1E 62	(Beaconsfield Ter.)	Bankside La. NE34: S Shi 1J 87
NE8: Gate 5G 83	Bk. Heaton Pk. Rd.	NE17: C'wl 7K 93	Bankside Rd. NE15: Newc T 1F 81
NE36: W Bol 7G 87	NE6: Newc T 7K 63 (3N 5)	(Frederick St.)	Bankside Wlk. NE62: Chop 7K 11
Avonlea Way NE5: Newc T 2J 61	Bk. High Mkt. NE63: Ash 3J 11	Balgonie Cotts. NE40: Ryton ...1G 79	Bank, The SR6: Whit 6H 89
Avonmouth Rd. SR3: E Her 2K 131	Bk. High St. NE3: Gos 1E 62	Baliol Rd. NE43: Stoc 7J 75	BANK TOP 3G 59
Avonmouth Sq. SR3: E Her 2K 131	Bk. Hylton Rd. SR4: Sund ...1D 118 (3F 7)	Baliol Sq. DH1: Dur 5J 165	Bank Top NE25: Well 5A 38
Avon Rd. DH9: Stly 4F 125	Bk. John St. Nth. DH7: B'don ...1F 175	Balkwell Av. NE29: N Shi 6D 48	NE30: N Shi 1J 49
NE31: Heb 2J 85	Back La. DH3: Gt Lum 1E 142	Balkwell Grn. NE29: N Shi 6E 48	NE40: G'sde 3F 79
SR8: Pet 7A 172	DH4: Pen 1B 130	Ballast Hill NE24: Bly 1K 23	NE40: Ryton 3C 78
Avon St. NE8: Gate 5J 83	DH7: Lan 4K 137	Ballast Hill Rd. NE29: N Shi ...2G 67	Bank Top Hamlet NE16: Whi 7G 81
SR1: Sund 2H 119	DH8: Con 1D 136	Ballater Cl. DH9: Stly 3H 125	Bannatyne's Health & Squash Club ..1F 167
SR8: Eas 7C 160	NE21: Bla T 4B 80	Balliol Av. NE12: Longb 3A 46	Bannerman Ter. DH6: Sher 3C 168
Avon Ter. NE38: Wash 4J 115	NE25: Whit B 6E 38	Balliol Bus. Pk. NE12: Longb ...4J 45	DH7: Ush M 2B 164
Awnless Ct. NE34: S Shi 1J 87	Bk. Lodge Ter. SR1: Sund 2H 119	(not continuous)	Bannister Dr. NE12: Longb 4D 46
Axbridge Cl. NE62: Chop 1J 17	Bk. Loud Ter. DH9: Ann P 5H 123	Balliol Cl. SR8: Pet 7K 171	Bannockburn NE12: Kil 7A 36
Axbridge Gdns. NE4: Newc T ...1A 82	Bk. Maling St. NE6: Newc T 6M 5	Balliol Gdns. NE7: Longb 7K 45	Barbara St. SR2: Sund 6H 119
Axford Ter. NE17: Ham C 3K 107	Bk. Middle St. TS27: B Col 2H 183	Ballston Cl. NE38: Wash 5J 115	Barbary Cl. DH2: Pelt 2G 127
Axminster Cl. NE23: Cra 1A 26	Bk. Mitford St. NE4: Newc T ..3D 82 (10B 4)	Balmain Rd. NE3: Ken 1A 62	Barbary Dr. SR6: Monk 5H 105
Axwell Dr. NE24: Cow 2F 23	Bk. Mount Joy DH1: Dur 4B 166 (6E 6)	Balmlaw NE9: Gate 3B 100	Barbondale Lonnen NE5: Cha P ...3C 60
AXWELL PARK 5E 80	Bk. Mowbray St. NE6: Chop 1H 17	Balmoral DH3: Gt Lum 2E 142	Barbor Ct. DH1: Dur 2B 166 (1D 6)
Axwell Pk. Cl. NE16: Whi 7G 81	Bk. New Bri. St. NE1: Newc T ..7H 63 (4J 5)	Balmoral Av. NE3: Gos 1G 63	Barbour Av. NE34: S Shi 6C 68
Axwell Pk. Rd. NE21: Bla T 5E 80	Bk. North Bri. St. SR5: Monk ..7F 105 (1J 7)	NE32: Jar 3E 86	Barclay Pl. NE5: Newc T 4H 61
Axwell Pk. School Ho's. NE21: Bla T ..5B 80	Bk. Nth. Railway St. SR7: S'hm 2B 148	Balmoral Ct. SR5: C'twn 4G 103	Barclay St. SR6: Monk 7F 105 (1J 7)
Axwell Pk. Vw. NE15: Newc T ...1H 81	Bk. North Ter. SR7: S'hm 2B 148	Balmoral Cres. DH5: Hou S 3E 144	Barcusclose La. DH9: Tan L 2C 110
Axwell Ter. NE16: Swa 5G 81	Bk. Palmerston St. DH8: Con 7H 121	Balmoral Ct. NE25: H'wll 1K 37	NE16: Burn 2C 110
Axwell Vw. NE16: Whi 7G 81	Bk. Percy Gdns. NE30: N Shi 4K 49	Balmoral Dr. NE10: Gate 6A 84	Bardolph Rd. NE29: N Shi 6D 48
NE21: Bla T 5C 80	Bk. Prudhoe Ter. NE30: N Shi 4K 49	SR8: Pet 2J 181	Bardon Cl. NE5: Newc T 1F 61
Aycliffe Av. NE9: Gate 3B 100	(off Percy Pk. Rd.)	Balmoral Gdns. NE26: Whit B ...5F 39	Bardon Ct. NE34: S Shi 1A 88
Aycliffe Cres. NE9: Gate 3B 100	Bk. Prudoe St. NE29: N Shi 7G 49	NE29: N Shi 5F 49	Bardon Cres. NE25: H'wll 1K 37
			Bardsey Pl. NE12: Longb 5K 45

Barehirst St.—Bedford Pl.

Barehirst St. NE33: S Shi 6H 67
Barents Cl. NE5: Newc T 3F 61
Baret Rd. NE6: Walk 5C 64
Barford Ct. NE9: Gate 5J 99
Barford Dr. DH2: Ches S 1J 141
Baring St. NE33: S Shi 1J 67
Barkers Haugh DH1: Dur 1B 166
Barker St. NE2: Newc T 7H 63 (3J 5)
Barking Cres. SR5: C'twn 4F 103
Barking Sq. SR5: C'twn 4F 103
Barkwood Rd. NE39: Row G 5G 95
Barleycorn Pl. SR1: Sund 2G 119 (5K 7)
Barley Mill Cres. DH8: Con 5D 120
Barley Mill Rd. DH8: Con, Shot B 5D 120
BARLEY MOW 7B 114
BARLOW 1G 95
Barlow Cres. NE21: Bla T 1G 95
Barlow Fell Rd. NE21: Bla T 2G 95
Barlowfield Cl. NE21: Bla T 6A 80
Barlow La. NE21: Bla T 7J 79
Barlow La. End NE40: G'sde 5F 79
Barlow Rd. NE21: Bla T 1G 95
Barlow Vw. *NE40: G'sde 5F 79*
(off Dyke Heads La.)
BAR MOOR 1F 79
BARMOOR 3K 15
Barmoor Bank NE61: Hep 3K 15
Barmoor Dr. NE3: Gos 3B 44
Barmoor La. NE40: Ryton 1F 79
Barmoor Ter. NE40: Ryton 1E 78
Barmouth Cl. NE28: W'snd 7H 47
Barmouth Rd. NE29: N Shi 7C 48
BARMSTON 2K 115
Barmston Cen. NE38: Wash 2K 115
Barmston Cl. NE38: Wash 4K 115
Barmston Ct. NE38: Wash 4K 115
Barmston Ferry NE38: Wash 5B 116
Barmston La. NE37: Wash 6A 102
NE38: Wash 4B 116
(not continuous)
SR5: Wash 1B 116
Barmston Mere Training Cen.
SR5: Wash 1B 116
Barmston Rd. NE38: Wash 4A 116
Barmston Way NE38: Wash 2K 115
(not continuous)
Barnabas Pl. SR2: Sund 3H 119
Barnard Av. DH6: Shad 5J 169
Barnard Cl. DH1: Dur 4B 154
NE22: Bed 7G 17
Barnard Ct. DH4: Hou S 1H 143
Barnard Cres. NE31: Heb 6J 65
Barnard Grn. NE3: Ken 5A 44
Barnard Gro. NE32: Jar 2D 86
Barnard Pk. DH5: Hett H 6G 145
Barnard St. NE24: Bly 2J 23
SR4: Sund 3B 118
Barnard Wynd SR8: Pet 2K 181
Barnesbury Rd. NE4: Newc T 1A 82
Barnes Ct. SR4: Sund 3B 118
Barnes Pk. Rd. SR4: Sund 4C 118
Barnes Rd. NE33: S Shi 6H 67
SR7: Mur 7D 146
Barnes St. DH5: Hett H 6G 145
Barnes Vw. SR4: Sund 4B 118
Barnett Ct. SR5: S'wck 5D 104
Barnett Sq. DH6: Has 2A 170
Barn Hill DH9: Stly 2E 124
Barn Hollows SR7: Eas 3A 160
Barningham NE38: Wash 3A 116
Barningham Cl. SR3: Sund 6D 118
Barns Cl. NE32: Jar 2A 86
Barnstaple Cl. NE28: W'snd 7G 47
Barnstaple Rd. NE29: N Shi 3C 48
Barns, The DH9: Stly 1E 124
Barnston NE63: N Sea 4F 13
Barnton Rd. NE10: Gate 1C 100
BARNWELL 1B 130
Barnwood Cl. NE28: W'snd 7G 47
Baroness Dr. NE15: Newc T 6G 61
Barons Quay Rd. SR5: C'twn 7H 103
Baronswood NE3: Gos 1D 62
Barrack Ct. NE4: Newc T 7E 62 (4C 4)
Barrack Rd. NE2: Newc T 6C 62 (2A 4)
NE4: Newc T 7E 62 (2A 4)
Barrack Row DH4: Hou S 3A 130
Barrack St. SR1: Sund 7H 105
Barrack Ter. NE11: Kib 2F 113
Barras Av. NE23: Dud 2K 35
NE24: News 4H 23
Barras Av. W. NE24: News 5H 23
Barras Bri. NE1: Newc T 7F 63 (3F 4)
Barras Dr. SR3: Sund 5D 118
Barrasford Cl. NE3: Gos 1C 62
NE63: Ash 5J 11
Barrasford Dr. NE13: Wide O 6E 34
Barrasford Rd. DH1: Dur 5B 154
NE23: Cra 5A 26
Barrasford St. NE28: W'snd 4C 66
Barras Gdns. NE23: Dud 2K 35
Barras M. NE23: Seg 2D 36
Barrass Av. NE23: Seg 2C 36
Barr Cl. NE28: W'snd 7J 47
Barr Hills DH8: Con 6H 121
Barr Ho. Av. DH8: Con 6H 121
Barrie Sq. SR5: S'wck 5D 104
Barrington Av. NE30: N Shi 2F 49
Barrington Ct. DH5: Hett H 6G 145
NE22: Bed 1J 21
Barrington Dr. NE38: Wash 3H 115
Barrington Ind. Est. NE22: Bed 4J 17
Barrington Pk. NE22: E Sle 5D 18
Barrington Pl. NE4: Newc T 7D 62 (3A 4)
NE8: Gate 4F 83
(Chester Pl.)
NE8: Gate 4G 83
(off Bensham Rd.)
Barrington Rd. NE22: Bed, Sco G 4H 17
Barrington St. NE33: S Shi 2J 67
Barrington Way DH6: Bow 4H 177
Barron St. Sth. SR5: C'twn 6J 103
Barrons Way DH7: B'hpe 5D 138
Barrowburn Pl. NE23: Seg 2E 36
Barrow St. SR5: C'twn 3F 103
Barry St. NE8: Gate 7F 83
NE11: Dun 5B 82
Barsloan Gro. SR8: Pet 4K 171
Barton Cl. NE28: W'snd 7H 47
NE30: N Shi 3H 49
NE37: Usw 5K 101
Barton Ct. SR6: Monk 2E 104
Barton Pk. SR2: Ryh 2F 133
Bartram Gdns. NE8: Gate 7G 83
Bartram St. SR5: Monk 4E 104
Barwell Cl. NE28: W'snd 7H 47
Barwell Ct. NE7: Newc T 3C 64
Barwick St. SR7: Mur 2F 159
SR8: Eas 7D 160
Basildon Gdns. NE28: W'snd 7G 47
Basil Way NE34: S Shi 3A 88
Basingstoke Pl. NE12: Longb 5A 46
Basingstoke Rd. SR8: Pet 5A 172
Baslow Gdns. SR3: Sund 5D 118
Bassenfell Ct. NE37: Wash 2F 115
Bassenthwaite Av. DH2: Ches S 1K 141
Bassington Av. NE23: Cra 3G 25
Bassington Cl. NE4: Newc T 7D 62 (3B 4)
Bassington Dr. NE23: Cra 2F 25
Bassington Ind. Est. NE23: Cra 3G 25
Bassington La. NE23: Cra 2F 25
Bates Ho's. NE21: Bla T 5F 81
Bates La. NE21: Bla T 4F 81
Batey St. DH9: Ann P 4J 123
Bath Cl. NE28: W'snd 7J 47
Bathgate Av. SR5: C'twn 3F 103
Bathgate Cl. NE28: W'snd 7J 47
Bathgate Sq. SR5: C'twn 4F 103
Bath La. DH8: Con 6H 121
NE4: Newc T 1E 82 (5C 4)
NE24: Bly 2K 23
Bath La. Ter. NE4: Newc T 1E 82 (5C 4)
Bath Rd. NE10: Gate 4B 84
NE31: Heb 3J 85
Bath Sq. NE32: Jar 5A 86
Bath St. NE6: Walk 7F 65
Bath St. Ind. Est. NE6: Walk 7F 65
Bath Ter. NE3: Gos 7F 45
NE24: Bly 2K 23
NE30: N Shi 5K 49
SR7: S'hm 2B 148
Batley St. SR5: C'twn 4F 103
Batt Ho. Rd. NE43: Stoc 2H 91
BATTLE FIELD 1H 83 (5K 5)
Battle Grn. DH2: Pelt 4G 127
BATTLE HILL 7H 47
Battle Hill NE46: Hex 2D 70
Battle Hill Dr. NE28: W'snd 1G 65
Battle Hill Est. NE28: W'snd 6K 47
Baugh Cl. NE37: Wash 1E 114
Baulkham Hills DH4: Pen 3B 130
Bavington NE10: Gate 2E 100
Bavington Dr. NE5: Newc T 4J 61
Bavington Gdns. NE30: N Shi 3G 49
Bavington Rd. NE25: Sea D 7H 27
Bawtry Ct. NE28: W'snd 7G 47
Bawtry Gro. NE29: N Shi 7E 48
Baxter Av. NE4: Newc T 7A 62
SR5: C'twn 3F 103
Baxter Pl. NE25: Sea D 7H 27
Baxter Rd. SR5: C'twn 3F 103
Baxters Bldgs. NE25: Sea D 7H 27
Baxter Sq. SR5: C'twn 3F 103
Baxterwood Ct. NE4: Newc T 7C 62 (4A 4)
Baxterwood Gro.
NE4: Newc T 7C 62 (4A 4)
Bay Av. SR8: Pet 6F 173
Baybridge Rd. NE5: Newc T 2E 60
Bay Ct. DH7: Ush M 3D 164
Bayfield Gdns. NE8: Gate 5K 83
Baysdale DH4: Pen 1J 129
Bayswater Av. SR5: C'twn 4G 103
Bayswater Rd. NE2: Newc T 3G 63
NE8: Gate 6K 83
Bayswater Sq. SR5: C'twn 4G 103
Baytree Gdns. NE25: Whit B 1F 49
Baytree Ter. DH2: Beam 2D 126
Bay Vw. E. NE64: Newb S 2J 13
Bay Vw. W. NE64: Newb S 3J 13
Baywood Gro. NE28: W'snd 7G 47
Beach Av. NE26: Whit B 6G 39
Beachborough Cl. NE29: N Shi 3F 49
Beach Cft. Av. NE30: N Shi 2H 49
Beachcross Rd. SR4: Sund 3D 118
Beachdale Cl. TS28: Win 7H 181
Beach Gro. SR8: Pet 5F 173
Beach Rd. NE29: N Shi 5E 48
NE30: N Shi 4G 49
NE33: S Shi 3K 67
Beach St. SR4: Sund 7D 104 (1F 7)
Beach Ter. NE64: Newb S 4H 13
Beachville St. SR4: Sund 3D 118
Beach Way NE30: N Shi 3G 49
Beachway NE24: Bly 5K 23
Beacon Ct. NE9: Gate 2K 99
NE13: Wide O 5C 34
Beacon Dr. NE13: Wide O 5C 34
SR6: Monk 6H 105
Beacon Glade NE34: S Shi 1E 88
BEACON HILL 5D 178
Beacon Ho. NE26: Whit B 3F 39
Beacon La. NE23: Cra, Dud 4F 25
BEACON LOUGH 2K 99
Beacon Lough Rd. NE9: Gate 3H 99
Beacon M. NE23: Cra 4G 25
Beacon Ri. NE9: Gate 2K 99
Beaconsfield Av. NE9: Gate 2J 99
Beaconsfield Cl. NE25: Whit B 4D 38
Beaconsfield Cres. NE9: Gate 2J 99
Beaconsfield Rd. NE9: Gate 2H 99
Beaconsfield St. DH8: Con 5H 121
DH9: Stly 2F 125
NE4: Newc T 1C 82 (3A 4)
NE24: Bly 2K 23
Beaconsfield Ter. DH3: Bir 4K 113
NE17: C'wl 6K 93
Beacon Shop. Cen. NE29: N Shi 7H 49
Beaconside NE34: S Shi 7E 68
Beacon St. NE9: Gate 2H 99
NE30: N Shi 6J 49
NE33: S Shi 1J 67
Beadling Gdns. NE4: Newc T 7A 62
Beadnell Av. NE29: N Shi 1D 66
Beadnell Cl. DH2: Ches S 1J 141
NE21: Bla T 6A 80
Beadnell Ct. NE28: W'snd 7J 47
Beadnell Gdns. NE27: Shir 1K 47
Beadnell Pl. NE2: Newc T 7H 63 (4J 5)
Beadnell Rd. NE24: Bly 4F 23
Beadnell Way NE3: Gos 7C 44
Beagle Sq. SR3: New S 2C 132
Beal Cl. NE24: Bly 2G 23
Beal Dr. NE12: Longb 3D 46
Beal Gdns. NE28: W'snd 7K 47
Beal Grn. NE3: Ken 1J 61
Beal Rd. NE27: Shir 1K 47
Beal Ter. NE6: Walk 2D 84
Beal Wlk. DH1: H Shin 7F 167
Beal Way NE3: Gos 7D 44
Beaminster Way NE3: Ken 7J 43
Beaminster Way E. NE3: Ken 7J 43
BEAMISH 1A 126
Beamishburn Rd. DH9: Beam, Stly 7G 111
NE16: Sun 4H 111
Beamish Cl. DH7: Lang P 5H 151
NE28: W'snd 7G 47
Beamish Ct. DH2: Pelt 3E 126
DH9: Stly 3E 124
NE25: Whit B 1E 48
Beamish Gdns. NE9: Gate 3B 100
Beamish Hills DH9: Beam 2K 125
Beamish
(North of England Open Air Mus., The)
6K 111
Beamish Red Row DH9: Beam 5H 111
Beamish St. DH9: Stly 3E 124
Beamish Vw. DH3: Bir 3B 114
DH9: Stly 2H 125
Beamsley Ter. NE63: Ash 4B 12
Beaney La. DH2: Plaw 3H 141
Beanley Av. *NE15: Lem 7C 60*
(off Shirley St.)
NE31: Heb 2H 85
Beanley Cres. NE30: N Shi 5K 49
Beanley Pl. NE7: Newc T 2J 63
BEARL 1H 75
Bearl Vw. NE43: Mic 6A 76
BEARPARK 1D 164
Beatrice Av. NE24: News 5F 23
Beatrice Gdns. NE34: S Shi 7B 68
NE36: E Bol 7K 87
Beatrice Ho. SR2: Sund 6G 7
Beatrice Rd. NE6: Newc T 4K 63
Beatrice St. NE63: Hir 3C 12
SR6: Monk 5G 105
Beatrice Ter. DH4: Hou S 3B 130
DH4: Pen 7J 115
Beattie St. NE34: S Shi 1H 87
Beatty Av. NE2: Gos 2G 63
SR5: C'twn 4F 103
Beatty Rd. NE22: Bed 1K 21
Beatty St. SR8: Eas 7D 160
Beaufort Cl. DH4: Hou S 4B 130
NE5: Newc T 2K 61
Beaufort Gdns. NE28: W'snd 7H 47
Beaufront Av. NE46: Hex 2E 70
Beaufront Cl. NE10: Gate 1F 101
Beaufront Gdns. NE5: Newc T 4J 61
NE8: Gate 5K 83
Beaufront Ter. NE32: Jar 3B 86
NE33: S Shi 5J 67
NE36: W Bol 7H 87
Beauly NE38: Wash 5H 115
Beaumaris DH4: Hou S 6H 129
Beaumaris Ct. NE12: Longb 6J 45
Beaumaris Gdns. SR3: E Her 2J 131
Beaumaris Way NE5: Newc T 1H 61
Beaumont Cl. DH1: Dur 4J 153
DH6: Bow 4H 177
Beaumont Ct. NE25: Whit B 5D 38
NE42: Pru 4D 76
Beaumont Cres. SR8: Pet 3C 172
Beaumont Dr. NE25: Whit B 4C 38
NE38: Wash 3H 115
Beaumont Ho. NE5: Newc T 3J 61
Beaumont Mnr. NE24: Cow 2D 22
Beaumont Pl. SR8: Pet 6C 172
Beaumont St. NE4: Newc T 3B 82
NE24: Bly 1H 23
NE29: N Shi 7G 49
NE46: Hex 2C 70
SR2: Sund 4G 119
SR5: S'wck 4C 104
SR7: S'hm 4B 148
Beaumont Ter. NE3: Gos 7F 45
NE5: Newc T 3F 61
NE13: Bru V 5C 34
NE32: Jar 1A 86
NE42: Pru 4C 76
Beaumont Way NE42: Pru 5D 76
Beaurepaire DH7: Ush M 1C 164
Beaver Cl. DH1: Dur 3A 154
Bebdon Ct. NE24: Bly 4G 23
BEBSIDE 2B 22
Bebside Furnace Rd. NE24: Cow 7B 18
Bebside Rd. NE24: Cow 2A 22
Beckenham Av. NE36: E Bol 6K 87
Beckenham Cl. NE36: E Bol 6A 88
Beckenham Gdns. NE28: W'snd 1G 65
Beckett St. NE8: Gate 2J 83 (8M 5)
Beckfoot Cl. NE5: Newc T 4H 61
Beckford NE38: Wash 4A 116
Beckford Cl. NE28: W'snd 7G 47
Beck Pl. SR8: Pet 5B 172
Beckside Gdns. NE5: Cha P 4B 60
Beckwith Rd. SR3: E Her 1J 131
Beda Hill NE21: Bla T 3C 80
Bedale Cl. DH1: Carr 7H 155
NE28: W'snd 7G 47
Bedale Ct. NE9: Gate 5K 99
NE34: S Shi 1G 87
Bedale Cres. SR5: C'twn 4G 103
Bedale Dr. NE25: Whit B 1F 49
Bedale Grn. NE5: Newc T 2K 61
Bedale St. DH5: Hett H 1G 157
Bedburn NE38: Wash 7D 114
Bedburn Av. SR5: C'twn 5J 103
Bede Av. DH1: Dur 3E 166
(not continuous)
Bedeburn Foot NE5: Newc T 7F 43
Bedeburn Rd. NE5: Newc T 1F 61
Bede Burn Rd. NE32: Jar 7B 66
Bede Burn Vw. NE32: Jar 1B 86
Bede Cl. DH9: Stly 2H 125
NE12: Longb 4G 47
Bede Ct. DH3: Ches S 6A 128
NE8: Gate 4J 83
NE30: N Shi 1J 49
Bede Cres. NE28: W'snd 1H 65
NE38: Wash 2G 115
Bede Gallery 2B 86
Bede Ho. NE8: Gate 4H 83
SR3: E Her 2K 131
(off Castle Grn.)
Bede Ind. Est. NE32: Jar 7E 66
Bede Pct. NE32: Jar 6B 66
Bede Station (Metro) 7E 66
Bede St. SR6: Monk 5G 105
SR8: Eas 7D 160
Bedesway NE32: Jar 7E 66
Bede's World Mus. 6D 66
Bede Ter. DH2: Ches S 6K 127
DH6: Bow 3H 177
NE32: Jar 1C 86
NE36: E Bol 7K 87
Bede Twr. SR2: Sund 3F 119 (7K 7)
Bede Trad. Est. NE32: Jar 7E 66
Bede Wlk. NE3: Gos 7G 45
NE31: Heb 1K 85
Bede Way DH1: Dur 5A 154
Bedeway SR8: Pet 6B 172
Bedewell Ind. Pk. NE31: Heb 1A 86
Bedford Av. DH3: Bir 1A 128
(not continuous)
NE28: W'snd 2E 64
NE33: S Shi 4J 67
Bedford Ct. NE30: N Shi 7H 49
Bedford Ho. *NE29: N Shi 7H 49*
(off Saville St.)
Bedford Pl. NE5: Cha P 4C 60
NE8: Gate 4G 83

Bedford Pl.—Bethany Gdns.

Bedford Pl. SR3: New S 1C **132**
SR8: Pet 4A **172**
Bedfordshire Dr. DH1: Carr 1H **167**
Bedford St. DH5: Hett H 6F **145**
NE29: N Shi 6G **49**
SR1: Sund 1F **119** (2K **7**)
Bedford Ter. *NE29: N Shi 7G 49*
(off Bedford St.)
Bedford Way NE29: N Shi 7H **49**
BEDLINGTON 1H **21**
Bedlington Bank NE22: Bed 1J **21**
Bedlington Country Pk. 3K **21**
BEDLINGTON STATION 6A **18**
Bedson Bldg. NE1: Newc T 2E **4**
Beech Av. DH4: Hou S 1D **144**
NE3: Ken 6B **44**
NE13: Din 4H **33**
NE16: Whi 6J **81**
NE23: E Cram 5B **26**
NE46: Hex 1A **70**
NE61: Mor 1J **15**
SR6: Whit 5H **89**
SR7: Mur 7F **147**
TS27: B Col 3J **183**
Beechbrooke SR2: Ryh 3H **133**
Beechburn Wlk.
NE4: Newc T 1D **82** (5A **4**)
Beech Cl. DH1: Bras 3C **154**
NE3: Gos 3F **45**
Beech Ct. DH7: Lang P 5J **151**
NE20: Pon 3E **40**
NE29: N Shi 3E **48**
(Cedar Ct.)
NE29: N Shi 6F **49**
(Chase, The)
Beech Cres. SR7: S'hm 4A **148**
Beech Crest DH1: Dur 3K **165** (4A **6**)
Beechcroft NE3: Gos 3D **62**
NE37: Usw 5F **101**
Beechcroft Av. DH7: B'don 2B **174**
NE3: Ken 2C **62**
Beechcroft Cl. DH1: Dur 1E **166**
Beechdale Rd. DH1: Carr 7H **155**
DH8: Con 6J **121**
Beech Dr. NE11: Dun 5A **82**
NE45: Cor 7F **53**
Beecher St. NE24: Cow 1F **23**
Beeches La. DH8: C'sde 4B **134**
Beeches, The NE4: Newc T 3C **82**
NE12: Longb 6B **46**
NE20: Pon 5H **31**
Beechfield Gdns. NE28: W'snd 2E **64**
Beechfield Rd. NE3: Gos 1D **62**
Beech Gdns. NE9: Gate 1H **99**
Beech Gro. DH7: B'hpe 6D **138**
DH7: Ush M 3D **164**
DH9: Dip 2G **123**
NE9: Spri 6D **100**
NE12: Longb 6A **46**
NE17: C'wl 2K **107**
NE22: Bed 7J **17**
NE26: Whit B 6F **39**
NE28: W'snd 3F **65**
NE34: S Shi 2B **88**
NE42: Pru 4D **76**
TS29: Trim S 7C **180**
Beech Gro. Ct. NE40: Ryton 2D **78**
Beechgrove La. DH7: Edm 7B **126**
DH9: Edm 7B **126**
Beech Gro. Rd. NE4: Newc T 2C **82**
Beech Gro. Sth. NE42: Pru 4E **76**
Beech Gro. Ter. NE40: Ryton 2D **78**
Beechgrove Ter. DH7: Edm 1A **140**
Beech Gro. Ter. Sth. NE40: Ryton 2D **78**
Beech Hill NE46: Hex 1A **70**
Beech M. NE3: Ken 4B **44**
Beecholm Ct. SR2: Sund 5F **119**
Beech Pk. DH7: B'don 2C **174**
Beech Rd. DH1: Dur 6K **153**
DH6: Sher 2K **167**
DH8: Lead 6B **122**
Beech Sq. NE38: Wash 4J **115**
Beech St. NE4: Newc T 1A **82**
NE8: Gate 5K **83**
NE16: Sun 5H **97**
NE32: Jar 6A **66**
NE43: Mic 6A **76**
Beech Ter. DH9: Ann P 4J **123**
DH9: Stly 5E **124**
(Hustledown Rd.)
DH9: Stly 6H **125**
(Oak Ter.)
NE16: Burn 2C **110**
NE21: Bla T 4C **80**
NE63: Hir 5C **12**
SR8: Pet 6E **172**
Beech Vw. DH1: Sher 5H **167**
Beech Way NE12: Kil 7A **36**
Beechway NE10: Gate 2D **100**
NE63: N Sea 4E **12**
Beechways DH1: Dur 1H **165**
Beechwood NE39: H Spen 4E **94**
Beechwood Av. NE3: Gos 6G **45**
NE9: Gate 4J **99**
NE25: Whit B 7D **38**
Beechwood Av. NE40: Ryton 1G **79**
NE62: Chop 7J **11**
Beechwood Cl. NE32: Jar 7D **66**
Beechwood Cres. SR5: S'wck 4B **104**
Beechwood Gdns. NE11: Gate 1D **98**
Beechwood Ho. NE7: Newc T 1J **63**
Beechwood Pl. NE20: Pon 4J **31**
Beechwoods DH2: Ches S 4K **127**
Beechwood St. SR2: Sund 3D **118** (6F **7**)
Beechwood Ter. DH4: Hou S 6C **130**
SR2: Sund 3D **118** (6F **7**)
Beehive Workshops DH1: Dur 2F **167**
Beeston Av. SR5: C'twn 4F **103**
Beetham Cres. NE5: Newc T 5G **61**
Beethoven St. NE33: S Shi 3K **67**
Beggar La. NE61: Mor 6F **9**
Begonia Cl. NE31: Heb 3J **85**
Bek Rd. DH1: Dur 5A **154**
Beldene Dr. SR4: Sund 4A **118**
Belford Av. NE27: Shir 1K **47**
Belford Cl. NE28: W'snd 7H **47**
SR2: Sund 5F **119**
Belford Ct. NE24: Cow 2F **23**
Belford Gdns. NE11: Gate 2C **98**
Belford Rd. SR2: Sund 5G **119**
Belford St. SR8: Pet 3D **172**
Belford Ter. NE6: Walk 1C **84**
NE30: N Shi 5G **49**
Belford Ter. E. SR2: Sund 5G **119**
Belfry, The DH4: Hou S 5A **130**
Belgrade Cres. SR5: C'twn 3F **103**
Belgrade Sq. SR5: C'twn 4F **103**
Belgrave Ct. NE10: Gate 6B **84**
Belgrave Cres. NE24: Bly 3K **23**
Belgrave Gdns. NE34: S Shi 7B **68**
NE63: N Sea 5E **12**
Belgrave Pde. NE4: Newc T 2D **82** (8A **4**)
Belgrave Ter. NE10: Gate 6B **84**
NE33: S Shi 2K **67**
Bellamy Cres. SR5: C'twn 4F **103**
Bellburn Ct. NE23: Cra 2B **26**
Belle Gro. Pl. NE2: Newc T 6D **62** (2A **4**)
Belle Gro. Ter. NE2: Newc T 6D **62** (1B **4**)
Belle Gro. Vs. NE2: Newc T 6D **62** (1B **4**)
Belle Gro. W. NE2: Newc T 6D **62** (1A **4**)
Bellerby Dr. DH2: Ous 5G **113**
Belle St. DH9: Stly 3F **125**
Belle Vw. NE39: H Spen 2D **94**
Belle Vue DH6: Quar H 5D **178**
DH9: Tan L 3E **110**
Belle Vue Av. NE3: Gos 7F **45**
Belle Vue Bank NE9: Gate 2G **99**
Belle Vue Cotts. NE9: Gate 2G **99**
Belle Vue Cres. NE33: S Shi 7H **67**
SR2: Sund 4E **118**
Bellevue Cres. NE23: Cra 7K **21**
Belle Vue Dr. SR2: Sund 4E **118**
Belle Vue Gdns. DH8: Con 6H **121**
Belle Vue Gro. NE9: Gate 2H **99**
Belle Vue La. NE36: E Bol 1J **103**
Belle Vue Leisure Cen. 6J **121**
Belle Vue Pk. SR2: Sund 4E **118**
Belle Vue Pk. W. SR2: Sund 4E **118**
Belle Vue Rd. SR2: Sund 4E **118**
Belle Vue St. NE30: N Shi 1J **49**
Belle Vue Swimming Cen. 6J **121**
Belle Vue Ter. DH1: Dur 1F **167**
NE9: Gate 2G **99**
NE9: Spri 6D **100**
NE22: E Sle 1E **18**
NE29: N Shi 7G **49**
NE40: Ryton 2C **78**
Belle Vue Vs. NE36: E Bol 7J **87**
Bellfield Av. NE3: Ken 6B **44**
Bellgreen Av. NE3: Gos 3F **45**
Bell Gro. NE12: Kil 7K **35**
Bell Ho. Rd. SR5: S'wck 2C **104**
(not continuous)
Bellingham Cl. NE28: W'snd 1H **65**
Bellingham Ct. NE3: Ken 7K **43**
Bellingham Dr. NE12: Longb 5D **46**
Bellingham Ho. SR4: Sund 4H **117**
Bellingham Vs. NE22: Bed 7J **17**
Bellister Gro. NE5: Newc T 6J **61**
Bellister Pk. SR8: Pet 1C **182**
Bellister Rd. NE29: N Shi 6D **48**
Bell Mdw. DH7: B'don 2C **174**
Belloc Av. NE34: S Shi 3H **87**
Bellows Burn La. TS27: Cas E 7C **182**
Bell Rd. NE41: Wylam 7K **57**
Bells Bldgs. DH9: Ann P 4K **123**
Bellsburn Ct. NE63: Ash 5K **11**
BELL'S CLOSE 7E **60**
Bells Cl. NE15: Lem 1E **80**
NE24: Cow 1D **22**
Bells Cl. Ind. Est. NE15: Lem 1E **80**
Bell's Cotts. NE40: G'sde 5E **78**
Bell's Ct. NE1: Newc T 1G **83** (5G **4**)
Bell's Folly DH1: Dur 5J **165**
Bellshill Cl. NE28: W'snd 6J **47**
Bells Lonnen NE42: Pru 3F **77**
Bell's Pl. NE22: Bed 1J **21**
Bell St. DH4: Pen 1B **130**
NE30: N Shi 7H **49**
NE31: Heb 7H **65**
Bell St. NE38: Wash 4K **115**
SR4: Sund 2B **118**
Bell's Ville DH1: Dur 2E **166**
Bells Wood Ct. DH8: Con 5F **121**
Bell Vw. NE42: Pru 3H **77**
Bell Vw. Dr. DH8: C'sde 4C **134**
Bell Vs. NE20: Pon 5K **31**
Bellway Ind. Est. NE12: Longb 5D **46**
Bellwood Ter. DH8: Lead 6B **122**
BELMONT 1G **167**
Belmont NE10: Gate 2E **100**
Belmont Av. NE25: Whit B 7D **38**
SR7: Eas 3K **159**
Belmont Bus. Pk. DH1: Dur 7F **155**
Belmont Cl. NE28: W'snd 7H **47**
Belmont Cotts. NE5: Newc T 2F **61**
Belmonte Av. TS27: B Col 3K **183**
Belmont Ind. Est. DH1: Dur 7F **155**
Belmont Ri. DH5: Hett H 2G **157**
Belmont Rd. DH1: Carr, Dur 7E **154**
SR4: Sund 3B **118**
Belmont St. NE6: Walk 3D **84**
Belmont Ter. NE9: Spri 6C **100**
Belmont Wlk. NE6: Walk 3D **84**
Belmount Av. NE3: Gos 3F **45**
Belper Cl. NE28: W'snd 7G **47**
Belsay NE38: Wash 4D **114**
Belsay Av. NE13: Bru V 7C **34**
NE25: Whit B 7H **39**
NE34: S Shi 6C **68**
SR8: Pet 4D **172**
Belsay Cl. NE28: W'snd 7G **47**
NE61: Peg 4B **10**
Belsay Ct. NE24: Cow 2G **23**
Belsay Gdns. NE3: Ken 4B **44**
NE11: Gate 2C **98**
SR4: Sund 3B **118**
Belsay Gro. NE22: Bed 5A **18**
Belsay Pl. NE4: Newc T 7C **62**
Belsfield Gdns. NE32: Jar 2B **86**
Belsize Pl. NE6: Walk 5D **64**
Beltingham NE5: Newc T 4E **60**
Belvedere NE29: N Shi 5F **49**
Belvedere Av. NE25: Whit B 7F **39**
Belvedere Ct. NE6: Newc T 6A **64**
Belvedere Gdns. DH6: Shot C 5D **170**
NE12: Longb 6B **46**
Belvedere Ho. NE6: Newc T 3P **5**
Belvedere Parkway NE3: Ken 6K **43**
Belvedere Retail Pk.
NE3: Ken 6K **43**
Belvedere Rd. SR2: Sund 3E **118** (7H **7**)
Bemersyde Dr. NE2: Newc T 2G **63**
Benbrake Av. NE29: N Shi 3E **48**
Bendigo Av. NE34: S Shi 3F **87**
Benedict Rd. SR6: Monk 5H **105**
Benevente St. SR7: S'hm 4B **148**
Benfield Bus. Pk. NE6: Walk 5C **64**
Benfield Cl. DH8: Shot B 3E **120**
Benfield Gro. NE26: Sea S 3B **28**
Benfield Rd. NE6: Newc T 3B **64**
BENFIELDSIDE 3E **120**
Benfieldside Rd. DH8: Shot B 3E **120**
Benfleet Av. SR5: C'twn 4F **103**
Benjamin Rd. NE28: W'snd 2A **66**
Benjamin St. NE40: Ryton 3D **78**
Bennett Ct. NE15: Lem 7C **60**
SR2: Sund 5G **119**
Bennett Gdns. NE10: Gate 4B **84**
Bennett's Wlk. NE61: Mor 7G **9**
Benridge Bank DH4: W Rai 1A **156**
Benridge Pk. NE24: News 6F **23**
BENSHAM 5G **83**
Bensham Av. NE8: Gate 5F **83**
Bensham Ct. NE8: Gate 5F **83**
NE34: S Shi 1J **87**
Bensham Cres. NE8: Gate 5E **82**
Bensham Rd. NE8: Gate 6F **83** (10G **4**)
Bensham St. NE35: Bol C 5F **87**
Bensham Trad. Est. NE8: Gate 6E **82**
Benson Cl. NE46: Hex 2A **70**
Benson Pl. NE6: Newc T 7A **64**
Benson Rd. NE6: Walk 7B **64**
Benson St. DH3: Ches S 7A **128**
DH9: Stly 2E **124**
Benson Ter. NE10: Gate 6B **84**
Bentall Bus. Pk. NE37: Wash 1K **115**
Bent Ho. La. DH1: Dur 3F **167**
Bentinck Cres. NE4: Newc T 2B **82**
NE61: Peg 4A **10**
Bentinck Pl. NE4: Newc T 2B **82**
Bentinck Rd. NE4: Newc T 2B **82**
Bentinck St. NE4: Newc T 2B **82**
Bentinck Ter. NE4: Newc T 1B **82**
Bentinck Vs. NE4: Newc T 1B **82**
BENTON 6B **46**
Benton Av. SR5: C'twn 3F **103**
Benton Bank NE7: Newc T 4J **63**
(not continuous)
Benton Cl. NE7: Newc T 7K **45**
Benton Hall Wlk. NE7: Newc T 3B **64**
Benton La. NE12: Longb 3K **45**
(not continuous)
Benton Lodge Av. NE7: Newc T 7K **45**
Benton Pk. Rd. NE7: Longb, Newc T 7H **45**
Benton Rd. NE7: Newc T 7A **46**
NE27: Shir 2H **47**
NE34: S Shi 4J **87**
BENTON SQUARE 3F **47**
Benton Sq. Ind. Est. NE12: Kil 3F **47**
Benton Station (Metro) 6B **46**
Benton Ter. DH9: Stly 2F **125**
NE2: Newc T 6H **63** (1J **5**)
Benton Vw. NE12: Longb 4B **46**
Benton Way NE28: W'snd 4F **65**
(Brussels Rd.)
NE28: W'snd 5F **65**
(Neptune Rd.)
Bents Cotts. NE33: S Shi 3A **68**
Bents Cotts. App. NE33: S Shi 3A **68**
Bents Pk. Rd. NE33: S Shi 2A **68**
Bents, The SR6: Monk 7H **89**
Benville Ter. DH7: New B 4A **164**
BENWELL 1K **81**
Benwell Cl. NE15: Newc T 1K **81**
Benwell Dene Ter. NE15: Newc T 1J **81**
Benwell Grange NE15: Newc T 1K **81**
Benwell Grange Av. NE15: Newc T 1K **81**
Benwell Grange Rd. NE15: Newc T 1J **81**
Benwell Grange Ter. NE15: Newc T 1J **81**
Benwell Gro. NE4: Newc T 1A **82**
Benwell Hall Dr. NE15: Newc T 7H **61**
Benwell Hill Gdns. NE5: Newc T 6J **61**
Benwell Hill Rd. NE5: Newc T 6H **61**
Benwell La. NE15: Newc T 1H **81**
(not continuous)
Benwell Village NE15: Newc T 7H **61**
Benwell Village M. NE15: Newc T 7J **61**
Berberis Way *NE15: Thro 5J 59*
(off Lovaine St.)
Beresford Av. NE31: Heb 3H **85**
Beresford Ct. NE26: Sea S 4D **28**
Beresford Gdns. NE6: Newc T 1A **84**
Beresford Pk. SR2: Sund 3D **118** (6F **7**)
Beresford Rd. NE26: Sea S 4D **28**
NE30: N Shi 1G **49**
Beresford St. NE11: Dun 5C **82**
Bergen Cl. NE29: N Shi 1B **66**
Bergen Sq. SR5: C'twn 3F **103**
Bergen St. SR5: C'twn 3F **103**
Berkdale Rd. NE9: Gate 4G **99**
Berkeley Cl. NE12: Kil 7C **36**
NE35: Bol C 4F **87**
SR3: E Her 2J **131**
Berkeley Sq. NE3: Gos 5D **44**
Berkeley St. NE33: S Shi 3K **67**
Berkhampstead Ct. NE10: Gate 7G **85**
Berkley Av. NE21: Bla T 4E **80**
Berkley Cl. NE28: W'snd 7H **47**
Berkley Rd. NE29: N Shi 6D **48**
Berkley St. NE15: Thro 5K **59**
Berkley Ter. NE15: Thro 5K **59**
Berkley Way NE31: Heb 5K **65**
Berkshire Cl. DH1: Carr 1G **167**
NE5: Newc T 3F **61**
Berkshire Rd. SR8: Pet 4A **172**
Berksyde DH8: Con 1J **135**
Bermondsey St. NE2: Newc T 7H **63** (4K **5**)
Bernard Shaw St. DH4: Hou S 2D **144**
Bernard St. DH4: Hou S 2D **144**
NE6: Walk 2F **85**
Bernard Ter. DH2: Pelt 3G **127**
Berrington Dr. NE5: Newc T 2H **61**
Berrishill Gro. NE25: Whit B 5C **38**
Berry Cl. NE6: Walk 1E **84**
NE28: W'snd 7G **47**
Berry Edge Rd. DH8: Con 7H **121**
Berry Edge Vw. DH8: Con 6G **121**
Berryfield Cl. SR3: New S 4C **132**
Berry Hill NE40: G'sde 5F **79**
Berryhill Cl. NE21: Bla T 5D **80**
Berrymoor NE63: Hir 3C **12**
Berry Pk. Factories DH8: Con 7G **121**
Bertha St. DH8: Con 6H **121**
Bertha Ter. DH4: Hou S 5D **130**
Bertram Cres. NE15: Newc T 7J **61**
Bertram Pl. NE27: Shir 7K **37**
NE61: Peg 3B **10**
Bertram St. DH3: Bir 4A **114**
NE33: S Shi 5J **67**
Bertram Ter. *NE61: Peg 4B 10*
(off Bamburgh Pl.)
NE63: Hir 4B **12**
Berwick NE38: Wash 4D **114**
Berwick Av. SR5: C'twn 3F **103**
Berwick Chase SR8: Pet 2K **181**
Berwick Cl. NE15: Lem 6A **60**
Berwick Ct. NE20: Pon 4K **31**
Berwick Dr. NE28: W'snd 7H **47**
Berwick Hill Rd. NE20: Pon, Wool 3K **31**
Berwick Sq. SR5: C'twn 4F **103**
Berwick St. NE31: Heb 7H **65**
Berwick Ter. NE29: N Shi 1D **66**
Besford Gro. SR1: Sund 2G **119**
Bessemer Rd. DH6: S Het 4B **158**
Bessemer St. DH8: Con 6G **121**
Bessie Surtees Ho. 7G **4**
Best Ter. NE21: Bla T 4A **80**
Best Vw. DH4: Pen 3B **130**
Bethany Gdns. DH9: Ann P 4K **123**

Bethany Ter.—Blue Quarries Rd.

Bethany Ter. DH9: Ann P 4K **123**
Bethel Av. NE6: Walk 6B **64**
Bethune Av. SR7: S'hm 3J **147**
(not continuous)
Betjeman Cl. DH9: Stly 3G **125**
Bet's La. NE61: Tra W 7D **14**
Better Bodies Health & Fitness Club 5B **26**
Betts Av. NE15: Newc T 1H **81**
Bevan Av. SR2: Ryh 2G **133**
Bevan Cres. DH6: Whe H 4A **180**
Bevan Dr. NE12: Longb 6H **45**
Bevan Gdns. NE10: Gate 6E **84**
Bevan Gro. DH1: Dur 2F **167**
DH6: Shot C 6E **170**
Bevan Sq. SR7: Mur 6E **146**
Beverley Cl. DH6: Coxh 7J **177**
NE3: Gos 2D **44**
Beverley Ct. NE9: Gate 1J **99**
NE32: Jar 6B **66**
NE37: Wash 1H **115**
Beverley Cres. NE9: Gate 1J **99**
Beverley Dr. NE16: Swa, Whi 5J **81**
NE21: Bla T 6K **79**
NE62: Chop 7H **11**
Beverley Gdns. DH3: Ches S 7B **128**
DH8: Con 6H 121
(off Beverley Ter.)
DH8: Shot B 4F **121**
NE30: N Shi 1J **49**
NE40: Ryton 1E **78**
Beverley Pk. NE25: Whit B 7E **38**
Beverley Pl. NE28: W'snd 2K **65**
Beverley Rd. NE9: Gate 1J **99**
NE25: Whit B 7E **38**
SR2: Sund 6H **119**
Beverley Ter. DH8: Con 6H **121**
DH9: Ann P 4J **123**
NE6: Walk 1E **84**
NE15: Thro 3A **60**
NE30: N Shi 1J **49**
Beverley Vs. NE30: N Shi 1J **49**
Beverley Way SR8: Pet 5A **172**
Bevin Gro. TS27: B Col 3K **183**
Bevin Sq. DH6: S Het 4D **158**
Beweshill Cres. NE21: Bla T 5A **80**
Beweshill La. NE21: Bla T 4K **79**
(not continuous)
Bewick Cl. DH2: Ches S 2J **141**
Bewick Ct. NE1: Newc T 4G **4**
Bewick Cres. NE15: Lem 6D **60**
Bewicke Lodge NE28: W'snd 3A **66**
Bewicke Rd. NE28: W'snd 4A **66**
(not continuous)
Bewicke Rd. Ind. Est. NE28: W'snd 4A **66**
Bewicke St. NE28: W'snd 4B **66**
Bewicke Vw. DH3: Bir 3B **114**
Bewick Gth. NE43: Mic 5A **76**
Bewick La. NE42: O'ham 2D **76**
Bewick Main Cvn. Pk. DH2: Kib 3G **113**
Bewick Pk. NE28: W'snd 6K **47**
Bewick Rd. NE8: Gate 5G **83**
Bewick St. NE1: Newc T 2E **82** (7D **4**)
NE33: S Shi 5J **67**
Bewley Gro. SR8: Pet 2J **181**
Bewley Ter. DH7: New B 4A **164**
Bexhill Rd. SR5: C'twn 4F **103**
Bexhill Sq. NE24: News 4J **23**
SR5: C'twn 3F **103**
Bexley Av. NE15: Newc T 7G **61**
Bexley Gdns. NE28: W'snd 7H **47**
Bexley Pl. NE16: Whi 2G **97**
Bexley St. SR4: Sund 2B **118**
Biceps Fitness Cen. 5E **172**
Bickerton Wlk. NE5: Newc T 4E **60**
Bickington Ct. DH4: Hou S 6C **130**
BIDDICK HALL 4H **87**
Biddick Hall Dr. NE34: S Shi 2H **87**
Biddick Inn Ter. NE38: Wash 1J **129**
Biddick La. NE38: Wash 1H **129**
Biddick Ter. NE38: Wash 5J **115**
Biddick Vw. NE38: Wash 5J **115**
Biddick Village Cen. NE38: Wash 5H **115**
Biddick Vs. NE38: Wash 5J **115**
Biddlestone Cres. NE29: N Shi 7D **48**
Biddlestone Rd. NE6: Newc T 4A **64**
Bideford Gdns. NE9: Gate 4H **99**
NE26: Whit B 5F **39**
NE32: Jar 1E **86**
NE34: S Shi 4C **68**
Bideford Gro. NE16: Whi 2G **97**
Bideford Rd. NE3: Ken 1A **62**
Bideford St. SR2: Sund 6H **119**
Bigbury Cl. DH4: Hou S 5C **130**
Bigges Gdns. NE28: W'snd 1D **64**
BIGGES MAIN 3D **64**
Bigg Mkt. NE1: Newc T 1F **83** (6F **4**)
Big Waters Nature Reserve 4B **34**
Bilbrough Gdns. NE4: Newc T 2K **81**
BILL QUAY 4F **85**
Bill Quay Farm 4E **84**
Bill Quay Ind. Est. NE10: Gate 3F **85**
BILLY MILL 5D **48**
Billy Mill Av. NE29: N Shi 6E **48**
Billy Mill La. NE29: N Shi 4C **48**
Bilsdale SR6: Monk 7H **89**
Bilsdale Pl. NE12: Longb 6H **45**
Bilsmoor Av. NE7: Newc T 3K **63**
Bilton Hall Rd. NE32: Jar 7D **66**
Bilton's Ct. NE61: Mor 6F **9**
Binchester St. NE34: S Shi 2G **87**
Bingfield Gdns. NE5: Newc T 4J **61**
Bingley Cl. NE28: W'snd 7J **47**
Bingley St. SR5: C'twn 4F **103**
Bink Moss NE37: Wash 2E **114**
Binsby Gdns. NE9: Gate 5K **99**
Binswood Av. NE5: Newc T 4H **61**
Bircham Dr. NE21: Bla T 4D **80**
Bircham St. DH9: Stly 4D **124**
Birch Av. NE10: Gate 7E **84**
SR6: Whit 5H **89**
Birch Cl. NE46: Hex 3A **70**
Birch Ct. NE42: Pru 4C **76**
SR3: New S 3A **132**
Birch Cres. DH4: Hou S 7C **130**
NE16: Burn 2K **109**
BIRCHES NOOK 7J **75**
Birches Nook Cotts. NE43: Stoc 7J **75**
Birches Nook Rd. NE43: Stoc 7J **75**
Birches, The DH5: Eas L 2J **157**
DH9: Stly 1F **125**
(not continuous)
NE16: Sun 5J **97**
Birchfield NE16: Whi 1H **97**
NE38: Wash 6J **115**
Birchfield Gdns. NE9: Gate 5J **99**
NE15: Lem 6E **60**
Birchfield Rd. SR2: Sund 4D **118** (7F **7**)
Birchgate Cl. NE21: Bla T 5A **80**
Birch Gro. DH8: Con 3A **136**
NE28: W'snd 7G **47**
NE32: Jar 6A **66**
Birchgrove Av. DH1: Dur 1F **167**
Birchington Av. NE33: S Shi 6J **67**
Birch Pl. DH7: Esh W 4D **162**
Birch Rd. NE21: Bla T 4D **80**
Birch St. DH8: Con 7H **121**
NE32: Jar 6A **66**
Birch Ter. DH3: Bir 3K **113**
NE6: Walk 1E **84**
Birchtree Gdns. NE25: Whit B 1F **49**
Birchvale Av. NE5: Newc T 3G **61**
Birchwood Av. NE7: Newc T 2A **64**
NE13: Wide O 6D **34**
NE16: Whi 2G **97**
Birchwood Cl. DH9: Beam 1A **126**
NE23: Seg 2D **36**
Birchwood Dr. DH6: Shot C 7H **171**
Birdhill Pl. NE34: S Shi 1J **87**
Birds Nest Rd. NE6: Newc T, Walk 2B **84**
(not continuous)
Bird St. NE30: N Shi 6J **49**
Birkdale NE25: Whit B 6D **38**
NE33: S Shi 4A **68**
Birkdale Av. SR6: Monk 7G **89**
Birkdale Cl. NE7: Newc T 1A **64**
NE28: W'snd 1F **65**
NE37: Usw 5F **101**
Birkdale Dr. DH4: Hou S 5A **130**
Birkdale Gdns. DH1: Carr 1H **167**
Birkdene NE43: Stoc 1K **91**
Birkhead Cottages, Garden & Nursery 2K **111**
BIRKHEADS 2K **111**
Birkheads La. NE11: Kib, Sun 2K **111**
Birkland La. DH9: Beam 2A **112**
NE11: Beam, Kib 2A **112**
NE16: Kib, Sun 6J **97**
Birkshaw Wlk. NE5: Newc T 4E **60**
Birks Rd. NE15: Hed W, Thro 7F **41**
Birling Pl. NE5: Newc T 3K **61**
Birnam Gro. NE32: Jar 4E **86**
Birney Edge NE20: Pon 3G **41**
Birnham Pl. NE3: Ken 2B **62**
Birnie Cl. NE4: Newc T 2A **82**
Birrell Sq. SR5: C'twn 3F **103**
Birrell St. SR5: C'twn 3F **103**
BIRTLEY 4A **114**
Birtley Av. NE30: N Shi 4K **49**
(not continuous)
SR5: C'twn 3F **103**
Birtley Cl. NE3: Gos 1C **62**
Birtley Crematorium DH3: Bir 2K **113**
Birtley La. DH3: Bir 3A **114**
Birtley Leisure Cen. 5A **114**
Birtley Rd. NE38: Wash 7D **114**
Birtley Sports Complex 6A **114**
Birtley Vs. DH3: Bir 3A **114**
Birtwhistle Av. NE31: Heb 3H **85**
Biscop Ter. NE32: Jar 1C **86**
Bishopbourne Cl. NE29: N Shi 3F **49**
Bishop Cres. NE32: Jar 5C **66**
Bishopdale DH4: Pen 1J **129**
(not continuous)
NE28: W'snd 7D **46**
Bishopdale Av. NE24: Cow 3E **22**
Bishop Morton Gro. SR1: Sund 2G **119**
Bishop Ramsey Ct. NE34: S Shi 7C **68**
Bishop Rock Dr. NE12: Longb 6J **45**
Bishop's Av. NE4: Newc T 1C **82**
Bishops Cl. NE28: W'snd 3J **65**
Bishops Ct. DH1: H Shin 6D **166**
NE5: Newc T 5F **61**
Bishops Dr. NE40: Ryton 2H **79**
Bishops Hill NE46: Acomb 3C **50**
(not continuous)
Bishops Mdw. NE22: Bed 7G **17**
Bishop's Rd. NE15: Newc T 2K **81**
Bishops Way DH1: Dur 4K **153**
SR3: New S 4A **132**
Bishops Wynd DH5: Hou S 3E **144**
Bishopton St. NE24: Bly 3J **23**
SR2: Sund 2G **119**
Bishopton Way NE46: Hex 3A **70**
BISHOPWEARMOUTH 1E **118** (2G **7**)
Bisley Ct. NE28: W'snd 7H **47**
Bisley Dr. NE34: S Shi 6K **67**
Bittern Cl. NE11: Dun 4B **82**
NE28: W'snd 6A **48**
Biverfield Rd. NE42: Pru 3G **77**
Blackberries, The NE9: Spri 6D **100**
Black Boy Rd. DH4: Hou S 4H **143**
Black Boy Yd. NE1: Newc T 1F **83** (6F **4**)
Blackburn Cl. DH7: Ush M 7C **152**
Blackburn Grn. NE10: Gate 7A **84**
BLACK CALLERTON 4B **42**
Blackcap Cl. NE38: Wash 5D **114**
Blackcliff Way DH7: Ush M 7C **152**
Blackclose Bank NE63: Ash 7A **12**
Blackclose Est. NE63: Ash 7B **12**
Blackdene NE63: Ash 5K **11**
Blackdown Cl. SR8: Pet 7K **171**
Black Dr. DH3: Lam P 4F **129**
Blacketbridge NE1: Newc T 4E **4**
Blackett Cotts. NE41: Wylam 7J **57**
Blackett Ct. NE41: Wylam 7J **57**
Blackett Pl. NE1: Newc T 1F **83** (5F **4**)
Blackett St. DH9: Ann P 5J **123**
NE1: Newc T 1F **83** (5E **4**)
NE31: Heb 5K **65**
Blackett Ter. SR4: Sund 2C **118**
BLACKFELL 2E **114**
Blackfell Rd. NE37: Wash 2D **114**
Blackfell Village Cen. NE37: Wash 2E **114**
Blackfell Way DH3: Bir 3B **114**
Blackfriars 6D **4**
Blackfriars Ct. NE1: Newc T 6D **4**
Blackfriars Way NE12: Longb 6J **45**
BLACKFYNE 5G **121**
BLACKHALL COLLIERY 2H **183**
Blackhall Colliery Ind. Est.
TS27: B Col 1H **183**
BLACKHALL MILL 2K **107**
BLACKHALL ROCKS 3J **183**
Blackheath Cl. NE37: Usw 5G **101**
Blackheath Ct. NE3: Ken 7H **43**
BLACKHILL 5F **121**
Blackhill Av. NE28: W'snd 5J **47**
Blackhill Cres. NE9: Gate 3B **100**
Blackhills Rd. SR8: Pet 4E **172**
Blackhills Ter. SR8: Pet 5E **172**
BLACKHOUSE 1A **140**
Black Ho. La. DH7: Edm 2A **140**
Blackhouse La. NE40: Ryton 1F **79**
Black La. DH6: Whe H 2B **180**
NE5: Newc T 6F **43**
NE9: Gate 5K **99**
NE9: Spri 6K **99**
NE13: Wool 6F **43**
NE20: Mil 1A **30**
NE21: Bla T 5A **80**
Blackpool Pde. NE31: Heb 3A **86**
Black Rd. DH7: B'don 6G **165**
NE31: Heb 6K **65**
SR2: Ryh 2H **133**
Blackrow La. NE9: Gate 4J **99**
NE15: Hed W, Thro 2D **58**
Blackstone Ct. NE21: Bla T 4A **80**
Black Thorn Cl. DH7: B'don 2C **174**
Blackthorn Cl. NE16: Sun 5G **97**
Blackthorn Dr. NE24: News 5G **23**
NE28: W'snd 7G **47**
Blackthorne NE10: Gate 2D **100**
Blackthorne Av. SR8: Pet 6F **173**
Blackthorn Pl. NE4: Newc T 3D **82** (9A **4**)
Blackthorn Way DH4: Hou S 7A **130**
NE63: Ash 5K **11**
Blackwater Ho. SR3: New S 3C **132**
Blackwell Av. NE6: Walk 7D **64**
Blackwood Rd. SR5: C'twn 4F **103**
Bladen St. NE32: Jar 6A **66**
Bladen St. Ind. Est. NE32: Jar 6A **66**
Blagdon Av. NE34: S Shi 5A **68**
Blagdon Cl. NE1: Newc T 1H **83** (5J **5**)
NE61: Mor 7E **8**
Blagdon Ct. NE22: Bed 6A **18**
Blagdon Cres. NE23: Nel V 2G **25**
Blagdon Dr. NE24: News 6G **23**
Blagdon Ter. NE13: Sea B 3D **34**
NE23: Cra 4K **25**
Blaidwood Dr. DH1: Dur 7J **165**
Blair Cl. DH6: Sher 3K **167**
Blair Ct. DH7: B'don 7G **165**
Blake Av. NE16: Whi 7H **81**
Blake Cl. DH9: Stly 3G **125**
BLAKELAW 3J **61**
Blakelaw Rd. NE5: Newc T 3H **61**
(Bonnington Way)
NE5: Newc T 3J **61**
(Cragston Cl.)
Blakemoor Pl. NE5: Newc T 4J **61**
Blake St. SR8: Eas 7D **160**
Blaketown NE23: Seg 2E **36**
Blake Wlk. NE8: Gate 4J **83**
Blanche Gro. SR8: Pet 7B **172**
Blanche Ter. DH9: Tan L 6B **110**
Blanchland NE38: Wash 7J **115**
Blanchland Av. DH1: Dur 5C **154**
NE13: Wide O 5D **34**
NE15: Lem 6C **60**
Blanchland Cl. NE28: W'snd 1H **65**
Blanchland Dr. NE25: H'wll 1K **37**
SR5: S'wck 4E **104**
Blanchland Ter. NE30: N Shi 5H **49**
Blandford Ct. NE4: Newc T 2E **82** (7C **4**)
Blandford Pl. SR7: S'hm 3B **148**
Blandford Rd. NE29: N Shi 3D **48**
Blandford Sq. NE1: Newc T 2E **82** (7C **4**)
(not continuous)
Blandford St. NE1: Newc T 2E **82** (8C **4**)
SR1: Sund 2F **119** (4J **7**)
Blandford Way NE28: W'snd 7H **47**
Bland's Opening DH3: Ches S 6A **128**
Blaxton Pl. NE16: Whi 2F **97**
BLAYDON 3D **80**
Blaydon Av. SR5: C'twn 3G **103**
Blaydon Bank NE21: Bla T 5B **80**
BLAYDON BURN 4A **80**
Blaydon Bus. Cen. NE21: Bla T 3E **80**
Blaydon Bus. Pk. NE21: Bla T 2F **81**
Blaydon Haughs Ind. Est.
NE21: Bla T 2E **80**
Blaydon Highway NE21: Bla T 3C **80**
Blaydon Ind. Pk. NE21: Bla T 3D **80**
Blaydon Station (Rail) 2C **80**
Blaydon Swimming Pool 4E **80**
Blaydon Trade Pk. NE21: Bla T 3E **80**
Blaykeston Cl. SR7: S'hm 1G **147**
Blayney Row NE15: Thro 5G **59**
Bleachfeld NE10: Gate 1D **100**
BLEACH GREEN 5C **80**
Bleach Grn. DH5: Hett H 7G **145**
Bleasdale Cres. DH4: Pen 2B **130**
Bleheim Ct. NE24: News 6H **23**
Blencathra NE30: N Shi 2G **49**
NE37: Wash 2G **115**
Blencathra Way NE21: Bla T 6C **80**
Blenheim NE12: Kil 7B **36**
Blenheim Ct. NE10: Gate 1B **100**
Blenheim Dr. NE22: Bed 5A **18**
Blenheim Gdns. NE61: Peg 3A **10**
Blenheim Pl. NE11: Dun 5A **82**
Blenheim Wlk. NE33: S Shi 2K **67**
Blenkinsop Ct. NE34: S Shi 4H **87**
Blenkinsop Gro. NE32: Jar 3B **86**
Bleinburn M. NE3: Gos 3C **44**
Blenkinsopp Ct. SR8: Pet 2K **181**
Blenkinsop St. NE28: W'snd 3F **65**
Bletchley Av. SR5: C'twn 3F **103**
Blezard Bus. Pk. NE13: Sea B 2D **34**
Blezard Ct. NE21: Bla T 2E **80**
Blind La. DH1: Dur 3K **165** (4A **6**)
DH3: Ches S 3B **128**
DH4: Hou S 5A **130**
SR3: New S 1C **132**
SR8: Eas 5A **160**
Blindy La. DH5: Eas L 2J **157**
Bloemfontein Pl. *DH9: Stly 6H 125*
(off Middles Rd.)
Bloom Av. DH9: Stly 3E **124**
Bloomfield Ct. SR6: Monk 5H **105**
Bloomfield Dr. DH5: W Rai 7D **144**
Bloomsbury Ct. NE3: Gos 1D **62**
Blossomfield Way DH6: Has 1B **170**
Blossom Gro. DH4: Hou S 5B **130**
Blossom St. DH5: Hett H 5H **145**
Blount St. NE6: Walk 7B **64**
Blucher Colliery Rd. NE15: Thro 4B **60**
Blucher Rd. NE12: Kil 3A **46**
NE29: N Shi 2F **67**
Blucher Ter. NE15: Thro 4B **60**
BLUCHER VILLAGE 4B **60**
Blue Anchor Ct. NE1: Newc T 7H **5**
Bluebell Cl. DH8: Lead 6A **122**
NE9: Gate 2K **99**
NE41: Wylam 6J **57**
TS27: B Col 2H **183**
Bluebell Dene NE5: Newc T 7G **43**
Bluebell Way NE34: S Shi 1H **87**
Blueburn Dr. NE12: Kil 7D **36**
Blue Carpet, The 5G **4**
Blue Coat Bldgs. DH1: Dur 2B **166** (2D **6**)
Blue Coat Ct. DH1: Dur 2B **166** (2D **6**)
Blue Ho. Bank DH2: Edm, Pelt 6B **126**
DH9: Edm 6B **126**
Blue Ho. Ct. NE37: Usw 7F **101**
Blue Ho. La. NE37: Wash 7F **101**
SR6: Cle, S'wck 7B **88**
Blue Ho. Rd. NE31: Heb 3H **85**
Blue Quarries Rd. NE9: Gate 1K **99**

Blue Reef Aquarium—Brandling La.

Blue Reef Aquarium .2J 49
Blue Top Cotts. NE23: Cra .4B 26
Blumer St. DH4: Hou S .2A 144
BLYTH .1J 23
Blyth Cl. NE23: Dud .3H 35
Blyth Ct. NE15: Lem .6C 60
NE34: S Shi .1J 87
Blyth Crematorium NE24: Cow .1G 23
Blyth Dr. NE61: Hep .7A 16
Blythe Ter. DH3: Bir .4K 113
Blyth Ind. Est. NE24: Cow .7F 19
Blyth Rd. NE26: Sea S, Whit B .6E 28
Blyth Spartans AFC (Croft Pk.) .3J 23
Blyth Sports Cen. .2H 23
Blyth Sq. SR5: C'twn .4G 103
Blyth St. NE17: C'wl .6A 94
NE25: Sea D .6G 27
SR5: C'twn .4G 103
Blythswood NE2: Newc T .5G 63
Blyth Ter. NE63: Hir .3C 12
Blyton Av. NE34: S Shi .1F 87
SR2: Ryh .2G 133
Bobby Shafto Cvn. Pk. DH9: Beam .7C 112
Bodlewell Ho. SR1: Sund .1G 119 (off High St. E.)
Bodlewell La. SR1: Sund .1G 119
Bodley Cl. NE3: Ken .7K 43
Bodmin Cl. NE28: W'snd .7J 47
Bodmin Ct. NE9: Gate .5J 99
Bodmin Rd. NE29: N Shi .4C 48
Bodmin Sq. SR5: C'twn .3G 103
Bodmin Way NE3: Ken .6B 44
Body Line Health & Fitness Studio .6H 119 (off Ryhope Rd.)
Bodywork Health Club .2F 175
Body Zone Health & Fitness Club .5G 4
Bog Ho's. NE23: E Har .7A 22
Boghouse La. DH9: Stly .6G 111
Bognor St. SR5: C'twn .3F 103
Bog Row DH5: Hett H .7G 145
Bohemia Ter. NE24: Bly .3J 23
Boker La. NE36: E Bol .6H 87
Bolam NE38: Wash .4D 114
Bolam Av. NE24: Bly, Cow .2H 23
NE30: N Shi .3G 49
Bolam Bus. Cen. NE23: Cra .2G 25
Bolam Ct. NE15: Thro .4H 59
Bolam Coyne NE6: Newc T .1A 84 (6P 5)
Bolam Dr. NE63: Hir .5C 12
Bolam Gdns. NE28: W'snd .2B 66
Bolam Gro. NE30: N Shi .3G 49
Bolam Ho. NE4: Newc T .7D 62 (4B 4)
Bolam Pl. NE22: Bed .6A 18
Bolam Rd. NE12: Kil .1A 46
Bolams Bldgs. DH9: Tan L .7A 110
Bolam St. NE6: Newc T .1A 84
NE8: Gate .6D 82
SR8: Eas .7D 160
Bolam Way NE6: Newc T .1A 84 (6P 5)
NE25: Sea D .7G 27
Bolbec Rd. NE4: Newc T .6A 62
Bolburn NE10: Gate .7E 84
BOLDON .6J 87
Boldon Bus. Pk. NE35: Bol C .6E 86 (Brooklands Way)
NE35: Bol C .7E 86 (Didcot Way)
Boldon Cl. NE28: W'snd .7H 47
BOLDON COLLIERY .5E 86
Boldon Colliery Workshops .5F 87
Boldon Dr. NE36: W Bol .7F 87
Boldon Gdns. NE9: Gate .4A 100
Boldon Ho. DH1: Dur .2A 154
Boldon La. NE34: S Shi .7H 67 (not continuous)
NE36: E Bol .6J 87
NE36: S Shi .5J 87
SR6: Cle .5A 88
Boldon UGC Cinema .6E 86
Bolingbroke Rd. NE29: N Shi .6D 48
Bolingbroke St.
NE6: Newc T .7J 63 (3M 5)
NE33: S Shi .3K 67
Bollihope Dr. SR3: Sund .6D 118
Bolsover St. NE63: Hir .4B 12
Bolsover Ter. NE61: Peg .3B 10
NE63: Hir .4B 12
Bolton Cl. DH1: Dur .4A 154
Bolton's Bungs. NE17: C'wl .7K 93
BOMARSUND .3A 18
Bonaventure DH4: Pen .1C 130
Bonchester Cl. NE22: Bed .6H 17
Bonchester Ct. NE28: W'snd .7J 47
Bonchester Pl. NE23: Cra .2B 26
Bond Cl. SR5: S'wck .6E 104
Bond Ct. NE4: Newc T .1A 82
Bondene Av. NE10: Gate .6C 84
Bondene Av. W. NE10: Gate .6B 84
Bondene Way NE23: Cra .7K 21
Bondfield Cl. NE28: W'snd .2K 65
Bondfield Gdns. NE10: Gate .6E 84
Bondgate Cl. NE46: Hex .3D 70
Bondgate Ct. NE46: Hex .2D 70
Bondicarr Pl. NE5: Newc T .4K 61
Bondicar Ter. NE24: Bly .2H 23
Bond St. NE4: Newc T .1K 81
Bone La. DH9: Dip .7H 109
Bonemill La. NE38: Wash .1C 128
Bonner's Fld. SR6: Monk .7F 105 (1J 7)
Bonnington Way NE5: Newc T .3H 61
Bonnivard Gdns. NE23: Seg .2E 36
Bonsall Ct. NE34: S Shi .1K 87
Booths Rd. NE63: Ash .3J 11
Booth St. NE10: Gate .6B 84
SR4: Sund .2C 118
Bootle St. SR5: C'twn .4G 103
Bordeaux Cl. SR3: New S .3A 132
Border Rd. NE28: W'snd .4F 65
Boreham Cl. NE28: W'snd .7H 47
Borehole La. NE61: Mor .6G 9
Borodin Av. SR5: C'twn .4F 103
Borough and Scotch Gills Nature Reserve .7C 8
Borough Ct. SR1: Sund .1G 119
Borough Rd. NE29: N Shi .7G 49
NE32: Jar .7B 66
NE34: S Shi .1B 88
SR1: Sund .2F 119 (4K 7)
Borrowdale DH3: Bir .7B 114
DH8: Lead .5B 122
NE16: Whi .7K 81
NE37: Wash .7G 101
Borrowdale Av. NE6: Walk .6D 64
NE24: Cow .1E 22
SR6: Monk .2E 104
Borrowdale Cl. NE36: E Bol .6J 87
Borrowdale Cres. DH4: Pen .1A 130
NE21: Bla T .6B 80
Borrowdale Dr. DH1: Carr .7G 155
Borrowdale Gdns. NE9: Gate .4K 99
Borrowdale Ho. NE34: S Shi .1J 87
Borrowdale St. DH5: Hett H .1G 157
Boscombe Dr. NE28: W'snd .1G 65
Boston Av. NE7: Newc T .7K 45
NE38: Wash .2G 115 (not continuous)
Boston Cl. NE28: W'snd .7H 47
Boston Ct. NE12: Longb .4D 46
Boston Cres. SR5: C'twn .3E 102
Boston St. SR5: C'twn .3E 102
SR8: Eas .7D 160
Boswell Av. NE34: S Shi .3H 87
Bosworth NE12: Kil .7B 36
Bosworth Gdns. NE6: Newc T .3A 64
BOTHAL .5D 10
Bothal Av. NE62: Chop .1G 17
Bothal Bank NE61: Peg .5D 10
Bothal Cl. NE24: Bly .2G 23
NE61: Peg .4A 10
Bothal Cotts. NE63: Ash .3H 11
Bothal St. NE6: Newc T .7B 64
Bothal Ter. NE62: Chop .7K 11
NE63: Ash .3H 11
Botham Ho. NE29: N Shi .2D 66
Bottle Bank NE8: Gate .2G 83 (8H 5)
Bottlehouse St. NE6: Newc T .2A 84
Bottle Works Rd. SR7: S'hm .3C 148
Boulby Cl. SR3: New S .2E 132
Boulevard, The NE11: Dun .5J 81
NE12: Longb .6J 45
Boulmer Av. NE23: Cra .7K 21
Boulmer Cl. NE3: Ken .4B 44
Boulmer Ct. DH2: Ches S .7A 128
Boulmer Gdns. NE13: Wide O .5D 34
Boulsworth Rd. NE29: N Shi .3E 48
Boult Ter. DH4: Hou S .3B 130
Boundary Cl. DH7: Ush M .3C 164
Boundary Dr. NE61: Mor .1G 15
Boundary Gdns. NE7: Newc T .2J 63
BOUNDARY HOUSES .5A 130
Boundary Ho's DH4: Hou S .4K 129
Boundary La. DH8: Shot B, W'stll .5A 106
Boundary Mill Stores
NE27: Shir .2K 47
Boundary St. SR5: S'wck .5E 104
Boundary Way NE26: Sea S .4D 28
Bourdon Ho. SR1: Sund .2F 119 (5K 7)
Bourne Av. NE4: Newc T .6A 62
Bourne Ct. DH9: Stly .2G 125 (not continuous)
Bournemouth Ct. NE28: W'snd .7H 47
Bournemouth Dr. SR7: Mur .4H 147
Bournemouth Gdns. NE5: Newc T .2F 61
NE26: Whit B .5F 39
Bournemouth Pde. NE31: Heb .3A 86 (not continuous)
Bournemouth Rd. NE29: N Shi .7C 48
Bourne St. SR8: Eas .7D 160
Bourne Ter. DH9: Ann P .5K 123
Bourn Lea DH4: Hou S .4A 130
BOURNMOOR .6J 129
Bournmoor DH4: Hou S .6J 129
Bourtree Cl. NE28: W'snd .1G 65
Bowbank Cl. SR3: Sund .6D 118
BOWBURN .5H 177
Bowburn Av. SR5: C'twn .5J 103
Bowburn Cl. NE10: Gate .7G 85
Bowburn Nth. Ind. Est. DH6: Bow .4G 177
Bowburn Sth. Ind. Est. DH6: Bow .5G 177
Bower St. SR6: Monk .3F 105
Bower, The NE32: Jar .6B 86
Bowes Av. DH5: Eas L .2H 157
SR7: Mur .4G 147
Bowes Cl. NE16: Sun .5H 97
Bowes Ct. DH1: Dur .4B 154
NE3: Gos .7G 45
NE24: Bly .2J 23
Bowes Cres. NE16: Burn .7D 96
Bowes Ho. SR3: E Her .2K 131 (off Castle Grn.)
Bowes Lea DH4: Hou S .5K 129
Bowes Lyon Cl. NE39: Row G .7H 95
Bowes Lyon Ct. NE9: Gate .6H 83
Bowes Manor Equestrian Cen. .1B 114
Bowes Railway Cen. .5C 100
Bowes St. NE3: Gos .7G 45
NE24: Bly .2H 23 (not continuous)
Bowes Ter. DH9: Dip .1H 123
Bowesville NE16: Burn .3B 110
Bowes Wlk. NE12: Longb .5A 46
Bowfell Av. NE5: Newc T .1K 61
Bowfell Cl. NE5: Newc T .2K 61
Bowfell Gdns. NE62: Chop .7J 11
Bowfield Av. NE3: Gos .3E 44
Bowland Cres. NE21: Bla T .4C 80
Bowland Ter. NE21: Bla T .3C 80
Bow La. DH1: Dur .3A 166 (4C 6)
Bowler's Hill NE43: Mic .7B 76
Bowlynn Cl. SR3: New S .3A 132
Bowman Dr. NE23: Dud .3K 35
Bowman Pl. NE33: S Shi .4J 67
Bowman Sq. NE63: Hir .5B 12
Bowman St. SR6: Whit .5H 89
Bowmont Dr. DH9: Tan L .1C 124
NE23: Cra .2B 26
Bowmont Wlk. DH2: Ches S .1J 141
Bowness Av. NE28: W'snd .6J 47
Bowness Cl. NE36: E Bol .7J 87
SR8: Pet .5C 172
Bowness Pl. NE9: Gate .3K 99
Bowness Rd. NE5: Newc T .4G 61
NE16: Whi .7J 81
Bowness St. SR5: C'twn .3G 103
Bowness Ter. NE28: W'snd .7J 47
Bowsden Ct. NE3: Gos .7G 45
Bowsden Ter. NE3: Gos .7G 45
Bow St. DH6: Bow .4H 177
DH6: Thor .1K 179
Bow St. E. DH6: Thor .1K 179
Bow St. W. DH6: Thor .1K 179
Bowtrees SR2: Sund .5F 119
Boxlaw NE9: Gate .2A 100
Boyd Cres. NE28: W'snd .3G 65
Boyd Rd. NE28: W'snd .3G 65
Boyd St. DH1: Dur .4B 166 (5D 6)
DH8: Con .1J 135
NE2: Newc T .7H 63 (4K 5)
NE15: Thro .5J 59
SR8: Eas .7D 160
Boyd Ter. DH9: Stly .4E 124
NE5: Newc T .2F 61
NE15: Thro .4B 60
Boyne Ct. DH7: B'don .7F 165
NE24: Bly .1J 23 (off Regent St.)
Boyne Gdns. NE27: Shir .1J 47
Boyne Ter. NE37: Usw .7G 101
Boyntons DH2: Plaw .6H 141
Boystones Ct. NE37: Wash .2F 115
Brabourne Gdns. NE29: N Shi .3F 49
Brabourne St. NE34: S Shi .7J 67
Bracken Av. NE28: W'snd .7G 47
Brackenbeds Cl. DH2: Pelt .3G 127
Brackenbeds La. DH2: Ous, Pelt .2H 127 (not continuous)
Brackenburn Cl. DH4: Hou S .1C 144
Bracken Cl. DH9: Stly .3E 124
NE13: Din .5H 33
Bracken Ct. DH7: Ush M .1C 164 (not continuous)
Brackendale Ct. TS28: Win .7H 181
Brackendale Rd. DH1: Carr .1H 167
Brackendene Dr. NE9: Gate .2G 99
Brackendene Pk. NE9: Gate .2G 99
Bracken Dr. NE11: Dun .1B 98
Bracken Fld. Rd. DH1: Dur .6K 153
Brackenfield Rd. NE3: Gos .1D 62
Bracken Hill SR8: Pet .7H 171
Brackenhill Av. DH6: Shot C .6G 171
Bracken Hill Bus. Pk. SR8: Pet .7H 171
Brackenlaw NE9: Gate .3A 100
Brackenpath M. NE3: Gos .3D 44
Bracken Pl. NE4: Newc T .6K 61
Bracken Ridge NE61: Mor .5C 8
Brackenridge NE16: Burn .2J 109
Brackenside NE3: Gos .3E 44
Bracken Way NE40: Ryton .3E 78
Brackenway NE37: Wash .1F 115
Brackenwood Gro. SR2: Sund .6E 118
Brackley NE37: Usw .6J 101
Brackley Gro. NE29: N Shi .1D 66
Bracknell Cl. SR3: New S .1E 132
Bracknell Gdns. NE5: Cha P .4B 60
Brack Ter. NE10: Gate .4F 85
Bradbury Cl. DH9: Tan L .1C 124
NE10: Gate .7G 85
Bradbury Ct. NE20: Pon .5K 31 (off Thornhill Rd.)
NE25: Sea D .4H 27
Bradbury Pl. NE25: Sea D .4H 27
Bradford Av. NE28: W'snd .7H 47
SR5: C'twn .3G 103
Bradford Cres. DH1: Dur .1D 166
Bradley Av. DH5: Hou S .4E 144
NE34: S Shi .7C 68
Bradley Bungs. DH8: Lead .3A 122
Bradley Cl. DH2: Ous .6F 113
Bradley Cotts. DH8: Lead .3A 122
Bradley Fell La. NE41: Wylam .4A 78
Bradley Fell Rd. NE40: G'sde, Pru .6J 77
NE42: Pru .6J 77
Bradley Gdns. NE41: Wylam .2B 78
Bradley Lodge Dr. DH9: Dip .1J 123
Bradley Rd. NE42: Pru .3H 77
Bradley St. DH8: Lead .5A 122
SR8: Eas .7D 160
Bradley Ter. DH5: Eas L .2J 157
DH9: Dip .2J 123
Bradley Vw. NE40: Ryton .3D 78
Bradley Workshops Ind. Est.
DH8: Lead .5K 121
Bradman Dr. DH3: Ches S .7C 128
Bradman Sq. SR5: C'twn .3G 103
Bradman St. SR5: C'twn .3G 103
Bradshaw Sq. SR5: C'twn .4G 103
Bradshaw St. SR5: C'twn .4G 103
Bradwell Rd. NE3: Ken .7A 44
Bradwell Way DH4: Hou S .4C 130
Brady & Martin Ct.
NE1: Newc T .7G 63 (3G 4)
Brady Sq. NE38: Wash .4K 115
Brady St. SR4: Sund .1B 118
Braebridge Pl. NE3: Ken .2B 62
Braefell Ct. NE37: Wash .2F 115
Braemar Ct. DH8: Con .6E 120
NE10: Gate .4F 85
Braemar Dr. NE34: S Shi .5C 68
Braemar Gdns. NE25: Whit B .7C 38
SR3: E Her .3J 131
SR3: Sund .5D 118
Braemar Ter. SR8: Pet .6F 173
Braeside DH7: B'hpe .6D 138
DH7: Edm .3D 140
NE11: Dun .7B 82
SR2: Sund .4D 118
Braeside Cl. NE30: N Shi .1G 49
Braeside Ter. NE26: Whit B .7J 39
Braes, The DH8: C'sde .1E 134
Brae, The SR2: Sund .2D 118
Braham Rd. NE29: N Shi .1D 66
Braintree Gdns. NE3: Ken .1B 62
Braithwaite Rd. SR8: Pet .6D 172
Brakespeare Pl. SR8: Pet .7C 172
Brama Teams Ind. Pk. NE8: Gate .5D 82
Bramble Cl. NE24: News .5G 23
Bramble Dykes NE15: Newc T .1H 81
Bramblelaw NE9: Gate .3A 100
Brambles Leisure Cen. .2J 67
Brambles, The DH3: Bir .2B 114
NE40: Ryton .1F 79
Brambling Lea NE22: Bed .6A 18
Bramhall Dr. NE38: Wash .1F 129
Bramham Ct. NE34: S Shi .1A 88
Bramhope Grn. NE9: Gate .5K 99
Bramley Cl. SR4: Sund .5G 117
Bramley Ct. NE7: Newc T .2C 64
Brampton Av. NE6: Walk .2D 84
Brampton Ct. NE23: Cra .2A 26
SR8: Eas .1K 171
Brampton Gdns. NE9: Gate .4J 99
NE15: Thro .3H 59
NE28: W'snd .1A 66
Brampton Pl. NE29: N Shi .7D 48
Brampton Rd. NE34: S Shi .1G 87
Bramwell Ct. NE3: Gos .7F 45
Bramwell Rd. SR2: Sund .3G 119
Bramwell Ter. DH8: Con .5J 121
BRANCEPETH .5A 174
Brancepeth Av. DH4: Hou S .1A 144
NE4: Newc T .2A 82
Brancepeth Castle .5A 174
Brancepeth Chare SR8: Pet .2K 181
Brancepeth Cl. DH1: Dur .5B 154
DH7: Ush M .3E 164
NE15: Lem .6C 60
Brancepeth Rd. NE31: Heb .6K 65
NE38: Wash .4E 114
Brancepeth Ter. NE32: Jar .3B 86
Brancepeth Vw. DH7: B'don .2B 174
BRANCH END .7K 75
Branch End Ter. NE43: Stoc .7K 75
Branch St. NE21: Bla T .5B 80
Brand Av. NE4: Newc T .6A 62
Brandling Ct. NE2: Newc T .5H 63 (1J 5)
NE10: Gate .5B 84 (off William St.)
NE34: S Shi .2C 88
Brandling Dr. NE3: Gos .3F 45
Brandling La. NE10: Gate .5B 84

Brandling M.—Brooklands

Brandling M. NE3: Gos 3F 45
Brandling Pk. NE2: Newc T 5F 63 (1F 4)
Brandling Pl. NE10: Gate 5B 84
Brandling Pl. Sth.
NE2: Newc T 5G 63 (1F 4)
Brandling St. NE8: Gate 2G 83 (8J 5)
SR6: Monk 5G 105
(not continuous)
Brandling St. Sth. SR6: Monk 6G 105
Brandlings Way SR8: Pet 5B 172
Brandling Ter. NE30: N Shi 6H 49
BRANDLING VILLAGE 5G 63 (1G 4)
BRANDON 1D 174
Brandon Av. NE27: Shir 1J 47
Brandon Cl. DH2: Ches S 1H 141
DH4: Hou S 3D 144
NE21: Bla T 6A 80
NE24: Cow 1F 23
Brandon Gdns. NE9: Gate 4B 100
Brandon Gro. NE2: Newc T 6H 63 (1K 5)
Brandon Ho. DH7: B'don 2C 174
Brandon La. DH7: B'don 1C 174
DH7: New B 7F 163
DL15: New B 7F 163
(not continuous)
Brandon Rd. DH7: Esh W 4E 162
NE3: Ken 6B 44
NE29: N Shi 6D 48
Brandon Vw. DH7: Ush M 4E 164
BRANDON VILLAGE 7C 164
Brandy La. NE37: Wash 1F 115
Brandywell NE10: Gate 1D 100
Brannen St. NE29: N Shi 7G 49
Bransdale DH4: Pen 1J 129
Bransdale Av. SR6: Monk 7H 89
Branston St. SR5: S'wck 5D 104
Branton Av. NE31: Heb 3H 85
Brantwood DH2: Ches S 6H 127
Brantwood Av. NE25: Whit B 7D 38
Brantwood Ct. NE21: Bla T 4D 80
Branxton Cres. NE6: Walk 1D 84
Brasher St. NE33: S Shi 1J 67
BRASSIDE 3D 154
Brass Thill DH1: Dur 3K 165 (3A 6)
Braunespath Est. DH7: New B 4B 164
Bray Cl. NE28: W'snd 7H 47
Braydon Dr. NE29: N Shi 2E 66
Brayside NE32: Jar 5D 86
Breackneck Stairs NE1: Newc T 8F 4
Breamish Dr. NE38: Wash 7D 114
Breamish Ho. NE1: Newc T 1J 83 (5L 5)
Breamish Quays NE1: Newc T 1J 83 (5L 5)
Breamish St. NE1: Newc T 1J 83 (5K 5)
NE32: Jar 1A 86
Brearley Way NE10: Gate 6A 84
Breckenbeds Rd. NE9: Gate 3G 99
Brecken Ct. NE9: Gate 3G 99
Brecken Way DH7: B'don 1E 174
Brecon Cl. NE5: Newc T 1H 61
NE63: N Sea 6C 12
SR8: Pet 7K 171
Brecon Pl. DH2: Ous 1H 127
Brecon Rd. DH1: Dur 4C 154
Bredon Cl. NE38: Wash 5F 115
Brendale Av. NE5: Newc T 2D 60
Brendon Pl. SR8: Pet 5K 171
BRENKLEY 1K 33
Brenkley Av. NE27: Shir 2J 47
Brenkley Cl. NE13: Din 4H 33
Brenkley Ct. NE13: Sea B 3D 34
Brenkley Way NE13: Sea B 2D 34
Brenlynn Cl. SR3: New S 3A 132
Brennan Cl. NE15: Newc T 7H 61
NE63: N Sea 4E 12
Brentford Av. SR5: C'twn 4G 103
Brentford Sq. SR5: C'twn 4G 103
Brentwood Av. NE2: Newc T 3F 63
NE64: Newb S 2H 13
Brentwood Cl. NE25: Sea D 1J 37
Brentwood Ct. DH9: Stly 3J 125
Brentwood Gdns. NE2: Newc T 3F 63
NE16: Whi 2H 97
SR3: Sund 5D 118
Brentwood Gro. NE28: W'snd 4H 65
Brentwood Pl. NE33: S Shi 3K 67
Brentwood Rd. DH4: Hou S 4A 130
Brettanby Gdns. NE40: Ryton 7G 59
Brettanby Rd. NE10: Gate 7A 84
Brett Cl. NE7: Newc T 2B 64
Brettonby Av. NE43: Stoc 7K 75
Bretton Gdns. NE7: Newc T 3A 64
Brewers La. NE29: N Shi 3C 66
Brewer Ter. SR2: Ryh 3J 133
Brewery Bank NE16: Swa 5G 81
Brewery Bond NE29: N Shi 1H 67
Brewery La. NE10: Gate 4B 84
NE16: Swa 5G 81
(off Brewery Bank)
NE20: Pon 5J 31
NE33: S Shi 3H 67
Brewery Sq. DH9: Stly 2F 125
Brewery Stables *NE1: Newc T 6C 4*
(off Blandford Sq.)
Brewery St. *NE24: Bly 1K 23*
(off Sussex St.)
Brewhouse Bank NE30: N Shi 6J 49
Brian Ct. NE26: Whit B 6F 39
Briar Av. DH4: Hou S 2D 144
DH7: B'don 2C 174
NE26: Whit B 4F 39
Briar Bank DH1: Dur 3K 153
Briar Cl. DH2: Plaw 7H 141
DH4: Hou S 5K 129
(Boundary Houses)
DH4: Hou S 1J 143
(Woodstone Village)
NE21: Bla T 4A 80
NE28: W'snd 7G 47
Briar Dale DH8: Con 3K 135
Briardale NE13: Din 4H 33
NE22: Bed 7G 17
Briardale Rd. NE24: Cow 2E 22
Briardene DH1: Dur 3K 165 (4A 6)
DH7: Esh W 3C 162
DH7: Lan 7J 137
NE16: Burn 2J 109
NE63: Ash 5K 11
Briardene Cl. SR3: E Her 3J 131
Briardene Cres. NE3: Ken 2C 62
Briardene Dr. NE10: Gate 6H 85
Briar Edge NE12: Longb 4B 46
Briarfield NE38: Wash 7H 115
Briarfield Rd. NE3: Gos 1D 62
Briar Glen SR7: Mur 7B 146
Briarhill DH2: Ches S 4J 127
Briar La. NE15: Thro 4J 59
Briar Lea DH4: Hou S 5K 129
DH7: Wit G 2D 152
Briarlea NE61: Hep 4A 16
Briar M. DH8: Shot B 4F 121
Briar Pl. NE15: Newc T 1G 81
Briar Rd. DH1: Carr 7H 155
NE39: Row G 5H 95
Briarside DH8: Shot B 4F 121
NE5: Newc T 2G 61
Briars, The SR5: C'twn 6H 103
Briarsyde NE12: Longb 6C 46
Briarsyde Cl. NE16: Whi 2E 96
Briar Ter. NE16: Burn 2C 110
Briar Va. NE25: Whit B 1D 48
Briarwood NE23: Dud 3K 35
Briarwood Av. DH2: Pelt 6G 127
NE3: Gos 6G 45
Briarwood Cres. NE6: Walk 4D 64
NE11: Dun 6B 82
Briarwood Rd. NE24: Bly 3K 23
Briarwood St. DH4: Hou S 1J 143
Briary Gdns. DH8: Shot B 3E 120
Briary, The DH8: Shot B 3F 121
NE15: Thro 3G 59
Brick Gth. DH5: Eas L 3H 157
Brick Row SR2: Ryh 2G 133
Bridekirk NE37: Wash 1G 115
(not continuous)
Bridge App. SR5: Sund 6C 104
Bridge Cotts. NE23: Dud 3K 35
Bridge Ct. DH6: Shad 5E 168
Bridge Cres. SR1: Sund 1F 119 (2J 7)
BRIDGE END 7E 50
Bridge End DH3: Ches S 5A 128
DH6: Coxh 7K 177
Bri. End Ind. Est. NE46: B End 7E 50
BRIDGEHILL 5E 120
Bridge Ho. SR1: Sund 3J 7
Bridgemere Dr. DH1: Dur 5J 153
Bridge Pk. NE3: Gos 4E 44
Bridge Rd. DH6: Shot C 7E 170
Bridge Rd. Sth NE29: N Shi 1E 66
Bridge Row DH1: Carr 5H 155
Bridges Shop. Cen., The
SR1: Sund 2E 118 (4H 7)
Bridges, The SR1: Sund 3H 7
Bridge St. DH1: Dur 2K 165 (2A 6)
DH7: Lang P 4J 151
DH8: Con 6F 121
DH9: Stly 5E 124
NE8: Gate 2G 83 (8H 5)
NE13: Sea B 3D 34
NE21: Bla T 2B 80
NE24: Bly 1J 23
(not continuous)
NE61: Mor 7F 9
NE64: Newb S 3J 13
SR1: Sund 1F 119 (3J 7)
Bridges Vw. NE8: Gate 4F 83
Bridge Ter. NE22: Bed 5A 18
NE27: Shir 7K 37
NE62: Chop 7K 11
Bridgewater Cl. NE15: Lem 6C 60
NE28: W'snd 1G 65
Bridgewater Rd. NE37: Wash 1J 115
Bridge Way DH7: Lang P 5K 151
Bridle Path NE3: Gos 5G 45
NE36: E Bol 7J 87
SR3: E Her 1J 131
Bridle, The NE27: Shir 2B 48
Bridlington Av. NE9: Gate 4H 99
Bridlington Cl. NE28: W'snd 7H 47
Bridlington Pde. NE31: Heb 3A 86
Bridport Rd. NE29: N Shi 3D 48
Brier Av. SR8: Pet 4D 172
Brier Dene Cl. NE26: Whit B 3F 39
Brierdene Ct. NE26: Whit B 3E 38
Brier Dene Cres. NE26: Whit B 3E 38
Brierdene Rd. NE26: Whit B 2F 39
Brierdene Vw. NE26: Whit B 3E 38
Brierfield Gro. SR4: Sund 4K 117
Brierley Cl. NE24: Cow 2F 23
Brierley Rd. NE24: Cow 2F 23
Briermede Av. NE9: Gate 3H 99
Briermede Pk. NE9: Gate 3H 99
Brierville DH1: Dur 3K 165 (4A 6)
Brieryside NE5: Newc T 4K 61
Briery Va. Cl. SR2: Sund 3E 118 (7H 7)
Briery Va. Rd. SR2: Sund 3E 118 (7H 7)
Brigham Av. NE3: Ken 2A 62
Brigham Pl. NE33: S Shi 2J 67
Brightlea DH3: Bir 3C 114
Brightman Rd. NE29: N Shi 6G 49
Brighton Cl. NE28: W'snd 7J 47
Brighton Gdns. NE8: Gate 7G 83
Brighton Gro. NE4: Newc T 7C 62 (2A 4)
NE26: Whit B 5F 39
NE29: N Shi 6F 49
Brighton Pde. NE31: Heb 3A 86
Brighton Rd. NE8: Gate 5F 83
Brighton Ter. DH6: Sher 3D 168
Bright St. DH8: Con 5H 121
NE33: S Shi 3K 67
SR6: Monk 6F 105
Brignall Cl. DH3: Gt Lum 3F 143
Brignall Gdns. NE15: Newc T 6G 61
Brignall Ri. SR3: Sund 6D 118
Brigside Cotts. NE13: Sea B 3E 34
(not continuous)
Brindley Rd. NE37: Wash 2H 115
SR8: Pet 6H 171
Brinkburn DH2: Ches S 6J 127
NE38: Wash 6J 115
Brinkburn Av. NE3: Gos 6D 44
NE8: Gate 6G 83
NE16: Swa 6G 81
NE23: Cra 4A 26
NE24: Bly 3K 23
Brinkburn Cl. NE6: Newc T 1K 83 (4P 5)
NE21: Bla T 6A 80
Brinkburn Ct. NE6: Newc T 4P 5
NE30: N Shi 6H 49
Brinkburn Cres. DH4: Hou S 7C 130
NE63: Hir 3D 12
Brinkburn Gdns. NE62: Chop 7H 11
Brinkburn La. NE6: Newc T 4P 5
Brinkburn Pl. NE6: Newc T 7K 63 (4P 5)
Brinkburn Sq. NE6: Newc T 1K 83 (5P 5)
(not continuous)
Brinkburn St. NE6: Newc T 1K 83 (5P 5)
(not continuous)
NE28: W'snd 4C 66
NE34: S Shi 1H 87
SR4: Sund 3C 118
Brisbane Av. NE34: S Shi 3F 87
Brisbane Ct. NE8: Gate 3G 83 (10H 5)
Brisbane St. SR5: C'twn 4G 103
Brislee Av. NE30: N Shi 5J 49
(not continuous)
Brislee Gdns. NE3: Ken 1A 62
Bristlecone SR3: New S 4A 132
Bristol Av. NE37: Usw 7F 101
SR5: C'twn 4F 103
Bristol Dr. NE28: W'snd 7H 47
Bristol St. NE25: Sea D 5G 27
Bristol Ter. NE4: Newc T 2C 82
Bristol Wlk. NE25: Sea D 4H 27
Bristol Way NE32: Jar 5C 86
Britannia Ct. NE4: Newc T 2C 82
Britannia Pl. NE4: Newc T 1C 82
Britannia Rd. SR3: New S 2C 132
Britannia Ter. DH4: Hou S 2A 144
Briton Ter. DH8: Con 6G 121
Britten Cl. DH9: Stly 4G 125
Brixham Av. NE9: Gate 4H 99
Brixham Cl. SR7: Mur 4J 147
Brixham Cres. NE32: Jar 1D 86
Brixham Gdns. SR3: Sund 5D 118
Broadbank NE10: Gate 6F 85
Broad Chare NE1: Newc T 1G 83 (6H 5)
Broad Cl., The SR8: Pet 6B 172
Broadfield Pl. NE34: S Shi 1K 87
Broadfield Wlk. NE5: Newc T 1G 61
Broad Gth. NE1: Newc T 2G 83 (7H 5)
Broadgate Rd. DH7: Esh W 1J 163
Broadgates NE46: Hex 2D 70
Broad Landing NE33: S Shi 2H 67
Broadlands SR6: Cle 7C 88
Broadlea NE10: Gate 6F 85
Broadmayne Av. SR4: Sund 4K 117
Broadmayne Gdns. SR4: Sund 4K 117
Broad Mdws. NE3: Ken 2B 62
SR2: Sund 4D 118 (7F 7)
Broadmeadows DH6: Bow 5J 177
NE38: Wash 6J 115
SR3: E Her 3H 131
Broadmeadows Cl. NE16: Swa 5G 81
Broadmead Way NE15: Newc T 1F 81
Broadmires Ter. DH2: Plaw 6G 141
Broadoak NE10: Gate 5F 85
Broadoak Dr. DH7: Lan 6J 137
Broad Oak Ter. NE17: C'wl 6K 93
Broadpark NE10: Gate 6F 85
Broadpool Grn. NE16: Whi 1J 97
Broadpool Ter. NE16: Whi 1J 97
(Broom Ter.)
NE16: Whi 1J 97
(Southfield Ter.)
Broad Rd. TS27: B Col 3K 183
Broadshaw Wlk. NE15: Thro 4H 59
Broadsheath Ter. SR5: S'wck 6B 104
(not continuous)
Broadside NE10: Gate 6F 85
Broadstairs Ct. SR4: Sund 4K 117
Broadstone Gro. NE5: Cha P 4C 60
Broadstone Way NE28: W'snd 1G 65
Broadviews DH3: Gt Lum 2E 142
Broadview Vs. DH6: Sher 3A 168
Broadwater NE10: Gate 5F 85
Broadway DH3: Ches S 4A 128
DH8: Con 3K 135
NE9: Gate 1K 99
NE15: Lem 6D 60
NE16: Whi 2F 97
NE20: Pon 1G 41
NE24: Bly 3J 23
NE62: Chop 1H 17
Broadway Circ. NE24: Bly 2H 23
Broadway Cl. NE30: N Shi 1H 49
Broadway Ct. NE3: Gos 5E 44
NE28: W'snd 6J 47
Broadway Cres. NE24: Bly 3J 23
Broadway E. NE3: Gos 5E 44
Broadway Gdns. NE46: Hex 1B 70
Broadway, The DH4: Hou S 2E 144
NE30: N Shi 1H 49
NE33: S Shi 3B 68
SR4: Sund 5H 117
(not continuous)
SR5: C'twn 7G 103
Broadway Vs. NE15: Newc T 1H 81
Broadway W. NE3: Gos 5D 44
Broadwell Ct. NE3: Newc T 1H 63
Broadwood Rd. NE15: Newc T 6F 61
Broadwood Vw. DH3: Ches S 7B 128
DH8: Shot B 4E 120
Brockenhurst Dr. SR4: Sund 6G 117
Brock Farm Ct. NE30: N Shi 6G 49
Brockhampton Cl. NE35: Bol C 4E 86
Brock La. NE22: E Sle, W Sle 2D 18
Brockley Av. NE34: S Shi 2H 87
Brockley St. SR5: C'twn 4G 103
Brockley Ter. NE35: Bol C 5E 86
BROCKLEY WHINS 3F 87
Brockley Whins Station (Metro) 4F 87
Brock Sq. NE6: Newc T 1K 83 (5P 5)
Brock St. NE6: Newc T 1K 83 (5P 5)
Brockwade NE10: Gate 2D 100
Brockwell TS27: B Col 2G 183
Brockwell Cen., The NE23: Cra 2K 25
Brockwell Cl. NE21: Bla T 5A 80
Brockwell Ct. NE24: Bly 4G 23
Brockwell Dr. NE39: Row G 4J 95
Brockwell Ho. NE5: Newc T 3J 61
Brockwell La. DH8: Con 5G 121
Brockwell Rd. NE38: Wash 3D 114
Brockwell St. NE24: Bly 5G 23
Brockwood Cl. NE63: Ash 6K 11
Broderick Ter. DH4: Hou S 6D 130
Brodie Cl. NE34: S Shi 2J 87
Brodrick Cl. NE3: Ken 7K 43
Brodrick St. NE33: S Shi 2K 67
Brokenheugh NE5: Newc T 4F 61
Bromarsh Ct. SR6: Monk 6H 105
Bromford Rd. NE3: Ken 7K 43
Bromley Av. NE25: Whit B 1E 48
Bromley Cl. DH1: H Shin 1F 177
Bromley Ct. NE3: Ken 5K 43
Bromley Gdns. NE24: News 4J 23
NE28: W'snd 7H 47
Brompton Cl. DH2: Ous 6G 113
Brompton Pl. NE11: Dun 6C 82
Brompton Ter. DH4: Hou S 5D 130
Bromsgrove Cl. NE28: W'snd 7H 47
Bronte Pl. DH9: Stly 5H 125
Bronte St. NE8: Gate 5K 83
Brookbank Cl. SR3: New S 4B 132
Brook Ct. NE22: Bed 7J 17
Brookdale DH1: Carr 7J 155
Brooke Av. NE16: Whi 6G 81
NE35: Bol C 6H 87
Brooke Cl. DH9: Stly 3G 125
Brooke Ho. DH5: Hou S 3E 144
Brookes Ri. DH7: B'don 7F 165
Brooke St. SR5: Monk 7E 104 (1H 7)
Brookes Wlk. NE34: S Shi 4G 87
Brookfield NE3: Gos 3D 62
Brookfield Cres. NE5: Cha P 4C 60
Brookfield Ter. *NE10: Gate 5E 84*
(off Shields Rd.)
Brook Gdns. NE26: Whit B 5H 39
Brookland Dr. NE12: Kil 1C 46
Brookland Rd. SR4: Sund 2B 118
Brooklands NE20: Pon 1E 40

Brooklands Way—Buston Ter.

Brooklands Way NE35: Bol C 6D 86
Brookland Ter. NE29: N Shi 3B 48
(not continuous)
Brooklyn St. SR7: Mur 1F 159
Brooklyn Ter. SR7: Mur 1F 159
Brook Rd. SR4: Sund 3D 118
Brookside DH5: Hou S 4D 144
DH7: Sac 6E 140
DH7: Wit G 3D 152
NE23: Dud 4J 35
Brookside Av. NE13: Bru V 6C 34
NE24: Cow 2F 23
Brookside Cotts. SR2: Sund 4E 118
Brookside Cres. NE5: Newc T 4K 61
Brookside Gdns. SR2: Sund 4E 118 (7G 7)
Brookside Ter. SR2: Sund 4E 118 (7H 7)
Brookside Wood NE38: Wash 7H 115
Brookside Works DH9: Stly 7J 125
Brooksmead NE28: W'snd 1E 64
Brook St. NE6: Newc T 1B 84
NE26: Whit B 6H 39
Brookvale Av. NE3: Ken 1B 62
Brook Vw. DH7: Lan 7J 137
SR7: S'hm 2H 147
Brook Wlk. SR3: New S 4B 132
Broom Cl. DH9: Stly 2H 125
NE16: Whi 1J 97
NE21: Bla T 6B 80
NE61: Mor 1J 15
Broom Ct. NE9: Spri 7D 100
Broom Cres. DH7: Ush M 2C 164
Broome Cl. NE3: Ken 6B 44
Broome Ct. DH7: Ush M 4F 165
Broome Rd. DH1: Carr 7H 155
Broom Farm W. DH7: Ush M 4E 164
Broomfield NE32: Jar 4C 86
Broomfield Av. NE6: Walk 4C 64
NE28: W'snd 7G 47
Broomfield Cres. NE17: C'wl 7K 93
Broomfield Rd. NE3: Gos 1D 62
Broomfield Ter. NE40: Ryton 3C 78
Broom Grn. NE16: Whi 1J 97
Broom Hall Dr. DH7: Ush M 3D 164
BROOMHAUGH 7A 74
Broomhaugh Cl. NE46: Hex 2E 70
BROOM HILL 4F 145
Broom Hill DH9: Stly 2D 124
Broomhill Est. DH5: Hett H 4F 145
Broomhill Gdns. NE5: Newc T 4K 61
Broomhill Rd. NE42: Pru 3F 77
Broomhill Ter. DH5: Hett H 5F 145
DH8: M'sly 1J 121
Broomhouse La. NE42: Pru 3G 77
Broomhouse Rd. NE42: Pru 3G 77
Broom La. DH1: Dur 4E 164
DH7: Ush M 3C 164
NE16: Whi 2H 97
Broomlaw NE9: Gate 3A 100
Broomlea NE29: N Shi 3B 48
Broomlea Ct. NE21: Bla T 3C 80
Broomlee NE63: Hir 5C 12
Broomlee Cl. NE7: Newc T 2B 64
Broomlee Rd. NE12: Kil 1A 46
BROOMLEY 2D 90
Broomley Ct. NE3: Ken 5B 44
Broomley Wlk. NE3: Ken 5B 44
BROOMPARK 4E 164
Broomridge Av. NE15: Newc T 7K 61
Broomshields Av. SR5: S'wck 4D 104
Broomshields Cl. SR5: S'wck 4D 104
BROOMSIDE 7J 155
Broomside Ct. DH1: Carr 7H 155
Broomside La. DH1: Carr 7G 155
Broomside Pk. DH1: Dur 7E 154
Brooms La. DH8: Con, Lead 5C 122
Brooms, The DH2: Ous 6H 113
Broom Ter. NE16: Burn 2B 110
NE16: Whi 1J 97
Broom Wood Ct. NE42: Pru 5D 76
Broomy Hill Rd. NE15: Thro 3G 59
Broomylinn Pl. NE23: Cra 2A 26
Brotherlee Rd. NE3: Ken 5B 44
Brougham Ct. SR8: Pet 2J 181
Brougham St. SR1: Sund 2F 119 (4J 7)
Brough Ct. NE6: Newc T 6A 64
Brough Gdns. NE28: W'snd 1A 66
Brough Pk. Stadium (Speedway) 7B 64
Brough Pk. Way NE6: Walk 7B 64
Brough St. NE6: Newc T 6A 64
Broughton Rd. NE33: S Shi 3K 67
Brough Way NE6: Newc T 6A 64
Browbank DH7: Sac 1F 153
Brown Cres. NE9: Spri 6A 100
Browne Rd. SR6: Monk 4F 105
BROWNEY 2F 175
Browney La. DH6: Crox, Dur 2E 174
DH7: B'don 2E 174
Browning Cl. DH9: Stly 3H 125
NE34: S Shi 4H 87
(not continuous)
Browning Sq. NE8: Gate 4J 83
Browning St. SR8: Eas 7D 160
Brownlow Cl. NE7: Newc T 2C 64
Brownlow Rd. NE34: S Shi 7J 67
Brownney Ct. DH7: Lang P 4J 151
Brownrigg Dr. NE23: Cra 5A 26
Brownriggs Ct. NE37: Wash 2F 115
Brown Rd. SR5: C'twn 6H 103
Browns Bldgs. DH3: Bir 7A 114
NE22: Bed 1G 21
Brownsea Pl. NE9: Gate 7J 83
Brown's Ter. DH7: Lang P 5J 151
Browntop Pl. NE34: S Shi 1J 87
Brow, The NE6: Newc T 1A 84
Broxbourne Ter. SR4: Sund 2C 118
Broxburn Cl. NE28: W'snd 7J 47
Broxburn Ct. NE5: Newc T 2J 61
Broxholm Rd. NE6: Newc T 4K 63
Bruce Cl. NE5: Newc T 3F 61
NE34: S Shi 2J 87
Bruce Cres. TS28: Win 5F 181
Bruce Gdns. NE5: Newc T 6J 61
Bruce Glasier Ter. DH6: Shot C 7E 170
Bruce Kirkup Rd. SR8: Pet 4D 172
Bruce Pl. SR8: Pet 4A 172
Bruce St. DH7: Sac 4D 140
SR5: S'wck 5E 104
Brumell Dr. NE61: Mor 6D 8
Brumwell Ct. NE43: Stoc 7H 75
Brundon Av. NE26: Whit B 4F 39
Brunel Dr. SR6: Monk 5H 105
Brunel Lodge *NE4: Newc T 3C 82*
(off Brunel St.)
Brunel St. NE4: Newc T 3D 82 (9B 4)
NE8: Gate 6F 83
Brunel Ter. NE4: Newc T 3C 82
Brunel Wlk. NE4: Newc T 3C 82
Brunswick Gro. NE13: Bru V 5C 34
Brunswick Ind. Est. NE13: Bru V 5B 34
Brunswick Pk. Ind. Est.
NE13: Bru V 5B 34
Brunswick Pl. NE1: Newc T 1F 83 (4F 4)
Brunswick Rd. NE27: Shir 2K 47
SR5: C'twn 3G 103
Brunswick Sq. NE27: Shir 2K 47
Brunswick St. NE33: S Shi 4J 67
BRUNSWICK VILLAGE 5C 34
Brunton Av. NE3: Ken 6B 44
NE28: W'snd 2B 66
Brunton Cl. NE27: Shir 2K 47
Brunton Gro. NE3: Ken 6B 44
Brunton La. NE3: Gos 2K 43
NE3: Ken 7J 43
NE13: Bru V, Wide O, Wool 2K 43
Brunton M. NE13: Bru V 2B 44
Brunton Rd. NE13: Wool 5H 43
Brunton St. NE29: N Shi 2D 66
Brunton Ter. SR4: Sund 2C 118
Brunton Wlk. NE3: Ken 6J 43
(not continuous)
Brunton Way NE10: Gate 4F 85
NE23: Cra 7K 21
Brussels Rd. NE28: W'snd 4F 65
SR4: Sund 1K 117
BRYAN'S LEAP 2A 110
Bryans Leap NE16: Burn 1A 110
Bryden Ct. NE34: S Shi 1K 87
Brydon Cres. DH6: S Het 5D 158
Bryers St. SR6: Whit 5H 89
Buchanan Grn. NE11: Dun 5C 82
Buchanan St. NE31: Heb 1H 85
Buckham St. DH8: Con 5G 121
Buckingham SR3: E Her 1A 132
Buckingham Cl. SR6: Whit 6H 89
Buckingham Rd. SR8: Pet 4K 171
Buckinghamshire Rd. DH1: Carr 1G 167
Buckingham St. NE4: Newc T 1D 82 (6B 4)
Buckland Cl. DH4: Hou S 7C 130
NE38: Wash 5H 115
Buck's Hill DH1: Dur 6A 166
Buck's Hill Vw. NE16: Whi 1J 97
Buck's Nook La. NE40: G'sde, Pru 7K 77
Buckthorne Gro. NE7: Newc T 2A 64
Buddle Arts Cen. 3F 65
Buddle Cl. SR8: Pet 4B 172
Buddle Ct. NE4: Newc T 2A 82
Buddle Gdns. NE40: G'sde 5D 78
Buddle Ind. Est. NE28: W'snd 5G 65
Buddle Rd. NE4: Newc T 2K 81
Buddle St. DH8: Con 1J 135
NE28: W'snd 4G 65
Buddle Ter. NE27: Shir 3J 47
SR2: Sund 3G 119
Bude Ct. NE28: W'snd 7G 47
Bude Gdns. NE9: Gate 4H 99
Bude Gro. NE29: N Shi 3D 48
Bude Sq. SR7: Mur 6F 147
Budle Cl. NE3: Gos 6D 44
NE24: Bly 2G 23
Budleigh Rd. NE3: Ken 7B 44
Budworth Av. NE26: Sea S 5D 28
Bugatti Ind. Pk. NE29: N Shi 7C 48
Buller's Grn. NE61: Mor 6E 8
Bullfinch Dr. NE16: Whi 7G 81
Bullion La. DH2: Ches S 6K 127
Bull La. SR1: Sund 1G 119
Bulman Ho. NE3: Gos 7E 44
Bulman's La. NE29: N Shi 4G 49
Bulmer Ho. NE34: S Shi 6C 68
Bulmer Rd. NE34: S Shi 6C 68
Bungalows, The DH3: Bir 2K 113
DH5: Hett H 4F 145
DH6: S Het 5D 158
DH6: Thor 2J 179
DH7: Esh W 4E 162
DH7: New B 4B 164
DH8: C'sde 3D 134
DH8: Ebc 4G 107
DH9: Tan L 1C 124
NE10: Gate 6C 84
NE11: Kib 7G 99
NE17: Ham C 4K 107
NE21: Bla T 4A 80
NE28: W'snd 2K 65
SR8: Pet 4D 172
TS27: Hes 4H 183
Bunyan Av. NE34: S Shi 3G 87
Burdale Av. NE5: Newc T 4G 61
BURDON 6D 132
Burdon Av. DH5: Hou S 2G 145
NE23: Nel V 3H 25
Burdon Cl. SR6: Cle 5A 88
Burdon Cres. SR2: Ryh 3G 133
SR6: Cle 5A 88
SR7: S'hm 1H 147
TS28: Win 4G 181
Burdon Dr. SR8: Pet 5G 171
Burdon La. SR2: New S, Ryh 4E 132
SR3: New S 6B 132
Burdon Lodge NE16: Sun 5J 97
Burdon Main Row NE29: N Shi 1G 67
Burdon Pk. NE16: Sun 5J 97
Burdon Pl. NE2: Newc T 5G 63
SR8: Pet 6C 172
(not continuous)
Burdon Plain NE16: Sun 2H 111
Burdon Rd. SR1: Sund 2F 119 (6K 7)
SR2: Sund 3F 119 (7K 7)
SR3: New S 4D 132
SR6: Cle 5A 88
Burdon St. NE29: N Shi 2D 66
Burdon Ter. NE2: Newc T 5G 63
NE22: Bed 7G 17
Burford Ct. NE3: Newc T 1J 63
Burford Gdns. SR3: Sund 5D 118
Burghley Gdns. NE61: Peg 3B 10
Burghley Rd. NE10: Gate 1A 100
Burgoyne Ct. NE37: Usw 7H 101
Burgoyne Ter. NE41: Wylam 7J 57
Burke St. SR5: C'twn 4G 103
Burlawn Cl. SR2: Ryh 1H 133
Burleigh St. NE33: S Shi 4K 67
Burlington Cl. SR2: Sund 3G 119
Burlington Ct. NE2: Newc T 3H 63
NE28: W'snd 5J 47
Burlington Gdns. NE6: Newc T 5K 63
Burlison Gdns. NE10: Gate 4A 84
Burnaby Dr. NE40: Ryton 2F 79
Burnaby St. SR4: Sund 3C 118
Burn Av. NE12: Longb 4B 46
(not continuous)
NE28: W'snd 3F 65
Burnbank NE10: Gate 1E 100
NE13: Sea B 3D 34
SR5: S'wck 5D 104
Burnbank Av. NE25: Well 6B 38
Burnbridge NE13: Sea B 3D 34
Burn Closes Cres. NE28: W'snd 2J 65
Burn Cft. NE46: Hex 2C 70
Burn Crook DH5: Hou S 4D 144
Burnden Gro. DH4: Hou S 4K 129
Burnell Rd. DH7: Esh W 4E 162
Burnet Cl. NE28: W'snd 7G 47
Burnet Ct. NE63: Ash 6K 11
Burnett Cres. DH6: Kel 7E 178
Burney Vs. NE8: Gate 5J 83
Burnfoot NE42: O'ham 2C 76
Burnfoot Ter. NE26: Whit B 7H 39
Burnfoot Way NE3: Ken 2A 62
Burn Gdns. SR8: Eas 7A 160
Burnhall Dr. SR7: S'hm 1J 147
Burnham Av. NE15: Lem 6A 60
Burnham Cl. DH4: Pen 3B 130
NE24: News 4J 23
Burnham Gro. NE6: Walk 2C 84
NE36: E Bol 7K 87
Burnham St. NE34: S Shi 7J 67
Burn Heads Rd. NE31: Heb 2H 85
Burnhills Gdns. NE40: G'sde 5E 78
Burnhills La. NE21: G'sde 6F 79
BURNHOPE 5D 138
Burnhope Dr. SR5: S'wck 4D 104
Burnhope Gdns. NE9: Gate 4B 100
Burnhope Rd. NE38: Wash 2J 115
Burnhopeside Av. DH7: Lan 7A 138
Burnhope Way SR8: Pet 5K 171
Burnigill DH7: B'don 2E 174
Burnip Rd. SR7: Mur 6E 146
Burnland Ter. NE46: Hex 1B 70
Burn La. DH5: Hett H 7G 145
NE46: Hex 1C 70
Burnlea Gdns. NE23: Seg 1F 37
Burnley St. NE21: Bla T 4C 80
Burnmoor Gdns. NE9: Gate 4B 100
BURNOPFIELD 2K 109
Burnopfield Gdns. NE15: Newc T 7G 61
Burnopfield Rd. NE39: Row G 6K 95
Burnop Ter. NE39: Row G 5E 94
Burn Pk. Rd. DH4: Hou S 2C 144
SR2: Sund 3D 118 (6F 7)
Burn Prom. DH4: Hou S 1D 144
(not continuous)
Burn Rd. NE21: Bla T 5K 79
Burns Av. NE24: Bly 4G 23
NE35: Bol C 6H 87
TS27: B Col 1G 183
Burns Av. Nth. DH5: Hou S 3E 144
(not continuous)
Burns Av. Sth. DH5: Hou S 3E 144
Burns Cl. DH4: W Rai 1A 156
DH9: Stly 3G 125
NE16: Whi 2H 97
Burns Ct. NE34: S Shi 3H 87
Burns Cres. NE16: Swa 6G 81
BURNSIDE 7C 130
Burn Side SR8: Pet 6B 172
Burnside DH7: Esh W 3D 162
DH7: Lan 6J 137
DH7: Wit G 3D 152
NE2: Newc T 1B 4
NE10: Gate 7C 84
NE20: Pon 1F 41
NE22: Bed 5B 18
NE25: H'wll 2K 37
NE32: Jar 2C 86
NE36: E Bol 7A 88
NE42: O'ham 2K 75
NE46: Hex 3B 70
NE61: Mor 6G 9
NE63: N Sea 4E 12
Burnside Av. DH4: Hou S 1C 144
NE23: Dud 3K 35
SR8: Pet 6E 172
Burnside Cl. NE16: Whi 3G 97
NE23: Seg 2C 36
NE24: Cow 1F 23
NE42: O'ham 2C 76
Burnside Cotts. NE23: Dud 3K 35
NE43: Mic 5A 76
SR7: Mur 5J 147
Burnside Rd. NE3: Gos 5E 44
NE30: N Shi 1H 49
NE30: Whit B 1H 49
NE39: Row G 5H 95
Burnside, The NE5: Newc T 4E 60
Burnside Vw. NE23: Seg 2C 36
Burns St. DH6: Whe H 3A 180
NE32: Jar 6B 66
Burn's Ter. DH6: Shot C 6F 171
Burnstones NE5: Newc T 4E 60
Burn St. DH6: Bow 4H 177
Burn Ter. DH4: Hou S 3C 130
NE28: W'snd 3K 65
NE31: Heb 4G 85
Burnthouse Bank DH2: Pelt 5H 127
Burnt Ho. Cl. NE21: Bla T 6A 80
Burnthouse La. NE16: Sun, Whi 3G 97
(Rosewell Pl.)
NE16: Whi 2G 97
(Fairfield Av.)
Burnt Ho. Rd. NE25: Whit B 1E 48
Burntland Av. SR5: S'wck 5B 104
Burn Vw. NE23: Dud 3K 35
NE32: Jar 6C 86
Burnville NE6: Newc T 6J 63 (1M 5)
Burnville Rd. SR4: Sund 3D 118
Burnville Rd. Sth. SR4: Sund 3D 118
Burnway NE37: Wash 7F 101
SR7: S'hm 2J 147
Burnwood Cl. NE17: C'wl 6K 93
BURRADON 5A 36
Burradon NE23: Dud 6A 36
Burradon Rd. NE23: Dud 5A 36
(Cheviot Grange)
NE23: Dud 3A 36
(Seaton Cft.)
Burrow St. NE33: S Shi 2J 67
Burscough Cres. SR6: Monk 5F 105
Burstow Av. NE6: Walk 3C 84
Burswell Av. NE46: Hex 1B 70
Burswell Vs. NE46: Hex 1B 70
Burt Av. NE29: N Shi 7E 48
Burt Cl. DH6: Has 1A 170
SR8: Pet 4B 172
Burt Cres. NE23: Dud 3K 35
Burt Memorial Homes NE62: Sco G 3G 17
Burtree NE38: Wash 6F 115
Burt Rd. NE22: Bed 5C 18
Burt St. NE24: Bly 1J 23
Burt Ter. NE15: Thro 3A 60
NE61: Mor 7G 9
Burwell Av. NE5: Newc T 5F 61
Burwood Cl. NE6: Walk 3E 84
Burwood Rd. NE6: Walk 3D 84
NE29: N Shi 4C 48
Bushblades La.
DH9: Ann P, Dip, Tan L 1J 123
Bus. & Innovation Cen.
SR5: Sund 6B 104
Buston Ter. NE2: Newc T 4H 63

Busty Bank—Carnegie St.

Busty Bank NE16: Burn 6K 95
NE39: Burn 6K 95
Butcher's Bri. Rd. NE32: Jar 1B 86
Butcher's La. NE61: Peg 1B 10
Bute Cotts. NE11: Dun 5A 82
Bute Ct. SR3: New S 3C 132
Bute Dr. NE39: H Spen 3D 94
Buteland Rd. NE15: Newc T 6F 61
Buteland Ter. NE64: Newb S 3H 13
Bute Rd. Nth. NE39: H Spen 3D 94
Bute Rd. Sth. NE39: H Spen 4D 94
Bute St. DH9: Tan L 6A 110
Butler St. SR8: Eas 7D 160
Butsfield Gdns. SR3: Sund 6D 118
Butsfield La. DH8: Con 7K 135
Butterburn Cl. NE7: Newc T 1C 64
Butterfield Cl. NE40: Ryton 3D 78
Buttermere NE10: Gate 6E 84
SR6: Cle 5C 88
SR8: Pet 2J 181
Buttermere Av. DH5: Eas L 3J 157
NE16: Whi 7J 81
Buttermere Cl. DH2: Ches S 7A 128
NE5: Newc T 4H 61
NE12: Kil 1A 46
Buttermere Cres. DH6: S Het 3A 158
NE21: Bla T 6B 80
Buttermere Gdns. NE9: Gate 2J 99
NE34: S Shi 7A 68
Buttermere Rd. NE30: N Shi 2G 49
Buttermere St. SR2: Sund 6G 119
Buttermere Way NE24: Cow 7F 19
Butterwell Dr. NE61: Peg 4K 9
Button's Bank DH7: Wat 7B 162
DL15: Wat 7B 162
Buttsfield Ter. DH4: Pen 1B 130
Buxton Cl. NE28: W'snd 7H 47
NE32: Jar 1C 86
Buxton Gdns. NE5: Newc T 2F 61
SR3: Sund 5D 118
Buxton Grn. NE5: Newc T 2F 61
Buxton St. NE1: Newc T 1H 83 (5J 5)
Byer Bank DH5: Hou S 3G 145
BYERMOOR 1D 110
Byermoor Ind. Est. NE16: Burn 1D 110
Byers Ct. SR3: New S 1D 132
Byer Sq. DH5: Hett H 4G 145
Byer St. DH5: Hett H 4G 145
Bye, The DH8: C'sde 2E 134
Byeways, The NE12: Longb 6K 45
Bygate Cl. NE3: Ken 2A 62
Bygate Rd. NE25: Whit B 7E 38
BYKER 1A 84 (5P 5)
Byker Bank NE1: Newc T 1J 83 (5M 5)
NE6: Newc T 1J 83 (5M 5)
Byker Bri. NE1: Newc T 7H 63 (4K 5)
NE6: Newc T 7H 63 (4K 5)
Byker Bus. Development Cen.
NE6: Newc T 1K 83 (5N 5)
Byker Cres. NE6: Newc T 7A 64
Byker Lodge NE6: Newc T 1A 84 (6P 5)
Byker Station (Metro) 7K 63 (4P 5)
Byker St. NE6: Walk 7D 64
Byker Ter. NE6: Walk 7D 64
Byker Wall Baths 7K 63 (4P 5)
Byland Cl. DH4: Hou S 7C 130
Byland Ct. DH7: Ush M 1D 164
NE38: Wash 3G 115
Byland Rd. NE12: Longb 6H 45
Bylands Gdns. SR3: Sund 5D 118
Byony Toft SR2: Ryh 2J 133
Byrness NE5: Newc T 4E 60
Byrness Cl. NE3: Ken 1J 61
Byrness Ct. NE28: W'snd 7J 47
Byrness Row NE23: Cra 2A 26
Byrne Ter. W. SR3: New S 2D 132
Byron Av. DH2: Pelt 6G 127
NE24: Bly 4G 23
NE28: W'snd 4A 66
NE31: Heb 7K 65
NE35: Bol C 6G 87
TS27: B Col 1G 183
Byron Cl. DH2: Ous 7H 113
DH9: Stly 3G 125
NE62: Chop 1G 17
Byron Ct. NE5: Cha P 3C 60
NE16: Swa 6G 81
Byron Lodge Est. SR7: S'hm 2G 147
Byron Pl. NE63: Hir 5D 12
Byron Rd. SR5: S'wck 5C 104
Byrons Ct. SR7: S'hm 1A 148
Byron St. DH2: Ous 7H 113
DH6: Whe H 3B 180
NE2: Newc T 7G 63 (3H 5)
NE33: S Shi 5K 67
SR5: S'wck 6E 104
SR8: Eas 7D 160
Byron Ter. DH5: Hou S 3E 144
DH6: Shot C 6F 171
SR7: S'hm 1H 147
Byron Wlk. NE8: Gate 4J 83
By-Way, The NE15: Thro 4H 59
BYWELL 6F 75
Bywell Av. NE3: Ken 4B 44
NE15: Lem 6E 60
Bywell Av. NE34: S Shi 6C 68
NE46: Hex 2F 71
SR5: S'wck 4E 104
Bywell Castle (remains of) 6F 75
Bywell Cl. NE40: Ryton 3C 78
Bywell Dr. SR8: Pet 2A 182
Bywell Gdns. NE10: Gate 1K 99
NE11: Gate 2C 98
Bywell Gro. NE27: Shir 1A 48
Bywell Rd. NE63: Hir 5B 12
SR6: Cle 6B 88
Bywell St. NE6: Newc T 1B 84
(not continuous)
Bywell Ter. NE26: Sea S 4D 28
NE32: Jar 3B 86
Bywell Vw. NE43: Stoc 7K 75

C

Cadehill Rd. NE43: Stoc 1H 91
Cadger Bank DH7: Lan 7J 137
Cadlestone Ct. NE23: Cra 2B 26
Cadwell La. SR8: Eas 7K 159
Caedmon Live Theatre 6H 83
Caernarvon Cl. NE5: Newc T 1H 61
Caernarvon Dr. SR3: E Her 3J 131
Caer Urfa Cl. NE33: S Shi 1J 67
Caesar's Wlk. NE33: S Shi 1J 67
Caesar Way NE28: W'snd 1J 65
Cain Ter. DH6: Whe H 3A 180
Cairncross SR5: C'twn 6G 103
Cairnglass Grn. NE23: Cra 2B 26
Cairngorm Av. NE38: Wash 5E 114
Cairnhill Ter. DH4: Hou S 5D 130
Cairnside SR3: E Her 2J 131
SR7: Sea 1F 147
Cairnside Sth. SR3: E Her 2H 131
Cairnsmore Cl. NE6: Walk 5F 65
NE23: Cra 6K 25
Cairnsmore Dr. NE38: Wash 5F 115
Cairns Rd. SR5: Monk 3E 104
SR7: Mur 7C 146
Cairns Sq. SR5: Monk 3E 104
Cairns Way NE3: Ken 5B 44
Cairo St. SR2: Sund 4G 119
Caithness Rd. SR5: C'twn 5F 103
Caithness Sq. SR5: C'twn 5F 103
Calais Rd. SR5: C'twn 6F 103
Calandra Chase
NE2: Newc T 5D 62 (1B 4)
Caldbeck Av. NE6: Walk 3D 84
Caldbeck Cl. NE6: Walk 3D 84
Calderbourne Av. SR6: Monk 3G 105
Calder Ct. SR3: New S 3B 132
Calderdale NE28: W'snd 7D 46
Calderdale Av. NE6: Walk 6D 64
Calder Grn. NE32: Jar 4C 86
Calder's Cres. NE38: Wash 7H 115
Calder Wlk. NE16: Sun 5G 97
Calderwood Cres. NE9: Gate 4J 99
Calderwood Pk. NE9: Gate 4J 99
Caldew Ct. DH5: Eas L 1H 157
Caldew Cres. NE5: Newc T 5G 61
Caldwell Rd. NE3: Ken 4B 44
Caledonia DH3: Gt Lum 2E 142
NE21: Bla T 6A 80
Caledonian Rd. SR5: C'twn 4F 103
Caledonian St. NE31: Heb 6H 65
Caledonia St. NE6: Walk 2E 84
Calfclose Dr. NE32: Jar 4B 86
Calfclose La. NE32: Jar 4B 86
Calfclose Wlk. NE32: Jar 3C 86
California NE21: Bla T 5B 80
California Gdns. NE61: Mor 7G 9
Callaley Av. NE16: Whi 1F 97
Callaly Av. NE23: Cra 4A 26
Callaly Cl. NE61: Peg 4B 10
Callaly Way NE6: Walk 2B 84
Callander DH2: Ous 6J 113
Callendar Ct. NE9: Gate 2K 99
Callerdale Rd. NE24: Cow 1E 22
CALLERTON 6B 42
Callerton NE12: Kil 6B 36
Callerton Av. NE29: N Shi 6C 48
Callerton Cl. NE23: Cra 4A 26
NE63: Hir 5D 12
Callerton Ct. NE5: Newc T 2G 61
NE20: Pon 7J 31
Callerton La. NE5: Cal 3J 41
NE20: Cal, Pon 2J 41
CALLERTON LANE END 5J 41
Callerton La. End Cotts. NE5: Cal 5J 41
Callerton Parkway Station (Metro) 3E 42
Callerton Pl. DH9: Stly 7K 125
NE4: Newc T 1C 82
Callerton Rd. NE15: Thro 3H 59
Callerton Vw. NE5: Cha P 1B 60
Calley Cl. SR8: Pet 2A 182
Callington Cl. DH4: Hou S 7J 129
Callington Dr. SR2: Ryh 2H 133
Callum Dr. NE34: S Shi 5C 68
Calow Way NE16: Whi 2F 97
Calstock Cl. SR7: Mur 1F 159
Calthwaite Cl. SR5: C'twn 5G 103
Calver Ct. NE34: S Shi 1A 88
(not continuous)
Calvert Ter. SR7: Mur 7D 146
Calvus Dr. NE15: Hed W 3D 58
Camberley Cl. SR3: New S 1E 132
Camberley Dr. DH7: B'don 2B 174
Camberley Rd. NE28: W'snd 1A 66
Camberwell Cl. NE11: Gate 1D 98
Camberwell Way
SR3: E Her, New S 3K 131
Cambo Av. NE22: Bed 7A 18
NE25: Whit B 1D 48
Cambo Cl. NE3: Gos 7F 45
NE24: Bly 2G 23
NE28: W'snd 6H 47
Cambo Dr. NE23: Cra 5A 26
Cambo Grn. NE5: Newc T 3J 61
CAMBOIS 4H 19
Cambo Pl. NE30: N Shi 3G 49
Camborne Gro. NE8: Gate 5H 83
Camborne Pl. NE8: Gate 5H 83
Cambourne Av. SR6: Monk 3G 105
Cambria Grn. SR4: Sund 2G 117
Cambrian Cl. NE38: Wash 5F 115
Cambrian St. NE32: Jar 6C 66
Cambrian Way NE38: Wash 4F 115
Cambria St. SR4: Sund 2G 117
Cambridge Av. DH8: C'sde 3C 134
NE12: Longb 4B 46
NE26: Whit B 6G 39
NE28: W'snd 2E 64
NE31: Heb 7K 65
NE37: Usw 7F 101
Cambridge Cres. DH4: Hou S 3A 130
Cambridge Dr. DH3: Gt Lum 3E 142
Cambridge Pl. DH3: Bir 7A 114
Cambridge Rd. NE62: Chop 1J 17
SR3: New S 2C 132
SR8: Pet 4A 172
Cambridgeshire Dr. DH1: Carr 2G 167
Cambridge St. NE4: Newc T 3D 82 (9A 4)
Cambridge Ter. DH6: Bow 5H 177
NE8: Gate 5G 83
Camden Sq. NE30: N Shi 7H 49
SR7: S'hm 4A 148
Camden St. NE2: Newc T 7G 63 (3H 5)
NE30: N Shi 7H 49
SR5: S'wck, Sund 6C 104
Camelford Ct. NE15: Lem 5C 60
Camelot Cl. SR7: S'hm 2A 148
Cameron Cl. NE34: S Shi 3J 87
Cameron Rd. NE42: Pru 4F 77
Cameron Wlk. NE11: Dun 4J 81
Camerton Pl. NE28: W'snd 5J 47
Camilla Rd. NE15: Hed W 3D 58
Camilla St. NE8: Gate 5H 83
Cam Mead SR3: New S 5C 132
CAMPBELL PARK 1K 85
Campbell Pk. Rd. NE31: Heb 7J 65
Campbell Pl. NE4: Newc T 1C 82 (5A 4)
Campbell Rd. SR5: C'twn 5F 103
Campbell Sq. SR5: C'twn 5F 103
Campbell St. NE31: Heb 6J 65
SR8: Eas 7D 160
Campbell Ter. DH5: Eas L 2H 157
CAMPERDOWN 6K 35
Camperdown NE5: Newc T 4F 61
Camperdown Av. DH3: Ches S 4B 128
NE12: Kil 7K 35
Camperdown Ind. Est. NE12: Kil 6K 35
Campion Dr. DH9: Tan L 1D 124
Campion Gdns. NE10: Gate 2B 100
Campion Way NE63: Ash 5A 12
Campsie Cl. NE38: Wash 5F 115
Campsie Cres. NE30: N Shi 3G 49
Camp St. SR8: Eas 7D 160
Camp Ter. NE29: N Shi 6G 49
Campus Martius NE15: Hed W 3B 58
Campville NE29: N Shi 6G 49
Camsey Cl. NE12: Longb 6H 45
Camsey Pl. NE12: Longb 6H 45
CANADA 5A 128
Canberra Av. NE25: Whit B 1D 48
Canberra Dr. NE34: S Shi 2E 86
Canberra Rd. SR4: Sund 4K 117
Candelford Cl. NE7: Newc T 2B 64
Candlish St. NE33: S Shi 3K 67
Candlish Ter. SR7: S'hm 4C 148
Canning St. NE4: Newc T 1A 82
(Farndale Rd.)
NE4: Newc T 1A 82
(Wellfield Rd.)
NE31: Heb 1H 85
Cannock DH2: Ous 6H 113
NE12: Kil 7B 36
Cannock Dr. NE7: Newc T 1J 63
Cannon St. NE8: Gate 2G 83 (8H 5)
Cann Rd. SR8: Pet 4B 172
Cann St. SR8: Eas 7A 160
Canonbie Sq. NE23: Cra 2B 26
Canon Cockin St. SR2: Sund 4G 119
Canon Gro. NE32: Jar 6C 66
Canon Savage Dr. NE46: Hex 2A 70
Canonsfield Cl. NE15: Cha P 2B 60
SR3: New S 4B 132
Canterbury Av. NE28: W'snd 6H 47
Canterbury Cl. DH3: Gt Lum 4E 142
NE12: Longb 6J 45
NE63: N Sea 5D 12
Canterbury Rd. DH1: Dur 3B 154
SR5: C'twn 5G 103
Canterbury St. NE6: Walk 7B 64
(not continuous)
NE33: S Shi 5K 67
Canterbury Way NE13: Wide O 5D 34
NE32: Jar 5A 86
Capercaillie Lodge NE23: Dud 2A 36
Capetown Rd. SR5: C'twn 5F 103
Capetown Sq. SR5: C'twn 5F 103
Caplestone Cl. NE38: Wash 5F 115
Capstan La. NE9: Gate 5A 100
Captains Row, The NE33: S Shi 5H 67
Captains Wharf NE33: S Shi 2H 67
Capulet Gro. NE34: S Shi 1G 87
Capulet Ter. SR2: Sund 4G 119
Caradoc Cl. NE38: Wash 5F 115
Caragh Rd. DH2: Ches S 1K 141
Caraway Wlk. NE34: S Shi 4A 88
(not continuous)
Carden Av. NE34: S Shi 1D 88
Cardiff Sq. SR5: C'twn 6F 103
Cardiff St. SR8: Eas 7D 160
Cardigan Gro. NE30: N Shi 1G 49
Cardigan Rd. SR5: C'twn 5F 103
Cardigan Ter. NE6: Newc T 6K 63 (2N 5)
Cardinal Cl. NE12: Longb 6J 45
NE15: Cha P 2B 60
Cardinals Cl. SR3: New S 4B 132
Cardonnel St. NE29: N Shi 1G 67
Cardoon Rd. DH8: Con 7J 121
Cardwell St. SR6: Monk 6F 105
(not continuous)
Careen Cres. SR3: E Her 2H 131
Carew Ct. NE23: Cra 5K 25
Carey Cl. DH6: Bow 5H 177
Carham Av. NE23: Cra 4A 26
Carham Cl. NE3: Gos 6F 45
NE45: Cor 1E 72
Caribees DH8: Con 3A 136
Carisbrooke NE22: Bed 6H 17
Carisbrooke Cl. NE37: Usw 7H 101
Caris St. NE8: Gate 6J 83
Carlby Way NE23: Cra 7H 21
Carlcroft SR6: Monk 6G 105
Carlcroft Pl. NE23: Cra 5A 26
CARLEY HILL 3C 104
Carley Hill Rd. SR5: S'wck 4D 104
Carley Rd. SR5: S'wck 5D 104
Carley Sq. SR5: S'wck 5D 104
Carlile Ho NE4: Newc T 5A 4
Carlingford Rd. DH2: Ches S 1K 141
Carliol Pl. NE1: Newc T 1G 83 (5G 4)
Carliol Sq. NE1: Newc T 1G 83 (5G 4)
(not continuous)
Carliol St. NE1: Newc T 1G 83 (5G 4)
Carlisle Cl. NE27: Longb 4G 47
Carlisle Ct. NE10: Gate 5B 84
Carlisle Cres. DH4: Pen 2A 130
Carlisle Ho. *SR3: E Her* 2K 131
(off Ashford Rd.)
Carlisle Pl. NE9: Gate 3K 99
Carlisle Rd. DH1: Dur 4C 154
Carlisle St. NE10: Gate 5B 84
Carlisle Ter. NE27: Shir 3J 47
SR5: S'wck 5C 104
Carlisle Vw. *NE61: Mor* 7F 9
(off Waterside)
Carlisle Way NE27: Longb 3G 47
Carlow Dr. NE62: W Sle 7B 12
Carlton Av. NE24: News 6G 23
Carlton Cl. DH2: Ous 6G 113
NE3: Ken 2C 62
Carlton Ct. NE11: Gate 2E 98
NE29: N Shi 7F 49
Carlton Cres. SR3: E Her 2J 131
Carlton Gdns. NE15: Lem 6E 60
Carlton Grange NE3: Ken 2C 62
Carlton Gro. NE63: N Sea 6D 12
Carlton Ho. NE22: Bed 7H 17
Carlton Rd. NE12: Longb 6B 46
Carlton St. NE24: Bly 2K 23
Carlton Ter. NE9: Gate 2G 99
NE9: Spri 6D 100
NE24: Bly 1H 23
NE29: N Shi 7F 49
SR2: Sund 7K 7
SR8: Eas 1K 171
Carlyle Ct. NE28: W'snd 4A 66
Carlyle Cres. DH6: Shot C 6F 171
NE16: Swa 6G 81
Carlyle St. NE28: W'snd 4A 66
Carlyon St. SR2: Sund 3F 119 (7J 7)
Carmel Gro. NE23: Cra 1J 25
Carmel Rd. DH9: Stly 3D 124
Carnaby Cl. NE42: Pru 3F 77
Carnaby Rd. NE6: Walk 2D 84
Carnation Av. DH4: Hou S 6J 129
Carnation Ter. NE16: Whi 7H 81
Carnegie Cl. NE34: S Shi 2J 87
Carnegie St. SR2: Sund 6H 119

Chapel St.—Christchurch Ct.

Chapel St. NE29: N Shi 7E **48**
TS28: Win 7G **181**
Chapel Vw. DH4: W Rai 2K **155**
NE13: Bru V 5C **34**
NE39: Row G 4J **95**
Chapelville NE13: Sea B 3D **34**
Chaplin St. SR7: S'hm 5B **148**
Chapman St. SR6: Monk 3G **105**
Chapter Row NE33: S Shi 2J **67**
Chare La. DH6: Shad 5E **168**
Chare, The NE1: Newc T 7F **63** (4E **4**)
SR8: Pet 6B **172**
Chareway NE46: Hex 7C **50**
Chareway La. NE46: Hex 7C **50**
CHARLAW 6D **140**
Charlaw Cl. DH7: Sac 6D **140**
Charlaw La. DH7: Edm, Sac, Wit G 5K **139**
(not continuous)
DH7: Sac, Wit G 6A **140**
Charlaw Ter. DH7: Sac 7D **140**
Charlbury Cl. NE9: Spri 6D **100**
Charlcote Cres. NE36: E Bol 7K **87**
Charles Av. NE3: Ken 6A **44**
NE12: Longb 4B **46**
NE26: Whit B 6H **39**
NE27: Shir 7K **37**
Charles Baker Wlk.
NE34: S Shi 6D **68**
Charles Ct. *NE6: Newc T 6A* ***64***
(off Elvet Cl.)
Charles Dr. NE23: Dud 3K **35**
Charles Perkins Memorial Cott. Home
DH3: Bir 5A **114**
Charles St. DH4: Hou S 5D **130**
DH9: Stly 5E **124**
NE8: Gate 4H **83** (10J **5**)
NE13: Bru V 7C **34**
NE35: Bol C 6F **87**
NE61: Peg 4B **10**
SR1: Sund 2K **7**
SR2: Ryh 3J **133**
SR3: New S 1C **132**
SR6: Monk 7F **105** (1K **7**)
SR7: S'hm 3B **148**
SR8: Eas 7D **160**
Charles Ter. DH2: Pelt 4G **127**
Charleswood NE3: Gos 4F **45**
Charlie St. NE40: G'sde 5D **78**
Charlotte Cl. NE4: Newc T 3D **82** (9A **4**)
Charlotte M. NE1: Newc T 6D **4**
Charlotte Sq. NE1: Newc T 1E **82** (6D **4**)
Charlotte St. DH9: Stly 5E **124**
NE28: W'snd 3G **65**
(not continuous)
NE30: N Shi 7H **49**
NE33: S Shi 3J **67**
NE40: Ryton 3C **78**
Charlton Cl. NE46: Hex 4B **70**
Charlton Ct. NE25: Whit B 1E **48**
Charlton Gdns. NE61: Mor 1H **15**
Charlton Gro. SR6: Cle 6C **88**
Charlton Rd. SR5: Monk 4E **104**
Charlton St. NE15: Lem 7D **60**
NE24: Bly 2H **23**
NE63: Ash 3A **12**
Charlton Vs. *NE40: G'sde 5F* ***79***
(off Lead Rd.)
Charlton Wlk. NE8: Gate 5E **82**
Charman St. SR1: Sund 1F **119** (3J **7**)
Charminster Gdns. NE6: Newc T 3A **64**
Charnwood DH9: Stly 1E **124**
Charnwood Av. NE12: Longb 6J **45**
Charnwood Ct. NE33: S Shi 3A **68**
Charnwood Gdns. NE9: Gate 1K **99**
Charter Dr. SR3: E Her 2J **131**
Charters Cres. DH6: S Het 5B **158**
Chartwell Pl. DH8: Con 5H **121**
Chase Ct. DH6: Sher 3A **168**
NE16: Whi 7H **81**
Chasedale Cres. NE24: Cow 2E **22**
CHASE FARM 2D **22**
Chase Farm Dr. NE24: Cow 1D **22**
Chase Mdws. NE24: Cow 3D **22**
Chase M. NE24: Cow 2D **22**
Chase, The NE12: Kil 2J **45**
NE29: N Shi 6G **49**
NE38: Wash 7D **114**
NE46: Hex 3B **70**
Chatham Cl. NE25: Sea D 2H **37**
Chatham Rd. SR5: C'twn 5G **103**
Chathill Cl. NE25: Whit B 6D **38**
NE61: Mor 3G **15**
Chathill Ter. NE6: Walk 1D **84**
Chatsworth NE3: Gos 3E **62**
Chatsworth Ct. NE33: S Shi 2K **67**
Chatsworth Cres. SR4: Sund 4C **118**
Chatsworth Dr. NE22: Bed 5A **18**
Chatsworth Gdns. NE5: Newc T 2F **61**
NE6: Newc T 2B **84**
NE25: Whit B 1E **48**
Chatsworth Pl. NE16: Whi 2G **97**
Chatsworth Rd. NE32: Jar 1C **86**
Chatsworth St. SR4: Sund 3C **118**
Chatsworth St. Sth. SR4: Sund 4C **118**
Chatterton St. SR5: S'wck 5C **104**
Chatton Av. NE23: Cra 4A **26**
NE34: S Shi 5D **68**
Chatton Cl. DH2: Ches S 1J **141**
NE61: Hep 3J **15**
Chatton St. NE28: W'snd 4C **66**
Chatton Wynd NE3: Ken 5C **44**
Chaucer Av. NE34: S Shi 3G **87**
TS27: B Col 1G **183**
Chaucer Cl. DH9: Stly 3G **125**
NE8: Gate 4J **83** (10L **5**)
Chaucer Rd. NE16: Whi 6H **81**
Chaucer St. DH4: Hou S 2D **144**
Chaytor Gro. SR1: Sund 2G **119**
Chaytor Rd. DH8: Con 4D **120**
Chaytor St. NE32: Jar 5B **66**
Chaytor Ter. Nth. DH9: Stly 6H **125**
Chaytor Ter. Sth. DH9: Stly 6J **125**
Cheadle Av. NE23: Cra 7J **21**
NE28: W'snd 6H **47**
Cheadle Rd. SR5: C'twn 5G **103**
Cheam Cl. NE16: Whi 2H **97**
Cheam Rd. SR5: C'twn 5G **103**
Cheddar Gdns. NE9: Gate 4H **99**
Chedder Ct. DH9: Ann P 6K **123**
Cheeseburn Gdns. NE5: Newc T 5J **61**
Cheldon Cl. NE25: Whit B 5C **38**
Chelford Cl. NE28: W'snd 5J **47**
Chelmsford Gro. NE2: Newc T 6J **63** (2L **5**)
Chelmsford Rd. SR5: C'twn 5G **103**
Chelmsford Sq. SR5: C'twn 4G **103**
Chelmsford St. SR3: New S 1C **132**
Chelsea Gdns. NE8: Gate 6K **83**
Chelsea Gro. NE4: Newc T 1C **82**
Chelsea Ho. *DH9: Stly 2F* ***125***
(off Quarry Rd.)
Cheltenham Ct. NE63: Ash 5A **12**
Cheltenham Dr. NE35: Bol C 4E **86**
Cheltenham Rd. SR5: C'twn 5G **103**
Cheltenham Sq. SR5: C'twn 5G **103**
Cheltenham Ter. NE6: Newc T 6K **63** (1P **5**)
Chelton Cl. NE13: Bru V 7D **34**
Chepstow Cl. DH8: Shot B 2F **121**
Chepstow Gdns. NE8: Gate 7F **83**
Chepstow Rd. NE15: Newc T 7F **61**
Chepstow St. SR4: Sund 2D **118**
Cherribank SR2: Ryh 3G **133**
Cherry Av. SR8: Pet 6F **173**
Cherry Banks DH3: Ches S 4B **128**
Cherry Blossom Way SR5: Wash 6B **102**
Cherryburn Gdns. NE4: Newc T 5A **62**
Cherryburn
(Thomas Bewick Birthplace Mus.)
4B 76
Cherry Cotts. DH9: Tan L 6B **110**
Cherry Dr. DH6: Has 1B **170**
Cherry Gro. NE12: Kil 7A **36**
NE42: Pru 3D **76**
Cherry La. NE46: Hex 6B **50**
Cherry Pk. DH7: B'don 2C **174**
Cherrytree Cl. NE12: Kil 2D **46**
Cherrytree Ct. NE22: Bed 6B **18**
Cherry Tree Dr. NE22: Bed 7H **17**
Cherrytree Dr. DH7: Lang P 5H **151**
NE16: Whi 6J **81**
Cherry Tree Gdns. NE15: Hor 5E **56**
Cherrytree Gdns. NE9: Gate 3J **99**
NE25: Whit B 1F **49**
Cherry Tree La. NE41: Wylam 7J **57**
Cherrytree Rd. DH2: Ches S 4J **127**
Cherry Trees NE24: Bly 3H **23**
Cherrytree Sq. SR2: Ryh 1G **133**
Cherry Tree Wlk. NE31: Heb 2J **85**
Cherry Way DH4: Hou S 1B **144**
NE12: Kil 7A **36**
Cherrywood NE6: Walk 4C **64**
Cherrywood Gdns. SR3: New S 2D **132**
Cherwell NE37: Usw 7K **101**
Cherwell Rd. SR8: Pet 7K **171**
Cherwell Sq. NE12: Longb 3A **46**
Chesham Gdns. NE5: Cha P 3B **60**
Chesham Grn. NE3: Ken 7B **44**
Cheshire Av. DH3: Bir 7A **114**
Cheshire Cl. NE63: Ash 3J **11**
Cheshire Ct. NE31: Heb 1H **85**
Cheshire Dr. DH1: Carr 2G **167**
Cheshire Gdns. NE28: W'snd 2E **64**
Cheshire Gro. NE34: S Shi 6D **68**
Chesils, The NE12: Longb 7J **45**
Chesmond Dr. NE21: Bla T 3C **80**
Chessar Av. NE5: Newc T 3H **61**
Chester Av. NE28: W'snd 2K **65**
Chester Cl. NE20: Pon 7F **31**
Chester Cres. NE2: Newc T 6H **63** (2J **5**)
SR1: Sund 2D **118** (4F **7**)
Chesterfield Rd. NE4: Newc T 2B **82**
Chester Gdns. DH7: Wit G 2D **152**
NE34: S Shi 6A **68**
Chester Gro. NE23: Seg 2C **36**
NE24: Bly 3G **23**
Chesterhill NE23: Cra 6K **25**
CHESTER-LE-STREET 6A **128**
Chester-le-Street Leisure Cen. 6B 128
Chester-le-Street Station (Rail) 6A **128**
Chester M. SR4: Sund 3D **118**
CHESTER MOOR 3J **141**
Chester Oval SR1: Sund 5F **7**
Chester Pl. NE8: Gate 4F **83**
SR8: Pet 5K **171**
Chester Rd. DH3: Gt Lum, Lam P 4C **128**
DH4: Pen 3B **130**
DH8: C'sde 3C **134**
DH9: Stly 2G **125**
SR1: Sund 2D **118** (5F **7**)
SR2: Sund 2D **118**
SR4: Pen 5G **117**
SR4: Sund 5G **117**
(Sevenoaks Dr.)
SR4: Sund 3A **118**
(West Mt.)
Chester Rd. Est. DH9: Stly 2G **125**
Chesters Av. NE12: Longb 6H **45**
Chesters Ct. NE12: Longb 6K **45**
Chesters Dene DH8: Ebc 5G **107**
Chesters Gdns. NE40: Ryton 2C **78**
Chesters Pk. NE9: Gate 1H **99**
Chesters, The DH8: Ebc 5G **107**
NE5: Cha P 4C **60**
NE25: Whit B 5D **38**
Chester St. DH2: Ches S 1G **141**
DH4: Hou S 7D **130**
NE2: Newc T 6H **63** (2J **5**)
SR4: Sund 2C **118**
Chester St. E. SR4: Sund 2D **118**
Chester St. W. SR4: Sund 2C **118**
Chester Ter. SR1: Sund 2D **118** (4F **7**)
SR8: Eas 7B **160**
Chester Ter. Nth. SR4: Sund 2D **118**
Chesterton Rd. NE34: S Shi 2H **87**
Chester Way NE32: Jar 5A **86**
Chesterwood Dr. NE28: W'snd 3E **64**
Chesterwood Ter. NE10: Gate 4F **85**
Chestnut Av. NE5: Newc T 3K **61**
NE16: Whi 2H **97**
NE24: Bly 7H **19**
NE25: Whit B 7F **39**
NE38: Wash 7F **115**
Chestnut Cl. NE12: Kil 7K **35**
NE32: Jar 5D **86**
Chestnut Cres. SR5: S'wck 4B **104**
Chestnut Dr. DH6: Has 1C **170**
Chestnut Gdns. NE8: Gate 6E **82**
Chestnut Gro. DH7: Ush M 3C **164**
NE34: S Shi 2B **88**
Chestnut St. NE28: W'snd 4G **65**
NE63: Hir 4C **12**
(Fourth Av.)
NE63: Hir 3B **12**
(Woodhorn Rd.)
Chestnut Ter. DH4: Hou S 7C **130**
Cheswick Dr. NE3: Gos 6F **45**
Cheswick Rd. NE25: Sea D 1J **37**
Cheveley Pk. Shop. Cen. DH1: Carr 7H **155**
Cheveley Wlk. DH1: Carr 1H **167**
Chevin Cl. NE6: Walk 4E **64**
Chevington NE10: Gate 2E **100**
Chevington Cl. NE61: Peg 4K **9**
Chevington Gdns. NE5: Newc T 4K **61**
Chevington Gro. NE25: Whit B 4D **38**
Cheviot Cl. DH2: Ches S 2J **141**
NE21: Bla T 5C **80**
(not continuous)
NE29: N Shi 2F **49**
NE37: Wash 2E **114**
Cheviot Ct. DH9: Ann P 6K **123**
NE7: Newc T 1J **63**
NE21: Bla T 3C **80**
NE26: Whit B 7J **39**
NE61: Mor 2G **15**
SR7: S'hm 2J **147**
Cheviot Gdns. NE11: Gate 7C **82**
SR7: S'hm 2J **147**
Cheviot Grange NE23: Dud 5A **36**
Cheviot Grn. NE11: Dun 6C **82**
Cheviot Gro. NE61: Peg 4A **10**
Cheviot Ho. NE37: Wash 4G **115**
Cheviot La. SR2: Ryh 2F **133**
Cheviot Mt. NE6: Newc T 7A **64**
Cheviot Pl. SR8: Pet 5K **171**
(not continuous)
Cheviot Rd. DH2: Ches S 1K **141**
(not continuous)
NE32: Jar 2A **86**
NE34: S Shi 5C **68**
Cheviot St. SR4: Sund 1B **118**
Cheviot Ter. DH9: Stly 4G **125**
Cheviot Vw. NE10: Gate 1B **100**
NE12: Longb 6B **46**
NE13: Bru V 5C **34**
NE20: Pon 5A **32**
NE23: Seg 2D **36**
NE26: Whit B 7H **39**
NE27: Shir 3H **47**
NE42: Pru 4G **77**
NE63: Hir 2C **12**
Cheviot Way NE46: Hex 2C **70**
NE62: Chop 7K **11**
Chevron, The NE6: Newc T 5P **5**
Chevy Chase NE1: Newc T 4E **4**
Chevychase Ct. SR7: Sea 7H **133**
Cheyne Rd. NE42: Pru 3E **76**
Cheyne, The SR3: New S 4C **132**
Chichester Av. NE23: Nel V 2H **25**
Chichester Cl. NE3: Ken 5K **43**
NE8: Gate 4G **83**
NE63: N Sea 5E **12**
Chichester Gro. NE22: Bed 6H **17**
Chichester Pl. NE33: S Shi 5J **67**
Chichester Rd. DH1: Dur 4B **154**
NE33: S Shi 5J **67**
SR6: Monk 3G **105**
Chichester Rd. E. NE33: S Shi 4K **67**
Chichester Station (Metro) 5J **67**
Chichester Way NE32: Jar 5B **86**
Chicken Rd. NE28: W'snd 2E **64**
Chicks La. SR6: Whit 6H **89**
Chigwell Cl. DH4: Pen 2B **130**
Chilcote NE10: Gate 7B **84**
Chilcrosse NE10: Gate 1D **100**
(not continuous)
Childhood Memories Toy Mus. 3K 49
Chilham Ct. NE29: N Shi 4B **48**
NE38: Wash 4F **115**
Chillingham Cl. NE24: Bly 4F **23**
Chillingham Ct. NE6: Newc T 6A **64**
Chillingham Cres. NE63: Ash 4A **12**
Chillingham Dr. DH2: Ches S 2J **141**
NE29: N Shi 1D **66**
Chillingham Gro. SR8: Pet 2J **181**
Chillingham Ho. *SR6: Monk 7G* ***105***
(off Mulgrave Dr.)
Chillingham Ind. Est. NE6: Walk 6A **64**
Chillingham Rd. DH1: Dur 5B **154**
NE6: Newc T, Walk 4A **64**
Chillingham Road Station (Metro) 6B **64**
Chillingham Ter. NE32: Jar 2D **86**
Chilside Rd. NE10: Gate 7B **84**
Chiltern Av. DH2: Ches S 7K **127**
(not continuous)
Chiltern Cl. NE38: Wash 5F **115**
NE63: N Sea 6D **12**
Chiltern Dr. NE12: Longb 3K **45**
Chiltern Gdns. DH9: Stly 4H **125**
NE11: Gate 7C **82**
Chiltern Rd. NE29: N Shi 2E **48**
Chilton Av. DH4: Hou S 1K **143**
Chilton Gdns. DH4: Hou S 2A **144**
Chilton Gth. SR8: Pet 7D **172**
CHILTON MOOR 3A **144**
Chilton St. SR5: S'wck 6E **104**
Chimney Mills NE2: Newc T 5E **62** (1C **4**)
China St. SR2: Sund 4G **119**
Chingford Cl. DH4: Pen 2C **130**
Chipchase NE38: Wash 4D **114**
Chipchase Av. NE23: Cra 4K **25**
Chipchase Cl. NE22: Bed 7F **17**
NE61: Peg 4B **10**
Chipchase Ct. DH4: Hou S 1H **143**
NE25: Sea D 4G **27**
SR7: Sea 7H **133**
Chipchase Cres. NE5: Newc T 2E **60**
Chipchase M. NE3: Gos 3C **44**
Chipchase Ter. NE32: Jar 3B **86**
Chippendale Pl. NE2: Newc T 6D **62** (1A **4**)
Chip, The NE61: Loan 3F **15**
Chirdon Cres. NE46: Hex 2E **70**
Chirnside NE23: Cra 6K **25**
Chirnside Ter. DH9: Ann P 6J **123**
CHIRTON 7F **49**
Chirton Av. NE29: N Shi 7F **49**
NE34: S Shi 7E **68**
Chirton Dene Quay NE29: N Shi 3F **67**
Chirton Dene Way NE29: N Shi 3F **67**
Chirton Grn. NE24: Bly 4F **23**
NE29: N Shi 7F **49**
Chirton Gro. NE34: S Shi 7E **68**
Chirton Hill Dr. NE29: N Shi 5C **48**
Chirton La. NE29: N Shi 6E **48**
Chirton Lodge NE29: N Shi 7E **48**
Chirton W. Vw. NE29: N Shi 7F **49**
Chirton Wynd NE6: Newc T 1A **84**
Chislehurst Rd. DH4: Pen 2B **130**
Chiswick Gdns. NE8: Gate 6J **83**
Chiswick Rd. SR5: C'twn 5G **103**
Chiswick Sq. SR5: C'twn 5G **103**
Chollerford Av. NE25: Whit B 7H **39**
NE29: N Shi 6C **48**
Chollerford Cl. NE3: Gos 1C **62**
Chollerford M. NE25: H'wll 1K **37**
Chollerton Dr. NE12: Longb 4E **46**
NE22: Bed 7J **17**
CHOPPINGTON 3G **17**
Choppington Rd. NE22: Bed 7H **17**
NE61: Mor 2H **15**
NE62: Sco G 7H **17**
CHOPWELL 6K **93**
Chopwell Gdns. NE9: Gate 5B **100**
Chopwell Rd. NE17: C'wl 1A **108**
Chopwell Woods Rd. NE39: H Spen 5D **94**
Chorley Pl. NE6: Walk 1C **84**
CHOWDENE 4H **99**
Chowdene Bank NE9: Gate 5G **99**
NE11: Gate 5G **99**
Chowdene Ter. NE9: Gate 3H **99**
Christal Ter. SR6: Monk 4F **105**
Christchurch Ct. SR7: S'hm 2J **147**

Christchurch Pl.—Clockburnsyde Cl.

Christchurch Pl. SR8: Pet 7A **172**
Christie Ter. NE6: Walk 1D **84**
Christon Cl. NE3: Gos 7G **45**
Christon Rd. NE3: Gos 7E **44**
Christon Way NE10: Gate 4F **85**
Christopher Rd. NE6: Walk 6C **64**
Chudleigh Gdns. NE5: Cha P 3B **60**
Chudleigh Ter. NE21: Bla T 4C **80**
Church Av. NE3: Gos 7F **45**
NE62: Sco G 3G **17**
NE62: W Sle 1B **18**
Church Bank DH8: Shot B 3E **120**
DH9: Stly 2F **125**
NE15: Thro 6K **59**
NE28: W'snd 3H **65**
NE32: Jar 6D **66**
SR5: S'wck 6C **104**
Churchburn Dr. NE61: Loan 3F **15**
Church Chare DH3: Ches S 6B **128**
NE16: Whi 7H **81**
NE20: Pon 4K **31**
Church Cl. DH4: Hou S 5J **129**
DH8: Ebc 5G **107**
NE13: Din 4H **33**
NE22: Bed 1H **21**
NE25: Whit B 7C **38**
NE44: Rid M 7K **73**
SR7: S'hm 2A **148**
SR8: Pet 7C **172**
Church Ct. NE10: Gate 5B **84**
NE13: Bru V 7C 34
(off Church La.)
NE22: Bed 1H **21**
Churchdown Cl. NE35: Bol C 4E **86**
Church Dr. NE9: Gate 1J **99**
Churcher Gdns. NE28: W'snd 1E **64**
Church Flatt NE20: Pon 4K **31**
Church Grn. NE16: Whi 7H **81**
SR7: S'hm 2A **148**
Churchill Av. DH1: Dur 2D **166**
NE25: Whit B 1E **48**
SR5: S'wck 5C **104**
Churchill Cl. DH8: Shot B 3E **120**
Churchill Gdns. NE2: Newc T 4J **63**
Churchill M. NE6: Newc T 2A **84**
Churchill Sq. DH1: Dur 1D **166**
DH4: Hou S 2B **144**
Churchill St. NE1: Newc T 2E **82** (8C **4**)
NE28: W'snd 7K **47**
SR1: Sund 2G **119**
Churchill Ter. DH6: Sher 4E **168**
CHURCH KELLOE 7F **179**
Churchlands NE46: Hex 2F **71**
Church La. DH1: Dur 2C **166**
(Gilesgate)
DH1: Dur 4B **166** (5D **6**)
(Hallgarth St.)
DH6: Shad 5E **168**
NE3: Gos 7F **45**
NE9: Gate 1K **99**
NE22: Bed 1J **21**
NE44: Rid M 7J **73**
SR1: Sund 2E **118** (4H **7**)
SR6: Whit 6H **89**
SR7: Mur 7D **146**
Church La. Nth. SR7: Mur 7D **146**
Church Mdw. DH7: B'don 7F **165**
Church M. NE27: Back 6G **37**
Church Pde. DH7: Sac 6D **140**
Church Pk. DH6: Whe H 2B **180**
Church Pl. NE10: Gate 5B **84**
Chu. Point Cvn. Pk. NE64: Newb S 2K **13**
Church Ri. NE16: Whi 7H **81**
NE40: Ryton 1J **79**
(not continuous)
Church Rd. DH2: Pelt 3F **127**
DH5: Hett H 4G **145**
DH8: Con 5F **121**
NE3: Gos 7E **44**
NE9: Gate 2J **99**
NE15: Thro 6K **59**
NE27: Back, H'wll 6G **37**
NE41: Wylam 7J **57**
Church Row *NE10: Gate 1A 100*
(off Windy Nook Rd.)
NE46: Hex 1D **70**
Church Side DH3: Gt Lum 3E **142**
Churchside NE13: Din 4H **33**
Church St. DH1: Dur 4B **166** (5D **6**)
DH3: Bir 4A **114**
DH4: Hou S 2E **144**
DH4: W Rai 1A **156**
DH5: Hou S 2E **144**
DH6: Has 1A **170**
DH6: Quar H 5D **178**
DH6: Whe H 2B **180**
DH7: Lang P 5H **151**
DH7: Sac 7D **140**
DH8: C'sde 5B **134**
DH8: Con 7H **121**
DH8: Lead 5A **122**
DH9: Ann P 5K **123**
DH9: Stly 2F **125**
NE6: Walk 2E **84**
(Caledonia St.)
Church St. NE6: Walk 1E **84**
(Church Wlk.)
NE8: Gate 2G **83** (8H **5**)
NE10: Gate 6B **84**
NE11: Dun 5C **82**
NE16: Sun 7G **97**
NE21: Bla T 5B **80**
NE23: Cra 4K **25**
NE24: Bly 1J **23**
NE30: N Shi 6H **49**
NE31: Heb 6H **65**
NE32: Jar 6B **66**
SR4: Sund 2G **117**
SR5: S'wck 5D **104**
SR7: Mur 1E **158**
SR7: S'hm 3B **148**
TS27: Hes 4E **182**
TS28: Win 7H **181**
Church St. E. SR1: Sund 1G **119**
Church St. Head
DH1: Dur 4B **166** (6D **6**)
Church St. Nth. SR6: Monk 6F **105**
Church St. Vs. DH1: Dur 4B **166** (6D **6**)
Church Ter. NE21: Bla T 3C **80**
Church Va. DH6: H Pitt 7C **156**
Church Vw. DH1: Carr 7H **155**
DH2: Plaw 7J **141**
DH3: Bir 4A **114**
DH6: Has 1A **170**
DH6: Shot C 5E **170**
DH6: Thor 1K **179**
DH7: Esh W 3D **162**
DH7: Lan 7K **137**
DH7: Lang P 7B **150**
DH8: Con 7G **121**
NE25: Well 6K **37**
NE28: W'snd 3H **65**
NE35: Bol C 5E **86**
NE37: Wash 1H **115**
NE64: Newb S 2G **13**
SR3: New S 2C **132**
Church Vw. Vs. DH5: Hett H 5G **145**
Church Vs. DH6: Shad 5E **168**
Church Wlk. DH6: Thor 1J **179**
(not continuous)
NE6: Walk 1E **84**
(not continuous)
NE8: Gate 2G **83** (8H **5**)
NE61: Mor 7E **8**
SR1: Sund 1H **119**
Churchwalk Ho. NE6: Walk 1E **84**
Church Ward SR2: Ryh 3J **133**
Church Way NE25: Well 5A **38**
NE29: N Shi 6G **49**
NE33: S Shi 2J **67**
Church Wood NE23: Cra 4K **25**
Church Wynd DH6: Sher 3K **167**
Churston Cl. DH4: Hou S 5C **130**
Cicero Ter. SR5: S'wck 5C **104**
Cinderford Cl. NE35: Bol C 4E **86**
Circle Pl. NE46: Hex 1C **70**
Circle, The NE32: Jar 2B **86**
Cirencester St. SR4: Sund 1D **118**
Cirus Ho. SR3: New S 3C **132**
Citadel E. NE12: Kil 1B **46**
Citadel W. NE12: Kil 1B **46**
Citygate NE1: Newc T 1E **82** (5D **4**)
City Library 4K **7**
City Pool 7G **63** (3G **4**)
City Rd. NE1: Newc T 1G **83** (6G **4**)
City Stadium 7J **63** (3L **5**)
City Theatre (Durham) 3A **166** (3C **6**)
City Way SR3: E Her 4H **131**
Civic Ct. NE31: Heb 1K **85**
Clacton Rd. SR5: C'twn 6F **103**
Clanfield Ct. NE3: Newc T 1H **63**
Clanny Ho. SR4: Sund 2B **118**
Clanny St. SR1: Sund 2E **118** (4G **7**)
(St Michaels Way)
SR1: Sund 2D **118** (5F **7**)
(Westbourne Rd.)
Clapham Av. NE6: Newc T 1B **84**
Clappersgate SR8: Eas 1J **171**
Clara Av. NE27: Shir 7K **37**
Clarabad Ter. NE12: Longb 3E **46**
Clara St. NE4: Newc T 2K **81**
NE21: Bla T 5B **80**
SR7: S'hm 2K **147**
CLARA VALE 7C **58**
Clara Va. Complex
NE40: Ryton 7C **58**
Clare Lea NE43: Hed 4C **92**
Claremont Av. NE15: Lem 5D **60**
SR6: Monk 4G **105**
Claremont Bri. NE2: Newc T 2F **4**
Claremont Ct. *NE26: Whit B 3E 38*
(off Claremont Cres.)
Claremont Cres. NE26: Whit B 4E **38**
Claremont Dr. DH4: Hou S 3A **130**
Claremont Gdns. NE26: Whit B 5F **39**
NE36: E Bol 7K **87**
Claremont Ho. NE1: Newc T 6E **62** (1D **4**)
Claremont Nth. Av. NE8: Gate 4G **83**
Claremont Pl. NE2: Newc T 6E **62** (1D **4**)
NE8: Gate 5G **83**
Claremont Rd. NE2: Newc T 5C **62** (1B **4**)
NE26: Whit B 3E **38**
SR6: Monk 4G **105**
Claremont Sth. Av. NE8: Gate 5G **83**
Claremont Sports Hall 6E **62** (1C **4**)
Claremont St. NE2: Newc T 6E **62** (1C **4**)
NE8: Gate 5G **83**
Claremont Ter. NE2: Newc T 6E **62** (1C **4**)
NE9: Spri 6D **100**
NE10: Gate 4F **85**
NE24: Bly 2H **23**
SR2: Sund 3E **118** (6H **7**)
Claremont Twr. NE1: Newc T 2E **4**
Claremont Wlk. NE8: Gate 5G **83**
(Bk. Woodbine St.)
NE8: Gate 5F **83**
(St Cuthbert's Pl.)
Claremount Ct. NE36: W Bol 7H **87**
Clarence Cres. NE26: Whit B 7H **39**
Clarence Gdns. DH8: Con 5G **121**
Clarence Ho. NE2: Newc T 7H **63** (3J **5**)
Clarence Pl. NE3: Gos 7G **45**
Clarence St. DH6: Bow 5H **177**
DH6: Coxh 7K **177**
DH9: Tan L 6B **110**
NE2: Newc T 7H **63** (4J **5**)
NE26: Sea S 5D **28**
SR5: S'wck 5B **104**
(not continuous)
SR7: S'hm 3B **148**
Clarence Ter. DH3: Ches S 6A **128**
Clarence Vs. DH6: Coxh 7K **177**
Clarence Wlk. NE2: Newc T 7H **63** (3J **5**)
Clarendon M. NE3: Gos 2E **44**
Clarendon Rd. NE6: Newc T 4A **64**
Clarendon Sq. SR5: S'wck 4D **104**
Clarendon St. *DH8: Con 6H 121*
(off George St.)
Clare Rd. SR8: Pet 7K **171**
Clarewood Av. NE34: S Shi 5C **68**
Clarewood Ct. NE4: Newc T 7C **62** (4A **4**)
Clarewood Grn. NE4: Newc T 7C **62** (4A **4**)
Clarewood Pl. NE5: Newc T 5J **61**
Clarke's Ter. NE23: Dud 4J **35**
Clarke Ter. NE10: Gate 6A **84**
SR7: Mur 7E **146**
Clarks Fld. NE61: Mor 2E **8**
Clarks Hill Wlk. NE15: Thro 6K **59**
Clark's Ter. SR7: S'hm 1G **147**
Clark Ter. DH8: Lead 3K **121**
DH9: Stly 1F **125**
Clarty La. NE11: Kib 4F **113**
NE46: Sand 4H **51**
Clasper Ct. NE33: S Shi 1J **67**
Clasper St. NE4: Newc T 3D **82** (10A **4**)
Clasper Way NE16: Swa 3G **81**
Claude Gibb Hall NE1: Newc T 2H **5**
Claude St. DH5: Hett H 7G **145**
NE40: Ryton 3D **78**
Claude Ter. SR7: Mur 7F **147**
Claudius Ct. NE33: S Shi 1J **67**
Claverdon St. NE5: Cha P 1B **60**
Clavering Cen. NE16: Whi 2F **97**
Clavering Pl. DH9: Ann P 6K **123**
NE1: Newc T 2F **83** (7F **4**)
Clavering Rd. NE16: Swa 6G **81**
NE21: Bla T 5C 80
(off Shibdon Bank)
Clavering Sq. NE11: Dun 6B **82**
Clavering St. NE28: W'snd 4B **66**
(not continuous)
Clavering Way NE21: Bla T 5E **80**
Claverley Dr. NE27: Back 6G **37**
Claxheugh Rd. SR4: Sund 1H **117**
Claxton St. SR8: Pet 5E **172**
Clay La. DH1: Dur 4J **165** (5A **6**)
(not continuous)
Claymere Rd. SR2: Sund 7G **119**
Claypath DH1: Dur 2B **166** (2D **6**)
NE10: Gate 3D **100**
Claypath Ct. DH1: Dur 2B **166** (2D **6**)
Claypath La. NE33: S Shi 3J **67**
(not continuous)
Claypath Rd. DH5: Hett H 1G **157**
Claypath St. NE6: Newc T 7J **63** (4M **5**)
Claypool Ct. NE34: S Shi 1J **87**
Clayside Ho. NE33: S Shi 4K **67**
Clayton Pk. Sq. NE2: Newc T 5G **63**
Clayton Rd. NE2: Newc T 5F **63**
Clayton St. NE1: Newc T 1F **83** (6E **4**)
NE22: Bed 6B **18**
NE23: Dud 3H **35**
NE32: Jar 6B **66**
Clayton St. W. NE1: Newc T 2E **82** (7D **4**)
Clayton Ter. NE10: Gate 5A **84**
Clayton Ter. Rd. NE17: C'wl 5A **94**
NE39: H Spen 5A **94**
Clayworth Rd. NE3: Gos 3D **44**
CLEADON 5C **88**
Cleadon Gdns. NE9: Gate 4B **100**
NE28: W'snd 7A **48**
Cleadon Hill Dr. NE34: S Shi 2C **88**
Cleadon Hill Rd. NE34: S Shi 2D **88**
Cleadon La. NE36: E Bol 5A **88**
SR6: Cle, Whit 5D **88**
Cleadon La. Ind. Est. NE36: E Bol 6K **87**
Cleadon Lea SR6: Cle 5B **88**
Cleadon Mdws. SR6: Cle 5C **88**
CLEADON PARK 2C **88**
Cleadon St. DH8: Con 6H **121**
NE6: Walk 7C **64**
Cleadon Towers NE34: S Shi 2D **88**
Cleasby Gdns. NE9: Gate 1H **99**
Cleasewell Ter. NE62: Chop 1J **17**
Cleaside Av. NE34: S Shi 2C **88**
Cleaswell Hill NE62: Chop 1H **17**
Cleehill Dr. NE29: N Shi 3F **49**
Cleeve Ct. NE38: Wash 3H **115**
Cleghorn St. NE6: Newc T 5A **64**
Clegwell Ter. NE31: Heb 7K **65**
Clematis Cres. NE9: Spri 5B **100**
Clement Av. NE22: Bed 7A **18**
Clementhorpe NE29: N Shi 5G **49**
Clementina Cl. SR2: Sund 3G **119**
Clement St. NE9: Gate 2H **99**
Clennel Ho. NE4: Newc T 1A **82**
Clennell Av. NE31: Heb 1H **85**
Clent Way NE12: Longb 6J **45**
Clephan St. NE11: Dun 5B **82**
Clervaux Ter. NE32: Jar 7C **66**
Cleveland Av. DH2: Ches S 7K **127**
NE29: N Shi 6F **49**
NE64: Newb S 3H **13**
Cleveland Ct. NE32: Jar 6A **66**
NE33: S Shi 1J **67**
Cleveland Cres. NE29: N Shi 6G **49**
Cleveland Dr. NE38: Wash 5F **115**
Cleveland Gdns. NE7: Newc T 2J **63**
NE28: W'snd 2B **66**
Cleveland Pl. SR8: Pet 6K **171**
Cleveland Rd. NE29: N Shi 6F **49**
SR4: Sund 4B **118**
Cleveland St. NE33: S Shi 1K **67**
Cleveland Ter. DH9: Stly 4G **125**
NE29: N Shi 6G **49**
NE64: Newb S 3H **13**
SR4: Sund 3C **118**
Cleveland Vw. SR6: Monk 1G **105**
Cliff Cotts. NE32: Jar 5D **66**
Cliffe Ct. SR6: Monk 3H **105**
Cliffe Pk. SR6: Monk 3H **105**
Clifford Gdns. NE40: Ryton 3D **78**
Clifford Rd. DH9: Stly 3E **124**
NE6: Newc T 1B **84**
Clifford's Bank DH7: Lang P 1B **162**
Clifford's Fort Moat NE30: N Shi 7J **49**
(not continuous)
Cliffords Ga. DH7: Esh W 3C **162**
Clifford St. DH3: Ches S 1A **142**
DH7: Lang P 5H **151**
NE6: Newc T 7K **63** (4N **5**)
NE21: Bla T 3C **80**
NE30: N Shi 6J **49**
SR4: Sund 2C **118**
Clifford Ter. DH3: Ches S 7A **128**
NE40: Ryton 2D **78**
Cliff Rd. SR2: Ryh 3J **133**
Cliff Row NE30: Whit B 7J **39**
Cliffside NE34: S Shi 7E **68**
Cliff Ter. SR2: Ryh 3J **133**
SR8: Eas 1K **171**
Cliff Vw. SR2: Ryh 3J **133**
CLIFTON 6G **15**
Clifton Av. NE28: W'snd 3F **65**
NE34: S Shi 6A **68**
Cliftonbourne Av. SR6: Monk 3G **105**
Clifton Cl. NE40: Ryton 2J **79**
NE62: Chop 7J **11**
Clifton Ct. NE3: Ken 5K **43**
NE9: Spri 6C **100**
NE25: Whit B 4E **38**
Clifton Gdns. NE9: Gate 7H **83**
NE24: News 5H **23**
NE29: N Shi 2E **66**
(not continuous)
Clifton Gro. NE25: Whit B 5E **38**
Clifton La. NE61: Tra W 7H **15**
Clifton Rd. NE4: Newc T 1A **82**
NE23: Cra 5A **26**
SR6: Monk 4G **105**
Clifton Sq. SR8: Pet 5B **172**
Clifton Ter. NE12: Longb 5B **46**
NE26: Whit B 6H **39**
NE33: S Shi 6J **67**
Cliftonville Av. NE4: Newc T 1A **82**
Cliftonville Gdns. NE26: Whit B 5G **39**
Clifton Wlk. NE5: Cha P 3B **60**
Climbing Tree Wlk. NE61: Peg 4A **10**
Clintburn Ct. NE23: Cra 2A **26**
Clinton Pl. NE3: Gos 2D **44**
SR3: E Her 3J **131**
Clipsham Cl. NE12: Longb 6K **45**
Clipstone Av. NE6: Walk 3C **84**
Clipstone Cl. NE15: Thro 3G **59**
Clitheroe Gdns. NE22: Bed 6F **17**
Clive Pl. NE6: Newc T 1K **83** (5N **5**)
Clive St. NE29: N Shi 7H **49**
NE34: S Shi 2G **87**
Clockburn Lonnen NE16: Whi 2D **96**
Clockburnsyde Cl. NE16: Whi 2E **96**

Clockmill Rd.—Conway Dr.

Clockmill Rd. NE11: Dun 5C **82**
Clockstand Cl. SR6: Monk 5G **105**
Clockwell St. SR5: S'wck 6B **104**
Cloggs, The NE20: Pon 4K **31**
Cloister Av. NE34: S Shi 1G **87**
Cloister Ct. NE8: Gate 3H **83** (10K **5**)
Cloister Gth. NE7: Newc T 7H **45**
Cloisters, The NE7: Newc T 7H **45**
NE34: S Shi 6B **68**
SR2: Sund 3F **119** (7J **7**)
TS28: Win 4G **181**
Cloister Wlk. NE32: Jar 6C **66**
Close NE1: Newc T 2F **83** (8F **4**)
Closeburn Sq. SR3: New S 3D **132**
Close E., The DH2: Ches S 4A **128**
Closefield Gro. NE25: Whit B 7E **38**
Close Ho. Est. NE15: Hed W 4B **58**
Close St. SR4: Sund 1C **118**
SR5: S'wck 6D **104**
Close, The DH1: Carr 1H **167**
DH2: Ches S 4A **128**
DH5: Hou S 2F **145**
DH7: Lan 6J **137**
DH7: New B 4A **174**
DH8: Shot B 3F **121**
NE5: Newc T 5E **60**
NE16: Burn 1C **110**
NE20: Pon 6J **31**
NE21: Bla T 5A **80**
NE23: Seg 2D **36**
NE24: Bly 7J **19**
NE42: O'ham 2B **76**
NE42: Pru 3G **77**
SR6: Cle 5B **88**
Cloth Mkt. NE1: Newc T 1F **83** (6F **4**)
CLOUGH DENE 5A **110**
Clough Dene NE16: Burn, Tan L 5A **110**
Clough La. NE1: Newc T 6F **4**
Clousden Dr. NE12: Longb 3C **46**
Clousden Grange NE12: Kil 3C **46**
Clousden Hill NE12: Longb 3C **46**
Clovelly Gdns. NE22: Bed 1H **21**
NE26: Whit B 5G **39**
Clovelly Pl. NE20: Pon 2G **41**
NE32: Jar 1E **86**
Clovelly Rd. SR5: C'twn 4F **103**
Clovelly Sq. SR5: C'twn 4G **103**
Clover Av. DH4: Hou S 4B **130**
NE10: Gate 4K **83**
NE21: Bla T 1C **96**
Cloverdale NE22: Bed 7G **17**
Cloverdale Gdns. NE7: Newc T 2K **63**
NE16: Whi 2H **97**
Cloverfield Av. NE3: Ken 6B **44**
Clover Hill NE16: Sun 5H **97**
(not continuous)
NE32: Jar 5C **86**
Cloverhill DH2: Ches S 7H **127**
Cloverhill Av. NE31: Heb 3H **85**
Cloverhill Cl. NE23: Dud 2J **35**
Cloverhill Dr. NE40: Ryton 2E **78**
Clover Laid DH7: B'don 2C **174**
Clowes Ter. DH9: Ann P 5K **123**
Clowes Wlk. DH9: Stly 2H **125**
Club La. DH1: Dur 1H **165**
Clumber St. NE4: Newc T 3C **82**
(not continuous)
Cluny Gallery, The 7J 63 (4L 5)
Clyde Av. NE31: Heb 3J **85**
Clyde Ct. SR3: New S 3B **132**
Clydedale Av. NE12: Longb 5A **46**
Clydesdale Av. DH4: Pen 2B **130**
Clydesdale Gth. DH1: Dur 3A **154**
Clydesdale Mt. NE6: Newc T 1A **84**
Clydesdale Rd. NE6: Newc T 1A **84**
Clydesdale St. DH5: Hett H 1G **157**
Clyde St. DH9: Stly 2H **125**
NE8: Gate 6J **83**
NE17: C'wl 6A **94**
Clyvedon Ri. NE34: S Shi 3C **88**
Coach La. DH7: Wit G 3C **152**
NE7: Newc T 7A **46**
NE12: Newc T 7A **46**
NE13: Bru V 7J **33**
NE29: N Shi 7G **49**
Coach Open NE28: W'snd 4B **66**
Coach Rd. NE11: Gate 2D **98**
NE15: Thro 3G **59**
NE28: W'snd 4G **65**
NE37: Usw 6G **101**
Coach Rd. Est. NE37: Usw 6G **101**
Coach Rd. Grn. NE10: Gate 4A **84**
Coalbank Rd. DH5: Hett H 1F **157**
Coalbank Sq. DH5: Hett H 1F **157**
COALBURNS 7B **78**
Coalburn Ter. NE61: Hep 4K **15**
Coaley La. DH4: Hou S 6C **130**
Coalford La. DH6: H Pitt 6C **156**
Coalford Rd. DH6: Sher 2K **167**
Coal La. NE42: O'ham 2K **75**
Coalway Dr. NE16: Whi 6H **81**
Coalway La. NE16: Swa, Whi 6H **81**
NE16: Whi 6H **81**
NE40: G'sde, Wylam 4B **78**
NE41: Wylam 4B **78**
Coalway La. Nth. NE16: Swa 5H **81**
Coanwood Bungs. NE23: Cra 5K **25**
Coanwood Dr. NE23: Cra 5K **25**
Coanwood Gdns. NE11: Gate 2D **98**
Coanwood Rd. NE15: Newc T 2H **81**
Coanwood Way NE16: Sun 4H **97**
Coast Rd. NE7: Newc T 4K **63**
NE28: W'snd 2F **65**
NE29: N Shi 6D **48**
NE34: S Shi 4C **68**
SR6: Whit 6F **69**
SR8: Pet 6E **172**
TS27: B Col 2J **183**
(Dene Rd.)
TS27: B Col 6E **172**
(Willow Gro.)
Coast Vw. TS27: B Col 3K **183**
Coates Cl. DH9: Stly 4G **125**
Coatsworth Ct. NE8: Gate 4G **83**
Coatsworth Rd. NE8: Gate 4G **83**
Cobalt Cl. NE15: Lem 5C **60**
Cobbett Cres. NE34: S Shi 3H **87**
Cobbler's La. NE18: Newt 2H **55**
NE18: Welt 2H **55**
Cobblestone Ct. NE6: Newc T 1K **83** (6P **5**)
Cobden Rd. NE23: Cra 6A **26**
Cobden St. DH8: Con 6J **121**
NE8: Gate 5J **83**
NE28: W'snd 3F **65**
Cobden Ter. NE8: Gate 5J **83**
Cobham Pl. NE6: Walk 2E **84**
Cobham Sq. SR5: S'wck 5D **104**
Cobledene NE29: N Shi 2E **66**
Coblehouse NE26: Whit B 7J **39**
Coble Landing NE33: S Shi 2H **67**
Coburg St. NE8: Gate 4H **83**
NE24: Bly 2K **23**
NE30: N Shi 6H **49**
Coburn Ct. NE23: Dud 6A **36**
Cochrane Ct. NE4: Newc T 1A **82**
Cochrane Pk. Av. NE7: Newc T 2A **64**
Cochrane St. NE4: Newc T 1A **82**
Cochrane Ter. DH7: Ush M 3C **164**
NE13: Din 4H **33**
Cochran St. NE21: Bla T 3C **80**
Cockburn Ter. NE29: N Shi 2D **66**
Cocken La. DH3: Gt Lum 3F **143**
Cocken Lodge Farm Cvn. Pk.
DH4: Leam 7G **143**
Cocken Rd. DH1: Gt Lum 7F **143**
DH3: Gt Lum, Leam, Plaw 7B **142**
DH4: Leam 7F **143**
Cockermouth Grn. NE5: Newc T 5G **61**
Cockermouth Rd. SR5: C'twn 4F **103**
Cockhouse La. DH7: Ush M 2J **163**
Cockshaw NE46: Hex 1C **70**
Cockshaw Ct. NE46: Hex 1C **70**
Cockshott Dean NE42: Pru 3E **76**
Cohen Ct. NE8: Gate 6G **83**
Cohort Cl. DH8: Ebc 5G **107**
Colbeck Av. NE16: Swa 5H **81**
Colbeck Ter. NE30: N Shi 5K **49**
Colbourne Av. NE23: Nel V 1G **25**
Colbourne Cres. NE23: Nel V 1G **25**
Colbury Cl. NE23: Cra 7J **21**
Colby Ct. NE4: Newc T 2D **82** (7A **4**)
Colchester St. NE34: S Shi 2G **87**
Colchester Ter. SR4: Sund 3B **118**
Coldbeck Ct. NE23: Cra 5A **26**
COLD HESLEDON 1J **159**
Cold Hesledon Ind. Est. SR7: Mur 7J **147**
Coldingham Ct. DH7: Sac 7D **140**
Coldingham Gdns. NE5: Newc T 3K **61**
Coldside Gdns. NE5: Cha P 2B **60**
Coldstream DH2: Ous 6J **113**
Coldstream Av. SR5: S'wck 5D **104**
Coldstream Cl. DH4: Hou S 4B **130**
Coldstream Dr. NE21: Bla T 6A **80**
Coldstream Gdns. NE28: W'snd 2K **65**
Coldstream Rd. NE15: Newc T 7H **61**
Coldstream Way NE29: N Shi 4C **48**
Coldwell Cl. DH6: S Het 4A **158**
Coldwell La. NE10: Gate 7A **84**
Coldwell Pk. Av. NE10: Gate 7A **84**
Coldwell Pk. Dr. NE10: Gate 7A **84**
Coldwell Rd. NE42: Pru 3H **77**
Coldwell St. NE10: Gate 6B **84**
Coldwell Ter. NE10: Gate 7A **84**
Colebridge Cl. NE5: Newc T 2J **61**
Colebrooke DH3: Bir 6B **114**
Cole Gdns. NE10: Gate 6E **84**
Colegate NE10: Gate 7D **84**
Colegate W. NE10: Gate 7D **84**
Colepeth NE10: Gate 7C **84**
Colepike Rd. DH7: Lan 7J **137**
Coleridge Av. NE9: Gate 3G **99**
NE33: S Shi 4A **68**
TS27: B Col 7G **173**
Coleridge Dr. NE62: Chop 1H **17**
Coleridge Gdns. DH9: Dip 1H **123**
Coleridge Pl. DH2: Pelt 6G **127**
Coleridge Rd. SR5: C'twn 5H **103**
Coleridge Sq. NE31: Heb 7J **65**
Coley Grn. NE5: Cha P 1B **60**
Coley Hill Cl. NE5: Cha P 1C **60**
Coley Ter. SR6: Monk 4G **105**
Colgrove Pl. NE3: Ken 7A **44**
Colgrove Way NE3: Ken 7B **44**
Colima Av. SR5: Sund 7H **103**
Colin Ct. NE21: Bla T 2E **80**
Colin Pl. NE6: Walk 5E **64**
Colin Ter. SR2: Ryh 3H **133**
College Burn Rd. SR3: New S 4A **132**
College Dr. NE33: S Shi 5A **68**
College Ho. NE1: Newc T 3G **4**
College La. NE1: Newc T 7G **63** (3G **4**)
NE12: Longb 6A **46**
College Pl. NE63: Hir 5C **12**
College Rd. DH7: Esh W 7J **151**
NE31: Heb 3H **85**
NE63: Hir 5C **12**
College St. NE1: Newc T 7G **63** (3G **4**)
College, The DH1: Dur 3A **166** (4B **6**)
College Vw. DH7: Esh W 5D **162**
DH7: Ush M 7C **152**
DH8: Con 2A **136**
SR5: S'wck 6E **104**
Collier Cl. NE15: Thro 4H **59**
Collierley La. DH9: Dip 7G **109**
Colliery La. DH5: Hett H 1H **157**
NE4: Newc T 1D **82** (5B **4**)
Colliery Rd. DH7: Ush M 7D **152**
NE11: Dun 4B **82**
NE46: Acomb 4B **50**
COLLIERY ROW 2B **144**
Collin Av. NE34: S Shi 1D **88**
Colling Av. SR7: S'hm 3J **147**
(not continuous)
Collingdon Grn. NE39: H Spen 3D **94**
Collingdon Rd. NE39: H Spen 3E **94**
Collingwood Av. NE28: W'snd 1F **65**
Collingwood Bldgs. *NE1: Newc T* *6F 4*
(off Collingwood St.)
Collingwood Cen. NE29: N Shi 3F **49**
Collingwood Cl. NE23: Nel V 2G **25**
Collingwood Cotts. NE20: Pon 4F **31**
Collingwood Ct. NE37: Usw 7K **101**
Collingwood Cres. NE20: Pon 7H **31**
Collingwood Dr. DH4: Hou S 3A **130**
NE46: Hex 3B **70**
Collingwood Gdns. NE10: Gate 4B **84**
Collingwood Mans. NE29: N Shi 1H **67**
Collingwood M. NE3: Gos 7E **44**
Collingwood Pl. NE62: Chop 1J **17**
Collingwood Rd. NE25: Well 6A **38**
NE64: Newb S 2G **13**
Collingwood St. DH5: Hett H 4G **145**
NE1: Newc T 2F **83** (7F **4**)
NE10: Gate 5B **84**
NE31: Heb 7A **66**
NE33: S Shi 5J **67**
SR5: S'wck 5D **104**
(not continuous)
Collingwood Ter. NE2: Newc T 4H **63**
NE11: Dun 5C **82**
NE24: Bly 2J **23**
NE26: Whit B 7J **39**
NE30: N Shi 5K **49**
NE61: Mor 6F **9**
Collingwood Vw. NE29: N Shi 7F **49**
Collingwood Wlk. *NE37: Usw* *7K 101*
(off Collingwood Ct.)
Collison St. DH8: Con 6H **121**
Collywell Bay Rd. NE26: Sea S 4D **28**
Collywell Ct. NE26: Sea S 4D **28**
Colman Av. NE34: S Shi 7G **67**
Colmet Ct. NE11: Gate 3F **99**
Colnbrook Cl. NE3: Ken 5K **43**
Colombo Rd. SR5: C'twn 6F **103**
Colpitts Ter. DH1: Dur 3K **165** (3A **6**)
Colston Pl. NE12: Longb 5B **46**
Colston Ri. SR8: Pet 5A **172**
Colston St. NE4: Newc T 1K **81**
Colston Way NE25: Whit B 4D **38**
Coltere Av. NE36: E Bol 7A **88**
Colton Gdns. NE9: Gate 4J **99**
Colt Pk. NE17: Ham C 3K **107**
Coltpark NE5: Newc T 4F **61**
Coltpark Pl. NE23: Cra 5K **25**
Coltsfoot Gdns. NE10: Gate 2A **100**
Coltspool NE11: Kib 2F **113**
Columba St. SR5: S'wck 5D **104**
Columba Wlk. NE3: Gos 7F **45**
(not continuous)
COLUMBIA 4K **115**
Columbia Grange NE3: Ken 7A **44**
Columbia Ter. NE24: Bly 3J **23**
Column of Liberty 4B **96**
Colville Ct. DH9: Stly 3H **125**
Colwell Pl. NE5: Newc T 6J **61**
Colwell Rd. NE27: Shir 2K **47**
NE29: N Shi 3F **49**
NE63: Hir 6D **12**
Colwyne Pl. NE5: Newc T 3H **61**
Colwyn Pde. NE31: Heb 4A **86**
Combe Dr. NE15: Lem 6B **60**
Comet Dr. SR8: Eas 7A **160**
Comet Row NE12: Kil 2A **46**
Comet Sq. SR3: New S 2C **132**
Comma Ct. NE11: Gate 7D **82**
Commerce Way DH4: Hou S 3C **144**
Commercial Bldgs. *NE24: Bly* *1J 23*
(off Church St.)
Commercial Pl. *NE46: Hex* *2D 70*
(off Priestpopple)
Commercial Rd. NE3: Gos 7G **45**
NE6: Newc T 1A **84**
NE24: Bly 1J **23**
NE32: Jar 5C **66**
(not continuous)
NE33: S Shi 4H **67**
SR2: Sund 3H **119**
Commercial Rd. E. DH6: Coxh 7K **177**
Commercial Sq. DH7: B'don 1E **174**
Commercial St. DH7: B'don 7E **164**
DH7: Lang P 7A **150**
NE21: Bla T 5B **80**
Commercial Way NE23: Cra 4J **25**
Commissioners Wharf NE29: N Shi 3G **67**
Community North Sports Complex 3J 103
Community Recreation Cen. 1D 60
Compton Av. NE34: S Shi 6K **67**
Compton Ct. NE38: Wash 3F **115**
Compton Rd. NE29: N Shi 7F **49**
CONCORD 6H **101**
Concorde Ho. NE25: H'wll 2J **37**
Concorde Sq. SR3: New S 2C **132**
Concorde Way NE32: Jar 7B **66**
Concord Ho. NE5: Newc T 3F **61**
NE37: Usw 7H **101**
Concordia Leisure Cen. 4J 25
Condercum Ct. NE15: Newc T 1J **81**
Condercum Ind. Est. NE4: Newc T 1K **81**
Condercum Rd. NE4: Newc T 1K **81**
Condercum Rd. Bk. NE4: Newc T 1K **81**
Cone St. NE33: S Shi 3H **67**
Cone Ter. DH3: Ches S 6B **128**
Conewood Ho. NE3: Ken 6B **44**
Congburn Bank DH7: Edm 2C **140**
Conhope La. NE4: Newc T 1K **81**
Conifer Cl. DH1: Dur 1E **166**
NE21: Bla T 6B **80**
Conifer Ct. NE12: Longb 4D **46**
Coningsby Cl. NE3: Gos 4F **45**
Coniscliffe Av. NE3: Ken 2B **62**
Coniscliffe Pl. SR6: Monk 6G **105**
Coniscliffe Rd. DH9: Stly 3D **124**
Coniscliffe Ter. *SR8: Eas* *1K 171*
(off Thorpe Rd.)
Conishead Ter. DH6: S Het 3B **158**
Coniston DH3: Bir 6B **114**
NE10: Gate 6E **84**
Coniston Av. DH5: Eas L 3J **157**
NE2: Newc T 3G **63**
NE16: Whi 7K **81**
NE31: Heb 1K **85**
NE64: Newb S 4G **13**
SR5: Monk 3E **104**
Coniston Cl. DH1: Carr 7J **155**
DH2: Ches S 7A **128**
NE12: Kil 1A **46**
NE15: Thro 6J **59**
SR8: Pet 6C **172**
Coniston Ct. NE5: Newc T 5H **61**
Coniston Cres. NE21: Bla T 6B **80**
Coniston Dr. DH7: Sac 6D **140**
NE32: Jar 3D **86**
Coniston Gdns. NE9: Gate 2K **99**
Coniston Grange NE36: E Bol 6H **87**
Coniston Ho. NE38: Wash 2G **115**
Coniston Pl. NE9: Gate 2K **99**
Coniston Rd. NE24: Cow 7D **18**
NE28: W'snd 1K **65**
NE30: N Shi 2F **49**
Coniston Way DH8: Lead 5B **122**
Connaught Cl. DH4: Hou S 4C **130**
Connaught Gdns. NE12: Longb 5B **46**
Connaught M. *NE2: Newc T* *4G 63*
(off Bk. St George's Ter.)
Connaught Ter. NE32: Jar 7B **66**
Conniscliffe Ct. NE46: Hex 3A **70**
Conniscliffe Rd. NE46: Hex 3B **70**
Connolly Ho. NE34: S Shi 3K **87**
Connolly Ter. NE17: C'wl 2A **108**
CONSETT 6H **121**
Consett Bus. Pk. DH8: Con 5K **121**
Consett La. DH8: C'sde 7D **120**
Consett Pk. Ter. DH8: C'sde 3D **134**
Consett Rd. DH7: Lan 5J **137**
DH8: C'sde 4B **134**
NE11: Gate 2B **98**
Consett Ter. DH7: Esh W 6G **151**
Constable Cl. DH9: Stly 3F **125**
NE40: Ryton 2G **79**
Constable Gdns. NE34: S Shi 3J **87**
Constables Gth. DH3: Bir 4A **114**
Constance St. DH2: Pelt 2G **127**
DH8: Con 7H **121**
Constitutional Hill DH1: Dur 2C **166**
Content St. NE21: Bla T 5C **80**
Convent Rd. NE4: Newc T 6K **61**
(not continuous)
Conway Cl. NE22: Bed 7F **17**
NE40: Ryton 2H **79**
Conway Dr. NE7: Newc T 1J **63**

Conway Gdns.—Cragside

Conway Gdns. NE28: W'snd 1E 64
SR3: E Her 2K 131
Conway Gro. NE26: Sea S 3B 28
Conway Pl. DH2: Ous 1H 127
Conway Rd. SR5: C'twn 5F 103
Conway Sq. NE9: Gate 6J 83
SR5: C'twn 5F 103
Conyers DH2: Plaw 6H 141
Conyers Av. DH2: Ches S 4K 127
Conyers Cres. SR8: Pet 3C 172
Conyers Gdns. DH2: Ches S 4K 127
Conyers Pl. DH2: Ches S 4K 127
Conyers Rd. DH2: Ches S 4K 127
NE6: Newc T 7K 63 (4P 5)
Cook Av. DH7: Ush M 1C 164
Cook Cl. NE33: S Shi 5H 67
Cook Cres. SR7: Mur 7D 146
Cooke's Wood DH7: Ush M 4E 164
Cook Gdns. NE10: Gate 6F 85
Cook Gro. SR8: Pet 3C 172
Cook's Cotts. DH7: Ush M 2B 164
Cookshold La. DH6: H Pitt, Sher 3A 168
Cookson Cl. NE4: Newc T 1D 82 (5A 4)
NE45: Cor 7D 52
Cookson Ho. NE33: S Shi 2J 67
Cookson Pl. DH9: Stly 4H 125
Cookson's La. NE1: Newc T 2F 83 (8E 4)
Cookson St. NE4: Newc T 1C 82 (5A 4)
Cookson Ter. DH2: Ches S 6K 127
Cook Sq. SR5: C'twn 5G 103
Cooks Wood NE38: Wash 5H 115
Cook Way SR8: Pet 4G 171
Coomassie Rd. NE24: Bly 2J 23
Coomside NE23: Cra 6A 26
Coop Bldgs. DH3: Bir 4A 114
Co-operative Bldgs. DH9: Dip 1G 123
NE25: Sea D 7H 27
Co-operative Cres. NE10: Gate 7A 84
Cooperative St. DH3: Ches S 5A 128
Co-operative Ter. DH2: Beam 2C 126
DH2: Pelt 5C 126
DH4: Hou S 1K 143
DH5: Hett H 6G 145
DH6: Shot C 6E 170
DH7: B'hpe 5E 138
DH7: New B 4A 164
DH8: M'sly 7K 107
DH8: Shot B 2E 120
DH9: Dip 1G 123
NE10: Gate 7A 84
NE12: Longb 3E 46
NE13: Bru V 5C 34
NE16: Burn 2B 110
NE27: Shir 3J 47
(Cramlington Ter.)
NE27: Shir 1J 47
(St Mark's Ct.)
NE37: Usw 7J 101
NE39: H Spen 2D 94
SR4: Sund 3C 118
Co-operative Ter. E. DH9: Dip 1H 123
Co-operative Ter. W. DH9: Dip 1G 123
Co-operative Vs. DH6: Sher 3D 168
DH7: B'don 7G 165
Cooperative Workshops *DH7: Sac* 7E 140
(off Plawsworth Rd.)
Coopers Cl. DH6: Thor 1K 179
Cooper Sq. DH1: Dur 1D 166
Cooper's Ter. DH6: Thor 1J 179
Cooper St. SR6: Monk 5G 105
Coopies Fld. NE61: Mor 1H 15
Coopies Haugh NE61: Mor 1J 15
Coopies La. NE61: Mor 1G 15
Coopies La. Ind. Est. NE61: Mor 7J 9
Coopies Way NE61: Mor 1J 15
Copeland Ct. DH1: Dur 4J 165
Copenhagen Ho. NE1: Newc T 6J 5
Copland Ter. NE2: Newc T 7H 63 (4J 5)
Copley Av. NE34: S Shi 4J 87
Copley Dr. SR3: Sund 6D 118
Copperas La. NE15: Newc T 6F 61
Copper Chare NE61: Mor 6F 9
Copperfield DH1: Dur 5J 165
Coppergate Ct. NE31: Heb 6K 65
Coppers Cl. NE11: Gate 7D 82
Coppice Hill DH7: Esh W 4F 163
Coppice, The NE26: Sea S 4C 28
Coppice Way NE2: Newc T 7H 63 (3J 5)
Coppy La. DH9: Beam 3H 111
NE16: Beam, Sun 3H 111
Copse, The NE3: Gos 4F 45
NE12: Longb 3C 46
NE16: Burn 2K 109
NE21: Bla T 4F 81
NE37: Usw 5F 101
NE42: Pru 4H 77
Coptleigh DH5: Hou S 3G 145
Coquet NE38: Wash 7D 114
Coquet Av. NE3: Gos 6D 44
NE24: News 4J 23
NE26: Whit B 6G 39
NE34: S Shi 5D 68
Coquet Bldgs. NE15: Thro 4B 60
Coquet Cl. SR8: Pet 7A 172
Coquetdale Av. NE6: Walk 7E 64
Coquetdale Cl. NE61: Peg 4A 10
Coquetdale Pl. NE22: Bed 7A 18
Coquetdale Vs. SR6: Monk 5G 105
Coquet Dr. DH2: Ous 1G 127
Coquet Gdns. DH9: Stly 5E 124
Coquet Gro. NE15: Thro 3G 59
Coquet Ho. SR3: New S 3B 132
Coquet St. NE1: Newc T 1H 83 (5K 5)
NE17: C'wl 6A 94
NE31: Heb 7H 65
NE32: Jar 1A 86
NE63: Hir 3C 12
Coquet Ter. NE6: Newc T 4A 64
NE23: Dud 3H 35
Corbett St. SR7: S'hm 2K 147
(not continuous)
SR8: Eas 7D 160
Corbiere Cl. SR3: New S 3A 132
Corbitt St. NE8: Gate 5E 82
CORBRIDGE 1D 72
Corbridge Av. NE13: Wide O 5D 34
Corbridge Cl. NE28: W'snd 6J 47
CORBRIDGE COMMON 7C 72
Corbridge Ct. NE12: Longb 6H 45
Corbridge Rd. DH8: Con, M'sly 1J 121
NE6: Newc T 7A 64
NE45: Cor 2D 70
NE46: Hex 2D 70
Corbridge Roman Site & Mus. 7C 52
Corbridge Station (Rail) 2D 72
Corbridge St. NE6: Newc T 7K 63 (4P 5)
Corby Gdns. NE6: Walk 7D 64
Corby Ga. SR2: Sund 4F 119
Corby Gro. SR8: Pet 2J 181
Corby Hall Dr. SR2: Sund 4F 119
Corby M. SR2: Sund 4F 119
Corchester Av. NE45: Cor 7D 52
Corchester La. NE45: Cor 6J 51
NE46: Ayd, B End 6J 51
Corchester Rd. NE22: Bed 6G 17
Corchester Towers NE45: Cor 6C 52
Corchester Wlk. NE7: Newc T 1K 63
Corcyra St. SR7: S'hm 4B 148
Corfu Rd. SR5: C'twn 5G 103
Corinthian Sq. SR5: C'twn 5G 103
Cork St. SR1: Sund 1G 119
Cormorant Cl. NE24: News 5K 23
NE38: Wash 5D 114
NE63: Hir 6C 12
Cormorant Dr. NE11: Dun 4C 82
Cornbank Cl. SR3: New S 4C 132
Corndean NE38: Wash 4A 116
Cornelia Cl. SR3: New S 2C 132
Cornelia St. SR3: New S 2C 132
Cornelia Ter. SR7: S'hm 3A 148
Cornel M. NE7: Newc T 2A 64
Cornel Rd. NE7: Newc T 2K 63
Corney St. NE33: S Shi 6H 67
Cornfield Gth. SR8: Pet 7D 172
Cornfields, The NE31: Heb 7J 65
Cornforth Cl. NE10: Gate 1G 101
NE63: Ash 5K 11
Cornhill NE5: Newc T 4F 61
NE32: Jar 5C 86
Cornhill Av. NE3: Ken 5B 44
Cornhill Cen., The *SR5: S'wck* 5D 104
(off Goschen St.)
Cornhill Cl. NE29: N Shi 5D 48
Cornhill Cres. NE29: N Shi 5D 48
(not continuous)
Cornhill Rd. NE23: Cra 4A 26
SR5: S'wck 5D 104
Corn Mill Dr. DH5: Hou S 4D 144
Cornmoor DH2: Ches S 7H 127
Cornmoor Gdns. NE16: Whi 2H 97
Cornmoor Rd. NE16: Whi 1H 97
CORNSAY COLLIERY 7A 150
Cornsay Cres. DH2: Ous 6H 113
Cornthwaite Dr. SR6: Whit 5G 89
Cornwall Ct. SR7: Mur 7F 147
Cornwallis NE37: Usw 6J 101
Cornwallis Sq. NE33: S Shi 4H 67
Cornwallis St. NE33: S Shi 2J 67
Cornwall Rd. NE31: Heb 3K 85
Cornwall St. SR8: Eas 7D 160
Cornwall Wlk. DH1: Carr 1H 167
Cornwell Ct. NE3: Newc T 1H 63
Cornwell Cres. NE22: Bed 1K 21
Coronation Av. DH1: Carr 7H 155
NE16: Sun 5H 97
SR2: Ryh 3H 133
SR8: Pet 6E 172
TS27: B Col 2J 183
Coronation Bungs. NE3: Gos 7F 45
Coronation Cl. SR1: Sund 1G 119
Coronation Cotts. DH6: Shot C 6E 170
Coronation Cres. DH4: Hou S 7C 130
DH6: H Pitt 5B 156
NE25: Whit B 6F 39
Coronation Grn. DH5: Eas L 3K 157
Coronation Homes DH7: Esh W 4F 163
Coronation Rd. NE5: Cha P 2B 60
NE16: Sun 5H 97
NE25: Sea D 7G 27
TS28: Win 4F 181
Coronation Sq. DH6: S Het 4D 158
Coronation St. DH2: Pelt 3E 126
DH3: Ches S 1B 142
NE23: Dud 2K 35
NE24: Bly 3J 23
NE28: W'snd 3G 65
NE29: N Shi 1G 67
NE33: S Shi 3J 67
NE40: Ryton 2J 79
NE64: Newb S 2J 13
SR1: Sund 1G 119 (3K 7)
(not continuous)
Coronation Ter. DH1: Dur 3G 167
DH2: Pelt 5D 126
DH3: Ches S 1A 142
DH5: Hett H 1G 157
DH9: Ann P 5B 124
NE9: Spri 6D 100
NE11: Kib 2E 112
NE29: N Shi 3B 48
NE35: Bol C 5E 86
NE63: Ash, Hir 6B 12
SR4: Sund 2H 117
TS29: Trim S 7B 180
Corporation Rd. SR2: Sund 4H 119
Corporation St. NE4: Newc T 1D 82 (6B 4)
Corporation Yd. NE15: Thro 5K 59
NE61: Mor 6F 9
Corriedale Cl. DH1: Dur 3A 154
Corrighan Ter. DH5: W Rai 6C 144
Corrofell Gdns. NE10: Gate 4C 84
Corry Cl. TS27: B Col 2J 183
(not continuous)
Corry Ct. SR4: Sund 4A 118
Corsair NE16: Whi 1F 97
Corsenside NE5: Newc T 4F 61
Corstophine Town NE33: S Shi 5H 67
Cortina Av. SR4: Sund 4K 117
Cortland Rd. DH8: Con 5E 120
Cort St. DH8: Con 6G 121
Corvan Ter. DH9: Tan L 6A 110
Cosford Ct. NE3: Ken 5J 43
Cossack Ter. SR4: Sund 1A 118
Cosserat Pl. NE31: Heb 6H 65
Cosser St. NE24: News 5F 23
Coston Dr. NE33: S Shi 2J 67
(not continuous)
Cosyn St. NE6: Newc T 1J 83 (5M 5)
Cotehill Dr. NE20: Pon 7F 31
Cotehill Rd. NE5: Newc T 4H 61
Cotemede NE10: Gate 1E 100
Cotemede Ct. NE10: Gate 1E 100
Cotfield Wlk. NE8: Gate 5F 83
Cotgarth, The NE10: Gate 7C 84
Cotherstone Cl. DH8: Con 1H 135
Cotherstone Ct. SR3: Sund 6D 118
Cotherstone Rd. DH1: Dur 5B 154
Cotman Gdns. NE34: S Shi 4K 87
Cotsford Cres. SR8: Pet 6E 172
Cotsford Grange SR8: Pet 6F 173
Cotsford La. SR8: Pet 6E 172
Cotsford Pk. Est. SR8: Pet 6F 173
Cotswold Av. DH2: Ches S 7J 127
(not continuous)
NE12: Longb 3K 45
Cotswold Cl. NE38: Wash 4F 115
Cotswold Dr. NE25: Whit B 1F 49
NE63: N Sea 6C 12
Cotswold Gdns. NE7: Newc T 2J 63
NE11: Gate 7C 82
Cotswold Pl. SR8: Pet 5K 171
Cotswold Rd. NE29: N Shi 2E 48
SR5: C'twn 5G 103
Cotswolds La. NE35: Bol C 5E 86
Cotswold Sq. SR5: C'twn 4G 103
Cotswold Ter. DH9: Stly 4G 125
Cottage Farm NE7: Newc T 2B 64
Cottage Gdns. SR6: Cle 5C 88
Cottage La. NE5: Newc T 4K 61
Cottages Rd. SR7: S'hm 4B 148
Cottages, The NE11: Kib 6G 99
SR8: Pet 3C 172
Cottenham Chare
NE4: Newc T 1D 82 (5B 4)
Cottenham St. NE4: Newc T 1D 82 (6B 4)
Cotterdale NE28: W'snd 7D 46
Cotterdale Av. *NE8: Gate* 6H 83
(off Patterdale Ter.)
Cotter Riggs Pl. NE5: Cha P 3B 60
Cotter Riggs Wlk. NE5: Cha P 3B 60
Cottersdale Gdns. NE5: Cha P 2B 60
Cottingham Cl. SR8: Pet 5K 171
Cottinglea NE61: Mor 6F 9
Cottingvale NE61: Mor 5F 9
Cottingwood Ct. NE4: Newc T 7D 62 (4A 4)
Cottingwood Gdns.
NE4: Newc T 7D 62 (4A 4)
NE61: Mor 6F 9
Cottingwood Grn. NE24: News 6G 23
Cottingwood La. NE61: Mor 5F 9
Cottonwood DH4: Hou S 3K 129
SR3: New S 4A 132
Coulson Cl. NE46: Hex 4B 70
Coulthards La. NE8: Gate 3H 83 (9K 5)
Coulthards Pl. NE8: Gate 2J 83 (8L 5)
Coulton Dr. NE36: E Bol 7K 87
Council Av. DH4: Hou S 3B 130
Council Rd. NE63: Ash 3A 12
Council Ter. NE37: Wash 1H 115
Counden Rd. NE5: Newc T 2E 60
Countess Av. NE26: Whit B 6G 39
Countess Cl. SR7: S'hm 2A 148
Countess Dr. NE15: Newc T 6G 61
Counts House 4A 166 (5C 6)
County Hall Bldgs. DH1: Dur 1K 165
County Mills *NE46: Hex* 2D 70
(off Priestpopple)
County Show Ground (Agricultural) 5H 129
Coupland Gro. NE32: Jar 3B 86
Coupland Rd. NE63: Ash 4A 12
Courtfield Rd. NE6: Walk 5D 64
Court La. DH1: Dur 3B 166 (4D 6)
Courtney Ct. NE3: Ken 5J 43
Courtney Dr. DH2: Ous 2H 127
SR3: New S 1B 132
Court Rd. NE22: Bed 7H 17
Court St. SR8: Eas 7D 160
Court, The NE16: Whi 1J 97
Courtyard, The DH9: Tan L 1C 124
Cousin St. SR1: Sund 1G 119
Coutts Rd. NE6: Walk 5C 64
Covent Gdn. NE64: Newb S 2J 13
Coventry Gdns. NE4: Newc T 2A 82
NE29: N Shi 1E 66
Coventry Rd. DH1: Dur 4C 154
Coventry Way NE32: Jar 4B 86
Coverdale NE10: Gate 1E 100
NE28: W'snd 7D 46
Coverdale Av. NE24: Cow 2E 22
NE37: Usw 7G 101
Coverdale Wlk. NE33: S Shi 6J 67
Coverley DH3: Gt Lum 2E 142
Coverley Rd. SR5: C'twn 5H 103
Covers, The NE12: Longb 6C 46
NE16: Swa 5F 81
NE28: W'snd 2F 65
NE61: Mor 1G 15
Cove, The DH4: Hou S 3B 130
Cowan Cl. NE21: Bla T 2A 80
Cowans Av. NE12: Kil 7A 36
Cowan Ter. SR1: Sund 2F 119 (5J 7)
Cowdray Ct. NE3: Ken 5J 43
Cowdray Rd. SR5: C'twn 5H 103
Cowdrey Ho. *NE29: N Shi* 2D 66
(off St John's Grn.)
Cowell Gro. NE39: Row G 5G 95
Cowell St. SR8: Pet 5D 172
Cowen Gdns. NE9: Gate 6J 99
Cowen Rd. NE21: Bla T 3D 80
Cowen St. NE6: Walk 7D 64
NE21: Bla T 6B 80
Cowen Ter. NE39: Row G 4K 95
Cowgarth NE46: Hex 1C 70
COWGATE 4K 61
Cowgate NE1: Newc T 1G 83 (6H 5)
Cowgate Leisure Cen. 2K 61
Cow La. NE45: Cor 7D 52
(not continuous)
Cowley Cres. DH5: W Rai 6C 144
Cowley Pl. NE24: Cow 1F 23
Cowley Rd. NE24: Cow 7F 19
Cowley St. DH6: Shot C 6F 171
Cowpath Gdns. NE10: Gate 5E 84
COWPEN 1E 22
Cowpen Hall Rd. NE24: Cow 1E 22
COWPEN NEW TOWN 7E 18
Cowpen Rd. NE24: Bly, Cow 1D 22
(not continuous)
Cowpen Sq. NE24: Bly 7H 19
Cowper Ter. NE12: Longb 3A 46
Cox Chare NE1: Newc T 1H 83 (6J 5)
Coxfoot Cl. NE34: S Shi 1J 87
COX GREEN 5B 116
Coxgreen Rd. DH4: Pen 1A 130
SR4: Pen 7A 116
COXLODGE 7C 44
Coxlodge Rd. NE3: Gos 7C 44
Coxlodge Ter. NE3: Gos 7C 44
Coxon St. NE10: Gate 4F 85
SR2: Sund 3G 119
Coxon Ter. NE10: Gate 5A 84
Crabtree Rd. NE43: Stoc 7J 75
Cradock Av. NE31: Heb 2H 85
Cragdale Gdns. DH5: Hett H 1F 157
Craggyknowe NE37: Wash 2D 114
Craghall Dene NE3: Gos 1G 63
Craghall Dene Av. NE3: Gos 1G 63
CRAGHEAD 6J 125
Craghead La. DH9: Stly 7J 125
Craghead Rd. DH2: Pelt 5G 127
Cragleas NE16: Burn 4A 110
Cragside DH2: Ches S 5J 127
DH7: Wit G 3D 152
NE7: Newc T 2K 63
NE13: Wide O 5D 34
NE23: Cra 6K 25
NE26: Whit B 4E 38
NE34: S Shi 1D 88
NE37: Wash 1E 114
NE45: Cor 6F 53

Cragside Av.—Cullercoats Rd.

Cragside Av. NE29: N Shi . . . 4D 48
Cragside Ct. DH5: Hou S . . . 2F 145
DH8: Con . . . 5E 120
DH9: Ann P . . . 6K 123
NE4: Newc T . . . 3A 82
Cragside Gdns. NE11: Gate . . . 2C 98
NE12: Kil . . . 7D 36
NE22: Bed . . . 5K 17
NE28: W'snd . . . 2K 65
Cragston Av. NE5: Newc T . . . 2J 61
Cragston Cl. NE5: Newc T . . . 3J 61
Cragston Ct. NE5: Newc T . . . 3J 61
Cragston Way NE5: Newc T . . . 3J 61
Cragton Gdns. NE24: Cow . . . 2F 23
Crag Works DH8: Lead . . . 3A 122
Craigavon Rd. SR5: C'twn . . . 6H 103
Craig Cres. NE23: Dud . . . 3J 35
Craigend NE23: Cra . . . 5A 26
Craighill DH4: Hou S . . . 3A 130
Craiglands, The *SR2: Sund* . . . *5E 118* (off Tunstall Rd.)
Craigland Vs. DH7: Sac . . . 1E 152
Craigmillar Av. NE5: Newc T . . . 2J 61
Craigmillar Cl. NE5: Newc T . . . 2H 61
Craigmill Pk. NE24: Cow . . . 1E 22
Craigmont Ct. *NE12: Longb* . . . *6B 46* (off West Av.)
Craigshaw Rd. SR5: C'twn . . . 4F 103
Craigshaw Sq. SR5: C'twn . . . 4F 103
Craigside Ct. NE11: Gate . . . 2C 98
Craig St. DH3: Bir . . . 4A 114
Craig Ter. SR8: Eas . . . 1K 171
Craigwell Dr. SR3: New S . . . 5C 132
Crake Way NE38: Wash . . . 6D 114
Cramer St. NE8: Gate . . . 5H 83
CRAMLINGTON . . . 4J 25
Cramlington Rd. NE23: Dud . . . 2J 35
SR5: C'twn . . . 6F 103
Cramlington Sports Cen. . . . 6J 25
Cramlington Sq. SR5: C'twn . . . 5F 103
Cramlington Station (Rail) . . . 3H 25
Cramlington Ter. NE24: News . . . 5G 23
NE27: Shir . . . 3J 47
CRAMLINGTON VILLAGE . . . 3K 25
Cramond Ct. NE9: Gate . . . 4G 99
Cramond Way NE23: Cra . . . 6K 25
Cranberry Dr. NE38: Wash . . . 5J 115
Cranberry Rd. SR5: C'twn . . . 5G 103
Cranberry Sq. SR5: C'twn . . . 5G 103
Cranborne SR3: E Her . . . 3J 131
Cranbourne Gro. NE30: N Shi . . . 1H 49
Cranbrook SR3: Sund . . . 5C 118
Cranbrook Av. NE3: Gos . . . 5E 44
Cranbrook Ct. NE3: Ken . . . 5A 44
Cranbrook Dr. NE42: Pru . . . 4D 76
Cranbrook Rd. NE15: Newc T . . . 2H 81
Cranemarsh Cl. NE63: Ash . . . 6A 12
Craneshaugh Cl. NE46: Hex . . . 2G 71
Cranesville NE9: Gate . . . 2A 100 (not continuous)
Craneswater Av. NE26: Whit B . . . 2F 39
Cranfield Pl. NE15: Lem . . . 6C 60
Cranford Gdns. NE15: Lem . . . 6E 60
Cranford St. NE34: S Shi . . . 7J 67
Cranford Ter. SR4: Sund . . . 3C 118
SR8: Eas . . . 7K 159
Cranham Cl. NE12: Kil . . . 7D 36
Cranlea NE3: Ken . . . 6J 43
Cranleigh DH3: Gt Lum . . . 3E 142
Cranleigh Av. NE3: Ken . . . 5J 43
Cranleigh Gro. NE42: Pru . . . 3F 77
Cranleigh Pl. NE25: Whit B . . . 5D 38
Cranleigh Rd. SR5: C'twn . . . 5G 103
Cranshaw Pl. NE23: Cra . . . 5K 25
Cranston Pl. SR2: Ryh . . . 3J 133
Crantock Rd. NE3: Ken . . . 7B 44
Cranwell Ct. NE3: Ken . . . 5J 43
Cranwell Dr. NE13: Wide O . . . 5D 34
Craster Av. NE12: Longb . . . 3D 46
NE27: Shir . . . 1J 47
NE34: S Shi . . . 5D 68
Craster Cl. DH2: Ches S . . . 1H 141
NE24: Bly . . . 2G 23
NE25: Whit B . . . 5D 38
Craster Ct. NE11: Gate . . . 1E 98
NE23: Cra . . . 4J 25
Craster Gdns. NE28: W'snd . . . 2K 65
Craster Rd. NE29: N Shi . . . 7D 48
Craster Sq. NE3: Gos . . . 2C 44
Craster Ter. NE7: Newc T . . . 3K 63
Crathie DH3: Bir . . . 1A 114
Craven Ct. SR6: Monk . . . 6H 105
CRAWCROOK . . . 3C 78
Crawcrook Ho's. *NE40: Ryton* . . . *3C 78* (off Old Main St.)
Crawcrook La. NE40: Ryton, Wylam . . . 2A 78
NE41: Wylam . . . 2A 78
Crawcrook Ter. NE40: Ryton . . . 3C 78
Crawfields Ct. NE12: Longb . . . 6H 45
Crawford Av. SR8: Pet . . . 4B 172
Crawford Av. W. SR8: Pet . . . 4A 172
Crawford Cl. DH6: Sher . . . 3K 167
Crawford Cotts. NE61: Mor . . . 6G 9
Crawford Ct. SR3: New S . . . 3B 132
Crawford Gdns. NE40: Ryton . . . 2E 78
Crawford Pl. NE25: Whit B . . . 7E 38
Crawford St. NE24: Bly . . . 7H 19
Crawford Ter. NE6: Walk . . . 1D 84
NE61: Mor . . . 6G 9
Crawhall Cres. NE61: Mor . . . 1E 14
Crawhall Rd. NE1: Newc T . . . 1H 83 (5K 5)
Crawlaw Bungs. SR8: Eas . . . 6C 160
Crawlaw Rd. SR8: Eas . . . 6B 160
Crawley Av. NE31: Heb . . . 3H 85
Crawley Gdns. NE16: Whi . . . 7J 81
Crawley Rd. NE28: W'snd . . . 4F 65
Crawley Sq. NE31: Heb . . . 3H 85
Craythorne Gdns. NE6: Newc T . . . 3A 64
Creeverlea NE38: Wash . . . 5G 115
Creighton Av. NE3: Ken . . . 2A 62
Creland Way NE5: Newc T . . . 2J 61
Crescent Av. NE46: Hex . . . 1B 70
Crescent Cl. DH6: Sher . . . 3K 167
Crescent, The DH2: Ches S . . . 3J 141 (Chester Moor)
DH2: Ches S . . . 6K 127 (Chester-le-Street)
DH2: Ous . . . 1H 127
DH2: Plaw . . . 6H 141
DH4: Hou S . . . 5D 130
DH4: W Rai . . . 1K 155
DH5: Hett H . . . 7G 145
DH6: Sher . . . 3K 167
DH7: Lan . . . 2A 138
DH7: Lang P . . . 5G 151
DH7: Wit G . . . 2D 152
DH8: Con . . . 5H 121 (Balfour St.)
DH8: Con . . . 5D 120 (Barley Mill Cres.)
DH8: Shot B . . . 4E 120
DH9: Tan L . . . 1D 124
NE7: Newc T . . . 7K 45
NE11: Dun . . . 6B 82
NE11: Kib . . . 2E 112
NE13: Wool . . . 6H 43
NE15: Thro . . . 3H 59
NE16: Sun . . . 5H 97
NE16: Whi . . . 1J 97
NE20: Pon . . . 1E 40
NE23: Seg . . . 2D 36
NE26: Whit B . . . 7H 39
NE28: W'snd . . . 2F 65
NE30: N Shi . . . 4J 49
NE32: Jar . . . 2A 86
NE34: S Shi . . . 2B 88
NE39: H Spen . . . 4D 94
NE39: Row G . . . 5K 95
NE40: Ryton . . . 1H 79
NE41: Wylam . . . 1K 77
NE61: Loan . . . 2F 15
SR3: New S . . . 7C 118
SR6: Cle . . . 6B 88
SR8: Eas . . . 6C 160
TS27: B Col . . . 2H 183
Crescent Va. *NE26: Whit B* . . . *7G 39* (off Jesmond Ter.)
Crescent Way NE12: Longb . . . 4C 46
Cres. Way Nth. NE12: Longb . . . 4C 46
Cres. Way Sth. NE12: Longb . . . 4C 46
Creslow NE10: Gate . . . 1D 100
Cressbourne Av. SR6: Monk . . . 3G 105
Cresswell Av. NE12: Longb . . . 3C 46
NE26: Sea S . . . 4C 28
NE29: N Shi . . . 5F 49
SR8: Pet . . . 6E 172
Cresswell Cl. NE21: Bla T . . . 6A 80
NE25: Whit B . . . 1E 48
Cresswell Dr. NE3: Ken . . . 5A 44
NE24: Bly . . . 4G 23
Cresswell Rd. NE28: W'snd . . . 4E 64
Cresswell St. NE6: Walk . . . 7B 64 (not continuous)
Cresswell Ter. NE63: Ash . . . 3A 12
SR2: Sund . . . 3E 118 (6H 7)
Cresthaven NE10: Gate . . . 1C 100
Crest, The NE13: Din . . . 4H 33
NE22: Bed . . . 7G 17
NE26: Sea S . . . 6D 28
Crewe Av. DH1: Dur . . . 3F 167
Crichton Av. DH3: Ches S . . . 1B 142
Cricket Ter. NE16: Burn . . . 2A 110
Cricklewood Dr. DH4: Pen . . . 2B 130
Cricklewood Rd. SR5: C'twn . . . 6F 103
Criddle St. NE8: Gate . . . 2J 83 (8L 5)
Crieff Gro. NE32: Jar . . . 3D 86
Crieff Sq. SR5: C'twn . . . 5F 103
Crigdon Hill NE5: Newc T . . . 4F 61
Crighton NE38: Wash . . . 3E 114
Crimdon Gro. DH4: Hou S . . . 3C 144
Crimea Rd. SR5: C'twn . . . 5F 103
Crime Rigg Bank DH6: Shad . . . 4D 168
Crindledykes NE38: Wash . . . 6J 115
Cripps Av. NE10: Gate . . . 6F 85
Crispin Ct. NE5: Newc T . . . 2F 61
Crocus Cl. NE21: Bla T . . . 4A 80
Croft Av. NE12: Longb . . . 5C 46
NE28: W'snd . . . 3G 65
SR4: Sund . . . 2C 118
Croft Cl. NE40: Ryton . . . 2H 79
Croft Ct. DH7: Lan . . . 6J 137
Croftdale Rd. NE21: Bla T . . . 4C 80
Crofter Cl. NE23: Dud . . . 2J 35
Crofthead Dr. NE23: Cra . . . 6K 25
Crofton Mill Ind. Est. NE24: Bly . . . 3K 23
Crofton St. NE24: Bly . . . 2J 23
NE34: S Shi . . . 7J 67
Crofton Way NE15: Lem . . . 6B 60
Croft Pk. . . . 3J 23
Croft Rigg DH7: B'don . . . 2C 174
Croft Rd. NE24: Bly . . . 2J 23
Crofts Av. NE45: Cor . . . 1E 72
Crofts Cl. NE45: Cor . . . 1E 72
Croftside DH3: Bir . . . 3A 114
Croftside Av. SR6: Whit . . . 5H 89
Croftside Ho. SR3: New S . . . 4B 132
Crofts La. NE15: Hor . . . 5E 56
Crofts Pk. NE61: Hep . . . 3A 16
Croft Stairs NE1: Newc T . . . 1G 83 (6H 5)
Crofts, The NE20: Pon . . . 5K 31
Croft St. DH7: Sac . . . 7E 140
NE1: Newc T . . . 1G 83 (5G 4)
Crofts Way NE45: Cor . . . 1E 72
Croftsway NE4: Newc T . . . 2B 82
Croft Ter. DH9: Ann P . . . 5A 124
NE15: Hor . . . 5E 56
NE32: Jar . . . 7B 66
NE46: Hex . . . 2C 70
Croft, The DH6: Sher . . . 3D 168
NE3: Ken . . . 1C 62
NE12: Kil . . . 7C 36
NE22: H Bri . . . 1C 20
NE40: Ryton . . . 2H 79
SR7: Mur . . . *1F 159* (off Grasmere Ter.)
Croft Vw. DH7: Lan . . . 6J 137
NE12: Kil . . . 2C 46
NE40: Ryton . . . 3C 78
NE42: O'ham . . . 2D 76
Croft Vs. NE40: G'sde . . . 4D 78
NE40: Ryton . . . 3C 78
Croftwell Cl. NE21: Bla T . . . 5D 80
Cromarty DH2: Ous . . . 6H 113
Cromarty St. SR6: Monk . . . 5F 105
Cromdale Pl. NE5: Newc T . . . 4H 61
Cromer Av. NE9: Gate . . . 4H 99
Cromer Ct. NE9: Gate . . . 4J 99
Cromer Gdns. NE2: Gos . . . 2G 63
NE26: Whit B . . . 5G 39
Crompton Rd. NE6: Newc T . . . 4K 63
Cromwell Av. NE21: Bla T . . . 4B 80
Cromwell Ct. *NE10: Gate* . . . *4G 85* (off Richmond Av.)
NE21: Bla T . . . 2A 80
Cromwell Pl. NE21: Bla T . . . 5A 80
Cromwell Rd. NE10: Gate . . . 4F 85
NE16: Whi . . . 6J 81
Cromwell St. NE8: Gate . . . 5J 83
NE21: Bla T . . . 2A 80
SR4: Sund . . . 1C 118
Cromwell Ter. NE10: Gate . . . 4F 85
NE29: N Shi . . . 6F 49
Crondall St. NE33: S Shi . . . 6K 67
Cronin Av. NE34: S Shi . . . 2H 87
Cronniewell NE17: Ham C . . . 3K 107
CROOKGATE BANK . . . 2C 110
CROOKHALL . . . 1K 135
Crook Hall Gardens . . . 1A 166
Crookhall La. DH8: Con, Lead . . . 7A 122 (not continuous)
Crookhall Rd. DH8: Con . . . 6J 121
Crookham Gro. NE61: Mor . . . 3H 15
Crookham Way NE23: Cra . . . 6A 26
CROOKHILL . . . 1J 79
Crookhill Ter. NE40: Ryton . . . 2J 79
Croome Gdns. NE61: Peg . . . 3B 10
Cropthorne NE10: Gate . . . 1F 101
Crosby Ct. SR2: Sund . . . 3H 119
Crosby Gdns. NE9: Gate . . . 4K 99
Crosland Pk. NE23: Nel V . . . 1H 25
Crosland Way NE23: Nel V . . . 7H 21
Cross Av. NE28: W'snd . . . 1D 64
Cross Bank NE46: Acomb . . . 3A 50
Crossbank Rd. NE5: Newc T . . . 2K 61
Crossbank Vw. NE46: Acomb . . . 4B 50
Crossbrook Rd. NE5: Newc T . . . 3K 61
Cross Carliol St. NE1: Newc T . . . 1G 83 (5G 4)
Cross Dr. NE40: Ryton . . . 7G 59
Crossfell NE20: Pon . . . 7G 31
Crossfell Gdns. NE62: Chop . . . 7J 11
Crossfield DH7: Sac . . . 1E 152
Crossfield Cres. DH6: Shot C . . . 5E 170
Crossfield Pk. NE10: Gate . . . 1A 100
Crossfield Ter. NE6: Walk . . . 2E 84
Crossgate DH1: Dur . . . 3K 165 (3A 6)
NE33: S Shi . . . 3J 67
CROSSGATE MOOR . . . 2J 165
Crossgate Moor Gdns. DH1: Dur . . . 1H 165
Crossgate Peth DH1: Dur . . . 3J 165 (3A 6)
Crossgate Rd. DH5: Hett H . . . 1G 157
Crossgill NE37: Wash . . . 1F 115
Crosshill Rd. NE15: Newc T . . . 2H 81
Cross Keys La. NE9: Gate . . . 2H 99
Cross La. DH7: Sac . . . 6D 140
NE11: Dun . . . 4K 81
Cross La. NE11: Gate . . . 4C 98
NE16: Dun, Swa, Whi . . . 6J 81
Crosslaw NE5: Newc T . . . 4F 61
Crosslea Av. SR3: Sund . . . 5D 118
Crossleas DH7: Sac . . . 7E 140
Crossley Ter. NE4: Newc T . . . 7B 62
NE12: Longb . . . 3D 46
Cross Morpeth St.
NE2: Newc T . . . 5D 62 (1B 4)
Cross Pde. NE4: Newc T . . . 2C 82 (7A 4)
Cross Pl. SR1: Sund . . . 1G 119
Cross Rigg Cl. DH4: Pen . . . 2A 130
Cross Row DH1: Dur . . . 4A 154
NE10: Gate . . . 5K 83
NE40: Ryton . . . 2J 79
Cross Sheraton St. NE2: Newc T . . . 1B 4
Cross St. DH4: Hou S . . . 2A 144 (Front St.)
DH4: Hou S . . . 1D 144 (Station Rd.)
DH6: Crox . . . 6K 175
DH6: H Pitt . . . 7D 156
DH8: Con . . . 5F 121
NE1: Newc T . . . 1E 82 (6D 4)
NE6: Newc T . . . 1J 83 (5M 5)
NE8: Gate . . . 5H 83
NE42: Pru . . . 3F 77
SR8: Eas . . . 7D 160
Cross Ter. NE39: Row G . . . 6H 95
NE40: Ryton . . . 7G 59
Cross Va. Rd. SR2: Sund . . . 4E 118 (7H 7)
Cross Valley Ct. DH1: Dur . . . 3J 165
Cross Vw. Ter. DH1: Dur . . . 4J 165
Cross Villa Pl. No. 2
NE4: Newc T . . . 1E 82 (6C 4)
Cross Villa Pl. No. 3
NE4: Newc T . . . 1E 82 (6C 4)
Cross Villa Pl. No. 4
NE4: Newc T . . . 1D 82 (6B 4)
Cross Villa Pl. No. 5
NE4: Newc T . . . 1D 82 (6B 4)
Crossway NE2: Newc T . . . 2G 63
NE9: Gate . . . 1K 99 (Broadway)
NE9: Gate . . . 1J 99 (Sheriff's Highway)
NE30: N Shi . . . 4J 49
Cross Way NE34: S Shi . . . 1C 88
Crossway NE62: Chop . . . 1H 17
Crossway Ct. NE3: Ken . . . 2B 62
Crossways DH7: Lang P . . . 5J 151
DH7: Sac . . . 1E 152
NE32: Jar . . . 5C 86
NE36: E Bol . . . 7A 88
SR3: New S . . . 2B 132
Crossways, The NE13: Bru V . . . 7C 34
Cross Way, The NE61: Loan . . . 2F 15
Crossway, The NE3: Ken . . . 1B 62
NE15: Lem . . . 6D 60
Crosthwaite Gro. SR5: C'twn . . . 6G 103
Croudace Row NE10: Gate . . . 6B 84
Crow Bank NE28: W'snd . . . 3G 65
Crow Hall La. NE23: Cra, Nel V . . . 7H 21
Crowhall La. NE10: Gate . . . 6B 84
Crow Hall Rd. NE23: Nel V . . . 1H 25
Crowhall Towers NE10: Gate . . . 6B 84
Crow La. SR3: E Her . . . 2H 131
Crowley Av. NE16: Whi . . . 7J 81
Crowley Gdns. NE21: Bla T . . . 4C 80
Crowley Rd. NE16: Swa . . . 5G 81
Crowley Vs. *NE16: Swa* . . . *5G 81* (off Crowley Rd.)
Crown Rd. SR5: Sund . . . 7C 104
Crown St. NE24: Bly . . . 2K 23
NE61: Mor . . . *7G 9* (off Castle St.)
Crown Ter. NE40: G'sde . . . 5F 79
Crowther Ind. Est. NE38: Wash . . . 3D 114
Crowther Rd. NE38: Wash . . . 3D 114
Crowtree Leisure Cen. . . . 2E 118 (4H 7)
Crowtree Rd. SR1: Sund . . . 2E 118 (3H 7) (not continuous)
Crowtrees La. DH6: Bow . . . 5H 177
CROXDALE . . . 6K 175
Croxdale Ct. NE34: S Shi . . . 1G 87
Croxdale Gdns. NE10: Gate . . . 5E 84
Croxdale Ter. NE10: Gate . . . 5E 84
NE40: G'sde . . . 5G 79
Croydon Rd. NE4: Newc T . . . 7C 62
Crozier St. SR5: S'wck . . . 6E 104
Cruddas Pk. Shop. Cen.
NE4: Newc T . . . 3C 82 (8A 4)
Crudwell Cl. NE35: Bol C . . . 4E 86
Crummock Av. SR6: Monk . . . 3E 104
Crummock Ct. NE28: W'snd . . . 1A 66
Crummock Rd. NE5: Newc T . . . 5H 61
Crumstone Ct. NE12: Kil . . . 7C 36
Crusade Wlk. NE32: Jar . . . 1B 86
Cuba St. SR2: Sund . . . 4G 119
Cuddy's La. *NE46: Hex* . . . *2C 70* (off Priestlands La.)
Cuillin Cl. NE38: Wash . . . 5F 115
Culford Pl. NE28: W'snd . . . 6J 47
CULLERCOATS . . . 1J 49
Cullercoats Rd. SR5: C'twn . . . 6F 103

Cullercoats Sq.—Dene Pk.

Cullercoats Sq. SR5: C'twn 6F **103**
Cullercoats Station (Metro) 1J **49**
Cullercoats St. NE6: Walk 7C **64**
(not continuous)
Culloden Ter. SR8: Eas 1D **172**
Culloden Wlk. NE12: Kil 7B **36**
Culzean Ct. DH8: Con 5F **121**
Cumberland Av. NE22: Bed 7G **17**
NE64: Newb S 3H **13**
Cumberland Pl. DH3: Bir 7B **114**
NE34: S Shi 6D **68**
Cumberland Rd. DH8: C'sde 3C **134**
NE29: N Shi 5B **48**
SR3: New S 1C **132**
Cumberland St. NE28: W'snd 4B **66**
(George St.)
NE28: W'snd 3G **65**
(Richardson St.)
SR1: Sund 1F **119** (2J **7**)
(not continuous)
Cumberland Wlk. NE7: Newc T 1K **63**
(not continuous)
Cumberland Way NE37: Usw 5H **101**
Cumbrian Av. DH2: Ches S 7A **128**
(not continuous)
SR6: Monk 2E **104**
Cumbrian Gdns. NE11: Gate 1C **98**
Cumbrian Way SR8: Pet 6C **172**
Cumbria Pl. DH9: Stly 2G **125**
Cumbria Wlk. NE4: Newc T 1C **82** (6A **4**)
Cummings Av. DH6: Sher 2K **167**
Cummings Sq. TS28: Win 5F **181**
Cummings St. NE24: Bly 1J **23**
Cunningham Pl. DH1: Dur 1D **166**
Curlew Cl. NE12: Longb 5J **45**
NE38: Wash 6E **114**
NE40: Ryton 2J **79**
NE63: Hir .7B **12**
Curlew Hill NE61: Mor 5D **8**
Curlew Rd. NE32: Jar 5C **66**
(not continuous)
Curlew Way NE24: News 5J **23**
Curly Kews NE61: Mor 7E **8**
Curran Ho. NE32: Jar 5C **66**
Curren Gdns. NE10: Gate 4A **84**
Curry's Bldgs. *NE61: Mor 6E 8*
(off Buller's Grn.)
Curtis Rd. NE4: Newc T 6B **62**
Curzon Pl. NE5: Newc T 3H **61**
NE8: Gate 2G **83** (8H **5**)
Curzon Rd. W. NE28: W'snd 4F **65**
Curzon St. NE8: Gate 6G **83**
Cushat Cl. NE6: Newc T 1A **84** (6P **5**)
Cushycow La. NE40: Ryton 2H **79**
Customs House, The 3H **67**
Cut Bank NE1: Newc T 1J **83** (5L **5**)
Cuthbert Av. DH1: Dur 3E **166**
Cuthbert Cl. DH1: Dur 3F **167**
(Cuthbert Av.)
DH1: Dur 3F **167**
(Dragon Villa)
Cuthbertson Ct. SR6: Monk 2G **105**
Cuthbert St. NE8: Gate 4F **83**
NE16: Sun 6G **97**
NE31: Heb 7H **65**
(not continuous)
Cuthbert Wlk. NE3: Gos 7G **45**
Cutlers Av. DH8: Shot B 4E **120**
Cutlers Hall Rd. DH8: Shot B 3E **120**
Cut Throat La. NE17: Ham C 4K **107**
Cutting St. SR7: S'hm 1H **147**
Cygnet Cl. NE5: Cha P 1D **60**
NE63: Hir .7B **12**
Cyncopa Way NE5: Newc T 3K **61**
Cypress Av. NE4: Newc T 5K **61**
Cypress Ct. DH7: B'don 2D **174**
Cypress Cres. NE11: Dun 6B **82**
NE24: Bly .2J **23**
Cypress Dr. NE24: Bly 2J **23**
Cypress Gdns. NE12: Kil 7A **36**
NE24: Bly .2J **23**
Cypress Gro. DH1: Dur 1E **166**
NE40: Ryton 7F **59**
Cypress Pk. DH7: Esh W 4D **162**
Cypress Rd. NE9: Spri 5B **100**
NE21: Bla T 4C **80**
Cypress Sq. SR3: New S 1C **132**
Cypress Vw. DH6: Whe H 2A **180**
Cyprus Gdns. NE9: Gate 1J **99**
Cyril St. DH8: Con 5H **121**

D

Dachet Rd. NE25: Whit B 4D **38**
Dacre Gdns. DH8: Con 7J **121**
Dacre Rd. SR6: Monk 3F **105**
Dacre St. NE33: S Shi 5J **67**
(not continuous)
NE61: Mor .6F **9**
Daffodil Av. SR8: Pet 5D **172**
Daffodil Cl. NE21: Bla T 4B **80**
TS27: B Col 2H **183**
Dahlia Ct. SR4: Sund 1D **118** (3F **7**)
Dahlia Cres. SR8: Eas 1B **172**
Dahlia Pl. NE4: Newc T 6K **61**
Dahlia Way NE31: Heb 2J **85**
(not continuous)
Dainton Cl. DH4: Hou S 5C **130**
Dairnbrook NE37: Wash 2E **114**
Dairy La. DH4: Hou S 2C **144**
NE2: Newc T 5D **62** (1B **4**)
Dairy Wlk. DH3: Lam P 3F **129**
Daisy Cotts. DH3: Bir 4A **114**
DAISY HILL 4D **140**
Dalamere Cl. NE38: Wash 2F **129**
Dalden Gro. SR7: S'hm 2B **148**
Dale Ct. NE46: Hex 2E **70**
Dalegarth Gro. SR6: Monk 2E **104**
Dale Rd. NE25: Whit B 7D **38**
Daleside DH7: Sac 5E **140**
Dales, The NE5: Newc T 3A **62**
Dale St. DH7: Lang P 4J **151**
DH7: Ush M 2B **164**
DH8: Con 6F **121**
NE24: Bly .7J **19**
NE33: S Shi 2K **67**
NE40: Ryton 2D **78**
Dale Ter. SR6: Monk 4G **105**
SR7: Mur .5J **147**
Dale Top NE25: H'wll 2J **37**
Dale Vw. Gdns. NE40: Ryton 3C **78**
Dalla St. SR4: Sund 1G **117**
Dally M. NE3: Gos 3D **44**
Dallymore Dr. DH6: Bow 3G **177**
Dalmahoy NE37: Usw 4H **101**
Dalmatia Ter. NE24: Bly 3J **23**
Dalston Pl. NE24: News 5J **23**
Dalton Av. SR7: S'hm 3K **147**
(not continuous)
Dalton Cl. NE23: Cra 4K **25**
Dalton Ct. NE28: W'snd 7D **46**
Dalton Cres. NE6: Newc T 7K **63** (4P **5**)
Dalton Hgts. SR7: Mur 4G **147**
(not continuous)
DALTON-LE-DALE 5H **147**
Daltonpark SR7: Mur 1G **159**
Dalton Pl. NE5: Cha P 2C **60**
Daltons La. NE33: S Shi 3H **67**
Dalton St. NE6: Newc T 7K **63** (4P **5**)
(not continuous)
Dalton Ter. DH6: Whe H 4A **180**
NE17: C'wl 7K **93**
SR7: Mur .1F **159**
Dalton Way DH4: Pen 2A **130**
Dame Dorothy Cres. *SR6: Monk 6G 105*
(off Dame Dorothy St.)
Dame Dorothy St.
SR6: Monk 7F **105** (1J **7**)
Dame Flora Robson Av.
NE34: S Shi 2F **87**
Damside NE61: Mor 6G **9**
Damson Way DH1: Dur 2F **167**
Danby Cl. NE38: Wash 1D **128**
SR3: New S 3D **132**
Danby Gdns. NE6: Newc T 3B **64**
Dance City .7D **4**
Danelaw DH3: Gt Lum 2E **142**
Danville Rd. SR6: Monk 3F **105**
Daphne Cres. SR7: S'hm 4A **148**
D'Arcy Ct. SR1: Sund 2G **119**
D'Arcy Sq. SR7: Mur 6G **147**
D'Arcy St. DH7: Lang P 4J **151**
SR1: Sund 2G **119**
Darden Cl. NE12: Kil 7D **36**
Darden Lough NE5: Newc T 4F **61**
Darenth St. NE34: S Shi 7J **67**
Darien Av. SR6: Monk 3F **105**
Dark La. NE61: Mor 6G **9**
Darley Ct. DH2: Plaw 6J **141**
SR3: New S 3B **132**
Darley Pl. NE15: Newc T 1G **81**
Darling Pl. DH9: Stly 4H **125**
Darlington Av. SR8: Pet 4D **172**
Darlington Rd. DH1: Dur 4J **165**
Darnell Pl. NE4: Newc T 7D **62** (4A **4**)
Darnley Rd. NE63: Ash 4A **12**
Darras Ct. NE33: S Shi 4K **67**
Darras Dr. NE29: N Shi 5C **48**
DARRAS HALL 1G **41**
Darras M. NE20: Pon 1G **41**
Darras Rd. NE20: Pon 1E **40**
Darrell St. NE13: Bru V 5C **34**
Dartford Cl. NE25: Sea D 7H **27**
Dartford Rd. NE33: S Shi 3B **68**
SR6: Monk 3F **105**
Dartmouth Av. NE9: Gate 4H **99**
Dartmouth Cl. SR7: Mur 4J **147**
Darvall Cl. NE25: Whit B 4D **38**
Darwin Cres. NE3: Ken 2B **62**
Darwin St. SR5: S'wck 6B **104**
Daryl Cl. NE21: Bla T 5A **80**
Daryl Way NE10: Gate 6H **85**
Davenport Dr. NE3: Gos 3D **44**
David Gdns. SR6: Monk 4H **105**
David Lloyd Tennis Cen. 2H **63**
Davidson Cotts. NE2: Gos 2G **63**
Davidson Rd. NE10: Gate 4F **85**
Davidson St. NE10: Gate 6B **84**
David St. NE28: W'snd 4F **65**
David Ter. DH6: Bow 3H **177**
DH6: Quar H 6D **178**
NE40: Ryton 3D **78**
Davies Hall NE31: Heb 6H **65**
Davies Wlk. SR8: Pet 4C **172**
Davis Cres. DH7: Lang P 4G **151**
Davison Av. NE26: Whit B 5F **39**
SR3: New S 2D **132**
Davison Cres. SR7: Mur 6D **146**
Davison St. NE15: Thro 5J **59**
NE24: Bly .1J **23**
NE35: Bol C 5E **86**
Davison Ter. DH7: Sac 6D **140**
SR5: S'wck 5C 104
(off Nth. Hylton Rd.)
Davis Ter. SR8: Eas 7B **160**
Davy Bank NE28: W'snd 4H **65**
Davy Dr. SR8: Pet 5H **171**
DAWDON .5B **148**
Dawdon Bus. Pk. SR7: S'hm 6C **148**
Dawdon Cres. SR7: S'hm 4B **148**
Dawlish Cl. NE29: N Shi 4D **48**
SR7: S'hm 4H **147**
Dawlish Gdns. NE9: Gate 4H **99**
Dawlish Pl. NE5: Cha P 2C **60**
Dawson Pl. NE61: Mor 6F **9**
Dawson Rd. TS28: Win 5G **181**
Dawson Sq. NE30: N Shi 5K **49**
Dawson St. NE6: Walk 7E **64**
Dawson Ter. SR4: Sund 1G **117**
Daylesford Dr. NE3: Newc T 1H **63**
Daylesford Rd. NE23: Cra 7J **21**
Dayshield NE5: Newc T 4F **61**
Deacon Cl. NE15: Cha P 3B **60**
Deacon Ct. NE12: Longb 6J **45**
Deaconsfield Cl. SR3: New S 4B **132**
Deadridge La. NE45: Cor 7E **52**
DEAF HILL 7C **180**
Deaf Hill Ter. TS29: Trim S 7B **180**
Deal Cl. NE24: News 5J **23**
Dean Cl. SR8: Pet 7D **172**
Deanery St. NE22: Bed 7H **17**
Deanery Vw. DH7: Lan 6K **137**
Deanham Gdns. NE5: Newc T 5J **61**
Dean Ho. NE6: Walk 5E **64**
Dean Rd. NE33: S Shi 6H **67**
DEANS 6J **67**
Deans Av. NE64: Newb S 2G **13**
Deans Cl. NE16: Whi 6H **81**
Deansfield Cl. SR3: New S 4B **132**
Deansfield Gro. NE15: Cha P 2B **60**
Deansgate Ho. DH1: Dur 3B **166** (4D **6**)
Dean St. DH7: Lang P 4K **151**
NE1: Newc T 1G **83** (6G **4**)
NE9: Gate 2H **99**
NE46: Hex 1E **70**
Deans Wlk. DH1: Dur 1D **166**
Dean Ter. NE33: S Shi 6H **67**
NE40: Ryton 1G **79**
SR5: S'wck 6B **104**
Dearham Gro. NE23: Cra 7J **21**
Debdon Gdns. NE6: Newc T 4A **64**
Debdon Pl. NE23: Cra 4K **25**
Debdon Rd. NE63: Hir 5D **12**
Debussy Ct. NE32: Jar 7C **66**
DECKHAM 6J **83**
Deckham St. NE8: Gate 6J **83**
Deckham Ter. NE8: Gate 6J **83**
Deepbrook Rd. NE5: Newc T 4J **61**
Deepdale NE28: W'snd 7D **46**
NE38: Wash 7E **114**
Deepdale Cl. NE16: Whi 3F **97**
Deepdale Cres. NE5: Newc T 3K **61**
Deepdale Gdns. NE12: Kil 1A **46**
Deepdale Grn. NE5: Newc T 3A **62**
Deepdale Rd. NE30: N Shi 2H **49**
Deepdale St. DH5: Hett H 1G **157**
Deepdene Gro. SR6: Monk 2G **105**
Deepdene Rd. SR6: Monk 2F **105**
Deerbolt Pl. NE12: Longb 5A **46**
Deerbush NE5: Newc T 4F **61**
Deerfell Cl. NE63: Ash 5K **11**
Deerness Ct. DH7: B'don 1E **174**
Deerness Gro. DH7: Esh W 2D **162**
Deerness Hgts. DH7: B'don 7D **164**
Deerness Leisure Cen. 3D **164**
Deerness Pl. DH7: Wat 6C **162**
Deerness Rd. SR2: Sund 3G **119**
DEERNESS VIEW 2K **163**
Deerness Vw. DH7: Ush M 2K **163**
Dee Rd. NE31: Heb 3K **85**
Deer Pk. Way NE21: Bla T 5E **80**
Dees Av. NE28: W'snd 2F **65**
Dee St. NE32: Jar 6C **66**
Defender Ct. SR5: Sund 7J **103**
Defoe Av. NE34: S Shi 3J **87**
De Grey St. NE4: Newc T 3C **82**
Deighton Wlk. NE5: Newc T 4F **61**
Delacour Rd. NE21: Bla T 3C **80**
Delamere Ct. SR3: New S 3C **132**
Delamere Cres. NE23: Cra 7J **21**
Delamere Gdns. SR8: Eas 7A **160**
Delamere Rd. NE3: Ken 7B **44**
DELAVAL 2H **81**
Delaval DH2: Ches S 6J **127**
Delaval Av. NE25: Sea D 7G **27**
NE29: N Shi 6E **48**
Delaval Ct. NE22: Bed 6A **18**
NE33: S Shi 4K **67**
Delaval Cres. NE24: News 5F **23**
Delavale Cl. SR8: Pet 6D **172**
Delaval Gdns. NE15: Newc T 2H **81**
NE24: News 5F **23**
Delaval Rd. NE12: Longb 4B **46**
NE15: Newc T 2H **81**
(not continuous)
NE26: Whit B 7J **39**
Delaval St. NE24: News 5F **23**
Delaval Ter. NE3: Gos 1C **62**
NE24: Bly .1H **23**
(not continuous)
Delaval Trad. Est.
NE25: Sea D 5G **27**
Deleval Ct. *NE12: Longb 3C 46*
(off Deleval Rd.)
Delhi Cres. NE40: G'sde 3E **78**
Delhi Gdns. NE40: G'sde 3E **78**
Delhi Vw. NE40: G'sde 3E **78**
Delight Bank DH9: Dip 2H **123**
Delight Ct. DH9: Dip 1H **123**
Delight Row DH9: Dip 1H **123**
Dellfield Dr. SR4: Sund 4G **117**
Dell, The DH4: Hou S 6D **130**
NE61: Mor 4E **8**
Delta Bank Rd. NE11: Dun 3J **81**
Delta Pk. NE11: Dun 3J **81**
Delton Cl. NE38: Wash 5J **115**
Delvedere DH8: Con 1K **135**
DELVES 2K **135**
Delves La. DH8: Con 7J **121**
Delves La. Ind. Est. DH8: Con 3K **135**
De Merley Rd. NE61: Mor 5F **9**
Demesne Dr. NE22: Bed 1H **21**
Demesne, The NE63: N Sea 5F **13**
De Mowbray Way NE61: Mor 5D **8**
Dempsey Rd. NE13: Bru V 7D **34**
Denbeigh Pl. NE12: Longb 5A **46**
Denbigh Av. NE28: W'snd 1A **66**
SR6: Monk 3F **105**
Denby Cl. NE23: Cra 7J **21**
Denby Wlk. NE5: Cha P 2C **60**
Dene Av. DH5: Hou S 3G **145**
DH6: Shot C 6F **171**
NE3: Gos .1G **63**
NE12: Kil .2J **45**
NE13: Bru V 5C **34**
NE15: Lem 7D **60**
NE39: Row G 6H **95**
NE46: Hex 2E **70**
SR8: Eas 5C **160**
Dene Bank DH7: Wit G 3C **152**
Denebank NE25: Whit B 6E **38**
Dene Bank Av. SR8: Pet 6E **172**
Dene Bank Vw. NE3: Ken 2A **62**
Deneburn NE10: Gate 7E **84**
Deneburn Ter. DH8: C'sde 2E **134**
Dene Cl. NE7: Newc T 4J **63**
NE40: Ryton 1H **79**
NE42: O'ham 1D **76**
NE44: Rid M 6K **73**
Dene Cotts. DH2: Ches S 1F **141**
Dene Ct. DH3: Bir 2A **114**
DH6: Shad 6E **168**
DH7: Wit G 2D **152**
NE7: Newc T 4K **63**
NE15: Lem 5E **60**
NE17: Ham C 2K **107**
NE38: Wash 2G **115**
Dene Cres. DH6: Shot C 6F **171**
DH7: Sac .7F **141**
NE3: Gos .1G **63**
NE26: Whit B 5F **39**
NE28: W'snd 3H **65**
NE39: Row G 6H **95**
NE40: Ryton 1H **79**
Denecrest DH8: M'sly 6J **107**
Denecroft NE41: Wylam 7J **57**
Dene Dr. DH1: Carr 6H **155**
Deneford NE9: Gate 6J **99**
Dene Gdns. DH5: Hou S 3F **145**
NE10: Gate 5F **85**
NE15: Lem 7D **60**
NE25: Whit B 6E **38**
Dene Gth. NE42: O'ham 1C **76**
Dene Gro. NE3: Gos 1G **63**
NE23: Seg 1E **36**
NE42: Pru 3D **76**
Deneholm NE25: Whit B 5E **38**
NE28: W'snd 2H **65**
Deneholme Ter. DH7: Edm 3K **139**
Dene Ho. Rd. SR7: S'hm 2A **148**
Denelands NE46: Hex 1E **70**
Dene La. DH6: Shad 6F **169**
SR6: Monk 3F **105**
(Dykelands La.)
SR6: Monk, Whit 7E **88**
(Moor La.)
Dene M. SR5: C'twn 6J **103**
Dene Pk. DH7: Esh W 4D **162**
NE20: Pon 1F **41**

Dene Pk.—Doreen Av.

Dene Pk. NE46: Hex 2E 70
SR5: C'twn 6J 103
Dene Rd. NE21: Bla T 3C 80
NE30: N Shi 4J 49
NE39: Row G 6H 95
NE41: Wylam 7K 57
NE62: Chop 1G 17
SR5: C'twn 6J 103
SR7: Mur, S'hm 5H 147
TS27: B Col 2J 183
DENESIDE 4J 147
Dene Side NE21: Bla T 4D 80
Deneside DH7: Lan 7K 137
DH7: Sac 6E 140
DH7: Wit G 3D 152
NE5: Newc T 1F 61
NE11: Dun 7B 82
NE15: Newc T 6G 61
NE17: Ham C 2K 107
NE23: Seg 1E 36
NE32: Jar 5C 86
NE34: S Shi 7E 68
Deneside Av. NE9: Gate 3G 99
Deneside Cl. NE15: Thro 3H 59
Deneside Ct. NE2: Newc T 5J 63 (1L 5)
NE26: Whit B 3E 38
Dene St. DH5: Hett H 4G 145
DH9: Stly 4D 124
NE25: H'wll 1K 37
NE42: Pru 3G 77
SR3: New S 7C 118
SR4: Sund 1B 118
SR8: Pet 5E 172
Denesyde DH8: M'sly 6J 107
Dene Ter. DH6: Shot C 6F 171
NE3: Gos 1G 63
NE15: Thro 4K 59
NE21: Bla T 4B 80
(off Park Av.)
NE32: Jar 2A 86
NE42: O'ham 2K 75
NE42: Pru 4C 76
NE44: Rid M 6K 73
(off Dene Cl.)
SR6: Monk 3F 105
SR7: S'hm 2B 148
SR8: Pet 6E 172
Dene Ter. E. *NE41: Wylam 7J 57*
(off Algernon Ter.)
Dene Ter. W. *NE41: Wylam 7J 57*
(off Algernon Ter.)
DENE, THE 6K 107
Dene, The DH2: Ches S 3K 141
DH4: W Rai 1A 156
DH8: M'sly 6J 107
NE25: Whit B 6E 38
NE41: Wylam 7K 57
SR7: Mur 5J 147
Dene Vw. DH6: Cass 3F 179
DH9: Stly 2J 125
NE3: Gos 1G 63
NE16: Burn 2A 110
NE22: Bed 7A 18
NE25: H'wll 1K 37
NE39: H Spen 4E 94
NE39: Row G 5G 95
NE42: O'ham 2K 75
NE63: Ash 4J 11
TS27: Cas E 6B 182
TS27: Hes 4G 183
Dene Vw. Ct. NE24: Cow 1F 23
Dene Vw. Cres. SR4: Sund 2H 117
Dene Vw. Dr. NE24: Cow 1F 23
Dene Vw. E. NE22: Bed 1A 22
Dene Vw. W. NE22: Bed 1K 21
Dene Vs. DH3: Ches S 1B 142
SR8: Pet 6F 173
Dene Wlk. NE29: N Shi 3E 66
Dene Way SR7: S'hm 2A 148
Deneway NE39: Row G 3A 96
Denewell Av. NE7: Newc T 2J 63
NE9: Gate 2H 99
Denewood NE12: Kil 2B 46
Denewood Ct. DH9: Stly 5H 125
NE28: W'snd 3A 66
Dene Wood (Nature Reserve) 5H 125
Denham Av. SR6: Monk 3F 105
Denham Dr. NE25: Sea D 1H 37
Denham Gro. NE21: Bla T 6K 79
Denham Wlk. NE5: Cha P 2B 60
Denhill Pk. NE15: Newc T 7K 61
Denholm Av. NE23: Cra 7J 21
Denholme Lodge NE11: Dun 5B 82
Denmark Cen. NE33: S Shi 2J 67
Denmark Ct. NE6: Newc T 6A 64 (2P 5)
Denmark St. NE6: Newc T 6A 64 (2P 5)
(not continuous)
NE8: Gate 4H 83
Dennison Cres. DH3: Bir 2A 114
Dennis St. DH6: Whe H 2B 180
Denshaw Cl. NE23: Cra 7J 21
Dent Cl. DH6: Has 1A 170
Dentdale DH4: Pen 1J 129
Denton Av. NE15: Lem 7D 60
NE29: N Shi 6C 48
DENTON BURN 5F 61
Denton Chare NE1: Newc T 2F 83 (7F 4)
Denton Ct. NE5: Newc T 6G 61
Denton Gdns. NE15: Newc T 1J 81
Denton Ga. NE5: Newc T 2G 61
Denton Gro. NE5: Newc T 2G 61
Denton Hall Turret 6F 61
Denton Pk. Ho. NE5: Newc T 3E 60
Denton Pk. Shop. Cen. NE5: Newc T 3E 60
Denton Park Swimming Pool 3E 60
Denton Rd. NE15: Newc T 7F 61
Denton Vw. NE21: Bla T 4B 80
Dent St. NE24: Bly 3K 23
SR6: Monk 3F 105
Denver Gdns. NE6: Walk 1C 84
Denway Gro. NE26: Sea S 3B 28
Denwick Av. *NE15: Lem 7C 60*
(off Shirley St.)
Denwick Cl. DH2: Ches S 2J 141
Denwick Ter. NE30: N Shi 5J 49
Depot Rd. NE6: Walk 6B 64
DEPTFORD 7D 104
Deptford Rd. NE8: Gate 2J 83 (7M 5)
SR4: Sund 1D 118 (2F 7)
Deptford Ter. SR4: Sund 7C 104
Derby Ct. NE4: Newc T 7D 62 (4B 4)
Derby Cres. DH8: C'sde 3C 134
NE31: Heb 1H 85
Derby Dr. DH8: C'sde 3C 134
Derby Gdns. NE28: W'snd 2E 64
Derby Rd. DH9: Stly 4E 124
Derbyshire Dr. DH1: Carr 2H 167
Derby St. NE4: Newc T 7D 62 (4B 4)
NE32: Jar 6C 66
NE33: S Shi 3J 67
SR2: Sund 2E 118 (5G 7)
Derby Ter. NE33: S Shi 3K 67
Dereham Cl. NE26: Sea S 5D 28
Dereham Ct. NE5: Newc T 1H 61
Dereham Rd. NE26: Sea S 6D 28
Dereham Ter. NE62: Chop 7A 12
Dereham Way NE29: N Shi 4B 48
Dere Pk. DH8: Lead 5A 122
Dere Rd. DH8: Con 1K 135
Dere St. DH7: Esh W 1C 162
Derry Av. SR6: Monk 3G 105
Derwent Av. NE11: Gate 2F 99
NE15: Thro 6J 59
NE31: Heb 3J 85
NE39: Row G 6J 95
Derwent Cen., The *DH8: Con 7H 121*
(off Trafalgar St.)
Derwent Cl. DH7: Sac 7D 140
SR7: S'hm 2A 148
Derwent Cote NE17: Ham C 3K 107
Derwentcote Steel Furnace 3B 108
Derwent Ct. NE7: Newc T 1J 63
NE11: Gate 2F 99
Derwent Cres. DH3: Gt Lum 3F 143
DH8: Lead 4B 122
NE16: Swa 6G 81
NE17: Ham C 3K 107
Derwent Crook Dr. NE9: Gate 2G 99
Derwent Crookfoot Rd. NE9: Gate 2G 99
Derwent Dale DH8: Shot B 4E 120
Derwentdale Ct. *DH8: Con 6F 121*
(off Meadowfield)
Derwentdale Gdns. NE7: Newc T 2K 63
Derwentdale Ind. Est. DH8: Con 6F 121
Derwent Gdns. NE9: Gate 2J 99
NE28: W'snd 1A 66
DERWENTHAUGH 4G 81
Derwenthaugh Ind. Est. NE16: Swa 3F 81
Derwenthaugh Marina NE21: Bla T 3G 81
Derwenthaugh Riverside Pk.
NE16: Swa 4G 81
Derwenthaugh Rd. NE21: Bla T, Swa 2F 81
Derwent Haven NE17: Ham C 3K 107
Derwent Ho. NE37: Wash 4F 115
Derwent M. DH8: Con 5F 121
Derwent Pk. NE39: Row G 5K 95
Derwent Pl. DH8: Shot B 3E 120
NE21: Bla T 5B 80
Derwent Rd. NE26: Sea S 4B 28
NE30: N Shi 2H 49
NE46: Hex 2E 70
SR8: Pet 5C 172
Derwentside NE16: Swa 6G 81
Derwent St. DH4: Hou S 3B 130
DH5: Eas L 1H 157
DH8: Con 5F 121
DH9: Stly 1E 124
NE15: Newc T 1H 81
NE17: C'wl 2K 107
(Blackhall Mill)
NE17: C'wl 6K 93
(Chopwell)
SR1: Sund 2E 118 (5H 7)
Derwent Ter. DH6: S Het 3A 158
DH9: Ann P 6J 123
NE16: Burn 2B 110
(not continuous)
NE38: Wash 4J 115
Derwent Tower NE11: Dun 5C 82
Derwent Valley Cotts. NE39: Row G 6K 95
Derwent Valley Vs. NE17: Ham C 2J 107
Derwent Vw. DH8: Con 3K 121
NE16: Burn 2B 110
NE17: C'wl 4A 94
NE21: Bla T 5B 80
Derwent Vw. Ter. DH9: Dip 7H 109
Derwentwater Av. DH2: Ches S 1K 141
Derwentwater Ct. NE8: Gate 5F 83
Derwentwater Gdns. NE16: Whi 7K 81
Derwentwater Rd. NE8: Gate 6D 82
NE64: Newb S 3G 13
Derwentwater Ter. NE33: S Shi 5J 67
Derwent Way NE12: Kil 1A 46
NE21: Bla T 5E 80
Deuchar Ho. NE2: Newc T 1J 5
Deuchar St. NE2: Newc T 5H 63
Devon Av. NE16: Whi 7J 81
Devon Cl. NE63: Ash 3H 11
Devon Cres. DH3: Bir 2K 113
DH8: C'sde 3D 134
Devon Dr. SR3: New S 1C 132
Devon Gdns. NE9: Gate 7H 83
NE34: S Shi 6D 68
Devonport DH4: Hou S 6C 130
Devon Rd. NE29: N Shi 3D 48
NE31: Heb 3K 85
Devonshire Dr. NE27: Kil 3G 47
Devonshire Gdns. NE28: W'snd 2E 64
Devonshire Pl. NE2: Newc T 4H 63
Devonshire Rd. DH1: Carr 1H 167
Devonshire St. NE33: S Shi 6H 67
SR5: S'wck 6E 104
Devonshire Ter. NE2: Newc T 6F 63 (1F 4)
NE26: Whit B 7H 39
Devonshire Twr. SR5: S'wck 6F 105
Devon St. DH4: Hou S 3C 130
DH5: Hett H 6F 145
Devon Wlk. NE37: Usw 6H 101
Devonworth Pl. NE24: Cow 2E 22
De Walden Sq. NE61: Peg 4A 10
De Walden Ter. NE61: Peg 4B 10
Dewhurst Ter. NE16: Sun 5H 97
Dewley NE23: Cra 5K 25
Dewley Ct. NE23: Cra 5K 25
Dewley Pl. NE5: Newc T 2E 60
Dewley Rd. NE5: Newc T 4G 61
Dewsgreen NE23: Cra 4K 25
Dexter Ho. NE29: N Shi 2E 66
Dexter Way NE10: Gate 6A 84
Deyncourt DH1: Dur 6J 165
NE20: Pon 2H 41
Deyncourt Cl. NE20: Pon 3H 41
Diamond Ct. NE3: Ken 7J 43
Diamond Sq. NE46: Hex 2D 70
Diamond St. NE28: W'snd 3F 65
Diamond Ter. DH1: Dur 2A 166 (1B 6)
Diana St. NE4: Newc T 1D 82 (5B 4)
Dibley Sq. NE6: Newc T 1K 83 (5P 5)
Dibley St. NE6: Newc T 1K 83 (5P 5)
Dickens Av. NE16: Swa 6G 81
NE34: S Shi 3H 87
Dickens St. DH4: Hou S 2D 144
SR5: S'wck 6C 104
Dickens Wlk. NE5: Cha P 2C 60
Dickens Wynd DH1: Dur 5J 165
Dickins Wlk. SR8: Pet 7C 172
Dickson Dr. NE46: Hex 3A 70
Dick St. NE40: Ryton 3D 78
Didcot Av. NE29: N Shi 1E 66
Didcot Way NE35: Bol C, W Bol 7E 86
Diggerland 4J 151
Dillon St. NE32: Jar 1A 86
SR7: S'hm 3B 148
DILSTON 3B 72
Dilston Av. NE25: Whit B 7H 39
NE46: Hex 2E 70
Dilston Castle 3B 72
Dilston Cl. NE27: Shir 2K 47
NE38: Wash 4E 114
NE61: Peg 4C 10
SR8: Pet 2A 182
Dilston Dr. NE5: Newc T 3E 60
NE63: Hir 5B 12
Dilston Gdns. SR4: Sund 3B 118
Dilston Rd. DH1: Dur 5B 154
NE4: Newc T 1C 82
(not continuous)
Dilston Ter. NE3: Gos 1G 63
NE32: Jar 3B 86
Dimbula Gdns. NE7: Newc T 3B 64
Dinmont Pl. NE23: Cra 5K 25
DINNINGTON 4H 33
Dinnington Rd. NE13: Bru V, Din 7J 33
NE13: Din 5J 33
NE29: N Shi 6C 48
Dinsdale Av. NE28: W'snd 1G 65
Dinsdale Cotts. SR2: Ryh 3H 133
Dinsdale Dr. DH1: Carr 7H 155
Dinsdale Pl. NE2: Newc T 6H 63 (2K 5)
Dinsdale Rd. NE2: Newc T 6H 63 (2K 5)
SR6: Monk 5G 105
Dinsdale St. SR2: Ryh 3H 133
Dinsdale St. Sth. SR2: Ryh 3H 133
Dinting Cl. SR8: Pet 7K 171
Dipe La. NE36: E Bol, W Bol 1G 103
DIPTON 1H 123
Dipton Av. NE4: Newc T 2A 82
Dipton Cl. NE46: Hex 2G 71
Dipton Gdns. SR3: Sund 6D 118
Dipton Gro. NE23: Cra 4K 25
DIPTONMILL 7B 70
Dipton Mill Rd. NE46: Hex 7B 70
Dipton Rd. NE25: Whit B 4D 38
Dipwood Rd. NE39: Row G 7H 95
Dipwood Way NE39: Row G 7H 95
Discovery Ct. SR3: New S 3B 132
Dishforth Grn. NE9: Gate 6K 99
Dispensary La. NE1: Newc T 1F 83 (6D 4)
Disraeli St. DH4: Hou S 2B 144
NE24: Bly 1H 23
(not continuous)
Disraeli Ter. NE17: C'wl 6K 93
DISSINGTON 7A 30
Dissington La. NE15: Hed W, Pon 5B 40
DISSINGTON MARCH 4F 41
Dissington Pl. NE5: Newc T 5J 61
NE16: Whi 2G 97
Ditchburn Ter. SR4: Sund 7B 104
Dixon Av. DH8: Ebc 5H 107
Dixon Est. DH6: Shot C 7E 170
Dixon Est. Bungs. DH6: Shot C 1E 180
Dixon Pl. NE11: Dun 6B 82
Dixon Ri. SR8: Pet 6F 173
Dixon Rd. DH5: Hou S 4D 144
Dixons Sq. SR6: Monk 6F 105
Dixon St. DH8: Con 5G 121
NE8: Gate 5E 82
NE33: S Shi 4J 67
Dobson Cl. NE4: Newc T 3D 82 (9A 4)
Dobson Cres. NE6: Newc T 2A 84
Dobson Ho. NE3: Gos 6E 44
NE12: Kil 2K 45
Dobson Ter. SR7: Mur 7E 146
TS28: Win 4F 181
Dockendale La. NE16: Whi 7J 81
Dockendale M. NE16: Whi 7J 81
Dock Rd. NE29: N Shi 1G 67
Dock Rd. Sth. NE29: N Shi 2G 67
Dock St. NE33: S Shi 7H 67
SR6: Monk 7G 105
Dockwray Cl. NE30: N Shi 7H 49
Dockwray Sq. NE30: N Shi 7H 49
Doctor Pit Cotts. NE22: Bed 7H 17
Doctor Ryan Ho. NE6: Walk 1E 84
Doctor Syntax Rd. NE42: Pru 4E 76
Doctor Winterbottom Hall
NE33: S Shi 4B 68
Doddfell Cl. NE37: Wash 2E 114
Doddington Cl. NE15: Lem 6B 60
Doddington Dr. NE23: Cra 4K 25
Doddington Vs. NE10: Gate 7A 84
Dodd's Bldgs. NE35: Bol C 5E 86
Dodds Cl. DH6: Whe H 2C 180
Dodd's Ct. SR5: C'twn 4G 103
Dodds Ter. DH3: Bir 2A 114
TS28: Win 4F 181
Dodd Ter. DH9: Ann P 6K 123
Dodsworth Nth. NE40: G'sde 5F 79
Dodsworth Ter. NE40: G'sde 5F 79
Dodsworth Vs. NE40: G'sde 5F 79
Dog Bank NE1: Newc T 2G 83 (7H 5)
Dogger Bank NE61: Mor 6E 8
Dog Leap Stairs NE1: Newc T 7G 4
Dolphin Ct. NE4: Newc T 1K 81
Dolphin Quay NE29: N Shi 7H 49
Dolphin St. NE4: Newc T 1K 81
Dolphin Vs. NE13: Bru V 7D 34
Dominies Cl. NE39: Row G 4K 95
Dominion Rd. DH7: B'don 2D 174
Donald Av. DH6: S Het 3A 158
Donald St. NE3: Gos 7G 45
Doncaster Rd. NE2: Newc T 6H 63 (2K 5)
Don Cres. DH3: Gt Lum 3F 143
Doncrest Rd. NE37: Usw 6F 101
Don Dixon Dr. NE32: Jar 5B 86
Donerston Gro. SR8: Pet 1J 181
Don Gdns. NE36: W Bol 7F 87
NE37: Usw 6H 101
Donkin Rd. NE37: Wash 1E 114
Donkins St. NE35: Bol C 5E 86
Donkin Ter. NE30: N Shi 5J 49
NE40: Ryton 3C 78
Donnington Cl. SR5: C'twn 6G 103
Donnington Ct. NE3: Newc T 1H 63
Donnini Ho. SR8: Eas 7A 160
Donnini Pl. DH1: Dur 1D 166
Donnison Gdns. SR1: Sund 1G 119
Donridge NE37: Usw 6F 101
Don Rd. NE32: Jar 6D 66
Donside NE10: Gate 3D 100
Don St. NE11: Gate 3E 98
Donvale Rd. NE37: Usw 6E 100
Don Vw. NE36: W Bol 7F 87
DONWELL 6F 101
Dorcas Av. NE15: Newc T 1J 81
Dorcas Ter. NE37: Usw 7H 101
Dorchester Cl. NE5: Cha P 2B 60
Dorchester Ct. NE25: Sea D 4G 27
Dorchester Gdns. NE9: Gate 5H 99
Doreen Av. SR7: Mur 4H 147

Dykelands Rd.—Edward Cain Ct.

Dykelands Rd. SR6: Monk 3F 105
Dykelands Way NE34: S Shi 3F 87
Dykenook Cl. NE16: Whi 3G 97
Dykes Way NE10: Gate 2B 100
Dymock Ct. NE3: Ken 7H 43

E

Eaglescliffe Dr. NE7: Newc T 3B 64
Eaglesdene DH5: Hett H 6G 145
Ealing Ct. NE3: Ken 6H 43
Ealing Dr. NE30: N Shi 3J 49
Ealing Sq. NE23: Cra 4F 25
Eardulph Av. DH3: Ches S 6B 128
Earl Grey's Monument 1F 83 (5F 4)
Earl Grey Way NE29: N Shi 2F 67
Earlington Ct. NE12: Longb 3C 46
Earls Cl. NE13: Wool 4F 43
Earls Ct. NE11: Gate 2F 99
NE42: Pru 2G 77
SR5: S'wck 3C 104
Earls Court Health Club 4J 7
(off Blandford St.)
Earls Dene NE9: Gate 3H 99
Earls Dr. NE9: Gate 3H 99
NE15: Newc T 6G 61
Earl's Gdns. NE24: Cow 1G 23
Earls Grn. DH5: W Rai 7D 144
Earls Pk. Nth. NE11: Gate 7E 82
Earlston St. SR5: S'wck 3C 104
Earlston Way NE23: Cra 7A 22
Earl St. DH9: Ann P 4K 123
SR4: Sund 2D 118
SR7: S'hm 2J 147
Earls Way NE1: Newc T 4F 4
Earlsway NE11: Gate 7E 82
Earlswood Av. NE9: Gate 3H 99
Earlswood Gro. NE24: News 6H 23
Earlswood Pk. NE9: Gate 3H 99
Earnshaw Way NE25: Whit B 4D 38
EARSDON 6A 38
Earsdon Cl. NE5: Newc T 4G 61
Earsdon Ct. NE25: Whit B 7D 38
Earsdon Grange Rd.
DH5: Hou S 1F 145
Earsdon Rd. DH5: Hou S 2F 145
NE3: Ken 2A 62
NE25: Well, Whit B 6A 38
NE27: Back, Shir 2H 47
Earsdon Ter. NE27: Shir 3J 47
SR2: Ryh 3H 133
Earsdon Vw. NE27: Shir 7K 37
Easby Cl. NE3: Gos 4F 45
Easby Rd. NE38: Wash 4H 115
Easedale NE26: Sea S 4C 28
Easedale Av. NE3: Gos 3E 44
Easedale Gdns. NE9: Gate 3J 99
EASINGTON 1K 171
Easington Av. NE9: Gate 4A 100
NE23: Cra 7A 22
EASINGTON COLLIERY 6C 160
Easington Greyhound Stadium 6K 159
EASINGTON LANE 2J 157
EASINGTON LEA 5B 160
Easington Rd. DH6: S Het 5E 158
Easington St. SR5: Monk 7E 104 (1H 7)
SR8: Eas 7B 160
Easington St. Nth. SR5: Monk 1H 7
East Acres NE13: Din 3J 33
NE21: Bla T 4D 80
E. Atherton St. DH1: Dur 3K 165 (3A 6)
East Av. DH2: Ches S 3J 141
NE12: Longb 6B 46
NE25: Whit B 6E 38
NE34: S Shi 7C 68
(not continuous)
NE38: Wash 7F 115
SR8: Eas 5C 160
E. Back Pde. SR2: Sund 3H 119
East Bailey NE12: Kil 7B 36
East Block DH7: Wit G 3C 152
EAST BOLDON 7A 88
E. Boldon Rd. SR6: Cle 6A 88
East Boldon Station (Metro) 7A 88
Eastbourne Av. NE6: Walk 7E 64
NE8: Gate 6G 83
Eastbourne Ct. NE6: Walk 7E 64
Eastbourne Gdns. NE6: Walk 7E 64
NE23: Cra 4F 25
NE26: Whit B 5F 39
Eastbourne Gro. NE33: S Shi 2K 67
Eastbourne Pde. NE31: Heb 4A 86
Eastbourne Sq. SR5: S'wck 3D 104
E. Bridge St. DH4: Pen 7J 115
Eastburn Gdns. NE10: Gate 4E 84
Eastcheap NE6: Newc T 4A 64
E. Cleft Rd. SR1: Sund 2D 118 (5F 7)
East Clere DH7: Lang P 5J 151
Eastcliffe Av. NE3: Ken 2C 62
E. Cliff Rd. SR7: S'hm 5C 148
East Cl. NE34: S Shi 7C 68
Eastcombe Cl. NE35: Bol C 4E 86
E. Coronation St. SR7: Mur 7F 147
Eastcote Ter. NE6: Walk 2D 84
EAST CRAMLINGTON 5B 26
E. Cramlington Ind. Est.
NE23: E Cram 6C 26
East Cramlington Pond (Nature Reserve)
6E 26
East Cres. NE22: Bed 6C 18
E. Cross St. SR1: Sund 2K 7
Eastdene Rd. SR7: S'hm 3H 147
Eastdene Way SR8: Pet 7D 172
EAST DENTON 5G 61
East Dr. NE24: News 5G 23
SR6: Cle 6B 88
E. Ellen St. SR7: Mur 1F 159
(off W. Ellen St.)
East End NE26: Sea S 6E 28
East End Swimming Pool 7A 64 (3P 5)
Easten Gdns. NE10: Gate 5B 84
Easterfield Ct. NE61: Mor 6G 9
Eastern Av. DH7: Lang P 5J 151
NE9: Gate 3F 99
NE11: Gate 3F 99
Eastern Ter. NE28: W'snd 4C 66
Eastern Way NE5: Newc T 3K 61
NE20: Pon 6H 31
E. Farm Ct. NE16: Sun 4J 97
NE23: Cra 4K 25
E. Farm M. DH8: M'sly 6A 108
E. Farm Ter. NE23: Cra 4K 25
Eastfield SR8: Pet 7D 172
Eastfield Av. NE6: Walk 5E 64
NE25: Whit B 7D 38
Eastfield Ho. NE6: Walk 5E 64
Eastfield Rd. NE12: Longb 6A 46
NE34: S Shi 5B 68
East Flds. SR6: Whit 6H 89
Eastfields DH9: Stly 4E 124
NE46: Hex 2F 71
Eastfield St. SR4: Sund 3B 118
Eastfield Ter. NE12: Longb 6B 46
E. Ford Rd. NE62: Chop 7A 12
E. Forest Hall Rd. NE12: Longb 4C 46
East Front NE2: Newc T 5G 63 (1G 4)
Eastgarth NE5: Newc T 7G 43
East Ga. NE61: Mor 1G 15
NE8: Gate 3H 83 (9J 5)
NE46: Hex 2D 70
NE62: Sco G 3G 17
Eastgate Bank NE43: Mic 6B 76
Eastgate Gdns. NE4: Newc T 2B 82
EAST GATESHEAD 3J 83 (10L 5)
E. George Potts St. NE33: S Shi 4K 67
E. George St. NE30: N Shi 6J 49
East Grange NE25: H'wll 1K 37
SR5: S'wck 4E 104
E. Grange Ct. SR8: Eas 1K 171
East Grn. DH6: Shot C 6F 171
NE62: Sco G 3H 17
East Gro. SR4: Sund 3H 117
EAST HARTFORD 6K 21
E. Hendon Rd. SR1: Sund 2H 119
EAST HERRINGTON 2H 131
East Hetton Aged Workmen's Homes
DH6: Kel 7E 178
E. Hill Rd. NE8: Gate 5K 83
E. Holburn NE33: S Shi 3H 67
EAST HOLYWELL 4H 37
EAST HOWDON 3C 66
E. Howdon By-Pass NE28: W'snd 4C 66
NE29: N Shi 4C 66
EAST JARROW 7D 66
EAST KYO 3B 124
Eastlands DH5: Hett H 7F 145
NE7: Newc T 2J 63
NE21: Bla T 5B 80
NE38: Wash 2C 128
East Law DH8: Ebc 7F 107
East Lea DH6: Thor 7J 169
NE21: Bla T 6C 80
NE64: Newb S 1J 13
Eastlea Cres. SR7: S'hm 3J 147
Eastlea Rd. SR7: S'hm 3H 147
Eastleigh Cl. NE35: Bol C 6E 86
East Loan NE61: Mor 5G 9
E. Moffett St. NE33: S Shi 4K 67
E. Moor Rd. SR4: Sund 1B 118
Eastmoor Rd. SR7: Mur 1G 159
E. Norfolk St. NE30: N Shi 7H 49
E. Oakwood NE46: Sand 5G 51
Easton Homes NE22: Bed 6A 18
East Pde. DH2: Plaw 7H 141
DH8: Con 7J 121
DH9: Stly 2G 125
NE26: Whit B 5H 39
E. Park Gdns. NE21: Bla T 5C 80
E. Park Rd. NE9: Gate 1G 99
E. Park Vw. NE24: Bly 2K 23
E. Pastures NE63: Ash 5K 11
E. Percy St. NE30: N Shi 6J 49
EAST RAINTON 6C 144
East Riggs NE22: Bed 1H 21
E. Sea Vw. NE64: Newb S 2K 13
E. Side Av. DH7: Ush M 1C 164
EAST SLEEKBURN 5D 18
East Sq. NE23: Cra 4J 25
E. Stainton St. NE33: S Shi 4K 67
EAST STANLEY 2G 125
E. Stanley By-Pass DH9: Stly 2H 125
E. Stevenson St. NE33: S Shi 4K 67
East St. DH2: Pelt 4C 126
DH6: Hett 7C 176
DH6: Shot C 6F 171
DH6: Thor 1A 180
DH7: Sac 6D 140
DH8: Con 7J 121
(Meadow Ri.)
DH8: Con 7K 121
(North St.)
DH9: Stly 2H 125
NE8: Gate 3H 83 (9J 5)
NE17: C'wl 6B 94
NE30: N Shi 4K 49
NE31: Heb 6K 65
(not continuous)
NE33: S Shi 2J 67
NE39: H Spen 3D 94
NE43: Mic 5B 76
SR4: Sund 1A 118
SR6: Whit 6H 89
TS27: B Col 1H 183
East Ter. NE17: C'wl 1A 108
NE62: Chop 1A 18
TS27: Hes 5E 182
TS28: Win 7H 181
East Thorp NE5: Newc T 7F 43
East Vw. DH2: Plaw 1H 153
DH6: Sher 3D 168
DH6: Whe H 4B 180
DH7: B'don 2E 174
DH8: Con 5H 121
DH9: Dip 1H 123
DH9: Stly 6E 124
NE10: Gate 1D 100
NE13: Wide O 4D 34
NE16: Burn 2A 110
NE21: Bla T 3D 80
NE22: Bed 5B 18
NE23: Seg 2D 36
NE25: Sea D 5G 27
NE31: Heb 2H 85
NE35: Bol C 6F 87
NE36: W Bol 7G 87
NE39: Row G 5G 95
NE40: Ryton 7C 58
NE61: Mor 7G 9
NE62: Chop 1A 18
SR2: Ryh 3G 133
SR5: C'twn 6J 103
SR6: Monk 4G 105
SR7: Mur 1F 159
SR7: S'hm 1H 147
SR8: Pet 5E 172
E. View Av. NE23: Cra 4K 25
E. View Sth. SR5: C'twn 6J 103
E. View Ter. NE10: Gate 1D 100
NE16: Swa 6H 81
NE23: Dud 3J 35
East Vs. DH6: Has 7B 158
East Vines SR1: Sund 1H 119
Eastward Grn. NE25: Whit B 7D 38
Eastway NE34: S Shi 1D 88
East-West Link Rd. NE23: Cra 3K 25
Eastwood DH7: Sac 1E 152
Eastwood Av. NE24: News 6H 23
Eastwood Cl. NE23: Dud 6A 36
Eastwood Ct. NE12: Longb 5B 46
Eastwood Gdns. NE3: Ken 1B 62
NE9: Gate 1J 99
NE10: Gate 5A 84
Eastwood Grange Ct. NE46: Hex 2G 71
Eastwood Grange Rd. NE46: Hex 2G 71
E. Woodlands NE46: Hex 2F 71
Eastwood Pl. NE23: Cra 7A 22
Eastwoods Rd. NE42: Pru 3H 77
Eastwood Ter. NE42: Pru 4H 77
Eastwood Vs. NE42: Pru 2H 77
Eaton Cl. NE38: Wash 1F 129
Eaton Pl. NE4: Newc T 1B 82
Eavers Ct. NE34: S Shi 1J 87
Ebba Wlk. NE3: Gos 7F 45
EBCHESTER 4G 107
Ebchester Av. NE9: Gate 4B 100
Ebchester Ct. NE3: Ken 7J 43
Ebchester Hill DH8: Ebc, M'sly 5G 107
Ebchester Roman Baths & Mus. 4G 107
Ebchester St. NE34: S Shi 1G 87
Ebdon La. SR6: Monk 3F 105
Ebor St. NE6: Newc T 5A 64
NE34: S Shi 2G 87
Eccles Ct. NE27: Back 6G 37
Eccles Ter. NE27: Shir 3J 47
Eccleston Cl. NE27: Back 7G 37
Eccleston Rd. NE33: S Shi 3A 68
Ecgfrid Ter. NE32: Jar 1C 86
Eco Cen., The NE31: Heb 5K 65
Eddison Rd. NE38: Wash 4K 115
Eddleston NE38: Wash 7E 114
Eddleston Av. NE3: Ken 2C 62
Eddrington Gro. NE5: Cha P 2C 60
Ede Av. NE11: Dun 6B 82
NE34: S Shi 7D 68
Eden Av. DH8: Lead 4B 122
NE16: Burn 2A 110
Edenbridge Cres. NE12: Longb 5K 45
Eden Cl. NE5: Cha P 3C 60
Eden Cotts. TS27: Hes 4E 182
Eden Ct. NE22: Bed 1J 21
NE28: W'snd 4F 65
Edencroft DH9: Stly 3C 126
Eden Dale NE40: Ryton 2D 78
Edendale Av. NE6: Walk 7E 64
NE12: Longb 5A 46
NE24: Cow 1F 23
Edendale Ct. NE24: Cow 1F 23
NE34: S Shi 2G 87
Edendale Ter. NE8: Gate 6H 83
SR8: Pet 6D 172
Edenfield DH9: Stly 2C 126
Edengarth NE30: N Shi 2F 49
Eden Gro. NE61: Mor 2G 15
Edenhill Rd. SR8: Pet 5C 172
Eden Ho. Rd. SR4: Sund 3D 118
Eden La. SR8: Pet 4B 172
Eden Pl. NE30: N Shi 3G 49
Eden Rd. DH1: Dur 5A 154
Eden St. NE28: W'snd 4F 65
SR8: Pet 5E 172
Eden St. W. SR1: Sund 1E 118 (3G 7)
Eden Ter. DH1: Dur 1G 167
DH4: Hou S 3B 130
DH9: Stly 4D 124
SR2: Sund 3D 118
Eden Va. SR2: Sund 3D 118
Edenvale Est. SR8: Pet 6D 172
Eden Vw. DH6: Shot C 6F 171
Eden Vs. NE38: Wash 4J 115
Eden Wlk. NE32: Jar 3C 86
Edgar St. NE3: Newc T 7H 45
Edgecote NE37: Usw 7K 101
Edge Ct. DH1: Dur 2D 166
(not continuous)
Edgefield Av. NE3: Ken 7B 44
Edgefield Dr. NE23: Cra 7A 22
Edge Hill NE20: Pon 3F 41
Edgehill NE61: Mor 2H 15
Edgehill Cl. NE20: Pon 3G 41
Edge La. DH7: B'hpe, Lan 2A 138
Edgemount NE12: Kil 7C 36
Edgeware Ct. SR5: S'wck 4C 104
Edgeware Rd. NE8: Gate 6J 83
Edgeware Wlk. NE4: Newc T 3A 82
Edgewell Av. NE42: Pru 5D 76
Edgewell Grange NE42: Pru 4E 76
Edgewell Ho. Rd. NE42: Mic 7C 76
Edgewell Rd. NE42: Pru 4D 76
Edgewell Rd. W. NE42: Pru 4D 76
(off Edgewell Rd.)
Edgewood NE20: Pon 2H 41
NE46: Hex 2F 71
Edgewood Av. NE22: Bed 7A 18
Edgewood Ct. DH7: Sac 6D 140
Edgeworth Cl. NE35: Bol C 4E 86
Edgeworth Cres. SR6: Monk 5F 105
Edgmond Ct. SR2: Ryh 1G 133
Edhill Av. NE34: S Shi 1F 87
Edhill Gdns. NE34: S Shi 2F 87
Edinburgh Ct. NE3: Ken 4K 43
Edinburgh Dr. NE22: Bed 6F 17
Edinburgh Rd. NE32: Jar 2E 86
Edinburgh Sq. SR5: S'wck 4C 104
Edington Gdns. NE40: Ryton 7C 58
Edington Gro. NE30: N Shi 3G 49
Edington Rd. NE30: N Shi 3G 49
Edison Gdns. NE8: Gate 7G 83
Edison St. SR7: Mur 7E 146
Edith Av. NE21: Bla T 4C 80
Edith Moffat Ho. NE29: N Shi 6G 49
(off Albion Rd.)
Edith St. DH8: Con 7H 121
NE30: N Shi 4J 49
NE32: Jar 6A 66
SR2: Sund 4G 119
SR7: S'hm 5C 148
Edith Ter. DH4: Hou S 5D 130
NE16: Whi 7G 81
(off Swalwell Bank)
Edlingham Cl. NE3: Gos 1H 63
Edlingham Ct. DH5: Hou S 2F 145
Edlingham Rd. DH1: Dur 6A 154
EDMONDSLEY 3D 140
Edmondsley La. DH7: Sac 4D 140
Edmondsley Rd.
DH2: Ches S, Edm, Plaw 3D 140
DH7: Edm, Plaw, Sac 3D 140
Edmonton Sq. SR5: S'wck 4C 104
E.D. Morel Ter. NE17: C'wl 7A 94
Edmund Ct. DH7: Ush M 7C 152
Edmund Pl. NE9: Gate 2H 99
Edmund Rd. NE27: Longb 3H 47
Edna St. DH6: Bow 5H 177
Edna Ter. NE5: Newc T 2G 61
Edrich Ho. NE29: N Shi 2E 66
Edward Av. DH6: Bow 4H 177
SR8: Pet 5D 172
Edward Burdis St. SR5: S'wck 5D 104
Edward Cain Ct. SR8: Pet 5E 172

Edward Ho.—Embankment Rd.

Edward Ho. SR2: Sund 5G 7
Edwardia Ct. DH8: Con 7G 121
Edward Pl. NE4: Newc T 1D 82 (5A 4)
Edward Rd. DH3: Bir 3K 113
NE22: Bed 6B 18
NE28: W'snd 2K 65
Edwardson Rd. DH7: B'don 2F 175
Edwards Rd. NE26: Whit B 7J 39
Edward St. DH1: Dur 2D 166
DH3: Ches S 6A 128
DH5: Hett H 6G 145
DH7: Esh W 4E 162
DH9: Stly 7J 125
NE3: Gos 7E 44
NE16: Burn 4A 110
NE24: Bly 1H 23
NE31: Heb 7G 65
NE40: Ryton 3C 78
NE61: Mor 7G 9
NE61: Peg 4B 10
SR3: New S 2C 132
SR7: S'hm 4B 148
Edwards Wlk. DH7: B'hpe 4E 138
NE1: Newc T 7F 63 (3E 4)
Edward Ter. DH2: Pelt 3E 126
DH7: New B 4B 164
DH9: Ann P 5B 124
Edwina Gdns. NE29: N Shi 5E 48
Edwin Gro. NE28: W'snd 2A 66
Edwin's Av. NE12: Longb 4C 46
Edwin's Av. Sth.
NE12: Longb 4C 46
Edwin St. DH5: Hou S 1E 144
NE6: Newc T 7K 63 (3P 5)
NE13: Bru V 5C 34
SR4: Sund 1A 118
Edwin Ter. NE40: G'sde 4G 79
Egerton Rd. NE34: S Shi 7J 67
Egerton St. NE4: Newc T 2K 81
(not continuous)
SR2: Sund 3G 119 (6K 7)
Eggleston Cl. DH1: Dur 5C 154
DH3: Gt Lum 3F 143
Eggleston Dr. DH8: Con 1H 135
SR3: Sund 6C 118
Egham Rd. NE5: Cha P 3C 60
Eglesfield Rd. NE33: S Shi 5J 67
Eglingham Av. NE30: N Shi 3J 49
Eglingham Cl. NE61: Hep, Mor 2H 15
Eglingham Way NE61: Hep 2H 15
Eglinton St. SR5: S'wck 6E 104
Eglinton St. Nth. SR5: S'wck 6E 104
Eglinton Twr. SR5: S'wck 6F 105
Egremont Dr. NE9: Gate 1J 99
Egremont Gdns. NE9: Gate 1J 99
Egremont Gro. SR8: Pet 2J 181
Egremont Pl. NE26: Whit B 7H 39
Egremont Way NE23: Cra 7A 22
Egton Ter. DH3: Bir 3A 114
Eider Cl. NE24: News 6J 23
Eider Wlk. NE12: Kil 7A 36
Eighteenth Av. NE24: Bly 4G 23
(not continuous)
Eighth Av. DH2: Ches S 6K 127
NE6: Newc T 5A 64 (1P 5)
NE11: Gate 4E 98
NE24: Bly 4H 23
NE61: Mor 1H 15
NE63: Hir 5C 12
Eighth Row NE63: Ash 3K 11
Eighth St. SR8: Pet 5E 172
TS27: B Col 1H 183
EIGHTON BANKS 5B 100
Eighton Ter. NE9: Gate 4C 100
Eilansgate NE46: Hex 1B 70
Eilansgate Ter. NE46: Hex 1C 70
Eilanville NE46: Hex 1C 70
Eishort Way NE12: Longb 6K 45
Eland Cl. NE3: Ken 7K 43
Eland Edge NE20: Pon 4K 31
Eland Grange NE20: Pon 4J 31
Eland La. NE20: Pon 5K 31
Eland Vw. NE20: Pon 5K 31
Elberfield Ct. NE32: Jar 7B 66
Elder Cl. DH7: Ush M 3D 164
Elder Gdns. NE9: Spri 6A 100
Elder Gro. NE9: Gate 2H 99
NE34: S Shi 3B 88
Elder Sq. NE63: Hir 5C 12
Elders Wlk. SR6: Whit 6H 89
Elderwood Gdns. NE11: Gate 2D 98
Eldon Cl. DH7: Lang P 5G 151
Eldon Ct. NE1: Newc T 7F 63 (4E 4)
NE28: W'snd 4B 66
(off Eldon St.)
Eldon Gdns. NE1: Newc T 7F 63 (4E 4)
Eldon Ho. NE3: Gos 6E 44
Eldon La. NE1: Newc T 1F 83 (5F 4)
Eldon Leisure Cen. 5E 4
Eldon Pl. NE1: Newc T 6F 63 (2F 4)
NE15: Lem 6D 60
NE33: S Shi 6H 67
Eldon Rd. NE15: Lem 6D 60
NE46: Hex 2F 71
Eldon Sq. NE1: Newc T 1F 83 (5E 4)
Eldon Sq. Bus Concourse
NE1: Newc T 4E 4
(off Percy St.)
Eldon Sq. Shop. Cen.
NE1: Newc T 7F 63 (4E 4)
Eldon St. NE8: Gate 3J 83 (10L 5)
NE28: W'snd 3A 66
NE33: S Shi 4H 67
SR4: Sund 2C 118
Eldon Way NE1: Newc T 7F 63 (4F 4)
Eleanor St. NE30: N Shi 7J 39
NE33: S Shi 2K 67
Eleanor Ter. NE16: Whi 7G 81
(off Swalwell Bank)
NE40: Ryton 2E 78
Electric Cres. DH4: Hou S 5C 130
Elemore Cl. DH7: Lang P 5H 151
Elemore La. DH5: Eas L 4G 157
(not continuous)
DH6: Eas L, H Pitt 6C 156
Elemore St. DH6: H Pitt 6B 156
ELEMORE VALE 3H 157
Elemore Vw. DH6: S Het 4B 158
Elenbel Av. NE22: Bed 7A 18
Eleventh Av. DH2: Ches S 6K 127
NE11: Gate 5F 99
NE24: Bly 3J 23
NE61: Mor 1H 15
Eleventh Av. Nth. NE11: Gate 4G 99
Eleventh Row NE63: Ash 3K 11
Eleventh St. SR8: Pet 5D 172
TS27: B Col 1G 183
(not continuous)
Elford Cl. NE25: Whit B 6D 38
Elfordleigh DH4: Hou S 5C 130
Elgar Av. NE5: Cha P 3C 60
Elgar Cl. DH9: Stly 4G 125
Elgen Vs. NE39: Row G 6H 95
Elgin Av. NE28: W'snd 1K 65
SR7: S'hm 3H 147
Elgin Cl. NE22: Bed 6B 18
NE23: Cra 4F 25
NE29: N Shi 4C 48
Elgin Ct. NE10: Gate 4F 85
Elgin Gdns. NE6: Walk 7D 64
Elgin Gro. DH9: Stly 3H 125
Elgin Pl. DH3: Bir 6B 114
Elgin Rd. NE9: Gate 7K 83
Elgin St. NE32: Jar 2E 86
Elgy Rd. NE3: Gos 2D 62
Elisabeth Av. DH3: Bir 2K 113
Elite Bldgs. DH9: Stly 2F 125
Elizabeth Ct. DH6: H Pitt 6C 156
NE12: Longb 4E 46
Elizabeth Cres. NE23: Dud 3J 35
Elizabeth Diamond Gdns.
NE33: S Shi 5H 67
Elizabeth Dr. NE12: Longb 4E 46
Elizabeth Pl. DH6: Shot C 6F 171
(off East St.)
Elizabeth Rd. NE28: W'snd 2A 66
Elizabeth St. DH5: Hou S 1E 144
DH9: Ann P 5A 124
NE6: Newc T 7J 63 (3M 5)
NE17: C'wl 6K 93
NE23: E Cram 5D 26
NE33: S Shi 3K 67
SR5: C'twn 6H 103
SR5: Monk 4E 104
SR7: S'hm 3A 148
TS27: B Col 3J 183
Elizabeth Woodcock Maritime
Almshouses, The SR2: Sund 7J 7
Eliza St. DH7: Sac 1D 152
Ella McCambridge Ho. NE6: Walk 1E 84
Ellam Av. DH1: Dur 4J 165
Ell-Dene Cres. NE10: Gate 7C 84
Ellen Ct. NE32: Jar 6B 66
Ellen Ter. NE37: Usw 7K 101
Ellerbeck Cl. NE10: Gate 6A 84
Ellerby Ho. NE6: Walk 3C 84
(off McCutcheon Ct.)
Ellersmere Gdns. NE30: N Shi 2H 49
Ellerton Way NE10: Gate 6A 84
NE23: Cra 7A 22
Ellesmere DH4: Hou S 6H 129
(not continuous)
Ellesmere Av. NE3: Gos 1G 63
NE5: Newc T 3G 61
NE6: Walk 6C 64
Ellesmere Ct. SR2: Sund 7G 119
Ellesmere Dr. SR7: S'hm 3H 147
Ellesmere Gdns. NE62: Chop 7A 12
Ellesmere Rd. NE4: Newc T 1A 82
Ellesmere Ter. SR6: Monk 4G 105
Ellie Bldgs. DH9: Stly 2E 124
(off Royal Rd.)
Elling Ct. NE23: Cra 7A 22
Ellington Cl. DH2: Ous 6G 113
NE15: Lem 6B 60
SR2: Ryh 4H 133
Ellington Rd. NE63: Ash 3H 11
Ellington Ter. NE63: Ash 3H 11
Elliot Rd. NE10: Gate 4K 83
(not continuous)
Elliot St. DH6: Thor 1K 179
Elliott Cl. DH4: Pen 2B 130
Elliott Ct. NE61: Mor 2H 15
Elliott Dr. NE10: Gate 6B 84
Elliott Gdns. NE28: W'snd 1E 64
NE34: S Shi 4K 87
Elliott Rd. SR8: Pet 5B 172
Elliott St. DH7: Sac 7E 140
NE24: Bly 5F 23
Elliott Ter. NE4: Newc T 1B 82
NE37: Usw 7J 101
Elliott Wlk. NE13: Bru V 7B 34
Ellis Leazes DH1: Dur 2C 166
Ellison Bldg. NE1: Newc T 4G 4
Ellison Pl. NE1: Newc T 7G 63 (4G 4)
NE9: Gate 3H 99
NE32: Jar 5B 66
Ellison Rd. NE11: Dun 6B 82
SR8: Pet 5C 172
Ellison St. NE8: Gate 3G 83 (10H 5)
NE31: Heb 6G 65
(not continuous)
NE32: Jar 5B 66
(not continuous)
Ellison Ter. NE1: Newc T 7G 63 (4G 4)
NE40: G'sde 5D 78
Ellison Vs. NE8: Gate 5J 83
Ellis Rd. SR5: S'wck 4C 104
Ellis Sq. NE61: Peg 4B 10
SR5: S'wck 4D 104
Ellwood Gdns. NE9: Gate 6H 83
Ellwoods Gym
Peterlee 6F 173
(off Windsor Ter.)
Sunderland 5K 7
(off Murton St.)
Elm Av. DH2: Pelt 3E 126
DH7: B'don 2D 174
NE11: Dun 6B 82
NE13: Din 4H 33
NE16: Whi 6J 81
NE34: S Shi 2B 88
TS27: B Col 3K 183
Elm Bank Rd. NE41: Wylam 1K 77
Elm Cl. NE23: Cra 7A 22
NE46: Hex 3A 70
Elm Ct. DH7: Sac 7E 140
NE16: Whi 2H 97
Elm Cres. DH2: Plaw 7H 141
Elm Cft. Rd. NE12: Longb 5C 46
Elmdale Rd. DH8: Con 6J 121
Elm Dr. NE22: Bed 1H 21
SR6: Whit 5J 89
Elmfield DH5: Hett H 4G 145
DH7: Lan 6J 137
Elmfield App. NE3: Gos 2E 62
Elmfield Av. DH1: Dur 1F 167
Elmfield Cl. SR3: E Her 3J 131
Elmfield Gdns. NE3: Gos 1D 62
NE25: Whit B 1D 48
NE28: W'snd 2D 64
Elmfield Gro. NE3: Gos 1D 62
Elmfield Pk. NE3: Gos 2D 62
Elmfield Rd. DH8: Con 5H 121
NE3: Gos 2D 62
NE15: Thro 3J 59
NE31: Heb 3K 85
Elmfield Ter. NE10: Gate 5E 84
NE31: Heb 2K 85
Elm Gro. DH4: Hou S 4C 130
DH7: Ush M 3D 164
NE3: Ken 5B 44
NE12: Kil 3B 46
NE16: Burn 2K 109
NE34: S Shi 2B 88
Elm Pk. Rd. DH8: Con, Shot B 2H 121
Elm Pk. Ter. DH8: Shot B 2G 121
Elm Pl. DH4: Hou S 6D 130
Elm Rd. NE20: Pon 6A 32
NE21: Bla T 4D 80
NE29: N Shi 5B 48
Elmsford Gro. NE12: Longb 6K 45
Elmsleigh Gdns. SR6: Cle 4C 88
Elms, The DH5: Eas L 3K 157
DH8: Shot B 2G 121
NE3: Gos 2D 62
SR2: Sund 3F 119 (7J 7)
SR4: Sund 2G 117
TS27: Hes 4H 183
Elm St. DH3: Ches S 6A 128
DH7: Lang P 4J 151
(not continuous)
DH8: Con 5H 121
DH9: Stly 5D 124
NE13: Sea B 3E 34
NE16: Sun 5H 97
NE32: Jar 6A 66
NE43: Mic 6A 76
Elm St. W. NE16: Sun 5H 97
Elms W. SR2: Sund 3F 119 (7J 7)
Elm Ter. DH3: Bir 3K 113
DH8: Lead 5B 122
DH9: Ann P 5J 123
DH9: Stly 6H 125
DH9: Tan L 6B 110
Elm Ter. NE28: W'snd 3G 65
SR8: Pet 6E 172
Elm Tree Ct. SR7: S'hm 5A 148
Elm Tree Dr. NE40: G'sde 5F 79
Elmtree Gdns. NE25: Whit B 1E 48
SR8: Pet 6D 172
Elmtree Gro. NE3: Gos 2D 62
Elm Trees NE24: Bly 3H 23
Elm Vs. NE13: Bru V 6C 34
Elmway DH2: Ches S 4J 127
Elmwood DH2: Ches S 7H 127
NE15: Lem 5C 60
Elmwood Av. NE13: Wide O 6E 34
NE28: W'snd 3K 65
(not continuous)
SR5: S'wck 4B 104
Elmwood Cres. NE6: Walk 4D 64
Elmwood Dr. NE20: Pon 4J 31
Elmwood Gdns. NE11: Gate 1D 98
Elmwood Gro. NE26: Whit B 5G 39
Elmwood Ho. NE7: Newc T 1J 63
Elmwood Rd. NE25: Whit B 7E 38
Elmwood Sq. SR5: S'wck 5B 104
Elmwood St. DH4: Hou S 1J 143
SR2: Sund 3D 118 (6F 7)
Elrick Cl. NE5: Cha P 3C 60
Elrington Gdns. NE5: Newc T 5H 61
Elsdon Av. NE25: Sea D 7G 27
Elsdonburn Rd. SR3: New S 4A 132
Elsdon Cl. DH2: Ches S 1H 141
NE24: Bly 2G 23
SR8: Pet 2A 182
Elsdon Ct. NE16: Whi 2G 97
Elsdon Dr. NE12: Longb 4D 46
NE63: Ash 4A 12
Elsdon Gdns. DH8: Con 4H 121
NE11: Dun 6C 82
Elsdon M. NE31: Heb 6K 65
Elsdon Pl. NE29: N Shi 1G 67
Elsdon Rd. DH1: Dur 5B 154
NE3: Gos 7E 44
NE16: Whi 1G 97
Elsdon St. NE29: N Shi 1G 67
Elsdon Ter. NE28: W'snd 4F 65
NE29: N Shi 1D 66
Elsham Grn. NE3: Ken 6A 44
Elsing Cl. NE5: Newc T 1H 61
Elstob Cotts. SR3: Sund 6C 118
Elstob Pl. NE6: Walk 2C 84
SR3: Sund 6C 118
Elston Cl. NE5: Cha P 3C 60
Elstree Ct. NE3: Ken 5H 43
Elstree Gdns. NE24: News 6H 23
Elstree Sq. SR5: S'wck 3C 104
ELSWICK 2B 82
Elswick Ct. NE1: Newc T 7F 63 (4F 4)
Elswick Dene NE4: Newc T 3C 82
Elswick E. Ter. NE4: Newc T 2D 82 (7B 4)
Elswick Rd. NE4: Newc T 2A 82 (7A 4)
NE37: Wash 1E 114
Elswick Row NE4: Newc T 1D 82 (6A 4)
Elswick St. NE4: Newc T 1D 82 (6A 4)
Elswick Swimming Pool 2C 82
Elswick Way NE34: S Shi 7G 67
Elswick Way Ind. Est. NE34: S Shi 7G 67
Elsworth Grn. NE5: Newc T 2J 61
Elterwater Rd. DH2: Ches S 1K 141
Eltham St. NE33: S Shi 5H 67
Elton St. E. NE28: W'snd 4F 65
Elton St. W. NE28: W'snd 4F 65
ELTRINGHAM 4C 76
Eltringham Cl. NE28: W'snd 3E 64
Eltringham Rd. NE42: Pru 4C 76
Elvaston Dr. NE46: Hex 3C 70
Elvaston Gro. NE46: Hex 3D 70
Elvaston Pk. Rd. NE46: Hex 3C 70
Elvaston Rd. NE40: Ryton 7G 59
NE46: Hex 2C 70
Elvet Bri. DH1: Dur 3B 166 (3C 6)
Elvet Cl. NE6: Newc T 6A 64 (2P 5)
NE13: Wide O 5C 34
Elvet Ct. NE6: Newc T 6A 64 (2P 5)
Elvet Cres. DH1: Dur 3B 166 (4D 6)
Elvet Grn. DH2: Ches S 7A 128
DH5: Hett H 2G 157
Elvet Hill Rd. DH1: Dur 5A 166 (7B 6)
Elvet Moor DH1: Dur 5J 165
Elvet Waterside DH1: Dur 3B 166 (3D 6)
Elvet Way NE6: Newc T 6A 64 (2P 5)
Elvington St. SR6: Monk 4G 105
Elwin Cl. NE26: Sea S 5D 28
Elwin Pl. DH2: Pelt 3G 127
NE26: Sea S 5D 28
Elwin St. DH2: Pelt 2G 127
Elwin Ter. SR2: Sund 3E 118 (5G 7)
Ely Cl. NE7: Newc T 1B 64
Ely Rd. DH1: Dur 3B 154
Ely St. NE8: Gate 5G 83
Ely Ter. DH9: Ann P 4C 124
Ely Way NE32: Jar 5B 86
Embankment Rd. SR7: S'hm 4B 148
(Cottages Rd.)
SR7: S'hm 2K 147
(Stanley St.)

Embassy Gdns.—Fairways, The

Embassy Gdns. NE15: Newc T 7H **61**
Emblehope NE37: Wash 2E **114**
Emblehope Dr. NE3: Gos 1C **62**
Emblehope Ho. SR3: E Her 1K **131**
Embleton Av. NE3: Gos 6C **44**
NE28: W'snd .7J **47**
NE34: S Shi .5D **68**
Embleton Cl. DH1: Dur 4B **154**
Embleton Cres. NE29: N Shi 4C **48**
Embleton Dr. DH2: Ches S 1H **141**
NE24: Bly 4G **23**
Embleton Gdns. NE5: Newc T 4K **61**
NE10: Gate .5B **84**
Embleton Rd. NE10: Gate 4F **85**
NE29: N Shi 4C **48**
Embleton St. SR7: S'hm 5B **148**
Embleton Wlk. *NE8: Gate 4F 83*
(off St Cuthbert's Rd.)
Emden Rd. NE3: Ken 6B **44**
EMERSON 6D 114
Emerson Ct. NE27: Shir 1J **47**
SR8: Pet 5E **172**
Emerson Pl. NE27: Shir 1J **47**
Emerson Rd. NE38: Wash 4D **114**
NE64: Newb S 2H **13**
Emily Davison Av. NE61: Mor 7E **8**
Emily St. DH4: Hou S 5D **130**
NE6: Walk .7C **64**
NE8: Gate 5K **83**
Emily St. E. SR7: S'hm 3B **148**
(not continuous)
Emlyn Rd. NE34: S Shi 7J **67**
Emma Ct. SR2: Sund 3G **119**
Emma St. DH8: Con 5H **121**
Emma Vw. NE40: Ryton 3D **78**
Emmaville NE40: Ryton 2E **78**
Emmbrook Cl. DH5: W Rai 6D **144**
Emmerson Sq. DH6: Thor 7J **169**
Emmerson Ter. NE38: Wash 3J **115**
Emmerson Ter. W. SR3: New S 2D **132**
Emperor Way SR3: E Her 4H **131**
Empire Bldgs. DH1: Dur 2E **166**
Empire Theatre
Consett 7H 121
Sunderland 1E 118 (3H 7)
Empress Rd. NE6: Walk 2F **85**
Empress St. SR5: S'wck 6E **104**
Emsworth Rd. SR5: S'wck 4C **104**
Emsworth Sq. SR5: S'wck 4C **104**
Enderby Dr. NE46: Hex 2A **70**
Enderby Rd. SR4: Sund 1D **118**
Enfield Av. NE16: Swa 5H **81**
Enfield Gdns. NE16: Whi 2H **97**
Enfield Rd. NE8: Gate 6H **83**
SR7: S'hm .3H **147**
Enfield St. SR4: Sund 1B **118**
Engels Ter. DH9: Stly 4G **125**
Engel St. NE39: Row G 5F **95**
Engine Inn Rd. NE28: W'snd 1K **65**
Engine La. NE9: Gate 3H **99**
Engine Rd. NE17: C'wl 3G **93**
NE42: Pru .2H **93**
Engleby Ho. *NE61: Mor 7F 9*
(off Oldgate)
Englefeld NE10: Gate 3D **100**
Englefield Cl. NE3: Ken 5K **43**
Englemann Way SR3: New S 4A **132**
Enid Av. SR6: Monk 4F **105**
Enid Gdns. TS27: B Col 2J **183**
Enid St. NE13: Bru V 7C **34**
Ennerdale DH3: Bir 6C **114**
NE10: Gate .6E **84**
NE37: Wash 1G **115**
SR2: Sund 4E **118** (7H **7**)
Ennerdale Cl. DH1: Carr 7J **155**
SR7: S'hm .3H **147**
SR8: Pet 5B **172**
Ennerdale Cres. DH4: Pen 1A **130**
NE21: Bla T 6B **80**
Ennerdale Gdns. NE9: Gate 2J **99**
NE28: W'snd 1A **66**
Ennerdale Pl. DH2: Ches S 1A **142**
Ennerdale Rd. NE6: Walk 7D **64**
NE24: Cow .7D **18**
NE30: N Shi 2G **49**
Ennerdale St. DH5: Hett H 1F **157**
Ennerdale Ter. NE17: Ham C 3J **107**
Ennerdale Wlk. NE16: Whi 3F **97**
Ennis Cl. NE62: W Sle 7B **12**
Ennismore Ct. NE12: Longb 6B **46**
Ensign Ho. NE30: N Shi 5K **49**
Enslin Gdns. NE6: Walk 3D **84**
Enslin St. NE6: Walk 3D **84**
Enterprise Ct. NE23: Nel V 1H **25**
SR7: Sea 7G **133**
Enterprise Ho. NE11: Gate 3F **99**
Eothen Rest Ho. NE26: Whit B 7G **39**
Epinay Wlk. NE32: Jar 7C **66**
Epping Cl. SR7: S'hm 4H **147**
Epping Ct. NE23: Cra 4F **25**
Epping Sq. SR5: S'wck 4C **104**
EPPLETON 5G 145
Eppleton Cl. DH7: Lang P 5H **151**
Eppleton Est. DH5: Hett H 5H **145**
Eppleton Hall Cl. SR7: S'hm 2G **147**
Eppleton Row DH5: Hett H 6H **145**
Eppleton Ter. DH2: Beam 2D **126**
Eppleton Ter. E. DH5: Hett H 6H **145**
Eppleton Ter. W. DH5: Hett H 6H **145**
Epsom Cl. DH8: Shot B 2G **121**
NE29: N Shi 1F **67**
Epsom Ct. NE3: Ken 5J **43**
Epsom Dr. NE63: Ash 5A **12**
Epsom Sq. SR5: S'wck 4C **104**
Epsom Way NE24: News 6H **23**
Epwell Gro. NE23: Cra 7A **22**
Epworth DH9: Tan L 1C **124**
Epworth Gro. NE8: Gate 5F **83**
Equitable St. NE28: W'snd 4F **65**
Erick St. NE1: Newc T 1G **83** (5G **4**)
(not continuous)
Erin Sq. SR5: S'wck 4D **104**
Erith Ter. SR4: Sund 2B **118**
Ermine Cres. NE9: Gate 1K **99**
Ernest Pl. DH1: Dur 2E **166**
Ernest St. DH2: Pelt 2G **127**
NE35: Bol C 6G **87**
SR2: Sund .4G **119**
Ernest Ter. DH3: Ches S 7A **128**
DH9: Stly .1F **125**
SR2: Ryh 3J **133**
Ernwill Av. SR5: C'twn 6H **103**
Errington Bungs. DH7: Sac 7D **140**
Errington Cl. NE20: Pon 2G **41**
Errington Dr. DH9: Tan L 1C **124**
Errington Pl. NE42: Pru 4E **76**
Errington Rd. NE20: Pon 2F **41**
Errington St. NE24: Cow 2C **22**
Errington Ter. NE12: Longb 3C **46**
Errol Pl. DH3: Bir 6B **114**
Erskine Ct. NE2: Newc T 3H **63**
Erskine Rd. NE33: S Shi 3K **67**
Erskine Way NE33: S Shi 3K **67**
Escallond Dr. SR7: Mur 4H **147**
Escombe Ter. *NE6: Newc T 1A 84*
(off St Peter's Rd.)
Esdale SR2: Ryh 3G **133**
ESH 6F 151
Esh Bank DH7: Esh W 6D **150**
Esher Ct. NE3: Ken 5J **43**
Esher Gdns. NE24: News 6H **23**
Esher Pl. NE23: Cra 4F **25**
Esh Hillside DH7: Lang P 5J **151**
Esh Laude DH7: Esh W 7E **150**
Eshmere Cres. NE5: Cha P 2C **60**
Eshott Cl. NE3: Ken 6C **44**
NE5: Newc T 4G **61**
Eshott Ct. NE5: Newc T 4G **61**
Esh Rd. DH7: Esh W 2H **163**
Esh Ter. DH7: Lang P 5J **151**
ESH WINNING 4E 162
Esh Winning Ind. Est. DH7: Esh W 3E **162**
Esh Wood Vw. DH7: Ush M 2B **164**
Esk Av. DH3: Gt Lum 3F **143**
Esk Ct. SR3: New S 3B **132**
Eskdale DH3: Bir 7C **114**
DH4: Pen .1A **130**
Eskdale Av. NE24: Cow 1E **22**
NE28: W'snd 7G **47**
Eskdale Cl. DH1: Carr 7J **155**
SR7: S'hm .3H **147**
Eskdale Ct. NE34: S Shi 7J **67**
Eskdale Cres. NE37: Usw 7F **101**
Eskdale Dr. NE32: Jar 3D **86**
Eskdale Gdns. NE9: Gate 3J **99**
Eskdale Mans. *NE2: Newc T 1G 4*
(off Eskdale Ter.)
Eskdale Rd. SR6: Monk 1H **105**
Eskdale St. DH5: Hett H 1F **157**
NE34: S Shi 1J **87**
Eskdale Ter. NE2: Newc T 5G **63** (1G **4**)
NE26: Whit B 7J **39**
NE30: Whit B 7J **39**
Eskdale Wlk. SR8: Pet 6C **172**
Esk St. NE9: Gate 7K **83**
Esk Ter. DH3: Bir 3A **114**
Eslington Ct. NE8: Gate 6D **82**
Eslington M. NE63: Hir 3D **12**
Eslington Rd. NE2: Newc T 6G **63** (1H **5**)
Eslington Ter. NE2: Newc T 5G **63** (1H **5**)
Esmeralda Gdns. NE23: Seg 2E **36**
Esplanade NE26: Whit B 6H **39**
Esplanade Av. NE26: Whit B 6H **39**
Esplanade M. SR2: Sund 3F **119** (6J **7**)
Esplanade Pl. NE26: Whit B 6H **39**
Esplanade, The SR2: Sund 6J **7**
Esplanade W. SR2: Sund 3F **119** (7J **7**)
Espley Cl. NE12: Longb 4E **46**
Espley Ct. NE3: Ken 5A **44**
Esporta
Silksworth 4K 131
Essen Way SR3: Sund 5D **118**
Essex Av. DH8: C'sde 4C **134**
Essex Cl. NE4: Newc T 3D **82** (9A **4**)
NE63: Ash .3J **11**
Essex Cres. SR7: S'hm 3H **147**
Essex Dr. NE37: Usw 5H **101**
Essex Gdns. NE9: Gate 7H **83**
NE28: W'snd 2J **65**
NE34: S Shi 6E **68**
Essex Gro. SR3: New S 1C **132**
Essex Pl. SR8: Pet 4A **172**
Essex St. DH5: Hett H 6F **145**
Essington Way SR8: Pet 3A **172**
Estate Ho's. DH4: Hou S 5J **129**
Esther Campbell Ct.
NE2: Newc T 6E **62** (1C **4**)
Esther Sq. NE38: Wash 4J **115**
Esthwaite Av. DH2: Ches S 1K **141**
Eston Ct. NE24: Cow 1F **23**
NE28: W'snd 7D **46**
Eston Gro. SR5: S'wck 4E **104**
Estuary Way SR4: Sund 1H **117**
Etal Av. NE25: Whit B 7H **39**
NE29: N Shi 1D **66**
Etal Cl. NE27: Shir 1K **47**
Etal Ct. NE29: N Shi 6G **49**
Etal Cres. NE27: Shir 1K **47**
NE32: Jar 2E **86**
Etal Ho. NE63: Hir 3D **12**
Etal La. NE5: Newc T 2G **61**
Etal Pl. NE3: Ken 5C **44**
Etal Rd. NE24: News 6F **23**
Etal Way NE5: Newc T 1H **61**
Ethel Av. NE21: Bla T 4C **80**
SR2: Ryh 3J **133**
Ethel St. NE4: Newc T 2K **81**
NE23: Dud .5J **35**
Ethel Ter. NE34: S Shi 1H **87**
NE39: H Spen 4D **94**
NE46: Hex .2C **70**
SR5: C'twn 6H **103**
Etherley Cl. DH1: Dur 4B **154**
Etherley Rd. NE6: Walk 6B **64**
Etherstone Av. NE7: Newc T 3A **64**
Eton Cl. NE23: Cra 7A **22**
Eton Sq. NE31: Heb 7K **65**
Ettrick Cl. NE12: Kil 7A **36**
Ettrick Gdns. NE8: Gate 6K **83**
SR4: Sund .4B **118**
Ettrick Gro. SR3: Sund 3A **118**
SR4: Sund .3A **118**
Ettrick Lodge NE3: Gos 1F **63**
Ettrick Rd. NE32: Jar 1A **86**
Ettrick Ter. Nth. DH9: Stly 6H **125**
Ettrick Ter. Sth. DH9: Stly 6H **125**
European Way SR4: Sund 1K **117**
Euryalus Ct. NE33: S Shi 4B **68**
Eustace Av. NE29: N Shi 7E **48**
Euston Ct. SR5: S'wck 3C **104**
Evanlade NE10: Gate 1F **101**
Evansleigh Rd. DH8: C'sde 2E **134**
Eva St. NE15: Lem 7C **60**
Evelyn St. SR2: Sund 3D **118** (7F **7**)
Evelyn Ter. DH9: Stly 3E **124**
NE21: Bla T 3C **80**
SR2: Ryh 3H **133**
Evenwood Gdns.
NE9: Gate .2K **99**
Evenwood Rd. DH7: Esh W 4E **162**
Everard St. NE23: E Har 6K **21**
Everest Gro. NE36: W Bol 7H **87**
Everest Sq. SR5: S'wck 3C **104**
Ever Ready Ind. Est.
DH9: Tan L 6E **110**
Eversleigh Pl. NE15: Thro 3J **59**
Eversley Cres. SR5: S'wck 4C **104**
(not continuous)
Eversley Pl. NE6: Newc T 6K **63** (1N **5**)
NE28: W'snd 2K **65**
Everton Dr. SR7: S'hm 3H **147**
Everton La. SR5: S'wck 4C **104**
Evesham SR4: Sund 2G **117**
Evesham Av. NE26: Whit B 5F **39**
Evesham Cl. NE35: Bol C 5F **87**
Evesham Gth. NE3: Ken 2A **62**
Evesham Pl. NE23: Cra 3F **25**
Evesham Rd. SR7: S'hm 3H **147**
Eve St. SR8: Pet 6F **173**
Evistones Gdns. NE6: Walk 3C **84**
Evistones Rd. NE9: Gate 1H **99**
Ewart Ct. NE3: Ken 5C **44**
Ewart Cres. NE34: S Shi 2E **86**
Ewbank Av. NE4: Newc T 6A **62**
Ewe Hill Cotts. DH4: Hou S 1K **143**
Ewe Hill Ter. DH4: Hou S 1K **143**
Ewe Hill Ter. W. DH4: Hou S 1K **143**
Ewehurst Cres. DH9: Dip 7J **109**
Ewehurst Gdns. DH9: Dip 7J **109**
Ewehurst Pde. DH9: Dip 7J **109**
Ewehurst Rd. DH9: Dip 7J **109**
(not continuous)
Ewen Ct. NE29: N Shi 4B **48**
Ewesley NE38: Wash 1E **128**
Ewesley Cl. NE5: Newc T 4G **61**
Ewesley Gdns. NE13: Wide O 5D **34**
Ewesley Rd. SR4: Sund 3B **118**
Ewing Pl. SR4: Sund 3C **118**
Ewing Rd. SR4: Sund 3D **118**
Exchange Bldgs. *NE1: Newc T 7H 5*
(off King St.)
NE26: Whit B 6H **39**
Exelby Cl. NE3: Gos 4F **45**
Exeter Av. SR7: S'hm 3K **147**
(not continuous)
Exeter Cl. DH3: Gt Lum 4E **142**
NE23: Cra .3G **25**
NE63: N Sea 5E **12**
Exeter Ct. NE31: Heb 1H **85**
Exeter Rd. NE28: W'snd 7E **46**
NE29: N Shi 3C **48**
Exeter St. NE6: Walk 2E **84**
NE8: Gate .5G **83**
SR4: Sund .1B **118**
Exeter Way NE32: Jar 4B **86**
Exhibition Pk. 5F 63 (1E 4)
Exmouth Cl. SR7: S'hm 4J **147**
Exmouth Rd. NE29: N Shi 7C **48**
Exmouth Sq. SR5: S'wck 4C **104**
Exmouth St. SR5: S'wck 4C **104**
Extension Rd. SR1: Sund 2H **119**
Eyemouth Ct. NE34: S Shi 1G **87**
Eyemouth La. SR5: S'wck 4C **104**
Eyemouth Rd. NE29: N Shi 7C **48**
Eyre St. DH9: Stly 4D **124**

F

Faber Rd. SR5: S'wck 4C **104**
Factory Rd. NE21: Bla T 2D **80**
Factory, The TS27: Cas E 4K **181**
Fairbairn Rd. SR8: Pet 4B **172**
Fairburn Av. DH5: Hou S 4E **144**
NE7: Newc T 1A **64**
Fairclough Ct. SR8: Pet 7K **171**
Fairdale Av. NE7: Newc T 1A **64**
Fairfalls Ter. DH7: New B 4A **164**
Fairfield DH2: Pelt 2F **127**
DH8: Con .1K **135**
DH9: Ann P 4K **123**
NE12: Longb 6H **45**
NE46: Hex .2B **70**
Fairfield Av. NE12: Longb 4B **46**
NE16: Whi .2G **97**
NE24: News 5H **23**
Fairfield Cl. NE11: Dun 5B **82**
Fairfield Cres. NE46: Sand 5G **51**
Fairfield Dr. NE25: Whit B 7C **38**
NE30: N Shi 2H **49**
NE63: N Sea 5E **12**
SR6: Whit .4H **89**
Fairfield Grn. NE25: Whit B 7C **38**
Fairfield Ind. Est.
NE10: Gate .4E **84**
Fairfield Rd. NE2: Newc T 4F **63**
Fairfields NE40: Ryton 2F **79**
Fairfield Ter. NE10: Gate 5E **84**
Fair Grn. NE25: Whit B 7C **38**
Fairgreen Cl. SR3: New S 4B **132**
Fairhaven NE9: Spri 5D **100**
Fairhaven Av. NE6: Walk 7E **64**
Fairhill Cl. NE7: Newc T 1A **64**
Fairhills Av. DH9: Dip 2G **123**
Fairholme Av. NE34: S Shi 7B **68**
Fairholme Rd. SR3: Sund 5E **118**
Fairholm Rd. NE4: Newc T 1A **82**
Fairisle DH2: Ous 7J **113**
Fairlands E. SR6: Monk 5F **105**
Fairlands W. SR6: Monk 5F **105**
Fairlawn Gdns. SR4: Sund 4A **118**
Fairlawns Cl. TS29: Trim S 7B **180**
Fairles St. NE33: S Shi 1K **67**
Fairmead Way SR4: Sund 3G **117**
Fairmile Dr. SR3: New S 4C **132**
Fairmont Way NE7: Newc T 1A **64**
FAIR MOOR 3C 8
Fairney Cl. NE20: Pon 5K **31**
Fairney Edge NE20: Pon 5K **31**
Fairnley Wlk. NE5: Newc T 3G **61**
Fairport Ter. SR8: Eas 1D **172**
Fairspring NE5: Newc T 3G **61**
Fair Vw. DH4: W Rai 1K **155**
DH7: B'hpe 7D **138**
DH7: Esh W 3E **162**
DH7: Wit G 2C **152**
NE16: Burn 2J **109**
NE42: Pru .4E **76**
(South Rd.)
NE42: Pru .4E **76**
(Swalwell Cl.)
Fairview Av. NE34: S Shi 6B **68**
Fairview Dr. DH8: Con 1J **121**
Fairview Grn. NE7: Newc T 1A **64**
Fairview Pk. DH5: Hett H 7H **145**
Fairview Ter. DH9: Ann P 6J **123**
Fairville Cl. NE23: Cra 7K **21**
Fairville Cres.
NE7: Newc T 1A **64**
Fairway NE21: Bla T 2A **80**
NE62: Chop 7J **11**
Fairway Cl. NE3: Gos 4D **44**
Fairways DH8: Con 4H **121**
NE25: Whit B 6C **38**
SR3: New S 2D **132**
Fairways Av. NE7: Newc T 7A **46**
Fairways, The DH9: Stly 3C **126**
(Green's Bank)
DH9: Stly .7E **124**
(New Acres Rd.)

Fairway, The—Finchale Av.

Fairway, The NE3: Gos 4D 44
NE37: Usw 4G 101
NE61: Loan 3F 15
Fairwood Rd. NE46: Hex 2F 71
Fairy St. DH5: Hett H 6G 145
Falconars Ct. NE1: Newc T 1F 83 (6E 4)
Falconar St. NE1: Newc T 7G 63 (4H 5)
NE2: Newc T 7G 63 (4H 5)
Falcon Ct. NE63: Ash 6K 11
Falcon Hill NE61: Mor 7D 8
Falcon Pl. NE12: Longb 5J 45
Falcon Ter. NE41: Wylam 7K 57
Falcon Way DH7: Esh W 3C 162
NE34: S Shi 2H 87
Faldonside NE6: Newc T 3B 64
Falkirk NE12: Kil 7B 36
Falkland Av. NE3: Ken 2B 62
NE31: Heb 7J 65
Falkland Rd. SR4: Sund 2A 118
Falkous Ter. DH7: Wit G 3C 152
Falla Pk. Cres. NE10: Gate 6A 84
Falla Pk. Rd. NE10: Gate 6A 84
Falloden Av. NE3: Ken 4B 44
Fallodon Gdns. NE5: Newc T 3K 61
Fallodon Rd. NE29: N Shi 7D 48
Fallowfeld NE10: Gate 1E 100
Fallowfield Av. NE3: Ken 6B 44
Fallowfield Dene Cvn. Pk.
NE46: Acomb 1D 50
Fallowfield Ter. DH6: S Het 5C 158
Fallowfield Way NE38: Wash 6J 115
NE63: Ash 5K 11
Fallow Pk. Av. NE24: Bly 3G 23
Fallow Rd. NE34: S Shi 7F 69
Fallsway DH1: Carr 6H 155
Falmouth Cl. SR7: Mur 4J 147
Falmouth Dr. NE32: Jar 1D 86
Falmouth Rd. NE6: Newc T 6K 63 (2N 5)
NE29: N Shi 3D 48
SR4: Sund 1A 118
Falmouth Sq. SR4: Sund 2A 118
Falmouth Wlk. NE23: Cra 2J 25
Falsgrave Pl. NE16: Whi 2F 97
Falstaff Rd. NE29: N Shi 6D 48
Falston Cl. NE12: Longb 4E 46
Falstone NE10: Gate 2D 100
NE38: Wash 6J 115
Falstone Av. NE15: Lem 5E 60
NE34: S Shi 7C 68
Falstone Ct. NE46: Hex 3B 70
Falstone Cres. NE63: Hir 6C 12
Falstone Dr. DH2: Ches S 1H 141
Falstone Sq. NE3: Ken 6C 44
Falstone Way NE46: Hex 3B 70
Falston Rd. NE24: Bly 4G 23
Faraday Cl. NE38: Wash 3B 116
Faraday Gro. NE8: Gate 7F 83
SR4: Sund 2A 118
Faraday Rd. SR8: Pet 3C 172
Faraday St. SR7: Mur 7E 146
Faraday Ter. DH6: Has 1A 170
Farbridge Cres. DH8: Ebc 5H 107
Farding Lake Ct. NE34: S Shi 7E 68
Farding Sq. NE34: S Shi 7F 69
Fareham Gro. NE35: Bol C 6D 86
Fareham Way NE23: Cra 3K 25
FAREWELL HALL 7K 165
Farewell Vw. DH7: B'don 6G 165
Farlam Av. NE30: N Shi 3G 49
Farlam Rd. NE5: Newc T 5H 61
Farleigh Ct. NE29: N Shi 4B 48
Farm Cl. NE16: Sun 5H 97
NE37: Usw 6F 101
Farm Cotts. DH6: Shot C 5F 171
Farmer Cres. SR7: Mur 7D 146
Farm Hill Rd. SR6: Cle 4C 88
Farm Rd. DH1: Dur 7B 166
NE23: E Har 6K 21
Farm St. SR5: S'wck 6D 104
Farm Wlk. SR3: New S 4C 132
Farm Well Pl. NE42: Pru 3F 77
Farnborough Cl. NE23: Cra 2K 25
Farnborough Dr. SR3: New S 1D 132
Farn Ct. NE3: Ken 4K 43
Farndale NE28: W'snd 7D 46
Farndale Av. NE62: Chop 6J 11
SR6: Monk 1H 105
Farndale Cl. NE13: Din 4H 33
NE21: Bla T 6K 79
Farndale Ct. NE24: News 5H 23
Farndale Rd. NE4: Newc T 1A 82
Farne Av. NE3: Ken 5C 44
NE34: S Shi 6D 68
NE63: Hir 5B 12
Farne Rd. NE12: Longb 4C 46
NE27: Shir 1K 47
Farne Sq. SR4: Sund 1K 117
Farne Ter. NE6: Walk 7C 64
Farnham Cl. DH1: Dur 6A 154
NE15: Lem 7D 60
Farnham Gro. NE24: News 5H 23
Farnham Lodge NE12: Longb 5K 45
Farnham Rd. DH1: Dur 5A 154
NE34: S Shi 7J 67
Farnham St. NE15: Lem 7D 60
Farnham Ter. SR4: Sund 3B 118
Farnley Hey Rd. DH1: Dur 3J 165
Farnley Mt. DH1: Dur 3J 165
Farnley Ridge DH1: Dur 3J 165
Farnley Rd. NE6: Newc T 4A 64
Farnon Rd. NE3: Gos 7C 44
Farnsworth Ct. NE2: Newc T 3H 63
Farquhar St. NE2: Newc T 5H 63
Farrfeld NE10: Gate 3D 100
Farrier Cl. DH1: Dur 3K 153
NE38: Wash 6J 115
Farriers Ct. NE22: Bed 3A 18
FARRINGDON 2K 131
Farringdon Av. SR3: E Her 1J 131
Farringdon Rd. NE30: N Shi 2G 49
Farringdon Row SR1: Sund 7D 104 (1F 7)
Farrington's Ct. NE1: Newc T 1F 83 (6F 4)
Farrow Dr. SR6: Whit 5G 89
Farthings, The NE37: Usw 5F 101
FATFIELD 7H 115
Fatfield Pk. NE38: Wash 6H 115
Fatfield Rd. NE38: Wash 4J 115
Fatherly Ter. DH4: Hou S 2B 144
Faversham Ct. NE3: Ken 5K 43
Faversham Pl. NE23: Cra 2K 25
Fawcett Hill Ter. DH9: Stly 7J 125
Fawcett St. SR1: Sund 1F 119 (3J 7)
Fawcett Ter. SR2: Ryh 3J 133
Fawcett Way NE33: S Shi 2J 67
FAWDON 6B 44
Fawdon Cl. NE3: Ken 4B 44
Fawdon Gro. NE61: Peg 4K 9
Fawdon Ho. NE3: Ken 4B 44
Fawdon La. NE3: Ken 5B 44
Fawdon Pk. Cen. NE3: Ken 6B 44
Fawdon Pk. Ho. *NE3: Ken 6B 44*
(off Fawdon Pk. Rd.)
Fawdon Pk. Rd. NE3: Ken 5A 44
Fawdon Pl. NE29: N Shi 6C 48
Fawdon Station (Metro) 6B 44
Fawdon Wlk. NE3: Ken 5K 43
Fawlee Grn. NE3: Ken 1J 61
Fawley Cl. NE35: Bol C 5E 86
Fawn Rd. SR4: Sund 2J 117
Fearon Wlk. DH1: Dur 3B 166 (3D 6)
Featherbed La. SR2: Ryh 3J 133
Featherstone DH3: Gt Lum 2F 143
NE38: Wash 3D 114
Featherstone Gro. NE3: Gos 3C 44
NE22: Bed 6G 17
NE32: Jar 3A 86
Featherstone Rd. DH1: Dur 6B 154
Featherstone St. SR6: Monk 5H 105
Featherstone Vs. SR6: Monk 5H 105
Federation Sq. SR7: Mur 1E 158
Federation Ter. DH9: Tan L 6B 110
Federation Way NE11: Dun 5A 82
Fee Ter. SR2: Ryh 3G 133
Feetham Av. NE12: Longb 4D 46
Feetham Ct. NE12: Longb 3E 46
Felixstowe Dr. NE7: Newc T 2A 64
Fell Bank DH3: Bir 4A 114
Fell Cl. DH3: Bir 5C 114
NE16: Sun 5H 97
NE37: Wash 1F 115
Fell Cotts. *NE9: Spri 6D 100*
(off Fell Rd.)
Fell Ct. NE9: Gate 2K 99
Fellcross DH3: Bir 3A 114
Fell Dyke NE10: Gate 1A 100
Felldyke NE10: Gate 2C 100
FELLGATE 5B 86
Fellgate Av. NE32: Jar 5C 86
Fellgate Gdns. NE10: Gate 6G 85
Fellgate Station (Metro) 4C 86
FELLING 6B 84
Felling Bus. Cen. NE10: Gate 4B 84
Felling By-Pass NE10: Gate 5C 84
(Abbotsford Rd.)
NE10: Gate 4A 84
(Grn. Lane Gdns.)
Felling Dene Gdns. NE10: Gate 5C 84
Felling Ga. NE10: Gate 5A 84
Felling Ho. Gdns. NE10: Gate 5B 84
Felling Ind. Est. NE10: Gate 4A 84
Felling Pool 1E 100
Felling Shore Ind. Est.
NE10: Gate 3B 84
Felling Station (Metro) 5B 84
Felling Vw. NE6: Walk 3D 84
Fellmere Av. NE10: Gate 6E 84
Fell Pl. NE9: Spri 6D 100
Fell Rd. DH2: Pelt 6G 127
NE9: Spri 6D 100
SR4: Sund 1K 117
Fellrose Ct. DH2: Pelt 5G 127
Fellsdyke Ct. NE10: Gate 1A 100
FELLSIDE 5E 96
Fell Side DH8: Con 2K 135
Fellside DH3: Bir 5B 114
NE20: Pon 3F 41
NE34: S Shi 1D 88
Fellside Av. NE16: Sun 4H 97
Fellside Cl. DH9: Stly 2H 125
NE20: Pon 3F 41
Fellside Ct. NE16: Whi 7G 81
NE37: Wash 2F 115
Fellside Gdns. DH1: Carr 7G 155
FELLSIDE PARK 1F 97
Fellside Rd. NE16: Burn 1C 110
NE16: Whi 5E 96
Fellside Ter. DH9: Stly 7D 124
Fell Side, The NE3: Ken 1B 62
Fell Sq. SR4: Sund 1J 117
Fells Rd. NE11: Gate 7F 83
Fells, The NE9: Gate 1J 99
Fell Ter. NE16: Burn 2B 110
Felltop DH8: Con 6F 121
Fell Vw. DH8: C'sde 1E 134
DH9: Stly 4E 124
NE39: H Spen 4E 94
NE40: Ryton 3D 78
Fell Vw. W. NE40: Ryton 3D 78
Fell Way, The NE5: Newc T 4D 60
Felsham Sq. SR4: Sund 2A 118
Felstead Cres. SR4: Sund 1K 117
Felstead Pl. NE24: News 5H 23
Felstead Sq. SR4: Sund 2K 117
Felthorpe Ct. NE5: Newc T 1H 61
Felton Av. NE3: Ken 6C 44
NE25: Whit B 7H 39
NE34: S Shi 7C 68
Felton Cl. NE27: Shir 1K 47
NE61: Mor 2H 15
Felton Cres. NE8: Gate 7G 83
Felton Dr. NE12: Longb 3D 46
Felton Grn. NE6: Newc T 7A 64
Felton Ter. *NE30: N Shi 4K 49*
(off Hotspur St.)
NE63: Hir 5B 12
Felton Wlk. NE6: Newc T 7A 64
Femwick Wlk. *NE8: Gate 4F 83*
(off St Cuthbert's Rd.)
FENCE HOUSES 1A 144
Fencer Ct. NE3: Gos 4E 44
Fencer Hill Pk. NE3: Gos 4E 44
Fence Rd. DH3: Lam P 3J 129
FENHALL 5J 137
Fenhall Pk. DH7: Lan 6J 137
FENHAM 5K 61
Fenham Chase NE4: Newc T 5K 61
Fenham Ct. NE4: Newc T 5A 62
Fenham Hall Dr. NE4: Newc T 5K 61
Fenham Rd. NE4: Newc T 7C 62
(not continuous)
Fenham Swimming Pool 5K 61
Fenkle St. NE1: Newc T 1F 83 (6D 4)
Fennel NE9: Gate 3A 100
Fennel Gro. NE34: S Shi 3A 88
SR8: Eas 7K 159
Fenning Pl. NE6: Newc T 2A 84
Fenside Rd. SR2: Ryh 1H 133
Fenton Cl. DH2: Ches S 7J 127
Fenton Sq. SR4: Sund 2K 117
Fenton Ter. DH4: Hou S 3D 130
Fenton Wlk. NE5: Newc T 3G 61
Fenton Well La. DH3: Gt Lum 3C 142
Fenwick Av. NE24: News 4H 23
NE34: S Shi 1G 87
Fenwick Cl. DH2: Ches S 1H 141
DH4: Pen 2B 130
NE2: Newc T 4H 63
Fenwick Gro. NE46: Hex 1C 70
NE61: Mor 6G 9
Fenwick St. DH4: Pen 1B 130
NE35: Bol C 5E 86
Fenwick Ter. DH1: Dur 4H 165
NE2: Newc T 4H 63
NE29: N Shi 6G 49
Fenwick Way DH8: Con 6F 121
Ferens Cl. DH1: Dur 1B 166 (1E 6)
Ferens Pk. DH1: Dur 1B 166 (1E 6)
Ferguson Cres. NE13: Bru V 7C 34
Ferguson's La. NE15: Newc T 7G 61
Ferguson St. SR2: Sund 2H 119
Fern Av. DH9: Stly 4D 124
NE2: Newc T 4G 63
NE3: Ken 5B 44
NE23: Cra 7K 21
NE26: Whit B 6H 39
NE29: N Shi 6F 49
SR5: S'wck 5C 104
SR6: Whit 4H 89
Fernbank NE26: Sea S 4B 28
Fern Ct. NE62: Chop 1G 17
SR8: Pet 1H 181
Fern Cres. SR7: S'hm 6A 148
Ferndale DH1: Carr 1H 167
Ferndale Av. NE3: Gos 3F 45
NE28: W'snd 3G 65
NE36: E Bol 7K 87
Ferndale Cl. NE24: Cow 1E 22
TS28: Win 7H 181
Ferndale Ct. DH8: Con 6J 121
Ferndale Gro. NE36: E Bol 7K 87
Ferndale La. NE36: E Bol 7K 87
Ferndale Rd. DH4: Pen 1A 130
Ferndale Ter. NE9: Spri 6D 100
SR4: Sund 7A 104
Fern Dene NE28: W'snd 1J 65
Ferndene Av. DH2: Pelt 6G 127
Ferndene Ct. NE3: Gos 1F 63
Ferndene Cres. SR4: Sund 2B 118
Ferndene Gro. NE7: Newc T 2K 63
NE40: Ryton 7H 59
Fern Dene Rd. NE8: Gate 6G 83
Ferndown Ct. NE10: Gate 7F 85
NE40: Ryton 2H 79
Fern Dr. NE23: Dud 3J 35
SR6: Cle 5B 88
Fern Gdns. NE9: Gate 1H 99
Ferngrove NE32: Jar 6C 86
Fernhill Av. NE16: Whi 7G 81
Fernlea NE23: Dud 3K 35
Fernlea Cl. NE38: Wash 6J 115
Fernlea Gdns. NE40: Ryton 2E 78
Fernlea Grn. NE3: Ken 7B 44
Fernleigh DH3: Gt Lum 3E 142
Fernley Vs. NE23: Cra 4A 26
Fernlough NE9: Gate 2A 100
Fern Rd. DH7: Sac 7F 141
Fern St. DH8: Con 6H 121
SR4: Sund 1D 118 (2F 7)
Fernsway SR3: Sund 5D 118
Fern Ter. DH9: Tan L 7K 109
Fernville Av. NE16: Sun 5H 97
Fernville Rd. NE3: Gos 2D 62
Fernville St. SR4: Sund 3D 118
Fernway NE61: Mor 7H 9
Fernwood DH7: Sac 1D 152
NE2: Newc T 5G 63
Fernwood Av. NE3: Gos 6F 45
Fernwood Cl. SR3: New S 4C 132
Fernwood Gro. NE39: Ham M 3D 108
Fernwood Rd.
NE2: Newc T 5G 63 (1H 5)
NE15: Lem 7D 60
Ferrand Dr. DH4: Hou S 2D 144
Ferriby Cl. NE3: Gos 4F 45
Ferrisdale Way NE3: Ken 5B 44
Ferry App. NE33: S Shi 2H 67
Ferryboat La. SR5: C'twn 4F 103
Ferrydene Av. NE3: Ken 1B 62
Ferry M. NE29: N Shi 1H 67
Ferry St. NE32: Jar 5B 66
NE33: S Shi 2H 67
Festival Cotts. NE12: Kil 6K 35
FESTIVAL PARK 7D 82
Festival Pk. Dr. NE11: Gate 7D 82
Festival Way NE11: Dun 5C 82
Fetcham Ct. NE3: Ken 5J 43
Fewster Sq. NE10: Gate 1E 100
Field Cl. NE2: Newc T 7H 63 (4K 5)
Fieldfare Cl. NE38: Wash 5D 114
Field Fare Ct. NE16: Burn 3C 110
Field Ho. NE33: S Shi 4B 68
Fieldhouse Cl. NE61: Hep 3A 16
Fieldhouse La. DH1: Dur 1J 165
NE61: Hep 3A 16
Field Ho. Rd. NE8: Gate 7G 83
Field Ho. Ter. DH6: Has 1B 170
Fieldhouse Ter. DH1: Dur 1K 165
Fielding Ct. NE5: Newc T 1G 61
NE34: S Shi 3G 87
Fielding Pl. NE9: Gate 6K 83
Field La. NE10: Gate 6D 84
Fieldside DH2: Pelt 2G 127
DH5: W Rai 7C 144
SR6: Whit 5G 89
Field Sq. SR4: Sund 2K 117
Field St. NE3: Gos 7G 45
NE10: Gate 5B 84
Field Ter. NE15: Thro 3H 59
NE32: Jar 1B 86
Field Vw. DH7: Ush M 1D 164
Fieldway NE32: Jar 5C 86
Fiennes Rd. SR8: Pet 5H 171
Fife Av. DH2: Ches S 6K 127
NE32: Jar 3E 86
Fife St. NE8: Gate 5J 83
SR7: Mur 1F 159
Fife Ter. NE17: C'wl 2K 107
Fifteenth Av. NE24: Bly 3H 23
Fifth Av. DH2: Ches S 6K 127
NE6: Newc T 6A 64 (1P 5)
NE11: Gate 2E 98
(Carlton Ct.)
NE11: Gate 2F 99
(Earlsway)
NE24: Bly 3H 23
NE61: Mor 1H 15
NE63: Hir 5B 12
Fifth Av. Bus. Pk. NE11: Gate 3F 99
Fifth Av. E. NE11: Gate 2F 99
Fifth St. DH8: Con 7K 121
SR8: Pet 5E 172
(not continuous)
TS27: B Col 1H 183
Filby Dr. DH1: Carr 6H 155
Filey Cl. NE23: Cra 2K 25
Filton Cl. NE23: Cra 2K 25
Finchale NE38: Wash 5G 115
Finchale Abbey Cvn. Pk.
DH1: Bras 1E 154
Finchale Av. DH1: Bras 3C 154

Finchale Cl.—Frederick Rd.

Finchale Cl. DH4: Hou S 2D 144
NE11: Dun 1B 98
SR2: Sund 3G 119
Finchale Ct. DH4: W Rai 1K 155
Finchale Gdns. NE9: Gate 5A 100
NE15: Thro 2H 59
Finchale Priory 7F 143
Finchale Rd. DH1: Dur 3B 154
(Canterbury Rd.)
DH1: Dur 6J 153
(Durham Moor)
NE31: Heb 4J 85
Finchale Ter. DH4: Hou S 1J 143
NE6: Newc T 1A 84
NE32: Jar 2D 86
Finchale Vw. DH1: Dur 3K 153
DH4: W Rai 1J 155
Finchdale Cl. NE29: N Shi 1F 67
Finchdale Ter. DH3: Ches S 6A 128
Finchley Ct. NE6: Walk 5E 64
Finchley Cres. NE6: Walk 5E 64
Findon Av. DH7: Sac 7E 140
DH7: Wit G 2D 152
Findon Gro. NE29: N Shi 1E 66
Findon Hill DH7: Sac 1E 152
Fine La. DH8: Ebc 4E 106
DH8: Shot B 7C 106
Fines Pk. DH9: Ann P 4A 124
Fines Rd. DH8: M'sly 1K 121
Finings Av. DH7: Lang P 5G 151
Finings St. DH7: Lang P 5H 151
Finney Ter. DH1: Dur 2B 166 (1D 6)
Finsbury Av. NE6: Walk 7C 64
Finsbury St. SR5: S'wck 6E 104
Finsmere Pl. NE5: Newc T 4H 61
Finstock Ct. NE3: Newc T 1H 63
Fir Av. DH1: Dur 3E 166
DH7: B'don 2D 174
Firbank Av. NE30: N Shi 2H 49
Firbanks NE32: Jar 5D 86
Fire Sta. Cotts. SR6: Monk 3F 105
Firfield Rd. NE5: Newc T 3J 61
Fir Gro. NE34: S Shi 1B 88
Fir Pk. DH7: Ush M 2D 164
First Av. DH2: Ches S 1K 127
NE6: Newc T 6A 64 (1P 5)
NE11: Gate 1E 98
NE24: Bly 3H 23
NE29: N Shi 1B 66
NE61: Mor 1H 15
NE63: Hir 3B 12
Firs Ter. DH7: Lang P 4K 151
Firs, The NE3: Gos 1D 62
Fir St. NE32: Jar 6A 66
First Row NE63: Ash 3J 11
First St. DH6: Whe H 2B 180
DH8: Con 7K 121
DH8: Lead 4A 122
(not continuous)
NE8: Gate 5F 83
SR8: Pet 5E 172
TS27: B Col 2H 183
Fir Ter. NE16: Burn 2B 110
Fir Terraces DH7: Esh W 3D 162
Firth Sq. SR4: Sund 1K 117
Firtree Av. NE6: Walk 4E 64
NE12: Longb 3B 46
NE38: Wash 7F 115
Fir Tree Cl. DH1: Dur 7E 154
Fir Tree Copse NE61: Hep 4A 16
Firtree Cres. NE12: Longb 3A 46
Firtree Gdns. NE25: Whit B 1F 49
Firtree Rd. NE16: Whi 1G 97
Firtrees DH2: Ches S 4K 127
NE10: Gate 2C 100
Firtrees Av. NE28: W'snd 2B 66
Firwood Cres. NE39: H Spen 4E 94
Firwood Gdns. NE11: Gate 2D 98
Fisher Ind. Est. NE6: Walk 7F 65
Fisher La. NE13: Sea B 1D 34
NE23: Cra, Nel V 5D 24
Fisher Rd. NE27: Back 6F 37
Fisher St. NE6: Walk 6F 65
Fisherwell Rd. NE10: Gate 4E 84
Fish Quay NE30: N Shi 7J 49
Fitzpatrick Pl. NE33: S Shi 3A 68
Fitzroy Ter. SR5: S'wck 5B 104
Fitzsimmons Av. NE28: W'snd 2F 65
Flag Chare NE1: Newc T 6J 5
Flagg Ct. NE33: S Shi 2K 67
Flagg Ct. Ho. NE33: S Shi 2K 67
Flake Cotts. DH3: Ches S 5B 128
Flambard Rd. DH1: Dur 6K 153
Flass Av. DH7: Ush M 2B 164
Flassburn Rd. DH1: Dur 1J 165
Flasshall La. DH7: Esh W 2H 163
Flass Hall Ter. DH7: Esh W 2G 163
Flass St. DH1: Dur 2K 165 (2A 6)
Flass Ter. DH7: Ush M 2B 164
Flaunden Cl. NE34: S Shi 1D 88
Flaxby Cl. NE3: Gos 4F 45
Flax Cotts. NE62: Sco G 3G 17
Flax Sq. SR4: Sund 1J 117
Fleece Cotts. DH7: Edm 4D 140
Fleece Ter. DH7: Edm 4D 140
Fleetham Cl. DH2: Ches S 1H 141
Fleet St. SR1: Sund 2H 119
Fleming Bus. Cen., The
NE2: Newc T 5F 63
Fleming Ct. DH6: Shot C 5D 170
NE8: Gate 4E 82
Fleming Fld. Farm Rd.
DH6: Shot C 5D 170
Fleming Gdns. NE10: Gate 7A 84
Fleming Pl. SR8: Pet 6B 172
Fletcher Cres. DH4: E Her 3E 130
Fletcher Ter. DH4: Hou S 5D 130
Flexbury Gdns. NE9: Gate 5J 99
NE10: Gate 6A 84
NE15: Lem 6E 60
Flight, The NE21: Bla T 5A 80
FLINT HILL 7J 109
Flint Hill Bank DH9: Dip 7J 109
Flixton DH4: Hou S 1B 144
Flock Sq. SR4: Sund 1K 117
Flodden NE12: Kil 7B 36
Flodden Cl. DH2: Ches S 1H 141
Flodden Rd. SR4: Sund 2K 117
Flodden St. NE6: Newc T, Walk 1B 84
Floral Dene SR4: Sund 2G 117
Floralia Av. SR2: Ryh 3J 133
Flora St. NE6: Newc T 7K 63 (3P 5)
Florence Av. NE9: Gate 1J 99
Florence Cres. SR5: S'wck 5B 104
Florence St. NE21: Bla T 5B 80
Florence Ter. DH5: Hett H 1G 157
Florida St. SR4: Sund 1B 118
Flotterton Gdns. NE5: Newc T 6J 61
Flour Mill Rd. NE11: Dun 4B 82
Flying Ho. SR3: New S 4B 132
Folds Cl. DH7: New B 5A 164
Folds, The DH4: Hou S 2B 144
DH5: W Rai 6D 144
(off North St.)
Fold, The DH7: Lang P 7C 150
NE6: Walk 5E 64
NE16: Burn 1A 110
NE25: Whit B 6E 38
SR3: New S 4D 132
Folldon Av. SR6: Monk 4F 105
FOLLINGSBY 2H 101
Follingsby Av. NE10: Gate 2H 101
Follingsby Cl. NE10: Gate 1H 101
Follingsby Dr. NE10: Gate 7G 85
Follingsby La.
NE10: Gate, Usw, W Bol 2G 101
NE36: W Bol 3C 102
Follingsby Pk. NE10: Gate 1H 101
(not continuous)
Follonsby La. NE36: W Bol 3D 102
Follonsby Ter. NE36: W Bol 7J 85
Folly Cotts. NE40: G'sde 5F 79
Folly La. NE40: G'sde 4E 78
Folly Ter. DH1: Dur 4J 153
FOLLY, THE 4G 79
Folly, The NE36: W Bol 7G 87
Folly Yd. NE40: G'sde 4G 79
Fondlyset La. DH9: Ann P, Dip 2H 123
Fontaine Rd. SR1: Sund 1E 118 (2H 7)
Fontburn Ct. NE29: N Shi 1E 66
SR5: S'wck 3B 104
Fontburn Cres. NE63: Hir 4D 12
Fontburn Gdns. NE61: Mor 1E 14
Fontburn Pl. NE7: Longb 7J 45
Fontburn Rd. NE22: Bed 7A 18
NE25: Sea D 7H 27
Fontburn Ter. NE30: N Shi 6H 49
Fonteyn Pl. DH9: Stly 4H 125
NE23: Cra 7K 21
Font Side NE61: Mit 6A 8
Fontwell Dr. NE8: Gate 7F 83
Forbeck Rd. SR4: Sund 2K 117
Forber Av. NE34: S Shi 7D 68
Forbes Ter. SR2: Ryh 3G 133
Ford Av. NE29: N Shi 1D 66
NE63: Hir 5B 12
SR4: Sund 2G 117
Ford Cres. DH7: Lan 7K 137
NE27: Shir 1J 47
NE32: Jar 3B 86
SR4: Sund 2G 117
Ford Dr. NE24: Bly 2G 23
Fordenbridge Cres. SR4: Sund 2K 117
Fordenbridge Rd. SR4: Sund 2K 117
Fordenbridge Sq. SR4: Sund 2A 118
FORD ESTATE 2A 118
Fordfield Rd. SR4: Sund 2J 117
Ford Gro. NE3: Gos 5D 44
Fordhall Dr. SR4: Sund 2A 118
Fordham Dr. DH7: Sac 6D 140
Fordham Rd. DH1: Dur 5A 154
SR4: Sund 1K 117
Fordham Sq. SR4: Sund 2A 118
Fordland Pl. SR4: Sund 2B 118
FORDLEY 3K 35
Fordmoss Wlk. NE5: Newc T 3G 61
Ford Oval SR4: Sund 1H 117
Ford Pk. NE62: Chop 7K 11
Ford Rd. DH1: Dur 4B 154
DH7: Lan 7K 137
Ford St. DH7: Lan 7K 137
DH8: Con 2K 135
NE6: Newc T 1J 83 (5M 5)
NE8: Gate 5K 83
Ford Ter. NE28: W'snd 3K 65
NE62: Chop 1H 17
SR4: Sund 2B 118
Ford, The NE42: Pru 3E 76
Ford Vw. NE23: Dud 2J 35
Forest Av. NE12: Longb 4C 46
Forestborn Ct. NE5: Newc T 3F 61
Forest Dr. NE38: Wash 1D 128
Forest Ga. NE12: Kil 3E 46
TS28: Win 5F 181
FOREST HALL 4B 46
Forest Hall Rd. NE12: Longb 4C 46
Fore St. NE2: Newc T 5J 63 (1M 5)
NE46: Hex 1D 70
Forest Rd. NE15: Newc T 2J 81
NE33: S Shi 3J 67
SR4: Sund 1K 117
Forest Rd. Ind. Est. NE33: S Shi 3J 67
Forest Vw. DH7: B'don 2B 174
Forest Way NE23: Seg 2D 36
Forfar St. SR6: Monk 5F 105
Forge Cl. NE17: C'wl 2K 107
Forge La. DH3: Gt Lum 1F 143
NE17: Ham C 2B 108
Forge Rd. NE8: Gate 6C 82
Forge, The DH1: Dur 3J 153
DH7: New B 4A 174
NE46: Acomb 4B 50
SR4: Sund 1B 118
Forge Wlk. NE15: Thro 4K 59
Forres Ct. DH9: Stly 3H 125
Forres Pl. NE23: Cra 2K 25
Forrest Rd. NE28: W'snd 4E 64
Forster Av. DH6: Sher 2K 167
NE22: Bed 7G 17
NE34: S Shi 6A 68
SR7: Mur 2G 159
Forster Ct. NE9: Gate 3H 99
Forster Cres. DH6: S Het 5D 158
Forster Sq. TS28: Win 5F 181
Forster St. DH8: Con 7J 121
NE1: Newc T 1H 83 (6J 5)
NE24: Bly 2K 23
SR6: Monk 5G 105
Forsyth Rd. NE2: Newc T 4F 63
Forsyth St. NE29: N Shi 3B 48
Forth Banks NE1: Newc T 2F 83 (8E 4)
Forth Cl. SR8: Pet 7B 172
Forth Ct. NE34: S Shi 1J 87
SR3: New S 3B 132
Forth La. NE1: Newc T 2F 83 (7E 4)
Forth Pl. NE1: Newc T 2E 82 (7D 4)
Forth St. NE1: Newc T 2E 82 (8D 4)
NE17: C'wl 6A 94
Fortrose Av. SR3: Sund 5C 118
Fort Sq. NE33: S Shi 1J 67
Fort St. NE33: S Shi 1K 67
Forum Cinema, The 1D 70
Forum Ct. NE22: Bed 7H 17
Forum, The NE15: Newc T 6F 61
NE28: W'snd 4F 65
Forum Way NE23: Cra 4H 25
Fossdyke NE10: Gate 2D 100
Fossefeld NE10: Gate 7E 84
Fosse Law NE15: Thro 4J 59
Fosse Ter. NE9: Gate 1J 99
Foss Way DH8: Ebc 5G 107
Fossway NE6: Walk 6B 64
Foss Way NE34: S Shi 1H 87
Foster Ct. NE11: Gate 4E 98
Foster Dr. NE8: Gate 4K 83 (10N 5)
Foster Memorial Homes NE24: Bly 2H 23
Foster St. NE6: Walk 7F 65
(not continuous)
Foster Ter. DH6: Crox 7K 175
Foundation 6H 5
Foundry Ct. NE6: Newc T 2A 84
Foundry Ind. Est. NE46: B End 7E 50
Foundry La. NE6: Newc T 7J 63 (4M 5)
NE16: Swa 5G 81
Foundry Rd. SR7: S'hm 3C 148
Foundry, The TS27: Cas E 5A 182
Fountain Cl. NE22: Bed 7H 17
Fountain Gro. NE34: S Shi 5B 68
Fountain Head Bank NE26: Sea S 4B 28
Fountain La. NE21: Bla T 3C 80
(not continuous)
Fountain Row NE2: Newc T 6D 62 (1A 4)
Fountains Cl. NE11: Dun 1B 98
NE38: Wash 4H 115
Fountains Cres. DH4: Hou S 7C 130
NE31: Heb 3J 85
Fouracres Rd. NE5: Newc T 3A 62
Four La. Ends DH5: Hett H 1H 157
Four Lane Ends Station (Metro) 7A 46
Fourstones NE5: Newc T 3G 61
Fourstones Cl. NE3: Ken 7K 43
Fourstones Rd. SR4: Sund 1A 118
Fourteenth Av. NE24: Bly 3H 23
Fourth Av. DH2: Ches S 6K 127
NE6: Newc T 6A 64
Fourth Av. NE11: Gate 2E 98
NE24: Bly 3H 23
NE61: Mor 1H 15
NE63: Hir 4B 12
Fourth St. DH8: Con 7K 121
DH8: Lead 3A 122
(not continuous)
DH9: Stly 7D 124
NE8: Gate 5F 83
SR8: Pet 5E 172
(not continuous)
TS27: B Col 2H 183
Fourway Ct. TS28: Win 4G 181
Fowberry Cres. NE4: Newc T 6A 62
Fowberry Rd. NE15: Newc T 2F 81
Fowler Cl. DH4: Hou S 5C 130
Fowler Gdns. NE11: Dun 5B 82
Fowler St. NE33: S Shi 2J 67
Fowlers Yd. DH1: Dur 3C 6
Fox & Hounds La. NE15: Newc T 7J 61
Fox & Hounds Rd. NE5: Newc T 6J 61
Fox Av. NE34: S Shi 2F 87
Fox Cover NE63: Hir 6D 12
Foxcover Ct. SR7: S'hm 5A 148
Foxcover La. SR3: E Her 2H 131
Foxcover Rd. SR3: E Her 6F 117
SR4: Sund 6F 117
Fox Covert La. NE20: Pon 5H 31
Foxes Row DH7: New B 5A 174
Foxglove DH2: Ches S 7H 127
DH4: Hou S 4K 129
Foxglove Cl. NE24: News 5G 23
Foxglove Ct. NE34: S Shi 2H 87
Foxhill Cl. NE63: Ash 6K 11
Foxhills Cl. NE38: Wash 6J 115
Foxhills Covert NE16: Whi 2E 96
Foxhills Cres. DH7: Lan 6H 137
Foxhills, The NE16: Whi 1E 96
Foxhomes NE32: Jar 6D 86
Foxhunters Light Ind. Est.
NE25: Whit B 1F 49
Foxhunters Rd. NE25: Whit B 1F 49
Foxlair Cl. SR3: New S 5C 132
Fox Lea Wlk. NE23: Seg 2C 36
Foxley NE37: Usw 7J 101
Foxley Cl. NE12: Kil 7D 36
Foxpit La. DH9: Stly 5G 111
Fox St. NE10: Gate 5A 84
SR2: Sund 3D 118 (7F 7)
SR7: S'hm 4B 148
Foxton Av. NE3: Ken 5B 44
NE30: N Shi 1H 49
Foxton Cl. NE29: N Shi 2E 66
Foxton Ct. SR6: Cle 5C 88
Foxton Grn. NE3: Ken 7A 44
Foxton Hall NE37: Usw 4H 101
Foxton Way DH1: H Shin 7F 167
NE10: Gate 4F 85
Foxwood Ct. DH7: Lan 5J 137
Foyle St. SR1: Sund 2F 119 (4K 7)
Framlington Ho. NE2: Newc T 6E 62 (1C 4)
Framlington Pl. NE2: Newc T 6E 62 (1C 4)
Framwelgate DH1: Dur 2A 166 (1B 6)
Framwelgate Bridge
DH1: Dur 3A 166 (3B 6)
Framwelgate Peth DH1: Dur 1K 165 (1A 6)
Framwelgate Waterside
DH1: Dur 2A 166 (2C 6)
FRAMWELLGATE MOOR 6J 153
Framwellgate School Sports Cen. 5K 153
Francesca Ter. *NE5: Newc T 5H 61*
(off Pooley Rd.)
Frances St. NE21: Bla T 4A 80
SR3: New S 2C 132
Frances Ville NE62: Sco G 3G 17
Francis St. SR6: Monk 5F 105
Francis Way DH5: Hett H 6G 145
NE27: Longb 3H 47
Frank Av. SR7: S'hm 3K 147
(not continuous)
Frankham St. NE5: Newc T 3F 61
Frankland Dr. NE25: Whit B 1E 48
Frankland La.
DH1: Bras, Dur 1A 166 (1C 6)
Frankland Mt. NE25: Whit B 1E 48
Frankland Rd. DH1: Dur 6K 153
Franklin Ct. NE37: Usw 7H 101
Franklin St. NE33: S Shi 3J 67
SR4: Sund 1C 118
Franklin Trad. Est. NE21: Bla T 2E 80
Franklyn Av. NE26: Sea S 3B 28
Franklyn Rd. SR8: Pet 5A 172
Frank Pl. DH3: Bir 5A 114
NE29: N Shi 6G 49
Frank St. DH1: Dur 2E 166
NE28: W'snd 4F 65
NE40: G'sde 5D 78
SR5: S'wck 5D 104
Fraser Cl. NE33: S Shi 5H 67
Frater Ter. NE28: W'snd 3C 66
Frazer Ter. NE10: Gate 5E 84
Freda St. SR5: S'wck 6B 104
Frederick Gdns. DH4: Pen 2A 130
Frederick Pl. DH4: Hou S 2E 144
Frederick Rd. SR1: Sund 1F 119 (3K 7)

Frederick St.—Gateshead Stadium Station (Metro)

Frederick St. NE17: C'wl 7K **93**
NE33: S Shi 5J **67**
SR1: Sund 1F **119** (3K **7**)
SR4: Sund 2G **117**
SR7: S'hm 3B **148**
Frederick St. Nth. DH7: B'don 2E **174**
Frederick St. Sth. DH7: B'don 2E **174**
Frederick Ter. DH5: Eas L 2H **157**
DH6: S Het 5B **158**
SR6: Whit 5H **89**
Fred Peart Sq. DH6: Whe H 3B **180**
Freehold Av. NE62: Chop 1H **17**
Freehold St. NE24: Bly 1K **23**
Freeman Rd. NE3: Gos 1H **63**
Freemans Pl. DH1: Dur 2A **166** (2C **6**)
Freeman Way NE26: Whit B 4E **38**
NE63: N Sea 6D **12**
Freesia Gdns. SR5: Monk 4E **104**
Freesia Grange NE38: Wash 5J **115**
Freezemoor Rd. DH4: Hou S 3D **130**
Freight Village NE13: Wool 2E **42**
Fremantle Rd. NE34: S Shi 1D **88**
French Gdn. Ind. Est. NE46: B End 7E **50**
Frenchmans Row NE15: Thro 3F **59**
Frenchmans Way NE34: S Shi 6D **68**
French St. NE24: Bly 1J **23**
Frensham NE38: Wash 4A **116**
Frensham Way DH7: B'don 1E **174**
Frenton Cl. NE5: Cha P 3C **60**
Friarage Av. SR6: Monk 4F **105**
Friar Rd. SR4: Sund 2K **117**
Friars *NE1: Newc T 6D **4***
(off Low Friar St.)
Friars Dene Rd. NE10: Gate 4A **84**
Friarsfield Cl. SR3: New S 4A **132**
Friars Ga. NE61: Mor 1D **14**
FRIARS GOOSE 3B **84**
Friars Goose Water Sports Club 3B **84**
Friarside DH7: Wit G 3D **152**
Friarside Cres. NE39: Row G 7H **95**
Friarside Gdns. NE16: Burn 2K **109**
NE16: Whi 1G **97**
Friarside Rd. NE4: Newc T 5A **62**
Friar Sq. SR4: Sund 2K **117**
Friars Row DH1: Dur 1D **166**
NE16: Burn 3K **109**
Friars St. NE1: Newc T 1E **82** (6D **4**)
Friar St. DH6: Shot C 6F **171**
Friars Way NE5: Newc T 5J **61**
Friar Way NE32: Jar 6C **66**
Friary Gdns. NE10: Gate 4A **84**
Friday Flds. La. NE2: Newc T 2G **63**
Friendly Bldgs. NE13: Din 4H **33**
Frinton Pk. SR3: Sund 5C **118**
Frobisher Ct. SR3: New S 3B **132**
Frobisher St. NE31: Heb 7K **65**
Frome Gdns. NE9: Gate 5H **99**
Frome Pl. NE23: Cra 2K **25**
Frome Sq. SR4: Sund 2J **117**
Front Rd. SR4: Sund 1K **117**
Front St. DH1: Dur 5J **153**
(Durham Ter.)
DH1: Dur, Sher 3E **166**
(Habgood Dr.)
DH2: Ous 1H **127**
DH2: Pelt 4D **126**
(Grange Villa Rd.)
DH2: Pelt 4F **127**
(North Vw.)
DH2: Pelt 2F **127**
(Station La.)
DH3: Ches S 5A **128**
DH3: Gt Lum 3E **142**
DH4: Hou S 2A **144**
(Cross St.)
DH4: Hou S 6D **130**
(Houghton Rd.)
DH4: Pen 1C **130**
DH5: Hett H 6G **145**
(Caroline St.)
DH5: Hett H 2E **156**
(York St.)
DH6: Crox 7K **175**
DH6: H Pitt 5A **156**
DH6: Has 1B **170**
DH6: Kel 7E **178**
DH6: S Het 3A **158**
DH6: Sher 3G **167**
DH6: Shot C 5F **171**
DH6: Whe H 2B **180**
DH7: B'don 6G **165**
DH7: B'hpe 5D **138**
DH7: Edm 3D **140**
DH7: Esh W 6F **151**
DH7: Lan 6J **137**
DH7: Lang P 4J **151**
(Langley Park)
DH7: Lang P 7B **150**
(Quebec)
DH7: Wit G 3B **152**
DH8: C'sde 3B **134**
DH8: Con 7H **121**
DH8: Ebc 5G **107**
DH8: Lead 5A **122**
DH8: Shot B 3E **120**
Front St. DH9: Ann P 5K **123**
DH9: Dip 2G **123**
(not continuous)
DH9: Stly 6J **125**
(Craghead)
DH9: Stly 2G **125**
(East Stanley)
DH9: Stly 3E **124**
(Stanley)
DH9: Tan L 6B **110**
DH9: Tan L 4D **110**
DL16: Crox 7K **175**
DL16: Tud V 7K **175**
(not continuous)
NE7: Longb, Newc T 7A **46**
NE12: Kil 6K **35**
NE12: Longb, Newc T 7A **46**
NE13: Din 4H **33**
NE13: Sea B 2D **34**
NE15: Lem 1E **80**
NE16: Burn 2J **109**
NE16: C Dene 5K **109**
NE16: Swa 5G **81**
NE16: Whi 7G **81**
NE21: Bla T 5B **80**
NE23: Cra 5B **26**
(High Pit Rd.)
NE23: Cra 4K **25**
(Station Rd.)
NE23: Dud 2K **35**
NE23: Seg 2C **36**
NE24: Cow 2B **22**
NE25: Well 6A **38**
NE25: Whit B 7E **38**
NE29: N Shi 4G **49**
(Bulman's La.)
NE29: N Shi 7E **48**
(Quadrant, The)
NE30: N Shi 5K **49**
(Bath Ter.)
NE30: N Shi 1J **49**
(Victoria Cres.)
NE35: Bol C 5E **86**
NE36: E Bol 7J **87**
NE37: Usw 7H **101**
NE39: H Spen 2D **94**
NE41: Pru 7H **57**
NE42: Pru 4F **77**
NE45: Cor 1D **72**
NE61: Peg 4B **10**
NE62: Chop 1G **17**
NE64: Newb S 3H **13**
SR6: Cle 5C **88**
SR6: Whit 6G **89**
TS27: Hes 4D **182**
TS28: Win 7H **181**
(Acclom St.)
TS28: Win 7G **181**
(Chapel St.)
Front St. E. DH4: Pen 1B **130**
DH6: Crox 7K **175**
*DH6: Has 1B **170***
(off Front St.)
NE22: Bed 1J **21**
TS28: Win 6F **181**
Front St. Ind. Est. DH6: Whe H 2B **180**
Front St. Nth. DH6: Cass, Quar H 6D **178**
Front St. Sth. DH6: Cass, Quar H 6D **178**
Front St. W. DH4: Pen 1B **130**
DH6: Has 7B **158**
NE22: Bed 1H **21**
TS28: Win 6F **181**
Frosterley Cl. DH1: Dur 5B **154**
DH5: Eas L 3K **157**
Frosterley Dr. DH3: Gt Lum 3F **143**
Frosterley Gdns. DH9: Ann P 5K **123**
SR3: Sund 6D **118**
Frosterley Pl. NE4: Newc T 7C **62** (4A **4**)
Frosterley Wlk. NE16: Sun 4H **97**
Froude Av. NE34: S Shi 3J **87**
Fuchsia Gdns. NE31: Heb 3J **85**
Fuchsia Pl. NE5: Newc T 3K **61**
FULBECK 4E **8**
Fulbrook Cl. NE23: Cra 7K **21**
Fulbrook Rd. NE3: Ken 7B **44**
Fulforth Cl. DH7: Ush M 7C **152**
Fulforth Way DH7: Sac 6D **140**
Fuller Rd. SR2: Sund 4G **119**
Fullerton Pl. NE9: Gate 6J **83**
Fulmar Dr. NE24: News 5J **23**
NE38: Wash 4D **114**
Fulmar Wlk. SR6: Whit 4H **89**
Fulton Pl. NE5: Newc T 3J **61**
FULWELL 3F **105**
Fulwell Av. NE34: S Shi 6D **68**
Fulwell Grn. NE5: Newc T 4H **61**
Fulwell Rd. SR6: Monk 3F **105**
SR8: Pet 6C **172**
Fulwell Windmill 4E **104**
Furnace Bank NE22: Bed 7B **18**
Furness Cl. SR8: Pet 6K **171**
Furness Ct. SR3: New S 3B **132**
Furrowfield NE10: Gate 2A **100**
Furzefield Rd. NE3: Gos 1D **62**
Fylingdale Dr. SR3: New S 2E **132**
Fyndoune DH7: Sac 1E **152**
Fyndoune Community College Sports Cen. 1E **152**
Fyndoune Way DH7: Wit G 2D **152**
Fynes Cl. SR8: Pet 4B **172**
Fynes St. NE24: Bly 1J **23**
Fynway DH7: Sac 1E **152**

G

Gables Ct. SR4: Sund 5J **117**
Gables, The DH6: Thor 1J **179**
DH7: B'hpe 6D **138**
NE13: Wool 6H **43**
NE24: Bly 1H **23**
*NE38: Wash 4J **115***
(off Fatfield Rd.)
Gable Ter. DH6: Whe H 2B **180**
Gadwall Rd. DH4: W Rai 4B **144**
Gainers Ter. NE28: W'snd 5G **65**
Gainford DH2: Ches S 6J **127**
NE9: Gate 5H **99**
Gainsborough Av. NE34: S Shi 3K **87**
NE38: Wash 4J **115**
Gainsborough Cl. NE25: Whit B 4C **38**
Gainsborough Cres. DH4: Hou S 4A **130**
NE9: Gate 7K **83**
Gainsborough Gro. NE4: Newc T 7B **62**
Gainsborough Pl. NE23: Cra 7K **25**
Gainsborough Rd. DH9: Stly 4F **125**
SR4: Sund 6J **117**
Gainsborough Sq. SR4: Sund 6J **117**
Gainsford Av. NE9: Gate 3G **99**
Gair Ct. DH2: Plaw 6H **141**
Gairloch Cl. NE23: Cra 1K **25**
Gairloch Dr. DH2: Ous 2H **127**
NE38: Wash 5E **114**
Gairloch Rd. SR4: Sund 5J **117**
Gairsay Cl. SR2: Ryh 1G **133**
Gala Bingo
Derwenthaugh 3H **81**
Newcastle upon Tyne 6E **4**
Sunderland 1C **118**
Willington Square 7K **47**
Galashiels Gro. DH4: Hou S 4B **130**
Galashiels Rd. SR4: Sund 5H **117**
Galashiels Sq. SR4: Sund 5J **117**
*Gala Theatre 2C **6***
(off Millennium Pl.)
Galen Ho. NE1: Newc T 6E **4**
Gale St. DH9: Stly 4D **124**
Galfrid Cl. SR7: Mur 4H **147**
Gallagher Cres. SR8: Pet 6D **172**
Gallalaw Ter. NE3: Gos 7H **45**
Gallant Ter. NE28: W'snd 4C **66**
Galleria, The NE11: Dun 5J **81**
Galleries Retail Pk.
NE38: Wash 2G **115**
Galleries Shop. Cen., The
NE38: Wash 3G **115**
Galley's Gill Rd. SR1: Sund 1E **118** (3G **7**)
Galloping Grn. Cotts. NE9: Spri 5B **100**
Galloping Grn. Farm Cl. NE9: Spri 5B **100**
Galloping Grn. Rd. NE9: Gate, Spri 4B **100**
Galloway Rd. SR8: Pet 5B **172**
Gallowgate NE1: Newc T 1E **82** (5D **4**)
Gallowhill La. NE15: Hor 1C **76**
NE42: O'ham 1C **76**
Gallows Bank NE46: Hex 3D **70**
Galsworthy Rd. NE34: S Shi 3G **87**
SR4: Sund 5J **117**
Galt St. DH6: Thor 1K **179**
Galway Rd. SR4: Sund 5H **117**
Galway Sq. SR4: Sund 5H **117**
Gambia Rd. SR4: Sund 6H **117**
Gambia Sq. SR4: Sund 6H **117**
Ganton Av. NE23: Cra 6K **25**
Ganton Cl. NE37: Usw 5G **101**
Ganton Ct. NE34: S Shi 3B **88**
Gaprigg Ct. NE46: Hex 2D **70**
Gaprigg La. NE46: Hex 2C **70**
Gaps, The NE46: Acomb 3C **50**
Garasdale Cl. NE24: News 5H **23**
Garcia Ter. SR6: Monk 3G **105**
(not continuous)
Garden Av. DH1: Dur 5J **153**
DH7: Lang P 5H **151**
Garden City Vs. NE63: Hir 4B **12**
Garden Cl. DH8: Con 6H **121**
NE13: Sea B 3D **34**
Garden Cotts. NE9: Gate 2J **99**
Garden Cres. DH8: Ebc 4H **107**
Garden Cft. NE12: Longb 4C **46**
Garden Dr. NE31: Heb 2H **85**
Gardener St. NE4: Newc T 3C **82**
Garden Est. DH5: Hett H 6H **145**
Garden Ho. Cres. NE16: Whi 6J **81**
Garden Ho. Dr. NE46: Acomb 4B **50**
Garden Ho. Est. NE40: Ryton 2C **78**
Garden La. NE33: S Shi 3J **67**
SR6: Cle 6B **88**
Garden Pk. NE28: W'snd 1K **65**
Garden Pl. DH4: Pen 2B **130**
*DH8: Con 6H **121***
(off George St.)
DH8: Lead 5A **122**
SR1: Sund 1E **118** (3H **7**)
Gardens, The DH2: Ches S 6K **127**
NE25: Whit B 7F **39**
NE38: Wash 4J **115**
Garden St. DH4: Hou S 6D **130**
NE3: Gos 7E **44**
NE21: Bla T 3C **80**
Garden Ter. DH4: Hou S 6D **130**
DH6: Thor 1K **179**
DH8: Lead 5A **122**
DH9: Stly 6H **125**
(Middles, The)
DH9: Stly 4E **124**
(Stanley)
*NE21: Bla T 5B **80***
(off Florence St.)
NE25: Well 6A **38**
NE40: G'sde 3E **78**
NE40: Ryton 2D **78**
NE46: Hex 1C **70**
Garden Wlk. NE11: Dun 4J **81**
Gardiner Cres. DH2: Pelt 5G **127**
Gardiner Rd. SR4: Sund 5G **117**
Gardiner Sq. NE11: Kib 3E **112**
SR4: Sund 5H **117**
Gardner Pk. NE29: N Shi 7F **49**
Gardner Pl. NE29: N Shi 7H **49**
Gardners Pl. DH7: B'don 7F **165**
Garesfield Gdns. NE16: Burn 2K **109**
NE39: Row G 4J **95**
Garesfield La. NE21: Bla T 2J **95**
Gareston Cl. NE24: Cow 2F **23**
Garfield St. SR4: Sund 1B **118**
Garforth Cl. NE23: Cra 6J **25**
Garland Ter. DH4: Hou S 2A **144**
Garleigh Cl. NE12: Kil 1E **46**
Garmondsway NE6: Newc T 1A **84**
Garner Cl. NE5: Cha P 2D **60**
Garnet St. SR4: Sund 1B **118**
Garnwood St. NE33: S Shi 5H **67**
Garrett Cl. NE28: W'snd 2K **65**
Garrick Cl. NE29: N Shi 5C **48**
Garrick St. NE33: S Shi 5J **67**
Garrigill NE38: Wash 7K **115**
Garron St. SR7: S'hm 4B **148**
(not continuous)
Garsdale DH3: Bir 7C **114**
Garsdale Av. NE37: Usw 7G **101**
Garsdale Rd. NE26: Whit B 2E **38**
Garside Av. DH3: Bir 2A **114**
Garside Gro. SR8: Pet 4K **171**
Garstin Cl. NE7: Newc T 2C **64**
Garth Cres. NE21: Bla T 5B **80**
NE34: S Shi 4C **68**
Gth. Farm Rd. NE21: Bla T 5B **80**
Garthfield Cl. NE5: Newc T 2G **61**
Garthfield Cnr. NE5: Newc T 2G **61**
Garthfield Cres. NE5: Newc T 2G **61**
Gth. Heads NE1: Newc T 1H **83** (6J **5**)
Garths, The DH7: Lan 7K **137**
Garth, The DH2: Pelt 2G **127**
DH8: M'sly 6A **108**
NE3: Ken 1B **62**
NE5: Newc T 4E **60**
NE21: Bla T 5B **80**
Gth. Thirteen NE12: Kil 7A **36**
Gth. Sixteen NE12: Kil 7B **36**
Gth. Twenty NE12: Kil 1C **46**
Gth. Twenty One NE12: Kil 7C **36**
Gth. Twenty Two NE12: Kil 1C **46**
Gth. Twenty Four NE12: Kil 1C **46**
Gth. Twenty Five NE12: Kil 1D **46**
Gth. Twenty Seven NE12: Kil 1D **46**
Gth. Thirty Two NE12: Kil 1C **46**
Gth. Thirty Three NE12: Kil 1B **46**
Gartland Rd. SR4: Sund 5G **117**
Garvey Vs. NE10: Gate 1K **99**
Gashouse Dr. DH3: Lam P 3G **129**
Gas Ho. La. NE61: Mor 7G **9**
Gaskell Av. NE34: S Shi 3H **87**
Gas La. NE21: Bla T 2C **80**
Gas Works Rd. SR7: S'hm 4C **148**
Gatacre St. NE24: Bly 1J **23**
Gatehouse Factories DH8: Con 7G **121**
Gateley Av. NE24: News 5H **23**
Gatesgarth NE9: Gate 2J **99**
Gatesgarth Gro. SR6: Monk 2F **105**
GATESHEAD 3G **83** (9H **5**)
Gateshead FC 3A **84** (10P **5**)
Gateshead Highway
NE8: Gate 3H **83** (9J **5**)
Gateshead Indoor Bowling Cen. 5H **83**
Gateshead International Stadium 3A **84** (10P **5**)
Gateshead Leisure Cen. 6H **83**
Gateshead Millennium Bridge (Footbridge) 1H **83** (7J **5**)
Gateshead Quay Vis. Cen. 8H **5**
Gateshead Rd. NE16: Sun 6H **97**
Gateshead Station (Metro) 3G **83** (10H **5**)
Gateshead Stadium Station (Metro) 4J **83**

Gateshead Western By-Pass—Goldstone Ct.

Gateshead Western By-Pass
NE9: Gate, Kib 6H 99
NE11: Gate 5A 82
NE16: Dun, Swa 5J 81
Gate, The 1F 83 (5E 4)
Gatwick Ct. NE3: Ken 5H 43
Gatwick Rd. SR4: Sund 5H 117
Gaughan Cl. NE6: Walk 3D 84
Gaweswell Ter. *DH4: Hou S* 5D 130
(off North St.)
Gayfield Ter. SR8: Eas 1D 172
Gayhurst Cres. SR3: New S 3C 132
Gayton Rd. NE37: Usw 6J 101
Geddes Rd. SR4: Sund 5H 117
Gellesfield Chare NE16: Whi 3H 97
Gelt Cres. DH5: Eas L 1H 157
General Graham St. SR4: Sund 3C 118
General Havelock Rd. SR4: Sund 1A 118
General's Wood, The NE38: Wash 1F 129
Genesis Way DH8: Con 7G 121
Geneva Rd. SR4: Sund 5H 117
Genister Pl. NE4: Newc T 5K 61
Geoffrey Av. DH1: Dur 4J 165
Geoffrey St. NE34: S Shi 3J 87
SR6: Whit 5H 89
Geoffrey Ter. DH9: Stly 4D 124
George Av. SR8: Eas 6C 160
(not continuous)
George Pit La. DH3: Gt Lum 4F 143
George Pl. NE1: Newc T 7F 63 (3E 4)
George Rd. NE22: Bed 6B 18
NE28: W'snd 5F 65
George Scott St. NE33: S Shi 1K 67
George Smith Gdns. NE10: Gate 4A 84
George Sq. DH6: Shad 6E 168
DH6: Shot C 6F 171
NE30: N Shi 6H 49
Georges Rd. NE4: Newc T 2B 82
(not continuous)
George Stephenson's Birthplace 7B 58
George Stephenson Way NE29: N Shi 2F 67
George St. DH1: Dur 3J 165
DH3: Bir 4K 113
DH3: Ches S 7B 128
DH5: Hett H 5G 145
DH6: Bow 3G 177
DH6: Has 1B 170
DH6: Sher 4E 168
(Durham La.)
DH6: Sher 3K 167
(Hallgarth St.)
DH7: Esh W 4E 162
DH7: Lang P 4J 151
DH8: Con 6H 121
DH8: Shot B 5F 121
DH9: Dip 1H 123
DH9: Stly 7J 125
NE3: Gos 7C 44
NE4: Newc T 2E 82 (7B 4)
NE10: Gate 5D 84
NE13: Bru V 5C 34
NE15: Thro 3K 59
NE16: Whi 7G 81
NE21: Bla T 3D 80
NE24: Bly 3J 23
NE28: W'snd 4B 66
NE30: N Shi 6H 49
NE40: Ryton 3D 78
NE63: Hir 3C 12
SR2: Ryh 3J 133
SR7: Mur 1F 159
SR7: S'hm 3A 148
George St. E. SR3: New S 1C 132
George St. Ind. Est. SR7: S'hm 3A 148
George St. Nth. SR6: Monk 7F 105
George St. W. SR3: New S 1C 132
George's Vw. NE23: Dud 4J 35
George Ter. DH7: Ush M 1E 164
George Way NE4: Newc T 2E 82 (8C 4)
Georgia Ct. DH8: Con 7G 121
Georgian Ct. NE12: Longb 3K 45
SR4: Sund 4C 118
Gerald St. NE4: Newc T 2K 81
NE34: S Shi 3J 87
Gerrard Cl. NE23: Cra 6K 25
NE26: Whit B 2E 38
Gerrard Rd. NE26: Whit B 2E 38
SR4: Sund 5H 117
Gertrude St. DH4: Hou S 7D 130
Ghyll Edge NE61: Mor 6D 8
Ghyll Fld. Rd. DH1: Dur 6K 153
Gibbons Wlk. NE34: S Shi 4G 87
Gibbs Ct. DH2: Ches S 7A 128
GIBSIDE 6C 96
Gibside 5B 96
Gibside DH2: Ches S 6J 127
Gibside Cl. DH9: Stly 2H 125
Gibside Ct. NE11: Dun 1B 98
Gibside Cres. NE16: Burn 7D 96
Gibside Gdns. NE15: Newc T 7H 61
Gibside Ter. NE16: Burn 2B 110
Gibside Vw. NE21: Bla T 5B 80
Gibside Way NE11: Dun, Swa 4H 81
Gibson Ct. NE35: Bol C 6F 87
(not continuous)
Gibson Flds. NE46: Hex 2D 70
Gibson Ho. *NE46: Hex* 2C 70
(off Battle Hill)
Gibson Pl. NE46: Hex 1C 70
Gibsons Bldgs. *NE40: Ryton* 2E 78
(off Main St.)
Gibson St. DH8: Con 6H 121
NE1: Newc T 1H 83 (5J 5)
NE28: W'snd 7J 47
NE64: Newb S 4H 13
Gibson Street Leisure Cen. 1H 83 (5K 5)
Gibson Ter. *NE40: Ryton* 2E 78
(off Main St.)
Gifford Sq. SR4: Sund 4J 117
Gilberdyke NE10: Gate 2E 100
Gilbert Rd. SR4: Sund 5H 117
SR8: Pet 5A 172
Gilbert Sq. SR4: Sund 6H 117
Gilbert St. NE33: S Shi 5J 67
Gilderdale DH4: Pen 1J 129
Gilderdale Way NE23: Cra 7J 25
GILESGATE 1E 166
Gilesgate DH1: Dur 2B 166 (2E 6)
NE46: Hex 1C 70
Gilesgate Cl. DH1: Dur 2B 166 (1E 6)
GILESGATE MOOR 2E 166
Gilesgate Rd. DH5: Eas L 1H 157
Gilhurst Grange SR1: Sund 2D 118 (4F 7)
Gilhurst Ho. SR1: Sund 1D 118 (3F 7)
Gillas La. DH5: Hou S 3G 145
Gillas La. E. DH5: Hou S 3F 145
Gillas La. W. DH5: Hou S 4E 144
Gill Bri. Av. SR1: Sund 1E 118 (2H 7)
Gill Burn NE39: Row G 4J 95
Gill Cres. Nth. DH4: Hou S 7J 129
Gill Cres. Sth. DH4: Hou S 7J 129
Gill Cft. DH2: Ches S 7H 127
GILLEY LAW 1A 132
Gillies St. NE6: Newc T 7B 64
Gilliland Cres. DH3: Bir 2A 114
Gillingham Rd. SR4: Sund 5H 117
Gill Rd. SR1: Sund 1E 118 (2H 7)
Gillside Ct. NE34: S Shi 1G 87
Gill Side Gro. SR6: Monk 5G 105
Gill Side Vw. DH8: Con 5E 120
Gill St. DH8: Con 1H 135
NE4: Newc T 1A 82
Gill Ter. *SR4: Sund* 1G 117
(off Pottery La.)
Gill Vw. DH8: C'sde 2E 134
Gilmore Cl. NE5: Cha P 2D 60
Gilmore Ho. *NE8: Gate* 6G 83
(off Whitehall Rd.)
Gilpin Ho. DH4: Hou S 7C 130
Gilpin St. DH4: Hou S 2D 144
Gilsland Av. NE28: W'snd 2K 65
Gilsland Gro. NE23: Cra 1K 25
Gilsland St. SR4: Sund 2C 118
Gilwell Way NE3: Gos 3D 44
Gilwood Ct. DH4: Pen 3A 130
Gingler La. NE40: G'sde 4E 78
Girtin Rd. NE34: S Shi 4K 87
Girton Cl. SR8: Pet 7K 171
Girvan Cl. DH9: Stly 3H 125
Girven Ter. DH5: Eas L 2J 157
Girven Ter. W. DH5: Eas L 2H 157
Gisburn Ct. NE23: Cra 1K 25
Gishford Way NE5: Newc T 3H 61
Givens St. SR6: Monk 5G 105
Gladeley Way NE16: Sun 5G 97
Glade, The NE15: Cha P 3A 60
NE32: Jar 5B 86
Gladewell Ct. NE62: Chop 2G 17
Gladstonbury Pl. NE12: Longb 6A 46
Gladstone Av. NE26: Whit B 5F 39
Gladstone Gdns. DH8: Con 6J 121
Gladstone M. NE24: Bly 1H 23
Gladstone Pl. NE2: Newc T 6G 63 (2H 5)
Gladstone St. DH4: Hou S 2B 144
DH8: Con 6J 121
DH9: Beam 2K 125
DH9: Stly 4D 124
NE15: Lem 7C 60
NE24: Bly 1H 23
NE28: W'snd 4B 66
NE31: Heb 7A 66
NE61: Mor 7H 9
SR6: Monk 6F 105
Gladstone Ter. DH3: Bir 4K 113
DH4: Pen 1K 129
NE2: Newc T 6G 63 (2H 5)
NE8: Gate 5H 83
NE22: Bed 1J 21
NE26: Whit B 7H 39
NE35: Bol C 4E 86
NE37: Usw 7K 101
TS28: Win 7G 181
Gladstone Ter. W. NE8: Gate 5G 83
Gladstone Vs. DH1: Dur 4B 166 (6D 6)
Gladwyn Rd. SR4: Sund 6H 117
Gladwyn Sq. SR4: Sund 6H 117
Glaholm Rd. SR1: Sund 2H 119
Glaisdale Ct. NE34: S Shi 2G 87
Glaisdale Dr. SR6: Monk 1G 105
Glaisdale Rd. NE7: Longb 7J 45
Glamis Av. NE3: Gos 2E 44
SR4: Sund 4J 117
Glamis Ct. DH4: Hou S 1H 143
NE34: S Shi 3B 88
Glamis Cres. NE39: Row G 3A 96
Glamis Ter. NE16: Sun 6G 97
Glamis Vs. DH3: Bir 2A 114
Glanmore Rd. SR4: Sund 5H 117
Glantlees NE5: Newc T 3G 61
Glanton Av. NE25: Sea D 7G 27
Glanton Cl. DH2: Ches S 7J 127
NE6: Newc T 2A 84
NE10: Gate 7G 85
NE28: W'snd 2J 65
NE61: Hep 3H 15
Glanton Ct. NE11: Dun 5C 82
Glanton Rd. NE29: N Shi 5D 48
NE46: Hex 2F 71
Glanton Sq. SR4: Sund 5J 117
Glanton Ter. SR8: Pet 6F 173
Glanton Wynd NE3: Gos 5D 44
Glanville Cl. NE11: Gate 7D 82
Glanville Rd. SR3: E Her 4K 131
Glasbury Av. SR4: Sund 4J 117
Glasgow Rd. NE32: Jar 2E 86
Glassey Ter. NE22: Bed 7B 18
Glasshouse Bri. NE1: Newc T 1J 83 (6M 5)
NE6: Newc T 1J 83 (6M 5)
Glasshouse St. NE6: Newc T 2A 84
Glastonbury NE38: Wash 4H 115
Glastonbury Gro. NE2: Newc T 3H 63
Glaston Ho. NE24: Cow 1F 23
Glazebury Way NE23: Cra 1K 25
Gleaston Ct. SR8: Pet 2K 181
GLEBE 3H 115
Glebe Av. NE12: Longb 5B 46
NE16: Whi 7H 81
SR8: Eas 7B 160
Glebe Cen. NE38: Wash 3H 115
Glebe Cl. NE5: Cha P 2D 60
NE20: Pon 4J 31
Glebe Ct. NE22: Bed 7H 17
Glebe Cres. NE12: Longb 3B 46
NE38: Wash 2J 115
SR8: Eas 7B 160
Glebe Dr. SR7: S'hm 7H 133
Glebe Est. SR7: S'hm 7H 133
Glebe Farm NE62: Chop 7G 11
Glebelands NE45: Cor 7E 52
Glebe M. NE22: Bed 7H 17
Glebe Mt. NE38: Wash 2J 115
Glebe Ri. NE16: Whi 7G 81
Glebe Rd. NE12: Longb 3B 46
NE22: Bed 7H 17
Glebeside DH5: Hett H 5G 145
DH7: Wit G 3D 152
Glebe Ter. DH4: Hou S 1D 144
NE11: Dun 6B 82
NE12: Longb 3B 46
NE62: Sco G 4G 17
SR8: Eas 7A 160
(not continuous)
Glebe Vw. SR7: Mur 6G 147
(not continuous)
Glebe Vs. NE12: Longb 3A 46
Glebe Wlk. NE16: Whi 7H 81
Glenallen Gdns. NE30: N Shi 3J 49
Glenamara Ho. NE2: Newc T 3H 5
Glen Av. NE43: Stoc 7J 75
Glenavon Av. DH2: Ches S 5K 127
Glen Barr DH2: Ches S 5K 127
Glenbrooke Ter. NE9: Gate 3H 99
Glenburn Cl. NE38: Wash 5D 114
Glencarron Cl. NE38: Wash 5E 114
Glen Cl. NE39: Row G 4J 95
Glencoe NE12: Kil 7B 36
Glencoe Av. DH2: Ches S 5K 127
NE23: Cra 7K 25
Glencoe Ri. NE39: Row G 6G 95
Glencoe Rd. SR4: Sund 6H 117
Glencoe Sq. SR4: Sund 5H 117
Glencoe Ter. NE39: Row G 6G 95
Glencot Gro. SR7: Eas 4J 159
Glencourse NE36: E Bol 7A 88
Glen Ct. NE31: Heb 7H 65
Glendale Av. NE3: Gos 1C 62
NE16: Whi 1G 97
NE24: Cow 1C 22
NE26: Whit B 4G 39
NE28: W'snd 1F 65
NE29: N Shi 6E 48
NE37: Usw 7G 101
NE62: Chop 7J 11
Glendale Cl. NE5: Cha P 2D 60
NE21: Bla T 6K 79
SR3: E Her 3J 131
Glendale Gdns. NE9: Gate 2K 99
NE62: Chop 7J 11
Glendale Gro. NE29: N Shi 6F 49
Glendale Rd. NE27: Shir 1A 48
NE63: N Sea 5E 12
Glendale Ter. NE6: Newc T 7A 64
Glendford Pl. NE24: News 5H 23
Glendower Av. NE29: N Shi 6D 48
Glendyn Cl. NE7: Newc T 4J 63
Gleneagle Cl. NE5: Cha P 2D 60
Gleneagles NE25: Whit B 6D 38
NE33: S Shi 4B 68
Gleneagles Cl. NE7: Newc T 7A 46
Gleneagles Ct. NE25: Whit B 6D 38
Gleneagles Dr. NE37: Usw 5F 101
Gleneagles Rd. NE9: Gate 4G 99
SR4: Sund 6H 117
Gleneagles Sq. SR4: Sund 6H 117
Glenesk Gdns. SR2: Sund 6E 118
Glenesk Rd. SR2: Sund 5E 118
Glenfield Av. NE23: Cra 1K 25
Glenfield Rd. NE12: Longb 5A 46
(Hailsham Av.)
NE12: Longb 5K 45
(Ongar Way)
Glengarvan Cl. NE38: Wash 5E 114
Glenholme Cl. NE38: Wash 5D 114
Glenholme Ter. TS27: B Col 2J 183
Glenhurst Cotts. SR8: Eas 7B 160
Glenhurst Dr. NE5: Cha P 2D 60
NE16: Whi 3F 97
Glenhurst Gro. NE34: S Shi 7B 68
Glenhurst Rd. SR8: Eas 7B 160
Glenhurst Ter. SR7: Mur 7F 147
Glenkerry Cl. NE38: Wash 5E 114
Glenleigh Dr. SR4: Sund 4J 117
Glenluce DH3: Bir 5C 114
(not continuous)
Glenluce Ct. DH8: Con 6E 120
NE23: Cra 6K 25
Glen Luce Dr. SR2: Sund 6H 119
Glenluce Dr. NE23: Cra 7J 25
Glenmeads DH2: Plaw 6H 141
Glenmoor NE31: Heb 6H 65
Glenmore DH8: Con 2A 136
Glenmore Av. DH2: Ches S 5A 128
Glenmuir Av. NE23: Cra 7J 25
Glenorrin Cl. NE38: Wash 5E 114
Glen Path SR2: Sund 5F 119
Glenridge Av. NE6: Newc T 4K 63
Glenroy Gdns. DH2: Ches S 5K 127
Glens Flats DH6: H Pitt 6B 156
Glenshiel Cl. NE38: Wash 5E 114
Glenside DH8: Shot B 3F 121
NE32: Jar 4C 86
Glenside Ct. NE9: Gate 3G 99
Glenside Ter. DH2: Pelt 5H 127
Glen St. NE31: Heb 1H 85
Glen Ter. DH2: Ches S 5J 127
DH4: Pen 1B 130
(off Rainton St.)
NE38: Wash 4J 115
NE46: Hex 1B 70
Glen, The SR2: Sund 5F 119
Glenthorne Rd. SR6: Monk 5G 105
Glenthorn Rd. NE2: Newc T 3G 63
Glen Thorpe Av. SR6: Monk 5G 105
Glenthorpe Ho. NE33: S Shi 4K 67
Glenwood NE63: Ash 5A 12
Glenwood Wlk. NE5: Cha P 2D 60
Gloria Av. NE25: Sea D 4H 27
Glossop St. NE39: H Spen 3D 94
Gloucester Av. SR6: Monk 3G 105
Gloucester Cl. DH3: Gt Lum 4E 142
Gloucester Ct. NE3: Ken 4J 43
Gloucester Pl. NE34: S Shi 1C 88
SR8: Pet 5K 171
Gloucester Rd. DH8: Con 1J 135
NE4: Newc T 1C 82 (6A 4)
NE29: N Shi 5B 48
Gloucestershire Dr. DH1: Carr 1G 167
Gloucester St. NE25: Sea D 5H 27
Gloucester Ter. DH6: Has 3A 170
NE4: Newc T 2C 82 (7A 4)
Gloucester Way NE4: Newc T 2D 82 (8A 4)
NE32: Jar 5B 86
Glover Ind. Est. NE37: Wash 1J 115
Glover Network Cen. NE37: Wash 1A 116
Glover Rd. NE37: Usw 7K 101
SR4: Sund 6H 117
Glovers Pl. NE46: Hex 1C 70
Glover Sq. SR4: Sund 6H 117
Glue Gth. DH1: Dur 2D 166
Glynfellis NE10: Gate 2D 100
Glynfellis Ct. NE10: Gate 2D 100
Glynwood Cl. NE23: Cra 1K 25
Glynwood Gdns. NE9: Gate 2J 99
Goalmouth Cl. SR6: Monk 5G 105
Goatbeck Ter. DH7: B'don 7F 165
Goathland Av. NE12: Longb 6K 45
Goathland Dr. SR3: New S 2D 132
Godfrey Rd. SR4: Sund 5H 117
Gofton Wlk. NE5: Newc T 3G 61
Goldcrest Rd. NE38: Wash 5D 114
Goldcrest Way NE15: Lem 1C 80
Golden Acre DH8: Shot B 3F 121
Goldfinch Cl. NE4: Newc T 3B 82
Goldlynn Dr. SR3: New S 3A 132
Goldsborough Ct. TS28: Win 4G 181
Goldsbrough Ct. NE2: Newc T 6E 62 (1C 4)
Goldsmith Rd. SR4: Sund 6H 117
Goldspink La. NE2: Newc T 6H 63 (1K 5)
Goldstone NE9: Gate 3H 99
Goldstone Ct. NE12: Kil 7C 36

Goldthorpe Cl.—Green La.

Goldthorpe Cl. NE23: Cra 1K 25
Golf Course Rd. DH4: Hou S 5K 129
Gompertz Gdns. NE33: S Shi 5H 67
Goodrich Cl. DH4: Hou S 4C 130
Good St. DH9: Stly 1E 124
Goodwell Lea DH7: New B 4A 174
Goodwood NE12: Kil 1C 46
Goodwood Av. NE8: Gate 6E 82
Goodwood Cl. DH8: Shot B 3F 121
NE5: Cha P 2D 60
Goodwood Ct. NE63: Ash 5B 12
Goodwood Rd. SR4: Sund 5G 117
Goodwood Sq. SR4: Sund 5G 117
Goodyear Cres. DH1: Dur 3E 166
Goole Rd. SR4: Sund 5J 117
Goose Hill NE61: Mor 7G 9
Gordon Av. NE3: Gos 1E 62
SR5: C'twn 7G 103
SR8: Pet 5D 172
Gordon Ct. *NE10: Gate 5B 84*
(off Church Pl.)
Gordon Dr. NE36: E Bol 7K 87
Gordon Ho. NE6: Newc T 5P 5
Gordon Rd. NE6: Newc T 1K 83 (5P 5)
NE24: Bly 4K 23
NE34: S Shi 7J 67
SR4: Sund 6H 117
Gordon Sq. NE6: Newc T 1K 83 (5P 5)
NE26: Whit B 7J 39
Gordon St. NE33: S Shi 5J 67
Gordon Ter. DH4: Pen 1C 130
DH9: Stly 1F 125
NE22: Bed 1J 21
NE26: Whit B 6J 39
NE42: Pru 4F 77
NE62: Chop 1A 18
SR2: Ryh 3J 133
SR5: S'wck 5C 104
Gordon Ter. W. NE62: Chop 1A 18
Gorecock La. DH8: Con 2F 137
DH9: Ann P, Con, Lan 2F 137
Gore Hill Est. DH6: Thor 1J 179
Gore La. DH6: Thor 1J 179
Gorleston Way SR3: New S 5C 132
Gorse Av. NE34: S Shi 1B 88
Gorsedale Gro. DH1: Carr 1H 167
Gorsedene Av. NE26: Whit B 2F 39
Gorsedene Rd. NE26: Whit B 2E 38
Gorsehill NE9: Gate 2A 100
Gorse Hill Way NE5: Newc T 2J 61
Gorse Rd. SR2: Sund 3F 119 (7J 7)
Gorseway NE61: Mor 1D 14
Gort Pl. DH1: Dur 1D 166
Goschen St. NE8: Gate 6F 83
NE24: Bly 1H 23
(not continuous)
SR5: S'wck 5C 104
GOSFORTH 1E 62
Gosforth Av. NE34: S Shi 2J 87
Gosforth Bowling Club 1E 62
Gosforth Bus. Pk. NE12: Longb 5H 45
Gosforth Cen., The NE3: Gos 1E 62
Gosforth Ind. Est. NE3: Gos 7G 45
Gosforth Pk. Vs. NE13: Wide O 7E 34
Gosforth Pk. Way NE12: Longb 5H 45
Gosforth St. NE2: Newc T 7H 63 (3J 5)
(not continuous)
NE10: Gate 5B 84
Gosforth Swimming Pool 6E 44
Gosforth Ter. NE3: Gos 7G 45
NE10: Gate 5D 84
Gosport Way NE24: News 5H 23
Gossington NE38: Wash 3A 116
Goswick Av. NE7: Newc T 3K 63
Goswick Dr. NE3: Ken 4B 44
Gouch Av. NE22: Bed 4J 17
Goundry Av. SR2: Ryh 3J 133
Gourock Sq. SR4: Sund 5G 117
Gowanburn NE23: Cra 7J 25
NE38: Wash 6K 115
Gowan Ter. NE2: Newc T 4H 63
Gower Rd. SR5: S'wck 5C 104
Gower St. NE6: Walk 2E 84
Gower Wlk. NE8: Gate 6A 84
Gowland Av. NE4: Newc T 7A 62
(not continuous)
Gowland Sq. SR7: Mur 7D 146
Grace Ct. DH9: Ann P 6J 123
Gracefield Cl. NE5: Cha P 2D 60
Grace Gdns. NE28: W'snd 1E 64
Grace Ho. NE29: N Shi 2E 66
Grace St. NE6: Newc T 7A 64
(not continuous)
NE11: Dun 6B 82
Gradys Yd. NE15: Thro 2H 59
Grafton Cl. NE6: Newc T 7K 63 (3P 5)
Grafton Ho. NE6: Newc T 7K 63 (3N 5)
Grafton Pl. NE6: Newc T 7K 63 (3N 5)
Grafton Rd. NE26: Whit B 7J 39
Grafton St. NE6: Newc T 7K 63 (3P 5)
SR4: Sund 1D 118
Gragareth Way NE37: Wash 2E 114
Graham Av. NE16: Whi 6G 81
Graham Ct. DH7: Sac 7E 140
Graham Pk. Rd. NE3: Gos 2E 62
Graham Rd. NE31: Heb 1H 85
Grahamsley St. NE8: Gate 4H 83 (10J 5)
Graham St. NE33: S Shi 3K 67
Graham Ter. DH6: H Pitt 6B 156
SR7: Mur 7F 147
Graham Way, The SR7: Mur, S'hm 4H 147
Grainger Arc. NE1: Newc T 1F 83 (5E 4)
Grainger Mkt. NE1: Newc T 1F 83 (5E 4)
Grainger Pk. Rd. NE4: Newc T 2B 82
Grainger St. NE1: Newc T 2F 83 (7E 4)
Graingerville Nth. *NE4: Newc T 1C 82*
(off Westgate Rd.)
Graingerville Sth. *NE4: Newc T 1C 82*
(off Westgate Rd.)
Grampian Av. DH2: Ches S 7K 127
(not continuous)
Grampian Cl. NE29: N Shi 3F 49
Grampian Ct. DH9: Ann P 6J 123
Grampian Dr. SR8: Pet 7K 171
Grampian Gdns. NE11: Gate 1D 98
Grampian Gro. NE36: W Bol 7H 87
Grampian Pl. NE12: Longb 3K 45
Granaries, The NE39: H Spen 3D 94
Granary, The DH4: Hou S 2B 144
Granby Cl. NE16: Sun 4H 97
SR3: Sund 5D 118
Granby Ter. NE16: Sun 5H 97
TS28: Win 4G 181
Grand Pde. NE30: N Shi 2J 49
Grandstand Rd. NE2: Gos, Newc T 4C 62
NE4: Newc T 5B 62
NE5: Gos, Newc T 4C 62
Grand Vw. DH6: Sher 5K 167
Grange Av. DH4: Hou S 1A 144
NE12: Longb 6C 46
NE22: Bed 5C 18
NE27: Shir 7K 37
SR8: Eas 1K 171
Grange Cl. NE24: News 5H 23
NE25: Whit B 7D 38
NE28: W'snd 3G 65
NE30: N Shi 2H 49
SR8: Pet 4A 172
Grange Ct. DH2: Pelt 4D 126
NE10: Gate 6E 84
NE32: Jar 6B 66
NE40: Ryton 2G 79
NE42: Pru 4F 77
NE61: Mor 1G 15
Grange Cres. NE10: Gate 7E 84
NE40: Ryton 2G 79
SR2: Sund 3F 119 (6J 7)
Grange Dr. NE40: Ryton 2G 79
Grange Est. NE11: Kib 2E 112
Grange Farm DH1: H Shin 1F 177
Grange Farm Dr. NE16: Whi 2G 97
Grange La. NE16: Whi 2G 97
Grange Lonnen NE40: Ryton 1F 79
Grange Mnr. NE16: Whi 2H 97
Grangemere Cl. SR2: Sund 7G 119
Grange Nook NE16: Whi 2G 97
GRANGE PARK 5C 18
Grange Pk. NE25: Whit B 1C 48
Grange Pk. Av. NE22: Bed 5B 18
SR5: S'wck 4E 104
Grange Pk. Cres. DH6: Bow 5J 177
Grange Pl. NE32: Jar 6B 66
Grange Rd. DH1: Carr 7G 155
DH9: Stly 3D 124
NE3: Gos 5E 44
NE4: Newc T 7J 61
NE10: Gate 7E 84
NE15: Thro 5J 59
NE20: Pon 4J 31
NE32: Jar 6B 66
(not continuous)
NE40: Ryton 1G 79
NE61: Mor 1G 15
SR5: C'twn 7G 103
Grange Rd. W. NE32: Jar 6A 66
Grange St. DH2: Pelt 2G 127
DH8: Con 2K 135
Grange St. Sth. SR2: Sund 6H 119
Grange Ter. DH2: Pelt 5F 127
DH6: Shot C 5E 170
DH8: M'sly 7K 107
NE9: Gate 6J 83
NE11: Kib 2E 112
NE36: E Bol 7K 87
NE42: Pru 4F 77
SR2: Sund 3E 118 (6H 7)
SR5: S'wck 5D 104
Grange, The DH9: Tan L 1C 124
NE22: H Bri 1C 20
NE25: Whit B 7C 38
NE36: E Bol 7K 87
GRANGETOWN 6H 119
Grange Vw. DH4: Hou S 6D 130
DH5: W Rai 5D 144
NE40: Ryton 2G 79
SR5: S'wck 4E 104
GRANGE VILLA 4C 126
Grange Villa Rd. DH2: Pelt 4D 126
Grange Vs. NE28: W'snd 3G 65
Grange Wlk. NE16: Whi 2G 97
Grangeway NE29: N Shi 3F 49
Grangewood Cl. DH4: Hou S 4A 130
Grangewood Ct. DH4: Hou S 3A 130
Grantham Av. SR7: S'hm 4K 147
(not continuous)
Grantham Dr. NE9: Gate 3G 99
Grantham Pl. NE23: Cra 6J 25
(not continuous)
Grantham Rd. NE2: Newc T 6H 63 (1J 5)
SR6: Monk 5G 105
Grantham St. NE24: Bly 3K 23
Grants Cres. SR7: S'hm 3A 148
Grant St. NE32: Jar 6A 66
SR8: Pet 5E 172
Granville Av. DH9: Ann P 5K 123
NE12: Longb 3C 46
NE26: Sea S 5D 28
Granville Ct. NE2: Newc T 5H 63 (1H 5)
Granville Cres. NE12: Longb 5C 46
Granville Dr. DH4: Hou S 4C 130
NE5: Cha P 2D 60
NE12: Longb 5C 46
Granville Gdns. NE2: Newc T 5J 63
NE62: Chop 7J 11
Granville Lodge NE12: Longb 4C 46
Granville Rd. NE2: Newc T 5H 63 (1J 5)
NE3: Gos 5F 45
SR8: Pet 7D 172
Granville St. NE8: Gate 5H 83
SR4: Sund 1D 118
Granville Ter. DH6: Whe H 2B 180
Grape La. DH1: Dur 3A 166 (3B 6)
(not continuous)
Grasmere DH3: Bir 6C 114
SR6: Cle 5C 88
Grasmere Av. DH5: Eas L 3J 157
NE6: Walk 1C 84
NE10: Gate 6D 84
NE15: Thro 6J 59
NE32: Jar 3D 86
Grasmere Ct. NE12: Kil 1A 46
NE15: Thro 6J 59
Grasmere Cres. DH4: Hou S 3B 130
NE21: Bla T 6B 80
NE26: Whit B 4F 39
SR5: Monk 4E 104
Grasmere Gdns. NE34: S Shi 7A 68
NE38: Wash 4J 115
Grasmere Ho. NE6: Walk 1C 84
Grasmere M. DH8: Lead 5B 122
Grasmere Pl. NE3: Gos 5E 44
Grasmere Rd. DH2: Ches S 1K 141
NE16: Whi 7J 81
NE28: W'snd 4E 64
NE31: Heb 1K 85
SR8: Pet 5C 172
Grasmere St. NE8: Gate 5G 83
Grasmere St. W. NE8: Gate 5G 83
Grasmere Ter. DH6: S Het 4D 158
DH9: Stly 5D 124
NE38: Wash 4J 115
NE64: Newb S 3H 13
SR7: Mur 1F 159
Grasmere Way NE24: Cow 1E 22
Grasmoor Pl. NE15: Lem 6B 60
Grassbanks NE10: Gate 1F 101
Grassdale DH1: Carr 1H 167
Grassholme Cl. DH8: Con 1J 135
Grassholm Mdws. SR3: Sund 6D 118
Grassholm Pl. NE12: Longb 5J 45
Grassington Dr. NE23: Cra 6J 25
Grasslees NE38: Wash 1D 128
GRASSWELL 7D 130
Grasswell Cvn. Pk. DH4: Hou S 7D 130
Grasswell Dr. NE5: Newc T 2K 61
Grasswell Ter. DH4: Hou S 7D 130
Gravel Walks DH5: Hou S 1E 144
Gravesend Rd. SR4: Sund 6H 117
Gravesend Sq. SR4: Sund 6J 117
Gray Av. DH1: Dur 6K 153
DH2: Ches S 7K 127
DH6: Sher 2K 167
NE13: Wide O 4E 34
SR7: Mur 7E 146
TS27: Hes 4D 182
Gray Ct. SR2: Sund 4F 119 (7K 7)
SR8: Eas 7B 160
Graylands NE38: Wash 1C 128
Grayling Ct. SR3: E Her 4J 131
Grayling Rd. NE11: Gate 7D 82
Gray Rd. SR2: Sund 4F 119 (7K 7)
Grays Cross *SR1: Sund 1G 119*
(off High St. E.)
Gray Sq. TS28: Win 5G 181
Grays Ter. DH1: Dur 3J 165
NE35: Bol C 5E 86
Graystones NE10: Gate 7F 85
Gray St. DH8: Con 6G 121
NE24: Bly 7J 19
NE32: Jar 6C 66
Gray's Wlk. NE34: S Shi 4G 87
Gray Ter. DH9: Ann P 4C 124
Graythwaite DH2: Ches S 6H 127
GREAT EPPLETON 5K 145
Greathead St. NE33: S Shi 6H 67
Gt. Lime Rd.
NE12: Dud, Gos, Kil, Longb 1J 45
(not continuous)
GREAT LUMLEY 3F 143
Gt. North Rd. DH1: Dur 5J 153
NE2: Gos, Newc T 2F 63 (1F 4)
NE3: Gos 3E 44
NE13: Wide O 5E 34
NE61: Tra W 6G 15
Great Pk. NE13: Wide O 1C 44
Grebe Cl. NE11: Dun 4C 82
NE24: News 4J 23
NE63: Hir 6C 12
Grebe Ct. NE2: Newc T 4H 63
Greely Rd. NE5: Newc T 3F 61
Greenacre Pk. NE9: Gate 4H 99
Green Acres NE61: Mor 1E 14
Greenacres DH2: Pelt 2F 127
NE20: Pon 2G 41
Greenacres Cl. NE40: Ryton 3E 78
Greenacres Rd. DH8: Shot B 4F 121
Green Av. DH4: Hou S 5D 130
Green Bank NE46: Hex 2E 70
Greenbank NE21: Bla T 4C 80
NE32: Jar 6B 66
Greenbank Dr. SR4: Sund 3G 117
Greenbank St. DH3: Ches S 5B 128
Greenbank Ter. DH3: Ches S 5A 128
Greenbourne Gdns. NE10: Gate 7A 84
Green Cl. NE25: Whit B 7D 38
NE30: N Shi 3H 49
Green Ct. DH1: Dur 2D 166
DH7: Esh W 7F 151
Green Cres. NE23: Dud 3G 35
GREENCROFT 6J 123
Greencroft DH6: S Het 4C 158
NE63: Ash 5A 12
Greencroft Av. NE6: Walk 5E 64
NE45: Cor 7E 52
Greencroft Ind. Est. DH9: Ann P 7J 123
Greencroft Ind. Pk. DH9: Ann P 7J 123
GREENCROFT PARK 2J 137
Greencroft Parkway DH9: Ann P 1J 137
Greencroft Rd. DH8: Con 2A 136
Greencroft School Sports Cen. 5J 123
Greencroft Ter. DH9: Ann P 6H 123
Greendale Cl. NE24: Cow 1E 22
Greendale Gdns. DH5: Hett H 1F 157
Green Dr. SR7: S'hm 5B 148
Greendyke Ct. NE5: Newc T 7G 43
Greener Ct. NE42: Pru 5D 76
Greenesfield Bus. Cen.
NE8: Gate 3G 83 (10G 4)
Greenfield Av. NE5: Newc T 3G 61
Greenfield Dr. NE62: Chop 2G 17
Green Fld. Pl. NE4: Newc T 1E 82 (6C 4)
Greenfield Pl. NE40: Ryton 1G 79
Greenfield Rd. NE3: Gos 2D 44
Green Flds. NE40: Ryton 1F 79
Greenfields DH2: Ous 6J 113
Greenfield Ter. DH9: Ann P 5K 123
NE10: Gate 5D 84
Greenfinch Cl. NE38: Wash 5D 114
Greenford NE11: Kib 2F 113
Greenford La. DH2: Bir, Kib 2H 113
NE11: Kib 7G 99
Greenford Rd. NE6: Walk 3D 84
Green Gro. NE40: G'sde 3F 79
Greenhall Vw. NE5: Newc T 3A 62
Greenhaugh NE12: Longb 3K 45
Greenhaugh Rd. NE25: Well 6B 38
Greenhead NE38: Wash 4D 114
Greenhead Rd. NE17: C'wl 4J 93
Greenhead Ter. NE17: C'wl 5K 93
Greenhill SR7: Mur 7F 147
Greenhills DH9: Stly 6E 124
NE12: Kil 6A 36
Greenhills Est. TS28: Win 4G 181
Greenhills Ter. DH6: Whe H 2B 180
Greenhill Vw. NE5: Newc T 3A 62
Grn. Hill Wlk. NE34: S Shi 7E 68
Greenholme Cl. NE23: Cra 1K 25
Greenhow Cl. SR2: Ryh 4H 133
Greenland Rd. DH7: Lang P 7C 150
Greenlands DH9: Stly 5D 124
NE32: Jar 4C 86
Greenlands Ct. NE25: Sea D 6H 27
Green La. DH1: Dur 2D 166
(McNally Pl., not continuous)
DH1: Dur 3C 166
(Old Elvet)
DH1: Sher 3J 167
DH6: Eas L, Has 7G 157
DH7: B'hpe, Stly 2E 138
NE10: Gate 4B 84
(Bath Rd.)
NE10: Gate 5E 84
(Shields Rd.)
NE10: Gate 5A 84
(Sunderland Rd.)
NE12: Kil 7C 36
(not continuous)
NE13: Wool 4F 43
NE23: Dud 3H 35
NE34: S Shi 2G 87

Green La.—Halstead Sq.

Green La. NE36: E Bol 1K **103**
NE61: Mor 1H **15**
(Charlton Gdns.)
NE61: Mor 7H **9**
(Salisbury St.)
NE61: Peg 3J **9**
NE63: Ash 4K **11**
SR7: Sea 4A **146**
TS29: Trim S 5K **179**
Green La. Gdns. NE10: Gate 4A **84**
Greenlaw NE5: Newc T 5E **60**
Greenlaw Rd. NE23: Cra 7J **25**
Green Lea DH7: Wit G 2D **152**
Greenlea NE29: N Shi 3B **48**
Greenlea Cl. NE39: H Spen 4E **94**
SR4: Sund 5J **117**
Greenlee NE63: Hir 5C **12**
Greenlee Dr. NE7: Newc T 2B **64**
Greenmarket NE1: Newc T 1F **83** (5E **4**)
Greenmount DH4: Hou S 1B **144**
Green Pk. NE28: W'snd 2C **64**
Greenrigg NE21: Bla T 5D **80**
(not continuous)
NE26: Sea S 4C **28**
Greenrigg Gdns. SR3: Sund 5D **118**
Greenriggs Av. NE3: Gos 3F **45**
Greenrising NE42: O'ham 2K **75**
Green's Bank DH9: Stly 2C **126**
Greenshields Rd. SR4: Sund 6H **117**
Greenshields Sq. SR4: Sund 6H **117**
GREENSIDE 5D **78**
Greenside NE34: S Shi 7D **68**
NE63: Ash 3A **12**
Greenside Av. NE13: Bru V 5C **34**
NE28: W'snd 2K **65**
SR8: Pet 5D **172**
Greenside Ct. SR3: Sund 6J **117**
Greenside Cres. NE15: Newc T 6G **61**
Greenside Rd. NE40: G'sde 4D **78**
NE40: Ryton 3C **78**
Green's Pl. NE33: S Shi 1J **67**
(not continuous)
Green Sq. NE25: Whit B 7D **38**
Green St. DH8: Con 6H **121**
DH8: Lead 5A **122**
DH8: Shot B 2E **120**
SR1: Sund 1F **119** (3J **7**)
SR7: S'hm 3B **148**
Green Ter. SR1: Sund 2E **118** (4H **7**)
Green, The DH1: H Shin 1F **177**
DH2: Ches S 6K **127**
DH2: Plaw 6H **141**
DH5: Hou S 1F **145**
DH6: Hett 7C **176**
DH6: Thor 2J **179**
NE3: Ken 2B **62**
NE10: Gate 6C **84**
NE15: Thro 4K **59**
NE17: C'wl 7K **93**
NE20: Pon 3K **31**
NE25: Whit B 5E **38**
NE28: W'snd 3F **65**
NE38: Wash 2J **115**
NE39: Row G 5G **95**
NE42: O'ham 2J **75**
NE46: Acomb 4C **50**
SR5: S'wck 6C **104**
SR7: Eas 4K **159**
SR8: Pet 1J **181**
Greentree La. DH9: Ann P 4J **123**
Greentree Sq. NE5: Newc T 3H **61**
Green Way NE25: Whit B 7D **38**
Greenway NE4: Newc T 5K **61**
NE5: Cha P 1C **60**
Greenway Ct. DH8: Con 2A **136**
Greenways DH8: Con 3A **136**
Greenway, The SR4: Sund 4J **117**
Greenwell Cl. NE21: Bla T 5A **80**
Greenwell Dr. NE42: Pru 2F **77**
Greenwell Pk. DH7: Lan 7K **137**
Greenwell Ter. NE40: Ryton 2C **78**
Greenwich Pl. NE8: Gate 2J **83** (8M **5**)
Greenwood NE12: Kil 1D **46**
Greenwood Av. DH4: Hou S 2C **144**
DH7: B'hpe 6D **138**
NE6: Walk 4E **64**
NE22: Bed 5B **18**
Greenwood Cl. DH6: Whe H 2C **180**
NE38: Wash 5K **115**
Greenwood Cotts. DH6: Thor 1J **179**
Greenwood Gdns. NE10: Gate 5B **84**
NE11: Gate 2C **98**
Greenwood Rd. SR4: Sund 5H **117**
Greenwood Sq. SR4: Sund 6H **117**
Greetlands Rd. SR2: Sund 6E **118**
Gregory Rd. SR4: Sund 6H **117**
Gregory Ter. DH4: Hou S 1A **144**
Gregson St. DH7: Sac 7E **140**
NE15: Newc T 2G **81**
Gregson Ter. DH6: S Het 5D **158**
SR7: S'hm 1H **147**
Grenada Cl. NE26: Whit B 3F **39**
Grenada Dr. NE26: Whit B 3F **39**
Grenada Pl. NE26: Whit B 3F **39**
Grenfell Sq. SR4: Sund 6H **117**
Grenville Ct. NE20: Pon 7E **30**
NE23: Cra 5J **25**
Grenville Dr. NE3: Gos 3D **44**
Grenville Ter. NE1: Newc T 1H **83** (5J **5**)
Grenville Way NE26: Whit B 4E **38**
Gresford St. NE33: S Shi 7J **67**
Gresham Cl. NE23: Cra 6K **25**
Gresley Rd. SR8: Pet 6J **171**
Greta Av. DH4: Pen 3A **130**
Greta Gdns. NE33: S Shi 5K **67**
Greta St. Nth. DH2: Pelt 3E **126**
Greta St. Sth. DH2: Pelt 3E **126**
Greta Ter. SR4: Sund 3C **118**
Gretna Dr. NE32: Jar 4F **87**
Gretna Rd. NE15: Newc T 6H **61**
Gretna Ter. NE10: Gate 6A **84**
Gretton Pl. NE7: Newc T 2J **63**
Grey Av. NE23: Cra 7J **25**
Greybourne Gdns. SR2: Sund 6E **118**
Greyfriars La. NE12: Longb 6J **45**
Grey Gables DH7: B'don 1E **174**
Grey Lady Wlk. NE42: Pru 3F **77**
Greylingstadt Ter. DH9: Stly 6G **125**
Grey Pl. *NE61: Mor 7G 9*
(off Noble Ter.)
Grey Ridges DH7: B'don 1E **174**
Grey's Ct. NE1: Newc T 1F **83** (6F **4**)
Greystead Cl. NE5: Cha P 2D **60**
Greystead Rd. NE25: Well 6B **38**
Greystoke Av. NE2: Newc T 6J **63** (1L **5**)
NE16: Whi 1H **97**
SR2: Sund 6E **118**
Greystoke Gdns. NE2: Newc T 5J **63** (1L **5**)
NE9: Gate 5K **99**
NE16: Whi 2H **97**
NE61: Mor 6F 9
(off Howard Rd.)
SR2: Sund 5E **118**
Greystoke Pk. NE3: Gos 4D **44**
Greystoke Pl. NE23: Cra 7J **25**
(not continuous)
Greystoke Wlk. NE16: Whi 2G **97**
Greystone Pl. SR5: S'wck 5C **104**
Greystones DH6: Shad 5J **169**
Grey St. DH4: Hou S 1D **144**
NE1: Newc T 1F **83** (5F **4**)
NE13: Bru V 5C **34**
NE28: W'snd 3G **65**
NE30: N Shi 6H **49**
Grey Ter. SR2: Ryh 3H **133**
Greywood Av. NE4: Newc T 6A **62**
Grieves Bldgs. DH4: Hou S 3C **130**
Grieves' Row NE23: Dud 2J **35**
Grieve's Stairs *NE29: N Shi 7H 49*
(off Bedford St.)
Grieve St. NE24: Bly 7H **19**
Griffith Ter. NE27: Shir 3H **47**
Grimsby St. NE24: Bly 3J **23**
Grindleford Ct. NE34: S Shi 1A **88**
GRINDON 5H **117**
Grindon Av. SR4: Sund 3H **117**
Grindon Cl. NE23: Cra 7J **25**
NE25: Whit B 2E **48**
Grindon Ct. SR4: Sund 5J **117**
Grindon Gdns. SR4: Sund 5J **117**
Grindon La. SR3: Sund 5J **117**
SR4: Sund 5J **117**
(Glenleigh Dr.)
SR4: Sund 3H **117**
(Rowan Cl.)
Grindon Pk. SR4: Sund 5J **117**
Grindon Ter. SR4: Sund 3C **118**
Grinstead Cl. NE34: S Shi 6B **68**
Grinstead Way DH1: Carr 6H **155**
Grisedale Gdns. NE9: Gate 3J **99**
Grisedale Rd. SR8: Pet 6C **172**
Grizedale NE37: Wash 2F **115**
Grizedale Ct. SR6: Monk 1E **104**
Groat Mkt. NE1: Newc T 1F **83** (6F **4**)
Grosmont DH3: Gt Lum 2E **142**
Grosvener Ter. DH8: Con 6J **121**
Grosvenor Av. NE2: Newc T 4H **63**
NE16: Swa 6H **81**
Grosvenor Cl. NE23: Cra 7J **25**
Grosvenor Ct. NE5: Cha P 2D **60**
Grosvenor Cres. NE31: Heb 2K **85**
Grosvenor Dr. NE26: Whit B 7G **39**
NE34: S Shi 5B **68**
SR6: Cle 5A **88**
Grosvenor Gdns. NE2: Newc T 5J **63**
NE28: W'snd 2A **66**
NE34: S Shi 7B **68**
Grosvenor M. NE29: N Shi 6G **49**
NE33: S Shi 5A **68**
Grosvenor Pl. NE2: Newc T 4G **63**
NE24: Cow 3D **22**
NE29: N Shi 6G **49**
Grosvenor Rd. NE2: Newc T 4H **63**
NE33: S Shi 5A **68**
Grosvenor St. SR5: S'wck 5B **104**
Grosvenor Vs. NE2: Newc T 4H **63**
Grosvenor Way NE5: Cha P 3D **60**
Grotto Gdns. NE34: S Shi 6F **69**
Grotto Rd. NE34: S Shi 7F **69**
Grousemoor NE37: Wash 1E **114**
Grousemoor Dr. NE63: Ash 5A **12**
Grove Av. NE3: Gos 1F **63**
Grove Cotts. DH3: Bir 4A **114**
NE40: Ryton 2D **78**
Grove Ct. DH6: Hett 7C **176**
DH6: Shot C 7E **170**
Grove Ho. Dr. DH1: Dur 2C **166**
Grove Ind. Est., The DH8: C'sde 1F **135**
Grove Rd. DH7: B'don 2C **174**
NE9: Gate 1J **99**
NE15: Thro 4K **59**
Grove Rd. Shop. Units DH7: B'don 2D **174**
Grove St. DH1: Dur 3K **165** (4A **6**)
Grove Ter. DH7: B'don 6G **165**
NE16: Burn 2B **110**
GROVE, THE 1E **134**
Grove, The DH1: Dur 1J **165**
DH5: Hou S 4D **144**
DH7: B'hpe 6D **138**
NE2: Newc T 3H **63**
(not continuous)
NE3: Gos 1E **62**
NE5: Newc T 4D **60**
NE12: Longb 6B **46**
NE16: Whi 1J **97**
NE20: Pon 6H **31**
NE25: Whit B 7F **39**
NE32: Jar 5B **86**
NE39: Row G 6K **95**
NE43: B'ley 4J **91**
NE61: Mor 6F **9**
SR2: Ryh 3H **133**
SR2: Sund 4F **119** (7J **7**)
SR5: C'twn 6H **103**
SR8: Eas 7J **159**
Guardians Ct. NE20: Pon 4K **31**
Gubeon Wood NE61: Tra W 6B **14**
Guelder Rd. NE7: Newc T 2A **64**
Guernsey Rd. SR4: Sund 6H **117**
Guernsey Sq. SR4: Sund 6H **117**
Guessburn NE43: Stoc 7G **75**
GUIDE POST 1G **17**
Guildford Pl. NE6: Newc T 6K **63** (2P **5**)
Guildford St. SR2: Sund 4G **119**
Guillemot Cl. NE24: News 4J **23**
Guillemot Row NE12: Kil 7A **36**
Guisborough Dr. NE29: N Shi 4B **48**
Guisborough St. SR4: Sund 3B **118**
Gulbenkian Studio Theatre 3F **4**
Gullane NE37: Usw 4H **101**
Gullane Cl. DH9: Stly 3H **125**
NE10: Gate 4G **85**
Gully Rd. TS28: Win 5G **181**
Gunnerston Gro. NE3: Ken 7K **43**
Gunnerton Cl. NE23: Cra 7K **25**
Gunnerton Pl. NE29: N Shi 6D **48**
Gunn St. NE11: Dun 6B **82**
Gut Rd. NE28: W'snd 3K **65**
Guyzance Av. NE3: Gos 6C **44**
Gypsies Green Sports Ground 3B **68**

H

Habgood Dr. DH1: Dur 3E **166**
Hackwood Pk. NE46: Hex 3D **70**
Hackworth Gdns. NE41: Wylam 7K **57**
Hackworth Rd. SR8: Eas, Pet 3H **171**
TS27: B Col 1H **183**
Hackworth Way NE29: N Shi 2F **67**
Haddington Rd. NE25: Whit B 4C **38**
Haddon Cl. NE25: Whit B 6B **38**
Haddon Grn. NE25: Well 6B **38**
Haddon Rd. SR2: Sund 6H **119**
Haddricksmill Ct. NE3: Gos 1G **63**
Haddricks Mill Rd. NE3: Gos 1G **63**
Hadleigh Ct. DH4: Hou S 3B **130**
Hadleigh Rd. SR4: Sund 3K **117**
Hadrian Av. DH3: Ches S 4B **128**
Hadrian Ct. NE12: Kil 1C **46**
NE15: Lem 5E **60**
NE20: Pon 3F **41**
Hadrian Gdns. NE21: Bla T 5D **80**
Hadrian Ho. NE15: Thro 3H **59**
Hadrian Lodge NE34: S Shi 1F **87**
Hadrian Pl. NE9: Gate 7J **83**
NE15: Thro 3H **59**
Hadrian Rd. NE4: Newc T 6K **61**
NE24: News 6G **23**
NE28: W'snd 4G **65**
NE32: Jar 2D **86**
(Finchale Ter.)
NE32: Jar 3D **86**
(Lindisfarne Rd.)
NE32: Jar 2E **86**
(Newcastle Rd.)
Hadrian Road Station (Metro) 4J **65**
Hadrians Ct. NE11: Gate 3F **99**
Hadrian Sq. NE6: Newc T 7A **64** (3P **5**)
Hadrian St. SR4: Sund 1C **118**
Hadrians Way DH8: Ebc 5G **107**
Hadstone Pl. NE5: Newc T 4J **61**
Hagan Hall NE32: Jar 5C **86**
Haggerston Cl. NE5: Newc T 1H **61**
Haggerston Ct. NE5: Newc T 1H **61**
Haggerston Cres. NE5: Newc T 2H **61**
Haggerstone Dr. SR5: C'twn 6G **103**
Haggerston Ter. NE32: Jar 2E **86**
Haggie Av. NE28: W'snd 2H **65**
Haggs La. NE11: Kib 7C **98**
Hahnemann Ct. SR5: S'wck 5D **104**
Haig Av. NE25: Whit B 7E **38**
Haig Cres. DH1: Dur 3E **166**
NE15: Newc T 1G **81**
Haigh Ter. NE9: Spri 6A **100**
Haig Rd. NE22: Bed 1K **21**
Haig St. NE11: Dun 6B **82**
Hailsham Av. NE12: Longb 5A **46**
Hailsham Pl. SR8: Pet 6B **172**
HAINING 6H **131**
Haininghead NE38: Wash 6J **115**
Hainingwood Ter. NE10: Gate 4F **85**
Haldane Ct. NE2: Newc T 5G **63**
Haldane St. NE63: Ash 3A **12**
Haldane Ter. NE2: Newc T 5G **63**
Haldon Pl. SR8: Pet 7K **171**
Hale Ri. SR8: Pet 6C **172**
Halewood Av. NE3: Ken 1A **62**
Half Flds. Rd. NE21: Bla T 5B **80**
Half Moon La. NE8: Gate 3G **83** (9H **5**)
(Hudson St.)
NE8: Gate 3G **83** (10H **5**)
(Mulgrave Ter.)
NE30: N Shi 5K 49
(off Front St.)
Half Moon St. NE62: Chop 7K **11**
Half Moon Yd. NE1: Newc T 1F **83** (6F **4**)
Halidon Rd. SR2: Sund 7F **119**
Halidon Sq. SR2: Sund 7F **119**
Halifax Pl. NE11: Dun 5A **82**
SR2: Ryh 3H **133**
Halifax Rd. NE11: Dun 5A **82**
Halkirk Way NE23: Cra 1J **25**
Hallam Rd. SR8: Pet 5B **172**
Hall Av. DH7: Ush M 2B **164**
NE4: Newc T 7A **62**
Hall Cl. DH4: W Rai 1A **156**
SR7: Sea 1F **147**
TS27: B Col 2H **183**
Hall Cres. SR8: Pet 3D **172**
Hall Dene Way SR7: Sea 1G **147**
Hall Dr. NE12: Kil 6A **36**
Halleypike Cl. NE7: Newc T 2B **64**
Hall Farm DH1: H Shin 6D **166**
Hall Farm Cl. NE43: Stoc 7H **75**
Hall Farm Rd. SR3: New S 4B **132**
Hallfield Cl. SR3: New S 4C **132**
Hallfield Dr. SR8: Eas 1J **171**
Hall Gdns. DH6: Sher 3A **168**
NE10: Gate 7B **84**
NE36: W Bol 7G **87**
HALLGARTH 7B **156**
Hall Gth. NE3: Gos 4E **44**
Hallgarth DH8: C'sde, Con 1E **134**
NE10: Gate 7E **84**
(not continuous)
Hallgarth Bungs. DH5: Hett H 1G **157**
Hallgarth Ct. SR6: Monk 6H **105**
Hallgarth Ho. NE33: S Shi 5J **67**
Hallgarth La. DH6: H Pitt 7B **156**
Hallgarth Rd. NE21: Bla T 4B **80**
Hallgarth St. DH1: Dur 3B **166** (4D **6**)
DH6: Sher 3K **167**
Hallgarth Ter. DH7: Lan 7K **137**
Hallgarth, The DH1: Dur 4B **166** (5E **6**)
Hallgarth Vw. DH1: Dur 4B **166** (5E **6**)
DH6: H Pitt 6C **156**
Hallgarth Vs. DH6: Sher 3A **168**
Hallgate NE46: Hex 1D **70**
Hall Grn. NE24: Cow 2F **23**
Halliday Gro. DH7: B'don 7F **165**
Halling Cl. NE6: Walk 2E **84**
Hallington Dr. NE25: Sea D 7H **27**
Hallington M. NE12: Kil 1A **46**
Halliwell St. DH4: Hou S 1D **144**
Hall La. DH1: H Shin 7D **166**
DH4: W Rai 1A **156**
DH5: Hou S 2E **144**
DH6: Has 1B **170**
Hallorchard Rd. NE46: Hex 1D **70**
Hallow Dr. NE15: Thro 4G **59**
Hall Pk. NE21: Bla T 2A **80**
Hall Rd. DH7: Esh W 7F **151**
DH8: C'sde 7E **120**
NE17: C'wl 6A **94**
NE31: Heb 1J **85**
NE37: Usw 7J **101**
Hall Rd. Bungs. NE17: C'wl 5K **93**
Hallside Rd. NE24: Cow 3F **23**
Hallstile Bank NE46: Hex 1D **70**
Hall St. DH6: S Het 4B **158**
Hall Ter. NE10: Gate 4F **85**
NE24: Bly 1J **23**
Hall Vw. SR6: Whit 6H **89**
Hall Wlk. SR8: Eas 7J **159**
Hall Walks SR8: Eas 7H **159**
Hallwood Cl. NE22: H Bri 1C **20**
Halstead Pl. NE33: S Shi 3K **67**
(not continuous)
Halstead Sq. SR4: Sund 3K **117**

Halterburn Cl.—Haven, The

Halterburn Cl. NE3: Gos 1C 62
HALTON 1F 53
Halton Castle (remains of) 1F 53
Halton Cl. NE43: Stoc 1K 91
Halton Dr. NE13: Wide O 5D 34
NE27: Back 1H 47
Halton Rd. DH1: Dur 6B 154
Halton Way NE3: Gos 3C 44
Hamar Cl. NE29: N Shi 1C 66
Hambard Way NE38: Wash 4H 115
Hambledon Av. DH2: Ches S 7K 127
(not continuous)
NE30: N Shi 1G 49
Hambledon Cl. NE35: Bol C 6E 86
Hambledon Gdns. NE7: Newc T 2J 63
Hambledon Pl. SR8: Pet 7J 171
Hambledon St. NE24: Bly 1H 23
Hambleton Ct. NE63: N Sea 6D 12
Hambleton Dr. SR7: S'hm 2K 147
Hambleton Grn. NE9: Gate 6K 99
Hambleton Rd. NE38: Wash 5F 115
Hamilton Ct. DH6: Shot C 6E 170
NE8: Gate 6J 83
SR6: Monk 5H 105
Hamilton Cres. NE4: Newc T 7D 62 (4A 4)
NE29: N Shi 4C 48
Hamilton Dr. NE26: Whit B 3F 39
Hamilton Pl. NE4: Newc T 7D 62 (4A 4)
HAMILTON ROW 6B 162
Hamilton Row St. DH7: Wat 6B 162
Hamilton St. SR8: Pet 5D 172
Hamilton Ter. DH7: Sac 4D 140
NE36: W Bol 1G 103
(off Dipe La.)
NE61: Mor 7G 9
(off Jackson Ter.)
Hamilton Way NE26: Whit B 3F 39
Hammer Sq. Bank DH9: Beam 1A 126
Hampden Rd. SR6: Monk 5G 105
Hampden St. NE33: S Shi 5J 67
Hampshire Ct. NE4: Newc T 4C 82 (10A 4)
Hampshire Gdns. NE28: W'snd 1J 65
Hampshire Pl. NE37: Usw 6H 101
SR8: Pet 5K 171
Hampshire Rd. DH1: Carr 1G 167
Hampshire Way NE34: S Shi 6E 68
Hampstead Cl. NE24: News 6G 23
Hampstead Gdns. NE32: Jar 4D 86
Hampstead Rd. NE4: Newc T 1A 82
SR4: Sund 4K 117
Hampstead Sq. SR4: Sund 4J 117
Hampton Cl. DH9: Ann P 5J 123
NE23: Cra 3B 26
Hampton Ct. DH3: Ches S 2B 128
NE16: Swa 5H 81
Hampton Dr. NE10: Gate 6A 84
Hampton Rd. NE30: N Shi 2F 49
Hamsteels Bank DH7: Lang P 5A 150
Hamsteels La. DH7: Lang P 5A 150
(not continuous)
HAMSTERLEY 2K 107
Hamsterley Cl. DH3: Gt Lum 3F 143
Hamsterley Ct. SR3: New S 3C 132
Hamsterley Cres. DH1: Dur 5B 154
NE9: Gate 4A 100
NE15: Lem 6B 60
Hamsterley Dr. NE12: Kil 7A 36
Hamsterley Gdns. DH9: Ann P 5J 123
HAMSTERLEY MILL 3E 108
Hanby Gdns. SR3: Sund 5C 118
Hancock Mus. 6F 63 (2F 4)
Hancock St. NE2: Newc T 6F 63 (2F 4)
Handel St. NE33: S Shi 3K 67
Handel Ter. DH6: Whe H 3A 180
Handley Cres. DH5: W Rai 6C 144
Handley Cross DH8: M'sly 6A 108
Handley St. SR8: Pet 5D 172
Handy Dr. NE11: Dun 4K 81
Handyside Pl. NE1: Newc T 7F 63 (4E 4)
Hangingstone La. DH9: Ann P 6F 123
Hangmans La. DH5: Hou S 7A 132
SR3: New S 7A 132
Hanlon Ct. NE32: Jar 5K 65
Hannington Pl. NE6: Newc T 7J 63 (3M 5)
Hannington St. NE6: Newc T 7J 63 (3M 5)
Hann Ter. NE37: Usw 7K 101
Hanover Cl. NE5: Cha P 3C 60
Hanover Ct. DH1: Dur 3K 165 (3A 6)
(not continuous)
NE9: Gate 5J 99
NE23: Dud 2K 35
Hanover Dr. NE21: Bla T 5A 80
Hanover Gdns. *NE28: W'snd 4A 66*
(off Station Rd.)
Hanover Ho. NE32: Jar 2B 86
Hanover Pl. NE23: Cra 7J 21
SR4: Sund 7D 104 (1F 7)
Hanover Sq. NE1: Newc T 2F 83 (8F 4)
NE21: Bla T 5A 80
(off Waterloo St.)
Hanover Stairs NE1: Newc T 8F 4
Hanover St. NE1: Newc T 2F 83 (8F 4)
Hanover Wlk. NE5: Cha P 3C 60
NE21: Bla T 6A 80
Harbord Ter. NE26: Sea D 5K 27
Harbottle Av. NE3: Gos 6C 44
NE27: Shir 2K 47
Harbottle Ct. NE6: Newc T 2A 84
Harbottle Cres. NE32: Jar 4B 86
Harbottle St. NE6: Newc T 2A 84
Harbour Dr. NE33: S Shi 1K 67
(not continuous)
Harbour, The DH4: Hou S 3B 130
Harbour Vw. NE22: E Sle 5F 19
NE30: N Shi 7H 49
(off Lit. Bedford St.)
NE33: S Shi 7J 49
SR6: Monk 5H 105
Harbour Wlk. SR7: S'hm 2A 148
Harcourt Pk. NE9: Gate 2J 99
Harcourt Rd. SR2: Sund 7F 119
Harcourt St. NE9: Gate 2J 99
Hardgate Rd. SR2: Sund 7F 119
Hardie Av. NE16: Whi 6G 81
Hardie Dr. NE36: W Bol 7G 87
Hardman Cl. NE40: Ryton 1H 79
Hardman Gdns. NE40: Ryton 1H 79
Hardwick Ct. NE8: Gate 5J 83
TS27: B Col 2H 183
(off Middle St.)
Hardwick Pl. NE3: Ken 2C 62
Hardwick Ri. SR6: Monk 7G 105
Hardwick St. SR8: Pet 6E 172
TS27: B Col 2G 183
Hardyards Ct. NE34: S Shi 1J 87
Hardy Av. NE34: S Shi 3H 87
Hardy Ct. NE30: N Shi 6H 49
Hardy Gro. NE28: W'snd 7E 46
Hardy Sq. SR5: S'wck 5C 104
Hardy St. SR7: S'hm 3B 148
Hardy Ter. DH9: Ann P 5C 124
Harebell Rd. NE9: Gate 2A 100
Harehills Av. NE5: Newc T 2K 61
Harehills Twr. NE3: Ken 2A 62
Hareholme Ct. DH7: New B 3J 163
HARELAW 3J 123
Harelaw Cl. DH2: Pelt 3F 127
Harelaw Dr. NE63: Ash 6K 11
SR6: Monk 6G 105
Harelaw Gdns. DH9: Ann P 3J 123
Harelaw Gro. NE5: Newc T 4D 60
Harelaw Ind. Est.
DH9: Ann P 2J 123
Hareshaw Rd. NE25: Well 6B 38
Hareshaw Ter. *NE6: Newc T 2A 84*
(off St Peter's Rd.)
Hareside NE23: Cra 5J 25
Hareside Cl. NE15: Thro 5K 59
Hareside Ct. NE15: Thro 5K 59
Hareside Foot Path NE15: Thro 6K 59
Hareside Wlk. NE15: Thro 5K 59
Harewood Cl. NE16: Whi 3G 97
NE25: Whit B 7B 38
Harewood Ct. NE25: Whit B 7B 38
Harewood Cres. NE25: Whit B 7B 38
Harewood Dr. NE22: Bed 6A 18
Harewood Gdns. NE61: Peg 3A 10
SR3: Sund 5C 118
Harewood Grn. NE9: Gate 5K 99
Harewood Rd. NE3: Gos 6E 44
Hareydene NE5: Newc T 6F 43
Hargill Dr. NE38: Wash 7E 114
Hargrave Ct. NE24: Bly 3G 23
Harland Way NE38: Wash 3H 115
Harlebury NE27: Back 6F 37
Harle Cl. NE5: Newc T 4E 60
Harlequin Lodge NE10: Gate 6B 84
Harle Rd. NE27: Back 1H 47
Harleston Way NE10: Gate 1C 100
Harle St. DH7: B'don 2F 175
NE28: W'snd 3F 65
Harley Ter. DH6: Sher 2K 167
NE3: Gos 7F 45
Harlow Av. NE3: Ken 5B 44
NE27: Back 1H 47
Harlow Cl. NE23: Cra 1K 25
HARLOW GREEN 5J 99
Harlow Grn. La. NE9: Gate 5J 99
Harlow Pl. NE7: Newc T 2K 63
Harlow St. SR4: Sund 2D 118
Harnham Av. NE29: N Shi 7D 48
Harnham Gdns. NE5: Newc T 5J 61
Harnham Gro. NE23: Cra 5J 25
Harold Sq. SR2: Sund 3G 119
Harold St. NE32: Jar 6C 66
Harold Wilson Dr. TS27: Hes 4D 182
Harper Bungs. *DH6: Whe H 4A 180*
(off Bevan Cres.)
HARPERLEY 3A 124
Harperley Dr. SR3: Sund 6D 118
Harperley Gdns. DH9: Ann P 4J 123
Harperley La. DH9: Tan L 7B 110
Harperley Rd. DH9: Ann P 4K 123
Harper St. NE24: Bly 2H 23
Harraby Gdns. NE9: Gate 4J 99
Harras Bank DH3: Bir 5A 114
HARRATON 7F 115
Harraton Ter. DH3: Bir 4A 114
DH3: Lam P 2G 129
Harriet Pl. NE6: Newc T 7A 64
Harriet St. NE6: Newc T 7B 64
NE21: Bla T 4C 80
Harrington Gdns. NE62: Chop 7K 11
Harrington St. *NE28: W'snd 3F 65*
(off Blenkinsop St.)
Harriot Dr. NE12: Kil 2J 45
Harrison Cl. SR8: Pet 7C 172
Harrison Ct. DH3: Bir 5A 114
NE23: Dud 3K 35
Harrison Gdns. NE8: Gate 7F 83
Harrison Gth. DH6: Sher 2K 167
Harrison Pl. NE2: Newc T 6G 63 (2H 5)
Harrison Rd. NE28: W'snd 2A 66
Harrison Ter. SR8: Eas 7B 160
Harrogate St. SR2: Sund 3G 119
Harrogate Ter. SR7: Mur 7E 146
Harrow Cres. DH4: Hou S 3A 130
Harrow Gdns. NE13: Wide O 6E 34
Harrow Sq. SR4: Sund 3K 117
Harrow St. NE27: Shir 7J 37
Hartburn NE10: Gate 2E 100
Hartburn Dr. NE5: Cha P 2D 60
Hartburn Pl. NE4: Newc T 6B 62
Hartburn Rd. NE30: N Shi 3F 49
Hartburn Ter. NE25: Sea D 7H 27
Hartburn Wlk. NE3: Ken 7K 43
(not continuous)
Hart Ct. SR1: Sund 1F 119 (2K 7)
Hart Cres. TS27: B Col 4K 183
Hartford NE12: Kil 6B 36
Hartford Bank NE22: H Bri 5E 20
NE23: H Bri 5E 20
HARTFORD BRIDGE 4E 20
Hartford Bri. Farm NE22: H Bri 4D 20
Hartford Cvn. Site NE22: H Bri 3D 20
Hartford Ct. NE22: Bed 1G 21
Hartford Cres. NE22: Bed 1G 21
NE63: Hir 5B 12
Hartford Dr. NE22: H Bri 4E 20
Hartford Ho. NE4: Newc T 3B 4
Hartford Rd. NE3: Gos 5F 45
NE22: Bed, H Bri 4E 20
NE34: S Shi 1G 87
SR4: Sund 3K 117
Hartford Rd. E. NE22: Bed 1H 21
Hartford Rd. W. NE22: Bed 1H 21
Hartford St. NE6: Newc T 5A 64
Hartforth Cres. NE10: Gate 4F 85
Harthope Av. SR5: C'twn 4J 103
Harthope Cl. NE38: Wash 1D 128
Harthope Dr. NE29: N Shi 2E 66
Hartington Rd. NE30: N Shi 3G 49
Hartington St. DH8: Con 6H 121
NE4: Newc T 1C 82
NE8: Gate 5H 83
SR6: Monk 5G 105
Hartington Ter. NE33: S Shi 5K 67
Hartland Dr. DH3: Bir 5B 114
Hartlands NE22: Bed 1G 21
Hartleigh Pl. NE24: Cow 2E 22
Hartlepool Av. SR8: Pet 4D 172
Hartlepool St. DH6: Thor 1K 179
Hartlepool St. Nth. DH6: Thor 1K 179
Hartlepool St. Sth. DH6: Thor 1K 179
HARTLEY 6D 28
Hartley Av. NE26: Whit B 6E 38
Hartleyburn Av. NE31: Heb 3H 85
HARTLEYBURN ESTATE 3H 85
Hartley Ct. NE13: Bru V 5B 34
NE25: Sea D 4H 27
Hartley Gdns. NE25: Sea D 7G 27
SR5: S'wck 4E 104
Hartley La. NE25: Well, Whit B 5A 38
NE26: Sea S, Whit B 1C 38
Hartley Sq. NE26: Sea S 6D 28
Hartley St. NE25: Sea D 7G 27
SR1: Sund 1H 119
Hartley St. Nth. NE25: Sea D 7G 27
Hartley Ter. NE24: News 5G 23
Hartoft Cl. DH4: Hou S 6D 130
HARTON 7B 68
Harton Gro. NE34: S Shi 6A 68
Harton Ho. Rd. NE34: S Shi 6A 68
Harton Ho. Rd. E. NE34: S Shi 6C 68
Harton La. NE34: S Shi 1J 87
HARTON NOOK 1B 88
Harton Quay NE33: S Shi 3H 67
Harton Ri. NE34: S Shi 6B 68
Harton Vw. NE36: W Bol 7G 87
HARTSIDE 3F 153
Hartside DH3: Bir 7B 114
NE15: Lem 6C 60
Hartside Cotts. DH9: Ann P 5K 123
Hartside Cres. NE21: Bla T 6A 80
NE23: Cra 7J 21
NE27: Back 7H 37
Hartside Gdns. DH5: Eas L 2J 157
NE2: Newc T 4H 63
Hartside Pl. NE3: Gos 3E 44
Hartside Rd. SR4: Sund 4K 117
Hartside Sq. SR4: Sund 4K 117
Hartside Vw. DH1: Dur 4J 153
DH7: Ush M 7C 152
Hart Sq. SR4: Sund 3A 118
Hartswood NE9: Gate 6J 99
Hart Ter. SR6: Monk 1H 105
Harvard Rd. NE3: Ken 7A 44
Harvest Cl. SR3: New S 4B 132
Harvey Cl. NE38: Wash 3D 114
NE63: N Sea 4E 12
SR8: Pet 5B 172
Harvey Combe NE12: Kil 1K 45
Harvey Cres. NE10: Gate 6F 85
Harwood Cl. NE23: Cra 5J 25
NE38: Wash 7E 114
Harwood Ct. NE23: Cra 5J 25
Harwood Dr. NE12: Kil 1D 46
Harwood Grn. NE3: Ken 6A 44
Hascombe Cl. NE25: Whit B 5D 38
Haslemere Dr. SR3: Sund 5C 118
Hassop Way NE22: Bed 6H 17
Hastings Av. DH1: Dur 5J 165
NE3: Ken 5K 43
NE12: Longb 5B 46
NE26: Sea S 3B 28
NE26: Whit B 3E 38
Hastings Ct. NE22: Bed 6A 18
NE25: Sea D 4H 27
Hastings Dr. NE30: N Shi 4J 49
Hastings Gdns. NE25: Sea D 4H 27
HASTINGS HILL 6G 117
Hastings Pde. NE31: Heb 3A 86
Hastings St. NE23: Cra 5A 26
SR2: Sund 4G 119
Hastings Ter. NE23: Cra 7B 22
NE25: Sea D 3H 27
SR2: Sund 5H 119
Hastings Wlk. *NE37: Usw 7J 101*
(off Hastings Ct.)
HASWELL 1B 170
Haswell Cl. NE10: Gate 7H 85
Haswell Gdns. NE30: N Shi 6G 49
Haswell Ho. NE30: N Shi 5K 49
HASWELL PLOUGH 3A 170
Haswell Rd. TS28: Win 4F 181
Hatfield Av. NE31: Heb 7K 65
Hatfield Cl. DH1: Dur 5J 153
Hatfield Dr. NE23: Seg 1D 36
Hatfield Gdns. NE25: Whit B 6B 38
SR3: Sund 5C 118
Hatfield Ho. NE29: N Shi 7G 49
Hatfield Pl. SR8: Pet 7C 172
Hatfield Sq. NE33: S Shi 2K 67
Hatfield Vw. DH1: Dur 3B 166 (4D 6)
Hathaway Gdns. SR3: Sund 5C 118
Hatherley Gro. TS27: B Col 2H 183
Hatherley Sq. *TS27: B Col 2H 183*
(off Hatherley Gro.)
Hathersage Gdns. NE34: S Shi 1K 87
Hatherton Av. NE30: N Shi 1H 49
Hathery La. NE24: Bly, Cow 2B 22
Hatton Gallery 2E 4
Haugh La. NE21: Bla T 1A 80
NE21: Thro 7J 59
NE46: Hex 1C 70
Haugh La. Ind. Est. NE46: Hex 7C 50
Haughs, The NE42: Pru 3F 77
Haughton Ct. NE4: Newc T 3C 82
Haughton Cres. NE5: Newc T 4E 60
NE32: Jar 4B 86
Haughton Ter. NE24: Bly 2J 23
Hautmont Rd. NE31: Heb 2K 85
Hauxley NE12: Kil 6B 36
Hauxley Dr. DH2: Ches S 2H 141
NE3: Ken 5A 44
NE23: Cra 7H 21
Hauxley Gdns. NE5: Newc T 3K 61
Havanna NE12: Kil 6A 36
Havannah Cres. NE13: Din 4H 33
Havannah Nature Reserve 7A 34
Havannah Rd. NE37: Wash 1F 115
Havant Gdns. NE13: Wide O 4D 34
Havelock Cl. NE8: Gate 4G 83
Havelock Ct. SR4: Sund 2K 117
Havelock Cres. NE22: E Sle 5D 18
Havelock Ho. SR4: Sund 2K 117
Havelock M. NE22: E Sle 4D 18
Havelock Pl. NE4: Newc T 1D 82 (6A 4)
Havelock Rd. NE27: Back 1H 47
SR4: Sund 2A 118
Havelock St. NE24: Bly 1J 23
NE33: S Shi 4J 67
(Frederick St.)
NE33: S Shi 4H 67
(Rekendyke La.)
SR1: Sund 1H 119
Havelock Ter. *DH9: Stly 2F 125*
(off High St.)
DH9: Tan L 6B 110
NE8: Gate 4G 83
NE17: C'wl 6K 93
NE32: Jar 1B 86
SR2: Sund 3D 118 (6F 7)
Havelock Vs. NE22: E Sle 5D 18
Haven Ct. DH1: Dur 3A 154
NE24: Bly 3G 23
SR6: Monk 6H 105
Haven Ho. DH8: Lead 6A 122
Haven, The DH4: Hou S 3B 130
DH7: B'hpe 6D 138

Haven, The—Hensby Ct.

Haven, The DH7: Lang P 4G 151
DH8: Lead 5A 122
NE29: N Shi 2G 67
NE42: Pru 4F 77
NE64: Newb S 3J 13
Haven Vw. NE64: Newb S 3J 13
Havercroft NE10: Gate 7F 85
Haverley Dr. SR7: S'hm 1G 147
Haversham Cl. NE7: Newc T 7J 45
Haversham Pk. SR5: Monk 2E 104
Hawarden Cres. SR4: Sund 3C 118
Hawes Av. DH2: Ches S 1A 142
Hawes Ct. SR6: Monk 2E 104
Hawesdale Cres. NE21: Bla T 6B 80
Hawes Rd. SR8: Pet 5B 172
Haweswater Cl. NE34: S Shi 7K 67
Haweswater Cres.
NE64: Newb S 3G 13
Hawick Ct. DH9: Stly 3H 125
Hawick Cres. NE6: Newc T 2K 83 (7P 5)
Hawick Cres. Ind. Est.
NE6: Newc T 2K 83 (7P 5)
Hawkesley Rd. SR4: Sund 3K 117
Hawkey's La. NE29: N Shi 6F 49
Hawkhill Cl. DH2: Ches S 2J 141
Hawkhills Ter. DH3: Bir 3A 114
Hawkhurst NE38: Wash 6J 115
Hawkins Ct. SR3: New S 3B 132
Hawkins Rd. SR7: Mur 2G 159
Hawksbury NE16: Whi 7G 81
Hawksfeld NE10: Gate 3C 100
Hawkshead Ct. NE3: Ken 5K 43
Hawkshead Pl. NE9: Gate 2K 99
Hawkshill Ter. DH7: Lang P 1A 162
Hawksley NE5: Newc T 3F 61
Hawksmoor Cl. NE63: Ash 6A 12
Hawks Rd. NE8: Gate 2H 83 (8J 5)
Hawks St. NE8: Gate 2J 83 (8M 5)
Hawk Ter. DH3: Bir 5C 114
Hawkwell Ri. NE15: Thro 4H 59
Hawsker Cl. SR3: New S 2E 132
HAWTHORN 4K 159
Hawthorn Av. NE13: Bru V 6C 34
SR3: New S 1D 132
Hawthorn Cl. DH2: Plaw 7H 141
NE16: Whi 2H 97
SR7: Mur 1F 159
Hawthorn Cotts. DH6: S Het 4D 158
DH8: Con 5F 121
Hawthorn Ct. DH2: Plaw 7H 141
NE61: Mor 7E 8
Hawthorn Cres. DH1: Dur 1E 166
DH6: Quar H 6C 178
NE38: Wash 7F 115
SR8: Pet 6E 172
Hawthorn Dr. NE11: Dun 6B 82
Hawthorne Av. NE31: Heb 7K 65
NE34: S Shi 2B 88
TS27: B Col 2J 183
Hawthorne Cl. DH7: Lang P 5H 151
Hawthorne Dr. NE32: Jar 4D 86
Hawthorne Gdns. NE9: Gate 1H 99
Hawthorne Rd. NE24: Bly 3K 23
Hawthorne Ter. DH6: Shot C 6E 170
DH7: Lang P 4K 151
DH9: Tan L 5C 110
Hawthorne Vw. DH6: Thor 2J 179
Hawthorn Gdns. NE3: Ken 1B 62
NE10: Gate 5B 84
NE26: Whit B 6F 39
NE29: N Shi 5F 49
NE40: Ryton 2J 79
Hawthorn Gro. NE28: W'snd 3F 65
Hawthorn M. NE3: Gos 1E 62
Hawthorn Pk. DH7: B'don 1D 174
Hawthorn Pl. DH1: Dur 3K 153
NE4: Newc T 2D 82 (8A 4)
NE12: Kil 7A 36
Hawthorn Rd. DH1: Carr 6H 155
DH6: S Het 4E 158
NE3: Gos 1E 62
NE21: Bla T 4C 80
NE63: Hir 3B 12
Hawthorn Rd. W. NE3: Gos 1E 62
Hawthorn Sq. SR7: S'hm 2B 148
Hawthorns, The DH9: Ann P 4K 123
NE3: Gos 1E 62
NE4: Newc T 3C 82 (9A 4)
NE9: Spri 6B 100
NE36: E Bol 7K 87
Hawthorn St. DH4: Hou S 7C 130
DH8: Con 5F 121
NE15: Thro 3K 59
NE32: Jar 6A 66
SR4: Sund 2C 118
SR8: Eas 6B 160
Hawthorn Ter. DH1: Dur 3K 165 (3A 6)
DH2: Pelt 4G 127
DH3: Ches S 7B 128
DH7: New B 4A 164
DH8: Con 5F 121
DH9: Ann P 5B 124
NE4: Newc T 2C 82 (7A 4)
NE9: Spri 6B 100
(Sandy La.)
Hawthorn Ter. NE9: Spri 6D 100
(Peareth Hall Rd.)
NE15: Thro 3K 59
NE40: Ryton 3C 78
(off Mitchell St.)
SR6: Monk 1G 105
Hawthorn Vs. NE23: Cra 4A 26
NE28: W'snd 3F 65
Hawthorn Wlk.
NE4: Newc T 2D 82 (8A 4)
Hawthorn Way NE20: Pon 1H 41
Haydn St. NE8: Gate 6H 83
Haydock Dr. NE10: Gate 7G 85
Haydon NE38: Wash 7J 115
Haydon Cl. NE3: Ken 4B 44
Haydon Dr. NE25: Whit B 1F 49
Haydon Gdns. NE27: Back 1H 47
Haydon Pl. NE5: Newc T 5G 61
Haydon Rd. NE63: Hir 5B 12
Haydon Sq. SR4: Sund 3K 117
Hayes Wlk. NE13: Wide O 5D 34
Hayfield La. NE16: Whi 1H 97
Hayhole Rd. NE29: N Shi 3E 66
Haylands Sq. NE34: S Shi 1A 88
Hayleazes Rd. NE15: Newc T 6F 61
Haymarket NE1: Newc T 7F 63 (4F 4)
Haymarket La. NE1: Newc T 7F 63 (3E 4)
Haymarket Station (Metro) 7F 63 (3F 4)
Haynyng, The NE10: Gate 7C 84
Hayricks, The DH9: Tan L 4D 110
Hay St. SR5: Monk 7E 104 (1H 7)
Hayton Av. NE34: S Shi 1C 88
Hayton Cl. NE23: Cra 3A 26
Hayton Rd. NE30: N Shi 3F 49
Hayward Av. NE25: Sea D 7H 27
Hayward Pl. NE5: Newc T 3H 61
Hazard La. DH5: Hett H, W Rai 7D 144
Hazel Av. DH4: Hou S 2C 144
DH6: Quar H 6D 178
DH7: B'don 2C 174
NE29: N Shi 5F 49
SR3: New S 1D 132
Hazel Cres. SR8: Eas 1B 172
Hazeldene NE25: Whit B 6D 38
NE32: Jar 6C 86
Hazeldene Av. NE3: Ken 1J 61
Hazeldene Ct. NE30: N Shi 5J 49
Hazel Dr. TS27: Hes 4D 182
Hazeley Gro. NE3: Ken 7K 43
Hazeley Way NE3: Ken 7K 43
Hazel Gro. DH2: Ches S 4J 127
NE12: Kil 2K 45
NE16: Burn 2C 110
NE34: S Shi 2B 88
Hazelgrove NE10: Gate 7F 85
Hazel Leigh DH3: Gt Lum 3E 142
Hazelmere Av. NE3: Gos 3F 45
NE22: Bed 7G 17
Hazelmere Cres. NE23: Cra 2A 26
Hazelmere Dene NE23: Seg 2C 36
Hazelmoor NE31: Heb 6H 65
Hazel Rd. NE8: Gate 6E 82
NE21: Bla T 4D 80
Hazel St. NE32: Jar 6A 66
Hazel Ter. DH4: Hou S 7C 130
DH6: Shot C 6E 170
DH9: Stly 6H 125
Hazelwood NE12: Kil 1D 46
NE32: Jar 7D 66
Hazelwood Av. NE2: Newc T 3G 63
NE64: Newb S 2H 13
SR5: S'wck 5B 104
Hazelwood Cl. NE9: Spri 5B 100
Hazelwood Ct. DH7: Lang P 5J 151
Hazelwood Gdns. NE38: Wash 7F 115
Hazelwood Ter. NE28: W'snd 2A 66
Hazledene Ter. SR4: Sund 2B 118
HAZLERIGG 7C 34
Hazlitt Av. NE34: S Shi 3H 87
Hazlitt Pl. NE23: Seg 2E 36
Headlam Gdns. *NE6: Newc T 7B 64*
(off Grace St.)
Headlam St. NE6: Newc T 7A 64 (3P 5)
Headlam Vw. NE28: W'snd 3A 66
Healey Dr. SR3: Sund 6D 118
HEALEYFIELD 5A 134
Healeyfield La. DH8: C'sde 5A 134
Health Connection, The 7A 44
Healthlands Fitness & Leisure Cen.
Washington 7H 101
Whickham 7H 81
Heartsbourne Dr. NE34: S Shi 3B 88
Heath Cl. DH6: Bow 5H 177
NE11: Gate 7D 82
SR8: Pet 7C 172
(not continuous)
Heathcote Grn. NE5: Newc T 2H 61
Heath Ct. NE1: Newc T 1G 83 (6G 4)
Heath Cres. NE15: Newc T 2G 81
Heathdale Gdns. NE7: Newc T 2K 63
Heather Cl. SR6: Cle 4C 88
Heatherdale Cres. DH1: Carr 7H 155
Heatherdale Ter. NE9: Gate 4K 99
Heather Dr. DH5: Hett H 5G 145
Heather Hill NE9: Spri 6D 100
Heatherlaw NE9: Gate 2A 100
NE37: Wash 2D 114
Heather Lea DH9: Dip 6J 109
Heatherlea Gdns. NE62: Chop 7J 11
SR3: Sund 5D 118
Heather Lea La. NE42: Pru 3F 77
Heatherlea Pl. NE37: Usw 6H 101
Heather Pl. NE4: Newc T 5A 62
NE40: Ryton 2E 78
Heatherslaw Rd. NE5: Newc T 5J 61
Heather Ter. NE16: Burn 2B 110
Heather Way DH9: Stly 3D 124
Heatherwell Grn. NE10: Gate 7A 84
Heathery La. NE3: Gos 5G 45
Heathfield DH2: Ches S 7H 127
NE61: Mor 2G 15
SR2: Sund 6E 118
Heathfield Cres. NE5: Newc T 2K 61
Heathfield Farm NE40: G'sde 5E 78
Heathfield Gdns. DH9: Ann P 4K 123
NE40: G'sde 5E 78
Heathfield Pl. NE3: Gos 3F 45
NE9: Gate 1H 99
Heathfield Rd. NE9: Gate 1H 99
Heath Grange DH5: Hou S 1E 144
Heathlands Fitness & Leisure Cen. *7B 128*
(off Front St.)
Heathlands Ladies Leisure Cen.
South Gosforth 7G 45
Whitley Bay 4E 38
Heathmeads DH2: Pelt 3F 127
Heath Sq. SR4: Sund 3A 118
Heath Vw. TS28: Win 7J 181
Heathway NE32: Jar 4C 86
SR7: S'hm 6A 148
Heathways DH1: H Shin 7F 167
Heathwell Gdns. NE16: Swa 6H 81
Heathwell Rd. NE15: Newc T 6F 61
Heathwood Av. NE16: Whi 7G 81
HEATON 4A 64
Heaton Cl. NE6: Newc T 6K 63 (2P 5)
Heaton Gdns. NE34: S Shi 4J 87
Heaton Gro. NE6: Newc T 6K 63 (2N 5)
Heaton Hall Rd. NE6: Newc T 6K 63 (2P 5)
Heaton Pk. Ct. NE6: Newc T 6K 63 (3N 5)
Heaton Pk. Rd. NE6: Newc T 6K 63 (2N 5)
Heaton Pk. Vw. NE6: Newc T 6K 63 (1N 5)
Heaton Pl. NE6: Newc T 6K 63 (2P 5)
Heaton Rd. NE6: Newc T 4K 63 (1P 5)
Heaton Swimming Pool 4A 64
Heaton Ter. NE6: Newc T 7J 63 (3M 5)
NE29: N Shi 6E 48
Heaton Wlk. NE6: Newc T 7K 63 (3P 5)
Heaviside Pl. DH1: Dur 2C 166
HEBBURN 1H 85
Hebburn Baths 7K 65
HEBBURN COLLIERY 6K 65
HEBBURN NEW TOWN 1G 85
Hebburn Station (Metro) 7H 65
Hebburn St. SR8: Eas 7A 160
Heber St. NE4: Newc T 1E 82 (5C 4)
Hebron Av. NE61: Peg 3K 9
Hebron Pl. NE63: Hir 4D 12
Hebron Way NE23: Cra 4J 25
Hector St. NE27: Shir 7K 37
Heddon Av. NE13: Bru V 7C 34
Heddon Banks NE15: Hed W 4B 58
Heddon Cl. NE3: Ken 6C 44
NE40: Ryton 1H 79
HEDDON-ON-THE-WALL 3C 58
Heddon Vw. NE21: Bla T 4B 80
NE40: Ryton 1H 79
Heddon Way NE34: S Shi 7G 67
Hedge Cl. NE11: Gate 7D 82
HEDGEFIELD 1K 79
Hedgefield Av. NE21: Bla T 1K 79
Hedgefield Cotts. NE21: Bla T 1K 79
Hedgefield Ct. NE21: Bla T 1K 79
Hedgefield Gro. NE24: News 6G 23
Hedgefield Vw. NE23: Dud 2J 35
Hedgehope NE37: Wash 2E 114
Hedgehope Rd. NE5: Newc T 1G 61
Hedgelea NE40: Ryton 1F 79
Hedgelea Rd. DH5: W Rai 7C 144
Hedgeley Rd. NE5: Newc T 5E 60
NE29: N Shi 5D 48
NE31: Heb 7H 65
Hedgeley Ter. NE6: Walk 7D 64
Hedgerow M. NE63: Ash 5K 11
Hedley Av. NE24: Bly 3J 23
Hedley Cl. NE33: S Shi 1J 67
Hedley Ct. DH7: Ush M 7C 152
NE24: Bly 3K 23
Hedleyhill La. DH7: Lang P 2A 162
Hedley Hill Rd. DH7: Wat 6A 162
Hedley Hill Ter. DH7: Wat 6A 162
Hedley La. NE16: Sun 2H 111
HEDLEY ON THE HILL 4B 92
Hedley Pl. NE28: W'snd 4F 65
(Equitable St.)
NE28: W'snd 4F 65
(York Dr.)
Hedley Rd. NE25: H'wll 1J 37
NE29: N Shi 2F 67
NE41: Wylam 7K 57
Hedley St. NE3: Gos 7E 44
NE8: Gate 6F 83
NE33: S Shi 1J 67
Hedley Ter. DH6: S Het 4B 158
DH7: Lang P 4J 151
(off Front St.)
DH9: Dip 3E 122
NE3: Gos 7E 44
SR2: Ryh 3J 133
HEDWORTH 4D 86
Hedworth Av. NE34: S Shi 2G 87
Hedworth Ct. SR1: Sund 2G 119
Hedworth La. NE32: Jar 3C 86
NE35: Bol C 5D 86
Hedworth Pl. NE9: Gate 4A 100
Hedworth Sq. SR1: Sund 2G 119
Hedworth St. DH3: Ches S 5A 128
Hedworth Ter. DH4: Hou S 3B 130
SR6: Whit 6H 89
(off North Guards)
Hedworth Vw. NE32: Jar 3D 86
Heighley St. NE15: Newc T 1F 81
Helena Av. NE26: Whit B 6H 39
Helena Ho. SR2: Sund 6F 7
Helen St. NE21: Bla T 4A 80
NE23: E Cram 5D 26
SR6: Monk 3G 105
Helford Rd. SR8: Pet 1A 182
Hellpool La. NE46: Hex 1B 70
Hellvellyn Ct. DH9: Ann P 6K 123
Helmdon NE37: Usw 7J 101
Helmsdale Av. NE10: Gate 5B 84
Helmsdale Rd. SR4: Sund 3K 117
Helmsley Cl. DH4: Pen 3A 130
Helmsley Ct. SR5: S'wck 4A 104
Helmsley Dr. NE28: W'snd 3K 65
Helmsley Grn. NE9: Gate 5K 99
Helmsley Rd. DH1: Dur 4A 154
NE2: Newc T 6H 63 (2J 5)
Helston Ct. NE15: Lem 6B 60
Helvellyn Av. NE38: Wash 5E 114
Helvellyn Cl. NE21: Bla T 6C 80
Helvellyn Rd. SR2: Sund 7F 119
Hemel St. DH3: Ches S 7A 128
Hemlington Cl. SR2: Ryh 3H 133
Hemmel Courts DH7: B'don 7E 164
Hemming St. SR2: Sund 6H 119
Hemsley Rd. NE34: S Shi 4B 68
Hencotes NE46: Hex 2C 70
Hencote's Ct. *NE46: Hex 2C 70*
(off St Cuthbert's Ter.)
Hencotes M. NE46: Hex 2C 70
Henderson Av. DH6: Whe H 3A 180
NE16: Whi 6G 81
Henderson Cl. NE46: Hex 3B 70
Henderson Ct. NE29: N Shi 2F 67
Henderson Gdns. NE10: Gate 6F 85
Henderson Rd. NE28: W'snd 1F 65
NE34: S Shi 2F 87
SR4: Sund 2B 118
Hendersons Bldgs. *NE64: Newb S 2J 13*
(off Vernon Pl.)
Hendersyde Cl. NE5: Newc T 2H 61
HENDON 4G 119
Hendon Burn Av. SR2: Sund 3G 119
Hendon Burn Av. W. SR2: Sund 4G 119
Hendon Cl. NE29: N Shi 2G 67
SR1: Sund 2G 119
Hendon Gdns. NE32: Jar 4D 86
Hendon Rd. NE8: Gate 6K 83
SR1: Sund 1G 119
(not continuous)
SR2: Sund 2G 119
Hendon St. SR1: Sund 2H 119
Hendon Valley Ct. SR2: Sund 4G 119
Hendon Valley Rd. SR2: Sund 3G 119
Henley Av. DH2: Pelt 6G 127
Henley Cl. NE23: Cra 3B 26
Henley Gdns. DH8: Con 7J 121
NE28: W'snd 1B 66
Henley Rd. NE30: N Shi 3J 49
SR4: Sund 3K 117
Henley St. NE6: Walk 6A 64
Henley Way NE35: Bol C 6E 86
Henlow Rd. NE15: Lem 6C 60
Henry Av. DH6: Bow 3H 177
(not continuous)
Henry Nelson St. NE33: S Shi 1K 67
Henry Robson Way NE33: S Shi 3J 67
Henry Sq. NE2: Newc T 7H 63 (4J 5)
Henry St. DH4: Hou S 3B 130
DH5: Hett H 4G 145
DH5: Hou S 1E 144
DH8: Con 6G 121
NE3: Gos 7E 44
NE15: Thro 3A 60
NE29: N Shi 7G 49
NE33: S Shi 1K 67
SR7: S'hm 2B 148
Henry St. E. SR2: Sund 2H 119
Henry St. Nth. *SR7: Mur 7F 147*
(off Henry St. Sth.)
Henry St. Sth. SR7: Mur 7F 147
Henry Ter. DH4: Hou S 7K 129
Hensby Ct. NE5: Newc T 1H 61

Henshaw Ct.—Hillhead Rd.

Henshaw Ct. NE63: Ash .5J **11**
Henshaw Gro. NE25: H'wll .1K **37**
Henshaw Pl. NE5: Newc T .6H **61**
Henshelwood Ter. NE2: Newc T .4G **63**
Henson Cl. NE38: Wash .4H **115**
Hepburn Gdns. NE10: Gate .5A **84**
Hepburn Gro. SR5: C'twn .6F **103**
Hepple Ct. NE24: Bly .3G **23**
Hepple Rd. NE64: Newb S .4G **13**
Hepple Way NE3: Gos .6C **44**
HEPSCOTT .3A **16**
Hepscott Av. TS27: B Col .2J **183**
Hepscott Dr. NE25: Whit B .5D **38**
HEPSCOTT PARK .7A **16**
Hepscott Ter. NE33: S Shi .6K **67**
Hepscott Wlk. NE61: Peg .4A **10**
Herbert St. DH8: Con .6H **121**
NE8: Gate .5J **83**
Herbert Ter. SR5: S'wck .2D **104**
SR7: S'hm .3B **148**
Herd Cl. NE21: Bla T .5A **80**
Herd Ho. La. NE21: Bla T .4K **79**
Herdinghill NE37: Wash .2D **114**
Herdlaw NE23: Cra .4J **25**
Hereford Ct. NE3: Ken .4K **43**
SR2: Sund .7F **119**
Hereford Rd. SR2: Sund .7F **119**
Herefordshire Dr. DH1: Carr .1G **167**
Hereford Sq. SR2: Sund .7F **119**
Hereford Way NE32: Jar .5B **86**
(not continuous)
Heritage Cl. NE8: Gate .5E **82**
Hermiston NE25: Whit B .6E **38**
Hermiston Retail Pk. DH8: Con .1H **135**
Hermitage Gdns. DH2: Ches S .1K **141**
Hermitage Pk. DH3: Ches S .1A **142**
Hermitage, The DH2: Ches S .2K **141**
Heron Cl. NE24: News .5J **23**
NE38: Wash .6E **114**
NE63: Hir .6C **12**
Heron Dr. NE33: S Shi .1J **67**
Heron Pl. NE12: Longb .5J **45**
Heron Vs. NE34: S Shi .2H **87**
Heron Way NE16: Whi .7H **81**
Herrick St. NE5: Newc T .2G **61**
Herring Gull Cl. NE24: News .6J **23**
Herrington Cl. DH7: Lang P .5H **151**
Herrington M. DH4: E Her .3E **130**
Herrington Rd. DH4: E Her .3F **131**
SR3: E Her .2H **131**
Herschel Bldg. NE1: Newc T .3E **4**
Hersham Cl. NE3: Ken .5K **43**
Hertburn Gdns. NE37: Wash .1H **115**
Hertburn Ind. Est. NE37: Wash .1J **115**
Hertford NE9: Gate .5H **99**
Hertford Av. NE34: S Shi .6E **68**
Hertford Cl. NE25: Whit B .5C **38**
Hertford Cres. DH5: Hett H .6F **145**
Hertford Gro. NE23: Cra .3A **26**
Hertford Pl. SR8: Pet .4A **172**
Herton Cl. SR8: Pet .5A **172**
(not continuous)
Hesket Ct. NE3: Ken .5A **44**
HESLEDEN .4E **182**
Hesleden Rd. TS27: B Col, Hes .3E **182**
Hesledon La. SR7: Eas .2K **159**
Hesledon Wlk. SR7: Mur .6G **147**
Hesleyside NE63: Hir .5D **12**
Hesleyside Dr. NE5: Newc T .5H **61**
Hesleyside Rd. NE25: Well .6B **38**
Hessewelle Cres. DH6: Has .3A **170**
Hester Av. NE25: Sea D .4H **27**
Hester Bungs. *NE25: Sea D* .*4H* ***27***
(off Hester Av.)
Hester Gdns. NE25: Sea D .4J **27**
Heswall Rd. NE23: Cra .7J **21**
HETT .7C **176**
Hett La. DH6: Crox, Hett .5K **175**
HETTON DOWNS .4H **145**
HETTON-LE-HOLE .6G **145**
Hetton Lyons Country Pk. .6H **145**
Hetton Lyons Ind. Est. DH5: Hett H .7H **145**
Hetton Rd. DH5: Hou S .3E **144**
Hetton Sports Complex .6G **145**
Heugh Edge DH7: Sac .5D **140**
Heugh Hall Row DH6: Quar H .5K **177**
Heugh Hill NE9: Spri .5E **100**
Hewitson Ter. NE10: Gate .7A **84**
Hewitt Av. SR2: Ryh .1G **133**
Hewley Cres. NE15: Thro .4H **59**
HEWORTH .6C **84**
Heworth Av. NE10: Gate .5E **84**
Heworth Burn Cres. NE10: Gate .6C **84**
Heworth Ct. NE34: S Shi .1G **87**
Heworth Cres. NE37: Usw .7H **101**
Heworth Dene Gdns. NE10: Gate .5C **84**
Heworth Gro. NE37: Usw .7G **101**
Heworth Rd. NE37: Usw .5H **101**
Heworth Station (Metro) .5D **84**
Heworth Station (Rail) .6D **84**
Heworth Way NE10: Gate .6E **84**
Hewson Pl. NE9: Gate .1K **99**
HEXHAM .1D **70**
Hexham NE38: Wash .4D **114**
Hexham Abbey .1D **70**
Hexham Av. NE6: Walk .1D **84**
NE23: Cra .3A **26**
NE31: Heb .4J **85**
SR7: S'hm .4K **147**
(not continuous)
Hexham Cl. NE29: N Shi .5C **48**
Hexham Ct. DH7: Sac .7D **140**
NE6: Walk .7E **64**
NE11: Dun .1B **98**
Hexham Dr. DH9: Ann P .4K **123**
Hexham Ho. NE6: Walk .7E **64**
Hexham Moothall & Gallery .1D **70**
Hexham Old Rd. NE40: Bla T, Ryton .1G **79**
Hexham Race Course .6A **70**
Hexham Race Course Cvn. Site
NE46: Hex .5A **70**
Hexham Rd. NE15: Hed W, Thro .3C **58**
NE16: Swa .5F **81**
SR4: Sund .3K **117**
Hexham Station (Rail) .1E **70**
Hexham Swimming Pool .1C **70**
Hextol Ct. NE46: Hex .2B **70**
Hextol Cres. NE46: Hex .2C **70**
Hextol Gdns. NE15: Newc T .6F **61**
Hextol Ter. NE46: Hex .2B **70**
Heybrook Av. NE29: N Shi .4F **49**
Heyburn Gdns. NE15: Newc T .1K **81**
Heywood's Ct. NE1: Newc T .1F **83** (6F **4**)
Hibernian Rd. NE32: Jar .6B **66**
Hibernia Rd. NE6: Walk .2E **84**
Hickling Ct. NE5: Newc T .1J **61**
Hickstead Cl. NE28: W'snd .5J **47**
Hickstead Gro. NE23: Cra .3B **26**
Hiddleston Av. NE7: Newc T .7K **45**
HIGHAM DYKES .1C **30**
Higham Pl. NE1: Newc T .7G **63** (4G **4**)
High Axwell NE21: Bla T .4D **80**
High Back Cl. NE32: Jar .2A **86**
HIGH BARNES .3B **118**
High Barnes DH3: Gt Lum .3E **142**
High Barnes Ter. SR4: Sund .3C **118**
High Beacon Stairs *NE30: N Shi* .*7J* ***49***
(off Union Quay)
High Bri. NE1: Newc T .1F **83** (6F **4**)
Highbridge NE3: Gos .5E **44**
Highburn NE23: Cra .6J **25**
High Burn Ter. NE10: Gate .7C **84**
High Burswell NE46: Hex .1B **70**
Highbury NE2: Newc T .4F **63**
NE10: Gate .6C **84**
NE25: Whit B .6E **38**
Highbury Av. NE9: Spri .5E **100**
Highbury Cl. NE9: Spri .5E **100**
Highbury Pl. NE29: N Shi .7E **48**
HIGH CALLERTON .2J **41**
High Carr Cl. DH1: Dur .6K **153**
High Carr Rd. DH1: Dur .6J **153**
High Chare DH3: Ches S .6A **128**
HIGH CHURCH .1F **15**
Highcliffe Gdns. NE8: Gate .6J **83**
High Cl. NE42: Pru .3H **77**
High Croft DH7: B'don .7D **164**
NE37: Usw .6F **101**
High Cft. Cl. NE31: Heb .2H **85**
Highcroft Dr. SR6: Whit .5G **89**
Highcroft Pk. SR6: Whit .5H **89**
(not continuous)
Highcrofts NE15: Hor .5E **56**
Highcross Rd. NE30: N Shi .1G **49**
High Cross St. DH6: Cass .4F **179**
High Dene NE7: Newc T .4J **63**
NE34: S Shi .1H **87**
High Dewley Burn NE15: Thro .2H **59**
High Downs Sq. DH5: Hett H .5G **145**
HIGH DUBMIRE .2B **144**
HIGH FELL .1J **99**
HIGHFIELD .5G **95**
Highfield DH3: Bir .2A **114**
DH7: Sac .7E **140**
NE16: Sun .4H **97**
NE24: Cow .2D **22**
NE42: Pru .4E **76**
Highfield Av. NE12: Longb .4B **46**
Highfield Cl. NE5: Newc T .2F **61**
Highfield Ct. NE10: Gate .7C **84**
Highfield Cres. DH3: Ches S .4A **128**
Highfield Dr. DH4: Hou S .2B **144**
NE34: S Shi .5B **68**
NE63: N Sea .5D **12**
Highfield Gdns. DH3: Ches S .4A **128**
Highfield Grange DH4: Hou S .3B **144**
Highfield La. NE42: Pru .5E **76**
Highfield Pl. NE13: Wide O .6C **34**
SR4: Sund .2B **118**
Highfield Ri. DH3: Ches S .4A **128**
Highfield Rd. DH4: Hou S .3A **130**
NE5: Newc T .3F **61**
NE8: Gate .5J **83**
NE33: S Shi .4B **68**
NE34: S Shi .4B **68**
NE39: Row G .5G **95**
Highfield Ter. DH7: Ush M .3B **164**
NE6: Walk .2D **84**
NE42: Pru .4D **76**
High Flatworth NE29: N Shi .6B **48**
Highford Gdns. NE61: Mor .1E **14**
Highford La. NE46: Hex .3A **70**
High Friar La. NE1: Newc T .1F **83** (5F **4**)
High Friars NE1: Newc T .5E **4**
HIGH FRIARSIDE .2J **109**
High Gth. *SR1: Sund* .*1G* ***119***
(off High St. E.)
Highgate DH1: Dur .2A **166** (1B **6**)
Highgate Gdns. NE32: Jar .4D **86**
Highgate Rd. SR4: Sund .3K **117**
High Ga., The NE3: Ken .1A **62**
High Graham St. DH7: Sac .1E **152**
Highgreen Chase NE16: Whi .3G **97**
High Grindon Ho. SR4: Sund .5J **117**
High Gro. NE4: Newc T .1C **82** (7A **4**)
NE40: Ryton .2H **79**
Highgrove NE5: Cha P .3D **60**
Highgrove Ct. SR8: Eas .2A **172**
High Hamsterley Rd. NE39: Ham M .3E **108**
HIGH HANDENHOLD .2D **126**
Highheath NE37: Wash .2D **114**
HIGH HEATON .3K **63**
High Hedgefield Ter. NE21: Bla T .1J **79**
High Hermitage Cvn. Pk.
NE42: O'ham .1F **77**
HIGH HESLEDEN .4H **183**
HIGH HEWORTH .7C **84**
High Heworth La. NE10: Gate .7C **84**
High Horse Cl. NE39: Row G .3A **96**
High Horse Cl. Wood NE39: Row G .3A **96**
High Ho. Cl. NE61: Mor .7D **8**
High Ho. Gdns. NE10: Gate .6C **84**
(not continuous)
High Ho. La. DH8: Con .7G **135**
High Ho. Rd. NE61: Mor .7C **8**
Highland Rd. NE5: Newc T .2K **61**
High La. DH4: E Her, Hou S .5E **130**
DH6: Has .7A **158**
High La. Row NE31: Heb .5K **65**
High Lanes NE10: Gate .7D **84**
High Laws NE3: Gos .1H **63**
Highlaws Gdns. NE9: Gate .5K **99**
High Level Rd. NE8: Gate .3G **83** (9G **4**)
High Mkt. NE63: Ash .3H **11**
High Mdw. NE34: S Shi .5B **68**
High Mdws. DH7: B'don .7C **164**
NE3: Ken .2A **62**
HIGH MICKLEY .7B **76**
High Mill Rd. NE39: Ham M .3E **108**
Highmoor NE61: Mor .1D **14**
High Moor Ct. NE5: Newc T .3A **62**
High Moor Pl. NE34: S Shi .1J **87**
HIGH MOORSLEY .3D **156**
HIGH NEWPORT .1C **132**
High Pk. NE61: Mor .1F **15**
High Pk. La. NE61: Mor .1G **15**
High Pasture NE38: Wash .7J **115**
High Pit Rd. NE23: Cra .5B **26**
HIGH PITTINGTON .6B **156**
High Primrose Hill DH4: Hou S .6H **129**
High Quay NE1: Newc T .1J **83** (6L **5**)
High Reach NE10: Gate .4E **84**
High Ridge NE13: Bru V .7D **34**
NE22: Bed .7G **17**
Highridge DH3: Bir .3A **114**
DH8: Con .6E **120**
High Rd., The NE34: S Shi .7B **68**
High Row DH4: Hou S .1J **143**
NE15: Lem .7C **60**
NE37: Usw .6H **101**
NE40: Ryton .2J **79**
High Sandgrove SR6: Cle .5C **88**
High Shaw NE42: Pru .5D **76**
High Shaws DH7: B'don .7E **164**
HIGH SHIELDS .4J **67**
HIGH SHINCLIFFE .7F **167**
Highside Dr. SR3: Sund .5C **118**
HIGH SOUTHWICK .4C **104**
HIGH SPEN .3D **94**
High Spen Ct. NE39: H Spen .3E **94**
High Spen Ind. Est. NE39: H Spen .2D **94**
HIGH STANNERS .6F **9**
High Stanners NE61: Mor .6E **8**
Highstead Av. NE23: Cra .1J **25**
Highsteads DH8: M'sly .7K **107**
High Stobhill NE61: Mor .2G **15**
High St. DH1: Carr .7G **155**
DH1: Dur .2A **166** (2C **6**)
DH1: H Shin .7F **167**
(High Shincliffe)
DH1: H Shin .6D **166**
(Shincliffe)
DH5: Eas L .2J **157**
DH6: H Pitt .5B **156**
DH6: Thor .1J **179**
DH7: B'don .7G **165**
DH9: Stly .2F **125**
NE3: Gos .7E **44**
NE8: Gate .2G **83** (8H **5**)
(Bottle Bank)
NE8: Gate .3H **83** (9J **5**)
(Nelson St.)
NE9: Gate .4A **100**
NE10: Gate .6B **84**
NE15: Thro .6K **59**
High St. NE24: Bly .2H **23**
(Edward St.)
NE24: Bly .2J **23**
(Thoroton St.)
NE32: Jar .6D **66**
(Church Bank)
NE32: Jar .6C **66**
(Monkton Rd.)
NE62: Chop .2G **17**
NE64: Newb S .2J **13**
SR4: Sund .2G **117**
High St. E. NE28: W'snd .4G **65**
SR1: Sund .1G **119**
High St. Nth. DH1: H Shin .6E **166**
DH7: B'don .7F **165**
(not continuous)
High St. Sth. DH1: H Shin .6E **166**
DH7: B'don .7G **165**
High St. Sth. Bk. DH7: B'don .7G **165**
High St. W. NE6: W'snd .4E **64**
SR1: Sund .2E **118** (4G **7**)
(St Michael's Way)
SR1: Sund .1E **118** (3H **7**)
(West St.)
High Swinburne Pl.
NE4: Newc T .1E **82** (6C **4**)
Hightree Cl. SR3: New S .4B **132**
HIGH URPETH .1D **126**
High Vw. DH7: Ush M .2B **164**
NE20: Pon .2H **41**
NE28: W'snd .2F **65**
NE43: Hed .4B **92**
High Vw. Nth. NE28: W'snd .1E **64**
High Wlk. DH3: Lam P .3G **129**
High Well Gdns. NE10: Gate .5C **84**
Highwell La. NE5: Newc T .4E **60**
High W. La. SR7: Eas .4J **159**
High W. St. NE8: Gate .4H **83** (10J **5**)
HIGH WESTWOOD .4K **107**
High Winning Cotts. *TS28: Win* .*4H* ***181***
(off Wellfield Rd.)
Highwood Rd. NE15: Newc T .6F **61**
High Wood Ter. DH1: Dur .6D **6**
High Wood Vw. DH1: Dur .4B **166** (6D **6**)
Highworth Dr. NE7: Newc T .2B **64**
NE9: Spri .6D **100**
High Yd. DH1: Dur .3B **166** (4D **6**)
Hilda Av. DH1: Dur .3E **166**
Hilda Cl. DH1: Dur .3F **167**
Hilda Pk. DH2: Ches S .4K **127**
Hilda St. DH9: Ann P .4J **123**
NE8: Gate .5F **83**
SR6: Monk .4F **105**
(not continuous)
Hilda Ter. DH2: Ches S .4K **127**
(not continuous)
NE15: Thro .3H **59**
Hilden Bldgs. NE7: Newc T .3A **64**
Hilden Gdns. NE7: Newc T .3A **64**
Hillary Av. NE12: Longb .4C **46**
Hillary Pl. NE5: Newc T .2G **61**
Hill Av. NE23: Seg .1E **36**
Hill Brow SR3: New S .3D **132**
Hill Ct. NE4: Newc T .1E **82** (5C **4**)
Hill Cres. SR7: Mur .7D **146**
SR7: S'hm .5C **148**
Hill Crest DH7: B'hpe .6D **138**
DH7: Esh W .7F **151**
DH7: Sac .1F **153**
NE16: Burn .2B **110**
Hillcrest DH1: Dur .2B **166** (1E **6**)
DH1: H Shin .7F **167**
DH8: C'sde .4B **134**
NE10: Gate .1C **100**
NE25: Whit B .6E **38**
NE32: Jar .4D **86**
NE34: S Shi .1D **88**
NE42: Pru .4F **77**
NE63: N Sea .5E **12**
SR3: E Her .2H **131**
Hillcrest Av. NE62: Chop .7H **11**
Hillcrest Ct. NE42: Pru .4F **77**
Hillcrest Dr. NE11: Dun .7A **82**
NE46: Hex .2E **70**
Hill Crest Gdns. NE2: Gos .1G **63**
Hillcrest M. DH1: Dur .2B **166** (1D **6**)
Hillcrest Pl. TS27: Hes .4D **182**
Hill Cft. NE15: Hor .4E **56**
Hillcroft DH3: Bir .3A **114**
NE9: Gate .1J **99**
Hillcroft NE39: Row G .5G **95**
Hill Dyke NE9: Gate, Spri .5A **100**
Hillfield DH8: Con .6F **121**
NE25: Whit B .6D **38**
Hillfield Gdns. SR3: Sund .5D **118**
Hillfield St. NE8: Gate .4G **83**
Hillford Ter. NE17: C'wl .6K **93**
Hillgarth DH8: C'sde .4D **134**
Hillgate NE8: Gate .2G **83** (8H **5**)
NE61: Mor .7F **9**
Hill Head Dr. NE5: Newc T .4D **60**
Hillhead Gdns. NE11: Dun .1C **98**
Hillhead La. NE16: Burn .6D **96**
Hillhead Parkway NE5: Cha P .3C **60**
Hillhead Rd. NE5: Cha P, Newc T .4D **60**

Hillheads Ct.—Horsley Ter.

Hillheads Ct. NE25: Whit B 7G 39
Hillheads Rd. NE25: Whit B 1F 49
Hillhead Way NE5: Newc T 2E 60
Hill Ho. Rd. NE15: Thro 3G 59
Hillingdon Gro. SR4: Sund 6G 117
Hill La. DH4: Pen 7C 116
Hill Mdws. DH1: H Shin 7E 166
Hillmeads DH2: Plaw 6H 141
Hill Pk. NE20: Pon 2H 41
HILL PARK ESTATE 1C 86
Hill Pk. Rd. NE32: Jar 1C 86
Hill Ri. NE38: Wash 2H 115
NE40: Ryton 3D 78
Hillrise Cres. SR7: Sea 2F 147
Hill Rd. NE46: Hex 7D 70
Hills Ct. NE21: Bla T 2E 80
Hillsden Rd. NE25: Whit B 4D 38
Hillside DH3: Bir 4B 114
DH3: Ches S 5A 128
DH7: Wit G 2D 152
NE11: Dun 7A 82
NE12: Kil 2C 46
NE20: Pon 3G 41
NE21: Bla T 4B 80
NE34: S Shi 2D 88
NE36: W Bol 7G 87
NE61: Mor 1F 15
NE63: Ash 3A 12
SR3: Sund 5E 118
Hillside Av. NE15: Lem 6E 60
Hillside Cl. NE39: Row G 4J 95
TS27: B Col 3J 183
Hillside Cres. NE15: Newc T 2G 81
Hillside Dr. SR6: Whit 5G 89
Hillside Gdns. DH9: Stly 1G 125
(not continuous)
SR2: Sund 5E 118
Hillside Gro. DH6: H Pitt 6B 156
Hillside Pl. NE9: Gate 1J 99
Hillside Rd. NE46: Hex 2F 71
Hillside Vw. DH6: Sher 2K 167
Hillside Vs. SR8: Pet 5D 172
Hillside Way DH4: Hou S 1E 144
Hillsleigh Rd. NE5: Newc T 2K 61
Hills St. NE8: Gate 3G 83 (9H 5)
Hill St. NE32: Jar 6A 66
NE33: S Shi 4H 67
NE45: Cor 1D 72
SR3: New S 2C 132
SR7: S'hm 4B 148
Hillsview Av. NE3: Ken 7A 44
Hillsyde Cres. DH6: Thor 1J 179
Hill Ter. DH4: E Her 3E 130
Hill, The NE42: O'ham 2D 76
Hillthorne Cl. NE38: Wash 4J 115
Hill Top DH3: Bir 4B 114
DH7: Esh W 6K 151
NE21: Bla T 5B 80
Hilltop DH9: Stly 2H 125
Hill Top Av. NE9: Gate 2J 99
Hilltop Bungs. DH6: Thor 2H 179
Hill Top Cl. NE62: Chop 7H 11
Hill Top Gdns. NE9: Gate 2J 99
Hilltop Gdns. SR3: New S 2E 132
Hilltop Ho. NE5: Newc T 3G 61
Hilltop Rd. DH7: Ush M 7C 152
Hill Top Vw. DH7: Lang P 5K 151
Hilltop Vw. SR6: Whit 4G 89
Hill Vw. DH7: Esh W 4E 162
DH7: Ush M 4E 164
DH9: Beam 2K 125
Hillview SR3: E Her 2H 131
Hillview Cres. DH4: Hou S 6D 130
Hill Vw. Gdns. SR3: Sund 5D 118
Hillview Gro. DH4: Hou S 6D 130
Hill Vw. Rd. SR2: Sund 6F 119
Hillview Rd. DH4: Hou S 6D 130
Hill Vw. Sq. SR2: Sund 6F 119
Hilton Av. NE5: Newc T 3H 61
Hilton Cl. NE23: Cra 7J 21
Hilton Dr. SR8: Pet 7B 172
HINDLEY 4F 91
Hindley Cl. NE40: Ryton 3C 78
Hindley Gdns. NE4: Newc T 6K 61
Hindmarch Dr. NE35: Bol C 6H 87
NE36: W Bol 7G 87
Hindson's Cres. Nth. DH4: Hou S 4A 130
Hindson's Cres. Sth. DH4: Hou S 4A 130
Hind St. SR1: Sund 2E 118 (4G 7)
Hinkley Cl. SR3: New S 3D 132
Hippingstones La. NE45: Cor 7D 52
Hipsburn Dr. SR3: Sund 5C 118
Hiram Dr. NE36: E Bol 7K 87
HIRST 4C 12
Hirst Head NE22: Bed 7J 17
Hirst Ter. Nth NE22: Bed 7J 17
Hirst Vs. NE22: Bed 7J 17
Hirst Yd. NE63: Hir 3B 12
Histon Ct. NE5: Newc T 2H 61
Histon Way NE5: Newc T 2H 61
Hi-Tec Village NE35: Bol C 7D 86
Hither Grn. NE32: Jar 4D 86
HMP Durham DH1: Dur 3B 166 (4E 6)
HMP Frankland DH1: Bras 3D 154
HMP Low Newton DH1: Bras 3D 154
Hobart NE26: Whit B 4F 39
Hobart Av. NE34: S Shi 3F 87
Hobart Gdns. NE7: Longb 7K 45
HOBSON 3A 110
Hobson Ind. Est. NE16: Burn 3A 110
Hodgkin Pk. Cres.
NE15: Newc T 1J 81
Hodgkin Pk. Rd. NE15: Newc T 1J 81
Hodgson's Rd. NE24: Bly 1H 23
Hodgson Ter. NE37: Usw 7K 101
Hodkin Gdns. NE9: Gate 1K 99
Hogarth Cotts. NE22: Bed 1J 21
Hogarth Dr. NE38: Wash 5J 115
Hogarth Rd. NE34: S Shi 4J 87
Holbein Rd. NE34: S Shi 3J 87
Holborn Cl. DH7: Esh W 4E 162
Holborn Ct. DH7: Ush M 3D 164
Holborn Pl. NE5: Newc T 4E 60
Holborn Rd. SR4: Sund 4K 117
Holborn Sq. SR4: Sund 4K 117
Holburn Cl. NE40: Ryton 1H 79
Holburn Cres. NE40: Ryton 1J 79
Holburn Gdns. NE40: Ryton 1J 79
Holburn La. NE40: Ryton 7H 59
Holburn La. Ct. NE40: Ryton 7G 59
Holburn Ter. NE40: Ryton 1J 79
Holburn Wlk. NE40: Ryton 1J 79
Holburn Way NE40: Ryton 1H 79
Holden Pl. NE5: Newc T 3K 61
Holder Ho. Way NE34: S Shi 3A 88
Holderness Rd. NE6: Newc T 4K 63
NE28: W'snd 2A 66
Hole La. NE16: Sun, Whi 3F 97
Holeyn Hall Rd. NE41: Wylam 4H 57
Holeyn Rd. NE15: Thro 4G 59
Holland Dr. NE2: Newc T 6D 62 (2A 4)
Holland Pk. NE2: Newc T 6D 62 (1A 4)
NE28: W'snd 2C 64
Holland Pk. Dr. NE32: Jar 4D 86
Hollinghill Rd. NE25: H'wll 1J 37
Hollings Cres. NE28: W'snd 1F 65
Hollingside La. DH1: Dur 5A 166
Hollingside Way NE34: S Shi 1K 87
Hollings Ter. NE17: C'wl 6J 93
Hollington Av. NE12: Longb 6K 45
Hollington Cl. NE12: Longb 6K 45
Hollinhill NE39: Row G 3A 96
Hollinhill La. NE39: Row G 2K 95
Hollin Hill Rd. NE37: Wash 1J 115
Hollinhill Ter. NE44: Rid M 6K 73
Hollinside Cl. NE16: Whi 2G 97
Hollinside Gdns. NE15: Newc T 7H 61
Hollinside Rd. NE11: Dun 5H 81
NE16: Dun, Swa 5H 81
SR4: Sund 3K 117
Hollinside Sq. SR4: Sund 3J 117
Hollinside Ter. NE39: Row G 5H 95
Hollon St. NE61: Mor 6E 8
Hollowdene DH5: Hett H 7G 145
Hollow Mdws. NE46: Hex 1E 70
Hollow, The NE32: Jar 5B 86
NE63: N Sea 5F 13
Holly Av. DH5: Hou S 2E 144
NE2: Newc T 4G 63
NE3: Ken 6B 44
NE11: Dun 7B 82
NE12: Longb 3B 46
NE21: Bla T 1C 96
NE25: Well 6B 38
NE26: Whit B 6G 39
NE28: W'snd 4G 65
NE34: S Shi 1C 88
NE40: Ryton 7G 59
NE61: Mor 1E 14
NE64: Newb S 2G 13
SR3: New S 1D 132
SR6: Whit 5H 89
Holly Av. W. NE2: Newc T 4G 63
Holly Bush Gdns. NE40: Ryton 2J 79
Hollybush Rd. NE10: Gate 6A 84
Hollybush Vs. NE40: Ryton 1J 79
Hollycarrside Rd. SR2: Ryh 1G 133
Holly Cl. NE12: Kil 7K 35
NE46: Hex 3A 70
Holly Ct. NE5: Newc T 3H 61
NE26: Whit B 6F 39
SR4: Sund 2C 118
Holly Cres. DH7: Sac 7E 140
NE38: Wash 7G 115
Hollycrest DH2: Ches S 4K 127
Hollydene NE11: Kib 2F 113
NE39: Row G 5K 95
Holly Gdns. DH8: C'sde 2E 134
NE9: Gate 1H 99
Holly Gro. NE42: Pru 3D 76
Holly Haven DH5: W Rai 6D 144
Holly Hill NE10: Gate 6B 84
Holly Hill Gdns. DH9: Stly 4F 125
Holly Hill Gdns. E. DH9: Stly 4G 125
Holly Hill Gdns. W. DH9: Stly 5F 125
(not continuous)
Hollyhock NE38: Wash 6J 115
Hollyhock Gdns. NE31: Heb 3J 85
Hollyhock Ter. DH6: Coxh 7J 177
Holly M. NE26: Whit B 6G 39
Hollymount Av. NE22: Bed 1J 21
Hollymount Sq. NE22: Bed 1J 21
Hollymount Ter. NE22: Bed 1J 21
Hollyoak Ho. NE24: Bly 4F 23
Holly Pk. DH7: B'don 1D 174
DH7: Ush M 2C 164
Holly Pk. Vw. NE10: Gate 6B 84
Holly Rd. NE29: N Shi 5F 49
Hollyside Cl. DH7: Ush M 7C 152
Hollys, The DH3: Bir 1K 113
Holly St. DH1: Dur 3K 165 (3A 6)
NE32: Jar 6A 66
NE63: Hir 4B 12
Holly Ter. DH9: Ann P 4J 123
DH9: Stly 4D 124
NE16: Burn 2C 110
Holly Vw. NE10: Gate 6A 84
Hollywell Ct. DH7: Ush M 3D 164
Hollywell Gro. NE13: Wool 4F 43
Hollywell Rd. NE29: N Shi 6D 48
Hollywood Av. NE3: Gos 6F 45
NE6: Walk 4E 64
SR5: S'wck 5B 104
Hollywood Cres. NE3: Gos 6F 45
Hollywood Gdns. NE11: Gate 2D 98
Holman Ct. NE33: S Shi 3J 67
Holmcroft NE64: Newb S 2J 13
Holmdale NE46: Hex 2E 70
NE63: Ash 5A 12
Holme Av. NE6: Walk 4D 64
NE16: Whi 7G 81
Holme Gdns. NE28: W'snd 3A 66
SR3: Sund 5D 118
Holme Ri. NE16: Whi 7H 81
Holmesdale Rd. NE5: Newc T 4K 61
Holmeside SR1: Sund 2F 119 (4J 7)
Holmeside Ter. NE16: Sun 5J 97
Holmewood Dr. NE39: Row G 7H 95
Holmfield Av. NE34: S Shi 6A 68
Holmfield Vs. DH6: Coxh 7J 177
Holm Grn. NE25: Whit B 7C 38
Holmhill La. DH2: Ches S 3A 142
DH3: Ches S, Plaw 3A 142
SR8: Eas 6B 160
Holmland NE15: Newc T 2J 81
Holmlands NE25: Whit B 6E 38
Holmlands Cl. NE25: Whit B 6E 38
Holmlands Cres. DH1: Dur 6J 153
Holmlands Pk. DH3: Ches S 7B 128
Holmlands Pk. Nth. SR2: Sund 4E 118
Holmlands Pk. Sth. SR2: Sund 4E 118
Holmlea DH7: B'hpe 6D 138
HOLMSIDE 3K 139
Holmside Av. DH7: Lan 7K 137
NE11: Dun 6C 82
Holmside Hall Rd. DH7: B'hpe 1G 139
DH9: B'hpe, Edm, Stly 1G 139
Holmside La. DH7: B'hpe, Edm 6C 138
Holmside Pl. NE6: Newc T 6K 63 (1N 5)
Holmside Ter. DH9: Stly 7J 125
Holmsland Vs. DH7: Sac 1E 152
Holmwood Av. NE25: Whit B 7D 38
NE64: Newb S 2H 13
Holmwood Gro. NE2: Newc T 3F 63
Holwick Cl. DH8: Con 1J 135
NE38: Wash 6E 114
HOLY CROSS 2H 65
Holy Cross Cemetery NE28: W'snd 2H 65
Holy Cross Church (remains of) 2H 65
Holyfields NE27: Shir 2H 47
(not continuous)
Holy Ho. *SR1: Sund 1H 119*
(off Adelaide Pl.)
Holy Island NE46: Hex 1C 70
Holy Jesus Bungs.
NE2: Newc T 5D 62 (1A 4)
Holylake Sq. SR4: Sund 3K 117
Holyoake Gdns. DH3: Bir 4A 114
NE9: Gate 6H 83
Holyoake St. DH2: Pelt 3E 126
NE42: Pru 3F 77
Holyoake Ter. DH9: Stly 5E 124
NE37: Usw 7H 101
SR6: Monk 4G 105
Holyrood DH3: Gt Lum 2E 142
Holyrood Rd. SR2: Sund 6H 119
HOLYSTONE 3G 47
Holystone Av. NE3: Gos 6D 44
NE24: Bly 4G 23
NE25: Whit B 7H 39
Holystone Cl. DH4: Hou S 7B 130
NE24: Bly 4F 23
Holystone Ct. NE8: Gate 5F 83
Holystone Cres. NE7: Newc T 2K 63
Holystone Dr. NE27: Kil 2G 47
Holystone Gdns. NE29: N Shi 4D 48
Holystone Grange NE27: Longb 3G 47
Holystone St. NE31: Heb 7H 65
Holystone Trad. Est. NE31: Heb 7H 65
Holystone Way NE12: Longb 4F 47
NE27: Longb 4F 47
HOLYWELL 1K 37
Holywell Av. NE6: Walk 3C 84
NE25: H'wll 1K 37
NE26: Whit B 5E 38
Holywell Cl. NE4: Newc T 7D 62 (3B 4)
NE21: Bla T 5D 80
NE25: H'wll 1K 37
Holywell Dene Rd. NE25: H'wll 1K 37
Holywell La. NE16: Sun 4H 97
Holywell M. NE26: Whit B 5F 39
Holywell Ter. NE27: Shir 3H 47
Home Av. NE9: Gate 3H 99
Homedale NE42: Pru 4G 77
Homedale Pl. NE42: Pru 5G 77
Homedale Ter. *NE42: Pru 4G 77*
(off Homedale)
Homedowne Ho. NE3: Gos 7E 44
Home Farm Cl. NE63: Ash 3H 11
Homeforth Ho. NE3: Gos 7E 44
Homelea DH4: Hou S 5J 129
Home Pk. NE28: W'snd 2C 64
Homeprior Ho. NE25: Whit B 7E 38
Homer Ter. DH1: Dur 4J 165
Homestall Cl. NE34: S Shi 1K 87
Home Vw. NE38: Wash 3J 115
Honeycomb Cl. SR3: New S 4B 132
Honeycrook Dr. NE7: Newc T 2C 64
Honeysuckle Av. NE34: S Shi 2H 87
Honeysuckle Cl. SR3: New S 4C 132
Honister Av. NE2: Gos 2G 63
Honister Cl. NE15: Lem 6D 60
Honister Dr. SR5: Monk 4E 104
Honister Pl. NE15: Lem 6D 60
Honister Rd. NE30: N Shi 2H 49
Honister Way NE24: News 6G 23
Honiton Cl. DH4: Hou S 5C 130
Honiton Ct. NE3: Ken 6H 43
Honiton Way NE29: N Shi 4B 48
Hood Cl. SR5: S'wck 6E 104
Hood Sq. NE21: Bla T 5A 80
Hood St. NE1: Newc T 1F 83 (5F 4)
NE16: Swa 5G 81
NE61: Mor 6F 9
HOOKER GATE 4E 94
Hookergate La. NE39: H Spen 3D 94
(Ashtree La.)
NE39: H Spen, Row G 4E 94
(Woodlands Cl.)
Hope Av. SR8: Pet 6E 172
Hopedene NE10: Gate 2E 100
Hope Shield NE38: Wash 7D 114
Hope St. DH6: Sher 3K 167
DH8: Con 5G 121
NE32: Jar 6C 66
SR1: Sund 2E 118 (4G 7)
Hope Vw. SR2: Ryh 2H 133
Hopgarth Ct. DH3: Ches S 5B 128
Hopgarth Gdns. DH3: Ches S 5B 128
Hopkins Ct. SR4: Sund 1B 118
Hopkins Wlk. NE34: S Shi 4G 87
Hopper Pl. DH1: Dur 6A 154
NE8: Gate 3H 83 (10J 5)
Hopper Rd. NE10: Gate 7A 84
Hoppers Ct. *NE16: Swa 5G 81*
(off Quality Row Rd.)
Hopper St. NE8: Gate 3H 83 (10J 5)
NE28: W'snd 3E 64
NE29: N Shi 7G 49
SR8: Eas 7K 159
Hopper St. W. NE29: N Shi 7F 49
Hopper Ter. DH6: Shot C 6E 170
Horatio Ho. NE30: N Shi 5K 49
Horatio St. NE1: Newc T 1J 83 (6L 5)
SR6: Monk 6G 105
HORDEN 5E 172
Hornbeam DH4: Hou S 4K 129
Hornbeam Pl. NE4: Newc T 3D 82 (9A 4)
Horncliffe Gdns. NE16: Swa 6J 81
Horncliffe Pl. NE15: Thro 3F 59
Horncliffe Wlk. NE15: Lem 6A 60
Horning Ct. NE5: Newc T 1H 61
Hornsea Cl. NE13: Wide O 6D 34
Hornsey Cres. DH5: Eas L 2H 157
Hornsey Ter. DH5: Eas L 2H 157
Horse Crofts NE21: Bla T 3C 80
Horsegate Bank NE17: C'wl 3B 94
NE40: C'wl, G'sde 3B 94
Horsham Gdns. SR3: Sund 5C 118
Horsham Gro. NE29: N Shi 1E 66
Horsham Ho. NE29: N Shi 1E 66
HORSLEY 5E 56
Horsley Av. NE27: Shir 2K 47
NE40: Ryton 3C 78
Horsley Bldgs. NE61: Mor 7G 9
Horsley Cl. NE62: Chop 7H 11
Horsley Ct. NE3: Ken 6A 44
Horsley Gdns. NE11: Dun 6C 82
NE25: H'wll 1K 37
SR3: Sund 5C 118
HORSLEY HILL 5C 68
Horsley Hill Rd. NE33: S Shi 4A 68
Horsley Hill Sq. NE34: S Shi 6D 68
(not continuous)
Horsley Ho. NE3: Gos 6E 44
Horsley Rd. NE7: Newc T 4K 63
NE38: Wash 2A 116
NE42: O'ham 1C 76
Horsley Ter. NE6: Walk 1D 84
NE30: N Shi 5K 49

Horsley Va. NE34: S Shi 6B 68
Horsley Vw. NE42: Pru 3H 77
Horsley Wood Cotts. NE15: O'ham 6F 57
Horton Av. NE22: Bed 1H 21
NE27: Shir 2K 47
NE34: S Shi 3K 87
Horton Cres. DH6: Bow 3H 177
NE13: Din 4H 33
Hortondale Gro. NE24: Cow 2F 23
Horton Dr. NE23: Cra 1J 25
Horton Mnr. NE24: Cow 2B 22
Horton Pl. NE24: News 5F 23
Horton Rd. NE22: Bed, Cow 2K 21
NE24: Cow 2K 21
Horton St. NE24: Bly 2K 23
Horwood Av. NE5: Newc T 3E 60
Hospital Dr. NE31: Heb 2H 85
Hospital La. NE15: Lem, Thro 6A 60
Hospital of St Mary the Virgin, The
NE4: Newc T 2D 82 (8B 4)
Hospital Rd. DH7: Lang P 5H 151
Hotch Pudding Pl. NE5: Newc T 5F 61
Hotspur Av. NE22: Bed 1H 21
NE25: Whit B 7G 39
NE34: S Shi 6A 68
Hotspur Rd. NE28: W'snd 7E 46
Hotspur St. NE6: Newc T 6J 63 (2L 5)
NE30: N Shi 4K 49
Hotspur Way NE1: Newc T 7F 63 (4E 4)
HOUGHALL 7B 166
HOUGHTON 3B 58
Houghton Av. NE5: Newc T 2A 62
NE30: N Shi 1H 49
Houghton Cut DH5: Hou S 1E 144
Houghton Ent. Cen. DH5: Hou S 2E 144
Houghton Ga. DH3: Gt Lum 6F 129
HOUGHTON-LE-SPRING 1D 144
Houghton Rd. DH4: Hou S 6D 130
DH5: Hett H 4F 145
Houghton Rd. W. DH5: Hett H 6G 145
Houghtonside DH4: Hou S 1E 144
Houghton Sports Complex 1D 144
Houghton St. SR4: Sund 2C 118
Houghwell Gdns. DH9: Stly, Tan L 1D 124
Houlet Gth. NE6: Newc T 1A 84 (6P 5)
Houlskye Cl. SR3: New S 2E 132
Hoults Estates NE6: Newc T 1K 83 (6P 5)
Houndelee Pl. NE5: Newc T 4J 61
Houndslow Dr. NE63: Ash 5K 11
Hounslow Gdns. NE32: Jar 4D 86
Housesteads Gdns. NE12: Longb 6H 45
House Ter. NE37: Usw 7H 101
Housing La. DH8: M'sly 7A 108
DH9: M'sly 7A 108
Houston Ct. NE4: Newc T 2D 82 (7B 4)
Houston St. NE4: Newc T 2D 82 (7B 4)
Houxty Rd. NE25: Well 6B 38
Hovingham Cl. SR8: Pet 7C 172
Hovingham Gdns. SR3: Sund 5C 118
Howard Cl. NE27: Longb 3G 47
Howard Ct. NE30: N Shi 7H 49
Howard Gro. NE61: Peg 4A 10
Howardian Cl. NE38: Wash 5F 115
Howard Pl. NE3: Gos 7E 44
Howard Rd. NE61: Mor 6G 9
Howard St. NE1: Newc T 1H 83 (5K 5)
NE8: Gate 5K 83
NE10: Gate 1A 100
NE30: N Shi 7H 49
NE32: Jar 7C 66
SR5: S'wck 6F 105
Howard Ter. NE39: H Spen 3D 94
NE61: Mor 6F 9
Howarth St. SR4: Sund 2C 118
Howarth Ter. DH6: Has 1B 170
Howat Av. NE5: Newc T 4A 62
Howburn Cres. NE61: Peg 4A 10
Howden DH8: Con 6F 121
Howden Bank DH7: Lan 4K 137
Howden Bank Cotts. DH7: Lan 3A 138
Howden Cl. NE45: Cor 1F 73
Howdene Rd. NE15: Newc T 7F 61
Howden Gdns. TS28: Win 5G 181
Howden Grn. Ind. Est. NE28: W'snd 3B 66
Howden Rd. NE28: W'snd 4C 66
HOWDON 1A 66
Howdon La. NE28: W'snd 2A 66
HOWDON PANS 4C 66
Howdon Rd. NE28: W'snd 3C 66
NE29: N Shi 2F 67
Howdon Station (Metro) 3A 66
Howe Sq. SR4: Sund 3J 117
Howe St. NE8: Gate 5K 83
NE31: Heb 7A 66
Howford La. NE46: Acomb 4A 50
Howick Av. NE3: Ken 5C 44
Howick Pk. SR6: Monk 7F 105 (1K 7)
Howick Rd. SR6: Monk 7F 105 (1K 7)
Howlcroft Vs. DH1: Dur 4J 165
Howletch La. SR8: Pet 6A 172
Howlett Hall Rd. NE15: Newc T 6F 61
Howley Av. SR5: C'twn 5J 103
Hownam Cl. NE3: Gos 1C 62
Hownsgill Dr. DH8: Con 3K 135
Hownsgill Ind. Est. DH8: Con 2H 135
Hoy Cres. SR7: S'hm 1H 147
Hoylake Av. NE7: Newc T 7A 46
Hoyle Av. NE4: Newc T 7A 62
Hoyle Fold SR3: New S 5C 132
Hoyson Vs. NE10: Gate 4F 85
Hubert St. NE35: Bol C 6F 87
Hucklow Gdns. NE34: S Shi 1K 87
Huddart Ter. DH3: Bir 3A 114
Huddlestone Ri. SR6: Monk 7G 105
Huddleston Rd. NE6: Walk 6B 64
Hudleston NE30: N Shi 7J 39
Hudshaw NE46: Hex 2F 71
Hudshaw Gdns. NE46: Hex 2F 71
Hudson Av. NE22: Bed 7K 17
NE23: Dud 3K 35
SR8: Pet 5D 172
Hudson Pl. NE61: Mor 6F 9
Hudson Rd. SR1: Sund 2G 119
Hudson St. NE8: Gate 3G 83 (9H 5)
NE30: N Shi 6H 49
NE34: S Shi 7H 67
(not continuous)
Hudspeth Cres. DH1: Dur 4J 153
Hugar Rd. NE39: H Spen 4D 94
Hugh Av. NE27: Shir 7K 37
Hugh Gdns. NE4: Newc T 2A 82
Hugh St. NE28: W'snd 4F 65
NE38: Wash 4K 115
SR6: Monk 3G 105
Hull St. NE4: Newc T 1B 82
Hulme Ct. SR8: Pet 7A 172
Hulne Av. NE30: N Shi 5K 49
Hulne Ter. NE15: Lem 7C 60
Humber Ct. SR3: New S 3B 132
Humber Gdns. NE8: Gate 5K 83
Humber Hill DH9: Stly 4G 125
Humberhill Dr. DH7: Lan 7J 137
Humberhill La. DH7: Lan 5C 136
Humber St. NE17: C'wl 6A 94
Humbert St. NE32: Jar 7B 66
Humbleburn La. DH7: Edm 1A 140
Humbledon Pk. SR3: Sund 5C 118
Humbledon Vw. SR2: Sund 4E 118 (7H 7)
Hume St. NE6: Newc T 1J 83 (5M 5)
SR4: Sund 2C 118
Humford Grn. NE24: Cow 2D 22
Humford Way NE22: Bed 2J 21
Humsford Gro. NE23: Cra 2A 26
Humshaugh Cl. NE12: Longb 4E 46
Humshaugh Rd. NE29: N Shi 6C 48
Hunns Bldgs. NE62: Sco G 3G 17
Hunstanton Ct. NE9: Gate 4G 99
Huntcliffe Av. SR6: Monk 1G 105
Huntcliffe Gdns. NE6: Newc T 4A 64
Hunter Av. DH7: Ush M 2B 164
NE24: Bly 3K 23
Hunter Cl. NE36: E Bol 1K 103
Hunter Ho. NE6: Walk 2E 84
Hunter Pl. SR8: Eas 7B 160
Hunter Rd. SR8: Pet 7J 171
Hunters Cl. DH8: M'sly 7A 108
Hunters Ct. NE3: Gos 7G 45
NE28: W'snd 3G 65
Hunters Hall Rd. SR4: Sund 3D 118
Hunters Lodge NE28: W'snd 3G 65
Hunters Moor Cl. NE2: Newc T 6D 62 (1A 4)
Hunters Pl. NE2: Newc T 5D 62 (1A 4)
Hunters Rd. NE2: Newc T 6C 62 (1A 4)
NE3: Gos 7H 45
Hunter's Ter. *NE9: Spri* *6D 100*
(off Peareth Hall Rd.)
NE33: S Shi 4K 67
Hunter St. DH4: Hou S 4A 130
NE33: S Shi 4K 67
Hunter Ter. SR2: Sund 4G 119
Huntingdon Cl. NE3: Ken 4J 43
Huntingdon Dr. NE23: Cra 3A 26
Huntingdon Gdns. SR3: Sund 5C 118
Huntingdon Pl. NE30: N Shi 5K 49
Huntingdon Rd. SR8: Pet 4A 172
Huntingdonshire Dr. DH1: Carr 1H 167
Hunt Lea NE16: Whi 2E 96
Huntley Av. SR7: Mur 7D 146
Huntley Cres. NE21: Bla T 6A 80
Huntley Sq. SR4: Sund 3K 117
Huntley Ter. SR2: Ryh 3H 133
Huntly Rd. NE25: Whit B 4C 38
Huntscliffe Ho. NE34: S Shi 3J 87
Hurbuck Cotts. DH7: Lan 4C 136
Hurst Ter. NE6: Walk 7C 64
Hurstwood Rd. SR4: Sund 4C 118
Hurworth Av. NE34: S Shi 7C 68
Hurworth Pl. NE32: Jar 7B 66
Hustledown Gdns. DH9: Stly 5F 125
Hustledown Ho. DH9: Stly 3F 125
Hustledown Rd. DH9: Stly 5E 124
Hutchinson Av. DH8: Con 6H 121
Hutton Cl. DH3: Ches S 1C 142
DH4: Hou S 2C 144
NE38: Wash 3D 114
HUTTON HENRY 7B 182
Hutton Ho. NE29: N Shi 2E 66
Hutton St. NE3: Gos 7C 44
NE35: Bol C 5F 87
SR4: Sund 3D 118
Hutton Ter. NE2: Newc T 6H 63 (1J 5)
NE9: Gate 3H 99
Huxley Cl. NE34: S Shi 4H 87
Huxley Cres. NE8: Gate 7G 83
Hyacinth Ct. SR4: Sund 1D 118
Hybrid Cl. DH4: Hou S 4K 129
Hydenside DH8: C'sde 2E 134
Hyde Pk. NE28: W'snd 2D 64
Hyde Pk. St. NE8: Gate 6F 83
Hyde St. NE33: S Shi 3K 67
SR2: Sund 4H 119
Hyde Ter. NE3: Gos 7F 45
Hylton Av. NE34: S Shi 7D 68
Hylton Bank SR4: Sund 2H 117
HYLTON CASTLE 5G 103
Hylton Castle (restored) 5H 103
Hylton Castle Rd. SR5: C'twn 6H 103
Hylton Cl. DH7: Lang P 5H 151
NE22: Bed 7F 17
Hylton Ct. NE38: Wash 3F 115
Hylton La. NE36: W Bol 1G 103
Hylton Pk. SR5: Sund 6A 104
Hylton Pk. Rd. SR5: Sund 6K 103
HYLTON RED HOUSE 5J 103
Hylton Riverside Retail Pk.
SR5: Sund 6K 103
Hylton Rd. DH1: Dur 5A 154
NE32: Jar 2B 86
SR4: Sund 4G 117 (3F 7)
Hylton St. DH4: Hou S 7D 130
NE8: Gate 5K 83
NE29: N Shi 1G 67
SR4: Sund 2C 118
Hylton Ter. DH2: Pelt 2G 127
NE10: Gate 4F 85
NE29: N Shi 7G 49
SR2: Ryh 3G 133
Hylton Wlk. SR4: Sund 3G 117
(not continuous)
Hymers Av. NE34: S Shi 2F 87
Hyperion Av. NE34: S Shi 1G 87
Hysehope Ter. *DH8: Con* *7J 121*
(off Sherburn Ter.)

I

Ilchester St. SR7: S'hm 4B 148
Ilderton Pl. NE5: Newc T 5E 60
Ilford Av. NE23: Cra 1J 25
Ilford Pl. NE8: Gate 6J 83
Ilford Rd. NE2: Gos 2F 63
NE28: W'snd 2K 65
Ilford Road Station (Metro) 2F 63
Ilfracombe Av. NE4: Newc T 1A 82
Ilfracombe Gdns. NE9: Gate 4H 99
NE26: Whit B 5F 39
Illingworth Ho. NE29: N Shi 2E 66
Ilminster Ct. NE3: Ken 6J 43
Imeary Gro. NE33: S Shi 4K 67
Imeary St. NE33: S Shi 4K 67
Imex Bus. Cen. DH3: Bir 4K 113
Imperial Bldgs. DH4: Hou S 2E 144
Inchberry Cl. NE4: Newc T 2A 82
Inchcape Ter. SR8: Eas 1D 172
Inchcliffe Cres. NE5: Newc T 3J 61
Independence Sq. NE38: Wash 3G 115
Industrial Rd. NE37: Usw 7J 101
NE37: Wash 1J 115
Industrial St. DH2: Pelt 3E 126
Industry Rd. NE6: Newc T 3B 64
Ingham Grange NE33: S Shi 4K 67
Ingham Gro. NE23: Cra 1J 25
Ingham Pl. NE2: Newc T 7H 63 (4K 5)
Ingham Ter. NE41: Wylam 7K 57
Ingleborough Cl. NE37: Wash 2E 114
Ingleby Ter. SR4: Sund 3C 118
Ingleby Way NE24: News 6G 23
Inglemere Pl. NE15: Newc T 7G 61
Ingleside NE16: Whi 1F 97
NE34: S Shi 7D 68
Ingleside Rd. NE29: N Shi 5F 49
Ingleton Ct. SR4: Sund 3D 118
Ingleton Dr. NE15: Thro 3F 59
Ingleton Gdns. NE24: News 6G 23
Inglewood Cl. NE24: Cow 2D 22
Inglewood Pl. NE3: Gos 3E 44
Ingoe Av. NE3: Ken 5B 44
Ingoe Cl. NE24: Bly 2G 23
Ingoe St. NE15: Lem 7C 60
Ingoldsby Ct. SR4: Sund 4A 118
Ingram Av. NE3: Ken 4B 44
Ingram Cl. DH2: Ches S 1J 141
NE28: W'snd 7K 47
Ingram Dr. NE5: Cha P 1D 60
NE24: Bly 2F 23
Ingram Ter. NE6: Walk 7E 64
Ingram Way TS28: Win 4G 181
Inkerman Rd. NE37: Usw 6H 101
Inkerman St. SR5: S'wck 6C 104
Inleborough Dr. NE40: Ryton 2H 79
Innesmoor NE31: Heb 6H 65
Inskip Ho. NE34: S Shi 1J 87
Inskip Ter. NE8: Gate 6H 83
Institute Rd. NE63: Ash 3K 11
Institute Ter. DH7: Ush M 1E 164
Institute Ter. E. DH2: Ous 1H 127
Institute Ter. W. DH2: Ous 1H 127
Interchange Cen. NE8: Gate 3G 83 (10H 5)
International Cen. for Life, The
. . . . 2E 82 (7D 4)
Inverness Rd. NE32: Jar 3E 86
Inverness St. SR6: Monk 5F 105
Invincible Dr. NE4: Newc T 3C 82 (10A 4)
Iolanthe Cres. NE6: Walk 6C 64
Iolanthe Ter. NE33: S Shi 3A 68
Iona Ct. NE28: W'snd 1K 65
Iona Pl. NE6: Walk 7E 64
Iona Rd. NE10: Gate 7K 83
NE32: Jar 3E 86
Irene Av. SR2: Sund 7H 119
Irene Ter. DH7: Lang P 5J 151
Iris Cl. NE21: Bla T 4A 80
Iris Cres. DH2: Ous 6H 113
Iris Pl. NE4: Newc T 6K 61
Iris Steadman Ho. NE4: Newc T 4A 4
Iris Ter. DH4: Hou S 6J 129
NE40: Ryton 3D 78
Ironside St. DH5: Hou S 1E 144
Irthing Av. NE6: Newc T 2B 84
Irton St. NE3: Gos 7E 44
Irvine Ho. NE12: Longb 4B 46
Irwin Av. NE28: W'snd 2G 65
Isabella Cl. NE4: Newc T 3A 82
Isabella Colliery Rd. NE24: Bly 3G 23
ISABELLA PIT 3G 23
Isabella Rd. NE24: Bly 3G 23
Isabella Wlk. NE15: Thro 4H 59
Isis Rd. SR8: Pet 7A 172
Islay Ho. SR3: New S 3C 132
Islestone NE9: Gate 3H 99
Ivanhoe NE25: Whit B 6E 38
Ivanhoe Cres. SR2: Sund 4D 118
Ivanhoe Ter. DH3: Ches S 7B 128
DH9: Dip 7J 109
Ivanhoe Vw. NE9: Gate 5K 99
Iveagh Cl. NE4: Newc T 2K 81
Ivesley Cotts. DH7: Wat 6A 162
Ivesley La. DH7: Lang P, Wat 4A 162
Iveson Rd. NE46: Hex 3A 70
Iveson Ter. DH7: Sac 7D 140
IVESTON 1D 136
Iveston La. DH8: Con 1D 136
Iveston Rd. DH8: Con 2K 135
(not continuous)
Iveston Ter. DH9: Stly 2F 125
Ivor St. SR2: Sund 6J 119
Ivy Av. NE40: Ryton 7G 59
NE64: Newb S 2G 13
SR7: S'hm 4K 147
(not continuous)
Ivy Cl. NE4: Newc T 3D 82 (9B 4)
NE40: Ryton 7G 59
Ivy La. NE9: Gate 4J 99
Ivymount Rd. NE6: Newc T 4K 63
Ivy Pl. DH9: Tan L 5C 110
Ivy Rd. NE3: Gos 7E 44
NE6: Walk 5D 64
NE12: Longb 4C 46
Ivy St. NE13: Sea B 3E 34
Ivy Ter. DH4: Hou S 3B 130
DH7: Lang P 5J 151
DH9: Stly 6H 125
(Middles, The)
DH9: Stly 5D 124
(South Moor)
NE40: Ryton 3C 78
Ivyway DH2: Pelt 2G 127

J

Jack Common Ho.
NE6: Newc T 6K 63 (1P 5)
Jack Crawford Ho. SR2: Sund 4H 119
Jack Lawson Ter. DH6: Whe H 3A 180
Jackson Av. NE20: Pon 4K 31
Jackson Rd. NE41: Wylam 7K 57
Jackson St. NE6: Walk 7D 64
NE8: Gate 3H 83 (10J 5)
NE30: N Shi 6H 49
SR4: Sund 3C 118
Jackson St. W. NE30: N Shi 6H 49
Jackson Ter. NE61: Mor 7G 9
Jack's Ter. NE34: S Shi 1J 87
Jacobins Chare NE1: Newc T 1E 82 (5D 4)
Jacques St. SR4: Sund 1B 118
Jacques Ter. DH2: Ches S 5K 127
Jade Cl. NE15: Lem 5C 60
James Armitage St. SR5: S'wck 5D 104
James Av. NE27: Shir 1K 47
James Bowman Ho. NE12: Kil 1C 46
James Clydesdale Ho. NE15: Newc T 6G 61
James Mather St. NE33: S Shi 2K 67
Jameson Dr. NE45: Cor 6F 53
Jameson St. DH8: Con 6H 121
James Pl. St. NE6: Newc T 7J 63 (4M 5)
James St. DH9: Ann P 5A 124
DH9: Dip 2F 123

James St.—Kent Wlk.

James St. DH9: Stly 7F **111**
NE4: Newc T 2B **82**
NE5: Newc T 3F **61**
NE16: Whi 7G **81**
SR5: S'wck 5C **104**
SR7: S'hm 4B **148**
SR8: Eas 6B **160**
James St. Nth. *SR7: Mur* *7F 147*
(off Nth. Coronation St.)
James St. Sth. SR7: Mur 7F **147**
James Ter. DH4: Hou S 2A **144**
DH5: Eas L 3H **157**
NE28: W'snd 4F **65**
James Williams St. SR1: Sund 1G **119**
Jamieson Ter. DH6: S Het 5D **158**
Jane Eyre Ter. NE8: Gate 5K **83**
Jane St. DH5: Hett H 4G **145**
DH9: Stly 5D **124**
NE6: Newc T 7A **64**
Jane Ter. NE6: Walk 1E **84**
Janet Sq. NE6: Newc T 1A **84**
Janet St. NE6: Newc T 1A **84** (6P **5**)
(Bolam Way)
NE6: Newc T 2A **84**
(St Peter's Rd., not continuous)
Janus Cl. NE5: Cha P 1C **60**
JARROW 6B **66**
Jarrow Riverside Pk. NE32: Jar 5C **66**
Jarrow Rd. NE34: Jar, S Shi 7F **67**
Jarrow Station (Metro) 6B **66**
Jarvis Rd. SR8: Pet 4B **172**
Jasmin Av. NE5: Cha P 1C **60**
Jasmine Cl. NE6: Walk 4C **64**
Jasmine Ct. NE63: Ash 6A **12**
SR4: Sund 1D **118** (3F **7**)
Jasmine Cres. SR7: S'hm 5A **148**
Jasmine Ter. DH3: Bir 4B **114**
Jasmine Vs. *NE16: Whi* *7G 81*
(off Front St.)
Jasper Av. NE40: G'sde 5F **79**
SR7: S'hm 4K **147**
(not continuous)
Jaycroft Ct. *NE30: N Shi* *7H 49*
(off Stephenson St.)
Jedburgh Cl. NE5: Cha P 1C **60**
NE8: Gate 5H **83**
NE29: N Shi 4E **48**
SR7: Mur 1C **158**
Jedburgh Ct. NE11: Gate 5G **99**
Jedburgh Gdns. NE15: Newc T 7H **61**
Jedburgh Rd. DH4: Hou S 3B **130**
NE2: Newc T 4A **62** (1C **4**)
NE4: Newc T 4A **62**
NE5: Newc T 4A **62**
Jedmoor NE31: Heb 6H **65**
Jefferson Cl. SR5: Monk 3E **104**
Jefferson Pl. NE4: Newc T 7D **62** (3B **4**)
Jellicoe Rd. NE6: Walk 3C **84**
Jellico Ter. DH4: Leam 7H **143**
Jenifer Gro. NE7: Newc T 2J **63**
Jenison Av. NE15: Newc T 1J **81**
Jennifer Av. SR5: C'twn 6H **103**
Jervis St. NE31: Heb 7K **65**
JESMOND 5G **63**
Jesmond Dene Rd.
NE2: Gos, Newc T 3F **63**
Jesmond Dene Ter. NE2: Newc T 4J **63**
Jesmond Gdns. NE2: Newc T 4H **63**
NE34: S Shi 3J **87**
Jesmond Pk. Ct. NE7: Newc T 4K **63**
Jesmond Pk. E. NE7: Newc T 3K **63**
Jesmond Pk. M. NE7: Newc T 4J **63**
Jesmond Pk. W. NE7: Newc T 3J **63**
Jesmond Pl. NE2: Newc T 4G **63**
Jesmond Rd. NE2: Newc T 6G **63** (1H **5**)
Jesmond Rd. W. NE2: Newc T 6F **63** (2F **4**)
Jesmond Station (Metro) 6G **63** (1H **5**)
Jesmond Swimming Pool 3G **63**
Jesmond Ter. NE26: Whit B 7H **39**
JESMOND VALE 6J **63**
Jesmond Va. NE2: Newc T 6J **63** (1L **5**)
(not continuous)
Jesmond Va. La.
NE6: Newc T 5K **63** (1N **5**)
Jesmond Va. Ter. NE6: Newc T 5K **63**
(not continuous)
Jessel St. NE9: Gate 3H **99**
Jetty, The NE10: Gate 4E **84**
Joan Av. SR2: Sund 7H **119**
Joannah St. SR5: Monk 4E **104**
Joan St. NE4: Newc T 2K **81**
(not continuous)
Jobling Av. NE21: Bla T 4A **80**
Jobling Cres. NE61: Mor 1H **15**
Joel Ter. NE10: Gate 4F **85**
John Av. NE40: G'sde 5F **79**
John Brown Ct. NE22: Bed 7H **17**
John Candlish Rd. SR4: Sund 1C **118**
John Clay St. NE33: S Shi 5K **67**
(Dean Rd.)
NE33: S Shi 4K **67**
(Victoria Rd.)
John Dobson St. NE1: Newc T 7F **63** (3F **4**)
John F Kennedy Est. NE38: Wash 3J **115**
(not continuous)
John George Joicey Mus. 1G **83** (6G **4**)
John Reid Rd. NE34: S Shi 2E **86**
(not continuous)
Johnson Cl. SR8: Pet 4B **172**
Johnson Est. DH6: Whe H 3B **180**
Johnson's Bldgs. DH8: Con 1C **136**
Johnson's St. TS28: Win 7G **181**
Johnson St. NE8: Gate 5D **82**
NE11: Dun 5B **82**
NE15: Lem 7C **60**
NE33: S Shi 6J **67**
SR1: Sund 1D **118** (3F **7**)
Johnson Ter. DH6: Crox 6K **175**
DH9: Ann P 6A **124**
NE37: Usw 7K **101**
NE39: H Spen 3D **94**
Johnson Vs. NE62: Chop 1D **16**
Johnston Av. NE31: Heb 3H **85**
John St. DH1: Dur 3K **165** (3A **6**)
DH4: Hou S 2A **144**
DH5: Hett H 6G **145**
DH5: Hou S 2F **145**
DH7: Sac 7E **140**
DH8: Con 7H **121**
DH8: Shot B 5F **121**
DH9: Beam 2K **125**
DH9: Stly 7J **125**
(Craghead)
DH9: Stly 5D **124**
(South Moor)
NE3: Gos 7G **45**
(Bowes St.)
NE3: Gos 7C **44**
(Kenton Rd.)
NE8: Gate 5K **83**
NE10: Gate 5D **84**
NE24: Cow 1F **23**
NE25: Well 6A **38**
NE28: W'snd 3F **65**
NE30: N Shi 7J **39**
NE35: Bol C 6F **87**
NE42: Pru 3G **77**
NE61: Peg 4B **10**
NE63: Ash 3A **12**
SR1: Sund 1F **119** (3K **7**)
SR2: Ryh 3J **133**
SR4: Sund 1G **117**
SR8: Eas 6C **160**
John St. Nth. DH7: B'don 1F **175**
John St. Sth. DH7: B'don 1F **175**
John St. Sq. DH8: Con 6H **121**
John Taylor Ct. SR5: S'wck 4C **104**
John Wesley Ct. NE42: Pru 4F **77**
John Williamson St.
NE33: S Shi 6H **67**
John Wilson Ct. SR8: Pet 5E **172**
Joicey Gdns. DH9: Stly 2F **125**
Joicey Pl. NE9: Gate 1J **99**
Joicey Rd. NE9: Gate 1H **99**
Joicey St. NE10: Gate 5E **84**
Joicey Ter. DH9: Tan L 1D **124**
Jolliffe St. DH3: Ches S 1B **142**
Jonadab Rd. NE10: Gate 4E **84**
Jonadab St. NE10: Gate 5E **84**
Jones Ct. DH6: Bow 4H **177**
Jones St. DH3: Bir 4A **114**
Jonquil Cl. NE5: Cha P 1C **60**
Joseph Cl. NE4: Newc T 2A **82**
Joseph Hopper Aged Miners Homes
DH3: Bir 1A **114**
Joseph Hopper Memorial Homes 1K **99**
Joseph St. DH9: Stly 4E **124**
Joseph Ter. NE17: C'wl 6K **93**
Jowett Sq. SR5: S'wck 5C **104**
Joyce Cl. NE10: Gate 6H **85**
Joyce Gro. SR8: Pet 2J **181**
Joyce Ter. DH7: Ush M 2K **163**
SR5: C'twn 6H **103**
Jubilee Av. NE9: Spri 6A **100**
SR7: Mur 4H **147**
Jubilee Bldgs. *NE46: Hex* *2D 70*
(off Cattle Mkt.)
Jubilee Cen. SR7: S'hm 3B **148**
Jubilee Cl. DH7: Edm 3D **140**
DH7: New B 5B **164**
Jubilee Cotts. DH4: Hou S 2D **144**
NE40: G'sde 7B **78**
Jubilee Ct. DH8: C'sde 3C **134**
NE8: Gate 6E **82**
NE23: Dud 2K **35**
NE24: Bly 3H **23**
NE31: Heb 7A **66**
Jubilee Cres. DH6: Sher 3D **168**
(not continuous)
NE3: Gos 7C **44**
Jubilee Est. NE63: Ash 6B **12**
Jubilee Ho. DH5: Eas L 2J **157**
Jubilee Ind. Est. NE63: Ash 5A **12**
Jubilee Lodge NE23: Cra 6K **25**
Jubilee M. NE3: Gos 7D **44**
Jubilee Pl. DH1: H Shin 6D **166**
DH6: Shot C 5E **170**
Jubilee Rd. NE1: Newc T 1H **83** (5J **5**)
NE3: Ken 6C **44**
NE24: Bly 3J **23**
Jubilee Sq. DH5: Eas L 3J **157**
DH6: S Het 4B **158**
NE38: Wash 3G **115**
Jubilee St. NE28: W'snd 3F **65**
Jubilee Ter. DH9: Ann P 5B **124**
DH9: Tan L 6A **110**
NE6: Newc T 7B **64**
(not continuous)
NE13: Sea B 3D **34**
NE16: Swa 5G **81**
NE22: Bed 6B **18**
NE38: Wash 6A **116**
NE40: Ryton *3C 78*
(off Greenside Rd.)
NE64: Newb S 3J **13**
Jude Pl. SR8: Pet 4A **172**
Jude St. SR8: Eas 7A **160**
Judson Rd. SR8: Pet 5H **171**
Julian Av. NE6: Walk 6C **64**
NE33: S Shi 1K **67**
Julian Rd. NE10: Gate 6H **85**
Julian St. NE33: S Shi 1K **67**
Juliet Av. NE29: N Shi 6D **48**
Juliet St. NE63: Hir 3C **12**
Julius Caesar St. SR5: S'wck 5C **104**
June Av. NE21: Bla T 1C **96**
Juniper Cl. NE3: Gos 3E **44**
NE24: News 5G **23**
SR2: Sund 4G **119**
Juniper Ct. NE21: Bla T 3C **80**
Juniper Wlk. NE5: Cha P 1D **60**
Jupiter Ct. SR8: Eas 7A **160**
Jupiter Health & Fitness Cen. 7K **159**
Jutland Av. NE31: Heb 7J **65**
Jutland Ter. DH9: Tan L 1D **124**

K

Kane Gdns. NE10: Gate 1A **100**
Karting North East (Go-Kart Track) 7A **132**
Kascada Bowl 2A **166** (1C **6**)
Kateregina DH3: Bir 4B **114**
Katherine St. NE63: Hir 3C **12**
Katrine Cl. DH2: Ches S 7K **127**
Katrine Ct. SR3: New S 4C **132**
Kayll Rd. SR4: Sund 2B **118**
KAYSBURN 3A **152**
Kay's Cotts. NE10: Gate 7A **84**
Kay St. DH9: Stly 2F **125**
Kearsley Cl. NE25: Sea D 7H **27**
Kearton Av. NE5: Cha P 2C **60**
Keating Cl. TS27: B Col 2H **183**
Keats Av. NE24: Bly 4G **23**
NE35: Bol C 6H **87**
SR5: S'wck 5C **104**
Keats Cl. DH9: Stly 3G **125**
Keats Gro. NE63: Hir 4D **12**
Keats Rd. NE15: Lem 7A **60**
Keats Wlk. NE8: Gate 4J **83**
NE34: S Shi 3G **87**
Keeble Ct. NE63: N Sea 4F **13**
Keebledale Av. NE6: Walk 6D **64**
Keele Dr. NE23: Cra 4F **25**
Keelman's Ho. *NE24: Bly* *1J 23*
(off Summers St.)
Keelmans La. SR4: Sund 1J **117**
Keelman Sq. NE1: Newc T 6J **5**
Keelman's Rd. SR4: Sund 1H **117**
Keelmans Ter. NE24: Bly 1J **23**
Keelman's Way NE8: Gate 4E **82**
Keelmen's Hospital
NE1: Newc T 1H **83** (6J **5**)
Keel Row NE11: Swa 3H **81**
NE24: Bly 1J **23**
Keighley Av. SR5: C'twn 3H **103**
Keighley Sq. SR5: C'twn 3G **103**
Keir Hardie Av. DH9: Stly 4F **125**
NE10: Gate 6E **84**
Keir Hardie Ct. NE64: Newb S 2J **13**
Keir Hardie St. DH4: Hou S 2B **144**
NE39: Row G 5F **95**
Keir Hardie Ter. DH3: Bir 2K **113**
Keith Cl. NE4: Newc T 2A **82**
Keith Sq. SR5: C'twn 3H **103**
Keldane Gdns. NE4: Newc T 1A **82**
Kelfield Gro. NE23: Cra 7K **21**
Kelham Sq. SR5: C'twn 3G **103**
Kell Cres. DH6: Sher 3C **168**
Kellfield Av. NE9: Gate 1J **99**
Kellfield Rd. NE9: Gate 2J **99**
KELLOE 7D **178**
Kell Rd. SR8: Pet 6D **172**
Kells Bldgs. DH1: Dur 4H **165**
Kells Gdns. NE9: Gate 2J **99**
Kells La. NE9: Gate 3H **99**
Kell's Way NE39: Row G 6J **95**
Kellsway NE10: Gate 2D **100**
Kellsway Ct. NE10: Gate 2D **100**
Kelly Cl. DH8: Con 5F **121**
Kelly Rd. NE31: Heb 3J **85**
Kelpie Gdns. SR6: Monk 6G **105**
Kelsey Way NE23: Cra 7K **21**
Kelso Cl. NE5: Cha P 1C **60**
Kelso Dr. NE29: N Shi 4E **48**
Kelso Gdns. NE15: Newc T 7H **61**
NE22: Bed 7A **18**
NE28: W'snd 1A **66**
Kelso Gro. DH4: Hou S 3A **130**
Kelson Way NE5: Cha P 1C **60**
Kelso Pl. NE8: Gate 5D **82**
Kelston Way NE5: Newc T 3J **61**
Kelvin Gdns. *DH8: Con* *7H 121*
(off Palmerston St.)
NE11: Dun 5B **82**
Kelvin Gro. NE2: Newc T 6H **63** (1K **5**)
NE8: Gate 6F **83**
NE29: N Shi 4G **49**
NE33: S Shi 4B **68**
SR6: Cle 5A **88**
SR6: Monk 5G **105**
Kelvin Pl. NE12: Longb 3E **46**
Kemble Cl. NE23: Cra 7K **21**
Kemble Sq. SR5: C'twn 3H **103**
Kemp Rd. SR8: Pet 5A **172**
Kempton Cl. DH8: Shot B 2F **121**
Kempton Gdns. NE8: Gate 7E **82**
Kenber Dr. TS27: B Col 2H **183**
Kendal DH3: Bir 6C **114**
(not continuous)
Kendal Av. NE24: Bly 3H **23**
NE30: N Shi 2H **49**
Kendal Cl. SR8: Pet 2J **181**
Kendal Cres. NE9: Gate 3K **99**
Kendal Dr. NE23: Cra 2A **26**
NE36: E Bol 7J **87**
Kendale Wlk. NE5: Newc T 2E **60**
Kendal Gdns. NE28: W'snd 7A **48**
Kendal Grn. *NE6: Newc T* *5P 5*
(off Kendal St.)
Kendal Ho. NE6: Newc T 4P **5**
Kendal Pl. NE6: Newc T 1K **83** (4P **5**)
Kendal St. NE6: Newc T 1K **83** (5P **5**)
Kendor Gro. NE61: Mor 2F **15**
Kenilworth DH3: Gt Lum 2E **142**
NE12: Kil 7B **36**
Kenilworth Ct. NE4: Newc T 2C **82**
NE37: Usw 7K **101**
Kenilworth Rd. NE4: Newc T 2C **82**
NE25: Whit B 6F **39**
NE63: Ash 3A **12**
Kenilworth Sq. SR5: C'twn 3J **103**
Kenilworth Vw. NE9: Gate 5J **99**
Kenley Rd. NE5: Newc T 5G **61**
SR5: C'twn 3H **103**
Kenmoor Way NE5: Cha P 2C **60**
Kenmore Cl. NE10: Gate 6F **85**
Kenmore Cres. NE40: G'sde 4F **79**
Kennersdene NE30: N Shi 3J **49**
Kennet Av. NE32: Jar 3C **86**
Kennet Sq. SR5: C'twn 3H **103**
Kennford NE9: Gate 5J **99**
Kennington Gro. NE6: Walk 1C **84**
Kenny Pl. DH1: Dur 1D **166**
Kensington Av. NE3: Gos 5E **44**
Kensington Cl. NE25: Whit B 6F **39**
Kensington Cotts. NE61: Mor 7H **9**
Kensington Ct. NE10: Gate 6A **84**
NE31: Heb 1H **85**
NE33: S Shi 5A **68**
Kensington Gdns. NE25: Whit B 6F **39**
NE28: W'snd 2C **64**
NE30: N Shi 6H **49**
Kensington Gro. NE30: N Shi 5H **49**
Kensington Ter. NE2: Newc T 6F **63** (1F **4**)
NE11: Dun 6B **82**
Kensington Vs. NE5: Newc T 2E **60**
Kent Av. NE11: Dun 6C **82**
NE28: W'snd 3K **65**
NE31: Heb 1H **85**
Kentchester Rd. SR5: C'twn 3J **103**
Kent Cl. NE63: Ash 3J **11**
Kent Ct. NE3: Ken 4K **43**
Kent Gdns. DH5: Hett H 6F **145**
Kentmere DH3: Bir 7B **114**
Kentmere Av. NE6: Walk 7D **64**
SR6: Monk 2E **104**
Kentmere Cl. NE23: Seg 1E **36**
Kentmere Ho. DH4: Hou S 7C **130**
Kentmere Pl. SR8: Pet 6C **172**
KENTON 1A **62**
Kenton Av. NE3: Ken 2C **62**
KENTON BANKFOOT 6H **43**
KENTON BAR 1K **61**
Kenton Ct. NE33: S Shi 4K **67**
Kenton Cres. DH6: Thor 2J **179**
NE3: Ken 1B **62**
Kenton Gro. SR6: Monk 6F **105**
Kenton La. NE3: Ken, Newc T 1K **61**
Kenton Pk. Shop. Cen.
NE3: Ken 2C **62**
Kenton Rd. NE3: Gos, Ken 7C **44**
NE29: N Shi 5C **48**
Kent Pl. NE34: S Shi 7C **68**
Kent Rd. DH8: C'sde 2D **134**
Kent St. NE32: Jar 7A **66**
Kent Ter. DH6: Has 3A **170**
Kentucky Rd. SR5: C'twn 3G **103**
Kent Vs. NE32: Jar 7A **66**
Kent Wlk. SR8: Pet 4A **172**

Kyo Bog La.—Lawn Ct.

Kyo Bog La. NE41: Wylam 6J 77
NE42: Pru 6J 77
Kyo Cl. NE41: Wylam 5K 77
Kyo Heugh Rd. DH9: Ann P, Tan L 3A 124
Kyo La. DH9: Tan L 3B 124
NE40: G'sde 7B 78
Kyo Rd. DH9: Ann P 4K 123

L

Laburnum Av. DH1: Dur 3K 165
DH8: Con 5G 121
NE6: Walk 5D 64
NE10: Gate 7E 84
NE24: Bly 1H 23
NE26: Whit B 6G 39
NE28: W'snd 3F 65
NE38: Wash 7F 115
Laburnum Cl. SR4: Sund 2G 117
Laburnum Ct. DH7: Sac 7D 140
DH7: Ush M 2D 164
NE12: Kil 7A 36
NE62: Chop 1G 17
(off Sheepwash Bank)
Laburnum Cres. NE11: Kib 2E 112
SR7: S'hm 6A 148
SR8: Eas 7A 160
Laburnum Gdns. NE9: Gate 1H 99
NE10: Gate 5B 84
NE32: Jar 2A 86
Laburnum Gro. NE16: Sun 4H 97
NE16: Whi 7G 81
NE31: Heb 3J 85
NE34: S Shi 1B 88
SR5: C'twn 7G 103
SR6: Cle 5C 88
Laburnum Ho. NE28: W'snd 4G 65
Laburnum Pk. DH7: B'don 2B 174
Laburnum Rd. NE21: Bla T 4C 80
SR6: Monk 4F 105
Laburnum Sq. TS29: Trim S 7D 180
Laburnum Ter. DH6: Shot C 6E 170
DH9: Ann P 4J 123
NE41: Wylam 7J 57
(off Main Rd.)
NE63: Hir 3B 12
Lacebark DH4: Hou S 3K 129
SR3: New S 5A 132
Ladock Cl. SR2: Ryh 1J 133
Lady Anne Rd. DH6: Sher 2K 167
Ladybank NE5: Cha P 2B 60
Lady Beatrice Ter. DH4: E Her 2E 130
Ladycutters La. NE45: Cor 3C 72
Lady Durham Cl. DH6: Sher 3J 167
Ladyhaugh Dr. NE16: Whi 3G 97
Lady in Leisure
Kingston Park 6J 43
Ladykirk Rd. NE4: Newc T 1A 82
Ladykirk Way NE23: Cra 4G 25
LADY PARK 5E 98
Ladyrigg NE20: Pon 7H 31
Ladysmith Ct. DH9: Stly 4G 125
(not continuous)
Ladysmith St. NE33: S Shi 3K 67
Ladysmith Ter. DH7: Ush M 2B 164
Lady's Piece La. DH6: H Pitt 5A 156
Lady St. DH5: Hett H 5G 145
Lady's Wlk. NE33: S Shi 1J 67
NE61: Mor 6E 8
(not continuous)
Ladywell NE43: Stoc 1K 91
Ladywell Rd. DH8: Con 2A 136
NE21: Bla T 4C 80
Ladywell Way NE20: Pon 4H 31
Ladywood Pk. DH4: Pen 1K 129
Laet St. NE29: N Shi 7H 49
Laider Cl. TS27: B Col 2H 183
Laindon Av. SR6: Monk 3F 105
Laing Art Gallery 7G 63 (4G 4)
Laing Gro. NE28: W'snd 2A 66
Laing Ho. NE37: Wash 4F 115
Laing Sq. TS28: Win 4F 181
Laing St. DH8: Con 5H 121
Laith Rd. NE3: Ken 7A 44
Lake App. NE21: Bla T 5E 80
Lake Av. NE34: S Shi 7E 68
Lake Bank Ter. TS28: Win 7G 181
Lake Ct. SR3: New S 3C 132
Lakeland Dr. SR8: Pet 5C 172
Lakemore SR8: Pet 7A 172
Lake Rd. DH5: Hou S 2E 144
Lakeside NE21: Bla T 5F 81
NE34: S Shi 7F 69
Lakeside Ct. NE11: Gate 2F 99
Lake Vw. NE31: Heb 2H 85
TS28: Win 7G 181
Laleham Ct. NE3: Ken 5K 43
Lamara Dr. SR5: Monk 4E 104
Lambden Cl. NE29: N Shi 2E 66
Lambert Rd. NE37: Wash 1D 114
Lambert Sq. NE3: Gos 7C 44
Lambeth Pl. NE8: Gate 6J 83
Lamb Farm Cl. NE12: Kil 3C 46
Lambley Av. NE30: N Shi 2H 49
Lambley Cl. NE16: Sun 5G 97
Lambley Cres. NE31: Heb 3H 85
Lambourn Av. NE29: N Shi 1D 66
Lambourne Av. NE12: Longb 5A 46
Lambourne Cl. DH4: Hou S 6J 129
Lambourne Rd. SR2: Sund 5E 118
Lambs Arms Bldgs. *NE40: Ryton 3C 78*
(off Greenside Rd.)
Lamb's Cl. TS27: Cas E 7C 182
Lamb's Pl. DH6: Bow 5H 177
Lamb St. NE6: Walk 1E 84
NE23: E Cram 5C 26
Lamb Ter. NE27: Shir 3H 47
LAMBTON 5F 115
Lambton Av. DH8: Con 2K 135
NE16: Whi 7J 81
Lambton Cen. NE38: Wash 5F 115
Lambton Cl. NE40: Ryton 3D 78
Lambton Ct. NE22: Bed 6A 18
NE38: Wash 1C 128
SR3: E Her 2J 131
SR8: Pet 2A 182
Lambton Dr. DH5: Hett H 1G 157
Lambton Gdns. NE16: Burn 3J 109
(not continuous)
Lambton La. DH4: Hou S 7K 129
Lambton Lea DH4: Hou S 5A 130
LAMBTON PARK 3F 129
Lambton Pl. DH4: Pen 1B 130
Lambton Rd. NE2: Newc T 5G 63 (1F 4)
NE31: Heb 6K 65
Lambton St. DH1: Dur 2K 165 (2A 6)
DH3: Ches S 7B 128
DH7: Lang P 4H 151
NE8: Gate 3G 83 (9J 5)
SR1: Sund 1F 119 (2K 7)
Lambton Ter. DH4: Pen 1K 129
DH9: Stly 6K 125
NE32: Jar 2B 86
Lambton Twr. *SR1: Sund 1G 119*
(off High St. E.)
Lambton Wlk. DH1: Dur 3B 6
LAMESLEY 7G 99
Lamesley Rd. DH3: Bir, Kib 6G 99
NE11: Kib 6G 99
Lamonby Way NE23: Cra 6J 25
Lampeter Cl. NE5: Newc T 2H 61
Lamplight Arts Cen. 3E 124
Lamport St. NE31: Heb 6G 65
Lanark Cl. NE29: N Shi 4C 48
Lanark Dr. NE32: Jar 3E 86
Lancashire Dr. DH1: Carr 1H 167
Lancaster Ct. NE3: Ken 5K 43
Lancaster Dr. NE28: W'snd 5H 47
Lancaster Hill SR8: Pet 4K 171
(not continuous)
Lancaster Ho. NE4: Newc T 3C 82 (10A 4)
NE23: Cra 5B 26
Lancaster Pl. NE11: Dun 5A 82
Lancaster Rd. DH8: C'sde 3C 134
NE11: Dun 5A 82
Lancaster St. NE4: Newc T 1D 82 (6B 4)
Lancaster Ter. DH3: Ches S 7B 128
NE61: Mor 6G 9
(off Bennett Wlk.)
Lancaster Way NE32: Jar 5A 86
(not continuous)
Lancastrian Rd. NE23: Cra 5J 25
Lancefield Av. NE6: Walk 2D 84
Lancet Ct. NE8: Gate 4H 83 (10K 5)
LANCHESTER 6K 137
Lanchester NE38: Wash 6J 115
Lanchester Av. NE9: Gate 4B 100
Lanchester Cl. NE10: Gate 1G 101
Lanchester Grn. NE22: Bed 6H 17
Lanchester Rd. DH1: Dur 4F 153
DH7: Lan 2A 138
DH9: Ann P, Lan 7A 124
Lancing Ct. NE3: Ken 5J 43
Land of Green Ginger
NE30: N Shi 5K 49
(off Front St.)
Landsale Cotts. NE40: G'sde 5E 78
Landscape Ter. NE40: G'sde 5F 79
Landsdowne Gdns. NE62: Chop 7J 11
Landseer Cl. DH9: Stly 3F 125
Landseer Gdns. NE9: Gate 6K 83
NE34: S Shi 4K 87
Landswood Ter. NE21: Bla T 7D 80
Lane Cnr. NE34: S Shi 1J 87
Lane Head NE40: Ryton 1G 79
Lanercost NE38: Wash 3H 115
Lanercost Av. NE21: Bla T 4B 80
Lanercost Dr. NE5: Newc T 5H 61
Lanercost Gdns. NE10: Gate 1A 100
NE15: Thro 3H 59
Lanercost Pk. NE23: E Cram 5B 26
Lanercost Rd. NE29: N Shi 7E 48
Lanesborough Ct. NE3: Gos 1C 62
Lane, The NE42: Pru 4F 77
Langdale DH3: Bir 7C 114
NE25: Whit B 6E 38
NE37: Wash 1G 115
Langdale Cl. DH8: Lead 5B 122
NE12: Longb 6J 45
Langdale Cres. DH1: Carr 6G 155
NE21: Bla T 6B 80
Langdale Dr. NE23: Cra 3G 25
Langdale Gdns. NE6: Walk 7E 64
NE28: W'snd 7A 48
Langdale Pl. SR8: Pet 6C 172
Langdale Rd. DH4: Pen 1A 130
NE9: Gate 2J 99
Langdale St. DH5: Hett H 1F 157
Langdale Ter. NE17: Ham C 3J 107
Langdale Way NE36: E Bol 6J 87
Langdon Cl. NE29: N Shi 3F 49
Langdon Gdns. DH9: Ann P 4J 123
Langdon Rd. NE5: Newc T 3D 60
Langeeford Pl. SR6: Monk 6G 105
Langford Dr. NE35: Bol C 4F 87
Langham Rd. NE15: Newc T 1F 81
Langholm Av. NE29: N Shi 4C 48
Langholm Ct. *NE36: E Bol 7A 88*
(off Station Rd.)
Langholm Rd. NE3: Gos 5E 44
NE36: E Bol 6K 87
Langhorn Cl. NE6: Newc T 6K 63 (2P 5)
Langhurst SR2: Ryh 1G 133
Langleeford Rd. NE5: Newc T 1G 61
Langley Av. DH7: B'hpe 5D 138
NE10: Gate 1F 101
NE24: Cow 1F 23
NE25: Whit B 1D 48
NE27: Shir 2A 48
NE46: Hex 2F 71
Langley Cl. DH7: Lan 3A 138
NE38: Wash 4F 115
Langley Cres. DH7: B'don 7F 165
Langley Gro. SR8: Pet 1J 181
Langley La. DH7: B'hpe, Lan, Wit G 6C 138
Langley Mere NE12: Longb 4B 46
LANGLEY MOOR 6G 165
Langley Moor Ind. Est. DH7: B'don 7G 165
(not continuous)
LANGLEY PARK 5J 151
Langley Pk. Ind. Est. DH7: Lang P 4J 151
Langley Pk. Nth. Ind. Est.
DH7: Lang P 3J 151
Langley Rd. DH1: Dur 5A 154
NE5: Newc T 5F 61
NE6: Walk 7D 64
NE29: N Shi 6C 48
NE63: Ash 4A 12
SR3: Sund 6D 118
Langley St. DH4: Hou S 3D 130
DH7: Lang P 4J 151
Langley Tarn NE29: N Shi 1G 67
Langley Ter. DH7: B'hpe 5D 138
DH9: Ann P 5A 124
NE32: Jar 3B 86
Langley Vw. DH9: Ann P 6C 124
Langport Rd. SR2: Sund 5F 119
Langthorne Av. SR8: Pet 6F 173
Langton Cl. SR4: Sund 2D 118
Langton Ct. NE20: Pon 7F 31
Langton Dr. NE23: Cra 7A 22
Langton Lea DH1: H Shin 7F 167
Langton St. NE8: Gate 4H 83
(not continuous)
Langton Ter. DH4: Hou S 7J 129
NE7: Newc T 3K 63
Langwell Cres. NE63: Ash 3A 12
Langwell Ter. NE61: Peg 3B 10
Lanivet Cl. SR2: Ryh 1H 133
Lannerwood *NE29: N Shi 1G 67*
(off Coach La.)
Lansbury Cl. DH3: Bir 2K 113
Lansbury Ct. NE12: Longb 7J 45
Lansbury Dr. DH3: Bir 2K 113
SR7: Mur 7E 146
Lansbury Gdns. NE10: Gate 6E 84
Lansbury Rd. NE16: Whi 1J 97
Lansbury Way SR5: C'twn 6H 103
Lansdowne SR2: Ryh 2G 133
Lansdowne Ct. NE3: Gos 7E 44
NE46: Hex 3B 70
Lansdowne Cres. DH6: Bow 5J 177
NE3: Gos 6E 44
Lansdowne Gdns. NE2: Newc T 5J 63
Lansdowne Pl. NE3: Gos 7E 44
Lansdowne Pl. W. NE3: Gos 7E 44
Lansdowne Rd. NE12: Longb 4B 46
Lansdowne St. SR4: Sund 1D 118
Lansdowne Ter. NE3: Gos 7E 44
NE29: N Shi 6F 49
Lansdowne Ter. E. NE3: Gos 7E 44
Lansdowne Ter. W. NE29: N Shi 6E 48
Lanthwaite Rd. NE9: Gate 2J 99
Lanton St. DH4: Hou S 3D 130
Lapford Dr. NE23: Cra 1A 26
Lapwing Cl. NE24: News 5J 23
NE38: Wash 5D 114
Lapwing Ct. NE16: Burn 3C 110
NE34: S Shi 1A 88
L'Arbre Cres. NE16: Whi 7F 81
Larch Av. DH4: Hou S 1C 144
NE34: S Shi 1C 88
SR6: Whit 5J 89
Larch Cl. NE9: Spri 5B 100
Larches Rd. DH1: Dur 1J 165
Larches, The DH7: Esh W 4D 162
NE4: Newc T 3C 82 (9A 4)
NE16: Burn 1B 110
Larch Gro. NE24: News 5G 23
Larchlea NE20: Pon 2G 41
Larchlea Sth. NE20: Pon 2G 41
Larch Rd. NE21: Bla T 3D 80
Larch St. DH8: Con 6H 121
NE16: Sun 5H 97
Larch Ter. DH7: Lang P 5J 151
DH9: Stly 6H 125
DH9: Tan L 7A 110
Larchwood NE38: Wash 7F 115
Larchwood Av. NE3: Ken 5B 44
(not continuous)
NE6: Walk 5C 64
NE13: Wide O 6E 34
Larchwood Dr. NE63: Ash 6A 12
Larchwood Gdns. NE11: Gate 2D 98
Larchwood Gro. SR2: Sund 6E 118
Larkfield Cres. DH4: Hou S 4A 130
Larkfield Rd. SR2: Sund 5E 118
Larkhill SR2: Ryh 2H 133
Larkrise Cl. NE7: Newc T 2B 64
Larkspur NE9: Gate 2A 100
Larkspur Cl. DH9: Tan L 1D 124
Larkspur Rd. NE16: Whi 7H 81
Larkspur Ter. NE2: Newc T 4G 63
Larkswood NE34: S Shi 6D 68
Larne Cres. NE9: Gate 2J 99
Larriston *NE42: Pru 5D 76*
(off Simonside)
Larriston Pl. NE23: Cra 4H 25
Lartington Cl. DH8: Con 2H 135
Lartington Ct. DH3: Gt Lum 4F 143
Lartington Gdns. NE3: Newc T 7H 45
Larwood Ct. DH3: Ches S 1C 142
DH9: Ann P 6J 123
Lascelles Av. NE34: S Shi 1A 88
Laski Gdns. NE10: Gate 6F 85
Lassells Rigg NE42: Pru 3F 77
Latimer St. NE30: N Shi 4K 49
Latrigg Ct. SR3: New S 3B 132
Latton Cl. NE23: Cra 6J 25
Laude Bank DH7: Esh W 7C 150
Lauderdale Av. NE28: W'snd 1F 65
Launceston Cl. NE3: Ken 4K 43
Launceston Ct. SR3: E Her 2K 131
Launceston Dr. SR3: E Her 2J 131
Laura St. SR1: Sund 2F 119 (4K 7)
SR7: S'hm 4B 148
Laurel Av. DH1: Dur 3E 166
NE3: Ken 6C 44
NE12: Kil 3E 46
SR7: S'hm 3K 147
Laurel Ct. DH2: Ches S 4K 127
NE30: N Shi 7H 49
Laurel Cres. DH2: Beam 2D 126
DH4: Hou S 7C 130
DH6: Thor 2J 179
NE6: Walk 4D 64
Laurel Dr. DH8: Lead 6B 122
NE63: Ash 6A 12
Laurel End NE12: Kil 3E 46
Laurel Gro. SR2: Sund 6E 118
Laurel Pl. NE12: Kil 3D 46
NE23: Cra 3K 25
Laurel Rd. NE21: Bla T 4D 80
Laurels, The *SR3: New S 1C 132*
(off Chelmsford St.)
Laurel St. NE15: Thro 2H 59
NE28: W'snd 4G 65
Laurel Ter. DH7: Lang P 5K 151
NE16: Burn 2K 109
NE25: H'wll 1J 37
Laurel Wlk. NE3: Gos 7E 44
Laurel Way NE40: Ryton 3E 78
Laurelwood Gdns. NE11: Gate 2D 98
Lauren Ct. SR8: Eas 7A 160
Laurens Ct. NE37: Usw 7H 101
Lavender Ct. NE63: Ash 6A 12
Lavender Gdns. DH7: Sac 7F 141
NE2: Newc T 4F 63
NE9: Gate 1H 99
Lavender Gro. SR5: C'twn 6G 103
Lavender La. NE34: S Shi 1H 87
Lavender Rd. NE16: Whi 1G 97
Lavender Row NE9: Gate 2K 99
Lavender St. SR4: Sund 2G 117
Lavender Wlk. NE31: Heb 3J 85
Lavendon Cl. NE23: Cra 6J 25
Laverick NE10: Gate 1D 100
Laverick La. NE36: W Bol 7K 85
Laverick Ter. DH9: Ann P 6A 124
Laverock Ct. NE6: Newc T 1A 84 (6P 5)
Laverock Hall Rd. NE24: Bly, News 7C 22
Laverock Pl. NE3: Ken 7K 43
NE24: News 6F 23
Lavers Rd. DH3: Bir 3A 114
Lavington Rd. NE34: S Shi 5A 68
Lawe Rd. NE33: S Shi 1K 67
LAWE, THE 1K 67
Lawn Cotts. SR3: New S 3B 132
Lawn Ct. NE63: Ash 4K 11

Lawn Dr.—Lindsey Cl.

Lawn Dr. NE36: W Bol 1F 103
Lawnhead Sq. SR3: New S 3D 132
Lawnside SR7: S'hm 4J 147
Lawns, The DH5: Eas L 2J 157
SR3: New S 3B 132
SR6: Whit 6H 89
SR7: S'hm 4J 147
Lawnsway NE32: Jar 5C 86
Lawnswood DH5: Hou S 3F 145
Lawn, The NE40: Ryton 7G 59
Lawrence Av. NE21: Bla T 3C 80
NE34: S Shi 3K 87
Lawrence Ct. NE21: Bla T 3C 80
Lawrence Hill Ct. NE10: Gate 6F 85
Lawrence St. SR1: Sund 2G 119
Lawson Av. NE32: Jar 3C 86
Lawson Ct. DH2: Ches S 7A 128
DH9: Stly 3C 126
NE35: Bol C 7F 87
Lawson Cres. SR6: Monk 3F 105
Lawson Rd. DH6: Bow 4H 177
Lawson St. NE28: W'snd 4G 65
NE29: N Shi 1G 67
Lawson St. W. NE29: N Shi 1G 67
Lawson Ter. DH1: Dur 3K 165
DH5: Eas L 2H 157
NE4: Newc T 2A 82
Laws St. SR6: Monk 3F 105
Laxey St. DH9: Stly 3E 124
Laxford DH3: Bir 6B 114
Laxford Ct. SR3: New S 4C 132
Laybourn Gdns. NE34: S Shi 2G 87
(not continuous)
Layburn Gdns. NE15: Lem 5E 60
Layburn Pl. SR8: Pet 5A 172
Laycock Gdns. NE23: Seg 2C 36
Layfield Rd. NE3: Gos 3E 44
Laygate NE33: S Shi 4H 67
(not continuous)
Laygate Pl. NE33: S Shi 4J 67
Laygate St. NE33: S Shi 4H 67
Lea Av. NE32: Jar 4C 86
Leabank NE15: Lem 5D 60
Leaburn Ter. NE42: Pru 4D 76
LEADGATE
Consett 5A 122
Newcastle upon Tyne 3J 93
Leadgate Cotts. NE17: C'wl 3J 93
Leadgate Ind. Est. DH8: Con 7C 122
Leadgate Rd. DH8: Con 6J 121
(not continuous)
Lead La. DH8: W'stll 3E 106
NE15: Hor 4E 56
Lead Rd. NE17: C'wl 4G 93
NE21: Bla T, G'sde 4G 79
NE40: G'sde 7B 78
NE43: B'ley 4H 91
Leafield Cres. NE34: S Shi 5C 68
Lea Grn. DH3: Ches S 7C 114
Leagreen Ct. NE3: Gos 7C 44
Leaholme Cres. NE24: Bly 3G 23
Leaholme Ter. TS27: B Col 3J 183
Lea La. SR8: Eas 5K 159
Lealholm Rd. NE7: Longb 7J 45
Leam Gdns. NE10: Gate 6G 85
Leamington St. SR4: Sund 2D 118
Leam La. NE10: Gate 4C 100
NE10: Gate 6J 85
NE32: Jar 4B 86
NE32: S Shi 1E 86
LEAM LANE ESTATE 2E 100
LEAMSIDE 1J 155
Leamside NE10: Gate 1D 100
NE32: Jar 2C 86
Leander Av. DH3: Ches S 1B 128
NE62: Chop 7J 11
Leander Ct. NE62: Chop 7K 11
Leander Dr. NE35: Bol C 6E 86
Leander M. NE62: Chop 7K 11
Leaplish NE38: Wash 6K 115
Leap Mill 1B 110
Lea Rigg DH4: W Rai 1A 156
(not continuous)
Lea Side DH8: Con 2K 135
Leas, The DH4: Hou S 6D 130
NE25: Whit B 7D 38
Leasyde Wlk. NE16: Whi 2E 96
Leatham SR2: Ryh 1G 133
Leat Ho. NE38: Wash 4B 116
Lea Vw. NE34: S Shi 5D 68
Leaway NE42: Pru 4D 76
LEAZES 2K 109
Leazes Arc. NE1: Newc T 4E 4
Leazes Ct. DH1: Dur 2B 166 (2D 6)
NE4: Newc T 7D 62 (3A 4)
Leazes Cres. NE1: Newc T 7E 62 (4D 4)
NE46: Hex 1B 70
Leazes La. DH1: Dur 2C 166
NE1: Newc T 7F 63 (4E 4)
NE45: Ayd 5E 52
NE46: Hex 1A 70
Leazes Pde. NE2: Newc T 7D 62 (3A 4)
Leazes Pk. NE46: Hex 1A 70
Leazes Pk. Rd. NE1: Newc T 7E 62 (4D 4)
Leazes Parkway NE15: Thro 4G 59
Leazes Pl. DH1: Dur 2B 166 (2D 6)
Leazes Ri. SR8: Pet 6D 172
Leazes Rd. DH1: Dur 2A 166 (2B 6)
Leazes Sq. NE1: Newc T 7F 63 (4E 4)
Leazes Ter. NE1: Newc T 7E 62 (3D 4)
NE45: Cor 7D 52
NE46: Hex 1B 70
Leazes, The DH6: Bow 5H 177
NE15: Thro 4G 59
NE16: Burn 2K 109
NE34: S Shi 7B 68
SR1: Sund 2D 118 (4F 7)
Leazes Vw. NE39: Row G 5H 95
NE42: O'ham 2K 75
Leazes Vs. NE16: Burn 2A 110
Lecondale NE10: Gate 3D 100
Lecondale Ct. NE10: Gate 3D 100
Ledbury Rd. SR2: Sund 5F 119
Leechmere Cres. SR7: S'hm 1G 147
Leechmere Ind. Est.
SR2: Sund 7G 119
Leechmere Rd. SR2: Sund 6E 118
Leechmere Vw. SR2: Ryh 1H 133
Leechmere Way SR2: Ryh 1G 133
(not continuous)
Lee Cl. NE38: Wash 3B 116
Leeds St. SR6: Monk 5F 105
Lee Hill Ct. DH7: Lan 6J 137
Leeholme DH5: Hou S 3F 145
Leeholme Ct. DH9: Ann P 6A 124
Leeman's La. DH6: Hett 7C 176
Leeming Gdns. NE9: Gate 1K 99
Leesfield Dr. DH7: B'don 2E 174
Leesfield Gdns. DH7: B'don 2E 174
Leesfield Rd. DH7: B'don 2E 174
Lees St. DH9: Stly 2F 125
Lee St. SR5: S'wck 6D 104
SR6: Monk 3F 105
Lee Ter. DH5: Hett H 1G 157
DH6: Shot C 6E 170
SR8: Eas 7A 160
Legg Av. NE22: Bed 5C 18
Legion Gro. NE15: Newc T 6F 61
Legion Rd. NE15: Newc T 6F 61
Leicester Cl. NE28: W'snd 7E 46
Leicestershire Dr.
DH1: Carr 2H 167
Leicester St. NE6: Walk 1C 84
Leicester Wlk. SR8: Pet 4A 172
Leicester Way NE32: Jar 5A 86
Leighton Rd. SR2: Sund 6F 119
Leighton St. NE6: Newc T 7J 63 (4M 5)
NE33: S Shi 3A 68
Leighton Ter. DH3: Bir 3K 113
Leith Ct. NE34: S Shi 1J 87
Leith Gdns. DH9: Tan L 7D 110
Leland Pl. NE61: Mor 1D 14
LEMINGTON 7C 60
Lemington Gdns. NE5: Newc T 6J 61
Lemington Rd. NE15: Lem 6A 60
Lemon St. NE33: S Shi 7H 67
Lena Av. NE25: Whit B 7E 38
Lenin Ter. DH9: Stly 5F 125
NE17: C'wl 7A 94
Lenore Ter. NE40: G'sde 4F 79
Leominster Rd. SR2: Sund 6F 119
Leonard Ho. SR3: New S 2C 132
Leopold Ho. SR2: Sund 6F 7
Leopold St. NE32: Jar 7B 66
Lesbury Av. NE27: Shir 1J 47
NE28: W'snd 2K 65
NE62: Chop 6J 11
NE63: Hir 5B 12
Lesbury Chase NE3: Gos 5D 44
Lesbury Cl. DH2: Ches S 1H 141
Lesbury Gdns. NE13: Wide O 5E 34
Lesbury Rd. NE6: Newc T 4K 63
Lesbury St. NE15: Lem 7C 60
NE28: W'snd 4C 66
Lesbury Ter. NE17: C'wl 7K 93
Leslie Av. NE31: Heb 1J 85
Leslie Cl. NE40: Ryton 2J 79
Leslie Cres. NE3: Gos 2E 62
Leslie's Vw. NE61: Mor 5E 8
Letch Av. SR7: Eas 3J 159
Letch Path NE15: Lem 6C 60
Letch, The NE12: Longb 3B 46
Letch Way NE15: Lem 6C 60
Letchwell Vs. NE12: Longb 3C 46
Leuchars Ct. DH3: Bir 5A 114
Leven Av. DH2: Ches S 1K 141
Leven Ho. SR3: New S 3C 132
Levens Wlk. NE23: Cra 3G 25
Leven Wlk. SR8: Pet 1A 182
Levisham Cl. SR3: New S 2E 132
Lewis Cres. SR2: Sund 3H 119
Lewis Dr. NE4: Newc T 7B 62
Lewis Gdns. NE34: S Shi 3J 87
Lexington Ct. DH7: B'don 3C 174
Leybourne Av. NE12: Kil 3B 46
Leybourne Dene NE12: Kil 2B 46
Leybourne Hold DH3: Bir 2A 114
Leyburn Cl. DH2: Ous 7F 113
DH4: Hou S 1D 144
Leyburn Ct. NE23: Cra 6J 25
Leyburn Dr. NE7: Newc T 2J 63
Leyburn Gro. DH4: Hou S 1C 144
Leyburn Pl. DH3: Bir 2K 113
Leyfield Cl. SR3: New S 4D 132
Leyland Cl. DH6: Bow 3J 177
Leyton Pl. NE8: Gate 6J 83
Liberty Ter. DH9: Tan L 6B 110
Liberty Way SR6: Monk 7G 105
Library Stairs NE30: N Shi 7H 49
Library Ter. DH9: Ann P 5K 123
Library Wlk. DH9: Ann P 4K 123
Lichfield Av. NE6: Walk 2C 84
Lichfield Cl. DH3: Gt Lum 4E 142
NE3: Ken 5A 44
NE63: N Sea 5D 12
Lichfield Ho. SR5: S'wck 4D 104
Lichfield Rd. DH1: Dur 3B 154
SR5: S'wck 4C 104
Lichfield Way NE32: Jar 5A 86
(not continuous)
Lidcombe Cl. SR3: New S 2D 132
Liddell Ct. SR6: Monk 5H 105
Liddells Fell Rd. NE21: Bla T 4K 79
Liddell St. NE30: N Shi 7H 49
SR6: Monk 7F 105 (1K 7)
Liddell Ter. NE8: Gate 5F 83
NE11: Kib 2E 112
Liddle Av. DH6: Sher 3K 167
Liddle Cl. SR8: Pet 4K 171
Liddle Ct. NE4: Newc T 1C 82 (5A 4)
Liddle Rd. NE4: Newc T 1C 82 (5A 4)
Liddles St. NE22: Bed 5B 18
Lidell Ter. DH6: Whe H 4A 180
Lieven St. NE13: Bru V 7C 34
Lifeboat Station
Newbiggin-by-the Sea 2K 13
(off Promenade)
Life Science Cen. 2E 82 (8D 4)
Liffey Rd. NE31: Heb 3K 85
Lightbourne Rd. NE6: Walk 7E 64
Lightfoot Sports Cen. 2D 84
Lightwood Av. NE15: Newc T 2G 81
Lilac Av. DH1: Dur 6K 153
DH5: Hou S 2F 145
DH7: Sac 1E 152
NE12: Longb 4D 46
NE24: Bly 1H 23
NE34: S Shi 1B 88
SR3: New S 1D 132
SR6: Whit 3H 89
TS27: B Col 3K 183
Lilac Cl. NE5: Cha P 1B 60
Lilac Ct. NE63: Ash 6A 12
Lilac Cres. NE16: Burn 2A 110
Lilac Gdns. DH2: Beam 2D 126
NE9: Gate 1H 99
NE16: Whi 7G 81
NE38: Wash 7G 115
SR6: Cle 4C 88
Lilac Gro. DH2: Ches S 4J 127
SR6: Monk 4F 105
Lilac Pk. DH7: Ush M 3C 164
Lilac Pl. DH8: Lead 6B 122
Lilac Rd. NE6: Walk 4E 64
Lilac Sq. DH4: Hou S 6J 129
Lilac St. SR4: Sund 2G 117
Lilac Ter. DH6: Shot C 6E 170
DH9: Ann P 4J 123
Lilac Wlk. NE31: Heb 3J 85
Lilburn Cl. DH2: Ches S 2J 141
NE6: Newc T 2A 84
NE36: E Bol 6J 87
Lilburne Cl. SR1: Sund 1G 119
Lilburn Gdns. NE3: Newc T 1H 63
Lilburn Pl. SR5: S'wck 6C 104
Lilburn Rd. NE27: Shir 2J 47
Lilburn St. NE29: N Shi 7F 49
Lilian Av. NE28: W'snd 4E 64
SR2: Ryh 1G 133
Lilian Ter. DH7: Lang P 5J 151
Lilleycroft NE39: Row G 5K 95
Lilley Gro. SR5: C'twn 6H 103
Lilley Ter. NE39: Row G 4K 95
Lily Av. NE2: Newc T 4G 63
NE22: Bed 1K 21
Lily Bank NE28: W'snd 3F 65
Lily Bungs. DH9: Dip 1J 123
Lily Cl. NE21: Bla T 4A 80
Lily Cres. NE2: Newc T 4G 63
SR6: Whit 3H 89
Lily Est. NE15: Thro 2H 59
Lily Gdns. DH9: Dip 1J 123
Lily St. SR4: Sund 1D 118 (2F 7)
Lily Ter. DH4: Hou S 5D 130
NE5: Newc T 2G 61
Lilywhite Ter. DH5: Eas L 1H 157
Lime Av. DH4: Hou S 1C 144
TS27: B Col 2J 183
Limecrag Av. DH1: Dur 1F 167
Limecroft NE32: Jar 5C 86
Lime Gro. NE40: Ryton 1F 79
NE42: Pru 3D 76
Limekiln Rd. NE28: W'snd 3H 65
Lime Pk. DH7: B'don 1D 174
Limes Av. NE24: Bly 7H 19
Limes, The DH4: Pen 1B 130
NE61: Mor 6F 9
(off Cottingwood La.)
SR2: Sund 4F 119 (7J 7)
SR6: Whit 6G 89
(off Front St.)
Limestone La. NE18: Pon 5C 30
NE20: Pon 5C 30
Lime St. DH2: Ches S 1G 141
DH9: Stly 6D 124
NE1: Newc T 7J 63 (4L 5)
NE15: Thro 2H 59
NE21: Bla T 5D 80
SR4: Sund 1D 118
Lime Ter. DH7: Lang P 5K 151
Limetree NE38: Wash 6J 115
Limetrees Gdns. NE9: Gate 7H 83
Limewood Ct. NE2: Newc T 5D 62 (1B 4)
Limewood Gro. NE13: Wide O 6D 34
Linacre Cl. NE3: Ken 6H 43
Linacre Ct. SR8: Pet 7K 171
Linbridge Dr. NE5: Newc T 4D 60
Linburn NE38: Wash 1F 129
Lincoln Av. NE28: W'snd 2E 64
SR3: New S 1C 132
Lincoln Ct. NE31: Heb 1H 85
Lincoln Cres. DH5: Hett H 6F 145
Lincoln Grn. NE3: Gos 3E 44
Lincoln Pl. DH8: C'sde 3C 134
Lincoln Rd. DH1: Dur 4B 154
DH8: C'sde 3C 134
NE23: Cra 7A 22
NE34: S Shi 6D 68
Lincolnshire Cl. DH1: Carr 1G 167
Lincoln St. NE8: Gate 5G 83
SR4: Sund 1B 118
Lincoln Wlk. DH3: Gt Lum 3E 142
SR8: Pet 4A 172
Lincoln Way NE32: Jar 5B 86
(not continuous)
Lincrest Ct. NE5: Newc T 3F 61
Lindale Av. NE16: Whi 2G 97
Lindale Rd. NE4: Newc T 5A 62
Lindean Pl. NE23: Cra 4H 25
Linden NE9: Gate 3B 100
Linden Av. NE3: Gos 1E 62
NE4: Newc T 6K 61
Linden Cl. NE62: Chop 7J 11
Linden Gdns. SR2: Sund 5E 118
Linden Gro. DH4: Hou S 2D 144
DH8: Lead 6B 122
NE11: Dun 6C 82
Linden Pk. DH7: B'don 1D 174
Linden Rd. DH7: Ush M 1D 164
NE3: Gos 1E 62
NE12: Longb 6B 46
NE21: Bla T 4D 80
NE25: Sea D 7F 27
SR2: Sund 5E 118
Linden Ter. NE9: Spri 6D 100
NE12: Longb 5B 46
NE26: Whit B 6H 39
Linden Way DH8: Con 5G 121
NE9: Spri 5A 100
(not continuous)
NE20: Pon 1G 41
Lindfield Av. NE5: Newc T 4H 61
Lindisfarne DH1: H Shin 7F 167
NE38: Wash 4G 115
SR2: Ryh 3G 133
SR8: Pet 1A 182
Lindisfarne Av. DH3: Ches S 6B 128
NE62: Chop 1G 17
(off Morpeth Rd.)
Lindisfarne Cl. DH2: Ches S 1J 141
DH4: Hou S 7C 130
NE2: Newc T 3H 63
NE5: Newc T 4F 61
NE61: Mor 2G 15
NE61: Peg 3C 10
Lindisfarne Ct. NE32: Jar 7F 67
Lindisfarne Dr. NE8: Gate 4H 83 (10K 5)
Lindisfarne La. NE61: Mor 2G 15
Lindisfarne Nursing Home
DH2: Ches S 6J 127
Lindisfarne Pl. NE28: W'snd 2H 65
Lindisfarne Recess NE32: Jar 2D 86
Lindisfarne Ri. DH1: Dur 6B 154
Lindisfarne Rd. DH1: Dur 6B 154
NE2: Newc T 3H 63
NE31: Heb 3J 85
NE32: Jar 2D 86
Lindisfarne Ter. NE30: N Shi 5G 49
Lindom Av. DH3: Ches S 6B 128
Lindon Mnr. NE12: Kil 7A 36
Lindon Rd. DH9: Stly 4E 124
Lindrick Ct. NE10: Gate 7G 85
Lindrick Pk. DH5: Hett H 7H 145
Lindsay Av. NE24: Cow 1G 23
Lindsay Cl. SR2: Sund 3G 119
Lindsay Ct. SR6: Whit 4H 89
Lindsay Rd. SR1: Sund 2G 119
SR2: Sund 2G 119
Lindsay St. DH5: Hett H 4H 145
Lindsey Cl. NE23: Cra 4G 25

Lindum Rd.—Low Rd. W.

Lindum Rd. NE9: Gate 6H 83
Linfield SR2: Ryh 2G 133
Lingcrest NE9: Gate 2A 100
Lingdale DH1: Carr 1H 167
Lingdale Av. SR6: Monk 1G 105
Lingey Cl. DH7: Sac 6D 140
Lingey Gdns. NE10: Gate 6G 85
Lingey La. NE10: Gate 7F 85
Lingfield DH5: Hou S 3F 145
Lingfield Rd. DH8: Con 6H 121
Lingholme DH2: Ches S 5J 127
Lingmell NE37: Wash 2F 115
Lingshaw NE10: Gate 7F 85
Lingside NE32: Jar 4C 86
Linhope Av. NE3: Ken 5B 44
Linhope Rd. NE5: Newc T 3F 61
Link Av. NE22: Bed 7F 17
Link Rd. NE5: Newc T 3A 62
NE13: Bru V 7C 34
Links Av. NE26: Whit B 4F 39
NE30: N Shi 2J 49
Links Ct. NE26: Whit B 4G 39
Links Dr. DH8: Con 4G 121
Links Grn. NE3: Gos 6F 45
Links Grn. Wlk. NE3: Gos 6F 45
Links Ho. Gdns. Cvn. Pk. NE24: Bly 5K 23
Links Rd. NE24: Bly 1A 28 & 5K 23
NE26: Sea S 4C 28
NE30: N Shi 1J 49
Links, The DH1: Carr 7H 155
NE26: Sea S 4C 28
NE26: Whit B 2F 39
Links Vw. NE24: News 5G 23
NE63: N Sea 7E 12
Links Wlk. NE5: Newc T 3F 61
Link, The NE46: Hex 1B 70
Linkway DH7: Sac 7E 140
NE32: Jar 5D 86
Linley Hill NE16: Whi 2E 96
Linnel Dr. NE15: Lem 6E 60
Linnels Bank NE46: Hex 6H 71
Linnet Cl. NE38: Wash 5E 114
Linnet Ct. NE63: Ash 5K 11
Linnet Gro. SR5: C'twn 6J 103
Linnetsfield *NE6: Walk* *5D 64*
(off Northmoor Rd.)
Linney Gdns. NE34: S Shi 2G 87
Linnheads NE42: Pru 5D 76
Linshiels Gdns. NE63: Hir 5D 12
Linskell SR2: Ryh 1G 133
Linskill Pl. NE3: Ken 2B 62
NE30: N Shi 5H 49
Linskill St. NE30: N Shi 7H 49
Linskill Ter. NE30: N Shi 6H 49
Linslade Wlk. NE23: Cra 4H 25
Lintfort NE38: Wash 2C 128
Linthorpe Ct. NE34: S Shi 1G 87
Linthorpe Rd. NE3: Gos 5E 44
NE30: N Shi 3H 49
Linton NE12: Kil 6B 36
Linton Rd. NE9: Gate 4H 99
NE26: Whit B 2E 38
Lintonville Parkway NE63: Wood 2A 12
Lintonville Ter. NE63: Ash 3A 12
NE63: Wood 2A 12
LINTZ 2K 109
LINTZFORD 1G 109
Lintzford Cl. NE39: Row G 7H 95
Lintzford Gdns. NE15: Lem 6E 60
NE39: Row G 7H 95
Lintzford La. NE39: C'wl, Row G 5E 94
Lintzford Rd. NE39: Ham M, Row G 3D 108
LINTZ GREEN 3G 109
Lintz Grn. La. NE39: Ham M 2G 109
Lintz La. NE16: Burn 3G 109
Lintz Ter. DH9: Stly 4C 124
NE16: Burn 2K 109
Linum Pl. NE4: Newc T 5A 62
Linwood Pl. NE3: Gos 3E 44
Lion Wlk. NE29: N Shi 2F 67
Lipman Bldg. NE1: Newc T 2G 4
Lisa Av. SR4: Sund 3G 117
Lisburn Ter. SR4: Sund 1C 118
Lish Av. NE26: Whit B 7J 39
Lishman Cotts. *NE40: Ryton* *2C 78*
(off Main St.)
Lishman Ter. NE40: Ryton 2E 78
Lisle Ct. NE28: W'snd 3F 65
Lisle Gro. NE28: W'snd 2A 66
Lisle Rd. NE34: S Shi 6B 68
Lisle St. NE1: Newc T 7F 63 (4F 4)
NE28: W'snd 3F 65
Lismore Av. NE33: S Shi 6K 67
Lismore Pl. NE15: Newc T 7K 61
Lismore Ter. NE9: Spri 6D 100
Lister Av. NE11: Dun 5B 82
NE40: G'sde 6D 78
Lister Cl. DH5: Hou S 4D 144
Lister Rd. SR8: Pet 4J 171
Listers La. NE9: Gate 6J 83
Lister St. NE15: Newc T 2F 81
Litchfield Cres. NE21: Bla T 5B 80
Litchfield La. NE21: Bla T 5B 80
Litchfield St. NE21: Bla T 5B 80
Litchfield Ter. NE21: Bla T 5B 80
Lit. Bedford St. NE29: N Shi 7G 49
Littlebridge Ct. DH1: Dur 4J 153
Little Bldgs. NE42: O'ham 2K 75
LITTLEBURN 7G 165
Littleburn Cl. DH4: Hou S 7C 130
Littleburn Ind. Est. DH7: B'don 1H 175
Littleburn La. DH7: B'don 7G 165
Littleburn Rd. DH7: B'don 7G 165
Little Dene NE2: Gos 2F 63
Littledene NE9: Gate 7H 83
Little Eden SR8: Pet 5B 172
Little Mus. of Gilesgate, The 2D 166
Little Theatre, The 6H 83
LITTLE THORPE 2A 172
LITTLETOWN 1E 168
Littletown La. DH6: H Pitt 2D 168
Lit. Villiers St. SR1: Sund 1G 119 (3K 7)
(not continuous)
Little Way NE15: Newc T 2H 81
Litton Ct. SR3: New S 3B 132
Littondale NE28: W'snd 1D 64
Liverpool St. NE1: Newc T 7F 63 (4E 4)
Live Theatre 7H 5
Livingstone Pl. NE33: S Shi 1J 67
Livingstone Rd. SR1: Sund 1E 118 (3G 7)
Livingstone St. DH8: Con 6H 121
NE33: S Shi 1K 67
Livingstone Vw. NE30: N Shi 5J 49
Lizard La. NE34: S Shi 7F 69
SR6: Whit 3G 89
Lizard La. Cvn. & Camping Site
NE34: S Shi 7F 69
Lizard Vw. SR6: Whit 3G 89
Lloyd Av. DH5: W Rai 6C 144
Lloyd Ct. NE11: Dun 4A 82
Lloyds Ter. DH7: Lang P 5J 151
Lloyd St. NE40: Ryton 3D 78
LOANING BURN 7H 159
LOANSDEAN 3F 15
Lobban Av. NE31: Heb 3H 85
Lobelia Av. NE10: Gate 4K 83
Lobelia Cl. NE5: Cha P 2B 60
Lobley Gdns. NE11: Dun 1C 98
LOBLEY HILL 1C 98
Lobley Hill DH7: B'don 1F 175
Lobley Hill Rd. NE8: Gate 1C 98
NE11: Gate 1C 98
Lobleyhill Rd. NE16: Burn, Sun 1C 110
Local Av. DH6: Sher 3C 168
Locarno Ct. *NE64: Newb S* *2J 13*
(off Locarno Pl.)
Locarno Pl. NE64: Newb S 3J 13
Lochcraig Pl. NE23: Cra 4G 25
Lochfield Gdns. NE11: Kib 2E 112
Lochmaben Ter. SR5: Monk 5F 105
Lockerbie Gdns. NE15: Lem 6E 60
Lockerbie Rd. NE23: Cra 4H 25
LOCKHAUGH 3A 96
Lockhaugh Rd. NE39: Row G 4K 95
Locksley Cl. NE29: N Shi 3B 48
Locomotion Way NE12: Kil 6K 35
NE29: N Shi 2G 67
Locomotive Ct. NE42: Pru 4E 76
Lodge Cl. NE39: Ham M 3E 108
Lodgeside Mdw. SR3: New S 4D 132
Lodges Rd., The NE9: Gate 4G 99
Lodge Ter. NE28: W'snd 3H 65
Lodore Ct. SR3: New S 3B 132
Lodore Gro. NE32: Jar 3D 86
Lodore Rd. NE2: Gos 2F 63
Lodsworth Dr. NE23: Cra 6J 25
Loefield DH3: Gt Lum 2E 142
Lofthill SR3: New S 4A 132
Logan Rd. NE6: Walk 4D 64
Logan St. DH5: Hett H 7G 145
DH7: Lang P 4J 151
Logan Ter. *DH6: S Het* *3A 158*
(off Front St.)
Lola St. NE13: Bru V 7B 34
Lombard Dr. DH3: Ches S 2A 128
Lombard Pl. DH3: Gt Lum 3E 142
Lombard St. NE1: Newc T 2G 83 (7H 5)
SR1: Sund 1G 119
Lomond Cl. NE38: Wash 5F 115
Lomond Ct. SR3: New S 3C 132
Lomond Pl. DH2: Ches S 1K 141
London Av. NE37: Usw 6F 101
Londonderry Bungs. SR8: Eas 7B 160
Londonderry Ct. SR7: S'hm 2B 148
Londonderry St. SR3: New S 2C 132
SR7: S'hm 5C 148
Londonderry Ter. SR3: New S 2D 132
SR8: Eas 7B 160
Londonderry Way DH4: Pen 2A 130
Longacre DH4: Hou S 2C 144
NE38: Wash 7J 115
Long Acres DH1: Dur 1D 166
Long Bank DH3: Bir 1A 114
NE9: Gate, Spri 7K 99
LONGBENTON 6J 45
Longbenton Station (Metro) 7J 45
Longborough Ct. NE3: Newc T 1J 63
Long Burn Dr. DH2: Ches S 7H 127
Longclose Bank DH8: M'sly 6A 108
DH9: M'sly 6B 108
Longclose Bank NE17: Ham C 6B 108
NE39: Ham M 6B 108
Long Cl. Rd. NE39: Ham M 3D 108
Long Crag NE37: Wash 3E 114
Long Dale DH2: Ches S 7H 127
Longdean Cl. NE31: Heb 1G 85
Longdean Pk. DH3: Ches S 3A 128
Long Dr. NE61: Loan 3F 15
Long Edge DH7: B'hpe, Wit G 7E 138
Longedge La. DH8: C'sde, Con 6D 134
Longfellow St. DH5: Hou S 3E 144
Long Fld. Cl. NE34: S Shi 2K 87
Longfield Rd. SR6: Monk 4F 105
Longfield Ter. NE6: Walk 2E 84
Long Gair NE21: Bla T 6A 80
Long Gth. DH1: Dur 7H 153
Long Headlam NE6: Newc T 7A 64
LONGHIRST 1B 10
Longhirst NE5: Newc T 3F 61
NE10: Gate 7E 84
NE12: Kil 6B 36
Longhirst Dr. NE13: Wide O 6D 34
NE23: Cra 6J 25
Longhirst Rd. NE61: Peg 4B 10
Longhirst Village NE61: Peg 1A 10
Longlands NE46: Hex 2C 70
Longlands Dr. DH5: Hou S 3E 144
Longleat Gdns. NE33: S Shi 2K 67
NE61: Peg 3A 10
Longley St. NE4: Newc T 7C 62 (4A 4)
Long Mdw. Cl. NE40: Ryton 3D 78
Longmeadows NE20: Pon 1F 41
SR3: E Her 3J 131
Longnewton St. SR7: S'hm 5B 148
Longniddry NE37: Usw 4G 101
Longniddry Ct. NE9: Gate 4G 99
Long Pk. NE64: Newb S 3H 13
Longridge NE21: Bla T 5A 80
Longridge Av. NE7: Newc T 2B 64
NE38: Wash 5E 114
Longridge Dr. NE26: Whit B 4E 38
Longridge Rd. NE21: Bla T, G'sde 4G 79
Longridge Sq. SR2: Sund 6F 119
Longridge Way NE22: Bed 4J 17
NE23: Cra 4H 25
Longrigg NE10: Gate 7D 84
NE16: Swa 4G 81
Longriggs, The NE44: Rid M 7J 73
Long Row NE33: S Shi 1H 67
Long Row Cl. NE40: G'sde 6D 78
LONG SANDS 3K 49
Longsdale Ct. NE17: Ham C 4K 107
Longshank La. DH3: Bir 2J 113
Longstaff Gdns. NE34: S Shi 2K 87
Long Stairs NE1: Newc T 2G 83 (7G 4)
Longston Av. NE30: N Shi 1H 49
Longstone NE9: Gate 3H 99
Longstone Ct. NE12: Kil 7C 36
Longstone Sq. NE5: Newc T 4D 60
Longwood Cl. NE16: Sun 4H 97
Lonnen Av. NE4: Newc T 5K 61
Lonnen Dr. NE16: Swa 6G 81
Lonnen, The NE34: S Shi 1D 88
NE40: Ryton 1J 79
Lonsdale DH3: Bir 7C 114
Lonsdale Av. NE24: Cow 1C 22
SR6: Monk 1G 105
Lonsdale Ct. NE2: Newc T 3G 63
NE34: S Shi 2G 87
Lonsdale Gdns. NE28: W'snd 1A 66
Lonsdale Rd. SR6: Monk 5G 105
Lonsdale Ter. NE2: Newc T 3G 63
Lookout Farm NE26: Sea S 4B 28
Lope Hill Rd. DH8: Con 7C 122
Loraine Ter. NE15: Lem 7C 60
Lord Armstrong Memorial 2F 4
Lord Byrons Wlk. SR7: S'hm 1H 147
Lordenshaw NE5: Newc T 3F 61
Lord Gort Cl. SR5: S'wck 6C 104
Lord Nelson St. NE33: S Shi 7H 67
Lord St. NE1: Newc T 2E 82 (7C 4)
NE33: S Shi 4A 68
SR3: New S 2D 132
SR7: S'hm 3B 148
Lorimers Cl. SR8: Pet 1K 181
Lorne St. DH5: Eas L 3H 157
Lorne Ter. SR2: Sund 3E 118 (7H 7)
Lorrain Rd. NE34: S Shi 4K 87
Lort Ho. NE2: Newc T 7H 63 (3J 5)
Lorton Av. NE30: N Shi 2G 49
Lorton Rd. NE9: Gate 3J 99
Losh Ter. NE6: Walk 1D 84
Lossiemouth Rd. NE29: N Shi 7C 48
Lothian Cl. DH3: Bir 7B 114
Lothian Ct. NE5: Newc T 2J 61
Lotus Cl. NE5: Cha P 2B 60
Lotus Pl. NE4: Newc T 6K 61
Loudon St. NE34: S Shi 1J 87
Loud Ter. DH9: Ann P 5H 123
Loud Vw. Ter. DH9: Ann P 6J 123
Loughborough Av. NE30: N Shi 3J 49
SR2: Sund 5E 118
Loughbrow Pk. NE46: Hex 4D 70
Lough Ct. NE9: Gate 2K 99
Loughrigg Av. NE23: Cra 4G 25
Louie Ter. NE9: Gate 2J 99
Louisa Cen., The 3E 124
Louisa Ter. DH7: Wit G 3D 152
DH9: Stly 3E 124
Louis Av. SR6: Monk 4F 105
Louise Ho. SR2: Sund 6G 7
Louise Ter. DH3: Ches S 6A 128
Louisville NE20: Pon 4K 31
Loup St. NE21: Bla T 3C 80
Loup Ter. NE21: Bla T 3C 80
Louvain Ter. DH5: Hett H 5G 145
NE62: Chop 1H 17
Louvain Ter. W. DH5: Hett H 5G 145
Lovaine Av. NE25: Whit B 7G 39
NE29: N Shi 7G 49
Lovaine Hall NE1: Newc T 2H 5
Lovaine Pl. NE29: N Shi 7G 49
Lovaine Pl. W. NE29: N Shi 7F 49
Lovaine Row NE30: N Shi 4K 49
Lovaine St. DH2: Pelt 3E 126
NE15: Thro 5J 59
Lovaine Ter. NE29: N Shi 6G 49
Love Av. NE23: Dud 4K 35
Love Av. Cotts. NE23: Dud 3K 35
Lovelady Ct. *NE30: N Shi* *5K 49*
(off St Oswin's Pl.)
Love La. NE1: Newc T 1H 83 (6J 5)
NE21: Bla T 5B 80
Loveless Gdns. NE10: Gate 6F 85
Lovett Wlk. NE8: Gate 4E 82 (10D 4)
Lowbiggin NE5: Newc T 7E 42
Low Bri. NE1: Newc T 1G 83 (6G 4)
Low Burswell NE46: Hex 1B 70
Low Carrs Cvn. Pk.
DH1: Dur 4K 153
Low Chare DH3: Ches S 6A 128
Low Chu. St. DH9: Ann P 4K 123
Low Cl. NE42: Pru 3G 77
Lowden Ct. NE2: Newc T 6E 62 (1C 4)
Lowdham Av. NE29: N Shi 1E 66
Low Downs Rd. DH5: Hett H 4G 145
Low Downs Sq. DH5: Hett H 4H 145
Lwr. Crone St. *NE27: Shir* *7K 37*
(off Up. Crone St.)
Lwr. Dundas St. SR6: Monk 7F 105
Lower Prom. NE30: N Shi 4K 49
Lwr. Rudyerd St. NE29: N Shi 7H 49
Lowerson Av. DH4: Hou S 4A 130
Lowery La. DH9: Edm, Stly 7K 125
LOWE'S BARN 5H 165
Lowe's Barn Bank DH1: Dur 5H 165
Lowes Ct. DH1: Dur 4J 165
Lowes Fall DH1: Dur 4J 165
Lowes Ri. DH1: Dur 4J 165
Loweswater Av. DH2: Ches S 1K 141
DH5: Eas L 3J 157
Loweswater Cl. NE24: Cow 7D 18
Loweswater Rd. NE5: Newc T 5H 61
NE9: Gate 3J 99
Loweswood Cl. NE7: Newc T 4J 63
Lowes Wynd DH1: Dur 4J 165
LOW FELL 2H 99
Lowfield Ter. NE6: Walk 2D 84
Lowfield Wlk. NE16: Whi 7G 81
Low Flatts Rd. DH3: Ches S 3A 128
Low Fold NE6: Newc T 1K 83 (5N 5)
LOW FRIARSIDE 1H 109
Low Friar St. NE1: Newc T 1F 83 (6E 4)
Lowgate NE15: Thro 4H 59
Low Gosforth Ct. NE3: Gos 3F 45
Low Graham St. *DH7: Sac* *7E 140*
(off Front St.)
Low Grn. DH1: H Shin 6D 166
LOW GREENSIDE 4E 78
Low Haugh NE20: Pon 4K 31
Low Heighley Dr. NE61: Fair M 1B 8
Low Heworth La. NE10: Gate 4D 84
Lowhills Rd. SR8: Pet 4K 171
Lowick Cl. DH3: Bir 7B 114
Lowick Ct. NE3: Gos 1G 63
Lowland Cl. SR3: New S 4C 132
Lowland Ho. DH7: B'don 1D 174
Lowland Rd. DH7: B'don 1D 174
Low La. NE34: S Shi 1J 87
Lowleam Ct. NE5: Newc T 4F 61
Low Level Bri. NE1: Newc T 1J 83 (6M 5)
NE6: Newc T 1J 83 (6M 5)
LOW LIGHTS 6J 49
Low Mann Pl. NE23: Cra 4K 25
Low Mdws. SR6: Cle 5C 88
Low Moor Cotts. DH1: Dur 2B 154
Low Moor Rd. DH7: Lang P 6D 150
LOW MOORSLEY 2E 156
Lownds Ter. NE6: Walk 7C 64
LOW PITTINGTON 5B 156
LOW PRUDHOE 2G 77
Low Prudhoe Ind. Est.
NE42: Pru 2F 77
(Princess Ct.)
NE42: Pru 1H 77
(Regents Dr.)
Lowrey's La. NE9: Gate 2H 99
Low Rd. DH1: H Shin 6D 166
Low Rd. E. DH1: H Shin 6D 166
Low Rd. W. DH1: H Shin 6D 166

Low Row—Mansfield Pl.

Low Row NE40: Ryton 3J 79
SR1: Sund 2E 118 (4G 7)
SR8: Eas 7K 159
Lowry Gdns. NE34: S Shi 4K 87
Lowry Rd. SR6: Monk 2G 105
LOW SOUTHWICK 6D 104
Low Sta. Rd. DH4: Leam 1J 155
Low Stobhill NE61: Mor 1G 15
Low St. SR1: Sund 1G 119
Lowther Av. DH2: Ches S 7K 127
(not continuous)
Lowther Cl. NE63: N Sea 6D 12
SR8: Pet 5B 172
Lowther Ct. SR8: Pet 3K 181
Lowther Sq. NE23: Cra 4G 25
Lowthian Cres. NE6: Walk 1C 84
Lowthian Ter. NE38: Wash 4K 115
LOW WALKER 7F 65
Low Well Gdns. NE10: Gate 5C 84
Low W. Av. NE39: Row G 6G 95
LOW WESTWOOD 3J 107
Loxton Sq. NE23: Cra 7J 25
Lucknow St. SR1: Sund 1H 119
Lucock St. NE34: S Shi 1H 87
Lucombe Cl. DH4: Hou S 4K 129
Lucy St. DH3: Ches S 5A 128
NE21: Bla T 3D 80
Ludlow Av. NE29: N Shi 4E 48
Ludlow Ct. NE3: Ken 5A 44
Ludlow Dr. NE25: Whit B 6B 38
Ludlow Rd. SR2: Sund 6F 119
LUDWORTH 5J 169
Luffness Dr. NE34: S Shi 3B 88
Luke Av. DH6: Cass 4E 178
Luke Ct. SR8: Pet 1B 182
Luke Cres. SR7: Mur 7D 146
Lukes La. NE31: Gate, Heb 4K 85
Luke Ter. DH6: Whe H 3A 180
Lulsgate SR5: C'twn 6G 103
Lulworth Av. NE32: Jar 1D 86
Lulworth Ct. SR3: E Her 2J 131
Lulworth Gdns. SR2: Sund 5E 118
Lumley Av. NE16: Swa 5H 81
NE34: S Shi 7D 68
Lumley Cl. DH2: Ches S 6K 127
NE38: Wash 3F 115
Lumley Ct. NE22: Bed 6A 18
NE31: Heb 5K 65
SR3: E Her 2J 131
Lumley Cres. DH4: Hou S 5C 130
Lumley Dr. DH8: Con 2A 136
SR8: Pet 2B 182
Lumley Gdns. NE8: Gate 5K 83
NE16: Burn 3J 109
(not continuous)
Lumley New Rd.
DH3: Ches S, Gt Lum 7D 128
DH3: Gt Lum 1F 143
DH4: Hou S 1F 143
Lumley Rd. DH1: Dur 4A 154
Lumley Sixth Pit
DH4: Hou S 7H 129
Lumley's La. NE42: Mic 7C 76
Lumley St. DH4: Hou S 7D 130
SR4: Sund 2C 118
Lumley Ter. DH3: Ches S 7B 128
NE32: Jar 3B 86
SR2: Ryh 3H 133
LUMLEY THICKS 1G 143
Lumley Twr. SR1: Sund 1G 119
Lumley Wlk. NE11: Dun 5C 82
Lumley Way NE3: Gos 3C 44
Lumsden's La. NE61: Mor 6F 9
Lumsden Sq. SR7: Mur 7D 146
Lumsden Ter. DH9: Ann P 4J 123
Lund Av. DH1: Dur 5K 153
Lund Ct. DH1: Dur 5K 153
Lund's La. DH8: Con 1E 136
Lunedale Av. SR6: Monk 2E 104
Lunedale Cl. DH3: Gt Lum 4F 143
Lune Grn. NE32: Jar 4C 86
Lunesdale St. DH5: Hett H 1G 157
Lupin Cl. NE5: Cha P 1C 60
Luss Av. NE32: Jar 3E 86
Luton Cres. NE29: N Shi 1D 66
Lutterworth Cl. NE12: Longb 7K 45
Lutterworth Pl. NE12: Longb 7K 45
Lutterworth Rd. NE12: Longb 7K 45
SR2: Sund 5E 118
Luxembourg Rd. SR4: Sund 1K 117
Lychgate Ct. NE8: Gate 3H 83 (10K 5)
Lydbury Cl. NE23: Cra 1A 26
Lydcott NE38: Wash 3B 116
Lydford Ct. DH4: Hou S 6C 130
NE3: Ken 6J 43
Lydford Way DH3: Bir 5B 114
Lydney Cl. NE15: Thro 4G 59
Lymington DH7: Esh W 5E 162
Lyncroft NE63: Ash 5A 12
Lyncroft Rd. NE29: N Shi 6E 48
Lyndale NE23: Cra 1A 26
Lynden Gdns. NE5: Newc T 2G 61
Lynden Ga. NE9: Gate 4J 99
Lynden Rd. SR2: Ryh 1H 133
LYNDHURST 3H 99
Lyndhurst Av. DH3: Ches S 3A 128
NE2: Newc T 3G 63
NE9: Gate 3H 99
Lyndhurst Cl. NE21: Bla T 6A 80
Lyndhurst Cres. NE9: Gate 3J 99
Lyndhurst Dr. DH1: Dur 3J 165
NE9: Gate 3J 99
Lyndhurst Gdns. NE2: Newc T 3F 63
Lyndhurst Grn. NE9: Gate 3H 99
Lyndhurst Gro. NE9: Gate 3J 99
Lyndhurst Rd. DH9: Stly 3D 124
NE12: Longb 5B 46
NE25: Whit B 6E 38
NE63: N Sea 6D 12
Lyndhurst St. NE33: S Shi 3K 67
Lyndhurst Ter. NE16: Swa 5G 81
SR4: Sund 7A 104
Lyndon Cl. NE36: E Bol 7H 87
Lyndon Dr. NE36: E Bol 7H 87
Lyndon Gro. NE36: E Bol 7H 87
Lyndon Wlk. NE24: Cow 1D 22
Lyne Cl. DH2: Ous 1H 127
Lyne's Dr. DH7: B'don 7F 165
Lynfield NE26: Whit B 4E 38
Lynfield Ct. NE5: Newc T 2H 61
Lynfield Pl. NE5: Newc T 2H 61
Lynford Gdns. SR2: Sund 5E 118
Lyngrove SR2: Ryh 1H 133
Lynholm Gro. NE12: Longb 4B 46
Lynmouth Pl. NE7: Newc T 2K 63
Lynmouth Rd. NE9: Gate 4H 99
NE29: N Shi 7C 48
Lynn Cres. DH6: Cass 4E 178
(not continuous)
Lynndale Av. NE24: Cow 2E 22
Lynneholm Ct. NE8: Gate 6J 83
Lynnholm Cl. NE7: Newc T 3K 63
Lynnholme Gdns. NE9: Gate 6H 83
(not continuous)
Lynn Rd. NE28: W'snd 4E 64
NE29: N Shi 5D 48
Lynn St. DH3: Ches S 7A 128
NE24: Bly 2H 23
Lynn Ter. DH6: Whe H 1C 180
Lynnwood Av. NE4: Newc T 1B 82
Lynnwood Bus. Development Cen.
NE4: Newc T 1C 82
Lynnwood Ter. NE4: Newc T 1B 82
Lynthorpe SR2: Ryh 1H 133
Lynthorpe Gro. SR6: Monk 3G 105
Lynton Av. NE32: Jar 1E 86
Lynton Ct. DH4: Hou S 6C 130
NE5: Newc T 2H 61
Lynton Pl. NE5: Newc T 2H 61
Lynton Way NE5: Newc T 2H 61
Lynwood Av. NE21: Bla T 3C 80
NE64: Newb S 2H 13
SR4: Sund 6G 117
Lynwood Cl. NE20: Pon 2G 41
LYONS 1H 157
Lyons Av. DH5: Eas L 1H 157
Lyons La. DH5: Eas L 2J 157
Lyons, The DH5: Eas L 1H 157
Lyon St. NE31: Heb 7H 65
Lyric Cl. NE29: N Shi 4C 48
Lysdon Av. NE25: Sea D 4H 27
Lyster Cl. SR7: S'hm 1G 147
Lytchfeld NE10: Gate 7E 84
(not continuous)
Lytham Cl. DH8: Con 4G 121
NE23: Cra 4G 25
NE28: W'snd 5J 47
NE37: Usw 5G 101
Lytham Dr. NE25: Whit B 6D 38
Lytham Grange DH4: Hou S 5A 130
Lytham Grn. NE10: Gate 4F 85
Lytham Pl. NE6: Walk 1C 84
Lythe Way NE12: Longb 6A 46

M

Mabel St. NE21: Bla T 3C 80
Macadam St. NE8: Gate 7F 83
McAnany Av. NE34: S Shi 1K 87
McAteer Ct. DH6: Has 3A 170
Macbeth Wlk. SR8: Pet 6F 173
McClaren Way DH4: E Her 2F 131
McCracken Cl. NE3: Gos 4E 44
McCracken Dr. NE13: Wide O 4E 34
McCutcheon Ct. NE6: Walk 3C 84
McCutcheon St. SR7: S'hm 1G 147
MacDonald Rd. NE4: Newc T 2K 81
McErlane Sq. NE10: Gate 5E 84
McEwan Gdns. NE4: Newc T 1B 82
McEwans Indoor Cricket Cen. 4D 144
McGowen Ct. NE6: Newc T 1A 84
McGuinness Av. SR8: Pet 3C 172
(not continuous)
McIlvenna Gdns. NE28: W'snd 1E 64
McIntyre Hall NE31: Heb 6K 65
McIntyre Rd. NE31: Heb 6K 65
McKendrick Vs. NE5: Newc T 4K 61
MacKintosh Ct. DH1: Dur 2D 166
McLennan Ct. NE38: Wash 2H 115
Maclynn Cl. SR3: New S 3A 132
Macmerry Cl. SR5: C'twn 7F 103
Macmillan Gdns. NE10: Gate 6E 84
McNally Pl. DH1: Dur 2D 166
McNamara Rd. NE28: W'snd 2J 65
McNulty Ct. NE23: Dud 3H 35
Maddison Ct. SR1: Sund 1H 119
Maddison Gdns. NE23: Seg 2C 36
Maddison St. NE24: Bly 1J 23
Maddox Rd. NE12: Longb 6B 46
Madeira Av. NE26: Whit B 4F 39
Madeira Cl. NE5: Cha P 1C 60
Madeira Ter. NE33: S Shi 4K 67
Madras St. NE34: S Shi 2G 87
Madrona Cl. DH4: Hou S 4K 129
Mafeking Pl. NE29: N Shi 3B 48
Mafeking St. NE6: Walk 3D 84
NE9: Gate 6J 83
SR4: Sund 1B 118
Mafeking Ter. DH7: Sac 1D 152
Magdalene Av. DH1: Carr 7G 155
Magdalene Ct. *DH1: Dur 2C 166*
(off Leazes La.)
DH8: M'sly 7K 107
(off Nth. Magdalene)
NE2: Newc T 6D 62 (1B 4)
SR7: S'hm 2B 148
Magdalene Hgts. *DH1: Dur 2C 166*
(off Leazes La.)
Magdalene Pl. SR4: Sund 1B 118
Magdalene St. DH1: Dur 2C 166
Magenta Cres. NE5: Cha P 7C 42
Maglona St. SR7: S'hm 4B 148
Magnolia Cl. NE4: Newc T 6K 61
Magnolia Dr. NE63: Ash 6A 12
Magnolia Gro. NE16: Burn 2B 110
Magpie Ct. NE63: Ash 5K 11
Mahogany Row DH9: Beam 7K 111
Maidenhair DH4: Hou S 4K 129
Maiden La. NE40: G'sde 4E 78
MAIDEN LAW 2A 138
Maiden Law DH4: Hou S 3A 144
Maidens Cft. NE46: Hex 2B 70
Maiden St. NE4: Newc T 3D 82 (9B 4)
Maidens Wlk. NE8: Gate 2H 83 (8J 5)
NE46: Hex 2D 70
Maidstone Cl. SR3: New S 3K 131
Maidstone Ter. DH4: Hou S 5D 130
Main Cres. NE28: W'snd 1D 64
Maingate NE11: Gate 7E 82
Main Rd. NE13: Din 4H 33
NE13: Wool 5H 43
NE40: Ryton 1E 78
NE41: Wylam 7J 57
NE42: O'ham 2D 76
NE43: Stoc 7G 75
Mains Ct. DH1: Dur 6J 153
Mainsforth Ter. SR2: Sund 3H 119
Mainsforth Ter. W. SR2: Sund 4G 119
Mains Pk. Rd. DH3: Ches S 6B 128
Mains Pl. NE61: Mor 6F 9
Mainstone Cl. NE23: Cra 4J 25
Main St. DH8: Con 7K 121
NE20: Pon 5J 31
NE40: Ryton 2D 78
NE45: Cor 1E 72
NE46: Acomb 4B 50
Main St. Nth. NE23: Seg 2D 36
Main St. Sth. NE23: Seg 2D 36
Maitland Ter. NE64: Newb S 3H 13
Makendon St. NE31: Heb 6J 65
Makepeace Ter. NE9: Spri 6D 100
Malaburn Way SR5: S'wck 6C 104
Malaga Cl. NE5: Cha P 1B 60
Malaya Dr. NE6: Walk 1F 85
Malcolm Av. DH6: Quar H 6D 178
Malcolm Ct. NE25: Whit B 7D 38
Malcolm St. NE6: Newc T 7J 63 (3M 5)
SR7: S'hm 4B 148
Malden Cl. NE23: Cra 4H 25
Maling Pk. SR4: Sund 1H 117
Malings Cl. SR1: Sund 2H 119
Maling St. NE6: Newc T 1J 83 (5M 5)
Mallard Cl. NE38: Wash 4D 114
NE63: Ash 7B 12
Mallard Ct. NE12: Kil 7A 36
Mallard Lodge NE10: Gate 6B 84
Mallard Way DH4: W Rai 4B 144
NE24: News 6K 23
NE28: W'snd 6A 48
Mallowburn Cres. NE3: Ken 1J 61
Malmo Cl. NE29: N Shi 7B 48
Malone Gdns. DH3: Bir 2A 114
Malory Pl. NE8: Gate 4H 83
Maltby Cl. NE38: Wash 4H 115
SR3: New S 4A 132
Malt Cres. SR8: Pet 5D 172
Malthouse Way NE5: Newc T 1H 61
Maltings, The DH1: Dur 3B 6
SR3: New S 2E 132
TS28: Win 4G 181
Maltkiln NE46: Hex 2C 70
Malton Cl. NE15: Lem 7E 60
NE24: Cow 2F 23
Malton Ct. NE32: Jar 6A 66
Malton Cres. NE29: N Shi 1E 66
Malton Gdns. NE28: W'snd 1F 65
Malton Grn. NE9: Gate 6K 99
Malvern Av. DH2: Ches S 7K 127
(not continuous)
Malvern Cl. NE63: N Sea 6D 12
SR8: Pet 7K 171
Malvern Ct. NE11: Gate 1C 98
NE15: Lem 6B 60
SR6: Cle 5B 88
Malvern Cres. SR7: S'hm 3J 147
TS29: Trim S 7C 180
Malvern Gdns. NE11: Gate 1C 98
(not continuous)
SR6: Monk 4G 105
Malvern Rd. NE26: Sea S 5D 28
NE28: W'snd 2K 65
NE29: N Shi 4E 48
NE38: Wash 5F 115
Malvern St. NE4: Newc T 2C 82
NE33: S Shi 6J 67
Malvern Ter. DH9: Stly 4G 125
Malvern Vs. DH1: Dur 2D 166
Malvins Cl. Rd. NE24: Cow 2G 23
Malvins Rd. NE24: Cow 1F 23
Manchester St. NE61: Mor 6F 9
Mandale Cres. NE30: N Shi 1G 49
Mandarin Cl. NE5: Cha P 1B 60
Mandarin Lodge *NE10: Gate 6B 84*
(off Crowhall La.)
Mandarin Way NE38: Wash 2B 116
Mandela Cl. DH9: Stly 4D 124
SR1: Sund 1H 119
Mandela Way NE11: Dun 3J 81
Manderville Pk. DH5: Hett H 7H 145
Mandeville NE37: Usw 7K 101
Manet Gdns. NE34: S Shi 2K 87
Mangrove Cl. NE5: Cha P 1B 60
Manila St. SR2: Sund 4G 119
Manisty Ho. NE4: Newc T 2A 82
Manisty Ter. SR8: Eas 7A 160
Manley Vw. NE63: N Sea 5E 12
Mann Cres. SR7: Mur 6F 147
Manners Gdns. NE25: Sea D 6G 27
Manningford Cl. NE23: Cra 5J 25
Manningford Dr. SR3: New S 4A 132
Manor Av. NE7: Newc T 7A 46
NE15: Thro 5K 59
Manor Chare NE1: Newc T 1G 83 (6H 5)
Manor Cl. DH1: H Shin 6E 166
DH8: C'sde 1E 134
NE3: Gos 7F 45
NE44: Rid M 7K 73
Manor Cotts. NE45: Cor 7D 52
Manor Ct. NE33: S Shi 4B 68
Manor Dr. DH9: Ann P 4K 123
NE7: Newc T 7A 46
NE64: Newb S 2J 13
Manor Farm NE23: Dud 1J 35
Manorfields NE12: Newc T 6B 46
Manor Gdns. NE7: Newc T 7A 46
NE10: Gate 6F 85
Manor Grange DH7: Lan 7A 138
Manor Gro. DH4: E Her 2F 131
NE7: Newc T 7A 46
NE15: Thro 6K 59
Manor Hall Cl. SR7: S'hm 2G 147
Manor Ho. Cl. NE6: Newc T 1A 84
Manor Ho. Est. TS27: Cas E 7B 182
(No's 19-30)
TS27: Cas E 7K 181
(No's 5-18)
Manor Ho. Farm Cotts. NE3: Ken 1K 61
Manor Ho. Rd. NE2: Newc T 4H 63
Manor Pk. NE37: Usw 7H 101
NE45: Cor 7D 52
Manor Pl. NE7: Newc T 7A 46
Manor Rd. DH8: M'sly 7K 107
DH9: Stly 2F 125
NE7: Newc T 1A 64
NE30: N Shi 4K 49
NE37: Usw 7H 101
Manors Station (Metro) 1G 83 (5H 5)
Manors Station (Rail) 1G 83 (5H 5)
Manors, The NE42: Pru 3G 77
Manor Ter. NE21: Bla T 5A 80
(Winlaton)
NE21: Bla T 7C 80
(Winlaton Moor)
Manor Vw. DH6: H Pitt 7B 156
NE37: Usw 7J 101
NE64: Newb S 2J 13
Manor Vw. E. NE37: Usw 7J 101
Manor Wlk. NE7: Newc T 7A 46
Mnr. Walks Shop. Cen. NE23: Cra 4J 25
Manor Way SR8: Pet 7C 172
Manorway NE30: N Shi 4K 49
NE32: Jar 5C 86
Mansell Cres. SR8: Pet 5C 172
Mansell Pl. NE3: Ken 2A 62
Mansel Ter. NE24: Cow 2C 22
Manse St. DH8: Con 5G 121
Mansfield Ct. NE36: W Bol 7G 87
Mansfield Cres. SR6: Monk 4G 105
Mansfield Pl. NE4: Newc T 1D 82 (5B 4)

Mansfield St.—Meadow Cl.

Mansfield St. NE4: Newc T 1D 82 (5A 4)
Mansion Ho. NE36: W Bol 7G 87
Manston Cl. SR3: New S 3K 131
Manx Sq. SR5: S'wck 4D 104
Maple Av. DH1: Dur 2E 166
NE11: Dun 7C 82
NE25: Whit B 1F 49
SR3: New S 1D 132
Maplebeck Cl. SR3: New S 4K 131
Maple Cl. NE15: Lem 7E 60
NE22: Bed 7H 17
Maple Ct. DH7: B'don 2B 174
NE12: Kil 7A 36
NE25: Sea D 4H 27
Maple Cres. NE24: Cow 1D 22
SR7: S'hm 6A 148
Mapledene NE38: Wash 6J 115
Mapledene Rd. NE3: Ken 6B 44
Maple Gdns. DH8: Con 5E 120
DH9: Stly 5E 124
Maple Gro. DH9: Stly 5D 124
NE8: Gate 7G 83
NE10: Gate 6C 84
NE34: S Shi 2B 88
NE42: Pru 4D 76
SR6: Whit 5H 89
Maple Pk. DH7: Ush M 3D 164
Maple Rd. NE21: Bla T 4C 80
Maple Row NE11: Dun 4H 81
Maple St. DH8: Con 6H 121
DH9: Stly 5D 124
NE4: Newc T 2D 82 (8B 4)
NE32: Jar 6A 66
NE63: Hir 4B 12
(Third Av.)
NE63: Hir 3B 12
(Woodhorn Rd.)
Maple Ter. DH4: Hou S 4A 130
DH9: Ann P 4J 123
(off Pine Ter.)
NE4: Newc T 2D 82 (8A 4)
NE16: Burn 2K 109
Maplewood DH2: Ches S 4J 127
NE6: Walk 5C 64
Maplewood Av. SR5: S'wck 4B 104
Maplewood Ct. DH7: Lang P 5H 151
Maplewood Cres. NE38: Wash 7F 115
Maplewood Dr. DH6: Has 1B 170
Maplewood St. DH4: Hou S 1J 143
Mapperley Dr. NE15: Lem 6E 60
Marblet Ct. NE11: Gate 7D 82
Marbury Cl. SR3: New S 3K 131
Marchburn La. NE44: Rid M 7J 73
March Rd. NE23: Dud 3K 35
March Ter. NE13: Din 4G 33
Marcia Av. DH6: Shot C 5E 170
SR6: Monk 4F 105
Marconi Way NE11: Dun, Swa 5H 81
Marcross Cl. NE15: Cha P 3B 60
Marcross Dr. SR3: New S 4K 131
Mardale NE37: Wash 1F 115
Mardale Gdns. NE9: Gate 4J 99
Mardale Rd. NE5: Newc T 4H 61
Mardale St. DH5: Hett H 1G 157
MARDEN 7G 39
Marden Av. NE30: N Shi 1J 49
Marden Bridge Sports Cen. 7G 39
Marden Cl. NE61: Mor 1D 14
Marden Ct. NE26: Sea S 3B 28
Marden Cres. NE26: Whit B 7J 39
Marden Farm Dr. NE30: N Shi 1H 49
Marden Quarry Nature Reserve 1G 49
Marden Rd. NE26: Whit B 6G 39
(not continuous)
Marden Rd. Sth. NE25: Whit B 7G 39
(not continuous)
Marden Ter. NE30: N Shi 1J 49
Mareburn Cres. NE10: Gate 6C 84
Mare Cl. NE23: Seg 7E 26
Maree Cl. SR3: New S 4A 132
Margaret Alice St. SR4: Sund 1A 118
Margaret Collins Ho. NE6: Walk 7C 64
Margaret Cotts. *NE25: N Shi 2F 49*
(off Zetland Dr.)
Margaret Ct. DH6: Bow 4H 177
Margaret Dr. NE12: Longb 4E 46
Margaret Gro. NE34: S Shi 1G 87
Margaret Rd. NE26: Whit B 7J 39
Margaret St. DH6: Shad 5J 169
SR2: Sund 6J 119
SR7: S'hm 4B 148
Margaret Ter. DH4: Hou S 3C 130
DH9: Tan L 7C 110
NE39: Row G 6G 95
Margate St. SR3: New S 1C 132
Margery La. DH1: Dur 3K 165 (4A 6)
Marguerite Ct. SR4: Sund 1D 118 (3F 7)
Marian Ct. NE8: Gate 5F 83
Marian Dr. NE10: Gate 4F 85
Marian Way NE20: Pon 2F 41
NE34: S Shi 3B 88
Maria St. NE4: Newc T 2A 82
SR3: New S 2C 132
SR7: S'hm 3B 148
Marie Curie Dr. NE4: Newc T 2B 82
Marigold Av. NE10: Gate 4K 83
Marigold Ct. SR4: Sund 1D 118
Marigold Cres. DH4: Hou S 6J 129
Marigold Wlk. NE34: S Shi 1H 87
Marina Av. SR6: Monk 4E 104
Marina Ct. SR6: Monk 4F 105
Marina Dr. NE25: Whit B 7B 38
NE33: S Shi 2A 68
Marina Gro. SR6: Monk 4F 105
Marina Ter. SR2: Ryh 3H 133
SR6: Whit 5H 89
Marina Vw. NE28: W'snd 3K 65
NE31: Heb 7G 65
Marine App. NE33: S Shi 3K 67
Marine Av. NE26: Whit B 6F 39
Marine Cotts. NE64: Newb S 3H 13
Marine Ct. E. NE26: Whit B 5G 39
Marine Ct. W. NE26: Whit B 5G 39
Marine Cres. TS27: B Col 3K 183
Marine Dr. NE31: Heb, Jar 3A 86
SR2: Ryh 1H 133
Marine Gdns. NE26: Whit B 6G 39
Mariner's Cotts. NE33: S Shi 2A 68
(not continuous)
Mariners' La. NE30: N Shi 5J 49
Mariners Point NE30: N Shi 5K 49
Mariner Sq. SR1: Sund 7H 105
Mariners Wharf NE1: Newc T 1J 83 (6L 5)
Marine St. NE64: Newb S 2J 13
Marine Ter. NE24: Bly 2J 23
Marine Ter. E. NE24: Bly 2J 23
Marine Vw. NE26: Sea S 3B 28
Marine Wlk. SR6: Monk 4H 105
Marion St. SR2: Sund 4G 119
Maritime Cres. SR8: Eas 2D 172
Maritime Pl. NE61: Mor 6F 9
Maritime St. SR1: Sund 2F 119 (4J 7)
Maritime Ter. SR1: Sund 2E 118 (4H 7)
Marius Av. NE15: Hed W 3D 58
Mariville E. SR2: Ryh 4J 133
Mariville W. SR2: Ryh 4J 133
Marjorie St. NE23: E Cram 5C 26
Markby Cl. SR3: New S 4A 132
Market Cres. DH4: Hou S 3C 130
TS28: Win 7G 181
Market Hall DH9: Stly 2E 124
Market La. NE1: Newc T 1G 83 (6G 4)
NE11: Dun 6A 82
NE16: Dun, Swa, Whi 5G 81
Market Pl. DH1: Dur 2C 6
DH3: Ches S 5A 128
DH5: Hou S 2F 145
DH7: Esh W 4E 162
NE22: Bed 1H 21
NE24: Bly 1J 23
NE33: S Shi 2J 67
NE45: Cor 1D 72
NE46: Hex 1D 70
NE61: Mor 6F 9
Market Pl. Ind. Est. DH5: Hou S 1F 145
Market Pl. W. NE61: Mor 7F 9
Market Sq. NE32: Jar 6B 66
SR1: Sund 2F 119 (4J 7)
Market St. DH5: Hett H 5H 145
DH8: Shot B 5F 121
(off Queen's Rd.)
NE1: Newc T 1F 83 (5F 4)
NE23: Dud 3H 35
NE24: Bly 1J 23
NE46: Hex 1D 70
Market Way NE11: Gate 1F 99
Mark Gdns. NE41: Wylam 7J 57
Markham Av. SR6: Whit 6J 89
Markham St. SR2: Sund 6H 119
Markington Dr. SR2: Ryh 3H 133
Markle Gro. DH5: W Rai 5D 144
Mark Ri. DH5: Hett H 5G 145
Mark's La. DH4: Leam, W Rai 6J 143
Marlboro Av. NE16: Swa 6H 81
Marlborough SR7: S'hm 3B 148
Marlborough App. NE3: Gos 5E 44
Marlborough Av. NE3: Gos 5D 44
Marlborough Ct. DH5: Hou S 4E 144
NE3: Ken 5K 43
NE32: Jar 1B 86
Marlborough Cres.
NE1: Newc T 2E 82 (7D 4)
NE9: Gate 4A 100
SR8: Pet 6F 173
Marlborough Ho. NE26: Whit B 5F 39
Marlborough Rd. NE37: Usw 6J 101
SR4: Sund 5F 117
Marlborough St. Nth. NE33: S Shi 5K 67
Marlborough St. Sth. NE33: S Shi 5K 67
Marlborough Ter. NE62: Sco G 4H 17
Marlbro Health & Fitness Club *2B 148*
(off Vane Ter.)
Marleen Av. NE6: Newc T 5A 64
Marleen Ct. NE6: Newc T 5A 64
Marlene Av. DH6: Bow 3G 177
Marlesford Cl. SR3: New S 3K 131
Marley Cres. SR5: S'wck 4B 104
MARLEY HILL 6G 97
MARLEY POTS 4B 104
Marleys Cotts. DH7: Lang P 7A 150
Marlfield Ct. NE5: Newc T 2H 61
Marlow Dr. SR3: New S 4K 131
Marlowe Gdns. NE8: Gate 5H 83
Marlowe Pl. DH5: Hou S 3E 144
Marlowe Wlk. NE34: S Shi 3G 87
Marlow Pl. NE12: Longb 6A 46
Marlow St. NE24: Bly 2H 23
Marlow Way NE16: Whi 2F 97
Marmion Rd. NE6: Walk 5D 64
Marmion Ter. NE25: Whit B 7F 39
Marne St. DH4: Hou S 3C 130
Marondale Av. NE6: Walk 6D 64
Marquis Av. NE5: Cha P 7C 42
Marquis Cl. NE12: Newc T 7B 46
Marquis Ct. NE11: Gate 4F 99
NE42: Pru 2G 77
Marquisway NE11: Gate 4F 99
Marquisway Cen. NE11: Gate 4E 98
Marr Rd. NE31: Heb 1K 85
MARSDEN 1E 88
Marsden Av. SR6: Whit 3H 89
Marsden Cl. DH4: Hou S 2C 144
Marsden Gro. NE9: Gate 4B 100
SR6: Whit 5H 89
Marsden La. NE5: Newc T 2G 61
NE34: S Shi 6D 68
Marsden Rd. NE34: S Shi 6B 68
SR6: Cle 6B 88
Marsden St. NE33: S Shi 5K 67
Marsden Vw. SR6: Whit 3H 89
Marshall's Ct. NE1: Newc T 1F 83 (6E 4)
Marshall St. SR6: Monk 3F 105
Marshall Ter. DH1: Dur 1F 167
Marshall Wallis Rd. NE33: S Shi 5J 67
(not continuous)
Marsham Cl. NE15: Lem 6E 60
SR6: Cle 4C 88
Marsham Rd. NE5: Newc T 2E 60
Marsh Ct. NE11: Gate 7D 82
Marshes Ho's. NE62: W Sle 1B 18
Marshmont Av. NE30: N Shi 3J 49
Marske Ter. NE6: Walk 7C 64
Marston NE12: Kil 7B 36
Marston Wlk. NE16: Whi 2F 97
Martello Gdns. NE7: Newc T 3B 64
Martha St. DH9: Tan L 6B 110
Martin Ct. NE38: Wash 6D 114
Martindale Av. SR6: Monk 3E 104
Martindale Pk. DH5: Hou S 2E 144
Martindale Pl. NE25: Sea D 7J 27
Martindale Wlk. NE12: Kil 1A 46
TS28: Win 4G 181
Martin Hall NE32: Jar 7C 66
Martin Rd. NE28: W'snd 3K 65
Martin Ter. SR4: Sund 1B 118
Martin Way NE13: Bru V 5C 34
Marwell Dr. NE37: Usw 5J 101
Marwood Ct. NE25: Whit B 5D 38
Marwood Gro. SR8: Pet 2A 182
Marx Cres. DH9: Stly 4F 125
(not continuous)
Marx Ter. NE17: C'wl 7A 94
Mary Agnes St. NE3: Gos 7C 44
Mary Av. DH3: Bir 2K 113
Mary Cres. DH6: Kel 7E 178
Maryhill Cl. NE4: Newc T 2A 82
Mary Magdalene Bungs.
NE2: Newc T 5D 62
Maryside Pl. NE40: Ryton 6D 58
Mary's Pl. NE6: Walk 7F 65
Mary St. DH9: Ann P 5A 124
DH9: Stly 3E 124
NE21: Bla T 4A 80
(Black La.)
NE21: Bla T 3C 80
(Murray St.)
SR1: Sund 2E 118 (5H 7)
SR3: New S 1C 132
SR7: S'hm 3C 148
Mary Ter. DH6: Bow 4G 177
NE5: Newc T 3G 61
Masefield Av. NE16: Swa 5H 81
Masefield Cl. DH9: Stly 2H 125
Masefield Dr. NE34: S Shi 3G 87
Masefield Pl. NE8: Gate 4H 83
Masefields DH2: Pelt 6G 127
Maslin Gro. SR8: Pet 2J 181
MASON 3H 33
Mason Av. NE26: Whit B 6H 39
Mason Cres. SR8: Pet 6D 172
Mason Rd. NE28: W'snd 1E 64
Mason St. DH8: Con 7H 121
NE6: Newc T 1A 84 (5P 5)
NE13: Bru V 5C 34
Mason Vw. NE13: Sea B 3D 34
Massingham Way NE34: S Shi 1H 87
Master Mariner's Homes NE30: N Shi 5J 49
Master's Cres. NE42: Pru 4D 76
Mast La. NE30: N Shi 1H 49
Matamba Ter. SR4: Sund 2D 118
Matanzas St. SR2: Sund 5G 119
Matfen Av. NE13: Bru V 7C 34
NE27: Shir 2A 48
Matfen Cl. NE15: Lem 7E 60
NE24: Bly 2G 23
Matfen Ct. DH2: Ches S 6J 127
Matfen Dr. SR3: New S 3K 131
Matfen Gdns. NE28: W'snd 7K 47
Matfen Pl. NE3: Ken 6C 44
NE4: Newc T 6B 62
Matfen Ter. NE64: Newb S 4H 13
Mather Rd. NE4: Newc T 2D 82 (8A 4)
Mathesons Gdns. NE61: Mor 7F 9
Matlock Gdns. NE5: Newc T 2F 61
Matlock Rd. NE32: Jar 1C 86
Matlock St. SR1: Sund 1F 119 (2J 7)
Matterdale Rd. SR8: Pet 6D 172
Matthew Bank NE2: Gos 2G 63
Matthew Cl. NE6: Newc T 7K 63 (3P 5)
Matthew Rd. NE24: Bly 4K 23
Matthews Cres. DH6: S Het 5D 158
Matthews Rd. SR7: Mur 2G 159
Matthew St. NE6: Newc T 7K 63 (3P 5)
Maude Gdns. NE28: W'snd 4F 65
Maudlin Pl. NE5: Newc T 4K 61
Maudlin St. DH5: Hett H 4H 145
Mauds La. SR1: Sund 1G 119
Mauds Ter. NE64: Newb S 2J 13
Maud St. NE15: Lem 7C 60
SR6: Monk 3G 105
Maud Ter. DH9: Tan L 5D 110
NE27: Shir 3J 47
Maudville DH8: C'sde 4C 134
Maughan St. NE24: Bly 2K 23
Maureen Av. TS27: B Col 3J 183
Maureen Ter. DH1: Dur 5G 155
SR7: S'hm 3A 148
Maurice Rd. NE28: W'snd 5F 65
Maurice Rd. Ind. Est.
NE28: Walk 5F 65
Mautland Sq. DH4: Hou S 1E 144
Mautland St. DH4: Hou S 1E 144
Mavin St. DH1: Dur 4B 166 (5E 6)
Maxton Cl. SR3: New S 4K 131
Maxwell St. NE8: Gate 7F 83
NE33: S Shi 3J 67
SR4: Sund 1B 118
May Av. NE21: Bla T 7C 80
NE40: Ryton 7G 59
NE64: Newb S 2G 13
Maybury Vs. NE12: Longb 7J 45
May Cres. TS29: Trim S 7D 180
Maydown Cl. SR5: C'twn 7F 103
Mayfair Ct. NE31: Heb 1H 85
Mayfair Gdns. NE8: Gate 6J 83
NE20: Pon 5K 31
NE34: S Shi 6A 68
Mayfair Health Club *3D 118*
(off Durham Rd.)
Mayfair Rd. NE2: Newc T 3F 63
Mayfield NE16: Whi 2H 97
NE61: Mor 1E 14
Mayfield Av. NE15: Thro 4J 59
NE23: Cra 4A 26
Mayfield Ct. SR6: Monk 4F 105
Mayfield Dr. SR6: Cle 6D 88
Mayfield Gdns. NE15: Thro 4J 59
NE28: W'snd 2D 64
NE32: Jar 7A 66
Mayfield Gro. SR4: Sund 6G 117
Mayfield Pl. NE13: Wide O 6C 34
Mayfield Rd. NE3: Gos 1D 62
SR4: Sund 2G 117
Mayfield Ter. NE5: Newc T 4A 62
May Gro. SR6: Whit 3H 89
May Lea DH7: Wit G 2D 152
Maynards Row DH1: Dur 2D 166
Maynes Way DH9: Stly 2H 125
Mayo Dr. SR3: New S 4A 132
Mayoral Way NE11: Gate 4F 99
Mayorswell Cl. DH1: Dur 2B 166 (1E 6)
Mayorswell Fld. DH1: Dur 2C 166 (1E 6)
Mayorswell St. DH1: Dur 2B 166 (1E 6)
Maypole Cl. SR5: S'wck 6D 104
May St. DH1: Dur 3K 165
DH3: Bir 4A 114
NE21: Bla T 5B 80
NE33: S Shi 4K 67
SR4: Sund 1D 118 (3F 7)
Mayswood Rd. SR6: Monk 4F 105
May Ter. DH7: Lang P 5J 151
Maythorne Dr. DH6: S Het 5D 158
Maytree Ho. NE4: Newc T 2C 82 (8A 4)
Maywood Cl. NE3: Ken 1A 62
Mazine Ter. DH6: Has 3A 170
Meaburn St. SR1: Sund 2G 119
Meaburn Ter. SR1: Sund 2G 119
Meacham Way NE16: Whi 2G 97
Mead Av. NE12: Longb 4C 46
Mead Cres. NE12: Longb 4C 46
Meadow Av. TS27: B Col 3J 183
Meadowbank DH7: Lang P 5H 151
NE23: Dud 3J 35
Meadowbank Dr. NE62: Chop 1G 17
Meadowbrook Dr. NE10: Gate 7G 85
Mdw. Brook Dr. NE17: C'wl 5A 94
Meadow Cl. DH5: Hou S 3F 145
NE11: Dun 5A 82
NE12: Longb 5K 45
NE21: Bla T 5K 79

Meadow Cl.—Miller's La.

Meadow Cl. NE23: Seg 1D 36
NE40: Ryton 1H 79
Meadow Ct. NE20: Pon 6J 31
NE22: Bed 7G 17
Meadowcroft M. NE8: Gate 5F 83
Meadowdale Cres. NE5: Newc T 2K 61
NE22: Bed 7F 17
Meadow Dr. DH2: Ches S 7H 127
NE13: Sea B 3E 34
SR3: E Her 3H 131
SR4: Sund 3H 117
MEADOWFIELD 2E 174
Meadowfield DH8: Con 6F 121
NE9: Spri 6D 100
NE20: Pon 4J 31
NE25: Whit B 6D 38
NE63: N Sea 5E 12
Meadowfield Av. NE3: Ken 6C 44
Meadowfield Ct. NE20: Pon 4H 31
Meadowfield Cres. NE40: Ryton 2E 78
Meadowfield Dr. SR6: Cle 5C 88
Meadowfield Gdns. NE6: Walk 4E 64
Meadowfield Ind. Est.
DH7: B'don 2F 175
(Edwardson Rd.)
DH7: B'don 2G 175
(St John's Rd.)
NE20: Pon 5J 31
Meadowfield Leisure Cen. 1F 175
Meadowfield Pk. *NE20: Pon* *5J 31*
(off Meadowfield)
Meadowfield Pk. Sth. NE43: Stoc 2J 91
Meadowfield Pl. DH7: B'don 1F 175
Meadowfield Rd. NE3: Gos 1D 62
NE43: Stoc 1H 91
Meadowfield Ter. NE12: Longb 3D 46
NE43: Stoc 7K 75
Meadowfield Way DH9: Tan L 1C 124
Meadow Gdns. SR3: Sund 5D 118
Meadow Grange DH4: Hou S 7J 129
Meadow Gro. SR4: Sund 3H 117
Meadow La. DH1: Dur 6G 155
NE11: Dun 5A 82
NE40: Ryton 2E 78
SR3: E Her 3H 131
Meadow Laws NE34: S Shi 2C 88
Meadow Pk. NE44: Rid M 7K 73
Meadow Ri. DH8: Con 7J 121
NE5: Newc T 1H 61
NE9: Gate 2A 100
Meadow Rd. NE15: Lem 5D 60
NE25: Whit B 7D 38
NE26: Sea S 4B 28
NE28: W'snd 3K 65
Meadows Crest NE43: Hed 4C 92
Meadowside SR2: Sund 4D 118
Meadows La. DH4: W Rai 6B 144
Meadows, The DH4: Hou S 6H 129
DH4: W Rai 1A 156
NE3: Ken 6B 44
NE16: Burn 4A 110
NE40: Ryton 1H 79
Meadow St. DH5: W Rai 7C 144
Meadowsweet Cl. DH8: Con 7J 121
NE24: News 5G 23
Meadow Ter. DH4: Hou S 3C 130
Meadow Va. SR2: Sund 4E 118
Meadowvale NE20: Pon 2E 40
Meadow Vw. DH7: Sac 7E 140
DH8: Con 3A 136
DH9: Dip 7J 109
NE25: Sea D 4H 27
NE29: N Shi 1E 66
NE32: Jar 6D 86
NE40: G'sde 4E 78
SR3: E Her 3H 131
Meadow Wlk. NE40: Ryton 1H 79
SR3: New S 4B 132
Meadow Way DH7: Lan 7J 137
Meadow Well Station (Metro) 1E 66
Mdw. Well Way NE29: N Shi 1E 66
Mead Wlk. NE6: Walk 7D 64
Mead Way NE12: Longb 4C 46
Meadway Dr. NE12: Longb 5D 46
Meadway Ho. NE12: Longb 4D 46
Meal Mkt. *NE46: Hex* *1D 70*
(off Fore St.)
Means Ct. NE23: Dud 5K 35
Means Dr. NE23: Dud 5K 35
Mecca Bingo
Blyth 1K 23
Gateshead 3H 83 (9J 5)
Sunderland 2F 119 (4J 7)
MEDBURN 2C 40
Medburn Av. NE30: N Shi 2J 49
Medburn Rd. NE15: Lem 6B 60
NE25: H'wll 1J 37
Medina Cl. SR3: New S 4A 132
Mediterranean Village *NE11: Dun* *4J 81*
(off Metro Cen.)
Medlar NE9: Gate 3A 100
Medlar Cl. DH4: Hou S 3K 129
MEDOMSLEY 7A 108
Medomsley Gdns. NE9: Gate 3C 100
Medomsley Rd. DH8: Con 6H 121
Medomsly St. SR4: Sund 1C 118
Medway DH3: Gt Lum 3E 142
NE32: Jar 4C 86
Medway Av. NE31: Heb 3J 85
Medway Cl. SR8: Pet 1A 182
Medway Cres. NE8: Gate 5K 83
Medway Gdns. DH9: Stly 5E 124
NE29: N Shi 5G 49
SR4: Sund 4K 117
Medway Pl. NE23: Cra 1A 26
Medwood Ct. NE3: Ken 7A 44
Medwyn Cl. DH4: Hou S 6J 129
NE24: News 4H 23
Megstone NE9: Gate 3H 99
Megstone Av. NE23: Cra 5J 25
Megstone Ct. NE12: Kil 7C 36
Melbeck Dr. DH2: Ous 6G 113
Melbourne Ct. NE1: Newc T 1H 83 (5K 5)
NE8: Gate 3G 83 (9H 5)
Melbourne Cres. NE25: Whit B 1E 48
Melbourne Gdns. NE34: S Shi 3F 87
Melbourne Pl. SR4: Sund 4A 118
Melbourne St. NE1: Newc T 1G 83 (6H 5)
Melbourne Ter. DH7: Sac 5D 140
Melbury NE25: Whit B 5C 38
Melbury Ct. SR6: Monk 4F 105
Melbury Rd. NE7: Newc T 4J 63
Melbury St. SR7: S'hm 5B 148
Meldon Av. DH6: Sher 3A 168
NE3: Ken 5B 44
NE34: S Shi 7A 68
Meldon Cl. NE28: W'snd 2J 65
Meldon Ct. NE40: Ryton 3C 78
Meldon Gdns. NE11: Gate 2C 98
NE62: Chop 7H 11
Meldon Ho. NE24: Cow 1F 23
Meldon Rd. SR4: Sund 1B 118
Meldon St. NE4: Newc T 2C 82
NE28: W'snd 4C 66
Meldon Ter. NE6: Newc T 5K 63
NE40: G'sde 5D 78
NE64: Newb S 4H 13
Meldon Way DH1: H Shin 7F 167
DH9: Ann P 5B 124
NE21: Bla T 6K 79
Melgarve Dr. SR3: New S 4A 132
Melkington Ct. NE5: Newc T 2H 61
Melkridge Gdns. NE7: Newc T 2B 64
Melkridge Pl. NE23: Cra 5H 25
Mellendean Cl. NE5: Newc T 2H 61
Melling Rd. NE23: Cra 4H 25
Melmerby Cl. NE3: Gos 5F 45
Melness Rd. NE13: Bru V 6C 34
Melock Ct. NE13: Bru V 6C 34
Melrose NE38: Wash 5H 115
Melrose Av. NE9: Gate 2J 99
NE22: Bed 7B 18
NE25: Sea D 1H 37
NE25: Whit B 7F 39
NE27: Back 6G 37
NE30: N Shi 2G 49
NE31: Heb 3J 85
SR7: Mur 1C 158
Melrose Cl. NE3: Gos 2D 44
NE15: Lem 7E 60
Melrose Ct. DH8: Con 5E 120
NE22: Bed 6B 18
Melrose Cres. SR7: S'hm 2H 147
Melrose Gdns. DH4: Hou S 6C 130
NE28: W'snd 7A 48
SR6: Monk 4G 105
Melrose Gro. NE32: Jar 2E 86
Melrose Ter. NE22: Bed 6B 18
NE64: Newb S 4H 13
Melrose Vs. NE22: Bed 6B 18
Melsonby Cl. SR3: New S 3K 131
Meltham Ct. NE15: Cha P 3B 60
Meltham Dr. SR3: New S 4A 132
Melton Av. NE6: Walk 1D 84
Melton Cres. NE26: Sea S 6D 28
Melton Dr. NE25: Sea D 4H 27
Melton Ter. NE25: Sea D 4H 27
Melvaig Cl. SR3: New S 4A 132
Melville Av. NE24: News 4H 23
Melville Gdns. NE25: Whit B 7C 38
Melville Gro. NE7: Newc T 2J 63
Melville St. DH3: Ches S 7A 128
Melvin Pl. NE5: Newc T 3H 61
Melvyn Gdns. SR6: Monk 4G 105
Membury Cl. SR3: New S 4A 132
Memorial Av. SR8: Eas 7C 160
Memorial Homes DH9: Tan L 1D 124
Memorial Sq. NE64: Newb S 2H 13
Menai Ct. SR3: New S 3B 132
Menceforth Cotts. DH2: Ches S 5K 127
Mendham Cl. NE10: Gate 1C 100
Mendip Av. DH2: Ches S 7K 127
(not continuous)
Mendip Cl. NE29: N Shi 3F 49
NE63: N Sea 6C 12
SR8: Pet 6K 171
Mendip Dr. NE38: Wash 5F 115
Mendip Gdns. NE11: Gate 1D 98
Mendip Ho. DH2: Ches S 7A 128
Mendip Ter. DH9: Stly 4G 125
Mendip Way NE12: Longb 6H 45
Mentieth Cl. NE38: Wash 5F 115
Menvill Pl. SR1: Sund 2G 119
Mercantile Rd. DH4: Hou S 3C 144
Merchants Wharf NE6: Newc T 3A 84
Mercia Retail Pk. DH1: Dur 3A 154
Mercia Way NE15: Lem 1E 80
Meredith Gdns. NE8: Gate 5H 83
Mere Dr. DH1: Dur 4K 153
Mere Knolls Rd. SR6: Monk 2G 105
Meresyde NE10: Gate 1E 100
Meresyde Ct. NE10: Gate 7E 84
Merevale Cl. NE37: Usw 5J 101
Merganser Lodge *NE10: Gate* *6B 84*
(off Crowhall La.)
Meridian Way NE7: Newc T 2B 64
Merlay Dr. NE13: Din 5H 33
Merlay Hall NE6: Walk 2E 84
Merle Gdns. NE6: Newc T 1A 84 (6P 5)
NE61: Mor 5D 8
Merle Ter. SR4: Sund 7B 104
Merley Cft. NE61: Mor 2G 15
Merley Ga. NE61: Mor 2G 15
Merlin Cl. SR7: S'hm 2A 148
Merlin Ct. DH7: Esh W 4C 162
NE10: Gate *6B 84*
(off High St.)
Merlin Cres. NE28: W'snd 2K 65
Merlin Dr. DH3: Ches S 2B 128
Merlin Pl. NE12: Longb 5J 45
Merlin Way NE27: Shir 3A 48
Merrick Ho. SR3: New S 3B 132
Merrington Cl. NE25: Sea D 3H 27
SR3: New S 3K 131
Merrion Cl. SR3: New S 3K 131
Merryfield Gdns. SR6: Monk 4G 105
MERRYOAKS 5J 165
Mersey Ct. SR3: New S 3B 132
Mersey Pl. NE8: Gate 6K 83
Mersey Rd. NE8: Gate 6K 83
NE31: Heb 3J 85
Mersey St. DH8: Lead 4B 122
NE17: C'wl 6A 94
Merton Ct. NE4: Newc T 2A 82
Merton Rd. NE6: Walk 3D 84
NE20: Pon 5J 31
Merton Sq. *NE24: Bly* *1J 23*
(off Regent St.)
Merton Way NE20: Pon 5J 31
Merz Ct. NE1: Newc T 2E 4
Messenger Bank DH8: Shot B 3E 120
Metcalfe Cres. SR7: Mur 7D 146
Metcalfe Ho. DH1: Dur 2K 165 (2A 6)
Metcalfe Rd. DH8: Con 1K 135
Method Ho's. DH9: Beam 1A 126
Methuen St. NE9: Gate 6J 83
Methven Way NE23: Cra 7A 22
Metro Cen. NE11: Dun 4J 81
Metrocentre E. Bus. Pk. NE11: Dun 4A 82
Metro Centre Station (Rail) 4K 81
Metroland & Superbowl 4J 81
Metro Pk. W. NE11: Dun 4H 81
Metro Retail Pk. NE11: Dun 4H 81
Mews Ct. DH5: Hou S 2E 144
Mews, The DH1: H Shin 6D 166
DH2: Plaw 5J 141
DH4: Hou S 3A 144
NE1: Newc T 7F 63 (4E 4)
NE3: Gos 3F 45
NE10: Gate 6F 85
NE21: Bla T 4E 80
NE30: N Shi 4K 49
SR3: E Her 2H 131
Michaelgate NE6: Newc T 1A 84
Mickle Cl. NE37: Wash 2E 114
Mickle Hill Rd. TS27: B Col, Hes 4E 182
Mickleton Cl. DH3: Gt Lum 3F 143
DH8: Con 1H 135
Mickleton Gdns. SR3: Sund 6D 118
Micklewood Cl. NE61: Peg 1A 10
MICKLEY SQUARE 5B 76
Mid Cross St. NE4: Newc T 3D 82 (9B 4)
Middlebrook NE20: Pon 1F 41
Middle Chare DH3: Ches S 6A 128
Middle Cl. NE38: Wash 7F 115
Middle Ct. DH8: Con 7H 121
Middle Dr. NE13: Wool 2F 43
(not continuous)
NE20: Pon 2F 41
Middle Engine La. NE27: N Shi 5A 48
NE28: N Shi, W'snd 7K 47
NE29: N Shi, W'snd 5A 48
Middlefield DH2: Pelt 2G 127
Middlefields Ind. Est.
NE34: S Shi 7H 67
Middlefield Ter. DH7: Ush M 3B 164
Middle Garth NE5: Newc T 3K 61
Middle Ga. NE5: Newc T 4D 60
NE61: Loan 2F 15
Middle Grn. NE25: Whit B 7C 38
Middle Gro. DH7: B'don 2C 174
Middleham Cl. DH2: Ous 7F 113
Middleham Ct. SR5: S'wck 4A 104
Middleham Rd. DH1: Dur 4B 154
MIDDLE HERRINGTON 1J 131
MIDDLE RAINTON 7B 144
Middle Row DH4: Hou S 1J 143
NE40: Ryton 3J 79
Middles Rd. DH9: Stly 5F 125
MIDDLES, THE 6H 125
Middle St. DH8: Con 7H 121
NE6: Walk 7D 64
NE24: News 5F 23
NE30: N Shi 5K 49
(not continuous)
NE45: Cor 1D 72
SR1: Sund 1E 118 (3H 7)
(not continuous)
TS27: B Col 1H 183
Middle St. E. NE6: Walk 7E 64
Middleton Av. NE4: Newc T 7A 62
NE39: Row G 6K 95
Middleton Cl. DH8: Con 1J 135
SR7: S'hm 1G 147
Middleton Ct. NE2: Newc T 6H 63 (1J 5)
Middleton St. NE24: Bly 2J 23
Middlewood DH7: Ush M 2C 164
Middlewood Pk. NE4: Newc T 6A 62
Middlewood Rd. DH7: Lan 7J 137
Middridge Rd. DH7: Lang P 5G 151
Mid Farm Ct. NE23: Cra 3K 25
Midfield Dr. SR6: Monk 5G 105
Midgley Dr. SR3: New S 4A 132
Midhill Cl. DH7: B'don 1D 174
DH7: Lang P 5J 151
Midhurst Av. NE34: S Shi 5B 68
Midhurst Cl. SR3: New S 3K 131
Midhurst Rd. NE12: Longb 5B 46
Midmoor Rd. SR4: Sund 1A 118
Midsomer Cl. SR3: New S 4K 131
Midway NE6: Walk 7E 64
Milbanke Cl. DH2: Ous 7H 113
Milbanke St. DH2: Ous 7H 113
Milbank Ter. DH6: Shot C 6E 170
MILBOURNE 1A 30
Milburn Cl. DH3: Ches S 7C 128
NE46: Hex 4B 70
Milburn Dr. NE15: Newc T 7H 61
Milburn Rd. NE63: Hir 4B 12
Milburn St. SR4: Sund 1D 118
Milburn Ter. NE62: Chop 2A 18
Milcombe Cl. SR3: New S 3K 131
Mildmay Rd. NE2: Newc T 3F 63
Mildred St. DH5: Hou S 1E 144
Milecastle Ct. NE5: Newc T 3D 60
Mile End Rd. NE33: S Shi 1J 67
(not continuous)
Milfield Av. NE27: Shir 1K 47
NE28: W'snd 1G 65
Milford Gdns. NE3: Gos 3D 44
Milford Rd. NE15: Newc T 1J 81
Military Rd. NE15: Hed W 1J 57
NE30: N Shi 6H 49
Military Vehicle Mus. 5F 63
Milk Mkt. NE1: Newc T 6J 5
Milkwell NE45: Cor 7E 52
Milkwell La. NE45: Ayd, Cor 5E 52
Millais Gdns. NE34: S Shi 4J 87
Mill Bank SR5: Monk 3E 104
Millbank Ct. DH1: Dur 2K 165
Millbank Cres. NE22: Bed 7J 17
Millbank Ho. SR7: S'hm 2H 147
Millbank Ind. Est. NE33: S Shi 3J 67
Millbank Pl. NE22: Bed 1K 21
Millbank Rd. NE6: Walk 2E 84
NE22: Bed 7K 17
Millbank Ter. NE22: Bed 7J 17
TS28: Win 7H 181
Millbeck Gdns. NE9: Gate 4K 99
Millbeck Gro. DH5: Hou S 4D 144
Millbrook NE10: Gate 7C 84
NE29: N Shi 7E 48
Millbrook Rd. NE23: Cra 1A 26
Millburngate DH1: Dur 2A 166 (2B 6)
Millburngate Shop. Cen.
DH1: Dur 2A 166 (2B 6)
Millburn Ho. NE5: Newc T 3A 62
Millburn Ter. DH4: Hou S 3B 130
Mill Cl. NE29: N Shi 7E 48
NE44: Rid M 7K 73
Mill Ct. DH4: Hou S 7J 129
NE17: C'wl 2K 107
Mill Cres. DH4: Pen 3B 130
NE31: Heb 4G 85
Milldale SR7: S'hm 2H 147
Milldale Av. NE24: Cow 2E 22
MILL DAM 3H 67
Milldam NE33: S Shi 3H 67
Milldene Av. NE30: N Shi 4J 49
Mill Dene Vw. NE32: Jar 1C 86
Milldyke Cl. NE25: Whit B 5C 38
Millennium Pl. DH1: Dur 2A 166 (2C 6)
Millennium Way SR5: Monk 7E 104 (1H 7)
Miller Gdns. DH2: Pelt 5F 127
Millers Bank NE28: W'snd 3K 65
Millersfield NE46: Acomb 3B 50
(not continuous)
Millers Hill DH4: Hou S 3C 130
Millershill La. DH8: C'sde, Con 7F 135
Miller's La. NE16: Swa 5H 81

Millers Rd.—Moorsley Rd.

Millers Rd. NE6: Walk 6A 64
Miller St. NE8: Gate 6F 83
Miller Ter. SR3: New S 1C 132
Mill Farm Cl. NE4: Newc T 1D 82 (6A 4)
Mill Farm Rd. NE39: Ham M 2E 108
MILLFIELD 1C 118
Millfield DH7: Lan 6J 137
DH8: Con 2H 135
NE22: Bed 2J 21
NE26: Sea S 5D 28
Millfield Av. NE3: Ken 2A 62
Millfield Cl. DH2: Ches S 1J 141
NE15: Thro 6K 59
Millfield Ct. DH8: Con 6E 120
NE16: Whi 7J 81
NE22: Bed 1J 21
NE26: Sea S 5D 28
NE46: Hex 1B 70
Millfield E. NE22: Bed 2J 21
Millfield Gdns. NE10: Gate 6A 84
NE24: Bly 7H 19
NE30: N Shi 4J 49
NE46: Hex 1B 70
Millfield Gro. NE30: N Shi 3J 49
Millfield La. NE15: Thro 5K 59
Millfield Nth. NE22: Bed 1J 21
Millfield Rd. NE16: Whi 1H 97
NE44: Rid M 7K 73
Millfield Sth. NE22: Bed 2J 21
Millfield Station (Metro) 1C 118
Millfield Ter. NE17: C'wl 6K 93
NE46: Hex 1B 70
SR6: Whit 3H 89
Millfield W. NE22: Bed 1J 21
Millford NE10: Gate 7F 85
Millford Ct. NE10: Gate 1F 101
Millford Way DH6: Bow 4J 177
Mill Grange NE44: Rid M 6A 74
Mill Gro. NE30: N Shi 4J 49
NE34: S Shi 2D 88
Millgrove Vw. NE3: Ken 2B 62
Mill Hill DH5: Hou S 4D 144
SR8: Eas, Pet 4H 171
Mill Hill La. DH1: Dur 5J 165
Mill Hill Rd. NE5: Newc T 5F 61
SR3: New S 3B 132
Mill Hill Wlk. SR3: New S 3C 132
Mill Ho. NE2: Newc T 5D 62 (1B 4)
Mill Ho. Ct. DH1: Dur 2E 166
Milling Ct. NE8: Gate 4E 82
Mill La. DH1: Dur 2E 166
(St Josephs Cl.)
DH1: Dur, H Shin 5E 166
(Willow Tree Av.)
DH2: Plaw 6J 141
DH3: Plaw 6J 141
DH6: Sher 3A 168
DH7: New B 4C 164
DH8: Ebc 4G 107
DH9: Beam 6F 113
NE4: Newc T 2C 82
NE15: Hed W 2D 58
NE21: Bla T 7B 80
NE23: Seg 2A 36
NE29: N Shi 1H 67
NE31: Heb 3H 85
SR6: Whit 2H 89
Mill La. Nth NE4: Newc T 1C 82
Millne Ct. NE22: Bed 7H 17
Millom Ct. SR8: Pet 2J 181
Millom Pl. NE9: Gate 3K 99
Mill Pit DH4: Hou S 3B 130
Mill Race Cl. NE17: C'wl 2K 107
Mill Ri. NE3: Gos 1G 63
Mill Rd. DH7: B'don 7G 165
NE8: Gate 2H 83 (8K 5)
NE17: C'wl 6K 93
SR7: S'hm 2H 147
Mills Gdns. NE28: W'snd 2F 65
Millside NE61: Mor 7F 9
Mill St. DH8: Con 2K 135
SR4: Sund 2D 118
Mill Ter. DH4: Hou S 3B 130
SR8: Eas 7J 159
Millthorp Cl. SR2: Sund 7J 119
Millum Ter. SR6: Monk 6G 105
Mill Vw. NE10: Gate 7A 84
NE36: W Bol 7G 87
Mill Vw. Av. SR6: Monk 4F 105
Millview Dr. NE30: N Shi 3H 49
Mill Vw. Ri. NE42: Pru 2F 77
Mill Vs. NE36: W Bol 7G 87
Mill Way NE15: Hor, O'ham 5F 57
Millway NE9: Gate 7J 83
NE26: Sea S 5D 28
Millway Gro. NE26: Sea S 5D 28
Millwood Grn. NE21: Bla T 1C 96
Milner Cres. NE21: Bla T 5A 80
Milner St. NE33: S Shi 3A 68
Milne Way NE3: Ken 7B 44
Milrig Cl. SR3: New S 4A 132
Milsted Cl. SR3: New S 4K 131
Milsted Ct. NE15: Cha P 3B 60
Milton Av. DH5: Hou S 3E 144
(not continuous)
Milton Av. NE31: Heb 7J 65
TS27: B Col 7G 173
Milton Cl. DH9: Stly 3H 125
NE2: Newc T 6H 63 (2J 5)
SR7: S'hm 3J 147
Milton Grn. NE2: Newc T 6H 63 (2J 5)
Milton Gro. DH6: Shot C 6F 171
NE29: N Shi 6F 49
(not continuous)
NE42: Pru 5D 76
NE63: Hir 4D 12
(not continuous)
Milton La. SR8: Eas 7A 160
Milton Pl. NE2: Newc T 6H 63 (2J 5)
NE9: Spri 6D 100
NE29: N Shi 6F 49
Milton Rd. NE16: Swa, Whi 6G 81
Milton Sq. NE8: Gate 4J 83
(not continuous)
Milton St. NE32: Jar 5B 66
NE33: S Shi 5K 67
NE40: G'sde 5C 78
SR4: Sund 1C 118
Milton Ter. DH2: Pelt 6G 127
NE29: N Shi 6F 49
Milvain Av. NE4: Newc T 7A 62
Milvain Cl. NE8: Gate 5H 83
Milvain St. NE8: Gate 5H 83
Milverton Ct. NE3: Ken 6J 43
Mimosa Dr. NE31: Heb 3J 85
Mimosa Pl. NE4: Newc T 5K 61
Minden St. NE1: Newc T 1G 83 (5H 5)
Mindrum Ter. NE6: Walk 2D 84
NE29: N Shi 1D 66
Mindrum Way NE25: Sea D 7H 27
Minehead Gdns. SR3: New S 1C 132
Miners Cotts. NE15: Newc T 6G 61
Miners' Vs. DH6: Whe H 2C 180
Minerva Cl. NE5: Cha P 1C 60
Mingarry DH3: Bir 6C 114
Mingary Cl. DH5: W Rai 6C 144
Minorca Cl. SR1: Sund 2G 119
Minorca Pl. NE3: Ken 2B 62
Minskip Cl. SR3: New S 4A 132
Minster Ct. DH1: Carr 1G 167
NE8: Gate 3H 83 (10K 5)
Minster Gro. NE15: Cha P 2B 60
Minsterley DH3: Gt Lum 3E 142
Minster Pde. NE32: Jar 6C 66
Minting Pl. NE23: Cra 4H 25
Minton Ct. NE29: N Shi 1F 67
Minton La. NE29: N Shi 1F 67
Minton Sq. SR4: Sund 1A 118
Mirlaw Rd. NE23: Cra 5H 25
Mistletoe Rd. NE2: Newc T 4G 63
Mistletoe St. DH1: Dur 3K 165 (3A 6)
Mitcham Cres. NE7: Newc T 2K 63
Mitchell Av. NE2: Newc T 2G 63
NE25: Whit B 7D 38
Mitchell Cl. SR8: Pet 4K 171
Mitchell Dr. NE63: N Sea 4F 13
Mitchell Gdns. NE34: S Shi 6B 68
Mitchell St. DH1: Dur 2K 165 (2A 6)
DH3: Bir 4K 113
DH9: Ann P 5A 124
DH9: Stly 5D 124
NE6: Walk 7E 64
(not continuous)
NE40: Ryton 3C 78
Mitchell Ter. DH9: Tan L 6B 110
MITFORD 7A 8
Mitford Av. NE24: Bly 3G 23
NE25: Sea D 7G 27
NE61: Peg 3A 10
Mitford Cl. DH1: H Shin 7F 167
DH3: Ches S 1B 128
NE38: Wash 4F 115
Mitford Ct. SR8: Pet 1B 182
Mitford Dr. DH6: Sher 3A 168
NE5: Newc T 2E 60
NE63: Hir 5B 12
Mitford Gdns. NE11: Gate 2C 98
NE13: Wide O 4E 34
NE28: W'snd 7K 47
NE62: Chop 7H 11
(not continuous)
Mitford Pl. NE3: Ken 6C 44
Mitford Rd. NE34: S Shi 7A 68
NE61: Mor 6E 8
Mitford St. NE28: W'snd 3C 66
SR6: Monk 3G 105
Mitford Ter. NE32: Jar 4B 86
Mitford Way NE13: Din 5H 33
Mithras Gdns. NE15: Hed W 3C 58
Mitre Pl. NE33: S Shi 5H 67
Moat Gdns. NE10: Gate 6G 85
Moatside Ct. DH1: Dur 3A 166 (3C 6)
Moatside La. DH1: Dur 3A 166 (3C 6)
Modder St. NE6: Walk 3D 84
Model Dwellings NE38: Wash 4J 115
Model Ter. DH4: Pen 1A 130
Modigars La. NE43: Stoc 3A 92
Moffat Av. NE32: Jar 2E 86
Moffat Cl. NE29: N Shi 4C 48
Moine Gdns. SR6: Monk 4G 105
Moir Ter. *SR2: Ryh 3J 133*
(off Robson Pl.)
Molesdon Cl. NE30: N Shi 3G 49
Molineux Cl. NE6: Newc T 7K 63 (3N 5)
Molineux Ct. NE6: Newc T 7K 63 (3N 5)
Molineux St. NE6: Newc T 7K 63 (3N 5)
Mollyfair Cl. NE40: Ryton 2D 78
Monarch Av. SR3: E Her 4J 131
Monarch Rd. NE4: Newc T 3C 82 (10A 4)
Monarch Ter. NE21: Bla T 4C 80
Monastery Ct. NE32: Jar 6B 66
Mona St. DH9: Stly 2F 125
Moncreiff Ter. SR8: Eas 7B 160
Monday Cres. NE4: Newc T 7D 62 (3A 4)
(not continuous)
Monday Pl. NE4: Newc T 7D 62 (3A 4)
Money Slack DH1: Dur 7K 165
Monkchester Grn. NE6: Walk 1C 84
Monkchester Rd. NE6: Walk 1C 84
Monk Ct. NE8: Gate 4H 83 (10K 5)
SR8: Pet 2K 181
Monkdale Av. NE24: Cow 3E 22
MONK HESLEDEN 6H 183
Monkhouse Av. NE30: N Shi 3G 49
Monkridge NE15: Cha P 3B 60
NE26: Whit B 4E 38
Monkridge Ct. NE3: Gos 1G 63
Monkridge Gdns. NE11: Dun 7B 82
Monks Av. NE25: Whit B 1D 48
Monks Cres. DH1: Dur 1D 166
MONKSEATON 6F 39
Monkseaton Dr. NE25: Whit B 6C 38
NE26: Whit B 4F 39
Monkseaton Rd. NE25: Well 6A 38
Monkseaton Station (Metro) 6F 39
Monkseaton Ter. NE63: Hir 6C 12
Monksfeld NE10: Gate 7C 84
Monksfield Cl. SR3: New S 4B 132
Monkside NE6: Newc T 5B 64
NE23: Cra 5H 25
Monkside Cl. NE38: Wash 6E 114
Monks Mdws. NE46: Hex 2F 71
Monks Pk. Way NE12: Longb 6J 45
Monks Ridge NE61: Mor 1D 14
Monks Rd. NE25: Whit B 1C 48
Monk's Ter. NE46: Hex 2F 71
Monkstone Av. NE30: N Shi 4J 49
Monkstone Cl. NE30: N Shi 4J 49
Monkstone Cres. NE30: N Shi 4J 49
Monkstone Grange
NE30: N Shi 3H 49
Monk St. NE1: Newc T 1E 82 (6D 4)
SR6: Monk 6F 105
Monks Way NE30: N Shi 3J 49
Monksway NE32: Jar 7E 66
Monks Wood NE29: N Shi 4E 48
Monkswood Sq. SR3: New S 3D 132
Monk Ter. NE32: Jar 7C 66
MONKTON 3A 86
Monkton NE10: Gate 1D 100
Monkton Av. NE34: S Shi 2F 87
Monkton Bus. Pk. NE31: Heb 4J 85
Monkton Dene NE32: Jar 2A 86
Monkton Hall NE31: Heb 2K 85
Monkton La. NE31: Heb 4J 85
NE32: Jar 3K 85
Monkton Rd. NE32: Jar 6B 66
(not continuous)
Monkton Stadium 2A 86
Monkton Ter. NE32: Jar 6C 66
MONKWEARMOUTH 7F 105
Monkwearmouth Station Mus.
7F 105 (1J 7)
Monmouth Gdns. NE28: W'snd 1A 66
Monroe Pl. NE5: Newc T 3K 61
Mons Av. NE31: Heb 7J 65
Mons Cres. DH4: Hou S 3C 130
Montagu Av. NE3: Ken 2C 62
Montagu Ct. NE3: Ken 3C 62
Montague Ct. NE9: Gate 6H 83
Montague St. NE15: Lem 7D 60
SR6: Monk 4F 105
Monteigne Dr. DH6: Bow 4H 177
Monterey NE37: Usw 6H 101
SR3: New S 4A 132
Montfalcon Cl. SR8: Pet 6A 172
Montford Cl. SR3: New S 4K 131
Montgomery Rd. DH1: Dur 1D 166
Montorosso NE20: Wool 6C 32
Montpelier Ter. SR2: Sund 4G 119
Montpellier Pl. NE3: Ken 2B 62
Montrose Cl. NE25: Sea D 4H 27
Montrose Cres. NE9: Gate 7K 83
Montrose Dr. NE10: Gate 7F 85
Montrose Gdns. NE61: Mor 1F 15
SR3: Sund 5C 118
Monument Ct. DH1: Dur 4J 165
Monument Mall Shop. Cen.
NE1: Newc T 1F 83 (5F 4)
Monument Station (Metro) 1F 83 (5F 4)
Monument Ter. DH3: Bir 4A 114
DH4: Pen 1A 130
Monument Vw. DH4: Pen 1B 130
Moonfield NE46: Hex 2D 70
MOOR 4D 46
Moor Cl. NE29: N Shi 4C 48
SR1: Sund 1H 119
Moor Ct. DH4: Hou S 6J 129
NE3: Gos 3D 62
SR6: Whit 6G 89
Moor Cres. DH1: Dur 1E 166
DH6: Shad 5H 169
NE3: Gos 3E 62
Moor Crest Ter. *NE29: N Shi 4F 49*
(off Walton Av.)
Moor Cft. NE64: Newb S 2J 13
Moorcroft Cl. NE15: Lem 6D 60
Moorcroft Rd. NE15: Lem 6E 60
Moor Cft. Vw. NE64: Newb S 2J 13
Moordale Av. NE24: Cow 3E 22
Moore Av. NE11: Dun 6B 82
NE34: S Shi 7A 68
Moore Ct. NE15: Thro 6G 59
Moore Cres. DH3: Bir 2A 114
Moore Cres. Nth. DH5: Hou S 3E 144
Moore Cres. Sth. DH5: Hou S 3E 144
Moor Edge DH1: Dur 2H 165
DH7: B'don 2D 174
Moor Edge Rd. NE27: Shir 7J 37
MOOR END 7G 155
Moor End Ter. DH1: Carr 7G 155
Moor End Vs. NE64: Newb S 2K 13
Moore Pk. NE8: Gate 5J 83
Moore Sq. TS28: Win 4F 181
Moore St. DH6: Whe H 3B 180
DH9: Stly 4E 124
NE8: Gate 5J 83
Moore St. Vs. *NE8: Gate 5J 83*
(off Moore St.)
Moore Ter. DH6: Shot C 7F 171
Moorfield NE2: Gos 2F 63
Moorfield Gdns. SR6: Cle 7C 88
Moorfields NE61: Mor 2G 15
Moorfoot Av. DH2: Ches S 7A 128
(not continuous)
Moorfoot Gdns. NE11: Gate 7C 82
Moor Gdns. NE29: N Shi 4C 48
Moor Grange NE42: Pru 5F 77
Moorhead NE5: Newc T 4A 62
Moorhead Ct. NE5: Newc T 4A 62
Moorhead M. NE5: Newc T 4A 62
Moorhouse Cl. NE34: S Shi 1K 87
Moorhouse Est. NE63: Hir 3C 12
Moorhouse Gdns. DH5: Hett H 1G 157
(not continuous)
Moorhouse La. NE63: Hir 4D 12
Moorhouses Rd. NE29: N Shi 4C 48
Moorings, The NE6: Newc T 2A 84
Moorland Av. NE22: Bed 5C 18
Moorland Cotts. NE22: Bed 5B 18
Moorland Ct. NE22: Bed 5C 18
Moorland Cres. DH8: C'sde 4B 134
NE6: Walk 6C 64
NE22: Bed 5C 18
Moorland Dr. NE22: Bed 6C 18
Moorlands DH8: Shot B 4E 120
DH9: Dip 7J 109
NE32: Jar 5D 86
NE42: Pru 5G 77
Moorlands Cres. DH8: Shot B 5E 120
Moorlands, The DH1: Dur 2E 166
Moorland Vw. DH8: C'sde 4B 134
NE17: C'wl 7K 93
Moorland Vs. NE22: Bed 5C 18
Moorland Way NE23: Nel V 1G 25
Moor La. NE3: Ken 1K 61
NE20: Pon 7F 31
NE34: S Shi 7A 68
NE36: E Bol 6A 88
SR6: Cle 7C 88
TS28: Win 6G 181
Moor La. E. NE34: S Shi 7B 68
Moormill NE11: Kib 2E 112
Moormill La. NE11: Kib 2F 113
Moor Pk. Ct. NE29: N Shi 5C 48
Moor Pk. Rd. NE29: N Shi 5B 48
(not continuous)
Moor Pl. NE3: Gos 2E 62
Moor Rd. NE42: Pru 5F 77
Moor Rd. Nth NE3: Gos 7F 45
Moor Rd. Sth. NE3: Gos 2F 63
Moorsburn Dr. DH4: Hou S 1C 144
Moors Cl. DH4: Hou S 2B 144
Moorsfield DH4: Hou S 2B 144
MOORSIDE
Consett 3D 134
Sunderland 4A 132
Moorside NE12: Longb 2K 45
NE32: Jar 5C 86
NE37: Wash 1F 115
Moorside Community College Sports Cen.
2D 134
Moorside Ct. NE5: Newc T 4A 62
Moorside Ind. Est. SR3: E Her 4K 131
Moorside Nth. NE4: Newc T 4A 62
Moorside Pl. NE4: Newc T 5B 62
Moorside Rd. SR3: E Her, New S 3K 131
Moorside Sth. NE4: Newc T 6B 62
Moorsley Rd. DH5: Hett H 2E 156
DH5: Hett H, H Pitt 4B 156

Moor St.—Nevilles Ct.

Moor St. SR1: Sund 1G 119
(Coronation St.)
SR1: Sund 2H 119
(Woodbine St.)
Moor Ter. SR1: Sund 1H 119
Moorvale La. NE5: Newc T 3A 62
Moor Vw. DH6: Thor 1A 180
DH6: Whe H 2B 180
NE3: Ken 1K 61
NE12: Kil 6A 36
NE40: Ryton 2E 78
NE64: Newb S 2J 13
SR6: Whit 6G 89
Moorview DH8: Con 5G 121
Moor Vw. Cl. NE61: Peg 4K 9
Moorview Cres. NE5: Newc T 3A 62
Moor Vw. Ter. DH9: Ann P 6J 123
Moor Vw. Wlk. NE12: Kil 7A 36
Moorway NE37: Wash 1F 115
Moorway Dr. NE15: Lem 6E 60
Moraine Cres. NE17: C'wl 2K 107
Moralee Cl. NE7: Newc T 2B 64
Moran St. SR6: Monk 3F 105
Moray Cl. DH3: Bir 7B 114
SR8: Pet 7A 172
Moray St. SR6: Monk 5F 105
Morcott Gdns. NE29: N Shi 1E 66
Morden St. NE1: Newc T 7F 63 (4E 4)
Mordey Cl. SR2: Sund 3G 119
Mordue Ter. DH9: Ann P 6A 124
Morecambe Pde. NE31: Heb 4A 86
Moreland Rd. NE34: S Shi 3K 87
Moreland St. SR6: Monk 5F 105
Moresby Rd. NE23: Cra 7A 22
Morgan Bus. Cen. NE12: Kil 6K 35
Morgan St. SR5: S'wck 5D 104
Morgans Way NE21: Bla T 4A 80
Morgan Vs. NE28: W'snd 3G 65
(off North Vw.)
Morgy Hill E. NE40: Ryton 3D 78
Morgy Hill Sth. NE40: Ryton 3D 78
Morgy Hill W. NE40: Ryton 2C 78
Morinda Cl. DH4: Hou S 4K 129
Morland Av. NE38: Wash 5J 115
Morland Gdns. NE9: Gate 7K 83
Morley Av. NE10: Gate 4F 85
Morley Ct. NE6: Newc T 6A 64
Morley Cres. DH6: Kel 7E 178
Morley Gdns. DH8: Con 5H 121
Morley Hill Rd. NE5: Newc T 5F 61
Morley La. DH7: New B 7K 163 & 1A 174
Morley Pl. NE27: Shir 7K 37
Morley Ter. DH4: Hou S 1A 144
NE10: Gate 6B 84
Morningside DH7: Sac 6E 140
NE38: Wash 1C 128
Morningside Ct. DH3: Ches S 5A 128
Mornington Av. NE3: Ken 2B 62
MORPETH 7F 9
Morpeth Av. NE13: Wide O 4E 34
NE32: Jar 3B 86
NE34: S Shi 6K 67
NE61: Peg 3K 9
Morpeth Castle 7G 9
Morpeth Chantry Bagpipe Mus. 7G 9
(off Bridge St.)
Morpeth Clocktower 7F 9
(off New Market)
Morpeth Cl. NE38: Wash 4E 114
NE62: Chop 2G 17
Morpeth Cricket, Hockey & Tennis Club 1K 9
Morpeth Dr. SR3: New S 3K 131
Morpeth Rd. NE62: Chop 1C 16
(not continuous)
NE63: Ash 3H 11
Morpeth Station (Rail) 1G 15
Morpeth St. NE2: Newc T 5D 62 (1B 4)
SR8: Pet 3D 172
Morpeth Ter. NE29: N Shi 1D 66
Morris Av. NE34: S Shi 3H 87
Morris Ct. NE23: Dud 3K 35
Morris Cres. DH6: Thor 1J 179
NE35: Bol C 6G 87
Morris Gdns. NE10: Gate 6F 85
Morrison Ind. Est. DH9: Ann P 6A 124
Morrison Rd. DH9: Ann P 7A 124
NE61: Mor 6F 9
Morrison Rd. Nth. Ind. Est.
DH9: Ann P 6A 124
Morrison St. NE8: Gate 4E 82
Morrison Ter. NE46: Acomb 4B 50
Morris Rd. NE16: Whi 6H 81
Morris Sq. SR8: Eas 1A 172
Morris St. DH3: Bir 4K 113
NE8: Gate 6E 82
NE37: Usw 7G 101
Morris Ter. DH5: Hou S 3F 145
Morrit Ct. NE7: Newc T 7A 46
Morston Dr. NE15: Lem 7E 60
Mortimer Av. NE5: Newc T 2F 61
NE29: N Shi 6D 48
Mortimer Chase NE23: E Har 6K 21
Mortimer Rd. NE33: S Shi 5K 67
NE34: S Shi 5K 67
Mortimer St. DH8: Con 6F 121
SR4: Sund 1B 118
Mortimer Ter. NE25: H'wll 1J 37
(off Laurel Ter.)
NE61: Peg 3B 10
Morton Cl. NE38: Wash 4H 115
Morton Cres. DH4: Hou S 1K 143
NE5: Cal 6B 42
Morton Grange Ter. DH4: Hou S 1J 143
Morton Sq. SR8: Pet 5A 172
Morton St. NE6: Newc T, Walk 7B 64
NE33: S Shi 1J 67
Morton Wlk. NE33: S Shi 1J 67
Morval Cl. SR3: New S 4K 131
Morven Dr. NE10: Gate 5F 85
Morven Lea NE21: Bla T 4B 80
Morven Pl. NE63: Ash 3K 11
Morven Ter. NE63: Ash 3K 11
Morwick Cl. NE23: Cra 5H 25
Morwick Pl. NE5: Newc T 4K 61
Morwick Rd. NE29: N Shi 4D 48
Mosley St. NE1: Newc T 1F 83 (6F 4)
Mossbank NE9: Gate 4K 99
Moss Cl. NE15: Lem 5C 60
Moss Cres. NE40: Ryton 2E 78
Mossdale DH1: Carr 7J 155
Mosspool NE21: Bla T 4A 80
Moss Side NE9: Gate 4A 100
Mossway DH2: Pelt 2F 127
MOSSWOOD 7A 120
Mostyn Grn. NE3: Ken 7B 44
Motcombe Way NE23: Cra 7A 22
Moulton Ct. NE5: Newc T 3J 61
Moulton Pl. NE5: Newc T 3J 61
Mountbatten Av. NE31: Heb 2J 85
Mount Cl. NE12: Kil 7B 36
NE25: Whit B 1D 48
SR4: Sund 2H 117
Mt. Cottage NE9: Spri 7C 100
NE9: Spri 7C 100
Mount Ct. DH3: Bir 3B 114
Mountfield Gdns. NE3: Ken 7B 44
Mountford Rd. NE25: Sea D 3H 27
Mount Gro. NE11: Dun 7B 82
SR4: Sund 4C 118
Mt. Joy Cres. DH1: Dur 4B 166 (6E 6)
Mount La. NE9: Spri 7C 100
Mt. Lonnen NE9: Spri 7C 100
Mt. Park Dr. DH7: Lan 6J 137
MOUNT PLEASANT
Gateshead 5K 83
Houghton-le-Spring 1J 129
Mt. Pleasant DH3: Bir 3A 114
DH5: Hou S 2F 145
DH7: B'hpe 6D 138
DH7: Lan 6J 137
DH7: Sac 6D 140
DH9: Dip 7J 109
NE21: Bla T 5B 80
SR5: S'wck 6C 104
Mt. Pleasant Bungs. DH3: Bir 3A 114
Mt. Pleasant Ct. NE15: Thro 3H 59
Mt. Pleasant Gdns. NE8: Gate 5J 83
Mt. Pleasant Rd. DH3: Bir 3A 114
Mount Rd. DH3: Bir 3A 114
NE9: Spri 7C 100
SR4: Sund 4B 118
Mountsett Crematorium DH9: Dip 6J 109
Mountside DH8: Shot B 3F 121
Mountside Gdns. NE11: Dun 7B 82
Mt. Stewart St. SR7: S'hm 5B 148
Mount Ter. NE33: S Shi 3J 67
Mount, The DH8: Shot B 3F 121
NE15: Thro 3G 59
NE40: Ryton 1G 79
Mount Vw. DH7: Lan 6J 137
NE16: Swa 6H 81
NE40: Ryton 3D 78
Mt. View Ter. NE43: Stoc 7G 75
Mourne Gdns. NE11: Gate 1C 98
Moutter Cl. SR8: Pet 4C 172
Mowbray Cl. SR2: Sund 3F 119 (7K 7)
Mowbray Rd. NE12: Longb 4B 46
NE29: N Shi 6D 48
NE33: S Shi 4K 67
SR2: Sund 4F 119 (7J 7)
Mowbray St. DH1: Dur 2K 165 (2A 6)
NE6: Newc T 7J 63 (3L 5)
Mowbray Ter. DH4: Hou S 7D 130
NE62: Chop 1H 17
Mowlam Dr. DH9: Stly 3G 125
Moyle Ter. NE16: Burn 4A 110
Mozart St. NE33: S Shi 3K 67
Muirfield NE25: Whit B 6D 38
NE33: S Shi 4B 68
Muirfield Cl. DH8: Con 4G 121
Muirfield Dr. NE10: Gate 1B 100
NE37: Usw 5G 101
Muirfield Rd. NE7: Newc T 7A 46
Muirston Av. NE23: Cra 7A 22
Mulben Cl. NE4: Newc T 2A 82
Mulberry Cl. NE24: News 5H 23
Mulberry Gdns. NE10: Gate 4A 84
Mulberry Gro. NE16: Burn 4A 110
Mulberry Pk. NE9: Gate 2H 99
Mulberry Pl. NE4: Newc T 3D 82 (9A 4)
Mulberry St. NE10: Gate 5A 84
Mulberry Ter. DH9: Ann P 5B 124
Mulberry Trad. Est. NE10: Gate 5A 84
Mulberry Way DH4: Hou S 1B 144
Mulcaster Gdns. NE28: W'snd 2E 64
Mulgrave Dr. SR6: Monk 7G 105
Mulgrave Ter. NE8: Gate 3G 83 (10H 5)
Mulgrave Vs. NE8: Gate 4G 83 (10H 5)
Mullen Dr. NE40: Ryton 2G 79
Mullen Gdns. NE28: W'snd 1E 64
Mullen Rd. NE28: W'snd 1E 64
Mull Gro. NE32: Jar 3E 86
Mullin Cl. DH7: Ush M 1D 164
Muncaster M. SR8: Pet 2J 181
Mundella Ter. NE6: Newc T 6K 63 (1P 5)
Mundell St. DH9: Stly 5E 124
Mundle Av. NE21: Bla T 1C 96
Mundles La. NE36: E Bol 7K 87
Municipal Ter. NE37: Wash 2H 115
Munslow Rd. SR3: E Her 1J 131
Muriel St. DH9: Stly 6E 124
Murphy Gro. SR2: Ryh 2G 133
Murray Av. DH4: Hou S 1A 144
Murray Ct. DH2: Ches S 6K 127
DH8: Shot B 4F 121
Murrayfield NE23: Seg 1D 36
Murrayfield Dr. DH7: B'don 2C 174
Murrayfield Rd. NE5: Newc T 3K 61
Murrayfields NE27: Shir 3H 47
Murray Gdns. NE11: Dun 7C 82
Murray Pl. DH2: Ches S 6K 127
Murray Rd. DH2: Ches S 6K 127
NE28: W'snd 2K 65
Murray St. NE21: Bla T 3C 80
SR8: Pet 6E 172
Murray Ter. DH9: Dip 1G 123
Murtagh Diamond Ho.
NE34: S Shi 1J 87
MURTON
Houghton-le-Spring 7E 146
Newcastle upon Tyne 2B 48
Murton Ho. NE29: N Shi 3C 48
Murton La. DH5: Eas L 2J 157
NE27: N Shi, Shir 3A 48
Murton St. SR1: Sund 2G 119 (5K 7)
SR7: Mur 1F 159
Muscott Gro. NE15: Newc T 7G 61
Mus. of Antiquities 3E 4
Musgrave Gdns. DH1: Dur 2E 166
Musgrave Rd. NE9: Gate 1H 99
Musgrave Ter. NE6: Walk 7C 64
NE10: Gate 5E 84
NE38: Wash 2H 115
Muswell Hill NE15: Newc T 1G 81
Mutual St. NE28: W'snd 4F 65
Mylord Cres. NE12: Kil 6K 35
Myra Av. TS27: Hes 4E 182
Myre Hall DH5: Hou S 2E 144
Myrella Cres. SR2: Sund 6E 118
Myreside Pl. NE12: Longb 5K 45
Myrtle Av. NE11: Dun 6B 82
SR6: Whit 5H 89
Myrtle Cres. NE12: Longb 3B 46
Myrtle Gro. NE2: Newc T 3G 63
NE9: Gate 2H 99
NE16: Burn 2K 109
NE28: W'snd 4H 65
NE34: S Shi 2B 88
Myrtle Rd. NE21: Bla T 5C 80
Myrtles DH2: Ches S 4K 127
Myrtle St. NE63: Hir 3B 12

N

Nafferton Pl. NE5: Newc T 5J 61
Nailor's Bank NE8: Gate 2J 83 (7L 5)
Nailsworth Cl. NE35: Bol C 4E 86
Nairn Cl. DH3: Bir 7B 114
NE37: Usw 5G 101
Nairn Rd. NE23: Cra 3K 25
Nairn St. NE32: Jar 3E 86
Naisbitt Av. SR8: Pet 4C 172
Nansen Cl. NE5: Newc T 3F 61
Nansen St. DH8: Con 6J 121
Napier Cl. DH3: Ches S 1B 128
Napier Ct. NE16: Whi 3H 97
Napier Rd. NE16: Swa 5G 81
SR7: S'hm 2J 147
Napier St. NE2: Newc T 7H 63 (3J 5)
NE32: Jar 6B 66
(not continuous)
NE33: S Shi 7H 67
Napier Way NE21: Bla T 4E 80
Napoleon Cl. SR2: Ryh 2H 133
Narvik Way NE29: N Shi 7B 48
Nash Av. NE34: S Shi 3K 87
Nater's Bank NE30: N Shi 7J 49
(off Union Quay)
Naters St. NE26: Whit B 7J 39
National Glass Cen. 7G 105
Natley Av. NE36: E Bol 7A 88
Nattress Ter. TS28: Win 5F 181
Navan Cl. NE62: W Sle 7B 12
Navenby Cl. NE3: Gos 4F 45
SR7: S'hm 1J 147
Naworth Av. NE30: N Shi 3G 49
Naworth Ct. SR8: Pet 2K 181
Naworth Dr. NE5: Newc T 2D 60
Naworth Ter. NE32: Jar 2D 86
Nawton Av. SR5: S'wck 5E 104
Nayland Rd. NE23: Cra 3J 25
Naylor Av. NE21: Bla T 1C 96
Naylor Ct. NE21: Bla T 2E 80
Naylor Pl. NE26: Sea S 3B 28
Nazareth M. NE2: Newc T 5H 63 (1K 5)
Neale St. DH9: Ann P 5A 124
DH9: Tan L 6B 110
NE42: Pru 3F 77
SR6: Monk 4F 105
Neale Ter. DH3: Bir 4A 114
Neale Wlk. NE3: Ken 2A 62
Nearlane Cl. NE13: Sea B 3E 34
Neasdon Cres. NE30: N Shi 3H 49
Neasham Rd. SR7: S'hm 1J 147
NEDDERTON 1C 20
Nedderton Cl. NE5: Cha P 1B 60
Needham Pl. NE23: Cra 3K 25
Neighbourhood Cen., The
NE5: Newc T 1G 61
Neil Cres. DH6: Quar H 6D 178
Neill Dr. NE16: Sun 5H 97
Neilson Rd. NE10: Gate 4K 83 (10P 5)
Neil St. DH5: Eas L 2J 157
Nellie Gormley Ho. NE12: Kil 2K 45
Nell Ter. NE39: Row G 6G 95
Nelson Av. NE3: Gos 7C 44
NE23: Nel V 2G 25
NE33: S Shi 2A 68
Nelson Cl. NE63: Hir 5C 12
SR2: Sund 3G 119 (6K 7)
SR8: Pet 5E 172
(not continuous)
Nelson Cres. NE29: N Shi 2D 66
Nelson Dr. NE23: Cra, Nel V 3F 25
Nelson Ho. NE30: N Shi 5K 49
Nelson Ind. Est. NE23: Nel V 1G 25
Nelson Pk. NE23: Nel V 1G 25
Nelson Pk. E. NE23: Nel V 1H 25
Nelson Pk. W. NE23: Nel V 1F 25
Nelson Rd. NE6: Walk 2F 85
NE23: Nel V 1F 25
NE25: Well 6B 38
NE62: Chop 1J 17
Nelson St. DH3: Ches S 7A 128
DH5: Hett H 7G 145
DH8: Con 7H 121
DH8: Lead 5A 122
NE1: Newc T 1F 83 (5F 4)
NE8: Gate 3G 83 (9H 5)
NE29: N Shi 7G 49
NE33: S Shi 2J 67
NE38: Wash 4J 115
NE40: G'sde 5D 78
SR2: Ryh 2H 133
SR7: S'hm 2K 147
Nelson Ter. DH6: Sher 3A 168
NE17: C'wl 7K 93
NE29: N Shi 2D 66
NELSON VILLAGE 2G 25
Nelson Way NE23: Nel V 7F 21
Nene Ct. NE37: Usw 7J 101
Nent Gro. NE46: Hex 2E 70
Nenthead Cl. DH3: Gt Lum 3F 143
Neptune Rd. NE15: Lem 6E 60
NE28: W'snd 5F 65
Neptune Way SR8: Eas 7A 160
Nesbit Rd. SR8: Pet 7C 172
Nesburn Rd. SR4: Sund 4C 118
Nesham Pl. DH5: Hou S 2E 144
Nesham St. NE4: Newc T 3C 82
Nesham Ter. SR1: Sund 1H 119
Ness Ct. NE21: Bla T 4A 80
Nest Rd. NE10: Gate 4B 84
Netherburn Rd. SR5: S'wck 5E 104
Netherby Ct. NE5: Newc T 5K 61
Netherby Dr. NE5: Newc T 5J 61
Netherdale NE22: Bed 7F 17
Nether Farm Rd. NE10: Gate 5D 84
Nether Riggs NE22: Bed 1H 21
Netherton NE12: Kil 6A 36
Netherton Av. NE29: N Shi 4D 48
Netherton Cl. DH2: Ches S 7H 127
DH7: Lang P 5H 151
Netherton Gdns. NE13: Wide O 5D 34
Netherton Gro. NE29: N Shi 5D 48
Netherton La. NE22: Bed 6E 16
Netherwitton Way NE3: Gos 3D 44
Nettleham Rd. SR5: S'wck 5E 104
Nettles La. SR3: New S 3D 132
NETTLESWORTH 6H 141
Neville Ct. NE37: Usw 7K 101
Neville Cres. DH3: Bir 2A 114
Nevilledale Ter. DH1: Dur 4A 6
Neville Dene DH1: Dur 3H 165
Neville Rd. NE15: Lem 6D 60
SR4: Sund 6B 118
SR8: Pet 5A 172
Nevilles Ct. DH1: Dur 3J 165

Neville's Cross Bank DH1: Dur 5H 165
Neville's Cross Rd. NE31: Heb 1K 85
Neville's Cross Vs. DH1: Dur 4J 165
Neville Sq. DH1: Dur 5J 165
Neville St. DH1: Dur 3A 166 (3B 6)
NE1: Newc T 2E 82 (7D 4)
Neville Ter. DH1: Dur 2J 165
DH6: Bow 5J 177
Neville Wlk. NE37: Usw 6K 101
(off Marlborough Rd.)
Nevill Rd. NE43: Stoc 7K 75
Nevinson Av. NE34: S Shi 3K 87
Nevis Cl. NE26: Whit B 3E 38
Nevis Ct. NE26: Whit B 3E 38
Nevis Gro. NE36: W Bol 7H 87
Nevis Way NE26: Whit B 4E 38
New Acres DH7: Ush M 2C 164
New Acres Rd. DH9: Stly 7E 124
Newark Cl. NE22: Bed 6F 17
SR8: Pet 5A 172
(not continuous)
Newark Cres. SR7: S'hm 1J 147
Newark Dr. SR6: Whit 6H 89
Newark Sq. NE29: N Shi 1F 67
Newarth Cl. NE15: Lem 6E 60
Newbank Wlk. NE21: Bla T 5A 80
NEWBIGGIN
Durham 6F 137
Hexham 7F 71
NEWBIGGIN-BY-THE-SEA 2J 13
NEWBIGGIN HALL ESTATE 1F 61
Newbiggin La. DH7: Lan 6D 136
NE5: Newc T 1F 61
Newbiggin Rd. NE63: Hir, N Sea 6B 12
Newbiggin Sports & Community Cen. 2H 13
New Blackett St. DH9: Ann P 4J 123
Newbold Av. SR5: S'wck 5E 104
Newbold St. NE6: Walk 1B 84
Newbolt Ct. NE8: Gate 4J 83
NEWBOTTLE 6D 130
Newbottle La. DH4: Hou S 3K 143
Newbottle St. DH4: Hou S 1D 144
NEW BRANCEPETH 5B 164
Newbridge Av. SR5: S'wck 5E 104
Newbridge Bank DH3: Lam P 4D 128
Newbridge Banks DH2: Pelt 5C 126
New Bri. St. NE1: Newc T 1G 83 (5H 5)
New Bri. St. W. NE1: Newc T 1F 83 (5F 4)
(not continuous)
Newbrough Cres. NE2: Newc T 3G 63
Newburgh Av. NE25: Sea D 1G 37
NEWBURN 5K 59
New Burn Av. DH6: Bow 4H 177
Newburn Av. SR5: S'wck 5E 104
Newburn Bri. Rd. NE21: Bla T, Thro 7J 59
Newburn Ct. NE33: S Shi 4K 67
Newburn Cres. DH4: Hou S 1D 144
Newburn Hall Motor Mus. 5K 59
Newburn Haugh Ind. Est. NE15: Lem 7B 60
Newburn Ind. Est. NE15: Lem 7A 60
Newburn La. End NE15: Thro 3H 59
Newburn Leisure Cen. 5J 59
Newburn Riverside Ind. Pk.
NE15: Lem 2C 80
Newburn Rd. DH9: Stly 1F 125
NE15: Thro 3H 59
Newbury NE12: Kil 7B 36
Newbury Av. NE8: Gate 6F 83
(not continuous)
Newbury Cl. NE15: Lem 6D 60
Newbury Dr. DH8: Shot B 2G 121
Newbury St. NE33: S Shi 6K 67
SR5: Monk 4E 104
Newby Cl. NE22: Bed 5A 18
Newby La. DH6: H Pitt 6C 156
Newby Pl. NE9: Gate 3K 99
Newcastle Arts Cen. 2F 83 (7E 4)
Newcastle Av. SR8: Pet 4D 172
Newcastle Bank DH3: Bir 1K 113
Newcastle Bus. Pk.
NE4: Newc T 3B 82 (10A 4)
(not continuous)
Newcastle Coll. NE1: Newc T 2G 4
Newcastle Discovery Mus. 2E 82 (7C 4)
Newcastle Falcons Rugby Football Ground
(Kingston Pk.) 5H 43
Newcastle Football Cen. 7H 61
NEWCASTLE INTERNATIONAL AIRPORT 1D 42
Newcastle Opera House 1E 82 (6D 4)
Newcastle Playhouse 6F 63 (2F 4)
Newcastle Race Course 2F 45
Newcastle Rd. DH1: Dur 7H 153
DH3: Bir 2A 114
DH3: Ches S 5A 128
DH4: Hou S 2C 144
NE24: News 5G 23
NE34: S Shi 2E 86
(not continuous)
NE36: W Bol 7J 85
NE45: Cor 1F 73
SR5: Monk 3E 104
SR5: S'wck 2C 104
Newcastle Road Baths 5F 105

Newcastle Science Pk.
NE1: Newc T 1G 83 (5H 5)
Newcastle Station (Rail) 2F 83 (7E 4)
Newcastle St. NE29: N Shi 7G 49
Newcastle Ter. DH1: Dur 5J 153
NE30: N Shi 5K 49
Newcastle United FC (St James' Pk.) 7E 62 (4D 4)
NEWCASTLE UPON TYNE 1F 83 (5E 4)
Newcastle Western By-Pass
NE3: Gos 3B 44
NE5: Newc T 1J 61
NE13: Bru V 3B 44
NE15: Lem, Newc T 7E 60
New Coliseum Cinema 6H 39
New Cotts. NE62: Chop 1E 16
New Cross Row TS28: Win 5F 181
NEW DELAVAL 5F 23
Newdene Wlk. NE15: Lem 6D 60
New Dr. SR7: S'hm 1K 147
New Durham Rd. DH9: Ann P 6A 124
SR2: Sund 2D 118 (5F 7)
New Elvet DH1: Dur 3B 166 (2D 6)
NEWFIELD 4E 126
Newfield Rd. DH2: Pelt 4E 126
Newfield Ter. DH2: Pelt 4E 126
Newfield Wlk. NE16: Whi 1G 97
New Front St. DH9: Ann P 5K 123
DH9: Tan L 7D 110
Newgate NE1: Newc T 1F 83 (6E 4)
Newgate St. NE1: Newc T 1F 83 (5E 4)
NE61: Mor 6F 9
New George St. NE33: S Shi 5J 67
New Grange Ter. DH2: Pelt 5F 127
New Grn. St. NE33: S Shi 4J 67
Newham Av. NE13: Bru V 7C 34
NEW HARTLEY 4H 27
Newhaven Av. SR5: S'wck 5E 104
NEW HERRINGTON 3D 130
New Herrington Country Pk. 1D 130
New Herrington Ind. Est.
DH4: Hou S 3D 130
Newhouse Av. DH7: Esh W 3D 162
Newhouse Rd. DH7: Esh W 3D 162
Newington Ct. NE37: Usw 7G 101
SR5: S'wck 6E 104
Newington Dr. NE29: N Shi 3F 49
Newington Rd. NE2: Newc T 6H 63 (2K 5)
(not continuous)
NE6: Newc T 6J 63 (2L 5)
New King St. NE64: Newb S 2K 13
NEW KYO 5B 124
NEW LAMBTON 7J 129
Newland Ct. NE34: S Shi 1J 87
NEWLANDS 4E 106
Newlands DH8: Shot B 4F 121
NE30: N Shi 2G 49
Newlands Av. NE3: Gos 3E 44
NE24: Bly 4H 23
NE25: Whit B 1D 48
SR3: Sund 5D 118
Newlands Pl. NE24: Bly 4H 23
Newlands Rd. DH1: Carr 7G 155
NE2: Gos 2F 63
NE24: Bly 4H 23
Newlands Rd. E. SR7: S'hm 2K 147
Newlands Rd. W. SR7: S'hm 2J 147
Newlyn Cres. NE29: N Shi 7E 48
Newlyn Dr. NE23: Cra 3J 25
NE32: Jar 7D 66
Newlyn Rd. NE3: Ken 7A 44
Newman La. NE38: Wash 5J 115
Newman Pl. NE8: Gate 6J 83
Newman Ter. NE8: Gate 6J 83
Newmarch St. NE32: Jar 6A 66
New Market NE61: Mor 7F 9
Newmarket St. DH8: Con 6H 121
Newmarket Wlk. NE33: S Shi 3J 67
(not continuous)
New Mills NE4: Newc T 7D 62 (3A 4)
Newminster Abbey (remains of) 7D 8
Newminster Cl. DH4: Hou S 7B 130
Newminster Rd. NE4: Newc T 7J 61
Newmin Way NE16: Whi 2F 97
Newport Gro. SR3: New S 1C 132
New Quay NE29: N Shi 1H 67
Newquay Gdns. NE9: Gate 5H 99
New Queen St. NE64: Newb S 2J 13
New Rainton DH4: Pen 1B 130
(off Rainton St.)
New Rainton St. DH4: Pen 1B 130
(off Rainton St.)
New Redheugh Bri. Rd.
NE1: Newc T 3E 82 (9D 4)
NE8: Gate 3E 82 (9D 4)
NEW RIDLEY 4H 91
New Ridley Rd. NE43: B'ley, Stoc 7K 75
Newriggs NE38: Wash 6H 115
New Rd. DH2: Beam 2B 126
DH6: Shad, Thor 5J 169
DH9: Beam 2B 126
NE11: Gate 1D 98
NE16: Burn 1A 110
NE35: Bol C 6F 87
NE36: E Bol 6F 87

New Rd. NE38: Wash 1G 129
(not continuous)
New Sandridge NE64: Newb S 2K 13
(off Sandridge)
NEWSHAM 5H 23
Newsham Cl. NE5: Cha P 1B 60
Newsham Rd. NE24: Bly 4G 23
NEW SILKSWORTH 2B 132
New Sth. Ter. DH3: Bir 4B 114
Newstead Ct. NE38: Wash 3G 115
Newstead Ri. DH8: Shot B 4E 120
Newstead Rd. DH4: Hou S 7C 130
Newsteads Cl. NE25: Whit B 6D 38
Newsteads Dr. NE25: Whit B 6C 38
Newsteads Farm Cotts. NE25: Whit B 7C 38
Newstead Sq. SR3: New S 3C 132
New Strangford Rd. SR7: S'hm 2K 147
New St. DH1: Dur 2K 165 (2A 6)
DH6: Sher 3A 168
SR4: Sund 2G 117
NEWTON 7D 54
Newton Av. NE28: W'snd 2K 65
NE30: N Shi 1H 49
Newton Cl. NE15: Lem 6E 60
Newton Dr. DH1: Dur 6K 153
Newton Gro. NE34: S Shi 1G 87
NEWTON HALL
Durham 4A 154
Stocksfield 6D 54
Newton Hall NE7: Newc T 3K 63
Newton Ho. NE4: Newc T 3B 4
Newton Pl. NE7: Newc T 3K 63
Newton Rd. NE7: Newc T 2J 63
Newton St. DH7: Wit G 3C 152
NE8: Gate 6F 83
NE11: Dun 5B 82
Newton Ter. NE43: Mic 5A 76
Newton Vs. DH6: Coxh 7J 177
NEW TOWN
Boldon Colliery 6F 87
Houghton-le-Spring 2F 145
Newtown Ind. Est. DH3: Bir 6A 114
Newtown Vs. DH7: Sac 7E 140
New Watling St. DH8: Lead 5A 122
NEW YORK 3B 48
New York By-Pass NE29: N Shi 3B 48
New York Ind. Pk. NE27: N Shi 4A 48
NE27: Shir 3A 48
New York Rd. NE27: Back, Shir 1J 47
(not continuous)
NE29: N Shi 3A 48
New York Way NE27: N Shi 4A 48
(not continuous)
Nicholas Av. SR6: Whit 6H 89
Nicholas St. DH5: Hett H 5H 145
Nichol Ct. NE4: Newc T 1K 81
Nicholson Cl. SR1: Sund 2G 119
Nicholson's Ter. DH9: Beam 1B 126
Nicholson Ter. NE12: Kil 3C 46
Nichol St. NE4: Newc T 1K 81
Nickleby Chare DH1: Dur 5K 165
Nidderdale Av. DH5: Hett H 1F 157
Nidderdale Cl. NE24: Cow 1E 22
Nidsdale Av. NE6: Walk 6E 64
Nightingale Cl. SR4: Sund 4G 117
Nightingale Pl. DH9: Stly 4H 125
Nile Cl. NE15: Lem 5C 60
Nile Ct. NE8: Gate 5J 83
Nile St. DH8: Con 7H 121
NE29: N Shi 6G 49
NE33: S Shi 3H 67
SR1: Sund 1G 119 (3K 7)
Nilverton Av. SR2: Sund 5F 119
Nimbus Ct. SR3: New S 3C 132
Nine Lands DH4: Hou S 2C 144
Nine Pins NE8: Gate 7F 83
NE9: Gate 1G 99
Ninnian Ter. DH9: Dip 1G 123
Ninth Av. DH2: Ches S 6K 127
NE6: Newc T 5A 64 (1P 5)
NE11: Gate 4F 99
NE24: Bly 3H 23
NE61: Mor 1H 15
Ninth Av. E. NE11: Gate 4F 99
Ninth Row NE63: Ash 3J 11
Ninth St. SR8: Pet 5E 172
TS27: B Col 1H 183
Nissan Way SR5: Wash 1B 116
Nithdale Cl. NE6: Walk 5F 65
Nixon St. NE8: Gate 2J 83 (8L 5)
Nixon Ter. NE21: Bla T 5B 80
NE24: Bly 3K 23
Noble Gdns. NE34: S Shi 2F 87
Noble's Bank Rd. SR2: Sund 3H 119
Noble St. NE4: Newc T 3B 82
NE10: Gate 5B 84
SR2: Sund 3H 119
SR8: Eas 6C 160
Noble St. Ind. Est. NE4: Newc T 3B 82
Noble Ter. NE61: Mor 7G 9
SR2: Sund 3H 119
Noel Av. NE21: Bla T 1C 96
Noel St. DH9: Stly 2H 125
Noel Ter. NE21: Bla T 7D 80
Noirmont Way SR3: New S 3A 132

Nookside SR4: Sund 4J 117
Nookside Ct. SR4: Sund 4J 117
Nook, The NE25: Whit B 7F 39
NE29: N Shi 7F 49
NO PLACE 2K 125
Nora St. NE34: S Shi 1J 87
SR4: Sund 4B 118
Norburn La. DH7: Wit G 7B 140
Norburn Pk. DH7: Wit G 2C 152
Norbury Gro. NE6: Newc T, Walk 1B 84
Nordale Way NE24: Cow 1E 22
Norfolk Av. DH3: Bir 7A 114
SR3: New S 1B 132
Norfolk Cl. NE63: Ash 3J 11
SR7: S'hm 1J 147
Norfolk Dr. NE37: Usw 5H 101
Norfolk Gdns. NE28: W'snd 1J 65
Norfolk M. NE30: N Shi 6G 49
Norfolk Pl. DH3: Bir 7B 114
Norfolk Rd. DH8: C'sde 3D 134
NE8: Gate 2J 83 (8L 5)
NE34: S Shi 6E 68
Norfolk Sq. NE6: Newc T 7K 63 (4P 5)
Norfolk St. DH5: Hett H 6F 145
NE30: N Shi 6H 49
SR1: Sund 1F 119 (3K 7)
Norfolk Wlk. SR8: Pet 4A 172
Norfolk Way NE15: Lem 6E 60
Norgas Ho. NE12: Kil 2A 46
Norham Av. Nth. NE34: S Shi 5C 68
Norham Av. Sth. NE34: S Shi 5C 68
Norham Cl. NE13: Wide O 6C 34
NE24: Bly 2G 23
Norham Ct. DH4: Hou S 1H 143
NE38: Wash 4F 115
Norham Dr. NE5: Newc T 2E 60
NE61: Hep, Mor 2H 15
SR8: Pet 2A 182
Norham Gdns. NE62: Chop 6J 11
Norham Pl. NE2: Newc T 4G 63
Norham Rd. DH1: Dur 4B 154
NE3: Gos 6D 44
NE26: Whit B 6F 39
NE29: N Shi 6C 48
NE63: Hir 5B 12
Norham Rd. Nth. NE29: N Shi 4A 48
Norham Ter. NE21: Bla T 4B 80
NE32: Jar 2B 86
Norhurst NE16: Whi 2E 96
Norland Rd. NE15: Newc T 7F 61
Norley Av. SR5: S'wck 5E 104
Norma Cres. NE26: Whit B 7J 39
Norman Av. SR3: New S 2D 132
Normanby Cl. SR7: S'hm 1J 147
Normanby Ct. SR6: Monk 6H 105
Normandy Cres. DH5: Hou S 2F 145
Norman Rd. NE39: Row G 6J 95
Norman Ter. DH6: H Pitt 6C 156
DH8: Con 6G 121
NE28: W'snd 3B 66
NE61: Mor 7G 9
Normanton Ter. NE4: Newc T 1C 82
Normount Av. NE4: Newc T 1A 82
Normount Gdns. NE4: Newc T 1A 82
Normount Rd. NE4: Newc T 1A 82
Northampton Rd. SR8: Pet 4A 172
Northamptonshire Dr. DH1: Carr 1H 167
North App. DH2: Ches S 5K 127
North Av. NE3: Gos 1D 62
NE5: Newc T 3F 61
NE12: Longb 6B 46
NE34: S Shi 7B 68
NE37: Usw 6G 101
NE62: Chop 1G 17
SR8: Pet 5D 172
North Bailey DH1: Dur 3A 166 (4C 6)
Nth. Balkwell Farm Ind. Est.
NE29: N Shi 5B 48
Nth. Bank Ct. SR5: S'wck 5D 104
NORTH BLYTH 7J 19
Northbourne Av. NE61: Mor 5F 9
Northbourne Rd. NE32: Jar 7A 66
Northbourne St. NE4: Newc T 2B 82
NE8: Gate 6H 83
Nth. Brancepeth Cl. DH7: B'don 6G 165
Nth. Brancepeth Ter. DH7: B'don 6G 165
Nth. Bridge St. SR5: Monk 7F 105 (1J 7)
North Burns DH3: Ches S 5A 128
Nth. Church St. NE30: N Shi 6H 49
North Cl. NE6: Newc T 6A 64 (2P 5)
NE34: S Shi 7B 68
NE40: Ryton 1G 79
Nth. Coronation St. SR7: Mur 7F 147
Northcote NE16: Whi 2G 97
Northcote Av. NE5: Cha P 4C 60
NE25: Whit B 7D 38
SR1: Sund 2G 119
Northcote St. NE4: Newc T 1C 82 (5A 4)
NE33: S Shi 5K 67
Northcott Gdns. NE23: Seg 2C 36
North Ct. NE32: Jar 6B 66
North Cres. DH1: Dur 1J 165
NE38: Wash 7F 115
NE62: Chop 7K 11
SR8: Eas 1K 171

Nth. Croft—Oak St.

Nth. Croft NE12: Longb 5C 46
Nth. Cross St. DH8: Lead 5A 122
NE3: Gos 7E 44
Northdene DH3: Bir 1A 114
Northdene Av. SR7: S'hm 2B 148
North Dr. NE31: Heb 1G 85
NE38: Ches S, Wash 2B 128
SR6: Cle 5A 88
Nth. Durham St. SR1: Sund 1G 119
North East Aircraft Mus. 4E 102
Nth. Eastern Ct. NE11: Dun 7A 82
North East Exhibition Cen. 1F 45
Nth. E. Fruit & Vegetable Mkt.
NE11: Gate 1F 99
Nth. East Ind. Est. SR8: Pet 3B 172
NORTH END 1J 165
North End DH1: Dur 1J 165
DH7: B'don 7C 164
Northern Gallery for Contemporary Art
. . . . 4K 7
Northern Prom. NE26: Whit B 3G 39
Northern Ter. NE23: Dud 2J 35
Northern Way SR5: S'wck 5C 104
North Farm NE22: H Bri 1C 20
Nth. Farm Av. SR4: Sund 6H 117
Nth. Farm Rd. NE31: Heb 1H 85
Northfield NE22: E Sle 4F 19
Northfield Cl. NE16: Whi 2F 97
Northfield Dr. NE12: Kil 2K 45
SR4: Sund 6H 117
Northfield Gdns. NE34: S Shi 5B 68
Northfield Rd. NE3: Gos 1D 62
NE33: S Shi 4B 68
Northfields Cl. NE6: Newc T 6A 64
Northfields Ho. *NE6: Newc T 6A 64*
(off North Vw.)
Northfield Vw. DH8: Con 6J 121
Northgate DH9: Ann P 6K 123
NE12: Kil 7B 36
North Grange NE20: Pon 3J 31
North Gro. NE40: Ryton 1H 79
SR6: Monk 4G 105
North Guards SR6: Whit 6G 89
Nth. Hall Rd. SR4: Sund 4K 117
North Haven SR7: S'hm 2K 147
North Holm DH8: Lead 5A 122
NORTH HYLTON 1G 117
Nth. Hylton Rd. SR5: C'twn, S'wck 5K 103
Nth. Hylton Rd. Ind. Est.
SR5: C'twn 5K 103
Nth. Jesmond Av. NE2: Newc T 2G 63
Nth. King St. NE30: N Shi 6H 49
Northland Cl. SR4: Sund 6H 117
Northlands DH3: Ches S 4A 128
NE21: Bla T 5B 80
NE30: N Shi 3H 49
Northlands Rd. NE61: Mor 5F 9
North La. DH5: Hett H 4A 146
NE36: E Bol 7J 87
NORTHLEA 2K 147
Northlea NE15: Lem 5E 60
(not continuous)
Northlea Rd. SR7: S'hm 2J 147
North Leech NE61: Mor 5D 8
North Leigh DH9: Tan L 7D 110
NORTH LODGE 2A 128
North Lodge DH3: Ches S 2A 128
Nth. Magdalene DH8: M'sly 7K 107
Nth. Mason Lodge NE13: Din 3H 33
North Mdws. NE42: O'ham 1D 76
Nth. Milburn St. SR4: Sund 1D 118
Nth. Moor Cotts. SR3: E Her 7A 118
Nth. Moor Ct. SR3: Sund 7A 118
Nth. Moor La.
SR3: E Her, New S, Sund 7A 118
Northmoor Rd. NE6: Walk 5C 64
Nth. Moor Rd. SR3: Sund 7A 118
Nth. Nelson Ind. Est.
NE23: Nel V 7G 21
Northolt Av. NE23: Cra 3K 25
North Pde. NE26: Whit B 6H 39
NE29: N Shi 3E 66
NE62: Chop 2G 17
Nth. Railway St. SR7: S'hm 3B 148
Nth. Ravensworth St. SR4: Sund 1D 118
North Ridge NE22: Bed 7G 17
(Forster Av.)
NE22: Bed 7F 17
(Meadowdale Cres.)
NE25: Whit B 6C 38
North Rd. DH1: Dur 1K 165 (1A 6)
DH3: Ches S 2A 128
DH5: Hett H, Hou S 4D 144
DH9: Ann P, Dip 2J 123
NE13: Wide O 5E 34
NE20: Pon 2J 31
NE28: W'snd 3F 65
NE29: N Shi 4F 49
NE35: Bol C 5E 86
(Boldon Colliery)
NE35: Bol C, W Bol 6F 87
(New Town)
NE36: E Bol 7J 87
(not continuous)
NE36: W Bol 6F 87
North Rd. SR7: S'hm 1B 148
TS28: Win 4F 181
North Rd. E. TS28: Win 6F 181
North Rd. W. TS28: Win 6F 181
North Row NE42: Pru 4C 76
Nth. Sands Bus. Cen. SR6: Monk 7G 105
NORTH SEATON 5E 12
NORTH SEATON COLLIERY 7E 12
Nth. Seaton Ind. Est. NE63: N Sea 6D 12
Nth. Seaton Rd. NE63: Ash 3B 12
NE64: Newb S 4H 13
NORTH SHIELDS 7G 49
North Shields Station (Metro) 7G 49
North Side DH3: Bir 2B 114
(not continuous)
DH6: Shad 6E 168
Northside Pl. NE25: H'wll 1J 37
Nth. Stead Dr. DH8: Shot B 4E 120
North St. DH3: Bir 5C 114
DH4: Hou S 5D 130
DH4: W Rai 1K 155
DH5: W Rai 6D 144
DH6: Hett 7C 176
DH8: Con 7K 121
NE1: Newc T 7F 63 (4F 4)
NE21: Bla T 4A 80
NE32: Jar 6B 66
NE33: S Shi 2J 67
SR3: New S 1C 132
SR5: S'wck 6E 104
SR6: Cle 5C 88
TS27: B Col 2H 183
North St. Ct. NE1: Newc T 4G 4
North St. E. NE1: Newc T 7G 63 (4G 4)
North Ter. DH1: Dur 5J 153
DH7: Wit G 3C 152
DH9: Ann P 4C 124
NE2: Newc T 6E 62 (1C 4)
NE17: C'wl 5K 93
NE27: Shir 3J 47
NE28: W'snd 3H 65
NE46: Hex 2D 70
SR3: New S 1D 132
SR7: S'hm 2B 148
SR8: Eas 1K 171
North Thorn DH9: Stly 2F 125
Nth. Tyne Ind. Est. NE12: Longb 4E 46
Northumberland Annexe
NE1: Newc T 3G 4
Northumberland Av. NE3: Gos 1C 62
NE12: Longb 5B 46
NE22: Bed 7G 17
NE28: W'snd 3K 65
NE64: Newb S 4H 13
Northumberland Bldg. NE1: Newc T 3G 4
Northumberland Cl. NE63: Ash 3J 11
Northumberland County Cricket Club
. . . . 5H 63
Northumberland County Tennis Ground
. . . . 3G 63
Northumberland Ct. NE42: Pru 2G 77
NE46: Acomb 3C 50
Northumberland Dock Rd.
NE28: W'snd 4C 66
Northumberland Gdns. NE2: Newc T 5J 63
NE5: Cha P 2B 60
Northumberland Ho. NE23: Cra 3A 26
Northumberland Pl. DH3: Bir 7B 114
NE1: Newc T 7F 63 (4F 4)
NE30: N Shi 6G 49
SR8: Pet 4K 171
Northumberland Rd.
NE1: Newc T 7F 63 (4F 4)
NE15: Lem 7C 60
NE40: Ryton 7G 59
Northumberland Sq. NE26: Whit B 6G 39
NE30: N Shi 6G 49
Northumberland St.
NE1: Newc T 7F 63 (3F 4)
NE8: Gate 5E 82
NE28: W'snd 3G 65
NE30: N Shi 6J 49
SR8: Pet 4D 172
Northumberland Ter.
NE6: Newc T 7K 63 (4N 5)
NE28: W'snd 3K 65
(off Northumberland Av.)
NE30: N Shi 5K 49
Northumberland Vs. NE28: W'snd 3J 65
Northumberland Way
NE37: Gate, Usw, Wash 3G 101
NE38: Wash 2J 115
Northumbria Birds of Prey Cen. 1J 45
Northumbria Cen. 4J 101
Northumbria Ho. NE3: Gos 6E 44
Northumbria Lodge NE5: Newc T 4A 62
Northumbrian Rd. NE23: Cra 2J 25
Northumbrian Way NE12: Kil 1K 45
NE29: N Shi 2G 67
Northumbria Pl. DH9: Stly 2H 125
Northumbria Wlk. NE5: Newc T 4F 61
North Vw. DH1: Dur 2E 166
DH2: Pelt 4F 127
DH4: Hou S 7J 129
DH5: Eas L 2J 157
North Vw. DH6: Has 1B 170
(Haswell)
DH6: Has 3A 170
(Haswell Plough)
DH6: Shad 5J 169
DH6: Sher 3D 168
DH7: B'don 2E 174
DH7: Ush M 1C 164
DH8: M'sly 7K 107
DH8: Shot B 5F 121
DH9: Stly 6H 125
NE6: Newc T 7K 63 (3N 5)
(not continuous)
NE9: Gate 4K 99
NE12: Longb 4B 46
NE13: Bru V 7C 34
NE13: Din 4H 33
NE16: Whi 7G 81
NE22: Bed 5B 18
NE24: Camb 2G 19
NE26: Whit B 7J 39
NE28: W'snd 3G 65
NE29: N Shi 4F 49
NE30: N Shi 7J 39
NE32: Jar 7A 66
NE34: S Shi 5B 68
NE37: Usw 7H 101
NE39: H Spen 4D 94
NE40: Ryton 1E 78
(Main Rd.)
NE40: Ryton 6C 58
(Stannerford Rd.)
NE43: Mic 5A 76
NE62: Chop 7A 12
NE63: Ash 3A 12
NE64: Newb S 4H 13
SR2: Ryh 3H 133
(off Stockton Rd.)
SR4: Sund 3G 117
SR5: C'twn 6J 103
SR6: Monk 4F 105
SR7: Mur 1E 158
SR8: Eas 6C 160
TS27: Cas E 4K 181
Nth. View E. NE39: Row G 5G 95
Nth. View Ter. DH4: Hou S 2B 144
NE10: Gate 5A 84
NE42: Pru 4D 76
NE43: Stoc 7J 75
Nth. View W. NE39: Row G 5F 95
North Vs. NE23: Dud 2J 35
NORTH WALBOTTLE 2B 60
Nth. Walbottle Rd. NE5: Cha P 3A 60
NE15: Cha P, Thro 3A 60
(not continuous)
North Way DH2: Ous 7G 113
Northway NE9: Gate 7K 83
NE15: Thro 2H 59
NE62: Chop 1H 17
Nth. West Ind. Est. SR8: Pet 5J 171
Nth. W. Radial NE2: Newc T 5D 62
Northwood Ct. SR5: S'wck 5E 104
Northwood Rd. SR7: S'hm 2K 147
Nth. Wylam Vw. NE42: Pru 2G 77
Norton Av. DH6: Bow 4H 177
SR7: S'hm 1J 147
Norton Cl. DH2: Ches S 1H 141
Norton Rd. SR5: S'wck 4C 104
Norton Way NE15: Lem 7E 60
Norway Av. SR4: Sund 4A 118
Norwich Av. NE13: Wide O 6D 34
Norwich Cl. DH3: Gt Lum 3F 143
NE63: N Sea 5E 12
Norwich Rd. DH1: Dur 4B 154
Norwich Way NE23: Cra 3J 25
(not continuous)
NE32: Jar 5B 86
Norwood Av. NE3: Gos 3E 44
NE6: Newc T 4K 63
Norwood Ct. NE9: Spri 5A 100
NE12: Longb 6B 46
Norwood Cres. NE39: Row G 5K 95
Norwood Gdns. NE9: Gate 6J 83
Norwood Rd. NE11: Gate 7D 82
NE15: Lem 5D 60
Nottingham Ct. NE22: Bed 6F 17
Nottingham Pl. SR8: Pet 4K 171
Nottinghamshire Rd. DH1: Carr 1G 167
Number One Ind. Est. DH8: Con 5J 121
Numbers Gth. SR1: Sund 1G 119
Nuneaton Way NE5: Cha P 1B 60
Nunn St. DH4: Hou S 4A 130
Nunnykirk Cl. NE42: O'ham 2C 76
Nuns La. NE1: Newc T 1F 83 (6E 4)
NE8: Gate 3H 83 (10J 5)
NUNS MOOR 4A 62
Nuns Moor Cres. NE4: Newc T 6A 62
Nuns Moor Rd. NE4: Newc T 6A 62
Nuns' Row DH1: Dur 1D 166
Nun St. NE1: Newc T 1F 83 (5E 4)
Nunthorpe Av. SR2: Sund 7H 119
Nunwick Gdns. NE29: N Shi 6C 48
Nunwick Way NE7: Newc T 2B 64
Nurseries, The SR6: Cle 5C 88
Nursery Cl. SR3: Sund 6C 118
Nursery Cotts. DH1: Dur 3K 165
Nursery Ct. NE17: C'wl 2K 107
Nursery Gdns. NE5: Newc T 5H 61
SR8: Eas 1K 171
Nursery Grange NE46: Hex 3B 70
Nursery La. NE10: Gate 7A 84
SR6: Cle 5C 88
(not continuous)
Nursery Pk. NE63: Hir 7C 12
Nursery Rd. SR3: Sund 6C 118
Nursery, The NE20: Pon 3C 40
Nutley Pl. NE15: Newc T 1G 81
Nye Bevan Ho. NE24: Bly 3K 23
Nye Dene SR5: C'twn 6H 103

O

Oakapple Cl. NE22: Bed 7H 17
Oak Av. DH1: Dur 3E 166
DH4: Hou S 1D 144
NE11: Dun 7B 82
NE13: Din 4J 33
NE34: S Shi 1C 88
TS27: B Col 2J 183
Oak Cl. NE46: Hex 3A 70
Oak Ct. DH7: Sac 7E 140
Oak Cres. DH2: Plaw 6J 141
SR6: Whit 5J 89
Oakdale NE22: H Bri 1D 20
Oakdale Cl. NE15: Lem 7D 60
Oakdale Rd. DH8: Con 6J 121
Oakdale Ter. DH2: Pelt 4E 126
DH3: Ches S 7A 128
Oakenshaw NE15: Lem 7E 60
Oakerside Dr. SR8: Pet 7A 172
OAKERSIDE PARK 2A 182
Oakey's Rd. DH9: Tan L 1F 125
Oakfield DH2: Ches S 7H 127
Oakfield Av. NE16: Whi 1H 97
Oakfield Cl. NE16: Whi 1H 97
SR3: E Her 3J 131
Oakfield Ct. SR3: E Her 3J 131
Oakfield Cres. DH6: Bow 4J 177
Oakfield Dr. NE12: Kil 1D 46
NE16: Whi 1H 97
Oakfield Gdns. NE15: Newc T 1K 81
NE28: W'snd 2D 64
Oakfield Grange NE13: Din 4H 33
Oakfield La. DH8: C'sde 1E 134
Oakfield Nth. NE40: Ryton 1F 79
Oakfield Pk. NE42: Pru 4F 77
Oakfield Rd. NE3: Gos 2D 62
NE11: Gate 1C 98
NE16: Whi 2F 97
Oakfields NE16: Burn 1B 110
Oakfield Ter. NE3: Gos 1D 62
NE10: Gate 5E 84
NE12: Kil 3C 46
NE42: Pru 4F 77
Oakfield Way NE23: Seg 2D 36
Oak Grn. Flats DH7: B'don 1D 174
Oak Gro. NE12: Longb 4B 46
NE28: W'snd 4H 65
Oakham Av. NE16: Whi 1F 97
Oakham Dr. DH1: Carr 6H 155
Oakham Gdns. NE29: N Shi 1E 66
Oakhurst Dr. NE3: Ken 2C 62
Oakhurst Ter. NE12: Longb 6B 46
Oakland Rd. NE2: Newc T 3F 63
NE25: Whit B 7D 38
Oaklands NE3: Gos 2E 62
NE16: Swa 5H 81
NE20: Pon 7H 31
NE44: Rid M 7K 73
NE46: B End 7F 51
Oaklands Av. NE3: Gos 2E 62
Oaklands Ct. NE20: Pon 7H 31
Oaklands Cres. SR5: S'wck 5B 104
Oaklands Pl. NE42: Pru 4G 77
Oaklands Ri. NE44: Rid M 7K 73
Oaklands Ter. SR4: Sund 3C 118
Oakland Ter. NE63: Ash 3A 12
Oak La. DH8: Shot B 2E 120
Oak Lea DH7: Wit G 2D 152
Oaklea DH2: Ches S 4J 127
Oakleigh Gdns. SR6: Cle 4C 88
Oakley Cl. NE23: Dud 3K 35
Oakley Dr. NE23: Cra 3A 26
Oakmere Cl. DH4: Pen 3B 130
Oakridge NE16: Whi 1F 97
Oakridge Rd. DH7: Ush M 2C 164
Oak Rd. NE29: N Shi 5B 48
SR8: Eas 7A 160
Oak Sq. NE8: Gate 5E 82
Oaks, The DH4: Pen 1B 130
DH7: Esh W 5D 162
NE40: G'sde 5F 79
NE46: Hex 3B 70
SR2: Sund 3G 119 (7K 7)
Oak St. DH2: Ches S 1G 141
DH4: Hou S 1J 143
DH7: Lang P 4J 151
DH8: Con 7H 121
NE13: Sea B 3E 34

Oxford Sq.—Paton Sq.

Oxford Sq. SR4: Sund 1A 118
Oxford St. DH9: Ann P 4K 123
NE1: Newc T 7G 63 (4G 4)
NE24: Bly 2K 23
NE26: Whit B 6G 39
NE30: N Shi 5K 49
NE33: S Shi 5K 67
SR4: Sund 1A 118
SR7: S'hm 3J 147
Oxford Ter. DH4: Hou S 3A 130
DH6: Bow 5H 177
NE8: Gate 5G 83
Oxford Way NE32: Jar 5B 86
OXHILL 3D 124
Oxhill Vs. DH9: Ann P 4B 124
Oxley St. DH8: Con 5F 121
Oxley Ter. DH1: Dur 4J 153
Oxnam Cres. NE2: Newc T 6D 62 (1A 4)
Oxted Cl. NE23: Cra 3B 26
Oxted Pl. NE6: Walk 3C 84
Oystershell La. NE4: Newc T 1E 82 (6C 4)
Oyston St. NE33: S Shi 3J 67
Ozanan Cl. NE23: Dud 4K 35

P

Pacific Hall Cl. SR7: S'hm 2G 147
Packham Rd. SR4: Sund 3J 117
Paddock Cl. DH4: Hou S 4K 129
NE42: Pru 4G 77
SR6: Cle 5A 88
Paddock Hill NE20: Pon 4K 31
Paddock La. NE18: Pon 6A 30
SR3: New S 2D 132
Paddock Ri. NE63: Ash 5K 11
Paddock, The DH4: E Her 2F 131
DH7: Lan 7J 137
DH7: Wat 6B 162
DH9: Tan L 1C 124
NE10: Gate 1D 100
NE12: Kil 1C 46
NE13: Wool 4F 43
NE15: Thro 4K 59
NE23: E Cram 5B 26
NE24: Cow 2G 23
NE25: Sea D 7J 27
NE39: H Spen 3D 94
NE43: Stoc 2J 91
Paddock Wood NE42: Pru 4G 77
Pader Cl. NE13: Bru V 6C 34
Padgate Rd. SR4: Sund 2J 117
Padonhill SR3: New S 4A 132
Padstow Cl. SR2: Ryh 1H 133
Padstow Gdns. NE9: Gate 5H 99
Padstow Rd. NE29: N Shi 1E 66
Page Av. NE34: S Shi 6A 68
Page's Bldgs. NE35: Bol C 6E 86
Page St. NE31: Heb 6K 65
Paignton Av. NE4: Newc T 1A 82
NE25: Whit B 7D 38
Paignton Sq. SR3: Sund 6A 118
PAINSHAWFIELD 1J 91
Painshawfield Rd. NE43: Stoc 1J 91
Painter Heugh NE1: Newc T 1G 83 (7G 4)
Paisley Sq. SR3: Sund 6A 118
Palace Grn. DH1: Dur 3A 166 (4C 6)
Palace Rd. NE22: Bed 6B 18
Palace St. NE4: Newc T 2D 82 (7B 4)
Palatine St. NE33: S Shi 1J 67
Palatine Vw. *DH1: Dur 4A 6*
(off Margery La.)
DH6: Sher 3C 168
Palermo St. SR4: Sund 7B 104
Paley St. SR1: Sund 1E 118 (3G 7)
Palgrove Rd. SR4: Sund 3J 117
Palgrove Sq. SR4: Sund 3J 117
Palladian Chapel 6A 96
Pallinsburn Ct. NE5: Newc T 2H 61
PALLION 7B 104
Pallion Ind. Est. SR4: Sund 1K 117
Pallion New Rd. SR4: Sund 7B 104
Pallion Pk. SR4: Sund 1B 118
Pallion Quay SR4: Sund 7B 104
Pallion Retail Pk. SR4: Sund 7A 104
Pallion Rd. SR4: Sund 2B 118
Pallion Station (Metro) 7A 104
Pallion Subway SR4: Sund 7A 104
Pallion Way SR4: Sund 1K 117
Pallion W. Ind. Est.
SR4: Sund 7K 103
Palm Av. NE4: Newc T 6A 62
NE34: S Shi 1C 88
Palm Ct. NE12: Kil 3D 46
Palmer Cres. NE31: Heb 7K 65
Palmer Gdns. NE10: Gate 6G 85
Palmer Rd. DH9: Dip 7J 109
SR8: Pet 7J 171
Palmers Gth. DH1: Dur 3B 166 (4D 6)
Palmers Grn. NE12: Kil 3D 46
Palmer's Hill Rd. SR6: Monk 1K 7
Palmerston Av. NE6: Walk 6C 64
Palmerstone Rd. SR4: Sund 4J 117
Palmerston Rd. SR4: Sund 5G 117
Palmerston Sq. SR4: Sund 4J 117
Palmerston St. DH8: Con 7H 121
NE33: S Shi 5J 67
Palmerston Wlk. NE8: Gate 4E 82
Palmer St. DH6: S Het 5D 158
DH9: Stly 4D 124
NE32: Jar 6A 66
PALMERSVILLE 3D 46
Palmersville NE12: Kil 3D 46
(not continuous)
Palmersville Station (Metro) 4E 46
Palm Lea DH7: B'don 1C 174
Palmstead Rd. SR4: Sund 3H 117
Palmstead Sq. SR4: Sund 3J 117
Palm St. DH7: Lang P 4K 151
DH8: Con 6H 121
Palm Ter. DH9: Stly 6H 125
DH9: Tan L 5C 110
Panatta Fitness Cen. *5E 82*
(within church)
Pancras Rd. SR3: Sund 6A 118
Pandon NE1: Newc T 1G 83 (6H 5)
Pandon Bank NE1: Newc T 1G 83 (6H 5)
Pandon Bldg. NE2: Newc T 3H 5
Pandon Ct. NE2: Newc T 7H 63 (3J 5)
Panfield Ter. DH4: Hou S 7J 129
Pangbourne Cl. NE15: Lem 5C 60
Pankhurst Gdns. NE10: Gate 6E 84
Pankhurst Pl. DH9: Stly 4H 125
Pann La. SR1: Sund 1F 119 (3J 7)
Panns Bank SR1: Sund 1F 119 (2J 7)
Pantiles, The NE37: Usw 5H 101
Parade Cl. NE6: Walk 1E 84
Parade, The DH2: Pelt 3E 126
(not continuous)
DH3: Ches S 1B 142
NE6: Walk 1E 84
NE11: Dun 4J 81
NE28: W'snd 7H 47
NE38: Wash 4J 115
SR2: Sund 2H 119
PARADISE 2J 81
Paradise Cres. SR8: Eas 7B 160
Paradise La. SR8: Eas 7B 160
Paradise Row NE23: Cra 4K 25
Paradise St. SR8: Pet 5F 173
Paramount Fitness Cen. 7H 17
Park & Ride
Callerton Parkway 3E 42
East Boldon 7A 88
Four Lane Ends 6A 46
Heworth 6D 84
Kingston Park 6J 43
Regent Centre 6E 44
Park Av. DH6: Coxh 7J 177
DH8: Con 6J 121
DH9: Stly 2F 125
NE3: Gos 6C 44
(not continuous)
NE3: Ken 5B 44
NE11: Dun 7A 82
NE21: Bla T 4B 80
(Blaydon Bank)
NE21: Bla T 4C 80
(Widdrington Rd.)
NE22: Bed 5C 18
NE26: Whit B 6G 39
NE27: Shir 1K 47
NE28: W'snd 3F 65
NE30: N Shi 5J 49
NE34: S Shi 2B 88
NE37: Usw 6H 101
NE42: Pru 5G 77
NE46: Hex 1B 70
SR3: New S 2D 132
SR6: Monk 4G 105
TS27: B Col 2H 183
Park Chare NE38: Wash 3H 115
Park Cl. DH7: Lang P 5K 151
DH9: Ann P 6A 124
NE4: Newc T 2C 82
Park Cotts. NE17: C'wl 2K 107
Park Ct. NE6: Walk 4E 64
NE8: Gate 10J 5
NE11: Gate 4F 99
Park Cres. NE27: Shir 1K 47
(not continuous)
NE30: N Shi 5H 49
Park Cres. E. NE30: N Shi 5J 49
Parkdale Ri. NE16: Whi 7F 81
Park Dr. DH7: Lang P 4J 151
NE3: Gos 3E 44
NE12: Longb 4C 46
NE16: Whi 7J 81
NE24: News 5F 23
NE61: Hep 7K 15
NE61: Mor 1F 15
Parker Av. NE3: Gos 1D 62
Parker Ct. NE11: Dun 4A 82
Parker's Bldgs. DH8: Con 1C 136
Pk. Farm Vs. NE24: News 7G 23
Park Fld. NE40: Ryton 1F 79
Parkfield DH6: Coxh 7J 177
NE26: Sea S 4C 28
NE32: Jar 5C 86
Parkfield Ter. DH9: Ann P 3J 123
Park Gdns. NE26: Whit B 6G 39
Park Ga. SR6: Monk 4G 105
Parkgate DH5: Hett H 7J 145
Parkgate La. NE21: Bla T 6B 80
Park Gro. NE27: Shir 1K 47
NE37: Usw 6H 101
Parkham Cl. NE23: Cra 1K 25
Parkhead DH9: Ann P 7J 123
Parkhead Gdns. NE21: Bla T 6B 80
Pk. Head Rd. NE7: Newc T 3J 63
NE7: Newc T 4J 63
Parkhead Sq. NE21: Bla T 5C 80
Park Hill DH6: Coxh 7J 177
Parkhouse Av. SR5: C'twn 7H 103
Pk. House Cl. DH6: Sher 2K 167
Pk. House Gdns. DH6: Sher 2K 167
(not continuous)
Pk. House Rd. DH1: Dur 5J 165
Parkhurst Rd. SR4: Sund 4H 117
Parkin Gdns. NE10: Gate 7C 84
Parkinson Cotts. NE40: Ryton 2J 79
Parkland NE12: Longb 6B 46
NE21: Bla T 2A 80
Parkland Av. NE21: Bla T 6B 80
Parkland Ct. SR7: S'hm 2K 147
Parklands NE10: Gate 6G 85
NE20: Pon 2F 41
NE39: Ham M 3D 108
Parklands Ct. NE10: Gate 5G 85
TS27: Cas E 4K 181
Parklands Dr. TS27: Cas E 4K 181
Parklands Gro. DH6: S Het 5D 158
Parklands Way NE10: Gate 6G 85
Parkland Ter. SR7: S'hm 2K 147
Park La. NE8: Gate 3H 83 (10K 5)
NE21: Bla T 6B 80
NE27: Shir 1K 47
NE42: Pru 5F 77
(not continuous)
SR1: Sund 2E 118 (4H 7)
SR7: Mur 7D 146
SR8: Pet 5E 172
Park La. Interchange SR1: Sund 5H 7
Park Lane Station (Metro) 2F 119 (5J 7)
Park Lea SR3: E Her 3G 131
Parklea NE26: Sea S 4C 28
Pk. Lea Rd. SR6: Monk 4G 105
Parkmore Rd. SR4: Sund 5G 117
Park Pde. NE26: Whit B 6G 39
SR6: Monk 5G 105
Park Pl. DH3: Ches S 4B 128
DH5: Hett H 7G 145
Park Pl. E. SR2: Sund 3F 119 (6K 7)
Park Pl. W. SR2: Sund 3F 119 (6K 7)
Park Ri. NE15: Lem 6C 60
Park Rd. DH5: Hett H 6G 145
DH6: Sher 2K 167
DH8: Con 6F 121
DH9: Stly 4D 124
NE4: Newc T 2C 82 (8A 4)
NE8: Gate 3J 83 (10M 5)
NE10: Gate 3J 83 (10M 5)
NE15: Thro 5K 59
NE22: Bed 7J 17
NE24: Bly 2K 23
NE25: Sea D 7G 27
NE26: Whit B 5G 39
NE27: Shir 1K 47
NE28: W'snd 3F 65
NE31: Heb 1J 85
NE32: Jar 7A 66
NE39: Row G 5H 95
NE63: Ash 4K 11
SR2: Sund 3F 119 (6J 7)
SR8: Pet 4D 172
Park Rd. Central DH3: Ches S 6B 128
Park Rd. E. NE63: Ash 4A 12
Park Rd. Ind. Est. DH8: Con 6F 121
Park Rd. Nth. DH3: Ches S 3A 128
Park Rd. Nth. Ind. Est. DH8: Con 6F 121
Park Rd. Sth. DH3: Ches S 1A 142
Park Row NE10: Gate 6B 84
SR5: S'wck 6B 104
Parkshiel NE34: S Shi 2C 88
PARKSIDE 5A 148
Park Side NE61: Hep 3B 16
Parkside DH1: Dur 2K 165 (2A 6)
DH7: B'hpe 5D 138
DH7: Sac 7E 140
DH8: Con 6G 121
DH9: Tan L 7C 110
NE11: Dun 6B 82
NE12: Kil 2J 45
NE15: Thro 4J 59
NE22: Bed 5C 18
NE28: W'snd 2H 65
NE30: N Shi 3K 49
NE31: Heb 2G 85
SR3: E Her 3H 131
Parkside Av. NE7: Newc T 7K 45
NE21: Bla T 5C 80
Parkside Cotts. DH9: Tan L 7C 110
Parkside Ct. NE13: Wide O 5E 34
Parkside Cres. NE30: N Shi 4K 49
SR7: S'hm 5A 148
Parkside Rd. SR7: S'hm 4A 148
Parkside Sth. SR3: E Her 3H 131
Parkside Ter. NE28: W'snd 1E 64
Parks Leisure Cen. 1F 67
Parks, The DH3: Ches S 1C 142
Parkstone Cl. SR4: Sund 6G 117
Park St. DH8: Con 5G 121
SR7: S'hm 4B 148
Park St. Sth. SR5: C'twn 6J 103
Park Ter. DH8: C'sde 4C 134
DH8: Lead 5B 122
NE2: Newc T 6F 63 (1E 4)
NE11: Dun 6B 82
NE12: Kil 2K 45
NE16: Burn 2A 110
NE16: Swa 5G 81
NE21: Bla T 5D 80
NE22: Bed 5B 18
NE26: Whit B 5G 39
NE28: W'snd 3F 65
NE30: N Shi 5J 49
NE37: Usw 6H 101
SR5: S'wck 5B 104
SR8: Pet 6E 172
Park Vw. DH2: Ches S 4K 127
DH2: Plaw 6H 141
DH4: Hou S 3B 130
DH4: Hou S 5H 129
DH5: Hett H 7G 145
DH7: B'don 6G 165
DH7: Wit G 3B 152
DH8: Con 5H 121
NE6: Walk 1E 84
NE10: Gate 6B 84
NE12: Longb 4B 46
NE13: Wide O 5E 34
NE16: Burn 2B 110
NE16: Swa 5F 81
NE21: Bla T 6C 80
NE23: Cra 4K 25
(off Station Rd.)
NE24: Bly 2K 23
NE25: Sea D 7H 27
(not continuous)
NE26: Whit B 6G 39
NE28: W'snd 3F 65
NE32: Jar 2B 86
NE63: Ash 3K 11
SR7: S'hm 2H 147
SR8: Pet 5E 172
Pk. View Cl. NE40: Ryton 1H 79
Pk. View Ct. NE3: Ken 7A 44
NE12: Longb 2K 45
NE26: Whit B 6G 39
Pk. View Gdns. NE40: Ryton 1H 79
Pk. View Sports Complex 7A 44
Park Vs. *DH8: Lead 5B 122*
(off Dunelm Way)
DH9: Dip 2G 123
NE3: Gos 3D 62
NE28: W'snd 3F 65
NE63: Ash 3K 11
Parkville NE6: Newc T 6J 63 (1M 5)
Park Wlk. SR3: New S 4C 132
Parkway NE38: Wash 3G 115
NE62: Chop 1H 17
Parkwood Av. DH7: Ush M 1C 164
NE42: Pru 3H 77
Parliament St. DH8: Con 7G 121
NE31: Heb 6G 65
Parmeter St. DH9: Stly 5E 124
Parmontley St. NE15: Newc T 1F 81
Parnaby St. DH8: Con 7H 121
Parnell St. DH4: Hou S 2B 144
Parry Dr. SR6: Whit 5G 89
Parson Rd. NE41: Wylam 7K 57
Parson's Av. NE6: Walk 1D 84
Parsons Dr. NE40: Ryton 1G 79
Parsons Gdns. NE11: Dun 5B 82
Parsons Ind. Est. NE37: Wash 1F 115
Parsons Rd. NE37: Wash 1F 115
SR8: Pet 3B 172
Parsons St. *NE24: Bly 1J 23*
(off Union St.)
Partick Rd. SR4: Sund 4H 117
Partick Sq. SR4: Sund 4J 117
Partnership Ct. SR7: Sea 7G 133
Partridge Cl. NE38: Wash 4D 114
Partridge Ter. TS28: Win 5F 181
Passfield Sq. DH6: Thor 1J 179
SR8: Eas 1A 172
Passfield Way SR8: Pet 1J 181
Pasteur Rd. DH6: S Het 4B 158
Paston Rd. NE25: Sea D 1H 37
Pastures, The NE24: News 5H 23
NE43: Stoc 6H 75
NE61: Mor 1D 14
PATH HEAD 3A 80
Path Head Water Mill 2A 80
Pathside NE32: Jar 4C 86
Path, The NE9: Gate 3J 99
Patience Av. NE13: Sea B 3E 34
Patina Cl. NE15: Lem 5C 60
Paton Rd. SR3: Sund 6B 118
Paton Sq. SR3: Sund 6B 118

Patrick Cain Ho.—Pier Pavilion Theatre

Patrick Cain Ho. NE33: S Shi 5H 67
Patrick Cres. DH6: S Het 3A 158
Patrick Ter. NE23: Dud 4K 35
Patterdale Cl. DH1: Carr 7J 155
NE36: E Bol .7J 87
Patterdale Gdns. NE7: Newc T 2K 63
Patterdale Gro. SR5: Monk 3E 104
Patterdale M. DH8: Lead 5B 122
Patterdale Rd. NE24: Cow 1E 22
Patterdale St. DH5: Hett H 1G 157
Patterdale Ter. NE8: Gate 6H 83
Patterson Cl. NE46: Hex 3A 70
Patterson Ho. NE24: Bly 3J 23
Patterson St. NE21: Bla T 2E 80
Pattinson Gdns. NE9: Gate 7K 83
NE10: Gate 4A 84
Pattinson Ind. Est. NE38: Wash 4A 116
(Barmston Rd.)
NE38: Wash 2B 116
(Mandarin Way)
Pattinson Nth. Ind. Est. NE38: Wash . . .3B 116
Pattinson Rd. NE38: Wash 5K 115
Pattinson Sth. Ind. Est. NE38: Wash . . .5K 115
Pattison Cres. TS27: B Col 3K 183
Pattison Gdns. TS27: B Col 3K 183
Patton Wlk. DH6: Whe H 2C 180
Patton Way NE61: Peg 4A 10
Pauline Av. SR6: Monk 4F 105
Pauline Gdns. NE15: Newc T 6G 61
Paul Lea DH9: Beam 1A 126
Pauls Grn. DH5: Hett H 4G 145
Paul's Rd. SR1: Sund 2G 119
Paulsway NE32: Jar 7E 66
Pavilion M. NE2: Newc T 5H 63
Pavilion Ter. DH5: Hett H 7G 145
DH7: B'hpe 5D 138
Pavilion, The NE16: Swa 5F 81
Pavillion Ct. SR1: Sund 5K 7
Pawston Rd. NE21: Bla T, H Spen 2E 94
NE39: H Spen 2E 94
Paxford Cl. NE7: Longb 7J 45
Paxton Ter. SR4: Sund 1C 118
Peacehaven Ct. NE37: Usw 5G 101
Peacock Ct. NE11: Gate 7D 82
Peacock La. NE61: Mor 5D 8
Peacock St. W. SR4: Sund 2B 118
Pea Flatts La. DH3: Gt Lum 3G 143
Peak Body Fitness Club 6H 83
Peak Fitness
Jesmond *5H 63*
(off Jesmond Rd.)
Whitley Bay *6G 39*
(off Park Vw.)
Peareth Ct. *NE8: Gate 10J 5*
(off Hopper St.)
Peareth Edge NE9: Spri 6D 100
Peareth Gro. SR6: Monk 4H 105
Peareth Hall Rd. NE9: Spri 6D 100
NE37: Usw 5F 101
Peareth Rd. SR6: Monk 3G 105
Peareth Ter. DH3: Bir 4A 114
Pear Lea DH7: B'don 1C 174
Pearl Rd. SR3: Sund 6B 118
Pea Rd. DH9: Stly 3D 124
Pearson Ct. NE21: Bla T 2E 80
Pearson Pl. NE30: N Shi 6H 49
NE32: Jar 5C 66
Pearson's Ter. NE46: Hex 1C 70
Pearson St. DH9: Stly 1F 125
NE33: S Shi 1K 67
Peart Cl. DH6: Sher 3A 168
Peartree Bungs. NE17: C'wl 2A 108
Peartree Ct. NE17: C'wl 2A 108
Peartree Gdns. NE6: Walk 4E 64
Peartree M. SR2: Sund 4E 118
Pear Tree Ter. DH3: Gt Lum 1F 143
NE17: C'wl 7K 93
Peartree Ter. DH7: B'hpe 4H 139
Peary Cl. NE5: Newc T 3F 61
Pease Av. NE15: Newc T 7J 61
Peasemore Rd. SR4: Sund 3H 117
Pease Rd. SR8: Pet 4H 171
Pebble Beach SR6: Monk 7H 89
Pecket Cl. NE24: Bly 4E 22
Peddars Way NE34: S Shi 1H 87
Peebles Cl. NE29: N Shi 4C 48
Peebles Rd. SR3: Sund 6A 118
Peel Av. DH1: Dur 2F 167
Peel Cen., The NE37: Wash 1K 115
Peel Ct. NE13: Sea B 3D 34
Peel Gdns. NE34: S Shi 2E 86
Peel Ho. NE1: Newc T 6D 4
Peel La. NE1: Newc T 2E 82 (7D 4)
Peel Retail Pk. NE37: Wash 1K 115
Peel St. NE1: Newc T 1E 82 (7D 4)
SR2: Sund 3G 119 (6K 7)
Peggy's Wicket DH9: Beam 1B 126
PEGSWOOD 4B 10
Pegswood Ho. NE4: Newc T 3B 4
Pegswood Ind. Est. NE61: Peg 3B 10
Pegswood Station (Rail) 4B 10
Pegwood Rd. SR4: Sund 3J 117
Peile Ct. DH8: Shot B 3E 120
Peile Pk. DH8: Shot B 3E 120
PELAW 5E 84
Pelaw Av. DH2: Ches S 4K 127
DH9: Stly .1G 125
NE64: Newb S 2H 13
Pelaw Bank DH3: Ches S 5A 128
Pelaw Cres. DH2: Ches S 4K 127
(not continuous)
Pelaw Grange Ct. DH3: Ches S 1A 128
Pelaw Grange Stadium 1A 128
Pelaw Ind. Est. NE10: Gate 5E 84
Pelaw Leazes La. DH1: Dur 2B 166 (2E 6)
Pelaw Pl. DH2: Ches S 4A 128
Pelaw Rd. DH2: Ches S 4A 128
Pelaw Sq. DH2: Ches S 4K 127
SR4: Sund .1J 117
Pelaw Station (Metro) 5E 84
Pelaw Ter. DH2: Ches S 4K 127
Pelaw Way NE10: Gate 6E 84
Peldon Cl. NE7: Longb 7H 45
Pelham Ct. NE3: Ken 5K 43
PELTON 2G 127
Peltondale Av. NE24: Cow 3E 22
PELTON FELL 5G 127
Pelton Fell Rd. DH2: Ches S, Pelt 5G 127
Pelton Ho. Farm Est.
DH2: Pelt .3G 127
Pelton La. DH2: Pelt 2E 126
(Beamish Ct.)
DH2: Pelt .2G 127
(Fieldside)
DH2: Pelt .5C 126
(Newbridge Banks)
PELTON LANE ENDS 3E 126
Pelton M. DH2: Pelt 3E 126
Pelton Rd. SR4: Sund 4J 117
Pemberton Av. DH8: C'sde 2E 134
Pemberton Bank DH5: Eas L 2H 157
Pemberton Cl. SR5: S'wck 6D 104
Pemberton Gdns. SR3: Sund 5D 118
Pemberton Rd. DH8: C'sde, Con 1B 134
Pemberton St. DH5: Hett H 6G 145
Pemberton Ter. Nth. DH9: Stly 6H 125
Pemberton Ter. Sth. DH9: Stly 6H 125
Pembridge NE38: Wash 3E 114
Pembroke Av. DH3: Bir 7B 114
(not continuous)
NE6: Walk .5C 64
SR3: New S 3D 132
Pembroke Ct. NE3: Ken 5K 43
NE24: Bly .2K 23
NE64: Newb S 2J 13
SR5: C'twn 3G 103
Pembroke Dr. NE20: Pon 6E 30
Pembroke Gdns. NE28: W'snd 1A 66
NE63: N Sea 6E 12
Pembroke Pl. SR8: Pet 4K 171
Pembroke Ter. NE33: S Shi 6J 67
Pendeford NE38: Wash 4A 116
Pendle Cl. NE38: Wash 5F 115
SR8: Pet 7K 171
Pendle Grn. SR4: Sund 3C 118
Pendleton Dr. NE23: Cra 1J 25
Pendower Way NE15: Newc T 7J 61
Pendragon DH3: Gt Lum 2F 143
Penfold Cl. NE7: Newc T 1A 64
Penhale Dr. SR2: Ryh 2H 133
Penhill Cl. DH2: Ous 7H 113
Penistone Rd. SR4: Sund 4G 117
Penman Pl. NE29: N Shi 1G 67
Penman Sq. SR4: Sund 4H 117
Pennant Sq. SR4: Sund 2J 117
Pennine Av. DH2: Ches S 7K 127
(not continuous)
Pennine Ct. DH9: Ann P 6K 123
SR3: New S 3B 132
Pennine Dr. NE63: N Sea 6C 12
SR8: Pet 7J 171
Pennine Gdns. DH9: Stly 4G 125
NE11: Gate 7C 82
Pennine Gro. NE36: W Bol 7H 87
Pennine Ho. NE37: Wash 4F 115
Pennine Vw. NE17: C'wl 7K 93
Pennine Way NE12: Longb 6J 45
Penn Sq. SR4: Sund 2J 117
Penn St. NE4: Newc T 3D 82 (10A 4)
Pennycross Rd. SR4: Sund 4G 117
Pennycross Sq. SR4: Sund 3G 117
Pennyfine Cl. NE29: N Shi 4G 49
Pennyfine Rd. NE16: Sun 4J 97
Pennygate Sq. SR4: Sund 3G 117
Pennygreen Sq. SR4: Sund 3G 117
Pennymore Sq. SR4: Sund 4G 117
PENNYWELL 4H 117
Pennywell Bus. Cen. SR4: Sund 3J 117
Pennywell Ind. Est. SR4: Sund 4G 117
Pennywell Rd. SR4: Sund 4J 117
Pennywell Shop. Pct. SR4: Sund 4H 117
Penrith Av. NE30: N Shi 2G 49
Penrith Ct. NE22: Bed 6F 17
Penrith Gdns. NE9: Gate 3K 99
Penrith Gro. NE9: Gate 3K 99
Penrith Rd. NE31: Heb 2K 85
SR5: Monk 3E 104
Penrose Grn. NE3: Ken 7B 44
Penrose Rd. SR4: Sund 4H 117
Penryn Av. SR7: Mur 7F 147
Penryn Way DH7: B'don 1E 174
Pensford Ct. NE3: Ken 6J 43
PENSHAW 1B 130
Penshaw Cl. DH7: Lang P 5H 151
Penshaw Gdns. DH9: Stly 2H 125
(not continuous)
Penshaw Grn. NE5: Newc T 2K 61
Penshaw La. DH4: Pen 1B 130
Penshaw Monument 7C 116
Penshaw Vw. DH3: Bir 5C 114
DH7: Sac .1F 153
NE10: Gate 6G 85
NE31: Heb .2H 85
NE32: Jar 2B 86
Penshaw Way DH3: Bir 4C 114
Pensher St. NE10: Gate 5A 84
SR4: Sund 2D 118
Pensher St. E. NE10: Gate 5A 84
Pensher Vw. NE37: Usw 6K 101
Pentland Cl. NE23: Cra 1K 25
NE29: N Shi 3F 49
NE38: Wash 5F 115
NE63: N Sea 7C 12
SR8: Pet 7J 171
Pentland Ct. DH2: Ches S 7A 128
Pentland Gdns. NE11: Gate 7C 82
Pentland Gro. NE12: Longb 3K 45
Pentlands Ter. DH9: Stly 4G 125
Pentridge Cl. NE23: Cra 3A 26
Penwood Rd. SR4: Sund 3J 117
Penyghent Way NE37: Wash 2E 114
Penzance Bungs. SR7: Mur 6F 147
Penzance Ct. SR7: Mur 6F 147
Penzance Pde. NE31: Heb 4A 86
Penzance Rd. SR4: Sund 4H 117
Peoples Theatre 4K 63
Peplow Sq. SR4: Sund 1J 117
Peppercorn Ct. NE1: Newc T 7H 5
Peppermires DH7: New B 4C 174
Percival St. SR4: Sund 1B 118
Percy Av. DH9: Ann P 4J 123
NE26: Whit B 6F 39
NE30: N Shi 7J 39
Percy Bldg. NE1: Newc T 2E 4
Percy Cl. NE46: Hex 4B 70
Percy Cotts. NE25: Sea D 7J 27
(not continuous)
Percy Ct. NE29: N Shi 2D 66
Percy Cres. DH7: Lan 7K 137
NE29: N Shi 2D 66
Percy Gdns. DH8: Con 1K 135
(not continuous)
NE11: Dun .7C 82
NE12: Longb 4B 46
NE25: Whit B 7G 39
NE30: N Shi 4K 49
NE62: Chop 7J 11
Percy Gdns. Cotts. *NE30: N Shi 4K 49*
(off Percy Gdns.)
Percy La. DH1: Dur 3J 165
Percy Lonnen NE42: Pru 3F 77
PERCY MAIN .2D 66
Percy Main Station (Metro) 2D 66
Percy Pk. NE30: N Shi 4K 49
Percy Pk. Rd. NE30: N Shi 4K 49
Percy Rd. NE26: Whit B 6H 39
Percy Scott St. NE34: S Shi 3J 87
Percy Sq. DH1: Dur 5J 165
Percy St. DH5: Hett H 6H 145
DH6: Thor 1K 179
DH6: Whe H 2B 180
DH9: Stly .4D 124
NE1: Newc T 7F 63 (4E 4)
NE12: Longb 3E 46
NE15: Lem .7C 60
NE23: Cra .5A 26
NE24: Bly .1K 23
NE28: W'snd 3G 65
NE30: N Shi 5K 49
(East St.)
NE30: N Shi 5K 49
(Percy Pk. Rd.)
NE32: Jar 6C 66
NE33: S Shi 3K 67
NE63: Hir .3C 12
Percy St. Sth. NE24: Bly 2K 23
Percy Ter. DH1: Dur 3J 165
DH4: Pen .1A 130
DH8: Con .1K 135
DH9: Ann P 5B 124
NE3: Gos 7G 45
NE15: Thro 6K 59
NE25: Whit B 6E 38
SR2: Sund 4G 119
(not continuous)
SR6: Whit .5H 89
Percy Ter. Sth. SR2: Sund 5G 119
Percy Way NE15: Thro 4A 60
Peregrine Ct. NE29: N Shi 6F 49
Peregrine Pl. NE12: Longb 5J 45
Perivale Rd. SR4: Sund 4H 117
PERKINSVILLE 1H 127
Perrycrofts SR3: New S 5C 132
(not continuous)
Perry St. NE9: Gate 6H 83
Perth Av. NE32: Jar 3E 86
NE34: S Shi 3E 86
Perth Cl. NE28: W'snd 1K 65
NE29: N Shi 4C 48
Perth Ct. NE11: Gate 5G 99
SR3: Sund 7A 118
Perth Gdns. NE28: W'snd 1K 65
Perth Grn. NE32: Jar 3E 86
Perth Rd. SR3: Sund 7A 118
Perth Sq. SR3: Sund 6B 118
Pescott Ct. NE46: Hex 2D 70
Pesspool Av. DH6: Has 1B 170
Pesspool Bungs. DH6: Has 1B 170
Pesspool La. DH6: Eas, Has, S Het . . .1B 170
SR8: S Het 1E 170
Pesspool Ter. DH6: Has 1B 170
Peterborough Cl. NE8: Gate 4G 83
Peterborough Rd. DH1: Dur 4C 154
Peterborough Way NE32: Jar 5B 86
PETERLEE 6B 172
Peterlee Cl. SR8: Pet 5A 172
Peter Lee Cotts. DH6: Whe H 3A 180
Peterlee Leisure Cen. 7B 172
Peter's Bank DH9: Tan L 2A 124
Petersfield Rd. SR4: Sund 4H 117
Petersham Rd. SR4: Sund 2J 117
Peter Stracey Ho. SR6: Monk 3F 105
Peth Bank DH7: Lan 7K 137
Petherton Ct. NE3: Ken 6J 43
Peth Grn. DH5: Eas L 2H 157
PETH HEAD 1E 70
Peth Head NE46: Hex 1E 70
Peth La. DH7: B'hpe, Lan 6A 138
NE40: Ryton, Thro 7H 59
Pethside DH7: Lan 7A 138
Petrel Cl. NE33: S Shi 2J 67
Petrel Way NE24: News 5K 23
Petteril NE38: Wash 7E 114
Petwell Cres. SR8: Eas 7A 160
Petwell La. SR8: Eas 7K 159
Petworth Cl. NE33: S Shi 2K 67
Petworth Gdns. NE61: Peg 3A 10
Pevensey Cl. NE29: N Shi 3F 49
Pexton Way NE5: Newc T 5G 61
Phalp St. DH6: S Het 5D 158
Pheasantmoor NE37: Wash 1E 114
PHILADELPHIA 5D 130
Philadelphia Complex DH4: Hou S . . .4D 130
Philadelphia La. DH4: Hou S 3B 130
Philip Av. DH6: Bow 3H 177
DH8: Con .2K 135
Philip Ct. NE9: Gate 2K 99
Philiphaugh NE28: Walk, W'snd 5F 65
Philip Pl. NE4: Newc T 7C 62 (3A 4)
Philipson St. NE6: Walk 7D 64
Philip Sq. SR3: Sund 6A 118
Philip St. NE4: Newc T 7C 62
Phillips Av. NE16: Whi 6G 81
Phillips Cl. DH6: Has 1A 170
Phoebe Grange Cotts. NE42: Pru 4F 77
Phoenix Chase NE29: N Shi 4B 48
Phoenix Cl. DH7: Lang P 5H 151
Phoenix Ct. DH8: Con 6E 120
NE29: N Shi 4C 48
NE61: Mor .7F 9
(off New Market)
Phoenix Hot Glass Studio and Gallery
. . . . .2A 166 (2C 6)
Phoenix Rd. NE38: Wash 2C 114
SR4: Sund 2J 117
Phoenix St. NE24: Bly 5F 23
Phoenix Theatre, The 2K 23
Phoenix Way DH4: Hou S 3C 144
Phoenix Workshops SR8: Pet 4E 172
Physique Health Club 1K 99
Piccadilly SR3: E Her 1A 132
Picherwell NE10: Gate 7B 84
Pickard Cl. SR8: Pet 5C 172
Pickard St. SR4: Sund 1C 118
Pickering Ct. NE32: Jar 6A 66
Pickering Grn. NE9: Gate 5K 99
PICKERING NOOK 4A 110
Pickering Rd. SR4: Sund 5G 117
Pickering Sq. SR4: Sund 4H 117
Pickering St. TS28: Win 7F 181
Pickersgill Ho. SR5: C'twn 4J 103
Pickhurst Rd. SR4: Sund 5G 117
Pickhurst Sq. SR4: Sund 5H 117
PICKTREE 2C 128
Picktree Cotts. DH3: Ches S 5B 128
Picktree Cotts. E. DH3: Ches S 5B 128
Picktree Farm Cotts.
NE38: Ches S, Wash 2C 128
Picktree La. DH3: Ches S 5B 128
(Hopgarth Gdns.)
DH3: Ches S, Lam P 3C 128
(Chester Rd.)
NE38: Ches S, Wash 1C 128
Picktree Lodge DH3: Ches S 1B 128
Picktree M. DH3: Ches S 5B 128
Picktree Ter. DH3: Ches S 5B 128
Pickwick Cl. DH1: Dur 5K 165
Pier Amusement Cen. 1A 68
Pier Pde. NE33: S Shi 1A 68
Pier Pavilion Theatre 1A 68

Pier Rd.—Priestlands Av.

Pier Rd. NE30: N Shi 5K **49**
Pier Vw. SR6: Monk 5H **105**
Pike Hill DH8: Shot B 7A **106**
Pikestone Cl. NE38: Wash 5E **114**
Pikesyde DH9: Dip 2F **123**
Pilgrim Cl. SR5: S'wck 6E **104**
Pilgrims Ct. NE2: Newc T 5G **63**
Pilgrim St. NE1: Newc T 1F **83** (5F **4**)
(New Bri. St. W.)
NE1: Newc T 2G **83** (7H **5**)
(Tyne Bri.)
Pilgrims Way DH1: Dur 1D **166**
NE61: Mor 1D **14**
Pilgrimsway NE9: Gate 7J **83**
NE32: Jar 7E **66**
Pilton Rd. NE5: Newc T 2F **61**
Pilton Wlk. NE5: Newc T 2F **61**
Pimlico DH1: Dur 4A **166** (5B **6**)
Pimlico Ct. NE9: Gate 3H **99**
Pimlico Rd. DH5: Hett H 2H **157**
SR4: Sund 4H **117**
Pinders Way DH6: Sher 3D **168**
Pine Av. DH1: Dur 3E **166**
DH4: Hou S 2D **144**
NE3: Ken 5B **44**
NE13: Din 4J **33**
NE16: Burn 2K **109**
NE34: S Shi 1C **88**
NE62: Chop 1F **17**
Pinedale Dr. DH6: S Het 4B **158**
Pinegarth NE20: Pon 2G **41**
Pine Lea DH7: B'don 1C **174**
Pine Pk. DH7: Ush M 3D **164**
Pine Rd. NE21: Bla T 4C **80**
Pines, The NE4: Newc T 3C **82** (9A **4**)
NE40: G'sde 5F **79**
Pine St. DH2: Beam 2D **126**
DH2: Ches S 1G **141**
(not continuous)
DH2: Pelt 4C **126**
DH3: Bir 3A **114**
DH3: Ches S 6A **128**
DH7: Lang P 4J **151**
DH9: Stly 5D **124**
NE13: Sea B 3E **34**
NE15: Thro 2H **59**
NE32: Jar 7A **66**
NE40: G'sde 5F **79**
SR4: Sund 1B **118**
Pinesway SR3: Sund 5D **118**
Pine Ter. DH9: Ann P 4J **123**
Pine Tree DH7: Esh W 4D **162**
Pinetree Cen. DH3: Bir 5A **114**
Pinetree Gdns. NE25: Whit B 1E **48**
Pinetree Way NE11: Dun 4H **81**
Pine Vw. DH9: Stly 5D **124**
Pine Vw. Vs. DH7: Esh W 4F **163**
Pinewood NE31: Heb 6G **65**
Pinewood Av. NE13: Wide O 6E **34**
NE23: Cra 1K **25**
NE38: Wash 7G **115**
Pinewood Cl. NE3: Ken 6H **43**
NE6: Walk 4D **64**
NE38: Wash 5K **115**
Pinewood Dr. NE61: Mor 6C **8**
Pinewood Gdns. NE11: Gate 2C **98**
Pinewood Rd. SR5: S'wck 5B **104**
Pinewoods NE21: Bla T 1K **95**
Pinewood Sq. SR5: S'wck 5B **104**
Pinewood St. DH4: Hou S 1J **143**
Pinewood Vs. NE34: S Shi 7C **68**
Pink La. NE1: Newc T 1E **82** (6D **4**)
(not continuous)
Pinner Pl. NE6: Walk 2C **84**
Pinner Rd. SR4: Sund 3J **117**
Pintail Ct. NE34: S Shi 2G **87**
Pioneer Ter. NE22: Bed 6A **18**
Piper Rd. NE42: O'ham 1D **76**
Pipershaw NE37: Wash 2D **114**
Pipe Track La. NE4: Newc T 2K **81**
Pipewell Ga. NE8: Gate 3F **83** (10F **4**)
Pitcairn Rd. SR4: Sund 3H **117**
Pit Ho. La. DH4: Leam 6J **143**
Pithouse Rd. DH8: Con 1K **121**
Pit La. DH1: Dur 5K **153**
DH7: B'don 7K **163**
NE23: Seg 2C **36**
Pit Row SR3: New S 1B **132**
PITTINGTON 4A **156**
Pittington La. DH1: Carr 6J **155**
DH6: Carr, H Pitt 6J **155**
Pittington Rd. DH5: H Pitt, W Rai 3K **155**
DH6: H Pitt 3K **155**
Pitt St. DH8: Con 7H **121**
NE4: Newc T 7D **62** (4B **4**)
PITY ME 4J **153**
Pity Me By-Pass DH1: Dur 6H **153**
Pixley Dell DH8: Con 3A **136**
PLAINS FARM 6B **118**
Plains Rd. SR3: Sund 6B **118**
Plaistow Sq. SR4: Sund 2J **117**
Plaistow Way NE23: Cra 1K **25**
Plane St. DH8: Con 7J **121**
Planesway NE10: Gate 2C **100**
Planetarium, The 5A **68**
Planet Ho. SR1: Sund 4J **7**
Planet Pl. NE12: Kil 2A **46**
Planetree Av. NE4: Newc T 5K **61**
Plane Tree Ct. SR3: New S 3A **132**
Plantagenet Av. DH3: Ches S 7B **128**
Plantation Av. DH6: H Pitt 1D **168**
NE16: Swa 6G **81**
Plantation Gro. NE10: Gate 4F **85**
Plantation Rd. SR4: Sund 1A **118**
Plantation Sq. SR4: Sund 1A **118**
Plantation St. DH8: Lead 5B **122**
NE28: W'snd 5F **65**
Plantation, The NE9: Gate 2J **99**
Plantation Vw. DH9: Stly 3B **126**
Plantation Wlk. DH6: S Het 4B **158**
PLAWSWORTH 6J **141**
Plawsworth Gdns. NE9: Gate 4B **100**
Plawsworth Rd. DH7: Sac 7E **140**
Pleasant Pl. DH3: Bir 3A **114**
Pleasant Vw. DH7: B'hpe 6D **138**
DH8: Con 5D **120**
(Barley Mill Rd.)
DH8: Con 3K **121**
(Corbridge Rd.)
Plenmeller Pl. NE16: Sun 4G **97**
Plessey Av. NE24: Bly 3K **23**
Plessey Ct. NE24: News 5F **23**
Plessey Cres. NE25: Whit B 7H **39**
Plessey Gdns. NE29: N Shi 7D **48**
Plessey Old Waggonway NE24: Bly 6C **22**
Plessey Rd. NE24: Bly, News 5F **23**
(not continuous)
Plessey St. NE23: E Har 6K **21**
Plessey Ter. NE7: Newc T 3K **63**
Plessey Woods Country Pk. Vis. Cen. 4D **20**
Plough Rd. SR3: New S 4B **132**
Plover Cl. NE24: News 5J **23**
NE38: Wash 5D **114**
Plover Dr. NE16: Burn 3C **110**
Ploverfield Cl. NE63: Ash 5A **12**
Plover Lodge DH3: Bir 2A **114**
Plummer Chare NE1: Newc T 2G **83** (7H **5**)
Plummers Tower 1G **83** (5G **4**)
Plummer St. NE4: Newc T 3E **82** (9C **4**)
Plumtree Av. SR5: C'twn 5J **103**
(not continuous)
Plunkett Rd. DH9: Dip 7J **109**
Plunkett Ter. DH2: Pelt 5F **127**
Plymouth Cl. SR7: Mur 4H **147**
Plymouth Sq. SR3: Sund 6A **118**
POINT PLEASANT 3K **65**
Point Pleasant Ind. Est. NE28: W'snd 3K **65**
Point Pleasant Ter. NE28: W'snd 3J **65**
Polden Cl. SR8: Pet 7J **171**
Polden Cres. NE29: N Shi 3F **49**
Polebrook Rd. SR4: Sund 2J **117**
Polemarch St. SR7: S'hm 4B **148**
Police Ho's. SR8: Pet 6A **172**
NE64: Newb S 2H **13**
Pollard St. NE33: S Shi 2K **67**
Polmaise St. NE21: Bla T 4C **80**
Polmuir Rd. SR3: Sund 6A **118**
Polmuir Sq. SR3: Sund 6A **118**
Polpero Cl. DH3: Bir 5B **114**
Polperro Cl. SR2: Ryh 2H **133**
Polton Sq. SR4: Sund 2J **117**
Polwarth Cres. NE3: Gos 4E **44**
Polwarth Dr. NE3: Gos 3D **44**
Polwarth Pl. NE3: Gos 4E **44**
Polwarth Rd. NE3: Gos 3E **44**
Polworth Sq. SR3: Sund 6B **118**
Ponds Cotts. NE40: G'sde 5D **78**
Ponds Ct. DH8: Con 7G **121**
Ponds Ct. Bus. Pk. DH8: Con 7G **121**
Pond St. DH1: H Shin 1F **177**
PONT 4K **121**
Pont Bungs. DH8: Lead 3K **121**
Pontdyke NE10: Gate 3D **100**
Pontefract Rd. SR4: Sund 5H **117**
PONTELAND 5J **31**
Ponteland Cl. NE29: N Shi 5C **48**
NE38: Wash 4D **114**
Ponteland Leisure Cen. 5K **31**
Ponteland Rd. NE2: Newc T 5C **62** (1A **4**)
NE3: Ken 6H **43**
NE4: Newc T 4B **62**
NE5: Newc T 4A **62**
NE13: Wool 1D **42**
NE15: Thro 1H **59**
NE15: Thro 1H **59**
Pont Haugh NE20: Pon 4K **31**
Ponthaugh NE39: Row G 4K **95**
Ponthead M. DH8: Lead 5B **122**
Pont La. DH8: Con 2K **121**
PONTOP 3E **122**
Pontop Ct. DH9: Ann P 5K **123**
Pontop Pike La. DH9: Ann P, Dip 4F **123**
Pontop Sq. SR4: Sund 1J **117**
Pontop St. DH5: W Rai 6C **144**
Pontopsyde DH9: Dip 2G **123**
Pontop Ter. DH9: Ann P 6J **123**
Pontop Vw. DH8: Con 2K **135**
DH9: Dip 2F **123**
NE39: Row G 5H **95**
Pont Pk. NE20: Wool 1A **32**
Pont Rd. DH8: Lead 4B **122**
Pont St. NE63: Hir 4B **12**
Pont Ter. DH8: Lead 5A **122**
Pont Vw. DH8: Lead 3K **121**
NE20: Pon 4K **31**
Pool Bri. NE10: Gate 7J **85**
Poole Cl. NE23: Cra 3A **26**
Poole Rd. SR4: Sund 2J **117**
Pooley Cl. NE5: Newc T 4H **61**
Pooley Rd. NE5: Newc T 5H **61**
Poplar Av. DH4: Hou S 2D **144**
NE6: Walk 4D **64**
NE13: Din 4J **33**
NE16: Burn 2K **109**
NE24: Bly 7H **19**
TS27: B Col 3J **183**
Poplar Cl. NE31: Heb 3J **85**
Poplar Ct. DH3: Ches S 6A **128**
Poplar Cres. DH3: Bir 3K **113**
NE8: Gate 5G **83**
NE11: Dun 7B **82**
Poplar Dr. DH1: Dur 1E **166**
SR6: Whit 5H **89**
Poplar Gro. DH9: Dip 1J **123**
NE22: Bed 7K **17**
NE34: S Shi 1B **88**
SR2: Ryh 1G **133**
Poplar Lea DH7: B'don 1C **174**
Poplar Pl. NE3: Gos 7E **44**
Poplar Rd. DH1: Carr 7H **155**
NE21: Bla T 5C **80**
Poplars, The DH3: Ches S 7B **128**
DH4: Pen 1B **130**
DH5: Eas L 2J **157**
NE3: Gos 2E **62**
NE4: Newc T 3C **82**
NE38: Wash 4H **115**
SR4: Sund 2G **117**
SR5: S'wck 5B **104**
Poplar St. DH2: Beam 2D **126**
DH2: Ches S 1G **141**
(not continuous)
DH3: Ches S 6A **128**
DH7: Sac 7E **140**
DH9: Stly 5D **124**
NE15: Thro 3H **59**
NE63: Hir 3B **12**
Poplar Ter. DH3: Ches S 5B **128**
Popplewell Gdns. NE9: Gate 3J **99**
Popplewell Ter. NE29: N Shi 4G **49**
Poppyfields DH2: Ches S 7H **127**
Porchester Dr. NE23: Cra 2A **26**
Porchester St. NE33: S Shi 6H **67**
Porlock Ct. NE23: Cra 1J **25**
Porlock Ho. NE32: Jar 1D **86**
Porlock Rd. NE32: Jar 1D **86**
Portadown Rd. SR4: Sund 5H **117**
Portberry St. NE33: S Shi 5H **67**
Portberry St. Ind. Est. NE33: S Shi 4H **67**
Portberry Way NE33: S Shi 4H **67**
(not continuous)
Portchester Gro. NE35: Bol C 6E **86**
Portchester Rd. SR4: Sund 3J **117**
Portchester Sq. SR4: Sund 4J **117**
Porter Ter. SR7: Mur 7E **146**
Porthcawl Dr. NE37: Usw 5G **101**
Portia St. NE63: Hir 3C **12**
Portland Av. SR7: S'hm 3J **147**
Portland Cl. DH2: Ches S 1J **141**
NE28: W'snd 7A **48**
Portland Gdns. NE9: Gate 5H **99**
NE23: Cra 3A **26**
NE30: N Shi 5G **49**
Portland M. NE2: Newc T 6H **63** (2J **5**)
Portland Rd. NE2: Newc T 6H **63** (2J **5**)
(not continuous)
NE15: Thro 3J **59**
SR3: Sund 6B **118**
Portland Sq. SR3: Sund 5B **118**
Portland St. NE4: Newc T 2B **82**
NE10: Gate 5E **84**
NE24: Bly 7H **19**
Portland Ter. NE2: Newc T 6H **63** (1H **5**)
NE46: Hex 1B **70**
NE63: Ash 2H **11**
Portman M. NE2: Newc T 3K **5**
Portman Pl. NE6: Walk 3C **84**
Portman Sq. SR4: Sund 3J **117**
Portmarnock NE37: Usw 5F **101**
PORTMEADS 5B **114**
Portmeads Ri. DH3: Bir 4B **114**
Portmeads Rd. DH3: Bir 3B **114**
PORTOBELLO 5C **114**
Portobello Ind. Est. DH3: Bir 4C **114**
Portobello La. SR6: Monk 6F **105**
(not continuous)
Portobello Rd. DH3: Bir 3C **114**
Portobello Ter. DH3: Bir 5C **114**
Portobello Way DH3: Bir 4B **114**
Portree Cl. DH3: Bir 7B **114**
Portree Sq. SR3: Sund 6A **118**
Portrush Cl. NE37: Usw 5G **101**
Portrush Rd. SR4: Sund 2J **117**
Portrush Way NE7: Newc T 7A **46**
Portslade Rd. SR4: Sund 4H **117**
Portsmouth Rd. NE29: N Shi 7C **48**
SR4: Sund 3H **117**
Portsmouth Sq. SR4: Sund 3H **117**
Portugal Pl. NE28: W'snd 4F **65**
Postern Cres. NE61: Mor 1F **15**
Post Office La. *NE29: N Shi* *4G 49*
(off Orchard Ct.)
Post Office Sq. *NE24: Bly* *1K 23*
(off Post Office St.)
Post Office St. NE24: Bly 1K **23**
Potterhouse La. DH1: Dur 3G **153**
Potterhouse Ter. DH1: Dur 3J **153**
Potteries, The NE33: S Shi 4A **68**
Potter Pl. DH9: Stly 4H **125**
Potters Bank DH1: Dur 5J **165** (7A **6**)
Potters Cl. DH1: Dur 5K **165**
Potter Sq. SR3: Sund 6B **118**
Potter St. NE28: W'snd 4A **66**
NE32: Jar 6A **66**
Pottersway NE9: Gate 7J **83**
Pottery Bank NE6: Walk 3D **84**
NE61: Mor 5E **8**
SR1: Sund 7H **105**
Pottery Bank Ct. NE61: Mor 5E **8**
Pottery La. NE1: Newc T 3E **82** (9D **4**)
SR4: Sund 2G **117**
Pottery Rd. SR5: S'wck 6C **104**
Pottery Yd. DH4: Hou S 2E **144**
Potto St. DH6: Shot C 6F **171**
Potts St. NE6: Newc T 7A **64**
Poulton Cl. NE38: Wash 1F **129**
Poultry Farm DH4: Hou S 3C **130**
Powburn Cl. DH2: Ches S 1J **141**
Powburn Gdns. NE4: Newc T 5A **62**
Powerleague 5D **82**
Powis Rd. SR3: Sund 6B **118**
Powis Sq. SR3: Sund 6B **118**
Powys Pl. NE4: Newc T 7C **62** (3A **4**)
Poynings Cl. NE3: Ken 7J **43**
Praetorian Dr. NE28: W'snd 4F **65**
Prebend Row DH2: Pelt 3F **127**
Prebends Fld. DH1: Dur 7D **154**
Prebends' Wlk. DH1: Dur 4A **166** (5B **6**)
Precinct, The NE21: Bla T 3D **80**
SR2: Sund 2D **118** (5F **7**)
(Chester Rd.)
SR2: Sund 6E **118**
(Leechmere Rd.)
Prefect Pl. NE9: Gate 7J **83**
Premier Health & Fitness *2C 118*
(off Hylton Rd.)
Premier Rd. SR3: Sund 6A **118**
Prendwick Av. NE31: Heb 3H **85**
Prendwick Cl. DH2: Ches S 2J **141**
Prendwick Ct. NE31: Heb 3H **85**
Prengarth Av. SR6: Monk 4F **105**
Prensgarth Way NE34: S Shi 3F **87**
Prescot Rd. SR4: Sund 2J **117**
Press La. SR1: Sund 1F **119** (3K **7**)
Prestbury Av. NE23: Cra 1J **25**
Prestbury Rd. SR4: Sund 4G **117**
Prestdale Av. NE24: Cow 2E **22**
Presthope Rd. SR4: Sund 4G **117**
Prestmede NE10: Gate 7C **84**
PRESTON 5G **49**
Preston Av. NE30: N Shi 5G **49**
Preston Ct. *NE29: N Shi* *4G 49*
(off Rosebery Av.)
Preston Ga. NE29: N Shi 3F **49**
PRESTON GRANGE 3F **49**
Prestonhill SR3: New S 4A **132**
Preston Nth. Rd. NE29: N Shi 2F **49**
Preston Pk. NE29: N Shi 5G **49**
Preston Rd. NE29: N Shi 4G **49**
SR2: Sund 4H **119**
Preston Ter. NE27: Shir 3J **47**
NE29: N Shi 4F **49**
Preston Towers NE29: N Shi 5G **49**
Preston Wood NE30: N Shi 3G **49**
PRESTWICK 6C **32**
Prestwick NE10: Gate 2C **100**
Prestwick Av. NE29: N Shi 5C **48**
Prestwick Carr Rd. NE13: Din 4G **33**
Prestwick Cl. NE37: Usw 5G **101**
Prestwick Dr. NE10: Gate 7G **85**
Prestwick Gdns. NE3: Ken 1B **62**
Prestwick Ho. NE4: Newc T 3B **4**
Prestwick Ind. Est. NE20: Wool 1C **42**
Prestwick Pit Ho's. NE20: Wool 7C **32**
Prestwick Rd. NE13: Din 4G **33**
SR4: Sund 2J **117**
PRESTWICK ROAD END 7C **32**
Prestwick Ter. NE20: Wool 1C **42**
Pretoria Av. NE61: Mor 7F **9**
Pretoria Sq. SR3: Sund 6A **118**
Pretoria St. NE15: Newc T 1G **81**
Price St. NE31: Heb 6G **65**
NE61: Mor 6E **8**
Priestburn Cl. DH7: Esh W 3D **162**
Priestclose Cotts. NE42: Pru 4H **77**
Priestclose Rd. NE42: Pru 4F **77**
Priestclose Wood Nature Reserve 4H **77**
Priestfield Gdns. NE16: Burn 2K **109**
Priestlands Av. NE46: Hex 2C **70**

Priestlands Cl.—Railway Cl.

Priestlands Cl. NE46: Hex 3C 70
Priestlands Cres. NE46: Hex 2C 70
Priestlands Dr. NE46: Hex 2C 70
Priestlands Gro. NE46: Hex 3C 70
Priestlands La. NE46: Hex 2C 70
Priestlands Rd. NE46: Hex 2C 70
Priestley Ct. NE34: S Shi 3G 87
Priestley Gdns. NE10: Gate 6F 85
Priestly Cres. SR4: Sund 7D 104 (1F 7)
Priestman Av. DH8: C'sde 1E 134
Priestman Ct. SR4: Sund 2K 117
Priestpopple NE46: Hex 2D 70
Priestsfield Cl. SR3: New S 4B 132
Primary Gdns. SR2: Sund 3H 119
Primate Rd. SR3: Sund 7A 118
PRIMROSE 3C 86
Primrose Av. NE34: S Shi 1H 87
SR8: Pet 5D 172
Primrose Cl. NE23: Dud 3J 35
Primrose Ct. NE63: Ash 6K 11
TS27: B Col 2H 183
Primrose Cres. DH4: Hou S 6J 129
SR6: Monk 4F 105
Primrose Gdns. DH2: Ous 6H 113
NE28: W'snd 1E 64
Primrose Hill DH4: Hou S 7J 129
NE9: Gate 2J 99
NE32: Jar 3C 86
Primrose Hill Ter. NE32: Jar 3C 86
Primrose Pl. NE9: Gate 2H 99
Primrose Pct. SR6: Monk 4F 105
Primrose St. SR4: Sund 2G 117
Primrose Ter. DH3: Bir 4B 114
NE32: Jar 2B 86
Prince Albert Ter.
NE2: Newc T 7H 63 (4J 5)
Prince Charles Av. DH6: Bow 3H 177
Prince Consort Ind. Est. NE31: Heb 6G 65
Prince Consort La. NE31: Heb 7H 65
(not continuous)
Prince Consort Rd.
NE8: Gate 4G 83 (10H 5)
NE31: Heb 7G 65
NE32: Jar 7C 66
Prince Consort Way NE29: N Shi 2G 67
Prince Edward Ct. NE34: S Shi 1C 88
Prince Edward Gro. NE34: S Shi 7E 68
Prince Edward Rd. NE34: S Shi 1B 88
Prince George Av. SR6: Monk 3F 105
Prince George Sq. NE33: S Shi 2K 67
Prince of Wales Cl. NE34: S Shi 1A 88
Prince Philip Cl. NE15: Newc T 1J 81
Prince Rd. NE28: W'snd 2F 65
Princes Av. NE3: Gos 6D 44
SR6: Monk 2G 105
Princes Cl. NE3: Gos 4D 44
Princes Gdns. NE24: Cow 1G 23
NE25: Whit B 6E 38
SR6: Monk 2G 105
Princes Mdw. NE3: Gos 7C 44
Princes Pk. NE11: Gate 2D 98
(not continuous)
Princes Rd. NE3: Gos 3D 44
Princess Av. DH8: Shot B 4F 121
Princess Cl. TS27: B Col 3J 183
Princess Ct. NE29: N Shi 2F 67
NE42: Pru 2F 77
Princess Dr. NE8: Dun 5C 82
Princess Gdns. DH5: Hett H 5G 145
Princess Louise Rd. NE24: Bly 2H 23
Princess Mary Ct. NE2: Newc T 5F 63
Princess Rd. SR7: S'hm 3A 148
Princess Sq. NE1: Newc T 7G 63 (4G 4)
Princess St. NE10: Gate 5E 84
NE16: Sun 5H 97
SR2: Sund 3E 118 (6H 7)
Princes St. DH1: Dur 2K 165 (1A 6)
DH4: Hou S 4A 130
DH9: Ann P 4J 123
NE30: N Shi 5H 49
NE45: Cor 1D 72
Princess Way NE42: Pru 3D 76
Prince St. NE17: C'wl 6K 93
SR1: Sund 1F 119 (3J 7)
Princesway NE11: Gate 3E 98
Princesway Central NE11: Gate 3E 98
Princesway Nth. NE11: Gate 1E 98
Princesway Sth. NE11: Gate 3E 98
(not continuous)
Princetown Ter. SR3: Sund 6A 118
Princeway NE30: N Shi 4K 49
Pringle Cl. DH7: New B 5A 164
Pringle Gro. DH7: New B 5B 164
Pringle Pl. DH7: New B 5B 164
Prinn Pl. NE16: Sun 5H 97
Priors Cl. DH1: Dur 2J 165
Priors Grange DH6: H Pitt 6B 156
Prior's Ho. NE30: N Shi 5K 49
Priors Path DH1: Dur 3K 165
Prior's Ter. NE30: N Shi 5K 49
Priors Wlk. NE61: Mor 1E 14
Priors Way NE28: W'snd 3J 65
Prior Ter. NE45: Cor 7D 52
(off Cookson Cl.)
NE46: Hex 7C 50
Priory Av. NE25: Whit B 7F 39
Priory Cl. DH8: Shot B 4E 120
Priory Cotts. NE26: Whit B 5G 39
Priory Ct. DH7: Sac 1E 152
NE8: Gate 9J 5
NE10: Gate 6F 85
NE30: N Shi 4K 49
NE33: S Shi 7K 49
Priory Dr. NE25: B End 6E 50
Priory Gdns. NE45: Cor 6D 52
Priory Grange NE24: Cow 2G 23
Priory Grn. NE6: Newc T 7K 63 (4P 5)
Priory Gro. SR4: Sund 3B 118
Priory M. NE30: N Shi 5K 49
Priory Orchard DH1: Dur 3K 165 (4A 6)
Priory Pl. NE6: Newc T 1A 84 (5P 5)
NE13: Wide O 6C 34
NE62: Chop 7J 11
Priory Rd. DH1: Dur 6K 153
NE32: Jar 5C 66
Priory Way NE5: Newc T 1F 61
Proctor Ct. NE6: Walk 1E 84
Proctor Sq. SR3: Sund 6B 118
Proctor St. NE6: Walk 1E 84
Promenade NE26: Whit B 5G 39
NE33: S Shi 1A 68
(Harbour Dr.)
NE33: S Shi 3C 68
(Sth. Foreshore)
NE64: Newb S 4H 13
SR6: Monk 3H 105
Promenade Ter. NE30: N Shi 5K 49
Promenade, The DH8: Con 5H 121
Promontory Ter. NE26: Whit B 7J 39
Promotion Cl. SR6: Monk 5G 105
Prospect Av. NE25: Sea D 7G 27
NE28: W'snd 2F 65
Prospect Av. Nth. NE28: W'snd 1F 65
Prospect Bus. Pk. DH8: Lead 6A 122
Prospect Cotts. NE9: Spri 6D 100
NE22: Bed 3A 18
Prospect Ct. NE4: Newc T 1C 82 (5A 4)
Prospect Cres. DH5: Eas L 3J 157
Prospect Gdns. NE36: W Bol 7G 87
Prospect Pl. DH7: New B 4A 164
DH8: Con 6H 121
NE4: Newc T 1C 82 (5A 4)
NE64: Newb S 2K 13
Prospect Row SR1: Sund 1H 119
Prospect St. DH3: Ches S 5A 128
DH8: Con 6H 121
Prospect Ter. DH1: Dur 4J 165
DH1: H Shin 6E 166
DH3: Ches S 5A 128
DH7: Lan 7J 137
DH7: New B 4B 164
DH9: Ann P 5B 124
NE9: Spri 5D 100
(Springwell Rd.)
NE9: Spri 6B 100
(Thomas St.)
NE11: Kib 2E 112
NE16: Burn 4A 110
NE30: N Shi 6J 49
NE36: E Bol 7J 87
NE42: Pru 4D 76
Prospect Vw. DH4: W Rai 1K 155
Providence Cl. DH1: Dur 1D 6
Providence Pl. DH1: Dur 3F 6
DH1: Dur 1F 167
NE10: Gate 5B 84
Providence Row DH1: Dur 2B 166 (2D 6)
Provident St. DH2: Pelt 3E 126
Provident Ter. DH9: Stly 6K 125
NE28: W'snd 3E 64
Provost Gdns. NE15: Newc T 2K 81
PRUDHOE 4F 77
Prudhoe Castle 3E 76
Prudhoe Chare
NE1: Newc T 7F 63 (4F 4)
Prudhoe Ct. NE3: Ken 5A 44
Prudhoe Gro. NE32: Jar 3A 86
Prudhoe Pl. NE1: Newc T 7F 63 (4E 4)
Prudhoe Station (Rail) 2D 76
Prudhoe St. NE1: Newc T 7F 63 (4E 4)
NE29: N Shi 7G 49
SR4: Sund 1B 118
Prudhoe Ter. NE29: N Shi 7G 49
NE30: N Shi 4K 49
Pudding Chare NE1: Newc T 1F 83 (6F 4)
Pudding M. NE46: Hex 1D 70
Pudsey Ct. DH1: Dur 5A 154
Puffin Cl. NE24: News 6K 23
Pullman Ct. NE9: Gate 2G 99
Puma Sunderland Tennis Cen. 7C 118
Pump La. NE6: Newc T 1K 83 (5N 5)
Purbeck Cl. NE29: N Shi 2F 49
Purbeck Gdns. NE23: Cra 3A 26
Purbeck Rd. NE12: Longb 6K 45
Purley NE38: Wash 4A 116
Purley Cl. NE28: W'snd 1K 65
Purley Gdns. NE3: Ken 1B 62
Purley Rd. SR3: Sund 6A 118
Purley Sq. SR3: Sund 6A 118
Putney Sq. SR4: Sund 4H 117
Pykerley M. NE25: Whit B 7E 38
Pykerley Rd. NE25: Whit B 6E 38

Q

Quadrant, The NE29: N Shi 7E 48
SR1: Sund 1H 119
QUAKING HOUSES 7D 124
Quality Row DH6: Cass 4E 178
NE6: Newc T 1J 83 (5M 5)
Quality Row Rd. NE16: Swa 5G 81
Quality St. DH1: H Shin 7F 167
Quantock Av. DH2: Ches S 7J 127
(not continuous)
Quantock Cl. NE29: N Shi 2E 48
Quantock Pl. SR8: Pet 6J 171
QUARRINGTON HILL 6D 178
Quarrington Hill Ind. Est.
DH6: Quar H 6D 178
Quarry Bank Ct. NE4: Newc T 1D 82 (6A 4)
Quarry Cotts. NE13: Din 4H 33
NE23: Dud 5A 36
Quarry Cres. DH7: Ush M 1C 164
Quarry Edge NE46: Hex 3E 70
Quarryfield Rd. NE8: Gate 2H 83 (8K 5)
Quarryheads La. DH1: Dur 4K 165 (5A 6)
Quarry Ho. Gdns. DH5: W Rai 6C 144
Quarry Ho. La. DH1: Dur 3H 165
DH5: W Rai 6D 144
Quarry La. NE34: S Shi 1C 88
(not continuous)
Quarry Rd. DH9: Stly 2F 125
NE15: Lem 7C 60
NE31: Heb 1J 85
SR3: New S 2D 132
Quarry Row NE10: Gate 5B 84
Quarry St. SR3: New S 2C 132
Quatre Bras NE46: Hex 1B 70
Quay Rd. NE24: Bly 1K 23
(not continuous)
Quaysgate NE8: Gate 2H 83 (8J 5)
QUAYSIDE 2G 83 (7H 5)
Quayside NE1: Newc T 2G 83 (7H 5)
(not continuous)
NE6: Newc T 2K 83 (7N 5)
NE24: Bly 1K 23
Quayside Bus. Development Cen.
NE6: Newc T 1K 83 (5N 5)
Quayside Ct. NE24: Bly 1K 23
NE30: N Shi 7H 49
Quayside Ho. *NE1: Newc T* 1H 83 (6J 5)
(off Quayside)
Quay, The DH5: Hett H 7G 145
Quay Vw. NE28: W'snd 3A 66
QUEBEC 7C 150
Quebec St. DH7: Lang P 5H 151
Queen Alexandra Bri. SR5: Sund 7C 104
Queen Alexandra Rd. NE29: N Shi 5F 49
SR2: Sund 5E 118
SR3: Sund 4C 118
SR7: S'hm 4B 148
Queen Alexandra Rd. W.
NE29: N Shi 5E 48
Queen Anne Ct. NE6: Newc T 6A 64
Queen Anne St. *NE6: Walk* 6A 64
(off Shields Rd.)
Queen Elizabeth Av. NE9: Gate 2K 99
Queen Elizabeth Ct. NE34: S Shi 3F 87
Queen Elizabeth Dr. DH5: Eas L 3K 157
Queen's Av. SR6: Monk 2G 105
SR7: Mur 4H 147
Queensberry St. SR4: Sund 1D 118 (3F 7)
Queensbridge NE12: Longb 5H 45
Queensbury Dr. NE15: Cha P 2A 60
Queensbury Ga. NE12: Longb 6J 45
Queensbury Rd. SR7: S'hm 3J 147
Queens Cl. NE46: Acomb 4C 50
Queens Ct. NE3: Gos 2E 44
NE4: Newc T 7D 62 (4B 4)
NE8: Gate 5E 82
NE15: Thro 4A 60
Queen's Cres. NE28: W'snd 2E 64
NE31: Heb 2H 85
SR4: Sund 3C 118
Queens Dr. NE16: Sun 5H 97
NE16: Whi 2J 97
NE26: Whit B 6G 39
Queens Gdns. NE12: Longb 6B 46
NE23: Dud 2K 35
NE24: Cow 1G 23
NE61: Mor 1E 14
Queens Gth. DH6: Crox 6K 175
Queens Ga. DH8: Con 6H 121
Queens Gro. DH1: Dur 5J 165
Queens Hall Bldgs. *NE25: Sea D* 7H 27
(off Hayward Av.)
Queensland Av. NE34: S Shi 2F 87
Queens La. NE1: Newc T 2G 83 (7F 4)
Queensmere DH3: Ches S 2A 128
Queens Pde. DH9: Ann P 5K 123
SR6: Monk 2H 105
Queens Pk. DH3: Ches S 7B 128
NE11: Gate 1E 98
Queens Pl. NE64: Newb S 2J 13
Queens Rd. DH8: Shot B 5G 121
NE2: Newc T 4G 63
(not continuous)
NE5: Newc T 2G 61
NE15: Thro 4A 60
NE22: Bed 6B 18
NE23: Dud 2K 35
NE26: Sea S 4D 28
NE26: Whit B 5F 39
SR5: S'wck 6C 104
TS28: Win 5F 181
Queens Sq. NE1: Newc T 7F 63 (4F 4)
Queens Ter. NE2: Newc T 4H 63
NE28: W'snd 2F 65
Queen St. DH2: Pelt 4C 126
DH3: Bir 4K 113
DH5: Hett H 5G 145
DH8: Con 7H 121
NE1: Newc T 2G 83 (7H 5)
NE8: Gate 6E 82
NE30: N Shi 6H 49
NE33: S Shi 2J 67
NE61: Mor 7G 9
NE63: Hir 3C 12
NE64: Newb S 2J 13
(not continuous)
SR1: Sund 1E 118 (2H 7)
(Gill Rd.)
SR1: Sund 1F 119 (3J 7)
(St Mary's Way)
SR2: Ryh 1H 133
SR7: S'hm 3A 148
Queen St. E. SR1: Sund 1G 119
Queens Way DH8: Shot B 4E 120
Queensway DH5: Hou S 3F 145
NE3: Gos 3D 44
NE4: Newc T 5K 61
NE20: Pon 1H 41
NE30: N Shi 4K 49
NE38: Wash 4J 115
NE46: Hex 1A 70
NE61: Mor 1D 14
Queensway Ct. NE11: Gate 1E 98
Queensway Nth. NE11: Gate 7E 82
Queensway Sth. NE11: Gate 3F 99
Queen Victoria Rd.
NE1: Newc T 7F 63 (3E 4)
Queen Victoria St. NE10: Gate 5D 84
Quentin Av. NE3: Ken 7K 43
Que Sera DH5: Hett H 7G 145
Quetlaw Rd. DH6: Whe H 3A 180
Quigley Ter. DH3: Bir 2K 113
Quilstyle Rd. DH6: Whe H 3A 180
Quin Cres. TS28: Win 5F 181
Quinn Cl. SR8: Pet 7B 172
Quinn's Ter. DH1: Dur 4J 165
Quin Sq. DH6: S Het 4C 158

R

Rabbit Banks Rd. NE8: Gate 3F 83 (10F 4)
Raby Av. SR8: Eas 6C 160
Raby Cl. DH4: Hou S 1A 144
NE22: Bed 7F 17
Raby Cres. NE6: Newc T 7A 64 (4P 5)
Raby Cross NE6: Newc T 1A 84 (6P 5)
Raby Dr. SR3: E Her 2J 131
Raby Gdns. NE16: Burn 2J 109
NE32: Jar 2B 86
Raby Ga. NE6: Newc T 7A 64
Raby Rd. DH1: Dur 4A 154
NE38: Wash 3D 114
Raby St. NE6: Newc T 7K 63 (3P 5)
(not continuous)
NE8: Gate 6H 83
SR4: Sund 2D 118
Raby Wlk. NE6: Newc T 7A 64 (3P 5)
Raby Way NE6: Newc T 7A 64 (4P 5)
Rachel Cl. SR2: Ryh 2E 132
Rackley Way SR6: Whit 6H 89
(not continuous)
Radcliffe Pl. NE5: Newc T 3K 61
Radcliffe Rd. NE46: Hex 2E 70
SR5: C'twn 5A 104
Radcliffe St. DH3: Bir 5A 114
Radlett Rd. SR5: C'twn 5K 103
Radnor Gdns. NE28: W'snd 2A 66
Radnor St. NE1: Newc T 7G 63 (3H 5)
Radstock Pl. NE12: Longb 5A 46
Rae Av. NE28: W'snd 1F 65
Raeburn Av. NE38: Wash 4J 115
Raeburn Gdns. NE9: Gate 7K 83
Raeburn Rd. NE34: S Shi 4K 87
SR5: C'twn 4J 103
Raey Ct. DH2: Ches S 7A 128
Raglan NE38: Wash 3E 114
Raglan Av. SR2: Sund 5G 119
Raglan Pl. NE16: Burn 1B 110
Raglan Row DH4: Hou S 4C 130
Raglan St. DH8: Con 7H 121
NE32: Jar 6C 66
Raich Carter Sports Cen. 4H 119
Railton Gdns. NE9: Gate 1K 99
Railway Cl. DH6: Sher 3J 167

Railway Cotts.—Reynolds Cl.

Railway Cotts. DH1: Dur 3H 165
DH2: Ches S 4J 127
DH3: Bir 4K 113
DH4: Hou S 2K 143
DH4: Pen 1A 130
DH6: Shot C 6E 170
NE24: Cow 1C 22
NE24: News 7G 23
NE44: Rid M 6A 74
SR4: Sund 2G 117
TS27: B Col 3K 183
TS28: Win 4H 181
(off Wellfield Rd.)
Railway Gdns. DH9: Ann P 5K 123
Railway Pl. DH8: Con 6F 121
Railway Row SR1: Sund 2D 118 (4F 7)
Railway St. DH4: Hou S 7D 130
DH5: Hett H 6G 145
DH7: Lan 7K 137
DH7: Lang P 4J 151
DH8: Con 7H 121
DH8: Lead 5B 122
DH9: Ann P 6A 124
DH9: Stly 7J 125
NE4: Newc T 3D 82 (10B 4)
NE11: Dun 5C 82
(Ravensworth Vw.)
NE11: Dun 4B 82
(St Omers Rd.)
NE29: N Shi 7G 49
NE31: Heb 6K 65
NE32: Jar 6A 66
SR1: Sund 2H 119
SR4: Sund 1B 118
Railway Ter. DH4: E Her 3D 130
DH4: Pen 1A 130
DH5: Hett H 5G 145
NE4: Newc T 3D 82 (10A 4)
NE24: Bly 2H 23
NE28: W'snd 4H 65
NE29: N Shi 7G 49
NE38: Wash 4K 115
SR4: Sund 2G 117
Railway Ter. Nth. DH4: E Her 2D 130
Raine Gro. SR1: Sund 2G 119
Rainford Av. SR2: Sund 5G 119
Rainhill Cl. NE37: Usw 6K 101
Rainhill Rd. NE37: Usw 6J 101
Rainton Bank DH5: Hou S 4F 145
Rainton Bri. Nth. Ind. Est.
DH4: Hou S 3C 144
Rainton Bri. Sth. Ind. Est.
DH4: W Rai 4B 144
Rainton Cl. NE10: Gate 1G 101
RAINTON GATE 2K 155
Rainton Gro. DH5: Hou S 4E 144
Rainton Meadows Nature Reserve 4B 144
Rainton St. DH4: Pen 1B 130
SR4: Sund 2C 118
SR7: S'hm 4B 148
Rainton Vw. DH4: W Rai 1K 155
Rake La. NE29: N Shi 3C 48
Raleigh Cl. NE33: S Shi 5H 67
Raleigh Rd. SR5: C'twn 5K 103
Raleigh Sq. SR5: C'twn 5K 103
Ralph Av. SR2: Ryh 1G 133
Ralph St. NE31: Heb 6K 65
Ramilies SR2: Ryh 3F 133
Ramillies Rd. SR5: C'twn 4J 103
Ramillies Sq. SR5: C'twn 4J 103
Ramona Av. DH6: Kel 7C 178
Ramparts, The NE15: Lem 5E 60
Ramsay Rd. NE17: C'wl 5K 93
Ramsay Sq. SR5: C'twn 4A 104
Ramsay St. NE21: Bla T 5B 80
NE39: H Spen 2E 94
Ramsay Ter. DH8: Con 2K 135
Ramsey Cl. DH1: Dur 2E 166
SR8: Pet 4B 172
Ramsey St. DH3: Ches S 7A 128
Ramsgate Rd. SR5: C'twn 4A 104
Ramshaw Cl. DH7: Lang P 5G 151
NE7: Newc T 2C 64
Ramside Vw. DH1: Carr 6H 155
Randolph St. NE32: Jar 6C 66
Range Vs. SR6: Whit 5H 89
Rangoon Rd. SR5: C'twn 4J 103
Ranksborough St. SR7: S'hm 2K 147
(not continuous)
Ranmere Rd. NE15: Newc T 1H 81
Ranmore Cl. NE23: Cra 3K 25
Rannoch Av. DH2: Ches S 1K 141
Rannoch Cl. NE10: Gate 6G 85
Rannoch Rd. SR5: C'twn 4J 103
Ranson Cres. NE34: S Shi 1F 87
Ranson St. SR2: Sund 4D 118
SR4: Sund 4D 118
Raphael Av. NE34: S Shi 3J 87
Rapperton Ct. NE5: Newc T 2F 62
Rathmore Gdns. NE30: N Shi 5G 49
Ratho Ct. NE10: Gate 1C 100
Ravel Ct. NE32: Jar 7C 66
Ravenburn Gdns. NE15: Newc T 7F 61
Raven Ct. DH7: Esh W 4C 162
Ravenna Rd. SR5: C'twn 4H 103
Ravensbourne Av. NE36: E Bol 6K 87
Ravensburn Wlk. NE15: Thro 3G 59
Ravenscar Cl. NE16: Whi 2E 96
Ravenscourt Pl. *NE8: Gate 5F 83*
(off Airey Ter.)
Ravenscourt Rd. SR5: C'twn 4J 103
Ravensdale Cres. NE9: Gate 1J 99
Ravensdale Gro. NE24: Cow 2E 22
Ravens Hill Dr. NE63: Ash 5J 11
Ravenshill Rd. NE5: Newc T 4D 60
Ravenside Rd. NE4: Newc T 5A 62
Ravenside Ter. DH8: Shot B 5F 121
NE17: C'wl 6J 93
Ravenstone NE37: Wash 1F 115
Ravenswood Cl. NE12: Longb 4C 46
Ravenswood Gdns. NE9: Gate 4H 99
Ravenswood Rd. NE6: Newc T 4A 64
SR5: C'twn 4H 103
Ravenswood Sq. SR5: C'twn 4H 103
Ravensworth SR2: Ryh 3E 132
Ravensworth Av. DH4: Hou S 1A 144
NE9: Spri 5A 100
Ravensworth Castle 4C 98
Ravensworth Cl. NE28: W'snd 3K 65
Ravensworth Ct. DH6: S Het 3B 158
NE3: Ken 5K 43
NE11: Dun 5C 82
NE22: Bed 5B 18
Ravensworth Cres. NE16: Burn 7D 96
Ravensworth Gdns. DH3: Bir 3K 113
Ravensworth Pk. Est.
NE11: Gate 3B 98
Ravensworth Rd. DH3: Bir 3K 113
NE11: Dun 6C 82
Ravensworth St. NE22: Bed 5B 18
NE28: W'snd 3K 65
SR4: Sund 1D 118
Ravensworth Ter. DH1: Dur 2B 166 (2E 6)
NE4: Newc T 1D 82 (6B 4)
NE11: Dun 6C 82
NE16: Sun 5H 97
NE22: Bed 5B 18
NE32: Jar 3B 86
NE33: S Shi 5J 67
Ravensworth Vw. NE11: Dun 4C 82
Ravensworth Vs. NE9: Gate 4A 100
Raven Ter. DH3: Bir 3A 114
Ravine Ter. SR6: Monk 4H 105
(not continuous)
Rawdon Rd. SR5: C'twn 4A 104
Rawling Rd. NE8: Gate 6F 83
Rawlston Way NE5: Newc T 2J 61
Rawmarsh Rd. SR5: C'twn 4J 103
Raydale SR5: C'twn 4A 104
Raydale Av. NE37: Usw 7F 101
Raylees Gdns. NE11: Dun 7C 82
Rayleigh Dr. NE13: Wide O 4D 34
Rayleigh Gro. NE8: Gate 7F 83
Raynes Cl. NE61: Mor 1D 14
Raynham Cl. NE23: Cra 7H 25
Raynham Ct. NE33: S Shi 4J 67
Readhead Av. NE33: S Shi 4A 68
Readhead Dr. NE6: Walk 2D 84
Readhead Rd. NE34: S Shi 5A 68
Reading Rd. NE33: S Shi 6K 67
SR5: C'twn 4K 103
Reading Sq. SR5: C'twn 4J 103
Reasby Gdns. NE40: Ryton 1F 79
Reasby Vs. NE40: Ryton 1F 79
Reavley Av. NE22: Bed 5C 18
Reay Cres. NE35: Bol C 6H 87
Reay Gdns. NE5: Newc T 2G 61
Reay Pl. NE3: Gos 7C 44
NE34: S Shi 1H 87
Reay St. NE10: Gate 4F 85
Rectory Av. NE3: Gos 1F 63
Rectory Bank NE36: W Bol 7G 87
Rectory Cotts. NE40: Ryton 7G 59
Rectory Ct. NE16: Whi 7H 81
Rectory Dene NE61: Mor 2F 15
Rectory Dr. NE3: Gos 1G 63
Rectory Grn. NE36: W Bol 7F 87
Rectory Gro. NE3: Gos 7F 45
Rectory La. DH8: Ebc 5G 107
NE16: Whi 1H 97
NE21: Bla T 5B 80
Rectory Pk. NE61: Mor 1F 15
Rectory Pl. NE8: Gate 5F 83
Rectory Rd. DH5: Hett H 7G 145
NE3: Gos 2F 63
NE8: Gate 5F 83
NE10: Gate 7A 84
Rectory Rd. E. NE10: Gate 7B 84
(not continuous)
Rectory Ter. NE3: Gos 1G 63
NE36: W Bol 1F 103
Rectory Vw. DH6: Shad 5E 168
Red Admiral Ct. NE11: Gate 7D 82
Red Banks DH2: Ches S 7H 127
Red Barns NE1: Newc T 1H 83 (5K 5)
Redberry Way NE34: S Shi 2H 87
Red Briar Wlk. DH1: Dur 4J 153
Red Bungs. NE9: Spri 6C 100
Redburn Cl. DH4: Hou S 2C 144
Redburn Cres. NE46: Acomb 4B 50
Redburn Rd. DH4: Hou S 3B 144
DH4: W Rai 3B 144
NE5: Newc T 1F 61
Redburn Row DH4: Hou S 3B 144
Redby Cl. SR6: Monk 5F 105
Redcar Rd. NE6: Newc T 4B 64
NE28: W'snd 2A 66
SR5: C'twn, S'wck 5K 103
Redcar Sq. SR5: C'twn 5A 104
Redcar Ter. NE36: W Bol 1G 103
Redcliffe Way NE5: Newc T 2H 61
Red Courts DH7: B'don 1E 174
Redcroft Grn. NE5: Newc T 2H 61
Redditch Sq. SR5: C'twn 4K 103
Rede Av. NE31: Heb 7J 65
NE46: Hex 2E 70
Redemarsh NE10: Gate 1D 100
Redesdale Av. NE3: Ken 6C 44
NE21: Bla T 6K 79
Redesdale Cl. NE12: Longb 4A 46
NE15: Lem 6E 60
Redesdale Gdns. NE11: Dun 7B 82
Redesdale Gro. NE29: N Shi 6D 48
Redesdale Pl. NE24: Cow 2F 23
Redesdale Rd. DH2: Ches S 1J 141
NE29: N Shi 6C 48
SR5: C'twn 4J 103
Rede St. NE11: Gate 2E 98
NE32: Jar 1A 86
Rede Ter. *NE46: Hex 2E 70*
(off Rede Av.)
Redewater Gdns. NE16: Whi 1G 97
Redewater Rd. NE4: Newc T 5A 62
Redewood Cl. NE5: Newc T 4G 61
Red Firs DH7: B'don 1D 174
Redford Pl. NE23: Dud 6A 36
Redgrave Cl. NE8: Gate 4K 83 (10N 5)
Red Hall Dr. NE7: Newc T 2B 64
REDHEUGH 4E 82
Redheugh Bri. Rd.
NE4: Newc T 3E 82 (9D 4)
Redheugh Ct. NE8: Gate 6D 82
Redheugh Rd. NE25: Well 6B 38
Redhill SR6: Whit 6G 89
Redhill Dr. NE16: Whi 3E 96
Redhill Rd. SR5: C'twn 4K 103
Redhills La. DH1: Dur 2J 165 (2A 6)
Red Hills Ter. DH1: Dur 3J 165
Redhills Way DH5: Hett H 1G 157
Red Hill Vs. DH1: Dur 2K 165
Redhill Wlk. NE23: Cra 3K 25
Redhouse Cl. DH7: Sac 1F 153
Red Ho. Dr. NE25: Whit B 5C 38
Red Ho. Farm Est. NE22: Bed 1F 21
Red Ho. Rd. NE31: Heb 7K 65
Redland Av. NE3: Ken 6K 43
Redlands DH4: Pen 2A 130
NE16: Sun 7G 97
Red Lion Bldg. NE9: Spri 6B 100
Red Lion La. NE37: Usw 5G 101
Redmayne Ct. NE10: Gate 6B 84
Redmires Cl. DH2: Ous 7G 113
Redmond Rd. SR5: C'twn 4A 104
Redmond Sq. SR5: C'twn 4A 104
Rednam Pl. NE5: Newc T 3H 61
Red Ridges DH7: B'don 7E 164
Red Rose Ter. DH3: Ches S 7B 128
Red Row NE22: Bed 4A 18
Red Row Ct. NE22: Bed 4A 18
Red Row Dr. NE22: Bed 5A 18
Redruth Gdns. NE9: Gate 5H 99
Redruth Sq. SR5: C'twn 4K 103
Redshank Cl. NE38: Wash 6D 114
Redshank Dr. NE24: News 5J 23
Redstart Ct. NE39: Row G 6H 95
Red Wlk. NE2: Gos 2H 63
NE7: Newc T 2H 63
Redwell Ct. NE34: S Shi 6E 68
NE42: Pru 4F 77
Redwell Hills DH8: Lead 5C 122
Redwell La. NE34: S Shi 6F 69
Redwell Rd. NE42: Pru 4F 77
Redwing Cl. NE38: Wash 5D 114
Redwing Ct. NE6: Walk 6C 64
Redwood Cl. DH5: Hett H 7F 145
NE12: Kil 7A 36
Redwood Ct. DH8: Con 5G 121
Redwood Flats DH7: B'don 1D 174
DH7: Esh W 5D 162
Redwood Gdns. NE11: Gate 2D 98
Redwood Gro. SR3: New S 2D 132
Reed Av. NE12: Kil 6A 36
Reedham Ct. NE5: Newc T 1H 61
Reedling Ct. SR5: C'twn 3J 103
Reedside NE40: Ryton 1H 79
Reedsmouth Pl. NE5: Newc T 5H 61
Reed St. NE30: N Shi 6H 49
NE33: S Shi 5H 67
Reedswood Cres. NE23: E Cram 5B 26
Reestones Pl. NE3: Ken 7K 43
Reeth Rd. SR5: C'twn 5K 103
Reeth Sq. SR5: C'twn 5K 103
Reeth Way NE15: Thro 4G 59
Regal Bus. Cen. NE4: Newc T 2B 82
Regal Rd. SR4: Sund 1C 118
Regal Sunderland Greyhound Stadium
....1B 104
Regency Ct. NE2: Newc T 5H 63
SR7: S'hm 3B 148
Regency Dr. NE16: Whi 1F 97
SR3: New S 1D 132
Regency Gdns. NE29: N Shi 6E 48
Regency Way NE20: Pon 6E 30
Regent Av. NE3: Gos 7D 44
Regent Centre Station (Metro) 6E 44
Regent Cen., The NE3: Gos 6E 44
Regent Ct. NE8: Gate 4H 83 (10J 5)
NE24: Bly 2H 23
NE31: Heb 1H 85
NE33: S Shi 4J 67
Regent Dr. NE16: Whi 3F 97
Regent Farm Ct. NE3: Gos 7E 44
Regent Farm Rd. NE3: Gos 6C 44
Regent Rd. NE3: Gos 7E 44
NE28: W'snd 2E 64
NE32: Jar 7C 66
SR2: Ryh 4J 133
Regent Rd. Nth. NE3: Gos 7E 44
Regents Cl. NE12: Longb 3K 45
Regents Ct. NE28: W'snd 1C 64
Regents Dr. NE30: N Shi 3J 49
NE42: Pru 2G 77
Regents Pk. NE28: W'snd 2C 64
Regent St. DH5: Hett H 5G 145
DH9: Ann P 4K 123
NE8: Gate 4G 83 (10H 5)
NE24: Bly 7J 19
NE33: S Shi 4H 67
Regent Ter. NE8: Gate 4G 83 (10H 5)
NE29: N Shi 5E 48
SR2: Sund 6H 119
Reginald St. NE10: Gate 5K 83
NE35: Bol C 6F 87
(not continuous)
SR4: Sund 1B 118
Regina Sq. SR5: C'twn 4K 103
Reg Vardy Arts Foundation Gallery 4F 119
Reid Av. NE28: W'snd 2F 65
Reid Pk. Cl. NE2: Newc T 3H 63
Reid Pk. Ct. NE2: Newc T 3H 63
Reid Pk. Rd. NE2: Newc T 3H 63
Reid's La. NE23: Seg 2C 36
Reid St. NE61: Mor 6G 9
Reigate Sq. NE23: Cra 3K 25
Reins Ct. NE46: Hex 1A 70
Reiverdale Rd. NE63: Hir 3B 12
Rekendyke Ind. Est. NE33: S Shi 5H 67
Rekendyke La. NE33: S Shi 4H 67
Relley Gth. DH7: B'don 7F 165
Relly Cl. DH7: Ush M 3D 164
Relly Path DH1: Dur 4J 165
Relton Av. NE6: Newc T 2B 84
Relton Cl. DH4: Hou S 3A 144
Relton Ct. NE25: Whit B 6E 38
Relton Pl. NE25: Whit B 6E 38
Relton Ter. DH3: Ches S 7A 128
NE25: Whit B 6E 38
Rembrandt Av. NE34: S Shi 3J 87
Remscheid Way NE63: Ash 5A 12
Remus Av. NE15: Hed W 3B 58
Remus Cl. NE13: Wide O 6D 34
Renaissance Point NE30: N Shi 6J 49
Rendel St. NE11: Dun 5B 82
Rendle Rd. NE6: Walk 2F 85
Renforth Cl. NE8: Gate 4K 83 (10N 5)
Renforth St. NE11: Dun 6B 82
Renfrew Cl. NE29: N Shi 4C 48
Renfrew Grn. NE5: Newc T 2H 61
Renfrew Pl. DH3: Bir 6B 114
Renfrew Rd. SR5: C'twn 4K 103
Rennie Rd. SR5: C'twn 4H 103
Rennie Sq. SR5: C'twn 4H 103
Rennington NE10: Gate 2D 100
Rennington Av. NE30: N Shi 3J 49
Rennington Cl. NE30: N Shi 3J 49
NE61: Mor 3H 15
Rennington Pl. NE5: Newc T 3K 61
Renny's La. DH1: Dur 2E 166
(not continuous)
Renny St. DH1: Dur 2C 166
Renoir Gdns. NE34: S Shi 4K 87
Renwick Av. NE3: Ken 6A 44
Renwick Rd. NE24: Bly 2H 23
Renwick St. NE6: Walk 7B 64
Renwick Ter. NE8: Gate 6E 82
Renwick Wlk. NE61: Mor 7E 8
Rescue Sta. Cotts. DH5: Hou S 4F 145
Resida Cl. NE15: Lem 5C 60
Retail World NE11: Gate 5F 99
Retford Rd. SR5: C'twn 4K 103
Retford Sq. SR5: C'twn 4K 103
Retreat, The NE15: Thro 6K 59
SR2: Sund 2D 118 (5F 7)
Revell Ter. NE5: Newc T 4A 62
Revelstoke Rd. SR5: C'twn 4H 103
Revesby St. NE33: S Shi 7J 67
Reynolds Av. NE12: Kil 2K 45
NE34: S Shi 3K 87
NE38: Wash 4J 115
Reynolds Cl. DH9: Stly 3F 125

Reynolds Ct.—Romsey Cl.

Reynolds Ct. SR8: Pet 6F 173
Reyrolle Ct. NE31: Heb 1H 85
Rheims Ct. SR4: Sund 1K 117
Rheydt Av. NE28: W'snd 3C 64
Rhoda Ter. SR2: Sund 7H 119
Rhodesia Rd. SR5: C'twn 4K 103
Rhodes St. NE6: Walk 1E 84
Rhodes Ter. DH1: Dur 4H 165
Rhondda Rd. SR5: C'twn 4H 103
Rhuddlan Ct. NE5: Newc T 1H 61
Rhyl Pde. NE31: Heb 4A 86
Rhyl Sq. SR5: C'twn 4A 104
Ribbledale Gdns. NE7: Newc T 2K 63
Ribble Rd. SR5: C'twn 5J 103
Ribblesdale DH4: Pen 2B 130
NE28: W'snd 1D 64
Ribblesdale Av. NE24: Cow 1E 22
(not continuous)
Ribble Wlk. NE32: Jar 3C 86
Richard Av. SR4: Sund 4C 118
Richard Browell Rd. NE15: Thro 4H 59
Richard Hollon Ct. NE61: Mor 7F 9
Richardson Av. NE34: S Shi 2F 87
(not continuous)
Richardson Rd. NE2: Newc T 6D 62 (1B 4)
Richardsons Bldgs. NE62: Sco G 3G 17
Richardson St. NE6: Newc T 5A 64
NE28: W'snd 3G 65
NE63: Hir 5C 12
Richardson Ter. NE17: C'wl 6J 93
NE37: Usw 7H 101
(not continuous)
SR2: Ryh 3J 133
Richard St. DH5: Hett H 7G 145
NE24: Bly 2J 23
Richmond SR2: Ryh 2E 132
Richmond Av. NE10: Gate 5G 85
NE16: Swa 5H 81
NE38: Wash 2H 115
Richmond Cl. NE22: Bed 6G 17
Richmond Ct. DH1: Dur 4B 154
NE8: Gate 5H 83
NE9: Gate 3H 99
NE32: Jar 6A 66
Richmond Dr. DH4: Hou S 1H 143
Richmond Flds. NE20: Pon 6E 30
Richmond Gdns. NE28: W'snd 2J 65
Richmond Gro. NE29: N Shi 7E 48
Richmond M. NE3: Gos 2D 62
Richmond Pk. NE28: W'snd 1C 64
Richmond Pl. DH3: Bir 6A 114
Richmond Rd. DH1: Dur 4B 154
NE34: S Shi 7J 67
Richmond St. SR5: Monk 7E 104 (1H 7)
Richmond Ter. DH6: Has 1B 170
NE8: Gate 5G 83
NE10: Gate 6B 84
NE15: Thro 4K 59
NE26: Whit B 4F 39
Richmond Way NE20: Pon 6E 30
NE23: Cra 7H 25
Rickaby St. SR1: Sund 7H 105
Rickgarth NE10: Gate 2D 100
(not continuous)
RICKLETON 1C 128
Rickleton Av. DH3: Ches S 4B 128
Rickleton Village Cen.
NE38: Wash 1D 128
Rickleton Way NE38: Wash 7D 114
Riddell Av. NE15: Newc T 1J 81
Riddell Ct. DH2: Ches S 7A 128
Riddell Ter. NE3: Gos 7C 44
Ridding Ct. DH7: Esh W 4D 162
Ridding Rd. DH7: Esh W 5D 162
Riddings Rd. SR5: C'twn 4K 103
Riddings Sq. SR5: C'twn 4K 103
Ridge Ct. NE13: Bru V 7D 34
Ridgely Cl. NE20: Pon 5A 32
Ridgely Dr. NE20: Pon 5A 32
Ridge Ter. NE22: Bed 7G 17
Ridge, The NE40: Ryton 2G 79
Ridge Vs. NE22: Bed 7G 17
Ridgeway DH3: Bir 2A 114
DH7: Lan 6J 137
NE4: Newc T 5A 62
NE10: Gate 7F 85
NE25: H'wll 2J 37
NE62: Chop 7J 11
NE63: N Sea 5E 12
SR2: Ryh 3E 132
Ridgeway Cres. SR3: Sund 5D 118
Ridge Way, The NE3: Ken 1B 62
Ridgeway, The DH5: Hett H 7G 145
NE34: S Shi 3B 88
Ridgewood Cres. NE3: Gos 7H 45
Ridgewood Gdns. NE3: Gos 7G 45
Ridgewood Vs. NE3: Gos 7G 45
Riding Bank NE46: Acomb 4C 50
Riding Barns Way NE16: Sun 5G 97
Riding Cl. NE40: Ryton 3C 78
NE44: Rid M 6K 73
Riding Dene NE43: Mic 5B 76
Riding Grange NE44: Rid M 6J 73
Riding Hill DH3: Gt Lum 3E 142
Riding Hill Rd. DH9: Ann P 4A 124
Riding La. NE11: Beam, Kib 3C 112
NE61: Chop 6F 11
RIDING LEA 6H 73
Riding Lea NE21: Bla T 5A 80
RIDING MILL 7K 73
Riding Mill Station (Rail) 6K 73
Ridings Ct. NE40: Ryton 3C 78
Ridings, The NE25: Whit B 5C 38
Riding Ter. *NE43: Mic 5A 76*
(off Station Bank)
Riding, The NE3: Ken 2A 62
Ridley Av. DH2: Ches S 7K 127
NE24: Bly 2K 23
NE28: W'snd 1A 66
SR2: Ryh 2H 133
Ridley Bldg. NE2: Newc T 1E 4
Ridley Cl. NE3: Ken 4B 44
NE46: Hex 3B 70
NE61: Mor 7E 8
Ridley Ct. NE1: Newc T 1F 83 (6F 4)
Ridley Gdns. NE16: Swa 5G 81
Ridley Gro. NE34: S Shi 6C 68
Ridley Ho. NE3: Gos 7E 44
Ridley Mill Cotts. NE43: Stoc 1H 91
Ridley Mill Rd. NE43: Stoc 1H 91
Ridley Pl. NE1: Newc T 7F 63 (3F 4)
Ridley St. DH9: Stly 2F 125
NE8: Gate 6F 83
NE23: Cra 5A 26
NE24: Bly 1K 23
SR5: S'wck 5C 104
Ridley Ter. DH8: Lead 5B 122
NE10: Gate 6C 84
NE24: Camb 4H 19
NE46: Hex 7C 50
(off Tyne Grn. Rd.)
SR2: Sund 3H 119
Ridsdale NE42: Pru 4D 76
Ridsdale Av. NE5: Newc T 4D 60
Ridsdale Cl. NE25: Sea D 7G 27
NE28: W'snd 1G 65
Ridsdale Ct. NE8: Gate 5F 83
Ridsdale Sq. NE63: Ash 4A 12
Rievaulx NE38: Wash 5G 115
Riga Sq. SR5: C'twn 4J 103
Riggs, The DH5: Hou S 2F 145
DH7: B'don 7E 164
NE45: Cor 6D 52
Rignall NE38: Wash 3A 116
Riley St. NE32: Jar 6A 66
Ringlet Cl. NE11: Gate 7D 82
Ringmore Ct. SR2: Sund 6E 118
Ringway NE62: Chop 6H 11
SR5: C'twn 7F 103
Ringwood Dr. NE23: Cra 3K 25
Ringwood Grn. NE12: Longb 5A 46
Ringwood Rd. SR5: C'twn 4K 103
Ringwood Sq. SR5: C'twn 4K 103
Rink St. NE24: Bly 1K 23
Rink Way NE25: Whit B 1F 49
Ripley Av. NE29: N Shi 7E 48
(Tonbridge Av.)
NE29: N Shi 1E 66
(Waterville Rd.)
Ripley Cl. NE22: Bed 6F 17
Ripley Ct. DH7: Sac 7E 140
NE9: Gate 6K 99
Ripley Dr. NE23: Cra 7H 25
Ripley Ter. NE6: Walk 7C 64
Ripon Cl. NE23: Cra 7H 25
Ripon Ct. DH7: Sac 7D 140
Ripon Gdns. NE2: Newc T 5J 63
NE28: W'snd 2J 65
Ripon Rd. DH1: Dur 3B 154
Ripon Sq. NE32: Jar 5B 86
Ripon St. DH3: Ches S 1A 142
NE8: Gate 5G 83
SR6: Monk 5G 105
Ripon Ter. DH2: Plaw 7J 141
SR7: Mur 7E 146
Rise, The DH8: C'sde 4C 134
NE3: Ken 1A 62
NE8: Gate 5K 83
(off Duncan St.)
NE20: Pon 1F 41
NE21: Bla T 2A 80
NE26: Sea S 6D 28
Rishton Sq. SR5: C'twn 4J 103
Rising Sun Cotts. NE28: W'snd 7F 47
Rising Sun Countryside Cen. 4G 47
Rising Sun Vs. NE28: W'snd 7F 47
Ritson Av. DH7: Ush M 1C 164
Ritson Cl. NE29: N Shi 5E 48
Ritson's Rd. DH8: Shot B 4F 121
Ritson St. DH8: Shot B 5F 121
DH9: Stly 3F 125
SR6: Monk 3G 105
Ritz Bingo 4C 46
River Bank NE62: Chop 7A 12
River Bank E. NE62: Chop 7A 12
Riverbank Rd. SR5: C'twn 5K 103
Riverdale SR5: C'twn 7H 103
River Dr. NE33: S Shi 2J 67
River Gth. *SR1: Sund 1G 119*
(off High St. E.)
River La. NE40: Ryton 7G 59
Rivermead NE38: Wash 7J 115
Rivermede NE20: Pon 4K 31
Riversdale Av. NE62: Chop 7J 11
Riversdale Ct. NE15: Lem 7C 60
NE17: C'wl 2K 107
NE62: Chop 1J 17
Riversdale Ho. *NE62: Chop 1J 17*
(off Riversdale Av.)
Riversdale Rd. NE8: Gate 3F 83 (10F 4)
Riversdale Ter. SR2: Sund 3D 118
Riversdale Way NE15: Lem 7B 60
Riverside DH3: Ches S 7C 128
DH8: Shot B 3E 120
NE20: Pon 5J 31
NE61: Mor 7F 9
(off Waterside)
Riverside Av. NE62: Chop 1F 17
Riverside Bus. Pk. NE28: W'snd 4A 66
Riverside Ct. NE11: Dun 5C 82
NE21: Bla T 2D 80
NE33: S Shi 3H 67
Riverside E. Ind. Est.
NE6: Newc T 2A 84 (7P 5)
Riverside Ind. Est. DH7: Lang P 4J 151
Riverside Leisure Cen. 7F 9
Riverside Leisure Pk. NE46: Hex 7B 50
Riverside Pk. SR4: Sund 1H 117
Riverside Rd. SR5: S'wck 5K 103
Riverside Sth. SR4: Sund 7A 104
Riverside Sports Complex 7C 128
Riverside Studios NE4: Newc T 3B 82
Riverside, The NE31: Heb 6G 65
Riverside Vw. NE6: Walk 3D 84
Riverside Way NE11: Dun, Swa 3G 81
NE16: Swa 3G 81
NE39: Row G 7H 95
River St. NE33: S Shi 5G 67
River Ter. DH3: Ches S 5B 128
River Vw. NE17: C'wl 2K 107
NE21: Bla T 4B 80
NE22: Bed 7B 18
NE30: N Shi 6J 49
NE40: Ryton 1J 79
NE42: O'ham 2C 76
NE42: Pru 4E 76
NE61: Mor 6G 9
(off Howard Rd.)
River Vw. Cl. NE22: Bed 7B 18
Riverview Lodge NE4: Newc T 2K 81
Roachburn Rd. NE5: Newc T 3E 60
Roadside Cotts. NE21: Bla T 1K 79
Robert Allen Ct. NE13: Bru V 5C 34
Robert Owen Gdns. NE10: Gate 7A 84
Robertson Ct. DH3: Ches S 7A 128
Robertson Rd. SR5: C'twn 5H 103
Robertson Sq. SR5: C'twn 4H 103
Robert Sq. SR7: S'hm 4C 148
Roberts St. NE15: Newc T 2G 81
Roberts Ter. NE32: Jar 1B 86
Robert St. NE24: Bly 2J 23
NE33: S Shi 4K 67
SR3: New S 2D 132
SR4: Sund 1C 118
SR7: S'hm 4C 148
Robert Ter. DH6: Bow 3H 177
DH9: Stly 1F 125
NE39: H Spen 3D 94
Robert Ter. Cotts. NE39: H Spen 3D 94
Robert Westall Way NE29: N Shi 2G 67
Robert Wheatman Ct. SR2: Sund 6G 119
Robin Ct. DH5: W Rai 7C 144
Robin Gro. SR5: C'twn 6J 103
Robin La. DH5: W Rai 2A 156
Robinson Gdns. NE28: W'snd 2A 66
SR6: Whit 5H 89
Robinson Ho. SR8: Pet 5E 172
Robinson Sq. *NE64: Newb S 2J 13*
(off High St.)
Robinson St. DH8: Con 5G 121
NE6: Newc T 7A 64
NE33: S Shi 4K 67
Robinson Ter. NE16: Burn 4A 110
NE38: Wash 4K 115
SR2: Sund 4H 119
Robinswood NE9: Gate 2H 99
Robsheugh Pl. NE5: Newc T 5J 61
Robson Av. SR8: Pet 5B 172
Robson Cres. DH6: Bow 3H 177
Robson Dr. NE46: Hex 3B 70
Robson Pl. SR2: Ryh 3J 133
Robson St. DH8: Con 6J 121
NE6: Newc T 7K 63 (3N 5)
NE9: Gate 2H 99
Robson Ter. DH1: H Shin 6D 166
DH9: Dip 6K 109
NE9: Spri 6B 100
NE39: Row G 4E 94
Rochdale Rd. SR5: C'twn 4K 103
Rochdale St. DH5: Hett H 1G 157
NE28: W'snd 4E 64
Rochdale Way SR5: C'twn 4K 103
Roche Ct. NE38: Wash 4G 115
Rochester Cl. NE63: N Sea 5E 12
Rochester Gdns. NE11: Dun 6C 82
Rochester Rd. DH1: Dur 4B 154
Rochester Sq. NE32: Jar 5B 86
Rochester St. NE6: Walk 2E 84
Rochester Ter. NE10: Gate 6C 84
Rochford Gro. NE23: Cra 7J 25
Rochford Rd. SR5: C'twn 4J 103
Rockcliffe *NE26: Whit B 6J 39*
(off Promenade)
NE33: S Shi 4B 68
Rockcliffe Av. NE26: Whit B 7J 39
Rockcliffe Gdns. NE15: Newc T 6F 61
NE26: Whit B 6J 39
Rockcliffe St. NE26: Whit B 6J 39
Rockcliffe Way NE9: Spri 5A 100
Rocket Way NE12: Longb 4D 46
Rock Gro. NE9: Gate 2H 99
Rockingham Rd. SR5: C'twn 4J 103
Rockingham Sq. SR5: C'twn 4J 103
Rock Lodge Gdns. SR6: Monk 4G 105
Rock Lodge Rd. SR6: Monk 4H 105
Rockmore Rd. NE21: Bla T 5C 80
Rock Ter. DH7: New B 4B 164
NE2: Newc T 7H 63 (3J 5)
NE37: Usw 7J 101
Rockville SR6: Monk 3G 105
Rock Wlk. DH3: Lam P 3F 129
Rockwood Gdns. NE40: G'sde 5C 78
Rockwood Hill Est. NE40: G'sde 6C 78
Rockwood Hill Rd. NE40: G'sde 6C 78
Rockwood Ter. NE40: G'sde 5D 78
Rodham Ter. DH9: Stly 1F 125
Rodin Av. NE34: S Shi 4K 87
Rodney Cl. NE30: N Shi 5K 49
SR2: Ryh 3E 132
Rodney Ct. *NE26: Whit B 4D 38*
(off Woodburn Sq.)
Rodney St. NE6: Newc T 1K 83 (6N 5)
Rodney Way NE26: Whit B 4D 38
Rodridge Pk. TS28: Win 7G 181
Rodsley Av. NE8: Gate 6G 83
Roeburn Way NE3: Ken 2B 62
Roedean Rd. SR5: C'twn 4A 104
Roehedge NE10: Gate 1F 101
Rogan Av. *NE37: Wash 2E 114*
(off Thirlmoor)
Rogerley Ter. DH9: Ann P 4J 123
Rogers Cl. SR8: Pet 6E 172
Rogerson Cl. DH6: Crox 6K 175
Rogerson Ter. DH6: Crox 6K 175
NE5: Newc T 3E 60
Roger St. DH8: Con 6G 121
NE6: Newc T 7K 63 (3N 5)
Rogues La. NE39: H Spen 1E 94
Rokeby Av. NE15: Lem 7D 60
Rokeby Dr. NE3: Ken 1B 62
Rokeby Sq. DH1: Dur 5J 165
Rokeby St. NE15: Lem 7D 60
SR4: Sund 2D 118
Rokeby Ter. NE6: Newc T 4A 64
(not continuous)
Rokeby Vw. NE9: Gate 5J 99
Rokeby Vs. NE15: Lem 7D 60
ROKER 4G 105
Roker Av. NE25: Whit B 7E 38
SR6: Monk 7F 105
Roker Baths Rd. SR6: Monk 5F 105
Rokerby Av. NE16: Whi 1J 97
Roker Pk. Cl. SR6: Monk 5G 105
Roker Pk. Rd. SR6: Monk 5G 105
Roker Pk. Ter. SR6: Monk 5H 105
Roker Ter. SR6: Monk 4H 105
Roland Rd. NE28: W'snd 3J 65
Roland St. NE38: Wash 4J 115
Rollesby Ct. NE5: Newc T 1H 61
Rolley Way NE42: Pru 3G 77
Rolling Mill Rd. NE32: Jar 5A 66
Romaldkirk Cl. DH8: Con 1H 135
SR4: Sund 3H 117
Roman Av. DH3: Ches S 6B 128
NE6: Walk 6C 64
Roman Ct. NE28: W'snd 1J 65
Roman Forum *NE11: Dun 4J 81*
(off Metro Cen.)
Roman Rd. DH7: B'don 3C 174
NE32: Jar 4B 86
(not continuous)
NE33: S Shi 1K 67
Roman Rd. Nth. NE33: S Shi 7J 49
Roman Way NE45: Cor 7D 52
Roman Way, The NE5: Newc T 4D 60
Romany Dr. DH8: Con 7G 121
Romford Cl. NE23: Cra 7J 25
Romford Pl. NE9: Gate 6J 83
Romford St. SR4: Sund 2B 118
Romiley Gro. NE10: Gate 7H 85
Romilly St. NE33: S Shi 3K 67
Romney Av. NE34: S Shi 3K 87
NE38: Wash 4J 115
SR2: Sund 5G 119
Romney Cl. DH4: Hou S 4C 130
NE26: Whit B 7J 39
Romney Dr. DH1: Carr 6H 155
Romney Gdns. NE9: Gate 7K 83
Romney Vs. NE38: Wash 4J 115
Romsey Cl. NE23: Cra 3K 25

Romsey Dr.—Rydal M.

Romsey Dr. NE35: Bol C 6D 86
Romsey Gro. NE15: Lem 5C 60
Ronald Dr. NE15: Newc T 7G 61
Ronald Gdns. NE31: Heb 2H 85
Ronaldsay Cl. SR2: Ryh 1G 133
Ronald Sq. SR6: Monk 4F 105
Ronan M. DH4: W Rai 1A 156
Ronsdorf Ct. NE32: Jar 7B 66
Rookery Cl. NE24: Cow 2F 23
Rookery La. NE16: Whi 3E 96
Rookery, The NE16: Burn 2K 109
Rookhope NE38: Wash 1D 128
Rooksleigh NE21: Bla T 5B 80
Rookswood NE61: Mor 2G 15
Rookswood Gdns. NE39: Row G 4J 95
Rookwood Dr. NE13: Sea B 3E 34
Rookwood Rd. NE5: Newc T 5G 61
Roosevelt Rd. DH1: Dur 1D 166
Ropery La. DH3: Ches S, Gt Lum 7B 128
NE28: W'snd 3J 65
NE31: Heb 7H 65
Ropery Rd. NE8: Gate 6D 82
SR4: Sund 7C 104
Ropery Stairs NE30: N Shi 7H 49
Ropery, The NE6: Newc T 2B 84
Ropery Wlk. SR7: S'hm 4B 148
Rosalie Ter. SR2: Sund 4H 119
Rosalind Av. NE22: Bed 1J 21
Rosalind St. NE63: Hir 3B 12
(First Av.)
NE63: Hir 4C 12
(Fourth Av.)
Rosamond Pl. NE24: Bly 2K 23
Rosa St. NE33: S Shi 3K 67
Rose Av. DH4: Hou S 1K 143
DH9: Stly 4D 124
NE16: Whi 7H 81
NE23: Nel V 2H 25
Rosebank Cl. SR2: Ryh 1G 133
Rosebank Hall NE28: W'snd 3J 65
Rosebay Rd. DH7: B'don 7G 165
Roseberry Ct. NE37: Usw 7J 101
Roseberry Cres. DH6: Thor 1J 179
Roseberry Grange NE12: Longb 3E 46
Roseberry St. DH9: Beam 2K 125
Roseberry Ter. DH8: Con 7H 121
NE35: Bol C 5E 86
Roseberry Vs. DH2: Pelt 4E 126
Rosebery Av. NE8: Gate 6J 83
NE24: Bly 2H 23
NE29: N Shi 4G 49
NE33: S Shi 4A 68
Rosebery Ct. NE25: Whit B 6E 38
Rosebery Cres. NE2: Newc T 5J 63
Rosebery Pl. NE2: Newc T 5H 63
Rosebery St. SR5: S'wck 6F 105
Rosebud Cl. NE16: Swa 5G 81
Rosebury Dr. NE12: Longb 7J 45
Roseby Rd. SR8: Pet 5D 172
Rose Cotts. DH6: S Het 4C 158
NE16: Burn 3J 109
Rose Ct. DH7: Esh W 2C 162
NE31: Heb 1H 85
SR8: Pet 2K 181
Rose Cres. DH4: Hou S 6H 129
DH7: Sac 7F 141
SR6: Whit 4H 89
(not continuous)
Rosedale NE22: Bed 7G 17
NE28: W'snd 1D 64
Rosedale Av. DH8: Shot B 4F 121
SR6: Monk 1G 105
Rosedale Ct. NE5: Newc T 3D 60
Rosedale Cres. DH4: Hou S 7B 130
Rosedale Gdns. *DH7: Edm* *3D 140*
(off Tyzack St.)
Rosedale Rd. DH1: Carr 7H 155
NE40: Ryton 3D 78
Rosedale St. DH5: Hett H 2E 156
SR1: Sund 2D 118 (4F 7)
Rosedale Ter. DH4: Hou S 6E 130
NE2: Newc T 6H 63 (2J 5)
NE30: N Shi 5H 49
SR6: Monk 3G 105
SR8: Pet 5D 172
Roseden Ct. NE12: Longb 5A 46
Rosedene Vs. NE23: Cra 4B 26
Rosefinch Lodge NE9: Gate 2H 99
Rose Gdns. NE11: Kib 2E 112
NE28: W'snd 1F 65
Rosegill NE37: Wash 2F 115
ROSEHILL 2J 65
Rosehill Bank NE28: W'snd 3J 65
Rosehill Rd. NE28: W'snd 3K 65
Rosehill Ter. *NE28: W'snd* *3J 65*
(off Willington Ter.)
Rosehill Way NE5: Newc T 4J 61
Rose Lea DH7: Wit G 2D 152
Roselea DH6: Thor 1J 179
NE32: Jar 5C 86
Roselea Av. SR2: Ryh 2H 133
Rosemary Cl. DH8: Con 7J 121
Rosemary Gdns. NE9: Spri 5B 100
Rosemary La. NE1: Newc T 1F 83 (6F 4)
SR8: Eas 7K 159
Rosemary Rd. SR5: C'twn 4K 103
Rosemary Ter. NE24: Bly 3K 23
Rosemount DH1: Dur 3B 154
DH6: Has *7B 158*
(off Pesspool La.)
DH9: Stly 2C 126
NE5: Newc T 3F 61
NE61: Mor 1G 15
SR4: Sund 3G 117
Rosemount Av. NE10: Gate 7F 85
Rosemount Cl. NE37: Usw 5G 101
Rosemount Ct. NE36: W Bol 7H 87
Rosemount Way NE7: Newc T 7A 46
NE25: Whit B 6C 38
Roseneath Ct. NE63: Ash 4B 12
Rose Pk. NE23: Seg 2C 36
Rose St. DH4: Hou S 2D 144
NE8: Gate 4E 82
NE31: Heb 1H 85
SR4: Sund 1D 118 (3F 7)
Rose St. E. DH4: Pen 1B 130
Rose St. W. DH4: Pen 1B 130
Rose Ter. DH2: Pelt 4G 127
DH7: Lang P 5J 151
NE5: Newc T 4A 62
NE40: G'sde 5G 79
Rosetown Av. SR8: Pet 6E 172
Rose Villa La. NE16: Whi 7H 81
Rose Vs. NE4: Newc T 1B 82
Roseville St. SR4: Sund 3D 118
Rosewell Pl. NE16: Whi 2G 97
Rosewood NE12: Kil 1D 46
Rosewood Av. NE3: Gos 6F 45
Rosewood Cl. DH7: Sac 7E 140
Rosewood Cres. NE6: Walk 4D 64
NE26: Sea S 6D 28
Rosewood Gdns. DH2: Ches S 4K 127
NE3: Ken 1B 62
NE9: Gate 2K 99
Rosewood Sq. SR4: Sund 6G 117
Rosewood Ter. DH3: Bir 3K 113
NE28: W'snd 3A 66
Rosewood Wlk. DH7: Ush M 2B 164
Roseworth Av. NE3: Gos 2E 62
Roseworth Cl. NE3: Gos 1F 63
Roseworth Cres. NE3: Gos 2F 63
Roseworth Ter. NE3: Gos 1E 62
NE16: Whi 7H 81
Roslin Pk. NE22: Bed 7A 18
Roslin Way NE23: Cra 7J 25
Ross DH2: Ous 6J 113
Ross Av. NE11: Dun 5B 82
Rossdale *NE40: Ryton* *3C 78*
(off Bank Top)
Rosse Cl. NE37: Wash 7F 101
Rossendale Pl. NE12: Longb 6H 45
Ross Gth. DH5: Hou S 3E 144
Ross Gro. NE23: Nel V 3H 25
Ross Lea DH4: Hou S 5A 130
Rosslyn Av. NE3: Ken 7A 44
NE9: Gate 1J 99
SR2: Ryh 2H 133
Rosslyn M. SR4: Sund 2C 118
(not continuous)
Rosslyn Pl. DH3: Bir 6B 114
Rosslyn St. SR4: Sund 2C 118
Rosslyn Ter. SR4: Sund 2C 118
Ross St. SR5: S'wck 6E 104
SR7: S'hm 3B 148
Ross Way NE3: Ken 4B 44
NE26: Whit B 4E 38
Rosyth Rd. SR5: C'twn 4A 104
Rosyth Sq. SR5: C'twn 4A 104
Rotary Parkway NE63: Ash 3J 11
Rotary Way DH1: Dur 3K 153
NE20: Pon 7J 31
NE24: Bly, News 3J 23
NE29: N Shi 2E 66
NE46: B End, Hex 7E 50
Rothay Pl. NE5: Newc T 3J 61
Rothbury SR2: Ryh 3F 133
Rothbury Av. NE3: Gos 6C 44
NE10: Gate 5E 84
NE24: Bly 3F 23
NE32: Jar 2A 86
SR8: Pet 4D 172
Rothbury Cl. DH2: Ches S 1J 141
NE12: Kil 1A 46
Rothbury Gdns. NE11: Gate 2C 98
NE13: Wide O 5E 34
NE28: W'snd 2K 65
Rothbury Rd. DH1: Dur 4A 154
SR5: C'twn 4K 103
Rothbury Ter. NE6: Newc T 5K 63
NE29: N Shi 1C 66
Rotherfield Cl. NE23: Cra 3K 25
Rotherfield Gdns. NE9: Gate 5J 99
Rotherfield Rd. SR5: C'twn 5J 103
Rotherfield Sq. SR5: C'twn 4J 103
Rotherham Cl. DH5: Hou S 4D 144
Rotherham Rd. SR5: C'twn 4J 103
Rothesay DH2: Ous 7H 113
Rothesay Ter. NE22: Bed 7K 17
Rothlea Gdns. NE62: Chop 7J 11
Rothley NE38: Wash 6K 115
Rothley Av. NE5: Newc T 6J 61
NE63: Hir 5B 12
SR8: Pet 4D 172
Rothley Cl. NE3: Gos 7F 45
NE20: Pon 4H 31
Rothley Ct. NE12: Kil 1A 46
SR5: S'wck 3B 104
Rothley Gdns. NE30: N Shi 3H 49
Rothley Gro. NE25: Sea D 7G 27
Rothley Ter. DH8: M'sly 7K 107
Rothley Way NE26: Whit B 4E 38
Rothsay Ter. NE64: Newb S 4H 13
Rothwell Rd. NE3: Gos 7E 44
SR5: C'twn 5J 103
Rotterdam Ho. NE1: Newc T 6K 5
ROUND HILL 6D 54
Roundhill NE32: Jar 5D 86
Roundhill Av. NE5: Newc T 3J 61
Roundstone Cl. NE7: Newc T 1B 64
Roundway, The NE12: Longb 5K 45
Routledge's Bldgs.
NE22: Bed 5A 18
Rowan Av. NE38: Wash 7G 115
Rowanberry Rd. NE12: Longb 6K 45
Rowan Cl. NE22: Bed 6H 17
SR4: Sund 3H 117
Rowan Ct. DH7: Esh W 5C 162
NE12: Longb 4D 46
NE16: Burn 2B 110
NE24: Bly 3H 23
Rowan Dr. DH1: Bras 3C 154
DH5: Hett H 7F 145
NE3: Ken 6A 44
NE20: Pon 4J 31
Rowan Gro. NE23: E Cram 5B 26
NE42: Pru 4D 76
Rowan Lea DH7: B'don 1D 174
Rowans, The NE9: Spri 5B 100
(not continuous)
Rowan Tree Av. DH1: Dur 7E 154
Rowantree Rd. NE6: Walk 4E 64
Rowanwood Gdns.
NE11: Gate 2C 98
Rowedge Wlk. NE5: Newc T 3G 61
Rowell Cl. SR2: Ryh 3E 132
Rowes M. NE6: Newc T 2A 84
Rowland Burn Way
NE39: Row G 5J 95
Rowlands Bldgs. NE23: Dud 2J 35
ROWLANDS GILL 6K 95
Rowlandson Ter. NE10: Gate 6B 84
SR2: Sund 4G 119
Rowlands Ter. TS28: Win 7G 181
ROWLEY 5D 134
Rowley Bank DH8: C'sde 4B 134
Rowley Cl. DH7: New B 5A 164
Rowley Cres. DH7: Esh W 3D 162
Rowley Dr. DH7: Ush M 3D 164
Rowley Link DH7: Esh W 3D 162
Rowley St. NE24: Bly 2J 23
Rowlington Ter. NE63: Hir 5B 12
Rowntree Way NE29: N Shi 2G 67
Rowsley Rd. NE32: Jar 1C 86
Row's Ter. NE3: Gos 7G 45
Roxborough Ho. NE26: Whit B 6G 39
Roxburgh Cl. NE21: Bla T 6A 80
Roxburgh Pl. NE6: Newc T 6K 63 (1P 5)
Roxburgh St. SR6: Monk 5F 105
Roxburgh Ter. NE26: Whit B 6G 39
Roxby Gdns. NE29: N Shi 7E 48
Roxby Wynd TS28: Win 4G 181
Royal Arc. NE1: Newc T 1G 83 (6G 4)
Royal Cres. NE4: Newc T 5A 62
Royal Ind. Est. NE32: Jar 6K 65
Royal Northumberland Yacht Club 4K 23
Royal Quays Outlet Shop.
NE29: N Shi 3E 66
Royal Rd. DH9: Stly 2E 124
Royalty, The SR2: Sund 2D 118 (5F 7)
Royalty Theatre, The 5F 7
Roydon Av. SR2: Sund 5G 119
Royle St. SR2: Sund 6H 119
Royston Ter. NE6: Walk 2E 84
Ruabon Cl. NE23: Cra 7J 25
Rubens Av. NE34: S Shi 3K 87
Ruby St. DH4: Hou S 7D 130
Rudby Cl. NE3: Gos 4F 45
Rudchester Pl. NE5: Newc T 5J 61
Ruddock Sq. NE6: Newc T 1A 84 (7P 5)
Rudyard Av. SR2: Sund 5G 119
Rudyerd Ct. NE29: N Shi 7H 49
Rudyerd St. NE29: N Shi 7G 49
Rugby Gdns. NE9: Gate 4A 100
NE28: W'snd 2J 65
Ruislip Pl. NE23: Cra 7H 25
Ruislip Rd. SR4: Sund 3G 117
Runcie Rd. DH6: Bow 5H 177
Runcorn SR2: Ryh 2E 132
Runcorn Rd. SR5: C'twn 4J 103
Runhead Est. NE40: Ryton 2H 79
Runhead Gdns. NE40: Ryton 1H 79
Runhead Ter. NE40: Ryton 1J 79
RUNNING WATERS 7C 168
Runnymede DH3: Gt Lum 2E 142
SR2: Ryh 2F 133
Runnymede Gdns. NE17: C'wl 1K 107
Runnymede Rd. NE16: Whi 1G 97
NE20: Pon 7E 30
SR5: C'twn 4K 103
Runnymede Way NE3: Ken 1A 62
SR5: C'twn 4K 103
Runswick Av. NE12: Longb 6H 45
Runswick Cl. SR3: New S 2E 132
Rupert Sq. SR5: C'twn 4A 104
Rupert St. SR6: Whit 5H 89
Rupert Ter. NE15: Thro 5K 59
Rushall Pl. NE12: Longb 6K 45
Rushbury Ct. NE27: Back 6G 37
Rushcliffe SR6: Monk 4F 105
Rushey Gill DH7: B'don 1C 174
Rushford SR2: Ryh 2F 133
Rushie Av. NE15: Newc T 1J 81
Rushley Cres. NE21: Bla T 3C 80
Rushsyde Cl. NE16: Whi 2E 96
Rushton Av. SR2: Sund 5G 119
Rushyrig NE37: Wash 2E 114
Ruskin Av. DH2: Pelt 6G 127
DH5: Eas L 3J 157
NE11: Dun 5B 82
NE12: Longb 3A 46
NE63: Hir 5D 12
Ruskin Cl. DH9: Stly 2H 125
NE42: Pru 5D 76
Ruskin Cres. DH6: Thor 1J 179
NE34: S Shi 3H 87
Ruskin Dr. NE7: Newc T 3B 64
NE35: Bol C 6G 87
Ruskin Rd. DH3: Bir 4A 114
NE10: Gate 7K 83
NE16: Swa 6G 81
Russel Ct. NE2: Newc T 3H 63
Russell Av. NE34: S Shi 7C 68
Russell Cl. DH7: New B 4A 174
DH8: Con 6J 121
Russell Ct. NE8: Gate 5E 82
Russell Cres. TS29: Trim S 7D 180
Russell Sq. NE13: Sea B 3D 34
Russell St. DH7: Wat 6C 162
NE29: N Shi 7G 49
NE32: Jar 6C 66
NE33: S Shi 2J 67
NE37: Usw 7G 101
SR1: Sund 1G 119
Russell Ter. DH3: Bir 2K 113
(not continuous)
NE1: Newc T 7H 63 (4J 5)
NE22: Bed 1H 21
Russell Way NE11: Dun 4J 81
Rustic Ter. NE64: Newb S 2J 13
Ruswarp Dr. SR3: New S 3D 132
Ruth Av. NE21: Bla T 4C 80
Rutherford Av. SR7: S'hm 2H 147
Rutherford Cl. NE62: Chop 1G 17
Rutherford Ct. DH7: Lang P 4H 151
Rutherford Hall NE1: Newc T 3G 4
Rutherford Ho. SR8: Eas 7B 160
Rutherford Pl. NE61: Mor 1F 15
Rutherford Rd. NE37: Usw 6J 101
SR5: C'twn 4H 103
Rutherford Sq. SR5: C'twn 4H 103
Rutherford St. NE4: Newc T 1E 82 (6D 4)
NE24: Bly 2H 23
NE28: W'snd 2B 66
Rutherglen Rd. SR5: C'twn 4A 104
Rutherglen Sq. SR5: C'twn 4A 104
Rutland Av. NE6: Walk 6E 64
SR3: New S 2B 132
Rutland Pl. DH8: C'sde 3D 134
NE29: N Shi 6E 48
NE37: Usw 5H 101
Rutland Rd. DH8: C'sde 3C 134
NE28: W'snd 4E 64
NE31: Heb 3K 85
Rutland Sq. DH3: Bir 3A 114
Rutland St. DH5: Hett H 6F 145
NE34: S Shi 7H 67
NE63: Ash 4A 12
SR4: Sund 1B 118
SR7: S'hm 2K 147
(not continuous)
Rutland Ter. DH6: Has 3K 169
Rutland Wlk. SR8: Pet 4A 172
Ryal Cl. NE24: Bly 2G 23
NE25: Sea D 7H 27
Ryall Av. NE13: Bru V 7C 34
Ryal Ter. NE6: Walk 1D 84
Ryal Wlk. NE3: Ken 1K 61
Ryan Ter. DH6: Whe H 4A 180
Rydal NE10: Gate 6E 84
Rydal Av. DH5: Eas L 3J 157
DH9: Stly 4D 124
NE30: N Shi 2G 49
Rydal Cl. DH7: Sac 7D 140
NE12: Kil 1D 46
NE36: E Bol 6J 87
Rydal Cres. NE21: Bla T 6B 80
SR8: Pet 6C 172
Rydale Ct. TS29: Trim S 7C 180
Rydal Gdns. NE34: S Shi 7A 68
Rydal M. DH8: Lead 5B 122

Seaburn Cl.—Shilton Cl.

Seaburn Cl. SR6: Monk 3G 105
Seaburn Ct. SR6: Monk 3G 105
Seaburn Dr. DH4: Hou S 2C 144
Seaburn Fun Pk. 2G 105
Seaburn Gdns. NE9: Gate 4B 100
SR6: Monk 3G 105
Seaburn Gro. NE26: Sea S 4C 28
Seaburn Hill SR6: Monk 3G 105
Seaburn Station (Metro) 3E 104
Seaburn Ter. SR6: Monk 3H 105
Seaburn Vw. NE25: Sea D 4H 27
Seacombe Av. NE30: N Shi 1H 49
Seacrest Av. NE30: N Shi 1H 49
Sea Crest Rd. NE64: Newb S 1J 13
Seafield Rd. NE24: News 4J 23
Seafields SR6: Monk 2G 105
Seafield Ter. NE33: S Shi 2K 67
Seafield Vw. NE30: N Shi 4K 49
Seaforth Rd. SR3: Sund 5C 118
Seaforth St. NE24: Bly 1J 23
SEAHAM 3B 148
Seaham Cl. NE34: S Shi 7D 68
Seaham Gdns. NE9: Gate 5A 100
Seaham Grange Ind. Est.
SR7: Sea 7H 133
Seaham Leisure Cen. 3K 147
Seaham Rd. DH5: Hou S 2F 145
SR2: Ryh 3J 133
Seaham Station (Rail) 2A 148
Seaham St. SR3: New S 2C 132
SR7: S'hm 5C 148
Sea La. SR6: Monk 3G 105
SR6: Whit 7H 89
SEAL, THE 1C 70
Sea Rd. NE33: S Shi 1J 67
SR6: Monk 3F 105
Seascale Pl. NE9: Gate 3K 99
Seaside La. SR8: Eas 7K 159
Seaside La. Sth. SR8: Eas 7C 160
Seatoller Ct. SR3: New S 3B 132
SEATON
Seaham 2F 147
Whitley Bay 5K 27
Seaton Av. DH5: Hou S 2F 145
NE22: Bed 7K 17
NE23: Dud 2K 35
NE24: News 5G 23
NE64: Newb S 3H 13
SEATON BURN 3D 34
Seaton Cl. NE10: Gate 1F 101
Seaton Cres. NE25: H'wll 1K 37
NE25: Whit B 6E 38
SR7: S'hm 1G 147
Seaton Cft. NE23: Dud 3A 36
SEATON DELAVAL 7G 27
Seaton Delaval Hall 5A 28
Seaton Gdns. NE9: Gate 4A 100
Seaton Gro. SR7: Sea 2F 147
Seaton Holme (Discovery/Exhibition Cen.) 7J 159
Seaton La. SR7: Sea 1F 147
Seaton Pk. SR7: S'hm 2H 147
Seaton Pl. NE6: Walk 3C 84
NE13: Wide O 6C 34
Seaton Rd. NE27: Shir 7A 38
SR3: Sund 5K 117
SEATON SLUICE 4D 28
SEATON TERRACE 7H 27
Seatonville Cres. NE25: Whit B 1E 48
Seatonville Gro. NE25: Whit B 1E 48
Seatonville Rd. NE25: Whit B 7D 38
Sea Vw. NE63: N Sea 7E 12
SR2: Ryh 3J 133
SR8: Eas 1K 171
TS27: B Col 3K 183
Sea Vw. Cotts TS27: Hes 4D 182
Sea Vw. E. SR2: Sund 6H 119
Sea Vw. Gdns. SR6: Monk 4G 105
SR8: Pet 4E 172
Seaview Ind. Est. SR8: Pet 3E 172
Sea Vw. La. NE64: Newb S 2J 13
Sea Vw. Pk. NE23: Cra 4B 26
SR6: Whit 6F 89
Sea Vw. Rd. SR2: Sund 6G 119
Sea Vw. Rd. W. SR2: Sund 6F 119
Sea Vw. St. SR2: Sund 6H 119
Seaview Ter. NE33: S Shi 2A 68
Sea Vw. Ter. NE64: Newb S 2J 13
Sea Vw. Vs. NE23: Cra 4B 26
Sea Vw. Wlk. SR7: Mur 6G 147
Sea Way NE33: S Shi 2A 68
Second Av. DH2: Ches S 1K 127
(Drum Rd.)
DH2: Ches S 7K 127
(Gray Av.)
NE6: Newc T 5A 64 (1P 5)
NE11: Gate 1D 98
NE24: Bly 3H 23
NE29: N Shi 1B 66
NE61: Mor 1H 15
NE63: Hir 4B 12
Second St. DH8: Con 7K 121
DH8: Lead 3A 122
(not continuous)
DH9: Stly 7D 124
Second St. NE8: Gate 5F 83
TS27: B Col 2H 183
Secretan Way NE33: S Shi 3J 67
Sedbergh Rd. NE30: N Shi 2G 49
Sedgefield Ct. NE12: Kil 1A 46
SEDGELETCH 7B 130
Sedgeletch Ind. Est. DH4: Hou S 7A 130
Sedgeletch Rd. DH4: Hou S 1A 144
Sedgemoor NE12: Kil 7B 36
Sedgemoor Av. NE15: Newc T 1G 81
Sedgewick Pl. NE8: Gate 5G 83
Sedley Rd. NE28: W'snd 4F 65
Sedling Rd. NE38: Wash 6F 115
Sefton Av. NE6: Newc T 4A 64
Sefton Ct. NE23: Cra 1A 26
Sefton Sq. SR3: Sund 5A 118
Segedunum Cres. NE28: W'snd 1J 65
Segedunum Roman Fort, Baths & Mus. 5G 65
Segedunum Way NE28: W'snd 4F 65
SEGHILL 2D 36
Seghill Ind. Est. NE23: Seg 1D 36
Seine Ct. NE32: Jar 7C 66
Selborne Av. NE9: Gate 3G 99
Selborne Gdns. DH8: Shot B 3F 121
NE2: Newc T 5J 63
Selbourne Cl. NE23: Cra 4G 25
Selbourne St. NE33: S Shi 3K 67
SR6: Monk 6F 105
(not continuous)
Selbourne Ter. NE24: Camb 5H 19
Selby Cl. NE23: Cra 1K 25
Selby Ct. NE6: Walk 2D 84
NE32: Jar 6B 66
Selby Gdns. DH8: C'sde 1E 134
NE6: Walk 5D 64
NE28: W'snd 2F 65
Selby Sq. SR3: Sund 5A 118
Selina Pl. SR6: Monk 6G 105
Selkirk Cres. DH3: Bir 2A 114
Selkirk Gro. NE23: Cra 1A 26
Selkirk Sq. SR3: Sund 5K 117
Selkirk St. NE32: Jar 3E 86
Selkirk Way NE29: N Shi 4C 48
Selsdon Av. SR4: Sund 6G 117
Selsey Ct. NE10: Gate 1C 100
Selwood Ct. NE34: S Shi 1B 88
Selwyn Av. NE25: Whit B 1D 48
Selwyn Cl. NE5: Newc T 2K 61
Senet Ent. Cen. NE63: Ash 5B 12
Serin Ho. NE5: Newc T 2G 61
Serlby Cl. NE37: Usw 6G 101
Serlby Pk. DH5: Hett H 7H 145
Seton Av. NE34: S Shi 2F 87
Seton Wlk. NE34: S Shi 2F 87
Setting Stones NE38: Wash 1E 128
Settlingstone Cl. NE7: Newc T 2B 64
Sevenacres DH3: Gt Lum 2F 143
Sevenoaks Dr. SR4: Sund 5G 117
Seventh Av. DH2: Ches S 6K 127
NE6: Newc T 6A 64 (1P 5)
NE11: Gate 3F 99
NE24: Bly 3H 23
(not continuous)
NE61: Mor 1H 15
NE63: Hir 5C 12
Seventh Row NE63: Ash 3K 11
Seventh St. SR8: Pet 5E 172
(not continuous)
TS27: B Col 1H 183
Severn Av. NE31: Heb 3J 85
Severn Cl. SR8: Pet 1A 182
Severn Ct. SR3: New S 3B 132
Severn Cres. DH9: Stly 4E 124
Severn Dr. NE32: Jar 4C 86
Severn Gdns. NE8: Gate 5K 83
Severn Ho's. NE37: Wash 7A 102
Severn St. NE17: C'wl 6A 94
Severs Ter. NE5: Cal 6B 42
Severus Rd. NE4: Newc T 6A 62
Seymour Ct. NE11: Dun 5C 82
NE63: N Sea 4F 13
Seymour Sq. SR3: Sund 5A 118
Seymour St. DH8: Con 7H 121
NE11: Dun 5C 82
NE29: N Shi 1G 67
SR8: Pet 6F 173
Seymour Ter. DH5: Eas L 2H 157
NE40: Ryton 1E 78
Shadfen Cres. NE61: Peg 4A 10
Shadfen Pk. Rd. NE30: N Shi 1G 49
SHADFORTH 5E 168
Shadforth Cl. SR8: Pet 1J 181
Shadon Way DH3: Bir 5C 114
Shaftesbury Av. NE26: Whit B 4F 39
NE32: Jar 7D 66
NE34: S Shi 7D 66
SR2: Ryh 2G 133
TS27: B Col 1H 183
Shaftesbury Cres. NE30: N Shi 1G 49
SR3: Sund 5B 118
TS27: B Col 1G 183
Shaftesbury Gro.
NE6: Newc T 6K 63 (1N 5)
Shaftesbury Rd. TS27: B Col 7G 173
Shaftesbury Wlk. NE8: Gate 4E 82
Shafto Cl. DH8: Con 2K 135
Shafto Ct. NE15: Newc T 1H 81
Shaftoe Cl. NE40: Ryton 3D 78
Shaftoe Ct. NE3: Ken 5C 44
NE12: Kil 1B 46
Shaftoe Cres. NE46: Hex 1C 70
Shaftoe Leazes NE46: Hex 1B 70
Shaftoe Rd. SR3: Sund 6K 117
Shaftoe Sq. SR3: Sund 6K 117
Shaftoe Way NE13: Din 4H 33
Shafto St. NE15: Newc T 1G 81
NE28: W'snd 2J 65
Shafto St. Nth. NE28: W'snd 2J 65
Shafto Ter. DH9: Stly 6K 125
(Craghead La.)
DH9: Stly 1F 125
(Newburn Rd.)
NE37: Wash 1H 115
Shaftsbury Dr. DH7: B'don 3C 174
Shakespeare Av. NE31: Heb 7J 65
TS27: B Col 7G 173
Shakespeare Cl. DH9: Stly 2H 125
(not continuous)
Shakespeare St. DH5: Hou S 3E 144
DH6: Whe H 3B 180
NE1: Newc T 1F 83 (5F 4)
NE8: Gate 4J 83
NE28: W'snd 2K 65
NE32: Jar 5B 66
NE33: S Shi 4K 67
SR5: S'wck 5D 104
SR7: S'hm 3B 148
Shakespeare Ter. DH2: Pelt 6G 127
SR2: Sund 3E 118 (6G 7)
SR8: Eas 7A 160
Shalcombe Cl. SR3: New S 3C 132
Shallcross SR2: Sund 4D 118
Shallon Ct. NE63: Ash 5A 12
Shalstone NE37: Usw 6K 101
Shamrock Cl. NE15: Lem 5C 60
Shandon Way NE3: Ken 7A 44
SHANKHOUSE 7A 22
Shanklin Pl. NE23: Cra 4G 25
Shannon Cl. SR5: C'twn 6G 103
Shannon Ct. NE3: Ken 5J 43
Shap Cl. NE38: Wash 5H 115
Shap Ct. SR3: New S 3B 132
Shapers *2D 118*
(off Chester Rd.)
Shap La. NE5: Newc T 4G 61
Shap Rd. NE30: N Shi 2G 49
Sharnford Cl. NE27: Back 6H 37
Sharon Cl. NE12: Kil 2K 45
Sharp Cres. DH1: Dur 1E 166
(not continuous)
Sharpendon St. NE31: Heb 6J 65
Sharperton Dr. NE3: Gos 3C 44
Sharpley Dr. SR7: S'hm 1G 147
Shaw Av. NE34: S Shi 2H 87
Shawbrow Cl. NE7: Newc T 2C 64
Shawdon Cl. NE5: Newc T 1H 61
Shaw Gdns. NE10: Gate 6F 85
Shaw La. DH8: Ebc 5G 107
NE17: Ham C 4J 107
Shaws La. NE46: Hex 2A 70
(not continuous)
Shaws Pk. NE46: Hex 7A 50
Shaw St. SR7: S'hm 3B 148
Shaw Wood Cl. DH1: Dur 1J 165
Shearlegs Rd. NE8: Gate 3J 83 (9M 5)
Shearwater SR6: Whit 3H 89
Shearwater Av. NE12: Longb 5J 45
Shearwater Cl. NE5: Newc T 1H 61
Shearwater Way NE24: News 5J 23
Sheelin Av. DH2: Ches S 1A 142
Sheen Cl. DH4: W Rai 1A 156
Sheen Ct. NE3: Ken 7H 43
Sheepfolds Nth. SR5: Monk 7F 105 (1J 7)
Sheepfolds Rd. SR5: Monk 7F 105 (1J 7)
SHEEP HILL 2B 110
Sheep Hill NE16: Burn 2B 110
SHEEPWASH 7G 11
Sheepwash Av. NE62: Chop 1G 17
Sheepwash Bank NE62: Chop 1G 17
Sheepwash Rd. NE61: Chop, Peg 4G 11
NE62: Chop 4G 11
Shefton Mus. of Greek Art & Archaeology, The 2E 4
Sheldon Ct. NE12: Longb 3A 46
Sheldon Gro. NE3: Ken 2C 62
NE23: Cra 1K 25
Sheldon Rd. NE34: S Shi 4B 68
Sheldon St. NE32: Jar 6B 66
Shelford Gdns. NE15: Lem 6E 60
Shellbark DH4: Hou S 3K 129
Shelley Av. DH5: Eas L 3K 157
NE9: Spri 6D 100
NE34: S Shi 1D 88
NE35: Bol C 6G 87
Shelley Cl. DH9: Stly 3G 125
Shelley Ct. DH2: Pelt 6H 127
Shelley Cres. NE24: Bly 4G 23
Shelley Dr. NE8: Gate 4J 83
Shelley Gdns. DH2: Pelt 6G 127
Shelley Rd. NE15: Thro 6K 59
Shelley Sq. SR8: Eas 1A 172
Shelley St. SR7: S'hm 3B 148
Shepherd Cl. NE23: Dud 5A 36
Shepherd's Quay NE29: N Shi 1H 67
Shepherd St. SR4: Sund 1C 118
Shepherds Way NE36: W Bol 7G 87
Shepherd Way NE38: Wash 6J 115
Sheppard Ter. SR5: C'twn 6H 103
Sheppey Ct. SR3: New S 3C 132
Shepton Cotts. NE16: Sun 4J 97
Sheraton NE10: Gate 2E 100
Sheraton St. NE2: Newc T 5D 62 (1B 4)
Sherborne DH3: Gt Lum 2F 143
Sherborne Av. NE29: N Shi 4D 48
SHERBURN 3K 167
Sherburn Grange Nth. NE32: Jar 1A 86
Sherburn Grange Sth. NE32: Jar 1A 86
Sherburn Grn. NE39: Row G 4K 95
Sherburn Gro. DH4: Hou S 1C 144
SHERBURN HILL 3C 168
SHERBURN HOUSE 5H 167
Sherburn Pk. Dr. NE39: Row G 4J 95
Sherburn Rd. DH1: Dur 2D 166
Sherburn Rd. Est. DH1: Dur 3E 166
Sherburn Rd. Flats *DH1: Dur 2D 166*
(off Sherburn Rd.)
Sherburn Sports Cen. 2K 167
Sherburn Ter. DH8: Con 7J 121
NE9: Gate 5A 100
NE17: Ham C 3H 107
Sherburn Vs. *DH8: Con 6H 121*
(off Maple St.)
Sherburn Way NE10: Gate 1G 101
Sherfield Dr. NE7: Newc T 3B 64
Sheridan Dr. DH9: Stly 3G 125
Sheridan Grn. NE38: Wash 7E 114
Sheridan Rd. NE34: S Shi 3G 87
Sheridan St. SR4: Sund 1B 118
SHERIFF HILL 2J 99
Sheriff Mt. Nth. NE9: Gate 7J 83
Sheriff Mt. Sth. NE9: Gate 7J 83
Sheriffs Cl. NE10: Gate 6K 83
Sheriffs Hall Vs. NE9: Gate 1J 99
Sheriff's Highway NE9: Gate 1J 99
Sheriff's Moor Av. DH5: Eas L 3J 157
Sheringham Av. NE29: N Shi 5D 48
Sheringham Cl. SR3: New S 5C 132
Sheringham Dr. NE23: Cra 4G 25
Sheringham Gdns. NE15: Thro 3F 59
Sheringham Ho. NE38: Wash 4K 115
Sherringham Av. NE3: Ken 7A 44
Sherwood NE27: Shir 2B 48
Sherwood Cl. DH8: Shot B 2G 121
NE27: Shir 2B 48
NE38: Wash 3H 115
Sherwood Ct. SR3: New S 3C 132
Sherwood Pl. NE3: Gos 2E 44
Sherwood Vw. NE28: W'snd 1E 64
Shetland Ct. SR3: New S 3C 132
Shibdon Bank NE21: Bla T 5C 80
Shibdon Bus. Pk. NE21: Bla T 3E 80
Shibdon Ct. *NE21: Bla T 3C 80*
(off Shibdon Rd.)
Shibdon Cres. NE21: Bla T 4D 80
Shibdon Pk. Vw. NE21: Bla T 4D 80
Shibdon Rd. NE21: Bla T 3C 80
Shibdon Way NE21: Bla T 4F 81
Shield Av. NE16: Swa 5H 81
Shieldclose NE37: Wash 2E 114
Shield Ct. NE2: Newc T 6H 63 (2J 5)
NE46: Hex 3D 70
SHIELDFIELD 7H 63 (4J 5)
Shieldfield Ho. NE2: Newc T 7H 63 (3J 5)
Shieldfield Ind. Est.
NE2: Newc T 7H 63 (4K 5)
Shieldfield La. NE2: Newc T 7H 63 (4K 5)
Shield Gro. NE3: Gos 6F 45
SHIELD ROW 1G 125
Shield Row DH9: Stly 2F 125
Shield Row Gdns. DH9: Stly 1F 125
Shieldrow La. DH9: Ann P 6A 124
Shields La. NE6: Newc T 7A 64
Shields Pl. DH5: Hou S 1E 144
Shields Rd. DH3: Ches S, Gt Lum 4B 128
NE6: Newc T 7K 63 (4N 5)
NE6: Walk 6A 64
NE10: Gate 5E 84
(Cartmel Pk.)
NE10: Gate 6D 84
(St Mary's Ter.)
NE22: H Bri 4D 20
NE25: Whit B 1F 49
NE61: Mor 1G 15
SR6: Cle, S Shi 3B 88
SR6: Monk, S'wck 1D 104
Shields Rd. By-Pass
NE6: Newc T 7K 63 (4N 5)
Shields Rd. W. NE6: Newc T 7J 63 (4M 5)
Shield St. NE2: Newc T 7H 63 (4J 5)
Shiel Gdns. NE23: Cra 4G 25
Shillaw Pl. NE23: Dud 5K 35
Shillmoor Cl. DH2: Ches S 1H 141
Shilmore Rd. NE3: Ken 7B 44
Shilton Cl. NE34: S Shi 1C 88

Shincliffe—South Hetton

SHINCLIFFE . . . 6E 166
Shincliffe Av. SR5: C'twn . . . 5J 103
Shincliffe Gdns. NE9: Gate . . . 4A 100
Shincliffe La. DH1: H Shin, Sher . . . 5F 167
SHINEY ROW . . . 4A 130
Shinwell Cres. DH6: Thor . . . 1J 179
(not continuous)
Shinwell Ter. DH6: Whe H . . . 3A 180
SR7: Mur . . . 7D 146
Shipby SR3: New S . . . 2B 132
SHIPCOTE . . . 6G 83
Shipcote La. NE8: Gate . . . 6H 83
Shipcote Ter. NE8: Gate . . . 6H 83
Shipley Art Gallery . . . 6H 83
Shipley Av. NE4: Newc T . . . 7A 62
SR6: Monk . . . 3G 105
Shipley Ct. NE8: Gate . . . 5H 83
Shipley Pl. NE6: Newc T . . . 7K 63 (4P 5)
Shipley Ri. NE6: Newc T . . . 7A 64 (4P 5)
Shipley Rd. NE30: N Shi . . . 5J 49
Shipley St. NE15: Lem . . . 7C 60
Shipley Wlk. NE6: Newc T . . . 7K 63 (4P 5)
Shipton Cl. NE35: Bol C . . . 5E 86
Shire Chase DH1: Dur . . . 3B 154
Shire Farm Gro. NE63: Ash . . . 5J 11
SHIREMOOR . . . 1K 47
Shiremoor By-Pass NE27: Back . . . 1G 47
Shiremoor Station (Metro) . . . 1K 47
Shirlaw Cl. NE5: Newc T . . . 1F 61
Shirley Gdns. SR3: Sund . . . 5D 118
Shirwood Av. NE16: Whi . . . 2G 97
Shop Row DH4: Hou S . . . 4C 130
Shop Spouts NE21: Bla T . . . 3C 80
Shoreham Ct. NE3: Ken . . . 6J 43
Shoreham Sq. SR3: Sund . . . 5A 118
Shorestone Av. NE30: N Shi . . . 1H 49
Shore St. SR6: Monk . . . 6F 105
Shoreswood Dr. SR3: New S . . . 2D 132
Short Gro. SR7: Mur . . . 7C 146
Shortridge St. NE33: S Shi . . . 2K 67
Shortridge Ter. NE2: Newc T . . . 4H 63
Short Row DH4: Hou S . . . 5J 129
NE5: Cal . . . 6B 42
Shot Factory La. NE4: Newc T . . . 3E 82 (9D 4)
Shotley Av. SR5: S'wck . . . 4D 104
SHOTLEY BRIDGE . . . 2F 121
Shotley Ct. NE63: Ash . . . 5J 11
Shotley Gdns. NE9: Gate . . . 7J 83
Shotley Gro. Rd. DH8: Con, Shot B . . . 4D 120
SHOTTON . . . 1A 24
Shotton Av. NE24: Bly . . . 3J 23
Shotton Bank SR8: Pet . . . 3H 181
SHOTTON COLLIERY . . . 6F 171
Shotton Colliery Ind. Est.
DH6: Shot C . . . 5F 171
SHOTTON EDGE . . . 4A 24
Shotton La. DH6: Pet, Shot C . . . 5F 171
(not continuous)
NE23: Cra, Nel V . . . 7D 20
NE61: Sea B . . . 1A 24
SR8: Pet . . . 7J 171
Shotton Rd. SR8: Pet . . . 5D 172
(Rosedale Ter.)
SR8: Pet, Shot C . . . 5G 171
(Burdon Dr.)
Shotton St. NE23: E Har . . . 6K 21
Shotton Way NE10: Gate . . . 1J 101
Shrewsbury Cl. NE7: Newc T . . . 1B 64
SR8: Pet . . . 7K 171
Shrewsbury Cres. SR3: Sund . . . 5A 118
Shrewsbury Dr. NE27: Back . . . 6G 37
Shrewsbury St. NE11: Dun . . . 6B 82
SR7: S'hm . . . 5B 148
Shrewsbury Ter. NE33: S Shi . . . 6J 67
Shrigley Cl. NE38: Wash . . . 1F 129
Shrigley Gdns. NE3: Ken . . . 7B 44
Shropshire Dr. DH1: Carr . . . 2G 167
Shummard Cl. DH4: Hou S . . . 4K 129
Shunner Cl. NE37: Wash . . . 2E 114
Sibthorpe St. NE29: N Shi . . . 7H 49
Side NE1: Newc T . . . 2G 83 (7G 4)
(not continuous)
Side Cliff Rd. SR6: Monk . . . 4F 105
Side Gallery . . . 7G 4
Sidegate DH1: Dur . . . 2A 166 (1B 6)
Side La. NE61: Hep . . . 3A 16
Sidgate NE1: Newc T . . . 4F 4
(off Eldon Sq.)
Sidings, The DH1: Dur . . . 2C 166
Sidlaw Av. DH2: Ches S . . . 7J 127
NE29: N Shi . . . 3F 49
Sidlaw Ct. NE63: N Sea . . . 6C 12
Sidmouth Cl. DH4: Hou S . . . 5C 130
SR7: Mur . . . 4H 147
Sidmouth Rd. NE9: Gate . . . 4H 99
NE29: N Shi . . . 6C 48
Sidney Cl. DH9: Stly . . . 3H 125
Sidney Cres. NE64: Newb S . . . 4H 13
Sidney Gro. NE4: Newc T . . . 7C 62
NE8: Gate . . . 5F 83
Sidney St. NE24: Bly . . . 2H 23
NE29: N Shi . . . 7G 49
NE35: Bol C . . . 6F 87
Sidney Ter. DH9: Tan L . . . 1D 124
Silent Bank DH6: Cass . . . 1E 178
Silkeys La. NE29: N Shi . . . 7F 49
Silkstun Ct. SR3: New S . . . 2C 132
SILKSWORTH . . . 3A 132
Silksworth Cl. SR3: New S . . . 1B 132
Silksworth Gdns. NE9: Gate . . . 5A 100
Silksworth Hall Dr. SR3: New S . . . 3B 132
Silksworth La. SR3: E Her . . . 2J 131
(not continuous)
SR3: New S . . . 2A 132
SR3: Sund . . . 5C 118
SR3: Sund . . . 4D 118
Silksworth Rd. SR3: E Her . . . 2J 131
SR3: New S . . . 2A 132
Silksworth Row SR1: Sund . . . 1E 118 (3G 7)
(not continuous)
Silksworth Sports Complex . . . 7B 118
Silksworth Ter. SR3: New S . . . 2C 132
Silksworth Way SR3: New S . . . 3A 132
Silkwood Cl. NE23: Cra . . . 1K 25
Silloth Av. NE5: Newc T . . . 5G 61
Silloth Dr. NE37: Usw . . . 5G 101
Silloth Pl. NE30: N Shi . . . 2H 49
Silloth Rd. SR3: Sund . . . 6K 117
Silvas Ct. NE61: Mor . . . 6G 9
Silverbirch Ind. Est. NE12: Kil . . . 7K 35
Silverbriar SR5: Sund . . . 6B 104
Silver Ct. NE9: Gate . . . 6J 83
Silver Courts DH7: B'don . . . 1D 174
Silverdale SR3: New S . . . 5C 132
Silverdale Av. NE10: Gate . . . 6H 85
Silverdale Dr. NE21: Bla T . . . 5K 79
Silverdale Rd. NE23: Cra . . . 1K 25
Silverdale Ter. NE8: Gate . . . 6H 83
Silverdale Way NE16: Whi . . . 2F 97
NE34: S Shi . . . 3F 87
Silver Fox Way NE27: N Shi, Shir . . . 4J 47
SILVER HILL . . . 2F 51
Silverhill Dr. NE5: Newc T . . . 6G 61
Silverlink Bus. Pk. NE27: N Shi . . . 4A 48
NE28: W'snd . . . 5K 47
Silverlink Nth., The NE27: Shir . . . 3J 47
Silverlink, The NE28: W'snd . . . 5A 48
Silver Lonnen NE5: Newc T . . . 6G 61
Silvermere Dr. NE40: Ryton . . . 2H 79
Silverstone NE12: Kil . . . 1C 46
Silverstone Way NE37: Usw . . . 7J 101
Silver St. DH1: Dur . . . 3A 166 (3B 6)
DH8: Con . . . 5F 121
NE30: N Shi . . . 5K 49
SR1: Sund . . . 7H 105
Silvertop Gdns. NE40: G'sde . . . 5E 78
Silvertop Ter. NE40: G'sde . . . 5D 78
Silverwood Gdns. NE11: Gate . . . 2D 98
Simonburn NE38: Wash . . . 4D 114
Simonburn Av. NE4: Newc T . . . 5A 62
NE29: N Shi . . . 6C 48
Simonburn La. NE63: Hir . . . 5D 12
Simon Pl. NE13: Wide O . . . 6C 34
SIMONSIDE . . . 1G 87
Simonside NE26: Sea S . . . 6D 28
NE34: S Shi . . . 1G 87
NE42: Pru . . . 5D 76
Simonside Av. NE28: W'snd . . . 1K 65
NE62: Chop . . . 7J 11
Simonside Cl. NE26: Sea S . . . 6D 28
NE61: Mor . . . 1D 14
Simonside E. Ind. Est. NE32: Jar . . . 1E 86
Simonside Hall NE34: S Shi . . . 1F 87
Simonside Ind. Est. NE32: Jar . . . 1D 86
Simonside Pl. NE9: Gate . . . 4A 100
Simonside Rd. NE21: Bla T . . . 5C 80
SR3: Sund . . . 5K 117
Simonside Ter. NE6: Newc T . . . 5K 63
NE64: Newb S . . . 3J 13
Simonside Vw. NE16: Whi . . . 7G 81
NE20: Pon . . . 4H 31
NE32: Jar . . . 2C 86
Simonside Wlk. NE11: Gate . . . 2C 98
Simonside Way NE12: Kil . . . 7D 36
Simpson Cl. NE35: Bol C . . . 6E 86
(not continuous)
Simpson Ct. NE63: N Sea . . . 4E 12
Simpsons Memorial Homes
NE40: Ryton . . . 2E 78
Simpson St. DH9: Stly . . . 2F 125
NE24: Bly . . . 1J 23
NE29: N Shi . . . 7E 48
NE30: N Shi . . . 7J 39
NE40: Ryton . . . 2J 79
SR4: Sund . . . 7D 104
Simpson Ter. NE2: Newc T . . . 7H 63 (4J 5)
NE15: Thro . . . 4B 60
Sinclair Ct. NE13: Bru V . . . 5C 34
Sinclair Dr. DH3: Ches S . . . 1B 128
Sinclair Gdns. NE25: Sea D . . . 7H 27
Sinderby Cl. NE3: Gos . . . 4F 45
Sir Godfrey Thomson Ct.
NE10: Gate . . . 6A 84
Sitwell Rd. DH9: Stly . . . 3G 125
Sixth Av. DH2: Ches S . . . 6K 127
NE6: Newc T . . . 6A 64 (1P 5)
NE11: Gate . . . 3E 98
NE24: Bly . . . 4H 23
NE61: Mor . . . 1H 15
NE63: Hir . . . 5B 12
Sixth St. DH8: Con . . . 1K 135
SR8: Pet . . . 5E 172
TS27: B Col . . . 1H 183
Skaylock Dr. NE38: Wash . . . 5E 114
Skegness Pde. NE31: Heb . . . 4A 86
Skelder Av. NE12: Longb . . . 6K 45
Skelton Ct. NE3: Ken . . . 4A 44
Skerne Cl. SR8: Pet . . . 1A 182
Skerne Gro. DH8: Lead . . . 4B 122
Skiddaw Cl. SR8: Pet . . . 6C 172
Skiddaw Ct. DH9: Ann P . . . 6K 123
Skiddaw Dr. SR6: Monk . . . 2E 104
Skiddaw Pl. NE9: Gate . . . 3K 99
Skinnerburn Rd.
NE4: Newc T . . . 4D 82 (10A 4)
Skipper Cl. NE11: Gate . . . 7D 82
Skippers Mdw. DH7: Ush M . . . 3D 164
(not continuous)
Skipsea Vw. SR2: Ryh . . . 2F 133
(not continuous)
Skipsey Ct. NE29: N Shi . . . 2D 66
Skipton Cl. NE22: Bed . . . 6F 17
NE23: Cra . . . 1A 26
Skipton Grn. NE9: Gate . . . 5K 99
Skirlaw Cl. NE38: Wash . . . 4H 115
Ski Vw. SR3: New S . . . 2B 132
Skye Ct. SR3: New S . . . 3C 132
Skye Gro. NE32: Jar . . . 4E 86
Slaidburn Rd. DH9: Stly . . . 2F 125
Slake Rd. NE32: Jar . . . 5D 66
Slake Ter. NE34: S Shi . . . 6H 67
Slaley NE38: Wash . . . 7J 115
Slaley Cl. NE10: Gate . . . 7G 85
Slaley Ct. NE22: Bed . . . 7J 17
SR3: New S . . . 3C 132
Slater Pl. DH6: Bow . . . 5H 177
Slater's Row DH3: Gt Lum . . . 3E 142
(not continuous)
Slatyford La. NE5: Newc T . . . 5G 61
Sled La. NE41: Wylam . . . 2A 78
Sledmere Cl. SR8: Pet . . . 4B 172
Sleekburn Av. NE22: Bed . . . 5B 18
Sleekburn Ho. NE22: Bed . . . 5B 18
Sleetburn La. DH7: B'don . . . 6F 165
Slingley Cl. SR7: S'hm . . . 1G 147
Slingsby Gdns. NE7: Newc T . . . 2B 64
Slipway, The NE10: Gate . . . 4E 84
Sloane Ct. NE2: Newc T . . . 6G 63 (2G 4)
Smailes La. NE39: Row G . . . 5G 95
Smailes St. DH9: Stly . . . 4E 124
SMALLBURN . . . 2H 31
Smallholdings NE64: Newb S . . . 1G 13
Smallhope Dr. DH7: Lan . . . 7K 137
Smeaton Ct. NE28: W'snd . . . 4A 66
Smeaton St. NE28: W'snd . . . 4A 66
Smillie Cl. SR8: Pet . . . 5B 172
Smillie Rd. SR8: Pet . . . 3C 172
Smithburn Rd. NE10: Gate . . . 7B 84
Smith Cl. DH6: Sher . . . 3K 167
Smithfield DH1: Dur . . . 3K 153
Smith Gro. SR2: Ryh . . . 3G 133
Smith's Ter. DH5: Eas L . . . 2H 157
Smith St. NE33: S Shi . . . 5H 67
SR2: Ryh . . . 3H 133
Smith St. Sth. SR2: Ryh . . . 3H 133
Smithyford NE9: Gate . . . 6J 99
Smithy La. NE9: Gate, Kib . . . 6G 99
NE11: Kib . . . 6G 99
Smithy Sq. NE23: Cra . . . 4K 25
Smithy St. NE33: S Shi . . . 2J 67
Smuggler's Cave . . . 1K 49
Smyrna Pl. SR1: Sund . . . 2G 119
Snaith Ter. TS28: Win . . . 5F 181
Sniperley Gro. DH1: Dur . . . 6H 153
Snipes Dene NE39: Row G . . . 4J 95
Snowdon Ct. DH9: Ann P . . . 6J 123
Snowdon Gdns. NE11: Gate . . . 1C 98
Snowdon Gro. NE36: W Bol . . . 7H 87
Snowdon Pl. SR8: Pet . . . 7J 171
Snowdon Ter. NE39: H Spen . . . 2D 94
SR2: Ryh . . . 2H 133
Snowdrop Av. SR8: Pet . . . 5D 172
Snowdrop Cl. NE21: Bla T . . . 4A 80
Snow's Grn. Rd. DH8: Shot B . . . 3E 120
Soane Gdns. NE34: S Shi . . . 3K 87
Softley Pl. NE15: Newc T . . . 6F 61
Solar Ho. SR1: Sund . . . 4J 7
Solingen Est. NE24: Bly . . . 4K 23
Solway Av. NE30: N Shi . . . 2G 49
Solway Rd. NE31: Heb . . . 2K 85
Solway Sq. SR3: Sund . . . 5A 118
Solway St. NE6: Newc T . . . 2A 84
Somerford NE9: Spri . . . 5D 100
Somersby Dr. NE3: Ken . . . 7A 44
Somerset Cl. NE63: Ash . . . 3J 11
Somerset Cotts. SR3: New S . . . 7C 118
Somerset Gdns. NE28: W'snd . . . 2E 64
Somerset Gro. NE29: N Shi . . . 4D 48
Somerset Pl. NE4: Newc T . . . 2D 82 (6A 4)
Somerset Rd. DH8: C'sde . . . 3C 134
NE31: Heb . . . 3K 85
SR3: Sund . . . 5K 117
Somerset Sq. SR3: Sund . . . 5K 117
Somerset St. SR3: New S . . . 1C 132
Somerset Ter. NE36: E Bol . . . 7K 87
Somerton Ct. NE3: Ken . . . 6J 43
Somervyl Av. NE12: Longb . . . 6H 45
Somervyl Ct. NE12: Longb . . . 5H 45
Sophia SR7: S'hm . . . 3B 148
Sophia St. SR7: S'hm . . . 3B 148
Sophy St. SR5: S'wck . . . 5E 104
Sorley St. SR4: Sund . . . 2C 118
Sorrel Cl. NE63: Ash . . . 5A 12
Sorrel Gdns. NE34: S Shi . . . 3A 88
Sorrell Cl. NE4: Newc T . . . 6K 61
Soulby Ct. NE3: Ken . . . 4K 43
Sourmilk Hill La. NE9: Gate . . . 1J 99
Souter Point Lighthouse . . . 1H 89
Souter Rd. NE3: Gos . . . 7C 44
Souter Vw. SR6: Whit . . . 4H 89
South App. DH2: Ches S . . . 6K 127
South Av. DH6: Shad . . . 4E 168
NE16: Whi . . . 2H 97
NE34: S Shi . . . 1B 88
NE37: Usw . . . 7G 101
NE40: Ryton . . . 1G 79
South Bailey DH1: Dur . . . 4A 166 (5C 6)
South Bend NE3: Gos . . . 3D 44
SOUTH BENTS . . . 1H 105
Sth. Bents Av. SR6: Monk . . . 1G 105
SOUTH BENWELL . . . 2A 82
Sth. Benwell Rd. NE15: Newc T . . . 2J 81
SOUTH BOLDON . . . 7H 87
Southburn Cl. DH4: Hou S . . . 2C 144
South Burns DH3: Ches S . . . 5A 128
Sth. Burn Ter. DH4: Hou S . . . 3C 130
South Cliff SR6: Monk . . . 5H 105
Southcliff NE26: Whit B . . . 7J 39
South Cl. DH5: Eas L . . . 3K 157
NE34: S Shi . . . 1B 88
NE40: Ryton . . . 2G 79
SR2: Ryh . . . 3H 133
(off Stockton Rd.)
Sth. Coronation St. SR7: Mur . . . 1F 159
(off George St.)
Southcote NE16: Whi . . . 2G 97
Sth. Cramlington Ind. Est. NE23: Dud . . . 1H 35
South Cres. DH1: Dur . . . 1K 165
DH4: Hou S . . . 1K 143
NE35: Bol C . . . 6F 87
NE38: Wash . . . 1F 129
SR7: S'hm . . . 3C 148
SR8: Pet . . . 3C 172
South Cft. NE12: Longb . . . 5C 46
Southcroft NE38: Wash . . . 7H 115
Sth. Cross St. DH8: Lead . . . 5A 122
NE3: Gos . . . 7E 44
South Dene NE34: S Shi . . . 1H 87
Southdowns DH2: Ches S . . . 7A 128
South Dr. NE13: Sea B . . . 4A 24
NE13: Wool . . . 4G 43
NE31: Heb . . . 2G 85
NE43: Newt . . . 6E 54
SR6: Cle . . . 5B 88
Sth. Durham Ct. SR1: Sund . . . 2G 119
Sth. East Vw. SR8: Pet . . . 5F 173
Sth. Eldon St. NE33: S Shi . . . 6H 67
South End DH6: H Pitt . . . 6C 156
SR6: Cle . . . 6A 88
Southend Av. NE24: Bly . . . 3G 23
Southend Pde. NE31: Heb . . . 4A 86
Southend Rd. NE9: Gate . . . 3J 99
SR3: Sund . . . 6A 118
Southend Ter. NE9: Gate . . . 1K 99
Southern Cl. NE63: N Sea . . . 4F 13
Southern Prom. NE26: Whit B . . . 6J 39
Southern Rd. NE6: Walk . . . 2D 84
Southern Way NE40: Ryton . . . 2G 79
Southernwood DH8: Con . . . 7J 121
NE9: Gate . . . 6J 99
Southey St. NE33: S Shi . . . 5J 67
(not continuous)
Southfield DH2: Pelt . . . 2G 127
NE61: Mor . . . 2F 15
Southfield Gdns. NE16: Whi . . . 7J 81
Southfield Grn. NE16: Whi . . . 1J 97
Southfield La. NE17: Ham C, Ham M . . . 5C 108
Southfield Rd. NE12: Longb . . . 6A 46
NE16: Whi . . . 1J 97
NE34: S Shi . . . 5B 68
Southfields DH9: Stly . . . 5E 124
NE23: Dud . . . 4J 35
Southfields Ho. NE6: Newc T . . . 3P 5
(off Heaton Rd.)
Southfield Ter. NE6: Walk . . . 2E 84
NE16: Whi . . . 1J 97
Southfield Way DH1: Dur . . . 7J 153
Sth. Foreshore NE33: S Shi . . . 3B 68
Southfork NE15: Lem . . . 5C 60
Sth. Frederick St. NE33: S Shi . . . 6H 67
South Front NE2: Newc T . . . 5G 63 (1G 4)
Southgate NE12: Kil . . . 2A 46
Southgate Ct. NE12: Longb . . . 6H 45
Southgate Wood NE61: Mor . . . 3G 15
SOUTH GOSFORTH . . . 1G 63
South Gosforth Station (Metro) . . . 1G 63
South Grn. DH6: Hett . . . 7C 176
South Gro. NE40: Ryton . . . 2H 79
South Harbour NE24: Bly . . . 3K 23
SOUTH HETTON . . . 4C 158

Stanhope Way—Stratford Cl.

Stanhope Way NE4: Newc T 7D **62** (4A **4**)
Stank La. DH1: Dur 2J **153**
STANLEY 3E **124**
Stanleyburn Ct. DH9: Ann P 5B **124**
Stanleyburn Vw. DH9: Ann P 5B **124**
Stanley By-Pass DH9: Stly 4D **124**
Stanley Cl. DH6: Sher 3K **167**
Stanley Ct. DH9: Stly 3G **125**
Stanley Cres. *NE26: Whit B 7H 39*
(off Alma Pl.)
NE42: Pru 3G **77**
Stanley Gdns. DH8: Con 6H **121**
NE9: Gate 5A **100**
NE23: Seg 2D **36**
Stanley Gro. NE7: Newc T 2J **63**
NE22: Bed 7K **17**
Stanley Indoor Bowling Cen. 3E **124**
Stanley St. DH5: Hou S 1E **144**
DH8: Con .6H **121**
NE4: Newc T 2B **82**
NE24: Bly .1K **23**
NE28: W'snd 2K **65**
NE29: N Shi 7G **49**
NE32: Jar .6C **66**
NE34: S Shi 1H **87**
SR5: C'twn 6H **103**
SR7: S'hm 2K **147**
Stanley St. W. NE29: N Shi 7G **49**
Stanley Ter. DH3: Ches S 7B **128**
DH4: Pen .3B **130**
DH6: Thor .1J **179**
Stanmore Rd. NE6: Newc T 4A **64**
Stannerford Rd. NE40: Ryton 7C **58**
Stanners, The NE45: Cor 1D **72**
Stanners Vw. NE40: Ryton 6C **58**
Stannington Av. NE6: Newc T . . .6K **63** (1P **5**)
Stannington Gdns. SR2: Sund 6E **118**
Stannington Gro.
NE6: Newc T 6K **63** (1N **5**)
SR2: Sund 5E **118**
Stannington Pl. NE6: Newc T . . .6A **64** (1P **5**)
NE20: Pon 3J **31**
Stannington Rd. NE29: N Shi 7C **48**
Stannington Sta. Rd. NE61: Hep 1A **20**
Stannington St. NE24: Bly 2K **23**
Stansfield St. SR6: Monk 6G **105**
Stanstead Cl. SR5: C'twn 7G **103**
Stanton Av. NE24: Bly 4F **23**
NE34: S Shi 6A **68**
Stanton Cl. NE10: Gate 7H **85**
Stanton Dr. NE61: Peg 4K **9**
Stanton Gro. NE30: N Shi 3G **49**
Stanton Rd. NE27: Shir 1J **47**
NE30: N Shi 3F **49**
Stanton St. NE4: Newc T 7C **62**
Stanway Dr. NE7: Newc T 2J **63**
Stanwick St. NE30: N Shi 4K **49**
Stapeley Ct. NE3: Ken 7K **43**
Stapeley Vw. NE3: Ken 7K **43**
Stapleford Cl. NE5: Newc T 4H **61**
Staple Rd. NE32: Jar 6C **66**
Stapylton Dr. SR2: Sund 4D **118**
Starbeck Av. NE2: Newc T 6H **63** (1J **5**)
Starbeck M. NE2: Newc T 6H **63** (1J **5**)
Stardale Av. NE24: Cow 3E **22**
STARGATE 2H **79**
Stargate Cl. DH7: Lang P 5G **151**
Stargate Gdns. NE9: Gate 5A **100**
Stargate Ind. Est. NE40: Ryton 3H **79**
Stargate La. NE21: Bla T, G'sde 1J **79**
NE40: Ryton 1J **79**
Starlight Cres. NE25: Sea D 7G **27**
Starling Wlk. NE16: Sun 5J **97**
Startforth Cl. DH3: Gt Lum 3F **143**
Stately Pk. DH5: Hett H 7H **145**
Station App. DH1: Dur 2K **165** (2A **6**)
NE11: Gate 3F **99**
NE12: Longb 6B **46**
NE33: S Shi 2J 67
(off Queen St.)
NE33: S Shi 2J **67**
NE36: E Bol 6A **88**
Station Av. DH5: Hett H 7G **145**
DH7: B'don 1E **174**
DH7: Esh W 4E **162**
Station Av. Nth. DH4: Hou S 1K **143**
Station Av. Sth. DH4: Hou S 1K **143**
Station Bank DH1: Dur 2A **166** (2B **6**)
NE40: Ryton 7G **59**
NE43: Mic .4A **76**
Station Bri. NE63: Ash 3A **12**
Station Cl. NE44: Rid M 6K **73**
Station Cotts. DH9: Beam 1A **126**
NE3: Ken .6B **44**
NE12: Longb 6B **46**
NE20: Pon 5J **31**
NE23: Seg 2E **36**
NE34: S Shi 7H **67**
NE39: Ham M 2G **109**
NE61: Mor .1G **15**
SR8: Pet .6G **173**
Station Cres. SR7: S'hm 2K **147**
Station Est. E. SR7: Mur 7C **146**
Station Est. Nth. SR7: Mur 7C **146**
(not continuous)
Station Est. Sth. SR7: Mur 7C **146**
Station Fld. Rd. DH9: Tan L 7F **111**
Station Ho's. DH2: Pelt 4G **127**
Station Ind. Est. NE42: Pru 3D **76**
Station La. DH1: Dur 2C **166**
DH2: Bir 4K **113**
DH2: Pelt .2F **127**
DH3: Bir 4A **114**
TS28: Win 7G **181**
Station M. NE30: N Shi 5K **49**
Station Rd. DH3: Ches S 6A **128**
DH4: Hou S 1D **144**
DH4: Leam, W Rai 1J **155**
DH4: Pen .7J **115**
DH5: Hett H 7G **145**
DH6: H Pitt 5A **156**
DH6: Shot C 5D **170**
DH7: B'don 1E **174**
DH7: Lan .7K **137**
DH7: Ush M 3B **164**
DH8: Con .7J **121**
DH9: Ann P 6K **123**
DH9: Beam 1A **126**
DH9: Stly .2F **125**
NE3: Gos .7G **45**
NE6: Walk 2E **84**
NE9: Gate 2G **99**
NE10: Gate 4F **85**
(Reay St.)
NE10: Gate 4F **85**
(South Pde.)
NE12: Kil .6K **35**
NE12: Longb 4B **46**
NE13: Wool 6H **43**
NE15: Hed W 3D **58**
(not continuous)
NE15: Thro 6K **59**
NE22: Bed 6A **18**
NE23: Cra .3H **25**
NE23: Dud 3H **35**
NE23: Seg 2D **36**
NE24: News 5G **23**
NE25: Sea D 6E **26**
NE26: Whit B 7H **39**
NE27: Back 7G **37**
NE28: W'snd 4A **66**
(Armstrong Rd.)
NE28: W'snd 2E **64**
(Queen's Cres.)
NE29: N Shi 1D **66**
NE30: N Shi 1J **49**
NE31: Heb .7H **65**
NE33: S Shi 3J **67**
NE35: Bol C 4E **86**
NE36: E Bol 7K **87**
NE38: Wash 3J **115**
NE39: Row G 6J **95**
NE41: Wylam 7K **57**
NE42: Pru .3D **76**
NE45: Cor .2D **72**
NE46: Hex .1D **70**
NE63: Ash .3K **11**
SR2: Ryh .3J **133**
SR6: Monk 3E **104**
SR7: Mur .7C **146**
SR7: S'hm 2H **147**
SR8: Eas .7D **160**
TS27: B Col 3K **183**
TS27: Hes 4E **182**
TS28: Win 7G **181**
TS29: Trim S 7B **180**
Station Rd. Bungs. TS27: B Col 3K **183**
Station Rd. E. TS29: Trim S 7B **180**
Station Rd. Nth. DH5: Hett H 7G **145**
NE12: Longb 4B **46**
NE28: W'snd 6D **46**
SR7: Mur .7C **146**
Station Rd. Sth. SR7: Mur 7C **146**
Station Rd. W. TS29: Trim S 7B **180**
Station Sq. NE26: Whit B 7H **39**
Station St. DH6: Has 1B **170**
DH7: Wat .6C **162**
NE22: Bed 5B **18**
NE24: Bly .1J **23**
NE32: Jar .6B **66**
SR1: Sund 1F **119** (3J **7**)
Station Ter. DH4: Hou S 1K **143**
DH8: Con .7J **121**
NE30: N Shi 5K **49**
NE36: E Bol 7A **88**
NE37: Usw 7J **101**
STATION TOWN 7H **181**
Station Vw. DH2: Ches S 6A **128**
DH5: Hett H 7G **145**
DH7: Esh W 5E **162**
Station Vs. DH9: Stly 1F **125**
Staveley Rd. SR6: Monk 2E **104**
SR8: Pet .6C **172**
Stavordale St. SR7: S'hm 4B **148**
(not continuous)
Stavordale St. W. SR7: S'hm 5B **148**
Stavordale Ter. NE9: Gate 7J **83**
Staward Av. NE25: Sea D 1H **37**
Staward Ter. NE6: Walk 2D **84**
Staynebrigg NE10: Gate 1D **100**
Steadings, The DH1: Dur 5J **165**
NE40: G'sde 5D **78**
NE63: Ash .5J **11**
Steadlands Sq. NE22: Bed 7A **18**
Stead La. NE22: Bed 7K **17**
Steadling Ct. DH8: Con 6J **121**
Steadman's La. DH7: Lang P 7A **150**
Steads, The NE61: Mor 2G **15**
Stead St. NE28: W'snd 2A **66**
Steavenson St. DH6: Bow 5H **177**
Stedham Cl. NE37: Usw 5J **101**
Steel St. DH8: Con 6H **121**
Steep Hill SR3: E Her 2J **131**
Steetley Ter. DH6: Quar H 6D **178**
STELLA 2A **80**
Stella Bank NE21: Bla T 1K **79**
Stella Cotts. NE21: Bla T 2A **80**
Stella Gill Ind. Est. DH2: Pelt 4H **127**
Stella Hall Dr. NE21: Bla T 2A **80**
Stella La. NE21: Bla T 2K **79**
Stella Rd. NE21: Bla T 1A **80**
Stephen Ct. NE32: Jar 7C **66**
Stephenson Bldg. NE2: Newc T 3K **5**
NE2: Newc T 1E 4
(off Stoddart St.)
Stephenson Cl. DH5: Hett H 6G **145**
Stephenson Ct. *NE30: N Shi 7H 49*
(off Stephenson St.)
NE41: Wylam 7A **58**
Stephenson Ho. NE12: Kil 2A **46**
NE46: Hex 1C 70
(off Haugh La.)
Stephenson Ind. Est. NE12: Kil 2A **46**
NE37: Usw 5J **101**
Stephenson Railway Mus. 5A **48**
Stephenson Rd. NE7: Newc T 4K **63**
NE37: Usw 5H **101**
SR8: Pet .3A **172**
Stephenson's La.
NE1: Newc T 2F **83** (8F **4**)
Stephenson Sq. SR8: Eas 1A **172**
Stephenson St. NE8: Gate 6F **83**
NE28: W'snd 4A **66**
NE30: N Shi 5K **49**
(Percy St.)
NE30: N Shi 6H **49**
(Suez St., not continuous)
SR7: Mur .7E **146**
Stephenson Ter. NE10: Gate 7B **84**
NE15: Thro 4B **60**
(Blucher Colliery Rd.)
NE15: Thro 3G **59**
(Hexham Rd.)
NE41: Wylam 7K **57**
Stephenson Trail, The NE12: Kil 3D **46**
Stephenson Way NE21: Bla T 6D **80**
NE22: Bed 4J **17**
Stephens Rd. SR7: Mur 7D **146**
Stephen's Ter. DH6: Whe H 2B **180**
Stephen St. DH8: Con 6H **121**
NE6: Newc T 7J **63** (4M **5**)
NE23: E Har 6K **21**
NE24: Bly .1J **23**
Stepney Bank NE1: Newc T 7H **63** (4K **5**)
Stepney La. NE1: Newc T 1H **83** (5J **5**)
Stepney Rd. NE2: Newc T 7H **63** (3K **5**)
Sterling St. SR4: Sund 2C **118**
Stevens Cl. NE5: Newc T 3D **60**
Stevenson Rd. DH9: Stly 3G **125**
Stevenson St. DH4: Hou S 2D **144**
NE33: S Shi 4K **67**
Steward Cres. NE34: S Shi 6D **68**
Stewart Av. SR2: Ryh 3G **133**
Stewart Dr. NE36: W Bol 7H **87**
TS28: Win 4G **181**
Stewartsfield NE39: Row G 5H **95**
Stewart St. SR3: New S 2C **132**
SR4: Sund 3D **118**
SR7: S'hm 4C **148**
SR8: Eas .7B **160**
Stewart St. E. SR7: S'hm 4C **148**
Stileford NE10: Gate 7E **84**
Stillington Cl. SR2: Ryh 4H **133**
Stirling Av. NE32: Jar 2E **86**
NE39: Row G 6J **95**
Stirling Cl. NE38: Wash 4A **116**
Stirling Cotts. NE10: Gate 7A **84**
Stirling Ct. NE11: Gate 5G **99**
Stirling Dr. NE22: Bed 6A **18**
NE29: N Shi 4C **48**
Stirling La. NE39: Row G 6J **95**
Stobart St. DH7: Edm 3D **140**
SR5: Monk 7E **104** (1H **7**)
Stobb Ho. Vw. DH7: B'don 7C **164**
STOBHILL 3H **15**
STOBHILLGATE 1H **15**
Stobhill Vs. NE61: Mor 1G **15**
Stock Bri. NE1: Newc T 1G **83** (6H **5**)
Stockdale Gdns. *NE6: Walk 2E 84*
(off Rochester St.)
Stockerley La. DH8: Con 4C **136**
Stockerley Rd. DH8: Con 1K **135**
Stockfold NE38: Wash 6J **115**
Stockholm Cl. NE29: N Shi 7B **48**
Stockley Av. SR5: C'twn 5J **103**
Stockley Ct. DH7: Ush M 3E **164**
Stockley Gro. DH7: New B 6A **174**
Stockley La. DH7: New B 6A **174**
Stockley Rd. NE38: Wash 2K **115**
STOCKSFIELD 7G **75**
Stocksfield Av. NE5: Newc T 6J **61**
Stocksfield Gdns. NE9: Gate 5J **99**
Stocksfield Station (Rail) 7G **75**
Stockton Av. SR8: Pet 4D **172**
Stockton Rd. DH1: Dur 4B **166** (6D **6**)
NE29: N Shi 2F **67**
SR1: Sund 2E **118** (5H **7**)
SR2: Ryh .5H **133**
SR2: Sund 2E **118** (6J **7**)
SR7: Mur, S'hm, Sea 6H **133**
SR8: Eas .2J **171**
TS27: Cas E 4K **181**
Stockton Rd. E. SR7: Eas 3K **159**
Stockton Rd. W. SR7: Eas 3K **159**
Stockton St. SR7: S'hm 2K **147**
Stockton Ter. SR2: Sund 6H **119**
Stockwell Grn. NE6: Walk 5D **64**
Stoddart Ho. NE2: Newc T 7H **63** (3J **5**)
Stoddart St. NE2: Newc T 7H **63** (3K **5**)
NE34: S Shi 7H **67**
Stoker Av. NE34: S Shi 2F **87**
Stoker Cres. DH6: Whe H 4A **180**
Stoker Ter. NE39: H Spen 4E **94**
Stokesley Gro. NE7: Newc T 2J **63**
Stokoe Dr. NE63: N Sea 4E **12**
Stokoe St. DH8: Con 5G **121**
Stone Cellar Rd. NE37: Usw 5F **101**
Stonechat Cl. NE38: Wash 5D **114**
Stonechat Mt. NE21: Bla T 1A **80**
Stonechat Pl. NE12: Longb 5J **45**
Stonecroft Gdns. NE7: Newc T 2B **64**
Stonecrop NE9: Gate 2A **100**
Stonecross NE63: Ash 5A **12**
Stonefold Cl. NE5: Newc T 2H **61**
Stonegate NE15: Hor 4F **57**
Stonehaugh Way NE20: Pon 2F **41**
Stonehills NE10: Gate 5F **85**
Stoneleigh NE61: Hep 4A **16**
Stoneleigh Av. NE12: Longb 6H **45**
Stoneleigh Cl. DH4: Hou S 1C **144**
Stoneleigh Pl. NE12: Longb 6J **45**
Stone Row DH2: Pelt 4C **126**
Stonesdale DH4: Pen 1J **129**
Stone St. NE10: Gate 1A **100**
Stonethwaite NE29: N Shi 2D **66**
Stoney Bank NE28: W'snd 3J **65**
Stoneycroft E. NE12: Kil 2C **46**
Stoneycroft W. NE12: Kil 2C **46**
STONEYGATE 5G **131**
Stoneygate Cl. NE10: Gate 5C **84**
Stoney Ga. Gdns. NE10: Gate 5C **84**
Stoneygate La. NE10: Gate 6C **84**
Stoneyhurst Av. NE15: Newc T 1H **81**
Stoneyhurst Rd. NE3: Gos 1G **63**
Stoneyhurst Rd. W. NE3: Gos 1F **63**
Stoney La. DH9: Beam 2C **126**
NE9: Spri .6D **100**
SR5: S'wck 6C **104**
Stoneylea Cl. NE40: Ryton 3C **78**
Stoneylea Rd. NE5: Newc T 5F **61**
Stoneyways NE40: G'sde 6C **78**
Stonybank Way NE43: Mic 6K **75**
Stonycroft NE37: Wash 1G **115**
Stonyflat Bank NE42: Pru 4G **77**
STONY HEAP .6F **123**
Stonyheap La. DH8: Con 7F **123**
DH9: Ann P 6F **123**
Store Bldgs. NE35: Bol C 6E **86**
Store Cotts. DH7: Sac 4D **140**
Store Farm Rd. NE64: Newb S 2G **13**
Store St. DH8: Con 6H **121**
NE15: Lem 7C **60**
NE21: Bla T 5B **80**
Store Ter. DH5: Eas L 2H **157**
Storey Ct. NE21: Bla T 2E **80**
Storey Cres. NE64: Newb S 2G **13**
Storey La. NE21: Bla T 2A **80**
Storey St. NE23: Cra 5A **26**
Stormont Grn. NE3: Ken 2B **62**
Stormont St. NE29: N Shi 7G **49**
Stotfold Cl. SR7: S'hm 2G **147**
Stothard St. NE32: Jar 6C **66**
Stotts Rd. NE6: Walk 5E **64**
Stowe Gdns. NE61: Peg 3A **10**
Stowell Sq. NE1: Newc T 1E **82** (6D **4**)
Stowell St. NE1: Newc T 1E **82** (6D **4**)
Stowell Ter. NE10: Gate 6C **84**
Straker Dr. NE46: Hex 3A **70**
Straker St. NE32: Jar 7D **66**
Straker Ter. NE34: S Shi 1H **87**
NE61: Peg .1D **10**
Strand, The SR3: E Her 1A **132**
Strangford Av. DH2: Ches S 1K **141**
Strangford Rd. SR7: S'hm 3K **147**
Strangways St. SR7: S'hm 4B **148**
Stranton Ter. SR6: Monk 5F **105**
Stratfield St. SR4: Sund 1A **118**
Stratford Av. SR2: Sund 5G **119**
Stratford Cl. NE12: Kil 1C **46**
NE23: Cra .3G **25**

Tamerton Dr. DH3: Bir ... 6B 114
Tamerton St. SR4: Sund ... 2B 118
Tamworth Rd. NE4: Newc T ... 7C 62
Tamworth Sq. SR3: Sund ... 7J 117
Tanbark DH4: Hou S ... 3K 129
TANFIELD ... 5D 110
Tanfield Comprehensive School Sports Cen. ... 1D 124
Tanfield Gdns. NE34: S Shi ... 7D 68
TANFIELD LEA ... 1D 124
Tanfield Lea Nth. Ind. Est.
DH9: Tan L ... 7D 110
Tanfield Lea Sth. Ind. Est.
DH9: Tan L ... 7F 111
Tanfield Pl. NE9: Gate ... 5A 100
Tanfield Railway ... 7H 97
Tanfield Rd. NE9: Gate ... 5A 100
NE15: Newc T ... 7G 61
SR3: Sund ... 6K 117
Tanfield St. SR4: Sund ... 1A 118
Tangmere Cl. NE23: Cra ... 3A 26
TAN HILLS ... 6H 141
Tankerville Pl. NE2: Newc T ... 4G 63
Tankerville Ter. NE2: Newc T ... 5G 63
Tanmeads DH2: Plaw ... 6H 141
Tanners Bank NE30: N Shi ... 6J 49
Tanners Ct. *NE1: Newc T ... 6D 4*
(off Friars St.)
Tanners Row NE46: Hex ... 1C 70
Tanners Yd. NE46: Hex ... 1C 70
Tantallon DH3: Bir ... 6B 114
(not continuous)
Tantallon Ct. DH4: Hou S ... 1H 143
TANTOBIE ... 6B 110
Tantobie Rd. NE15: Newc T ... 7G 61
Tarlton Cres. NE10: Gate ... 6A 84
Tarn Cl. SR8: Pet ... 6C 172
Tarn Dr. SR2: Sund ... 1H 133
Tarragon Way NE34: S Shi ... 3A 88
Tarrington Cl. NE28: W'snd ... 7K 47
Tarset Dr. NE42: Pru ... 4F 77
Tarset Pl. NE3: Ken ... 6C 44
Tarset Rd. NE25: Well ... 6B 38
Tarset St. NE1: Newc T ... 1J 83 (5L 5)
Tasmania Rd. NE34: S Shi ... 3F 87
Tasman Rd. SR3: Sund ... 1J 131
Tate St. NE24: Bly ... 1K 23
Tatham St. SR1: Sund ... 2G 119 (4K 7)
Tatham St. Bk. SR1: Sund ... 2G 119 (4K 7)
Tattershall SR2: Sund ... 4D 118
Taunton Av. NE29: N Shi ... 3D 48
NE32: Jar ... 1E 86
Taunton Cl. NE28: W'snd ... 7K 47
Taunton Pl. NE23: Cra ... 2K 25
Taunton Rd. SR3: Sund ... 7K 117
Taunton Sq. SR3: Sund ... 6K 117
Tavistock Ct. DH4: Hou S ... 6C 130
Tavistock Pl. NE32: Jar ... 1E 86
SR1: Sund ... 2F 119 (4K 7)
Tavistock Rd. NE2: Newc T ... 3G 63
Tavistock Sq. SR3: New S ... 1C 132
Tavistock Wlk. NE23: Cra ... 2K 25
Taylor Av. DH7: Ush M ... 1D 164
NE13: Wide O ... 5E 34
NE39: Row G ... 6K 95
NE63: N Sea ... 4F 13
Taylor Gdns. NE10: Gate ... 5E 84
NE26: Sea S ... 4D 28
SR2: Sund ... 4G 119
Taylor Gro. TS28: Win ... 4F 181
Taylor's Bldgs. NE22: Bed ... 6B 18
Taylors Ter. DH8: C'sde ... 1E 134
Taylor St. DH8: Con ... 7H 121
DH9: Ann P ... 4J 123
NE24: Cow ... 1E 22
NE33: S Shi ... 5H 67
Taylor Ter. NE27: Shir ... 3H 47
NE34: S Shi ... 2F 87
Taynton Gro. NE23: Seg ... 1D 36
Tay Rd. SR3: Sund ... 6J 117
Tay St. DH5: Eas L ... 3K 157
NE17: C'wl ... 6A 94
Teal Av. NE24: News ... 5K 23
Teal Cl. NE7: Longb ... 7A 46
NE38: Wash ... 5D 114
TEAMS ... 6E 82
Team St. NE8: Dun, Gate ... 5C 82
Team Va. Vs. NE11: Gate ... 1D 98
TEAM VALLEY ... 4F 99
Team Valley Bus. Cen.
NE11: Gate ... 1F 99
Team Valley Trad. Est. NE11: Gate ... 4F 99
(Seventh Av.)
NE11: Gate ... 1E 98
(Third Av.)
Teasdale Ho. NE5: Newc T ... 7G 43
Teasdale St. DH8: Con ... 6J 121
SR2: Sund ... 3H 119
Teasdale Ter. DH1: Dur ... 2F 167
Tebay Dr. NE5: Newc T ... 5F 61
Tedco Bus. Cen. NE32: Jar ... 5K 65
Tedco Bus. Works NE33: S Shi ... 3J 67
Teddington Cl. NE3: Ken ... 5H 43
Teddington Rd. SR3: Sund ... 6J 117
Teddington Sq. SR3: Sund ... 6J 117
Tedham Rd. NE15: Lem ... 6C 60
Tees Cl. SR8: Pet ... 1A 182
Tees Ct. NE34: S Shi ... 7J 67
NE37: Wash ... 3B 132
Tees Cres. DH9: Stly ... 4F 125
Teesdale Av. DH4: Pen ... 1A 130
Teesdale Gdns. NE7: Newc T ... 2K 63
Teesdale Gro. NE12: Longb ... 4B 46
Teesdale Pl. NE24: Cow ... 1D 22
Teesdale Ter. DH9: Ann P ... 5A 124
Tees Gro. DH8: Lead ... 4B 122
Tees Rd. NE31: Heb ... 3J 85
Tees St. DH5: Eas L ... 3K 157
NE17: C'wl ... 6A 94
SR7: S'hm ... 2B 148
SR8: Pet ... 5E 172
Tees Ter. NE37: Usw ... 7H 101
Teign Cl. SR8: Pet ... 7A 172
Teikyo University of Japan in Durham ... 5A 166 (7C 6)
Teindland Cl. NE4: Newc T ... 2A 82
Tel-el-Kebir Rd. SR2: Sund ... 4G 119
Telewest Arena Newcastle ... 3E 82 (9C 4)
Telford Cl. DH1: H Shin ... 1F 177
NE27: Back ... 6G 37
Telford Ct. NE28: W'snd ... 3C 66
NE61: Mor ... 2F 15
Telford Rd. SR3: Sund ... 6K 117
Telford St. NE8: Gate ... 7F 83
NE28: W'snd ... 3C 66
Temperance Ter. DH7: Ush M ... 2B 164
Temperley Pl. NE46: Hex ... 2C 70
Tempest Rd. SR7: S'hm ... 3A 148
Tempest St. NE21: Bla T ... 2A 80
SR3: New S ... 2C 132
Templar M. DH8: M'sly ... 1J 121
Templar St. DH8: Con ... 5F 121
Temple Av. NE24: Cow ... 1G 23
Temple Gdns. DH8: Con ... 1H 135
Temple Grn. NE8: Gate ... 6E 82
NE34: S Shi ... 1A 88
Temple Park Leisure Cen. ... 2A 88
Temple Pk. Rd. NE33: S Shi ... 7K 67
NE34: S Shi ... 7K 67
Temple St. NE1: Newc T ... 2E 82 (7D 4)
NE10: Gate ... 5B 84
NE33: S Shi ... 6H 67
Temple St. W. NE33: S Shi ... 6H 67
TEMPLETOWN ... 1H 135
Temple Town NE33: S Shi ... 5H 67
Tenbury Cres. NE12: Longb ... 5A 46
NE29: N Shi ... 3E 48
Tenby Rd. SR3: Sund ... 1J 131
Tenby Sq. NE23: Cra ... 2A 26
Ten Flds. DH5: Hett H ... 7F 145
Tennant St. NE31: Heb ... 1H 85
NE34: S Shi ... 2G 87
Tennyson Av. NE31: Heb ... 7K 65
NE35: Bol C ... 6H 87
TS27: B Col ... 7G 173
Tennyson Ct. NE8: Gate ... 4J 83
NE42: Pru ... 5D 76
Tennyson Cres. NE16: Swa ... 6G 81
Tennyson Gdns. DH9: Dip ... 2G 123
Tennyson Grn. NE3: Ken ... 2A 62
Tennyson Rd. DH2: Pelt ... 6G 127
SR8: Eas ... 7B 160
Tennyson St. NE33: S Shi ... 3K 67
SR5: S'wck ... 5C 104
Tennyson Ter. NE29: N Shi ... 1G 67
Tenter Gth. NE15: Thro ... 3G 59
Tenter Ter. DH1: Dur ... 2A 166 (2B 6)
NE61: Mor ... 7G 9
Tenth Av. DH2: Ches S ... 6K 127
NE6: Newc T ... 5A 64 (1P 5)
NE11: Gate ... 5F 99
NE24: Bly ... 4H 23
NE61: Mor ... 2H 15
Tenth Av. W. NE11: Gate ... 5E 98
Tenth St. SR8: Pet ... 5E 172
TS27: B Col ... 1G 183
Tern Cl. NE24: News ... 5K 23
Terrace Pl. NE1: Newc T ... 7E 62 (4D 4)
Terrace, The DH6: Shot C ... 5F 171
DH7: B'don ... 1F 175
DH8: Shot B ... 3E 120
NE35: Bol C ... 5E 86
NE36: E Bol ... 7K 87
NE42: O'ham ... 2D 76
NE46: Acomb ... 4B 50
SR4: Sund ... 2G 117
Terrier Cl. NE22: Bed ... 7A 18
Territorial La. DH1: Dur ... 3B 166 (3E 6)
Tesla St. DH4: Hou S ... 5D 130
Tetford Pl. NE12: Longb ... 5A 46
Teviot NE38: Wash ... 7E 114
Teviotdale Gdns. NE7: Newc T ... 2K 63
Teviot St. DH5: Eas L ... 3J 157
NE8: Gate ... 6J 83
Teviot Way NE32: Jar ... 1A 86
Tewkesbury NE12: Kil ... 7B 36
Tewkesbury Rd. NE15: Lem ... 5C 60
Thackeray Rd. SR3: Sund ... 6K 117
Thackeray St. DH4: Hou S ... 2D 144
Thames Av. NE32: Jar ... 3C 86
Thames Cres. DH4: Hou S ... 2A 144
DH9: Stly ... 5F 125
Thames Gdns. NE28: W'snd ... 4F 65
(not continuous)
Thames Rd. NE31: Heb ... 2K 85
SR3: Sund ... 1J 131
SR8: Pet ... 7A 172
Thames St. DH5: Eas L ... 3J 157
NE8: Gate ... 6J 83
NE17: C'wl ... 6A 94
Thanet Rd. SR3: Sund ... 7K 117
Tharsis Rd. NE31: Heb ... 1H 85
Thatcher Cl. NE16: Whi ... 3G 97
Theatre Pl. NE29: N Shi ... 7G 49
Theatre Royal ... 1F 83 (5F 4)
Thelma St. SR4: Sund ... 2D 118
Theme Rd. SR3: Sund ... 1J 131
Theresa Russell Ho.
NE6: Newc T ... 7A 64 (3P 5)
Theresa St. NE21: Bla T ... 3C 80
(not continuous)
SR7: S'hm ... 5C 148
(off Queen Alexandra Rd.)
Thetford NE38: Wash ... 4H 115
Thieves Bank NE61: Chop ... 6G 11
Third Av. DH2: Ches S ... 6K 127
(Bullion La.)
DH2: Ches S ... 2K 127
(Drum Rd.)
NE6: Newc T ... 6A 64 (1P 5)
NE11: Gate ... 1E 98
NE24: Bly ... 3H 23
NE29: N Shi ... 7B 48
NE61: Mor ... 1H 15
NE63: Hir ... 4B 12
Third St. DH8: Con ... 7K 121
DH8: Lead ... 3A 122
(not continuous)
DH9: Stly ... 7D 124
NE28: W'snd ... 4H 65
SR8: Pet ... 5E 172
TS27: B Col ... 2H 183
Thirkeld Pl. DH4: Pen ... 2A 130
Thirlaway Ter. NE16: Sun ... 5J 97
Thirlington Cl. NE5: Newc T ... 2H 61
Thirlmere DH3: Bir ... 6C 114
NE10: Gate ... 6E 84
SR6: Cle ... 5C 88
Thirlmere Av. DH2: Ches S ... 1K 141
DH5: Eas L ... 3J 157
NE30: N Shi ... 2G 49
Thirlmere Cl. NE12: Kil ... 1D 46
Thirlmere Ct. NE31: Heb ... 1K 85
Thirlmere Cres. DH4: Hou S ... 3B 130
NE21: Bla T ... 6B 80
Thirlmere Rd. SR8: Pet ... 5C 172
Thirlmere Ter. NE64: Newb S ... 3H 13
Thirlmere Way NE5: Newc T ... 4H 61
NE24: Cow ... 7E 18
Thirlmoor NE37: Wash ... 2E 114
Thirlmoor Pl. NE62: Chop ... 7J 11
Thirlwell Gro. NE32: Jar ... 3A 86
Thirlwell Rd. NE8: Gate ... 3J 83 (9L 5)
Thirsk Rd. SR3: Sund ... 6K 117
Thirston Dr. NE23: Cra ... 4A 26
Thirston Pl. NE29: N Shi ... 5D 48
Thirston Way NE3: Ken ... 7K 43
Thirteenth St. SR8: Pet ... 5D 172
Thistle Av. NE40: Ryton ... 2E 78
Thistle Ct. NE31: Heb ... 1H 85
Thistlecroft DH5: Hou S ... 3E 144
Thistledale SR2: Sund ... 3H 119
Thistledon Av. NE16: Whi ... 1F 97
Thistle Rd. DH7: B'don ... 1H 175
SR3: Sund ... 7J 117
Thistley Cl. NE6: Walk ... 5C 64
Thistley Grn. NE10: Gate ... 5F 85
Thomas Bell Ho. NE34: S Shi ... 2G 87
Thomas Bewick Sq.
NE1: Newc T ... 2F 83 (7E 4)
Thomas Dr. NE31: Heb ... 7H 65
Thomas Ferguson Ct. NE30: N Shi ... 6J 49
Thomas Hawksley Pk. SR3: Sund ... 5C 118
Thomas Holiday Homes *NE22: Bed ... 5B 18*
(off Burnside)
Thomas Horsley Ho. NE15: Newc T ... 1H 81
Thomas St. DH3: Ches S ... 7A 128
DH5: Hett H ... 5H 145
(not continuous)
DH7: Lang P ... 5J 151
DH7: Sac ... 1D 152
DH8: Con ... 6H 121
(off Gibson St.)
DH8: Shot B ... 5F 121
DH9: Ann P ... 5A 124
DH9: Stly ... 7J 125
(not continuous)
NE5: Newc T ... 3F 61
NE9: Spri ... 6B 100
NE16: Whi ... 7G 81
NE33: S Shi ... 2J 67
NE37: Usw ... 7K 101
SR2: Ryh ... 3H 133
SR8: Eas ... 6C 160
Thomas St. Nth. SR6: Monk ... 7F 105
Thomas St. Sth. SR2: Ryh ... 3H 133
SR5: Sund ... 6C 104
Thomas Taylor Cotts. NE27: Back ... 6G 37
Thompson Av. NE12: Kil ... 7A 36
Thompson Cres. SR5: C'twn ... 6H 103
Thompson Gdns. NE28: W'snd ... 3F 65
Thompson Pl. NE10: Gate ... 6B 84
Thompson Rd. SR5: S'wck ... 5D 104
Thompson's Bldgs. DH4: Hou S ... 4C 130
Thompson St. NE22: Bed ... 5B 18
NE24: Bly ... 7H 19
SR8: Pet ... 5E 172
Thompson Ter. SR2: Ryh ... 3J 133
Thorburn St. SR6: Monk ... 3F 105
Thoresby Ho. *NE6: Walk ... 3C 84*
(off McCutcheon Ct.)
Thornbank Cl. SR3: New S ... 5C 132
Thornbridge NE38: Wash ... 3A 116
Thornbury Av. NE23: Seg ... 1E 36
Thornbury Cl. NE3: Ken ... 7H 43
NE35: Bol C ... 5E 86
Thornbury Dr. NE25: Whit B ... 5C 38
Thornbury St. SR4: Sund ... 1C 118
Thorncliffe Pl. NE29: N Shi ... 7E 48
Thorn Cl. NE13: Wide O ... 6C 34
Thorndale Pl. NE24: Cow ... 1E 22
Thorndale Rd. DH1: Carr ... 7H 155
NE15: Newc T ... 1F 81
SR3: Sund ... 7J 117
Thorne Av. NE10: Gate ... 6F 85
Thornebrake NE10: Gate ... 7E 84
Thorne Rd. SR3: Sund ... 7J 117
Thornes Cl. SR8: Pet ... 6D 172
Thorne Sq. SR3: Sund ... 7J 117
Thorne Ter. NE6: Walk ... 6C 64
Thorneyburn Av. NE25: Well ... 6B 38
Thorneyburn Cl. DH4: Hou S ... 7C 130
Thorneyburn Way NE24: Cow ... 1F 23
THORNEY CLOSE ... 7K 117
Thorney Cl. Rd. SR3: Sund ... 7K 117
Thorneyfield Dr. NE12: Kil ... 2K 45
Thorneyford Pl. NE20: Pon ... 4J 31
Thorneyholme Ter. DH9: Stly ... 3F 125
NE21: Bla T ... 3C 80
Thornfield Gro. SR2: Sund ... 6G 119
Thornfield Pl. NE39: Row G ... 4J 95
Thornfield Rd. DH8: C'sde ... 2E 134
NE3: Gos ... 1D 62
Thorngill NE37: Wash ... 2G 115
Thornhaugh Av. NE16: Whi ... 2F 97
Thornhill Cl. NE11: Gate ... 6C 82
NE25: Sea D ... 1H 37
Thornhill Cres. SR2: Sund ... 2E 118 (5H 7)
Thornhill Gdns. NE16: Burn ... 3K 109
NE62: Chop ... 7J 11
SR2: Sund ... 4E 118 (7G 7)
Thornhill Pk. NE20: Pon ... 4J 31
SR2: Sund ... 3E 118 (7G 7)
Thornhill Reach SR7: S'hm ... 2K 147
Thornhill Rd. DH6: Shot C ... 6E 170
NE12: Longb ... 6B 46
NE20: Pon ... 4J 31
Thornhill St. DH4: Hou S ... 2D 144
Thornhill Ter. SR2: Sund ... 3E 118 (6G 7)
Thornholme Av. NE34: S Shi ... 7D 68
Thornholme Rd. SR2: Sund ... 4D 118 (7F 7)
Thornhope Cl. NE38: Wash ... 2K 115
Thornlaw Nth. DH6: Thor ... 1H 179
Thornlea NE61: Hep ... 4A 16
Thornlea Gdns. NE9: Gate ... 1H 99
Thornlea Gro. DH7: Lan ... 6J 137
Thornleigh Gdns. SR6: Cle ... 4C 88
Thornleigh Rd. NE2: Newc T ... 4G 63
THORNLEY ... 1J 179
Thornley Av. NE10: Gate ... 1F 101
NE23: Cra ... 4A 26
Thornley Cl. DH7: Ush M ... 3D 164
NE16: Whi ... 3G 97
Thornley La. NE21: Bla T, Row G ... 1A 96
NE39: Row G ... 1A 96
Thornley Rd. DH6: Whe H ... 2A 180
NE5: Newc T ... 5F 61
TS29: Trim S ... 7B 180
Thornley Sta. Ind. Est. DH6: Shot C ... 1F 181
Thornley Ter. NE22: Bed, Chop ... 3A 18
Thornley Vw. NE39: Row G ... 5K 95
Thornley Wood Country Pk. ... 1B 96
Thornley Wood Country Pk. Vis. Cen. ... 2B 96
Thornton Av. NE33: S Shi ... 6H 67
Thornton Cl. DH4: Pen ... 2B 130
DH6: Shad ... 5J 169
NE61: Mor ... 2H 15
Thornton Cotts. *NE40: Ryton ... 7G 59*
(off Northumberland Rd.)
Thornton Ct. NE1: Newc T ... 7D 4
NE38: Wash ... 3G 115
Thornton Cres. NE21: Bla T ... 3C 80
Thornton Lea DH2: Pelt ... 2F 127
Thorntons Cl. DH2: Pelt ... 2F 127
Thornton St. NE1: Newc T ... 2E 82 (7D 4)
Thornton Ter. NE12: Longb ... 3E 46
TS27: B Col ... 2J 183
Thorntree Av. NE13: Sea B ... 2D 34
Thorntree Cl. NE25: Whit B ... 7B 38

Tweed Cl.—Victoria Pl.

Tweed Cl. DH2: Ous 1H 127
SR2: Sund 1H 133
SR8: Pet 7A 172
Tweed Dr. NE61: Hep 7A 16
Tweed Gro. NE15: Lem 6C 60
Tweedmouth Ct. NE3: Gos 1G 63
Tweed St. DH5: Eas L 3J 157
NE4: Newc T 1B 82
NE8: Gate 5J 83
NE17: C'wl 6A 94
NE31: Heb 7H 65
NE32: Jar 1A 86
NE38: Wash 4K 115
NE63: Hir 2C 12
(not continuous)
Tweed Ter. DH9: Stly 4F 125
Tweedy's Bldgs. NE40: Ryton 1F 79
Tweedy St. NE24: Cow 1E 22
Tweedy Ter. NE6: Walk 1D 84
Twelfth Av. DH2: Ches S 5K 127
NE24: Bly 3H 23
Twelfth St. SR8: Pet 5D 172
Twentieth Av. NE24: Bly 4G 23
Twentyfifth Av. NE24: Bly 4H 23
Twentysecond Av. NE24: Bly 4G 23
Twentysixth Av. NE24: Bly 4G 23
Twentythird Av. NE24: Bly 4G 23
Twickenham Ct. NE23: Seg 1D 36
Twickenham Rd. SR3: Sund 6J 117
Twizell Av. NE21: Bla T 4B 80
Twizell La. DH9: Stly 4B 126
Twizell Pl. NE20: Pon 4J 31
Twizell St. NE24: Bly 3K 23
Two Ball Lonnen NE4: Newc T 6J 61
Twyford Cl. NE23: Cra 2K 25
Tyldesley Sq. SR3: Sund 7J 117
Tyndal Gdns. NE11: Dun 5B 82
Tyne App. NE32: Jar 5A 66
Tyne Av. DH8: Lead 4B 122
Tynebank NE21: Bla T 4B 80
Tyne Bri. NE1: Newc T 2G 83 (7G 4)
NE8: Gate 2G 83 (7G 4)
Tyne Bri. Twr. NE8: Gate 8H 5
Tyne Ct. NE46: Hex 7C 50
Tynedale Av. NE26: Whit B 5F 39
NE28: W'snd 1F 65
Tynedale Bus. Cen. NE46: Hex 7C 50
Tynedale Cl. NE41: Wylam 7K 57
Tynedale Ct. NE28: W'snd 1A 66
Tynedale Cres. DH4: Pen 2B 130
Tynedale Dr. NE24: Cow 1D 22
Tynedale Gdns. NE43: Stoc 1K 91
Tynedale Ho. NE15: Newc T 1H 81
Tynedale Rd. NE34: S Shi 5A 68
SR3: Sund 7J 117
Tynedale St. DH5: Hett H 2E 156
Tynedale Ter. DH9: Ann P 5A 124
NE12: Longb 6B 46
NE46: Acomb 4B 50
NE46: Hex 2B 70
Tynedale Vw. NE46: Hex 2B 70
Tynedale Vs. NE46: Hex 2B 70
TYNE DOCK 6H 67
Tyne Dock Station (Metro) 7H 67
Tyne Gdns. NE37: Usw 6H 101
NE40: Ryton 2J 79
NE42: O'ham 2D 76
Tynegate Pct. NE8: Gate 4H 83
Tyne Grn. NE46: Hex 7C 50
Tyne Green Country Pk. 7D 50
Tyne Grn. Rd. NE46: Hex 7C 50
Tyne Ho. SR3: New S 3B 132
Tynell Wlk. NE3: Ken 7H 43
Tyne Main Rd. NE10: Gate 3A 84 (9P 5)
Tyne Mills Ind. Est. NE46: Hex 7E 50
TYNEMOUTH 5K 49
Tynemouth Castle 5K 49
Tynemouth Cl. NE6: Newc T 7K 63 (3P 5)
Tynemouth Ct. NE6: Newc T 2P 5
NE29: N Shi 6F 49
Tynemouth Crematorium NE29: N Shi 5F 49
Tynemouth Pl. NE30: N Shi 5K 49
Tynemouth Pool 4F 49
Tynemouth Priory Theatre 4K 49
Tynemouth Rd. NE6: Newc T 6A 64 (2P 5)
(not continuous)
NE28: W'snd 3K 65
NE30: N Shi 6H 49
NE32: Jar 4B 86
Tynemouth Sq. SR3: Sund 7K 117
Tynemouth Squash Rackets Club 5D 48
Tynemouth Station (Metro) 5K 49
Tynemouth Ter. NE30: N Shi 5K 49
Tynemouth Way NE6: Newc T 6A 64
Tynepoint Ind. Est. NE32: Jar 1E 86
Tyne Riverside Country Pk. 3D 76
Tyne Rd. DH9: Stly 4E 124
Tyne Rd. E. DH9: Stly 4F 125
NE8: Gate 4E 82 (10E 4)
Tyneside Cinema 1F 83 (5F 4)
Tyneside Rd. NE4: Newc T 3D 82 (9B 4)
Tyneside Works NE32: Jar 5B 66
Tyne St. DH5: Eas L 3J 157
DH8: Con 7J 121
NE1: Newc T 1J 83 (6M 5)
Tyne St. NE10: Gate 4C 84
NE17: C'wl 6K 93
(off Derwent St.)
NE21: Bla T 2C 80
(Blaydon)
NE21: Bla T 5B 80
(Winlaton)
NE30: N Shi 7H 49
NE31: Heb 6H 65
NE32: Jar 5B 66
NE63: Hir 3C 12
SR7: S'hm 3B 148
Tyne Ter. NE34: S Shi 1J 87
SR8: Eas 7B 160
Tyne Tunnel NE32: Jar, W'snd 5C 66
Tyne Tunnel Trad. Est.
NE29: N Shi 1B 66
(Narvik Way)
NE29: N Shi 7B 48
(Tromso Cl.)
Tynevale Av. NE21: Bla T 5C 80
Tynevale Ter. NE8: Gate 5E 82
NE15: Lem 7C 60
(not continuous)
Tyne Vw. NE15: Lem 7C 60
NE16: Whi 6J 81
NE21: Bla T 5C 80
NE31: Heb 7G 65
NE40: Ryton 6D 58
NE41: Wylam 7K 57
Tyne Vw. Gdns. NE10: Gate 5D 84
Tyneview Pk. NE12: Newc T 7B 46
Tyne Vw. Pl. NE8: Gate 5E 82
Tyne Vw. Ter. NE28: W'snd 4C 66
NE42: Pru 3F 77
Tyneview Ter. NE46: Hex 3E 70
Tyne Wlk. NE15: Thro 4H 59
Tynewold Cl. NE8: Gate 5E 82
Tynside Retail Pk. NE28: W'snd 6A 48
Tyzack Cres. SR6: Monk 5F 105
Tyzack St. DH7: Edm 3D 140

U

UCI Cinema
Derwenthaugh 4K 81
UCI Silverlink Cinema 6A 48
Ugly La. DH2: Plaw 6H 141
Uldale Ct. NE3: Ken 5K 43
Ullerdale Cl. DH1: Carr 7J 155
Ullswater Av. DH5: Eas L 3J 157
NE32: Jar 3D 86
Ullswater Cl. NE24: Cow 1C 22
Ullswater Cres. NE21: Bla T 6B 80
Ullswater Dr. NE12: Kil 1D 46
Ullswater Gdns. NE34: S Shi 6K 67
Ullswater Gro. SR5: Monk 3E 104
Ullswater Rd. DH2: Ches S 1K 141
NE64: Newb S 4G 13
Ullswater Ter. DH6: S Het 3A 158
Ullswater Way NE5: Newc T 4H 61
Ulverstone Ter. NE6: Walk 6C 64
Ulverston Gdns. NE9: Gate 3K 99
Umfraville Dene NE42: Pru 3F 77
Underhill NE9: Gate 1J 99
Underhill Dr. NE62: Chop 2G 17
Underhill Rd. SR6: Cle 6B 88
Underhill Ter. NE9: Spri 6E 100
Underwood NE10: Gate 1E 100
Underwood Gro. NE23: Cra 1J 25
Unicorn Ho. NE30: N Shi 6H 49
Union Alley NE33: S Shi 2J 67
Union Ct. DH3: Ches S 7A 128
Union Hall Rd. NE15: Lem 7C 60
Union La. DH2: Ches S 3K 141
SR1: Sund 1G 119
Union Pl. DH1: Dur 6D 6
Union Quay NE30: N Shi 7J 49
Union Rd. NE6: Newc T 7A 64
NE6: Walk 7A 64
NE30: N Shi 6J 49
Union Stairs NE30: N Shi 7H 49
Union St. DH5: Hett H 6G 145
NE2: Newc T 7H 63 (4K 5)
(not continuous)
NE24: Bly 1J 23
NE28: W'snd 5F 65
NE30: N Shi 7H 49
NE32: Jar 5B 66
NE33: S Shi 7H 67
SR1: Sund 1F 119 (3J 7)
SR4: Sund 2G 117
SR7: S'hm 4B 148
Unity Ter. DH9: Ann P 5B 124
DH9: Dip 2J 123
DH9: Tan L 6B 110
NE24: Camb 4H 19
University Gallery 7G 63 (3G 4)
University of Durham
Botanic Gardens 6A 166
Graham Sports Cen., The 5D 166
Hatfield College 3B 166 (4D 6)
Palace Grn. 3A 166 (3C 6)
St Chad's College 4A 166 (5C 6)
University of Durham
St John's College 4A 166 (5C 6)
Trevelyan College 5A 166 (7B 6)
University of Newcastle upon Tyne
Botanical Grounds 5C 62
Queen Victoria Rd. 6F 63 (2E 4)
University of Northumbria at Newcastle
City Campus 6G 63 (2G 4)
Coach Lane Campus 1A 64
(not continuous)
University of Sunderland
City Campus 2E 118 (4G 7)
University Station (Metro) 2E 118 (5G 7)
Unsworth Gdns. *DH8: Con 7H 121*
(off Unsworth St.)
Unsworth St. DH8: Con 7H 121
Uphill Dr. DH7: Sac 7F 141
Uplands NE25: Whit B 6D 38
Uplands, The DH3: Bir 3B 114
NE3: Ken 1B 62
Uplands Way NE9: Spri 5D 100
Up. Camden St. NE30: N Shi 6G 49
Up. Chare SR8: Pet 6B 172
Up. Crone St. NE27: Shir 7K 37
Up. Elsdon St. NE29: N Shi 1G 67
Up. Fenwick Gro. NE61: Mor 5F 9
Up. Nile St. SR1: Sund 2G 119
Up. Norfolk St. NE30: N Shi 6H 49
Up. Pearson St. NE30: N Shi 6H 49
Up. Penman St. NE29: N Shi 1G 67
Up. Queen St. NE30: N Shi 6H 49
Up. Sans St. SR1: Sund 1G 119
Up. Yoden Way SR8: Pet 6B 172
Upton St. NE8: Gate 5D 82
Urban Gdns. NE37: Wash 1H 115
Urfa Ter. NE33: S Shi 1K 67
URPETH 6G 113
Urpeth Ter. DH2: Beam 2C 126
NE6: Newc T 1A 84
(off St Peter's Rd.)
Urpeth Vs. DH9: Beam 2B 126
Urswick Ct. NE3: Ken 7H 43
Urwin St. DH5: Hett H 7H 145
USHAW MOOR 2C 164
Ushaw Rd. NE31: Heb 7K 65
Ushaw Ter. DH7: Ush M 2B 164
Ushaw Vs. DH7: Ush M 2B 164
(not continuous)
Usher Av. DH6: Sher 2K 167
Usher St. DH6: Shad 5J 169
SR5: S'wck 6D 104
Usk Av. NE32: Jar 3C 86
Uswater Sta. Rd. NE37: Usw 7J 101
(not continuous)
USWORTH 6G 101
Usworth Hall NE37: Usw 5J 101
Uxbridge Ter. NE10: Gate 5B 84

V

Valebrook NE46: Hex 2B 70
Valebrooke SR2: Sund 7H 7
Valebrooke Av. SR2: Sund 3E 118 (7H 7)
Valebrooke Gdns.
SR2: Sund 3E 118 (7H 7)
Valehead NE25: Whit B 6D 38
Vale Ho. NE2: Newc T 5J 63 (1M 5)
Valentia Av. NE6: Walk 6C 64
Valeria Cl. NE28: W'snd 6H 47
Valerian Av. NE15: Hed W 3D 58
Valerian Ct. NE63: Ash 6K 11
Valeshead Ho. NE28: W'snd 3F 65
Valeside DH1: Dur 2K 165
NE15: Thro 3G 59
(not continuous)
Vale St. DH5: Eas L 3H 157
SR4: Sund 3D 118
Vale St. E. SR4: Sund 3D 118
Vale Wlk. NE2: Newc T 6J 63 (1M 5)
Valley Ct. SR2: Sund 3G 119
Valley Cres. NE21: Bla T 4A 80
Valley Dene NE17: C'wl 7K 93
Valley Dr. DH7: Esh W 2C 162
NE9: Gate 7H 83
NE11: Dun 7B 82
NE16: Swa 6G 81
Valley Forge NE38: Wash 2H 115
Valley Gdns. DH8: Con 5E 120
NE9: Gate 7J 83
NE25: Whit B 6D 38
NE28: W'snd 2H 65
(not continuous)
Valley Gth. DH7: Esh W 2C 162
Valley Grn. NE40: Ryton 3D 78
Valley Gro. DH7: Lan 7K 137
Valley La. NE34: S Shi 7E 68
Valley Rd. DH2: Pelt 5G 127
NE25: H'wll 1K 37
Valley Shop. Village NE11: Gate 2E 98
Valley Vw. DH3: Bir 2K 113
DH5: Hett H 2D 156
DH6: Crox 7K 175
DH7: Sac 1D 152
DH7: Ush M 3D 164
Valley Vw. DH8: Con 4D 120
(Chaytor Rd.)
DH8: Con 4A 136
(Hownsgill Dr.)
DH8: Lead 6A 122
DH9: Ann P 4K 123
DH9: Stly 5E 124
NE2: Newc T 4H 63
NE15: Lem 6B 60
NE16: Burn 1K 109
NE32: Jar 2B 86
NE38: Wash 7J 115
NE39: Row G 5G 95
NE42: Pru 5G 77
NE46: Hex 2E 70
Vallum Ct. NE4: Newc T 1D 82 (5A 4)
Vallum Pl. NE9: Gate 1K 99
Vallum Rd. NE6: Walk 7C 64
NE15: Thro 3H 59
Vallum Way NE4: Newc T 1D 82 (5A 4)
Vanburgh Ct. NE25: Sea D 1H 37
Vanburgh Gdns. NE61: Mor 7D 8
Vance Bus. Pk. NE11: Gate 6D 82
Vance Ct. NE21: Bla T 2E 80
Vancouver Dr. NE7: Newc T 3B 64
Vane St. SR3: New S 2C 132
(not continuous)
SR8: Eas 7C 160
Vane Ter. SR2: Sund 3H 119
SR7: S'hm 2B 148
Vane Vs. DH1: Dur 3F 167
Vanguard Ct. SR3: New S 3B 132
(not continuous)
Vanmildert Cl. SR8: Pet 1K 181
Vardy Ter. DH4: E Her 3E 130
Vauxhall Rd. NE6: Walk 5E 64
Vedra St. SR5: S'wck 6D 104
Velville Ct. NE3: Ken 6H 43
Ventnor Av. NE4: Newc T 1B 82
Ventnor Cres. NE9: Gate 2G 99
Ventnor Gdns. NE9: Gate 1G 99
NE26: Whit B 5G 39
Vera St. NE40: G'sde 6D 78
Verdun Av. NE31: Heb 7J 65
Vermont NE37: Usw, Wash 7H 101
Verne Rd. NE29: N Shi 7C 48
Vernon Cl. NE33: S Shi 5H 67
Vernon Dr. NE25: Whit B 7E 38
Vernon Pl. NE64: Newb S 2J 13
Vernon St. NE37: Usw 7H 101
Veryan Gdns. SR3: Sund 5D 118
Vespasian Av. NE33: S Shi 1K 67
Vespasian St. NE33: S Shi 1K 67
Viador DH3: Ches S 5A 128
Viaduct St. NE28: W'snd 3J 65
Vicarage Av. NE34: S Shi 7A 68
Vicarage Cl. DH2: Pelt 2G 127
SR3: New S 2B 132
Vicarage Ct. NE10: Gate 6D 84
Vicarage Est. TS28: Win 5G 181
Vicarage Flats DH7: B'don 1D 174
Vicarage Gdns. NE22: Bed 1J 21
Vicarage La. SR4: Sund 2G 117
Vicarage Rd. SR3: New S 2C 132
Vicarage St. NE29: N Shi 7G 49
Vicarage Ter. NE22: Bed 1J 21
SR7: Mur 1E 158
Vicarsholme Cl. SR3: New S 4A 132
Vicars La. NE7: Longb 7J 45
Vicars Pele 1D 72
Viceroy St. SR7: S'hm 3B 148
Victoria Av. DH7: B'don 1E 174
NE10: Gate 6A 84
NE12: Longb 5B 46
NE26: Whit B 6H 39
NE28: W'snd 3F 65
SR2: Sund 6G 119
SR4: Sund 2H 117
Victoria Av. W. SR2: Sund 6G 119
Victoria Bldgs. SR1: Sund 4G 7
Victoria Cen. DH8: Con 7H 121
Victoria Cotts. DH1: Dur 5J 153
Victoria Ct. DH7: Ush M 2C 164
DH8: Con 7H 121
NE8: Gate 5E 82
NE12: Longb 3A 46
NE25: Sea D 7H 27
NE30: N Shi 1J 49
NE31: Heb 1H 85
SR2: Sund 5G 7
Victoria Cres. NE29: N Shi 7F 49
NE30: N Shi 1J 49
(Beverley Ter.)
NE30: N Shi 7J 39
(Eskdale Ter.)
Victoria Gro. NE42: Pru 2G 77
Victoria Ho. NE4: Newc T 3D 82 (10A 4)
NE8: Gate 5E 82
Victoria Ind. Est. NE31: Heb 3G 85
Victoria M. NE2: Newc T 5J 63
NE24: Bly 2H 23
NE26: Whit B 6H 39
Victoria Parkway NE7: Newc T 2C 64
Victoria Pl. DH3: Ches S 7A 128
DH7: Edm 1A 140

Victoria Pl.—Warwick St.

Victoria Pl. NE25: Whit B .7E 38
NE37: Usw .7H 101
SR1: Sund .2G 119 (5K 7)
SR4: Sund .2D 118
Victoria Rd. DH8: Con .7H 121
(not continuous)
NE8: Gate .6E 82
NE33: S Shi .4J 67
NE37: Usw .7H 101
Victoria Rd. E. NE31: Heb .1J 85
Victoria Rd. W. NE31: Heb .4G 85
Victoria Sq. NE2: Newc T .6G 63 (1G 4)
NE10: Gate .6B 84
Victoria St. DH5: Hett H .6G 145
DH6: Shot C .6E 170
DH7: Lan .6J 137
DH7: Sac .7E 140
DH8: Con .6G 121
NE4: Newc T .2D 82 (7B 4)
NE11: Dun .5C 82
NE29: N Shi .1G 67
NE31: Heb .6G 65
NE40: Ryton .2D 78
SR7: S'hm .3A 148
Victoria Ter. DH1: Dur .2K 165 (1A 6)
DH2: Beam .2C 126
DH2: Pelt .3E 126
(Parade, The)
DH2: Pelt .4G 127
(Wesley Ter.)
DH4: Pen .2C 130
DH7: Lan .6J 137
DH9: Ann P .5K 123
NE9: Gate .4A 100
NE9: Spri .6D 100
NE10: Gate .6B 84
NE15: Thro .3H 59
NE17: Ham C .2K 107
NE22: Bed .7K 17
(not continuous)
NE26: Whit B .6H 39
NE32: Jar .7A 66
NE36: E Bol .7J 87
NE39: Row G .6G 95
NE42: Pru .4F 77
NE64: Newb S .3J 13
SR7: Mur .1F 159
Victoria Ter. Bk. NE15: Thro .3H 59
Victoria Ter. Sth. *SR5: S'wck .6F 105*
(off Warwick St.)
Victoria Vs. NE22: Bed .7K 17
Victor St. DH3: Ches S .6A 128
SR6: Monk .6G 105
(off Brandling St. Sth.)
Victor Ter. DH7: Ush M .1D 164
Victory Cotts. NE23: Dud .2J 35
Victory Ho. NE30: N Shi .5K 49
Victory St. SR4: Sund .7A 104
Victory St. E. DH5: Hett H .6H 145
Victory St. W. DH5: Hett H .6H 145
Victory Way SR3: E Her .4J 131
Viewforth Dr. SR5: S'wck .4E 104
Viewforth Grn. NE5: Newc T .4J 61
Viewforth Rd. SR2: Ryh .4H 133
Viewforth Ter. SR5: S'wck .4D 104
(not continuous)
Viewforth Vs. DH1: Dur .2H 165
Viewlands NE63: Hir .3B 12
View La. DH9: Stly .2F 125
View Tops DH9: Beam .1B 126
VIGO .6C 114
Vigodale DH3: Bir .7C 114
Vigo La. DH3: Bir, Ches S .1A 128
DH3: Ches S .7C 114
NE38: Wash .1D 128
Vigour Gym .3G 83 (9H 5)
Viking Ind. Est. NE32: Jar .5K 65
Viking Pct. NE32: Jar .6B 66
Viking Shop. Cen., The NE32: Jar .6B 66
Villa Cl. SR4: Sund .2B 118
Village Ct. NE26: Whit B .6F 39
Village E. NE40: Ryton .7G 59
Village Farm NE15: Thro .4A 60
Village Hgts. NE8: Gate .4F 83
Village La. NE38: Wash .2G 115
Village Pl. NE6: Newc T .1A 84
Village Rd. NE23: Cra .4A 26
VILLAGE, THE .4B 182
Village, The DH7: New B .5A 174
SR2: Ryh .3J 133
Village W. NE40: Ryton .7G 59
Villa Pl. NE8: Gate .5G 83
Villa Real Bungs. DH8: Lead .5K 121
Villa Real Ct. DH8: Con .5J 121
Villa Real Est. DH8: Con .5J 121
Villa Real Rd. DH8: Con .5J 121
Villas, The DH6: Thor .1J 179
DH7: B'hpe .5D 138
DH9: Ann P .6J 123
NE13: Wide O .6E 34
SR2: Ryh .4H 133
SR5: C'twn .6J 103
Villa Vw. NE9: Gate .1J 99
Villette Brooke St. SR2: Sund .4G 119
Villette Path SR2: Sund .4G 119
Villette Rd. SR2: Sund .4G 119
Villettes, The DH4: Hou S .6D 130
Villiers Pl. DH3: Ches S .5A 128
Villiers St. SR1: Sund .1G 119 (3K 7)
Villiers St. Sth. SR1: Sund .2G 119
Vimy Av. NE31: Heb .7J 65
Vincent St. SR7: S'hm .4B 148
SR8: Eas .7C 160
Vincent Ter. DH9: Ann P .6A 124
Vindomora Rd. DH8: Ebc .5G 107
Vindomora Vs. DH8: Ebc .4G 107
Vine Cl. NE8: Gate .4E 82
Vine Ct. NE46: Hex .2D 70
Vine La. NE1: Newc T .7F 63 (3F 4)
Vine La. E. NE1: Newc T .7G 63 (3G 4)
Vine Pl. DH4: Hou S .2E 144
SR1: Sund .2E 118 (5H 7)
Vine St. NE28: W'snd .4G 65
NE33: S Shi .7H 67
Vine Ter. NE46: Hex .2D 70
Viola Cres. DH2: Ous .6H 113
DH7: Sac .1E 152
Viola St. NE37: Usw .7H 101
Viola Ter. NE16: Whi .7H 81
Violet Cl. NE4: Newc T .2K 81
Violet St. DH4: Hou S .2D 144
SR4: Sund .1D 118 (3F 7)
(Deptford Rd.)
SR4: Sund .2G 117
(Primrose St.)
Violet Ter. DH4: Hou S .6H 129
Viscount Rd. SR3: New S .2C 132
Vivian Cres. DH2: Ches S .7A 128
Vivian Sq. SR6: Monk .4F 105
Voltage Ter. DH4: Hou S .5D 130
Vue Cinemas .7G 63 (4H 5)
Vulcan Pl. NE22: Bed .1J 21
SR6: Monk .6F 105
Vulcan Ter. NE12: Longb .3C 46

W

Waddington St. DH1: Dur .2K 165 (2A 6)
Wadham Cl. SR8: Pet .7K 171
Wadham Ct. SR2: Ryh .2G 133
Wadham Ter. NE34: S Shi .1H 87
Wadsley Sq. SR2: Sund .5G 119
Waggonway, The NE42: Pru .3E 76
Wagon Way NE28: W'snd .3H 65
Wagonway Ind. Est. NE31: Heb .5J 65
Wagonway Rd. NE31: Heb .6H 65
Wagtail Cl. NE21: Bla T .6C 80
Wagtail La. DH9: Stly .1E 138
Wagtail Ter. DH9: Stly .7J 125
Wakefield Av. NE34: S Shi .1D 88
Wakenshaw Rd. DH1: Dur .1D 166
WALBOTTLE .4K 59
Walbottle Hall Gdns. NE15: Thro .4A 60
Walbottle Rd. NE15: Thro .4K 59
Walden Cl. DH2: Ous .6F 113
Waldo St. NE29: N Shi .7H 49
WALDRIDGE .1G 141
Waldridge Cl. NE37: Wash .2E 114
Waldridge Fell Country Pk. .2G 141
Waldridge Gdns. NE9: Gate .4B 100
Waldridge La. DH2: Ches S, Plaw .1G 141
Waldridge Rd. DH2: Ches S .1G 141
Waldron Sq. SR2: Sund .5G 119
WALKER .1D 84
Walkerburn NE23: Cra .7K 25
Walker Ct. *NE16: Whi .7G 81*
(off Fellside Rd.)
Walkerdene Ho. NE6: Walk .5F 65
WALKERGATE .5C 64
Walkergate DH1: Dur .2C 6
Walker Ga. Ind. Est. NE6: Walk .7F 65
Walkergate Station (Metro) .5C 64
Walker Gro. NE6: Walk .5D 64
Walker Pk. Cl. NE6: Walk .2E 84
Walker Pk. Gdns. NE6: Walk .2E 84
Walker Pl. NE30: N Shi .6J 49
WALKER RIVERSIDE .2F 85
Walker Riverside Ind. Pk. NE6: Walk .1F 85
Walker Rd. NE6: Newc T .1K 83 (6N 5)
NE6: Walk .2B 84
Walker St. DH6: Bow .5H 177
Walker Swimming Pool .1E 84
Walker Ter. NE8: Gate .4G 83 (10H 5)
Walker Vw. NE10: Gate .6B 84
WALKERVILLE .4E 64
Wallace Av. NE16: Whi .6J 81
Wallace Gdns. NE9: Gate .4C 100
Wallace St. DH4: Hou S .2D 144
NE2: Newc T .6D 62 (1B 4)
NE11: Dun .5C 82
SR5: S'wck .6E 104
Wallace Ter. *NE25: Sea D .7J 27*
(off Astley Rd.)
NE40: Ryton .1G 79
Wallaw Cinema .2J 23
Wall Cl. NE3: Gos .7C 44
Waller Ter. DH5: Hou S .3E 144
(not continuous)
Wallflower Av. SR8: Pet .5D 172
Wallinfen NE10: Gate .2D 100
Wallingford Av. SR2: Sund .6G 119
Wallington Av. NE13: Bru V .5C 34
NE30: N Shi .3G 49
Wallington Cl. NE22: Bed .6A 18
Wallington Ct. NE3: Ken .5K 43
NE12: Kil .1A 46
NE25: Sea D .7H 27
NE30: N Shi .3H 49
Wallington Dr. NE15: Lem .5E 60
Wallington Gro. NE33: S Shi .2K 67
Wallington Rd. NE63: Hir .5D 12
Wallis St. DH4: Pen .1B 130
NE10: Gate .6B 84
NE33: S Shi .2J 67
WALL NOOK .4K 151
Wallnook La. DH7: Lang P .4K 151
Wallridge Dr. NE25: H'wll .1J 37
WALLSEND .4F 65
Wallsend Rd. NE29: N Shi .2C 66
(not continuous)
Wallsend Sports Cen. .3D 64
Wallsend Station (Metro) .4G 65
Wall St. NE3: Gos .7C 44
Wall Ter. NE6: Walk .6C 64
Walmer Ter. NE9: Spri .6B 100
Walnut Gdns. NE8: Gate .6E 82
Walnut Pl. NE3: Ken .2B 62
Walpole Cl. SR7: S'hm .4H 147
Walpole Ct. SR4: Sund .2B 118
Walpole St. NE6: Walk .5C 64
NE33: S Shi .4H 67
Walsham Cl. NE24: Bly .4F 23
Walsh Av. NE31: Heb .6J 65
Walsingham NE38: Wash .5G 115
Walter St. NE13: Bru V .5C 34
NE32: Jar .5B 66
Walter Ter. DH5: Eas L .2H 157
NE4: Newc T .7C 62 (3A 4)
Walter Thomas St. SR5: S'wck .5B 104
Waltham NE38: Wash .4H 115
Waltham Cl. NE28: W'snd .2D 64
Waltham Pl. NE5: Newc T .3H 61
Walton Av. NE24: Cow .1G 23
NE29: N Shi .5F 49
SR7: S'hm .4H 147
Walton Cl. DH9: Stly .4G 125
Walton Dr. NE62: Chop .1H 17
Walton La. SR1: Sund .1G 119
Walton Pk. NE29: N Shi .4F 49
Walton Rd. NE5: Newc T .4G 61
NE38: Wash .2A 116
Walton's Bldgs. DH7: Ush M .2B 164
Walton's Ter. DH7: New B .4B 164
Walton Ter. DH8: C'sde .4C 134
DH8: Con .5J 121
TS28: Win .4F 181
Walwick Av. NE29: N Shi .6D 48
Walwick Rd. NE25: Well .6B 38
Walworth Av. NE34: S Shi .7E 68
Walworth Gro. NE32: Jar .3B 86
Walworth Way SR1: Sund .1E 118 (3H 7)
Wandsworth Rd.
NE6: Newc T .6K 63 (2N 5)
Wanless La. NE46: Hex .2D 70
Wanless Ter. DH1: Dur .2B 166 (1D 6)
Wanley St. NE24: Bly .1J 23
Wanlock Cl. NE23: Cra .7A 26
Wanny Rd. NE22: Bed .7K 17
Wansbeck NE38: Wash .7E 114
Wansbeck Av. DH9: Stly .4F 125
NE24: News .3J 23
NE30: N Shi .1J 49
NE62: Chop .7J 11
Wansbeck Bus. Cen. NE63: Ash .3K 11
Wansbeck Bus. Pk. NE63: Ash .2K 11
Wansbeck Cl. DH2: Ous .2H 127
NE16: Sun .4G 97
Wansbeck Ct. *NE61: Mor .7G 9*
(off Wansbeck St.)
SR3: New S .3B 132
SR8: Pet .1A 182
Wansbeck Cres. NE61: Peg .4A 10
Wansbeck Gro. DH8: Lead .4B 122
NE25: Sea D .4H 27
Wansbeck M. NE63: Ash .3K 11
Wansbeck Pl. NE61: Mor .6E 8
Wansbeck Riverside Cvn. Pk.
NE63: Ash .6H 11
Wansbeck Rd. NE23: Dud .3H 35
NE32: Jar .1A 86
NE63: Ash .3J 11
Wansbeck Rd. Nth. NE3: Gos .6C 44
Wansbeck Rd. Sth. NE3: Gos .6C 44
Wansbeck Road Station (Metro) .6C 44
Wansbeck Sq. NE63: Ash .3A 12
Wansbeck St. NE17: C'wl .6A 94
NE61: Mor .7G 9
NE63: N Sea .7E 12
Wansbeck Ter. NE23: Dud .3H 35
NE62: W Sle .1B 18
Wansbeck Vw. NE62: Chop .7K 11
Wansdyke NE61: Mor .6C 8
Wansfell Av. NE5: Newc T .2K 61
Wansford Av. NE5: Newc T .4H 61
Wansford Way NE16: Whi .3F 97
Wantage Av. NE29: N Shi .1D 66
Wantage Rd. DH1: Carr .6H 155
Wantage St. NE33: S Shi .6K 67
Wapping Rd. NE24: Bly .1K 23
Wapping St. NE33: S Shi .1H 67
Warbeck Cl. NE3: Ken .6H 43
Warburton Cres. NE9: Gate .6J 83
Warcop Ct. NE3: Ken .5A 44
Ward Ct. SR2: Sund .3G 119
Warden Gro. DH5: Hou S .3F 145
WARDEN LAW .1K 145
Wardenlaw NE10: Gate .2D 100
Warden Law La. SR3: New S .3A 132
Wardill Gdns. NE9: Gate .7K 83
Ward La. NE43: Mic .7B 76
Wardle Av. NE33: S Shi .4A 68
Wardle Dr. NE23: Dud .3K 35
Wardle Gdns. NE10: Gate .7C 84
Wardles Ter. DH1: Dur .3A 6
Wardle St. DH9: Stly .6E 124
NE3: Gos .7G 45
Wardle Ter. NE40: Ryton .2D 78
WARDLEY .6G 85
Wardley Ct. NE10: Gate .6H 85
Wardley Dr. NE10: Gate .6H 85
Wardley Grn. NE10: Gate, Heb .4G 85
Wardley La. NE10: Gate .6H 85
(not continuous)
Wardroper Ho. NE6: Walk .2E 84
Ward St. SR2: Sund .3G 119
Warenford Cl. NE23: Cra .6A 26
Warenford Pl. NE5: Newc T .6J 61
Warenmill Cl. NE15: Lem .6B 60
Warennes St. SR4: Sund .1A 118
Warenton Pl. NE29: N Shi .3B 48
Waring Av. NE26: Sea S .3B 28
Waring Ter. SR7: Mur .4H 147
Wark Av. NE27: Shir .7K 37
NE29: N Shi .6C 48
Wark Ct. NE3: Gos .1G 63
Wark Cres. NE32: Jar .4B 86
Warkdale Av. NE24: Cow .2E 22
Wark St. DH3: Ches S .1A 142
Warkworth Av. NE24: News .4J 23
NE26: Whit B .6G 39
NE28: W'snd .1G 65
NE34: S Shi .6D 68
SR8: Pet .4D 172
Warkworth Cl. NE38: Wash .4F 115
Warkworth Cres. NE3: Gos .6D 44
NE15: Thro .6K 59
(off Newburn Rd.)
NE63: Ash .4A 12
SR7: S'hm .3G 147
Warkworth Dr. DH2: Ches S .1J 141
NE13: Wide O .4E 34
NE61: Peg .4B 10
Warkworth Gdns. NE10: Gate .6A 84
Warkworth Rd. DH1: Dur .4A 154
Warkworth St. NE15: Lem .7C 60
Warkworth Ter. NE30: N Shi .4K 49
(not continuous)
NE32: Jar .3B 86
Warkworth Woods NE3: Gos, Wide O .2D 44
Warnbrook Av. *SR7: Mur .1F 159*
(off E. Coronation St.)
Warnbrook Cres. TS27: B Col .3K 183
Warnham Av. SR2: Sund .6G 119
Warnhead Rd. NE22: Bed .7K 17
Warren Av. NE6: Walk .5E 64
Warren Cl. DH4: Hou S .5C 130
Warren Ct. NE63: Ash .5A 12
Warrenmor NE10: Gate .7E 84
Warren Sq. SR1: Sund .7H 105
SR8: Pet .6E 172
Warren St. SR8: Pet .5E 172
Warrens Wlk. NE21: Bla T .5A 80
Warrington Rd. NE3: Ken .6A 44
NE4: Newc T .2C 82
Warton Ter. NE6: Newc T .5A 64
Warwick Av. DH8: C'sde .3C 134
NE16: Whi .2G 97
Warwick Cl. NE16: Whi .2G 97
NE23: Seg .2C 36
Warwick Ct. DH1: Dur .5J 165
NE3: Ken .5K 43
NE8: Gate .4H 83 (10J 5)
Warwick Dr. DH5: Hou S .4E 144
NE16: Whi .2H 97
NE37: Usw .5H 101
SR3: E Her .2J 131
Warwick Gro. NE22: Bed .7F 17
Warwick Hall Wlk. NE7: Newc T .2B 64
Warwick Pl. SR8: Pet .5K 171
Warwick Rd. NE5: Newc T .5E 60
NE28: W'snd .4F 65
NE31: Heb .3K 85
NE33: S Shi .5K 67
NE34: S Shi .5K 67
Warwickshire Dr. DH1: Carr .2G 167
Warwick St. NE2: Newc T .7H 63 (2K 5)
NE8: Gate .4H 83
NE24: Bly .5G 23
SR5: S'wck .6F 105

Warwick Ter.—Westbourne Av.

Warwick Ter. SR3: New S 1C **132**
Warwick Ter. Nth. *SR3: New S 1C 132*
(off Warwick Ter.)
Warwick Ter. W. SR3: New S 1C **132**
Wasdale Cl. NE23: Cra 7A **26**
SR8: Pet .6C **172**
Wasdale Ct. SR6: Monk 2E **104**
Wasdale Cres. NE21: Bla T 6B **80**
Wasdale Rd. NE5: Newc T 5H **61**
WASHINGTON 3J **115**
Washington Arts Cen. 6H 115
Washington 'F' Pit Mus. 1G 115
Washington Gdns. NE9: Gate 4A **100**
Washington Highway DH4: Pen 5G **115**
NE37: Wash 7E **100**
NE38: Wash 7G **115**
Washington Leisure Cen. 4G 115
Washington Old Hall 2J 115
Washington Rd. NE36: W Bol 3E **102**
NE37: Wash, W Bol 7A **102**
SR5: C'twn 4F **103**
SR5: W Bol 5D **102**
SR5: Wash 5D **102**
Washington Sq. SR8: Eas 1K **171**
WASHINGTON STAITHES 5A **116**
Washington St. SR4: Sund 2B **118**
Washington Ter. NE30: N Shi 5J **49**
WASHINGTON VILLAGE 2H **115**
Washington Wildfowl & Wetlands Trust
. . . . .3C 116
Washingwell La. NE16: Whi 7J **81**
Washingwell Pk. NE16: Whi 1J **97**
Waskerley Cl. NE16: Sun 4G **97**
Waskerley Dr. DH6: Shot C 5D **170**
Waskerley Gdns. NE9: Gate 4B **100**
Waskerley Rd. NE38: Wash 3K **115**
Watch Ho. Cl. NE29: N Shi 2G **67**
Watcombe Cl. NE37: Usw 5K **101**
Water Activities Cen. 7K 49
Waterbeach Pl. NE5: Newc T 3H **61**
Waterbeck Cl. NE23: Cra 7A **26**
Waterbury Cl. SR5: S'wck 4B **104**
Waterbury Rd. NE3: Gos 3D **44**
Waterfield Rd. NE22: E Sle 4F **19**
Waterford Cl. DH5: W Rai 6D **144**
NE26: Sea S 4D **28**
Waterford Cres. NE26: Whit B 7H **39**
Waterford Grn. NE63: Hir 7B **12**
Waterford Pk. NE13: Bru V 5B **34**
Watergate NE1: Newc T 2G **83** (7G **4**)
Watergate Bank NE11: Gate 3A **98**
WATERGATE ESTATE 1J **97**
Watergate Rd. DH8: C'sde 4B **134**
Water Ho. Rd. DL15: New B 7E **162**
WATERHOUSES 6B **162**
Waterloo Ct. NE37: Usw 7J **101**
Waterloo Pl. NE29: N Shi 6G **49**
SR1: Sund 2F **119** (4J **7**)
Waterloo Rd. NE24: Bly 2H **23**
NE25: Well 6A **38**
NE37: Usw 6J **101**
(Manor Rd.)
NE37: Usw 5K **101**
(Rutherford Rd.)
Waterloo Sq. NE33: S Shi 2J **67**
Waterloo St. NE1: Newc T 2E **82** (7D **4**)
NE21: Bla T 5A **80**
Waterloo Va. NE33: S Shi 2J **67**
Waterloo Wlk. *NE37: Usw 7J 101*
(off Waterloo Ct.)
Waterlow Cl. SR5: S'wck 3B **104**
Watermark, The NE11: Dun, Swa 3H **81**
Watermill NE40: Ryton 1G **79**
Watermill La. NE10: Gate 6C **84**
Watermill Pk. NE10: Gate 7B **84**
Water Row NE15: Thro 6J **59**
Waterside NE61: Mor 7F **9**
Waterside Dr. NE11: Dun 4A **82**
Waterside Pk. NE31: Heb 7G **65**
Waterson Cres. DH7: Wit G 2D **152**
Water St. DH7: Sac 7E **140**
NE4: Newc T 3D **82** (10A **4**)
Waterview Pk. NE38: Wash 3C **116**
Waterville Pl. NE29: N Shi 7G **49**
Waterville Rd. NE29: N Shi 1D **66**
Waterville Ter. NE29: N Shi 7G **49**
Waterworks Rd. SR1: Sund 2D **118** (4F **7**)
SR2: Ryh 4G **133**
Waterworks, The SR2: Ryh 4G **133**
Waterworld 4G 77
Watford Cl. SR5: S'wck 3B **104**
Watkin Cres. SR7: Mur 7E **146**
Watling Av. SR7: S'hm 4G **147**
Watling Pl. NE9: Gate 1K **99**
Watling St. DH8: Lead 5B **122**
NE45: Cor 7D **52**
Watling St. Bungs. DH8: Lead 4A **122**
Watling Way DH7: Lan 7J **137**
Watson Av. NE23: Dud 3H **35**
NE34: S Shi 1D **88**
Watson Cl. DH6: Whe H 2C **180**
SR7: Mur 4H **147**
Watson Cres. TS29: Trim S 7C **180**
Watson Gdns. NE28: W'snd 2A **66**
Watson Pl. NE34: S Shi 1D **88**
Watson's Bldgs. DH7: Edm 3D **140**
Watson St. DH8: Con 5G **121**
DH9: Stly 1F **125**
NE8: Gate 5E **82**
NE16: Burn 2B **110**
NE32: Jar 5C **66**
NE39: H Spen 2E **94**
Watson Ter. NE35: Bol C 7F **87**
NE61: Mor 7G **9**
Watt's La. NE64: Newb S 2J **13**
Watts Moses Ho. *SR1: Sund 1H 119*
(off High St. E.)
Watt's Slope NE26: Whit B 5G **39**
Watts St. SR7: Mur 7E **146**
Watt St. NE8: Gate 7F **83**
Wave Health & Fitness Cen. 3F 105
(off Sea Rd.)
Wavendon Cres. SR4: Sund 4K **117**
Waveney Gdns. DH9: Stly 5E **124**
Waveney Rd. SR8: Pet 1K **181**
Waverdale Av. NE6: Walk 6E **64**
Waverdale Way NE33: S Shi 7H **67**
Waverley Av. NE22: Bed 7A **18**
(Roslin Pk.)
NE22: Bed 6A **18**
(Waverley Dr.)
NE25: Whit B 7F **39**
Waverley Cl. DH6: Shot C 5D **170**
NE21: Bla T 6K **79**
Waverley Ct. NE22: Bed 6A **18**
Waverley Cres. NE15: Lem 6D **60**
Waverley Dr. NE22: Bed 6A **18**
(not continuous)
Waverley Lodge NE2: Newc T 1J **5**
Waverley Pl. NE64: Newb S 2J **13**
Waverley Rd. NE4: Newc T 2D **82** (8A **4**)
NE9: Gate, Spri 5J **99**
Waverley Ter. DH9: Dip 7J **109**
SR4: Sund 1A **118**
Waverton Cl. NE23: Cra 7K **25**
Wawn St. NE33: S Shi 5K **67**
Wayfarer Rd. SR5: S'wck 6C **104**
Waygood Gallery 1F 83 (6F 4)
Wayland Sq. SR2: Sund 7G **119**
Wayman St. SR5: S'wck 6E **104**
Wayside DH6: Crox 7K **175**
DH6: Whe H 4A **180**
NE15: Newc T 1H **81**
NE34: S Shi 7D **68**
SR2: Sund 4D **118**
Wayside Ct. DH7: Ush M 1D **164**
Wealcroft NE10: Gate 3D **100**
Wealcroft Ct. NE10: Gate 2D **100**
Wealleans Cl. NE63: N Sea 4F **13**
WEAR 6F **115**
Wear Av. DH8: Lead 4B **122**
Wear Ct. NE34: S Shi 1J **87**
Wear Cres. DH3: Gt Lum 3F **143**
Weardale Av. NE6: Walk 6E **64**
NE12: Longb 4A **46**
NE24: Cow 1D **22**
NE28: W'snd 1F **65**
NE37: Usw 7G **101**
SR6: Monk 1G **105**
Weardale Cres. DH4: Pen 2B **130**
Weardale Ho. NE37: Wash 4F **115**
Weardale Pk. DH6: Whe H 2C **180**
Weardale St. DH5: Hett H 2E **156**
Weardale Ter. DH3: Ches S 7B **128**
DH9: Ann P 5A **124**
Weardale Way DH3: Gt Lum 4E **142**
Wearfield SR5: Sund 6A **104**
Wearhead Dr. SR4: Sund 4D **118**
Wear Ind. Est. NE38: Wash 6F **115**
Wear Lodge DH3: Ches S 2A **128**
Wearmouth Av. SR5: Sund 5F **105**
Wearmouth Dr. SR5: Monk 5E **104**
Wearmouth St. SR6: Monk 6F **105**
Wear Rd. DH9: Stly 3F **125**
NE31: Heb 2J **85**
Wearside Dr. DH1: Dur 2B **166** (1D **6**)
Wear St. DH3: Ches S 7B **128**
DH4: Hou S 3A **144**
DH5: Hett H 7G **145**
DH8: Con 7J **121**
NE17: C'wl 6K **93**
NE32: Jar 6B **66**
SR1: Sund 2H **119**
SR4: Sund 1G **117**
SR5: Sund 6C **104**
SR7: S'hm 3B **148**
Wear Ter. NE38: Wash 4K **115**
SR8: Eas .7B **160**
Wear Vw. DH1: Dur 2B **166** (1E **6**)
SR4: Sund 1H **117**
Weathercock La. NE9: Gate 2H **99**
Weatherside NE21: Bla T 5B **80**
Webb Av. SR7: Mur 6E **146**
SR7: S'hm 3G **147**
Webb Gdns. NE10: Gate 6E **84**
Webb Sq. SR8: Pet 3C **172**
Wedderburn Sq. NE63: Ash 4A **12**
Wedder Law NE23: Cra 7K **25**
Wedgewood Cotts. NE15: Lem 7D **60**
Wedgewood Rd. SR7: S'hm 4H **147**
Wedmore Rd. NE5: Newc T 3D **60**
Weetman St. NE33: S Shi 4H **67**
Weetslade Cres. NE23: Dud 4J **35**
Weetslade Ind. Est. NE23: Gos 6H **35**
Weetslade Rd. NE23: Dud 3H **35**
Weetslade Ter. NE23: Dud 6K **35**
Weetwood Rd. NE23: Cra 6A **26**
Weidner Rd. NE15: Newc T 7K **61**
Welbeck Grn. NE6: Walk 1C **84**
Welbeck Rd. NE6: Newc T, Walk 1A **84**
NE62: Chop 1G **17**
Welbeck Ter. NE61: Peg 3B **10**
NE63: Hir 5B **12**
Welburn Cl. NE42: O'ham 1D **76**
Welbury Way NE23: Cra 7K **25**
Welby Dr. DH7: Ush M 2B **164**
Weldon Av. SR2: Sund 6G **119**
Weldon Cl. DH6: Shot C 5D **170**
Weldon Cres. NE7: Newc T 3K **63**
Weldon Pl. NE29: N Shi 4D **48**
Weldon Rd. NE12: Longb 6K **45**
NE23: E Cram 5B **26**
Weldon Ter. DH3: Ches S 7B **128**
Weldon Way NE3: Gos 6D **44**
Welfare Cl. SR8: Eas 7C **160**
Welfare Cres. DH6: S Het 5D **158**
NE63: Hir 3D **12**
NE64: Newb S 3G **13**
TS27: B Col 2G **183**
Welfare Rd. DH5: Hett H 6F **145**
(not continuous)
Welford Av. NE3: Gos 7C **44**
Welford Rd. DH8: C'sde 2E **134**
Welland Cl. SR8: Pet 1A **182**
Wellands Cl. SR6: Whit 5G **89**
Wellands Ct. SR6: Whit 5G **89**
Wellands Dr. SR6: Whit 5G **89**
Wellands La. SR6: Whit 5G **89**
Well Bank NE45: Cor 7D **52**
Well Bank Rd. NE37: Usw 6F **101**
Wellburn Cl. DH6: Shot C 5D **170**
Wellburn Pk. NE2: Newc T 4J **63**
Wellburn Rd. NE37: Usw 6F **101**
Well Cl. Wlk. NE16: Whi 1G **97**
Well Dean NE42: Pru 3F **77**
Wellesley Ct. NE33: S Shi 1J **67**
Wellesley St. NE32: Jar 1B **86**
Wellesley Ter. NE4: Newc T 1C **82**
WELLFIELD
Whitley Bay 6B **38**
Wingate 4G **181**
Wellfield Cl. NE15: Thro 4G **59**
Wellfield Ct. NE40: Ryton 3C **78**
Wellfield La. NE5: Newc T 3G **61**
Wellfield M. SR2: Ryh 4G **133**
Wellfield Rd. NE4: Newc T 1K **81**
(not continuous)
NE39: Row G 6G **95**
SR7: Mur 7D **146**
TS28: Win 4G **181**
Wellfield Rd. Nth. TS28: Win 4G **181**
Wellfield Rd. Sth. TS28: Win 4G **181**
Wellfield Ter. NE10: Gate 7A **84**
NE10: Gate 5F 85
(off Shields Rd.)
SR2: Ryh 4G **133**
TS28: Win 4H 181
(off Wellfield Rd.)
Wellgarth Rd. NE37: Usw 6F **101**
Wellhead Dean Rd. NE61: Ash 5H **11**
NE63: Ash 5H **11**
Wellhead Ter. NE63: Ash 3J **11**
Wellhope NE38: Wash 1D **128**
Wellington Av. NE25: Well 6A **38**
Wellington Ct. NE10: Gate 6A **84**
NE37: Usw 7J **101**
Wellington Dr. NE33: S Shi 1J **67**
Wellington La. SR4: Sund 7D **104** (1F **7**)
Wellington Rd. NE11: Dun 5K **81**
(not continuous)
NE62: Chop 1J **17**
Wellington Row DH4: Hou S 4C **130**
Wellington St. DH6: H Pitt 6B **156**
NE4: Newc T 7E **62** (4B **4**)
NE8: Gate 2G **83** (8H **5**)
NE10: Gate 6A **84**
NE15: Lem 7D **60**
NE24: Bly 2K **23**
(not continuous)
NE31: Heb 1H **85**
Wellington St. E. NE24: Bly 1K **23**
Wellington St. W. NE29: N Shi 7G **49**
Wellington Wlk. *NE37: Usw 7J 101*
(off Wellington Ct.)
Well La. NE27: Shir 2B **48**
(not continuous)
Wellmere Rd. SR2: Sund 7H **119**
Well Ridge Cl. NE25: Whit B 5C **38**
Well Ridge Pk. NE25: Whit B 4C **38**
Well Rd. NE43: Stoc 2H **91**
Wells Cl. NE7: Newc T 1B **64**
Wells Cres. SR7: S'hm 3H **147**
Wells Gdns. NE9: Gate 5H **99**
Wells Gro. NE34: S Shi 6C **68**
Wellshede NE10: Gate 7F **85**
Wells St. NE35: Bol C 5E **86**
Well St. SR4: Sund 1B **118**
Well Way NE61: Mor 6F **9**
Wellway NE32: Jar 4B **86**
Wellway Ct. NE61: Mor 6F **9**
Wellwood Gdns. NE61: Mor 7G **9**
Welsh Ter. DH9: Ann P 6A **124**
WELTON 2H **55**
Welton Cl. NE43: Stoc 1K **91**
Welwyn Av. NE22: Bed 5B **18**
Welwyn Cl. NE28: W'snd 1D **64**
SR5: C'twn 7G **103**
Wembley Av. NE25: Whit B 7E **38**
Wembley Cl. SR5: S'wck 4B **104**
Wembley Gdns. NE24: Camb 2F **19**
Wembley Rd. SR5: S'wck 4B **104**
Wembley Ter. NE24: Camb 2F **19**
Wendover Cl. SR5: S'wck 3A **104**
Wendover Way SR5: S'wck 3A **104**
Wenham Sq. SR2: Sund 4D **118**
Wenlock NE38: Wash 4G **115**
Wenlock Dr. NE29: N Shi 4E **48**
Wenlock Lodge NE34: S Shi 1G **87**
Wenlock Pl. NE34: S Shi 2G **87**
Wenlock Rd. NE34: S Shi 1F **87**
Wensley Cl. DH2: Ous 7G **113**
NE5: Newc T 1J **61**
Wensleydale NE28: W'snd 7D **46**
Wensleydale Av. DH4: Pen 2A **130**
NE37: Usw 7G **101**
Wensleydale Dr. NE12: Longb 4B **46**
Wensleydale Ter. NE24: Bly 3K **23**
Wensley Ho. SR3: New S 4B **132**
Wentworth NE33: S Shi 4A **68**
Wentworth Cl. NE10: Gate 7B **84**
Wentworth Ct. NE20: Pon 7G **31**
Wentworth Dr. NE37: Usw 5G **101**
Wentworth Gdns. NE25: Whit B 7C **38**
Wentworth Grange NE3: Gos 1F **63**
Wentworth Leisure Cen. 1D 70
Wentworth Pl. NE46: Hex 1D **70**
Wentworth Ter. SR4: Sund 1D **118** (4F **7**)
Werdohl Way DH8: Con 4J **121**
Werhale Grn. NE10: Gate 6B **84**
Wesley Cl. DH9: Stly 2G **125**
Wesley Ct. DH9: Ann P 4K **123**
NE10: Gate 5A **84**
NE21: Bla T 3D **80**
Wesley Dr. NE12: Kil 3F **47**
Wesley Gdns. DH8: C'sde 4C **134**
Wesley Gro. NE40: Ryton 3C **78**
Wesley Mt. NE40: Ryton 3C **78**
Wesley Sq. NE1: Newc T 2H **83** (7J **5**)
Wesley St. DH8: Con 7H **121**
DH8: Shot B 5F **121**
NE2: Newc T 7H **63** (3J **5**)
NE9: Gate 2H **99**
NE33: S Shi 2J **67**
NE42: Pru 4F **77**
Wesley Ter. DH2: Pelt 4G **127**
DH3: Ches S 6A **128**
DH6: Sher 3C **168**
DH8: C'sde 4D **134**
DH9: Ann P 5K **123**
DH9: Dip .7H **109**
NE42: Pru 4F **77**
Wesley Way NE12: Kil 3F **47**
NE15: Thro 3H **59**
SR7: S'hm 3H **147**
Wessex Cl. SR5: S'wck 3B **104**
Wessington Ind. Est. SR5: C'twn 6J **103**
Wessington Ter. NE37: Wash 1H **115**
Wessington Way SR5: Sund 1F **117**
West Acre DH8: Shot B 4E **120**
Westacre Gdns. NE5: Newc T 6J **61**
West Acres NE13: Din 4H **33**
NE21: Bla T 4D **80**
W. Acres Av. NE16: Whi 2H **97**
Westacres Cres. NE15: Newc T 7J **61**
WEST ALLOTMENT 3J **47**
W. Allotment By-Pass NE27: Shir 2H **47**
West Av. DH2: Ches S 3J **141**
NE3: Gos .1E **62**
NE5: Newc T 3F **61**
NE12: Longb 6B **46**
(Thornhill Rd.)
NE12: Longb 3D **46**
(Young Rd.)
NE25: Whit B 6E **38**
NE29: N Shi 7D **48**
NE34: S Shi 7A **68**
NE38: Wash 7F **115**
NE39: Row G 6H **95**
NE62: Chop 1F **17**
SR6: Whit 5G **89**
SR7: Mur 1E **158**
SR8: Eas .6C **160**
TS27: B Col 1H **183**
West Bailey NE12: Kil 7K **35**
West Bank *NE40: Ryton 3C 78*
(off Bank Top)
West Block DH7: Wit G 3C **152**
WEST BOLDON 7G **87**
Westbourne Av. NE3: Gos 5E **44**
NE6: Walk 5D **64**

Westbourne Av.—Westwood St.

Westbourne Av. NE8: Gate 6G 83
NE62: Chop 6J 11
Westbourne Cotts. DH4: Hou S 3A 130
Westbourne Dr. DH4: Hou S 3A 130
Westbourne Gdns. NE6: Walk 7E 64
Westbourne Gro. NE46: Hex 1B 70
Westbourne Rd. SR1: Sund 2D 118 (5F 7)
Westbourne Ter. DH4: Hou S 4A 130
NE25: Sea D 7J 27
WEST BRANDON 7F 163
W. Bridge St. DH4: Pen 1J 129
NE24: Camb 5H 19
Westbrooke Ho. SR2: Sund 4F 119
W. Brunton Farm Cotts. NE13: Bru V 2K 43
Westburn NE40: Ryton 3C 78
(not continuous)
Westburn Cotts. NE40: Ryton 3C 78
Westburn Gdns. NE28: W'snd 1D 64
Westburn M. NE40: Ryton 3C 78
Westburn Ter. SR6: Monk 5G 105
Westbury Av. NE6: Walk 5E 64
Westbury Ct. NE12: Longb 7J 45
Westbury Rd. NE29: N Shi 4F 49
Westbury St. SR4: Sund 1D 118
WEST CHIRTON 7D 48
W. Chirton Ind. Est. NE29: N Shi 6C 48
W. Chirton (Middle) Trad. Est.
NE29: N Shi 5B 48
W. Chirton Nth. Ind. Est. NE29: N Shi 5A 48
WEST CHOPWELL 5K 93
Westcliff Cl. SR8: Eas 1J 171
Westcliffe Rd. SR6: Monk 3H 105
Westcliffe Way NE34: S Shi 3F 87
W. Clifton NE12: Kil 7A 36
West Copperas NE15: Lem 6E 60
(not continuous)
W. Coronation St. SR7: Mur 7F 147
Westcott Av. NE33: S Shi 4A 68
Westcott Dr. DH1: Dur 6J 153
Westcott Rd. NE34: S Shi 1J 87
SR8: Pet 5B 172
Westcott Ter. DH4: Pen 1C 130
West Ct. DH1: Dur 5A 166 (7B 6)
NE3: Gos 7C 44
NE24: Bly 3G 23
West Cres. NE10: Gate 6G 85
NE17: C'wl 1K 107
SR8: Eas 7A 160
Westcroft Pk. SR6: Whit 5G 89
Westcroft Rd. NE12: Longb 5C 46
W. Dene Dr. NE30: N Shi 4G 49
W. Denton Cl. NE15: Lem 5D 60
W. Denton Retail Pk. NE5: Newc T 3G 61
W. Denton Rd. NE15: Lem 5D 60
W. Denton Way NE5: Newc T 3D 60
West Dr. DH2: Ches S 7H 127
DH7: Lan 7J 137
NE24: News 5G 23
SR6: Cle 5A 88
W. Ellen St. SR7: Mur 1F 159
West End NE26: Sea S 6D 28
W. End Ter. NE46: Hex 2C 70
Wester Ct. SR3: New S 4B 132
Westerdale DH4: Pen 1J 129
NE28: W'snd 1D 64
Westerdale Pl. NE6: Walk 7F 65
Westerham Cl. SR5: S'wck 3B 104
WESTERHOPE 3F 61
Westerhope Gdns. NE5: Newc T 4K 61
Westerhope Rd. NE38: Wash 3K 115
Westerhope Small Bus. Pk.
NE5: Newc T 1E 60
Westerkirk NE23: Cra 7A 26
Western App. NE33: S Shi 6H 67
Western App. Ind. Est. *NE33: S Shi 4J 67*
(off Western App.)
Western Av. DH7: Esh W 3D 162
NE4: Newc T 1A 82
NE5: Newc T 4D 60
NE11: Gate 3E 98
NE25: Sea D 7F 27
NE42: Pru 4D 76
Western Ct. *NE26: Whit B 3F 39*
(off Western Way.)
Western Dr. NE4: Newc T 1B 82
Western Highway DH3: Wash 6C 114
NE38: Wash 6C 114
WESTERN HILL 1J 165
Western Hill DH8: Shot B 4E 120
SR2: Ryh 2G 133
SR2: Sund 2D 118 (5F 7)
Westernmoor NE37: Wash 2D 114
Western Rd. NE28: W'snd 3K 65
NE32: Jar 6A 66
Western Ter. NE23: Dud 3H 35
NE36: E Bol, W Bol 7G 87
NE37: Wash 1H 115
Western Ter. Nth. SR7: Mur 7F 147
Western Ter. Sth. SR7: Mur 7F 147
Western Vw. NE9: Spri 6A 100
Western Way NE20: Pon 7E 30
NE21: Bla T 4E 80
NE26: Whit B 3F 39
NE40: Ryton 2G 79
West Farm DH8: M'sly 6A 108
W. Farm Av. NE12: Longb 6H 45
W. Farm Ct. DH7: Ush M 4E 164
NE12: Kil 2C 46
NE23: Cra 3K 25
W. Farm La. DH8: M'sly 6A 108
W. Farm Rd. NE6: Walk 6C 64
NE28: W'snd 2J 65
SR6: Cle 6D 88
W. Farm Wynd NE12: Longb 7H 45
Westfield NE3: Gos 3D 62
NE10: Gate 1C 100
NE23: Dud 3H 35
NE32: Jar 5C 86
NE61: Mor 1E 14
Westfield Av. NE3: Gos 2E 62
NE13: Bru V 5C 34
NE25: Whit B 7D 38
NE40: Ryton 3D 78
Westfield Cl. NE46: Hex 1B 70
Westfield Ct. NE28: W'snd 5F 65
NE32: Jar 7B 66
SR4: Sund 4A 118
Westfield Cres. NE9: Spri 6D 100
NE40: Ryton 3D 78
NE64: Newb S 3H 13
Westfield Dr. NE3: Gos 2E 62
Westfield Gro. NE3: Gos 2D 62
SR4: Sund 4A 118
Westfield La. NE40: Ryton 7F 59
Westfield Pk. NE3: Gos 2E 62
NE28: W'snd 3E 64
Westfield Rd. NE8: Gate 6G 83
NE15: Newc T 1J 81
Westfields DH9: Stly 4D 124
Westfield Ter. NE8: Gate 6G 83
NE9: Spri 6C 100
(off Windsor Rd.)
NE46: Hex 1B 70
W. Ford Rd. NE62: Chop 7K 11
Westgarth NE5: Newc T 1E 60
Westgarth Gro. DH6: Shot C 5D 170
Westgarth Ter. NE37: Usw 7J 101
Westgate NE61: Mor 1D 14
Westgate Av. SR3: New S 1C 132
Westgate Cen. for Sport 7K 61
Westgate Cl. NE25: Whit B 5C 38
Westgate Ct. NE4: Newc T 5A 4
Westgate Gro. SR3: New S 1C 132
Westgate Hill Ter.
NE4: Newc T 1E 82 (6C 4)
Westgate Rd. NE1: Newc T 1E 82 (6D 4)
NE4: Newc T 7B 62 (5A 4)
W. George Potts St. NE33: S Shi 4J 67
West Grange SR5: S'wck 4E 104
West Grn. NE62: Sco G 3G 17
West Greens NE61: Mor 7G 9
West Gro. SR4: Sund 3H 117
SR7: S'hm 3H 147
W. Hartford Bus. Cen. NE23: E Har 6H 21
WEST HARTON 1J 87
W. Haven DH8: Con 6G 121
Westheath Av. SR2: Sund 7F 119
WEST HERRINGTON 2F 131
W. Hextol NE46: Hex 2B 70
W. Hextol Cl. NE46: Hex 2B 70
W. High Horse Cl. NE39: Row G 3A 96
West Hill NE61: Mor 1E 14
SR4: Sund 4A 118
Westhills DH9: Tan L 6A 110
Westhills Cl. DH7: Sac 5D 140
W. Holborn NE33: S Shi 4H 67
Westholme Gdns. NE15: Newc T 7K 61
Westholme Ter. *SR2: Sund 6H 119*
(off Ryhope Rd.)
WEST HOLYWELL 5H 37
Westhope Cl. NE34: S Shi 6C 68
Westhope Rd. NE34: S Shi 6C 68
WEST JESMOND 3G 63
W. Jesmond Av. NE2: Newc T 3G 63
West Jesmond Station (Metro) 3G 63
WEST KYO 4K 123
Westlands DH6: Coxh 7J 177
NE5: Cha P 4C 60
NE7: Newc T 3J 63
NE26: Sea S 4B 28
NE30: N Shi 3H 49
NE32: Jar 5D 86
Westlands, The SR4: Sund 3B 118
West La. DH3: Ches S 7A 128
DH6: S Het 4D 158
NE12: Kil 3B 46
NE16: Burn 6C 96
NE17: Ham C 4K 107
NE21: Bla T 6A 80
SR7: Eas 4H 159
West Lawn SR2: Sund 4F 119
W. Lawrence St. SR1: Sund 2G 119
W. Law Rd. DH8: Shot B 2F 121
WESTLEA 3H 147
West Lea DH4: E Her 3D 130
DH7: Wit G 3D 152
NE21: Bla T 6C 80
Westlea NE22: Bed 1F 21
Westlea Rd. DH4: Hou S 6C 130
SR7: S'hm 3H 147
West Leigh DH9: Tan L 1D 124
Westley Av. NE26: Whit B 2E 38
Westley Cl. NE26: Whit B 2E 38
Westline Ind. Est. DH2: Bir 6K 113
Westlings DH5: Hett H 7G 145
Westloch Rd. NE23: Cra 7K 25
Westmacott St. NE15: Thro 5J 59
West Mdws. NE5: Cha P 1D 60
West Mdws. Dr. SR6: Cle 7C 88
West Mdws. Rd. SR6: Cle 6D 88
WEST MICKLEY 6A 76
Westminster Av. NE29: N Shi 4B 48
(not continuous)
Westminster Cl. NE26: Whit B 7J 39
Westminster Cres. NE31: Heb 4J 85
Westminster Dr. NE11: Dun 1B 98
Westminster St. NE8: Gate 6F 83
SR2: Sund 6H 119
Westminster Way NE7: Newc T 1B 64
W. Moffett St. NE33: S Shi 4K 67
WEST MONKSEATON 7D 38
West Monkseaton Station (Metro) 7D 38
WEST MOOR 3K 45
W. Moor Ct. NE12: Longb 3K 45
Westmoor Dr. NE12: Longb 3K 45
W. Moor Dr. SR6: Cle 7C 88
Westmoor Rd. SR4: Sund 1K 117
Westmorland Av. NE22: Bed 7G 17
NE28: W'snd 3B 66
NE37: Usw 6H 101
NE64: Newb S 3H 13
Westmorland Ct. NE31: Heb 1H 85
Westmorland Gdns. NE9: Gate 2H 99
Westmorland La. NE1: Newc T 2E 82 (7D 4)
Westmorland Retail Pk. NE23: Cra 4H 25
Westmorland Ri. SR8: Pet 4K 171
Westmorland Rd.
NE1: Newc T 2E 82 (7D 4)
NE4: Newc T 2B 82 (8A 4)
NE29: N Shi 5B 48
NE34: S Shi 6E 68
Westmorland St. NE28: W'snd 3G 65
Westmorland Wlk. NE4: Newc T 3B 82
Westmorland Way NE23: Cra 4K 25
West Mt. NE12: Kil 1A 46
SR4: Sund 3A 118
WESTOE 4A 68
Westoe Av. NE33: S Shi 4A 68
Westoe Dr. NE33: S Shi 4A 68
Westoe Fitness Cen. 5K 67
Westoe Rd. NE33: S Shi 3K 67
Westoe Village NE33: S Shi 5A 68
Weston Av. NE16: Whi 2F 97
Weston Vw. SR8: Pet 5A 172
W. Ousterley Rd. DH9: Stly 5F 125
Westover Gdns. NE9: Gate 7H 83
West Pde. DH8: Con 7J 121
DH8: Lead 5A 122
NE4: Newc T 2D 82 (7A 4)
NE31: Heb 1H 85
West Pk. *NE11: Dun 5B 82*
(off Meadow La.)
NE61: Mor 1E 14
SR3: E Her 3H 131
W. Park Gdns. NE21: Bla T 5C 80
W. Park Rd. NE8: Gate 7G 83
NE33: S Shi 5J 67
SR6: Cle 5C 88
W. Park Vw. NE23: Dud 3H 35
W. Pastures NE36: W Bol 3C 102
NE63: Ash 5K 11
WEST PELTON 3C 126
W. Percy Rd. NE29: N Shi 1E 66
W. Percy St. NE29: N Shi 7G 49
Westport Cl. SR5: S'wck 3B 104
W. Quay Rd. SR5: Sund 6B 104
WEST RAINTON 1K 155
Westray DH2: Ches S 1J 141
Westray Cl. SR2: Ryh 1F 133
West Riggs NE22: Bed 1H 21
West Rig, The NE3: Ken 1A 62
West Rd. DH8: Con 5E 120
DH9: Ann P 6K 123
DH9: Tan L 7A 110
NE5: Newc T 5F 61
NE15: Newc T 5F 61
NE20: Pon 5H 31
NE22: Bed 6B 18
NE42: O'ham 2C 76
NE42: Pru 5C 76
NE46: Hex 7A 50
West Rd. Crematorium NE5: Newc T 6H 61
West Row DH3: Bir 5C 114
W. Salisbury St. NE24: Bly 1H 23
W. Shield Row Vs. DH9: Stly 1E 124
WEST SLEEKBURN 1B 18
W. Sleekburn Ind. Est. NE22: W Sle 2B 18
W. Sleekburn Rd. NE22: W Sle 2C 18
W. Spencer Ter. NE15: Thro 4B 60
W. Stainton St. NE33: S Shi 4J 67
(not continuous)
W. Stevenson St. NE33: S Shi 4K 67
West St. DH2: Pelt 4C 126
DH3: Bir 4A 114
DH6: Hett 7C 176
West St. DH6: Shot C 6E 170
DH8: Lead 5A 122
DH9: Tan L 1D 124
NE8: Gate 3G 83 (9H 5)
NE16: Whi 7G 81
NE27: Shir 3H 47
NE28: W'snd 2E 64
NE31: Heb 6K 65
NE39: H Spen 3D 94
SR1: Sund 1E 118 (3H 7)
SR3: New S 1C 132
SR7: S'hm 3B 148
TS27: B Col 1G 183
West St. Cotts. TS27: B Col 2G 183
W. Sunniside SR1: Sund 1F 119 (3K 7)
Westsyde NE20: Pon 1E 40
West Ter. DH1: Dur 2K 165 (1A 6)
DH6: Coxh 7K 177
DH7: B'hpe 5D 138
NE26: Sea S 4D 28
NE62: Chop 1A 18
W. Thorns Wlk. NE16: Whi 1G 97
West Thorp NE5: Newc T 7F 43
West Va. NE15: Thro 3F 59
West Vallum NE15: Newc T 6F 61
W. Victoria St. DH8: Con 6H 121
West Vw. DH1: Dur 2C 166
DH3: Ches S 5A 128
DH4: Hou S 6J 129
(Bournmoor)
DH4: Hou S 5B 130
(Success)
DH4: Pen 1B 130
DH6: Has 3K 169
DH6: Sher 3C 168
DH7: B'don 2E 174
DH7: Esh W 4E 162
DH7: Sac 7D 140
DH8: M'sly 1J 121
DH8: Shot B 4F 121
DH9: Stly 6E 124
NE4: Newc T 2B 82
NE9: Gate 3A 100
NE9: Spri 6C 100
NE11: Kib 2F 113
NE12: Longb 4B 46
NE13: Wide O 4D 34
NE15: Lem 7C 60
NE16: Burn 2A 110
NE17: C'wl 5A 94
NE21: Bla T 3C 80
NE22: Bed 5A 18
NE23: Cra 5A 26
NE23: Dud 3J 35
NE23: Seg 2D 36
NE24: Camb 2G 19
NE25: Well 6A 38
NE35: Bol C 5D 86
NE37: Usw 7H 101
NE40: Ryton 7C 58
NE41: Wylam 7K 57
NE46: Acomb 4C 50
NE61: Fair M 2C 8
NE61: Peg 4A 10
NE63: Ash 3A 12
NE64: Newb S 2J 13
SR2: Ryh 3G 133
(off Blackhills Rd.)
SR5: C'twn 6H 103
SR6: Monk 4F 105
SR7: Mur 1E 158
(Church St.)
SR7: Mur 5H 147
(Overdene)
SR8: Eas 1K 171
SR8: Pet 5E 172
W. View Bldgs. NE30: N Shi 1J 49
W. View Gdns. DH9: Stly 2E 124
W. View Ter. NE11: Dun 4A 82
NE46: Hex 3E 70
Westview Ter. DH9: Ann P 6J 123
West Vs. DH9: Stly 3B 126
West Wlk. DH3: Lam P 3E 128
West Walls NE1: Newc T 1E 82 (6D 4)
W. Walpole St. NE33: S Shi 4H 67
Westward Ct. NE5: Newc T 2E 60
Westward Grn. NE25: Whit B 7C 38
Westward Pl. NE38: Wash 7F 115
West Way NE11: Dun 6C 82
NE33: S Shi 6H 67
Westway NE15: Thro 2H 59
NE21: Bla T 4B 80
SR8: Pet 7A 172
Westway Ind. Pk. NE15: Thro 2H 59
W. Wear St. SR1: Sund 1F 119 (2K 7)
Westwell Ct. NE3: Newc T 1H 63
Westwood Av. NE6: Newc T 4K 63
Westwood Cl. NE16: Burn 1B 110
Westwood Gdns. NE3: Ken 1A 62
NE9: Gate 4B 100
NE38: Wash 3J 115
NE62: Chop 6H 11
Westwood La. NE17: Ham C 3J 107
Westwood Rd. NE3: Gos 3E 44
Westwood St. SR4: Sund 2B 118

Westwood Ter.—Willoughby Dr.

Westwood Ter. DH3: Ches S 7A 128
Westwood Vw. DH3: Ches S 1A 142
DH7: Sac 1D 152
NE40: Ryton 3C 78
Westwood Wlk. NE8: Gate 4E 82
WEST WYLAM 3G 77
W. Wylam Dr. NE42: Pru 4G 77
West Wynd NE12: Kil 1A 46
Wetheral Gdns. NE9: Gate 4J 99
Wetheral Ter. NE6: Walk 2D 84
Wetherburn Av. SR7: Mur 7D 146
Wetherby Cl. DH8: Shot B 2F 121
NE63: Ash 5A 12
Wetherby Gro. NE8: Gate 7F 83
Wetherby Rd. SR2: Sund 7J 119
Wet 'n' Wild Water Pk. 3F 67
Wettondale Av. NE24: Cow 2E 22
Weybourne Sq. SR2: Sund 6G 119
Weyhill Av. NE29: N Shi 1D 66
Weymouth Dr. DH4: Hou S 4K 129
SR7: Mur, S'hm 4H 147
Weymouth Gdns. NE9: Gate 5H 99
Weymouth Ho. NE4: Newc T 4C 82
Weymouth Rd. NE29: N Shi 7C 48
SR3: New S 4A 132
Whaggs La. NE16: Whi 1H 97
Whalebone La. NE61: Mor 7F 9
Whalton Av. NE3: Ken 6C 44
Whalton Cl. DH6: Sher 3A 168
NE10: Gate 7G 85
NE61: Hep 3H 15
Whalton Ct. NE3: Ken 6C 44
NE34: S Shi 7A 68
Whalton Rd. NE61: Loan, Mor, Tra W 6A 14
Wharfedale DH4: Pen 1A 130
NE28: W'snd 7D 46
Wharfedale Av. NE37: Usw 7F 101
Wharfedale Dr. NE33: S Shi 6J 67
Wharfedale Gdns. NE24: Cow 1E 22
Wharfedale Grn. NE9: Gate 6K 99
Wharfedale Pl. NE6: Walk 7F 65
Wharmlands Gro. NE15: Newc T 6F 61
Wharmlands Rd. NE15: Newc T 6F 61
Wharncliffe St. SR1: Sund 2D 118 (4F 7)
Wharnley Way DH8: C'sde 4B 134
Wharrier Sq. DH6: Whe H 4A 180
Wharrier St. NE6: Walk 2D 84
Wharton Cl. DH5: W Rai 6D 144
Wharton St. NE24: Bly 4F 23
NE33: S Shi 3K 67
Wheatall Dr. SR6: Whit 3H 89
Wheatall Way SR6: Whit 4H 89
Wheat Cl. DH8: Shot B 2G 121
Wheatear Cl. NE38: Wash 5D 114
Wheatfield Cl. NE42: O'ham 1D 76
Wheatfield Gro. NE12: Longb 5K 45
Wheatfield Rd. NE5: Newc T 2F 61
Wheatfields NE25: Sea D 6F 27
Wheatlands Way DH1: Dur 3A 154
Wheatley Gdns. NE36: W Bol 7G 87
Wheatley Grn. La. DH7: Edm 2K 139
WHEATLEY HILL 2B 180
Wheatley Ter. DH6: Whe H 3A 180
Wheatleywell La. DH2: Plaw 6J 141
DH3: Ches S, Plaw 5K 141
Wheatridge NE25: Sea D 6F 27
Wheatridge Row NE25: Sea D 6F 27
Wheatsheaf Ct. SR6: Monk 6H 105
Wheldon Ter. DH2: Pelt 2G 127
Wheler St. DH4: Hou S 1D 144
Whernside Cl. NE37: Wash 2E 114
Whernside Ct. SR3: New S 3B 132
Whernside Pl. NE23: Cra 7K 25
Whernside Wlk. NE40: Ryton 2H 79
Whetstone Bri. Rd. NE46: Hex 2B 70
Whetstone Grn. NE46: Hex 2B 70
WHICKHAM 7H 81
Whickham Bank NE16: Swa 7G 81
Whickham Cl. DH4: Hou S 2C 144
Whickham Gdns. NE6: Newc T 1A 84
Whickham Glebe Sports Club 7H 81
Whickham Highway NE11: Dun, Gate 7K 81
NE16: Whi 7K 81
Whickham Ind. Est. NE16: Swa 6F 81
Whickham Lodge NE16: Whi 7J 81
Whickham Lodge Ri. NE16: Whi 7J 81
Whickham Pk. NE16: Whi 7J 81
(Dockendale M.)
NE16: Whi 7J 81
(Heron Way)
Whickham Rd. NE31: Heb 1H 85
Whickham St. SR6: Monk 6G 105
SR8: Eas 7B 160
Whickham St. E. SR6: Monk 6G 105
Whickham Thorns Outdoor Activity Cen. 6K 81
Whickham Vw. NE9: Gate 2J 99
NE15: Newc T 6G 61
Whickhope NE38: Wash 6J 115
Whinbank NE20: Pon 2H 41
Whinbrooke NE10: Gate 1E 100
Whinbush Pl. NE15: Newc T 1G 81
Whindyke TS27: B Col 2G 183
Whinfell NE37: Wash 1F 115
Whinfell Cl. NE23: Cra 7A 26
Whinfell Ct. SR3: New S 3B 132
Whinfell Rd. NE20: Pon 1H 41
Whinfield Av. DH6: Shot C 6E 170
Whinfield Ind. Est. NE39: Row G 6G 95
Whinfield Ter. NE39: Row G 5H 95
Whinfield Way NE39: Row G 6G 95
Whinham Way NE61: Mor 3H 15
Whinlatter Gdns. NE9: Gate 3J 99
Whinlaw NE9: Gate 3A 100
Whinmoor Pl. NE5: Newc T 4A 62
Whinney Cl. NE21: Bla T 6A 80
Whinneyfield Rd. NE6: Walk 6D 64
Whinney Hill DH1: Dur 4B 166 (5E 6)
Whinney Leas NE17: C'wl 7J 93
Whinny La. DH8: Ebc, M'sly, Shot B 7G 107
Whinny Pl. DH8: C'sde 4C 134
Whinshaw NE10: Gate 7D 84
Whinside DH9: Stly 2D 124
Whinstone M. NE12: Longb 6B 46
Whinway NE37: Wash 1F 115
Whistler Gdns. NE34: S Shi 3K 87
Whitbeck Ct. NE5: Newc T 4G 61
Whitbeck Rd. NE5: Newc T 5F 61
Whitbourne Cl. NE37: Usw 5J 101
Whitbrey Ho. *NE6: Walk* *3C 84*
(off Oval, The)
WHITBURN 6H 89
Whitburn Bents Rd.
SR6: Monk, Whit 1H 105
Whitburn Cl. DH7: Lang P 5H 151
WHITBURN COLLIERY 4H 89
Whitburn Gdns. NE9: Gate 4B 100
Whitburn Pl. NE23: Cra 7K 25
Whitburn Rd. NE36: E Bol 6A 88
SR6: Cle 6A 88
SR6: Monk 2H 105
Whitburn Rd. E. SR6: Cle 5D 88
Whitburn St. SR6: Monk 7F 105
Whitburn Ter. NE36: E Bol 7K 87
SR6: Monk 3F 105
Whitby Av. NE46: Hex 1B 70
SR6: Monk 1H 105
Whitby Cl. NE8: Gate 5H 83
Whitby Cres. NE12: Longb 6A 46
Whitby Dr. NE38: Wash 5H 115
Whitby Gdns. NE28: W'snd 1J 65
Whitby St. NE30: N Shi 6H 49
Whitchester Ho. NE4: Newc T 3A 4
Whitchurch Cl. NE35: Bol C 5E 86
SR5: S'wck 3B 104
Whitchurch Rd. SR5: S'wck 3B 104
Whitdale Av. NE24: Cow 3E 22
Whiteacres NE61: Mor 1G 15
Whitebark SR3: New S 5A 132
Whitebeam Pl. NE4: Newc T 3D 82 (9A 4)
Whitebridge Cl. NE3: Gos 4F 45
Whitebridge Ct. NE3: Gos 5E 44
Whitebridge Pk. NE3: Gos 4F 45
Whitebridge Parkway NE3: Gos 4F 45
Whitebridge Wlk. NE3: Gos 4F 45
Whiteburn NE42: Pru 5D 76
White Cedars DH7: B'don 2C 174
Whitecliff Cl. NE29: N Shi 4F 49
White Cl. DH7: Lan 6K 137
White Cotts. NE32: Jar 2A 86
White Cres. TS27: Hes 4E 182
Whitecroft Rd. NE12: Kil 2K 45
White Cross NE46: Hex 2E 70
Whitecross Way NE1: Newc T 1F 83 (5E 4)
Whitefield Cres. DH4: Pen 2A 130
NE61: Peg 4A 10
Whitefield Gdns. NE40: G'sde 6D 78
Whitefield Gro. NE10: Gate 6B 84
Whitefield Ter. NE6: Newc T 4B 64
Whiteford Pl. NE23: Seg 1E 36
Whitefriars Pl. *NE1: Newc T* *8F 4*
(off Hanover Sq.)
Whitegate Cl. NE11: Dun 4B 82
White Gates Dr. DH5: Eas L 1H 157
Whitegates Rd. DH6: Sher 1K 167
Whitehall La. DH8: Con 1D 136
Whitehall Rd. NE8: Gate 6F 83
NE15: Thro 4K 59
Whitehall St. NE33: S Shi 7J 67
Whitehall Ter. SR4: Sund 2B 118
White Hart Yd. NE1: Newc T 1F 83 (6F 4)
Whitehead St. NE33: S Shi 6H 67
(not continuous)
WHITEHILL 6G 127
Whitehill NE10: Gate 2D 100
Whitehill Cres. DH2: Pelt 5G 127
(not continuous)
Whitehill Dr. NE10: Gate 1A 100
Whitehill Hall Gdns. DH2: Ches S 5J 127
White Hill Rd. DH5: Eas L 3J 157
Whitehill Rd. NE23: Cra 1J 25
WHITEHILLS 2D 100
Whitehill Way DH2: Ches S 7H 127
White Horse Vw. NE34: S Shi 7E 68
Whitehouse Av. DH7: B'hpe 5D 138
DH7: Ush M 2B 164
Whitehouse Ct. DH7: Ush M 1C 164
(not continuous)
SR8: Eas 1K 171
SR8: Pet 4K 171
Whitehouse Cres. NE9: Gate 3C 100
SR8: Shot C 6H 171
Whitehouse Ent. Cen. NE15: Newc T 2J 81
Whitehouse Farm Cen., The 7E 14
Whitehouse Ind. Est. NE15: Newc T 2J 81
Whitehouse Ind. Pk. SR8: Shot C 6G 171
Whitehouse La. DH7: Ush M 2B 164
NE9: Gate 3A 100
(Bramblelaw)
NE9: Gate 3B 100
(Harebell Rd.)
NE29: N Shi 4D 48
(not continuous)
Whitehouse M. NE28: W'snd 3G 65
White Ho. Pl. SR2: Sund 2H 119
Whitehouse Rd. NE15: Newc T 2H 81
White Ho. Rd. SR2: Sund 2G 119
(not continuous)
Whitehouse Ter. DH7: B'hpe 5D 138
White Ho. Way NE10: Gate 2C 100
Whitehouse Way SR8: Pet 6H 171
White Ladies Cl. NE38: Wash 2H 115
Whitelaw Pl. NE23: Cra 6A 26
Whitelea Cl. SR8: Pet 7D 172
WHITELEAS 4K 87
Whiteleas Way NE34: S Shi 2J 87
WHITE-LE-HEAD 7A 110
White-le-Head Gdns. DH9: Tan L 6A 110
Whiteley Cl. NE40: G'sde 5E 78
Whiteley Rd. NE21: Bla T 2E 80
Whitemere Cl. SR2: Sund 7G 119
White Mere Gdns. NE10: Gate 6G 85
Whiteoak Av. DH1: Dur 1F 167
White Oaks NE10: Gate 2C 100
White Rocks Gro. SR6: Whit 3H 89
White Rose Way NE10: Gate 2J 101
Whites Gdns. NE31: Heb 7H 65
Whiteside NE44: Rid M 7K 73
WHITESMOCKS 1H 165
Whitesmocks DH1: Dur 7J 153
Whitesmocks Av. DH1: Dur 1H 165
White St. NE6: Walk 1F 85
Whitethorn Cres. NE5: Newc T 3K 61
Whitethroat Cl. NE38: Wash 5D 114
Whitewell Cl. NE40: Ryton 1G 79
Whitewell La. NE40: Ryton 1G 79
Whitewell Rd. NE21: Bla T 4C 80
Whitewell Ter. NE40: Ryton 7G 59
Whitfield Dr. NE12: Longb 6A 46
Whitfield Rd. NE12: Longb 4B 46
NE15: Newc T 1F 81
NE25: Sea D 7H 27
Whitfield St. DH8: Con 6J 121
Whitfield Vs. NE33: S Shi 7H 67
Whitgrave Rd. NE5: Newc T 2K 61
Whithorn Ct. NE24: Cow 2G 23
Whitlees Ct. NE3: Ken 5A 44
WHITLEY BAY 6H 39
Whitley Bay Crematorium
NE26: Whit B 2E 38
Whitley Bay Holiday Pk.
NE26: Whit B 1E 38
Whitley Bay Ice Rink 1F 49
Whitley Bay Leisure Pool 4F 39
Whitley Bay Playhouse 5G 39
Whitley Bay Station (Metro) 7H 39
Whitley Ct. NE9: Gate 4B 100
Whitley Pl. NE25: H'wll 1J 37
Whitley Rd. NE12: Kil, Longb 5E 46
NE12: W'snd, Longb, Newc T 6B 46
NE25: Well 6A 38
NE26: Whit B 6H 39
NE27: Kil, Longb 3G 47
WHITLEY SANDS 4E 38
Whitley Ter. NE22: Bed 5B 18
NE25: H'wll 1J 37
Whitmore Rd. NE21: Bla T 3C 80
Whitsun Av. NE22: Bed 7J 17
Whitsun Gdns. NE22: Bed 7J 17
Whitsun Gro. NE22: Bed 7J 17
Whitticks, The NE36: E Bol 7H 87
Whittingham Cl. NE30: N Shi 2J 49
NE63: Ash 5J 11
Whittingham Ct. *NE8: Gate* *5F 83*
(off Second St.)
Whittingham Rd. NE5: Newc T 1F 61
NE30: N Shi 2J 49
Whittingham Rd. Bungs.
NE5: Newc T 1G 61
Whittington Gro. NE5: Newc T 6J 61
Whittleburn NE10: Gate 2D 100
Whitton Av. NE24: Bly 4F 23
Whitton Gdns. NE29: N Shi 5D 48
Whitton Pl. NE7: Newc T 1K 63
NE25: Sea D 7H 27
WHITTONSTALL 1A 106
Whittonstall NE38: Wash 7K 115
Whittonstall Rd. NE17: C'wl 6J 93
Whittonstall Ter. NE17: C'wl 6G 93
Whitton Way NE3: Gos 6D 44
Whitwell Acres DH1: H Shin 7F 167
Whitworth Cl. NE6: Walk 1E 84
NE8: Gate 7F 83
Whitworth La. DH7: New B 6A 174
DL16: New B 6A 174
Whitworth Pl. NE6: Walk 1E 84
Whitworth Rd. NE37: Wash 1D 114
SR8: Pet 6H 171
Whoral Bank NE61: Mor 5H 9
WHORLTON 1E 60
Whorlton Grange NE5: Newc T 1E 60
Whorlton Grange Cotts.
NE5: Newc T 1E 60
Whorlton La. NE5: Newc T, Wool 5B 42
Whorlton Pl. NE5: Newc T 2E 60
Whorlton Ter. NE5: Cha P 1B 60
Whyndyke NE10: Gate 2D 100
Whytrigg Cl. NE25: Sea D 6F 27
Wickham Av. NE11: Dun 6B 82
Wicklow Ct. NE62: W Sle 1B 18
Widdrington Av. NE34: S Shi 5D 68
Widdrington Gdns. NE13: Wide O 5E 34
Widdrington Rd. NE21: Bla T 4C 80
Widdrington Ter. NE21: Bla T 2A 80
NE29: N Shi 7G 49
(not continuous)
WIDE OPEN 5E 34
Widnes Pl. NE12: Longb 5A 46
Wigeon Cl. NE38: Wash 6E 114
Wigham Chare NE2: Newc T 3J 5
Wigham Ter. DH4: Pen 2B 130
NE16: Burn 4A 110
Wigmore Av. NE6: Walk 2C 84
Wilber Ct. SR4: Sund 1B 118
Wilberforce St. NE28: W'snd 5F 65
NE32: Jar 6C 66
Wilberforce Wlk. NE8: Gate 4E 82
Wilber St. SR4: Sund 2B 118
Wilbury Pl. NE5: Newc T 3J 61
Wildbriar NE38: Wash 6H 115
Wilden Ct. SR3: Sund 6C 118
Wilden Rd. NE38: Wash 4K 115
Wildshaw Cl. NE23: Cra 7A 26
Wilfred St. DH3: Bir 5A 114
DH3: Ches S 7A 128
NE6: Newc T 7J 63 (4M 5)
NE35: Bol C 7F 87
SR4: Sund 1A 118
Wilkes Cl. NE5: Newc T 3F 61
Wilkinson Av. NE31: Heb 3H 85
Wilkinson Ct. NE32: Jar 6B 66
Wilkinson Rd. SR8: Pet 3C 172
Wilkinson St. NE34: S Shi 1H 87
Wilkinson Ter. SR2: Ryh 3G 133
WILK'S HILL 6A 150
Wilkwood Cl. NE23: Cra 6A 26
Willans Bldgs. DH1: Dur 2D 166
Willerby Ct. NE9: Gate 6K 99
Willerby Dr. NE3: Gos 4F 45
Willerby Gro. SR8: Pet 5K 171
William Allan Homes NE22: Bed 7F 17
William Armstrong Dr. NE4: Newc T 3A 82
William Cl. NE12: Longb 4E 46
William Doxford Cen. SR3: New S 3B 132
William Johnson St. SR7: Mur 1F 159
William Leech Bldg. NE2: Newc T 2D 4
William Morris Av. NE39: Row G 5F 95
William Morris Ter. DH6: Shot C 7E 170
William Pl. DH1: Dur 2D 166
William Roberts Ct. NE12: Kil 3B 46
Williams Cl. DH9: Stly 3G 125
Williamson Sq. TS28: Win 5F 181
Williamson Ter. SR6: Monk 7F 105 (1K 7)
Williams Pk. NE12: Longb 6A 46
Williams Rd. SR7: Mur 7E 146
William's Ter. SR2: Ryh 3G 133
William St. DH2: Pelt 4E 126
DH3: Ches S 5A 128
DH6: Bow 4H 177
DH9: Ann P 6A 124
DH9: Stly 7J 125
(Edward St.)
DH9: Stly 5D 124
(Grasmere Ter.)
NE3: Gos 7G 45
NE10: Gate 5B 84
NE16: Whi 7G 81
NE17: C'wl 6K 93
NE24: Bly 2J 23
NE29: N Shi 7G 49
NE31: Heb 6H 65
(not continuous)
NE33: S Shi 2J 67
NE61: Peg 4B 10
SR1: Sund 1F 119 (2K 7)
SR4: Sund 2G 117
William St. W. NE29: N Shi 7G 49
NE31: Heb 7H 65
William Ter. DH4: Hou S 6D 130
NE31: Heb 7H 65
William Whiteley Homes
NE40: G'sde *5E 78*
(off Whiteley Cl.)
WILLINGTON 1K 65
WILLINGTON QUAY 4A 66
WILLINGTON SQUARE 7K 47
Willington Ter. NE28: W'snd 2J 65
Willis St. DH5: Hett H 5G 145
Willmore St. SR4: Sund 2C 118
Willoughby Dr. NE26: Whit B 4E 38

Willoughby Rd.—Woodkirk Cl.

Willoughby Rd. NE29: N Shi . . . 6D 48
Willoughby Way NE26: Whit B . . . 4E 38
Willow Av. NE4: Newc T . . . 5K 61
NE11: Dun . . . 6B 82
NE24: Bly . . . 7H 19
Willowbank Gdns. NE2: Gos . . . 1G 63
Willow Bank Rd. SR2: Sund . . . 5E 118
Willow Cl. DH7: B'don . . . 1D 174
NE16: Whi . . . 1H 97
NE61: Mor . . . 7H 9
Willow Ct. NE29: N Shi . . . 5F 49
NE40: Ryton . . . 7H 59
NE62: Chop . . . 1K 17
Willow Cres. DH8: Lead . . . 6B 122
NE24: News . . . 5G 23
Willowdene NE12: Kil . . . 3C 46
NE23: Dud . . . 4H 35
Willow Dyke NE45: Cor . . . 7E 52
Willowfield Av. NE3: Ken . . . 6B 44
Willow Gdns. NE12: Kil . . . 7A 36
Willow Grange NE32: Jar . . . 6A 66
Willow Grn. SR2: Sund . . . 4E 118
Willow Gro. NE10: Gate . . . 6B 84
NE28: W'snd . . . 3H 65
NE34: S Shi . . . 1B 88
SR8: Pet . . . 6F 173
Willow Lodge NE29: N Shi . . . 5G 49
Willow Pk. DH7: Lang P . . . 5G 151
Willow Pl. NE20: Pon . . . 7J 31
Willow Rd. DH4: Hou S . . . 2C 144
DH7: Esh W . . . 3D 162
NE21: Bla T . . . 4D 80
Willows Bus. Cen., The
NE21: Bla T . . . 1K 79
Willows Cl. NE13: Wide O . . . 6C 34
NE38: Wash . . . 4K 115
Willows, The DH1: Carr . . . 6H 155
NE4: Newc T . . . 3C 82
NE15: Thro . . . 4H 59
NE31: Heb . . . 2J 85
NE32: Jar . . . 5C 86
NE38: Wash . . . 4K 115
NE61: Mor . . . 7G 9
Willow Tree Av. DH1: H Shin . . . 6E 166
Willowtree Av. DH1: Dur . . . 7E 154
Willowvale DH2: Ches S . . . 4J 127
Willow Vw. NE16: Burn . . . 2A 110
Willow Way NE20: Pon . . . 2H 41
Wills Bldg. NE7: Newc T . . . 3C 64
Wills M. NE7: Newc T . . . 3C 64
Wills Oval NE7: Newc T . . . 3C 64
Wilmington Cl. NE3: Ken . . . 6H 43
Wilson Av. DH3: Bir . . . 3A 114
NE22: E Sle . . . 4F 19
Wilson Cres. DH1: Dur . . . 1E 166
Wilson Dr. NE36: W Bol . . . 6H 87
Wilson Gdns. NE3: Ken . . . 2D 62
Wilson Pl. SR8: Pet . . . 4B 172
Wilson's Ct. NE1: Newc T . . . 1F 83 (6F 4)
Wilson's La. NE9: Gate . . . 2H 99
Wilson St. NE11: Dun . . . 6B 82
NE28: W'snd . . . 3F 65
NE33: S Shi . . . 4J 67
SR4: Sund . . . 2B 118
Wilson St. Nth. SR5: Monk . . . 7E 104 (1H 7)
Wilson Ter. NE12: Longb . . . 4B 46
SR3: New S . . . 1C 132
Wilsway NE15: Thro . . . 3G 59
Wilton Av. NE6: Walk . . . 1C 84
Wilton Cl. NE23: Cra . . . 7A 26
NE25: Whit B . . . 6C 38
Wilton Dr. NE25: Whit B . . . 7B 38
Wilton Gdns. Nth. NE35: Bol C . . . 5E 86
Wilton Gdns. Sth. NE35: Bol C . . . 5E 86
Wilton Manse NE25: Whit B . . . 7B 38
Wilton Sq. SR2: Sund . . . 7G 119
Wiltshire Cl. DH1: Carr . . . 1G 167
SR5: S'wck . . . 3A 104
Wiltshire Dr. NE28: W'snd . . . 1D 64
Wiltshire Gdns. NE28: W'snd . . . 2D 64
Wiltshire Pl. NE37: Usw . . . 5H 101
Wiltshire Rd. SR5: S'wck . . . 4A 104
Wimbledon Cl. SR5: S'wck . . . 4B 104
Wimborne Cl. NE35: Bol C . . . 6E 86
Wimbourne Av. SR4: Sund . . . 4A 118
Wimbourne Grn. NE5: Newc T . . . 2F 61
Wimbourne Quay NE24: Bly . . . 7J 19
Wimpole Cl. NE37: Usw . . . 5J 101
Wimslow Cl. NE28: W'snd . . . 2D 64
Winalot Av. SR2: Sund . . . 6G 119
Wincanton Pl. NE29: N Shi . . . 1E 66
Winchcombe Pl. NE7: Newc T . . . 2J 63
Winchester Av. NE24: Bly . . . 2J 23
Winchester Cl. DH3: Gt Lum . . . 3E 142
NE63: N Sea . . . 5D 12
Winchester Ct. NE32: Jar . . . 5B 86
Winchester Dr. DH7: B'don . . . 3C 174
SR8: Pet . . . 7H 171
Winchester Rd. DH1: Dur . . . 4C 154
Winchester St. NE33: S Shi . . . 2K 67
Winchester Ter. NE4: Newc T . . . 1D 82 (6B 4)
Winchester Wlk. NE13: Wide O . . . 6D 34
Winchester Way NE22: Bed . . . 6H 17
Wincomblee NE6: Walk . . . 1E 84
Wincomblee Rd. NE6: Walk . . . 3E 84
Wincomblee Workshops *NE6: Walk . . . 1F 85*
(off White St.)
Windburgh Dr. NE23: Cra . . . 7K 25
Windermere DH3: Bir . . . 6B 114
SR6: Cle . . . 5C 88
Windermere Av. DH2: Ches S . . . 1A 142
DH5: Eas L . . . 3J 157
NE10: Gate . . . 6D 84
Windermere Cl. NE23: Cra . . . 7K 25
Windermere Cres. DH4: Hou S . . . 3B 130
NE21: Bla T . . . 6B 80
NE31: Heb . . . 1K 85
NE32: Jar . . . 3D 86
NE34: S Shi . . . 7A 68
Windermere Dr. NE12: Kil . . . 1A 46
Windermere Gdns. NE16: Whi . . . 7J 81
Windermere Rd. DH6: S Het . . . 3D 158
NE5: Newc T . . . 5H 61
NE64: Newb S . . . 4G 13
SR7: S'hm . . . 3G 147
Windermere St. NE8: Gate . . . 5G 83
SR2: Sund . . . 6H 119
Windermere St. W. NE8: Gate . . . 5G 83
Windermere Ter. DH9: Stly . . . 5D 124
NE29: N Shi . . . 6F 49
Windhill Rd. NE6: Walk . . . 3D 84
Winding, The NE13: Din . . . 4H 33
Windlass Ct. NE34: S Shi . . . 1J 87
Windlass La. NE37: Wash . . . 1G 115
Windmill Ct. NE2: Newc T . . . 5E 62 (1C 4)
Windmill Gro. NE24: Cow . . . 1E 22
Windmill Hill DH1: Dur . . . 5K 165 (7A 6)
NE33: S Shi . . . 4H 67
NE46: Hex . . . 1C 70
Windmill Ind. Est. NE23: Nel V . . . 7E 20
Windmill Sq. SR5: Monk . . . 3E 104
Windmill Way NE8: Gate . . . 4F 83
NE31: Heb . . . 5J 65
NE61: Mor . . . 7H 9
Winds La. SR7: Mur . . . 1C 158
(not continuous)
Winds Lonnen Est. SR7: Mur . . . 7C 146
Windsor Av. NE3: Gos . . . 1G 63
NE8: Gate . . . 6G 83
NE26: Whit B . . . 7J 39
Windsor Cl. NE16: Whi . . . 3G 97
NE28: W'snd . . . 1A 66
Windsor Cnr. SR8: Pet . . . 6F 173
Windsor Cotts. NE28: W'snd . . . 1A 66
Windsor Ct. DH6: Crox . . . 6K 175
NE3: Gos . . . 1G 63
NE3: Ken . . . 5A 44
NE10: Gate . . . 6A 84
NE22: Bed . . . 1H 21
NE23: Cra . . . 1J 25
NE39: Row G . . . 5K 95
NE45: Cor . . . 7E 52
SR8: Eas . . . 1J 171
Windsor Cres. DH5: Hou S . . . 2F 145
NE5: Newc T . . . 2G 61
NE26: Whit B . . . 7J 39
NE31: Heb . . . 7K 65
NE42: O'ham . . . 1D 76
Windsor Dr. DH5: Hou S . . . 4E 144
DH6: S Het . . . 3B 158
DH9: Ann P . . . 4K 123
NE24: News . . . 6H 23
NE28: W'snd . . . 2K 65
SR3: New S . . . 2C 132
SR6: Cle . . . 5B 88
Windsor Gdns. DH8: Con . . . 7J 121
NE10: Gate . . . 6K 83
NE22: Bed . . . 1H 21
NE26: Whit B . . . 5F 39
NE29: N Shi . . . 5G 49
NE34: S Shi . . . 6A 68
NE64: Newb S . . . 3H 13
Windsor Gdns. W. NE26: Whit B . . . 5F 39
Windsor Pk. NE28: W'snd . . . 2D 64
Windsor Pl. DH6: Shot C . . . 6F 171
NE2: Newc T . . . 6G 63 (1G 4)
NE20: Pon . . . 7F 31
NE27: Kil . . . 3G 47
Windsor Rd. DH3: Bir . . . 2K 113
(not continuous)
NE9: Spri . . . 6C 100
NE25: Whit B . . . 6E 38
NE64: Newb S . . . 3H 13
SR7: S'hm . . . 3H 147
Windsor St. NE6: Newc T . . . 7K 63 (4N 5)
NE28: W'snd . . . 3F 65
Windsor Ter. DH3: Gt Lum . . . 3F 143
DH6: Crox . . . 6K 175
DH6: Has . . . 1A 170
DH8: Lead . . . 5B 122
DH9: Ann P . . . 5B 124
DH9: Dip . . . 2F 123
NE2: Newc T . . . 6F 63 (1F 4)
NE3: Gos . . . 1G 63
NE9: Spri . . . 6D 100
NE26: Whit B . . . 7J 39
NE40: Ryton . . . 2E 78
NE45: Cor . . . 7E 52
NE46: Hex . . . 1B 70
NE62: Sco G . . . 4H 17
Windsor Ter. NE64: Newb S . . . 3J 13
SR2: Sund . . . 6H 119
SR3: E Her . . . 3J 131
SR7: Mur . . . 7F 147
SR8: Pet . . . 6F 173
Windsor Vs. NE62: Chop . . . 1J 17
Windsor Wlk. NE3: Ken . . . 5K 43
NE63: N Sea . . . 5E 12
Windsor Way NE3: Ken . . . 5J 43
Windt St. NE13: Bru V . . . 6C 34
Windy Gyle NE63: Hir . . . 3C 12
Windyhill Carr NE16: Whi . . . 2F 97
WINDY NOOK . . . 1A 100
Windy Nook Rd. NE9: Gate . . . 1K 99
NE10: Gate . . . 1A 100
Windy Ridge NE10: Gate . . . 7A 84
Windy Ridge Vs. NE10: Gate . . . 7A 84
WINGATE . . . 5G 181
Wingate Cl. DH4: Hou S . . . 2D 144
NE15: Lem . . . 7E 60
Wingate Gdns. NE9: Gate . . . 4B 100
Wingate Grange Ind. Est.
TS28: Win . . . 6F 181
Wingate La. DH6: Whe H . . . 3J 179
Wingrove NE39: Row G . . . 6H 95
Wingrove Av. NE4: Newc T . . . 7B 62
SR6: Monk . . . 4G 105
Wingrove Cl. TS28: Win . . . 4G 181
Wingrove Gdns. NE4: Newc T . . . 7B 62
Wingrove Ho. NE5: Newc T . . . 4A 62
NE33: S Shi . . . 7J 67
Wingrove Rd. NE4: Newc T . . . 7B 62
Wingrove Rd. Nth. NE5: Newc T . . . 4A 62
(not continuous)
Wingrove Ter. DH8: Lead . . . 5B 122
NE9: Spri . . . 6D 100
NE10: Gate . . . 5F 85
Winifred Gdns. NE28: W'snd . . . 4G 65
Winifred St. SR6: Monk . . . 3G 105
Winifred Ter. SR1: Sund . . . 2G 119
WINLATON . . . 5B 80
WINLATON MILL . . . 1C 96
Winsford Av. NE29: N Shi . . . 3F 49
Winshields NE23: Cra . . . 6A 26
Winshields Wlk. NE15: Thro . . . 4G 59
Winship Cl. NE34: S Shi . . . 3J 87
Winship Gdns. *NE6: Newc T . . . 7B 64*
(off Grace St.)
Winship St. NE24: Bly . . . 5G 23
Winship Ter. NE6: Newc T . . . 7A 64
Winskell Rd. NE34: S Shi . . . 2F 87
Winslade Cl. SR3: New S . . . 1D 132
Winslow Cl. NE6: Walk . . . 7E 64
NE35: Bol C . . . 4F 87
SR5: S'wck . . . 3B 104
Winslow Cres. SR7: S'hm . . . 3G 147
Winslow Gdns. NE9: Gate . . . 2G 99
Winslow Pl. NE6: Walk . . . 7E 64
Winson Grn. DH4: Pen . . . 1K 129
Winster NE38: Wash . . . 7E 114
Winster Pl. NE23: Cra . . . 7K 25
Winston Ct. NE9: Spri . . . 6D 100
Winston Cres. SR4: Sund . . . 4A 118
Winston Way NE43: B'ley . . . 4H 91
Winter Gardens . . . 5K 7
Winters Bank DH4: Hou S . . . 2B 144
Winton Cl. NE23: Seg . . . 1E 36
Winton Ct. NE21: Bla T . . . 6C 80
Winton Way NE3: Ken . . . 7B 44
Wirralshir NE10: Gate . . . 1E 100
Wiseton Ct. NE7: Longb . . . 7H 45
Wishart Ho. NE4: Newc T . . . 2A 82
Wishart Ter. NE39: H Spen . . . 3D 94
Wishaw Cl. NE23: Cra . . . 6A 26
Wishaw Ri. NE15: Lem . . . 6E 60
Witham Grn. NE32: Jar . . . 4C 86
Witham Rd. NE31: Heb . . . 3K 85
Witherington Cl. NE7: Newc T . . . 2C 64
Withernsea Gro. SR2: Ryh . . . 2F 133
WITHERWACK . . . 3A 104
Witney Cl. SR5: S'wck . . . 3A 104
Witney Way NE35: Bol C . . . 7E 86
Witton Av. DH7: Sac . . . 7E 140
NE34: S Shi . . . 7C 68
Witton Ct. NE3: Ken . . . 6A 44
NE38: Wash . . . 4F 115
SR3: Sund . . . 6D 118
Witton Gdns. NE9: Gate . . . 5B 100
NE32: Jar . . . 3B 86
Witton Gth. SR8: Pet . . . 2A 182
WITTON GILBERT . . . 3C 152
Witton Gro. DH1: Dur . . . 6H 153
DH4: Hou S . . . 3C 144
Witton Rd. DH7: Sac . . . 1D 152
NE27: Shir . . . 1K 47
NE31: Heb . . . 5K 65
Wittonstone Ho. NE4: Newc T . . . 3A 4
Witton St. DH8: Con . . . 2K 135
Witty Av. NE31: Heb . . . 1K 85
Woburn NE38: Wash . . . 4H 115
Woburn Cl. NE23: Cra . . . 1J 25
NE28: W'snd . . . 2D 64
Woburn Dr. NE22: Bed . . . 6A 18
SR3: New S . . . 3C 132
Woburn Way NE5: Newc T . . . 3G 61
Wolmer Rd. NE24: Bly . . . 4K 23
Wolseley Cl. DH6: Bow . . . 4H 177
NE8: Gate . . . 5E 82
Wolseley Gdns. NE2: Newc T . . . 5J 63
Wolseley Ter. SR4: Sund . . . 3C 118
Wolsey Ct. NE34: S Shi . . . 7J 67
Wolsey Rd. SR7: S'hm . . . 4G 147
Wolsingham Ct. NE23: Nel V . . . 3H 25
Wolsingham Dr. DH1: Dur . . . 5B 154
Wolsingham Gdns. NE9: Gate . . . 4B 100
Wolsingham Rd. DH7: New B . . . 4A 174
DH7: Wat . . . 6B 162
NE3: Gos . . . 1D 62
Wolsingham Ter. DH9: Ann P . . . 5K 123
Wolsington St. NE4: Newc T . . . 3C 82
Wolsington Wlk. NE4: Newc T . . . 3B 82
Wolsley Rd. NE24: Bly . . . 2J 23
Wolveleigh Ter. NE3: Gos . . . 7F 45
Wolviston Gdns. NE9: Gate . . . 4B 100
Woodbine Av. NE3: Gos . . . 1E 62
NE28: W'snd . . . 3F 65
SR8: Pet . . . 4D 172
Woodbine Cl. NE4: Newc T . . . 2B 82
Woodbine Cotts. DH2: Ches S . . . 5J 127
Woodbine Pl. NE8: Gate . . . 5G 83
Woodbine Rd. DH1: Dur . . . 4J 153
NE3: Gos . . . 1E 62
Woodbine St. NE8: Gate . . . 5G 83
NE33: S Shi . . . 2K 67
(Anderson St.)
NE33: S Shi . . . 2K 67
(Ocean Rd.)
SR1: Sund . . . 2H 119
Woodbine Ter. DH3: Bir . . . 4B 114
DH7: New B . . . 4A 164
DH9: Ann P . . . 5B 124
NE8: Gate . . . 6K 83
(Balmoral Dr.)
NE8: Gate . . . 5G 83
(Bewick Rd.)
NE10: Gate . . . 5E 84
NE24: Bly . . . 2K 23
NE45: Cor . . . 7E 52
NE46: Hex . . . 1B 70
NE63: Ash . . . 3H 11
SR4: Sund . . . 7B 104
WOODBRIDGE . . . 2D 12
Woodbrook Av. NE5: Newc T . . . 5G 61
Woodburn DH9: Tan L . . . 1C 124
NE10: Gate . . . 2C 100
Woodburn Av. NE4: Newc T . . . 4A 62
Woodburn Cl. DH4: Hou S . . . 7J 129
NE21: Bla T . . . 6A 80
Woodburn Dr. DH4: Hou S . . . 1C 144
NE26: Whit B . . . 4E 38
Woodburn Gdns. NE11: Dun . . . 7C 82
Woodburn Sq. NE26: Whit B . . . 4D 38
Woodburn St. NE15: Lem . . . 6C 60
Woodburn Ter. NE42: Pru . . . 4D 76
Woodburn Way NE26: Whit B . . . 4E 38
Woodchurch Cl. NE7: Newc T . . . 1B 64
Woodcock Rd. SR3: New S . . . 4C 132
Woodcroft Cl. NE23: Dud . . . 2K 35
Woodcroft Rd. NE41: Wylam . . . 7J 57
Woodend NE20: Pon . . . 2H 41
Woodend Way NE13: Ken . . . 4J 43
Wood Fld. SR8: Pet . . . 6A 172
Woodfields NE20: Pon . . . 5K 31
Woodford NE9: Gate . . . 5H 99
Woodford Cl. SR5: S'wck . . . 3B 104
Woodgate Gdns. NE10: Gate . . . 5F 85
Woodgate La. NE10: Gate . . . 4F 85
Wood Grn. NE10: Gate . . . 5G 85
Wood Gro. NE15: Newc T . . . 6F 61
Woodhall Cl. DH2: Ous . . . 6G 113
Woodhall Ct. NE25: Sea D . . . 7G 27
Woodhall Spa DH4: Hou S . . . 5A 130
Woodham Ct. DH7: Lan . . . 6J 137
Woodhead Rd. NE6: Walk . . . 5C 64
NE42: Pru . . . 3H 77
Woodhill Dr. NE61: Mor . . . 1E 14
Woodhill Rd. NE23: Cra . . . 6A 26
WOODHORN . . . 1F 13
Woodhorn Church Mus. . . . 1G 13
Woodhorn Colliery Ho's.
NE63: Wood . . . 2D 12
Woodhorn Colliery Mus. . . . 2D 12
Woodhorn Ct. NE63: Hir . . . 3C 12
Woodhorn Cres. *NE64: Newb S . . . 2H 13*
(off Woodhorn Rd.)
WOODHORN DEMESNE . . . 2H 13
Woodhorn Dr. NE62: Chop . . . 7H 11
Woodhorn Gdns. NE13: Wide O . . . 5D 34
Woodhorn La. NE63: Hir . . . 2D 12
NE64: Newb S . . . 2J 13
Woodhorn Pk. NE63: Hir . . . 3B 12
Woodhorn Rd. NE63: Hir . . . 3B 12
NE64: Newb S . . . 2H 13
Woodhorn Vs. NE63: Hir . . . 2D 12
(not continuous)
Woodhouse Ct. NE34: S Shi . . . 6E 68
Woodhouses La. NE16: Swa . . . 6G 81
NE16: Whi . . . 2E 96
Woodhurst Gro. SR4: Sund . . . 6G 117
Woodkirk Cl. NE23: Seg . . . 1E 36

HOSPITALS and HOSPICES
covered by this atlas.

N.B. Where Hospitals and Hospices are not named on the map, the reference
given is for the road in which they are situated.

BENSHAM HOSPITAL 7F **83**
Fontwell Drive
GATESHEAD
NE8 4YL
Tel: 0191 4820000

BLYTH COMMUNITY HOSPITAL 1H **23**
Thoroton Street
BLYTH
NE24 1DX
Tel: 01670 396400

CHERRY KNOWLE HOSPITAL 5G **133**
Stockton Road
Ryhope
SUNDERLAND
SR2 0NB
Tel: 0191 5656256

CHESTER-LE-STREET COMMUNITY HOSPITAL 7A **128**
Front Street
CHESTER LE STREET
DH3 3AT
Tel: 0191 3336262

COUNTY HOSPITAL (DURHAM) 2K **165** (2A **6**)
North Road
DURHAM
DH1 4ST
Tel: 0191 3336262

DRYDEN ROAD DAY HOSPITAL 7J **83**
134 Dryden Road
GATESHEAD
NE9 5BY
Tel: 0191 4036600

DUNSTON HILL HOSPITAL 7K **81**
Whickham Highway
GATESHEAD
NE11 9QT
Tel: 0191 4820000

EARLS HOUSE HOSPITAL 4G **153**
Lanchester Road
DURHAM
DH1 5RD
Tel: 0191 3336262

FLEMING NUFFIELD UNIT, THE 5G **63**
Burdon Terrace
NEWCASTLE UPON TYNE
NE2 3AE
Tel: 0191 2196400

FREEMAN HOSPITAL 1J **63**
Freeman Road
High Heaton
NEWCASTLE UPON TYNE
NE7 7DN
Tel: 0191 2843111

HEXHAM GENERAL HOSPITAL 2E **70**
Corbridge Road
HEXHAM
NE46 1QJ
Tel: 01434 655655

HUNTERS MOOR HOSPITAL 5D **62** (1A **4**)
Hunter's Road
NEWCASTLE UPON TYNE
NE2 4NR
Tel: 0191 2195661

MARIE CURIE HOSPICE CENTRE 2B **82**
Marie Curie Drive
NEWCASTLE UPON TYNE
NE4 6SS
Tel: 0191 2191000

MONKWEARMOUTH HOSPITAL 5E **104**
Newcastle Road
SUNDERLAND
SR5 1NB
Tel: 0191 5656256

MORPETH COTTAGE HOSPITAL 2F **15**
Loansdean
MORPETH
NE61 2BT
Tel: 01670 395600

NEWCASTLE GENERAL HOSPITAL 7B **62**
Westgate Road
NEWCASTLE UPON TYNE
NE4 6BE
Tel: 0191 2738811

NEWCASTLE NUFFIELD HOSPITAL, THE 5G **63**
Clayton Road
NEWCASTLE UPON TYNE
NE2 1JP
Tel: 0191 2816131

NEWCASTLE UPON TYNE DENTAL HOSPITAL 6E **62** (1C **4**)
Richardson Road
NEWCASTLE UPON TYNE
NE2 4AZ
Tel: 0191 2325131

NORTH TYNESIDE GENERAL HOSPITAL 3E **48**
Rake Lane
NORTH SHIELDS
NE29 8NH
Tel: 0191 2596660

NORTHGATE HOSPITAL 3D **8**
Fair Moor
MORPETH
NE61 3BP
Tel: 01670 394000

PALMER COMMUNITY HOSPITAL 6B **66**
Wear Street
JARROW
NE32 3UX
Tel: 0191 4516000

PETERLEE COMMUNITY HOSPITAL 7B **172**
O'Neil Drive
PETERLEE
SR8 5TZ
Tel: 0191 5863474

PRIMROSE HILL HOSPITAL 2C **86**
Primrose Terrace
JARROW
NE32 5HA
Tel: 0191 4516375

PRIORY DAY HOSPITAL 6F **49**
Hawkeys Lane
NORTH SHIELDS
NE29 0SF
Tel: 0191 2196629

PRUDHOE HOSPITAL 6G **77**
Moor Road
PRUDHOE
NE42 5NT
Tel: 01670 394000

QUEEN ELIZABETH HOSPITAL 2K **99**
Queen Elizabeth Avenue
GATESHEAD
NE9 6SX
Tel: 0191 4820000

ROYAL VICTORIA INFIRMARY 6E **62** (2D **4**)
Queen Victoria Road
NEWCASTLE UPON TYNE
NE1 4LP
Tel: 0191 2325131

RYHOPE GENERAL HOSPITAL 4H **133**
Stockton Road
Ryhope
SUNDERLAND
SR2 0LY
Tel: 0191 5656256

ST BENEDICT'S HOSPICE 5E **104**
Monkwearmouth Hospital
Newcastle Road
SUNDERLAND
SR5 1NB
Tel: 0191 5699191

ST CLARE'S HOSPICE 2C **86**
Primrose Hill Hospital
Primrose Terrace
JARROW
NE32 5HA
Tel: 0191 4516378

ST CUTHBERT'S HOSPICE 5J **165**
Park House Road
DURHAM
DH1 3QF
Tel: 0191 3861170

ST GEORGE'S HOSPITAL 4F **9**
Whorral Bank
MORPETH
NE61 2NU
Tel: 01670 512121

ST NICHOLAS HOSPITAL 7C **44**
Jubilee Road
Gosforth
NEWCASTLE UPON TYNE
NE3 3XT
Tel: 0191 2130151

ST OSWALD'S HOSPICE 7E **44**
Regent Avenue
NEWCASTLE UPON TYNE
NE3 1EE
Tel: 0191 2850063

SHOTLEY BRIDGE COMMUNITY HOSPITAL 3G **121**
Woodlands Road
CONSETT
DH8 0NB
Tel: 01207 214444

SIR G.B. HUNTER MEMORIAL HOSPITAL 3G **65**
The Green
WALLSEND
NE28 7PB
Tel: 0191 2205953

SOUTH MOOR HOSPITAL 5G **125**
Middles Road
STANLEY
DH9 6AD
Tel: 0191 3336262

SOUTH TYNESIDE DISTRICT HOSPITAL 1K **87**
Harton Lane
SOUTH SHIELDS
NE34 0PL
Tel: 0191 4548888

SUNDERLAND EYE INFIRMARY 5F **119**
Queen Alexandra Road
SUNDERLAND
SR2 9HP
Tel: 0191 5656256

SUNDERLAND ROYAL HOSPITAL 2C **118**
Kayll Road
SUNDERLAND
SR4 7TP
Tel: 0191 5656256

UNIVERSITY HOSPITAL OF NORTH DURHAM 7J **153**
Southfield Way
DURHAM
DH1 5TW
Tel: 0191 3332333

WALKERGATE HOSPITAL 5C **64**
Benfield Road
NEWCASTLE UPON TYNE
NE6 4QD
Tel: 0191 2194300

WANSBECK GENERAL HOSPITAL 3E **12**
Woodhorn Lane
ASHINGTON
NE63 9JJ
Tel: 01670 521212

WASHINGTON BUPA HOSPITAL 1C **128**
Picktree Lane
WASHINGTON
NE38 9JZ
Tel: 0191 4151272

WILLOW BURN HOSPICE 4K **137**
Lanchester Road
Maiden Law
DURHAM
DH7 0QS
Tel: 01207 214732